Secretaries of Defense Historical Series

McNamara, Clifford,

and the

Burdens of Vietnam

1965-1969

SECRETARIES OF DEFENSE HISTORICAL SERIES

Erin R. Mahan and Stuart I. Rochester, *General Editors*

Volume I: Steven L. Rearden, *The Formative Years, 1947-1950* (1984)
Volume II: Doris M. Condit, *The Test of War, 1950-1953* (1988)
Volume III: Richard M. Leighton, *Strategy, Money, and the New Look, 1953-1956* (2001)
Volume IV: Robert J. Watson, *Into the Missile Age, 1956-1960* (1997)
Volume V: Lawrence S. Kaplan, Ronald D. Landa, and Edward J. Drea,
    The McNamara Ascendancy, 1961-1965 (2006)

SECRETARIES OF DEFENSE HISTORICAL SERIES

Volume VI

McNamara, Clifford,
and the
Burdens of Vietnam
1965-1969

Edward J. Drea

Historical Office
Office of the Secretary of Defense
Washington, D.C. • 2011

Library of Congress Cataloging-in-Publication Data

    Includes bibliography and index.
    Contents: v. l. The formative years, 1947-1950 / Steven L. Rearden – v. 2. The
test of war, 1950-1953 / Doris M. Condit – v. 3. Strategy, money, and the new look,
1953-1956 / Richard M. Leighton – v. 4. Into the missile age, 1956-1960 / Robert
J. Watson – v. 5. The McNamara ascendancy, 1961-1965 / Lawrence S. Kaplan,
Ronald D. Landa, and Edward J. Drea.
    1. United States. Dept. of Defense—History. I. Goldberg, Alfred, 1918-   .
II.   Rearden, Steven L., 1946-   . III. Condit, Doris M., 1921-   . IV.
Leighton, Richard M., 1914-2001. V. Watson, Robert J., 1920- 2010. VI. Kaplan,
Lawrence S., 1924-   ; Landa, Ronald D., 1940-   ; Drea, Edward J., 1944-   .
VII. United States. Dept. of Defense. Historical Office.
UA23.6.R4   1984   353.6'09   84-601133

For sale by the Superintendent of Documents, U.S. Government Printing Office
Internet: bookstore.gpo.gov   Phone: toll free (866) 512-1800;   DC area (202) 512-1800
Fax: (202) 512-2104 Mail: Stop IDCC, Washington, DC 20402-0001

ISBN 978-0-16-088135-0

Foreword

Volume VI of the Secretaries of Defense Historical Series covers the last four years of the Lyndon Johnson administration—March 1965–January 1969, which were dominated by the Vietnam conflict. The escalating war tested Robert McNamara's reforms and abilities and shaped every aspect of Defense Department planning, programming, and budgeting. The demands posed by Vietnam weakened U.S. conventional forces for Europe, forced political compromises on budget formulation and weapons development, fueled an inflationary spiral, and ultimately led to McNamara's resignation. The credibility gap grew, dissipating public confidence in government and left the Johnson administration to confront massive civil disobedience and domestic rioting—much of it directed against the Pentagon. Vietnam also eclipsed major crises in the Dominican Republic, the Middle East, Korea, and Czechoslovakia. McNamara's successor, Clark Clifford, operating under President Johnson's new guidelines, spent much of his 11-month tenure as secretary attempting to disengage the United States from the Vietnam fighting.

Vietnam held center stage and frustrated McNamara's plans to reduce Defense budgets or downsize the military services and soured the secretary's workings with Congress. It cast a long shadow over U.S.-Soviet relations, alienated to a greater or lesser degree the NATO allies, and eroded congressional support for defense programs as well as military assistance. For the foreseeable future, it remains an emotionally charged issue that challenges Americans' views of themselves. Yet throughout these four years OSD still had to deal with a wide range of policy matters, international instability, and other contingencies. Beginning in the spring of 1965 with the intervention in the Dominican Republic and ending in late 1968 with the release of U.S. Navy crewmen held captive by the North Koreans, McNamara and Clifford handled a series of international crises and threats, defusing some, making the best of others. The final four years also witnessed extensive and repeated contacts between Washington and Moscow on matters of mutual interest such as nuclear proliferation, arms control, and a Middle East settlement. Dramatic changes in the composition and strategy of NATO's military alliance tested the durability of U.S. and European commitment. War between superpower surrogates in the Middle East threatened to expand from a regional conflict to a global one. The role that McNamara and Clifford played in often neglected subtexts of the period provides readers with a wider perspective in which to place Vietnam and to appreciate the ramifications of the war on national security policy.

The author organized and shaped his account of these years around the Vietnam conflict and its influence on Defense budgets, the national economy, national military strategy, technology, civil-military relations, and the home front. Budget formulation received much attention not only to analyze charges of manipulation and deception but also to clarify OSD's funding approach to competing defense and social programs. Paying for Vietnam impacted the non-Vietnam portion of the Defense budget and occasioned bitter struggles that pitted OSD against the Joint Chiefs of Staff and Congress over weapon systems, procurement policies, military strategy, and McNamara's credibility.

Edward J. Drea holds a Ph.D. in history from the University of Kansas and served as a historian with the U.S. Army. He taught at the U.S. Army Command and General Staff College and the U.S. Army War College. Subsequently, he was a branch and division chief at the U.S. Army Center of Military History. Dr. Drea is a prolific writer. Most notably, he is a co-author of *The McNamara Ascendancy, 1961–1965,* and author of *Japan's Imperial Army: Its Rise and Fall, 1853-1945,* as well as many other books and articles on military history.

Dr. Drea wrote most of this manuscript under General Editor Alfred Goldberg and his successor, Stuart Rochester, whose tragic and untimely death prevented him from witnessing the publication of this volume in the series. This volume is in small part a testament to Dr. Rochester's tremendous skills as an editor and writer. The profession has suffered a grievous loss.

This volume is the first in the series to be published under its new name, Secretaries of Defense Historical Series, a change meant to reflect a new sharper focus on the Secretary of Defense and his immediate staff and to explain how they contributed to the larger national security policies of the presidents under which they served.

Interested government agencies reviewed Volume VI and declassified and cleared its contents for public release. Although the text has been declassified, some of the official sources cited in the volume may remain classified. The volume was prepared in the Office of the Secretary of Defense, but the views expressed are those of the author and do not necessarily represent those of the Office of the Secretary of Defense.

ERIN R. MAHAN
Chief Historian, OSD

Preface

Victory has a hundred fathers and defeat is an orphan,* so runs a popular aphorism, but the tumultuous mid-1960s passage of the United States turned the saying on its head. Accounts of the period indict a wide variety of culprits—politicians, generals, reporters, demonstrators—for the disaster in Vietnam and its associated repercussions in the economic, social, political, and military spheres of American life. Yet perhaps more than anyone else, Secretary of Defense Robert S. McNamara is regularly singled out as cause and symbol of a lost war and all its dire consequences. Vietnam remains "McNamara's War," although it began long before his appointment as secretary of defense and continued long after he left office.

Beyond Vietnam, McNamara's legacy is almost as bitter and the charges as varied. He mismanaged the military services, leaving them under-funded, understrength, and discredited in the eyes of the nation. He routinely disregarded military advice, particularly on strategic matters, leaving the United States weaker before the Soviet Union. He unilaterally implemented programs and disregarded their consequences, leaving the larger society poorer for it. Even now, McNamara remains a vilified man, and attempts to rehabilitate his reputation during the 1990s only served to reopen the raw emotions of the contentious Vietnam era. Such accusations cannot be easily dismissed and many are accurate or nearly so. Still, Robert McNamara and the Office of the Secretary of Defense (OSD) operated in a broader context and by describing that setting one may derive a more balanced view of McNamara's, and by extension OSD's, successes and failures. That is my purpose in this book.

The volume is a policy history of OSD and its leaders covering almost four years from March 1965 through January 1969. It concentrates on OSD's role in creating and shaping defense policy, recognizing that Robert McNamara, who served from 21 January 1961 to 29 February 1968, and his successor as secretary of defense Clark M. Clifford, who served from 1 March 1968 to 20 January 1969,

---

* Galeazzo Ciano, *The Ciano Diaries, 1939-43*, 521, entry for 9 Sept. 1942. President Kennedy is quoted as having made a similar remark in the wake of the Bay of Pigs invasion in April 1961.

exerted great influence far beyond the doors of the Pentagon. Both men were involved, at presidential direction, in the major economic, diplomatic, domestic, and political issues of the day. Both were closely involved with national and international crises of the time. And, while both left their imprint on the Department of Defense (DoD), without question McNamara's legacy, both for good and for ill, is the more enduring. McNamara's long tenure made it so, but besides mere longevity McNamara set DoD on a new course and made OSD the unquestioned authority in the Pentagon.

The volume treats a wide variety of subjects from OSD's perspective, many of them overlapping. For those reasons, I have grouped chapters topically and connected them with both the broad policy themes of the period and specific areas where redundancy affected DoD decisions and policies. Chapter I sets the scene by describing DoD's senior leadership, OSD officials, and the workings of the Defense Department and the national security policymaking apparatus. The next eight chapters treat Vietnam policy formulation and its effect on ground and air operations in Southeast Asia as well as DoD budget development because this financial process was closely related to, indeed eventually dominated by, the far-away Asian battlefields. Next follows a discussion of the turmoil on the home front, particularly during 1967 and 1968, which frayed the national consensus over the war, race relations, and military service. OSD's role in the Dominican Republic crisis of 1965 is covered in chapter XI. Individual chapters on nuclear non-proliferation, strategic arms control, and two on the North Atlantic Treaty Organization (NATO) provide the wider context for OSD's often controversial decisions on strategic issues involving nuclear weapons initiatives and European allies. Chapter XVI is devoted to the Middle East War, 1967, while the succeeding chapter examines the fundamental shifts in military assistance policy that occurred under McNamara. Chapter XVIII relates the multiple crises of 1968 to Vietnam policy and budget considerations. Chapter XIX evaluates the effects of the McNamara tenure on the U.S. military establishment and the concluding chapter analyzes the performance of OSD and the respective secretaries of defense during the period.

From 1965 through 1969 OSD was involved in developments all over the globe. Space limitations alone make it is impossible to cover all of them. Thus, like any written history, the material in this volume involves selection, and I opted to discuss the important events of the four-year span that most involved DoD. To reiterate, this is an OSD policy history, and that fact determined my coverage. Subjects not treated or lightly touched upon include the Indo-Pakistan War of 1965, relations with Indonesia and other South Asian nations, relations with Latin America (excepting the Dominican Republic), intelligence, and OSD administrative procedures.

Many people assisted me in bringing this book to publication, but I am especially indebted to Alfred Goldberg, who as then OSD Chief Historian and series General Editor gave me the opportunity to write this volume. He offered constructive criticism and encouragement all along the way and invariably improved the work's many shortcomings. He is that rare combination of highly skilled government official and first-rate historian whose dedication to accuracy, research, and scholarship is responsible for the superb quality of this series. Stuart Rochester also deserves special mention. He applied his editorial expertise to the volume first as Deputy Historian and then, in succeeding Dr. Goldberg, as OSD Chief Historian and General Editor. As Acting OSD Chief Historian, Diane Putney, like her predecessors, provided unwavering support and ensured the resources necessary to complete the project, as has Erin Mahan, the current OSD Chief Historian and series General Editor.

I am likewise grateful to the editors of the OSD Historical Office who meticulously read and re-read my chapters, always pointing out ways to improve the manuscript. Nancy Berlage, who late in the process assumed the role of series Chief Editor, provided editorial guidance and prepared the final version for publication. Elaine Everley, John Glennon, Max Rosenberg, David Humphrey, and Winifred Thompson, each in his or her own way, greatly contributed to the final manuscript. Dr. Everley also deserves thanks for organizing the OSD archives into a user-friendly retrieval system. Fellow authors Richard Hunt, Lawrence Kaplan, Ronald Landa, and Richard Leighton always responded to my questions and shared their insights with me. Alice Cole, Roger Trask, Dalton West, and Rebecca Welch read chapters, made suggestions, and provided support. I am grateful for the administrative and technical assistance provided by Ruth Sharma, Josephine Dillard, Carolyn Thorne, Pamela Bennett, Renada Eldridge, and Ryan Carpenter as I worked through drafts of the manuscript. Catherine Zickafoose and her team at OSD Graphics, especially Stephen Sasser, wielded outstanding technical expertise in preparing the volume for print. I am also thankful to James Andrews, Defense Logistics Agency, and staff of the Government Printing Office for key assistance with production matters.

I enjoyed the good fortune of working at the Lyndon Baines Johnson Library, whose staff located documents, shared their expertise, unfailingly responded to my numerous inquiries, and made research a pleasure. Among an outstanding group of professionals, I must single out John Wilson who guided me through the archives and was always a source of sound advice and wise counsel. At the National Archives and Records Administration, Timothy Nenninger, Richard Boylan, Susan Francis-Houghton, Herb Rawlings-Milton, Jeannine Swift, and Victoria Washington deserve special mention as do John Carland, David Humphrey and Ted Keefer at the State Department Historian's Office. David Armstrong and Graham Cosmos of the Joint Chiefs of Staff Historical Office were always helpful; Susan Lemke and Robert Montgomery shepherded me through the valuable holdings of the Special Collections Library, National Defense University; Joel Meyerson, Terrence Gough, Robert Wright, and Jim Knight assisted me with the U.S. Army Center of Military History's extensive holdings; Thomas Hendrix, David Keough, and Randy Rakers helped me at the U.S. Army Military History Institute; Kathy Lloyd was of great assistance at the Naval Historical Center, and at the Marine Corps History and Museums Division Fred Graboske enabled me to see the extremely significant Wallace Greene collection. Lena M. Kaljot, Photo Historian, Marine Corps History Division, promptly provided digital images for the volume. Deborah Shapley took time from her busy schedule to show me her personal archives of Robert McNamara materials. Finally I owe deep gratitude to Pentagon Library staff who endured the September 11, 2001 attack on the Pentagon and its aftermath and throughout it all were still able to find that elusive congressional reference, odd journal article, or special report that had escaped me.

EDWARD J. DREA

Contents

CHARTS & MAPS

TABLES

Secretaries of Defense Historical Series

McNamara, Clifford,
and the
Burdens of Vietnam
1965-1969

CHAPTER I

MOVERS AND SHAKERS

As Robert McNamara began his fifth year in office in January 1965 the United States stood on the brink of being engulfed by the quicksand that was the Vietnam War. After four remarkably successful years as secretary of defense, McNamara endured three years of increasingly painful suffering and regret that left him drained in body and spirit. Along with President Lyndon Johnson, McNamara came to bear much of the blame for the unpopular Vietnam War that tore the country apart. The war eclipsed the great achievements of the early years, leaving McNamara greatly diminished in public reputation and stature.

By 1965 Vietnam had emerged as a flashpoint of the Cold War, but the rivalry between the United States and the Soviet Union (and a rising Communist China) played out on a stage larger than Southeast Asia. Even as the Johnson administration sought to improve relations with Moscow and build on the October 1963 partial nuclear test ban treaty by seeking further talks on arms control and limiting the proliferation of nuclear weapons, regional points of friction between the two nuclear superpowers abounded. Continuing Soviet support of Cuban President Fidel Castro proved a constant irritant, as did expanding Soviet influence in Africa, the Mediterranean, and the Middle East, especially among the more radical Arab regimes. Communist China—the People's Republic of China (PRC)—posed its own significant threat; Pentagon strategists pondered ways to contain a seemingly implacable and, judging from its rhetoric, sometimes bellicose regime. In one bright spot, Northeast Asia, DoD considered reducing U.S. forces in South Korea as that nation's economic prospects improved.

The perception of unrelenting Soviet aggressive behavior placed continuing pressure on the United States to defend Europe, frustrating U.S. plans for NATO allies to assume a greater share of the burden for their own defense. In the meantime, NATO suffered from France's growing alienation from the alliance and the deep-seated differences among the allies over command, control, and use of nuclear weapons. Closer to home, the administration had weathered the Cuban missile

1

crisis in 1962, but Castro persisted in his energetic efforts to export communism throughout Latin America, much to Washington's concern. In a further act of defiance the Cuban leader had cut off water supplies to the U.S. base at Guantanamo in February 1964.

At home, the great civil rights struggle of the 1960s created its own ferment and made additional demands on the Defense Department. African-American riots in New York and New Jersey during July 1964 had required National Guard troops to quell disturbances and restore order. They were a harbinger of more to come. DoD meanwhile gave special attention to the future of the Selective Service System, racial integration of National Guard and Reserve units, reorganization of reserve forces, and development of new weapons. By January 1965 the department had completed a major buildup of U.S. conventional, counterinsurgency, and nuclear forces and planned to reduce the Defense budget and military strength. The escalating war in Vietnam quickly ended such expectations.

While FY 1965 witnessed some retrenchment in Defense costs and personnel, in subsequent years the expanding war in Indochina and mounting troubles elsewhere necessitated continual increases. As of 30 June 1965, the armed services had 2,624,779 men and 30,610 women on active duty, altogether some 32,020 fewer than a year earlier. Major force elements included 16 Army and 3 Marine divisions, 880 Navy ships, 78 Air Force combat air wings, and 22 intercontinental ballistic missile squadrons. DoD employed more than 1,164,000 civilians. The FY 1965 Defense budget amounted to $49.7 billion in new obligational authority (NOA),* $1.2 billion less than the previous year. Three years later, 30 June 1968, the 3,509,505 men and 38,397 women in the active forces supported 18 Army and 4 Marine divisions, 932 Navy ships, 67 combat air wings,† and 26 intercontinental ballistic missile squadrons. DoD civilians numbered 1,436,000. The FY 1968 Defense budget with supplements amounted to $76.8 billion (NOA).[1]

Between 1965 and 1968 the Office of the Secretary of Defense (OSD) experienced similar growth. As of 30 June 1965, OSD had 1,729 civilian and 621 military personnel, a total of 2,350. Three years later that number had increased to 2,867—2,052 civilians and 815 military. In mid-1965 Defense agencies independent of the services and reporting to OSD employed 48,786 civilian and military personnel, the majority, just over 35,000, being in the Defense Supply Agency. The employees of the Defense agencies consisted almost entirely of men and women transferred from the military services. Three years later the agencies employed more than 84,000 people, most of the newcomers also from the services and the balance from new hires.[2]

---

* NOA is the sum of all new budget authority granted by Congress for a specific fiscal year.
† Although the Air Force reduced its number of combat air wings, it increased its aircraft inventory and the number of combat air squadrons.

DEPARTMENT OF DEFENSE
SEPTEMBER 1965

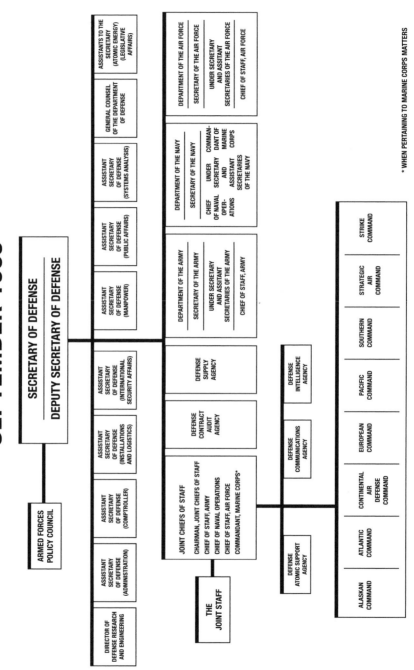

SECRETARY OF DEFENSE

DEPUTY SECRETARY OF DEFENSE

ARMED FORCES POLICY COUNCIL

DIRECTOR OF DEFENSE RESEARCH AND ENGINEERING

ASSISTANT SECRETARY OF DEFENSE (ADMINISTRATION)

ASSISTANT SECRETARY OF DEFENSE (COMPTROLLER)

ASSISTANT SECRETARY OF DEFENSE (INSTALLATIONS AND LOGISTICS)

ASSISTANT SECRETARY OF DEFENSE (INTERNATIONAL SECURITY AFFAIRS)

ASSISTANT SECRETARY OF DEFENSE (MANPOWER)

ASSISTANT SECRETARY OF DEFENSE (PUBLIC AFFAIRS)

ASSISTANT SECRETARY OF DEFENSE (SYSTEMS ANALYSIS)

GENERAL COUNSEL OF THE DEPARTMENT OF DEFENSE

ASSISTANTS TO THE SECRETARY (ATOMIC ENERGY) (LEGISLATIVE AFFAIRS)

JOINT CHIEFS OF STAFF

CHAIRMAN, JOINT CHIEFS OF STAFF
CHIEF OF STAFF, ARMY
CHIEF OF NAVAL OPERATIONS
CHIEF OF STAFF, AIR FORCE
COMMANDANT, MARINE CORPS*

THE JOINT STAFF

DEFENSE CONTRACT AUDIT AGENCY

DEFENSE SUPPLY AGENCY

DEPARTMENT OF THE ARMY
SECRETARY OF THE ARMY
UNDER SECRETARY AND ASSISTANT SECRETARIES OF THE ARMY
CHIEF OF STAFF, ARMY

DEPARTMENT OF THE NAVY
SECRETARY OF THE NAVY
CHIEF OF NAVAL OPER- ATIONS
UNDER SECRETARY AND ASSISTANT SECRETARIES OF THE NAVY
COMMAN- DANT OF MARINE CORPS

DEPARTMENT OF THE AIR FORCE
SECRETARY OF THE AIR FORCE
UNDER SECRETARY AND ASSISTANT SECRETARIES OF THE AIR FORCE
CHIEF OF STAFF, AIR FORCE

DEFENSE ATOMIC SUPPORT AGENCY

DEFENSE COMMUNICATIONS AGENCY

DEFENSE INTELLIGENCE AGENCY

ALASKAN COMMAND

ATLANTIC COMMAND

CONTINENTAL AIR DEFENSE COMMAND

EUROPEAN COMMAND

PACIFIC COMMAND

SOUTHERN COMMAND

STRATEGIC AIR COMMAND

STRIKE COMMAND

* WHEN PERTAINING TO MARINE CORPS MATTERS

DoD's Senior Leadership

Head of the vast DoD establishment from 21 January 1961 through February 1968, Robert McNamara powerfully filled the role of deputy commander-in-chief to the president. He had imprinted his aggressive management style and techniques on the department during his first four years in office.* By January 1965 he stood near a peak of success and influence. In taking command of the largest department in the government, he had improved its military capabilities, firmly established civilian control over the military services, swept away many outmoded practices and organizations, and forced the services and bureaucracy to adapt to a new, more analytical approach to defense management.

The transformation wrought by the McNamara ascendancy did not come without strong opposition and resentment. Controversy swirled around McNamara and OSD during his first four years as he applied managerial principles of cost efficiency and economy to every aspect of DoD and pushed the military services to change entrenched habits. What set McNamara apart was not only a far-reaching agenda but the depth and breadth of his involvement in all Defense affairs. He not only strove to manage a major war in Southeast Asia, he also involved himself deeply in preparation, coordination, and justification of the DoD budget, conceptualized a radical shift in strategic arms policy, including arms control, and planned and approved the specifics of the administration's Military Assistance Programs. Added to this impressive list McNamara had key roles in reorienting NATO's strategy, recasting the process of military procurement and weapon research and development, and responding to domestic disorders. As the president's chief adviser on defense matters he served on task forces responding to emergencies in the Dominican Republic, the Middle East, and elsewhere. A military assistant who worked with McNamara on a daily basis for years marveled at his "immense capacity" and energy to handle a wide variety of matters simultaneously.[3]

Throughout his early career, McNamara had demonstrated the same sort of drive and energy. Born in June 1916, he attended the University of California (Berkeley) and the Harvard Business School. During World War II he served for three years in the Army Air Forces, then following the war joined Ford Motor Company as a manager of planning and financial analysis. In November 1960 he became the first president of the company selected from outside the Ford family. After a strikingly successful business career he brought his formidable talents to the Pentagon in 1961. McNamara had both the intellect and the temperament to master the complexities of the Department of Defense. Journalist Theodore H. White exclaimed that "a man with a steel grip and a diamond-hard mind has seized control of the Pentagon."[4]

---

* See Kaplan et al, *McNamara Ascendancy*.

To the general public, the secretary's combed-back dark hair, rimless glasses, and business suit and tie bespoke a no-nonsense executive, brimming with self-confidence. His television appearances reinforced the impression of a brilliant mind in total command of a vast store of information. Over time the self-assurance and undaunted perseverance became a double-edged sword, as detractors accused him of arrogance, obstinacy, and rigidity. Both his performance and reputation would suffer under the strains of an unwinnable war and deteriorating relations with Congress, the president, and the press. When McNamara stepped down on 29 February 1968, he had served a record 85 months in office, the second half of his tenure far less successful than the first. But at the outset of 1965, even with his stature and trademark confidence beginning to erode, he was still firmly in control.

McNamara surrounded himself with able subordinates, relying on a highly capable and trusted team of top OSD civilian staff to implement his principles and agenda. No one senior OSD official could claim preponderant influence with the secretary, but for the most part all enjoyed a status belying their relative youth and limited Pentagon experience. McNamara treated them as his alter egos—delegating to them much responsibility while he attended to framing policy and strategy and advising the president, meeting with him often and conferring with him frequently by telephone. For a secretary, McNamara exercised unusual power and authority.[5]

In January 1964 McNamara selected Cyrus R. Vance to succeed Roswell Gilpatric as his deputy secretary of defense. A Yale graduate and New York lawyer, Vance joined DoD in 1961 as general counsel and later served as secretary of the Army. Soon after becoming deputy secretary he proved himself a deft troubleshooter during the Panama riots[*] of early 1964, a role he reprised during U.S. intervention in the Dominican Republic crisis in 1965.[†] He earned McNamara's confidence, performed smoothly and unobtrusively, shared the DoD leader's positions on national defense and initially on the use of military force, and acted as secretary during McNamara's absences.[6]

McNamara had originally assembled in 1961 a staff of assistant secretaries who served him exceptionally well during his first term as secretary. By the end of 1965 some of these had departed and others had moved on to higher or other positions in the department. Their replacements proved to be of equally high caliber, testifying to McNamara's ability to identify and attract talent.

The secretary considered the position of assistant secretary of defense (ASD) for international security affairs (ISA) "one of the two or three most significant posts in the whole department." ISA had responsibility for supporting DoD participation in National Security Council (NSC) affairs and for identifying and analyzing international political-military concerns with the aim of developing national military strategy. The office also directed the Military Assistance Program (MAP)

---

[*] See Kaplan et al, *McNamara Ascendancy,* 226.
[†] See Chapter XI.

and participated in arms control initiatives.[7] John T. McNaughton had headed ISA since July 1964, after having previously served as the DoD general counsel. A Rhodes scholar with a Harvard law degree, McNaughton had been a professor at the Harvard Law School. Even among equals he gained importance because of ISA's key role and his unstinting loyalty to McNamara. He shared McNamara's detached, impersonal style and analytical approach to decisionmaking. By at least one account, he also shared the secretary's impatience with opposing viewpoints. According to Thomas L. Hughes, director of the State Department's Bureau of Intelligence and Research, McNaughton "took to vilifying the purveyors of skeptical analysis."[8] Following McNaughton's tragic death at age 45 in a commercial airline accident, Paul C. Warnke, a Washington lawyer, succeeded him as ISA assistant secretary on 1 August 1967.

From February 1961 through July 1965, ASD (Comptroller) Charles J. Hitch supervised and directed preparation of the annual budget estimates for Defense. With McNamara's backing, he had revolutionized DoD's financial management process through the introduction of the Planning, Programming, and Budgeting System (PPBS). The ASD (Comptroller) office also provided systems analyses and reports useful in identifying overlapping programs and questionable spending.[9] In July 1965, with Hitch's departure, McNamara divided the office into two, retaining the comptroller title for preparation of the budget, the Five Year Force Structure and Financial Program, and the conduct of audit and statistical functions. He designated Robert N. Anthony, a Harvard Business School professor, as the new comptroller effective 10 September.

The new office, assistant secretary of defense for systems analysis, had been the comptroller's former directorate of systems analysis. Upgraded and formally chartered on 17 September, the office, under Alain C. Enthoven, produced analytical reports, cost estimates for forces and weapon systems, and special studies as directed by the secretary. Just turned 35, Enthoven, by the fall of 1965 had already emerged as a lightning rod for congressional and military discontent with OSD. Providing the quantitative data that "proved" the cost-effectiveness and strategic soundness of the secretary's plans and decisions, Systems Analysis, in the words of a McNamara aide, furnished the "numbers to back up his [McNamara's] position." Attesting to Enthoven's clout, one congressman labeled him "the most dangerous man we have in Government today."[10]

Enthoven and his stable of "whiz kids," exuding cocky assurance about the objectivity and efficacy of their methodology, often ignored military expertise and opinion, dismissing service dissent as a product of parochialism and resistance to both civilian authority and change. Not given to compromise, they sought to reshape programs through rational, quantifiable decisionmaking. But however scientific and sophisticated the new methodology, it had its limitations and biases. Critics pointed to subjective factors such as McNamara's favoring missiles over bombers and administration ceilings on troop strength that narrowed options and rendered the number-crunching less independent and less objective than Enthoven proclaimed. Further, rational analysis often clashed with empirical reality. Paul Nitze, McNamara's first assistant secretary for ISA and subsequently secretary of the Navy and deputy secretary of defense, later declared that he had no confidence in the organization because each analyst "saw himself as being the top strategist and secretary of defense." George Elsey, who served as special assistant to McNamara's successor Clark Clifford, complained that his boss would "never get an objective view from present [Systems Analysis] Staff. All are emotionally bound to defend S. A. as totally correct in *all* it does."[11]

Since 1958 the Director, Defense Research & Engineering (DDR&E) had served as principal adviser to the secretary of defense on all scientific and technical matters. DDR&E supervised all Defense research and engineering activities and coordinated service research and development programs, assuming an especially important role in evaluating the potential of strategic nuclear weapons and identifying the possible military application of new technologies. John S. Foster, Jr., became DDR&E on 1 October 1965, succeeding Harold Brown, who along with Vance selected Foster after others had turned down McNamara's offer of the position. Foster was a physicist, director of Livermore Laboratory, and a consultant to the President's Science Advisory Committee. He served as DDR&E until June 1973.[12] DDR&E's scientists often found themselves at odds with Systems Analysis staffers over weapon systems, particularly the antiballistic missile system (ABM).

Much of the day-to-day management functions of the department fell to the ASD (Administration), a position established on 1 July 1964 after McNamara combined several separate administrative elements within OSD under Solis Horwitz, a Harvard-trained lawyer, former counsel to Lyndon Johnson's Senate Defense Appropriations Subcommittee, and since 1961 director of Organizational and Management Planning in OSD. Beyond the functions it inherited, the new office supervised development of improved managerial practices to promote economy and eliminate duplication of effort. Additionally, Horwitz managed the national communications system and a newly created (15 July 1964) inspection service to conduct investigations within OSD, the Joint Chiefs of Staff, and other DoD components, including assessing the operational readiness and efficiency of military units, previously an exclusive prerogative of the military.[13]

The ASD (Installations and Logistics) handled DoD's logistical requirements, including production, procurement, and supply management and had responsibility as well for military construction, family housing, and real property upkeep. Paul R. Ignatius, under secretary of the Army, replaced Thomas D. Morris as assistant secretary in December 1964, remaining until 31 August 1967. Ignatius was succeeded by none other than his predecessor, Morris, who remained until the 1969 change in administrations.[14]

Under the ASD (Manpower) fell a potpourri of responsibilities, including personnel and reserve affairs, information and education programs, health, sanitation, medical care, military participation in civil and domestic emergencies, Armed Forces Radio and Television, and promotion of equal opportunity in the armed forces. With a background in government and management consulting, the hard-working Morris served as ASD (Manpower), which he regarded as "a secondary kind of job," from 1 October 1965 to 31 August 1967 between his stints at I&L. Perhaps his most important contribution during this period was implementing McNamara's Project 100,000.*[15] Alfred B. Fitt replaced Morris in October 1967 and served until February 1969.

The position of the ASD (Public Affairs) encompassed a wide range of activities that included dealing with the press, releasing information to the public, reviewing official statements for security, and coordinating public affairs within DoD and with other governmental departments and agencies.[16] Besides these functions, the forceful head of the office, Arthur Sylvester, presided over secretary of defense press conferences and background briefings until February 1967 when his deputy, Philip G. Goulding, replaced him.

As the legal adviser to the secretary, the general counsel ranked as an assistant secretary. A member of the secretary's immediate staff, he had a voice in a variety of complex legal and legislative matters, including those raised by the Joint Chiefs. McNamara clearly had a high regard for his legal advisers. Cyrus Vance (January 1961–June 1962), John McNaughton (July 1962–June 1964), and Paul Warnke (October 1966–July 1967) all initially served as general counsel before moving to other important positions in OSD. During the interval between July 1964 and September 1966 and after Warnke's departure in August 1967, career civil servant Leonard Niederlehner, deputy general counsel since November 1953, ably anchored the office as acting general counsel.[17]

Jack L. Stempler, assistant to the secretary of defense for legislative affairs, occupied the position from 13 December 1965 to 4 January 1970, advising the secretary and other top officials on congressional actions and issues relating to DoD legislative programs. The office served as liaison with Congress, keeping it informed on defense matters, replying to its inquiries and requests for information, and scheduling DoD witnesses for hearings.[18]

As presidentially appointed chairman of the Military Liaison Committee, William J. Howard also served as special assistant to the secretary of defense for atomic energy from January 1964 to June 1966; Carl Walske held the position from October 1966 until 1973. They advised the secretary on DoD atomic weapon policy, planning, and development, evaluated atomic weapon programs, and worked closely with the Atomic Energy Commission and the congressional Joint Committee on Atomic Energy.[19]

A "personal" special assistant to the secretary of defense and the deputy secretary served as aide, adviser, and, as required, troubleshooter. The position de-

---

* See Chapter X.

manded discretion, prudence, and resourcefulness in dealing with often politically sensitive or administratively complicated issues as the secretary's representative in high-level contacts with cabinet officers and their staffs, White House officials, members of Congress, and senior foreign officials. John M. Steadman held the position from October 1965 to March 1968, followed by George M. Elsey who, beginning in April 1968, performed similar duties for Secretary Clifford. In late 1965 McNamara also designated Henry Glass as a special assistant to the secretary. Previously an economic adviser to the ASD (Comptroller), Glass continued to prepare the secretary's annual "posture statements"[*] to Congress. He also edited McNamara's congressional testimony and provided knowledgeable advice on a variety of issues.[20]

The secretary and deputy secretary each had two military assistants. The most influential and longest serving, Colonel (later Lieutenant General) Robert E. Pursley, served under three secretaries from 1966 to August 1972. Military assistants functioned as executive officers, arranging meetings, preparing agendas, taking notes, and when requested or appropriate, offering advice. Pursley also became intimately involved in the policymaking process, helping to draft major recommendations concerning Vietnam during Clifford's tenure.[21]

McNamara deemed that the chief job of the service secretaries was to see to the logistics, procurement, and training necessary to provision and prepare the military services for their operational missions. Probably because of his tendency to limit the secretaries to a support role and restrict their involvement in the formulation of policy and strategy, McNamara went through no fewer than 10 departmental secretaries between 1961 and 1968. Judging the several departmental civilian staffs as generally weak, he preferred to rely primarily on his OSD team.[22]

Stanley R. Resor, secretary of the Army from July 1965 to June 1971, was the fourth to hold that position under McNamara. A decorated World War II veteran and roommate of Vance at Yale Law School, Resor, a corporate lawyer, served a few months as under secretary of the Army before stepping up to the top post. He worked closely with McNamara, especially in scheduling Army deployments to Vietnam. Paul H. Nitze, who served as secretary of the Navy from November 1963 to June 1967, did not want the job initially, having been promised the deputy secretary of defense position by President Kennedy. After slowly feeling his way along for a few months, Nitze became a forceful proponent of Navy proposals to the point of sometimes taking issue with McNamara and encountering "serious problems" with the Systems Analysis staff. His successor, Paul Ignatius, moved from ASD (Installations and Logistics) to become secretary of the Navy in September 1967 following the death of McNaughton, who had been scheduled to replace Nitze. Harold Brown, secretary of the Air Force from October 1965 to February 1969, had served previously as McNamara's first DDR&E. Brown's personality, by his own admission "introverted and likely to come across as cold," left him open to criticism that he was an ivory tower theoretician without practical experience. Nevertheless, he proved a forceful advocate for the Air Force even if it meant sometimes taking an adversarial stance toward former colleagues in OSD.[23]

McNamara favored internal promotions, advancing his original appointees and filling vacancies with care. He rewarded talent and ensured that new appointees acquired a wide range of experience. Vance, for example, moved from general counsel to secretary of the Army to deputy secretary of defense and Nitze from International Security Affairs to secretary of the Navy to deputy secretary of defense. Only a few senior officials—Enthoven in Systems Analysis and Horwitz in Administration—would serve in the same position throughout the period 1965–69. Others, like Ignatius or Morris, shifted positions within OSD or between OSD and elsewhere in DoD. Still others—for example, Vance and Public Affairs chief Sylvester—left before McNamara or shortly after him; Anthony left the comptroller position in July 1968. The largest turnover of senior personnel occurred in early and mid-1967.

The Civilian-Military Divide

The Joint Chiefs of Staff, composed of the heads of the military services and a chairman, were the "principal military advisers" to the secretary of defense, the president, and the NSC. Congress in June 1967 established four-year terms for members of the JCS. The chairman, appointed for two years and eligible for one reappointment, had no command authority over the military forces. The Chiefs' statutory duties included preparing strategic and logistics plans, reviewing requirements, and providing strategic direction of the military forces. A Joint Staff, responsible to the chairman, assisted the Chiefs. President Johnson's orders went to McNamara who passed them via the JCS to the eight unified commands—seven regional commands with forces from one or more services,* and the U.S. Air Force Strategic Air Command, denominated a specified command because, although part of the Air Force, it came under the operational control of the JCS.[24]

The chairman of the Joint Chiefs of Staff, General Earle G. Wheeler, had made his mark as a staff officer known for his intelligence and administrative ability. Highly regarded by the president and secretary, he served from July 1964 to July 1970, the only chairman to serve more than four years. He often acted as a buffer between his fellow Chiefs and McNamara. Some military people regarded him as McNamara's man, too close to the secretary to be a genuine spokesman for the JCS and the services.

Army Chief of Staff General Harold K. Johnson, who as a prisoner of war during World War II had survived the Bataan death march and years in a Japanese

---

* The seven regional unified commands were: European, Pacific, Southern, Strike, Atlantic, Alaskan, and Continental Air Defense.

POW camp, served from July 1964 to July 1968. A serious, religious man of integrity, Johnson was protective of his service and conservative in defining his JCS role. Given to reticence, he could be outspoken when it came to the Army; several times he toyed with the notion of resigning only to conclude he could do more good by remaining on the job. His successor, General William C. Westmoreland, a protégé of General Maxwell D. Taylor, had served under Taylor in World War II and as the secretary of the general staff when Taylor was Army chief of staff in the 1950s. Westmoreland had been a combat commander, a key staff officer, and commandant of West Point. Regarded as one of the most competent Army generals, he served as commander of U.S. Military Assistance Command, Vietnam (MACV) from June 1964 until becoming Army chief of staff on 3 July 1968.[25]

After holding important staff and command positions, General John P. McConnell headed the Air Force between February 1965 and July 1969. As deputy commander of the European Command he had favorably impressed McNamara and came recommended in 1964 by General Taylor, then chairman of the Joint Chiefs. In mid-1964, the president interviewed McConnell before naming him Air Force vice chief of staff with the understanding that he would succeed General Curtis LeMay as chief of staff.[26]

Chief of naval operations between 1963 and 1967, Admiral David L. McDonald had never wanted the job and was reluctant to serve in the Pentagon. A naval pilot, McDonald saw action in the Pacific as an aircraft carrier executive officer; his postwar career brought him a steady succession of senior staff positions and sea commands. Although increasingly frustrated over civilian disregard of JCS advice about Vietnam, he stayed until the end of his term. His successor, Admiral Thomas H. Moorer, a more opinionated officer and a strong airpower advocate, disliked McNamara and his OSD civilian "field marshals"; he regarded Clifford as a "political animal" whose early tough words were not matched by later deeds.[27]

General Wallace Greene served from 1 January 1964 to 31 December 1967 as commandant of the Marine Corps. A staff planner for operations in the Pacific during World War II, Greene gained extensive high-level staff experience in the postwar era. He chafed at the micromanagement of President Johnson and McNamara. Like his JCS colleagues he suspected that the OSD staff civilians would dump Vietnam on the generals as they happily returned to private life "where they can sit and kibitz and watch the JCS straighten out this mess." The selection of his successor, General Leonard F. Chapman, Jr., proved complicated. In mid-August 1967, Greene recommended Chapman, the assistant commandant and preferred choice of a majority of Marine generals. A few weeks later, however, Wheeler proposed General Victor H. Krulak, and McNamara endorsed the selection. In mid-September Nitze recommended Krulak to the president. Johnson procrastinated over the conflicting advice; finally, in mid-December, he selected Chapman. Neither flamboyant nor political, the new commandant, a straightforward, common-sense officer with a reputation as an effective manager, later said that the president never regretted his decision.[28]

The five officers comprising the JCS in 1965 all possessed recognized staff abilities, experience, and political savvy; they professed support for the reforms and policies instituted by McNamara even as they often disagreed with the secretary. Accustomed to following orders once a decision was reached, they promoted their respective service interests by working within the system, keeping their frustrations with DoD civilians private rather than airing them publicly.[29]

Despite the Chiefs' dutiful acquiescence and the long, constitutionally ingrained tradition of military deference to civilian authority, in the view of some Chiefs President Johnson had an innate distrust of the JCS and of the military generally. His guarded attitude toward the professional military mirrored McNamara's own misgivings. The defense secretary harbored special disdain toward the JCS as a corporate body, later calling it "a miserable organization" intent on protecting individual service interests and acting collegially only when expedient. The description was severe but unfortunately not far from the mark in the 1960s, when, under the pressure of tight budgets, interservice rivalry and competition even more than usual hampered consensus. The Air Force clamored for a new advanced bomber that the Army looked on as rendered obsolete by missiles; the Navy sought more aircraft carriers, which the Army and Air Force believed had a limited role; and the Army wanted more ground divisions, which the Air Force found archaic. Unsurprisingly, sharp differences surfaced also over what military options—both tactical and strategic—to pursue in Vietnam.[30]

During the first half of McNamara's tenure, under Taylor's chairmanship in particular, the Chiefs came to realize that if they forwarded split positions, they were inviting the secretary of defense to make decisions for them. Between 1961 and 1964, they averaged 1,479 decisions annually of which about 30, or two percent, were splits sent to McNamara for final determination. In 1965, an especially difficult year, they registered more than 3,000 decisions and 40 splits (1.3 percent); thereafter splits declined markedly to 7 in 1966 and just 4 in 1967. By then they had learned that McNamara took advantage of disagreement among them to have his way, that to preserve their own influence over policy decisions it was best to minimize their internal differences and develop unified positions, mainly where there were contentious issues such as the bombing campaign in Vietnam. Unresolved JCS splits not decided by the secretary of defense fluctuated from two in 1961 to five in 1965 and one per year thereafter. All of these unresolved splits involved major budget matters, not Vietnam; the president eventually made the final decision.[31]

On the day he retired as JCS chairman, 1 July 1964, Taylor informed McNamara that he considered the supporting Joint Staff only "marginally effective" because its inherent slowness adversely affected the timeliness of Joint Chiefs' views, thereby diminishing their impact. Taylor went on to warn that neither International Security Affairs nor Systems Analysis should be "in the business of military planning," nor should they become rival sources of military advice competing with the JCS.[32] McNamara was predisposed to listen to complaints about the Joint Staff but not about OSD, and certainly not criticism disparaging OSD's core activities. While willing to seek JCS advice on military tactics, he was not about to relinquish OSD authority over the crafting of the nation's military strategy.

As the situation in Vietnam became more problematic through 1964, Johnson faced the prospect of either losing South Vietnam or getting the United States mired in a faraway war before the November election. He relied less and less on the military for advice and excluded the Chiefs from policymaking. The exclusion may have helped muffle internal dissent and foster the illusion of administration unity and consensus but at the price of exacerbating the underlying tensions. By early autumn, reports of "considerable unhappiness" among the military over their lack of participation in policy planning reached White House Special Assistant for National Security Affairs McGeorge Bundy. In mid-November White House aide Jack Valenti advised Johnson to have the Joint Chiefs "sign on" before making any formal decisions on Vietnam because their inclusion in presidential decisions would shield the administration from possible congressional recriminations. If the Chiefs participated in pertinent NSC meetings "they could have their views expounded to the Commander-in-Chief, face to face. That way, they will have been heard, they will have been part of the consensus, and our flank will have been covered in the event of some kind of flap or investigation later." Subsequently, at a 19 November White House meeting the president informed his top civilian advisers that in the future no decisions on Vietnam "would be made without participation by the military"; otherwise he could not make his case to the congressional leadership on issues. Johnson followed Valenti's counsel and let the Chiefs be heard, but he consigned them to a token role, either by slight or calculation or continuing to shut them out of key aspects of policymaking. To cite but one example, in early 1965 the White House denied the Chiefs access to cables passed between the State Department and the U.S. ambassador in Saigon.[33]

Indeed as the war in Vietnam escalated, the Joint Chiefs as a group seldom met with their commander in chief—only on 10 occasions between 15 March 1965 and 8 June 1967. A March 1965 meeting and two sessions the following month involved substantive exchanges about the course of action in South Vietnam but had little effect on policy. A 22 July 1965 meeting confirmed previous decisions by the civilian leadership about Vietnam. The budget meetings of December 1965 and 1966 respectively and a session on 4 January 1967 recorded meaningful discussions that appeared to help shape policy, though in a direction to which Johnson seemed predisposed anyway. On the other occasions the Chiefs ratified policies already decided by the White House. Rather than deal with the Chiefs in an open deliberative process where agreement could be elusive and leaks and other mischief could occur, Johnson and McNamara preferred to work their will through Wheeler, considered by the defense secretary "as the directing officer—the CEO, if you will—of the Joint Chiefs."[34]

The Commander in Chief

The powerful and ever-increasing impact of the Vietnam War on the Johnson administration brought McNamara into an even closer relationship with the president, who involved himself to an unusual degree in determining policy and making decisions about the military conduct of the war. Volumes have been written attempting to explain the complexities of Lyndon Johnson's character. A man of enormous energy and boundless ambition, Johnson achieved the pinnacle of success and power yet remained insecure and thin-skinned. Often coarse and bullying, he was also compassionate, kind, and generous. "He could be altruistic and petty, caring and crude, generous and petulant, bluntly honest and calculatingly devious—all within the same few minutes," recalled Special Assistant Joseph A. Califano.[35] Johnson's moods seemed to swing from one extreme to another almost seamlessly, the contradictions concealing his innermost motivations. Emotions, however, seldom overrode political judgment.

As president, Johnson appears to have employed the same techniques that he had developed in the Senate, where deals were made one-on-one behind closed doors, compromises struck, favors exchanged, and consensus achieved with much exertion but little transparency. Years later Clifford wrote of Johnson, "I often had the feeling that he would rather go through a side door even if the front door were open."[36] At Johnson's "side door" stood a coterie of senior officials and advisers—inside and outside of government—who participated in the most sensitive and far-reaching policy decisions.

Johnson gathered information voraciously from a wide variety of trusted friends from whom he sought opinions and advice and with whom he "had those damned telephones of his going all the time." His compulsive attention to detail matched McNamara's penchant for data—both believing that the more a problem underwent vigorous analysis the more uncertainty could be removed from the final decision. "The appetite of Washington for details is insatiable," protested General Krulak in 1967. "The idea . . . is to take more and more items of less and less significance to higher and higher levels so that more and more decisions on smaller and smaller matters may be made by fewer and fewer people."[37]

For Johnson knowledge was power. He collected and stored information but never shared it entirely with subordinates, seeking to reserve to himself possession of the entire picture and thus dominate policy formulation. His obsession with leaks reinforced his compulsion for secrecy, so he carefully limited his advisory circle to prevent unauthorized disclosures of policy discussions to the media and his political foes. It was not just the JCS who were relegated to the sidelines but others too who would ordinarily be key players by virtue of their position or need to know.

Further complicating the policymaking process, Johnson delayed making binding decisions, indeed considered no "important decision irrevocable until it has been announced and acted upon." He consequently demanded information right up to the very moment of his decision, thinking it "simple prudence" to keep his options open.[38] It also allowed him to keep control of the situation, or so he thought, sometimes changing his mind at the last minute, reversing what senior aides believed were firm commitments, such as the mobilization of reserve forces in 1965 or the pursuit of a nonproliferation treaty the same year.

As rough-hewn and mercurial as his predecessor had been poised and coolly detached, Johnson had both prodigious flaws and talents, and an inimitable political style that historian Eric Goldman likened to "Machiavelli in a Stetson." He could no more shake that distinctive persona than he could change his lanky frame, so often caricatured in the political cartoons of the day.

The National Security Policymaking Apparatus

Over the course of his presidency (1963–1969), Johnson met with the National Security Council 75 times, a far cry from the regular weekly session chaired by President Eisenhower but consistent with President Kennedy's record.* Thirty-three of Johnson's NSC meetings had Vietnam or Southeast Asia on the agenda. The NSC met 16 times at irregular intervals from early 1965 until mid-1966 to ratify presidential decisions regarding Vietnam; 11 from February through August 1965, 2 more in January 1966, and the other 3 during May and June of that year. Thereafter, until November 1968 the NSC discussed complex, broader international issues exclusive of Vietnam, enabling Johnson to silence critics who asserted that he was preoccupied with the war. The president also convened the NSC during emergencies such as the June 1967 Middle East War, the *Pueblo* incident of January 1968, and the Czech crisis of August 1968. The objective, according to historian David Humphrey, being not so much to receive advice as to "project an image of effective leadership during a crisis." One reason for Johnson's diminishing use of the NSC was the large number of attendees. With an average of 21 persons attending council meetings, Johnson worried about leaks.[39]

On the subject that mattered most, Vietnam, neither the White House nor DoD followed a smoothly integrated policymaking process. The exclusion of the JCS from key OSD and White House deliberations, particularly during 1965, marginalized a principal stakeholder and knowledge base. McNamara did meet with the Joint Chiefs weekly, but by mid-September 1965 Wheeler had concluded that the last few meetings were not only "sterile," but had degenerated almost to the point where McNamara appeared to be hazing the military officers. To improve communication, Wheeler initiated regular Monday afternoon executive sessions between the Chiefs and the secretary, but by mid-1967 these too had become increasingly infrequent and somewhat pro forma affairs.[40]

---

* Kennedy met with the NSC 15 times during his first six months in office and about once a month thereafter for a total of 49 meetings.

McNamara's departmental staff meetings began as occasions to exchange ideas, provide guidance, and shape Pentagon policy. By late 1964 the meetings, attended by the secretary, his deputy, the JCS, service secretaries, assistant secretaries of defense, and military assistants to the secretary, had become more sporadic and usually involved single-issue briefings related to long-term service-related interests, not current policy concerns. No meetings occurred, for example, from 21 June through 6 September 1965, arguably the period during which the administration made its most fateful decisions on Vietnam. True, McNamara would still occasionally use the gathering to assign responsibilities, perhaps most notably in early December 1965 regarding Vietnam projects after his November visit there and again in mid-February 1966 after a major conference in Honolulu.* In between, the conferees heard a discussion on naval mine warfare. The usual agenda included a set briefing about such varied topics as the military sales program (21 November 1966), spending for Defense research (24 October 1966), Navy pilot requirements (17 October 1966), and DoD space programs (12 December 1966),[41] important issues but not crucial. After succeeding McNamara as secretary of defense on 1 March 1968, Clifford rejuvenated the staff meeting to encompass a substantive exchange of opinions, guidance, and information more focused on matters of immediate DoD concern requiring resolution.

For the most part, coordination at the upper policymaking levels in the administration was surprisingly poor. Civilian and military strategists often talked past each other. In late 1965, for instance, Lt. Gen. Andrew J. Goodpaster, assistant to the JCS chairman, advocated heavier air attacks on North Vietnam. When a high-ranking State Department official asked Goodpaster how widespread such ideas were in military circles, he was nonplussed by the general's reply that such views were "obvious at all echelons from the battlefield to the Joint Chiefs of Staff."[42] It appeared that two cultures existed side by side almost independently of one another.

Johnson's preference for informal channels played havoc with the normal policymaking apparatus. According to one scholar, the execution of policy "was largely organized around personal contacts and ad hoc arrangements, with no overarching, authoritative body to give effective coordination and strategic direction to what was being done. Policy thus tended to lurch along, addressing minor problems more or less successfully, but leaving the bigger ones—Vietnam especially—to grow only bigger and less manageable as time went on."[43] The Johnson approach thus focused on short-term gains that often produced serious long-range consequences.

While the written record is voluminous and remains indispensable for understanding the administration's policymaking process, McNamara and other key Defense officials conducted much of their business by phone or in unrecorded

---

* See Chapter V for a discussion of the Honolulu Conference.

meetings. The president likewise often dealt with his secretary of defense by tele-phone or in completely private sessions. During Johnson's lengthy absences from Washington, senior officials remained in contact with him via phone or lengthy teletypewriter cables dispatched from the White House communications center to his Texas ranch. McNamara used all these means of communication to reach John-son privately in order to lay the groundwork in advance for approval of actions he supported, and never hesitated to approach the president directly to reverse deci-sions that he did not like.

The so-called Tuesday luncheon at the White House, the epitome of this high-ly personalized and makeshift policy process, did not necessarily meet either on Tuesday or over lunch. The luncheons began in February 1964, met periodically to March 1965, and then became routine through the summer months. They lapsed during the fall of 1965, resumed sporadically between January and May 1966, then met regularly through October. Dropped again, the luncheons recommenced in January 1967, occurring regularly until Johnson left office two years later. Hav-ing used a similar luncheon format as Senate majority leader to manage affairs in the upper house, Johnson adapted it to the White House. Attended mainly by the president and his three top civilian advisers—McGeorge Bundy (after April 1966, Walt W. Rostow), McNamara, and Secretary of State Dean Rusk—Johnson in large part relied on these informal brainstorming sessions among his "inner circle" to shape national security policy and manage the Vietnam War, particularly the bombing campaign. As Admiral U.S. Grant Sharp, Jr., commander of U.S. forces in the Pacific (PACOM), acidly pointed out, "no professional military man, not even the Chairman of the JCS, was present at these luncheons until late in 1967." Wheeler became a regular at the luncheons only in October of that year.[44]

The private, intimate meetings allowed the most influential civilian deci-sionmakers to speak frankly directly to the president on major issues. McNamara thought the luncheons "extremely useful" because the informal exchanges let the president "probe intensively" the views of his key national security advisers with a candor impossible in a larger group. Rusk agreed on the president's right "to have a completely private conversation" to debate and discuss freely and fully sensitive issues. He felt his role was "to stand as a buffer between the President and the bu-reaucracy with respect to matters of considerable controversy."[45] Both Rusk and Rostow came to see the lunch meetings as the real NSC.

While permitting candor, the lunches did not necessarily guarantee clarity. Participants could walk away with contradictory understandings of what trans-pired, leading William P. Bundy, assistant secretary of state for Far Eastern affairs,* to describe the process as "an abomination." This overstated the case. Although perceptions occasionally varied, sometimes wildly, leaving mystified participants to wonder if they had attended the same luncheon, in general individual accounts

---

* After 1 November 1966, assistant secretary of state for East Asian and Pacific affairs.

of what had occurred were quite similar.[46]

McNamara always briefed Wheeler on the results of the luncheon deliberations; sometimes he reported the outcome to the Joint Chiefs as a body. However, when the president's decision ran contrary to McNamara's advice, which he at times had shared with the JCS in advance, he typically announced the result without further elaboration, leaving the Chiefs in the dark as to how the recommended position got changed and why.[47] The secretary's firm belief that the president was entitled to confidentiality left even senior OSD staff members frustrated, much like their JCS counterparts, because, according to Warnke, McNamara never told them "what he said to the President or what the President said to him." Frequent discrepancies between McNamara's public and private utterances added to the general confusion. One critic complained there was McNamara's public position, his classified position, his personal views expressed privately to the president, his views disclosed to friendly journalists, his position with peers, "his daytime views as war manager at the Pentagon, and his nighttime views" with the Kennedys or Washington society.[48]

Mastering the Pentagon

Whatever clarity or coordination the overall policymaking process lacked, once a decision was made, McNamara took pains to enforce unanimity within DoD. He strove to ensure that "there would be no way that the press or anybody else could drive a wedge between the President and me." McNamara believed that indications of policy disagreement at the top level, particularly in writing, could "be disastrous." For example, should discussions about a draft memorandum be leaked, "you would have evidence of conflict in the upper echelons of the administration and it would reduce the effectiveness of the administration."[49]

For sure, McNamara was master of his own domain. A military observer identified three salient characteristics of the secretary of defense: "the distrust of emotion, the passion for being right, and his amazing intelligence." Those qualities might have put him on a collision course with Johnson but for an equally strong sense of loyalty and an ego that took greater satisfaction from institutional than personal success.[50]

McNamara's sense of loyalty extended down to those who worked for him as well as up to the president. Where Johnson saw the defense secretary "surrounded by a good many people" the president did not trust—including Enthoven, McNaughton, and Warnke, all of whom Johnson regarded as "pretty soft"—McNamara was quick to shield his subordinates from White House, as well as congressional, criticism. A demanding boss, he granted wide latitude to key civilian subordinates but expected of them the same long hours and attention to detail he imposed on himself. McNamara's towering intellect and the vigor of his arguments did not eliminate dissent, according to one high-ranking Defense official, it just made it difficult to make one's case with the secretary. The State Department's director of intelligence and research alleged that McNamara regularly intimidated challengers, "hobbling if not silencing" them.[51]

The force of McNamara's personality and intellect alone would not have mattered much had he not been an effective manager. He ruled the Pentagon most of all by methodically managing its purse. Decisively if not peremptorily, he determined service budgets, pronounced judgment on major weapon acquisitions, and set requirements for force structure and equipment. His chief budget tool, draft presidential memoranda or DPMs, were highly classified papers initially prepared by Systems Analysis and other OSD staffers as part of the department's budget formulation. Each communicated the secretary's five-year projection on the content and funding of a specific military program—strategic offensive, continental defense, airlift, etc.—and went first to the JCS and service secretaries for review and reclama. After receiving service and agency comments, a final draft containing the secretary's decisions and JCS comments on those decisions was prepared for the president. The inevitable cuts in service proposals that ensued enabled McNamara and OSD to take public credit for reducing the defense budget to manageable levels. A less apparent reason for the large discrepancies between initial service requests and final OSD decisions was McNamara's unwillingness to give the services initial budgetary ceilings.[52]

Although too detailed for presidential use—"completely useless for the President's purposes in view of their length and complexity," as one top NSC staffer wrote—DPMs were more than guidance for DoD agencies. The standard DPMs served as the basis for McNamara's lengthy annual January statement to Congress on the world situation as it related to DoD's budget request and his projection of costs over the next five years. This annual statement, usually prepared by Henry Glass, was popularly known as the Posture Statement, although McNamara did not like the term and would not use it. On Vietnam, as well as the antiballistic missile program, NATO, and other major policy issues, McNamara often communicated directly with the president through "out-of-cycle" memoranda—ultrasensitive DPMs seen by only a small handful of people, and very occasionally by only McNamara and the president.[53]

While it is true that much of the excitement associated with the McNamara ascendancy had faded by the second year of Johnson's presidency, mounting criticism of the defense secretary prior to 1965 entailed more an indictment of style than competence. Both the level of scrutiny and the nature of the criticism would change as McNamara's vaunted skills and mastery would be put to a sterner test. But that reckoning was still in the future.

By 1965 DoD's—and the administration's—once bright prospects had become shadowed by the continuing deterioration of the military and political situation in Vietnam. Each day seemed to bring news of another communist military victory, another Saigon coup d'etat, or another instance of the South Vietnamese government's incompetence and corruption. The men in the president's trusted inner circle knew that Johnson would soon have to make important decisions about the future course of U.S. involvement in Vietnam. Yet, at the start of that pivotal year, if McNamara and other leaders shared a conviction that a widening U.S. commitment could not be avoided, they shared an equal conviction that the United States could accomplish whatever might be required.

Chapter II

Vietnam:
Escalation Without Mobilization

Early in 1965 the days of the Republic of Vietnam seemed numbered. Racked by domestic political instability and a growing Viet Cong communist insurgency, the government teetered on the verge of collapse. Determined that the country should not fall into communist hands, the Johnson administration cautiously and incrementally improvised a succession of fateful decisions during 1965 that ultimately committed American combat forces to a large-scale ground and air war in Southeast Asia.

Viewing the Vietnam scene during the first six or seven months of 1965 was like peering into a kaleidoscope. The pervasive political and military instability in Vietnam and political unrest in the United States presented a shifting and perplexing set of options for decisionmakers. There emerged a strengthening intent to save South Vietnam from the communist yoke but no consistent policy or strategy to carry it out. The civilian and military leaders held different views, which shifted often, on recommended force levels and deployments. Gradually and reluctantly the administration found itself drawn deeper into the morass until it finally took the seemingly inescapable decision to commit the nation to the rescue of South Vietnam from communist domination.

That the administration approached the crossroads haltingly and in seeming disarray is not surprising. Involved in the decisionmaking process were Taylor and Westmoreland in Vietnam, Sharp at PACOM, the Joint Chiefs, McGeorge Bundy, Secretary of State Rusk, McNamara, and President Johnson. A host of supporting staff provided information, ideas, and exhortations that helped shape deliberations. The desultory nature of the process and the frequent postponement of decisions may be attributed in part to deficiencies in the policymaking apparatus described in Chapter I but also to the inability of the key actors to give their full attention to the matter at hand. While the military could devote much or most of their attention to Vietnam, Johnson, McNamara, Rusk, and others in the civilian leadership were distracted by other matters of importance. Johnson in particular was engaged in fashioning and securing approval of his Great Society vision, to which he gave as much priority as the national security challenge.

During these months of ambivalence and hesitation the administration sought to devise a strategy that would achieve its ends without the risk of a wider war or the fullest engagement by the United States. It was an attempt at a balancing act that took insufficient account of the do-or-die resolve of the North Vietnamese. It betrayed also the deep ignorance of Vietnam and its culture, acknowledged later by McNamara and others, from which leaders of the Johnson administration suffered in formulating policy and conducting the war. It was a handicap they were not able to surmount.

Pondering Escalation

By January 1965, many senior DoD officials regarded South Vietnam as a lost cause, barring a major change in policy. It was, McNamara and others informed the president, a time for a hard choice: escalate military support, reinforcing the 23,300 U.S. military in Vietnam, or withdraw. The secretary favored using increased military power, but he believed the grave consequences of this step merited careful study of alternatives preceding a presidential decision. Johnson dispatched a group headed by McGeorge Bundy to Saigon on 2 February for an intensive firsthand appraisal.* A deadly Viet Cong (VC) attack on the American base at Pleiku on 7 February caused the party to return to Washington early. In his report, Bundy warned the president that a South Vietnamese collapse by 1966 was inevitable without substantially increased American assistance, military and otherwise. In response to the Pleiku attack, President Johnson immediately authorized a retaliatory air strike against North Vietnam.[1]

The following day McNamara asked the Joint Chiefs to work with ISA on a plan for a two-month air campaign against North Vietnam. He estimated a one-in-three chance of ground force involvement, expecting that the graduated bombing would result in Hanoi either negotiating or escalating the conflict. Another Viet Cong attack against an Army base at Qui Nhon on 10 February prompted a second air strike against the North and gave added impetus to a wider policy review.

In response to McNamara's request and after debate between Air Force Chief of Staff General McConnell and his Army counterpart General Johnson about the size of an Air Force deployment and the requirement for large numbers of ground combat troops, the Joint Chiefs on 11 February recommended eight weeks of expand-

---

* Members of Bundy's mission included ASD(ISA) John McNaughton; Deputy Assistant Secretary of State Leonard Unger; Lt. Gen. Andrew Goodpaster, assistant to the chairman of the JCS; Chester Cooper of the NSC staff; and Col. Jack Rogers, ISA executive officer.

ing air strikes against North Vietnam south of the 19th parallel and the immediate deployment of two combat brigades—one Army to Thailand, one Marine to Da Nang for base security. They also proposed to place other ground and air units on alert for movement into Vietnam and elsewhere in the Western Pacific.[2]

McNamara discussed this proposal with the Chiefs at the weekly meeting on 15 February. He still regarded large-scale ground involvement as unlikely, but in the event preferred to err on the high side, favoring committing six to eight divisions if such intervention became necessary. Two days later MACV Commander General Westmoreland notified the JCS that he needed more troops to protect American lives and installations because the Vietnamese army could not.[3]

Although the president had authorized the two retaliatory air attacks on North Vietnam in response to the Pleiku and Qui Nhon incidents, he was not yet prepared to articulate a comprehensive policy for Vietnam. Fearing the domestic political effects of a broadened war, Johnson quietly sought advice from top administration officials, major congressional leaders, and especially from President Eisenhower during a two-and-a-half-hour meeting on 17 February. Seeking to build a consensus to support whatever decision he made, the president took the middle ground and kept his own counsel. By arranging numerous one-on-one sessions and requesting personal, as opposed to formally staffed, memoranda, Johnson made sure he understood all options as he considered key policy decisions. This process did not produce a policy, and without one McNamara realistically could neither plan nor issue military orders.[4] Presidential decisions were needed, especially about the protection of Da Nang, the principal base for U.S. air attacks against North Vietnam and Laos.

Westmoreland regarded Da Nang in the northern part of South Vietnam as the keystone to the U.S. effort against the North. The exposed base, packed with American planes, invited VC retaliation. About 1,300 marines were already at or near Da Nang, part of an earlier commitment of support troops. On 23 February, with the reluctant concurrence of Ambassador Taylor who deemed "white-faced" soldiers as unsuitable for fighting in Asian forests and jungles, Westmoreland recommended the immediate infusion of combat marines to defend the vulnerable base against overt assault. At a meeting with his top civilian advisers on 26 February, Johnson agreed to deploy some but not all of the requested security forces.[5]

Meanwhile, on 13 February, the president tentatively approved a limited version of the JCS-planned eight-week air campaign against the North. Dubbed Rolling Thunder, the actual attacks did not occur until 2 March, following four earlier strike cancellations. On the same day, the 2d, apparently at the suggestion of Mc-Naughton, the president directed a group headed by General Johnson to examine with Taylor, Westmoreland, and other American and Vietnamese officials "all possible additional actions—political, military, and economic—to see what more can be done in South Vietnam."* The Joint Chiefs and McNamara promised West-moreland everything needed to strengthen the Government of Vietnam (GVN) position. While General Johnson's group listened to briefings in Vietnam between 5 and 12 March, Rusk, McGeorge Bundy, and McNamara in Washington held a long, freewheeling discussion on 5 March about the future of South Vietnam. They met not with a sense of crisis, but more with a felt need for guidance and direction. Late the next morning, JCS Chairman General Wheeler conferred with McNamara, reported MACV's previous-day pessimistic assessment of the situation in Vietnam, and urged the immediate dispatch of more marines to Da Nang.[6]

Reporting to the president on the 5 March session, Bundy praised Johnson's policy and achievements to date but pointed out that "the brutal fact is that we have been losing ground at an increasing rate in the countryside in January and February." Thus the president's senior policy advisers needed to know what the United States would do if the enemy escalated the fighting or if South Vietnam collapsed. Would the president order large numbers of ground troops to South Vietnam, and when? Especially urgent was the question of possible deployments of substantial allied ground forces to the central and northern regions of South Vietnam. Given the president's well-known abhorrence of self-serving leaks, Bundy assured John-son that only an extremely limited circle of senior civilians would participate in the sensitive discussions and leave no written record of their sessions. McNamara excluded the Joint Chiefs from those deliberations and for a time dropped them from cable traffic passed between the State Department and Ambassador Taylor.[7]

The president had several factors to consider. At the time, pursuing the over-riding goal of securing approval of his Great Society social programs, the president did not want to provide Congress the excuse of Vietnam to divert action and funding from the domestic legislation. He also feared that the political right would demand greater and riskier military action in Vietnam that might provoke China or the Soviet Union into a wider, possibly even nuclear war. Yet, the conservative circles that had attacked President Harry S. Truman for "losing China" would surely level similar accusations against Johnson for "losing Vietnam" if he did not take action.[8]

As Johnson viewed it, failing to dispatch additional marines to Da Nang would likely result in the loss of more American lives and planes to communist attacks. Guessing the odds at "60-40 against [the start of] a big land war," the president worried about the psychological impact on public opinion of sending marines to Vietnam. Weighing these factors, on the afternoon of 6 March he reluctantly or-dered in 3,500 marines to Da Nang; McNamara then withheld public announce-ment until the following afternoon, a Sunday, to minimize newspaper headlines.[9]

---

* General Johnson's group included McNaughton and Goodpaster, who had been part of Bundy's inspection team of the previous month, as well as U.S. Information Agency Director Carl Rowan. They left Washington on 3 March, arrived in Vietnam on 5 March and departed on the 12th, and arrived back in Washington on the 14th. (Ed note, *FRUS 1964–68*, II:395-96.)

McNamara's trusted aide, John McNaughton, returned to Washington on 9 March, ahead of the rest of General Johnson's team, in a gloomy, even defeatist, mood. Before his departure McNaughton had looked on the ground war as a largely Vietnamese affair to be augmented by American air support within South Vietnam; a few U.S. ground troops plus sea and air patrols to seal Vietnam's coastline and rivers, combined with psychological operations, would serve to hamper VC effectiveness. The "grim prognosis" he heard in Vietnam, particularly at MACV headquarters, however, changed McNaughton's views. He now proposed three alternatives: pressure the North; sustain the South, which would require "lots of U.S. and if poss[ible] Allied troops"; or "get out with limited humiliation." Invited to attend the 9 March Tuesday luncheon, McNaughton repeated his assessment, causing the president, after much discussion, to remark, "I'd much prefer to stay in SVN—but after 15 mo[nths] we all agree we have to do more."[10]

Presidential discussions with McNamara and Rusk among others continued the next day at Camp David, Maryland. The ghost of the 1938 Munich appeasement added credence to the then prevalent domino theory, convincing the president that U.S. withdrawal from Vietnam would only encourage further aggression and endanger Thailand, presumably next in line for communist conquest. McNamara professed not to believe in the domino effect, but on 11 March his arguments before the House Committee on Foreign Affairs about the "probabilities" and "pressures" that would develop if the United States pulled out of Vietnam clearly enunciated the domino theory. Burma and Laos would go communist and Thailand would be threatened. Indonesia's Communist Party would soon take over that nation, pressuring Malaysia, Japan, and the Philippines to demand closure of U.S. bases on their soil.[11]

General Johnson returned from Vietnam on 14 March and reported that the rapid and extensive deterioration there required "major new remedial actions." He recommended 21 steps—military, political, financial, and civic—to arrest the decline, plus two additional ones that would free some of the Vietnamese forces for offensive operations. Finally, he offered several other measures to contain infiltration of North Vietnamese forces. These last steps envisioned the employment of four or five American or Southeast Asia Treaty Organization (SEATO) divisions. As Bundy noted, this report outlining the perilous state of South Vietnam and the increasing boldness of the communists reinforced the president's emerging conviction to stay in Vietnam "come hell or high water" and his call for increased U.S. military action.[12]

The next day, 15 March, McNamara's disinclination to do so notwithstanding, the president brought the Joint Chiefs to the White House to make certain they did not "feel left out" of the process. He carefully reviewed General Johnson's report with the JCS, McNamara, and Deputy Secretary Vance, after which he approved "in principle" the general's 21 measures but withheld an immediate decision on the proposed large-scale combat division deployments. Marine Corps Commandant Greene described the president as "'desperate' to do *something* in South Vietnam."[13]

While the president agreed with General Johnson that U.S. combat forces were needed to defeat the insurgents and appeared ready to send them, he rejected any action that he thought might lead to China's active intervention, reasoning that if the United States could not "lick" the Viet Cong, it should not take on the Chinese. He instructed the Chiefs to submit proposals to him through McNamara. Having put the JCS on notice and made them aware of his dissatisfaction with the war's progress, at his Tuesday luncheon on 16 March the president admonished his key civilian advisers to give him more ideas and recommendations on Vietnam. On the same day, Wheeler notified CINCPAC Commander Admiral Sharp and Westmoreland that the JCS were considering three options: (1) gradually escalate to arrest further deterioration; (2) deploy ground combat forces to Vietnam's central highlands; and (3) establish coastal enclaves from which to conduct offensive combat operations.[14]

Under continued presidential pressure, on 17 March McNamara conferred with the JCS about deploying a three-division force. Generals Johnson and Greene, though differing on where to deploy them, agreed it was time, in Greene's words, to "bite [the] bullet" and commit large numbers of combat troops. McConnell opposed a ground buildup prior to a wider, hard-hitting air campaign against North Vietnam. Admiral McDonald proposed a gradual deployment of ground forces but was leery of committing them initially to the guerrilla-infested central highlands. Wheeler wanted a review of all policies because "we are losing [the] war." At subsequent meetings on 18 and 19 March the Chiefs continued to air their disagreements. By cable Sharp expressed concern about placing the Army division inland, while Westmoreland insisted its deployment there was the linchpin of his strategy. The Air Force chief finally agreed to a compromise that recommended more air strikes against the North and the deployment of four fighter squadrons in conjunction with the three-division deployment. Fearing the war was being lost, on 20 March the Joint Chiefs recommended to McNamara stepping up air raids against North Vietnam and deploying three divisions (one U.S. Army, one U.S. Marine, and one Republic of Korea) to South Vietnam for offensive combat operations. This was a major about-face by the JCS within a two-week span, effectively calling for a change in the primary American role from adviser to active participant in the destruction of the Viet Cong.[15]

The president, aware such a policy lacked congressional and popular support, remained noncommittal. Wanting to negotiate, albeit from an unassailable position of military might, he hesitated to escalate the conflict by bombing Hanoi itself and did not even consider the idea of committing additional ground troops.[16] Estimates of North Vietnam's intentions remained clouded by uncertainty at NSC's 26 March meeting. The intelligence community informed the president that Hanoi, unconvinced that it could not win militarily and unwilling as yet to negotiate, was infiltrating regular North Vietnamese Army (NVA) combat units into the South. Westmoreland and Taylor were requesting more combat troops; U.S. casualties were increasing; the JCS were scheduled to meet in several days with Taylor in Washington about deploying even more combat troops. No one could predict what might happen next in the byzantine world of Saigon politics. The president then stated that he wanted to meet with the Joint Chiefs the next week "to discuss their new military plans."[17]

Taylor's return from Saigon launched a series of meetings within the White House, State and Defense Departments, and Congress. On 29 March he told McNamara and the Joint Chiefs that stepped-up communist activity notwithstanding, the JCS three-division plan was excessive. McNamara agreed, but if it became necessary he favored sending large-scale reinforcements to take the offensive and relieve South Vietnamese forces for pacification duties. This would be done "as rapidly as possible, considering what can be politically accepted, logistically supported, and usefully tasked." The identification of regular People's Army of North Vietnam (PAVN) units in South Vietnam's central highlands in early April and other intelligence indicating the threat of a major Viet Cong offensive added further pressure to either commit U.S. ground troops to forestall the communist seizure of central Vietnam or accept its imminent loss.[18]

According to McGeorge Bundy, McNamara and Taylor preferred a modest deployment for the moment—a U.S. Marine battalion and air squadron and a Korean battle group (3,500 men)—while preparing logistically for a much larger deployment, if it became necessary. At a late afternoon White House meeting on 1 April, Wheeler insisted that three divisions were required because, as he said again, "we are losing the war out there." He also wanted a reserve call-up to replenish the strategic reserve in the United States if active duty divisions deployed to Vietnam. In accord with recommendations that Bundy had made previously to the president, McNamara and Rusk suggested deferring any decision on the JCS proposals.[19]

At the meeting, the president agreed to the deployment of approximately 20,000 logistical troops plus the additional marines and the authorization for U.S. ground forces to participate in offensive counterinsurgency operations in South Vietnam, thus allowing them to engage officially in a shooting war. The next day the NSC was briefed on these decisions, ones that significantly altered the mission of U.S. ground forces, but was not asked to affirm them. NSAM No. 328, 6 April, codified the policy but, at the president's insistence, minimized "any appearance of sudden changes in policy."[20]

Also on 1 April Johnson authorized further approaches to Australia, New Zealand, and South Korea to seek combat forces for South Vietnam. Each had already supplied advisers—160 Australians, 30 New Zealanders, and about 2,400 Korean engineers and security personnel. Small military establishments precluded Australia or New Zealand from sending a division-size unit, leaving South Korea's 600,000-man army as the best source for large forces.* Furthermore, the administration's failure the previous year to enlist Asian members of SEATO for Vietnam service made Korean troops attractive precisely because they were Asians. Although McNamara wanted Korean forces to accompany further U.S. deployments in order to temper domestic reaction to the widening American role in the war, he was simultaneously considering major troop withdrawals from South Korea and reductions in Korean ground forces and military assistance.† The president finally resolved the problem in mid-May when he encouraged South Korean President Park Chung Hee to send a Korean infantry division to South Vietnam, assuring him that the United States would extend all possible aid to South Korea and maintain U.S. troop strength on the peninsula.[21]

On the evening of 7 April, from the Johns Hopkins University campus, Johnson spoke to the nation, expressing willingness to talk with Hanoi and offering it massive economic support if peace were restored. At the same time he insisted that U.S. reinforcements and heavier air attacks signaled no change in purpose—of deterring North Vietnamese aggression—only a change in requirements to achieve that purpose. When correspondents reported U.S. forces engaging in offensive operations even as the White House press secretary denied any mission change, the administration's credibility suffered.[22] Having gotten deeper into a war, McNamara and his advisers now had to articulate a coherent military strategy.

In this, as he later lamented, McNamara failed. His aggressive management style, his passion for personal scrutiny of projects, and his proclivity to "concentrate on what could be quantified" immersed him in day-to-day details better left to others and left him little time to ponder an effective strategy or long-term plan for the forces required to carry it out. Still, in his view, everything had a solution. "If we can learn how to analyze this thing," he said of Vietnam, "we'll solve it." To that end he marshaled a dazzling array of facts and figures that only tended to obscure the larger issues. Unfortunately the president's policymaking style exacerbated the defense secretary's own blind spots. Instead of developing a coordinative national strategy to inform and integrate the administration's diplomatic, political, military, and economic policies in Vietnam, Johnson compartmentalized the categories, held off making decisions as long as he could, and frequently changed his mind after apparently deciding on a course of action. As late as September 1966, White House Press Secretary Bill D. Moyers warned Johnson that though now at war in Vietnam, "the Government is not really organized for war"; consequently it was "fighting a war on a part-time basis."[23]

---

* Australian peak strength in Vietnam eventually reached about 7,000; New Zealand's about 500; and South Korea's about 50,000 (SecDef FY 1969 Budget Statement, Feb 68, 45, fldr Vietnam 1968, box 36, SecDef Bio files, OSD Hist).
† See Chapter XVII on the Military Assistance Program.

Hidden Escalation

Based on the 1 and 2 April meetings, Wheeler, for the JCS, informed Sharp and Westmoreland on 3 April that the approved logistic reinforcements were preparatory to a probable three-division combat deployment; Joint Staff planning proceeded on this basis. McNamara then asked the Chiefs on 5 April for a detailed scheduling plan to introduce a two-or three-division force into South Vietnam "at the earliest practicable date." And the quick and contemptuous dismissal of the president's Johns Hopkins appeal by the North Vietnamese seemed to leave him more sympathetic to the military's deployment proposals.[24]

In late March, Westmoreland had asked for an infantry division, airborne brigade, and Marine battalion. Informed of the decision for the more modest deployment of marines during Taylor's Washington visit, on 12 April Westmoreland insisted that he still needed the airborne brigade for airfield security and as a mobile reserve. On 8 April the Joint Chiefs had met with a president worried over his lack of popular and congressional support, frustrated by the inability to defeat the VC quickly, dissatisfied with the South Vietnamese leadership, and wanting advice on how "to kill more Viet Cong." Greene thought that Johnson did "not seem to grasp the military details of what can and cannot be done in Vietnam." The general believed that unless North Vietnam agreed to negotiate, the United States could only withdraw from Vietnam or escalate the fighting. Either way the United States would get hurt.[25]

Five days later, at the Tuesday luncheon of 13 April, the president continued to withhold a decision on the JCS recommendation to deploy three divisions and their supporting units (180,000 men) because he lacked congressional support and was concerned over Hanoi-Peking reaction to such escalation. He criticized McNamara, Rusk, and the Joint Chiefs, asserting that he was "tired of taking the blame" for advisers whose advice "hadn't apparently been very good because we were losing the game." And although Johnson did not agree to the three-division proposal, he concurred in Westmoreland's recent request for an airborne brigade and several more Marine battalions (33,000 men with supporting units) to protect the expanding logistical forces and to conduct counterinsurgency combat operations. Immediately thereafter McNamara explained to the Chiefs that political sensitivity made the administration reluctant to intervene with large forces. They agreed on the need for caution to avoid charges of reckless escalation. Once McNamara departed, however, Wheeler, apparently frustrated that the president did not authorize the three divisions, told his fellow officers that their civilian leaders had led them into a trap and were getting ready to shift the blame for any failure in Vietnam to the senior officers' shoulders.[26]

The next day (14 April), having been informed of this latest decision by a JCS message sent from Washington on the 13th, Ambassador Taylor cabled Rusk and expressed surprise, noting that during his recent visit in Washington it had been decided that "we would experiment with the Marines in a counterinsurgency role before bringing in other U.S. contingents." He recommended delay pending clarification. That confusion abounded was evident when Rusk phoned McNamara and stated that he was not quite sure what decisions the president had made at the previous day's luncheon. Moreover, Congress needed to be consulted. Stating that clearance from the Vietnamese government was equally necessary, McNamara indicated that "he would try to pull the pieces together this morning."

Rusk then called Bundy and asked "what the decisions were yesterday." Bundy claimed the JCS had "confused matters" with their cable and that he hoped that he, McNamara, and Rusk could meet with the president after OSD prepared a draft reply to Taylor. Rusk and McNamara later discussed the draft, during which the former observed that Taylor would not favor the proposed actions and should be consulted. McNamara replied that not only Taylor but "a lot of people" would not favor the proposed actions but added that "someone has to make a decision" and that it would be sent to Taylor specifically as a directive.[27]

As finally drafted, approved by the president, and sent to Taylor during the early evening of 15 April, the directive contained a preamble stating that in view of the deteriorating situation "something new must be added in the South to achieve victory." To that end the administration proposed seven individual actions, the first three of which involved combat operations. All were regarded as "experimental." The first called for encadrement, assigning U.S. troops to about 10 Vietnamese units and/or combined operations at battalion-level. The second would introduce a U.S. Army brigade to Bien Hoa to protect U.S. bases and conduct counterinsurgency operations. The third would deploy battalion-size or larger units at two or three coastal enclaves for the same purpose. If successful, these moves would be followed by requests for additional U.S. forces.[28]

Taylor was "greatly troubled" by the president's directive. In a series of four same-day cables to Washington, he vented his anger about being blindsided and set out his thinking on why some of the proposals should not be implemented and the reasons for his unwillingness to discuss them with the Vietnamese government. He obviously wanted far more consideration of what he deemed fundamental changes to U.S. policy and the American role in the war. Anxious to get Taylor on board, Johnson suspended implementation of his directive and called for a McNamara-led comprehensive review in Hawaii with Wheeler, Westmoreland, Sharp, McNaughton, and William Bundy. Taylor "was ordered to proceed" to the conference, as he noted in his diary.[29]

On the eve of McNamara's departure for Honolulu, the Joint Chiefs gave the secretary a deployment proposal in answer to his 5 April request. It was based largely on a CINCPAC plan for a three-division force, plus the 173d Airborne Brigade, to execute a four-stage operation: (1) securing coastal enclaves; (2) conducting offensive operations from the enclaves; (3) securing highland (inland) bases; and (4) launching offensive operations from the inland bases. The secretary was unenthusiastic about committing that many troops even though he had originally suggested a two- or three-division basis for the study.[30]

Two executive sessions held on 20 April in Honolulu aired fundamental disagreements between the participants. The military wanted two divisions and two brigades dispatched to Vietnam. The civilians, while accepting the need for reinforcements, generally opposed committing the two divisions. Taylor found his position opposing large-scale combat troop deployments generally untenable, undermined by South Vietnamese military incompetence. The participants compromised by proposing the two-brigade Army deployment plus three additional Marine battalions, less than half the Joint Chiefs' recommendation, plus numerous logistics support units. McNamara reported to the president that all conferees had agreed that another 48,000 U.S. service personnel should be deployed, raising the total in Vietnam to 82,000, with still more to follow, if needed.[*] He advised Johnson to notify congressional leaders of the contemplated deployments and the changed mission of U.S. forces and indicated that it might take at least six months and perhaps a year or two to demonstrate VC failure in the South. The compromise at Honolulu served to defer consideration of comprehensive future military requirements in favor of providing forces immediately to avoid defeat.[31]

At a White House meeting on 21 April the president listened to the pros and cons of McNamara's proposals for reinforcements. Several participants voiced skepticism. Under Secretary of State George W. Ball vigorously favored negotiation over military escalation; McGeorge Bundy wanted assessment of likely Soviet and Chinese reactions to large ground deployments; Central Intelligence Agency (CIA) Director John A. McCone, not a favorite of the president and due to leave office the following week, feared the incremental deployments "would drift into a combat situation where victory would be dubious and from which we could not extricate ourselves." Later that day in an interdepartmental intelligence report McCone warned that U.S. troops might get bogged down in Vietnam; on the other hand "intervention and military success" might convince the communists to opt for a temporary political settlement.[32]

The president made no decision, but the next day Rusk notified Taylor that Johnson was "inclined" to approve the deployments and, at the president's direction, added that the administration did not intend to publicize the entire program but rather to "announce individual deployments at appropriate times." This approach established a pattern of behavior about troop deployments that persisted throughout Johnson's tenure. First, formal military requests were severely pared or ignored when initially submitted, then eventually got fulfilled in piecemeal increments. Second, by not releasing news of the latest reinforcement, apparently to avoid public debate that might prove detrimental to his Great Society objectives, Johnson withheld from the American people information about the scope of his Vietnam commitment.[33]

---

[*] In addition, the conference recommended the deployment of 4,000 Korean troops and 1,250 Australians.

More Troops, More Money

The president now sought to orchestrate a public opinion campaign to gain greater popular support for administration policies. McNamara's 26 April press conference hammered on North Vietnamese infiltration into the South. On the 28th, he met with House leaders to suggest ways that Congress could mobilize public sentiment for the war and demonstrate near unanimous support for the president's policy. The next day in a closed executive session of the Senate Committee on Armed Services, McNamara reemphasized the threat to the South but equivocated about major U.S. reinforcements being sent to Vietnam.[34]

The president simultaneously pursued three parallel tracks. First, McNamara and Rusk worked to influence domestic and world opinion by proposing to suspend bombing of the North and to pursue a diplomatic solution in support of the U.S. position. Second, in Saigon Taylor met with Vietnamese officials in strictest secrecy about deploying additional U.S. and foreign combat troops to Vietnam. Third, on 30 April the Joint Chiefs provided the plan to meet the Honolulu deployment proposals, recommending to McNamara an increase of about 48,000 troops (raising the number in Vietnam to 82,000) with future additional reinforcements of 56,000—a total equivalent to their desired three-division force.[35]

McNaughton found the 30 April numbers proposed by the JCS, adding 56,000 to the 82,000 figure agreed on in Honolulu, far in excess. He advised McNamara to scale them back and approve the JCS proposal solely for planning purposes. On 15 May McNamara notified the Chiefs that there would be "continuing high-level deliberations" on the matter. Meanwhile, on 30 April the president approved the pending deployment of the Army brigade and three Marine battalions after Taylor assured him that the South Vietnamese prime minister agreed to the introduction of more U.S. forces.[36]

In the midst of these events, the Dominican Republic crisis erupted on 24 April, temporarily drawing attention away from Vietnam. Johnson had already made basic decisions about Vietnam regardless of events in the Caribbean, but he did use the emergency to extract from Congress an endorsement of the Southeast Asia policies. On 4 May, the president asked Congress for $700 million in additional funds to cover the unanticipated costs of operations in Vietnam and warned that he might need more. Johnson noted that a vote for the request would indicate congressional support for his actions against communist aggression. Unstated was that it would also avoid a public policy debate on Vietnam—he linked the appropriation to congressional support for U.S. operations in Vietnam. As anticipated, Congress approved the emergency appropriation by overwhelming majorities, 408 to 7 in the House on the 5th and 88 to 3 in the Senate on the 6th, and the president signed the bill the next day.[37]

The Enemy Dictates the Course of Action

On 11 May the Viet Cong launched the long predicted general offensive to split South Vietnam in half. The incompetence of Army of the Republic of South Vietnam (ARVN) forces during a prolonged battle (29 May–4 June) for Ba Gia painfully exposed the possibility of South Vietnam's early military collapse. All during June the president and his advisers wrestled with adjusting the size of the force to be sent to assist South Vietnam. The numbers varied greatly depending on the source of the estimate. From Saigon Taylor warned on 5 June that further VC victories might lead to a complete collapse of the ARVN and require additional U.S. ground troops. The assessment caused many of the administration's top civilians to meet the same day at State and, unexpectedly, the president joined them. They reached no decisions but the president foresaw "great danger" and the arrival of "a big problem any day." It arrived two days later in the form of a cable from Westmoreland. The MACV commander saw no alternative course of action but to bring in additional U.S. and allied forces as soon as possible. He wanted more marines, an army airmobile division, a Korean division, all with supporting units—an overall total in Vietnam of 123,000 Americans and possibly more to fight a large-unit war against the Viet Cong and the growing number of infiltrating North Vietnamese soldiers. McNamara later described the cable as the most disturbing he received during his seven-year DoD tenure. In starkest terms this meant the administration had to decide on war or withdrawal.[38] Characterized by agonizing indecision, the process would involve intensive study and daily or more frequent meetings before a choice was made some seven weeks later.

McNamara's concern reflected the administration's sense that the VC guerrillas and North Vietnamese troops were taking over the South Vietnamese countryside. Still, there was no military or political consensus on what to do. The Joint Chiefs split over the details of deployment and the use of both ground and air forces but agreed on the need to send reinforcements. McNamara, however, advocated deferring or limiting the size of the reinforcements. At a White House meeting on 10 June with top officials including Taylor, who had been called home once again for emergency consultations, McNamara recommended halving Westmoreland's request, which would still offer "a plan to cover us to end of year." That evening he expressed his apprehension to Johnson about the open-ended troop commitment the military was seeking.[39]

The Joint Chiefs wanted to meet Westmoreland's troop request and augment it with a more punishing air campaign against the North. They differed with Westmoreland on the placement and use of the reinforcements, preferring coastal enclaves instead of the central highlands that he favored. An NSC meeting on 11 June aired the overall deployment subject but reached no decision. Taylor returned to Vietnam with the understanding that the president would further review the differing recommendations at his ranch over the weekend.[40]

On 16 June during a televised press conference, McNamara announced that the 54,000 U.S. personnel in Vietnam would soon be increased to 70,000–75,000. However he did not say that the decision for this increase had been made more than two months previously and the president was already considering even larger additions. The troop mission, as defined by McNamara, was to protect U.S. bases, but Westmoreland could use them in combat if requested by the Vietnamese. He failed to mention that the president had made that decision in early April. At his 17 June press conference, the president vigorously defended his actions, asserting that the August 1964 Gulf of Tonkin resolution gave him the authority as commander in chief to take all necessary steps to protect American forces and counter aggression.[41]

Johnson tended to support McNamara's recommendations to send just enough forces to perhaps save South Vietnam but provoke neither Chinese intervention nor congressional scrutiny. By holding on through the summer and not irreversibly committing the United States to a major ground war, they hoped to keep U.S. options open, but what that policy meant in terms of future reinforcements the president neither spelled out nor decided. Johnson admitted to McNamara that he was "just praying and gasping to hold on during monsoon [May through October] and hope they'll quit."[42] Events in South Vietnam, however, outpaced the policy-making process in Washington.

On 12 June, South Vietnam's military took control of the government in a bloodless coup and later installed Generals Nguyen Cao Ky as prime minister and Nguyen Van Thieu as chief of state. Concurrently Westmoreland reported that the VC were destroying ARVN battalions (five in the past three weeks) faster than the units could be created and trained and again urged immediate and substantial U.S. reinforcements, including an airmobile division. Heeding Westmoreland's appeals, McNamara instructed the Chiefs to increase the overall U.S. commitment by the end of July from approximately 60,000 to 98,000 men. He shared with Johnson the view that additional military force might at best convince the communists that they could not win in Vietnam and at worst prevent for the time being the loss of South Vietnam. On 18 June the Joint Chiefs furnished McNamara their revised deployment schedule; the same day the president decided in principle to send the requested airmobile division to Vietnam and withdraw two brigades currently there by 1 September. This would raise the U.S. military ceiling in Vietnam to about 95,000; however, sometime before 1 September the president would reexamine the withdrawal portion of his decision and decide whether to retain the two brigades and thereby raise overall strength to 115,000.[43]

Secretly commissioned surveys to test public reaction to larger deployments indicated that half or more favored such action. Would the respondents have been as supportive of the president if he had informed the public about the precarious condition of South Vietnam and the likelihood of a drawn-out war? McNamara certainly did not intend to tell the American people that the administration's evolving strategy sought a military stalemate in South Vietnam accompanied by limited bombing of the North to produce at length a negotiated settlement, because he did not judge Americans tough enough to see such a policy through.[44]

McNamara's 180-Degree Turn

Doubts about the administration's candor and transparency contributed to a credibility gap. Some reporters, like Joseph Alsop, wrote that the rise to 75,000 had long been decided and further increases were pending. He accused the president of trying to stage-manage the news to fight a major war in "a furtive manner." Another columnist on 20 June noted that the 75,000 figure had been "gossiped about weeks ago" and dismissed by the administration. "Now the talk mentions 300,000. . . . That talk, too, is denied or disowned. But. . . ." By deploying the minimum force needed Johnson believed that he was not making irreversible decisions, thereby keeping options open.[45] If conditions worsened, he had the option of strengthening U.S. forces by using the airmobile division to reinforce, not re-place, U.S. units. Still uncertain exactly what course to pursue, Johnson wanted no public debate on his Vietnam policies.

On 18 June, Ball had warned Johnson to limit the U.S. military commitment in size and duration, thus keeping open the possibility of either greater involve-ment or disengagement. Five days later Johnson convened a White House meeting to assess the deepening U.S. military involvement. All agreed that more troops would be needed, but Ball wanted a cap at 100,000; if they were unable to tip the military balance then consideration should be given to withdrawal and a shift to using Thailand as the base of the anticommunist effort. On the other hand, McNamara and Rusk believed that Vietnam's defeat meant the loss of Thailand as well and McNamara argued for more reinforcements accompanied by greater diplomatic efforts. The president said little and concluded the meeting by direct-ing McNamara and Ball to make military and political recommendations for the next three months and report back to him in one week. Sixteen people attended the session, but they were not specialists on Vietnam and appear to have calculated their positions more from intuition than knowledge.[46]

McNamara second-guessed his earlier decisions at a 25 June session with the Joint Chiefs. He wondered aloud if a major commitment a year earlier might have turned the tide. This "180 degree turn" convinced Greene that the president and his "small coterie" of advisers, including Wheeler, were taking steps to address the Vietnam predicament while leaving the Chiefs "out of the stream of military actions," consulting them only after the civilians had made the decisions. Yet the JCS also remained divided over a military strategy for Vietnam. In a meeting of the service chiefs the same day, McConnell argued that they would be "criminally re-sponsible" if they sent more ground troops to the South before "completely knock-ing out the North Vietnamese with air power."[47]

On 26 June McNamara circulated for comment a draft memo prepared by McNaughton. In a radical policy shift, he proposed to increase the number of U.S. troops in South Vietnam to 200,000, mobilize 100,000 reserves, conduct intensified naval and air attacks on the North and, in an attempt to stop the shipment of all war supplies into North Vietnam, mine harbors, wreck all rail and highway bridges between China and North Vietnam, and destroy the enemy's warmaking supplies and facilities, airfields, and surface-to-air missile (SAM) sites. An intensified political effort to gain a negotiated settlement would accompany the expanded military campaign. McNamara later attributed his conversion to a troubling message on 24 June from Westmoreland that predicted a protracted war of attrition requiring numbers of U.S. combat troops well beyond those requested in his 7 June cable.[48]

Although McGeorge Bundy sharply disagreed with McNamara' proposals to double personnel strength in Vietnam, triple the air effort against the North, and impose a naval quarantine there and described them as "rash to the point of folly," it was apparent that the recent upsurge of communist attacks demanded action. Taylor described Generals Ky and Thieu as "sober-faced and depressed" over the series of recent battlefield reverses and asking for more U.S. combat troops. Emboldened by their success, the VC had also become more active around Da Nang. The administration responded by deploying more marines to the area despite the ongoing policy review and advice to avoid giving the impression the United States was taking over the war.[49]

As the Chiefs subsequently developed their plans, McConnell argued for heavier bombing of "worthwhile targets" in North Vietnam before introducing more troops. A few days later on 2 July, with South Vietnam falling apart, Greene counseled unanimity among the Chiefs, and Wheeler admonished that partisan disagreements along service lines harmed their image. Again the military men compromised to prevent McNamara from exploiting their differences but at the expense of forgoing a full airing of their concerns at the highest level. As requested by McNamara, their 2 July plan included more airpower and met MACV's request for 175,000 American troops (some 60,000 above the 18 June program), most to arrive by 1 October 1965.[50] The president never approved these recommendations as a single program, but Westmoreland's June request became the de facto basis for the piecemeal reinforcement that followed.

Anticipating the JCS, on 1 July McNamara forwarded to the president the revised version of his 26 June draft memorandum. It remained a hardline call for a much expanded ground war waged by 44 combat battalions (34 U.S.), mobilization of the reserves, and a dramatic escalation in the air and naval campaigns against North Vietnam as well as an intense effort to obtain a diplomatic solution through negotiation. Although anticipating increased casualties in a wider war sure to continue for some time, McNamara believed the American public would support this "combined military-political program" because it was "likely to bring about a favorable solution to the Vietnam problem."[51]

Conflicting Assessments

On 1 July McGeorge Bundy presented the McNamara memorandum and three other documents (one each from Rusk, Ball, and William Bundy) to the president in preparation for a White House meeting with them the next day. Bundy regarded McNamara as deadly serious about his hawkish recommendations for troop increases, but flexible on the bombing and blockade issues. A few hours before the meeting McNamara discussed his hardline approach with the president by phone. Johnson wanted some assurance that the United States could win and that domestic support for the war would remain solid in the absence of further congressional authority. He remarked that McNamara's proposal to commit large numbers of ground troops and to call up the reserves "makes sense."[52]

At the White House session, the president discussed the four memoranda: McNamara's call for simultaneous military and diplomatic offensives; Ball's proposal for holding on to secure a compromise settlement; William Bundy's paper expounding a "middle course" between the McNamara and Ball positions; and Rusk's direct warning that the United States could not abandon Vietnam. McNamara later recalled that Johnson "seemed deeply torn over what to do." Instead of resolution, the president postponed a major decision on Vietnam until the end of July because it might endanger the Medicare and voting rights bills currently before Congress. He ended the 2 July session by directing his defense secretary, along with Wheeler and Henry Cabot Lodge (newly appointed to replace Taylor as ambassador to South Vietnam),* to visit Saigon for another look at the political and military situation. The president also dispatched Ambassador at Large W. Averell Harriman to Moscow to explore reconvening the Geneva Conference and Ball to Paris in an attempt to reopen contact with Hanoi's representative there. McNamara's proposal had proven too extreme for a president who cherished compromise and consensus and, on Vietnam, wanted a middle course between the extremes of massive military escalation and humiliating withdrawal. As McGeorge Bundy later described it, Johnson adhered to the "principle of minimum necessary action."[53]

Meanwhile, McNamara had asked the Joint Chiefs and Westmoreland to reexamine their recommendations for more ground troops and airpower. Judging the ARVN unreliable for the task, he agreed that more U.S. troops were needed but he wanted to know what they expected 44 battalions would achieve. Over the next several weeks, McNamara repeatedly sought the answer; in turn Wheeler questioned Westmoreland. The MACV commander's reply was that with the reinforcements he expected to reestablish a military balance with the communists by year's end. More troops would be required in 1966, and a limited recall of reserves would send a strong signal of U.S. resolve to Hanoi and Peking. As to the clarity McNa-

---

* On 8 July the White House announced that Taylor would step down. Taylor had accepted the assignment in June 1964 with the understanding that for personal reasons it be limited to about one year. See Taylor, *Swords and Plowshares*, 313-14.

mara obviously wanted, Westmoreland stated, "We cannot now give SecDef the definitive answer he seeks. There are simply too many unknowns at this juncture."[54]

Unable to get assurances from military commanders that 44 battalions would suffice, McNamara posed the question differently to Wheeler. If the United States did everything it could in Vietnam, McNamara asked, what assurance was there of winning the war? Without notifying his fellow Chiefs, Wheeler tasked his special assistant, General Goodpaster, to work with McNaughton and a joint team to produce an estimate before the secretary left for Saigon in mid-July. McNaughton hoped the study would produce a strategy for winning the war in South Vietnam, by which he meant "demonstrating to the VC that they cannot win."[55]

During the interim, the CIA and the Defense Intelligence Agency (DIA) weighed in with their analyses. Both described the Viet Cong's summer offensive, abetted by infiltration of men and sophisticated weaponry from the North, as punishing ARVN forces and eroding popular confidence in the South Vietnamese government. The reports expected deepening U.S. military involvement in the fighting but acknowledged there was no way to measure its effect on the enemy at the time. Contrary to a MACV analysis, both CIA and DIA tended to believe that the conflict would remain a guerrilla war punctuated by occasional large-unit operations.[56]

Preparing for his visit to Saigon, McNamara cabled Taylor on 7 July requesting the ambassador's views and recommendations on a range of topics related to the deployment and use of U.S. reinforcements. Two days later McNamara met with top OSD officials to establish schedules, identify requirements as well as problems, and assign tasks and direct actions leading to buildup decisions upon his return from Vietnam. He also placed Vance in charge of the various working groups responsible for drafting appropriate messages, legislation, and background papers. There were to be no net reductions from NATO either in manpower or equipment to pay for the buildup in Vietnam. Moreover, it seemed preferable to seek a congressional authorization action similar to that obtained during the Berlin Crisis in 1961 rather than a presidential declaration of emergency. In order to deploy 175,000 troops by 1 November 1965 and even more in 1966, OSD planned to obtain a congressional resolution for a large call-up of selected Army Reserve units and the reserve 4th Marine Division and to request a supplemental budget appropriation.[57]

McNamara planned that after his return from Vietnam (scheduled for 22 July) there would be discussions with the State Department and White House concluding with a presidential decision about Vietnam on 26 July, followed two days later by a request to Congress for enabling legislation. As part of his legislative package, the secretary wanted authorization for the president to call up reserves and extend tours involuntarily as well as provision for budget supplements or amendments. He asked also for a program of public statements to prepare the American people for the grave commitment their leaders were about to undertake in Vietnam.[58]

It was at this time that many senior Pentagon people learned for the first time that large-scale intervention was even under consideration. One of his top civilian assistants asked McNamara later how he could have missed overhearing a single word about such an important and complex undertaking. The decision, McNamara replied, was made very secretly "across the river" (in the White House); it was never discussed in the Pentagon. According to Greene, the Joint Chiefs were especially discouraged by their exclusion from policy deliberations. When McNamara did explain his scenario to the Chiefs on 10 July, he left Greene with an impression of a "slightly condescending and impatient" executive informing them of decisions already made "only because he felt he had to." Since McNamara had not consulted the Joint Chiefs as a body beforehand, he had, in Greene's opinion, carefully thought through neither the requirements for additional forces nor deployment issues.[59]

McNamara met a few days later on 12 July with the service secretaries and his top staff members to discuss mobilization and overall increases in service strengths. He wanted preparation of a joint congressional resolution allowing for a 24-month call-up of reserves with the objective of releasing them after 12 months, if possible. He also wanted them to consider a plan to almost double the deployment in Vietnam from 34 to 63 U.S. combat battalions. Vance also planned to confer with Sen. John Stennis (D-Miss.), acting chairman of the Senate Appropriations Committee's DoD subcommittee, on the desirability of deferring any Vietnam supplemental appropriations until after passage of the FY 1966 Defense appropriations bill. He charged Vance to meet daily, beginning 15 July, with major DoD participants, complete a staff study on the buildup before McNamara's return from Vietnam, and report on problem areas in need of solution or clarification—all in the strictest secrecy. McNamara also informed Stennis on 14 July that a U.S. force increase in Vietnam would include a reserve call-up, higher draft calls, and a supplemental budget request.[60]

McNaughton's 13 July draft of "Analyses and Options for South Vietnam," prepared for McNamara's trip book, recommended committing 180,000 U.S. and more than 20,000 allied ground troops to fight a conventional war in South Vietnam. The scenario mobilized the reserves, considered constructing an electrified fence across the Ho Chi Minh Trail in Laos, and continued the bombing of the North more or less at current levels. These actions would likely achieve a stalemate and compromise settlement.[61] This separate conclusion by McNaughton differed sharply from the Goodpaster study group's report of 14 July presented to McNamara that day as he departed for Saigon.

The Goodpaster report also foresaw U.S. troops fighting large enemy units in South Vietnam away from population centers and it proposed greatly increased air attacks against North Vietnam on the assumption that China and the Soviet Union would stay out of the fighting. The study concluded, however, that there was no reason the United States could not win (defining victory as the destruction of at least 75 percent of the organized communist battalions), provided the will existed to sustain a considerable enlargement of the commitment. Goodpaster later remarked that McNamara took no "explicit action" on the study, and indeed the defense secretary never endorsed the report. McNamara did support recommendations for aggressive offensive operations to "locate and destroy" VC and NVA forces in South Vietnam.[62]

On 15 July Vance presided at the initial meeting of the service secretaries and OSD assistant secretaries, working against a 19 July deadline. At subsequent meetings the participants drafted a presidential statement and sent it to Saigon so that McNamara, Lodge, and Wheeler might review it before returning to Washington. Warning orders for possible deployment to Vietnam had already been issued to the airmobile division and its supporting units, a total of about 28,000 troops. To ensure confidentiality, only OSD Public Affairs personnel were to reply to media questions about any planned buildup. Vance issued guidance to the military services for their respective reserve mobilization and active force expansion in what came to be known as Plan I.[63]

Vance also learned from the president that he intended to approve Westmoreland's long-pending request for additional U.S. forces. The next day Vance sent a top-secret, "literally eyes only" back-channel cable informing McNamara in Saigon. He explained that on 16 July he had met three times with "Highest Authority" (the president) whose "current intention" was to approve the 34-battalion plan. Vance also stated that the president would not seek the required supplementary funds to cover both the deployment and the reserve recall for fear such a large request would "kill" his domestic legislative program. Instead, by using the May supplemental ($700 million), a small ($300–400 million) new supplemental, and deficit financing,* it would be possible to tell Congress that adequate authority and funds currently existed. The same cable informed McNamara that the president agreed to seek legislation for the reserve call-up.[64]

Meanwhile the daily Vietnam planning sessions to implement the presidential guidance continued in the Pentagon. At their third meeting, on 17 July, the conferees agreed to seek legislative authority to call up 250,000 reservists, chiefly for the Army and Marine Corps, for a period of two years and to extend enlistments by two years. DoD's acting general counsel, Leonard Niederlehner, was instructed to prepare draft legislation acceptable in principle to Sen. Richard B. Russell (D-Ga.) and Rep. L. Mendel Rivers (D-S.C.), respectively, chairmen of the Senate and House Committees on Armed Services.[65]

At the fifth and final of the Vance meetings, on 20 July, the committee agreed to change the draft legislation for both the reserve call-up and the enlistment extension to only 12 months. Budgetary submissions would stay at "minimum essential" requirements. A draft scenario envisioned the president briefing selected leaders of Congress at the White House about the administration's intentions,

---

* Existing legislation enabled the secretary of defense to cover costs of additional personnel for purposes of national defense. See Chapter IV.

while McNamara would do the same for members of the armed services and appropriations committees. To add to the impact of his address to the nation the president would also make public the large numbers of troops involved, with the listing of the reserve units to follow.[66]

During the secretary's trip to Vietnam, Vance and his committee worked long hours to prepare the budget and manpower numbers for the anticipated large-scale deployment of U.S. troops. Under their Plan I, the administration would deploy an additional 100,000 troops to Vietnam for a total of 175,000 by 1 November. The president would ask Congress to approve an extended enlistment period, a large reserve call-up, and a supplemental request for an addition to the pending DoD appropriation. Eventually the number would go higher, but for initial budgetary planning purposes the anticipated recall was for about 156,000 reservists,[*] of which 100,000 Army reservists would form infantry, combat service support, and training units to replace those deploying to Vietnam. The Vance committee left undone only filling in the blanks in the president's address with the final numbers of men and units to be recalled and the money appropriated.[67]

Funding the war without asking for an alarming amount of money presented a special problem. To preserve his Great Society programs the president further cut the already radically reduced service requests for supplemental funding. It did not help that in an assessment requested by State at the insistence of Vance, the CIA on 20 July concluded that larger U.S. ground forces and increased air attacks would not sway Hanoi from its course in the South. The Soviets and the Chinese Communists would remain adamantly opposed to U.S. intervention and "there would still be increased apprehension among non-communist countries."[68]

During the frenetic Washington activity, the secretary of defense was conducting his own whirlwind policy review in Saigon. The meetings, McNamara later wrote, "reinforced many of my worst fears and doubts." Later he faulted himself for not questioning fundamental assumptions about the nature of the war. When McNamara arrived in Saigon on 16 July he believed more U.S. troops were needed in Vietnam but still wanted assurance that sending them would achieve U.S. goals. Upon his arrival, he reviewed Taylor's and Westmoreland's written answers to his 7 July cable. Their replies told him that the enemy could match increases in U.S. forces and implicitly acknowledged that the communists held the initiative. The enemy could simply avoid large-scale decisive military confrontations by melting into the population or withdrawing to isolated areas firmly under its control. In short, the proposed military strategy would not eliminate the Viet Cong hold on important segments of the country. Even assuming that U.S. forces would destroy main enemy units, American battlefield success might mean little unless the South Vietnamese forces could reestablish a government presence in the cleared areas. Asked by McNamara for assurances on winning, Taylor only promised the costly

---

[*] Including 6,000 Navy personnel, 39,000 Marines, and 11,000 Air Force.

prospect of a "campaign of uncertain duration." By December 1965 the rate of U.S. casualties, admittedly based on guesswork, might run 500 killed and 2,100 wounded a month, an overall total of about 31,000 in 1966. (Actual U.S. casualties in 1966 were 5,008 killed and 30,093 wounded.)[69]

By any measure the war would have to be won in South Vietnam where all statistical indicators—rising desertion rates, mounting losses of weapons, increasing terrorism and growing inflation—pointed to an ARVN defeat. Over the past year, the Saigon government had steadily lost control over territory, population, and transportation networks while the military had lost the initiative to the communists and the people had lost confidence in their leaders. The minimum strength deemed necessary to reverse the current losing trend was more than 176,000 allied troops, predominantly U.S. ground forces (about 155,000) in Phase I, which would continue through 1965. Phase II, to convince the North Vietnamese that they could not win, would require an additional 95,000 personnel, again most of them ground troops, for a total of almost 271,000 allied personnel in Vietnam by the close of 1966.[70]

The afternoon of 16 July Thieu and Ky met with the secretary and his party and told them not to expect spectacular results from a government just three weeks old. Their "total war" against the communists would require both American economic and military assistance. Asked by McNamara about the number of allied troops needed, the Vietnamese mentioned the 44 battalions being planned plus another infantry division. This would raise the foreign military presence in Vietnam to more than 200,000, but Ky reassured the secretary that the Vietnamese people could accommodate such a rapid influx without fearing the possible imposition of a new colonial power. After all, the troops would be fighting far from the populated areas and by freeing the ARVN for pacification duties would contribute to the stable government everyone desired.[71]

Convinced of the seriousness of the military situation by MACV and embassy briefings that reinforced his predisposition to commit U.S. troops, McNamara accepted the Army's search-and-destroy approach and the requirements for large ground forces that went along with it. He also asked Westmoreland if he needed anything else. In response, MACV prepared a "shopping list," calling for even more troops.[72] Whatever his later disclaimers, McNamara had asked hard questions in Saigon and had gotten candid answers. Yet he remained optimistic, viewing the massive troop deployment as a carefully orchestrated prelude to an extended pause in the bombing of North Vietnam that might convince Hanoi to negotiate a settlement.

McNamara had listened carefully to what others told him; he forced officials to address difficulties squarely; and after gathering the data he analyzed the possible solutions. His 20 July report to the president minced no words when recounting the grave status of the Saigon regime and the conditions it faced. The situation was worse than a year ago, when it was even worse than the year before that. The

VC had the government forces on the run, and the Ky regime would likely not last out the year. Nor had U.S. airpower made Hanoi receptive to talks. Three options lay open to the United States: (1) a humiliating withdrawal; (2) holding on at current levels; or (3) escalating U.S. military pressure. Only the third alternative seemed acceptable, but it involved increasing the U.S. force of 75,000 in Vietnam to 175,000 men by October, contemplating another large deployment (perhaps 100,000 troops) that might be necessary in early 1966, and, depending on developments, sending in even more thereafter. To achieve this expansion, McNamara recommended an increase of 375,000 in the armed forces, a call-up of 235,000 from the Reserve and National Guard, and an expanded monthly draft. He also listed the need for a supplemental FY 1966 appropriation of a yet to be determined amount. The major participants in the Saigon meetings—Taylor, Lodge, Deputy Ambassador to Vietnam U. Alexis Johnson, Wheeler, Sharp, and Westmoreland— endorsed McNamara's proposal, which incorporated the DoD-produced Plan I.[73]

Assuming an imminent large deployment of U.S. combat forces to Vietnam, escalation and mobilization became central topics of discussion at a series of presidential meetings held between 21 and 27 July. Gathering once, twice, and even three times a day, the president's senior advisers reviewed the available options. The agenda, or "Checklist of Actions," closely followed McGeorge Bundy's and McNamara's scenarios for stretching out the policy deliberations to avoid giving the public the impression of a hastily made decision.[74]

On the 21st, McNamara initially met with senior officials from the White House, State and Defense Departments, CIA, and the NSC. Put simply, he reported that the war in South Vietnam was being lost and U.S. ground troops were needed to reverse the situation—a substantial policy change committing large numbers of ground forces to fight a conventional war in South Vietnam. President Johnson joined the group later, questioned the consequences of such a large call-up, and solicited alternatives. When Ball dissented from the McNamara proposal, the president called for another meeting that afternoon. At that time Ball again argued against McNamara and declared that the United States could not win a protracted war in Southeast Asia. In rebuttal, Bundy, Rusk, and McNamara argued that a unilateral withdrawal would only encourage further communist aggression.[75]

Meeting on 22 July with McNamara, Vance, the Joint Chiefs, and other top Pentagon officials, the president reviewed McNamara's recommendations and sought the participants' views. Withdrawal did not constitute an option because, as McNamara contended, and others agreed, South Vietnam's loss would start the dominos falling. President Johnson expressed concern that the North Vietnamese would simply match U.S. reinforcements, but Wheeler assured him that they could not match a U.S. buildup and, "from [a] military view," the United States could handle both North Vietnam and China. Greene told the president the military effort would take 500,000 troops and five years, and McNamara placed the cost of increased intervention at $12 billion in 1966. When the president suggested that hundreds of thousands of troops and billions of dollars might provoke China and Russia to intervene, General Johnson doubted either would enter the fighting. But what if they did? "If so," replied the general after a long silence, "we have another ball game." The president reminded him, "But I have to take into account they will."[76]

A few hours later Wheeler, fresh from another top-level White House meeting, notified the Chiefs that McNamara would meet with them on Saturday morning (24 July) to make final decisions. He also told them that the reserve Marine division would not be activated and that current thinking favored submitting two budget packages—an immediate supplemental request of $2 billion and a much larger one in January 1966 after Congress returned from its recess. McNamara subsequently issued new guidance to the service secretaries for preparing an option known as Plan II. This alternative still deployed large numbers of ground forces, but incrementally. It also deferred until September requests to Congress for the reserve call-up and supplemental funding.[77]

On 23 July, the president, McNamara, Rusk, Wheeler, Ball, Bundy, Press Secretary Moyers, and Special Presidential Assistant Horace Busby, Jr., assembled at the White House for a lengthy session. McNamara laid out three alternatives: the previously mentioned Plans I and II as well as a Plan III. The last would deploy the same numbers of forces but without a reserve call-up; request an immediate supplemental of only $1 billion; and in January request another $6 billion for FY 1966. It would meet the need for reinforcements and, hopefully, do so without provoking China or the Soviet Union. McNamara preferred Plan I, deploying 100,000 additional men in 1965 and another 100,000 in 1966, calling up the reserves, and adding $2 billion to the appropriations bill pending in the Senate. The president opted for Plan III.[78]

The President's Decision

Endless speculation has surrounded Johnson's change of mind about calling the reserves. Only a few days before, according to Vance on 17 July, the president was prepared to "bull it through." In his memoir Johnson explained that he did not wish to appear "too provocative and warlike" either to the American people or to China and the USSR. William Bundy believed Johnson's reluctance stemmed from his desire to fight the war with minimum disruption on the home front. McNamara shared that interpretation, later remembering that Johnson wanted "to avoid war hysteria, or fueling the fires of emotion in the nation" because of concern about triggering "a confrontation with the Chinese and/or the Soviets." Others argued that the sour aftertaste of the Berlin call-up of 1961, when people were summoned from their jobs to "sit in the can and go through some mickey-mouse drills," still lingered in politicians' memories. As the country's leader, Johnson did not want to do something "desperately unpopular," especially with those called up. Closer to the president's decision, on 26 July Johnson told Senator Russell, his longtime friend and mentor, that it would be "too dramatic" to call the reserves and it would make his position on Vietnam irreversible. Likewise he abhorred asking Congress for much money—a course recommended by McNamara—"because we don't want to blow this thing up."[79]

The twin specters of mobilization and higher taxes jolted Lyndon Johnson's ever sensitive political antenna. His sensibilities had already caused McGeorge Bundy to delete from his revised budget recommendation any mention of the potential threat that a large spending increase posed to the administration's domestic programs.[80] Not mobilizing the reserves saved money, but the trade-off was that a faster ground buildup in South Vietnam became impossible. Given the primitive logistics infrastructure in South Vietnam, a more rapid influx of U.S. combat forces was problematical. Such a course was acceptable to an administration that did not want a swift escalation that might spread into a wider conflict, but McNamara still had a war to fight.

After the 23 July decision, McNamara instructed the service secretaries to prepare a revised deployment and augmentation plan by the following morning. Without a reserve call-up, Plan III depended on higher draft calls to increase Army and Marine Corps end-strength. That evening the Joint Chiefs learned there would be no reserve call-up, with additional funding in the supplemental limited to $1 billion. Admiral McDonald, furious that the Joint Chiefs were "being four-flushed" by McNamara, speculated that the secretary was simply following the president's orders. McDonald observed that the absence of a call-up or large supplemental would only buttress the "national apathy" about Vietnam,[81] apparently what the president desired.

At his 24 July meeting with the Chiefs, McNamara discussed the implications of the president's decision. He explained there would be no reserve mobilization in order to reduce the "political 'noise level'" that might provoke China and the Soviet Union. When McDonald objected that it would "reduce [the] political noise level at home," McNamara "smilingly" replied that mobilization would create a divisive debate and give the communists the wrong impression. General Johnson recalled being "tongue-tied" because all Army contingency plans required a reserve call-up. He regained his voice to tell McNamara that the decision would erode the quality of the Army.[82]

On 26 July, Assistant Secretary of Defense for Manpower Norman S. Paul (Paul preceded Thomas Morris) notified McNamara that Army draft calls would rise significantly to obtain the 318,500 needed to fill the expanding ranks over the next 12 months, with increases from 16,500 in August 1965 to 27,400 the next month and then to 31,000 between November 1965 and January 1966. Paul provided the secretary with separate data regarding increased cost of readiness for selected reserve components plus associated costs.[83]

Meanwhile at Camp David on 25 July, Clark Clifford, a close friend and adviser to the president, restated his May warning that Vietnam could be a quagmire "without a realistic hope of ultimate victory" and counseled not deeper involvement but withdrawal. McNamara, however, insisted that without a rapid U.S. buildup South Vietnam would fall and, in turn, hurt the United States throughout the entire world.[84] Alone, Johnson pondered all that he had heard in recent days and apparently made his decision that evening at Camp David.

The NSC meeting of 27 July, expanded to include many other top administration leaders, merely affirmed what the president had already decided. Initially Rusk examined the international political scene and McNamara followed with a review of the alarming military situation in Vietnam, concluding that without additional armed support for the South a Hanoi triumph loomed inevitable. The president then summarized his alternatives: all-out aerial bombing; withdrawal; "hunker up," that is, just stay put at the current level; go on a war footing by calling the reserves, increasing the draft, and asking Congress for great sums of money; and, finally, "give our commanders in the field the men and supplies they say they need." Having stacked the deck, the president decided in favor of the last of these options, to the surprise of no one in the Cabinet Room. However, he promised to review the whole matter again in January. According to Johnson's account, when he asked each attendee if he agreed with his choice, each said "yes" or nodded approval.[85]

Ten minutes after the NSC meeting, Johnson, Rusk, McNamara, and others met with the joint congressional leadership, and the president recapitulated the alternatives. Johnson told them that he preferred to defer any major decision until January when the monsoon period would be over and the situation might be clearer; in the meantime he would consider several smaller reinforcement packages instead of a single large one. None of the legislators indicated opposition, although several implied their support rather than giving outright approval.[86]

McNamara had told NSC participants of plans to add 350,000 men to the armed forces over the next 15 months, almost double the troop commitment in Vietnam, but he made no mention of specific future deployment plans because the president had not approved any. Johnson spoke to legislators of perhaps sending three increments of 30,000 men each. McNamara's deployment scenario—originally known as the "July Plan" and later as Phase I—significantly modified the JCS recommendations of 2 July, added units from MACV's "shopping list" (about 7,000 men), and went to the president as an incremental buildup to about 195,000 U.S. troops (34 battalions and supporting units in Vietnam and another 17,000 troops in Thailand) by the end of December 1965. Although Johnson mentioned such an approach to congressional leaders on 27 July, he never formally approved MACV's and McNamara's recommendations as a single program.

While McNamara's Phase I proposal became the basis for DoD budgetary planning, he never furnished a copy to the Joint Chiefs.* Instead, following the president's preferences, McNamara would fill Westmoreland's requests directly and incrementally, bypassing the Chiefs and CINCPAC.[87]

At his press conference the next day (28 July), the president announced his decision to dispatch 50,000 more troops to Vietnam immediately, raising the authorization to 125,000, and promised to send additional forces as needed. Although draft calls would more than double, from 17,000 to 35,000 a month, he saw no need at this time to call up reserve units. He extended the olive branch to Hanoi, recalling his pledge "to begin unconditional discussions with any government, at any place, at any time."[88] North Vietnam's leader Ho Chi Minh was not swayed by Johnson's overtures.

Scarcely had the president spoken when on 30 July the Joint Chiefs presented McNamara with Westmoreland's request for 20,000 more troops during 1965. On 23 August, after another deployment planning conference in Hawaii earlier in the month, the Chiefs raised the troop requirement for Phase I to 210,000. To stay within the president's currently authorized 125,000 troop limit announced on 28 July, McNamara either had to request authorization for additional forces or halt scheduled movements to Vietnam by 1 September. On 1 September, McNamara requested 85,000 additional troops for a total of 210,000. The president did not approve the entire request for 210,000, but McNamara authorized, on an incremental basis, deployment of specific combat units as the Chiefs had recommended.[89]

Thus, three weeks later, on 22 September, the defense secretary tried again with a request for presidential approval of deployment of troops to the level of 210,000, describing this as "essential to our effort." After Johnson balked at exceeding 200,000, McNamara requested an interim deployment authorization of 20,000 beyond the total of 175,000 recommended in July (for an overall figure of 195,000) with the understanding that he would return in mid-November for the remaining 15,000 men. Johnson grudgingly agreed to the arrangement on 29 September, remarking that "he had no choice but to approve the increase."[90] Moreover, in keeping with current policy, there was no public announcement about the increase. Thus while the Joint Chiefs never received overall approval for their 23 August program of 34 battalions and 210,000 men, McNamara eventually gained presidential authority for such a commitment, albeit on a piecemeal basis.

---

* The JCS first learned of the existence of the Phase I deployment schedule in December 1965.

Table 1

U.S. Troop Deployments to South Vietnam, March–September 1965
(All figures rounded)

Date	Deployment	Remarks	Approved for Vietnam	Total Projected	Actually Deployed
31 Dec 1964		Already Present	23,000		23,000
6 Mar 1965	USMC		3,500		27,000 31 Mar
5 Apr 1965	USMC/ARMY	Army support units	23,500		
20 Apr 1965	JCS request additional 194,330 troops by Aug 1965	McNamara recommends 55,000 total (48,000 U.S.)	32,000	JCS 238,000 McNamara 82,000	33,000 20 Apr
SUBTOTAL			**82,300**	**82,000**	**42,000 5 May**
7 Jun 1965	Westmoreland requests 50,000 more troops (123,000 total)	McNamara reduces request	16,000 (from 48,000 recommended in April)	98,000 (projected end July)	53,000 8 Jun
1 Jul 1965	McNamara recommends 175,000 total	Becomes Phase I		175,000 (projected 1 Nov)	
	Wesmoreland Phase II adds 94,810 to Phase I	1966 requirements		270,972 (projected 31 Dec 66)	
28 Jul 1965	President approves 50,000 troops		50,000 (includes 16,000 above)	125,000 (projected 1 Sep 65)	80,000 29 Jul
20 Aug 1965	JCS request 210,000 total U.S. troops			210,000 (projected - most by 31 Dec)	
1 Sep 1965	McNamara recommends 85,000 more troops	President approves 50,000 (7 Sep)	50,000	Troop ceiling of 175,000	100,100 2 Sep
29 Sep 1965		President approves 35,000	35,000	Troop ceiling of 210,000	131,700 30 Sep
TOTAL			**217,000**	**210,000**	**131,700**

Sources: U.S. Military Buildup Strength in Vietnam, nd, c. Jan 1966, and NMCC, Deployments to Viet Nam Since 1 Jan 1965, 26 Jul 65: both fldr Build Up of U.S. Forces, box 369, Subj files, OSD Hist; memo SecDef for Pres, 21 Apr 65, *FRUS, 1964–68*, 2:575; DoD News Release, 405-65, 16 Jun 65; *McNamara Public Statements, 1965*, 5:1805-05A; Janicik, "Buildup," 122. The time required to prepare and transport units accounts for the strength differences between the approval date and the actual arrival in South Vietnam.

The policy decisions taken at this time clearly relied on the notion that the threat and use of escalating military force would prove too painful for the enemy and bring him to the negotiating table. This prevailing dictum did not take into account the impossibility of predicting with any precision the exact level of violence that would inflict more pain than Hanoi could endure. In the jargon of the day, "a pound of threat is worth an ounce of action—as long as we are not bluffing."

Yet neither threat nor action swayed Hanoi. U.S. civilian leaders in 1965, with the exception of Ball and Clifford, could not or would not contemplate the possibility that gradual escalation would degenerate into the commitment of massive military might without attaining the desired end.[91] They seem not to have realized the contradiction, not lost on Hanoi, between steadily upping the military ante and at the same time proclaiming willingness to negotiate an end to the conflict.

McNamara took pains to ensure the unanimity of the administration's position, thereby protecting the president. Air Force Secretary Eugene M. Zuckert (whom Harold Brown would succeed in October 1965) later described McNamara as "never more vigorous in defending a position than the one his boss had told him to take which he really didn't believe in, and he always overcompensated to make sure that his boss's position was the one that prevailed."[92] Still, in 1965 McNamara had become a leading proponent of massive military intervention in Vietnam. Once the president made his decision, McNamara showed no second thoughts and actively shaped the president's response to Vietnam critics.[93] His conduct exemplified his understanding of public service—expressing open disagreement would weaken not only the president but also the nation.

During the lengthy decisionmaking process the president relied on his immediate advisers but went his own way when his political antenna signaled to the contrary. Against McNamara's advice, in July 1965 Johnson deliberately played down the military and financial costs of intervention, preferring to cloak himself and his slow-emerging policy decisions in half-truths, evasions, and selective silence. In later years, McNamara rationalized that presidential deception was acceptable because the "deceit" grew from Johnson's desire to address the ills of American society.[94] Even granting that the end justified the means, such reasoning ignored the adverse military and budgetary ramifications of the president's decision, which resulted in reinforcements sent to Vietnam in piecemeal fashion, higher draft calls, an open-ended buildup, and mortgaging the cost of the intervention to ensure congressional approval of his Great Society legislation.

McNamara contributed to the deceit by dutifully concealing during 1965 the full extent and purpose of the administration's military intervention in Vietnam. But he made no attempt to hide the ever-expanding number of military personnel being deployed there and periodically reported accurately the growth from 23,000 in January, most of them advisers or training people, to more than 210,000 by December.[95] However, in keeping with the president's wishes, he was extremely sensitive and secretive about the planning for the future.

Not quite sure why the United States was in Vietnam, the American public grew increasingly confused and impatient with each passing day of the fighting. If all was going so well, why were draft calls so high and more and more American troops sent to that faraway little country? If all was not going well, why didn't the United States unleash all its military might on the aggressors? Unwilling to fully mobilize the nation to fight a war in Southeast Asia, Johnson turned to McNamara to control a rapidly escalating conflict without a comprehensive national strategy to utilize the full range of U.S. military power. In the absence of a coherent military strategy the contradictions in the administration's position were nowhere more glaring than in the conduct of the ongoing air war against North Vietnam.

CHAPTER III

THE AIR WAR AGAINST NORTH VIETNAM, 1965–1966

By the time President Johnson made the momentous decision in July 1965 to send U.S. troops in large numbers to fight a ground war in South Vietnam, the United States had already been engaged for five months in a steadily escalating air war against North Vietnam. The use of airpower had received increasing attention since the August 1964 Tonkin Gulf incidents when the United States responded with retaliatory air raids. Consideration of renewed air operations against the North had not progressed beyond discussions when on 1 November, just two days before the U.S. presidential election, Viet Cong forces attacked Bien Hoa Air Base. Johnson chose to ignore calls for retaliation, but in December he approved a policy of enhanced military action that included graduated air strikes. Beginning in February 1965 the administration undertook an air war against the North that, with intermittent cessations, would complement the ground war in the South through much of the course of the conflict.[1]

If it posed its own special dangers, the conduct of the air war presented much the same dilemma to the administration as that of the ground war. In both instances, of necessity civilian leaders paid heed to the geopolitical consequences as well as domestic political repercussions of a widening engagement. Where their military advisers for the most part advocated optimum use of force to achieve purely military objectives, Johnson and McNamara chose to rely on a measured, incremental exercise of power linked to progress on the diplomatic front. They viewed unrestricted air bombardment as a war-expanding, not a war-ending strategy, believing that an unleashed air offensive might provoke war with China, perhaps even a nuclear conflict. They worried, too, that the image of a strong-armed superpower pulverizing a tiny, backward nation would supply fresh fodder to critics at home and abroad, alienate neutrals, and discomfit even allies. While recognizing that national and international opinion would never tolerate a concerted air campaign

51

aimed at decimating North Vietnam, they could point out that the administration had shown restraint no doubt motivated in part by genuine humanitarian concern to minimize North Vietnamese civilian casualties.[2] Finally, the graduated response suited the president's preferred approach and time-tested political experience of seeking a middle course on the assumption that opponents would eventually come around to the bargaining table. Like McNamara and Rusk, the president had little confidence that airpower alone could ensure South Vietnam's survival, but leveraging it in conjunction with ground operations he hoped might cause sufficient pain to incline Hanoi toward an early settlement.[3]

As the civilian leadership learned with respect to the ground war, a tentative approach failed to grasp the depth of Hanoi's commitment to the reunification of Vietnam and its willingness to fight however long it might take to win. Moreover, since gradual escalation of the air war involved alternating pulses of moderation and escalation, suspension along with intensification, the policy drew constant criticism from both hawks and doves and confronted the administration with yet another set of vexing decisions that paralleled the difficult choices on the ground. To the extent even a limited aerial bombardment could be effective, the most promising targets lay within the densely inhabited cities of Hanoi and Haiphong, where air strikes were hazardous and casualties—both downed U.S. pilots and dead and injured among the civilian population—unpredictable and potentially high. By avoiding or deferring risky decisions involving attacks on those areas, the administration might keep an air campaign under control so as to retain domestic support for and international acceptance of the president's moderate war policies, yet jeopardize the larger goal of bringing sufficient pressure to bear on the enemy. Attempts to reconcile the multiple, often divergent military, political, tactical, and strategic aims complicated the formulation of a sound, consistent air plan. High-level indecision characterized the air war much as it had the ground war, and it took months to agree on and implement policy.

At the outset of the air war discussions, during the winter and spring of 1965, it seemed inconceivable to civilian and military leaders alike that Hanoi could long withstand the sustained application of U.S. airpower, even with constraints and stoppages, when combined with the flexing of muscles on the ground.[4] To an industry group McNamara expressed doubt that the North's political institutions could indefinitely absorb the punishment delivered by 400 bombing sorties a week;[5] at the very prospect, North Vietnam might quit the war before it happened. Among the services, as could be expected, the Army was the most skeptical about the efficacy of airpower, the Air Force the most sanguine. Still, one senior Army officer believed the Chiefs convinced themselves "that there was no harm in trying" the air option. To the extent there was consensus among the Chiefs, it was abetted by the conviction that to retain their limited influence they needed to take a unified position.[6] In the end the JCS, too, even as they pushed for a more robust air program, underestimated North Vietnam's tenacity and resiliency.

VIETNAM

CHINA

NORTH VIETNAM

★ **HANOI**

BURMA

GULF OF TONKIN

LAOS

20th Parallel

19th Parallel

■

VIENTIANE
★

■ ■

Udorn ●

● Nakhon
Phanom

Task Force 77

THAILAND

Ubon ●

● Da Nang
Chu Lai ●

● Takhli

● Korat

Pleiku ●

Phu Cat
●

Qui Nhon
●

Tuy
Hoa

● Don Muang
★ **BANKOK**

U-Tapao ●

CAMBODIA

**SOUTH
VIETNAM**

Nha Trang ●
Cam Ranh Bay ●

Phan Rang ●

Tan Son
Nhut
●
● Bien Hoa

★ **SAIGON**

PHNOM
PENH ★

GULF OF THAILAND

Binh Thuy ●

SOUTH CHINA SEA

SOUTHEAST ASIA
★ **NATIONAL CAPITAL**
● **PRINCIPAL U.S. AIR BASE**
■ **NAVY CARRIERS**

Targeting North Vietnam

Target selection, a critical function that itself had a significant political as well as military dimension, required careful calculation as the administration pursued a calibrated bombing campaign. Admiral U.S. Grant Sharp, commander in chief, Pacific, was in a difficult position in the target selection hierarchy. His vast Pacific Command, responsible for a region that stretched from the Aleutians to the Indian Ocean, included Military Assistance Command, Vietnam as one of his several major subordinate commands, but in practice McNamara exerted more direct control and influence there than Sharp. Indeed, McNamara initially wanted MACV to report directly to him.[7]

On organization charts, Sharp was the immediate superior of MACV commander Westmoreland, but the latter often circumvented him by dealing directly with McNamara and other senior OSD officials and exchanging extensive back-channel messages with JCS chairman Wheeler. Westmoreland also directed air operations in South Vietnam through the commander of the Seventh Air Force. Far removed from the war in South Vietnam, Sharp had to accord Westmoreland much latitude. Thus the admiral often served largely as an intermediary between MACV and the JCS.

Sharp controlled Rolling Thunder, the air war against North Vietnam, through his subordinates, the commander in chief of the Pacific Fleet and the commander in chief of the Pacific Air Forces, who issued operational directives to the carrier task force and until March 1966 the commander 2d Air Division and thereafter the commander Seventh Air Force in Saigon. Sharp was a forceful advocate of heavier bombing of the North, and his hawkish views did not sit well with McNamara. The secretary did not involve Sharp in major policy decisions and reduced his role to that of an executor of orders rather than an originator. Furthermore, Sharp's target recommendations were subject to Washington-imposed restrictions.[8]

After consultations with his subordinate commanders, Sharp would forward a list of recommended targets in North Vietnam to the JCS, usually for a one or two week period. Beginning in March 1965 a small team within the Joint Staff reviewed Sharp's nominations for Wheeler. Unless the proposals involved substantial changes to bombing policy, Wheeler routinely discussed the submissions with his fellow Chiefs at their weekly Friday afternoon meetings. The next morning the chairman personally delivered the JCS recommendations to McNamara's office where the two men reviewed the list of potential targets. Rusk and McNamara then discussed the bombing options, usually in the secretary of defense's office on Saturday afternoon or Sunday.*

---

* Originally the JCS forwarded copies of the proposals to State and the White House, but in October 1965 McNamara asked Wheeler to send him all copies for his decision on further distribution.

The JCS proposals underwent review from several levels of civilians in OSD, usually in International Security Affairs, and from officials in the State Department. After ISA and State agreed on their selections, or as might happen, disagreed, ISA's McNaughton informed McNamara of the results and the rationale for them. Benjamin H. Read, executive secretary of the Department of State, performed a similar function for Rusk by preparing short-notice staff papers to support the secretary's position on sensitive targets. The whole package then moved for final decision, customarily made at the White House Tuesday lunch.[9]

At the luncheons, McNamara presented the military view of the JCS and his own opinion as secretary of defense. In early 1965 he was "supremely confident and assertive," and his "forceful advocacy" dominated the targeting discussion. Occasionally, given the foreign policy implications, McNamara deferred to Rusk's judgment on target selection.[10] Though a recurring issue at Tuesday lunches, target selection was not a major focus. One participant estimated that nine of ten target lists that came up for discussion were approved. During periods when the Tuesday lunch group did not meet, or when the president felt the target list did not need his personal endorsement, McNamara had authority to approve or disapprove targets.[11]

In May 1965, with JCS concurrence, Sharp proposed to shift the target workup of the weekly program for the JCS from the Joint Staff in Washington to his CINCPAC headquarters. Following McNaughton's advice, McNamara rejected the proposal because the system in place was militarily effective and allowed "political considerations to be taken into account on a timely basis."[12]

Even after targets were authorized, it was not unusual for the secretary of state, the secretary of defense, or even the president to dictate minute changes, defer targets without explanation, pepper field commands with innumerable questions, and specify the day or even hour for attacks. Differences sometimes dictated compromise. To mollify the military, for instance, a highway ferry adjacent to a village might be swapped for a more isolated army cantonment. To accommodate the State Department, an ammunition storage area might replace a power plant.[13]

For all the erratic tendency of other aspects of the administration's Vietnam decisionmaking, the targeting system soon became institutionalized. Twice a month the Joint Staff revised the formalized Rolling Thunder target list (prepared and previously submitted by the JCS) to account for targets destroyed, under consideration, authorized, and recommended but not authorized. The staff forwarded the revisions to the ASD(ISA), who in turn sent them to the defense secretary. Every Tuesday and Friday the Joint Staff sent ISA a list of currently authorized, but not yet attacked, targets for review. Any new target recommendations by the JCS chairman in the restricted zones around Hanoi and Haiphong or in the Chinese buffer zone went to both ISA and McNamara's office. ISA coordinated the new targets with State and also evaluated the proposals for the secretary of defense. On those occasions when the chairman hand-carried new recommendations to the secretary of defense, the secretary might call ISA for an evaluation. Hence OSD, State Department, and White House approval were required before the JCS could authorize strikes against new targets. Clark Clifford inherited this system in March 1968 and continued it.[14]

Rolling Thunder

McGeorge Bundy regarded the Viet Cong attack on Pleiku on 7 February 1965 as a carefully timed and orchestrated communist provocation to coincide with his U.S. team's visit to Saigon; along with Ambassador Taylor and General Westmoreland, he urged immediate retaliatory air strikes. Ignoring the presence of Soviet Premier Alexei N. Kosygin in Hanoi, the president on the evening of 6 February (Washington time) authorized reprisal strikes, code named Flaming Dart I, against four pre-selected targets (military barracks) in North Vietnam. U.S. Navy aircraft hit one of the barracks on 7 February but bad weather forced cancellation of other strikes. The next day South Vietnamese and USAF aircraft attacked alternate targets. Meanwhile Bundy returned to Washington and proposed a sustained, graduated bombing of North Vietnam, something he had been predisposed to recommend anyway. Following a 10 February Viet Cong attack on a U.S. barracks at Qui Nhon, the three air forces again hit North Vietnamese targets.[15]

While alienating Kosygin, who believed the bombing intentionally coincided with his visit, Flaming Dart did not live up to optimistic expectations of destroying a high percentage of targets. Instead the Navy lost three aircraft while inflicting little damage and few casualties. McNamara publicly put the best face on the attacks, but on 17 February he made plain to the Joint Chiefs that unless future bombing inflicted far greater damage any such signals of U.S. resolve would carry "a hollow ring."[16]

At the NSC meeting of 8 February, after the president decided to implement the December policy for a phased air campaign against North Vietnam, McNamara directed the Joint Chiefs to prepare an escalating eight-week air offensive for the president's approval. The focus of operations would be the southern portion of North Vietnam, initially against targets beyond the operating radius of enemy MIG aircraft. The North Vietnamese MIG base of Phuc Yen (thought to be a flash point likely to bring China into the fighting) would remain off limits.[17]

Within three days, the JCS proposed an eight-week air campaign of attacks against low-risk targets south of the 19th parallel designed to persuade Hanoi to reduce its support of the Viet Cong by inflicting what the Chiefs deemed would be unacceptable levels of damage on the North. They conceded that the increasing severity of the strikes would probably bring Chinese "volunteers" into the war and oblige Moscow to equip North Vietnam with modern air defense systems, including surface-to-air missiles (SAMs). The CIA estimated Hanoi would likely try to secure respite from sustained air attacks by reducing, but never abandoning, its support of the Viet Cong. State's intelligence bureau declared the North would absorb the punishment and still carry on the fight. Others also questioned the Chiefs' strategy. Taylor believed the campaign unfolded too slowly, and Admiral Sharp at CINCPAC thought that it overemphasized "getting a message to Hanoi." Conversely, Rusk thought Hanoi got the message from previous raids that it could not expand the war into the South with impunity.[18] The president and McNamara, like Rusk, continued to worry about widening the war.

Without reconciling the contradictory views, on 13 February, three days after the Viet Cong attack on the U.S. base at Qui Nhon, the president approved in principle a limited air campaign designated Rolling Thunder, but withheld final authorization until 19 February; no public announcement followed. Thus began the sustained bombing of North Vietnam that, with interruptions, would continue until November 1968. Rolling Thunder's various phases gradually and steadily expanded the targets, scope, and intensity of the air war. Johnson's stubborn insistence that these policy shifts were not escalation eventually exposed him and his administration to charges of deceiving the American people. As the perceived architect of bombing policy, McNamara too would in time become reviled as a hypocrite and liar.[19]

The initial Rolling Thunder mission was scheduled for 20 February 1965, but the JCS had to scrub the first four missions because of an attempted coup d'etat and political turmoil in Saigon as well as bad weather over North Vietnam. While aircraft remained grounded, Wheeler counseled Westmoreland to be patient about political and military constraints and reminded him that the administration sought to steer a careful course to maximize the air campaign's effectiveness and minimize the likelihood of Chinese intervention. Getting the air campaign started mattered to the hawks because, based on experience in Laos and South Vietnam, they were confident that once bombing became routine the administration would relax restrictions. Henceforth the Joint Chiefs would push for more aggressive air operations, effectively setting the frame of reference for the war against North Vietnam.[20]

The initial strikes, actually labeled Rolling Thunder 5 and not executed until 2 March, lost six U.S. aircraft in attacks on two separate military targets—a naval base and a military depot. The next package of strikes, scheduled for 11 March, finally went ahead on 14 and 15 March after several weather delays and South Vietnamese air force failures. Hoping for the best and fearing the worst, the administration voiced satisfaction if not enthusiasm with the mixed results. Although Hanoi did not quit and South Vietnam did not unite behind its leaders, China did not intervene and Moscow did not sever relations with Washington. Perhaps most important for the president's cherished domestic agenda, the American public showed little awareness of the momentous shift he had directed in U.S. policy.[21] The desultory onset of the air campaign likely accounted for the indifference.

Taylor believed that Hanoi regarded Rolling Thunder as "merely a few isolated thunderclaps." Rusk appeared depressed by the continued fragile political situation in Saigon, particularly the lack of leadership there, and the surprising Viet Cong strength. McNamara thought the bombing had had little effect, that soon few worthwhile acceptable targets would remain, and that expanding the attacks would entail large-scale civilian casualties. As for the South, he was convinced that "guerrilla wars could not be won from the air"; clearly disappointed with the early results, he questioned CIA Director McCone's contention that heavier bombing might be productive when internal conditions continued to degrade. The president still hewed to a middle course of gradual escalation, neither wanting to run out of targets nor bomb Hanoi itself. Yet he too agonized over the course of events; by mid-March he had removed a number of tactical restraints. He neither intensified the air war as the Joint Chiefs wanted nor gave the military clear guidance. Instead he directed the avoidance of targets that might lead to clashes with North Vietnamese MIGs in the Hanoi area or provoke Chinese intervention; Wheeler interpreted this to mean that air strikes were confined to the area south of the 20th parallel. The president articulated his "urgent desire" to reverse the unfavorable tide in Vietnam but left the secretary and JCS to work out how to accomplish that goal.[22]

On 20 March McNamara asked the Joint Chiefs to plan a 12-week air campaign against the North, cautioning that strikes should stay away from urban areas to lessen civilian casualties and avoid direct attacks on North Vietnamese airfields to reduce the likelihood of escalation. The JCS reply, delivered a week later, outlined a 3-week aerial interdiction campaign south of the 20th parallel to impair North Vietnam's line of communication (LOC) by destroying roads, railroads, and bridges. The Chiefs recommended that approval of later phases—destroying rail lines throughout North Vietnam, mining its ports, and attacking industrial targets outside of Hanoi and Haiphong—await the outcome of the initial phase.[23]

On 29 March, Taylor, then in Washington for consultations, met with McNamara and the Joint Chiefs to review recent developments in Vietnam. The ambassador endorsed the gradually expanded bombing effort against the North. McNamara expected that the mining of Haiphong harbor would be "politically feasible" in 4 to 12 weeks. Anticipating also approval to destroy the two main bridges connecting North Vietnam with China at about the 12-week point in the campaign, he granted these actions would "bring very strong pressure" on Hanoi's leaders.[24] As the military situation in South Vietnam deteriorated and U.S. Marines landed at Da Nang, it seemed appropriate, the secretary's misgivings notwithstanding, to ratchet up Rolling Thunder to increase the cost of the war to the communists.

Rolling Thunder 9, launched 2 April, inaugurated the LOC interdiction phase south of the 20th parallel. The next day, after the loss of three U.S. planes to antiaircraft fire and the "intrusion of MIGs" (an inevitable consequence as the air campaign progressed northward), Wheeler feared that Washington's heightened apprehension over this latest escalation might result in new restrictions. The president's request the same day for an appraisal of the bombing added to the chairman's anxiety because the limited air strikes had little effect on North Vietnamese military and economic capabilities, except perhaps the destruction of three key bridges that created a LOC bottleneck. Indeed, battles with MIGs in North Vietnam's skies and the prospect of heavy U.S. aircraft losses to the surface-to-air missile (SAM) sites under construction around Hanoi alarmed Assistant Secretary of State William Bundy sufficiently that on 13 April he proposed to Rusk a leveling off of Rolling Thunder.[25]

With the direction of the air campaign against North Vietnam under scrutiny and differences over planned U.S. ground deployments unresolved, McNamara flew to Honolulu to discuss the future conduct of the war. At the 20 April conference, the bombing campaign came first on the agenda as the Washington contingent of McNamara, William Bundy, McNaughton, and Wheeler met with Taylor, Sharp, and Westmoreland. Years later Sharp, a proponent of heavier bombing, contended that McNamara had distorted his views by telling the president that all participants felt the tempo of limited air strikes against the North was about right and that South Vietnam should have first call on U.S. airpower.[26] According to the conference minutes, McNamara endorsed Sharp's proposal for more armed reconnaissance missions against North Vietnam and permitted the admiral to exceed the established daily quota of air sorties if pilots discovered lucrative targets of opportunity. The two diverged over the secretary's adamancy that operations over South Vietnam came first and that the air campaign against North Vietnam could consequently be scaled back as necessary. Sharp believed McNamara's emphasis on interdiction as a higher priority than attacking industrial facilities closer to Hanoi downgraded the air war against the North.[27]

On his return to Washington, McNamara proposed to the president at a meeting with officials from State, the CIA, OSD, and the White House on 21 April to extend the air war for a period of 6 to 12 months or more, but not to intensify it. The objective, he said, was to entice the North to seek a negotiated settlement rather than suffer a protracted interdiction campaign against its lines of infiltration and logistics. "The thrust of McNamara's statement and subsequent discussions," according to McCone's record of the meeting,

> was to change the purpose of the bombing attacks on North Vietnam from one of causing the DRV to seek a negotiated settlement to one of continual harassment of lines of supply, etc., while the combination of SVN forces and U.S. forces were engaging in defeating the Viet Cong to such a point that the DRV and other interested Communist States would realize the hopelessness of the Viet Cong effort and therefore would seek a peaceful negotiation.

The real purpose of the bombing, McNamara told Johnson, had been to lift morale in the South and push the North toward negotiations without provoking Chinese intervention. "We've done that."[28] Though the policy remained blurred and fluid, McNamara looked in essence to the ground war in the South rather than an aggressive air offensive over the North to bring Hanoi to the conference table, using air resources in the main to support the ground action, in particular through an interdiction campaign.

Others remained unconvinced of the efficacy of the strategy. Outgoing CIA Director McCone's parting letter to the president reiterated his advice to strike a wide range of military and industrial targets in the North. McCone's successor as of 28 April, Vice Adm. William F. Raborn, Jr. (USN Ret.), shared McCone's skepticism over McNamara's limited air campaign and very soon recommended its expansion to destroy or damage Hanoi's economic and military infrastructure. With U.S. Marines already fighting in South Vietnam and with planning under way to deploy major numbers of ground troops, McNamara anticipated expanding elements of the air war to complement the spreading ground conflict. Before its escalation, however, he wanted to send a strong diplomatic signal to Hanoi. Shortly after his return from Honolulu he had directed McNaughton to draft a bombing pause scenario, in the hope that a pause would trigger negotiations or reduce Hanoi's support of the insurgency while it bolstered domestic and international support for the administration's future course in Vietnam.[29]

Sustained bombing, however restricted, had already produced international appeals for restraint. In the United States stirrings of the peace movement had begun. In early April Canadian Prime Minister Lester Pearson, in a speech at a large American university, called for a bombing halt as a first step. U.S. military intervention in the Dominican Republic, ordered on 28 April, sparked another public outcry. Amidst mounting criticism, McNamara convinced a reluctant president to authorize an unpublicized bombing pause as part of an overture to Hanoi via the U.S. ambassador in Moscow, as much to defuse administration critics as to prepare the way for escalation of the war if Hanoi, as expected, rejected the gesture. Knowledge of the highly sensitive peace feeler, code-named Mayflower, was confined to the president's closest advisers. Regarding only Wheeler and Westmoreland as sufficiently "broad gauged" to appreciate the subtleties of the administration's position, the civilian leadership kept the information from other flag officers and did not share it with or deliberately misled even officials normally in the loop out of a concern over possible press leaks.[30]

On 11 May, the State Department attempted unsuccessfully to notify Hanoi privately through the Soviet ambassador in Washington and the North Vietnamese embassy in Moscow of the bombing pause. The message urged the North Vietnamese to respond by reducing their own military activities. The same day McNamara rather vaguely informed Sharp, who was calling for round-the-clock bombing, about the suspension, but stated the purpose was to "observe [the] reaction of DRV rail and road transportation systems." The negotiating ploy was never mentioned, although the president had earlier informed Taylor about it. Sharp was left in the odd position of knowing less than Moscow or Hanoi about Washington's diplomatic adventure, which likely reinforced his opinions about the naiveté of civilian leadership when dealing with communists.[31]

The 12–17 May bombing pause, overshadowed in the United States by the Dominican Republic crisis, came across in Hanoi as a charade, a smoke screen to divert attention from the continuing U.S. military buildup in South Vietnam. North Vietnam's refusal even to receive the proposal and its public denunciation of the overture left an unusually emotional McNamara sputtering, "Hanoi spit on our face."[32] Johnson, never comfortable with the pause for fear the North would use it to advantage and concerned that a longer delay risked losing public support, on 17 May ordered bombing resumed the next day. The combination of Washington's equivocation and Hanoi's intransigence also would hamper future negotiating initiatives.

Following the May pause, whether out of pique or frustration, McNamara moved to expand the air war. Rolling Thunder sorties gradually increased as pilots struck north of 20 degrees for the first time on 22 May and above the 21st parallel on 15 June. Although intensifying air operations against the North, McNamara still carefully controlled them by minimizing attacks against fixed targets on the JCS list—bridges, factories, barracks, etc.—and increasing armed reconnaissance sorties against vehicles, trains, and watercraft, so-called targets of opportunity discovered by the pilots. The stepped-up air campaign made it more difficult for North Vietnam to move men and supplies southward, but it reduced neither the regime's overall military capability noticeably nor its determination to persevere.[33] At this very time, communist military success in South Vietnam was forcing the administration to consider committing additional U.S. ground units to prop up the Saigon government.

To accompany any buildup of ground forces, the Joint Chiefs wanted an intensified air war against "militarily important targets" in the North. Confronted with an alarming military deterioration in the South Vietnamese forces, at a 23 June White House meeting McNamara also advocated applying greater force selectively against North Vietnam coupled with more serious negotiating overtures than those to date. His follow-up position, drafted at the president's request and formally submitted on 1 July, outlined, in addition to a buildup of ground forces, an expanded air war that now included destroying rail and road bridges leading from China to Hanoi, mining North Vietnamese harbors, destroying warmaking stockpiles and facilities, interdicting the enemy LOCs into South Vietnam, and, as required, knocking out enemy airfields and air defenses.[34]

Both McGeorge Bundy and the CIA demurred. Bundy informed the president that to triple air strikes against the North when the value of the air effort was sharply disputed and to mine the harbors regardless of the risks of further escalation seemed excessive. The CIA deemed the upgraded plan not substantial enough "to warrant the awkward international political complications such action would entail." The president deferred a decision and sent McNamara, Wheeler, and Lodge, recently designated as Taylor's replacement, to Saigon for a military assessment. During these mid-July consultations Taylor advised against rapid escalation, believing it was "psychologically unsound to get too far ahead in the air campaign while the ground campaign is lagging."[35] After returning, McNamara softened his stance and advised doing what the president was inclined to do—continue the gradually escalating air campaign against the North. Once U.S. ground troops deployed to South Vietnam and the air forces had accomplished a major goal in the North, such as destroying the important railway bridge north of Hanoi, a diplomatic initiative in the form of a six to eight week bombing pause might be considered.[36]

By late July McNamara professed satisfaction with the progress of the air campaign. No one, he explained to the president, had expected the bombing to promote a settlement until Hanoi recognized it could not win in the South. Interdiction had made resupply of its units slower, harder, and more costly for the North in terms of men and resources. The downside of the incremental air campaign was wide-ranging criticism of the administration, from the right for not bombing enough and from the left for bombing at all. The latter argued that the air offensive had damaged the United States internationally, strained U.S.-Soviet détente, and risked a wider war. Still not inclined to support a vastly more aggressive air war but running out of options, McNamara urged continued bombing as a bargaining chip in the bid for a settlement.[37]

Throughout August, while the buildup of U.S. ground forces proceeded, McNamara adhered to a moderate course, displaying on the one hand little interest in a bombing pause until the United States had made progress in the South, and on the other rejecting Sharp's proposal to attack POL (petroleum, oil, and lubricants) dumps at Hanoi and Haiphong. After appearing to have edged closer to the JCS position, he again took to rebuffing the Chiefs' recommendations for a more robust air campaign, deferring to Rusk's sensitivity over civilian casualties and his own trepidation about extending strikes northeast of Hanoi.[38] As the firewall between the Joint Chiefs demanding escalation and a president reluctant to make irrevocable decisions, McNamara took the heat for deteriorating civil-military relations.

By early September the policy of tightly controlled and limited air attacks embroiled McNamara in an ongoing debate with the Joint Chiefs, who wanted to bomb SAM sites, Phuc Yen airfield, LOCs in the northeast, and POL targets around Haiphong. On 2 September, Wheeler urged immediate approval of the strikes because the enemy grew stronger by the day and inaction would only increase U.S. losses. He requested that McNamara inform the president of the Chiefs' views "without delay," which he did. With the president's approval McNamara rejected the JCS proposals on 15 September because, he remained convinced, the military and political risks associated with the raids, especially the possibility of a U.S.-Chinese confrontation, outweighed any possible military advantages.[39]

The Joint Chiefs may have minimized the possibility and even the consequences of Chinese intervention, but as early as mid-April 1965 the fear of such action had become "gospel" among the administration's civilian leadership. Anxiety over Chinese intentions heightened after 1 June when Peking informed Washington through British channels that it supported North Vietnam "unconditionally" and would enter the conflict if the United States bombed Chinese soil.[40] Perhaps intending a warning to discourage U.S. military escalation against North Vietnam, the Chinese were deliberately vague about their reaction if escalation did not involve Chinese targets. As a consequence, after pondering the implications of the Chinese communiqué, no senior American official could determine at what point the Chinese might move into Vietnam and engage in open hostilities with the United States.[41]

This latest signal from China was consistent with Chinese military deployments to North Vietnam and a buildup of air defenses on its own border that began in late 1964, moves American intelligence deduced indicated China's determination to stand up to the United States. The loss of an F-104 near Hainan Island on 20 September 1965 and Chinese newsreel claims of destroying another American aircraft on 5 October were the kind of incidents, according to Thomas Hughes, director of State's Bureau of Intelligence and Research, that reinforced Rusk's "neuralgic apprehensions" about China.[42]

McNamara had no intention of risking a wider conflict by expanding the air war to the degree sought by the Chiefs; except for an occasional minor concession, he consistently tamped down JCS recommendations. In early October the Chiefs forwarded CINCPAC's proposals for Rolling Thunder 36/37, two weeks of operations targeting the northeast quadrant of North Vietnam, its most populous and industrialized area. With the exception of four bridges, McNamara deleted the proposed targets, directed that armed sorties be kept at current levels, and forbade them within 25 nautical miles of the Chinese border, 30 of Hanoi, and 10 of Haiphong. These restrictions persisted through the remainder of 1965, leaving the vital northeast quadrant virtually off limits to U.S. aircraft.[43]

Working Toward an Extended Bombing Pause

As the inconclusive air offensive continued, McNamara searched for other ways that might induce North Vietnam to negotiate. He tended to focus on evidence favorable to his position on the bombing campaign and dismissed or downplayed contrary information. He questioned the Special National Intelligence Estimate of 22 September that maintained attacks on key targets such as airfields, SAM defenses, and road and rail routes leading to China—that is, directed at the northeast quadrant—might move Hanoi toward negotiation. Repeated negotiating probes and pauses and avoidance of the northeast quadrant, the estimate stated, likely stiffened the North's resolution by creating doubts about U.S. determination to see the war through to a finish. The transparent criticism of OSD's management of the air war was troublesome enough, but McNamara insisted that by making its estimate "without the benefit of advice from experts" the intelligence community concluded wrongly that a hardening attitude in Hanoi resulted "largely because we were not rough enough in our bombing." At his urging, the president on 30 September appointed "experts"—all of them escalation opponents—to study the effects of the bombing campaign on North Vietnamese behavior.[44]

The resultant Thompson Report of 11 October, prepared under the direction of Ambassador at Large Llewellyn E. Thompson, Jr.,[*] predictably concluded that escalation would not affect Hanoi's will to continue the war and recommended leveling off the rate of attacks. Rather than increased bombing, the group suggested a second, more pronounced pause might bring about negotiations. State's William Bundy presented a plan that addressed the subject not only in a U.S.-North Vietnam context but considered the effect also on U.S. and North Vietnamese allies. Bundy proposed numerous domestic and worldwide political, diplomatic, and publicity measures to employ during a bombing suspension. Review of Bundy's "second pause" scenario was broadened the next day (23 October) to include discussions of MACV's plea for reinforcements and Ambassador Lodge's views on how negotiations with Hanoi might affect the weak South Vietnamese government, with the objectives of providing the president with policy choices for the next four to six weeks on the nature and length of any cessation and steps for swaying world opinion.[45]

Aware of the Thompson group's work as early as September, the Joint Chiefs, who viscerally opposed any letup in the air war, were certain that Hanoi would take advantage of any respite to reconstitute its air defenses to make future attacks more costly. They insisted on an immediate "sharp blow," an all-out air campaign against the North's airfields, LOCs, POL facilities, and air defenses.[46] For their part, the intelligence community (CIA and DIA) on 27 October again claimed that bombing to date had had little effect on the North because the attacked targets were not located in areas of major economic activity, and that it would be difficult to reduce North Vietnam's capabilities significantly so long as the most desirable targets—ports, POL facilities, power plants, airfields, and railroads—remained off limits.[47]

JCS and intelligence agency recommendations to continue and expand the bombing of North Vietnam notwithstanding, on 3 November McNamara drafted for the president's consideration several alternative plans—a soft-line pause, a hard-line pause, or no pause and either a graduated or a sharp-blow bombing program. His own preference was for a four-week pause followed, if necessary, by a graduated five-month Rolling Thunder campaign culminating in the mining of

---

[*] The report was largely put together in the State Department but reviewed by Taylor and McNaughton before its release. See *FRUS 1964–68*, 3:442 n1.

Haiphong harbor. McNamara declared that such a course did not assure success; in fact, "the harbor-mining aspect of Rolling Thunder" might cause "the Chinese or Russians to escalate the war." Nevertheless, he thought the proposed alternative provided "the best chance of achieving our objectives, and of avoiding a costly national political defeat."[48]

An important factor in McNamara's strong call for the bombing pause stemmed from his July 1965 briefings in Saigon. At that time he had learned that the communists needed only about 14 or 15 tons of supplies to meet their daily operational requirements in South Vietnam. Though the JCS questioned McNamara's subsequent use of the number, a Joint Staff study confirmed the figure. Stepped-up enemy operations and additional reinforcements might require as much as 165 tons per day, but McNamara believed the North Vietnamese capable of carrying that amount on their backs, if necessary. The small numbers convinced him that the North's infiltration system, even under constant bombing, could supply sufficient materiel to sustain combat operations in South Vietnam.[49] Accordingly, a bombing pause would not adversely affect U.S. military operations in the South and might jump-start negotiations with the North.

A consensus slowly emerged among OSD's senior civilians, White House advisers, and top-level State Department officials that a temporary cessation of the air attacks might lead to negotiations and a way out of Vietnam. President Johnson, however, still smarting from the Mayflower fiasco, remained skeptical, fearing the enemy would regard the pause as a sign of weakness and that a subsequent resumption of the bombing would further diminish domestic support for the war. Determined to seek a pause, after a one-and-a-half day trip to Vietnam on 28–29 November (along with Wheeler and Sharp) McNamara restated the pro-pause position in another lengthy memo to the president.[50] On the other hand, Taylor, now a special consultant to the president,[*] feared the communists would trap the United States into prolonged cease-fire negotiations as had happened during the Korean War. He also worried that a pause might create new domestic divisions rather than heal current ones.

McNamara informed the Joint Chiefs of his views, expressed in 3 and 30 November presidential memoranda, and of the slowly evolving consensus for a hiatus. The Chiefs, however, expected North Vietnam to exploit any pause and demanded heavy raids against industrial targets before any cessation. Perhaps for this reason, in early December the president approved attacks against a power plant and a highway bridge near Haiphong, in the words of an Air Force historian "two sensitive targets hardly calculated to make Hanoi more amenable to negotiations."[51] Johnson's balancing act thus set a pattern of heavy air attacks immediately preceding bombing pauses.

---

[*] On 1 September 1965, Johnson announced Taylor's appointment as a part-time presidential special consultant effective on or about 15 September (*Johnson Public Papers, 1965*, 2:962).

On 2 December McNamara again privately urged the president to endorse a bombing halt, cease-fire, or negotiations to defuse what was rapidly tending toward "further and further escalation, higher and higher risks, and a more and more uncertain outcome." To his colleagues the secretary reiterated the point that the air campaign could never completely prevent sufficient supplies from reaching the communists in South Vietnam; he promised that "qualified experts" would testify "that bombing the North doesn't help militarily."[52]

During a morning meeting at the White House on 17 December, with no JCS member present, McNamara, strongly supported by Ball and somewhat less by Rusk and McGeorge Bundy, pressed for an extended bombing pause. The president remained dubious, pointing out, "the Chiefs go through the roof when we mention this pause." McNamara agreed that "nothing will change their views" but suggested that "we decide what we want and impose it on them." Should the president concur on the pause, McNamara claimed, "I can deliver" the Chiefs. In the late afternoon of the same day, Johnson met with Wheeler and discussed the proposed scenario for an extended bombing pause while complaining about the pressure on him to order the cessation even though he was still unconvinced it would do any good.[53] The next day, the 18th, again with only his civilian advisers present,* after some four-and-one-half hours of discussion and deliberation Johnson agreed to extend the previously approved 30-hour across-the-board Christmas truce beginning at 6:00 p.m. on 24 December 1965 for several additional days. The same day Wheeler departed on his scheduled two-week Far East inspection tour without informing the service Chiefs about his White House meeting and the likely imposition of an extended pause. Also unbeknownst to them, the president had asked Wheeler to become his personal emissary to privately sound out Lodge and Westmoreland in Saigon about the proposed extended pause; both joined Wheeler in vehemently opposing any extension; their views were sent to the president through the Wheeler-Goodpaster back-channel communication.† Not until his return to Washington on 5 January 1966 did Wheeler inform "the disturbed and angry Chiefs" of his additional mission on the administration's behalf.[54]

Also feeding the Chiefs' resentment was Deputy Secretary Vance's cable of 24 December notifying Lodge, Sharp, and Westmoreland that the president forbade the restart of combat operations, including Rolling Thunder, until there were significant and confirmed instances of communist violence. Vance had drafted the message, sending it as a JCS message even after the acting JCS chairman, General McConnell, refused to sign and forward it. Vance also turned down McConnell's concurrent request to meet with the president on the matter.[55]

---

* At the request of the president, Abe Fortas, recently appointed to the Supreme Court, and Clark Clifford, "two old and trusted friends from outside the Executive branch," joined the meeting (Johnson, *Vantage Point*, 235).
† General Goodpaster was assistant to the chairman of the JCS.

Numerous Viet Cong violations of the truce in the South and obvious deployment of communist forces there and within the North convinced the Chiefs that they had been right all along. On 27 December Westmoreland called for a resumption of bombing against North Vietnam, which he labeled the "nerve center of direction, supply and manpower" for the war in the South. Sharp vigorously supported Westmoreland, stating that U.S. forces "should not be required to fight this war with one arm tied behind their backs." Rusk, Thompson, and William Bundy, among others at State, also favored immediate resumption with a longer pause coming later. To counter this sentiment, McNamara used his personal access to the president to outmaneuver those in favor of resuming the bombing. On 27 December he interrupted his Colorado vacation and, as earlier agreed to by the president, traveled to Johnson's Texas ranch, where he persuaded him to continue the bombing halt for an indefinite period.[56]

During the afternoon of the 28th, McNamara returned to the Pentagon where Admiral McDonald, dissatisfied with earlier Vance explanations, confronted him and laid out the Chiefs' case for opposing the pause. Possibly fearful that the military reaction to the pause might become public and embarrass the administration, McNamara immediately notified the four service chiefs of the indefinite extension as well as Westmoreland, Sharp, and Wheeler (now in Taiwan), explaining that it was meant to show that Washington was making "an honest attempt" to test Hanoi's willingness to enter into negotiations. If, as anticipated, North Vietnam failed to respond, the temporary cessation would serve to marshal public support for a huge increase in defense spending for ground operations in South Vietnam and an expanded air campaign against the North. Furthermore the pause would generate favorable world opinion and thus reduce the likelihood of a Soviet military response to such large-scale escalation. He concluded: "If at any time you believe the pause is seriously penalizing our operations in the south, please submit to me immediately the evidence backing up your belief." The next day, McNamara met with the disgruntled chiefs to explain again the rationale for the bombing halt and the curious handling of its extension. He appeared to cater to McDonald (perhaps attempting to divide the chiefs) by announcing he had put the Navy's sought-after construction of a nuclear carrier back into the FY 1967 budget. The promises and extra money failed to mollify them.[57]

A burst of diplomatic activity accompanied the pause: Rusk on 28 December issued a 14-point peace proposal; U.S. diplomats contacted at least 113 countries to demonstrate Washington's sincerity; and actual diplomatic contact with the North Vietnamese occurred the next day through their consul general in Rangoon, Burma. Dismissing the highly publicized U.S. search for a settlement as a ruse, China pressured the North Vietnamese leaders not to bargain with the Americans. Further undermining the peace initiative was the simple fact that although the bombing may have stopped, U.S. buildup of ground forces in South Vietnam continued, while, predictably, North Vietnam took advantage of the bombing halt to rush troops and supplies southward.[58]

Resuming Rolling Thunder

In the early days of the prolonged bombing hiatus over North Vietnam, during a White House meeting on 3 January 1966, McNamara reported that the Joint Chiefs still had not replied to his offer of 28 December to resume the bombing if they showed him that its absence affected U.S. operations in the South. He deemed the lack of a response "very encouraging." But five days later the JCS did reply. Based on aerial reconnaissance, they claimed that Hanoi was using the pause to increase infiltration, repair bomb damage, and strengthen its air defense network, nullifying the results of the pre-suspension strikes. The JCS recommended resuming intensified bombing within 48 hours of a visiting Soviet dignitary's scheduled departure on 12 January from Hanoi.[59]

At a 10 January White House meeting Wheeler, perhaps more assertive after the contretemps over the Vance message, disputed McNamara's contention that a few more days without bombing made little difference. On the contrary, Wheeler insisted, "every day makes a difference" because the North Vietnamese were working around the clock to improve their transportation network and air defenses. Taylor also thought the pause had about run its unsuccessful course. Two days later McConnell proposed that Rolling Thunder operations be resumed "dramatically by attacks more forceful than any heretofore." Field commanders were pressing for a renewed and much expanded bombing offensive against the North.[60]

McNamara preached patience, but as Hanoi remained unresponsive he, too, finally advised the president on 17 January and again a week later to resume an intensified bombing effort against North Vietnam to blunt the communist military buildup in the South. He assured the Joint Chiefs on 24 January that despite lagging public support the air attacks would begin soon. The following day the Chiefs proposed three alternatives for the renewed campaign: (1) a "maximum" surprise strike on perishable targets along the lines of communication, followed by the expanded campaign against POL and other targets recommended the previous week; (2) strikes beginning in southern North Vietnam and proceeding progressively northward; and (3) (which they favored) an all-out attack on the LOCs coupled with strikes against the POL system over a 24- to 72-hour period. The defense secretary took no immediate action, informing Wheeler later that the recommendations would receive full consideration as Rolling Thunder continued to evolve.[61]

After a series of daily White House meetings with top administration officials, congressional leaders, and civilian advisers between 24 and 28 January, and following Radio Hanoi's broadcast on the 28th of Ho Chi Minh's letter to several world leaders denouncing the "so-called search for peace" as a fraud, a frustrated Johnson, convinced the United States had done all it could to seek negotiations, declared, "I am not happy about Vietnam but we cannot run out—we have to resume bombing."[62] Clark Clifford concurred, insisting that bombing and airpower were the "most important weapons we have" to convince the North Vietnamese that they could not win militarily; he endorsed heavier bombing to show the world U.S. determination to see the conflict through. On 29 January the president ordered the bombing to resume as of the 31st, Saigon time, and he publicly announced it. Rusk summed up the pause and the elaborate diplomatic endeavor in this fashion: "The enormous effort made in the last 34 days has produced nothing—no runs, no hits, no errors."[63]

Bombing over North Vietnam resumed on 31 January 1966, after 37 days in all, but heavy rain and low visibility, along with a Washington-imposed lower level of sorties, thwarted Sharp's plans for a massive surprise air assault against the enemy's road network. Caution in Washington, specifically State's uneasiness over the international impact of a spectacular resumption of bombing, stymied the renewed air offensive that began slowly and without any new targets. Not until the president approved Rolling Thunder 49 on 26 February did the bombing plan return to the pre-pause level, but the target-rich northeast quadrant still remained forbidden to U.S. pilots.[64]

The POL Debate

Since the summer of 1965 Admiral Sharp had been recommending without success air attacks on North Vietnam's POL storage and distribution system. Early in November he received strong support from a Joint Staff study. Deprived of fuel, the staff argued, the enemy's transportation system would grind to a halt, choking off the southward flow of troops and supplies. The critical segment of the POL storage system, some 40 percent of total capacity, lay close to Haiphong and was therefore exempt from attack. In a 10 November memorandum to McNamara the Joint Chiefs explained that as the North grew ever more dependent on trucks to move supplies to its growing forces in the South, destroying the POL installations would be a crippling blow, more destructive than "an attack against any other single target system." In a second memo they urged an expanded air campaign starting with an "immediate sharp blow" against POL and electric power installations.[65]

These ill-timed JCS proposals came while the president's advisers were deep into exploring the merits of a temporary bombing cessation and in no mood to expand the air war. However, with the Joint Chiefs, in McNamara's words, "coming to a boiling point on bombing Haiphong," the secretary as a concession arranged for Wheeler to meet with the president. Contrary to McNamara's expectations Wheeler emerged from the 19 November meeting with the impression that Johnson favored the POL bombing. After learning this from Wheeler, McNamara advised the president to withhold a decision pending Rusk's return from abroad and a diplomatic and political evaluation of such attacks.[66]

McNamara's case against expanded bombing drew strength from a late November intelligence assessment he had requested from the CIA's Board of National Estimates and another issued on 2 December. The first explicitly stated that strikes against POL targets would represent "a conspicuous change in the ground rules," that is, attacking industrial rather than strictly military targets; the shift in targeting would probably not alter North Vietnam's policy but would cause considerable numbers of civilian casualties. In the second, the board also believed that heavier bombing alone would neither force Hanoi to quit nor stop infiltration southward because the communist regime was prepared for a long war and believed time was on its side.[67]

Wheeler strongly disagreed, claiming that the destruction of North Vietnam's POL facilities would drastically affect the enemy's military operations and significantly hamper a buildup of forces in South Vietnam. McNamara countered by asking for still another intelligence study—this one to estimate the effect of attacks on POL sites at Haiphong alone and on Haiphong plus other storage sites. The resulting study of 28 December slightly favored heavier air attacks because analysis indicated they would exacerbate economic difficulties in the North and the enemy's logistic problems in the South. Two days later, the Chiefs again pressed McNamara to authorize strikes against the POL system, initially near Haiphong and subsequently elsewhere. They reiterated that successful attacks would produce important military benefits, a conclusion ISA civilian officials disputed.[68]

After the bombing pause produced no tangible results, McNamara and McNaughton found themselves under enormous pressure to expand Rolling Thunder. Both harbored serious doubts that a renewed air campaign short of massed air attacks on North Vietnam's cities—a course they rejected as much for humanitarian reasons as for fear of provoking World War III—could halt infiltration into South Vietnam. Both looked on the war as stalemated. By late January 1966, after months of resistance, they finally considered a stepped-up offensive that included destruction of the POL network. McNaughton feared that any lowering of U.S. objectives would only give the communists the "smell of blood" and encourage them to finish off the decrepit Saigon regime. McNamara seemed to think that heavier bombing in conjunction with the massive U.S. troop reinforcement then under way might bring Hanoi to the conference table. He had also anticipated renewed pressure for escalation if the bombing suspension proved fruitless. Previously he had assured the president that in that event he would preempt the hawks by personally recommending attacks on POL targets and the mining of Haiphong harbor.[69]

The Joint Chiefs clamored to take out the POL system, but McNamara proposed only to double interdiction sorties. The secretary hoped that a six-month period of added thrust, together with a rapid increase in ground forces, might break Hanoi's will. When Johnson did not agree to bomb POLs, McNamara backed away from the idea. By early 1966, with preparations in motion to commit 400,000 American troops to South Vietnam, the administration needed to keep the pressure on the North by bombing or risk a public backlash for not supporting U.S. forces. McNamara remained preoccupied with focusing the expanded air campaign away from cities and lessening the risk of igniting a flash point that might bring China into the war. This approach disturbed the Chiefs, who wanted to destroy targets in the northeast quadrant that would reduce the North's ability to carry on the struggle.[70] Their position, now backed by the intelligence community, directly challenged McNamara's conduct of the air war.

CIA analysts in late February 1966, taking a more sanguine view of the application of airpower than the Board of Estimates had the previous fall, determined that with "drastically revised ground rules," particularly removing target and geographic restrictions, an air campaign against North Vietnam "could play an important role" in achieving U.S. objectives. Continuing the bombing under the existing restrictive "and militarily irrational" rules of engagement, however, "would result in a *virtually ineffective air attack program*." A revised estimate submitted in March took an even dimmer view of straitjacketing constraints, damning "self-imposed restrictions" that in effect granted immunity to the most lucrative targets in North Vietnam. The latest assessment conceded that concentrated and punishing attacks against Hanoi and Haiphong to destroy oil and industrial targets, mine harbors, and cut rail lines from China would not end the flow of infiltration southward, but noted they would make North Vietnam pay a steeper, and perhaps prohibitive, price. DIA generally concurred with the CIA's findings, adding that it supported the Joint Chiefs' position for an expanded air campaign with fewer restrictions.[71]

Beyond internal agency criticism of the air war's management, the administration had to take sober account of growing public disenchantment with the U.S. involvement itself. Johnson's centrist approach satisfied neither hawks who wanted him to do more to defeat the communists quickly nor doves who questioned the entire rationale for intervention. Those in between remained ambivalent. One poll conducted in late February and early March 1966 discovered the same majority who approved the president's handling of the war also favored deescalation. The president also suffered from a growing credibility gap largely of his own making. As *New York Times* pundit James Reston put it, "The imprecision—to use the polite diplomatic word—of the Administration's statements on this whole Vietnamese business is astonishing."[72]

The seeming disarray plus news reports that military officers in Vietnam anticipated the loosening of air war restrictions and favored attacking POL targets near Hanoi and Haiphong put McNamara on the defensive when he testified before the Senate Appropriations Committee in February 1966. Senator Russell remarked that civilian direction of DoD was fine, but the secretary should let professional soldiers run the war. He urged McNamara to reconsider POL targets because of the heavy reliance that the president placed on his judgment. McNamara understandably played down the disagreements between himself and the Chiefs over bombing POL facilities and mining Haiphong harbor. Still his attempt to obscure his differences with the JCS on the conduct of the war by claiming the bombing of North Vietnam was "in itself only a minor part of the program," only served to widen the credibility gap.[73] The air campaign became the most controversial aspect of a war that grew more problematic each passing day.

On 10 March the Chiefs resurrected the "sharp blow" strategy, proposing an expanded air campaign in the northeast quadrant, designated Rolling Thunder 50, to destroy POL storage. McNamara had previously promised his support to Wheeler and seemed sympathetic to the expanded air campaign and destruction of POL storage. A week later on 17 March, Westmoreland, worried about greatly increased enemy infiltration through Laos and the western portion of the DMZ, proposed shifting Rolling Thunder from attacks in northern North Vietnam to infiltration targets below the 19th parallel and in the Laotian panhandle. Informed of the recommendations, the president ordered a comprehensive study of how best to check infiltration.

Wheeler exploded at Westmoreland's attempt to reorient air operations because it undercut the case for a POL campaign by reinforcing McNamara's belief "that our air campaign against North Vietnam has had relatively little effect. . . . To say that this attitude disturbs me," declared Wheeler, "is to put it mildly because this conviction is used to argue against expansion of the air campaign against highly remunerative targets such as the POL system." He was especially perturbed because Westmoreland's proposal arrived just when McNamara seemed to be coming around to the JCS view that the destruction of POL facilities could significantly affect the course of the war. Indeed, after reviewing the Rolling Thunder 50 recommendations with Wheeler on 21 March, McNamara asked the Joint Chiefs to prepare an ambitious campaign against LOCs in the northeast quadrant, possibly including a cement plant and power facility in the Haiphong area and two or three important bridges.[74]

Several days later, on 26 March, the Joint Chiefs formally recommended initiating Rolling Thunder 50 on 1 April. State Department officials acquiesced to the heavier bombing of North Vietnam provided Washington carefully controlled any escalation, avoided targets in heavily populated urban areas, and did not mine Haiphong harbor. With the way now open to seek White House authorization, the Joint Chiefs relegated previously high-priority targets, such as ports and MIG bases, to secondary status to ensure nothing would stand in the way of the POL attacks.[75]

McNamara discussed Rolling Thunder 50 with the president on 31 March, emphasizing more forcefully than in January the need to intensify bombing to counter the enemy buildup in the South. Persuaded that Hanoi's ability to wage the war depended on having sufficient fuel for its growing infiltration effort and expanding air force, McNamara believed that destroying oil stocks would cause widespread shortages that would affect morale and "might eventually" aggravate "any differences which may exist within the regime as to the policies to be followed." His target recommendations echoed those of the JCS—seven POL storage facilities in the Hanoi-Haiphong area; the Haiphong cement plant; and roads, bridges, and rail lines in the northeast quadrant.

Coming full circle, McNamara in effect asked the president to approve a major escalation of the war. Wheeler described the secretary's apparent reversal as "one of his complete [flip-] flops," but in fact he had been moving in that direction, reluctantly but steadily, for months. But Johnson, as he had in July 1965, opted again for moderation, probably because of current widespread anti-government and anti-American activity occurring in South Vietnam.[76]

On 31 March the president approved a monthly increase of sorties from 700 to 900 within the northeast quadrant but limited the targets and disallowed attacks inside a Hanoi 30-mile circle, a Haiphong 10-mile circle, and a slightly enlarged buffer zone nearest China. Johnson did not reject more intensive strikes outright but instead deferred them, leaving McNamara with the impression that authorization was imminent; for that reason the secretary alerted the Chiefs to plan strikes in April against POL storage sites and other deferred targets. They in turn notified CINCPAC to execute, but only when directed. Some at State, however, believed such escalation risked provoking clashes with Chinese Communist fighter aircraft as well as causing civilian casualties and property damage that would offset any military advantage. Likely aware of State's reservations, Wheeler initially attributed the delay to a political decision not to escalate the bombing until a Communist Party world congress adjourned, but he expected presidential authorization soon after.[77] At this point, rising internal political discontent against the South Vietnamese government once more gave pause to U.S. decisionmakers.

Popular dissatisfaction with the Saigon military junta, uneasy relations among senior South Vietnamese officers, religious disaffection, and worsening inflation provided the tinder for the flareup. The spark was Prime Minister Ky's February decision to solidify his hold on power by reshuffling his cabinet followed in March by his firing of a popular military commander. From mid-March through mid-June internal political turmoil racked South Vietnam. Buddhist uprisings in Da Nang in May and Hue in June added to the combustion. Armed clashes in Da Nang during May between pro- and anti-government troops left 150 Vietnamese dead, 700 wounded, and the ringleaders under arrest. Martial law was declared in Hue on 16 June to suppress the opposition and quell rioting. A week later, Vietnamese troops and police rounded up hundreds of dissidents in Saigon and reasserted government control. Pending resolution of the crisis, the president withheld any decisions about escalating the air war. Meanwhile, McNamara and the Joint Chiefs wrestled with the details for the next large U.S. troop deployment to Southeast Asia, and Rusk explored with international sponsors ways to restart settlement negotiations.[78]

Among the latest peace initiatives, Canadian Premier Pearson's plan appeared to hold the most promise. Twice, in March and again in June, he sent retired diplomat Chester A. Ronning to Hanoi as his personal representative to attempt to arrange direct talks between North Vietnam and the United States. Both times

Ronning reported that Hanoi would talk only if the United States unconditionally ceased bombing. Unsure of the precise meaning of "talk" as opposed to negotiation, Washington remained wary of making any concessions when the situation in South Vietnam appeared so perilous.[79]

Throughout these diplomatic activities the Chiefs continued to press their case for destroying North Vietnam's oil reserves. At a White House luncheon on 2 May with the Joint Chiefs, Wheeler briefed the president on the need to attack the POL sites, particularly those located within the Hanoi-Haiphong off-limits areas; when asked his view by Johnson, McNamara concurred. General Greene thought the president had already made up his mind to strike the POL reserves and used the occasion to reinforce his determination. Hoping to forestall such attacks with an assumption that turned out to be unfounded, at a White House meeting three days later Rusk declared that hospitals, schools, and temples bordered the designated targets. When queried by Wheeler, DIA reported no such civilian buildings near the POL facilities.[80]

The continuing split over bombing policy within the administration showed little sign of resolution. Rusk, apparently influenced by Ball's aversion to the POL strikes, believed the attacks would increase international tension, a proposition recently installed national security adviser Walt Rostow, a strong supporter of POL bombing, challenged. Averell Harriman labeled any POL attack as ill-advised escalation, given the government's tenuous hold in the South. McNamara recognized that Saigon seemed to become weaker by the day but believed Hanoi and the Viet Cong were hurting as well. In discussions with Harriman he held out the hope that attacks on oil supplies might help set the stage for a settlement based on a coalition government in the South. The president thought, as he later explained to British Prime Minister Harold Wilson, that approving the POL attacks would stem infiltration from the North and likely minimize U.S. casualties in the expected heavy fighting in South Vietnam during the approaching monsoon season.[81]

On 24 May McNamara told Wheeler that the single obstacle to attacking the oil targets was the political turmoil in the South; if this were remedied, the president would authorize the POL attacks. On the 27th Sharp called for a quick decision since the enemy was dispersing POL inventories and the main storage areas would soon lose their target value. Amidst a growing consensus, three days later Rusk and McNamara agreed to include seven POL targets "along the edge of the restricted circles around Hanoi and Haiphong" in the Rolling Thunder package awaiting presidential approval.[82]

Sensing the "time of decision" to expand the air campaign against North Vietnam was at hand, Wheeler cabled Sharp and Westmoreland on 2 June that only Washington's concern over the continuing political disorder in South Vietnam delayed the attacks. The JCS chairman now proposed that if the political situation in Saigon remained stable, in about a week MACV and CINCPAC once again suggest to Washington inclusion of POL targets within Rolling Thunder. Westmoreland obliged with a 5 June cable that predicted the strikes on POL targets would inflict "a telling blow against a critical national resource." Sharp strongly seconded the general's recommendations the following day.[83]

By the time these cables arrived, however, the president had apparently decided he could delay no longer and tentatively authorized strikes against the POL infrastructure. Johnson thought, as he later recalled, that the serious disruption of POL supplies would make infiltration much more difficult and might cause Hanoi's leaders to negotiate. Simultaneously McNamara had a military officer brief British Prime Minister Harold Wilson about the decision. Wilson immediately urged Johnson not to escalate and warned that his government would have to publicly disassociate itself from the action. Nevertheless, on 6 June, at the president's direction, McNamara scheduled the raids to follow a 10 June meeting between Rusk and Wilson in London. On 8 June, however, at Rusk's urging, McNamara, despite his preferences to attack the POL targets, recommended that the president postpone the attacks until the results of the previously noted Ronning peace mission to Hanoi became known. Otherwise Washington risked denunciation for deliberately sabotaging a peace initiative it had endorsed. To further defuse anticipated criticism, McNamara directed Sharp to take precautions to ensure minimal North Vietnamese civilian casualties during the air strikes.[84]

At the 17 June NSC meeting the president described the POL attacks as a choice between accepting higher U.S. casualties and escalating the war. McNamara declared that while he had previously opposed hitting the POL targets he had changed his mind: such attacks would limit infiltration from the North, create anxiety among NVA troops in the South over their supplies, and exert pressure on the Hanoi regime by displaying U.S. determination. Army Chief of Staff General Johnson, representing Wheeler, expressed the JCS view that a sustained POL offensive might prove an important element in bringing an end to the war; Rostow claimed that it would seriously affect the infiltration rate. The president decided to await Rusk's return from Europe and Ronning's return from North Vietnam before making a final decision.[85]

Five days later, at the 22 June NSC meeting, the members heard that the Ronning mission had confirmed Hanoi's unyielding position. POL strikes might not stop infiltration, said Wheeler, but within a few months they would limit North Vietnam's "total infiltration effort." Retaining public support for the war by forcing Hanoi's hand and convincing himself that the raids represented no change to the policy of striking only military targets swayed Rusk. All other attendees, with one exception, Arthur J. Goldberg, U.S. Representative to the United Nations, in some degree went along with the proposal to destroy the POL targets. After the meeting, the president approved the attacks and so notified McNamara; the JCS then authorized CINCPAC to bomb seven key POL storage installations near Hanoi and Haiphong, beginning 24 June.[86]

Following Rostow's tactic of emphasizing policy continuity not change, the official rationale for the strikes emphasized the need to support U.S. ground troops as the enemy shifted to "a quasi-conventional military operation" involving heavy equipment and trucks. This would also help to explain why earlier attacks on POL sites had not been necessary. To deflect any criticism of procrastination, the administration instructed Public Affairs officers to admit that the targets had been considered for many months "but only recently did the JCS determine that they should be hit without further delay."[87] Then on 23 June (the 24th in Vietnam) bad weather and news leaks announcing the impending operations caused a postponement. Infuriated by the leaks, Johnson ordered an FBI investigation. During the anxious interlude McNamara assured the wavering president on 28 June that the bombing would keep up morale of U.S. troops in Vietnam as well as among supporters of the war on the home front.[88]

The same day, after Sharp reported that the weather on 29 June would be ideal for the attack, Wheeler notified McNamara, who quickly secured the president's approval. The defense secretary then directed Wheeler to authorize the attack, but not to inform the other Chiefs or any government officials and to avoid the normal Pentagon communications system. Initially only the president, McNamara, and Wheeler knew of the decision, although on the evening of the 28th McNamara informed Vance and together they disclosed the impending operation to Acting Secretary of State Ball and, in order to finalize post-strike announcements, to OSD press spokesman Sylvester and one of his deputies. The purpose of all this secrecy, Greene conjectured, was to avoid another leak that might disrupt the operation.[89]

After some six months of soul-searching at the highest administration levels, on 29 June Air Force and Navy aircraft struck POL installations located near Hanoi and Haiphong, catching the North Vietnamese flat-footed. Concerned about domestic and world reaction, both the president and McNamara kept close tabs on the operation, contacting CINCPAC by secure phone before and during the raids. In one roughly 75-minute period, Johnson phoned Rostow and Vance 11 times for mission updates. A spectacular plume of thick black smoke rising more than five miles into the sky over Haiphong appeared to confirm initial pilot reports of 80 percent destruction of Haiphong's POL installations. Subsequent photo reconnaissance revealed that only 40 percent had been destroyed, thereby requiring another strike on 5 July. The attack on the Hanoi tanks was far more effective, with about 90 percent of them destroyed.[90]

With the long-debated POL campaign finally under way, on 8 July McNamara, Sharp, and their staffs met in Honolulu to discuss future air operations. McNamara stressed at length the necessity of a sustained strangulation campaign against POL facilities coupled with destruction of the railroad bridges northeast of Hanoi leading to China. Returning to Washington, he told the Joint Chiefs that CINCPAC was placing "insufficient emphasis on destruction of the POLs" and indicated his willingness to remove restrictions on attacking rail lines running to China to accomplish the strangulation.[91] Wheeler, too, soon believed that CINCPAC had not sufficiently intensified the effort against the high-priority POL targets. Apprehensive that the secretary might impose a daily sortie quota, an action he deemed "would be regrettable," on 10 July Wheeler urged Sharp to step up the POL attacks. For his part, the JCS chairman kept McNamara apprised of the growing number of strikes against both fixed targets—a total of 225—and mobile targets—rolling stock, trucks, and watercraft—essential for POL distribution.[92]

As expected, bombing so close to the enemy's two main cities elicited loud protests and charges of escalation from the communist bloc, from neutral nations, and even from allies. Opponents of the war at home joined the chorus denouncing the attacks. But the criticism, though initially fierce, quickly subsided. Johnson's domestic popularity soared as did support for his Vietnam policy (jumping 12 points to 54 percent), propelled by hopes the bombing would soon end the war. It seemed that Americans wanted the war to end, even if escalation was the way to do it. Official intelligence assessments, though, now offered a far bleaker forecast.[93]

On 23 July the CIA concluded that two weeks of expanded air strikes had apparently not weakened North Vietnamese determination to carry on with the war. A subsequent report covering the period through 11 August judged the strangulation campaign had slowed POL imports and distribution, but communist resiliency and expediency allowed North Vietnam to continue its logistical support of operations in South Vietnam and Laos. About two weeks later DIA issued a similar assessment that cited North Vietnamese improvisations to circumvent damage at oil storage facilities and lack of evidence of reduced POL consumption in the North or indications of any direct effect on military operations in the South.[94] On 24 August, Wheeler reported slightly more favorable findings to McNamara but suggested that increased sorties might be required. No evidence of oil shortages affecting vital enemy operations appeared by mid-September, at which time forthcoming arms control talks with the Soviets precluded restrikes of Haiphong POL targets. After intelligence reports indicated movement of North Vietnamese army units southward toward the DMZ, CINCPAC on 4 September directed a balanced effort against men and materiel in the North Vietnamese panhandle region while continuing attacks against POL targets "on a selective basis." Five days later a "considerable buildup of enemy forces" in and just north of the DMZ caused Sharp to divert air strikes into that area.[95] The POL campaign thus effectively ended, with ramifications far greater in Washington than in Hanoi.

McNamara was displeased and disappointed with the failure of the POL campaign. He pointed out to both the Air Force and Navy the "glaring discrepancy" between their optimistic pre-strike assessments and the gloomy post-strike reality. "I think that we have proven at least to my satisfaction and I think the satisfaction of others that we cannot dry up the POL by bombing." Airpower's inability to impair significantly Hanoi's will and ability to continue supporting the war in the South led the secretary to consider other options, particularly a barrier proposed by a special study group in August 1966, as he groped for a long-range aerial strategy that would get a "big payoff elsewhere" other than the heavily defended northeast quadrant.[96] Conceding that his piecemeal, gradualist approach had failed, McNamara redirected DoD's energies into the construction of a network of manned and electronic obstacles to create a barrier reaching from the South China Sea across South Vietnam and Laos.* He resisted further aerial escalation until events in 1967 prompted him to advocate an intensification of the bombing once again.

Rolling Thunder: Indecision, Discord, and Escalation

As a follow-on to Rolling Thunder 50 and 51, on 22 August the JCS presented McNamara with their proposal for Rolling Thunder 52 based on the bombing plan that Sharp had recommended on 8 August: a formidable series of raids to destroy POL storage dumps at Phuc Yen and Kep airfields as well as numerous railroad shops, factories, power plants, and port warehouses. McNamara whittled down Sharp's list, which State still found too ambitious. The predilection now by both secretaries to limit the air campaign resulted in a mid-September decision by McNamara and Rusk against Rolling Thunder 52. A few days earlier, on 7 September, McNamara had rejected MACV and CINCPAC proposals for B-52 attacks against targets in North Vietnam or north of the demarcation line running through the DMZ because State believed that "many circles and the press" would see it as further escalation or even preparation for an invasion of North Vietnam. The man who had in the end invested so much in the POL attacks now counseled President Johnson to consider halting the bombing of the North after the fall congressional elections as part of a leveling off of the U.S. military commitment to South Vietnam.[97]

McNamara had come to recognize that bombing North Vietnam to induce a comprehensive settlement achieved results in inverse proportion to its intensity: the more bombing, the less possibility of negotiations. As early as May and June 1966, he had discussed with Harriman the idea of the United States stopping the bombing in exchange for Hanoi stopping infiltration. This reasoning permeated his latest assessment following his return from a visit to Saigon on 14 October. He told the president that Rolling Thunder had neither checked infiltration significantly nor cracked Hanoi's morale. Radical escalation was out of the question, for neither American nor world opinion would stomach the scale of bombing it entailed, and it might also draw the United States into war with China. The alternatives were to stop all bombing of North Vietnam or shift the bombing into its southern panhandle region as part of McNamara's newly requested barrier operation. The Joint Chiefs took sharp exception, insisting on the air campaign as indispensable to the overall war effort. Past failures, they maintained, resulted from McNamara's policy of gradualism, despite contrary military advice. Proper use of airpower could still overcome this strategic error; recommending approval of Rolling Thunder 52 they requested that their views be forwarded to the president.[98]

---

* The barrier strategy is discussed in Chapter V.

At a session on 15 October, the president, Vice President Hubert Humphrey, McNamara, Vance, and Wheeler discussed differences between the JCS and the secretary over the future course of the war. Wheeler thought Johnson favorably disposed toward Rolling Thunder 52, although some of the proposed targets, not further identified, gave the president "great difficulties." Johnson still opposed reducing the number of sanctuaries around Hanoi and Haiphong but would hit a few targets despite McNamara's advice to scale back the bombing campaign. Wheeler instructed Westmoreland to emphasize the importance of the air campaign against North Vietnam when he met with the president during the forthcoming Manila conference and at Cam Ranh Bay in South Vietnam during the latter's 23 October–2 November Asian trip.[99]

Westmoreland subsequently forwarded his recommendations for a change in strategy through Rostow. The MACV commander called for removal of current off-limit zones around Hanoi and Haiphong and permission to strike enemy air bases. He also reiterated what he had already told the president during his visit in August to the LBJ Ranch—pause or no pause, keep on bombing in the southern panhandle of North Vietnam to divert and debilitate enemy manpower and resources and disrupt enemy plans for a thrust en masse across the DMZ. The Joint Chiefs and Sharp chimed in, insisting the time had come to hit the enemy harder, not relax the pressure. On Johnson's return to the capital, the JCS urged McNamara to brief him, with Wheeler present, on the rationale for reducing restrictions on attacks against additional POL storage, ports, power plants, waterway locks, and SAM support facilities around Hanoi and Haiphong.[100]

A somewhat disparate CIA analysis of Rolling Thunder for the first nine months of 1966 supported escalation. Its summary declared that the cost-effectiveness of the campaign had diminished in 1966 despite the escalated bombing. Not only had the North Vietnamese continued to expand their support for the insurgency, they had also improved their overall capability to support the war effort because increased Chinese and Soviet military and economic aid had more than offset bombing losses. The body of the paper, however, reasoned that concentrated, repeated air attacks on target complexes, mining of principal North Vietnamese seaports, and bombing currently restricted targets—some 35 percent of all JCS-nominated targets—could inflict greater damage and create greater fear among Hanoi's leaders without provoking Chinese intervention.[101]

The latest policy debate over the air war pitted the Joint Chiefs and Rostow, who with certain exceptions favored an expanded bombing campaign, against McNamara and Rusk, who agreed to some but not dramatic escalation. Johnson meanwhile postponed any decision until after the 8 November midterm congressional elections. Then, typically, he sought a compromise by approving on 10 November targets selected by McNamara from the JCS recommendations, as well as authorizing strikes against a steel plant, a cement factory, and two thermal power plants, four targets not chosen by McNamara but on the Chiefs' list. McNamara conjectured that the president acted apparently feeling that he had world opinion on his side, but the next morning the secretary convinced Johnson to defer attacking the four specified targets for at least two weeks.[102] Wheeler attributed the postponement to an effort not to rock the boat during British Foreign Secretary George Brown's impending visit to Moscow and anticipated clearance to hit the four targets around 25 November, after the foreign secretary departed the Soviet Union. In any case, constant cloud cover delayed strikes on most Rolling Thunder 52 targets until December.[103]

Brown's visit and bad weather were not the only factors complicating the strikes. Marigold, an initiative under way for some months to seek negotiations with Hanoi, involved the Polish representative to the International Control Commission in Vietnam, and Lodge, with the Italian ambassador to Vietnam serving as an intermediary. As the talks continued, the State Department sent word to Hanoi that Washington would suspend the bombing if North Vietnam reciprocated with mutual forms of deescalation.[104] Meantime the JCS and the field forces prepared for Rolling Thunder 52, still uncertain of its content, timing, and duration.

McNamara worked to convince the president of the futility of increased bombing, arguing that the North Vietnamese had adapted their transportation system to life under the bombs. As long as North Vietnam could draw on its allies to make good its losses, the interdiction effort served no significant purpose. McNamara now touted the barrier system as holding greater promise, even though untested and unproved. With these competing and contradictory diplomatic and military initiatives simultaneously in motion, on 21 November State proposed to spread out any strikes as much as possible to cushion their effects on Marigold talks. The White House, preferring to complete Rolling Thunder 52 quickly (except for the deferred targets) to minimize its effects on Brown's trip to Moscow, leaned toward a single massive attack as soon as the weather permitted while insisting the strikes represented no major departure in policy.[105]

The separate diplomatic and military tracks converged on 1–2 December, predictably at cross-purposes: the first day, the Poles reported the North Vietnamese had agreed to start secret discussions in Warsaw; on the second, weather over North Vietnam broke, allowing upwards of 200 aircraft to bomb targets, most in the Hanoi environs. In some of the fiercest battles of the air war, eight planes were lost to intense SAM and AAA fire; the North Vietnamese had used the respite from bombing the Hanoi area to reconstitute and improve their air defense network.[106] Attacks against Haiphong POL storage facilities continued through 5 December.

Following these air strikes, on 6 and 9 December the president met with OSD, JCS, and White House advisers to consider the effects of the bombing on possible negotiations. On 9 December Johnson refused to decide on new targets "because of certain political problems," evidently a reference to Marigold, but said he would reconsider in about a week. Then fearing the North would interpret further delay as a sign of weakness, he rejected strong appeals from McNamara, Under Secretary of State Nicholas de B. Katzenbach, Lodge, and Llewellyn Thompson to cancel additional attacks; instead, he declined to halt strikes against two targets near Hanoi on 13 December and heavier follow-up raids the next day. Two days of concentrated attacks cost four more warplanes, including two downed during the 14 December restrike of the Yen Vien railway yard.[107]

These raids touched off an international uproar alleging that the American attacks in heavily populated areas had caused great property damage and many civilian casualties. On the 14th, the North Vietnamese informed Marigold's Polish contacts that they were terminating negotiation conversations. At a meeting with the president the same day, the participants supported suspending repeat strikes on the vehicle depot and railroad yards because of the "hue and cry" raised by Hanoi over bombing civilians.[108]

McNamara later lamented that these attacks deterred some political leaders in Hanoi who, he believed, favored negotiations, and caused Marigold's failure. Soviet Ambassador to the United States Anatoly F. Dobrynin subsequently told him that Moscow interpreted the timing of attacks as Washington's attempt to apply further military pressure on Hanoi at the start of any secret talks.[109] While the administration appeared to have bungled a serious peace initiative by failing to coordinate its military and diplomatic efforts, in fact the intimate group involved in Marigold knew fully about the proposed raids. Uncertainty also surrounded Hanoi's understanding of the Polish initiative, which may have misled North Vietnamese leaders into believing the United States was willing to stop the bombing without further military conditions—the fundamental communist demand that was never the American offer. The administration attempted to revive Marigold, and in line with this overture on 23 December the president forbade attacks on targets within 10 nautical miles of Hanoi's center. Sharp assumed that the White House's typical refusal to share with him the rationale for the latest prohibitions resulted from the enemy's latest furor over civilian casualties. He complained bitterly about the latest bombing ban when "we were just starting to put some real pressure on Hanoi."[110]

Further controversy erupted on 25 December when Harrison E. Salisbury of the *New York Times* prepared the first of 15 dispatches from Hanoi implying that U.S. aircraft regularly bombed civilian areas. Because the administration had always claimed that the aircrews attacked only military targets, the White House found itself struggling once again to repair its damaged credibility with the press and public. Deputy Assistant Secretary of Defense for Public Affairs Phil Goulding attributed the reaction to the administration's unwillingness to explain that bombing military targets also often claimed civilian lives and destroyed homes.

Despite 81,000 attack sorties, 48,000 other combat support sorties, $184 million in economic costs and damage to North Vietnam, destruction of 80 percent of the enemy's POL, and the loss of 280 U.S. aircraft, Rolling Thunder operations ended 1966 without substantially reducing Hanoi's military capability or will to continue the war and with many Americans, not least the secretary of defense, questioning their worth.[111]

It had taken the inner circle three months to decide to launch Rolling Thunder in February 1965, four months to initiate a meaningful bombing pause in December 1965, and seven months to agree on POL attacks in June 1966—a pattern of hesitation and indecision stemming from having to choose between several unpalatable alternatives but also owing to administration miscalculation and plain mismanagement. Tentativeness and ambivalence contributed to false starts and delays that undermined the timely achievement of goals and confused allies and enemies alike.[112]

The largely civilian direction of the air strategy failed the tests of both conception and execution. From the very first Rolling Thunder missions it became apparent that the bombing precision demanded during White House luncheon meetings exceeded the capacity of pilots flying against heavily defended targets. Aircrews had to contend with a landscape laced with antiaircraft guns and missiles and with abysmal flying weather over North Vietnam during the northeast monsoon season lasting from mid-October into mid-March. Severe weather conditions could prevent scheduled attacks for two or three weeks at a time.[113] There existed, indeed, a fog of war. But military leaders shared the blame, with an inflexibility and lack of appreciation for the political dimension of the conflict and with their own miscalculation—overstating the efficacy of airpower in an unconventional circumstance and hence reinforcing civilian mistrust of their judgment.

Lacking an integrated and coherent political-military strategic foundation, the air campaign proceeded by fits and starts, sputtering most of the time. Despite the great courage of the aviators and the expenditure of enormous resources, it proved inconclusive. Like the steady escalation of the ground war in South Vietnam, continued expansion of the air war against the North—Rolling Thunder operations recommenced in earnest in the spring of 1967 and, with further lulls and resumptions, would continue through November 1968—defied McNamara's intentions to contain the U.S. commitment. The widening intervention inflicted rising unanticipated costs that would render the defense secretary's methodically crafted DoD budget yet another casualty of a fatally flawed strategy.

Chapter IV

Paying for a War: Budgets, Supplements, and Estimates, 1965–1967

McNamara's annual budgeting process projected his vision of an efficiently managed, cost-effective Department of Defense. During the 1960s, the president transmitted to Congress each January his proposed budget for the 12-month period beginning the following 1 July. Crafting the DoD portion of the president's budget began more than a year before Congress received the final document in January. The process was guided by the Planning, Programming, Budgeting System (PPBS) introduced in DoD by McNamara in 1961. PPBS systematically employed cost-benefit analysis to determine program alternatives; the result became the Five Year Force Structure and Financial Program (FYFS&FP). The main JCS contribution to the PPBS, the Joint Strategic Objectives Plan, recommended the force structure and budgets needed to achieve mid-range (five-year) strategic goals.[1] The services used the OSD-approved JSOP force structure in budget planning for the five-year cycle.

Yearly budget planning was based on the secretary of defense's annual logistics guidance that provided the military services with a baseline force—the JSOP-derived number of Army and Marine divisions, Navy ships, and Navy and Air Force aircraft as well as operating and support assumptions—to use in determining fiscal year requirements. In March the JCS would normally send McNamara their recommended changes to the approved JSOP force. By 1 April, the secretary would issue tentative force guidance, and by 15 June the military departments would submit program change proposals (PCPs). These documents detailed cost and manpower effects of changes to the logistics guidance in the FYFS&FP and to the force structure in the JSOP as justified by international developments, new technology, or recent intelligence.

Budget and cost-benefit analysts in Systems Analysis* reviewed the PCPs to reconcile them with current force structure, procurement, and financial resource guidance. These evaluations went to McNamara for approval, after which he issued his tentative decisions to the services in the form of updated and revised versions of current Draft Presidential Memoranda (DPMs) prepared in Systems Analysis.[2] The Joint Chiefs, the military service secretaries, and OSD agencies used the DPM guidance for their program and budget reviews and for revisions in their original proposals as they prepared their budgets. They could also appeal OSD decisions and, if these were sustained, amend their budget submissions accordingly.

Formal budgeting commenced in mid-summer when the ASD (Comptroller) issued administrative guidance to the services and Defense agencies for budget submissions. McNamara initially imposed no monetary ceiling on service budget requests, insisting that he made decisions on the merits of Defense programs not budget ceilings. The comptroller, however, instructed the services to provide a basic budget request for those funds needed for approved programs and an addendum budget that contained PCPs not completed at the time the services prepared their budgets, and also requests not allowed in the basic budget, including those disapproved by McNamara. For instance, addenda for FY 1966 service budget submissions ran between seven and ten percent of basic budget requests. In practice, McNamara's unwillingness to give fiscal ceilings for overall budget totals encouraged the services and DoD agencies to inflate their requests for approved, but previously deferred, programs and to appeal OSD decisions. This accounted for the large discrepancies between the service budget requests and the final DoD budgets. The inevitable reductions then enabled McNamara and OSD to take public credit for reducing the Defense budget to manageable levels, signifying that the services did not need everything they requested.[3]

After completion of development of the internal DoD budget in late September, the interagency budget process commenced. In the frenetic period from early October, when the services and Defense agencies forwarded their revised budget estimates to OSD, to mid-January when the presidential budget went to Congress, Systems Analysis as well as Bureau of the Budget† and OSD budget experts carefully reviewed, evaluated, and formulated the budget submission for the next fiscal year.‡ Whereas previously the BoB had actively helped shape the DoD budget during its internal formulation in early spring, under its new director Charles L. Schultze, appointed 1 June 1965, it negotiated with OSD after the DoD budget estimates were drafted in the fall, but before they were finalized. Besides eliminat-

---

* Until September 1965 when McNamara elevated Systems Analysis to the level of Assistant Secretary of Defense (ASD), it was under the OSD Comptroller's office.

† The Bureau of the Budget, whose director was an important presidential adviser on expenditures, prepared the annual budget for the president.

‡ BoB staffers usually commenced their work after federal agencies had completed their internal budget reviews. The Defense budget was the exception. See Alain Enthoven, "Putting Together the Defense Department's Budget," nd but likely late 1968, 7, fldr #3, box 11, Enthoven Papers, LBJL.

ing requests deemed unnecessary, the interagency budget specialists also sought out "relatively low-priority" programs that OSD could defer in favor of approved projects that might need additional funding because of price increases, inflation, work slippages, or technical problems.[4] During the process, budget analysts presented recommendations and alternatives to the secretary of defense for tentative decision. The services also commented on or appealed the recommendations of the budget programmers.

From all of this information, McNamara drew together a summary statement of force structure and budget estimates in late November, in effect his decisions on funding for major Defense projects. He then discussed the budget proposals with the BoB director; after incorporating any modifications resulting from these sessions and from presidential guidance, he finalized DoD's budget estimates around 1 December. His approved DPMs, offering OSD's rationale for the Defense budget and explaining any significant differences between OSD and the Joint Chiefs over proposed funding, went to the White House where they could be used to prepare the president for his annual meeting with the Chiefs on the budget.

Between 15 November and 31 December, McNamara prepared his budget statement and rehearsed for his upcoming congressional testimony. During December he also drafted the Defense portion of the president's budget message. Shortly after Congress reconvened in January, the secretary normally appeared before four congressional committees to explain and defend the Defense budget. These appearances alone ate heavily into his time. Between 20 January and 5 October 1966, for instance, McNamara spent more than 100 hours testifying before congressional committees, almost a third of that time related specifically to budget issues discussed during nine appearances early in the year. By McNamara's own estimate, one hour of congressional testimony required four hours of preparation, and he believed the time devoted to Capitol Hill business took about 20 to 25 percent of his working hours.[5] Nevertheless, he judged his personal involvement throughout the budget cycle time well spent.

Congress acted on the DoD budget, a major part of the president's overall budget request, in two separate procedures—authorization (approval of the program) and appropriation (passage of a bill to provide the money). Four appropriation titles—(I) Personnel, (II) Operations & Maintenance, (III) Procurement, and (IV) Research Development Testing & Evaluation (RDT&E)—comprised the DoD bill. Military construction and family housing fell under the Military Construction Appropriation Bill, while civil defense and the Military Assistance Program (MAP) were treated in separate legislation.

Shortly after receiving the president's budget in January, the House and Senate Armed Services Committees and subcommittees considered the budget for defense and held hearings. During the 1960s, the committees were dominated by highly partisan Southern Democrats who were favorably disposed toward Defense but increasingly adversarial toward McNamara. Any differences in the Senate and House versions of a bill were resolved in a conference of members from both committees. The full House and Senate then voted to authorize specific amounts for each of the four appropriation titles. Military construction, civil defense, and military assistance were authorized separately.

Around June the Senate and House Appropriations Committees reviewed the approved authorization bill, held hearings, and resolved any differences in their respective versions of the legislation. The full House and Senate voted, usually during September, on the appropriation bill for procurement, personnel, operations and maintenance, and research and development. The president then signed or vetoed the DoD appropriation bill. Appropriations for military construction, civil defense, and the military assistance, as with the authorization actions, required separate legislation.

The appropriation act gave the government authority to obligate and pay out money from the appropriated funds. This was called New Obligational Authority (NOA): the sum of all new budget authority granted by Congress for a specific fiscal year and the amount that DoD could legally commit during the fiscal year 1 July–30 June, designated by the calendar year in which it ended. NOA, however, always included obligations for such long-term, multi-year projects as aircraft carrier construction; thus some NOA funds appropriated in one fiscal year carried over into successive fiscal years. These unspent balances, together with transfers, unused budget authority, reappropriations, and other moneys were added to current NOA to create a new category—Total Obligational Authority (TOA), the entire amount available to DoD to commit. The money DoD actually paid out in various forms during a fiscal year constituted expenditures. If expenditures exceeded appropriations, as often occurred, OSD would request a supplemental budget to cover the shortfall. The same congressional subcommittees or committees held hearings, and the full House and Senate passed authorizations and appropriated the additional NOA. Supplemental requests moved quickly; appropriations were passed usually within a few weeks.

The FY 1966 Defense Budget

Besides imposing fiscal responsibility on the military departments, McNamara's insistence on requirement-based budget requests enabled the secretary and his staff to monitor and control Defense spending closely, in particular to reduce significantly the amounts sought by the services. For example, the FY 1966 Defense budget, submitted to Congress on 25 January 1965, totaled about $48.6 billion dollars (NOA), almost $8 billion less than the services had requested and an overall reduction in NOA of $1.2 billion from the previous year. President Johnson trumpeted the accompanying reductions in Defense expenditures as a tribute to McNamara's effective stewardship of DoD, and the administration welcomed the lower Defense budget also because the Soviets responded by reducing their defense spending.[6]

In the brief period following the president's submission of the budget and McNamara's early February testimony on Capitol Hill in its behalf, however, events in Vietnam took a turn for the worse. Within days of the Viet Cong attack against Pleiku on 7 February 1965, the MACV commander requested more U.S. combat troops and the president authorized the bombing of North Vietnam. The "growing threat of trouble in Southeast Asia," to use Florida Democrat Robert L. F. Sikes's phrase, provoked recurring congressional questions about the adequacy of the proposed Defense budget which, after all, had been sent to Congress before the latest eruptions in South Vietnam. George H. Mahon (D-Tex.), head of the powerful House Appropriations Committee and chairman of the Subcommittee on DoD Appropriations, asked McNamara if he was "morally certain" that the budget was "reasonably adequate." For the moment, as McNamara had explained previously, additional money was unnecessary because the proposed budget would allow for increased conventional U.S. military strength as well as improved combat effectiveness and readiness.[7]

Congressional accommodation did not imply complete agreement with all of McNamara's budget proposals. In particular, the Special Training and Enlistment Program (STEP) and OSD's proposed merger of Army National Guard and Army Reserve units drew heavy criticism. STEP, a project dear to McNamara, would correct minor educational and physical deficiencies that otherwise barred a volunteer from enlisting in the Army. House critics contended the civilian sector or government agencies such as the Job Corps were better suited to such purposes; the Senate Appropriations Committee unanimously opposed the measure. The House committee markup of the DoD appropriations bill eliminated STEP, and language inserted into the appropriations legislation of 29 September 1965 excluded any use of appropriated funds for the program. As for merger of reserve forces, congressionally unpopular in any case, McNamara's decision to announce his plan publicly before consulting Congress only fueled lawmakers' ire over having to "read about it in the papers."[8]

Congressional committees also questioned the wisdom of reducing the request for additional nuclear-powered attack submarines from six to four and reinstated the original numbers. The Senate and House committee decisions significantly reduced the services' total RDT&E requests while inserting funds for an advanced manned bomber program that McNamara strongly disapproved. But overall the setbacks were relatively minor; an enthusiastic McNamara informed the president in mid-June that he thought it "absolutely fantastic" that the Defense budget had sailed through the House Appropriations Committee with so little change.[9]

The comptroller's mid-July review of the House report recommended acquiescing to committee action that accepted the funding for submarines and the advanced aircraft and did not propose appealing the RDT&E reductions. McNamara grudgingly agreed, though he still tried, unsuccessfully, to resuscitate

STEP and the reserve merger. He concurred with the RDT&E cuts, but appealed for flexibility to distribute the reductions throughout Title IV funds to minimize the detrimental effect on specific programs.[10]

When Congress enacted the general appropriation bill totaling more than $46.8 billion (NOA) for FY 1966, only $86 million less than requested, the legislation reflected the major decisions described above and included the $1.7 billion for Southeast Asia that OSD requested in an August 1965 budget amendment that appeared as Title V. DoD got slightly more than it requested in four of the appropriated titles, although a series of additions and reductions shifted the procurement accounts somewhat. Other separately enacted DoD appropriations fared poorly: military construction (PL 89-202) down 17 percent to slightly over $1 billion; family housing down nine percent to $665 million; and civil defense (PL 89-128) down 45 percent to $106 million. Finally, Congress also approved $1.17 billion for military assistance on 5 October.[11]

The 1965 Supplemental

Even as House and Senate committees deliberated over the FY 1966 budget, the escalating violence in Southeast Asia demanded additional funds to underwrite the costs of increasing U.S. involvement. During March 1965, McNamara promised the service secretaries "an unlimited appropriation" to finance assistance to South Vietnam; he separately reiterated to the Joint Chiefs that they should not "feel any constraints whatsoever—absolutely none" on proposing funding for South Vietnam.[12] Based on their experience in financing the Korean War (1950–53), the military services assumed that McNamara had issued them the customary blank check to pay for the war.

During the Korean conflict procurement on a huge scale proved so imprecise and prolonged that DoD ended up with over $32 billion in unexpended funds as of 30 June 1958, almost five years after hostilities ceased, even after spending almost $19 billion of such excess funds during 1954–1958. And this was after OSD had slashed initial service requests during the war years by as much as 38 percent. In 1965 the services expected that McNamara would also allow the military departments wide latitude in financial matters and an open-ended budget to accompany it. They were mistaken. The comptroller of the Army was quick to point out that peacetime restrictions not only limited the use of certain funds, but made large-scale (more than $2 million) reprogramming of authorizations cumbersome and required documentation for construction projects over $50,000.[13] Although the secretary of defense adopted certain budgetary techniques used during the Korean War, he never relinquished tight control over the budgets, believing PPBS as effective and efficient in time of war as in time of peace.

As war clouds thickened over Southeast Asia, a few senators called for negotiations with Hanoi and a few others urged the president to request new approval from Congress if he intended to expand U.S. involvement in Vietnam. Most, though, were discreetly silent, in part out of respect for the president's difficult position and in part because the administration had not informed them about any recent policy changes on Southeast Asia. If the president remained tight-lipped about his military strategy, he showed equal reticence to place a dollar figure on the cost of the steadily escalating war, complicating the job of administration economists.[14] Concerned that a public debate on his Vietnam policy would endanger his Great Society agenda, Johnson looked for an opportune moment to raise the issue. Such an occasion presented itself on 28 April 1965 when U.S. Marines landed in the Dominican Republic to protect American citizens and prevent an allegedly imminent communist takeover of its government.[*]

Faced with this latest international crisis, shortly after 10 a.m. on 4 May Johnson met in the White House with members of the House and Senate Appropriations, Foreign Relations, and Armed Services committees. "Before the day is over," his listeners learned, he would request that Congress appropriate a $700 million supplemental to the FY 1965 Defense budget, primarily to support the increasing tempo of fighting in Vietnam, but also to cover expenses arising from the recent intervention in the Dominican Republic. Reference to the Caribbean crisis disappeared from the president's special message to Congress sent later that day. He now linked the relatively small appropriation request exclusively to the need to halt communist aggression in South Vietnam, thereby transforming approval of his call for supplemental funding into a congressional endorsement of his Southeast Asia policy.[15]

McNamara's testimony that day before the House Committee on Armed Services in executive session buttressed the president's political agenda. The secretary reminded the representatives that existing legislation enabled the administration to use its emergency authority to spend beyond authorized budget levels, making the amount of the supplemental incidental. What mattered was congressional reappraisal and endorsement of U.S. policy in Southeast Asia. According to McNamara, a ringing vote of confidence on the appropriation would "eliminate some of the confusion of signals which have been given to Hanoi and Peking as to the intended purpose and will of this country." Conversely, extended debate might convey congressional displeasure with the president's Vietnam policy that in turn would signal a lack of U.S. resolve. By defining the issue in such terms, McNamara handed Congress a presidential ultimatum—either take "prompt action or no action" on the request, but do not debate it.[16]

A legitimate need for additional money existed because the U.S. presence in Vietnam had grown far beyond original expectations. American airpower in Southeast Asia had trebled during the past 90 days, to cite but one example, requiring more funds for airbase construction in Vietnam, ammunition and equip-

---

[*] See Chapter XI.

ment, and unanticipated costs of the U.S. deployments. Still the administration had no intention of underwriting a military spending spree. Rather than receiving the blank check they expected, the services discovered that McNamara, in characteristic fashion, had slashed their initial requests for $1.24 billion in supplemental funds to $700 million.[17]

McNamara's deepest cuts eliminated long-term spending for aircraft for the Navy and Air Force in favor of purchasing short-term necessities such as ammunition. He also held new spending to a minimum. Of the $286 million construction plan submitted by the services, for instance, he canceled $86 million outright, reprogrammed $20 million from the fiscal year 1965 construction budget, and financed $80 million from contingency appropriations requested for fiscal year 1966 construction, leaving only $100 million for the emergency supplemental to fund. He further reprogrammed $94 million for ammunition procurement over and above the $275 million supplemental request. The final distribution left little doubt the secretary still controlled the Defense checkbook. The services bought what he directed.[18]

McNamara's numbers had less to do with military considerations than the political realities of Johnson's White House. Determined neither to panic the American people nor disrupt their lives, the president personally proposed a deliberately low supplemental pegged at $700 million. His subsequent political maneuvering to minimize supplemental appropriations suggests that he regarded the $1 billion mark as a threshold which, if crossed, would open a policy debate on Vietnam that he so desperately wanted to avoid. An eye-catching figure like $1 billion might provoke questions about the magnitude of the growing U.S. military involvement in South Vietnam, but McNamara could stay well under the limit because the $700 million would pay only for those expenses incurred during the remaining two months of the 1965 fiscal year. Who knew what might happen in Southeast Asia after that? General Wheeler and the Joint Chiefs agreed the supplemental was helpful to permit a buildup "you might say, in anticipation of any escalation of the future." McNamara also made plain to congressional committees that if the administration needed more money for the Vietnam conflict he would again ask Congress for it.[19]

As Johnson anticipated, on 7 May Congress quickly approved the emergency supplemental by overwhelming majorities, 408 to 7 in the House and 88 to 3 in the Senate, since a "No" vote could be depicted as denying help to soldiers in combat. After receiving McNamara's official pro forma recommendation on 7 May for the extra funding, the president made a great show of transferring the $700 million appropriated by Congress for the Southeast Asia Emergency Fund to the regular DoD appropriation accounts. At a press conference the following day, the president equated the speedy congressional action on the supplemental with the American people's endorsement of the forces in Vietnam. Johnson assured reporters those U.S. troops had a "blank check" to draw on the very best support the nation could give them. Contrary to the rhetoric, however, the administration had no intention of allowing the services carte blanche to determine funding requirements for the Vietnam War. The president later put it bluntly: "[T]he Joint Chiefs of Staff . . . were not to receive one nickel without a plan."[20]

The administration's May supplemental request was a political device, "a gimmick" according to William Bundy, to mute potential congressional criticism of the Vietnam policy. In simplest terms, the president wanted much more than money; he coveted congressional legitimacy for his actions. Nevertheless, this "gimmick" set the tone for financing the Vietnam conflict. First, domestic political, not military, concerns exerted the paramount influence over DoD budget formulation. Second, responding to these political imperatives, McNamara always held Defense budgets to the lowest possible amount. Third, supplemental financing became the standard technique to pay for the escalating war. Many argued then and have argued since that McNamara deliberately used such methods to misrepresent the true financial cost of the war.[21] The actual process of budgetmaking during his wartime tenure became much more complex and reactive to events in Vietnam. After all, in May 1965 the administration had yet to make its major policy decisions about Vietnam, much less determine the financial implications of an expanded war. Johnson could still speak of having both guns and butter, although others were wondering about the price tag for the conflict.

While the president might vacillate about the size of future troop deployments to Vietnam, he could not hide the already obvious and expanding U.S. military presence in the small Asian nation. Wishing to appear supportive of the president yet wanting to know more about his Vietnam policy, Mahon questioned McNamara on 4 June 1965 about the adequacy of DoD's FY 1966 budget then before his committee. Thinking it better to err on the side of strength when providing funds for Defense, Mahon asked whether DoD was preparing another supplemental request or considering an extraordinary reprogramming of funds for Vietnam expenditures. McNamara responded that the Defense budget was divided into three parts: initial equipment and stocks; peacetime consumption; and wartime consumption. Requirements for the first two could be determined with great accuracy, but the third depended on whether and to what extent U.S. forces actually engaged in combat. Without such empirical data, it was better to submit war-related costs later in the fiscal year when the administration could "determine them with greater precision." In the meantime, the basic budget as submitted remained adequate.[22] McNamara's reply was accurate but incomplete: accurate because he insisted on identifying expenses in order to control costs and hold defense spending to a minimum; incomplete because the secretary's figures applied only to the current rather than future costs, which he publicly maintained were unknowable, even as estimates. This meant the budget was adequate—as long as U.S. involvement in Vietnam hovered around its current level.

Infusions of more money and additional combat troops failed to improve the military situation in South Vietnam. Barring a dramatic turnaround, during the early summer of 1965 it became apparent that the United States would have to do more of the fighting to achieve its goals. No one knew precisely how much an expanded war might cost, but everyone knew that with each passing day the bill for Vietnam operations was growing larger. Fiscal conservatives in Congress were already calling for a supplemental appropriation in the $2 billion range to fund the enlarged war.[23] Since the president intended to hold down the financial costs of U.S. involvement in Vietnam, he remained undecided, pending a policy review, about how large a supplemental to request.

As part of the major reevaluation, McNamara traveled to Saigon in mid-July 1965 for a firsthand examination of conditions in South Vietnam. In his absence, OSD principals prepared plans to support a greatly augmented U.S. military role in Southeast Asia. A key working assumption was that the president would approve a supplemental appropriation of $2 billion to $3 billion to pay for the additional personnel and materiel costs of the war.[24] Johnson, though, was having second thoughts about asking Congress for such a huge amount of money.

Concerned that such a request might kill the administration's Great Society domestic legislative program, on 16 July the president decided that through the use of the previously approved $700 million supplemental, and a "possible small current supplemental," by which he meant between $300 million and $400 million, sufficient funds were available to finance operations in Vietnam until January 1966 when more precise cost figures would become available. The plan relied on public funds obtained by borrowing rather than by taxation. McNamara learned of the president's decision on 17 July while in Saigon, when Vance informed him that he, OSD Comptroller Hitch, and I&L Assistant Secretary Ignatius were already at work to meet the president's goals.[25]

Two days later, on 19 July, Johnson asked McGeorge Bundy to draft a brief rebuttal to Senator Stennis's recent proposal on how to pay for the war. The Mississippi Democrat, a member of the Senate Appropriations Committee and later chairman of the Senate Armed Services Committee, wanted to increase the DoD FY 1966 budget immediately and handle early in 1966 a supplemental request for any additionally required funds. Bundy's memo, sent to Johnson the evening of 19 July, maintained that a billion-dollar appropriation would needlessly provoke the Soviets, stir worries at home about the health of the national economy, and engender a "guns or butter" debate harmful to the president's domestic legislative agenda. Bundy's logic intersected neatly with the president's "cardinal rule," in the words of biographer Doris Kearns, of keeping the war "as painless and concealed as possible," exemplified by his insistence on a small future supplemental request. It fell to McNamara to keep the Vietnam War costs at a reasonable level by combining budgetary restraint, reason, and responsibility with the tools of fiscal and monetary management.[26]

The August Supplemental Amendment to the 1966 Budget[*]

In planning a larger U.S. role in Vietnam, no matter the political calculations, OSD had to figure the monetary cost of the commitment. The overall price tag the services assigned to the buildup was more than $12.3 billion, or considerably more than 30 times the presidential guidance. In order to align the services' recommendations with political reality, Hitch reduced their original requests "to a minimum" by using the authority of Section 512(c)[†] to exclude from the August supplemental appropriation the military personnel ($1.8 billion) as well as operations and maintenance ($2.3 billion) accounts, and, where applicable, the equipment procurement associated with the increased strength requirements. Section 512(a) of the same legislation permitted the administration to spend on credit any money, appropriated or not, to fund these categories. This left only funding for procurement ($6.8 billion) and construction ($577 million) to consider. By further heavy use of his hatchet, Hitch arrived at a supplemental figure of about $1.75 billion—$1.6 billion for procurement and $150 million for construction.[27]

Despite all of Hitch's ingenuity, a supplemental of even that amount far exceeded the president's desires. Aware of Johnson's concern, McNamara had deliberately avoided precise figures by assigning an "x" cost to the Vietnam War. He did so for two reasons: he could not accurately compute the cost of the conflict because "during my trip to Vietnam, the x kept getting larger," and he wanted to avoid any differences over a figure between himself and the president from coming to light.[28] Nevertheless, a cleavage over disclosing the costs and means of financing the war had opened between Johnson and McNamara.

Realistic estimates of the proposed supplemental were far beyond Hitch's numbers and Johnson's preferences. Vance thought the price around $8 billion. Assuming more ground troops in South Vietnam, more air attacks on North Vietnam, and a reserve call-up, McNamara told the president at a 22 July meeting with the Joint Chiefs and the service secretaries that the war would cost $12 billion in 1966, but this additional spending would have little effect on the overall economy. Two hours later at a second meeting with only Wheeler and Vance joining him from DoD, McNamara passed on the services' estimates of $12 billion in 1966, but he informed the president the sum could be cut by half or more. Even Hitch's minimalist request would total at least $1.7 billion, or more than four times the amount that Johnson had set. McNamara concluded that asking for a supplemental of "another few hundred million" to pay the enormous costs of expanding the war was not politically credible. The amount required was too huge to conceal for

[*] Because Congress had not yet passed the FY 1966 appropriation bill (it was approved 29 September 1965 as PL 89-213), DoD had to request the additional $1.7 billion in the form of an amendment to the pending budget request.

[†] Reference is to Sec. 512 of the Department of Defense Appropriation Act, 19 August 1964; PL 88-446 (78 Stat 476).

long. Better, he thought, to ask for a $2 billion supplemental and come back to Congress for more money later as would have to be done in any event given the uncertainty of the x factor.[29]

The long-term financial issue involved taxes. Unless a tax increase raised new revenue to offset the ballooning costs of the war, inflationary pressures on the U.S. economy would mount. In July, around the time of his trip to Vietnam, McNamara had recommended a tax hike to Johnson to cover the expanded military operations in Vietnam. The president, however, saw no possibility of congressional support for raising taxes; furthermore he wanted to deny opponents in Congress any opportunity to shift his ambitious domestic spending to the military expenditures. When McNamara submitted his estimated spending and proposed tax increase to Johnson in a "highly classified draft memorandum," bypassing the treasury secretary and the chairman of the Council of Economic Advisors, the secretary's apparent political naiveté only exasperated the president. In the end though, Johnson agreed to ask Congress for a $1.7 billion supplemental appropriation, perhaps heeding his defense secretary's admonition to avoid appearances of "trying to pull a fast one."[30]

To cultivate legislative support for the extra funds, the president met with an 11-member bipartisan congressional delegation in the White House on the evening of 27 July. He discussed with his audience his reasons for requesting a supplemental appropriation of between $1 billion and $2 billion and, depending on what happened in Vietnam, coming back to Congress in January for additional money, "a few billion dollars." Presidential special assistants Califano and Valenti remembered things going so well at the meeting that the president opened up to his former colleagues by telling them there was enough money for now. "Then when you come back in January, you'll have a bill of several billion dollars." This admission may account for Senators Russell and Stennis remarking on national television that Vietnam might cost an additional $10–14 billion and Sen. Leverett Saltonstall (R-Mass.) later commenting that a January supplemental would range between $7 billion and $10 billion, at least.[31]

Three days after the White House meeting, McNamara requested that the Bureau of the Budget forward to Congress, as an amendment to the FY 1966 DoD budget then in the Senate, a request for an additional $1.7 billion for a new line-item appropriation—"Emergency Fund, Southeast Asia." This sum, not intended to cover the total costs of the buildup, would pay for gearing up production of new items, accelerating delivery of essential commodities to U.S. forces in Southeast Asia, and building new facilities in the war zone. McNamara left no doubt that he would have to return to Congress in January to ask for substantially more money to cover the larger forces and higher rates of consumption in Vietnam expected by December 1965.[32]

Now McNamara was asking Congress for a blank check. He told the Senate Armed Services and Appropriations Committees on 4 August of the plans to in-

crease force levels and air operations in Vietnam. Pressed by Senators Stennis and
Henry M. Jackson (D-Wash.) for a rough estimate of the costs, McNamara replied
he expected the buildup, that is adding 340,000 more men to the armed forces, to
be accomplished by September 1966 with a resulting additional annual cost from
that point of $1.7 billion. Beyond that figure, he could not estimate any operation
and maintenance or procurement and construction expenses because the services
were still developing their detailed plans. Precise expenditures depended, he said,
on what happened in Vietnam.[33]

Although technically correct, the secretary of defense was obfuscating the issue and misleading congressional committees. What happened in Vietnam would
determine future appropriation requests to a degree as yet uncertain. In contrast
to battlefield expenditures, one could estimate the price of expanding the military
base in support of the war effort. Indeed planners had already calculated personnel, O&M, procurement, and construction costs for the buildup at close to $3.6
billion during FY 1966. The figures originally accompanied McNamara's prepared
classified statement for the congressional hearings but got excised from the final
version and replaced with the innocuous sentence, "Detailed costs cannot be determined at this time and will be financed under Section 512." On 18 August, the
Senate Committee on Appropriations recommended the $1.7 billion appropria-
tion which became part of the 29 September DoD Appropriations Act.[34]

By August, however, events in Vietnam rather than in Washington were driving the cost of the United States commitment in Southeast Asia. This reality, as
much as the president's decision to downplay the financial burden of the war, accounted for the rapidly widening gap between the administration's projected costs
of the war and the actual spending needed for something no one in Washington
really wanted or expected—a full-scale conventional land war on the Asian continent.

The August amendment to the FY 1966 budget provided a stopgap solution
for expanding conventional U.S. forces to meet Vietnam requirements. It did not
address how to budget for a war which, by midsummer 1965, cast an ever dark-
ening shadow on the president's legislative agenda. The chairman of the Federal
Reserve Board hinted about hikes in interest rates to tighten credit, to slow the
economy, and to avoid inflation. On the other hand, Council of Economic Advisors Chairman Gardner Ackley discounted the effects of the war on the nation's
economy unless its costs neared $10 billion, a possibility he thought remote based
on McNamara's "super-confidential" explanation to him of a gradual and moderate buildup of military spending and manpower.[35]

In mid-August 1965, DoD projected $8.4 billion in additional costs for Viet-
nam, and those numbers held until recalculations in mid-November. Unspoken, as
always, was the assumption that costs were calculated as of the moment and could
increase or decrease depending on what happened in Vietnam. As BoB Director
Charles Schultze later put it, if the war continued, the "budget was understated

simply on technical grounds, but understated by an amount nobody knew." Mc-
Namara's warning at the NSC's 5 August meeting that the Republicans were "making political capital by overstating the effect on the U.S. economy of the cost of the
Vietnam war,"[36] suggested that at the time he believed the costs might not reach
the $10–12 billion range.

Even accounting for the "uncertainties about defense needs, private demand,
and Federal civilian programs," Ackley told the president on 30 July that the economy could absorb a buildup based on the Defense program Johnson had outlined
to him. While intensified concern about prices and wages was in order, if the expenditures followed the path McNamara believed likely, the additional spending
could provide a major stimulus to the economy during the first half of 1966. The
president's imposing presence always loomed behind McNamara's budget numbers. Insistent on enacting and funding Great Society measures "without a tax
increase and without inflation" as well as silencing congressional critics, Johnson
directed McNamara to hold the FY 1967 Defense budget to about $60 billion dol-
lars. On 20 August he reminded himself, "McNamara's got to find ways to drag his
feet on defense expenditures."[37]

The FY 1966 Supplemental

Without question the secretary strove to meet the president's desired budget
ceilings. Still, before the ink went dry on the August amendment, others in OSD
were already working the numbers for a much larger January supplemental to the
FY 1966 budget and for the basic FY 1967 budget. These had to go in tandem
because their influence on each other determined budget guidance throughout the
cycle. Vance had already put the FY 1967 budget process in motion on 19 July
when he issued guidance for changes to the FYFS&FP to account for the increased
costs of the Vietnam and Dominican Republic operations. He instructed recipients to assume for planning purposes combat rates of consumption and attrition
in Vietnam through 30 June 1967. Peacetime rates of consumption would apply
thereafter.[38] By assigning this arbitrary date for the war to end, McNamara's detractors asserted, he deliberately manipulated defense spending to conceal the real
costs of the war from Congress and the American people.

Indeed McNamara did drag his feet on the budget but not, as commonly supposed, by assigning an arbitrary date to the end of the Vietnam fighting. Instead
he reduced projected expenses in Vietnam through restrictive budget planning
assumptions. On 27 August, McNamara's budget guidance for the January 1966
supplemental appropriation provided that only Phase I deployments to Vietnam
(220,000 U.S. troops) and munitions for the ground forces computed at one and
one-half times the expected rates of consumption be the basis for programming
both the January supplemental and the FY 1967 basic budget requests. The secretary of the Army questioned the guidelines by suggesting they might create short-

ages if Phase II deployments (333,000 U.S. troops), then under serious consideration, were later approved. In response, on 4 October McNamara convened the service secretaries and Vance to discuss preparation of the upcoming budget on the assumption that Phase II deployments "are deferred indefinitely."[39]

Apparently as a result of this meeting, the secretary of defense issued formal budget guidance the following day. The consistent assumption underlying the FY 1966 supplemental and the FY 1967 budget, he stated, was that the war in Southeast Asia would end on 1 July 1967 and that manpower and consumption costs would return to peacetime levels after that date. Consumption for FYs 1966 and 1967 would be planned at the Phase I rates and the budget built accordingly— purely an administrative assumption for budget purposes that did "not imply anything, one way or the other, as to when SEA hostilities actually will cease." Neither did it suggest any decision regarding Phase II deployments. He reiterated this guidance in his 11 October memorandum on five-year programming assumptions.[40] The cutoff of the war at the end of FY 1967 constituted a budgetary tool that DoD had experience with, having used it during the Korean War.[*]

There were two ways to budget for the added war costs. First, OSD could assume the war would last indefinitely and finance everything, including combat attrition and consumption, through normal budget lead times. The JCS favored this method that would fund, for example, combat attrition of aircraft 18 months beyond the end of FY 1967. With this approach, if the fighting ended on 30 June 1966, DoD would still have funds authorized to replace aircraft combat losses through December 1968 even with the war long over. Besides being an unnecessary expenditure, such an authorization would introduce laxity into the rigorous financial order McNamara had constructed to account carefully for military procurement. Even for shorter lead-time consumables such as uniforms or small arms, DoD might end up buying items six months after the end of hostilities. The result would show surpluses and imbalances—items requiring long lead times, like aircraft, would be fully financed years in advance while short lead-time articles, like rifles, only months. Either way the procurement budget, because of gross overfunding, would replicate the unfortunate legacy of the post-Korean War era.

A second method would account for both long and short lead-time items uniformly in the original budget. This technique, however, required assumption of an arbitrary date for ending the war, the end of a fiscal year being the most con-

---

[*] During the Korean War, the administration and OSD assumed an early termination of hostilities, and since combat consumption rates were unpredictable preferred to fund them by supplemental appropriations late in the fiscal year or in the next year's budget. The JCS wanted the war funded on a regular fiscal year basis, moving the war's termination date year by year, and assuming the fighting would continue through any fiscal year then being considered. In other words, for the fiscal year 1954 budget submission, combat would be assumed to continue to 30 June 1954. The unobligated funds for the long lead-time items funded by the huge Defense budgets of fiscal years 1951 and 1952 would carry procurement for several years past 1953. (Condit, *The Test of War, 1950–1953*, 285-87.)

venient for planning purposes. As the fiscal year progressed, OSD could monitor expenditures versus requirements and, as necessary, refine the funding process by amending in mid-year the president's original budget request submitted in January or after congressional appropriations by presenting supplemental requests later, often in January, together with the new budget—as had occurred during the Korean War. A January request for a supplemental had the extra advantage of giving budget planners six additional months experience with combat-derived data and the chance to mesh the newly identified requirements with the following fiscal year's budget projections. Maintaining a strict financial accounting would avoid the pitfalls of the Korean War budgeting nightmare. Finally, assuming an arbitrary end to the Vietnam War became, in McNamara's words, a device to force Southeast Asia items into a supplemental that allowed him to retain control of current military spending, which, unlike in previous U.S. wars, had to compete for funds with the president's ambitious domestic budget.[41]

Nevertheless critics insisted McNamara used the arbitrary cut-off date as a means to misrepresent defense spending, and they further denounced Johnson for manipulating budget figures to ensure passage and funding of his Great Society plans. For a brief time during the late summer and fall of 1965, though, it appeared that with luck the war might end sooner rather than later. Between July and October, McNamara alternated between cautious optimism and growing skepticism about events in Vietnam. On the plus side, South Vietnam had survived communist offensives in June and July; Viet Cong activity had slowed; Washington regarded the marines' performance in Operation Starlite (18–24 August 1965) as "almost too good to be true"; and the State Department notified Ambassador Lodge in Saigon that the reinforced U.S. ground strength was forcing the Viet Cong to avoid large unit actions and revert to guerrilla warfare tactics. This period of good news from Southeast Asia coincided with McNamara's budget guidance on 27 August. The Phase I deployments seemed to have turned the communist tide and offered hope that the war might end by mid-1967. As long as McNamara had reason to believe the Phase I forces sufficient to achieve U.S. goals in South Vietnam, he could legitimately claim that its lengthy deployment period of 18 months would not involve excessive costs. When Rep. Leslie C. Arends (R-Ill.) asked in early August 1965 if it was "outlandish or reasonable" to think that the administration might seek an additional $10 billion to $14 billion the coming January, McNamara described such figures as both outlandish and shocking for the current program (Phase I).[42]

Aware that rumors of a major U.S. escalation had swept through Wall Street in late August, Ackley personally debunked press reports of a $12 billion increase in defense spending, describing them to the president as "highly exaggerated Viet Nam numbers." A week later, based on McNamara's assurances, Ackley again scotched such speculation by publicly announcing that Defense spending over the next 12 months would add only $2 billion to federal expenditures.[43]

Because government commitments to purchase (orders) always preceded expenditures (payment), it was likely DoD would spend (as opposed to order) no more than $2 billion during the period, although it would have much more on order awaiting future payment. As long as Phase I assumptions held true, McNamara could bring in budget numbers for Vietnam much lower than $10 billion. But as summer changed to fall, so too did the military presumptions of August. By October it had become obvious that Phase I forces were inadequate, and that more troops and more dollars would be required if the United States intended to remain in Vietnam. Like so much about the distant war, after today's successes came tomorrow's heartbreak.

Instead of backing off in the face of intensified U.S. air and ground operations, North Vietnam was apparently matching the American buildup. Surging infiltration of men and supplies from North Vietnam into the South led Westmoreland in mid-October to ask for 35,000 more U.S. troops. If OSD approved the MACV commander's proposal, then it also had to find money to pay the additional costs. Meanwhile on 8 October Johnson underwent a gall bladder operation that left him convalescing at his Texas ranch until early December, restricting his face-to-face contact with his senior policy advisers. Voluminous daily cables from Washington and regular visits to the ranch by his senior staff kept him fully informed of developments, including decisions about Westmoreland's troop requirements for 1966, the so-called Phase II and Phase IIa deployments.[44] By virtue of the president's confidence in him, his own towering abilities, and, to be sure, his self-assurance, McNamara had the central role in this process, one that led him to alter his own views on the Vietnam War.

At the Pentagon on 18 October, Brig. Gen. William E. DePuy, the MACV J-3 (Operations), presented the Washington civilians a sobering analytical, results-oriented approach to justify 115,000 additional troops during the course of 1966.* McNamara promptly ordered his Pentagon staff to translate DePuy's Phase II deployment proposals into personnel, unit, and budget figures. In a discussion following the briefing, the secretary outlined three options for implementing DePuy's recommendations. With customary decisiveness, McNamara said he wanted to know the implications of his alternatives in dollar terms within four days, and he summoned a meeting in his office early the next morning to mobilize the staff to obtain the numbers.[45]

At that meeting on 19 October, McNamara rescinded his previous budget guidance and instructed the service secretaries and JCS to assume approval of Phase II deployments and provide study requirements for the program. Subsequent reviews by the JCS and OSD lowered the service submissions for FYs 1966 and 1967 by cutting O&M and procurement requests, by not equipping newly raised units in the strategic reserve to full authorization, and by disallowing Navy

---

* These events are discussed in detail in Chapter V.

and Marine requests previously disapproved in force guidance. On 3 November McNamara recommended the president approve the reinforcements at a cost of $16 billion ($13 billion for Phase I and $3 billion for Phase II) through FY 1967.[46] Events in Vietnam, however, quickly outpaced OSD budget planning and forced continual changes in response to ever-increasing requirements from the field for more troops and material.

Citing the increased enemy strength figures and lackluster ARVN battlefield performance, Westmoreland continually pressed for accelerated deployment of Phase II combat forces. The president had already instructed McNamara to meet MACV's requests, and on 12 November, the secretary of defense informed the service secretaries and OSD principals that in the absence of a firm decision on Phase II deployments, he had decided "work should go ahead full speed now" to prepare the FY 1966 supplemental and the FY 1967 budgets to include funds for the Phase II deployments.[47]

A few days later McNamara handed the service secretaries deployment scenarios to use when revising their budgets. Although the FY 1966 supplemental request and the FY 1967 budget were to be based on Phase II deployment tables, because of the president's resistance to large increases McNamara loyally limited costs by reducing the latest service estimates by 12 percent to stay within the previous $16 billion projection. In mid-November, the president finally authorized McNamara to prepare the FY 1966 supplemental and the 1967 budgets on the assumption that the funds to meet Phase II deployments would become available.[48] After a month-long reappraisal, McNamara had finally aligned requirements for the troops needed in Vietnam and the cost of those forces. Then the latest battlefield estimates arrived at the Pentagon.

Westmoreland's 23 November request for still more troops obviously required more money. "The real problem centers on the budget," Wheeler told the service chiefs, because "the extent of the budget will horrify the president." To assess the situation personally McNamara and Wheeler flew to Saigon, where Wheeler had already relayed to Westmoreland the secretary's guidance to include the Phase II add-ons, known as Phase IIa, in MACV's briefing, because these extra forces would significantly influence resulting budget adjustments, funding, and programs for the increased force levels in Vietnam. During the 28–29 November visit DePuy's presentation, heavily laden with cost-benefit analysis jargon, convinced McNamara that more troops were needed in Vietnam.[49]

On his return to Washington on 1 December, McNamara instructed each service to expand its January supplemental to support the Phase IIa forces. The next day he alerted the president to a possible $11 billion supplemental to pay for Phase IIa programs. Moreover, DoD expenditures for FY 1967 would total $60–61 billion, "much higher than any [previous estimate] you've seen before." Bureau of Budget estimates of early November had led Johnson to expect a $9 billion supplemental, and, although he was distressed, in the end he and McNamara had to give in to the inevitable. If they wanted to fight a war they would have to pay for it. Even so, they continued to struggle against cost escalations. McNamara reduced the services' latest revised supplemental estimates of $15.8 billion by more than $2.6 billion, and still further over the next few weeks, despite their protests about substantial unfulfilled requirements, lack of Army support troops to meet the accelerated deployments, and degraded flexibility to meet NATO commitments.[50]

On 11 December, after canvassing members of Congress about a $10–12 billion supplemental and their views of Vietnam policy, the defense secretary forwarded a slightly modified Southeast Asia FY 1966 supplemental bill of $13.1 billion (NOA)* to the president. McNamara's working premises were: (1) the amount would support the Phase IIa schedule; (2) withdrawals of men and equipment from other areas might be necessary to meet the schedule; and (3) the funds would cover short lead-time items through 31 December 1966 and long lead-time ones through 30 June 1967. The 31 December date pared the total supplemental request for ground combat and air operations $4 billion by excluding the cost of six months (1 January–30 June 1967) worth of ammunition consumption, aircraft loss replacement, and other incremental costs. If it appeared that the war would continue beyond 31 December 1966, another supplemental, estimated at $9.8 billion, would be necessary. Also on 11 December McNamara approved, without public fanfare, speeding up deployment of combat forces to Vietnam as Westmoreland had repeatedly requested.[51]

On 17 January 1966, McNamara publicly announced the administration's intent to ask Congress for a $12.3 billion in FY 1966 supplemental funding. He hastened to add that expenditures, as opposed to new obligational authority, would increase by only $4.6 billion during fiscal year 1966, thereby allaying fears about inflation. Several weeks later, McNamara said that $3.9 billion represented the maximum amount of the $12.3 supplemental that DoD could spend in the remaining months of the 1966 fiscal year, although the bulk of the remainder would be obligated by 30 June 1966.[52]

On 19 January, the president formally transmitted to Congress his request for $12,345,719,000 in new obligational authority for DoD for the remainder of FY 1966, a staggering 25 percent increase over DoD's original and already amended $48.6 billion budget. Proposed supplemental procurement appropriations totaled $7 billion. Because budget planning was premised on hostilities ending on 30 June 1967, acquisition of items with a lead time exceeding one year—that is beyond the normal budget cycle—had to be funded in the FY 1966 supplemental. For example, planners estimated a total of 997 U.S. aircraft losses through 30 June 1967. Replacing so many aircraft had to be done incrementally, and McNamara argued that orders for the new planes had to be placed in FY 1966 to ensure production lines expanded sufficiently to meet requirements through June 1967. That, said

---

*The difference included adjustments of stock funds and a $75 million MAP reimbursement.

critics, amounted to increasing the FY 1966 budget to hold down the FY 1967 budget. Congressional skeptics also wondered if the process actually accelerated delivery of much needed equipment.[53]

To get defense production lines moving, DoD issued letter contracts, that is, commitments of intent to purchase as funds became available as opposed to authorized funds legally obligated to a contractor. In the third and fourth quarters of 1965 arms production soared because of letter contracts. Although no expenditures were yet involved, companies holding letter contracts moved to expand their work forces while borrowing money to improve productive capacity using the letter contract commitments as collateral. The resulting squeeze on the labor market and increased competition for available resources as well as capital were already pushing prices upward in the summer of 1965, thereby fueling inflation. In other words, defense procurement was picking up velocity before the nation's economists became fully aware of the effects on a superheated economy, already performing at near capacity levels, of a considerably larger investment in plant and equipment than anyone anticipated.[54] In part this was a function of the policies of the so-called "New Economics."

Just as senior civilians in OSD believed that they could control the tempo of a limited war in Vietnam, so too the "new economists" in the Johnson administration believed that they could control the business cycle by the way the government handled its tax collections and spending (that is, its fiscal policy). In lean economic times, greater spending by government and lower taxes would promote economic growth, and in boom times the opposite remedies would limit excessive growth and inflation. Thus they remained leery about a tax increase late into 1965, in part because the CEA's economic forecasts assumed no rapid jump in defense spending. Ackley and Schultze also worried about both inflation and recession, but Ackley, concerned about imposing higher taxes that might choke off economic growth, remained less sensitive to the dangers of inflation. It seemed that an administration with no coherent plan to fight a war likewise had no plan to pay for it.[55]

Without a comprehensive plan for Vietnam, future operational requirements were so uncertain that OSD's policy was to wait until the last possible moment to fund them, and then only through the end of FY 1967. This tactic, coupled with the requirement to start procurement immediately of long-term items such as aircraft in order to ensure their delivery during the next fiscal year, created an exquisite irony: the FY 1966 budget with amendment and January 1966 supplemental exceeded the proposed FY 1967 budget submitted on 24 January 1966. It also provoked angry charges of duplicity leveled against the administration for deliberately understating the costs of the Vietnam War. As late as mid-November 1965, however, any estimate of Vietnam costs remained highly conjectural because the requirement for additional money was tied to DoD's program of phased deployments—at that time, of course, still subject to the president's approval. In early December the picture became clearer, but even when the budget requests got finalized, the president still had made no decision on Phase II or Phase IIa augmentations, so no one could really know how much the Vietnam War would cost. Recollecting the Korean War's unrealistic Defense budgets—overestimated by 13 percent in FY 1953 and by 11 percent in FY 1954—economic advisers hesitated to take projected Vietnam expenditures too seriously.[56]

The FY 1967 Defense Budget

The crash effort during December 1965 to adjust and finalize the FY 1966 supplemental request coincided with the last-minute rush to complete the 1967 basic budget for submission to Congress in mid-January 1966. Based on previous guidance, the services had already submitted their estimates for FY 1967 to OSD on 1 October 1965. Their projections followed the January 1965 FYFS&FP, with increases for Southeast Asia included in the submission. OSD budget analysts completed their reviews in early November and then provided program issues to BoB Director Schultze for comment and coordination. Extra money for the stepped-up rate of deployments and additional troops would boost the FY 1967 administrative budget* to more than $115 billion. As of December, the president believed it impossible to get such a sum in the annual authorization from Congress. He thought it better for Defense to minimize its January 1967 budget submission and later go for a $10 billion supplemental instead. To accomplish this, the president established a $110 billion expenditure target for FY 1967. Both Schultze and McNamara labored to stay within Johnson's guideline as McNamara took the lead in translating the president's wishes into hard Defense budget numbers.[57]

Throughout the fall of 1965, the president had been kept aware that the economy showed signs of inflation. Late in the year his key economic advisers were warning him that the added military costs of Vietnam on an already near-capacity economy required stern financial measures—higher interest rates and increased taxes. Johnson's populist streak made the first alternative unacceptable, and he repeatedly urged William McChesney Martin, Jr., the chairman of the Federal Reserve Board, not to raise interest rates. In early October 1965, for instance, the president told Martin it was impossible to predict war costs. "It could be $10 billion, it could be $3 to $5 billion. . . . McNamara says it very likely will be less than $5 billion for the rest of [fiscal] 1966." At this time McNamara's projections were likely correct. It is likely also that Johnson believed, and wanted to believe, that the war would neither last more than a year or two at its current intensive rate nor hurt the economy. McNamara himself publicly insisted on 8 March 1966 that

---

* Administrative budget funds covered receipts and expenditures of the federal government subject to annual congressional authorization. In addition, Congress permanently authorized certain receipts to be set aside in trust funds for specified payments of programs like Social Security and administered in a fiduciary capacity. They were not part of the administrative budget. Thus the total budget was considerably larger than the administrative budget.

the nation could afford both guns and butter.[58] But other signs indicated that the economy was not running all that smoothly.

In mid-October 1965, Schultze had recommended, with McNamara's endorsement, that Johnson withhold the traditional fall budget review that would reveal an additional $4.5 billion in expenditures above the FY 1966 budget until Congress recessed. Even in late November Ackley saw defense purchases running below expectations during the first half of 1965, and, aware that the timing and pace of the buildup could not be precisely measured at the moment, he thought the uncertainty not of major proportions through mid-1966. By early December administration economists concluded the economy was overheating but disagreed about the extent and the cure. The Troika–the chairman of the CEA, the director of BoB, and the secretary of the treasury*—still regarded the Federal Reserve's proposed interest rate hike as premature and advised the president to defer all decisions on monetary policy, excise taxes, and fiscal policy until the shape of the 1967 budget became known. Johnson's senior staff assistants likewise counseled avoiding any dramatic tax increases while pushing the Defense budget as low as "is consistent with both your basic programs and your ability to withstand charges of concealment." Yet the latest figures for plant and equipment spending showed the rapid growth that outstripped economists' predictions and possibly created a strong inflationary strain early in 1966. Johnson reacted by asking selected advisers, including McNamara, Ackley, Treasury Secretary Henry H. Fowler, and Califano, to consider measures to deal more effectively with the problems of maintaining price stability and checking inflationary pressures.[59]

These developments and the Troika's new economic estimates announced on 17 December changed Ackley's views. He recommended raising taxes, but qualified his advice contingent upon the amount of the FY 1967 administrative budget. If it exceeded $115 billion, taxes had to rise; if it came in at $110 billion, higher taxes were less certain, though probably still necessary because inflationary pressures were already stronger than expected. Califano found Ackley's prognosis so gloomy that he recommended, and Johnson approved, that the Troika discreetly develop specific tax proposals, although he excluded their staffs from the process for fear of leaks to reporters.[60]

Troublesome economic news, compounded by reports from Vietnam, made the possibility of a short war without inflation seem less and less likely. In November McNamara had seemed to be recommending almost on a daily basis that ever more troops go to Vietnam. MACV cables resonated with calls for more troops. And the JCS always supported these requests. Fighting had intensified, and with it U.S. casualties. By December the economic competition between the demands

---

* The Troika prepared economic forecasts and provided economic advice to the president. The CEA was responsible for overall economic forecasting, the BoB for estimating expenditures, and the Treasury for estimating revenues. (Anderson and Hazleton, *Managing Macroeconomic Policy*, 47.)

of the Great Society on the one hand and the spiraling costs of the Vietnam War on the other for ever scarcer resources and money was becoming an open secret. Although the CEA did not have all the facts on the Vietnam buildup, "we knew what numbers were being talked about," recalled Ackley, "and we also knew very well that, whatever those numbers, they weren't nearly big enough in terms of what was going to happen to defense expenditures."[61]

Johnson's economic experts could explain the technical reasons for boosting taxes on their graphs and charts. Their arguments made sense, and Johnson understood them, but they remained too dry, too lifeless, and frankly too politically unsophisticated for a consummate politician. To assess what increased taxes meant to voters, the president drew on his former congressional colleagues. In late 1965, Rep. Wilbur Mills (D-Ark.), chairman of the formidable House Ways and Means Committee, simply opposed any tax increase in 1966. Congressional elections loomed just over the horizon, and no congressman in his right mind wanted to face the prospect of voting to raise taxes on his constituents. Realizing that a tax increase had no chance of passage, Johnson feared that even proposing higher taxes would give his congressional opponents the weapon to slay appropriations for his authorized Great Society programs. The intense political pressure from Congress to hold down the federal budget and avoid inflation squared with the president's own populist sentiments not to raise taxes or, for that matter, to acknowledge publicly the cost of the war, especially to the business community. Obviously, keeping the budget within limits meant checking the growth of Defense spending that, after all, constituted the major portion and greatest variable of the president's budget. If military costs could be held down, so too could inflationary pressure. This left McNamara with the task of holding Defense spending in the FY 1967 budget at no more than $57 billion, or $3 billion below his estimated total to cover the Vietnam buildup.[62]

On 8 November, Schultze forwarded to McNamara an agenda listing program issues for discussion at a meeting scheduled for the following afternoon. BoB's attention focused on DoD's strategic, big-ticket requests such as ballistic missile procurement, numbers of strategic bombers, Nike-X development, and anti-submarine warfare improvements. McGeorge Bundy, representing the NSC, and the senior leadership of BoB, the Office of Science and Technology (OST), as well as DoD attended the meeting. Both the secretary of defense and the BoB director were working to hold down the FY 1967 Defense budget to meet the president's $110 billion expenditure target. To accomplish this, they searched for ways to reduce costs either by stretching out procurement of such aircraft as the FB-111 and the Navy EA-6B; cutting fund allocations, as happened with air defense and the Nike-X developments; or deferring work, such as on the Navy's nuclear-powered aircraft carrier. BoB also proposed postponing construction of 10 destroyer escorts and building 3 instead of 5 new nuclear-powered submarines. Issues still unsettled after the meeting—R&D budgets, the Military Assistance

Program, and the nuclear carrier—were rescheduled for further discussion between McNamara and Schultze on 13 November. At that session, McNamara agreed to slip production of the FB-111 from 33 to 10 aircraft for FY 1966, but he insisted on maintaining stockages to support the planned force in combat, regardless of cost. OSD stood firm on funding for Nike-X development but accepted a $367 million reduction to hold the RDT&E budget to $6.9 billion. No final decisions were made about military assistance, but McNamara agreed to defer the nuclear-powered carrier to the FY 1968 budget. As Bundy later recalled, in such meetings McNamara's trump card was not arguing the merits of the issue but saying, "This is the smallest I can defend in the Congress."[63]

McNamara had to juggle the proposed supplemental and the FY 1967 budget until January. His proposed $59.8 billion FY 1967 Defense budget had trimmed almost $13 billion from service requests. He justified the reductions by assuming that combat support for Southeast Asia would cease on 30 June 1967, a point Mc-Namara emphasized to congressional committees early in 1966. Using the same rationale, the secretary made additional and larger reductions in aircraft, missile, and ammunition procurement on the grounds that a high level of production in FY 1966 had achieved the desired stockages for combat operations. He judged the service estimates excessive and likely to result in the vast surpluses characteristic of the post-Korean War period. The secretary had already programmed combat consumption of short lead-time items, like ammunition, only through December 1966, but long lead-time items through June 1967, and he had advised the president that if the war went beyond either date, additional funds would become necessary.[64]

Although warned by McNamara that the technique, while a "fair and square way," might leave the administration open to charges of sleight of hand and would damage credibility, Johnson was receptive because he wanted to keep the budget, inflation, and any deficit "as low as I can" to avoid a tax hike. Financing military personnel and operations and maintenance costs only through 31 December 1966 was the only way for McNamara to get a lower FY 1967 Defense budget aside from deliberately underestimating costs. That option, he admitted, would of course be far more difficult to explain to Congress.[65]

In this manner, cuts in the Army's budget requests came mainly in downward adjustments to personnel costs ($439 million), O&M ($926 million), and procurement ($1.756 million). The Air Force saw $278 million eliminated from its personnel account, $498 million from O&M, $2.486 million from aircraft and missile procurement, $461 million from munitions, and $639 million from research and development. The Navy, including the Marine Corps, took reductions of slightly more than $100 million in personnel accounts, $538 million from O&M, $350 million from shipbuilding, $584 million from procurement, and $104 million from research and development projects. Construction funds for the services declined $1.25 billion as McNamara delayed every project "that could possibly be postponed."[66] Nevertheless the Defense budget still hovered around $60 billion, which BoB deemed excessive.

McNamara incorporated the results of his discussions with BoB into his 9 December 1965 memorandum to the president on budget issues. Also finding expression in the document, albeit in muted tones, were the budgetary concerns of the JCS and service secretaries. The Joint Chiefs deemed the proposed budget insufficient at two levels. First, on a conceptual plane, they particularly objected to McNamara's assumption that the United States could fight a European war for six months and simultaneously continue operations in Vietnam. To the contrary, they claimed, funding was inadequate to support Southeast Asia operations and concurrently meet other U.S. global commitments. Furthermore, without a partial mobilization, the Chiefs asserted, the demands of the Vietnam War were eroding the general purpose forces, diminishing the training and rotation base, and creating shortages in certain types of ammunition, spare parts, and aircraft, further reducing overall capabilities.[67]

Second, the Chiefs desired more military hardware than the budget allowed. They wanted to delay the phaseout of B-52s in favor of slower production of the FB-111s; buy more SR-71 aircraft; and develop the advanced manned strategic aircraft (AMSA). McNamara did withdraw his projected FY 1967 reductions in the B-52 force, although this probably came more from the higher demand for B-52s in a tactical role over Vietnam than from the Chiefs' urgings and his inability to field the F-111Bs quickly enough to replace the aging bombers. On other programs he proved intractable, rejecting JCS arguments on the SR-71 and AMSA programs and refusing money for greater development of the Nike-X system as well as the Navy's shipbuilding program, including the construction of a nuclear-powered carrier in FY 1967.[68]

On 3 December the Joint Chiefs had requested McNamara to allow them to meet with the president and appeal among other issues, the Nike-X, the overall posture of conventional forces, and the Navy's shipbuilding program. Aware of the Chiefs' opposition to many of the budget decisions, McNamara and Vance had already arranged a meeting for 10 December at the president's Texas ranch to discuss the JCS budgetary requirements. They deliberately timed the session to ensure that Wheeler, who was leaving for Vietnam before Christmas, would be available to exert "a salutary influence on the Chiefs." On 8 December McNamara and Vance met with the Chiefs, explained the president's budget difficulties, and told them that McNamara intended to argue for his budget priorities at the Texas meeting. McNamara's memorandum the following day alerted Johnson to the major topics on the Chiefs' list. The same day, Admiral McDonald gave McNamara an advance copy of his proposed remarks before the president with particular reference to the need for the nuclear-powered carrier. A separate 9 December memo from McNamara to the president proposed a FY 1966 supplemental of $12.8 billion (NOA) and a FY 1967 Defense budget of $61.3 billion (NOA), the latter subject to further downward revision. The accompanying rationale for these figures served the president as background material for his meeting with the Chiefs.[69]

Although Johnson flattered the Chiefs by telling them how much he valued their advice, General Greene left convinced that the president either had already made up his mind on the Defense budget or he would rely, "as he normally appears to," on McNamara's recommendations. The president did appear troubled by the large Defense budget and its potential impact on his Great Society programs. He repeatedly mentioned his willingness to provide whatever was necessary in Vietnam, but he thought the proposed budget too high and wanted it reduced. Yet Johnson did force McNamara to reconsider the nuclear-powered carrier that McDonald deemed essential for the Navy. Indeed, as the admiral was leaving the president put his arm around McDonald's shoulder and whispered to him not to worry about the carrier.[70] The president's potent combination of remorse, flattery, and inveigling defused much of the Chiefs' resentment over the budget.

Still displeased with McNamara's budget, BoB's Schultze wanted Defense expenditures held to $57 billion. Together with McNamara, he devised two alternatives in mid-December to cut FY 1967 spending. Assuming the war would end on 31 December 1966 (not 30 June 1967) could reduce expenditures to $57 billion in FY 1967. Alternatively, McNamara could impose a two-week slippage on everything in the Defense budget, thereby reducing expenditures to $58 billion. Johnson felt uncomfortable with both approaches, but he favored the lower amount, agreeing with McNamara's observation that opponents would attack the higher figure to gut his Great Society. Schultze then proposed that if a large FY 1967 Defense supplemental request became necessary, accompanying it with a tax increase in May or June 1966 could make up any shortfalls. Not accepting Schultze's lower figure, McNamara insisted that only a higher figure of $60 billion would preserve the administration's "credibility both in budget terms and in terms of Vietnam." Despite Schultze's reservations, Johnson accepted McNamara's proposal for the higher amount. In so doing the president broke his self-imposed $110 billion expenditure ceiling and ultimately submitted total estimated expenditures of $112.8 billion (Defense coming in at an estimated $60.5 billion) and a total budget request for $121.9 billion (NOA), with $59.8 billion for Defense, including military assistance.[71]

Vietnam Spending and the Economy

McNamara had managed to keep his proposed FY 1967 budget expenditures close to the $60 billion target, but the ripple effects of the increased defense spending to date were beginning to appear as unsettling strains in the nation's economy. A mid-December memorandum from economist Walter W. Heller, a White House staff member, recommended the president switch from an expansive to a restrictive fiscal policy to ward off inflation, best accomplished by imposing a surtax specifically tied to Vietnam. On 27 December Ackley emphatically recommended that Johnson seek a tax increase that politically might come later but from an economic standpoint "needs to be done as soon as possible." The same day, also reacting to fears of inflation as demand outstripped available supply, Schultze informed the president that Defense expenditures in the $60 billion range necessitated a tax increase. For budget purposes, he again advised Johnson to assume expenditures of $57 billion in the January budget premised on U.S. forces returning from Vietnam by December 1966. Schultze estimated the cost of the war at $16 billion to $18 billion for fiscal year 1967, but advised the president to request $10 billion rather than ask for the full amount. If the fighting continued, the administration could then ask for a supplemental appropriation. This was consistent with Mills's advice to Fowler to keep the FY 1967 budget submission as low as possible by reflecting the current rate of expenditures for the war and, if need be, ask for a supplemental appropriation later. Schultze's originality lay not in the notion of a supplemental, which DoD had been planning since July, but in his "two-stage" strategy linking any tax increase to a supplemental Vietnam appropriation, not to the basic budget's expansion of Great Society programs.[72]

By early 1966, the president's overall budget forecast expenditures of $112.8 billion offset by revenues of $111 billion, a "mildly deflationary" and pleasantly surprising $1.8 billion deficit. Defense spending, McNamara now hopefully anticipated, would come to $58.3 billion, and he played down any fears of inflation before Congress, reasoning that Defense expenditures would increase over FY 1965 only marginally as percentages of GNP, by 0.4 percent in FY 1966 and 0.5 percent in FY 1967. Because the $12.3 supplemental would increase FY 1966 expenditures only $4.6 billion, McNamara estimated in January 1966 that the adjusted FY 1966 Defense expenditures would be $54.2 billion and those of FY 1967 $58.3, for what the *New York Times* termed "a relatively modest $4.1 billion" increase in federal spending.[73] Upon closer inspection, the amount of money available for Defense coffers far exceeded the $4.1 billion addition.

A month later, McNamara estimated that of the $12.3 billion (NOA) FY 1966 supplemental, DoD would likely spend only $3.9 billion during FY 1966 and obligate the remainder. That meant DoD would spend much of the 1966 supplemental during FY 1967, although it would not appear in that year's budget. Put another way, combining the "relatively modest" $4.1 billion spending increase to the FY 1967 budget with the $8.4 billion carryover from the FY 1966 supplemental added a potential $12.5 billion in new defense spending to the economy during FY 1967. Some of those additional defense dollars would get pumped into an overheated economy. To add to the inflationary pressure, although the administration projected the costs of the Vietnam War at $10.2 billion during fiscal year 1967, later estimates almost doubled that—$19.4 billion.[74] McNamara might possibly juggle the DoD budget figures; he could not control the spiraling costs of the war.

Did McNamara deliberately mislead Congress and the nation's economists about the cost of the war? The argument has persisted that the upward revision of his original projections proved the administration knew all along that the costs would go much higher than their initial estimates.[75] But budget planning guidance stayed fluid during the second half of 1965—that of July 1965 differed from that of November 1965, which in turn differed from that of December 1965. Revised deployment schedules to meet the changing circumstances in Southeast Asia occasioned new tables from which budget experts and cost analysts calculated the added price of the conflict. The voracious demands of the Vietnam War ran up the bill faster, and longer, than McNamara or anyone else had anticipated. Actual costs consistently outpaced DoD's constantly readjusted estimates. DoD's December 1965 projections of $22.6 billion still fell $6.5 billion short when compared to its October 1966 forecast.

TABLE 2

SOUTHEAST ASIA COST ESCALATION: DoD ESTIMATES, FY 66 AND FY 67
(IN BILLIONS)

Date	Event	Add-On Costs
13 Aug 65	FY 66 Amendment Estimate	$ 1.7
13 Aug 65	FY 66 Supplemental Estimate	$ 6.7
13 Aug 65	Subtotal (1)	$ 8.4
21 Nov 65	Preview forecast, 1967, Phase I	$ 5.1
21 Nov 65	Phase II, 1966 and 1967 Estimated	$ 2.4
13 Aug–23 Nov	Miscellaneous Growth Estimated	$ 1.0
23 Nov 65	Subtotal (1+2)	$ 16.9
4 Dec 65	Phase IIa Estimated	$ 2.8
4 Dec 65	Military Assistance Program	$ 0.7
23 Nov–4 Dec	Miscellaneous Growth Estimated	$ 1.9
	Subtotal (1+2+3)	$ 22.3
4–9 Dec 65	Miscellaneous Growth Estimated	$ 0.3
9 Dec 65	Total Add-On Estimated Forecast for FYs 66 and 67 (1+2+3+4)	$ 22.6
26 Oct 66	Estimated incremental costs for FY 66 and FY 67	$ 29.1

Sources: Southeast Asia Cost Escalation (DoD Estimates, FY 66 and FY 67), 9 Dec 65, fldr FY 67 Budget Summaries, box 5, Comptroller files, Acc 73-A-1389; memo SecDef for Pres, Southeast Asia Costs, 26 Oct 66, *FRUS 1964–68*, 4:786.

The president's domestic priorities and conflicting political pressures beyond question shaped the amounts of his proposed budgets and announced expenditures, but McNamara was not the first secretary of defense to labor under those Washington realities. His budget premises were on record, and he openly and repeatedly told Congress that the administration would need more money to prosecute the war. Both the secretary of defense and the president met with congressmen individually and collectively to alert them to likely price tags on the conflict. Economists understood the situation as evidenced by their calls for tax increases, interest rate hikes, and spending cuts. As Fortune magazine put it: "The budget is not misleading once its rather sophisticated underlying assumptions are understood; but the assumptions are not widely understood, and the Administration had not made much of an effort to see that they are."[76]

To McNamara's discredit, however, he misled Congress about the growing scope of American involvement and its actual cost to the U.S. taxpayer. His selective use of information, his obfuscation by detail, his repeated failure even to estimate future costs of the war, and his decision to place loyalty to the president above accuracy became more pronounced as the administration deployed more and more troops to Vietnam. Truth and transparency became the costs of his efficient control of the budget. McNamara knew the president's wishes; McNamara knew the dimensions of the Vietnam buildup; and only McNamara, it was reputed, understood the Defense budget. Paradoxically, at this critical juncture McNamara did not seem to fully appreciate the impact of a protracted war on the nation's economic health.

McNamara was not alone. The "new economists" guiding the administration overestimated their ability to control a cyclical economy. True, they too became victims of the same uncertainties that bedeviled OSD's civilian strategists, but even with growing awareness of inflationary pressures, they still pushed strong economic growth because they feared the real problem lay in recession, not inflation. The economy proved stronger than they suspected, too full in fact to absorb the wartime demands of the Vietnam buildup because plants were almost fully occupied with civilian production and operating at 90 percent of capacity. Unemployment was a very modest 4.5 percent (4 percent represented full employment), meaning fewer unemployed workers were available than, say, at the outbreak of the Korean War. Additional Defense requirements had to compete for scarce labor and materials, forcing up the demand and ultimately the cost for both. McNamara was right in believing that the increased Defense spending for Vietnam operations only affected the margins of the national economy, but wrong in thinking the already near-capacity industrial plant could absorb the additional demand even on the fringes. Though relatively marginal at three percent, the increase in total demand came at a time when it proved too much for the economy to accommodate without inflation.[77]

Added to federal spending for the Great Society, military expenditures should have set inflationary alarm bells ringing, but the economic impact of the increased spending was underestimates because of the time lag between government procurement orders and the federal payment for delivery of finished goods or services. The distribution of the FY 1966 supplemental over two fiscal years serves as an illustration. The majority of the supplemental was obligated during FY 1966, that is committed but not spent. By the time the obligated goods and services were delivered to the government, the inflationary impact had already entered the economy because contractors had produced goods and services; made payments for wages, rents, and interests; and taken profits using DoD obligations as collateral. Additionally the buildup itself was larger (and thus economically stronger) than economists realized at the time, largely because of the administration's lack of candor. The officially stated uncertainty about the extent of the U.S. commitment to the fighting in Vietnam and the delay in releasing budget information also contributed to the serious inflationary problems besetting the economy.[78]

As happened so often in this ill-begotten war, changing circumstances left otherwise seemingly rational and intelligent decisions foundering because their timing was inappropriate to the situation. If unemployment had been higher, if the economy had greater slack to increase production, if a tax cut in June 1965 had not reduced federal revenues, if the Great Society had not materialized coincidentally with massive escalation of the U.S. commitment in Southeast Asia—then deficit spending could have spurred full production and greater employment while keeping inflation in check. Instead, the additional expenses of the Vietnam War and the Great Society swelled the federal deficit, stoked rising inflation, and inevitably led to serious instability in the economy.[79]

Johnson later insisted that "moving step by step was not only the best way to plan the budget; it was the best way to save the Great Society." Perhaps, but by 1966 the administration was already cutting domestic spending to pay for the war. "Losing the Great Society was a terrible thought," recalled Johnson, "but not so terrible as the thought of being responsible for America's losing a war to the Communists. Nothing could possibly be worse than that."[80] Had the president given priority to either domestic reform or the war instead of trying to realize them simultaneously, he might have avoided the accusations then and later of mishandling both.

CHAPTER V

VIETNAM:
ESCALATING A GROUND WAR,
JULY 1965–JULY 1967

Lyndon Johnson's July–September 1965 decisions set in motion the Americanization of the war by an administration that remained extremely wary of an expanded U.S. military role in Southeast Asia.[1] Even while committing large numbers of U.S. ground troops to South Vietnam, the president rejected emergency mobilization, confined ground operations within South Vietnam's borders, proscribed the use of nuclear weapons, and restricted the air campaign against North Vietnam to ensure that the war, at least for the United States, would be a limited one. Within these guidelines, McNamara worked closely with General Westmoreland to determine the numbers of American troops sent to Vietnam and the timetables governing their deployment.

McNamara had to grapple with the problem of how to orchestrate a limited war so as to bring it to a reasonable conclusion in an acceptable period of time. Westmoreland's dilemma was how to correct a mismatch between the U.S. troops he had and the troops he needed to do his job. With both men unwilling to consider withdrawal and with each passing day aware that earlier, more optimistic estimates of South Vietnam's progress were wrong, their predicaments became intertwined, the more so because once the administration committed large numbers of troops to Vietnam it found the notion of an American defeat unthinkable. Still, North Vietnam's surprising resiliency and decision to match American reinforcements had altered the nature of the conflict, and as political and military circumstances in South Vietnam changed for the worse, the evolving views of U.S. civilian and military authorities on the war and the way ahead diverged. The military leaders repeatedly asked for more troops and their civilian counterparts repeatedly demurred. Even

113

as OSD and the administration eventually provided significant enhancements, demand continually outstripped what the civilians were willing to supply.

Like almost all senior policymakers, McNamara and Westmoreland originally underestimated Hanoi's determination, believing either that the communists would not persevere or, if they did, the military might of the United States would destroy them. Whereas Westmoreland remained optimistic, convinced that his tactics and strategy were steadily grinding down the enemy and that additional troops would accelerate MACV's progress toward winning the war, McNamara struggled to devise a war-winning strategy while wracked by doubts about the outcome. Until November 1965, McNamara remained cautiously optimistic that U.S. military intervention could decisively influence the conflict within presidentially imposed limitations. Thereafter he grew increasingly pessimistic that military means alone could produce a solution favorable to the United States. Nonetheless, as skeptical as he was in private, publicly he continued to express confidence.[2]

Although OSD originally approved MACV's steady demands for more troops with minimal alteration, by mid-1966 McNamara sharply questioned Westmoreland's requests. Their rapport remained cordial, though, as McNamara later put it, they increasingly differed in judgment on the course and conduct of the war.[3] Relations between McNamara and the Joint Chiefs deteriorated as he grew ever more convinced of the impossibility of a military victory in Vietnam while they chafed under political restraints they believed made a battlefield triumph unattainable. In the summer of 1965, however, any irreconciliation of the respective positions lay in the unpredictable future. ⌐

Planning a Ground War

Westmoreland had to fight more than an insurgency in South Vietnam. He had to fight an undeclared war against the large-unit forces that North Vietnam was sending into the uninhabited borderlands. The internal insurgency—the battle against the Viet Cong—he sought to leave to the South Vietnamese army. The results were less than satisfactory, as ARVN's deficiencies required Westmoreland to devote substantial U.S. forces to the effort. From the outset the MACV commander warned the administration to prepare the American public for a mobilization to fight a lengthy war of endurance. McNamara had to determine whether MACV possessed sufficient resources to accomplish its military goals in South Vietnam; knowing little about ground combat, he initially deferred to Westmoreland, rarely discussing the implications of the general's "search and destroy" strategy. With one major exception, he gave Westmoreland a free hand in the conduct of operations within South Vietnam.*[4] ⌐

---

* McNamara did rule on questions of employing CS (tear) gas or new types of ammunition in Vietnam, but these were incidental to Westmoreland's operational concept of carrying the war to the borders and his conventional search and destroy doctrine. The exception was the barrier strategy discussed below.

The U.S. buildup in Southeast Asia continued generally on schedule in the summer and fall of 1965. Allaying the administration's earlier fears, American troops had performed well in their baptism of fire. In particular, the Marines' August offensive into VC-held territory, Operation Starlite (18 to 19 August), the first big American ground operation of the war, met with resounding success. Such tactical victories did not automatically translate into grand strategy, requiring the Joint Chiefs of Staff in late August to "further formalize [their] concept for the future conduct of the war."[5]

The Chiefs saw the struggle as a test of U.S. determination to prevail over the communist concept of "wars of national liberation." Their strategy to defeat the indigenous Viet Cong forces in South Vietnam rested both on carrying the fight to the Viet Cong more aggressively in the South and on intensified air and naval operations to compel North Vietnam to cease its support of the southern insurgency. A U.S. strategic reserve in Thailand would serve to prevent China from entering the war. Promising rapid expansion of the war, the military's plan, transmitted to McNamara on 27 August, clashed with the predilection of the president and his senior civilian advisers for measured and gradual escalation of any fighting. McNamara followed McNaughton's recommendation and simply forwarded the Chiefs' proposal to the Department of State and the NSC "for use in future deliberations."[6]

Although McNamara pigeonholed the proposed JCS strategy, he heeded Westmoreland's calls for reinforcements. Rusk questioned the need for 200,000 U.S. troops (the Phase I requirement). Following informal policy discussions among State, DoD, and the White House, on 14 September Rusk asked Ambassador Lodge* about the role of U.S. reinforcements and what effect expanded U.S. military operations would have on South Vietnam. When he learned of Rusk's cable, Westmoreland regarded it as another attempt by Washington to "call all the shots, project all plans, and dictate how this war would be fought." Lodge, after consulting with Westmoreland, assured Rusk on 18 September that the full complement of Phase I deployments was needed. McNamara followed up on the 22nd, asking the president to approve the request; he agreed a week later to a ceiling of 195,000.[7]

Westmoreland and his J-3 (Operations), General DePuy, in part spurred by Rusk's cable, pressed forward with their plan to match increased forces with expanded operations. On 17 September Westmoreland issued a Phase II strategy for a sustained offensive, articulating a three-step plan of operations—halt the enemy offensive with Phase I forces (210,000 troops); take the initiative with the augmented Phase II units (an increase to 323,564 troops); and then restore govern-

---

* Lodge had previously served as ambassador to South Vietnam from August 1963 to June 1964. McNamara regarded him as a loner, averse to taking advice, and a poor administrator. To remedy these deficiencies, McGeorge Bundy recommended in July 1965 that Lodge be given two strong deputies to run the embassy and oversee pacification. (McNamara, *In Retrospect*, 106; memo Bundy for Pres, 21 Jul 65, *FRUS 1964–68*, 3:188–89.)

ment control of South Vietnam.[8] Preparations for Phase II reinforcements continued at a PACOM headquarters conference in Hawaii the last week of September.

At the conference, DePuy led the MACV planning group in sessions with teams representing PACOM and the services to work out the Phase II deployment schedule and briefed CINCPAC Admiral Sharp on how MACV's Phase II requirements complemented Westmoreland's concept of operations. Impressed, Sharp instructed DePuy to expand the presentation to include his views as well and offer it to the Joint Chiefs in Washington, an action Westmoreland also favored. Unknown to both officers, the timing was fortuitous because prior to DePuy's briefing in Washington, on 11 October McNamara received the Thompson Board report.[*] Although it concluded that air strikes would have no discernible effect on Hanoi's will to continue the war and called for a bombing pause over the North, the report observed that U.S. determination in the ground war coupled with progress in pacification would force the communists to switch from conventional tactics to a strategy of employing smaller units.[9] Headquarters MACV had independently reached a similar assessment about the ground war. As the command's spokesman, DePuy was about to make the case before the senior defense councils.

The Joint Chiefs proved extremely receptive to DePuy's presentation on 15 October and requested that McNamara hear what he had to say. Three days later the National Military Command Center, deep within the recesses of the Pentagon, served as DePuy's stage to present McNamara and his top assistants with MACV's Phase II goals, requirements, and estimates. The briefing, exactly the formula to appeal to the secretary—a model of precision, economy, and statistical analysis—became the prototype for future MACV briefings to McNamara. The general's full-color charts and graphs, displayed from overhead projectors, presented MACV's anticipated progress at the end of the Phase I deployments, a statistical analysis of the concept of operations, and a cost-benefit assessment of the Phase II reinforcements.[10]

DePuy promised no overnight success. He painted operations such as Starlite as "few and far between" as greater allied battlefield success made the communists less likely to stand and fight. The war, DePuy predicted, would be "fought and won in penny packets"—small-unit engagements requiring more time and more troops to break the back of the insurgency.[11]

Impressed, McNamara arranged for DePuy to brief senior White House and State officials, including Rusk, Maxwell Taylor, now special consultant to the president, and the Bundy brothers, McGeorge and William. Additional briefings followed for the various service staffs. Overall reaction was positive, although a few dissenters like Taylor voiced serious reservations about an implicitly open-ended military commitment that entailed a preponderant and time-consuming ground combat role with correspondingly heavier American casualties. Perhaps as an al-

---

[*] See Chapter III.

ternative, Rusk wondered if the communists had a "jugular vein" that could be severed quickly; both Wheeler and the Joint Staff agreed there was none.[12]

McNamara acted on DePuy's recommendations by initiating a planning exercise to determine the fiscal and political implications of Phase II deployments. McNamara told Pentagon staff officers to assume meeting the troop requirements for Phases I (210,000) and II (323,500) without recourse to a reserve mobilization. Believing it unlikely the administration would undertake Phase II without using reservists, however, he also ordered the preparation of specific plans for a mobilization likely to occur during the buildup. Finally, he wanted deployments for both phases completed as rapidly as possible, assuming a mid-November deadline for a decision on a call-up of reservists.[13]

The "sobering" DePuy briefing, the assessments of the Thompson Report, and a distressing 21 October cable from Lodge indicating the extreme weakness of the South Vietnamese government sparked a policy reexamination that became the basis for McNamara's 3 November memorandum for the president on future courses of action in Vietnam.[14] According to McNamara, the Phase I deployments had blunted the communist drive but were insufficient to achieve more than a compromise outcome likely to prove unpopular domestically and harmful internationally. To capitalize on initial success, as many as 410,000 troops (Phase I, Phase II, and perhaps add-on forces) might be needed. The danger was that the North Vietnamese could match the U.S. buildup, thereby nullifying the effects of the reinforcements. Yet to continue the ground war on the existing scale would result in a stalemate by March 1966 and perhaps a compromise settlement that would wreck the South Vietnamese government, prove unacceptable to the American public, and humiliate the United States.

Given the lack of progress, McNamara saw only two choices—cut American losses by leaving Vietnam or escalate the conflict by increasing the U.S. investment. He favored the second course—"the tandem, one-after-the-other scenario": a bombing pause, then heavier bombing of North Vietnam, and then Phase II deployments to place the United States in a stronger position should negotiations finally occur. McNamara believed a bombing pause vital to demonstrate that the United States desired peace while the administration laid the groundwork in preparing domestic and international opinion for future military escalation if necessary. His memorandum cautioned that none of his proposals ensured success; the odds were even that by 1967 the United States would still be fighting a war stalemated at a higher level and requiring additional (Phase III) forces.[15]

A worried President Johnson reviewed Vietnam policy on 11 November with his closest civilian advisers at his Texas ranch. They discussed additional deployments during 1966 and whether a bombing pause should precede them, but apparently reached no decisions. On 15 November McNamara told the Joint Chiefs that the president would consult with them before any bombing halt; on the 17th Navy Secretary Nitze informed Marine Corps Commandant Greene that the president would not decide on Phase II reinforcements until later. In the meantime, after DePuy's Pentagon briefing, the Chiefs had responded to the defense secretary's request for their Phase II deployment plans and a more detailed concept of operations. On 10 November they restated aims articulated in their August strategic plan—an expanded and generally unrestricted bombing campaign against North Vietnam, a selective reserve call-up, and the commitment of an additional 113,000 troops as Phase II reinforcements, raising the grand total to approximately 333,000 in Vietnam by December 1966.[16]

McNamara remained noncommittal about the Chiefs' Phase II estimates and their strategic recommendations, pending another visit to Vietnam later in the month. Taylor, however, balked at the JCS plan, seeing it again as placing the burden of heavier fighting and higher casualties on American troops. He favored joint U.S.-South Vietnamese ground operations to avoid the impression that the Americans were taking over the heavy combat and thereby shielding the South Vietnamese forces for less hazardous missions.[17] A drumbeat of distressing news from Vietnam forced the issue.

On 11 November, a long and gloomy cable from Lodge, endorsed by Westmoreland, reported that the Viet Cong were stepping up the fighting in the coastal provinces as well as in the central highlands and forming new units within South Vietnam. Northerners were infiltrating additional units into the South, perhaps two or more divisions, in the hope of restoring the strategic balance and regaining the initiative through a series of large-scale main force attacks supplemented by widespread guerrilla actions. The enemy evidently sought to inflict maximum casualties on U.S. and elite ARVN units, erode U.S. determination to continue the war, and weaken South Vietnamese morale. Until the enemy units were defeated, the ambassador believed, the Viet Cong would neither call off their war nor come to the conference table.[18]

As if to underline Lodge's foreboding analysis, the first major ground battle between U.S. and North Vietnamese troops, fought 14–19 November in South Vietnam's remote Ia Drang Valley near the Cambodian border, left more than 300 GIs and approximately 1,500 NVA dead. Additionally, a joint DIA-CIA assessment of 18 November concluded that U.S. air raids had neither lowered North Vietnamese popular morale nor altered the Hanoi regime's determination to continue the war in the South. Five days later, Westmoreland requested still more American troops—upward of 42,000 beyond the projected but as yet unapproved Phase II levels or a base force of more than 400,000—because the current pace of the enemy buildup would double that of U.S. forces. McNamara later described the cable as "a shattering blow," and reinforced his decision to go to Saigon for a firsthand assessment of the war's progress and a discussion of Phase II and other add-on deployments. The president also wanted him to visit Saigon, apparently hoping to avoid the publicity attendant to a major conference in Honolulu or summoning Westmoreland and Lodge to Washington for consultations.[19]

The MACV commander was well primed on what to ask for and what to expect during the secretary's visit. In mid-November Wheeler had notified Westmoreland of McNamara's support for the Phase II and add-on reinforcements, confiding his own belief that the president also favored additional deployments. Shortly afterward Sharp had privately informed Westmoreland that there was "high level consideration" about strengthening Phase II forces with another division; on 23 November Wheeler emphasized the importance of Westmoreland making his case with McNamara for the Phase II add-ons.[20]

Already committed to attend NATO meetings in Europe, McNamara proposed, as if it were perfectly natural, that on their return flight from Paris on 27 November he and his party make a brief—29-hour—stopover in Saigon. As usual before a visit, McNamara cabled questions to Lodge and Westmoreland asking about augmenting Phase II reinforcements, the need for additional troops for the Mekong Delta region, the adequacy of support forces, the role of the ARVN, and related issues.[21] Headquarters MACV, in the midst of revising its October presentation to account for the changing battlefield conditions, quickly adapted the latest briefing to accommodate the secretary's interests.

Arriving in Saigon on 28 November, McNamara moved directly from his aircraft to the MACV conference room for five hours of briefings interrupted by a single 15-minute break. He listened to MACV's estimate that the war was becoming a struggle of attrition with growing losses on both sides. DePuy, McNamara's personal choice as the primary briefer, projected that the surge in NVN reinforcements augured increasingly unfavorable force ratios unless 56,000 more troops (389,000 total) were added to the original Phase II goals. Without these "add-ons," the enemy would regain the strategic initiative and the conflict would drag on even longer. The next day, Westmoreland confided privately to McNamara that the United States had previously underestimated the capabilities of the enemy and overestimated those of the South Vietnamese.[22] MACV's reassessment, however, corrected that shortcoming.

The visit confirmed McNamara's "worst fears." For the first time in many months he heard that although South Vietnam was not falling apart, ensuring its survival carried a high price tag in reinforcements and casualties. The U.S. commitment of sizable air, ground, and naval forces had checked the communist campaign in the South, but the war seemed no nearer a resolution because more and more North Vietnamese units had joined the fighting. Without revealing his growing disillusionment, on leaving Saigon the next day he told American reporters at the airport that he foresaw "a long war." Lt. Col. George H. Sylvester, McNamara's Air Force aide who had accompanied him on the trip, thought too many uncertainties had gone unaddressed and privately wondered what U.S. troop morale would "be like in 2 years, when many will be back on their second (or third?) tours and there is no end in sight?"[23]

Returning to Washington on 30 November, McNamara immediately advised the president of the dramatic increase in NVA infiltration and the enemy's willingness to stand and fight, even in large-unit battles. To counter this threat and maintain the initiative, he counseled deploying MACV's Phase II add-ons, warning that as many as 600,000 American troops might be needed in 1967. The same day McNamara, according to Greene, appearing "bouncy, cocky, confident and arrogant," informed the Joint Chiefs that a major escalation would follow a yet-to-be determined bombing pause; he insisted that Westmoreland's latest requirements would be met on schedule without either reserve mobilizations or tour extensions, even if Army Chief of Staff General Johnson had "to rip the Army apart to do so!" Dismissing Johnson's protests that the Army needed to use its reserves for the reinforcement, the secretary insisted that all active-duty units worldwide, including forces in Europe, were eligible for Vietnam service.[24]

McNamara directed the service secretaries, assistant secretaries, JCS, and a handful of other staff members to begin planning for Phase IIa deployments and to schedule a conference in Honolulu in early 1966 to coordinate troop lists as well as deployment timetables for the reinforcements. Both Generals Wheeler and Johnson were enthusiastic about the secretary's approval of MACV's requests, although Johnson cautioned Westmoreland not to expect immediate reinforcements unless the administration declared a national emergency, something it was loath to do. While McNamara favored providing Westmoreland the reinforcements, on 2 December he reiterated to the president that implementation ought to be preceded by a bombing pause to seek a diplomatic end to the war. As McNaughton described it over a month later, the dilemma posed by Vietnam was that compromise would likely end in defeat, yet victory appeared unattainable; escalation would not necessarily avert military failure.[25]

During December 1965 and January 1966 McNamara queried congressional leaders and found they held widely varying views. He also met with senior presidential advisers, most of whom endorsed Westmoreland's approach. In the end, he favored widening the conflict by deploying the Phase IIa reinforcements, gradually expanding the air campaign, and accepting the devastating possibility of 12,000 Americans killed in action and more wounded each year. He believed, diplomatic initiatives notwithstanding, that the United States had to send the additional forces to avoid defeat.[26] In a sense, McNamara's concern thus shifted from convincing Hanoi it could not win to assuring that the United States would not lose.

He carried his proposals between the Texas ranch, where the president was recuperating from surgery, and the White House, always cautioning his listeners that military escalation alone did not guarantee victory. He could not assure the president that America's military power was hurting the North Vietnamese enough to promise certain victory or "to make them behave differently." If there were no military solution, then more U.S. reinforcements might only stalemate the war at a more costly level or, even worse, provoke the Chinese to join the fighting.

McNamara's views continued to vacillate during this volatile, pivotal period of policymaking. In general, he concluded that if the chances of military success in Vietnam were one-in-three and implementing Phase II ground operations made a heavier bombing campaign inevitable, then a political move had to accompany escalation.[27] A believer in the application of rational analysis to problem solving, he found himself bedeviled by the contradiction of having to prepare for a wider war and at the same time seeking an immediate end to it.

A growing feeling of powerlessness over the course of events took its toll on McNamara's legendary self-confidence. His sense of the war, as he later characterized it, "shifted from concern to skepticism to frustration to anguish"; yet he maintained what one contemporary described as "his usual tone of crisp authority and precision." Exuding the appearance of decisiveness could not have been easy. The administration's difficulties with the spiraling Defense budget and the likely need for tax increases or wage and price controls convinced McNamara that the president's effort to marshal public support for the massive deployments was fraught with pitfalls. He dreaded the possibility of a divisive national debate over Vietnam and told the JCS in early December that many Americans thought communist domination of Southeast Asia acceptable and South Vietnam not worth fighting for.[28]

McNamara shared with the JCS his gnawing fear of a stalemated war, but Wheeler believed the secretary's outlook unduly pessimistic. The Chiefs took solace in an early December joint State-Defense cable to U.S. embassies in the Pacific area as evidence of the administration's shift to a military hard line. The cable stated that because of the grave situation in South Vietnam U.S. ground troop strength there would be substantially increased as would air interdiction of infiltration routes while B-52 operations would grow to require another base in addition to the one at Guam. These activities necessitated support and cooperation from nearby countries.[29]

The Chiefs met with the president at his ranch on 10 December for their annual budget discussions, after which they turned to Vietnam matters. After Johnson affirmed that he had no intention of pulling out of Vietnam, Wheeler asked him to approve Westmoreland's request for reinforcements. Johnson sidestepped by assuring the Chiefs that he greatly valued their advice, and Greene left the ranch believing the meeting was "a cathartic" that enabled the JCS to state their views "and get it off their chests so to speak." But he already had an "uneasy feeling" that the president did not fully appreciate the dangers involved and had accepted McNamara's recommendations rather than those of the military experts.[30]

Hard Choices

Faced with the clear necessity to make decisions, on 20 January 1966 the president asked his senior civilian advisers for their assessment of enemy intentions and directed McNamara to obtain from Westmoreland his operational plans and expected results—"what happens [by] July—and next January." Four days later, McNamara's memorandum for the president restated DePuy's analysis of the military situation in South Vietnam. Unlike the optimistic views of the generals, McNamara's were more guarded: pacification was stalled, reinforcements might only produce a military standoff, and even success might invite Chinese intervention. Nevertheless, he advised the president to raise the U.S. force level in Vietnam to about 368,000 during 1966 while acknowledging that pacification was "hardly underway" and any meaningful success would likely require still more American troops. The Joint Chiefs regarded the secretary as overly glum; he seemed to ignore the uncertain yet probable effects of a devastating air campaign against the North and a punishing ground campaign in the South on enemy morale, capabilities, and will.[31]

After considering his advisers' various proposals and consulting with congressional leaders as well as outside counselors, on 31 January 1966 Johnson ordered a resumption of the bombing campaign against North Vietnam that he had halted on 24 December. He still procrastinated over deploying more troops to Vietnam during discussions in February and March. In early March he promised action on further reinforcements, believing it "a good psychological time" to "get some more men in there," but nothing happened.[32] Meanwhile McNamara planned for an expanded war, aware of the political and economic ramifications of such a course.

With the recent huge Defense budget requests and mounting casualties, more Americans were becoming apprehensive about the effects of a continually growing U.S. involvement. By February 1966 McNamara envisioned economists and businessmen questioning if the nation could afford the war. Rising inflation might mandate wage and price controls or tax increases, both anathema to a president with an ambitious social agenda. Others just wanted the United States out of Vietnam. Another constituency supported the war, but thought it mismanaged. Public confidence in the administration was eroding, a trend Taylor had warned about the previous December.[33]

Wheeler reported dissatisfaction even among otherwise stalwart supporters of U.S. policy. In January 1966, retired Army Lt. Gen. James M. Gavin, for instance, went public with his "enclave" strategy that, together with the current bombing halt, he asserted, would cap U.S. forces at about 200,000 troops, reduce American casualties, and avoid dangerous escalation that might lead to war with China. The Joint Chiefs rebutted these contentions, insisting that retreating into enclaves would sacrifice the military initiative and abandon national objectives. But to many, the mounting U.S. losses were "proof positive" that the South Vietnamese were content to let Americans do the fighting and dying while they "squabble pettily among themselves to achieve political advantage."[34] Against this confused backdrop, in early February the president and his entourage of cabinet secretaries and military leaders met with their Vietnamese counterparts in Honolulu to determine how many more U.S. troops would go to Vietnam.

To prepare for the sessions, CINCPAC had reviewed and forwarded Westmoreland's Phase IIa requirements to the JCS and OSD in mid-December. Sharp calculated a need for 443,000 U.S. troops in Vietnam by the end of 1966, an increase of almost 75,000 from the already pending Phase IIa request. Working from OSD guidance, staff members from the JCS, PACOM, and MACV met in Honolulu from mid-January to early February to prepare force structure and deployment schedules for 1966, developing three alternative programs—Case I, Case II, and Case III. They differed in the number and composition, source, and arrival dates of units in Vietnam. Case I tapped the standing forces in the United States, activated new units, drew on worldwide military assets, and called reservists to active duty. Case II was similar, but it excluded a reserve call-up, and Case III relied only on units in the existing force structure, with no worldwide drawdown and no reserve call-up.[35]

Critics claimed that the purpose of the 7–8 February Honolulu conference* was to divert attention from Senate hearings on Vietnam. But the session gave Johnson the opportunity to meet and talk with Westmoreland about force requirements and size up the Vietnamese leaders. The president stressed pacification and urged the Vietnamese to give priority to social and political programs. The day before the sessions, McNamara and Westmoreland agreed on the additional forces the general required, without calling the reserves and leaving it to MACV to make up the shortfall in logistical forces. By cross-servicing support units, contracting for civilian workers, and reducing requirements wherever possible, Westmoreland assured McNamara that he could make up any personnel deficit.[36]

Back in Washington on 9 February, McNamara notified the Joint Chiefs of the intention to deploy the additional forces according to the Case I scenario, but without calling up the reserves because it would disrupt the president's efforts to sustain public support. Briefly, Case I called for an additional 202,000 U.S. personnel (including 43 battalions) and 24,000 allied troops (13 battalions) by the end of 1966. Another 99,000 American troops would be added to PACOM forces outside of Vietnam. McNamara ignored General Johnson's protests that mobilization would demonstrate U.S. determination and disabuse China and the Soviet Union of any illusions that the nation lacked the will to prosecute a long war. On 10 March McNamara formally instructed the JCS to plan a Case I deployment without mobilization, despite impaired military readiness elsewhere, a diminished Army strategic reserve, and a lowered quality for newly raised units. If finally carried out as directed, the plan would place 425,000 U.S. troops in Vietnam by 30 June 1967 plus 49,100 in Thailand and 41,400 on off-shore Navy ships, a grand total of 516,100.[37]

---

* U.S. attendees included McGeorge Bundy, McNamara, Rusk, Secretary of Agriculture Orville L. Freeman, Secretary of Health, Education, and Welfare John W. Gardner, AID Administrator David E. Bell, Ambassadors Lodge and Harriman, Generals Wheeler and Westmoreland, Admiral Sharp, General Taylor, and numerous supporting staff members.

The JCS insisted on 4 April that the secretary's latest restrictions would force the services to meet Vietnam requirements with serious consequences for their NATO commitments. To implement Case I without a partial mobilization would oblige the Joint Chiefs to withdraw almost 60,000 soldiers and 10 fighter squadrons from Europe and reduce manning to one-third on 38 warships. Despite initial reservations, on 11 April McNamara agreed to several modifications, including the JCS request to stretch out the deployments over 16 months rather than the original 10 months. This decision completed the effort begun in Saigon in November 1965 to resolve the matter of force requirements. OSD formally issued SEA Deployment Plan #3 on 2 July, programming 431,000 U.S. servicemen in South Vietnam by 30 June 1967; by the end of the month this figure had increased by another 14,000.[38]

Culling 15,000 soldiers from U.S. Seventh Army in Germany, with an attendant decline in the Army's readiness, enabled OSD to meet the latest Vietnam levy in part without calling the reserves. Lengthening the deployment schedule, however, meant that Westmoreland never received as many troops as quickly as he needed them for his planned 1966 campaign and also allowed the North Vietnamese to match or exceed the slower rate of the American buildup.[39]

Cost-Effective Deployments

The constant demand for men and money impelled McNamara to seek to bring some measure of order out of the chaos surrounding the deployment process. Lack of adequate organizational arrangements had bred confusion and contention. Program requests often consisted of lumping together service demands for money, equipment, troops, and supplies from various components in Vietnam and rubber-stamping them through channels until they arrived in OSD without the vaguest information as to how, where, when, or why they would be used, or who would use them. To cite but one example, between late November 1965 and early January 1966, the number of combat support personnel requested by MACV jumped approximately 100,000 men without explanation or any justification. To provide a remedy, after the Honolulu conference in February 1966 McNamara created the Southeast Asia Programs Division (SEAPRO) to manage future deployments. SEAPRO, placed within Enthoven's Systems Analysis organization, originally functioned as an information clearinghouse for data related to the Vietnam buildup to keep McNamara and Vance fully informed of the effects of deployments on the overall force structure. Systems Analysis also used the information to validate PACOM, MACV, and JCS requests for additional forces. General Greene regarded SEAPRO as a way for OSD to bypass the Joint Chiefs, another sign of McNamara's disdain for the Chiefs and an indication that they were "being pushed back even further on the shelf."[40]

A further complication to deployment decisions was the internal political turmoil afflicting South Vietnam from mid-March through mid-June 1966. To solidify his hold on power, Prime Minister Ky reshuffled his cabinet in February and the next month fired a popular ARVN commander, igniting popular demonstrations against his government. When President Johnson met briefly with his advisers on 25 April to ascertain U.S. options in light of the civil strife racking South Vietnam, the alternatives were bleak: (1) continue as usual; (2) pressure Saigon to negotiate with the VC; (3) prepare to disengage. Johnson decided to stay on course, hoping, as McNamara later put it at a 10 May NSC meeting, that "heavy pressure by U.S. forces will carry us over the present period." During May armed clashes in Da Nang and Hue between pro- and antigovernment forces, according to U.S. estimates, resulted in 150 South Vietnamese killed, another 700 wounded, and scores arrested. The internal disarray further eroded public support in the United States for such a manifestly unstable, not to say undesirable, regime. The latest developments also convinced McNamara that the Saigon government would only grow weaker over time, fortifying his belief that only a political settlement, not a military victory, could end the fighting.[41] Military officials continued to think otherwise.

In mid-June 1966, Admiral Sharp submitted revised requirements asking for 475,000 U.S. and 46,000 allied troops in Vietnam by the end of 1966 plus a further increase of 84,000 during 1967. Sharp also wanted additional forces of 148,000 men by December 1966 and 172,000 by the end of 1967 elsewhere in the western Pacific to include a contingency corps (a theater reserve) either to shorten the war, if the opportunity appeared, or to offset future enemy buildups. Meanwhile Westmoreland was appealing for still more troops because of his growing concern about an enemy buildup in South Vietnam's central highlands. The president responded on 28 June by asking McNamara to expedite scheduled deployments to Southeast Asia.[42]

McNamara and Enthoven traveled to Hawaii for an 8 July briefing in another attempt to reconcile military strategy with the administration's political objectives. On arrival, McNamara told the press he was cautiously optimistic about military progress, an official attitude he maintained after returning to Washington, though advising reporters not to expect a short war. In crudest terms, the communists were fielding men faster than the allies could kill them. A National Intelligence Estimate issued in early July estimated the VC and NVA would gain 50,000 men during 1966 and grow to a force of about 125,000. So long as the enemy brought in these reinforcements, MACV would not likely meet goals developed after the February conference in Honolulu, such as securing population centers, opening lines of communication (LOCs), or denying base areas to the enemy. To achieve these agreed on objectives, PACOM had to have the additional forces requested in mid-June. The accompanying campaign plan would mass 65 percent of the ground forces in the northern provinces of South Vietnam to fight a war of attrition against NVA regulars. Total stated PACOM requirements by the end of 1967, including areas outside of South Vietnam, numbered nearly 800,000, including about 59,000 allied troops; with the desired contingency corps, the number would increase to more than 930,000 troops.[43]

Before his departure for Hawaii, McNamara passed the president's query about the pace of deployments to the JCS. Their 8 July reply pointed out that they had already hastened the diversion and deployment of units to Vietnam to meet MACV's February request for 389,000 troops in-country by year's end. Further significant surge deployments were impossible absent "emergency measures" (by which they meant mobilization of reservists). After returning from Hawaii, McNamara emphasized the positive for the president on 15 July, praising the Chiefs' "strenuous efforts" to quicken the dispatch of forces to Southeast Asia while omitting their assertion that the demands of the Vietnam War had stretched their services to the limits. The same day he requested presidential authorization to increase U.S. forces in South Vietnam to 355,000 by 1 October, noting that the number would grow to 395,000 by year's end, in line with Westmoreland's and Sharp's request of April. The latest (June) requests from the field for additional troops and plans for their use, however, came under increasingly critical OSD scrutiny.[44]

OSD's more exacting attitude became apparent when Westmoreland learned in early August that MACV-PACOM's latest request for a force increase had "gotten into trouble in the Washington arena." The JCS, reluctant to approve such increases without further rationale for their employment, forwarded the proposals to McNamara on 5 August solely "for information," adding that their recommendations would not be ready until late October or early November and only after considerable study. McNamara's reply the same day dismissed the logic for a more ambitious buildup and bluntly reminded the Chiefs that "excessive deployments weaken our ability to win by undermining the economic structure of the RVN and by raising doubts concerning the soundness of our planning." Citing the absence of "detailed, line-by-line analysis" of troop needs, McNamara appended Systems Analysis' initial challenges to the validity of some of the requests and asked the JCS to provide their recommendations by 15 September.[45]

Both Sharp and Westmoreland claimed that the war was entering a new phase that required the reinforcements. Now able to operate from secure bases, American troops would conduct sustained offensives to destroy enemy bases. The U.S. shield would allow the ARVN to turn its focus to pacification. Taylor thought the implications of Westmoreland's proposals merited thorough analysis, while McNamara felt that rather than another Washington-level review, the situation called for a reorganization of military and civil resources for the pacification effort in South Vietnam.[46]

During 1966, McNamara and his civilian cadre in OSD searched for alternatives to escalation of the war. In May and June McNamara had even considered direct negotiations with the North Vietnamese and Viet Cong. In September he asked for the CIA's assessment of whether communist officials thought U.S. negotiation overtures were "either insincere or unpalatably cast." McNamara also gave greater attention to the pacification objective, first articulated by the president at Honolulu in February and being vigorously implemented from the White House by Robert W. Komer, appointed 28 March as a special presidential assistant for supervising pacification support. Army staff officers briefed McNamara in mid-June on the so-called PROVN* study, outlining a long-term civic action program for the pacification of South Vietnam. In mid-August Komer proposed a sweeping reorganization of the pacification effort, and, with the assistance of McNaughton, got McNamara on 22 September to propose its consolidation under MACV headquarters. Westmoreland was cool to the idea and State and CIA opposed it. The president made no decision, but kept the Komer option open. In still another initiative to economize the use of U.S. forces, a month earlier McNamara had decided to give "highest priority" to constructing an "infiltration interdiction system"—a barrier of electronic sensors, mines, and manned "strong points" stretching across South Vietnam and Laos "to stop (or at a minimum to substantially reduce)" North Vietnamese infiltration of men and supplies into the South.[47]

The Barrier Concept

Creation of barrier controls to block enemy infiltration into the South had received attention as early as 1961. The concept of a physical ground barrier appeared in General Goodpaster's July 1965 Vietnam assessment and occasioned discussion by McNamara and Westmoreland of an obstacle system reaching from the South China Sea across South Vietnam and Laos to Thailand. The notion was resurrected in January 1966 by McNaughton as a possible alternative to bombing North Vietnam. A JCS study, prepared in April 1966 at the secretary's request, concluded that the three or more divisions needed to man a barrier could be put to better use elsewhere.[48] McNamara was undeterred.

Heightened interest in the concept grew out of a McNamara request to a group of distinguished scientists, working on contract with the JASON division of the Institute for Defense Analysis, to consider alternative methods of ending the war. Instead of the large-unit ground war so destructive of Vietnamese society and the air war that seemed unlikely to force Hanoi to quit, on 23 June the academics proposed a combination of technical devices, weapons, and manning to interdict designated choke points in a way that might reduce the flow of men and supplies sufficiently to deescalate the war. Relying more on technology than large troop commitments, the plan entailed installing an electronic fence, supplemented by mines and air and ground surveillance, across South Vietnam just south of the Demilitarized Zone separating the North and South and extending into Laos. Although admitting some uncertainty as to its feasibility and effectiveness, and concern over the installation time and cost, the JASON study concluded that the idea had enough merit to be pursued.[49]

* Program for the Pacification and Long Term Development of South Vietnam.

VIETNAM DMZ AND BARRIER

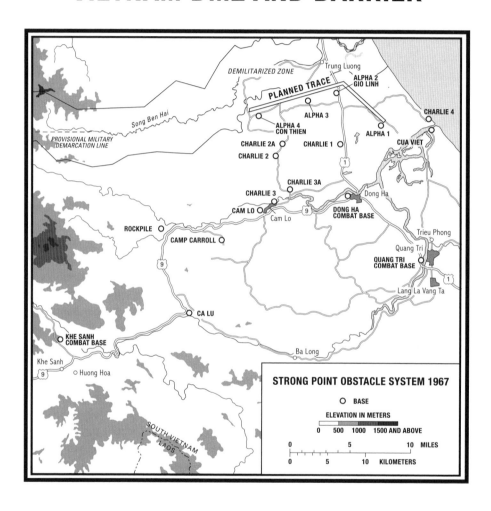

Moving rapidly, on 3 September McNamara requested the military's comments on the barrier proposal by mid-month, even though he had already made up his mind to proceed with it and have the "best possible barrier in place" within a year. On 8 September, the Joint Chiefs noted their reservations about such a system, questioning its impact on other items in the DoD budget and the authority to be accorded its manager. Given a preponderant Air Force involvement in the project, USAF Chief of Staff McConnell favored an airman as the director; the other Chiefs endorsed U.S. Army Lt. Gen. Alfred D. Starbird, director of the Defense Communications Agency, for the post. On the 15th, McNamara designated Starbird as the director of Joint Task Force 728 directly responsible to the secretary of defense and instructed him to have a system operational by September 1967. Despite a generally unfavorable MACV-PACOM position, on 17 September the Joint Chiefs half-heartedly endorsed the plan, pending further study, with the expectation that the system's high-tech hardware might have wider battlefield applications.[50] There were, however, skeptics.

William H. Sullivan, the U.S. ambassador in Laos, had been dismissive from the start when McNaughton broached the subject with him in Washington in the summer of 1966. He expressed "grave reservations" over the JASON proposals, particularly the reliability of acoustic sensors and other high-tech features. The portion of the system planned for Laos would be met he thought with "violent objection" by the Laotians and in any case was geographically wrongheaded, as "the best place to strike at infiltration is close to its source," (that is, on North Vietnamese soil). Sullivan regarded the JASON team as naive in matters of war and politics and disingenuous about the barrier's potential. One team member, for example, told him the concept was "totally impractical," yet, being unable to suggest anything better, he supported it. When asked by McNamara in early October for his comments on the proposed system, Sullivan returned a deflating critique.[51]

Despite the naysayers, in mid-October McNamara recommended an obstacle system to the president because "even the threat" of a viable barrier would work to U.S. advantage. As McNamara envisaged it, one section (to detect foot traffic) would be a conventional (linear) barrier placed just south of the DMZ and employ mines and sensors along with personnel. With the Marine base at Khe Sanh as its hub, this segment would link the linear strong points in South Vietnam to a high-tech electronic belt (to detect vehicular traffic) in Laos; here acoustic devices would relay signals of truck movement to monitoring aircraft that would then summon attack planes to hit the target. A third, low-tech section, in Wheeler's phrase, "something we have been doing for 2,000 years," placed troops at manning points near the easternmost part of the DMZ. In mid-November McNamara formally reported to the president preparations to install the ground foundations of the barrier.[52]

In the meantime, McNamara and Vance had also briefed Representative Mahon and Senator Russell on the system, explaining that its funding would be covered in the FY 1967 supplemental. Although agreeing readily to pour enormous amounts of dollars into the project—$1.5 billion for construction and $740 million for annual operating costs*–McNamara balked at authorizing additional soldiers to construct and defend the barrier. Westmoreland and Sharp complained that diverting troops currently in Vietnam would interfere with ongoing and planned combat operations, while the JCS expressed alarm at infrastructure, research, and resource costs. The Chiefs also seconded MACV's call for additional forces for Practice Nine, the barrier's latest cover name. Unable to tap reserve units for manpower, the JCS proposed to withdraw more than 8,300 Army troops from NATO reinforcing divisions to field the necessary forces for Practice Nine.[†53] Moreover, Westmoreland remained leery of any operational and tactical plan imposed on him. The constant bickering between field commanders and Washington forced McNamara in mid-December to send Starbird to consult personally with Westmoreland with the understanding that if MACV had to have an additional infantry brigade for the barrier, OSD would provide it. McNamara hoped the concession would win Westmoreland's support, allowing the secretary to avoid "ordering this to be done over the objection of all the military leaders" while simultaneously buying "a little insurance" in the absence of "a winning plan." On 13 January 1967 President Johnson approved the evolving barrier project and assigned it the highest national priority.[54]

More Troops, More Questions

The prospect of the barrier had no effect on continuing demands from MACV and PACOM for more troops, for which they received no quick reply. CINCPAC's mid-June 1966 augmentation request remained under review by the Joint Chiefs for months. In mid-September, McNamara advised the president to enforce a troop ceiling, fearing that unbridled escalation would have adverse effects on South Vietnam's economy and substitute U.S. soldiers to accomplish ARVN missions. Moreover, the JCS claimed it could no longer meet CINCPAC's stated requirements, even with six-to-eight month delays, unless they gutted the Army's strategic reserve, cut its NATO reinforcement capability until late 1968, and left it greatly understrength. The Navy's shortage of carrier pilots was worsening, and, although the Air Force was reducing its 22 NATO-based tactical fighter squadrons

---

* The two primary parts of the system—anti-personnel and anti-vehicle—each had substantial operating costs. The anti-personnel system cost more than $28 million a month to operate or roughly $340 million annually, while the anti-vehicle system ran $33 million a month or nearly $400 million annually. (Institute for Defense Analysis, JASON Division, "Air-Supported Anti-Infiltration Barrier," Study S-255, Aug 66, 40, fldr 728, box 4, ISA General files, Acc 70A-6649.)

† In June 1967 Practice Nine was dropped as a code name because of a security compromise. The barrier was known for a brief period as Illinois City and in mid-September as Dye Marker. Press reports compromised that name, too, so the project became known as SPOS (Strong-point-obstacle-system), also referred to as Dye Marker, with two sub-components, Dump Truck (anti-vehicle) and Mud River (anti-personnel) collectively called Muscle Shoals.

to 13, it could not rapidly deploy combat-ready tactical aircraft from the United States. Finally, the practice of drawing equipment from the reserves to outfit newly activated units scheduled for Vietnam had appreciably degraded reserve readiness.[55] With numerous personnel and equipment issues pending resolution, McNamara and Wheeler flew to Saigon on 8 October for another firsthand evaluation.

The ostensible purpose of the trip was to learn MACV's requirements in order to forecast DoD's future money requests, but the wide-ranging agenda covered such topics as MACV future deployments, the barrier system, pacification, and the South Vietnamese economy. The command estimated that a 520,000-man force would increase U.S. spending in South Vietnam to about $390 million annually, or 46 billion South Vietnamese piasters at the official exchange rate. Economists at the U.S. embassy feared that vast sum would wreck the country's already overheated and inflationary economy. Forewarned by Lodge, McNamara set 1967 end-strength at 463,000 at a less inflationary cost of 42 billion piasters ($364 million). Strategy by piaster drew immediate criticism from Westmoreland who insisted this would leave him short a combat division and its supporting units in 1967. Nonetheless, Westmoreland, after his private meeting with McNamara, agreed that between 480,000 and 500,000 troops by the end of 1967 would suffice and save about 1.4 billion piasters.[56]

Westmoreland firmly believed that the crossover point—the unknown figure at which casualties would exceed VC/NVA ability to replace losses—was near. Admitting that the enemy still held the initiative, he agreed with McNamara that the communist threat in the northern provinces was diverting more and more allied units to that region from other areas of the country. The MACV commander and the ambassador officially held out great hope for military success in 1967; privately Lodge seemed to question the worth of Westmoreland's search-and-destroy strategy, suggesting greater attention be given to pacification and the nonmilitary aspects of the war.[57] McNamara returned to Washington encouraged by the military success in blunting the possibility of communist victory in South Vietnam, discouraged by the enemy's stubborn persistence in continuing the war of attrition, disappointed by the regression in pacification, and unable to see any way to end the war soon.

On 14 October, McNamara recommended that the president stabilize the U.S. force in Vietnam at 470,000 (100,000 fewer than Westmoreland and Sharp wanted) and install the barrier system to choke off NVA infiltration through the DMZ. He emphasized pacification as the most effective means to achieve U.S. goals and believed that suspending or at least reducing the bombing campaign might lead to negotiations. Enacting these measures, however, did not guarantee that the fighting would end within the next two years. McNamara somberly concluded that it was time to gird openly for a longer war and convince the American public that sacrifices to save Vietnam were worth it.[58]

The JCS agreed with McNamara that it would be a long war but on little else. Preferring to "reserve judgment" until Westmoreland and Sharp evaluated the revised October deployment plans, the Chiefs expressed concern over OSD's substantial reductions to MACV's requests. They also faulted the secretary's inability to appreciate the cumulative effect of repeated military defeats on VC/NVA morale and his proposal to discard the bombing campaign, one of the president's "trump cards," with nothing in return. On 20 October, CINCPAC recommended that the JCS approve a force ceiling of slightly more than 384,000 troops by the end of 1966, rising to about 520,000 in 1968. On 24–25 October at the Manila Conference of the Chiefs of Governments, attended by national leaders contributing forces to Vietnam,[*] Westmoreland told McNaughton, as he had previously informed McNamara, that he could make do with between 480,000 and 500,000 U.S. troops, although he was anxious to have a theater reserve, the previously discussed corps contingency force, within quick-reaction distance of Vietnam. An apparent, if unmentioned, reason for such a force was MACV's developing proposal for three U.S. divisions to invade the Laotian panhandle beginning in 1968.[59]

On 4 November, the JCS proposed to McNamara force deployments for the rest of 1966 and for 1967 below CINCPAC's stated requirements, but argued that expanded and minimally restrained actions such as incursions into the southern half of the DMZ and cross-border operations to destroy communist bases in Cambodia and Laos could shorten the war and support nation-building in South Vietnam. They undercut their case, however, by dismissing OSD and State Department concerns about the inflationary effects the reinforcement costs would exert on the South Vietnamese economy as militarily unrealistic and statistically unreliable. In early November, McNamara and Wheeler met with the president three times, including two trips to his Texas ranch, to discuss the size of the next DoD budget and the implications of deploying additional U.S. troops to Vietnam. On 5 November McNamara announced to a waiting press corps that "the military victory which the North Vietnamese and Viet Cong sought . . . is now beyond their grasp." As a result, planned deployments as well as draft inductions would be reduced substantially, as would production of certain material, such as air ordnance.[60]

Four days later Enthoven drafted a McNamara reply to the JCS that noted Wheeler's recent report to the president that "the war . . . continues in a very favorable fashion. General Westmoreland retains the initiative and in every operation to date has managed to defeat the enemy." Additionally the memo pointed out that runaway inflation could undo these victories. It included the following table, listing a proposed Vietnam-based personnel level as Program #4.

---

[*] Attendees included President Johnson, President Ferdinand Marcos of the Philippines, Thieu and Ky, President Park of South Korea, and Prime Ministers Harold Holt of Australia, Keith Holyoake of New Zealand, and Thanom Kittikachorn of Thailand, plus their respective delegations.

TABLE 3

PROGRAM #4 PERSONNEL LEVELS PROPOSAL
(THOUSANDS OF PERSONNEL IN SVN)

Plan	December 1966	June 1967	December 1967	June 1968
JCS	395,000	456,000	504,000	522,000
CINCPAC	392,000	448,000	476,000	484,000
Program #4	391,000	440,000	463,000	469,000

Source: *Pentagon Papers*, bk 5, IV.C.6.(a), 101-03.

Accepting Enthoven's rationale and figures, on 11 November McNamara informed the JCS of a new ceiling of 463,300 U.S. troops in Vietnam for December 1967 (41,000 fewer than requested) and a June 1968 limit of 469,300 (53,000 below JCS projections). He asked that the JCS provide him with any proposed changes by 1 December. They replied on the 2d that they still preferred their proposal of 4 November but submitted a revised unit mix in the interest of a more balanced force without any substantial change to the secretary's total. McNamara accepted these revisions on 9 December.[61]

McNamara reinforced the logic for leveling off U.S. ground forces in his 17 November recommendation to the president for a Southeast Asia supplemental appropriation. He asserted that large-scale "seek out and destroy" operations had reached the point of diminishing returns and even sending 100,000 more U.S. troops would only increase VC/NVA losses by 70 casualties per week. Stabilizing American forces at a level sufficient to prevent interference with the pacification process by large enemy units would promote security and economic development and enable the United States to maintain forces in Vietnam indefinitely to nullify the Fabian tactics of the communists. The alternative—endless escalation—was unacceptable to the American people. Studies provided by Systems Analysis contributed to McNamara's recommendations, but his sense of urgency grew from his conviction that something had to be done and quickly in Vietnam. Otherwise, given the sour public mood, the president would probably lose the 1968 election.[62]

The Search for a Winning Formula

By late 1966 the administration could not help but be aware of the need to give more attention and harder thought to handling a war that was obviously not going well. There had to be a thorough rethinking of how to prosecute the conflict more effectively and to what end. Unfortunately, efforts to formulate firm overall policy direction proved no more successful than previous attempts. Direction of the war continued in the same day-to-day, ad hoc manner as before. Trying a new approach, the president approved on 15 November the formation of a small, secret kitchen cabinet, the so-called Non-Group. The original idea, proposed in late September by Komer and forwarded to the president by Bill Moyers, called for a handful of senior civilian policy officials just below the level of Secretaries McNamara and Rusk to monitor and coordinate the formulation of Vietnam policy. Members included Under Secretary of State Nicholas Katzenbach, who chaired the Thursday afternoon sessions, Rostow, Vance, Komer, and, at the insistence of the president, General Wheeler.[63]

In December, the Non-Group produced a draft national security action memorandum (NSAM) to coordinate 1967 military, civil, and political strategy in Vietnam. It emphasized a renewed commitment to pacification to strengthen the government of South Vietnam, hasten the erosion of VC support in the South, and convince the people of South Vietnam that the communists were losing. A weakened Hanoi and VC might then negotiate or at least understand U.S. determination to see the struggle through to conclusion. Such a strategy, the authors believed, would either resolve the war by December 1967 or position the United States for a longer pull. The NSAM was never issued.[64]

Commenting on the proposal, ISA favored pacification and rural development assistance over the dispatch of more U.S. troops to Vietnam, while the JCS insisted that nation building would follow logically in the wake of the destruction of communist forces in the South by military action. Field commanders believed that diverting forces to pacification duties reduced the operational flexibility MACV needed for offensive military operations. CINCPAC wanted to remove restrictions on the air war against the North and see the war in the South through to a military victory.[65] Many officials, including the president, straddled these extremes.

On New Year's Day 1967 Taylor, in his role as special consultant, described pacification as a poor second alternative to expanded U.S. military operations. He advised the president to revisit Westmoreland's troop requirements and strategy with an eye to limiting ground forces and providing operational guidance to the general. At the same time, Westmoreland concluded that the enemy intended to continue large-unit operations, despite heavy losses in 1966, in a protracted war of attrition. Komer believed the opposite, that the enemy was reverting to a small-unit guerrilla strategy.[66]

After the administration's efforts in early 1967 to open negotiations with the North Vietnamese failed to dent Hanoi's hardline attitude,* the Joint Chiefs sensed a chance to press their case. In mid-February Wheeler, reporting to the president

---

* See Chapter VIII for a detailed discussion of these initiatives.

after a visit to Vietnam, believed him "receptive to increasing our military pressure" in the air war against the North and ground operations in the South. Wheeler encouraged Westmoreland to request additional troops, anticipating that McNamara would speed up deployments.[67]

Despite his best efforts, Westmoreland responded, the ground war could not be accelerated beyond its current pace, given limitations imposed on MACV by available intelligence, troops, and helicopter support. Reminding Wheeler that he had asked for larger forces to counter enemy actions in the northern provinces, he maintained that his request for 550,000 U.S. troops remained valid. At a 17 February meeting with McNamara, Wheeler, Taylor, and Rostow, the president requested recommendations within five days on ways to accelerate military progress in South Vietnam. He felt current policy was "operating on borrowed time"; "he needed to get results" to solidify popular support for the war, from which Wheeler detected a new sense of urgency on the president's part.[68]

The JCS incorporated bombing strategy and ground campaign proposals into three alternative programs for Vietnam that the president, McNamara, Rusk, Taylor, and Wheeler discussed on 22 February: (1) continue the status quo but accelerate deployments; (2) escalate the conflict with significant policy changes, that is, destroy the MIG airfields in the North and expand ground operations into Laos to a 20-kilometer radius; or (3) elevate the engagement to an all-out war with major policy changes, that is, attack all NVN airfields, mine the ports, destroy dikes, conduct battalion-size operations in Laos, and deploy up to four additional U.S. divisions that would necessitate reserve mobilizations and increased draft calls. McNamara's contrary position paper, circulated at the meeting, opposed increased bombing and insisted that without the active involvement of the South Vietnamese government in pacification efforts the "real war" was unwinnable. Holding to his middle ground, Johnson opted to use greater, but still limited, force, approving among other proposals modified operations in Laos and acceleration of Program #4 deployments.[69]

The president's decision encouraged Wheeler and Westmoreland to push for more ground troops. Westmoreland had sound operational reasons for reinforcements. In order to mass multi-division forces for large-scale operations, MACV had to divert U.S. troops from other missions—providing security for populated areas, guarding bases, and defending lines of communication. Westmoreland also needed reinforcements in South Vietnam's northern provinces, where U.S. Marine offensives had sparked heavy fighting and casualties but had not quelled the NVN threat. Pressure in the northern areas forced Westmoreland to shift U.S. Army troops from other parts of the country; in April he redeployed his reserve northward to cope with the deteriorating situation.[70] In short, Westmoreland lacked troops to sustain large-scale combat operations against enemy base areas, or, for that matter, to continue operations on a reduced level to prevent the VC/NVA from returning to their old base camps.

Unable to implement his proposed large-scale operations with only the Program #4 forces, on 18 March Westmoreland described an unremitting campaign into communist-controlled areas that would require upwards of 200,000 more troops above the current ceiling of 470,000. With more troops, he could destroy the enemy main forces and give greater attention to rooting out the guerrilla infrastructure. Nonetheless, the general offered no assurance such a massive reinforcement, with its far-reaching international and domestic political ramifications, would win the war. On 21 March, the second day of the Guam Conference, an in-progress war review by Vietnamese and U.S. leaders,* the MACV commander announced that unless NVN infiltration could be stopped, "this war could go on indefinitely." According to Westmoreland, his evaluation left the high-level audience "painfully silent" wearing "looks of shock." McNaughton, in particular, "wore an air of disbelief." Reporters were also incredulous when McNamara on the 22d repeated MACV's contention that the war could go on indefinitely unless the military pressure being imposed against the enemy forces broke the will of the North, an accomplishment nowhere yet in sight.[71]

McNamara still entertained hopes of ending the war before the 1968 presidential election. According to Rostow, the secretary feared that political pressures during an election year might force the United States into an unsatisfactory settlement and was "thrashing about for a short cut" to end the war before that happened. Westmoreland was also looking for a way to end the war. At the request of the JCS shortly after the Guam Conference, Westmoreland on 28 March submitted his justification for the additional troops he had requested earlier in the month. His "minimum essential force" called for another 80,000 men; his "optimum force" required approximately 200,000 more troops. The "optimum force"—680,000 U.S. troops by July 1968—would enable Westmoreland to launch cross-border raids against communist base camps in Laos and Cambodia as well as threaten ground action against the southern part of North Vietnam.[72] The latest request for additional troops reached Washington at a time of growing dissatisfaction with both the ground and air strategies and resulted in a prolonged policy debate that the president did not resolve until July 1967.

At a 24 April OSD staff meeting, McNamara equated MACV's latest troop request to a "'65 type watershed," a major policy decision comparable to the 1965 choice to become fully engaged. Pouring cold water on the idea, he told his staff that a deployment of 200,000 more American troops to Vietnam might only leave the war stalemated at a higher level. The president likewise had little stomach for sending more U.S. troops to Southeast Asia unless the South Vietnamese government ordered a general mobilization to add substantially more men to carry a heavier load of the fighting.[73]

---

* Participants included the president, Ambassador-designate Ellsworth Bunker (who succeeded Lodge on 5 April), Harriman, Komer, Lodge, McNamara, McNaughton, Rostow, Rusk, Taylor, Sharp, Westmoreland, and Wheeler. Thieu and Ky led the high-ranking South Vietnamese delegation.

Mid-April found the Joint Chiefs divided over Westmoreland's proposals. McConnell doubted the additional ground forces would make any difference and advocated greater air and naval power to break North Vietnam's will. He agreed to the minimum essential force because of the communist threat to the northern provinces, and then only on condition that the Chiefs recommend expanding the air and naval war against North Vietnam. Moreover, the JCS contended that the services could meet MACV's FY 1968 minimum ground force requirements only by extending tours of duty and calling up reserves for two years of active service.[74]

In a separate initiative, on 24 April Non-Group chairman Katzenbach asked Defense and State as well as the CIA and White House for their respective evaluations of (1) the military and political actions that could bring the war to a successful conclusion; (2) the possibility of negotiations; and (3) the effects of escalation. The same day Komer, newly-appointed director of the U.S. pacification program in South Vietnam,* advised the president to make the South Vietnamese pull their weight and questioned sending large numbers of additional American reinforcements. Three days later, Rostow advocated military escalation, though at a level that would not bring other communist powers into the war. He saw no reason to call the reserves, a step that would, in any event, only create a domestic political uproar without promise of shortening the war.[75]

In late April Westmoreland returned to the United States to address the Associated Press annual convention in New York City and appear before Congress but also to participate in a probing policy review of his proposals. At a 27 April White House meeting that included McNamara, Wheeler, and others, Westmoreland maintained that his war of attrition was succeeding; except for the northern provinces, MACV had reached the crossover point where the enemy could no longer replace its losses. Without the reinforcements he had requested, the war would not be lost, but it would last longer, a point Wheeler later reiterated. At issue was what additional U.S. troops might accomplish and how long it would take them to do it. For an administration looking to scale back an increasingly costly ground war, another spiraling round of mutual escalation had no appeal. Where did it all end? Might Hanoi, like North Korea in 1950, call for outside volunteers to continue the struggle? To these presidential questions, Westmoreland had no answer.

According to Westmoreland's version of the meeting, Rostow suggested committing additional forces only to gain a spectacular advantage, such as an amphibious landing north of the DMZ. Despite Westmoreland's ready endorsement, the feeler died for lack of support, as did Wheeler's overture to extend operations into Laos and Cambodia to destroy communist bases and infiltration routes there. When the MACV commander estimated his present forces would take five years to finish the job, McNamara prodded the general to relate the alternative troop

---

* Komer became deputy to the commander, USMACV for civil operations and revolutionary development support and special assistant to the ambassador to Vietnam in May 1967.

plans to the time it would take to end the war. Reluctantly Westmoreland replied that with the minimum force it would take five years, with the maximum it would take three.[76]

MACV's call for reinforcements and the JCS demands for heavier bombing put pressure on OSD and State to examine alternative strategies, if only to explain their rejection. William Bundy opposed the increases because they might require calling the reserves, thus leading to a congressional debate of Vietnam strategy that would only benefit Hanoi. He rejected expanding the war into neighboring countries in favor of an accelerated pacification effort. Employing nimble, seemingly convincing, statistical analysis, Enthoven "demonstrated" enemy losses were unrelated to the size of U.S. forces. For example, during 1966 American forces had increased 23 percent but enemy losses increased by only 13 percent. Frustrated by Westmoreland's conduct of the war and his ever-increasing force requirements that lacked any analysis to show why they were needed, on 1 May Enthoven recommended holding firm to the current Program #4 ceiling of 470,000 men. Westmoreland would have to use them more effectively.[77]

McNaughton's 6 May rejoinder to Westmoreland's latest troop request went further, underscoring the lack of a coherent strategy. He assumed that Hanoi would not negotiate until after the November 1968 presidential election. By that time, however, a disgruntled American public might vent its growing dissatisfaction with the war on an incumbent president. No one, in McNaughton's view, had charge of the war, no one was coordinating military and diplomatic efforts efficiently, and no one really knew how the various executive components—OSD, State, White House, JCS, and by extension executive agents like MACV and PACOM—were fighting the war. Each followed its own meandering course "getting us in deeper and deeper" with no end in sight. "Since no pressure will have been put on anyone," he wrote, limiting deployments to Vietnam today merely postponed the issue of a reserve call-up, likely leading to one at a worse time politically for the administration. Someone (obviously the president) had to make an encompassing decision about the nature and future of the war or, at the very least, the president had to give Westmoreland a firm troop ceiling and make it clear to his field commander that whatever the number, that would be it.[78]

McNaughton's appraisal became the basis for McNamara's DPM of 19 May 1967. McNamara adopted the either-or approach: either Course A—escalate the war by honoring all of Westmoreland's requests; or Course B—try to stabilize it by limiting U.S. forces in Vietnam. The secretary concluded that the magnitude of the military's proposed escalation would necessitate a reserve call-up, a decision that might polarize national opinion and hand the prosecution of the war to the hawks, who would intensify it to a point, as he later wrote, that would "spin the war utterly out of control." More U.S. troops were not the answer because Hanoi would match any U.S. reinforcement. It would neither, at least not anytime soon, collapse under American military pressure nor seek a negotiated settlement. In brief, the war was unwinnable. This left Course B—to stabilize U.S. force levels in Vietnam and accept a stalemate by seeking neither military victory nor risking military defeat. The time had come to settle for a draw by restricting the bombing of North Vietnam, limiting further deployments, adhering to a firm troop ceiling, and actively seeking a political settlement. McNamara stopped short of recommending an outright pullout in the absence, he later recollected, of any "low cost means of withdrawal,"[79] apparently meaning that the domestic political consequences of such a decision would sink the administration.

The DPM offered stark alternatives, but Lyndon Johnson, true to form on Vietnam, deferred the decision, later rationalizing as "simple prudence" his insistence on exploring every element in depth, hearing every argument, and arraying every fact. Well before receiving the secretary's recommendations, the president had outlined his intention to dispatch McNamara, Katzenbach, and Wheeler to Saigon for yet another on-scene evaluation. In the midst of a major strategic reassessment, McNamara's memorandum of 19 May spurred Johnson to preside over a policy review through the remaining days of May and all of June. He also consulted members of Congress, private advisers, and others he respected.[80]

Unaware of the secretary's draft memorandum, on 20 May the JCS issued their worldwide posture statement, warning that the nation's military forces could no longer respond to other possible contingencies throughout the world in a timely fashion. Policies of restraint and gradualism in Vietnam had frittered away the opportunities for the United States to exploit its military superiority. It was time to deploy MACV's minimum essential force, time to expand the air and ground wars, and time to call up the reserves.[81]

The same day McNamara asked the JCS to comment on his DPM. Shortly afterward, Wheeler cautioned Sharp and Westmoreland that in the policy review then under way in Washington, OSD's conclusions were "at considerable variance with our own thinking and proposals." In addressing the DPM, the Chiefs singled out "five major areas of concern." First, the secretary did not appreciate fully the implications for the Free World of an unsuccessful outcome of the Southeast Asia conflict. Second, to "make do" with current military forces would unnecessarily lengthen the war. Third, restricting the air war against the North would allow the enemy to supply his forces in the South from all points of the compass— the DMZ, Laos, the coast, and Cambodia. Fourth, calling the reserve might well prompt a debate about national policy, but, unlike OSD, the JCS felt the American public would willingly accept escalation once properly informed about the issues. Fifth, the nation's military leaders questioned whether available intelligence estimates supported OSD's grim prognostications that Hanoi had no intention of negotiating until after the 1968 presidential election, that expanded military action would damage U.S. prestige, or that an intensified war effort would compel China to enter the fighting. The Chiefs insisted that McNamara's Course A did not accurately reflect JCS, PACOM, or MACV positions. As for Course B, adopting it would only prolong the war, reinforce Hanoi's belief in ultimate victory, and cost the United States more lives and treasure. They did not want the DPM sent to the president and again asked McNamara to approve the military strategy as proposed the previous April. Admiral Sharp regarded Course B as nothing more than "a blueprint for defeat," but he was resigned to losing the argument, believing the administration would not provide the forces called for in Course A nor activate the reserves. He sought a middle ground, but did not expect that it would be accepted.[82]

Others besides the military took issue with McNamara's 19 May DPM. Rostow advised an intermediate strategy somewhere between the McNamara and the JCS approaches, relying on greater military force and narrower political and diplomatic maneuvering less injurious to Saigon's morale. Calling the reserves, he sensed, would demonstrate Washington's resolve to Hanoi, but it required the administration to explain to the American people why such action had become necessary. The substantive policy debate, arguably the first soul-searching review since July 1965, was interrupted by the outbreak of the Arab-Israeli Six-Day War (5–10 June). The sudden crisis shifted Washington's attention away from Vietnam—McNamara scrapped the planned June trip to Saigon—and concerned Wheeler, who wanted the administration's focus "back to the war we are fighting." By early July, Vietnam reclaimed center stage as McNamara and his party arrived at Ton Son Nhut Air Base on the 7th for five days of firsthand assessment of the situation and to work out the latest schedule of reinforcements known as Program #5.[83]

The first two days of briefings offered an encouraging outlook. Neither the U.S. embassy nor the MACV staff considered the war stalemated, but they aired differing views on its future. While recently appointed Ambassador Bunker gave top priority to prosecuting the conflict, he opposed more U.S. reinforcements until Saigon's leaders showed that they were making maximum use of available Vietnamese manpower, a point McNamara underscored with considerable emotion. According to Westmoreland, political restraints had enabled Hanoi to seize the strategic initiative in South Vietnam, a complaint echoed in one form or another by all the generals and admirals present. The MACV commander again made his case for tens of thousands of U.S. reinforcements for his "optimum force." Westmoreland could then capitalize on previous battlefield successes, accelerate allied offensive efforts inside South Vietnam, and, political conditions permitting, carry the fight to the enemy outside South Vietnam's borders. Without the optimum force, the United States would still win, but victory would become a long, drawn-out process and lengthen the time before U. S. forces could leave Vietnam.[84]

Likewise, Sharp and Lt. Gen. William W. Momyer, Seventh Air Force commander, believed Hanoi was for the first time feeling the full effects of U.S. airpower (an argument Sharp had advanced the previous December). The timing appeared perfect for a massive, sustained, and intensive air campaign targeting the Hanoi-Haiphong area. McNamara seemed to accept their points, much to the relief of his military audience, who had anticipated a decision to level off troop commitments and further restrict the bombing campaign.[85]

During private discussions with Westmoreland and later, on 11 July, with General Creighton W. Abrams, deputy commander, MACV, McNamara agreed on a ceiling of 525,000 troops, thereby meeting their minimum force requirements. In exchange, MACV offered the secretary five reinforcement packages to meet its operational requirements with minimum increases in troop strength that would preclude either a call-up of the reserve or extension of service tours in Vietnam. Bunker's 12 July cable to the president described a meeting of minds on future actions to assure success in Vietnam.[86]

More U.S. servicemen could be sent to Vietnam without calling the reserves because Systems Analysis had identified more than 86,000 additional active-duty troops available for deployment. The price, however, was to reduce further the readiness of NATO-committed Strategic Army Forces (STRAF)* units and eliminate 50,000 positions from the Continental United States (CONUS) Sustaining Force that the Army insisted it needed to maintain its training and rotation base. An outraged Army Chief of Staff Johnson erupted, "Enthoven wants to do [it] with mirrors."[87]

Despite optimistic briefings about the war's progress, McNamara returned to a White House meeting on 12 July in an ambivalent mood. To the president's key question, "Are we going to be able to win this goddamned war?," McNamara answered that the war was no longer stalemated. He outlined Westmoreland's latest requests and rationale for additional troops, but added that by reducing waste and slippage "we can get by with less." Notes of the meeting observe that, "for the first time Secretary McNamara said he felt that if we follow the same program we will win the war and end the fighting." The president conceded the need for more troops but wanted the numbers shaved to the minimum. He would discuss the issue with Westmoreland later that day.[†][88] That evening Johnson met privately with Westmoreland. He recounted the day's meeting in detail and told the general that "he did not always accept the advice of his civilian advisors over that of his military advisors." At a session the next day with McNamara, Wheeler, and Westmoreland, the president restated his support for a troop increase.[89]

---

* The STRAF was a reserve of eight divisions and related combat support and service support units totaling approximately 207,000 troops, all stationed in the United States.

† Westmoreland had returned from Saigon on 10 July to attend his mother's funeral, following which the president called him to the White House for consultations.

Table 4

Deployment Ceilings for Vietnam and Dates of Approval

Program Number	Date Approved by Secdef	Maximum End Strength	Date Deployment Completed
1 (Phase I)	31 July 1965	190,100	June 1967
2 (Phase II)	10 November 1965	332,000	Later Revised
(Phase IIA)	28 November 1965	390,000	Later Revised
(Phase IIR)	11 December 1965	393,000	June 1967
3	2 July 1966	431,000	June 1967
4	18 November 1966	470,000	June 1968
5	14 August 1967	525,000	June 1969
6	4 April 1968	549,500	June 1969

Source: Fldr Miscellaneous 1968, box 65, Pentagon Papers Backup, Acc 330-75-062.

On 14 July, McNamara directed the preparation of a revised deployment plan (Program #5) to increase U.S. troop strength in South Vietnam to 525,000. Without calling the reserves, he had provided the additional troops Westmoreland said he needed to hasten the end of the war. He had imposed control of future deployments and kept restraints on ground forces. Yet the previous afternoon, McNamara had revealed to his OSD staff his worries over the continued breadth and depth of Viet Cong influence in the South, the slow pace of pacification, and the potential need for even more U.S. troops in the near future. These developments were especially discouraging because they augured even greater expenditures when McNamara was under intense criticism for his handling of the Defense budget. Like McNamara, Johnson harbored doubts about the success of the latest measures. On 14 July he decided to send Clark Clifford and Maxwell Taylor to confidentially solicit America's Asian allies to deploy more troops to Vietnam.[90] The president, too, was still looking for answers.

CHAPTER VI

More Than Expected:
Supplementals and Budgets,
1966–1968

Legislative stipulations and a fixed timetable governing the annual budget cycle made it normal to have budgets for three fiscal years—previous, current, and future—in play at one time.[1] When the administration closed the books on the FY 1966 budget on 30 June 1966, for example, DoD's FY 1967 budget, submitted to Congress on 24 January 1966, still remained unauthorized, unappropriated, and under congressional scrutiny, forcing the government to operate on the basis of a continuing resolution enacted by Congress on 30 June and subsequently twice extended until 15 October 1966. By that time, OSD and service staffers were well along in preparing the proposed FY 1968 budget. To further complicate matters, in August 1965 OSD budget analysts prepared an amendment to the FY 1966 budget;* this was followed by supplemental financing requests for FY 1966 and FY 1967 to underwrite the expanding military costs generated by the escalating warfare in Vietnam. Hovering over OSD's financial estimates were the president's domestic political agenda, a growing awareness about the threat of domestic inflation, an unexpectedly rapid increase in the number of American troops deployed to Vietnam, an increasingly restless and partisan Congress, and drawn-out political maneuvering over the merits of a tax increase—all influencing the formulation of Defense budget requests. It was, then, a time of political, military, economic, and social uncertainty that made extremely difficult the accurate forecasting of military budgeting and expenditures under the fixed legislative budget process.[2]

---

* The amendment, requested by the president on 4 August 1965, sought $1.7 billion for the Emergency Fund, Southeast Asia. It was approved along with the president's budget on 29 September 1965 (PL 89-213; 79 Stat 863).

Enacting the FY 1966 Supplemental

The FY 1966 Vietnam supplemental reached Congress on 19 January 1966 followed five days later by the president's FY 1967 budget request. Beginning on 20 January and continuing through August, OSD principals trooped up Capitol Hill to justify their budget prognostications before various House and Senate committees.

Well before his congressional testimony, McNamara had sounded out members of the Senate and House appropriations and armed services committees about a January supplemental for FY 1966 in the $10–12 billion range and a similar amount in the FY 1967 budget specifically for Vietnam to cover the "need for increased U.S. deployments if we were to avoid a military defeat or stalemate."[3] As with the August 1965 budget amendment, Deputy Secretary Vance served as McNamara's point man coordinating budget matters in advance with congressional leaders. Over lunch on 10 January, for instance, he informed Representative Sikes of the House Appropriations Committee that OSD would soon submit a $12–13 billion supplemental request that the administration hoped Congress would act upon before hearings commenced on the FY 1967 budget in mid-February. Sikes assured Vance this could be done, having already discussed the issue with George Mahon, chairman of the powerful appropriations panel. Sikes also suggested other influential congressmen for Vance to contact, recommended tactics to accelerate authorizations, and made plain the projects he favored for prosecution of the war. He concluded by telling Vance that "there will be a good deal of politics," but the administration "would get everything we asked for."[4] Republican Congressman Arends passed on a similar message. Beyond securing appropriations, OSD wanted congressional cooperation to avoid, as McNamara put it to Arends, "divisive action between the Legislative and the Executive branches when we were at war."[5]

McNamara's self-assurance and confidence were on full display throughout the hearings as he defended the president's request for $12.3 billion in supplemental funds (NOA). He dazzled the House Appropriations Committee with his command of figures: $1.6 billion for an additional 340,000 military and 36,000 direct-hire civilian personnel; $2.3 billion for increased operating expenses; $1.2 billion for expanded construction; $2.1 billion for higher ammunition costs. He reeled off estimates with striking facility. Ammunition consumption, for example, running at $100 million per month, was expected to rise to $170 million monthly by December 1966. The tonnage of bombs dropped on the enemy had climbed from 25,000 in June 1965 to 40,000 in December 1965 and was projected to average 75,000 per month during 1966. Anticipating losses of 500 fixed-wing aircraft and 500 helicopters during 1966, OSD forecast $1.8 billion in replacement costs and $1.2 billion more for spare parts and other equipment.[6] All of these estimates hinged on McNamara's assumption that increased deployments would suffice to convince Hanoi to desist from supporting the insurgents in South Vietnam.

Mahon, fearful of "a very considerable escalation of the war" that would raise associated costs beyond current projections, wondered if additional supplemental requests were in the cards. McNamara assured him that the funding OSD had requested presumed a rise from the approved level of 220,000-plus American servicemen in Southeast Asia by 1 March 1966, and, in fact, his recommended budget would sustain a force of between 375,000 and 400,000 U.S. troops in Vietnam without further funding increases.[7] Given the impossibility of estimating an opponent's intentions 18 months in advance (to June 1967, the end of the FY 1967 budget cycle), however, the secretary expected "our current estimate will prove to be at least partially in error," perhaps too high or too low.[8]

McNamara stood foursquare behind the administration's conduct of the war. Money was not the issue, he said. Instead, the American people lacked the will to fight a limited war. "We do not have any guts. That is what is wrong with us, as a people we are soft." In a testy exchange with Rep. Clarence D. Long (D-Md.) over war aims and national purpose, he dared Congress to withdraw its Tonkin Gulf Resolution of August 1964 if members disagreed with the president's Vietnam policy. Chinese expansion into Southeast Asia had to be checked now by confronting aggression in Vietnam. A policy of appeasement that allowed China to dominate the region would only carry a heavier price tag in the future.[9]

As Sikes had promised before the hearings, Congress was sympathetic to the supplemental request; as he had also predicted, there was a good deal of politics in play, as when the Republican minority members of the House Defense Appropriations Subcommittee went on record that McNamara had originally underestimated defense costs in the FY 1966 budget submission and had continued to understate them in his FY 1967 request. His manipulations, they argued, made additional supplemental requests a "virtual certainty" by late 1966 or early 1967.[10] Democrats, too, questioned the secretary's sincerity. Long bluntly admonished McNamara that the public was puzzled about the war, having been told many things that "didn't turn out to be true in the final analysis." Long blamed the confusion on the administration's penchant for operating "from 1 year's posture briefing to another" without squarely facing the overall implications of the Asian war.[11]

Despite questioning the administration's credibility, Congress remained steadfast in its support for the Vietnam War in general, if not for the way that McNamara chose to fight it. On 25 March 1966, Congress appropriated the entire $12.3 billion supplemental (NOA) the president had requested. OSD, however, had expected much swifter legislative action; consequently by the time of the bill's passage, OSD was running short of funds and was already involved with the FY 1967 appropriations hearings.[12]

The FY 1967 Defense Budget

The secretary of defense relied on the same rationale he employed in the 1966 supplemental request to defend DoD's FY 1967 NOA request of $58.936 billion submitted to Congress on 24 January 1966 as part of the president's budget. Of that amount, $57.688 billion was for the four major military appropriations titles—personnel, operations and maintenance (O&M), procurement, and research, development, test and evaluation (RDT&E).* As submitted, the budget could support troop deployments up to a level of between 375,000 to 400,000. If the war continued beyond 30 June 1967 or if combat operations intensified beyond current estimates, it might become necessary to seek a second FY 1966 supplement, but McNamara could not predict the timing or the amount of such a request at this time. Expressing disdain for the January 1966 "rush supplemental" presently under consideration as poor budgetary procedure, on 14 February Rep. Glenard P. Lipscomb (R-Calif.) pressed the secretary about the likelihood of another supplemental before the current session expired. McNamara insisted that waiting until January 1966 to ask for FY 1966 supplemental money had enabled OSD to present Congress with a more accurate appraisal of precise costs than was otherwise possible at an earlier date.[13] In fact, as early as July 1965 OSD had anticipated a FY 1966 supplemental request of $6.7 billion for Southeast Asia, about one-half of the actual amount finally requested in January 1966, suggesting that: (1) OSD had cost figures available but did not wish to make them public, and (2) initial estimates, though seemingly adequate at the beginning of the large-scale U.S. intervention during the summer of 1965, seriously underestimated future costs by disregarding the possibility that another massive escalation might prove necessary.[14]

Questions about the adequacy of the FY 1967 budget request were unrelenting, but McNamara remained unflappable during his numerous budget appearances before Senate and House committees. As for decisions on a supplemental appropriation, he explained that OSD would examine the 30 June 1967 assumption date in relation to lead times for item procurement, thus enabling the department to delay decisions on such short lead-time items as ammunition until November or December 1966 or even January 1967. With aircraft losses running less than forecast, if the trend held, OSD could postpone the June reexamination of this long-term procurement item until early fall or perhaps even next January.[15] McNamara informed Rep. Mendel Rivers on 10 March that he foresaw no need for a second supplemental for FY 1966 and perhaps none for FY 1967 because the rate of combat activity had been somewhat lower than expected.[16] The secretary, however, was less than candid with Rivers.

---

* Congress considered the remainder ($1.248 billion for military construction, family housing, and civil defense) in a separate bill.

About a week earlier an influential survey of business activity projected a whopping 19 percent increase over 1965 in planned 1966 capital spending for plant and equipment that threatened to generate inflationary backlogs of capital goods. Although the Council of Economic Advisors (CEA) forecast a lesser growth increase—16 percent—the additional capital spending still exceeded January estimates by $2 billion, portending labor shortages, larger inventory requirements, and higher incomes—classic symptoms of inflation. Earlier, in mid-January, BoB Director Schultze had cautioned the president that absent a settlement in Vietnam, there would be very little money available to finance the Great Society programs, for which the bulk of obligations would fall due in FY 1968. In response to the president's mid-February follow-up query, Schultze calculated that rising prices combined with added domestic outlays and increased defense spending would likely raise the level of total federal expenditures by almost $4 billion and necessitate a tax increase. Then in early March, CEA Chairman Ackley urged Johnson to call publicly for a tax increase.[17]

Instead Johnson approved Joseph Califano's proposal that the special assistant meet with the administration's financial troika—the directors of CEA and BoB and the secretary of the treasury[*]—to calm them down while a bill delaying excise tax reductions was before the Senate. McNamara also attended Califano's 5 March meeting where there emerged a general consensus to take no action that might jeopardize the pending tax bill; however, the attendees unanimously agreed that a tax increase later in the year was inevitable. McNamara was especially concerned about maintaining his credibility by delaying an additional supplemental request until June, the last month of the fiscal year. Faced with such disturbing forecasts, on 15 March the president ordered a slowdown in government spending, except for Vietnam, to protect the multitude of Great Society proposals then awaiting congressional action, and demanded austerity in government departments to guard against inflation.[18] Under these circumstances, McNamara could hardly tell Rivers that he was considering a second FY 1966 supplemental because the department was running out of money owing to the unanticipated expenses of Vietnam operations.

OSD budget experts and McNamara had assumed, as Vance told Sikes, that once Congress convened on 10 January, members would enact the supplemental by the end of February. As hearings dragged on, however, the diminished possibility of a supplemental funding bill during February held serious implications. For example, in the personnel and O&M accounts, the services were operating under the authority of Section 612(a),[†] incurring obligations at rates that would use up

---

[*] BoB estimated expenditures; CEA forecast overall economic performance; and the secretary of the treasury estimated revenues. See Anderson and Hazleton, *Managing Macroeconomic Policy*, 47.

[†] Section 612(a) of PL 89-213, 29 September 1965 (79 Stat 875), allowed the president to exempt DoD appropriations from the provisions of section 3679 of the Revised Statutes (31 USC 665). The chief executive could thus spend or obligate funds in excess of congressional appropriations whenever he deemed such action to be necessary in the interests of national defense.

appropriated funds within one to three months. Any further deferrals would be extremely disruptive and threaten readiness by requiring cutting non-SEA flying by 100,000 hours, deferring 62 ship overhauls, and curtailing Marine Corps recruitment.[19]

Procurement appropriations were likewise nearly exhausted. Because of the increased tempo of Vietnam operations, the Marine Corps would completely obligate its procurement funds by 1 March. Obligating authority to buy aircraft, missiles, tracked vehicles, and ships involved Procurement of Equipment and Missiles, Army (PEMA) accounts which required specific congressional authorization and appropriation action. The services could not legally initiate procurement actions to replace combat losses and consumption until Congress enacted supplemental legislation. Moreover, OSD had already programmed (earmarked for other purposes) its unobligated funds, so only through a time-consuming and paperwork-producing effort could it reprogram these funds to finance Southeast Asia accounts. Rather than continue to rely on Section 612(c)* authority to feed, clothe, house, and move the additional military personnel called to active duty because of the war, OSD Comptroller Robert Anthony urged McNamara to push for congressional action to provide additional, separate supplemental FY 1966 funding of roughly $3 billion. This amount also included $1.1 billion for "items requiring rapid [procurement] action," such as 500-pound bombs, aircraft spare parts, hand grenades, M-16 rifles, and ammunition.[20]

Indeed, on 2 March, eight days before the McNamara-Rivers exchange, Vance had issued guidance for a second FY 1966 supplemental request. The military services, JCS, and other Defense agencies were to include financial requirements, such as the additional Phase IIa costs associated with Vietnam operations, unforeseen before the January supplemental had been crafted in December 1965. Vance then expected to consolidate costs related to the Phase IIa revised deployment schedules by the end of March and arrange for additional FY 1966 financing to cover these unanticipated expenses.[21] The accelerated deployment timetables and the unwelcome delay in congressional action on the initial 1966 supplemental request led Vance to issue a follow-up memorandum on 19 March giving all agencies two weeks to submit their urgent but unfunded requirements for Southeast Asia.[22]

After consolidating service and Defense agency estimates totaling slightly more than $2 billion, McNamara decided neither to ask for a second supplemental 1966 appropriation nor to invoke Section 612(c) authority. Instead, in line with the president's anti-inflation drive, he enforced FY 1966 expenditures at the previously approved level of $54.2 billion.[23] His decision left unfunded a total of $700

---

* Section 612(c), PL 89-213 (79 Stat 875), allowed the president to fund the costs of additional military personnel on active duty beyond the appropriated amount in accordance with Section 3732 Revised (Statutes 641 USC 11). This permitted the services to provide for food, clothing, shelter, and transportation for the increased personnel.

million for personnel and O&M accounts, shortfalls the OSD comptroller had to cover in a variety of ways. McNamara eventually resorted to Section 3732 to legally over-obligate $336 million and used transfer authority under Section 636* to lop off another $200 million of the O&M account. The remaining $164 million was absorbed by so-called management actions—deferring the overhauling and rebuilding of vehicles, ships, and aircraft, postponing procurement of certain items, hiring freezes, and the like.

McNamara initialed the comptroller's proposals to handle FY 1966 obligations without a second supplemental on 25 April 1966. Then, following discussions between McNamara, Vance, and Representative Mahon, the comptroller on 5 May orally explained the policy to the service assistant secretaries for financial management, apportioning to each additional amounts of funding available under Section 636 transfer authority. Each service was to request relief formally under either Section 3732 or Section 636 as late in the 1966 fiscal year as feasible. In an effort to conceal costs as long as possible, OSD would issue no written instructions until the formal requests were received.[24]

Earlier, during congressional testimony on 8 March, McNamara actively promoted the president's agenda by insisting that not only could the nation enjoy both guns and butter, but also that no one in authority should hesitate to request or appropriate more money for guns.[25] He assuaged concerns about inflation by explaining that the Defense budget and supplemental, though huge, represented roughly the same percentage of America's gross national product (GNP) as in 1965 and proportionately less than Defense spending in relation to GNP between 1960 and 1964.[26] McNamara also downplayed the cost of the war, conceding that while *obligations* for that purpose would peak in FY 1966 at $15 billion to $16 billion, *expenditures* were spread over FY 1966 and 1967 and would total only about $10 billion per year.[27] The secretary's objective, as it had been since the previous summer, now reinforced by the latest economic news, was to hold defense expenditures to an absolute minimum in order to neither burden the public nor jeopardize the president's domestic programs.

McNamara's loyalty to Johnson, and, according to Gardner Ackley, the secretary's apprehension that if the public had to pay more for the war they might question its importance,[28] overrode whatever compunction he might have had about understating the effects of the Defense budget on the nation's economic prosperity. Congress, though, was becoming restive about the implications of the war for the national economy. Already tightened monetary policy (higher interest rates) and fiscal measures (reinstatement of certain excise tax reductions and speeding up collection of personal and corporate income taxes) proposed by the president in January 1966 and enacted by Congress in March as the Tax Adjustment Act ap-

---

* Section 636 of PL 89-213, 29 September 1965 (79 Stat 879), authorized the secretary of defense to transfer $200 million from the Emergency Fund during the current fiscal year for purposes vital to national security.

peared to restrain inflation and add revenue to government coffers. Asked by the House Committee on Armed Services during his 9 March testimony if higher taxes were also necessary to hold down inflation, McNamara, who was on record in the White House as approving higher taxes, replied that the president had indicated that he would consider raising taxes under certain circumstances, a view consistent with earlier official prognostications by the CEA.[29] After the hearings, House committees sent their markup authorizations to the House floor in late June. Congressional deliberations on the FY 1967 budget would continue into mid-October, by which time McNamara had requested supplemental funding.*

The Need for a FY 1967 Supplemental Budget

Belying McNamara's congressional testimony, expectations that OSD would need a FY 1967 amendment had shaped the FY 1967 budget request. On that assumption, Comptroller Anthony had deferred almost $1.9 billion, of which about half was for short lead-time items such as ammunition, spare parts, helicopters, and other essential materiel for the field forces in Vietnam.[30] The escalated fighting, however, created a greater demand for short lead-time items that caused still more spending. Relying on a continuing resolution authority, the services and Defense agencies were obligating funds at rates far in excess of the $58.9 billion (NOA) FY 1967 request. Operating appropriations (personnel and O&M) provided $34.4 billion, but the expected rate of obligation would be about $9.3 billion a quarter, meaning that DoD would exhaust those funds sometime in the spring of 1967. Moreover, funds in continuing appropriations accounts (procurement and construction) were being obligated at a pace that would deplete the entire $25.5 billion authorization before 1 April 1967 and leave a $1.5 billion shortfall. The combination of the current high rate of FY 1966 spending and the anticipated FY 1967 shortfalls forced the comptroller in April 1966 to assess their effects on the pending FY 1967 budget.

Anthony concluded that the requested FY 1967 budget would cover DoD's financial requirements only until April 1967 and, to avoid the imbroglio that had accompanied the passage of the FY 1966 supplemental, certain measures would have to be taken immediately. These included (1) carrying over $10 billion of obligating authority from the FY 1966 budget to FY 1967 to cover part of the continuing appropriation deficit; (2) letting two contracts for the same item, one for a quantity before 1 April and the other for the balance afterwards; (3) slowing Marine Corps procurement; (4) shortening reorder lead time on high production items; and (5) deferring letting contracts until the final quarter of the fiscal year.

Anthony based his financial projections on the assumption that a peak strength of 400,000 American troops would be deployed in Vietnam by December 1966,

---

* The 1967 budget passed the House on 20 July 1966; the Senate, where it was amended, on 18 August. After the House and Senate reached agreement on 11 October, the president signed PL 89-687 on 15 October (80 Stat 980).

requiring a $12.5 billion supplemental appropriation, of which $7.5 billion was needed for short-term procurement, assuming the war continued beyond 30 June 1967. Of course if the number of U.S. troops deployed in Southeast Asia increased beyond 400,000, so would the cost, an extra $3.5 billion to send 200,000 more, which would virtually dry up DoD appropriations by 1 April 1967. To hold costs to the absolute minimum, Anthony recommended that McNamara restrict requests for additional FY 1967 funds to items that had to be obligated before 1 April 1967, that fell under Section 412(b)* authority, or that otherwise required congressional authorization. In any event, Anthony urged McNamara to discuss "our FY 1967 financial problem" with the chairmen of the Senate and House appropriations committees, Russell and Mahon, respectively.[31]

At a 4 May meeting Mahon advised McNamara and Vance to submit an amendment to the pending 1967 budget. McNamara agreed that an amendment or a supplemental would be necessary but thought that requesting the former at the present time was undesirable. An amendment, Mahon observed, would take much of the heat off the secretary and silence many of his critics. Although conceding the correctness of the congressman's observation, McNamara told him such an amendment would "almost surely lead to substantial cuts in the President's Great Society Program," to which Mahon replied the program should be cut anyhow and that McNamara was "overly protective of the President."[32]

McNamara incorporated Anthony's ideas in his 22 June financial guidance for the start of FY 1967, a week hence. He instructed the services to obligate funds as necessary for long lead-time items to support Vietnam operations at existing levels through 30 June 1967 and beyond. Otherwise a peacetime level would be maintained. The military branches would obligate funds assuming that a FY 1967 supplemental funding request, to be submitted to Congress in January 1967, would be enacted by 31 March 1967. That meant spending could continue apace at current high rates because additional funds would be made available for obligation during the fourth quarter of the fiscal year. In such a scenario, Defense agencies would finance procurement in two increments—the first before 1 April and the second after that date when the supplemental became available. This practice limited to minimum quantities and amounts the contracts that OSD and the services had to place before 1 April 1967 (the beginning of the fourth quarter) to guarantee production lead times, maintain production lines, or meet operational requirements in Vietnam and elsewhere.[33] By dividing procurement orders into two parts, OSD could also recommend to Congress that funds planned for springtime procurement orders be used in the fall for other purposes. This would permit the department to shift or reprogram funds from one account to another.[34] The advantage was flexibility for OSD: the disadvantage was chronically underestimated Defense budgets.

---

* Section 412(b) stated that PEMA procurement, including tracked vehicles, must have congressional authorization (PL 89-37, 11 Jun 65, Section 304(b); 79 Stat 129).

Other measures to hold down the budget included deferring modernization, exclusive of replacement demanded by consumption or attrition, until the following fiscal year or until the end of hostilities in Southeast Asia. Peacetime consumption and attrition replenishment rates applied to forces not deployed in Vietnam; to further reduce cost estimates, OSD authorized the services to calculate replacement of reduced inventories at the lower FY 1966, not the higher FY 1967, prices. In addition, a change in the secretary's logistic guidance resulted in sizable reductions in munitions requirements with attendant savings.[35] By severely limiting funding for non-Southeast Asia needs, the savings could be applied to rising Vietnam munition costs without further requests to Congress.

Such budgetary techniques enabled the administration to hold to the letter of the president's 1967 budget. The financial plan, then, obligated funds, especially for procurement accounts, during the first three quarters of the fiscal year, in effect spending a 12-month budget in 9 months and relying on the supplemental to finance the fourth, and final, quarter of the fiscal year. Put differently, the potential existed to understate the FY 1967 Defense budget by 33 percent.

Facing distressing economic reports and an increasingly fractious tax debate, McNamara did not yet want to ask Congress for additional funding for FY 1967. Besides anticipating an adverse impact on public opinion, inflation, and the tax question, he believed that "in [the] environment of today" he would "be crucified" if he went to Capitol Hill for more money. He told Navy Secretary Nitze on 30 May that a supplemental request at this time might touch off an unfavorable debate on U.S. policy in Vietnam.[36] Unable to request additional funds but in need of extra money, OSD in effect borrowed appropriations from previously authorized projects. McNamara approved an additional series of proposals submitted by the military services to defer or stretch out certain programs during FY 1967. The reductions, amounting to $2 billion, would postpone modernization of some ships, National Guard and Reserve aircraft, 300 M-113 armored personnel carriers, five submarines, and some C-141 aircraft.[37] The "savings" were applied to more immediate service needs for Vietnam support—500-pound bombs, illumination flares, and rockets being three items in exceptionally high demand.

Few congressmen were willing to vote against Defense appropriations for the Vietnam War. Fewer still were willing to vote for a tax hike to pay for the war unless the administration took the initiative, and the blame, by originating a tax proposal. President Johnson was just as unwilling to take the lead. During 1966, he followed a familiar pattern. In economic affairs as in military matters, he preferred working issues through small, controlled groups, not tipping his hand in advance, and reaching conclusions only with painstaking deliberateness.[38] Johnson recognized the growing price of the Vietnam War but remained determined that the administration's economic policies would not interfere with his legislative agenda and the creation of the Great Society. He continued to balk at increasing taxes to pay for the added costs of the war, and chafed at the Federal Reserve Board's increase in interest rates to fend off the inflationary threat. As for Congress, the majority of its members made no secret that they supported funding for the war far more than for the president's domestic programs, many of which were awaiting congressional action and many more of which were on the way to Capitol Hill.* Nor were senators and representatives likely to advocate tax increases during an election year, a fact not lost on the president who, convinced he could not get a tax hike, believed that asking for one might boomerang into substantial cuts in his domestic programs.[39]

Formulation of Johnson's economic policies followed a pattern similar to that evidenced during America's military escalation in Vietnam in the summer of 1965. Policymakers worked behind the scenes on contentious issues while presenting a public facade of optimism and consensus. The president refused to make hard-and-fast decisions, insisting on further information from his economic advisers or congressional colleagues. Yet repeatedly and personally, he introduced "a series of piecemeal tax and expenditure changes that could be implemented quietly and easily,"[40] much like his policies of incremental deployments and gradual escalation in Vietnam. There were attempts to manipulate public opinion or orchestrate policy concurrence—such as Johnson's demand that his advisers collectively sign major recommendations affecting the economy—which in some instances seemed to take precedence over substantive analysis. As with the development of its military policy, the administration publicly claimed the economy was fine while privately considering further measures to stabilize it. In part the subterfuge resulted from the uncertainty of the war. While there were estimates about the price of the conflict in early 1966, accurate budget forecasts were impossible without knowing first how long it would last and how many U.S. troops would deploy to Southeast Asia. But there was also an intentional effort to minimize the Defense budget by resorting to accounting gimmicks and legislative language to mask or understate requirements. The increasing reliance on sleight of hand contributed to a growing credibility gap that steadily widened in 1966.

In the face of classic inflationary pressures, by early March the president's economic advisers and McNamara, over the objections of Treasury Secretary Fowler, counseled him to (1) discontinue the special tax stimulus that had been intended to spur capital investment but had fueled expansionary activity and (2) later in the year, raise taxes.[41] Ackley, already on record favoring tax increases, proposed on 12 March a presidential announcement of a tax hike of $4 billion to $7 billion. The president, however, following a meeting with his advisers in late March, decided—not surprisingly, given his attitude toward taxes, the mixed economic news, the weak support in Congress or in the commercial, business, and labor communities for a tax hike, and the lack of consensus even among his own fiscal brain trust—that it was premature to request a tax increase or curtail investment credit.[42]

---

* When the 89th Congress adjourned on 22 October 1966, it had passed 181 of 200 presidentially-initiated pieces of legislation.

In tactics reminiscent of his midsummer 1965 choreographing of an NSC meeting to secure ratification of his Vietnam decisions, Johnson sought to dramatize support for his economic policy through a series of stage-managed events. In one, he invited more than 150 leading businessmen to a White House dinner on 30 March. According to Johnson's colorful account, when he asked who favored a tax increase, not a hand went up. A former CEA member later informed Johnson that the businessmen believed that the president should take the lead and did not want to sign a blank check without knowledge of specific details. They were caught "flat footed with their tongues tied" by the president's abrupt, and seemingly impromptu, question. Johnson also sounded out labor and congressional leaders about a tax increase; the former opposed it because the burden fell on workers and the latter, reluctant to be seen as advocating higher taxes, wanted the president to lead the way.[43]

Despite some moderation after the first quarter, inflation for 1966 rose more rapidly than virtually anyone had expected. Consumer prices, up only one percent per year from 1961 to 1965, increased by more than 2.9 percent in 1966. Business demand for capital goods continued to rise rapidly throughout the spring and early summer and together with underestimated federal defense purchases spurred competition for increasingly scarce goods and labor, thereby contributing to higher prices.[44] On 10 and 11 May, reacting to the shifting economic sands, Ackley, Fowler, and Schultze separately recommended to Johnson an immediate ten percent increase in individual and corporate taxes; delay would risk throwing the economy into reverse and even recession by 1968. Only a Vietnam settlement within the next six months, Schultze warned, would obviate the need for a tax increase to offset strong inflationary pressures.[45] Then the economy seemed to reverse course as a second quarter slowdown reassured Ackley and provided "welcome relief from ominous imbalances"; by early June support for an immediate tax increase had evaporated. In mid-July Ackley viewed the economy as moving at a more moderate and sustainable rate after its late 1965 spurt, an interpretation endorsed by *Fortune* magazine, whose editors foresaw a $5 billion defense supplemental but predicted a slower rate of military spending accompanied by a slowdown in the U.S. economy.[46]

But spending for Vietnam was not slowing down. The federal deficit steadily mounted from the combination of Vietnam spending, an accompanying surge in demand for goods and labor, and Great Society funding. An obvious solution was to reduce federal expenditures, but Schultze in mid-June feared that announcing cutbacks while approval of the FY 1967 budget was still pending in congressional committees risked deeper reductions to domestic programs. He counseled deferring projects when possible to hold down spending and postponing formal budget reductions until after the crucial bills were through committee.[47] The flaw in Schultze's position was that the war was driving budget spending. Congressional Democrats were convinced and concerned that the war was hampering the administration's domestic programs and hurting their party.[48] Feeling already on the defensive, they were not amenable to initiating an increase in taxes during an election year despite the president's cajoling.

In meetings with congressional leaders on 18 July and with principals of the House and Senate appropriations committees the next day, Johnson informed them that the administration needed additional funding of between $5 billion and $10 billion to pay the costs of the Vietnam War. To justify his FY 1967 budget request that had asked for only part of the money to fight the war, he derided the defense secretary's earlier congressional testimony. "McNamara made a bad guess on bringing the troops home. I don't want to be caught like that."[49] Obviously, Johnson was indulging in political rhetoric; as often happened under his spell, congressional leaders were as willing as the president to suspend what one historian termed "any implication of the reality they both knew."[50] As one of Johnson's confidants put it, "he would quickly come to believe what he was saying even if it was clearly not true."[51]

Publicly touting cost reductions while privately crafting a supplemental request for additional funds strained credulity during the summer of 1966. At a news conference on 11 July, amidst great fanfare, McNamara announced that five years of his Cost Reduction Program* had saved taxpayers $14 billion. This responsible stewardship of the Defense budget, he maintained, enabled the administration to fight the Vietnam War without imposing wage and price controls or higher tax burdens on the American public. During the same conference, more good economic news followed as the secretary reported a cutback in the planned production of air ordnance that would reduce spending by another $1 billion.[52]

The savings were more apparent than real because the $1 billion came out of any *future* request for extra funds. As McNamara explained during his August 1966 testimony before the Senate Appropriations Committee, the FY 1967 budget contained $1.7 billion for various air ordnance, but adhering to the existing production schedule would have required spending an additional $1 billion in supplemental funds, or a total of $2.7 billion. By reducing the current rate of production, however, instead of costing $2.7 billion the entire program could be financed for some $1.8 billion, or about $130–140 million over the $1.7 billion budget.[53] In other words, $100 million spent became an extra $1 billion saved, or perhaps vice versa. These accounting contortions met growing congressional and media skepticism. Even accepting that McNamara's actions had saved money, the secretary seemed to be saying the more the government spent the more it saved, and the savings became the justification, in the words of one commentator, "for going ahead with the Great Society at home as if there were no war."[54] The effect was to undermine further the secretary's and the administration's credibility.

---

* See Chapter XIX for a discussion of the Cost Reduction Program. See, too, Kaplan et al., *McNamara Ascendancy*, 453-62.

On 1 August during hearings on the still pending FY 1967 Defense budget, Senator Russell grilled McNamara about a supplemental request, knowing full well the figures proposed by the president two weeks earlier. The secretary insisted that although the budget was based on the arbitrary war end date of 30 June 1967, this was not likely, but there were sufficient funds available to carry the war effort for several months beyond mid-1967. Admitting the likelihood of a supplemental request, he rejected one at the current time because of uncertainties about the duration of the conflict and the level of operations that needed to be financed. Where did Representative Mahon, Russell asked, get the idea that a supplemental in the neighborhood of $10 billion was in the offing? McNamara neither knew nor cared to comment.[55]

Both Mahon and Russell later in August announced that they expected a supplemental request of between $5 billion and $15 billion at the beginning of 1967.[56] Likewise, in early October the House Armed Services Committee conducted hearings on McNamara's request to reprogram funds in the not-yet-approved FY 1967 budget to allow an early start on increased production of several aircraft needed in the war. Rep. Otis Pike (D-N.Y.) lambasted the request as "just a way of getting more money until they have the guts to come in with their supplemental."[57] Congress was snapping at the secretary of defense because it dared not yet openly snap at the president.

The Price of Escalation

The Vietnam War continued to escalate more rapidly than anyone had expected. The deployment of 195,000 U.S. troops anticpated in July 1965 had ballooned to projections of 367,000 by late January 1966 and, a month later, to 429,000 with still no end in sight. Similarly, monthly air attack sorties jumped from the 23,500 anticipated in January 1966 to 27,600 monthly by year's end, including 600 by the enormously expensive B-52s that cost at least $30,000 per sortie.[58] More troops and more air raids consumed more munitions consistent with McNamara's policy of substituting, "to the maximum extent feasible, the expenditure of materiel in place of the expenditure of our manpower."[59] Projected munitions expenditures skyrocketed not only because of vastly increased battlefield requirements, but also because inadequate control procedures, larger than anticipated Vietnamese and Laotian needs, and huge amounts of defective ammunition combined to mock earlier forecasts.[60]

Throughout 1966 OSD was obligating and spending more and more procurement dollars than originally estimated for more and more bombs, small arms rounds, flares, and 2.75-inch rockets. Meeting MACV's requests for additional U.S. troops also added unfinanced requirements to OSD's personnel and O&M accounts. The reasons for the FY 1967 supplemental were the unforeseen requirements for more American troops to Vietnam (at least 100,000 more than projected in January 1966) and the enormous munitions outlays.

The less visible reason for a supplemental, as McNamara later admitted, was that OSD had concealed costs when preparing the FY 1967 budget.[61] McNamara could not know that events in Vietnam would overtake the deployments approved in January 1966 and necessitate increased force levels. Not until he recommended stabilizing the war at its current levels, a decision reached after his October 1966 meetings in Saigon, could he provide the president with accurate funding information. At that time, McNamara told the president that the incremental costs of Vietnam, that is the estimated additional amount over and above normal DoD expenses, totaled $19.7 billion for FY 1967. For FY 1968 estimates were running about $22.4 billion (because of the expected increase of the troop level to 470,000). These figures, as might be expected, exceeded by about $5.5 billion the OSD estimates forecast in November 1965 to support a 394,000-man deployment.[62]

After his return from Saigon in October, McNamara ignored an "open invitation" from Congress to present a "realistic estimate" of the price tag for the conflict based on his Saigon consultations. His reticence and delaying tactics irritated congressmen who later accused him of misrepresenting Vietnam costs.[63] Despite congressional caterwauling about being kept in the dark, the president had told congressional leaders in private what the war was costing but, locked in an increasingly bitter struggle with Congress over taxes, he refused to discuss costs publicly.

DoD's need for more funding had, of course, been obvious since late February 1966 when Anthony urged McNamara to ask for a second FY 1966 supplemental because Congress had not acted as rapidly as expected on the first supplemental request. Later, in mid-April, Anthony had marked out the range of a 1967 supplemental request. The OSD comptroller's midsummer review of FY 1967 budget requirements identified a shortfall of almost $10 billion, more than 50 percent of it for procurement, if the services had to submit their supplemental requests in early August.* Despite its magnitude, the figure was kept significantly below the earlier May estimate of a $14.3 billion supplemental by basing requirements on the 22 June guidance that deferred modernization, limited non-SEA inventories, and reduced ammunition stockpiles.[64] Although McNamara told the Senate Appropriations Subcommittee on 1 August that DoD had "sufficient funds to carry us on for several additional months," he also acknowledged that the spiraling war costs would require supplemental funds later in FY 1967.[65]

Under McNamara's June financial guidance for FY 1967 purchases of ammunition stockpiles and numerous other equipment stockages, units not directly

---

* The total was $9.852 billion. Of the $5.495 billion for procurement, $3.035 billion did not require further congressional authorization by virtue of not falling under Section 412(b) legislation that necessitated new authorization for procurement of aircraft, missiles, and naval vessels. In the event, the full amount slated for procurement appeared in the final 1967 supplemental request. See memo Anthony for McNamara, 9 Aug 66, fldr FY 1968 Budget Information, OASD(P&FC) Budget Estimates & Appropriations 1964–1970, box 5, Acc 73A-1389.

involved in Vietnam operations were limited to FY 1966 levels. As a result, the Marine Corps theoretically could outfit its recently activated 5th Marine Division[*] only by dividing the logistical support funds of its two non-Vietnam divisions among three divisions, leaving all of them short of their required inventories and jeopardizing their operational readiness. At least $60 million in additional procurement was needed.[66]

The 5th Marine Division's situation illustrated how paring non-Vietnam-related defense costs to pay for the war was becoming more and more difficult; after 18 months budget reductions in one area exerted ripple effects throughout the entire DoD budget. Just as the president insisted that the nation could afford a Great Society and a war simultaneously, McNamara maintained Vietnam costs could be absorbed elsewhere in the Defense budget. He seemed blind to the notion that escalating Vietnam expenses, not unrelated defense expenditures, had to be reduced to hold down budgets. Arkansas Sen. William Fulbright's July 1967 remark to the president during a meeting with the congressional leadership on the deficit offered an unacceptable resolution of the dilemma: "What you really need to do is to stop the war. That will solve all your problems."[67]

By midsummer 1966, the president realized the FY 1967 budget deficit would far outstrip his January projection of $1.8 billion. Moreover, consumer demand, temporarily restrained, again quickened, but it was the business demand for capital goods that was creating backlogs in orders, shortages of certain types of skilled labor, rising prices in capital goods industries, and intense demands on business credit.[68] Rising interest rates provoked a rare public warning from former President Harry S. Truman on 28 August that the deflationary effects of higher interest rates could lead to a "serious depression." A quickly issued White House statement decried such forecasts, but the president did acknowledge the need to restrain inflationary pressures. In typical fashion, Johnson, wishing to avoid a potentially embarrassing congressional debate on the administration's economic policies, asked Califano to explore on a close-hold basis whether the president had the authority to impose wage and price controls without congressional approval.[69]

The administration's economic advisers remained divided over the proper prescription for the feverish economy. Ackley favored a tax surcharge along with a reappraisal of defense expenditures and public acknowledgment of the need for supplemental funding. Fowler supported a surcharge on corporate profit taxes but opposed suspending the investment credit because it would not raise much revenue and might endanger economic growth. Schultze endorsed both taxing corporate profits and suspending the investment tax credit.[70]

---

[*] McNamara approved the reactivation of the 5th Marine Division in December 1965, and on 1 March 1966 DoD officially announced the formation of the division (*U.S. Marines in Vietnam, 1966*, 284).

House Ways and Means Committee Chairman Wilbur Mills continued to oppose any income tax hike unless the administration cut back expenditures and leveled with him on the budget. For his part, the president was not about to put his Great Society programs on the chopping block by asking for taxes he could not persuade Congress to enact.[71] With the stock market plunging—near the end of August the Dow Jones Industrial Average had fallen well below 800, down 21.6 percent from its all-time high in February, because of rising interest rates and rumors of major escalation in Vietnam—Johnson moved to shelve the investment credit. He again insisted his key advisers sign a memorandum recommending the action.[72]

The collective memorandum, signed on 2 September 1966 by Ackley, Schultze, Fowler, McNamara, and Califano among others, recommended the tax credit suspension, reduction of FY 1967 expenditures by $1.5 billion, preparations to reduce spending an additional $2 billion, and "at an appropriate time in the future" a request for "whatever tax measures are necessary" to cover add-ons to the budget by congressional action or by requests from the generals in Vietnam. Six days later Johnson asked that Congress temporarily suspend the seven percent investment tax credit, which it did. On 8 November Johnson signed the legislation, a move that cooled pressures on capital spending, undercut inflation, and slowed the climb in interest rates. It did not silence those vociferous advocates of tax increases who insisted that the unchecked deficit, fueled by military and domestic spending, made higher taxes unavoidable.[73]

The critics remained unconvinced, especially with the unsettled economic outlook during the autumn of 1966, and adopted a wait-and-see attitude about higher taxes. At a 22 November meeting, several administration officials, including McNamara and Califano, agreed on a tax increase, but not on its timing—Fowler and Schultze favored quick action, Ackley was uncertain, and McNamara advised delay.[74] Fall reports pointed to a softening of the nation's economy; by December several leading economic indicators, including housing starts, manufacturing orders, and retail sales, had dropped like the temperature. The economic troika foresaw sluggish growth during the first half of the coming year, hardly the time to further retard the economy with additional tax burdens.[75]

Confronted with unprecedented deficits, in mid-December Johnson asked for recommendations on fiscal and monetary policy. On 13 December, Federal Reserve Chairman Martin favored a temporary, moderate tax increase to demonstrate fiscal responsibility. McNamara also advised the president to apply surcharges to personnel and corporate income taxes as part of a broader fiscal package to reduce the deficit. The same day, however, Ackley forecast lower economic growth for 1967 and suggested postponing any tax increase because it might provoke a serious recession. Thus by the end of 1966 economic prospects were still uncertain. The economic advisers feared that tax surcharges by mid-1967 would stall the economy, increase unemployment, reduce corporate profits, and produce a recession. In short, the proposed cure was worse than the illness.[76]

Congress reacted to the FY 1967 Defense budget in much the same fashion. By late July 1966, the House completed action on it, adding almost a billion dollars to the original NOA request. More than half of the add-on was to pay for the fast-expanding military personnel strength. Other major items previously omitted by McNamara but now included were preproduction funding for Nike-X, the substitution of a nuclear-powered guided missile frigate for two conventionally powered guided missile destroyers, preparation for F-12 interceptor aircraft production, and additional funding for Advanced Manned Strategic Aircraft (AMSA) development. The resulting 15 October legislation appropriated $403 million (NOA) more than the administration had requested as legislators made clear their determination to fund Defense programs fully. More significantly, by earmarking the additional funding for the Cold War projects that McNamara had long opposed, Congress challenged the secretary's strategy regarding the Soviet Union and his stewardship of DoD.[77]

TABLE 5

CONGRESSIONAL ACTION ON THE FY 1967 DEFENSE BUDGET
(ALL FIGURES NOA IN BILLIONS)

Service/ Agency	President's FY 1967 Budget January 1966	Congressional Action on FY 1967 Budget October 1966
Army	$16.925	$17.165
Navy	$16.813	$16.826
Air Force	$20.686	$20.806
OSD	$3.239	$3.270
TOTAL	**$57.664**	**$58.067**

Sources: HCA, *Department of Defense Appropriation Bill, 1967*, H Rpt 1652, 24 Jun 66, 2; ASD(C), Cong Action on FY 67 Budget Requests, Section A, 7 Jun 67, vol III, Budget Data, FY 1966–68, ASD(C) files, OSD Hist.

During these months of action on the FY 1967 budget, economists outside of government challenged DoD's estimates of war costs, citing Commerce Department reports that the annual rate of Defense spending was running far ahead of budget projections. The Treasury Department's daily statement of expenditures also made explicit, too much so at times for McNamara, the amount DoD was spending.[78] Buffeted by the deadlock over a tax increase, the still escalating war, an uncertain economic outlook, growing public mistrust of administration policies, and a more militant and expanding antiwar movement, the credibility of the president and the secretary of defense steadily eroded. The announcement in late January 1967 of the FY 1967 supplemental request further diminished confidence in McNamara's numbers.

Enacting the FY 1967 Supplemental

Suspicions about McNamara's accounting techniques were well founded. On 30 August 1966, while the White House struggled to discover an effective and painless means of restraining the bursting economy and while Congress still had to decide on DoD's FY 1967 budget, the secretary's staff issued guidance for the preparation of FY 1967 supplemental requests. OSD directed that requests for funds be limited to Southeast Asia requirements on the assumption the war would continue through 30 June 1968; to military, civilian, and wage board pay raises, effective 1 July 1966; and to increased, liberalized moving expenses. Service estimates for the supplemental were due in OSD by 3 October.[79]

The Army requested a $7.65 billion supplemental, the Air Force $4.37 billion, the Navy $5.38 billion, and OSD agencies $.6 billion, a total of just over $18 billion in additional funds. McNamara struck almost $5.8 billion from that figure by reducing, reprogramming, and adjusting management funds, eliminating, revising, or deferring more than 60 major programs.[80] During a preliminary review of the departmental requests in mid-November, OSD proposed an FY 1967 Southeast Asia supplemental totaling $12.4 billion TOA. This amount would support the 469,000 U.S. troops anticipated to be in Vietnam by 30 June 1968. Specific cost recommendations included $5.4 billion for direct support of 385,000 Army and Marine combat forces (55,000 more than had been planned in December 1965) together with a higher, and thus more expensive, tempo of operations. Included in the $5.4 billion was the projected cost of mortar, artillery, and helicopter ordnance that would more than double—from $724 million to $1.7 billion. Dispatching six artillery battalions to Vietnam, for instance, increased ammunition consumption by $20 million per month or almost a quarter of a billion dollars annually. Another $4.3 billion was earmarked for increased B-52 and tactical air operations* throughout Southeast Asia, of which about half would go to replace

---

* In FY 1966 there were 278,000 sorties, including 231,000 attack sorties. In FY 1967 the planned numbers increased to 393,000 and 330,000 respectively.

fixed-wing and helicopter attrition, estimated at 1,200 aircraft. McNamara disapproved JCS requests to deploy seven additional Air Force tactical squadrons to the war theater because the $650 million annual price tag was too costly and included an estimated additional loss of 140 aircraft and a comparable number of lives. He rejected new air base construction and extra ordnance as tangential to the war effort. Instead he sought $1 billion to construct an interdiction barrier and $600 million for increased B-52 operations. Naval forces accounted for $330 million of the proposed supplemental, mainly for personnel and operating costs, ammunition, and small boat procurement. Additional support for the logistics base in South Vietnam claimed $1 billion.[81]

Since early September 1966 the president had used news conferences to portray his administration as fiscally responsible. Burdened with an impending large Vietnam supplemental, in late November Johnson announced a cutback of more than $5 billion in FY 1967 non-Defense programs. Insiders understood that the savings would be achieved by stretching out or deferring completion dates rather than by outright cancellation, but even the delays, the president believed, were painful. On 2 December, he encouraged McNamara to hold Defense costs to the minimum.[82] The publicity campaign appeared to backfire four days later when the president announced he would seek a supplemental appropriation of between $9 billion and $10 billion "in expenditures" to pay the costs of the Vietnam War for the balance of FY 1967. Even this enormous figure was an understatement. Only hours earlier, at the president's annual budget meeting with McNamara and the Joint Chiefs in Austin, the defense secretary had indicated the need for a supplemental of $14.7 billion (NOA).[83] An indignant press used the president's announcement to criticize McNamara for mismanagement or deception in concealing the true cost of the war, more so because the new funds would raise government expenditures to $127 billion against expected revenues of only $117 billion and create a $10 billion deficit.[84]

The administration appeared uncertain about the best means to counter the outbursts. Economist Walter Heller suggested the president launch a publicity campaign designed to convey that there was no "$10 billion error."[85] The official OSD response to a congressional inquiry noted that McNamara had repeatedly stressed to Congress the need for a supplemental and in no way had he misled the legislators or financial community.[86] This was not altogether untrue. The trouble, of course, was that the "$10 billion error" came as a surprise to the average citizen, who did not follow the economics of the war closely if at all.

The president's supplemental budget request, submitted to Congress on 24 January 1967, totaled almost $12.3 billion, less than the secretary of defense's November proposal, but more than the $9–10 billion projected at the 6 December news conference in Austin. The amounts for personnel, operations and maintenance, and procurement remained almost identical to the secretary's draft recommendations made in November. The major difference between the two proposals was that the presidential version shifted about $600 million, apparently from funds McNamara earmarked for rebuilding the strategic reserve, to pay for military construction in Vietnam.[87]

Although the press expressed shock and outrage over the size of the supplemental, Congress exhibited less concern about additional money for funding the conflict than it did about the conduct of the war, especially the administration's bombing policy. During mid-February 1967 House Appropriations Committee hearings, Rep. William Minshall (R-Ohio) put it succinctly: "I am talking about American lives. I do not care how much the cost in dollars, we want to get this war over with—soon and honorably."[88] One of the few congressional clashes over funding erupted at McNamara's earlier appearance before the House Armed Forces Committee authorization hearings. Rep. Robert Leggett (D-Calif.) told him that DoD's inability to estimate the costs of the war would have severe domestic repercussions. In a heated exchange McNamara insisted repeatedly that the nation was running not out of money but of will. On the contrary, asserted Leggett, raising taxes $4 billion, programming $4 billion more for sales certificates, increasing the national debt by $2 billion, and selling $1.5 billion from stockpiles still left $12 billion in federal red ink. The secretary dismissed these numbers by arguing the larger GNP not only supported increased defense spending but justified it.[89]

McNamara confidently defended the supplemental, telling congressional inquisitors during January and February hearings that he expected U.S. troop commitments in Vietnam to level off at 470,000 men. Did he anticipate a supplemental in 1968? "Barring unforeseen emergencies, definitely not." During later testimony the secretary reiterated that stand, insisting that he would not have to return for more money.[90] After minimal amendments to the O&M, Procurement, and RDT&E accounts that reduced the request by some $79 million, the supplemental in the amount of $12.196 billion overwhelmingly passed the House on 16 March, the Senate four days later, and was approved by the president on 4 April 1967.[91]

The FY 1968 Budget Request

In mid-March 1966, McNamara had issued his annual calendar memorandum, changing the name of the Five-Year Force Structure and Financial Plan (FYFS&FP) to the Five-Year Defense Program (FYDP). More importantly, the memo altered the decisionmaking process by differentiating in DoD's planning and programming efforts between "major force-oriented issues" and "other decisions."[92] A major force-oriented issue would be a proposal such as funding Poseidon missile deployment or a Nike-X antiballistic missile program that required resolution during the current budget year and which, if approved, would have a significant effect on military forces and budgets. The goal was to streamline the decisionmaking process by identifying such significant issues early in the planning-programming cycle. This approach would ensure focused effort by the secretary of defense, who had to "approve every individual program change proposal that breaks current thresholds." Under the new procedures, DoD components would submit a list of issues requiring resolution along with recommended solutions to the OSD comptroller who, in turn, would assign each issue to a primary OSD office for decision. After considering the recommendations, McNamara would in- corporate his tentative recommendations on major force-oriented issues into his DPMs and circulate them for comment to the JCS, appropriate assistant secretar- ies, and the military departments.[93]

On 18 July 1966 McNamara informally outlined to the service secretaries his budget guidance for preparation of their FY 1968 requests on the assumption that hostilities in Southeast Asia would continue at the June 1967 level throughout FY 1968 and cease on 30 June 1968. If it appeared the war might continue beyond 30 June 1968, OSD might require an amendment to the FY 1968 budget in the summer of 1967 or defer additional funding to a FY 1968 supplemental request. Force planning levels for FY 1968 assumed that forces during 1968 would remain at levels previously set for 30 June 1967.[94]

In early August the OSD comptroller forwarded the budget work schedule requiring DoD components to submit their FY 1968 budget estimates by early October. Initial comments on the narrative justification for 13 specific defense programs in the DPMs (later increased to 18) fell due between mid-June and early September 1966. Service and JCS comments on the preliminary budget markups likewise were staggered between late July and early October with final revisions to be completed by 20 October. The revised DPMs in turn became the basis of the secretary's detailed budget decisions made between mid-October and 25 Novem- ber. Simultaneously OSD would prepare the budget summary for the president, obtain other government agency inputs, coordinate the result with BoB, and sub- mit the revised summary to the White House around 30 November.[95]

McNamara's official budget guidance, issued by the comptroller on 30 August, confirmed earlier planning assumptions of mid-July and provided the services with the current and future military and civilian personnel strengths needed for budget computations.[96] Budget estimates would provide for the full support of operations in Southeast Asia through 30 June 1968; beyond that date, programmers would support the forces at a peacetime level of expenditures. On 19 November, McNa- mara altered the basic approach to budget formulation. Heretofore, OSD financial planners had assumed that the war would end coincidental with the conclusion of the fiscal year, but the secretary's latest change provided for Southeast Asia require- ments "through FY 1968 procurement lead time."[97]

Applying this guidance, the OSD comptroller crafted the FY 1968 budget to fund Vietnam consumption beyond the budget cycle ending 30 June 1968. For example, short-term procurement such as ammunition was funded through De- cember 1968 and long-term items such as aircraft were funded to January 1970.

McNamara's rationale, as detailed in his prepared statement of February 1967 before the House Appropriations Committee, was that a larger data base after two years of fighting enabled OSD to project Vietnam requirements more accurately and thus request sufficient money "to protect the production leadtime on all combat essential items until fiscal year 1969 funds would come available."[98]

He explained to Congress the inherent risk of overfunding if the war ended before 1 July 1968, but insisted that OSD's ability to raise or lower ongoing production—a so-called "hot line"—made the gamble acceptable.[99] The secretary also told reporters that OSD had prepared the FY 1968 budget "on the assumption that combat operations will continue indefinitely," but he was not asserting a belief that the fighting would continue forever. McNamara personally thought it "very unlikely" the fighting would continue to 1970. Rather the defense secretary's point was that U.S. operations in Southeast Asia had stabilized. If the war continued at the level of activity projected by OSD models, barring an unforeseen contingency elsewhere the FY 1968 budget covered foreseeable defense needs.[100] What McNamara left unsaid was that the new guidance enabled OSD to defer $9.5 billion that it might have included in FY 1968 procurement, thereby keeping the already swollen budget under presidential ceilings.[101]

The comptroller's "rough estimates" for the FY 1968 Defense budget came to $75.6 billion, including a minimum $4 billion supplemental. These cost figures supported 470,000 troops in Vietnam and paid for the emplacement of a physical barrier in northern I Corps and an electronic one in Laos.[102] Submissions from the military for their FY 1968 budgets, however, totaled about $98 billion, a figure McNamara told the president on 16 October he found "just unbelievable and there's no damned reason in the world for it and it won't come out that way" even if he had to work "every minute between now and Christmas to do it."[103]

On 1 November the comptroller provided McNamara with a rough "level-off" budget based on a peacetime FY 1965 budget of $51 billion plus the cost of the war ($24 billion), assuming the conflict continued indefinitely, with 440,000 deployed American troops, an unchanged sortie level, and no barrier—altogether a total of approximately $75 billion, the comptroller's high threshold for a desired budget.[104] Given a target in the low $70 billion range, by the January 1967 budget submission date OSD had pared service requests more than $15 billion—$5.6 billion from Navy procurement alone—which, together with financing adjustments of $1.2 billion and working capital accounts shifts of $1.1 billion, reduced the NOA total by almost $17.6 billion.[105] McNamara's role in this feat included personally resolving 436 Program/Budget Decision requests and another 94 Program Change Requests.[106]

Table 6

Comparison of Proposed Service Budgets with
President's FY 1968 Budget Request
(Figures in billions)

Service	Service Submission	President's Budget
Army	$27.741	$23.628
Navy	$28.862	$21.130
Air Force	$29.768	$24.890
DoD	$6.486	$5.616
TOTAL	**$92.857**	**$75.264**

Source: Comparison of DA, DN, DAF, and DoD Agencies Requests
for OSD With President's Budget for FY 1968, Back-up Book, FY
1968—Bk I, vol 1, Tab D, box 60, ASD(C) Files, OSD Hist.

During House Appropriations Committee hearings in early March 1967 several legislators, struck by the wide disparities between the original service requests and the OSD decisions, wondered if the services had intentionally overestimated their budgets in expectation of such massive reductions. Secretary of the Army Resor and Chief of Staff General Johnson testified, however, that changes to budget and logistic guidance during the budget preparation process as well as stretched out modernization programs, more precise consumption rates, and more specific planning data resulted in numerous changes to the original financial forecasts.[107] Air Force Secretary Brown also explained that budget differences often resulted from successive and sometimes alternative requests whose sums exceeded actual requirements. OSD's recalculated and lower attrition estimates, subsequently concurred in by the Air Force, offered another example of significant reductions to an initial budget request.[108] Navy Secretary Nitze attributed reductions to revised attrition computations and a munitions production base that was outstripping demand and consequently allowed cuts. As for ship construction, Nitze gave first priority to building the two approved guided missile destroyers, while, as "a matter of principle more than the immediate urgency," CNO McDonald wanted to reinstate the nuclear-powered guided missile frigate that OSD analysts had struck from the budget.[109]

DoD's final requests excluding Vietnam expenses came to about $51 billion (NOA) of the total $75.264 billion submitted for FY 1968. To pay the Vietnam-associated higher costs, McNamara opted to defer modernization and reduce operating and procurement expenses not directly related to Vietnam. Beyond the numbers, however, deferring, postponing, and extending major programs created genuine concerns among the Joint Chiefs about national security. As the war in Southeast Asia dragged on, more and more existing programs suffered. By late 1966, whipsawed between competing demands of the Southeast Asia conflict and worldwide commitments, the JCS believed that operational readiness and major defense initiatives such as optimum force structures and full development of an antiballistic missile system were falling dangerously behind schedule. The nub of the Chiefs' worries was the slowdown in modernization of the next generation of aircraft, missiles, and ships required to maintain military supremacy. Saving money in FY 1968 by deferring penetration aids for the Polaris A-3 missile ($215 million), reducing or cancelling new aircraft procurement ($1.5 billion), disapproving initial deployment of a light antiballistic missile system ($806 million), and holding off on construction of two nuclear-powered guided missile frigates ($135 million) had long-term consequences.[110]

Related and likely as important was military readiness. General Wheeler had recommended inserting a statement in McNamara's prepared testimony that supporting Vietnam operations made it necessary to withdraw resources and forces from other areas. It did not appear in the final version.[111] In his prepared statement for the 1968 budget hearings, McDonald warned that because of the war the Navy had to defer numerous fleet overhauls and conversions. Although this entailed no "unacceptable immediate risk," the cumulative effects on overall capabilities and readiness concerned him.[112] In short, the financial strains of the Vietnam War on service budgets were showing their global implications.

Disturbed by these trends, the JCS in December objected to 10 of the more than 20 decisions on major force-oriented issues found in McNamara's DPMs on strategic and non-Southeast-Asia-related general purpose forces. The defense secretary overruled the military's advice on matters that included deployment of the ABM system, Army force structure, advanced ICBM development, Navy ship and tactical aircraft procurement, Air Force tactical and strategic aircraft procurement, and logistics guidance.[113] He finally referred the five major outstanding differences (ABM, AMSA, Advanced ICBM, Army force structure, and Navy nuclear-guided missile ships) to the president for decision.[114]

Meanwhile McNamara prepared for his 19 November FY 1968 budget discussions with BoB officials. As was customary, BoB provided an advance agenda, whose major issues in this instance included Minuteman II/III conversions, range instrumentation ships for Poseidon missile testing, the main battle tank (MBT), and nuclear attack submarines (SSNs), among others. Working from these points and with service input, the assistant secretaries (primarily the ASD for Systems

Analysis) developed cost reducing alternatives for McNamara's consideration. Comparison of the ASD recommendations and OSD's subsequent budgetary adjustments indicates that BoB accepted McNamara's decisions regarding the major systems. Slipping the conversion of Minuteman II penetration aids and the fielding of Minuteman III/MIRVs, using existing ships for Poseidon tests, deferring development testing for the main battle tank, and funding three instead of five Navy ships saved more than $680 million in the FY 1968 budget.[115]

McNamara forwarded to the president on 5 December a proposed FY 1968 Defense budget that called for $77.6 billion (NOA) for FY 1968 and expenditures of $74.6 billion. McNamara's marginal note expressed his hope of further reducing these figures.[116] The next day, in Austin, at the annual budget meeting of McNamara, the JCS, and the president, the secretary identified, and the Chiefs confirmed, the five areas of difference, but Admiral McDonald added that otherwise they had never been "so close together" on the budget. Discussion focused on the five outstanding issues, but the president made no decisions. On three separate occasions during the session, however, Johnson asked the Chiefs if, aside from those matters, they were in general agreement on the budget. Each one answered positively.[117]

McNamara subsequently prevailed on four of the five controversial issues, the advanced ICBM, AMSA, Army force structure, and the nuclear-powered guided missile frigate, which accounted for adjustments of almost $500 million to the FY 1968 budget. After discussions with the president on 22 December about the politically explosive ABM issue, McNamara acceded in part to the JCS requests by approving the deployment of a light ABM system at a cost of $377 million in FY 1968.[118] The next day he reported, much to the president's delight, that he had reduced proposed FY 1968 expenditures to $73.1 billion and still hoped to squeeze $200–300 million more, if required.[119] On 24 January 1967, the president's annual budget message requested $75.5 billion (NOA) (including military construction and military assistance) for the Department of Defense, a figure that with adjustments left OSD anticipating FY 1968 expenditures of $73.1 billion.[120] Now the competition for money shifted to Congress.

Defending the FY 1968 Budget

As with the 1967 supplemental, McNamara testified in March 1967 during the House subcommittee hearings on DoD appropriations that, barring unforeseen circumstances, his FY 1968 budget was sufficient to finance the war without any 1968 supplemental.[121] The words came back to haunt him in the acerbic exchanges and in allegations congressmen hurled at him throughout the summer of 1967. House changes to the president's budget were numerous. Committee action on 9 June 1967, endorsed by the House four days later, reduced the FY 1968 request by $1.7 billion, but those cuts were partially offset by increases of slightly more than $.4 billion that added funding to retain the current B-52 inventory, buy more C-130s for the Air Force and EA-6A aircraft, desired by the Marine Corps, and restore the nuclear-powered guided missile frigate at the expense of the two conventionally powered guided missile destroyers. As a result, the NOA would total $70.3 billion instead of the requested $71.6 billion.*[122]

Besides reducing the president's recommended Defense appropriation, on 7 June the House refused to raise the debt ceiling to $365 billion to accommodate the administration's estimated $11 billion deficit, a sum that exceeded January projections by $3 billion. Since the government's outstanding debt was already close to the $336 billion ceiling, Johnson had to cut expenditures. The same day, bemoaning congressional unwillingness to believe his budget figures, he asked the JCS to reduce FY 1967 service expenditures by $500 million to "give us a stay of execution" until the new fiscal year started on 1 July. Following compromises by the White House, on 21 June the House approved a new debt limit; six days later the Senate followed suit, taking note of falling revenues and rising spending plus indications over the past two months that military outlays in Vietnam might be substantially higher than the latest administration estimates.[123]

In late July, Senator Russell asked in writing if OSD could foresee any changes in the FY 1968 budget then under Senate consideration. Reviews of additional costs were still in progress, McNamara replied, as was consideration of personnel increases in Vietnam. Rather than hold up the budget, the secretary urged Congress to enact the legislation with the understanding that he would inform the legislators of changes through normal reprogramming procedures.[124] In fact, the mid-course review of the yet unappropriated FY 1968 budget modified dozens of OSD programs and placed the potential funding in a sort of slush fund entitled Special Resources Set Aside to meet requirements otherwise unfinanced from available authority. Most of the savings came in O&M or procurement. Taken across the entire Defense budget, about $3.44 billion (TOA) was harvested for reprogramming.[125] Three years of such tactics had exasperated legislators and added to the administration's credibility gap. "I think you should try to avoid a supplemental," said House Appropriations Committee Chairman Mahon, "but don't try to kid us into believing that the chances are not very great that there will have to be one. . . . This is what shakes confidence in people."[126]

The reductions made by the House caused OSD to appeal for help to the Senate, which restored about 60 percent or $772 million of the House cuts, but in turn the Senate made even deeper cuts in certain programs, such as the funding for the FB-111 program, and lopped off almost $139 million more from the House figure. The appropriation bill was finally passed by the House on 12 September 1967, by the Senate a day later, and approved by the president on 29 September.[127] A comparison of the original request and congressional action follows:

---

* These figures do not include the requested military construction and military assistance funds, which Congress addressed with separate legislation.

Table 7

FY 1968 Budget
(Figures in billions)

Title	President's FY 1968 Budget January 1967	Final Appropriation 29 September 1967
Military Personnel	$22.0	$21.781
Operation and Maintenance	$19.136	$18.856
Procurement	$22.917	$22.000
RDT&E	$7.273	$7.108
Other	$ .257	$ .190
TOTAL	**$71.584**	**$69.936**

Does not include military construction, civil defense, or military assistance. Totals do not add up exactly due to rounding.

Source: Cong Action on FY 1968 Budget Requests by Appropriation Title (FAD 581), 4 Dec 67, Notebook Budget Data, 3, FY 1967–68, OSD Hist.

When signing the $69.9 billion FY 1968 Defense Appropriation Act, Johnson noted that the congressional cuts of $1.6 billion might well create an unavoidable requirement for additional Defense funds.[128] More bad blood was created when Congress, refusing to pass the construction portion of the budget, authorized a continuing resolution. The legislation's language, indicating that a majority wished to reduce non-defense spending by $5 billion, so infuriated the president that he instructed cabinet secretaries to "withhold and forego every possible commitment and expenditure" consistent with the nation's security and welfare until Congress acted on the remaining budget appropriations. McNamara responded by temporarily postponing all new awards for military construction as of 9 October because Congress had yet to issue its markup of the military construction report.[129] The standoff continued until 21 November when Congress passed a $1.4 billion military construction appropriation, one-third less than the president had requested.[130]

Developing and defending the FY 1966 and FY 1967 supplementals and the FY 1968 budget during 1967 was far more contentious and strident than the budget process in the previous year. Escalation of the Vietnam fighting outpaced OSD's projected funding in its FY 1967 and FY 1968 budgets, a misjudgment in part attributable to the inherent uncertainty of warfare. Withholding a supplemental request when one was clearly needed only hurt the administration's credibility in the midst of a tax fight with Congress, growing media skepticism about its policies, and changing public attitudes toward the war. Moreover, OSD's administrative guidance for the FY 1968 budget funded the war at the expense of non-Vietnam defense activities, incurring Defense obligations but postponing expenditures through deferrals, stretch-outs, or cancellations of previously authorized and funded DoD programs.

The administration's domestic agenda forced OSD to manipulate budgets to keep Defense requests at a bare minimum, an approach that invariably left DoD without enough money and McNamara in the awkward position of having to request huge supplementals from Congress, usually at the last minute, to cover the difference. As the president's standard-bearer McNamara defended the swollen yet inadequate Defense budget before Congress and the nation, but by mid-1966 legislators refused to rubber-stamp OSD's budget requests. The secretary's figures dazzled, his budget analysis shone, but in the end his numbers did not add up, leaving him open to charges of mismanagement or, far worse, deception.

The skyrocketing Defense budgets and the costs of the president's social programs stoked inflationary fires and fed a huge federal deficit. Uncertain of the nation's economic outlook, neither the White House nor Congress took the lead on a tax hike. The prolonged, increasingly bitter, and ultimately self-serving test of wills between the president and congressional leaders brought credit to neither side. The stalemate and growing deficit forced McNamara to hold Defense budgets to a minimum, but with fewer and fewer places to reduce spending this became more and more difficult to accomplish. McNamara's tactics left Defense budgets underfunded and understated, further misleading the public, if not the Congress, about the true costs of the war. Deferrals from previous years also skewed the preparation of the FY 1968 submission and future budgets. Sooner or later DoD would have to make good the funding difference that was straining its infrastructure to the limit.

All the conditions the president feared in the decisive summer of 1965—polarized debate on the administration's war policy, congressional opposition to domestic spending, the social and financial impacts of an open-ended conflict—came true by early 1967. Bookkeeping adjustments could no longer reconcile the dislocations that fighting a limited war imposed on the domestic economy, the defense infrastructure, the administration, and the military services. The cost of the conflict and its effect on the national economy and well being, like the war itself, proved beyond McNamara's control.

CHAPTER VII

VIETNAM:
AN ENDLESS WAR, 1967–1968

President Johnson, like McNamara, grappling with doubts about the progress of the Vietnam War, decided on 14 July 1967 to send Clark Clifford and Maxwell Taylor to press America's Asian allies to commit more troops. News reports heralding the purpose of the supposedly secret mission had only reinforced Clifford's initial skepticism about its chances of success. Although in effect their Asian hosts rejected the request, pleading that internal politics or external threats precluded sending more troops, the U.S. envoys, putting the best face on their visits, officially reported to the president that a foundation had been laid for further contributions. Clifford later recalled his dismay at the failure to elicit greater support from America's allies and privately told the president on 5 August that he was shocked by the indifference of those countries, whose security the United States believed it was defending, to do more for themselves. He also doubted that the course of the war would show much improvement through the coming year.[*][1]

Meanwhile, problems at home and mounting troubles abroad compounded the administration's anxiety. During 1967 antiwar protests, marked by acts of civil disobedience, increased in size and intensity; race riots tore through major American cities.[†] A potential budget deficit of $29 billion imperiled Great Society programs and mandated higher taxes. In August 1967 the president counted 15 national or international crises in the previous two months, ranging from a railroad strike to Westmoreland's latest troop requests.[2] The same month, hearings before the Senate Armed Services Committee's Preparedness Investigating Subcommittee,

---

[*] Taylor subsequently noted that allied forces actually increased from about 56,000 to more than 70,000 during the next two years. For comparative purposes, allied troops during the Korean War only totaled about 39,000. See Taylor, *Swords and Plowshares*, 376.
[†] See Chapter X.

the details of which were subsequently leaked to the press, exposed irreconcilable differences between McNamara and the Joint Chiefs of Staff over the efficacy of bombing North Vietnam.

It was also a difficult personal time for McNamara. Cyrus Vance, McNamara's alter ego within OSD, for health and financial reasons resigned as deputy secretary on 30 June 1967. In July McNamara's wife was hospitalized for ulcers and ISA Assistant Secretary John McNaughton, perhaps McNamara's closest confidant on Vietnam matters, died in a commercial airline crash in North Carolina. During this period, McNamara concluded that U.S. policies in Vietnam had failed; on 1 July he told Averell Harriman that it was impossible to win the war militarily. Anticipating, as he later stated, that the nation would need a record of how "we had gotten in such a hell of a mess," he commissioned in June what came to be called the *Pentagon Papers* as a documentary record for future generations.[3] Several observers believed the cumulative shocks and his increasing differences with the administration had left him on the verge of a nervous breakdown. McNamara later dismissed such speculation, but surely the personal turmoil and bleak Vietnam forecast took a terrible toll on a man used to being in control. Meanwhile, the air and ground wars droned on with an average of more than 1,300 Americans killed or wounded every week, with no end in sight.[4]

Accelerating Troop Deployments

The president's special budget message of 3 August 1967 called for another 45,000 troops for Vietnam, raising the authorized strength there to 525,000 men, and left the public with the impression of an open-ended commitment. Looking ahead to when Congress reconvened in January 1968, Johnson expected louder cries from hawks to escalate the war and from doves to end it. In early September, he wanted to keep the pressure on the enemy while minimizing domestic opposition, particularly from the doves, whom he regarded as "the major threat" to administration policy. Frustrated with the military's incessant demands for more troops and heavier bombing, on 12 September he told General Harold Johnson, the acting JCS chairman,* to come up with imaginative new ideas to end the war. Although McNamara and the president had agreed in July to cap deployment to Vietnam at 525,000 men, as of early September only 463,000 troops were actually there.[5] If the other 62,000 could be sent earlier than originally scheduled, Westmoreland might be able to bring greater pressure against the enemy in time to tamp down public discontent.

On 6 September, General Johnson was prodded, presumably by OSD, to speed up scheduled deployments. The proposed timing of the accelerated moves— one airborne brigade and one light infantry brigade to deploy before the key New

---

* General Wheeler was at Walter Reed Army Hospital recovering from a heart attack.

Hampshire presidential primary election on 12 March 1968—seemingly had as much to do with shaping domestic public opinion as it did with military requirements. The Joint Chiefs concluded that it was possible to meet the new schedule, but only by shortening stateside training. McNamara accepted the consequence and on 22 September he agreed to accelerate the deployment of 4,500 men of the 101st Airborne from February 1968 to December 1967.[6]

Through most of September, the North Vietnamese conducted heavy artillery bombardments of the U.S. Marine base at Con Thien, just two miles south of the DMZ and 14 miles inland, killing or wounding more than 2,000. Westmoreland then redeployed his forces to bolster Marines fighting in the northernmost provinces and to check the heavy enemy pressure there. His reassessment of planned operations led him to propose in a 28 September message a series of actions, including accelerated deployment of the remainder of his 525,000 troops to match the increased enemy threat to the DMZ as well as ease the burden on U.S. forces elsewhere in Vietnam.[7] At a White House luncheon on 3 October, McNamara informed the president that it was possible to increase the pace of deployments by curtailing stateside unit training and allowing MACV to conduct four weeks of unit training after the reinforcements arrived in South Vietnam. The following day he recommended that the president authorize the deployments; on 6 November the secretary officially approved accelerated movement of the 11th Infantry brigade to Vietnam during December 1967.[8]

Although the North Vietnamese broke off their attacks on Con Thien in early October, intense fighting continued in northernmost I Corps. Farther south, the enemy attacked South Vietnamese forces near the Cambodian frontier in III Corps. Elsewhere four North Vietnamese regiments, in an effort to draw U.S. units away from pacification duties in the coastal areas, massed astride the Cambodia-South Vietnam border. A mid-November spoiling attack by American troops against dug-in NVA positions on jungle-clad hills near Dak To led to severe losses on both sides, after which the North Vietnamese retreated into Cambodia. The increased level of fighting seemed to corroborate the growing U.S. public perception that the war was deadlocked.[9]

After the mid-October collapse of the Pennsylvania initiative,* with a prolonged stalemate now seeming likely, McNamara told the president that he believed the administration would not be able to maintain public support without a change in course. During this same period, on 17 October, the Joint Chiefs responded to the president's 12 September request to find ways to shorten the war. They proposed to expand the conflict outside of South Vietnam by heavier bombing of North Vietnam, increased ground operations against enemy sanctuaries in Laos and Cambodia, extended covert operations in North Vietnam, and mining of North Vietnamese harbors. The same day, McGeorge Bundy, now president of the Ford Foundation, recommended that the president follow a steady course

---

* The latest attempt to start negotiations with North Vietnam. See Chapter VIII.

without escalating the air or ground wars or suspending bombing operations in the North. On 31 October, after McNamara had voiced grave concerns about continuing the present approach the president suggested that he set his thoughts down in writing, thereby affording the secretary the opportunity to draft a sweeping reassessment of Vietnam policy entitled "A Fifteen Month Program for Military Operations in Southeast Asia."[10]

In his response of 1 November, McNamara expressed the view that adhering to the current path in Southeast Asia would lead to continued expansion of the fighting, result in correspondingly heavier U.S. casualties, and further erode public confidence. It was time to reassess MACV's ground strategy and stop the bombing of North Vietnam, which he was convinced would persuade Hanoi to negotiate or at least desist in military actions across the DMZ. McNamara would limit to its current level the U.S. military effort in South Vietnam in order to reduce American casualties, minimize further loss of U.S. domestic and international support, and compel South Vietnamese forces to assume more responsibility for the defense of their country. He believed that such a program would convince Hanoi of Washington's determination to wage a protracted war while gaining American domestic support.[11]

The day after McNamara submitted his memorandum, a bipartisan group of senior statesmen known as the "Wise Men"* addressed questions about Vietnam posed to them by the president. All felt that despite setbacks, recent progress was evident in South Vietnam; none recommended withdrawal. McNamara, present at the meeting, later wrote that the president had stacked the deck. Johnson neither invited advisers known to disagree with his Vietnam policy nor shared with the attendees an updated CIA analysis of 12 September. Although the paper concluded that a U.S. failure in Vietnam might encourage communist adventurism in Latin America and elsewhere, temporarily diminish U.S. prestige, and to some degree damage the security of the United States, overall, the authors observed, "such risks are probably more limited and controllable than most previous argument has indicated." Nor did the president circulate McNamara's memorandum to the gathering.[12] McNamara had ample opportunity to make his position clear both during preliminary background sessions and at the White House meeting, but, evidently not wanting to undercut the president, he did not speak his mind during the discussion.

The president did send a copy of the secretary's recommendations to Walt Rostow as well as Rusk for comment and made the substance of McNamara's memorandum available to several trusted confidants. With the exception of Rusk, all believed that capping the U.S. military commitment would eventually lead to a pullout and defeat in Vietnam. Clifford, for instance, predicted Hanoi would react with "chortles

---

* The term was used by McGeorge Bundy after the 1964 presidential campaign, when Johnson's team sought the backing of prominent members of the foreign policy and defense establishment. See Walter Isaacson and Evan Thomas, *The Wise Men*, 644-45; *U.S. Government and the Vietnam War*, pt 4: 872. The composition of the group varied. At this meeting the Wise Men were Clark Clifford, George Ball, Bundy, Maxwell Taylor, Omar Bradley, Robert Murphy, Henry Cabot Lodge, Averell Harriman, Dean Acheson, Abe Fortas, Arthur Dean, and Douglas Dillon (*FRUS 1964–68*, 5:954).

of unholy glee" to such an announcement. Rusk thought more troops might help, but he opposed expanding the ground war and counseled limiting it without announcing the policy shift.[13]

Johnson mulled over his defense secretary's recommendations for almost two months and, although he never replied to McNamara, on 18 December he recorded his personal views on the issue. The president discerned no reason to announce a policy of maintaining the war at its current level, but rejected increasing forces or expanding the ground war beyond South Vietnam's borders. To keep all his options open, he called for another review of military strategy with the aim of reducing American casualties by turning more of the operations over to the South Vietnamese.[14] Yet again he had postponed hard decisions about the conduct of the war.

Shaping Public Opinion

To combat the growing public disillusionment, disarm critics, and show that the United States was winning the war, Johnson brought Ambassador Bunker and General Westmoreland back to Washington in mid-November for a round of media events. They appeared on national television, spoke at the National Press Club, and testified before the House Armed Services Committee. Having been alerted by Wheeler to home front concerns that the South Vietnamese forces were not carrying their fair-share load, Westmoreland reassured his various audiences that his forces were "grinding down" the communists in South Vietnam, the South Vietnamese armed forces were improving, and, if these trends continued, in two years or less the South Vietnamese could shoulder the burden of the war and permit the beginning of a U.S. troop drawdown. This program justified the additional troops he had requested "based on the principle of reinforcing success."[15] At a White House meeting on 21 November the president emphasized expediting movement of scheduled troops to Vietnam, and Westmoreland expressed satisfaction with his "well balanced, hard-hitting" 525,000-man force. As the administration hoped, Johnson's popularity in the polls jumped 11 points following Westmoreland's optimistic pronouncements in the high-profile media appearances and Ambassador Bunker's equally confident, if lower-key, assessments of prospects in Vietnam.[16]

The president also used Westmoreland's visit to cultivate the general's support for his policies. In a long, private, after-dinner discussion on 20 November, Johnson told Westmoreland that McNamara was soon leaving the administration to "take advantage of a 'big job,'" and Clark Clifford would replace him. He further confided that for health reasons he did not plan to seek reelection in 1968.[17]

In line with presidential guidance, OSD urged Wheeler to do everything possible to deploy the scheduled troops at the earliest possible date. No matter how rapid the deployments, the Joint Chiefs insisted that the current policy provided no strategy for shortening the war. They counseled instead unrelenting pressure on the enemy and endorsed such initiatives as a clandestine multi-battalion ARVN foray into Laos (mentioned obliquely at the 21 November White House meeting).

For its part, MACV headquarters pushed for a large-scale invasion of the North Vietnamese panhandle above the DMZ involving two U.S. divisions and five ARVN battalions. State Department analysts, however, regarded such cross-border operations as a serious escalation of the war that would only lose international support for U.S. Southeast Asia policy without any lasting military benefits.[18]

The year 1967 ended on a discordant note in Washington. Although the president's personal popularity had risen in the polls, many Americans questioned his and the administration's credibility. A number of formerly pro-war Democrats had gone public with their opposition to the war, and others were sitting on the fence waiting to see which way to jump on the issue. The administration was in disarray over Vietnam. The president and his secretary of defense disagreed over fundamental issues, such as bombing policy and the conduct of ground operations. The Joint Chiefs and secretary of defense were at odds over much the same. McNamara's imminent departure to head the World Bank, announced 29 November, added to the uncertainty as rumors raced through the halls of the Pentagon about his replacement.[19]

In faraway Saigon, COMUSMACV's year-end appraisal graded allied progress from fair to excellent, citing heavy enemy casualties that required increasing numbers of NVA replacements for local VC units as evidence of the deterioration of the enemy's combat effectiveness. Moreover the Viet Cong had lost control over large areas of the countryside and still more of the population. Although the final three months of 1967 had witnessed a resurgence of communist activity, Westmoreland felt optimistic about 1968 because his solid logistic base and the accelerated flow of reinforcements would enable him to take the offensive. CINCPAC likewise noted the favorable shift to the allies militarily, leaving the enemy incapable of achieving a victory. Sharp, however, cautioned that the communists seemed willing to accept their losses; they continued a campaign of attacks, harassment, and terror throughout the countryside.[20]

To counter such moves, Westmoreland planned to carry the fight to the enemy near the borders where the VC/NVA were reorganizing and before they could do significant damage to the surrounding populated areas. These decisions caused more and more American troops to shift into northernmost I Corps. All eyes turned to that region early in 1968 when it appeared that thousands of North Vietnamese soldiers were massing in an attempt to overrun the remote Marine combat base at Khe Sanh, intended as a major linchpin in the oncoming barrier system.[21]

Manning the Barrier

Even after the president had assigned the anti-infiltration barrier the highest national priority in January 1967, Westmoreland worried that if it failed, critics would deride it as "McNamara's Folly" or "Westmoreland's Folly," especially because of its high cost in men as well as money, with little promise of return. It fell to the Marines at Khe Sanh to prevent the North Vietnamese from flanking the manned portion of the obstacle system, still under construction late in 1967 just south of the DMZ.[22]

The Joint Chiefs had split regarding the barrier. The service chiefs opposed it, but Wheeler favored it. He reasoned that troops would be operating in the area whether or not a barrier was constructed. He also expected that additional funds and forces would eventually become available for the system. McNamara accepted Wheeler's views, and discounted the service chiefs' proposals in late February (and subsequently) for more men, money, and field tests of the technology undergirding the barrier. In April the secretary insisted the operational date, already once postponed, remain fixed at 1 November 1967. Following coordination and agreement with South Vietnam and Thailand for basing, clearances for construction, expansion of air base and communications facilities, and so forth, Westmoreland assigned Marines to build the strong-point segment of the barrier.[23]

Work actually began on the trace in the summer of 1967. The North Vietnamese responded with the month-long shelling of Con Thien during September followed by the massing of troops against Khe Sanh. The increasing enemy threat near the DMZ, monsoon rains that hampered movement and construction, and the possibility of heavy casualties prompted Westmoreland to seek a scaling down of the original version. In mid-September he proposed, with Sharp's concurrence, reducing the trace and continuing ongoing operations from Marine combat bases that extended to the Laotian border. After considering MACV's rationale, ASD(ISA) Paul Warnke recommended that the Joint Chiefs examine the feasibility of moving the manned portion of the barrier system 10–15 kilometers farther south to reduce casualties and improve tactical flexibility. "Disinclined to start such a study now," McNamara took no action on the proposal.[24]

At his most optimistic in the summer of 1966, McNamara had hoped the barrier would preclude the need to bomb North Vietnamese territory, thus inducing Hanoi to negotiate. In July 1967 he told a MACV audience that he doubted if the barrier that required so much work and money would stop infiltration, but if it gave some benefit then the cost would really be quite small. In November of that year, with his resignation looming, he told the president and the Wise Men that while the work of scientists and engineers had improved the system (he refused to call it a barrier) and thus enhanced the effectiveness of the air campaign against the infiltration of vehicles and men, he did not want to overstate its potential. He insisted that if the system, which was to become operational in December, improved "the casualty ratio by even a few percent it will have been worth the effort."[25]

To his critics, the so-called McNamara Line was a metaphor for the secretary's arbitrary, highly personal, and aggressive management style that bypassed normal procedures and sometimes ignored experts to get things done. He had adopted an idea from civilian academics, forced a reluctant military to implement it, opted for technology over experience, launched the project quickly and with minimum coordination, rejected informed criticism, insisted available forces sufficed for the effort, and poured millions of dollars into a system that proceeded by fits and starts.

Years later, McNamara would note that the system "was intended to increase infiltration losses. And it did." A candid contemporary assessment in October 1968, however, concluded that the barrier had neither stopped nor materially diminished NVA infiltration into South Vietnam, although the system showed "great promise," particularly if finally completed as originally conceived.[26]

Khe Sanh

With Khe Sanh effectively isolated from overland supply, North Vietnamese troop concentrations in the vicinity of the base gave reason for grave concern. Since mid-November 1967, MACV had picked up indications of communist intentions; on 26 January 1968 the CIA forecast a major, countrywide enemy campaign around the Tet holidays (29–31 January) with the main pressure occurring in the northern provinces. Westmoreland increasingly viewed enemy probes against the remote Khe Sanh base as harbingers of the decisive battle of the war.[27]

Meanwhile, on 18 January, U.S. Marines reported a heavy increase in enemy sightings and activity near Khe Sanh. On the 20th, a captured North Vietnamese lieutenant revealed details of an imminent attack, which occurred that evening against hilltop outposts; more followed the next day with a shelling of the main base. On the 22nd, the enemy succeeded in capturing Khe Sanh village south of the base. By the end of January the Marines had restricted reconnaissance patrols to within 500 meters of the defense perimeter.[28]

Nervous civilian officials in Washington wondered if striking enemy rear areas in Laos might relieve the pressure on Khe Sanh or if a withdrawal from the base was still possible. Westmoreland ruled out a preemptive attack for logistical (the enemy had interdicted the surrounding roads, and poor visibility had grounded aerial transports), tactical (the enemy was in force and well supplied with artillery and antiaircraft weapons), and meteorological (the onset of the northeast monsoon) reasons. He insisted on holding Khe Sanh because of its tactical value as an advance staging base and as flank security for the barrier's strong-point obstacle system. Admiral Sharp added that withdrawal was "unthinkable" because it would hand the enemy a major propaganda victory with enormous psychological and political repercussions in the United States.[29] In truth, Westmoreland could neither withdraw from Khe Sanh nor attack the massing enemy forces. He could only defend.

The images of the beleaguered Marines surrounded by a fanatical enemy at Khe Sanh generated extensive publicity abetted by the dramatic backdrop the embattled camp offered for photo and film opportunities. Concern that Khe Sanh was another Dien Bien Phu* in the making stretched from Main Street to the

---

* In the spring of 1954 Vietnamese communist forces isolated and defeated French forces at Dien Bien Phu, a remote base in northwestern Vietnam, effectively ending the war in Indochina and leading to the Geneva Conference of 1954 that produced the independent nations of Cambodia, Laos, North Vietnam, and South Vietnam.

White House. With field commanders and senior military advisers warning of an imminent and widespread enemy offensive, President Johnson worried that the base might be overrun; beginning in early January he frequently called the White House situation room for the latest news from Khe Sanh. Military aides set up a command post in the White House basement complete with a terrain table and photo murals of Khe Sanh to enable the president to keep a close eye on the details of the siege. At an NSC meeting on the 24th, Johnson asked Wheeler to confirm that Westmoreland had been given all he had asked for and needed. Five days later, the president received verbal and written assurances from the individual service chiefs that everything had been done so that Westmoreland should, could, and would hold Khe Sanh. Johnson later described the two weeks before the Tet offensive (which began on 29 January) and the two months after as being as intense a period of activity as any of his presidency.[30]

Normally given to hyperbole, in this case Johnson might have succumbed to understatement. In mid-January North Korean commandos tried to assassinate the South Korean prime minister. While South Korean and American troops tracked down the infiltrators, half a world away on 21 January a B-52 bomber carrying four hydrogen bombs crashed about seven miles from Thule, Greenland. No one yet knew what had become of the lost plane and its thermonuclear cargo. Two days later attention snapped back to North Korea and its seizure of the USS *Pueblo*, an intelligence collection ship, in international waters off the peninsula's eastern port city of Wonsan. In Southeast Asia, U.S. troops had inadvertently strayed into Cambodia as the Khe Sanh situation was still simmering and threatened to boil over at any moment. In the midst of these emergencies McNamara joked to his successor-designate Clark Clifford on 23 January that this was a typical day around the White House. Clifford asked, "May I leave now?"[31] A few days later the defense secretary nominee may have wished that he had departed.

The Tet Offensive

The regularly scheduled Tuesday luncheon convened on 30 January to assess, among other topics, the latest disquieting reports of widespread, but apparently poorly coordinated, enemy rocket, mortar, and ground attacks against U.S. air bases and Vietnamese cities in I and II Corps; of particular concern was the growing threat to Khe Sanh. In the midst of the discussions, Walt Rostow returned from a call to report Saigon was under attack and the U.S. embassy had been hit. The participants regarded the latest assault as still another isolated example of VC terrorism—as Wheeler put it, "about as tough to stop as . . . an individual mugging in Washington, D.C."[32]

Unfortunately the blows against Saigon were part of the simultaneous nation-wide communist Tet offensive against a half dozen of South Vietnam's key cities, 36 provincial capitals, 64 district centers, and numerous villages and hamlets. Despite the magnitude and viciousness of the enemy attacks, or, more likely, because of the confusion and uncertainty generated by the multiple, synchronized thrusts, Westmoreland stayed focused on Khe Sanh. So did the president, concerned that the situation there might worsen enough to force him into a decision to use tactical nuclear weapons, one that he did not want to make. For reasons of "military prudence," in late January Sharp and Westmoreland had started "closely held" but "detailed planning" for the use of tactical nuclear weapons in the "highly unlikely" event that the Khe Sanh situation would become that desperate. As of 1 February, Westmoreland still regarded the Tet attacks as diversions to distract attention from Khe Sanh, where an enemy "capable of attack at any time" was readying to launch a major offensive.[33]

On 2 February Westmoreland told Wheeler that he expected the attack against Khe Sanh within the next day or two, prompting the president to ask Wheeler if MACV needed reinforcements. At a White House meeting the following day, Wheeler reported that Westmoreland did not need ground reinforcements, but wanted additional transport aircraft and helicopters. Unless the situation in the DMZ changed dramatically, preparations for the possible use of tactical nuclear weapons or chemical agents were unnecessary. Yet Maxwell Taylor, present at the meeting, described "an air of gloom" hanging over the discussion because of uncertainty that Khe Sanh could be held without suffering prohibitive losses. While no one suggested withdrawal from Khe Sanh, Taylor felt it "quite apparent" that most present wished U.S. troops were not there. He also recognized that the men in the room had done as much as anyone to build up the significance of Khe Sanh in the minds of the American people and would find it very difficult indeed to explain why the base was not important.[34]

Wheeler encouraged Westmoreland to think that the shock of the Tet offensive would force the administration into a policy review whose outcome would favor mobilization to replenish the strategic reserve as well as reinforce Vietnam. Perhaps to achieve those ends, on 7 February the chairman had painted a gloomy picture for the president of a hard-pressed South Vietnamese army teetering on the verge of defeat and the possibility of serious U.S. losses at Khe Sanh.[35] Hardly as pessimistic, Westmoreland hindered his own cause with his ambivalent cables. In a series of messages sent between 3 and 12 February, the MACV commander ruled out nuclear weapons, but noted that a dramatic unfavorable change might require their use; insisted Tet was an enemy defeat but that he needed reinforcements to retake the initiative; said he had to reinforce I Corps but could not redeploy any more forces from elsewhere in the country without taking an unacceptable risk; agreed the highest priority was clearing South Vietnam's cities, but declared the fall of Khe Sanh the single greatest threat and, if lost, the base would have to be retaken; praised ARVN units, but asserted they were spent and likely to experience high desertion rates; and expressed a determination to exploit enemy losses to shorten the war, but admitted that without needed reinforcements allied setbacks were possible.[36] Wheeler conveyed the MACV commander's views to Washington decisionmakers but rendered them through his own less sanguine lens.[37] Years later it remained impossible to determine with any certainty which officer's appraisal was more accurate, but the gap between their interpretations only confused the already divided civilian policymakers.[38]

What perplexed the president was how one week the service chiefs could say Westmoreland had what he needed and the next say he desperately required reinforcements. The week following Tet had seen no request from Westmoreland for more troops. Quite the contrary, on 8 February Bunker had cabled from Saigon that the enemy had suffered a major defeat. Wheeler felt differently and the same day sent Westmoreland two cables. The first suggested that MACV needed reinforcements and the second urged Westmoreland to request additional troops at this critical point in the war. The next day at the White House the Joint Chiefs addressed the possibility of a 40,000-man reinforcement and the mobilization of 120,000 reservists to support the deployment. After listening to the discussion, newcomer Clifford asked the obvious question: If the Tet offensive was a failure and the enemy had lost as many as 25,000 men, why were 40,000 additional troops and an emergency call-up of the reserves necessary?[39] No decisions came from the meeting.

Later that day, however, McNamara told the Joint Chiefs to submit three alternative deployment plans, of which only one would require reserve mobilization. He hoped to avoid a "prolonged and divisive debate" in Congress over a call-up and retain active forces at home to quell domestic civil disorders anticipated during the summer months. At a meeting on 10 February the president, wary of being blamed later for denying MACV's requests, seemed inclined toward sending Westmoreland whatever he required. At the same time, however, he announced that he wanted the 82nd Airborne Division (one of two units available for deployment) kept in the United States in the event of another summer of civil disturbances. He also appeared to heed McNamara's misgivings about sending more American troops as substitutes for the South Vietnamese.[40]

On 11 February, the president, his civilian advisers, and Wheeler reviewed Westmoreland's assessment of 9 February that the situation was stabilizing, except in northern I Corps where he was redeploying forces and welcomed additional reinforcements anytime they could be made available. Everyone concluded that since Westmoreland had not specifically requested additional reinforcements, he did not need them. McNamara particularly opposed any permanent augmentation beyond the earlier established 525,000-man limit, and Wheeler affirmed the president's observation that there was no need for additional troops, but Johnson also wanted to satisfy the 525,000-troop commitment, still short by 25,000 men.[41]

The following morning, McNamara reviewed Westmoreland's latest cable (12 February), requesting the immediate deployment of a brigade of the 82nd Airborne Division (3,800 men) and a Marine regimental landing team (RLT) (5,400 men)*

---

* Additional Air Force and Navy personnel brought the emergency reinforcement total to 10,644 troops.

over and above the 525,000-troop ceiling. The secretary notified the president by phone, recommending approval. At a hastily organized White House luncheon that afternoon, the president's civilian advisers and Wheeler debated the meaning of Westmoreland's recent cables. So great was the contrast between Friday's cable of 9 February welcoming more troops if they were available and Monday's of the 12th calling for "reinforcements, which I desperately need," the president remarked that it appeared to an unnamed person (actually Maxwell Taylor) that different people were writing Westmoreland's cables.[42]

"Scared about Khesanh," and more unsure of the appropriate action each day, a nervous president sought and received unanimous approval from his advisers for a crash program to get an additional 10,000 troops to Vietnam within 14 days, if possible. Clifford tried but failed to pin Wheeler down on exactly why Westmoreland needed such heavy reinforcements and remained silent during the approval exercise, deferring to McNamara until formally sworn in as secretary of defense. On 13 February, McNamara ordered the airborne brigade and a Marine RLT to deploy on a temporary basis, meaning that after the crisis passed they would be withdrawn and consequently would not count against the permanent troop ceiling. All of the designated troops reached Vietnam by 21 February.[43] These decisions did not, however, settle the reinforcement or reserve call-up issues.

Responding to McNamara's 9 February request, on the 12th the Joint Chiefs had actually proposed deferring reinforcements to Vietnam, though they would prepare the 82nd Airborne and the greater part of a Marine division for possible deployment and mobilize reservists both to replace units deployed to Southeast Asia and to reconstitute the CONUS strategic reserves. At the White House luncheon the next day, the president asked about the size of the mobilization and its legislative, financial, domestic, and international repercussions. McNamara's options ranged from deferring further reinforcements until again requested by Westmoreland to mobilizing about 130,000 troops and asking Congress for supplemental financing. The Joint Chiefs favored an immediate call-up of 44,000 reservists to support the roughly 10,000 Vietnam-bound emergency reinforcements and permission to mobilize another 138,000, should additional reinforcements became necessary.[*44]

Amidst intelligence reports of a planned "second wave" communist offensive and possibly responding to Taylor's 14 February suggestion that there remained time to withdraw from Khe Sanh, the president informed McNamara that he would rely on Westmoreland's judgment about withdrawal, but he added that he wanted to be forewarned so that he could "prepare the political defenses." About the same time, the president approved Wheeler's suggestion of the 11th to take a group to Saigon for an on-the-scene report. Pending Wheeler's report, Johnson deferred consideration of further reinforcement and a reserve call-up.[45]

---

[*] These numbers fluctuated as planners revised estimates. Two days later, for instance, these numbers had swelled to 46,300 immediate recalls and 137,000 to standby status (JCSM-99-68, 15 Feb 68). To avoid confusion, only those figures appearing in decisions are cited.

Wheeler met with Westmoreland, Bunker, senior military officers, and Vietnamese leaders between 23 and 25 February. Returning to Washington on the 28th, he informed the president that "the outcome is not at all clear." Despite massive personnel losses, the communists seemed determined to continue their offensive that had disabled South Vietnamese forces or driven them from the countryside into the towns and cities. Pacification was halted, the Viet Cong prowled the countryside, U.S. forces carried the bulk of the fighting, and MACV, operating on a "paper thin" margin without a strategic reserve, faced the possibility of some reverses. For these reasons, Westmoreland was requesting reinforcements beyond the 525,000 ceiling. Wheeler believed MACV needed a two-division theater reserve and recommended adding nearly 150,000 troops not later than 1 September, with a follow-up increment of 55,400 by December 1968, for an additional total of 205,400. The magnitude of these numbers frightened many of the civilian policymakers.[46]

Westmoreland would later claim that Wheeler had discounted MACV's more upbeat briefings in anticipation that the crisis atmosphere in Washington might produce a massive reinforcement that Wheeler thought justified. Still, Westmoreland was aware during Wheeler's visit of the apprehension in Washington and the two generals had outlined a plan on the assumption that the president would call up the reserves.[47] Westmoreland recollected that he was merely responding to the Joint Chiefs request for a contingency plan, and the figure of some 205,000 was a composite one to strengthen both his force and the virtually nonexistent strategic reserve. The generals expected their proposals to remain confidential, pending review at the highest levels in Washington. On 26 February, McNamara instructed the Joint Chiefs and service secretaries, neither group being comfortable with the magnitude of the numbers, to prepare alternative deployment plans to satisfy fully or partially the latest perceived levies for Vietnam.[48]

Whatever the facts, McNamara announced the next day during a meeting of top civilian advisers held at the State Department that the request for 205,000 reinforcements made no sense to him. The total was "neither enough to do the job, nor an indication that our role must change." To meet Westmoreland's requirements, McNamara foresaw a reserve mobilization, increased draft calls, and spending an additional $10 billion at a time when the president was fighting rising interest rates, a huge deficit, and congressional reluctance to support the administration's proposed tax package to pay for the war. McNamara's fears, indeed his entire torment over the war, broke open during the discussion. Tense, sarcastic, and deeply pessimistic, the secretary became visibly upset in a five-minute emotional appeal to other attendees, particularly to Clifford, to "end this thing. . . . It is out of control."[49]

On the 28th, a more composed McNamara explained to the president the implications—mobilization, larger draft calls, extended enlistments, a $10 billion budget increase—of sending the initial 105,000-man increment to Vietnam.

While Wheeler insisted that without the additional two divisions Westmoreland might have to abandon South Vietnam's northernmost provinces, McNamara concluded the North Vietnamese would likely match any U.S. reinforcement; he rejected anything beyond the emergency reinforcements already authorized. Before the meeting, Clifford had advised the president not to make any hasty decisions. Johnson complied, and during the discussions asked Clifford to head an interagency task force to make a fresh appraisal and report back by 4 March.[50]

Immediately following the meeting, in the presence of congressional leaders, members of the Supreme Court, friends, colleagues, and the press, the president presented McNamara the Medal of Freedom, the nation's highest civilian award. The man who had reorganized the Department of Defense, dominated America's national security decisionmaking, in large measure managed America's war in Vietnam—in short, the most powerful secretary of defense the office had known—was speechless. In front of the harsh glare of television lighting, holding back tears, his voice breaking, he stammered a few sentences. The following day, 29 February, Johnson presided over McNamara's farewell ceremony, conducted outdoors at the Pentagon in a storm of sleet and rain that seemed to fit the occasion. McNamara's contentious tenure was over; his most controversial legacy, the Vietnam War, was bequeathed to his successor.[51]

The New Secretary

Clark M. Clifford's selection as secretary of defense fueled speculation that Johnson had simply tapped a confidant he could depend on after his disappointment with McNamara. To Clifford his selection was a simple matter: the president wanted someone who supported his policy, could restore harmony between OSD and the Joint Chiefs, and could improve the administration's relations with Congress.[52]

Clifford, for better or worse, was no McNamara. McNamara dominated; Clifford consulted. McNamara, upon amassing information, often made decisions and then informed the Joint Chiefs; Clifford made decisions only after lengthy deliberation, explained his reasons to the Joint Chiefs, and addressed matters raised by them. McNamara delegated but never established a coherent system for control of the Vietnam War; Clifford established a control system before he delegated responsibility. McNamara administered the Pentagon and personally handled its relations with the White House and other government agencies; Clifford concentrated on external relationships (chiefly with the president and Congress), leaving the day-to-day administration to his deputy, Paul Nitze. If McNamara's regularly scheduled staff meetings were didactic, Clifford's were discursive; the new secretary involved his advisers in reviewing options and arriving at decisions. His Monday morning meeting, begun 6 March, served as "an invaluable bridge" to key staff assistants at times when the secretary was too busy to schedule individual appointments with them to evaluate policy issues.[53]

As noted, the president gave Clifford less than a week to examine alternatives and provide recommendations to address the military, political, and economic ramifications of meeting the Wheeler-Westmoreland troop request for Vietnam. He provided his new secretary with only draft instructions and large discretion, allowing Clifford to conduct a sweeping review as he saw fit in the best interests of the nation. The task force, composed of senior administration officials,* developed position papers based on common assumptions and then discussed their conclusions during frank and animated meetings held in Clifford's conference room.[54]

Alternatives ranged from giving MACV an additional 200,000 troops to standing pat. Systems Analysis and ISA argued that the 200,000 men would still not provide the military power to make the communists abandon their goal of taking over South Vietnam. It was up to the South Vietnamese, not the Americans, to develop the military and political institutions needed to survive. Taylor favored deployment of some reinforcements to demonstrate U.S. resolve; at the same time he thought Westmoreland's plan overly ambitious (even with all the requested troops) and in need of new strategic guidance from Washington. Proponents of a revised strategy, William Bundy and Nitze advocated pulling back U.S. troops from Vietnam's outlying borders to protect its populated areas and its major provincial capitals, in effect repudiating MACV's strategic concept. The Joint Staff recoiled at such recommendations, contending that the proper way to protect the populated areas was to defeat the enemy's main force units on the borders. Decrying the political constraints that had "prevented the most effective application of allied military power," a Joint Staff study endorsed deployment of another 194,000 troops, calling up the reserves, and lifting restraints on military operations in Laos, Cambodia, and North Vietnam.[55]

It was one thing for Clifford to hear a dispirited McNamara declare that 200,000 more troops would not make any difference, and quite another for him to listen to the Joint Chiefs—the nation's premier military strategists—say in so many words, according to Clifford, that they had no idea what effect 200,000 additional troops would have on the outcome of the war; had no indication the enemy's will was weakening; and, worst of all, within the political limitations, had no plan to win the war in the traditional sense. Their admissions, their lack of conviction, only confirmed Clifford's inclination not to send more troops. On 6 March, for instance, he explained to his staff the futility of expanding a limited war militarily or geographically. He sought an "honorable peace" that would enable the United States to withdraw and leave a government and military in South Vietnam capable of defending itself. In short, after less than a week in office, Clifford reversed his position on Vietnam.[56]

---

* Members included Clifford, Katzenbach, William Bundy, Nitze, Warnke, Taylor, Helms, Wheeler, and Treasury Secretary Fowler (*FRUS, 1964–68*, 6:276, n 2).

The task force, though, remained split over the question of immediate and future U.S. reinforcements to Vietnam. Unwilling to take on the powerful advisory hawks after only four days in office and aware of the president's desire to get more troops to Westmoreland, Clifford offered a compromise. His 4 March DPM recommended continued bombing of the North, sending Westmoreland 22,000 men (all that could be provided by 1 May), calling up 262,000 reservists (including more than 30,000 for the Korean crisis), extending terms of service, and increasing the draft to replenish the strategic reserve. Any future large deployments should depend on the developing military and political situations in Vietnam. Finally, Clifford noted the likely negative public reaction to increased troop deployments and a reserve call-up.[57]

At a late afternoon meeting on 4 March at the White House, Clifford described "a deep-seated concern" among some on the task force that sending even 205,000* more troops might only escalate the conflict with no end in sight. He restated his DPM's recommendations for reinforcements and reserves, adding that it was time to reassess in depth both the political and strategic aspects of the war, seek to reduce U.S. casualties, and no longer rely on the field commander whose appetite for more troops could be insatiable. The president told Wheeler to inform Westmoreland that only 22,000 reinforcements were available. He withheld comment on the remaining proposals, including the one for an in-depth study.[58]

Wheeler notified Westmoreland on 5 March of the "special committee" recommendations to the president, emphasized that no decisions had yet been made, and clarified that sending forces beyond the 22,000 troops depended on a reserve mobilization. The same day Johnson instructed Clifford and Wheeler to sound out Senator Russell about a call-up of the reserves to meet the *Pueblo* crisis and the Vietnam emergency. Two days later, Russell told Johnson that he opposed any mobilization until those without prior service (eligible draftees) and the South Vietnamese did their parts, views he and several colleagues reiterated to Clifford and Wheeler on 8 March.[59]

Also on 8 March, Westmoreland insisted that MACV lacked the logistic capability to sustain troops already in Vietnam; additional support forces would have to accompany all reinforcements. Faced with powerful congressional opposition, that afternoon the president again ruled out the 205,000 augmentation, but made no final decision on how many he would deploy. Wheeler warned MACV that any large increase was unlikely because of the "strong resistance from all quarters to putting more ground force units in South Vietnam" and to mobilizing the reserves.[60]

Even the remotest chance for large reinforcements disappeared following a lengthy article in the *New York Times* on 10 March that revealed not only the approximate number of troops requested but also extensive details of the intense

---

* Numbers vary according to source. The figure 205,000 was sometimes rounded to 200,000.

in-house policy debate in progress. White House meetings were "fairly inconclusive until about 11 March" when sentiment shifted to holding reinforcements to minimum levels. That evening the president indicated his intention to provide Westmoreland with 30,000 troops needed to get through the emergency period—all that could realistically be deployed—and to rebuild the strategic reserve.[61]

Two days later on 13 March, Johnson decided to deploy the 30,000, most to arrive by June 1968. This was in addition to the 10,500 dispatched on an emergency basis in mid-February. As for the reserves, the consensus within the Pentagon was to announce a call-up simultaneously with that of the deployment. Clifford informed the president on 15 March that he envisaged a mobilization of about 85,000 reservists, roughly 36,600 of whom would support the deployments with the remainder to reconstitute the strategic reserve. Presented at a White House meeting that evening, Clifford's revised figures involved two call-ups, one of 50,000, the other of 48,000, more or less equally divided between Vietnam and the strategic reserve. To head off media speculation that all 98,000 reservists were slated for Vietnam the president decided to announce that 50,000 reservists would go to Vietnam, but leave vague the total number to be recalled.[62]

Clifford's discussions with the Joint Chiefs on 18 March revealed that all the service chiefs preferred larger reinforcements and an expanded ground war into Laos or southern North Vietnam. Wheeler, however, while anxious to "beat up NVN from air and sea," would send no more U.S. troops beyond those under discussion; instead he would build up the South Vietnamese army to take over the war. The same day Warnke advised Clifford that without fundamental changes to U.S. strategy the war was unwinnable. U.S. forces had accomplished about as much as possible militarily, but the enemy retained the capability to fight. The real solution required South Vietnam to greatly improve its government and military forces.[63]

The next afternoon, 19 March, at the Tuesday luncheon, Clifford informed the president and his top advisers that Russell had agreed to the recall of 50,000 reservists, 43,000 of whom would deploy to Vietnam, plus a later mobilization of 48,000 to rebuild the strategic reserve. Three days later at another White House lunch, the president ruminated on the "dramatic shift in public opinion on the war." Clifford linked popular disenchantment to the perception that Vietnam was a "bottomless pit" and that the military had no winning plan. He suggested that the president call the reserves, but send no additional troops to Vietnam beyond those already promised. On Clifford's recommendation, the president agreed that Wheeler should meet Westmoreland in the Philippines to discuss strategy, reinforcement, and mobilization issues. Wheeler flew to Clark Air Base, where on 24 March he told Westmoreland that the administration had decided against a large-scale mobilization. Once more modifying a previous position, Westmoreland assured him that with the promised 24,500 reinforcements (11,000 combat plus 13,500 combat support) MACV could more than hold its own and pursue its current strategy.[64]

At the 19 March lunch Clifford had suggested reconvening the Wise Men to determine whether or not the events of the past four months had changed their views about the war. The president agreed and set the meeting for 26 March. Gathered at the State Department on 25 March for a series of background briefings and discussions,* the Wise Men listened to Clifford present three options: escalate the war, continue the status quo, or implement a "reduced strategy" contingent on curtailing both bombing of the North and U.S. ground operations in the South. During the after-dinner discussions, the group heard three presentations on the conduct of the war. Philip C. Habib from State, pessimistic and doubtful the war could be won, suggested a halt to the bombing and a start on negotiations. George A. Carver, the CIA's special assistant for Vietnamese affairs, acknowledged communist successes but believed the enemy had failed to achieve his objectives of defeating the ARVN, discrediting the Saigon government, and forcing a U.S. withdrawal. Heretofore optimistic about the progress of the war, Carver now saw the struggle as one for the South Vietnamese to win or lose. General DePuy, now the special assistant to the Joint Chiefs of Staff for counterinsurgency and special activities, described the Tet offensive as an allied victory. When questioned by Arthur Goldberg about the number of enemy casualties, DePuy asserted 80,000 killed and three times that number wounded. "Well," Goldberg demanded, "who the hell is there left for us to be fighting?" It was not an exchange that altered minds or swayed opinions. One participant, Cyrus Vance, thought most people came to the meeting "with their minds fairly well made up" on the future course of the war.[65]

Seeking a way to proceed, between 10:30 a.m. and 12:15 p.m. on 26 March the president met with Wheeler and General Abrams, the MACV deputy commander. Wheeler recounted his meeting with Westmoreland and the latter's assessment that the overall situation had improved, making additional reinforcements unnecessary. Feeling that Carver and DePuy "weren't up to par last night," Johnson then asked Wheeler and Abrams to give the Wise Men the whole picture, pro and con.[66]

One hour later Wheeler and Abrams briefed the Wise Men, explaining that Westmoreland had turned things around and was on the offensive. While both saw hard fighting ahead, Wheeler maintained that the greatest setback from Tet came in the United States, not Vietnam. Abrams commended the South Vietnamese forces, most of whom had fought hard, suffered heavy casualties, taken their objectives, and continued to improve. Unimpressed, a majority of the Wise Men felt that the time had come for the United States to begin to disengage from Vietnam. Taylor and Wheeler were surprised at their "defeatist attitude," but a growing sense that the war was unwinnable had convinced the Wise Men to reconsider their positions and recommend against further escalation.[67]

---

* The group included Dean Acheson, McGeorge Bundy, Douglas Dillon, Cyrus Vance, Arthur Goldberg, George Ball, Matthew Ridgway, Omar Bradley, Maxwell Taylor, Abe Fortas, Robert Murphy, Henry Cabot Lodge, John McCloy, and Arthur Dean. Acheson had been primed before the meeting by briefings at his Georgetown home (Kai Bird, *The Color of Truth*, 368).

That evening the president again met with Wheeler and Abrams as well as Clifford, Rusk, Walt Rostow, and others. Wheeler presented Westmoreland's assessment of the ground campaign. Westmoreland felt confident of MACV's ability to maintain the offensive given all the previously promised but as yet undeployed forces, up to the 525,000 ceiling (Program 5), along with the 24,500 tentatively approved (Program 6). The president also agreed to a call-up of 62,000 reservists, which included the support troops slated for Vietnam. In his long-planned 31 March television speech, the president announced that a portion of the 24,500 augmentation would be from the reserves. He made no mention of further call-ups, although the administration was still considering mobilizing another 48,500 reservists for the strategic reserve.[68]

Two days earlier on the 29th, Clifford had officially notified the Joint Chiefs that in his 31 March address the president would announce the limited deployment along with a reserve call-up. In response, on 2 April the services proposed to mobilize almost 57,000 reservists. Heeding Enthoven's caution that the nation's financial situation mandated a less expensive alternative, Clifford directed the Joint Chiefs to recall just 22,767. Instead of using reservists to reconstitute the strategic reserve, he opted to redesignate NATO-committed units in the United States, cancel their rotation plans to NATO, and make them available for use anywhere. The Joint Chiefs strongly objected, noting the originally proposed call-up was based on supporting Vietnam deployments and reconstituting the strategic reserve. Now OSD planned to change the U.S. strategic commitment to NATO, abrogate agreements with West Germany, and include NATO-designated units in the strategic forces.[69] Their arguments were fruitless.

Program 6, the latest, and, as it turned out, the last, Vietnam deployment plan, was formally issued by Deputy Secretary Nitze on 4 April 1968, to bring the end-strength total by 30 June 1969 to 549,500 men. Approximately 24,550 reservists were to be recalled to active duty with about 10,000 scheduled for Vietnam. The remainder would enter the strategic reserve but be available for rotation to Vietnam as comparable units returned to their home bases.[70] Thus, the resolution of reinforcement and mobilization issues that racked the administration into early April suggested an unstated reversal of the objective of winning the war. It pointed instead toward ending the war.

The Ground War Grinds On

The president's address of 31 March did not signal a radical departure from the overall ground strategy. Westmoreland launched the largest allied offensive operation of the war early in April, causing a spike in U.S. casualties. Nonetheless, the 31 March speech marked the end of the administration's willingness to support repeated demands from field commanders for additional personnel. Even earlier the secretary of defense had declared his intent to oversee more closely the ground war. During the next few months, Clifford insisted that MACV tone down its optimistic press releases; he instituted a tighter rein over General Abrams, who replaced Westmoreland on 11 June. He also encouraged fresh tactics designed to minimize the use and destructiveness of American firepower. Furthermore, he supported a new strategy to concentrate U.S. forces near populated areas and shift the burden of fighting to ARVN units in an effort to minimize American casualties that by May were running double those in the first two weeks of Tet.*[71]

Clifford was greatly heartened by North Vietnam's unexpected announcement of 3 April that under certain conditions it was willing to negotiate with the United States. Yet, he later described how Johnson's dilemma of wanting an honorable exit from Vietnam without becoming the first president to lose a foreign war had created conflicting signals and possibly lost opportunities to end the war during his administration. Perhaps more precisely, the administration had neither an exit strategy for Vietnam nor a coordinated approach with the Saigon regime. De-escalation had become an end in itself, so there existed no agreed upon negotiating strategy much less a consensus on what concessions the White House might make to end the conflict.[72]

In a 7 May speech and later 23 May congressional testimony, Clifford admitted that getting out of Vietnam meant getting out with honor and dignity; what that entailed defied easy definition. In a divided administration what one senior adviser considered honor and dignity might be another's shorthand for disgrace and defeat. Clifford predicted "lengthy, difficult, frustrating, and often stultifying" negotiations.[73] High hopes for an early settlement were further dampened as the United States, with very few bargaining chips, found itself mousetrapped by Hanoi and by Saigon into lengthy dickering over everything from the location of the preliminary talks—finally agreed upon as Paris—to the shape of the conference table.

In the weeks and months following the president's 31 March address, Clifford focused on extricating the United States from Vietnam. He explained to the Joint Chiefs in late April that the administration's basic policy was to start negotiations with North Vietnam while gradually turning over an increasingly larger share of the war effort to the South Vietnamese. These initiatives were put to the test early in May when North Vietnamese and Viet Cong forces launched their second general offensive of the year.[74]

Dubbed mini-Tet by the press, the May attacks failed to generate the spectacular headlines of their February namesake and had little impact on the rural pacification effort. The upsurge in fighting, however, left more Americans killed in action during the first half of 1968 than in all of 1967. Heavy fighting in Saigon and its suburbs wreaked enormous destruction and created tens of thousands of new refugees. While Ambassador Bunker remained optimistic the latest enemy

---

* More than one third each of the killed, the hospitalized wounded, and the non-hospitalized wounded for the period between 1961 and the end of June 1968 occurred in the first six months of 1968 (NMCC Operational Summary 156-68, 3 Jul 68, 16).

offensive would end in defeat, Clifford felt "a real crunch" was approaching in Vietnam that would force the "ultimate policy decision" on the future of the war. When that time arrived, he wanted to make the strongest case possible to the president for disengagement. On 18 May he assigned Warnke to prepare in utmost secrecy a position paper leading inexorably to the conclusion that the United States had to extricate itself from Vietnam.[75]

Aided by Col. Robert Pursley, Clifford's military assistant, and the secretary's special assistant, George Elsey, Warnke in a report delivered a few days later concluded that Westmoreland's strategy of attrition would only lead to higher U.S. and allied casualties and greater economic stress and political and social friction in the United States. The American public would not accept a weekly death toll of 400 to 500 U.S. soldiers and expenditures of $2 billion to $3 billion monthly to underwrite a strategy that Hanoi's willingness to sustain huge losses rendered irrelevant. Throwing more troops into the struggle and enlarging the ground war would only exacerbate the existing divisions in domestic public opinion, aggravate the already heavy economic burden of the conflict, and make disengagement that much more difficult.

Although an American military victory was deemed impossible, U.S. forces retained the capacity to deny success to the North Vietnamese. It followed that since neither side could win on the battlefield, both would be willing to accept a compromise settlement. Washington would maintain a security shield for the Saigon government, but at a reduced cost in American blood and treasure by scaling down its participation in the fighting, making clear to the enemy that it could not win, and negotiating an acceptable settlement. This close-hold policy estimate became Clifford's blueprint to get the United States out of Vietnam. The secretary articulated some telling points at a White House luncheon on 21 May, declaring that the limitations placed on the American military—no invasion of North Vietnam, no raids into cross-border sanctuaries, no mining of NVN's major ports—left the United States unable to win a stalemated war. With military victory impossible, only negotiations at Paris offered any hope of a settlement.[76]

Maxwell Taylor had concluded that the current low-key approach to reinforcing MACV and reconstituting the strategic reserve units diminished the international perception of U.S. deterrent strength. On 6 May he suggested that the president obtain a progress report from State, OSD, and the JCS on plans to reinforce American forces in Vietnam, to expand South Vietnamese forces, and to rebuild the strategic reserve.[77] At the president's direction, Clifford requested the JCS to address these matters, particularly the readiness of the diminished strategic reserves to respond to possible enemy pressure elsewhere around the globe.

They replied on 21 May that no Army forces based in the United States were available for deployment to Vietnam; sustaining additional Marine units necessitated mobilization. Increased Navy carrier support for Southeast Asia would denude naval units operating in the Mediterranean. Only four Air Force tactical squadrons based in the United States, two of them reserve units, were ready for immediate deployment. According to the Joint Chiefs, diminished readiness and reduced strategic capabilities limited U.S. responses to communist bloc initiatives outside of Southeast Asia. In no less than five instances in their reply, the Joint Chiefs reiterated that the recall of 56,877 reservists they had sought on 2 and 6 April had been turned down. Actual call-up of 24,550 was authorized on 11 April; this number was reduced by 1,262 on 7 May.[78]

Meanwhile the situation in Vietnam appeared to worsen. Wheeler's 20 May update for Clifford stressed that the enemy offensive showed no signs of diminishing, a massive infiltration from North Vietnam was under way, and an accompanying logistics buildup indicated Hanoi was strengthening its ability to fight in South Vietnam. At the president's request, the Joint Chiefs were quietly evaluating military options in late May should the Paris talks stall or collapse entirely. The options mulled by the Chiefs resembled those that Clifford had offered the Wise Men in late March: continue the current strategy; expand the ground war into Laos, Cambodia, or North Vietnam; revise strategy to minimize U.S. casualties; reinstitute the bombing of North Vietnam or cease all bombing of North Vietnam.[79]

The Joint Chiefs again called for expanding the air and ground wars. They opposed relinquishing territory as defeatist because any withdrawal would cede the battlefield initiative to the enemy and only prolong the war. Nitze disagreed, questioning their assumptions and lack of any end game should their recommendations be implemented. ISA Assistant Secretary Warnke prepared a draft presidential memorandum that refuted the JCS proposals and advocated continuing the current course in Vietnam, developing contingency plans to respond as needed to enemy actions directly endangering U.S. forces, attempting to broaden the talks to include South Vietnam and Viet Cong representatives, and informing Hanoi that under appropriate conditions the United States would halt the bombing of the North.[80]

The administration's team in Saigon, however, had reacted to the communists' May offensive with renewed fighting spirit. In a 10 May cable, Bunker called for a tough bargaining stance to dispel North Vietnamese illusions that the United States could not fight and negotiate simultaneously. Late in May he concurred with Westmoreland's plan to expand the ground war by allowing air and artillery strikes six miles deep into the tri-border area of Cambodia during hot pursuit of the enemy. Acknowledging that the North Vietnamese might respond to such a move by breaking off the Paris talks, Bunker assessed the payoff worth the risk. During a 30 May visit to the Texas ranch, Westmoreland also pressed on the president his views about hot pursuit.[*] In early June, MACV attributed the country-wide attacks to a concerted effort by the communists to create an "aura of success" in order to gain the upper hand in Paris. With the enemy bent on perpetuating

---

[*] Westmoreland had returned to the United States for congressional hearings on his appointment as chief of staff. He flew to the ranch to present a battlefield assessment to the president.

"the fiction of offensive momentum" and inflicting maximum casualties on U.S. forces, OSD proposals to open substantive negotiations with Hanoi and deescalate the fighting seemed to run against the tide.[81]

Dissension over Vietnam policy within the administration manifested itself in distrust and secretiveness. The State Department withheld from Clifford for a full day Soviet Premier Kosygin's cable of 5 June that implied an end to the bombing of North Vietnam might lead to a breakthrough and open the way to a peaceful solution. During the next four days, Rusk downplayed the Soviet initiative and, contrary to Clifford's position, sought guarantees before ending the bombing. Harriman later remonstrated with Rusk for undercutting Clifford, but the secretary of state replied that Clifford had "lost his nerve" since taking over the Pentagon. Similarly, during this period Walt Rostow told the executive secretary of the State Department, Benjamin Read, not to distribute to OSD the sensitive cables from the U.S. negotiating team in Paris. Read, after contacting Rusk and receiving approval for the distribution, established a private messenger service through Colonel Pursley to keep Clifford informed about events in Paris.[82] In the midst of the bureaucratic infighting, routine summertime reassignments and retirements proved fortuitous for Clifford's overall strategy.

With his 31 July retirement pending, Admiral Sharp, a vigorous proponent of heavier bombing of North Vietnam, was replaced as CINCPAC by Admiral John S. McCain, Jr., effective 2 July. Sharp had recommended McCain to the president as his successor, praising him as a decisive officer yet one able to work well with others and having political experience from his days as chief of the Navy's legislative liaison office.[83] Army Chief of Staff Harold Johnson had decided against a one-year extension and opted to retire on 30 June. His decision enabled the president to appoint Westmoreland chief of staff effective 3 July, a move long in the works.

The previous January, McNamara had urged the president either to extend both Generals Wheeler and Johnson for another year or to make Westmoreland the Army's chief of staff because "all of the chiefs" believed that after more than four years in Vietnam he should be reassigned. After discussing the issue with Senator Russell, the president informed Westmoreland on 23 March. Johnson initially wanted to meet the general in Hawaii on 5 April to explain his decision, but in the aftermath of the assassination of Dr. Martin Luther King, he requested Westmoreland proceed to Washington where he arrived 6 April. Johnson assured Westmoreland, disappointed and angry that he was being relieved of his command, that McNamara had recommended the appointment well before the Tet offensive erupted and showed him McNamara's memo. The president felt that Westmoreland showed "some bitterness," believing a lack of support in Washington made him the war's scapegoat. On 10 April General Creighton Abrams, a blunt-spoken soldier and in Taylor's words, "honest to the point of sometimes giving offense," was named the new COMUSMACV, effective 11 June.[84] During the interim, Abrams's outspokenness nearly cost him the assignment.

Bunker's reports of the enemy offensive, highlighting the effects of the devastation in Saigon on civilian morale, were relayed by Rusk at the 14 May Tuesday luncheon. Sometime later, Bunker forwarded to Clifford a 12 May report from a U.S. embassy foreign service officer in Saigon that ordinary Vietnamese civilians were bitterly resentful of the Americans for being the cause of so much death and destruction in the city. The president expressed concern about adverse press coverage that placed the blame for collateral damage on MACV's excessive use of force. On 4 June Clifford had Wheeler ask Abrams to change tactics against enemy infiltrators so as to minimize civilian casualties and property damage.[85]

Abrams's 5 June response dismissed most of the embassy report as unbalanced and asserted that despite unavoidable damage resulting from hostile operations, MACV activity had prevented the enemy from doing even more violence to the city. He denounced Washington's gullibility in accepting "raw data" from embassy sources and believing the accuracy of TV and newspaper reports. Coming on the heels of Warnke's advice that heavy-handed U.S. tactics might produce a backlash among the South Vietnamese, Abrams's temerity "sent Clifford into orbit." Was the MACV commander-designee, Clifford demanded of Wheeler, implying that he did not need the secretary's guidance and that the military commander was a better judge of evaluating State Department cables than the DoD secretariat? Was Abrams fit to take over command? On receiving a copy of Clifford's blistering memorandum through Wheeler, Abrams promptly apologized, admitted he was wrong, and gave reassurance that he had changed "tactics and techniques" to reduce collateral destruction and minimize civilian losses. As Clifford later put it, "the storm blew over."[86]

The tempest may have passed, but it left its mark on Clifford and on the relationship between the Defense boss and the field commander. Confronting Abrams on operational issues, Clifford made plain that he had no intention of relying solely on MACV's appreciation of the situation. He established even closer oversight of the ground war, in a way McNamara had never done. Further, he repudiated the firepower-intensive strategy endorsed by McNamara and Westmoreland. Finally, Clifford demanded total allegiance from his subordinates as he worked to extricate the United States from the Vietnam sinkhole. Firmly convinced the war could not be won militarily but only by political settlement, he stated before a Senate committee late in May, "I just don't want to go on fighting indefinitely in Vietnam."[87]

Settling In or Getting Out

At heavy cost to both sides, the allies blunted the communist May offensive, but Hanoi persisted in pushing fresh troops and supplies southward while building up its strength in the panhandle of North Vietnam along the DMZ. Abrams wanted to counter the enemy threat by using his maneuver units in a mobile role, not leaving them tied down defending fixed bases. In early June, he opted to aban-

don Khe Sanh, despite the adverse publicity sure to follow. Well aware of the political sensitivity, the president finally approved the withdrawal on 20 June, with
the stipulation that any public announcement be crafted to minimize unfavorable
publicity and triumphant enemy propaganda. Nonetheless, the official closing of
the Khe Sanh base on 5 July caused "incredulity and bewilderment in the United
States." If the base had been worth fighting and dying for a few months earlier,
what had changed to make it expendable? There was no sound-bite answer, although Abrams explained that it was "to get into a better position to meet the
increased enemy threat" by allowing mobile forces "to attack, intercept, reinforce,
or take whatever action is most appropriate."[88]

Beyond the political and psychological embarrassment of withdrawing from
Khe Sanh, Johnson worried that North Vietnam would capitalize on the U.S. self-
imposed bombing restrictions to jeopardize other American forces in I Corps. Hanoi's buildup north of the DMZ also troubled Wheeler, who warned the president
on 24 June that the full effects of communist preparations would not come until
the late summer and fall. On balance, however, he believed the enemy position in
South Vietnam had deteriorated markedly since 31 March 1968.[89]

Concerned over intelligence reports of another communist offensive in August, on 10 July the president instructed Clifford, during his coming visit to Vietnam, to query Abrams regarding the condition of the South Vietnamese forces, his
ability to meet the expected attacks, and MACV's urgent needs, if any. In subsequent guidance, he told Clifford to accomplish these tasks while simultaneously
identifying spending cuts in South Vietnam to help offset the $3 billion mandated
reduction in DoD expenditures.[90]

During Clifford's visit to Vietnam between 13–18 July, MACV described a
badly wounded foe, consistently thrown off balance by Abrams's mobile spoiling
operations, but one still determined to exploit the psychological success achieved
by Tet in the United States by conducting further opportunistic offensives. Abrams
assured Clifford that MACV had the resources to cope with the anticipated assault
now reckoned to commence as early as 25 July but more probably late in August
with attacks against Saigon and I Corps. Wheeler, who accompanied Clifford,
came away impressed by the progress in the five months since his last visit, con-
trasting the recovery of the South Vietnamese forces since Tet with the continuing heavy losses and lower quality of VC/NVA units. MACV forces, according
to Wheeler, had the confidence and capability to meet the next phase of enemy
attacks. Clifford, reflecting Johnson's concerns, told Abrams of the critical need
during a presidential election year to increase the use of South Vietnamese troops,
reduce American casualties, and defuse domestic criticism of the war.[91]

Much to Bunker's chagrin, Clifford also confronted President Thieu and Vice
President Ky at the presidential palace over several contentious issues, some longstanding, such as government corruption, and others potentially troublesome—for
example, Ky's ploy to strengthen South Vietnam's armed forces by diverting more

American dollars to pay for ARVN amenities and salaries. Clifford left Saigon sorely disappointed in the lack of progress in South Vietnamese units, Wheeler's estimation notwithstanding, and convinced that if he needed additional proof that the United States should get out of Vietnam, "this trip did it."[92]

Clifford's report to the president on 18 July stressed that U.S. commanders expected another large-scale enemy offensive but were prepared and confident they could defeat the attackers. South Vietnamese forces, however, despite some improvements, still lacked leadership, training, and equipment. Beyond his formal written report, Clifford made three points orally to the president. First, he reiterated that current political restrictions, particularly the defensive approach to U.S. military operations, made the war unwinnable. Wheeler, according to Clifford, shared that sentiment but felt constrained from saying so in front of his fellow Chiefs. Second, the secretary was convinced that the corrupt Saigon regime had no reason to end the war so long as it was protected by half a million U.S. troops and enjoyed a "golden flow of money." Third, he urged Johnson to let the South Vietnamese know that the president intended to do everything possible to end the war during his remaining months in office. Johnson found the proposals too radical at the moment; when a hawkish Rusk disagreed with Clifford's assessment, the president again found himself in the uncomfortable role of having to mediate between his senior advisers.[93]

On 30 July and again on 2 August, an apprehensive president discussed privately with Wheeler the possibility of resuming air and naval operations between the 19th and 20th parallels should the enemy strike South Vietnam's cities and warned publicly that Hanoi's preparations for new attacks made further restrictions on U.S. military action unthinkable. Sensing Johnson was reverting to a hard line, on 1 August Clifford ordered his immediate staff to prepare a position paper for his forthcoming meeting with the president in the hope of persuading him that further concessions to the North Vietnamese might produce results.[94]

Fighting While Negotiating

Abrams's decision to abandon static combat bases like Khe Sanh freed his troops to spoil the NVA/VC third general offensive launched 17–18 August. After an initial enemy success at Tay Ninh, ARVN and U.S. soldiers drove communist troops from the city in 24 hours using small arms fire to minimize loss of life and destruction of property. About two weeks into the attacks, Abrams estimated the enemy—badly off balance, his plans disrupted in I Corps, his losses heavy with little gain—was perhaps reconsidering his options. To exploit the advantage, Abrams requested authorization for American troops to pursue hostile units across the Cambodian border for a distance of 20 kilometers. These brigade-size infantry sweeps, designed to last up to five days with support by tactical air and B-52 strikes, would destroy NVA/VC base camps and supplies within the Cambodian sanctuaries, but the president turned down the proposal in mid-October.[95]

Abrams's timing was as inopportune as his plan was impractical. Far from being in a position to expand the war, the president found himself struggling to sustain support for the conflict at current levels. Nor could the depleted U.S. strategic reserve permit a meaningful response to crises elsewhere, such as the Soviet invasion of Czechoslovakia on 20 August. At home the overheated domestic economy demanded a $6 billion reduction in federal expenditures, with half coming from DoD spending; open revolt over the president's Vietnam policy was brewing in his own party. Johnson could hardly enlarge the ground war in Southeast Asia, but neither could he scale it down. Even Clifford, despite the apparent failure of the third Communist general offensive, could foresee no troop reductions "until there is some development that causes us to decide that we can bring some home."[96]

By early September both Abrams and Wheeler suspected that the enemy might try to offset battlefield reverses by seeking a cease-fire in place. On 15 September U.S. delegates in Paris learned that Hanoi, for whatever reasons, was prepared to begin peace discussions once the bombing of North Vietnam ended.[97] Wheeler expressed confidence in a solid U.S. military foundation for talks. Bunker in a cable of 24 September remained skeptical over Hanoi's seriousness of purpose in negotiating, citing its refusal to consider Saigon's participation. Several weeks later, the North Vietnamese delegates in Paris questioned whether the United States would stop bombing if Hanoi agreed to Saigon's participation in the talks. Abrams and Bunker interpreted this as additional evidence that the communist regime had abandoned hope of a battlefield victory and was shifting its attention to the conference table. In a series of meetings during 14 October, the president sought the advice of his civilian advisers and the Joint Chiefs on a bombing halt. Clifford, convinced that something had happened to weaken the enemy's resolve, believed that the United States could capitalize on the advantage by shifting its strategic position to test Hanoi's good faith. All agreed to a bombing halt provided aerial reconnaissance of North Vietnam continued; bombing would resume if the communists violated the understanding.[98]

Within days of agreeing to negotiate, however, Hanoi insisted on further concessions from the United States, leaving the president and secretary of defense fearful that agreed upon deals were coming undone. Intensive negotiations concluded on 27 October when North Vietnam acceded to the original U.S. conditions that the Saigon government be included in peace talks and that the North neither violate the DMZ nor shell or attack the South's cities. With a bargain struck, the president had Abrams return secretly to Washington to reaffirm his commitment to the bombing cessation, indicate the risks to American troops, and lend his support and credibility to the president's decision.[99]

Arriving in the dead of night on 29 October, Abrams was whisked from Andrews Air Force Base in nearby Maryland to the White House for a 2:30 a.m. meeting with the president and his political and military advisers. Why, the president asked, did Abrams favor a bombing halt now after having opposed one in August? The subsequent successful aerial interdiction campaign in the North Vietnam panhandle region and the enemy's inability to replace losses in I Corps had convinced him, Abrams replied, that the bombing could end without fear of creating additional American casualties. The MACV commander had full confidence in this new step. The decision to end the bombing, according to one historian, was stage-managed in "vintage Johnson" fashion.[100] But even Lyndon Johnson could not choreograph everything.

President Thieu, fully informed about the negotiations, had already agreed in principle to the American conditions, but he now reneged. During the course of the 29 October all-day meetings, Clifford expressed his outrage at Thieu's defiance of the "will of [the] President and [the] American people." He suggested Thieu's lame excuse that Saigon could not get a delegation to Paris in three days was possibly a cover for a more "ominous, even sinister" agenda.[101]

Clifford still insisted the negotiations go forward as planned because it was too late to turn back, but Johnson vacillated, sensitive to the charge that any such move before the elections could be construed as politically motivated. Reluctant to break with South Vietnam, he opted to postpone decisions "a day or two" to make the stakes clear to Thieu. Supposing the Saigon leader might stall in expectation that a Republican victory in the November presidential election would redound to South Vietnam's benefit, the president was quick to say, "I can't help him anymore, neither can anyone else who has my job." Exasperated by the "intolerable" situation brought on by Thieu's intransigence, Wheeler confessed, "For the first time I begin to wonder if I have been right for the past five and one half years." Unable to convince Thieu to support the forthcoming negotiations, on 31 October Johnson finally announced the bombing halt without the concurrence of the South Vietnamese government. The sorry episode exposed the futility of the administration's Vietnam policy. Despite the United States having "invested 29,000 dead and $75 billion,"[102] the conflict in South Vietnam seemed no nearer an acceptable resolution.

Prior to a planned nationwide address on 31 October, Johnson briefly assembled the NSC and other staff members in the cabinet room to announce his decision to stop all bombing of North Vietnam. Westmoreland described a meeting "conducted in considerable haste with a certain amount of emotion, and no voice of dissent . . . raised," despite lingering Joint Chiefs skepticism about North Vietnamese willingness to negotiate seriously. Westmoreland viewed the decision as an attempt to affect the 5 November presidential election as well as to place Johnson in the historical record as a peacemaker. That evening, to a national television and radio audience, the president declared that all air, naval, and artillery bombardment of North Vietnam would cease on 1 November at 8:00 a.m., Washington time, and talks with Hanoi would commence five days later.[103]

On 5 November 1968 Republican Richard M. Nixon, in a narrow victory over Democratic candidate Hubert H. Humphrey, was elected the 37th president of the United States. The next day, the United States announced the indefinite postponement of the Paris talks, ostensibly because the South Vietnamese needed more time to prepare for the sessions. Furious at South Vietnamese recalcitrance, at a 12 November press conference Clifford criticized Saigon's last-minute change of mind and warned that the president might decide to negotiate at Paris without them. On 27 November the Saigon government finally indicated that it would participate in the Paris talks, but soon after arriving in the French capital its delegation raised procedural questions, including the "famously stupid" argument over the configuration of the conference table that would not be resolved until 16 January.[104]

Although Abrams had supported a complete bombing halt, the aggressive commander still wanted to carry the war to the North Vietnamese be they in Cambodia or in the southern half of the DMZ. Abrams proposed in mid-October to take the war to Cambodia, and in mid-November he recommended small-unit operations to monitor the activity as well as verify the identity of the troops in the DMZ. After Clifford agreed, MACV probes between 24 November and 3 December resulted in the capture of prisoners who were plainly North Vietnamese. Consequently Abrams received approval to continue the patrols indefinitely, but his request for removal of restrictions on the size of the operations was turned down by the president.[105]

At a White House meeting on 3 December Rusk reminded the president that "we agreed to pour it on in South Vietnam after the bombing was halted." Over Clifford's objections Johnson sided with his secretary of state. Believing the North Vietnamese had failed the American test and afraid of being accused of a sellout, he even suggested that a resumption of the bombing would be justified. Two days later the president approved probes into the southern half of the DMZ for the purpose of driving enemy forces north of the demarcation line. On 13 December, the Joint Chiefs requested that Clifford authorize hot pursuit of the enemy as far as three miles deep into Cambodia, employing battalion-size forces. Clifford's 21 December reply deferred any action as he continued to oppose such potentially war-widening forays.[106]

Clifford worked behind the scenes for a "piecemeal disengagement" involving a mutual withdrawal of forces and trade-offs to reduce the level of violence, taking care to avoid leaks that would incense the president or harm the peace talks. His official pronouncements were vague, such as his statement to Congress in January 1969 that pullouts could come in FY 1971 provided the war ended "in such a way that we can withdraw our forces." The president's mood fluctuated during his final two months in office as he second-guessed his 31 October decision, blamed South Vietnamese President Thieu for his inability to end the war, and lashed out at his closest advisers.[107] To the very end of his presidency, Vietnam defied an American solution and thwarted Lyndon Johnson. A presidency that opened in tragedy closed on a similarly somber note.

Vietnam frustrated Clifford also. He sought a political exit but did not consider the consequences or indeed question how a divided, unpopular, and corrupt Saigon regime might carry on a war. Nor, at times, did Clifford seem to care. "If they can't hold themselves together," he told his staff in mid-December, "it's just too damn bad." His disgust with the South Vietnamese, exasperation with the president, and bitterness toward the State Department rendered him more and more pessimistic during the remainder of his stay in office.[108]

Neither escalation in 1965 nor de-escalation in 1968 produced the results the Johnson administration sought. Instead, as Lyndon Johnson turned over the presidency to Richard Nixon, the United States stayed locked in a stalemate in South Vietnam fighting a war that America's political and military leaders could neither win nor end.

Chapter VIII

The Air War Against North Vietnam: Escalation to Cessation, 1967–1968

Two years of a stop and start air war had proven as ineffective as the ground war in persuading North Vietnam to forsake its support of the insurgency in the South. It had become an open secret that the president and secretary of defense reviewed and approved all targets nominated by the Joint Chiefs, that they firmly controlled the air campaign, and that months of deliberation by civilian advisers preceded any bombing escalation; yet for all the micromanaging, the civilian-dictated air policy had achieved little in the way of decisive results. Advocates for intensifying the bombing took Johnson and McNamara to task for ignoring "the counsel of military professionals" and running the war "with a risky civilian dilettantism." Doves were equally impatient. McNamara, though he may have privately sympathized with them, believed that Washington could not unilaterally end the bombing without corresponding concessions from the other side; yet Hanoi repeatedly rejected negotiations while bombs were falling on its homeland.[1] By early 1967, with his earlier self-assured confidence long gone, a frustrated and anguished secretary of defense found his efforts to reorient bombing strategy hindered by few palatable options, diminished credibility, and increasingly open disagreement with his military advisers.

The State of the Air War at the Outset of 1967

The administration used a lull in the bombing at the start of 1967 to take stock and plan the next phase of the air war.[2] McNamara's testimony before Senate committees in January highlighted the growing divisiveness over the air campaign not only between OSD civilians and the JCS but also between the defense

202

secretary and Senate hawks. Skepticism, if not outright hostility, greeted many of McNamara's contentions. When he testified on 23 January that bombing the Haiphong docks would have little effect on North Vietnam's petroleum importation, Sen. Stuart Symington, who had been the first secretary of the Air Force, wondered sarcastically if McNamara "wouldn't want to go farther and say the more you hit the docks the better it would be for the North Vietnamese." Testifying alongside McNamara, General Wheeler contradicted the secretary's claims that airpower had not significantly reduced the southward movement of personnel and supplies. Paradoxically, McNamara also declared the bombing effort a success in that it had improved South Vietnamese morale, increased the cost that the North Vietnamese paid for infiltration, and, most importantly, provided a bargaining chip that Washington could play to its advantage. Yet the press reported a redacted version of McNamara's testimony made public in mid-February as an acknowledgment that the bombing of North Vietnam had failed.[3]

McNamara began 1967 as a reluctant advocate of continuing the bombing, if only because abandoning the air campaign would remove what little leverage the administration had as it groped for a solution to end the stalemate. Throughout 1967 his stance on the air war would periodically shift or seesaw out of loyalty to Johnson (when the president saw no way forward but escalation), lingering ambivalence, or a need to make concessions in order not to become marginalized as his attitude became more defeatist. But clearly McNamara had shed any illusions about the efficacy of the bombardment, and there was no mistaking that he and his military commanders were moving in fundamentally opposite directions even as their positions briefly converged early in the year.

In January Sharp and the Joint Chiefs proposed intensified and sustained bombing attacks in the Hanoi-Haiphong area against electric power, industrial, transportation, military, POL, and port targets. McNamara and Rusk, along with Rostow, endorsed nine targets having military significance but advised deferring the others, all industrial, until at least after the Tet holidays (8–12 February). Their advice took into account an ambitious diplomatic initiative on which the Joint Chiefs do not appear to have been consulted.* Named Sunflower, this latest effort to start up negotiations with North Vietnam consisted of three contacts: one through the embassies of the two countries in Moscow; a second via a direct personal appeal to Ho Chi Minh; and a third through British Prime Minister Wilson and Soviet Premier Kosygin.[4]

Johnson had earlier described for Wilson the so-called "Phase A-Phase B" formula: the United States would stop bombing (Phase A); in exchange Hanoi would cease infiltration (Phase B). During Kosygin's February visit to London, Wilson,

---

* The JCS were not asked for their views on any aspect of the initiative, and it is unclear whether they as a group, or the chairman separately, ever discussed the matter with McNamara or the president (*JCS and the War in Vietnam*, pt 3:40/13-14).

with White House approval, discussed the forthcoming proposal with the Soviet leader. On 8 February the president, in conjunction with the Tet bombing pause, informed Ho that he would stop the bombing after Hanoi quit its infiltration. This changed the conditions for talks and undercut the Kosygin-Wilson discussions. Once the differences became apparent, Wilson urged Washington to extend the pause according to the original terms.[5]

Johnson initially refused because the North Vietnamese were taking advantage of it to rush in troops and supplies. The president stated that a pilot reported the southbound traffic looked "like the New Jersey turnpike." Wheeler and McNamara were anxious to counteract the massive communist supply buildup and had opposed British requests to continue the suspension beyond the holiday. On 11 February, despite Kosygin's talks in London, Johnson approved McNamara's proposal to resume bombing as far north as the 20th parallel. Then came news that Ho would soon reply to the president's personal message; this together with the opposition of U.S. ambassador in London David K. E. Bruce to any bombing in the interim persuaded the president to continue the pause.[6] Wheeler objected that prolonging the suspension would increase the danger to allied forces, but after a flurry of last-minute activity on the 13th that Prime Minister Wilson thought productive, the JCS chairman agreed to another brief extension, feeling that a few more hours could do little harm since the North Vietnamese had completed their buildup. Having twice extended the pause, Johnson, even as he granted the short stay, grew convinced that the North Vietnamese had played him for a fool and that higher U.S. casualties might result.[7]

McNamara, equally disturbed by the North's buildup near the DMZ, interpreted Hanoi's actions as a de facto rejection of the U.S. proposal. On 13 February he insisted that the communists would only string out further talks, making it extremely difficult to justify renewed bombing. Deprived of its best bargaining chip, the administration, in McNamara's words, would be "in [a] hell of [a] fix." Wheeler described McNamara "fighting like a tiger to get operations cranked up again." Air strikes resumed over North Vietnam on 14 February; the next day Ho answered Johnson's personal letter by accusing the United States of aggression, war crimes, and endangering world peace. If the United States wanted direct talks, the communist leader stated, it must first stop the bombing.* Wheeler inferred from a conversation with McNamara that several factors—Ho's peremptory reply, Hanoi exploiting the Tet suspension to move additional supplies into the South, and turmoil in China† that offered a possible window of opportunity—may have swayed Johnson's thinking so that the president now seemed more receptive to increasing military pressure against North Vietnam, including expanding the air war.[8]

---

* The North Vietnamese Foreign Ministry released this high-level correspondence between Johnson and Ho on 21 March.

† Chinese officials were preoccupied with political and social upheaval related to the Cultural Revolution launched by Mao in May 1966.

The Targeting Debate

Once Rolling Thunder recommenced, the president sought views on the bombing's impact and whether and where to expand the number of targets. Mc-Naughton already regarded further escalation as pointless but thought intensive attacks against the southern panhandle of North Vietnam might be productive. On 17 February Rostow used a funnel metaphor to illustrate three options: interdict the top of the funnel to limit supplies coming into North Vietnam from China, hammer the Hanoi-Haiphong region in the middle of the funnel, or concentrate on targets in southern North Vietnam, the bottom of the funnel. On balance, Rostow favored the second option, particularly the destruction of North Vietnam's power plants. That afternoon the president discussed with Rostow, McNamara, Wheeler, and presidential consultant Maxwell Taylor the JCS recommendation to strike the power stations. Although extended deliberations did not result in any decisions, Johnson asked for several alternative courses of action by 22 February based on varying levels of risk outlined in Rostow's earlier proposals. Wheeler left convinced that there was "a new sense of urgency" about Rolling Thunder.[9]

At the follow-up White House meeting on 22 February, the president, Rusk, Wheeler, and McNamara discussed three levels of action proposed by the Chiefs: continue the status quo with minor escalation (for example, striking power plants); escalate the conflict with significant policy changes (for example, hitting MIG airfields); escalate the war with major policy changes (for example, unrestricted attacks on North Vietnam's airfields and dikes and the mining of ports). Frustrated as he was with maintaining the status quo, McNamara continued to believe that escalation would not stop NVA infiltration but only increase civilian casualties while unnecessarily risking a wider war. The president's compromise was Rolling Thunder 54, an incremental intensification of the air war that enabled him to hold to his middle ground by approving five new targets (one steel mill and four power plants) while maintaining the buffer zone along the China-North Vietnam border and restrictions in the Hanoi-Haiphong area.

Johnson downplayed the significance of the new attacks, portraying the impending strikes on North Vietnamese power plants and the mining of waterways south of the 20th parallel as a continuation, not an escalation, of military pressure against North Vietnam.[10] Two power plants far from heavily populated areas* were struck on 24 and 25 February, but the president minimized the raids at his 27 February news conference by describing them as a "more far-reaching" action but not a step-up of the war.[11]

Wheeler believed the president was now amenable to hitting the remaining electric power facilities. According to Wheeler, Johnson, convinced that the bomb-

---

* The Bac Giang power plant was about 25 nautical miles northeast of Hanoi and the Hon Gai facility about an equal distance northeast of Haiphong. Between them the facilities produced about 20 percent of North Vietnam's electricity.

ing was hurting Hanoi, felt a compelling sense "to get on with the war militarily" in order to silence his critics. His perception of recent battlefield success as the result of sound military advice disposed him to discount "contrary [civilian] advice which has not achieved similar success." Nonetheless, Wheeler cautioned his field commanders early in March not to complain publicly about restrictions; "escalation" was still a dirty word in Washington.[12]

On 2 March New York Sen. Robert Kennedy called for a halt to the bombing of North Vietnam without requiring up-front reciprocal concessions by Hanoi. Johnson solicited the views of his top aides—Rostow, McNamara, Rusk, and Taylor—as to the merits of Kennedy's proposal. To a man, they disagreed with the notion of a one-sided cessation of the bombing. McNamara, however, wrote to the president that a unilateral U.S. action, such as suspending the bombing north of 20 degrees, might induce Moscow to pressure its Hanoi client to enter into discussions. If talks progressed smoothly, the administration could suspend the bombing completely.[13]

Rostow reviewed McNamara's position and explained to Johnson that McNamara was "thrashing about for a short cut" to end the war before 1968 election-year politics forced the nation into an unsatisfactory settlement. According to Rostow, to get the war off dead center, McNamara would even risk a brief escalation by taking out all power and cement plants in North Vietnam by the end of March, then stop the bombing north of 20 degrees in hopes of encouraging the Soviets to mediate direct talks with Hanoi. The secretary believed—without hard evidence, noted Rostow—that bombing urban areas in the North only stiffened North Vietnam's will and poisoned public opinion in the United States as well as abroad, but he was willing to entertain a bold stroke—mining Haiphong harbor or striking the power plants—if it might force the issue.[14]

Confronted with conflicting proposals, the president gathered South Vietnamese leaders, U.S. military field commanders, embassy officials, and his principal staff members on Guam on 20–21 March to reevaluate the war. At McNamara's request, Sharp briefed the attendees on additional military measures that could be taken against North Vietnam. Advised by Wheeler to "avoid any semblance of putting pressure on the President" in the form of a "hard sell," Sharp was to lay out "logically and with no emotion the military advantages" of a seven-month campaign directed against 60 targets in five "target systems" (for example, POL, power facilities, military complexes, and so forth), gradually closing in on Hanoi and Haiphong. No decisions were expected, and there were none. But on the day he returned from Guam, 22 March, Johnson authorized one-time strikes against two Haiphong power plants, calling for extreme caution to avoid hitting foreign shipping in the harbor and prohibiting attacks on 26 March, Easter Sunday.*[15]

---

* Bad weather and the imposition of temporary restrictions prevented the precision attacks on the two Haiphong power plants until 20 April. There were just four operational flying days in March and six in April. See msg CINCPAC to JCS, 210430Z Jun 67, Cable files, OSD Hist.

Despite poor flying weather, by mid-March pilots had struck every originally authorized Rolling Thunder 54 target at least once. In mid-April Sharp called for reducing or eliminating some of the Haiphong-Hanoi restricted areas where no air strikes had occurred since the previous December. McNamara agreed, and on 14 April, aboard Air Force One, he and Johnson, apparently without consulting Rusk, approved renewed attacks on two Haiphong thermal power plants. Navy aircraft carried out the strikes six days later.[16]

On 22 April the president approved Rolling Thunder 55, a wide-ranging list of targets in North Vietnam's northeast quadrant, among them two MIG air bases as well as a cement plant and an ammunition dump in Haiphong; only the Hanoi power plant had been deleted from the JCS-proposed list. U.S. warplanes flew into the teeth of enemy MIG, AAA, and SAM air defenses as they attacked MIG fields, POL installations, and industrial or military targets in the northeast quadrant. During the week of 21–28 April, 16 U.S. aircraft were lost.[17] McNamara informed his staff members of the president's decision only on 24 April, revealing his underlying rationale for endorsing the latest target list by adding, "Let's get this behind us to show it won't solve the problem." He saw the administration at a "watershed," similar in magnitude to the major decisions of mid-1965, that demanded lengthy and "intense examination" of policy with no firm commitments anticipated before July.[18] Whatever McNamara may have had in mind, the reevaluation of the air campaign proved more ad hoc than comprehensive and less calculated than reactive as competing viewpoints vied for presidential approval.

Wheeler told the president at a 27 April top-level meeting that the bombing campaign was fast approaching the point where all worthwhile fixed targets except North Vietnam's ports would have been struck. Thus the administration would soon have to address attacking them. In the meantime Sharp was proposing still more new targets for Rolling Thunder 56 as the air campaign reached new levels of intensity. McNamara believed that escalation had to end, but it could stop only in the absence of suitable targets in North Vietnam. So at a 2 May presidential meeting that approved the Rolling Thunder 56 package, he supported short-term escalation in the belief that striking the power plants would eliminate the last significant targets in the Hanoi-Haiphong area, thereby enabling the administration to "cut back to the 20th parallel." The increasing intensity of the bombing and Sharp's proposals to strike still more new targets around Hanoi and Haiphong disturbed McNamara who, according to Rostow, felt "rational control over targeting was getting out of his hands."[19]

In early May a flurry of recommendations regarding the future direction of the air campaign reached the president. McGeorge Bundy, no longer a member of the administration, advised against escalation. He opposed suspending bombing without concessions by Hanoi, but, questioning the worth of hitting strategic targets such as electric power facilities or ports, he recommended concentrating on interdiction bombing along infiltration routes to the south. In response Wheeler insisted that air strikes against the North's power system had denied or disrupted electricity to war-supporting facilities and industries ranging from airfields to ports; he urged attacking yet unstruck power plants and ports. Among the administration's senior civilians, however, "the weight of opinion" had shifted against further intensification of the air war.[20]

McNaughton drafted a paper that declared the risks of attacking or mining Hanoi's ports unacceptable; he again recommended limiting the bombing to the North Vietnamese panhandle between 17 and 20 degrees. Lighter enemy defenses in that region would result in fewer aircraft and pilot losses while making possible some progress in disrupting infiltration. McNaughton sought to create the circumstances for an eventual positive North Vietnamese response to a clear U.S. signal of restraint. Rostow wanted to destroy the Hanoi power station and then switch the air offensive to the southern panhandle. On 9 May McNamara and Vance offered an approach that would allow bombing only south of the 20th parallel once the Hanoi power installation was taken out.[21]

The same day State Department experts, backed by CIA Director Richard Helms, advised Rusk that restricting operations primarily to south of the 20th parallel was generally the best strategy "strictly in terms of maximum effect in bringing Hanoi to change." In Rostow's view, the remaining presidential "gut decisions" concerned whether to hit the Hanoi power plant, the only "truly important" remaining target, to close enemy ports, and to cut the rail lines to China. Most other JCS-proposed targets could be attacked over time without exposing the administration to charges of reckless escalation.[22]

McNamara was ready to strike the Hanoi power facility as soon as possible in order to "get it over with"; then, according to Rostow, he could say to the JCS that "all the truly significant targets in the Hanoi/Haiphong area have been hit" and the air war should be deescalated. The president's civilian advisers requested a tactical plan to attack the Hanoi power station that included a clear statement of anticipated civilian damage. They also wanted a review of JCS targets, both approved and pending, and unanimously opposed attacks against airfields, ports, and rail lines to China. Taylor, though in overall agreement, thought their renewed doubts about the efficiency of bombing would generate a new wave of administration pessimism likely to lead to concessions that would make the enemy tougher to deal with. Unless Hanoi responded with a compensatory retrenchment in military activity, MACV, whose April request for 200,000 additional men was still pending, would probably ask for even more ground troops.[23]

On 16 May, after months of discussion and indecision, the president finally authorized an attack on the Hanoi power plant, persuaded that the Navy's new guided bomb, the Walleye, had sufficient accuracy to limit civilian casualties. The attack was to be completed before Buddha's birthday (23 May) and the beginning of an official visit to Moscow by the British foreign minister. Only two aircraft, each with a Walleye, struck the target on 19 May; one bomb fell short and the other hit one end of the complex. A more successful restrike two days later put the plant out of commission. The next day, the 22nd, Johnson and McNamara reimposed the longstanding 10-mile bombing restriction in the Hanoi area.[24]

On the same day that aircraft first struck the Hanoi power plant, 19 May, in a direct appeal to the president, McNamara attempted to force a decision on future war policy. In a lengthy draft presidential memorandum, largely prepared by McNaughton and forwarded without State or JCS coordination, he explained the futility of bombing and his conviction that Hanoi would not negotiate until after the 1968 presidential election. No significant targets remained in North Vietnam unless the administration wanted to go after a few unattacked airfields and ports, an action that would risk military confrontation with China and the Soviet Union. Acknowledging the damaging effect of a bombing rollback on American troop morale, McNamara proposed to concentrate air attacks on North Vietnam below the 20th parallel commencing by late May, warning that the war was acquiring a momentum of its own that the administration had to stop before it led to national disaster.[25]

As the bombing debate reached a critical juncture, Johnson's advisers displayed what Rostow on 19 May termed "dangerously strong feelings" in the "official family" over the issue. As portrayed by Rostow, Rusk felt the anti-American sentiment created by the bombing campaign outweighed any military advantage. McNamara maintained the air war was neither cost-effective nor worth the resultant adverse domestic and diplomatic consequences. Wheeler argued the bombing was productive but could muster no firm supporting evidence because no one really knew the cumulative and indirect costs of the air campaign to the Hanoi government. In a bid for consensus, Rostow proposed to destroy the Hanoi power plant and then cut back on attacks against the North's major cities for several weeks. The scenario would avert what McNamara and Rusk felt was a dangerous pattern of progressive bombing escalation, afford an opportunity to seek a diplomatic solution, and allow time for Wheeler to refine and restate his case.[26]

Rostow's attempt at a compromise satisfied no one. Decisions again got deferred, the principals having invested too much emotion and conviction in their respective proposals to yield ground. Endless meetings and position papers that often culminated in nondecisions sowed only more frustration and mistrust. Johnson himself, journalist Stanley Karnow would write, "swung from depths of doubt to peaks of ferocity" during this period. Meanwhile, the administration was losing the race, as Enthoven defined the stakes, between stemming the erosion of public support for the war and finding a winning exit strategy.[27]

The Rift Widens

McNamara's DPM of 19 May torpedoed Rostow's attempts to reconcile policy differences in the "official family," though by that time disagreements were likely too great anyway. Wheeler warned Sharp and Westmoreland on 25 May that "the current OSD thrust is at considerable variance with our own thinking and proposals" and informed them of OSD's preference for interdiction attacks south of 20 degrees as part of a comprehensive strategic review of U.S. policy in Southeast Asia then under way in Washington. The thorough reassessment was never completed. As happened in mid-1965 when the Dominican Republic intervention interrupted deliberations about Vietnam, the outbreak of the Arab-Israeli War on 5 June 1967 caused disruption. The Six Day War quickly captured attention, crowding out an orderly approach to Vietnam policy.[28] Rather than framing a systematic reexamination of Vietnam policy, McNamara's 19 May memo served only as the focus of another disjointed debate.

Faulting the DPM for errors, distortions, and misrepresentations, the JCS subsequently dismissed the funnel metaphor as less apt than one of a sieve, with supplies for communist forces pouring into South Vietnam from all sides—through the DMZ, Laos, the South China Sea, Cambodia, and the rivers of the Mekong Delta. Self-imposed U.S. restraints would allow the North Vietnamese to reconstitute their forces, rebuild their damaged economy, strengthen their air defenses, and continue to import war materiel with impunity. Unaware that McNamara had already shared his views with the president, the Joint Chiefs almost two weeks after the fact requested that he not send the DPM to the White House.[29]

Rostow thought the defense secretary had overreacted to the JCS position. The presidential assistant reiterated his previously advocated middle course: avoid "progressive and mindless escalation of the bombing in the Hanoi-Haiphong area" while not taking "the heat off that area without an adequate return." The CIA also reacted negatively to the McNamara memo, declaring that the interdiction approach alone would neither reduce the flow of supplies southward nor decrease Hanoi's determination to continue the war. Once it became apparent that a "virtual sanctuary" existed north of the panhandle region, the enemy would increase air defenses and move SAMs into the area, and, with Chinese encouragement, enjoy greater incentive to persist in its protracted war strategy.[30]

Whether swayed by McNamara's 19 May memo or Rostow's advice, Johnson, as mentioned, on 22 May halted all air attacks within 10 miles of the North Vietnamese capital following destruction of the Hanoi power plant. He later recorded his feeling that the air strikes in Route Pack VI cost more in U.S. losses than the results justified. The military thought otherwise. Citing the success of Rolling Thunder operations since mid-April, on 29 May Sharp voiced sentiments shared by the Joint Chiefs. He sought the abolition of restrictions on targets and thought it unfortunate that just when pressure on Hanoi was increasing and the operational weather over the North improving, "we must back off."[31]

Before learning of McNamara's DPM, the JCS on 20 May had urged bombing and mining the port of Haiphong, the entry point for most military imports and the North's principal logistic base, attacking rail lines to China, and destroying airfields to prevent the anticipated introduction of sophisticated Soviet-manufactured weapons—from SAMs to artillery and guided missile patrol boats—into North Vietnam. As they requested, McNamara forwarded their views to the president. Also on 20 May, McNamara asked the JCS and others for analyses of two alternatives with respect to bombing of the North. The first was straightforward: concentrate on targets in North Vietnam's panhandle region. The second would end the bombing of fixed targets in favor of a countrywide interdiction campaign (except for the Hanoi-Haiphong environs). The JCS reply several days later predictably insisted that the air and naval campaign in the north be expanded and intensified to deny the aggressor a sanctuary.[32]

When they later became aware of McNamara's minimalist proposals in his 19 May DPM, the JCS argued that curtailing infiltration was only one part of a larger effort designed to drain the North's resistance; sustained bombing of fixed targets was equally important. Rather than hand the communists a respite by restricting air attacks to below the 20th parallel, the Chiefs, although willing to forego mining major ports, would hit less prominent port facilities, focusing the bombing mainly against the Hanoi-Haiphong region and the buffer zone along the Chinese frontier.[33]

In another DPM, 21 pages long and dated 12 June, McNamara reacted sharply to the JCS criticisms. What would escalation accomplish? Concentrated attacks to date against southern North Vietnam had not prevented the flow of enemy forces into South Vietnam. Moreover, the slow progress made by friendly forces in South Vietnam, a corrupt and incompetent Saigon government, rising U.S. casualties, and declining American public support for the war all argued against further intensifying the air campaign. Still unable to recommend a total bombing halt, however, McNamara lamely proposed that destruction of NVN supplies near their destinations in South Vietnam as opposed to their departure points in the ports and on the rail lines in North Vietnam would lessen risks of enlarging the conflict, reduce losses of U.S. airmen, and perhaps induce Hanoi to negotiate.[34]

Meanwhile the president had tried to engage the Soviet Union, as co-chairman of the Geneva Conference on Southeast Asia, to broker a diplomatic end to the conflict. The effort continued in early June when Rostow drafted an overture to Moscow that involved Washington stopping the bombing in anticipation of North Vietnam reciprocating by deescalating the conflict. It was anticipated that the White House would dispatch the letter promptly after the next attack on the Hanoi thermal power plant. The letter was never sent because on 13 June the Kremlin announced that it would send a large delegation to New York for an emergency United Nations meeting on the Middle East crisis. The following day Kosygin privately informed U.S. officials that he would welcome a visit with President Johnson. Rostow then advised the president to hold off bombing the Hanoi-Haiphong area until the Soviets had time to get the North Vietnamese leaders to agree to serious negotiations.[35] Attempts to enlist Soviet assistance formed the core of the president's position on Vietnam for the summit meeting with Kosygin held in the small New Jersey town of Glassboro on 23 and 25 June 1967.[*]

At their first session Johnson informed Kosygin that the United States would end the air attacks over North Vietnam if aggression against the South ceased. Kosygin confided later that day that in anticipation of this meeting he had contacted North Vietnamese Prime Minister Pham Van Dong who promised that if the United States stopped the bombing, Hanoi would go to the conference table. After discussing the proposition with Rusk and McNamara, two days later the president handed the Soviet leader a proposal offering to stop the bombing on the assumptions that talks with the North Vietnamese would begin immediately, that Hanoi's forces deployed near the DMZ would not move southward, and that allied forces in I Corps would not advance northward.[36] Although the president dropped the previous condition that North Vietnam must stop all infiltration if the United States ended the bombing, freezing North Vietnamese forces in place above the 17th parallel would have served the same purpose. Hanoi never responded to the offer presumably because in June it approved in principle a strategy for what became the 1968 Tet offensive.[37]

Against this backdrop, the president soon dispatched McNamara to Saigon.[†] During the secretary's July visit, Sharp maintained that the air war had turned in favor of the United States; it was imperative to hit the northeast quadrant and hit it hard. If Washington eliminated the "only offensive element of our strategy," he concluded, "I do not see how we can expect to win." According to Sharp, this infuriated McNamara by contradicting the message he wanted to take back to Washington. The solid front presented by the military in Saigon, Sharp believed, was responsible for the continuation of Rolling Thunder.[‡][38]

McNamara reported to the president on 12 July that the field commanders favored intensification and escalation of the air war. He also disputed military claims of improved bombing results and questioned whether the interdiction effort against railways in the North affected the war in the South. Wheeler disagreed, lauded the air campaign, and wanted to enhance it by removing the restrictions around Hanoi and Haiphong.[39] With public support of the seemingly endless

---

[*] Mindful of the ill effects of the February 1965 raids against North Vietnam while Kosygin was visiting his communist allies, one week before the meeting McNamara asked Wheeler to ensure there would be no provocative incidents while the Soviet premier was in the United States (memrcd McNamara, 16 Jun 67, fldr MFRs, box 1, McNamara Papers, Acc 71-A-3470).

[†] On the eve of the secretary's departure, 29 June, U.S. Navy jets accidentally strafed a Soviet merchant ship in Haiphong harbor. Anxious to preclude future incidents that might adversely affect the U.S.-Soviet dialogue on the Mideast and valuing Moscow's willingness to serve as an intermediary between Hanoi and Washington, the president promptly ordered initiation of a four-nautical-mile prohibited area around Haiphong but was otherwise reluctant to change the pattern of bombing operations (msg Wheeler to Sharp, 291929Z Jun 67, fldr Goodpaster Chron Files [Jan 65] Tab 171, Wheeler Papers; msg CJCS to CINCPAC, 302108Z Jun 67, Cable files, OSD Hist).

[‡] But see Chapter IV for Westmoreland's views on the meeting.

struggle continuing to slip along with Johnson's approval ratings, McNamara had a tough time making the case for the status quo. Adding to his problem, the Senate Preparedness Investigating Subcommittee (Stennis Committee), preparing for its August hearings on the conduct of the war, knew that all commanders in Vietnam favored intensified attacks on North Vietnam and agreed that restrictions on the air campaign would allow the enemy to move more war materiel to the front.[40]

Ever sensitive to the domestic political climate, the president shifted ground to regain flagging support. At a mid-July discussion of bombing policy he underscored the public's belief that civilian officials ignored military advice in the bombing of the North. Apparently oblivious to Johnson's concern, McNamara then dismissed targets that Sharp recommended in restricted areas, including Phuc Yen airfield, as "largely unimportant," likely to inflict high civilian casualties, and "not worth the loss of a single U.S. plane or pilot." Generally disregarding his defense secretary's arguments, the president proceeded to authorize Rolling Thunder 57, which included several targets, mainly dispersed petroleum storage and surface-to-air missile support facilities, within the Hanoi-Haiphong restricted zones. By siding with his generals, Johnson expected to defuse the mounting congressional criticism of his war policies that was sure to emerge during the forthcoming hearings. Concurrently, in order to keep congressional doves quiet and minimize charges of escalation, he ordered no more than three attacks per day on the newly approved targets. Sharp regarded the decision as a continuation of the piecemeal expansion that again pushed the "increasingly divisive issue of the air war" to the back burner and satisfied no one.[41]

The president sought to use airpower to accomplish several not always complementary goals simultaneously. He wanted to keep the military pressure on North Vietnam, but without provoking China or the Soviet Union. He wanted to keep congressional hawks and administration critics at bay, but without imperiling ongoing secret pursuit of direct negotiations with Hanoi. Above all, he was looking for some way to win or at least end the war. Despite all that McNamara had told him, he still held out hope that escalating the bombing might do the trick. With these considerations in mind, between 22 July and 5 August the president had Clifford and Taylor lead a fact-finding mission and make the rounds of U.S. allies in Asia, beginning with South Vietnam.

Besides the mission's officially stated purposes, the president evidently wanted its assessment of the bombing controversy. During discussions with General Westmoreland on 24 July the Washington emissaries requested on a close-hold basis a list of important but as yet restricted targets along with an explanation of their value and the risks involved in attacking them. Unable to understand why certain targets such as Phuc Yen air base and all hydroelectric power plants were off-limits, and convinced aggressive moves against some untouched targets would weaken Hanoi's will or ability to continue the war, they recommended to the president a review of bombing policy. Both Taylor and Clifford understood the political objections to taking out the port of Haiphong but pointed out that such action was "the biggest card remaining unplayed in our political poker game with Ho Chi Minh." They reiterated these themes during a White House luncheon on 5 August where they urged the president to improve the interdiction effort by narrowing the restricted zones around Hanoi and Haiphong as well as opening selected targets within the Chinese buffer zone.[42] About the same time that the presidential envoys were advocating escalation, a negotiating channel to Hanoi seemed to hold out great promise. It was at this pivotal juncture that McNamara suffered the loss of his confidant and close adviser, John McNaughton, who died in the crash of a commercial airliner on 19 July.[*]

The Pennsylvania Initiative

From mid-June into October 1967, with Rusk's approval, McNamara oversaw the Pennsylvania initiative. The overture to North Vietnam enlisted two French intermediaries working with U.S. representative Henry A. Kissinger, then a Harvard professor and consultant to the Department of State, in the administration's first coordinated effort to establish mutually agreeable negotiating conditions with Hanoi. The secretary pursued the latest offer quietly, not wishing to embarrass the U.S. government with the unwanted or misleading publicity that had surrounded earlier negotiating proposals. By discussing Kissinger's progress at Tuesday luncheons, McNamara also expected to avoid the pitfalls of launching air strikes at sensitive moments during the talks, a circumstance he believed had wrecked the earlier Marigold offer. What intrigued McNamara was the report the Frenchmen conveyed in early August that Hanoi would not take advantage of a bombing cessation.[43]

With the president's consent, McNamara personally drafted instructions to Kissinger stating that the United States would stop bombing North Vietnam if such action would lead promptly to "productive discussions" and Hanoi promised not to take advantage of the moratorium. On 19 August, as the two Frenchmen prepared to return to Hanoi, the president agreed to suspend bombing within a 10-mile radius of Hanoi between 24 August and 4 September. The interval ensured the messengers' safety and added credibility to the proposal because Kissinger instructed them to tell the North Vietnamese that there would be a "noticeable change in the bombing pattern" beginning 24 August. Also on the 19th, the JCS passed the president's decision to CINCPAC—again without explanation—to stop bombing for the proscribed period within that area.[44]

While the Pennsylvania initiative was under way, the Stennis Committee prepared to open hearings. Anxious to deflect expected congressional criticism, the president on 8 August approved additional targets in North Vietnam, including

---

[*] Paul Warnke succeeded McNaughton as assistant secretary of defense for international security affairs on 1 August 1967.

some in the Hanoi restricted area and others in the sacrosanct Chinese buffer zone. In doing so, Johnson rejected McNamara's counsel to the contrary, noting, "We have got to do something to win. We aren't doing much now." On the other hand, he did not deem the action an escalation of the air war.[45]

The approval of heavier bombing coincident with the Pennsylvania negotiating initiative posed a seeming contradiction that required the administration to do some explaining. Sharp arrived in Washington on 8 August as the leadoff witness for the congressional hearings. Johnson ordered the admiral prepped on the political reasons for the general policy of not escalating the bombing, something the administration had never done previously. Sharp thought it obvious that authorization and release of the latest targets on the eve of his testimony was a McNamara maneuver to squelch criticism that the military were being ignored—"to spike my guns." A more willing collaborator was Wheeler, co-opted by a Rostow-inspired "roundup session" to review and evaluate all available targets and "generally get our ducks in a row for the congressional hearings on the subject." Wheeler was amenable, having made known that he could better deal with the committee if he could say that he had been fully and personally consulted on all major decisions. Such a statement would head off the argument that target selection had been made by civilians without benefit of military input.[46]

To prepare for the "roundup session," McNamara asked the Joint Chiefs to list additional fixed targets in North Vietnam for consideration. They responded with 70 new ones. McNamara, walking a thin line between disruption of the Pennsylvania talks because of escalation and appeasement of the JCS and congressional critics, on 11 August proposed only six be approved. Five days later, the president, again displaying concern over his diminishing domestic support, suggested striking "the least dangerous and the most productive targets," so that he could say "we have hit six out of every seven targets requested." McNamara promised he would get the president 20 more targets while Rusk advised spreading the air missions out over several days to avoid appearances of a "Roman holiday" that would provoke charges of escalation detrimental to the administration's cause.[47]

At the Rostow-instigated "roundup session," held on 18 August at the White House, McNamara thought there was a good chance of getting the selected targets "all out of the way by the 24th," just before his congressional testimony and the scheduled arrival of Kissinger's diplomatic contacts in Hanoi. Also rushing against the deadline, Wheeler proposed bombing the Phuc Yen and Cat Bi airfields, promising to provide the president justifications in time for his Tuesday luncheon on 22 August. Preoccupied with the Pennsylvania exercise, McNamara failed to heed the president's earlier admonition to "worry about the heat he [McNamara] has to take on the Hill about bombing limitations."[48]

To prepare for his testimony, McNamara had CIA Director Helms vet the draft of his prepared statement on the air war, relying on recent agency appraisals that the political risks of further escalation outweighed any likely military benefits.[49] It was in character that McNamara, certain that he was right, concluded that he could effectively counter the committee's manifest agenda: to establish that air and naval power alone could win the war and that the secretary and the Joint Chiefs were at odds over the conduct of the air war. McNamara also expected to use the hearings as a forum to express his views to the committee and eventually to a larger audience, but he failed to appreciate that the senators were after his scalp. He also foolishly hurt his case by his last-minute refusal of Chairman Stennis's request for several key JCS documents related to the conduct of the air war,[50] which may have fueled the committee's suspicion that the administration indeed had something to hide.

Preceding McNamara's appearance, each of the service chiefs, Admiral Sharp, and Lieutenant General Momyer, the Seventh Air Force commander, in individual testimony before a sympathetic committee, agreed that: (1) an expanded and intensified air campaign was necessary against the better and more lucrative targets as yet unstruck, especially the port of Haiphong; (2) reduction of the bombing effort would lead to increased U.S. casualties in South Vietnam; and (3) since early 1965, with the start of Rolling Thunder, the military had favored bombing of maximum intensity in the shortest feasible time as preferable to the strategy of gradualism that had allowed the North Vietnamese to adjust to the air campaign.[51] At the time, McNamara praised Wheeler's testimony, but years afterward he remembered the hearing as "one of the most stressful episodes of my life," because the Chiefs insisted that the bombing was effective "and this poor, inexperienced civilian didn't know what the hell was going on and had a different view."[52]

When McNamara's turn came on 25 August, his prepared statement addressed the objectives of the air war, JCS target recommendations, and the subject of escalation. Hostile senators dissected his remarks in minute detail, but McNamara gave as good as he got. Expanding the air war to strike all the JCS-recommended targets, he stated, would "not materially shorten the war," could not staunch the flow of supplies that the communists needed in the South, and would only harden North Vietnamese resistance to a settlement. No evidence existed to support claims that reduced bombing would increase American casualties. He totally disagreed that the political restrictions mandating gradualism had hampered the effective use of airpower.[53]

Throughout the adversarial questioning, McNamara resorted to evasion and obfuscation to ward off his critics. He addressed the issue of targets, for example, in quantitative terms, arguing that 95 percent of those recommended had been attacked. He simply dismissed as "not factual in this case" contentions that the remaining five percent might be more meaningful from a qualitative standpoint. He also invoked the constitution, pointing out that it made the president, a civilian, commander in chief; it did not require him to follow military advice blindly. Pressed by the staff counsel about bombing inconsequential targets, McNamara bridled: "If he [Sharp] doesn't consider them significant, why did he recommend them?" Reminded that the admiral had recommended many more targets than were approved, the defense secretary retorted: "That is not the issue."[54]

Above: Secretary McNamara hosts President Johnson and Deputy Secretary Cyrus Vance in his office, 12 Jul 1966.

Below: Secretary McNamara swears in Assistant Secretary of Defense for Systems Analysis Alain Enthoven (left) and Assistant Secretary of Defense Comptroller Robert Anthony (center), 10 Sep 1965.

Above: Following a ceremony on 1 Oct 1965, Secretary McNamara talks with (left to right) Undersecretary of the Air Force Norman Paul, Assistant Secretary of Defense for Manpower Thomas Morris, Director of Defense Research and Engineering John Foster, Jr., and Secretary of the Air Force Harold Brown.

Below: Marines go ashore at Da Nang, 8 Mar 1965. This marked a major turning point in American commitment in the Vietnam War.

Above: President Johnson and Secretary McNamara receive a CIA briefing on the situation in the Dominican Republic, 29 Apr 1965.
Below: Lieutenant General Bruce Palmer, Jr. (left rear), Deputy Secretary Vance (left front) and his executive officer Colonel DeWitt Smith (right rear) drive through Santo Domingo, May 1965.

Above: The president discusses Vietnam options with the Joint Chiefs and other senior officials, 22 Jul 1965.
Below: Assistant Secretary of Defense for International Security Affairs John McNaughton and General William Westmoreland confer at Manila, 24 Oct 1966.

The helicopter revolutionized battlefield mobility (*above*: troops deploy from a UH-1 Huey), but most infantrymen still fought on foot (*below*: soldiers of the 173d Airborne Brigade assault an enemy position).

Above: Senator Richard Russell, the president's friend, increasingly criticized McNamara.
Below: Secretary McNamara briefs selected members of Congress on Vietnam, 28 Jul 1965.

Above: Representatives Mendel Rivers and Edward Hébert at a hearing on the B-52, 6 Feb 1966.
Below: Representative Wilbur Mills, chairman of the House Ways and Means Committee, demanding spending reductions in exchange for supporting tax increases.

Above: Clark Clifford and General Maxwell Taylor report to the president on their Vietnam trip, 5 Aug 1967. Seated around the table clockwise from Johnson: Clifford, Paul Nitze, Nicholas Katzenbach, George Ball, Secretary Rusk (partly obscured) and Taylor.
Below: "Like the New Jersey Turnpike." North Vietnamese trucks en route south during the bombing pause, Feb 1967.

Above: The Joint Chiefs and Secretary McNamara wait to brief the president on plans to attack North Vietnam's fuel facilities, 12 Jun 1966.

Right: Flames rise from a fuel storage site near Hanoi after an air strike, 29 Jun 1966.

Below: Secretary McNamara announces the air campaign against fuel targets to the media.

Above: President Johnson and Secretary McNamara with key economic advisers, 1 Jun 1966.
Below: President Johnson, Clifford, and Secretary McNamara at LBJ Ranch, 6 Jul 1966.

BETTMANN/CORBIS

Above: A crowd of protesters at the Pentagon, Oct 1967.
Right: Michigan National Guard troops during the Detroit riots, Jul 1967.
Below: Secretary McNamara views the March on the Pentagon from the building roof, 21 Oct 1967.

Above: President Johnson at the Khe Sanh terrain model, White House, Jan 1968.
Left: A pall of smoke over Saigon during the Tet offensive, 1968.

Unmoved and unshaken by his toughest questioner, Senator Symington, McNamara obstinately insisted despite testimony by uniformed leaders to the contrary that no gulf existed between military and civilian officials over target selection.[55] This was the McNamara of old—supremely confident, certain of his mastery of the facts. Throughout the hearing, McNamara may have been on the defensive, but he was always forceful, opinionated, and unwilling to concede a single point to his inquisitors. Over and over he returned to his basic theme: expanding the air campaign would neither shorten the war nor check North Vietnamese infiltration. But three years of Vietnam had destroyed his credibility, discredited his policies, and shattered his aura of infallibility.

McNamara's testimony quickly became the stuff of legend. According to Roswell Gilpatric, the president summoned McNamara on his way back to the Pentagon from the hearings and upbraided him for three hours. McNamara did phone Johnson after his testimony, but there is no record of the secretary returning to the White House that evening, one which the president spent with guests aboard the presidential yacht Sequoia. Nor as has been alleged could the Joint Chiefs have gathered in Wheeler's office on 25 August for an emergency meeting to consider mass resignation; the chairman was en route home from Germany that day, having departed for Europe following his 22 August testimony.[56] When newspaper stories of a "generals' revolt" first surfaced in November, Wheeler told the president it was "absolutely untrue" that any JCS member had threatened to resign. Two of them, General Greene and Admiral Moorer, later denied the allegation, and Wheeler curtly dismissed it as "Bullshit!"[57]

Having earlier denied any "deep division" between his military and civilian advisers, Johnson explained any differences as a natural consequence of the policy-making process. He reminded reporters that six out of every seven recommended targets had been authorized. Still, the speculation refused to die. Certainly the military's stock rose after the hearings. On 5 September in the immediate aftermath the president, over the opposition of Rusk and McNamara, approved the JCS recommendation to bomb two minor ports if no ships were present. The following month Wheeler formally joined the Tuesday luncheons as a regular member. McNamara's testimony, made public on 11 October, reinforced the impression that, despite his attempts to minimize them, basic differences over the effectiveness of the bombing campaign persisted between him and the Joint Chiefs.*[58]

Simultaneously with the Stennis hearings and the imminent return to Hanoi of the Pennsylvania intermediaries (expected on or about 25 August), the air war reached a new level of fury. The 24th of August was scheduled as the deadline to suspend attacks in the Hanoi-Haiphong and Chinese border areas; however, the president and his advisers regarded operations before that day as unrelated to

---

* Rostow's military assistant, Col. Robert L. Ginsburgh, later claimed that after the hearings Johnson decided to back the JCS and ease McNamara out (Schandler, *The Unmaking of a President*, 61).

Pennsylvania, and proposed to hit as many authorized targets as possible before the French intermediaries arrived in Hanoi.[59] Previously planned but weather-postponed air strikes began on 20 August, a clear day, with 200 sorties. Intense air raids continued over three days. As had happened with Marigold, with their cities under heavy air bombardment, North Vietnamese officials initially refused to appear coerced and rejected the Frenchmen's visa applications on 21 August. This time, however, the communists kept the negotiating channel open.

North Vietnam's air defenses claimed six U.S. planes on the 21st and seven more plus a helicopter on the 23rd. Communist MIGs aggressively engaged U.S. aircraft in air-to-air combat, reconfirming for the Joint Chiefs the need to hit the MIG safe haven at Phuc Yen airfield.[60] On 24 August the president met with Rusk, McNamara, Nitze, and two of the service chiefs to decide whether to strike the airfield. Generals Johnson and McConnell explained that the elimination of the MIG threat would improve the chances of survival of American airmen. McNamara dissented, believing the operation a serious escalation that would add pressure on the Soviet Union and China to do more for their beleaguered ally, produce no lasting results, and cost more pilots than it would save. Rusk agreed that the political disadvantages outweighed the military advantages. Left with "two for and two against," the president, though inclined to hit Phuc Yen, did not authorize the attack; instead he stuck with his decision, effective 24 August, against bombing within 10 miles of Hanoi. On 1 September he changed it to an indefinite deadline that was not lifted until 23 October. [61]

Johnson's chronic vacillation reflected the administration's vexation over how to end the stalemate amid a "discernible polarization" of public sentiment about the war and the wisdom of U.S. intervention. As the CIA informed him, the intensified air strikes since May 1967 had increased the hardship of daily life in North Vietnam, destroyed a decade of economic growth, disrupted the transportation system, forced evacuations from targeted areas, and overburdened Haiphong port. Nonetheless, this had not prevented the communists from meeting their minimum needs in the North and moving essential military supplies to the South.[62] Nor for that matter had heavier bombing silenced hawkish critics, while proponents of a unilateral end to the attacks were angrier than ever and taking to the streets to protest the war.

Keenly aware of the unfavorable shift in public opinion about the war during the summer months of 1967, Johnson worried that when Congress reconvened in January it "will try to bring the war to a close either by getting out or by escalating significantly." To avoid those alternatives and to restore public confidence, the administration had to demonstrate progress in Vietnam. Otherwise, as the president put it, "no one can carry an election if he does not show hope of victory to his people." Searching for that victory, he asked General Johnson to have the Joint Chiefs come up with "imaginative ideas" to bring the war to a conclusion, but he also kept open the Pennsylvania channel.[63]

Throughout September the standoff over the future of the air war continued. The military pushed for fewer restraints and more targets, especially Phuc Yen and the port of Haiphong, but McNamara reconfirmed the bombing restrictions on 20 September, deeming escalation harmful to the Pennsylvania effort and without discernible military benefits. On 26 September, he and Rostow counseled a frankly skeptical president to give the negotiators more time. After several months of talks without results, however, the president, convinced the North Vietnamese were "playing us for suckers," wanted to strike targets inside the Hanoi circle, including Phuc Yen. He decided to allow one more week to produce results.[64]

During that grace period, on 29 September Johnson publicly offered his so-called "San Antonio formula."* This public articulation of the Pennsylvania propositions was the president's effort to disarm his critics, revive public confidence in his war policy, and offer Hanoi a meaningful proposal as the basis for negotiations. But proclaiming simultaneously steady progress in the war and a willingness to "stop all aerial and naval bombardment of North Vietnam when this will lead promptly to productive discussions," yet again, satisfied neither his domestic opponents nor his foreign enemies. On 3 October Hanoi rejected the president's offer as "a faked 'desire for peace'" that contained "nothing new."[65]

His patience exhausted even before Hanoi's announcement, Johnson now considered eliminating all targeting constraints. Moving in the opposite direction, McNamara, even more convinced that the bombing was ineffectual, inclined toward stopping it unilaterally. After Rusk and Rostow challenged this position at a 3 October meeting, the president requested the opponents to present in writing their respective views on a continued bombing campaign. This served as the origin of McNamara's controversial 1 November draft memorandum initially seen only by the president.[66]

With domestic support for the bombing declining, Johnson ignored the polling numbers and on 4 October overrode McNamara's objections in an effort "to pour the steel on" and hit everything except Hanoi's restricted zone. In response to the president's 12 September call for "imaginative ideas" to end the war, the JCS completed their reply on 17 October; McNamara forwarded it to the White House the next day. It recommended 10 additional actions, all against North Vietnam or its operations in Laos and Cambodia.[67]

The proposal was put on hold while senior administration officials and outside advisers (longtime trusted friend Justice Abe Fortas, Clifford, and Kissinger) debated the fate of the Pennsylvania plan. Deep-seated mistrust of the communists and fears that Hanoi would take advantage of a bombing halt to attack U.S. troops and installations effectively countered arguments for ending the bombing to induce negotiations. Clifford opposed any bombing suspension because he doubted the North Vietnamese were serious about negotiating and regarded Pennsylvania

---

* The president addressed the National Legislative Conference in San Antonio, Texas.

as a dead end. McNamara argued just as fiercely that if the bombing ended, talks would start quickly. Johnson had previously reminded his advisers, "If we cannot agree among ourselves we sure cannot get them to agree." Three weeks had passed and consensus still proved as elusive as ever.[68]

It may seem that U.S. disarray caused the breakdown of the Pennsylvania initiative, but it is just as apparent that Hanoi had little genuine interest in negotiations. In October North Vietnam was in the midst of preparations for the 1968 Tet offensive. While not rejecting either Pennsylvania or the San Antonio formula outright, Hanoi anticipated meaningful negotiations only after its attempt to win the war with a smashing military blow. Ignorant of all this, the president reluctantly agreed to one more attempt by Kissinger to start serious discussions. The North Vietnamese representative in Paris held stubbornly to the official line with predictable results. On 20 October North Vietnam closed down the channel.[69]

In the wake of Pennsylvania's demise and large-scale protests and demonstrations on 21–22 October at the Pentagon, a riled president reconvened his advisers on the 23rd and asked, "Are we now ready to take the wraps off the bombing?" They discussed the latest 10-point recommendation from the JCS, leading off with the proposal to hit Phuc Yen in retaliation for three U.S. aircraft recently lost to MIG fighters. The president noted that the airfield had already been authorized for attack subject to the winding up of the Pennsylvania talks. "Now we have gotten rid of all the excuses. Let's go with it." All present, including Rusk, Wheeler, and a conflicted McNamara, agreed that Phuc Yen plus numerous targets within the 10-mile Hanoi restricted zone should be struck. The president then lifted the ban that had been in effect since 24 August. Attacks on Phuc Yen on 24 and 25 October severely damaged the field and its MIG interceptors.[70]

Well before the latest escalation, senior administration officials were reassessing the bombing campaign from different angles. Wheeler, for example, greatly concerned over what might follow if North Vietnam accepted the San Antonio formula, with McNamara's guidance and approval on 19 October established an ad hoc study group composed of Joint Staff, DIA, and ISA members. He tasked them to consider the effects of a bombing halt, especially the dangers it posed to U.S. forces in South Vietnam and how to overcome them, and also to establish conditions to renew the bombing if necessary. This became the SEA CABIN* study.[71]

Meanwhile the CIA speculated that even though the bombing in the North had little effect on military operations in the South, a pause might yet induce Hanoi to open preliminary talks with Washington. The communists would, of course, take advantage of a halt to reconstitute their logistics network and improve their military capabilities. This analysis was shared by the CIA's George Carver, who headed a four-man team commissioned by McNamara to produce an "optimum

---

* SEA CABIN was an acronym for "Study of the Political-Military Implications in Southeast Asia of the Cessation of Aerial Bombardment and the Initiation of Negotiations."

fifteen month scenario" to end the conflict. Their consensus favored a unilateral bombing halt before the end of 1967 as a politically necessary step and as a possible path to talks. As Harry McPherson, the president's special counsel, pointed out, beyond the military aspects lay the political liability that the American people just did not understand the bombing program. Recapturing rapidly diminishing moderate support depended on the president's ability to explain the rationale for bombing as well as the conditions for stopping it.[72]

The "dangerously strong feelings" in the president's official family that had been building steadily since May spilled over when McNamara, verbally on 31 October and in writing on 1 November, urged the president to abandon the current U.S. course of action in Vietnam. Moving beyond his 19 May proposals, McNamara called for a unilateral bombing halt in hopes of eliciting reciprocal de-escalation and/or movement toward negotiations from Hanoi. Although Johnson never officially responded to his defense secretary's memorandum, in private he questioned McNamara's optimistic conclusion that the North Vietnamese would respond to a halt in kind by cutting back military activity across the DMZ. He worried that as usual the enemy would use any talks for propaganda purposes rather than serious negotiations.[*73]

Of the nine principal advisers to whom the president later circulated McNamara's memo for comment, only one, Under Secretary of State Katzenbach, agreed with McNamara's position on the bombing, but even he wondered if the administration would accept such a policy.[74] Clifford was especially outspoken that any unconditional halt would only convince Hanoi that the United States was tiring of the struggle, which in turn would lift enemy morale as well as enable the North to reconstitute its forces and economy. If Washington ever had to resume the bombing, a firestorm of national and international protest would erupt. Taylor interpreted a halt as a prelude to an eventual pullout and something that would encourage the enemy, discourage America's allies, and infuriate "the large majority" of Americans who supported the bombing.[75]

At a briefing held 1 November for the administration's senior officials and advisers, the invitees including the Wise Men,[†] McNamara stated that perhaps his and Rusk's efforts since 1961 had been a failure, but he did not disclose to the assembled group of senior statesmen that earlier in the day he had proposed to the president to stop the bombing in the North. Instead the secretary read from a month-old CIA estimate that bombing did not reduce the enemy's flow of supplies enough to hamper military operations. The Wise Men agreed but noted that the

---

[*] In his 1995 memoir McNamara wrote, "My November 1 memorandum did do one thing: it raised the tension between two men who loved and respected each other—Lyndon Johnson and me—to the breaking point. Four weeks later, President Johnson announced my selection as president of the World Bank. . . . I do not know to this day whether I quit or was fired. Maybe it was both" (McNamara, *In Retrospect*, 311).

[†] See Chapter VII.

bombing was a negotiating chip to stop enemy cross-the-DMZ operations. The following day at a White House meeting the same advisers unanimously proposed to moderate but not end the bombing. Although he later chastised the Wise Men for their conventional advice at the meeting, McNamara remained silent, neither enlightening the outside advisers about his shutdown proposal nor declaring his convictions.[76] So the bombing continued amidst calls from the JCS for escalation before the northeast quadrant was closed by bad weather.

The Joint Chiefs' latest plan, sent to McNamara on 27 November, proposed to mine Haiphong harbor and reduce the size of the restricted doughnut around Hanoi and Haiphong, thereby isolating the two cities from each other and the rest of North Vietnam. The president felt a strong need to placate his hawkish opponents by hitting all key targets as soon as possible, but it would be at the cost of a probable heavy loss in planes, pilots, and public opinion. The likelihood of large civilian casualties during such attacks plus the appearance of escalation caused State and OSD to recommend against the proposal. Furthermore the most recent CIA/DIA appraisal declared that even though heavy attacks against the transportation network had created the most serious disruptions to date, given the enemy's modest logistic requirements in the South, Hanoi could still support combat at current or increased levels.[77]

In response to McNamara's earlier request, in mid-December the ad hoc JASON group* concluded that the bombing of North Vietnam "had no measurable effect" on Hanoi's ability to conduct military operations in South Vietnam because the regime's allies were bearing the brunt of the economic and military materiel costs of the war. With the exception of a few targets in Hanoi and Haiphong, virtually all military and economic targets in North Vietnam had been struck without apparent diminution of national resolve or popular support for the communist government.[78]

McNamara received the report on 3 January 1968, with a notation from Assistant Secretary Warnke that it, like the SEA CABIN study of 22 November 1967, supported the position that a bombing pause, even for a significant period, would not appreciably affect enemy strength.[79] Warnke dwelt on SEA CABIN's assessment that despite the bombing North Vietnam had sufficient untapped manpower and capability to meet its logistic requirements in South Vietnam. Even without the bombing, a number of constraints would still limit the rate of infiltration. But SEA CABIN had also concluded that an extended pause (two to six months) would enable Hanoi to reconstitute its military and economic posture and greatly increase the flow of men and supplies to the South. More importantly, a bombing halt could be seen, especially in neighboring Asian nations, as "a display of weakness, lack of determination and unprincipled capitulation to world opinion" by the United States.[80]

---

* See Chapter V.

Following the enemy's countrywide Tet offensive launched on 31 January 1968, the JCS on 3 February again sought approval to reduce the restricted areas around Hanoi and Haiphong and expose critical supply and transportation nodes to attack. At the Tuesday luncheon three days later, the president overrode McNamara's objections and went along with the recommendations of secretary-designate Clifford by reducing the size of the restricted zones and authorizing strikes on 14 targets therein.[81]

After Tet

Although most attention at the next Tuesday lunch (13 February) focused on measures to repel the Viet Cong and North Vietnamese ground offensive in the South, the president and his advisers also discussed an expanded air offensive against the North. Rusk favored heavier bombing there in response to the Tet attacks and Hanoi's rejection of the administration's latest peace offer. Clifford, scheduled to take over from McNamara on 1 March, also advocated increased bombing. McNamara dissented, feeling the military worth of the targets small and the risks high. Faced with the split views, the president made no decision. Two weeks later at a 27 February meeting, according to participants a distraught and tense McNamara, eyes tearing and voice faltering, heatedly denounced the bombing of North Vietnam. Stunned by the outburst, listeners continued the charged discussions, with Clifford proposing a reassessment of "our entire posture in SVN" before making any decision on the future of the war. White House Special Assistant Joseph Califano, present to monitor the domestic implications of the deliberations, recalled the session as "the most depressing three hours in my years of public service."[82]

The subsequent sweeping but quick reevaluation of U.S.-Vietnam policy brought to the fore the conflicting perspectives in a fresh round of handwringing. The differences among the respective camps about bombing North Vietnam were "so profound" that their consideration had to be tabled while the group moved on to other issues. With the leaders at an impasse, Clifford's 4 March report to the president left undecided the fate of the air war against North Vietnam.[83]

In the meeting with his advisers on 4 March (absent the departed McNamara) the president was much taken by Rusk's comments that the bombing could be stopped during the rainy season in the North without major military risk. He directed that during this period the State Department "get on your horses" to bring about peace negotiations. Over the next month Rusk and Clifford drafted plans for a unilateral and unconditional end to the bombing north of the 20th parallel accompanied by an offer of talks with North Vietnam. Unlike past efforts, there would be no diplomatic fanfare or parsing of messages. Hanoi's actions, not words, would determine what happened next. If North Vietnam did not react after a month or so, the United States would resume the bombing.[84]

Others reinforced the limited bombing message. In mid-March Townsend W. Hoopes, under secretary of the Air Force, reiterated his February warning that further escalation was pointless because a U.S. military victory in Vietnam was not feasible. Warnke counseled that holding the war effort at its present level and restricting bombing primarily to south of the 19th parallel offered the only way to achieve a negotiated end to the war. The Joint Chiefs disagreed. At an 18 March discussion with Clifford they again called for an open-ended, unrestricted air offensive, but admitted that increased bombing alone could not end the war or appreciably reduce American casualties in South Vietnam. Clifford later acknowledged that the uncertainties at this and other meetings caused him to change his position from escalating the air war to limiting it as a more likely means of ending the conflict.[85]

The day after the 18 March session with the Joint Chiefs, Clifford attended the usual Tuesday luncheon, in this instance largely devoted to the war in South Vietnam and its costs. With the administration struggling to contain domestic opposition to the war, Clifford recommended and the president approved the reconvening of the Wise Men to seek their latest views and advice. On the following day, at another White House meeting, Clifford cautiously proposed to suspend operations north of 20 degrees and, if North Vietnam responded by stopping its use of the DMZ to launch artillery, rocket, and mortar attacks, further reduce the bombing. Although conceding that bombing around Hanoi and Haiphong "sure enrages the world," the president remained leery of a stand-down there, suspicious of the North Vietnamese, fearful of infuriating domestic hawks, and concerned about hurting the South Vietnamese war effort.[86]

Before the Wise Men could reassemble on 26 March, however, the White House, State, and OSD again reevaluated the air campaign. By mid-March Wheeler believed the bombing north of 20 degrees could be stopped because poor flying weather through mid-April precluded hitting many targets anyway. He expected Hanoi's response to be "tangible and measurable," that is a reciprocal curtailment of military action by North Vietnam and withdrawal of its regular forces from the DMZ in exchange for the bombing concessions. It was then that Clifford realized and suggested that the objective should be: "[W]e are not out to win the war—we are out to win the peace," to which the president replied, "That is right."[87]

Around the same time Clifford again suggested that de-escalation begin with a "limited cessation" of bombing north of the 20th parallel in expectation of reciprocal action by Hanoi in the vicinity of the DMZ. Rusk, while supportive, doubted Hanoi would reciprocate; William Bundy was skeptical but had no alternative to offer; and Rostow thought Hanoi would see through the charade of proclaiming a bombing halt in bad weather when few attacks could occur anyway. On 23 March, Harry McPherson sent Johnson a memo supporting the thrust of the Clifford-Rusk proposal, suggesting that the president announce his willingness to stop all bombing if Hanoi reciprocated by not attacking South Vietnamese cities or U.S. bases and not shelling the South from the DMZ. Two days later, Rusk told the president that he agreed with McPherson's approach, adding that if Hanoi mounted major attacks full bombing should be resumed; meanwhile, bombing "should be intensive and without wraps" in North Vietnam's panhandle region.[88]

The president met with the Wise Men contingent* on 26 March in the Cabinet Room. Some favored an immediate cessation of bombing, others a halt at some later point but not immediately because of the dangerous situation in the I Corps area along the DMZ. The recommendation apparently influenced the president's subsequent decision to restrict the bombing. On 29 March Clifford and Nitze informed the Joint Chiefs that the president had decided to halt the bombing north of the 20th parallel in order to shore up crumbling domestic support for the war and force the North Vietnamese to make the next move. Despite persisting misgivings about the effects of the pause, the Chiefs agreed to support the decision.[89]

On 31 March Johnson publicly announced his order to air and naval forces to make no attacks on North Vietnam, except in an undefined area north of the DMZ. If North Vietnam matched this restraint, he continued, even that limited bombing could end. Attempting to mollify Sharp, once again caught "completely unaware" of the major policy shift, Wheeler informed him that the duration of the bombing restrictions depended on North Vietnam's reaction to the president's peace offer. Johnson also told the nation that he would not seek reelection.[90]

The president's vagueness on the exact limitations of the bombing created a mini-tempest the next day when U.S. planes bombed targets more than 200 miles north of the DMZ, but still south of the 20th parallel. DoD spokesman Phil Goulding then announced that attacks were continuing south of that line.[91] In such circumstances, Hanoi's 3 April announcement of its willingness to open preliminary talks without an unconditional and complete bombing halt surprised not only Washington but Peking as well. Chinese Premier Chou En-lai twice rebuked Premier Pham Van Dong for accepting Washington's proposal for a limited bombing cessation and disappointing the "people of the world." Friction between communist allies perhaps validated U.S. speculation that Hanoi's subsequent rejection of proposed negotiating sites on 13 April came out of deference to China.[92]

To ensure that no incidents endangered the fresh initiative, after receipt of the North Vietnamese message the president ordered field commanders to schedule all attacks south of the 19th degree line unless otherwise directed by the Joint Chiefs. The administration, however, made no public announcement of this policy change, leaving it free to bomb farther north if necessary. As during previous bombing lulls, North Vietnam quickly set to work to repair its damaged military and port installations and embarked on a massive effort to shuttle supplies south. U.S. pilots frequently sighted convoys of as many as 200 trucks in the panhandle area during April, and intelligence indicated preparation for a new enemy offensive

---

* Present were Acheson, Ball, Bradley, McGeorge Bundy, Dean, Dillon, Fortas, Harriman, Lodge, Murphy, Taylor, Arthur Goldberg, Vance, and General (Ret.) Matthew Ridgway.

was well under way. Alarmed by this upsurge in activity, on 29 April Wheeler notified Clifford that CINCPAC believed the North Vietnamese, far from reciprocating the U.S. de-escalation, were once again taking advantage of the restrictions to improve their military position. Wheeler seconded Sharp's recommendation for renewed attacks between the 19th and 20th parallels to slow the enemy's progress.[93]

Heavy fighting near the DMZ raged throughout May. Concurrently on 4 May, the communists launched a series of attacks against South Vietnamese cities and U.S. bases, the so-called "Little Tet" offensive. By this time Clifford had grown convinced of two things: negotiations offered the only exit from Vietnam and "the gang around LBJ is turning [?] against settlement," thereby endangering the Paris talks in favor of just beating "the Hell out of them." Clifford spent the month parrying the counsel of the JCS who, supported by Rostow, would expand the bombing arena in order to offset the second major communist offensive of 1968. On 8 May, the Joint Chiefs proposed expanding air strikes to the 20th parallel to counter a growing North Vietnamese MIG threat against U.S. aircraft.[94]

Responding to the Joint Chiefs, on 14 May Warnke alerted Clifford that only a "most compelling military reason" could justify bombing north of the 19th parallel. Otherwise the administration would risk charges of escalation, dissipate support for its position that the next move toward de-escalation was up to Hanoi, and possibly jeopardize the Paris negotiations. Clifford made these arguments at a Tuesday luncheon the same day, concluding that the proposed targets were not worth the psychological problems they would create by escalating the air war while simultaneously asking the other side to scale down its attacks. Although the president rejected the JCS proposal, at a 15 May meeting he promised to reconsider it within a week or so.[95] Clifford took this as an ominous sign, recognizing the great appeal a military solution held for the president.

Clifford described the follow-on Tuesday luncheon on 21 May to his staff as "the grimmest affair we've had on V[iet] Nam & the bombing." The defense secretary was pitted against both Wheeler and Rusk. Wheeler hoped to expand the bombing, while Rusk, although opposed to a dramatic elevation of the air campaign, worried that overly rigid restrictions on attacks north of the 19th parallel were counterproductive in light of the large-scale North Vietnamese infiltration into the South. A skeptical president, also worried about getting locked into a policy that made it difficult to bomb north of 19 degrees, accused Clifford of "just carrying [?] me along from week-to-week." Characteristically, despite his inclination to hit everything below the 20th parallel, Johnson again decided to postpone action until the following week.[96]

These meetings highlighted the differences between Clifford and Rusk over ending the air offensive. Rusk insisted on reciprocity in advance, Clifford did not. Rusk would suspend bombing north of 19 degrees, but retain the option to attack above that line. Clifford, echoing McNamara's arguments of a few months before, wanted to ratchet down the air campaign on the way to ending the bombing completely. The two chief advisers also differed over the future course of the war. Rusk "charged that Clifford had lost his nerve," and Clifford claimed that Rusk regarded him as a threat because OSD had "won out" on the March debate. Clifford also directed his ire at the State Department for excluding OSD from receiving certain sensitive cables; in fact, however, it was the president, annoyed with the defense secretary's incessant clamoring to stop the bombing, who had withheld message traffic pertaining to the Paris talks.[97] What neither Clifford nor Rusk realized fully (or wanted to acknowledge) was that the president told them what they wanted to hear. In mid-July, for instance, Johnson shared with Rusk the view that there was little evidence of serious interest by Hanoi in meaningful discussions until the bombing ended. A few days later the president was telling Clifford how he had confronted South Vietnamese President Thieu in their Honolulu meeting with the defense secretary's criticism of the South's war efforts and the need for negotiations.[98]

To strengthen his arguments for de-escalation, Clifford in mid-May directed Colonel Pursley, his military aide, and Warnke to draft a policy paper that would make a convincing case for U.S. disengagement from Vietnam.* On the subject of the air war over North Vietnam, the authors depended on a recent CIA analysis that Hanoi could withstand an all-out, unrestricted air campaign and still sustain the war in the South. This was possible because the United States would neither attack the sources of North Vietnam's war-making materiel, the Soviet Union and Communist China, nor completely interdict the southward flow of supplies. They concluded that to reach the conference table the administration would ultimately have to stop the bombing campaign against the North without preconditions. Clifford realized this action was premature given the administration's lack of internal unity and the president's unwillingness heretofore to take such a step.[99] Nonetheless the document served as Clifford's benchmark in his efforts to end the bombing of North Vietnam.

As the vicious May fighting left the president apprehensive over the lack of progress in the negotiations, he asked Clifford to consider alternative actions if Hanoi should continue to reject U.S. demands for reciprocity. Clifford in turn directed the Joint Chiefs to prepare alternatives should North Vietnam prove inflexible or the Paris talks collapse. The Chiefs recited the standard litany: The North Vietnamese were stringing the United States along at the Paris talks to gain by negotiation what they could not win through aggression. Stopping the bombing only guaranteed higher U.S. casualties. Limiting the bombardment to 20 degrees continued the discredited policy of gradualism. The military solution, as it had been all along, was unrestricted attacks against all targets in the North, except the Chinese buffer zone, to force Hanoi into serious negotiations. In early June they cautioned the president that continued restraints on the use of U.S. military power during the protracted negotiations at Paris would result only in a deteriorating allied capability. Should

* See also Chapter VII.

the talks break down, they desired immediate resumption of unrestricted air and naval attacks on North Vietnam.[100] The JCS found little support.

The CIA felt a resumption of bombing to the 20th parallel would signal a hard-line U.S. policy but not likely lead to any North Vietnamese concessions. Opposition to a military solution remained strongest, however, within OSD. Nitze asked if there was evidence of increased movement south by enemy forces and what a bombing resumption might accomplish. Clifford counseled the president to continue the current course because renewed escalation would almost surely cause the breakdown of the Paris talks. He reminded Johnson that no one had expected the talks to be easy and results to date were about as anticipated.[101]

Two events in early June stifled talk of immediate escalation. The 3 June arrival in Paris of Le Duc Tho, North Vietnam's special adviser to the peace talks, caused the U.S. lead negotiators, Cyrus Vance and Averell Harriman, to recommend that further consideration of air strikes between the 19th and 20th parallels be deferred "to test the water" for any new proposals. Two days later, the president received a letter from Kosygin stating that he thought North Vietnam ready to negotiate if the United States stopped its air strikes completely.[102]

Rusk, suspicious of the Soviet overture, wanted a guarantee that Hanoi would do something concrete in response to a bombing halt. Vance was unsure what the letter meant, Harriman too favored clarification, and Wheeler saw nothing new in the proposal. Fearful that a pause might lead to higher American casualties and lower troop morale, the president, as usual, worried that communist violations might go unpunished because it would be difficult for him to restart the bombing. Clifford insisted the letter offered "a great opportunity" to bring the war to a conclusion and advocated that the president accept Kosygin's assurances. Having been burned by Moscow's similar guarantees in the 37-day pause in late 1965 and early 1966, the president greeted the latest Soviet proposal with understandable cynicism. Finally, on 9 June, he decided to ask Kosygin what specifically would happen if the bombing were stopped.[103]

Two days later, the president informed Kosygin that the United States stood prepared to end the bombing of North Vietnam "if we know it will lead to the de-escalation of the war." Hanoi, Johnson continued, must not take advantage of the cessation and must state what actions it would take to further reduce the violence. The next day Soviet Ambassador Dobrynin confessed that he was "disappointed" by the conditions the president had raised and did not feel he had been responsive to Kosygin's letter.[104] Once again Johnson had straddled the issue, willing neither to escalate nor end the air war. Like so many earlier peace moves, the Soviet initiative went nowhere.

With talks still stalled in late June, at the president's request Wheeler reported on the enemy's current military situation as compared with that of 31 March 1968: it had deteriorated in the South, but improved in the North. Augmented air defenses, advanced MIG-21 fighters, new airfields, more SAMs and AAAs deployed south of 20 degrees, plus restored roads, rail lines, and industrial facilities had enabled Hanoi to dispatch an unprecedented 80,000 troops southward since the 31 March bombing halt. Those numbers, Wheeler expected, would make themselves felt in combat during the late summer and fall of 1968. Increasingly restive over the enemy buildup in the southern portion of North Vietnam and convinced Hanoi had no intention of reducing the level of fighting, the Joint Chiefs again recommended air attacks between the 19th and 20th parallels.[105] To apprise the Joint Chiefs of the issues at stake, Vance during a return from Paris discussed with them the state of the negotiations. He addressed a variety of issues at a meeting on 17 July, explaining that bombing north of the 19th parallel would seriously hamper any chance for successful talks; moreover, the bombing south of the line was proving effective. Meanwhile Warnke had proposed to go even further—by ending the bombing unilaterally in the hope of producing meaningful negotiations.[106]

Beginning in mid-June, substantially diminished enemy-initiated offensive activity resulted in fewer rocket and mortar attacks against Saigon and the withdrawal of an NVA division to 170 miles above the DMZ. Amidst these hopeful military signs, Hanoi's diplomatic activity and public pronouncements also suggested restraint. But heavy fighting still raged in South Vietnam's northern provinces, so it was not clear whether there was genuine restraint or a pause to refit and regroup for future operations. Given this uncertainty, the JCS on 31 July urged the president to continue the bombing until Hanoi offered assurances of a reciprocal reduction in military activity. Johnson, concerned that without the air attacks against the North more enemy troops and supplies could reach South Vietnam, fumed that "the International Communists" were behind an "iniquitous campaign" to end the bombing and lent a sympathetic ear to Wheeler's arguments to reopen the area between the 19th and 20th parallels.[107]

Johnson's quandary over whether to bomb or not manifested itself over a *New York Times* editorial of late July that asserted that the only way to gauge Hanoi's restraint was to stop bombing the North entirely. To respond to what had become a "new wave of demands" to end the bombing, the president directed Taylor to prepare a report on the source of the pressure and what to do about it.[108] On 30 July Taylor reported the administration had three choices: (1) succumb to the critics and stop the bombing, (2) ignore the pressure and ride out the criticism, (3) link the level of bombing of the North to that of enemy violence in the South. Taylor favored the second course for the moment, while preparing to shift to tit-for-tat retaliation contingent on lifting geographical restrictions on potential targets. Rusk, Clifford, and Wheeler all agreed with the second alternative.[109] Clifford perceived no merit in escalation because the three-year air campaign had not forced Hanoi to cease military activity in the South. Moreover it might cause Hanoi to quit the Paris talks, with the United States blamed for the breakdown. Though still opposed to a unilateral bombing cessation absent "substantial restraint on the part of Hanoi," he did advise Johnson to develop initiatives that might make it possible to cease the bombing entirely, stating that he had "been considering" a plan that would allow resumption if necessary. In the meantime the secretary advocated staying the course. After five months of fruitless talks, however, Johnson was "exceedingly hostile" to any recommendations from Paris, caustically dismissing them as attempts to influence him as "part of [an] overall conspiracy," with the enemy using the president's own people as "dupes." Clifford thought this last reference was to him, Harriman, and Vance.[110]

Clifford spent the weekend of 3–4 August at the Texas ranch where the president was entertaining guests; on Sunday afternoon he managed a private meeting with Johnson to discuss his plan. Arguing that the war could not be won militarily, Clifford proposed an end to the bombing in exchange for Hanoi's agreement to mutually deescalate, stop violations in the DMZ, and end attacks on Saigon. He suggested Kosygin as an intermediary to bring Hanoi to the table. Playing on the president's vanity, he observed that a peace settlement would be the administration's greatest accomplishment. Johnson disagreed with his defense secretary's major points, claiming "he'd rather [leave] office with a 'fine military solution' than be craven." Still, the president left the door open to the initiative by asking Clifford to put his thoughts on paper and discuss them with Rusk.[111] Johnson was still unwilling to give up completely on the bombing campaign; to do so would admit a major policy failure and further encourage his domestic opponents.

The president blew hot and cold. In early September, he reckoned that if they could persevere a few more weeks "with our present posture" it could convince Hanoi that it would not get a better deal by waiting. But by mid-month, Clifford characterized the president's mood as impatient and more pugnacious: "It's: 'I'm Goddamned if I'll stop the bombing without something from the other side!'" Almost concurrently, in a 15 September cable from Paris, Harriman quoted North Vietnam's top negotiator as stating that his government was prepared to begin worthwhile discussions the day after the United States stopped bombing his country.[112]

Clifford was at Camp David with the president when the cable arrived. Johnson indicated that if the situation in Czechoslovakia* remained quiet, he would seek Kosygin's assurance of a quid pro quo: if North Vietnam ceased its violations in the DMZ, stopped attacking South Vietnamese cities, and entered into negotiations that included South Vietnamese representatives, then the United States would stop the bombing. Bright hopes for substantive negotiations soon dimmed as another lengthy round of procedural discussions ensued in Paris. By late September, Clifford, Ball, and Nitze favored a unilateral bombing cessation, while Rusk, Wheeler, and the president opposed such a step without some reciprocity.[113]

Talks remained deadlocked into early October when the CIA reported the withdrawal of numerous North Vietnamese units from South Vietnam into Laos or Cambodia. It also became clear that the communists' third offensive of 1968,

---

* See Chapter XVIII.

launched in mid-August, had failed, leaving MACV far less apprehensive about the consequences of a bombing halt. On 11 October North Vietnamese representatives in Paris showed signs of getting down to business; the following day the Soviet embassy in Paris informed Vance of Hanoi's willingness to enter substantive negotiations and to include the participation of Saigon representatives in such talks once the bombing stopped.[114]

On 14 October the president had a series of meetings with the JCS, congressional leaders, and his own senior advisers to discuss the recent developments before making a decision. Clifford, supposing that something had happened to weaken the resolve of the North Vietnamese, thought the administration had to test Hanoi's good faith by shifting its position on reciprocity. Wheeler noted that unlike with previous pauses North Vietnam had made an important move and agreed to honor the DMZ, not shell the South's cities, and accept South Vietnamese participation in the talks. However, it seemed to General Westmoreland, now Army chief of staff, that the political pressure of the approaching presidential election was "encouraging concessions to the enemy without due consideration to future implications." Nonetheless he too acquiesced in the president's course. Armed with a consensus, Johnson instructed Harriman to press the North Vietnamese for an agreement on a date to cease the bombing. Peace negotiations would begin a day later.[115]

The president also sought reassurance from General Abrams and Ambassador Bunker that Hanoi would not use any respite to reconstitute its battered forces for another round of attacks. Conceding that hard fighting lay ahead, on 14 October the general and the ambassador saw no possibility for another large-scale enemy offensive, were confident allied morale and fighting spirit could be maintained during negotiations, and believed the North serious about talks as evidenced by Hanoi's decision to include Saigon representatives in the discussions. Johnson also gained support from General Momyer, now back in the United States as commander of the Tactical Air Command, who agreed that a bombing halt over North Vietnam at the current time posed minimal risks to U.S. forces.[116]

As the administration prepared to announce the bombing cessation, however, the North Vietnamese delegates imposed new conditions such as a written statement committing Washington to an "unconditional" bombing halt, an interval between the end of the bombing and the beginning of talks, and the inclusion of the communist National Liberation Front representatives as a separate party at the negotiating table. Hanoi's backsliding may have stemmed from Peking's displeasure with its ally's decision to accept South Vietnamese representatives, thereby giving legal standing to the "puppet regime" in Saigon.[117]

Clifford remained unwilling to end the air campaign unless both sides agreed on a definite date to begin talks. To do otherwise would lay the president open to criticism that with nothing to show in exchange he had stopped the bombing solely to influence the November elections. On 27 October Hanoi conceded that it would open talks within four days of the bombing halt, agreed on as 29 October; it dropped all other proposals, thus eliminating Clifford's objections. Two days later, avoiding public attention, Abrams flew from Saigon to Washington to confer in the early morning hours with the president, on the verge of making his final decision. Abrams unconditionally supported a cessation, much to the relief of Clifford who had not been entirely sure how the field commander would respond.[118]

Clifford described the final days leading to the 31 October presidential announcement as "a roller-coaster" ride. Seemingly firm decisions collapsed, disagreements between Saigon's leaders and Washington flared, critics abounded, and rumors floated that leading Republicans were telling South Vietnam's President Thieu not to cooperate with Johnson who would soon be out of office. Despite the last-minute flurry of distractions and complications,* at the NSC meeting held 31 October the president announced that he would go ahead with a bombing suspension to test the good faith of the North Vietnamese. After listing all the military and civilian officials whose support he had requested and received, he asked each attendee if he disagreed; no one did. In a national radio and television address that evening,† Johnson announced an end to bombardment of North Vietnam of any kind as of 8:00 a.m., 1 November, Washington time; talks would commence five days later.[119] Rolling Thunder ended as it had unfolded—troubled, contentious, and inconclusive.

---

* The Saigon government first attempted to interject new demands into the negotiations and then on 28 October objected to beginning talks on 2 November. North Vietnamese negotiators in Paris agreed to resetting the bombing halt to 1 November and opening negotiations on the 6th.
† The president had recorded the address on 30 October for broadcast the following day.

CHAPTER IX

BILLS COME DUE:
BUDGETS AND SUPPLEMENTALS,
1968–1970

As the fighting in Vietnam escalated, domestic economic conditions worsened, exposing swollen Defense budgets as prime targets for congressional budget hawks and other critics of administration policies. In early 1967 the administration was struggling to contain growing Defense costs, sustain social welfare legislation, and obtain more tax revenues to accomplish its goals. On 9 January 1967, the eve of his State of the Union address, Johnson presented to his advisers a revised package of tax surcharges offset by higher Social Security benefits and tax credits that he found acceptable. The president typically insisted that each adviser initial a memorandum recommending the program, leading one, Clark Clifford, to quip, "Does he want it notarized and sworn to?" When the president announced that he would seek a six percent corporate and individual tax surcharge for at least the next two years, congressional reaction was predictably cool and, according to the Harris public opinion poll, nearly two-thirds of Americans opposed the idea.[1]

Confronting double-digit deficit numbers and projections of even higher Vietnam costs, estimated at $21.8 billion for FY 1968, the administration cautiously explored the longer-term postwar economic horizon. Here too the news was discouraging. A dramatic decrease in DoD spending in a post-Vietnam era was unlikely; in paying for the war to date OSD had deferred numerous requirements not directly related to the conflict, particularly force modernization and inventory replenishment. According to McNamara, "some extraordinary Defense procurement" would continue well beyond any settlement.[2] In the absence of a peace dividend, the president had to look elsewhere for revenue to pay for his cherished domestic social programs.

Immediate concern was triggered by a late February government survey of business investment suggesting that tight money and the suspension of the capital investment subsidy had worked too efficiently and seemed to be leading to an impending capital goods collapse. Following Ackley's advice, on 9 March the president requested reinstatement of the investment tax credit, and Congress quickly obliged. Fowler, Schultze, and Ackley maintained that the economy needed stimulation, not restraint, so a tax hike could wait until the economy shifted into anticipated high gear later in the year.[3]

Congress, though, was growing increasingly prickly over the lack of accurate information on Defense spending, especially because of April rumors that 50,000 or even 100,000 additional U.S. troops might be sent to Vietnam. By mid-1967 House Appropriations Committee chairman Mahon, for one, took for granted that supplemental funding would be needed to pay for any further reinforcements because McNamara had predicated the FY 1968 budget on supporting fewer than 500,000 men in Vietnam.[4] Talk about deepening U.S. involvement in the war was hardly confined to cocktail circuit gossip. At the highest levels deliberations were already under way about dispatching additional troops to Southeast Asia.

General Westmoreland's March 1967 request to deploy another 200,000 troops to Vietnam had avoided the question of whether the nation could afford the additional costs. Federal expenditures for Defense and the Great Society were rising while federal receipts remained flat. This created a post–World War II record deficit of $15 billion in the second quarter of 1967 that, without a tax increase, would hover around $12.5 billion for the year, barring further unanticipated increases in DoD expenditures.[5] But Defense spending continued to rise and along with it so did the deficit.

Southern Democrats, Republicans, and some doves united "to put the Administration on notice that Congress wants 'nonessential' domestic spending cut sharply." Westmoreland's latest troop request confronted the administration with the prospect that it would lead to substantially higher DoD spending and consequently greater deficits that in turn would sharply raise interest rates and inflate consumer prices. On 9 June Ackley recommended a six percent tax surcharge if the nation's strong economic performance continued and if Defense spending remained stable.[6]

OSD, BoB, Treasury, and the CEA, fearing that premature action might derail the expanding economy, could not agree on the timing to impose corrective measures. McNamara favored a tax hike to stem the growing deficit but thought the exact amount should depend on reinforcement decisions for Vietnam after his return from Saigon in early July. The economic troika concurred with McNamara's approach, although on 19 June Ackley warned that an upward drift of only $1 billion in defense outlays per quarter without a tax hike could put the economy "back in the soup of inflation and tight money" in 1968. Staring at the likelihood of another major troop escalation in Vietnam, on 10 July the president sought advice from his economists. Ackley and Schultze argued for a tax increase; along with Fowler they agreed that if major reinforcements were sent to Vietnam a considerably higher tax surcharge would be needed. The president opted to wait for McNamara's evaluation of Westmoreland's troop request because it would play a major part in determining FY 1968 defense expenditures, estimates for the FY 1969 DoD budget, and the proposed rate of the tax surcharge, somewhere between six and ten percent, then under consideration.[7]

Since mid-1965 McNamara had argued for higher taxes to pay for the war, so his 10 July 1967 cable from Saigon strongly supporting a tax surcharge was hardly surprising, but he opposed any expansion of U.S. forces in Vietnam if it would require calling up the reserves. This meant that the FY 1968 DoD budget should not be any larger than originally estimated and that a six or eight percent surtax was preferable to a ten percent hike. Furthermore, Systems Analysis had just identified excess troops in the active duty force structure whose availability for Vietnam duty by the end of 1968 made unnecessary any reserve call-up. Armed with these figures and agreement by Westmoreland and Wheeler, on his return from Vietnam on 12 July McNamara recommended a 55,000-man increase to U.S. forces in Southeast Asia without a reserve call-up. The president approved it the same day.[8]

On 21 July, McNamara conferred with senior economic advisers who, with the exception of Labor Secretary W. Willard Wirtz, anticipated federal expenditures reaching $138–139 billion because of increased defense spending. Opinions varied on the amount of a tax surcharge, McNamara now favoring nine percent. If additional taxes slowed the economy too much, he could always add another $2 billion in defense spending to reenergize it. The participants initialed a 22 July memorandum to Johnson that recommended, among other revenue raising devices, a ten percent tax surcharge on individuals and corporations.[9]

Two days later Johnson met with congressional leaders in an effort to convince them that a tax increase, cuts in DoD expenditures, and legislative restraint to hold down nondefense spending were necessary to control the growing deficit. He made the same approach to the Senate committee chairmen the following evening, further encouraging them to pass pending appropriation bills so he could judge what programs to cut. More arm-twisting ensued as the president met with Rep. Wilbur Mills, who made clear that he would not support higher taxes without corresponding reductions in spending. On 31 July Johnson again argued the urgency of the tax bill to Democratic congressional leaders. After weeks of persistent persuasion, on 3 August he finally sent his proposal for a ten percent tax surcharge to Capitol Hill where it ignited a long and bitter struggle.[10]

The Final FY 1968 Defense Budget

The president's proposed tax surcharge did not have any direct effect on the FY 1968 DoD budget, then in its final months of congressional massaging. Still, these final months proved as difficult and contentious as the preceding year of formulation.*

To reconcile the president's injunction to hold down federal spending yet pay for the soaring costs of the Vietnam War (now calculated at $3 billion above January estimates), in early June McNamara instructed OSD and the services to comb through their respective FY 1968 budgets and identify possible expenditure savings to offset the potential increases. OSD typically achieved most financial economies by deferring modernization projects and perpetuating maintenance backlogs of real property and equipment. Funding non-Vietnam related programs at the previous year's level left reduced inventories unreplenished as units steadily diminished their stockpiles merely to continue daily operations.[11]

When presenting his tax package on 3 August, the president announced his intention to send at least 45,000 more men to Vietnam during the fiscal year. Confronted by falling federal revenues (down $7 billion) and rising expenditures (up $8.5 billion, including $4 billion for DoD), Johnson called for frugality and specifically challenged McNamara to review defense spending with an eye "to withhold all such expenditures that are not now essential for national security." Meanwhile money-conscious House and Senate appropriations committees were making major reductions and some unasked-for additions to DoD's proposed FY 1968 budget. OSD found itself in the contradictory position of having to reclama congressional reductions to its FY 1968 budget submission while demanding the services "save" $3 billion from the same accounts. Furthermore, OSD expected the services to underwrite costly additional deployments to Southeast Asia that would exceed programmed FY 1968 expenditures by $275 million.[12] To resolve the multiple dilemmas, McNamara expected to tap accounts whose expenditures were running less than planned, thereby offsetting unforeseen increases in Vietnam spending.

The service and Defense agency revisions of the FY 1968 budget, showing both the corresponding increases and decreases to specific accounts, could not exceed the total NOA in the president's originally requested budget. In other words, the services and Defense agencies had to juggle existing accounts to pay the higher than projected costs of Vietnam, but they failed to meet McNamara's expectations. Under pressure from the president to hold down costs, McNamara reacted heatedly to service estimates that increased SEA requirements for operations, procurement, RDT&E, and military construction by as much as $4.5 billion in NOA

---

* See Chapter VI.

and almost $2 billion in expenditures. He dismissed many of the additional costs identified in the comptroller's projections as unjustifiable, adding curtly, "I don't understand this—where is our '3 billion' savings program."[13]

With Defense accounts being stretched in opposite directions, in August Nitze and Anthony had the unenviable task of explaining the status of the FY 1968 Defense budget to congressmen frustrated by the constantly changing numbers. Representative Mahon wondered what was wrong with asking for a supplemental appropriation, especially since the president had already announced defense spending might be $4 billion higher than previously estimated. Anthony and Nitze insisted that the $4 billion in spending was unrelated to DoD's FY 1968 request for $71.6 billion (NOA); that the department was also trying to stay within the original expenditure estimate of $73 billion; and, if Congress restored the full $1.4 billion in reductions it had imposed on OSD's original budget requests, a January 1968 supplemental would simply have the effect of revising the details of the FY 1968 budget without changing its overall total.[14] Through such an extensive reprogramming of funds initiated by McNamara, OSD was preparing the way for a "zero supplemental." This would be a request to Congress for permission to pay the growing Vietnam bills by shifting funds from certain appropriated DoD accounts to others, thereby making effective use of Defense outlays and avoiding asking for additional money.

Committee action approved by the House on 13 June reduced the FY 1968 NOA requests by $1.7 billion, offset by increases of slightly more than $.4 billion, including reinstating the nuclear-power guided missile frigate and additional Navy aircraft. The Senate concurred with most House recommendations on 22 August but only after reducing the House proposal by almost $139 million. After compromising its differences and lopping nearly $1.6 billion off the original DoD request, Congress sent the budget act to the White House. Almost three months after the beginning of the fiscal year, on 29 September the president signed the bill, but only after claiming that his version had been "austere," deploring the sizable reductions, and suggesting that additional funds would still be needed.[15]*

How Big a Tax Increase?

As congressional committees gave thought to the proposed DoD FY 1968 budget during most of 1967, the growing strain on the economy lent increasing urgency to the need to adopt tax legislation that would help ease the alarming condition. In early August, at the time of the president's request for surcharge tax legislation, and before congressional approval of the FY 1968 budget, Ackley warned that an unchecked deficit would drive interest rates so high that preventing a housing industry collapse and runaway inflation would require wage and

---

* For a snapshot of congressional action on the FY 1968 budget, see Chapter VI, p. 170.

price controls. Stable prosperity would be set back a decade. The administration's effort to cut spending in exchange for congressional passage of its tax legislation to reduce the deficit depended in large part on holding down the DoD budget. This meant that McNamara had to keep expenditures at the lowest levels consistent with national security. He understood that the American people were willing to pay higher taxes to ensure a strong defense, but, as he stated on a later occasion, it was a "great tragedy" that the public paid more than needed for defense "when we should be husbanding our resources for use elsewhere in our society where they are required." By mid-1967 McNamara had to maneuver between liberal Democrats in Congress demanding that additional tax revenues be used to underwrite expanded social programs and their conservative colleagues on both sides of the aisle just as willing to gut public works and antipoverty programs in favor of investing tax revenues in more Defense spending.[16]

Sundry proposals to borrow money, cut expenditures, and increase taxes floated between Capitol Hill and the White House from midsummer into fall 1967, but no resolution of the legislative impasse on taxes appeared imminent, even after Congress passed the FY 1968 DoD budget late in September. Johnson met repeatedly with congressional leaders in hopes of brokering a tax increase. The president prodded members of both parties in July and August to forego action on a federal pay raise, promised to push for tax reform after Congress passed his bill raising taxes, and pledged to make additional cuts in federal spending if Congress would only approve the numerous still-pending appropriation bills. He got nowhere, as hearings held by the Ways and Means Committee eventually tabled the administration's fiscal proposals. Chairman Mills was adamant that the president choose between guns and butter and just as strident in demanding that the choice should be guns. Exasperated by Mills's recalcitrance on tax legislation, in mid-September McNamara offered to decrease DoD spending proportionately if the president had to ask Congress to make a ten percent across-the-board reduction in appropriation bills. In early October, he informed Johnson that DoD FY 1968 financial needs had increased by $4.3 billion because of the war, that internal reprogramming could cover about three-fourths of it, and that he would be able to find yet another $1 billion in "savings" in order to submit a revised budget with zero NOA change.[17]

In the president's eyes, congressional insistence on chopping $5–10 billion from the national budget would undo three years of the administration's legislative accomplishments. Nevertheless, Congress continued to demand greater spending reductions, though not necessarily in DoD programs, before it would agree to support the tax package. Johnson in turn insisted that he had already spent "16–18 hours a day" in September to reduce the requests of all departments "to a bare minimum" and had saved $27 billion. Without a tax increase, however, the probable need of a $4 billion DoD supplemental for Vietnam could well cripple the social programs. At this point in mid-October, the president seemed to relent on his negotiating pressure, concerned that Congress would view such action as unfair arm-twisting to force through his agenda,[18] but also because he may have been mulling a revised strategy for a new tax initiative even if he judged it had no chance for passage. He asked McNamara for alternative measures should that occur.

His economic advisers pointed out that if nothing else, pursuing his tax effort would deny the Republicans a major election issue in 1968, force Congress to accept some responsibility with the electorate for its inaction, and, in McNamara's words, "pin the blame where it belongs, i.e., on the irresponsible Republican leadership in the House of Representatives." Later, in mid-November, a rejuvenated president was back doing his utmost for his tax package, energized by concern over "the heavy price of inaction"—rising federal debt, soaring interest rates, slumping home construction, growing inflation—and the new international threat to the American economy.[19]

On 18 November, the British government devalued the pound, creating a monetary crisis that directly affected the weakened American economy. Foreign holders of U.S. dollars could convert their holdings in gold at the fixed official price of $35 an ounce.* Currency speculators sensed an opportunity for enormous profits by gambling that Washington's inability to meet its commitments in bullion would force the administration to devalue the dollar, in effect raising the price it paid for gold. Among the consequences of devaluation would be increased overseas expenses of U.S. defense commitments, including the cost of the Vietnam War, and higher consumer prices for imported goods—both conditions the administration hoped to avoid. Only after European central banks pledged on 26 November to maintain the official gold price at $35 dollars did demand for the precious metal recede. During those eight days, however, the run on the international gold pool amounted to $1.5 billion, of which 60 percent was U.S. money.[†20]

Besides exposing the weakened American economy, the dramatic attack on the dollar revealed the additional strains that the Vietnam War, plus the political necessity to maintain troops in Korea and NATO, placed on the nation's balance of payments, problems previously downplayed by the administration. U.S. dollars flowing into South Vietnam accounted for about one-third of the running $3 billion balance of payments deficit, and paying for offshore procurement of war materiel from Japan, Korea, Australia, and the Philippines worsened the shortfall. To hold down overseas spending, the president tightened restrictions on American investment abroad, urged restraint on foreign travel, and imposed cutbacks in military and economic assistance to foreign countries.[21] The near unraveling of the

---

* The July 1944 Bretton Woods, New Hampshire, conference led to the establishment of an International Monetary Fund whose purpose was to restore an efficient international payments system. The linchpin of the system was the convertibility of the U.S. dollar into gold at $35 an ounce. See Collins, "The Economic Crisis of 1968 and the Waning of the 'American Century'," *American Historical Review*, 101:2 (Apr 1996).
† The gold pool had been established in London during the Kennedy administration to prevent undue speculation in gold and to channel gold to central banks in an orderly fashion.

worldwide monetary system added urgency to the tax issue. If the administration were to restore confidence in the dollar and slow down the rise of inflation, it had to reduce the deficit.

Quick to turn adversity into political advantage, Johnson wheeled out his big economic guns to force Democratic congressmen to move his tax package. Fowler and Federal Reserve Bank Chairman Martin told legislators that its enactment was "the single most important and indispensable step" to demonstrate fiscal responsibility, absolutely essential to check the accelerating deficit and curb runaway inflation. Schultze proposed a $4 billion cut in expenditures to accommodate Mills, and the president again pressured Congress for immediate action on the tax package. Meeting with congressional members of both parties on 20 November, Johnson offered to cut FY 1968 expenditures by $4 billion, half from non-Vietnam defense programs, to get his tax surcharge enacted. Earlier, anticipating the magnitude of possible cutbacks, on 2 November McNamara had again enjoined the services to hold expenditures within the FY 1968 budgeted level of $73.1 billion. It soon became apparent that they were not doing so, as November expenditures exceeded the forecast by $400 million; if continued, this would result in an overrun of $2 billion for the fiscal year. Mills resumed hearings on the tax bill on 29 November, but, unimpressed with the White House's latest proposal, he quickly adjourned them indefinitely. After four months of haggling and horse trading, the surtax proposal remained firmly stuck in congressional committee. Congress did, however, pass 12 of 14 pending FY 1968 appropriation bills, enabling Schultze to plan expenditure reductions.[22]

A sharp drop to a 3.9 percent unemployment rate, strong retail sales, expected higher interest rates, and huge gains in production and personal income were again heating up an economy badly in need of tax action. Ackley underscored for the president on 12 December the need to reduce FY 1968 expenditures, hold planned FY 1969 expenditures to around $140 billion, and restrain the predicted boom foreseen during 1968.[23] This again put the spotlight on the DoD budget as the most likely source of savings.

The Proposed FY 1969 Budget Submission

McNamara had to undertake preparation of the DoD FY 1969 budget request even as he juggled the other critical pieces of the fiscal puzzle facing the government—the FY 1968 budget, an assured FY 1968 supplemental, and the crucial tax policy. With the war looming ever menacingly in the background it must have been a wrenching time for the secretary. Nonetheless, inescapably, he had to "crunch the numbers."

In mid-June 1967, while MACV's request for more troops was still under consideration, McNamara's guidance for the preparation and submission of the FY 1969 budget assumed that the Vietnam conflict would continue indefinitely at its current level of intensity. The secretary directed the services to compute combat attrition and consumption data for reorder lead time on the basis of scheduled deployments authorized through 30 June 1968. Support of non-Vietnam committed forces was to be calculated at peacetime activity levels. Budget guidance also envisaged an overall decrease in Army strength of about 56,000 between 30 June 1968 and 30 June 1969, all the reductions coming from forces then committed in Southeast Asia. OSD again encouraged budget planners to defer materiel modernization in favor of using "all acceptable substitutes" to meet consumption and attrition requirements.[24] These guidelines remained in effect even after McNamara agreed in July to increase U.S. forces in Vietnam to 525,000 by June 1969.

Service and agency budget requests submitted to OSD for scrutiny in early October 1967 amounted to over $100 billion (NOA), a figure wholly unacceptable to McNamara. In mid-November, with unprogrammed requirements running about $4 billion over budget during the first quarter of FY 1968, the secretary saw the impasse over the tax increase auguring a possible $30 billion federal deficit that would put the country in an intolerable financial condition. On 20 November, he directed his service secretaries to review once more their respective programs and fund all requirements, but at substantially reduced levels; two days later he told the Joint Chiefs to eliminate or defer "everything that does not contribute to [the] war" in Vietnam. Even following this guidance and despite Anthony's best efforts to achieve reductions by slashing procurement, the revised service-proposed NOA budgets hovered near $85 billion. Growing more pessimistic about the passage of a tax bill with each passing week, McNamara insisted on a budget ceiling of $73 billion plus the congressionally mandated pay increases. In December he cancelled a long-scheduled trip to NATO headquarters in order to give his personal attention to reworking the budget request.[25]

After OSD further reduced the service and agency requests, it proposed an FY 1969 budget of $79.6 billion (NOA) with estimated expenditures of $77.1 billion. The services suffered severe cuts, with roughly two-thirds of the reductions coming from military construction and procurement requests. Three years of deferring new equipment, postponing ship conversions and overhauls, slowing military construction schedules, and drawing down inventories had exacted a toll on the military establishment. Reluctant to acknowledge that financial exigencies had compromised military readiness, McNamara directed the service secretaries and Joint Chiefs in mid-November to explicitly identify diminished readiness capabilities so that he could inform the president of the deteriorating conditions.[26]

Heeding his own guidance, the secretary took the unprecedented step of categorizing OSD's "adjustments" to the service requests according to their impact on national security. Paper changes such as revised pricing ($371 million), improved estimates ($3.2 billion), altered planning or guidance assumptions ($2.1 billion), and financial adjustments ($2.5 billion) accounted for much of the reduction and had little if any impact on defense posture. Deferring $10 billion in equipment modernization and construction made up most of the remaining "adjustments"; these categories, McNamara acknowledged, represented calculated risks with national security.[27]

Early in November, the Joint Chiefs expressed varying degrees of dissent with the secretary's proposed action on some 65 budget items. Their dissatisfaction applied to a whole host of programs: the strategic missile force, AMSA, F-12 interceptors, ABM deployment, Air Force and ground force structure, nuclear procurement related to anti-submarine warfare (ASW) programs, and major fleet escort construction. The Chiefs' resistance spoke directly to military apprehension about readiness and modernization issues. After considering their concerns, McNamara asked for their comments on a reworked version of his budget DPM before he sent it to the president. The secretary's latest decisions defused some but not all the disputes that still involved billions of defense dollars. In one such instance, McNamara continued to endorse a light (Chinese-oriented) antiballistic missile system over a heavy (Soviet-oriented) ABM favored by the Chiefs. The latter expressed their support for a light ABM, but they made it clear that it should be the first step in a much more ambitious and costly heavy system to protect U.S. cities against a Soviet missile attack.[28]

Before meeting with the president, McNamara conferred with the service secretaries and twice with the Joint Chiefs about major force issues.[29] His first meeting with the Chiefs, held 17 November, addressed strategic concerns, including their concept of limiting damage to the United States if deterrence policy failed to prevent a nuclear war. OSD's assured destruction doctrine gave priority to deterrence, precluding need of an extensive ABM system. The Joint Chiefs viewed this strategy as conceding a twofold advantage to the Soviets. First, Moscow did not have to contend with additional U.S. defensive measures, a plus for Soviet nuclear offensive strategy. Second, the USSR's continuing ABM deployment compelled U.S. strategic offensive forces to take costly measures to counter the Soviet defenses. McNamara saw the issue as a money pit—spending huge sums, more than $3.5 billion—to develop an apparently impractical system.

Discussions on conventional systems held the following week at the request of the Joint Chiefs failed to resolve disagreements over the size of the attack carrier force, the proper number of Navy and Air Force tactical aircraft, or the development of a next-generation multi-mission tactical airplane, a few of the more contentious topics. McNamara questioned the military's assertion that U.S. forces were growing increasingly obsolete. Other large issues identified by the Joint Chiefs, such as inconsistency in DPMs, the nation's ability (or lack thereof) to meet two simultaneous major contingencies, or the effect of technological improvements on force structure, were relegated to further study. Spurgeon M. Keeny, Jr., of the NSC staff, accurately observed that the Chiefs' meetings with McNamara were unlikely to change the secretary's mind on a series of budget-busting issues; he doubted, correctly as it turned out, whether OSD would even raise matters of JCS concern with BoB.[30]

As usual McNamara enumerated the differences between OSD and the JCS and service secretaries when he forwarded his budget recommendations to the president on 1 December. He also advised Johnson that it was unnecessary to read the details of the disagreements between himself and the Joint Chiefs because the Chiefs wished to discuss with the president three major matters affecting the budget: (1) AMSA, (2) modernization of the Fourth (Reserve) Marine Air Wing, and (3) development of a new FX/VFX tactical fighter. Almost as an afterthought the secretary wrote that while the uniformed leaders did not recommend FY 1969 budget action on a Soviet-oriented ABM defense, they wanted to repeat their views to the president on the ultimate need for the system.[31]

At their annual meeting with OSD, BoB officials had no clear indication of what ceiling McNamara might place on the FY 1969 budget. During their 17 November session, they opted to limit the discussion to strategic weapon systems, the main battle tank, logistics guidance for the Army in Europe, research and development, and nuclear test readiness. BoB favored a seven-month delay for the operational Minuteman III to save $500 million, which McNamara agreed to reconsider, though holding off on a final decision until later in the budget cycle. Budget officials suggested saving $800 million by initially limiting coverage by the light ABM-Sentinel system to the continental United States, adding coverage of Hawaii and Alaska later. McNamara balked, arguing that such action was not in accord with the decision to defend the entire nation. Conferees consented to ABM coverage for all 50 states, but also agreed to defer redundant defenses of Washington, D.C., and New York City for 12 months.[32]

Reluctant to replace the complex Spartan antimissile warhead with a simplified version to save $500 million as BoB proposed, the secretary insisted on the need for further study. Nor did he wish to limit funding for the new main battle tank only to development, test, and evaluation; because of German involvement in the project he demanded full funding in order to move to the production stage, if warranted. McNamara assented to study BoB's recommendation to draw down 75 days of the supply pipeline time for Army forces in Europe, and further agreed to try to hold down the R&D budget to BoB's $7.4 billion target, about $800 million below the DoD markup. But on 1 December his proposed R&D budget submitted to the president exceeded BoB's guidance by about $250 million; DoD ultimately would request slightly more than $8 billion for research and development programs.[33]

As agreed with BoB, McNamara slipped the Minuteman III operational date by six months and stretched out the proposed development of the Chinese-oriented ABM system. Changing his mind about building a new class of ASW escorts, McNamara eventually approved the Navy's proposal to construct five of the vessels in FY 1969. Likewise he reaffirmed his commitment to procure two nuclear attack submarines in FY 1969 and two more in FY 1970, left logistics guidance unaltered for Army forces in Europe, and gained the secretary of the Navy's tentative concurrence to build three nuclear-powered guided missile destroyers (DXGNs) in lieu of the JCS-recommended one nuclear frigate (DLGN) and two guided-missile destroyers (DDGs) in FY 1969.

Unlike previous years, McNamara's proposed FY 1969 budget offered the president a range of spending options by separating them into two parts, normal and Vietnam budgets. The normal budget would range between $54 billion and $57 billion, depending on presidential decisions about spending for such non-Vietnam programs as additional aircraft, helicopter, and submarine procurement as well as force modernization. Vietnam costs came to $25 billion, an amount covering the deployment of 525,000 troops in Vietnam and 46,700 more in Thailand, with their supporting equipment—3,608 helicopters, 2,646 aircraft of all types, and 707 ships and boats as of 30 June 1969. McNamara assured the president that the budget would allow for continuing the war indefinitely, "barring unforeseen contingencies," without recourse to an FY 1969 supplemental request. The resulting DoD budget proposal of between $79 billion and $82 billion NOA for FY 1969 in effect identified $3 billion in potential savings at the president's discretion.[34] Meeting with his designated successor Clark Clifford on 17 January 1968, McNamara expected that finalizing the budget would be his last DoD task. He added, however, that Clifford would be in a stronger position to defend the proposed budget because, mixing metaphors, the congressional knives were really out for the lame duck (McNamara).[35]

Juggling the Numbers

The incessant demands of the Vietnam War, the needs of the rest of the federal government other than DoD, the uncertainties of the national economy, and the resistance of Congress to increased appropriations and spending compelled the administration to seek budget and tax adjustments acceptable to Congress.

Accordingly, during his annual budget meeting with the Joint Chiefs and McNamara on 4 December 1967 President Johnson opted for fiscal austerity. With an overall deficit of $25–35 billion looming, Johnson told the military leaders that he planned to trim $4 billion in expenditures from the FY 1968 budget, with half coming from Defense. He urged the Chiefs to "sharpen up your lead pencils" and "forgo everything" but "pay increases and the men and materiel necessary." Still smarting from the summer tempest created by the conflicting congressional testimony of McNamara and the service leaders, Johnson coaxed the Joint Chiefs and the secretary to reconcile their differences in order to present a united front for looming congressional committee hearings. As far as the Chiefs were concerned, their objections on major issues still stood. Despite the president's cajoling, they later made known to McNamara their intent, if asked, to lay out before Congress their differences with the secretary.[36]

On 11–12 December, the House and Senate responded to the president's latest overture to cut federal spending when they passed a joint resolution directing him to reduce FY 1968 obligations and expenditures not less than $9 billion and $4 billion, respectively. The president signed the bill, PL 90-218, into law on 18 December and, true to his word to the JCS, ordered a FY 1968 spending cut of $4.3 billion. To meet the targeted cutbacks, civilian federal agencies had to reduce their personnel budgets by two percent and all other cost categories by ten percent; for DoD, the ten percent reduction applied only to non-Vietnam obligations.[37]

Anticipating the cutbacks, OSD had already frozen all civilian hires and curtailed civilian training, overtime, travel, printing, and building maintenance, moves, and alterations. Outside the halls of the Pentagon, a variety of savings accounted for more than $1.8 billion of the reductions imposed on DoD. In December the money was placed in a $3 billion DoD reserve established in compliance with PL 90-218.[38]

OSD resorted to a zero supplemental request as a device to fund additional personnel, operating, and materiel requirements for Vietnam as well as unforeseen expenses of non-SEA forces without requesting additional appropriations from Congress. In simplest terms, this involved maintaining financial equilibrium by increasing certain accounts and decreasing others. Of the total $6 billion so affected, the bulk of reprogramming, approximately $4.3 billion, appeared as changes within appropriation accounts; other accounting devices provided the rest of the money.[39]

The complex accounting transactions involving "literally thousands of individual increases and decreases" permitted OSD to move funds where needed and avoid spending money on overfunded or superfluous programs. Changes in ammunition requirements alone amounted to about one-quarter of the $6 billion total. Why, McNamara asked in mid-February 1968 testimony, continue to spend money to buy unneeded 81-mm. mortar ammunition when it was far better to shift those funds to purchase more 500- and 750- pound bombs needed for B-52 sorties that had doubled 1966 expectations? Slightly more than half the $6 billion in transfers would pay for a "different estimate of SEA force required to meet enemy capabilities," or, in plainer language, deploying more ground troops, flying more bombing sorties, spending more money for the McNamara barrier, and fighting a more intense war against a determined foe. The zero supplemental approach avoided asking Congress for additional money for Vietnam at a time of great political and financial sensitivity over federal spending in general as well as the conduct of the war. Moreover, despite numerous changes in the DoD program that increased financial requirements, this massive reprogramming allowed the department to remain within its FY 1968 budget authority and avoid increases to the troublesome deficit.[40]

Even the hint of additional funding angered the secretary of defense who insisted he was not recommending a budget supplement. He termed it a "financial miracle" that the changes held the line because the forecasts for the FY 1968 budget were made 21 months earlier. Others challenged McNamara for manipulating appropriations and authorizations and asking Congress to change wording on programs it favored, such as the Nike-X and F-12, that would allow him to spend money as he chose. Insisting this amounted to supplemental requests, on 16 February Rep. Glenard Lipscomb accused the defense secretary of "just playing on words." "If you want to say a 'zero' supplemental is what is meant by the word 'supplemental,' you use the term," McNamara shot back.[41]

By whatever name, the latest budget shifts yet again deferred non-Vietnam Defense projects to pay for the accelerated deployment of 55,000 reinforcements to Vietnam. As might be expected given its increased manpower costs and greater end strength, the Army gained $242 million in reprogramming via transfers from other DoD service appropriations. The Air Force internally reprogrammed $560 million. The Navy's decrease of $416 million was offset by transfers to a number of different programs.[42]

McNamara's economy drive, launched in mid-summer 1967, had examined the status of FY 1968 programs line-by-line, item-by-item to identify savings. This preliminary effort had later facilitated the 1968 mandatory readjustments imposed by legislative or executive directives. Yet once again the secretary's desire to control DoD outlays foundered because the earlier reviews were completed before the Tet offensive and the North Korean seizure of the intelligence vessel USS *Pueblo* created emergency demands for still more money.[43] There was something forlorn about McNamara's final appearances in defense of his budget. Vietnam, as it had since 1965, again mocked his cost projections, but he clung fast to his numbers as if figures determined actual expenses. Like him, his budgets were swept away by the whirlwind he helped to unleash in Southeast Asia.

The year 1968 proved the most trying and complicated for the DoD budget process during the Johnson presidency. The succession of emergencies beginning in January 1968 reinforced the president's need for a tax increase to cool off a rapidly accelerating wholesale price index (up three percent in 1967), stem other serious inflationary problems, and cover rising deficits. To hold down federal obligations, Johnson opted for the low range of McNamara's proposed FY 1969 budget; on 27 January the secretary requested $79.576 billion NOA (including military assistance) for DoD's share of the president's budget. Two days later, Johnson sent Congress his FY 1969 budget that once again proposed record outlays of more than $186 billion, including $79.8 billion for Defense. The president offered his financial plan as a combination of selective expansion of certain Great Society programs such as manpower training and wide-ranging reductions to other civilian programs, mostly by delaying or deferring federal construction projects. The reductions allowed for increases in DoD's budget to pay the cost of Vietnam.[44] It was not long before his proposed budget was in tatters.

McNamara estimated on 13 February that increasing the U.S. effort in Vietnam to meet the Tet emergency might add as much as $1 billion NOA to current FY 1968 estimates and two or three times that amount for FY 1969. Anticipated additional expenditures of $500 million in FY 1968 (ending 30 June 1968) and five times that amount the following year made the inflation threat even more worrisome. At a White House meeting two weeks later, MACV's request for 205,000 more troops was estimated to cost at least an extra $10 billion in FY 1969 and $15 billion additional in FY 1970. On 4 March Fowler and senior administration officials told the president that a new fiscal program involving higher taxes, a cut of $2–3 billion in social programs, wage and price controls, and other measures would be needed to pay for the six-figure troop request.[45]

BoB's shocking preliminary projections for DoD's FY 1970 budget, with which McNamara agreed, also forecast a rise of $10 billion each for non-Vietnam related obligations and expenditures. Procurement of major strategic systems—Sentinel, F-111, Minuteman III, Polaris/Poseidon, and shipbuilding—accounted for most of the increases. Absent tough decisions to reduce them, newly confirmed BoB Director Charles J. Zwick cautioned on 2 March, the president could face an FY 1970 Defense budget of $100 billion. By this time, FY 1968 DoD expenditures were running $3.5 billion over budget, making it difficult, even assuming no increase in current programs, to reach the end of the fiscal year (30 June) without asking for supplemental funding.[46]

A few weeks later the cost of the JCS recommendation to send an additional 200,000 reinforcements to South Vietnam, call up 250,000 reservists, and raise service end strength another 490,000 by 31 December 1968 became clear. On 20 March Anthony gave Clifford a price tag: an FY 1968 supplemental of $4 billion (NOA) with perhaps $3 billion extra in expenditures, increasing in FY 1969 to $10 billion additional NOA and $12 billion in expenditures. Moreover, removing so many potential workers from the labor pool for military service and spending the extra money on defense procurement would drive up the price of already scarce labor, fuel a 4.7 percent level of inflation (the highest since 1951), and deal a heavy blow to the U.S. balance of payments position. Such massive deployments, according to OSD Comptroller Anthony, would likely require substantial sacrifice of "the previous marginal Great Society programs which make the difference between domestic unrest and orderly progress toward established social goals."[47] In sum, the nation could not afford the ambitious plans of Westmoreland and Wheeler to reinforce Vietnam and reconstitute the strategic reserve without going on a wartime footing.

At a White House meeting with Democratic congressional leaders on 19 March, Johnson sought support for his tax legislation in exchange for reduced spending. Sketching out his fiscal program, he explained how his formula of raising $10 billion in taxes, eliminating $10 billion in appropriations, and reducing at least $4 billion in expenditures would avert a potential $20 billion deficit, prevent interest rates skyrocketing to 10 or 15 percent, and avoid devaluation of the dollar. Of the $4 billion in reduced spending, half would come from non-Vietnam DoD accounts; the president named the ABM and Minuteman III programs as likely candidates for retrenchment. Johnson assured his listeners that, sensational headlines to the contrary, he did not intend to ask Congress for legislation to call up hundreds of thousands of reservists. The next day Johnson sounded out his advisers on the economic effects of spending another $8.6 billion on Vietnam. To pay the additional cost, they recommended a bipartisan national unity package of $10 billion in tax increases coupled with a $10 billion decrease in government obligations and a $5 billion reduction in expenditures, measures that would also restore confidence in the dollar.[48] Pressures from inside and outside the administration and a realization that his guns and butter policies had overreached their limits forced the president to scale back his Vietnam program even further.

Even a much more modest JCS plan to call about 57,000 reservists to active duty was judged too costly in light of the deteriorating financial situation. Instead, on 3 April Clifford opted for the Systems Analysis proposal to restrict the reserve call-up to 23,000 men, a saving of $400 million. Nothing, including Vietnam, mattered more to Clifford than the nation's economic well-being; he told his staff on 18 March that deeper cuts in government spending were probably inevitable as the price of the president getting his long-sought-after tax bill. Following the president's dramatic announcement on 31 March of his decision not to seek reelection, the Senate did include a tax hike as a rider on an excise bill, but deliberations with the House on the proposal again ended in deadlock.[49]

Passage of the FY 1968 SEA Supplemental

By this time—March 1968—the compelling and not unexpected need for a large FY 1968 supplemental appropriation added another dimension to the numbers juggling. Actions taken and anticipated in Southeast Asia and Korea had added a minimum of $2.5 billion to Defense spending that could not be financed from available FY 1968 funds. Clifford, preoccupied with his Vietnam review, had left it to his deputy, Paul Nitze, to plan, manage, and, in 90 percent of the cases, decide necessary budget matters. Nitze notified the president on 6 March that DoD needed at least another $2.5 billion to pay for the 10,500 emergency reinforcements dispatched to Vietnam and the 14,600 reservists recalled to active duty in response to the *Pueblo* incident. Any additional call-ups or deployments would further enlarge these figures. Nitze requested the president to permit OSD to notify the chairmen of the House and Senate Armed Services and Appropriations committees of its intention to prepare a FY 1968 supplemental request separate and distinct from the "zero supplemental" currently under consideration.[50]

At a White House meeting on the 9th with Clifford, Nitze, Anthony, and BoB representatives, Johnson authorized in principle discussions with Congress on the tentative supplement. At the same time, the president instructed Clifford to plan for a further $3 billion expenditure reduction in the non-Southeast Asia portion of the DoD FY 1969 budget to enhance the possibilities of getting the administration's tax bill passed. Clifford moved quickly to restore a working relationship with congressional leaders, especially those on the Senate Armed Services Committee whose cooperation with the Pentagon, he believed, had virtually ceased during the past three years.[51] Then in rapid succession the contradictions of the past three years in Defense budgeting burst to the surface.

Responding to a formal BoB request for a contingency plan to cut $3 billion in non-Southeast Asia expenditures from the FY 1969 budget, OSD used the familiar tactic of defraying current costs by assigning them to later years. While notifying BoB how DoD might cut expenses in FY 1969, the OSD comptroller concurrently circulated procedures for requesting supplemental FY 1968 funds to cover contingency operations in Southeast Asia and Korea.[52]

By early April the question was less one of whether there would be a supplemental request than a matter of its timing. Nitze informed Zwick on 9 April of DoD's need for $3.9 billion in NOA supplemental FY 1968 funds that included the $1.7 billion reprogrammed in the zero supplemental sent to Congress in February. The next day Clifford officially notified the president of the $3.9 billion FY 1968 supplemental requirement, a combination of such newly identified expenses as those incurred by the Tet offensive and the *Pueblo* incident and additional requirements previously submitted to Congress in the zero supplemental (now being withdrawn).[53]

To pay for additional munitions, replace helicopter losses, purchase equipment, and pay the almost 38,000 reservists recalled to active duty by this time, OSD hoped to have the additional funds by 1 May. Clifford wanted to send the request immediately to enable Congress to act on it before its April midterm recess. However, the president, still trying to broker a compromise with congressional leaders on the tax increase, preferred to delay the request until after the legislators returned to Washington.[54] At that time, 21 May, he forwarded the $3.9 billion (NOA) FY 1968 Southeast Asia Supplemental as one of four supplementals, the others being for lesser amounts to fund military and civilian pay raises and related requirements; altogether DoD asked for a total of $7.3 billion.

The request was not as straightforward as it might appear. Of the $7.3 billion, $3.9 billion was NOA. Making up the $3.4 billion difference was primarily contingent on congressional release of $2.7 billion from the reserve established the previous December to comply with legislative requirements reducing FY 1968 obligations by ten percent; availability of the remaining $726 million depended on approval of civilian and military pay raises and related matters.[55]

Accounting legerdemain aside, the additional requirements in the largest of the supplementals were straightforward. Including the $341 million emergency fund for unforeseen events, the supplemental added up to $3.9 billion. By this time, DoD's financial condition had become so grave that on 23 May Clifford notified the Senate president, the House speaker, and the chairmen of the Defense Appropriation subcommittees that he would resort to recent R. S. 3732 legislation permitting deficit spending for clothing, subsistence, fuel, medical supplies and so forth.[56]

On 9 July the president signed PL 90-392, which appropriated $6.09 billion TOA for the Emergency Fund, SEA, including $3.75 billion NOA, or $125 million less than OSD requested; it also released $2.34 billion from the reserve, $284 million less than requested. The largest reduction occurred when both chambers rejected the $340 million proposed by OSD for an emergency account to fund unforeseen requirements.[57]

Enactment of the FY 1969 Budget

Meanwhile, the FY 1969 budget was making slow progress. In mid-March 1968 Zwick outlined for the president a $5 billion cutback in federal outlays, including $2 billion from DoD non-Vietnam FY 1969 expenditures, that would allow the administration to keep some momentum in Great Society programs and offer an acceptable tax program to Congress by holding down the FY 1970 DoD budget. In early April the president offered a modified $10 billion tax hike, $10 billion appropriations cut, and $4 billion expenditure reduction.[58]

By late April a more complete and accurate forecast of overall federal spending showed FY 1968 expenditures running within budget guidelines. For FY 1969, Zwick identified a possible decrease of $5 billion in expenditures ($2 billion from Defense) and possible reductions of $12 billion (NOA), Defense contributing more than one-third. These reductions in the FY 1969 budget, Zwick felt, would make it "difficult, if not impossible" for Mills and the Republicans to reject the president's latest tax package. As the political jockeying continued, Clifford told his staff that conditions remained too unsettled for him to issue written specific guidance for DoD cutbacks. Army Chief of Staff General Harold K. Johnson spoke out for laying "the cards on the table" to avoid antagonizing congressional committees, but the ensuing discussion only confirmed that without knowing how much and what to reduce, OSD's senior officials could do little until Congress acted on the FY 1969 budget request.[59]

On 9 May House-Senate conferees insisted that $6 billion be struck from FY 1969 federal expenditures. The president remained loath to make greater spending cuts because of opposition from organized labor and the unacceptable effect of wrecking popular programs such as poverty assistance, education, and the like in traditional Democratic voting strongholds. At a cabinet meeting five days later, he listened to details of the effects of the $6 billion reduction demand. Cutting FY 1969 expenditures by $2 billion, DoD's share of the overall reduction, would require eliminating 153,000 civilian positions from the department's rolls. OSD promptly notified congressional leaders of the harmful effects such reductions imposed on the war effort because 70,000 of the threatened jobs were overseas in Vietnam, Thailand, and Pacific supporting areas. DoD had also employed 72,000 civilians to replace or fill 75,000 military slots as part of its civilian-military substitution program, a McNamara-inspired effort to squeeze more troops from noncombat units into the field.[60] Unmoved by such appeals, Congress refused to act on the president's proposed tax package unless the administration made deeper cuts in federal spending.

Johnson tried to persuade House Speaker John W. McCormack (D-Mass.), Majority Leader Carl Albert (D-Okla.), and liberal Democrats to scale back overall cuts from $6 billion to $4 billion. He also asked McNamara for suggestions on reducing expenditures. On 13 May, the former defense secretary recommended $3 billion in DoD savings by disbanding the 6th Infantry Division, postponing construction of nuclear carriers, stretching out Minuteman III production, delaying the ABM (Sentinel) system, and withdrawing one Army division from Germany. Clifford and Wheeler dismissed McNamara's proposals, believing they seriously cut defense muscle.[61]

Doubts about the economy persisted. In early May CEA Chairman Arthur M. Okun thought higher taxes might "choke off economic growth," but the risk was "better for the economy than no tax bill at all." At a 14 May cabinet meeting, Fowler also endorsed an immediate tax increase, but the president doubted that liberals in Congress would agree to a House-Senate package calling for a $6 billion reduction in FY 1969 spending because of its effects on social programs. His economic advisers agreed that a $6 billion cut was excessive, but to get his tax bill he had to take the reduction or risk a "much more serious recession." A week later, in an unusually alarmist appraisal, Okun asserted that without a tax package another run on the dollar might result in a major global political defeat for the nation and deal a body blow to the international trade system that would cause financial panic and economic depression. Hanoi would interpret the financial calamity as evidence of U.S. inability to carry on the war in Vietnam and walk out of the Paris peace talks. Despite Okun's warning that his memo was highly sensitive, Johnson thought it too good not to use against his tax opponents. He privately called members of Congress and read them excerpts while denouncing Mills for stonewalling the administration's tax bill.[62]

In a final bid to enlist support for his program Johnson assembled 19 Democratic congressional members on 27 May to hear Okun preach the ruinous consequences to interest rates, home building, the gold flow, and credit if no tax bill was forthcoming. Unmoved, House members insisted on the $6 billion reduction in exchange for tax legislation. Keenly sensitive to warnings of a world financial crisis and the compelling need to cool demand and counteract inflation, on 29 May a reluctant president, unwilling to risk the potential damage to the economy over a difference of $2 billion, bowed to the congressional demand to cut $6 billion from FY 1969 government expenditures in exchange for early enactment of his tax bill. Johnson advised Clifford in mid-June to anticipate FY 1969 DoD spending reductions of $3 billion.[63]

PL 90-364, the Revenue and Expenditure Control Act of 1968 signed by Johnson on 28 June, imposed a temporary ten percent income tax surcharge and required a reduction of $10 billion in NOA and $6 billion in expenditures in the proposed FY 1969 budget. The act also restricted hiring until federal civilian employment was reduced to June 1966 levels; for DoD this meant freezing or eliminating some 150,000 DoD civilian slots. That same day Zwick informed executive departments of the legislative limitations and directed each agency head to prepare plans for budget reductions. Even though Vietnam operations would remain fully funded, DoD would have to reduce expenditures during FY 1969 by $3 billion.[64]

To make such major reductions, Clifford had to slash non-Vietnam programs, but where? An already frugal budget left nuclear superiority over the Soviets uncertain and cast doubt on the feasibility of expanding a thin ABM system against the Russian strategic threat. Reluctant to scale down strategic programs, yet anticipating severe cuts, Clifford had previously appointed a group, known as Project 693, to determine which programs to sacrifice when it became necessary.[65] Creating Project 693 proved fortuitous because it later enabled OSD to work closely with the House Appropriations Committee to mutually scale back programs in order to comply with PL 90-364.

Besides the members of Project 693, others were looking for future Defense savings, but with little success. In late July, a special committee devising scenarios for T-Day, the day hostilities in Vietnam ended, posited that, depending on timing assumptions, anywhere between 30,000 troops and a two-division corps (about 60,000 personnel) might have to remain in South Vietnam indefinitely. Furthermore, programs deferred because of the Vietnam War, including military construction and housing as well as force modernization, would have to be paid for as would upgrades for production facilities. As Nitze told Okun, significant DoD requirements "can be reasonably foreseen in the next few years" even if the war ended overnight. The T-Day group's findings only echoed what McNamara had learned a year earlier. Savings on national defense would not come from an illusory peace dividend, a view confirmed publicly in late June 1968 by Undersecretary of the Treasury Joseph W. Barr.[66]

On 2 July, four days after PL 90-364 took effect, Clifford decided not to activate the 6th Infantry Division, the first casualty of budget reductions. Other planned cutbacks made public in late August included the inactivation of eight naval air and seven Air Force F-101 squadrons plus the closure of 23 Nike-Hercules sites and their support infrastructure in 12 states. Even these relatively moderate actions brought glowers from Capitol Hill. For example, Rep. Mendel Rivers of the House Armed Services Committee indicated that congressional approval to close the Nike bases would depend on OSD inserting into the next military construction program $26 million to pay for relocation of 10 of the batteries "to compensate for the loss of effectiveness" due to the eliminations. Representative Sikes of the House Appropriations Committee emphasized that required reductions should be spread over several major programs to at least minimize the impact on any one program (and possibly any one congressional district). Legislators also expressed concern about the effect the cuts posed for both Vietnam operations and overall national security, though they offered no relief from the impending reductions.[67]

Following Project 693 guidance, Clifford felt decisions on which programs to cut should remain in DoD's hands, but the president wanted to place the onus for reductions squarely on Congress.[68] Accordingly, Clifford awaited congressional action on the FY 1969 authorization and appropriation bills before making any final decisions on further program reductions. In early July, Mahon notified Clifford and Nitze that Congress would impose substantial reductions in the DoD budget to meet PL 90-364 stipulations. Concurrently, Mahon's staff requested OSD to inform his committee about DoD plans to meet the $3 billion NOA reduction in the FY 1969 budget; they also questioned certain programs and their proposed funding as identified in the president's original budget request.

Mahon specifically challenged further funding for the Sentinel system, the F-111 and A-7 aircraft, and the Army's Cheyenne helicopter. In response, OSD furnished Mahon and Rivers with a list of possible non-Southeast Asia NOA reductions totaling $3.3 billion, suggesting that Clifford would discuss the particulars surrounding decisions and recommendations with them. A detailed list of specific line items for potential NOA reductions went also to the Senate Appropriations Committee.[69]

The 18 July House Committee Report, referred to the Senate Committee on Appropriations for review, recommended cuts of $4.8 billion in NOA from the president's January request for the FY 1969 DoD budget. Having worked closely with House leaders to identify possible reductions, OSD budget specialists had coordinated two-thirds of the total DoD cuts with program decreases identified in House authorization and appropriation bills reports. The $540 million OSD pruned from the Navy F-111B program, for example, matched House recommendations for reducing the project; the $677 million struck from the Air Force F-111A version of the aircraft dovetailed exactly with the House committee number. Saving $221 million by dropping the destroyer DX project provided another instance where Project 693 identified a reduction corresponding to a congressionally directed markdown. The services actually welcomed certain reductions. House rejection of further authorization for funding of the F-111B enabled the Navy to cancel the detested program that it had been trying to kill from inception. By dropping the F-111B, naval officials expected to open the way for a VFX-1 program (later to become the F-14A), a course they had been pushing since Clifford became defense secretary.[70]

To comply with the June 1968 Revenue and Expenditures Control Act, on 18 July the House Appropriations Committee recommended an FY 1969 Defense budget of $72.239 billion (NOA), striking $4.834 billion from DoD's request (not including military construction). Procurement accounts suffered heavily—almost $3 billion of the reductions. In general, however, the House followed OSD's recommendations, so OSD could quietly accept $4.3 billion, or about 90 percent, of the total reductions. But the House also cut another $95 million for minesweepers and pared general procurement and R&D accounts by almost $390 million over OSD's Project 693 guidance. OSD's reclama urged restoration of $520.7 million, including $183 million to buy four fast-deployment logistic ships and almost all of the $125 million for the otherwise eliminated Emergency Fund. Describing the latter as a matter of "highest urgency," on 24 July Nitze appealed the reductions to Chairman Russell of the Senate Committee on Appropriations, whose members would consider the bill as reported by the House.[71]

Clifford explained in closed testimony before the Senate Committee on Appropriations on 10 September that the $3 billion cutback in FY 1969 expenditures "postponed some actions" by shoving them into future years and warned of "real problems in 1970" because the program deferrals were a "temporary expedient" which, if continued indefinitely, would damage the nation's security. Nitze similarly cautioned that at least $300 million of the non-SEA expenditure reductions were deferrals that would enlarge current backlogs in aircraft rework and ship overhauls or further stretch out new weapons testing programs and construction projects. They would constitute an additional expenditure in FY 1970.[72]

After amending its July appropriations committee report, on 12 September the House finally approved an FY 1969 DoD budget that contained reductions of $3.7 billion NOA plus another $1.1 billion reduction from prior-year funds. The next day Nitze informed Senator Russell that DoD could accept more than 90 percent of the House-imposed reductions, but he urgently requested restoration of $340.8 million for five specific programs: $95.8 million to purchase 11 minesweepers; $20 million for Army RDT&E; $75 million for other RDT&E; an additional $100 million to achieve VFX-1 aircraft initial operating capability by early 1973; and $50 million for a DoD Emergency Fund to meet urgent, if unanticipated, requirements in Southeast Asia. Recounting his 17 September testimony before the Senate committee, Clifford told the president the same day that the Senate would "give us what we ask for," but the FY 1970 DoD budget would be in trouble.[73] OSD did get what it asked for, but at a cost far higher than Clifford first understood.

As in past years, congressional adjustments in recommended budgets were not zero-sum games but rather involved disproportionate decreases and increases within appropriation titles. Senators, for instance, struck $388.8 million for F-111B production while adding funds for congressionally favored programs such as the EA-6B and F-4J aircraft. Navy RDT&E accounts increased, primarily because of $130 million for the VFX-1 aircraft; the other services and OSD suffered decreases. Likewise, to pay for the minesweepers and other priorities pushed by Nitze, the Senate, pending flight testing of the Poseidon missile, sharply reduced conversion of Polaris boats to Poseidons from six to two by cutting $279 million from the $482.6 million requested.[74]

Unaware of the strategic implications of the Poseidon decision, Clifford accepted the swap of funds until Nitze explained the "frightful importance of getting back some of those boats." Delaying the conversions, Nitze explained, would cost the United States its hedge against a large Soviet ABM deployment in the mid-1970s. Clifford then appealed on 7 October to Mahon to reinstate the funds "as a matter of utmost gravity"; he urged the House to accept also Senate increases to RDT&E, VFX-1, and emergency fund accounts. Clifford also asked for relief from the restrictions on civilian employment in OSD in the Senate version of the bill.[75]

The House gave back $66 million to the Poseidon conversion program, bringing the appropriation to $269 million, far less than OSD wanted. As part of a compromise, the House signaled its willingness to exempt from PL 90-364 limitations* the 150,000 DoD civilian positions established since the end of FY 1966 in the Southeast Asia theater of operations. House action further provided $50 million for the emergency fund, furnished the full $130 million for the VFX, raised Army RDT&E by $6 million, but denied money for minesweepers. After conferring, on 10 October the House and Senate committees compromised their outstanding differences and the next day both chambers passed the appropriation, which the president signed on 17 October without public comment. After almost 10 months of negotiation, compromise, and occasional vilification by both sides, the Department of Defense Appropriation Act, 1969, chopped $5.2 billion (NOA) from the president's January budget request, bringing the final total, with financial adjustments, to $71.8 billion. Priorities mattered for little, appearances for much during the FY 1969 appropriations battle. As Arthur Okun later recalled, "the whole process was really screwy."[76]

The FY 1970 Defense Budget

When Clifford assumed office on 1 March 1968, the McNamara appointees administering the functioning PPBS process were already busy formulating the FY 1970 DoD budget. One month earlier, McNamara had circulated the calendar year schedule for program and budget reviews. According to his guidance, the services and OSD would prepare their FY 1970 budget submissions on the assumption that hostilities in Vietnam would continue through the FY 1970 funding lead time at the same levels and rates of activity as currently approved.[77]

Early in March, Nitze confirmed the continuity in DoD planning by circulating the timetable for DPMs and guidance memoranda, the standard tools instituted by McNamara to determine program funding allowances.[78] As in previous years, to keep non-SEA budget requests to a minimum, OSD guidance deferred modernization, stretched out production lead time for long-term items, and restricted actual production of short-term items to no more than 12 months.

---

* For PL 90-364 see above, p.32.

For planning purposes, OSD expected hostilities to continue indefinitely in Southeast Asia at a level of 549,000 troops, but this projection may have been a device to dispel the inevitable speculation that would occur if DoD presented a lower budget premised on de-escalation in Vietnam. The OSD civilian staff assumed that during FY 1970 costs for air and ground operational activity would decline by 20 percent from the average post-Tet 1968 levels with a corresponding ten percent decrease in bomb and ammunition expenditures. By late November and early December, Clifford, convinced that troop withdrawals were inevitable, spoke privately of a symbolic pullout of 5,000 U.S. troops from Vietnam by Inauguration Day 1969.[79] Washington's indecisiveness, Hanoi's hardheadedness, and Saigon's ineptness dashed these expectations during the waning days of the Johnson administration. Clifford, like McNamara, was discovering the frustration of a war seemingly impervious to American military power, diplomatic influence, and money.

Although the tentative target for the FY 1970 Defense budget was $85 billion, early estimates pointed toward a level of about $100 billion despite Clifford's admonition that forecasts in that range were "not within the order of practicability." The number of complex budget manipulations—reductions, additions, recisions, revisions, supplementals—made it appropriate for mid-August guidance to call for two FY 1970 budgets. The basic budget would encompass the "Approved Defense Program," part of the Five-Year Defense Program, as of 31 August. An addendum budget would display proposed additions or reductions not specifically related to DPM decisions and program change decision (PCD) reclamas—unanticipated and therefore unfinanced requirements. With acute financial problems hamstringing the administration, on 13 August OSD Comptroller Robert Moot* enjoined Defense agencies to hold any addendum submissions to the minimum, and then only for highest-priority requirements that could not otherwise be accommodated within the basic budget.[80]

The FY 1970 budget requests from the services in early October topped $100 billion, with the addendum budget accounting for $7 billion of the total. Clifford characterized these figures as "out of the ball park" and demanded that they "be brought back in line." The Navy's basic budget request totaled $27.2 billion and its addendum $3.2 billion, a total of almost $8 billion more than the previous year's appropriation. Major expenses included over $4.8 billion to buy more than 260 combat aircraft and $630 million in RDT&E and procurements funds for the VFX-1 (later the F-14A) aircraft. Navy officials also sought funding to replenish or refurbish the aging fleet—412 ships would be 25 years old by July 1970—by starting construction of 26 and modifying another 20 at a cost of $3.1 billion.[81]

---

* Moot replaced Anthony on 1 August.

The Air Force FY 1970 basic budget amounted to $30.6 billion (TOA) and the addendum portion another $2.2 billion. The major programs were aircraft procurement ($7 billion), missile and other procurement ($6 billion), and operations and maintenance ($14.7 billion). In addition to possible reductions in munitions costs, Air Force Secretary Harold Brown pointed to possible economies that could be obtained by early release of recalled National Guard and Reserve units and review of F-111/FB-111 spare parts requirements. He insisted that $879 million for aircraft modifications was a rock bottom estimate that might well require increases of between $150 million and $250 million.[82]

Even after an internal service review, which cut $5 billion, Army basic and addendum requests still totaled almost $30 billion. The basic budget, in addition to supporting the current force structure and the 369,000 Army soldiers committed to combat operations in Southeast Asia, requested $8.1 billion for equipment and missiles, $1.9 billion for the Sentinel system, and $8.6 billion for operations and maintenance.[83]

OSD ultimately reduced the Army request by $3.8 billion, the Navy by $6 billion, the Air Force by $7 billion, and Defense agencies by $350 million. Including the use of $1.8 billion in financing adjustments, NOA eventually fell by more than $19 billion to about $81 billion. Major decrements were easily predictable: operations and maintenance together with procurement accounted for most of the total. The proposed FY 1970 budget allotted $23 billion for Vietnam, a reduction of $4.6 billion from FY 1969. Lower operating rates, decreased ammunition requirements, diminished aircraft attrition, and reduced equipment and spare parts procurement would account for the major part of the savings. A 20 percent reduction in tactical air sorties because of restrictions on bombing North Vietnam targets and cutbacks in B-52 sorties, from the 1,800 already directed to 1,400 a month (not agreed to by the JCS), would also lessen demand for aerial munitions.[84] All of this, of course, was based on the expected start of the Paris negotiations.

The DoD-BoB budget review held on 12 November projected additional FY 1970 expenditures of $14 billion for the federal government, including $2 billion more for DoD, over the previous year's $185 billion. Nitze, representing Clifford, doubted, however, that DoD could hold its increase much under $4 billion unless he assumed a 20 percent reduction in Vietnam consumption of ammunition, aircraft, materiel, and so forth, or brought troops home from Southeast Asia. This extra spending threatened to swell the anticipated deficit despite projections of FY 1970 federal revenues at $195–196 billion with the tax surcharge and $185 billion without it. By late November expectations in OSD were that FY 1970 DoD spending would probably be held to $80–81 billion, although the president had not approved that figure nor had program decisions to reach that amount been made.[85]

Following discussions with BoB, on 21 November Nitze invited the Joint Chiefs to identify issues that warranted discussion in their annual budget meeting with the president. Instead of addressing individual issues, as in past years, the Chiefs proposed a posture briefing to dramatize "the decreasing readiness of U.S. military forces in light of our present and possible commitments." In a 45-minute meeting with the president on the morning of 26 December, Wheeler made a brief introductory statement pointing out that a growing Soviet strategic capability was eroding the once clearly superior U.S. strategic position. The other Chiefs in turn then registered their concerns that the Vietnam War was draining the readiness of American general purpose forces to reinforce NATO adequately in a timely manner and that deferred reconstitution of the strategic and general forces was generating an accumulation of unfunded requirements that threatened future force capabilities.[86] The hard fact remained that years of understating non-Vietnam Defense requirements could not be made good, especially in difficult economic times.

Clifford patterned his 2 December FY 1970 budget DPM on the format McNamara used the previous year. Like McNamara, he divided it into two parts: a so-called normal budget and one devoted to Vietnam. The normal budget asked for $58.2 billion (TOA), including about $700 million for military assistance and civil defense. Vietnam costs, pegged at $28.5 billion (TOA), covered 549,500 men in Vietnam and 48,700 more in Thailand along with such supporting equipment as 3,800 helicopters, more than 2,770 aircraft of all types, and 709 ships and boats through 30 June 1970. The proposed $86.7 billion (TOA) budget would underwrite the war at current levels and, "barring unforeseen contingencies," without an FY 1970 supplemental.[87]

The budget also called for increased expenditures of $1.2 billion to $2.2 billion above the $80–81 billion ceiling acceptable to the president. Clifford presented the Vietnam portion of the budget as the main area for possible savings—$4 billion in expenditures and $10 billion TOA. Assuming combat could not continue at the intensity level of 1968, he posed the possibility of a 20 percent reduction in consumption and attrition in FY 1970 and a 40 percent reduction in FY 1971 that would save $2.5 billion in outlays during fiscal years 1969 and 1970. Unlike McNamara, who had always found ways to pay for escalating the Vietnam War even as he played fast and loose with the figures, Clifford relied on radical and admittedly high-risk options that would save $4.8 billion (TOA) in FY 1970 funds by withdrawing 120,000 American troops, including one Marine and one Army division, and almost 400 tactical aircraft by 30 June 1970.[88]

Several days later, the administration's top economic advisers, somewhat surprised by the strong surges in consumer spending and homebuilding, informed Johnson that inflation might cause a pronounced slowdown of the economy in the first half of 1969. They offered four options, seeming to lean toward checking this trend by extending the surtax for another year to raise enough revenue to finance a $195 billion federal expenditure budget and still produce a surplus. Without the extra revenues, balancing a budget of $188.5 billion to $193.5 billion would require very hard decisions and drastic actions.[89]

In mid-December the president asked Clifford to hold down spending in the FY 1969 adjusted budget to $78 billion and in the proposed FY 1970 version to $79 billion. The secretary replied that it was impossible to do this without actually withdrawing troops from Vietnam. Complaining to his staff that OSD had successively cut the original $101 billion service requests for FY 1970 to $83 billion, then to $81 billion, and finally to $79.5 billion, he insisted that he would make no further reductions "without written orders" from the White House or BoB.[90]

Johnson pursued the matter with Zwick, telling him to review the draft DoD budget and list potential reductions to meet presidential targets of $78 billion and $79 billion in military expenditures for FY 1969 and FY 1970, respectively. Zwick found OSD's request for an additional $4 billion in non-Vietnam defense expenditures excessive and sure to provoke questions in Congress and the media. He recommended saving about $2 billion by reducing several non-SEA accounts including Sentinel, a program the president wanted, Poseidon conversion, already reclamaed by Clifford at Nitze's urging, and particularly shipbuilding. Having second thoughts, the president concluded after a long talk with Zwick that $79.3 billion for the DoD budget in FY 1970 was indeed too high. He proposed to cut RDT&E by $150 million and stretch out Sentinel deployment to save another $250 million. When on 30 December Clifford professed his inability to make such cuts, Zwick suggested he discuss the matter with the president.[91]

Johnson apparently relented; on 17 January 1969 the only Clifford-proposed budget went to BoB stipulating an outlay of $81.3 billion TOA (including military assistance) for FY 1969 and requesting $83 billion TOA for FY 1970. In the same document, Clifford notified BoB of DoD's FY 1969 supplemental requirement for $3 billion NOA, slightly more than half of it ($1.6 billion) earmarked to underwrite Southeast Asia operations. Noting that "neither law nor custom requires an outgoing Secretary of Defense to explain or justify the program and budget proposals for the forthcoming fiscal year," Clifford nonetheless submitted a lengthy and detailed posture statement to accompany the FY 1970 budget, being reluctant, he explained, to break the tradition of the annual posture statement "so firmly established" by McNamara.[92]

McNamara had managed the war account expecting to pay for the cost of the Vietnam conflict without short-term disruption of the military establishment or the national economy. As an accounting device his PPBS system worked to track four years of spending more than $80 billion on a futile war. It was less successful in containing Defense costs.[93]

Table 8

Four-Year Incremental Cost of SEA Conflict
(In billions of dollars)

FY 1966	FY 1967	FY 1968	FY 1969	**TOTAL**
$ 9.4	$ 19.4	$ 25.0	$ 27.0	**$ 80.8**

Source: ASD(C), Incremental Cost of SEA Conflict, 3 Jul 68, fldr Sec Clifford's Trip to Vietnam Jul 68, Vietnam Buildup Papers, TAB N, box 3, Pursley Correspondence file, Acc 73A-1934.

As fighting escalated far beyond Washington's initial expectations, DoD budgets skyrocketed and far surpassed OSD's carefully calculated projections. Politically motivated decisions to understate initial costs for the war haunted the administration as multi-billion dollar blockbuster supplementals strained the administration's credibility and the economy. McNamara had begun with a plausible concept to pay for the war, but his stubborn self-assuredness and manipulation of the system to conceal costs had a damaging effect on the military establishment and the nation's economic health.

Clifford inherited McNamara's budgets. To accommodate presidential and congressional pressures, Clifford oversaw steep reductions to Defense programs despite his misgivings about the cumulative effect on future needs. So long as the president insisted on fighting a major open-ended war and paying for his ambitious social programs without sacrifices on the home front, economic stability was impossible no matter what fiscal or monetary measures the administration devised. Holding down military budgets by deferring projects and squeezing funds from non-SEA accounts to cover shortfalls only mortgaged war debt into the future. Inextricably linked to the increasingly frustrating war, Defense budgets proved as difficult to control as the South Vietnamese countryside.

CHAPTER X

THE HOME FRONT

The growing and deadly U.S. entanglement in the Southeast Asia conflict exerted enormous pressures on domestic society. Beyond causing severe financial strains, the war bared glaring inequities in the military conscription system that further embittered the struggle over class and race discrimination that increasingly engulfed the nation. Antiwar sentiment allied itself with the civil rights movement in a volatile mixture of activism that challenged the prevailing orthodoxy on many counts, forcing the Department of Defense to deal with complicated and distracting social issues while fighting a demanding war.

The president's decision not to call the reserves to active duty during the Vietnam buildup in 1965 had broad ramifications across the home front, most obviously affecting the need for additional manpower to fill the much expanded active duty forces required to meet commitments abroad. McNamara's preliminary calculations in July 1965 called for about 350,000 additional men over the next 15 months. In line with that estimate, in August he proposed 235,000 for the Army, 30,000 for the Marines, 35,000 for the Navy, and 40,000 for the Air Force—a total of 340,000 new spaces, with another 7,000 for Air Force and Marine Corps Reserve units. He also wanted to add more than 35,000 to DoD's civilian force. Within a few months, in readying the FY 1966 supplemental budgetary request, McNamara increased these figures to about 379,000 by 30 June 1966 and 525,000 by early 1967.[1] Unable to recall reservists to fill these huge manpower levies even in part, he resorted to a sharp rise in draft calls, both to induct conscripts and to induce greater numbers of volunteers to enlist.

Draft law prescribed that every male in the United States between the ages of 18 and 26 had to complete a six-and-one-half-year military obligation. The National Advisory Commission on Selective Service reported in 1967 that in practice anywhere from one-fourth to one-third of the men in each draft call-up proved ineligible for military service because of educational or medical deficiencies or both.

Under the rigorous induction standards existing in FY 1965, for example, one of every two draft-age men was rejected.[2] The overly high induction standards, the luxury of a peacetime military, rendered African-Americans in particular less likely to be drafted than their white counterparts because substandard educational opportunities and poor medical care left many of them unfit for military service.

Draftees generally spent two years in the Army on active duty and the balance of their service in a reserve pool. Having no choice of assignment, they drew the bulk of infantry, armor, and field artillery jobs, in short, the most dangerous military occupational specialties. Other ways of meeting one's military obligation included voluntary enlistment for a three- or four-year active duty tour with two additional years in a standby reserve pool. Enlisting usually allowed the volunteer to choose his military specialty and often his assignment. One might also volunteer for the reserves or National Guard, spend six months on active duty for training, and spend the next six years in an organized reserve unit liable to be called to active duty in times of crisis. Finally, so long as the draft quota remained relatively small (between 3,000 and 8,600 in the months from August 1964 to February 1965, for example) and the available selection group relatively large, deferment to avoid induction and military service altogether was quite possible.[3]

Inductions began to rise significantly by April 1965 and increased steadily through December when 36,500 men were drafted, more than two-and-one-half times the April total. In gross terms, during FY 1966, 339,700 men were drafted as compared to 102,600 in FY 1965. Of these, more than 90 percent (317,500 men) went into the Army, 2,600 into the Navy, and 19,600 into the Marines, who also adopted two-year enlistments to meet their Vietnam buildup requirements. The rising draft calls in 1965 and 1966 clashed with the president's stated intention to meet military manpower needs "to the maximum extent possible with volunteers," thereby making the far-off war somewhat less painful for the home front. A sharp rise in voluntary enlistments did follow the president's July 1965 announcement of the expanded U.S. military role in Southeast Asia; between August and November volunteer enlistments increased 75 percent over the same period of the previous year. Manpower specialists in OSD attributed the increase to the "pressure of the draft."[4]

Voluntary enlistments in the reserves also soared. Besides recruitment to replace normal personnel turnover in the reserves, OSD added 4,500 spaces to the Air Force and 2,500 to the Marine Corps. More significantly, McNamara decided in September 1965 to reorganize the Army's reserve force structure by redistributing about 145,000 reserve personnel from 750 Army Reserve units that OSD deemed no longer necessary. OSD also authorized 18,500 new spaces for the Army National Guard with the intention that they be included in the new "Selected Reserve Force" of 150,000 men, composed mainly of Guard divisions and brigades, which would be 100 percent manned and equipped.[5]

McNamara's decision created two paradoxes. First, at a time when he was weakening the active duty forces in the United States by stripping them to augment outfits deploying to Vietnam, he was strengthening the stay-at-home National Guard units with additional men and equipment. Second, and concurrently, the Army National Guard intensified recruitment for the Selected Reserve Force, thus competing for volunteers with the active duty forces. Given a choice between possible combat duty and limited reserve service in the United States, many draft-eligible men enlisted in the reserve units. Furthermore, OSD's previous attempts to hold down the number of reservists in paid-drill status had prompted large numbers of obligated reserve enlistees to transfer out of organized units into the unpaid Individual Ready Reserve pool. This left many organized drill units under strength; to meet statutory end-strength requirements imposed by Congress, they too accepted new enlistees.[6]

As of 30 June 1965, the U.S. Army had far and away the largest reserve formations—695,263 paid personnel (more than twice the size of the other services' reserves combined)[*] divided between 316,278 Army Reservists and 378,985 Army National Guardsmen. To meet its much larger manpower needs, the Army offered volunteers for the Army Reserves or Army National Guard a Reserve Enlistment Program or REP. Under REP an individual served six months on active duty, mainly as a trainee, and for the next five-and-one-half years attended monthly drills and an annual two-week active duty summer camp. Law required REP volunteers to enter active duty within 120 days of enlistment. By midsummer 1965 the greatly increased numbers of volunteers and draftees had overwhelmed the Army's training facilities.[7]

The decision not to mobilize reserve forces aggravated the training backlog. Without reservist replacements the Regular Army had to expand by nearly 25 percent between 1 July 1965 and 30 June 1966 to make up the difference, forcing the training establishment to operate at close to full capacity to satisfy the Vietnam buildup requirements; this left little room for six-month trainees needed by the reserve components because the active duty recruits had priority.[8]

By the end of July 1966 when some 135,000 REPs were awaiting their call to active duty, at least 30,000 and perhaps many more were well past the 120-day benchmark. Two months later, more than 122,000 REPs still awaited active duty training—all of them, of course, exempt from the draft, having already enlisted. As early as mid-February 1966 McNamara admitted that thousands of enlisted reservists had yet to receive their six-month training, but he insisted to congressional critics that the specified end strengths they themselves established had forced DoD to recruit unneeded reservists.[9]

---

[*] The Naval Reserve counted 180,000 personnel, including Marines, and the Air Force Guard and Reserve, 126,000.

Besides the training fiasco, scandals involving bribes and blatant favoritism in enlisting men in the Reserves or National Guard further tarnished the public and congressional perception of the reserve units. Senator Russell and others in Congress came to view the Reserve and Guard as draft havens for many individuals. The House Armed Services Committee introduced legislation in mid-1966 that mandated, among other measures, a 100,000-man increase for the reserves and tightened authority on REP training; it also authorized the president to call to active duty individual reservists from paid-drill units. To remedy some of the more blatant abuses, the bill shifted responsibility for preferential treatment of reserve enlistees to the White House and OSD and directed the reserve components to improve their mobilization readiness requirements by correcting specified deficiencies. It further proposed to create an assistant secretary for reserve affairs in OSD and an assistant secretary for manpower and reserve affairs in each of the armed services. OSD opposed the bill, claiming the new assistant secretary position would duplicate responsibilities and confuse the roles of the other ASDs in reserve affairs. McNamara also rejected another 100,000 more men for the reserves, believing them unnecessary and likely to exacerbate the REP problem. The House passed the legislation, but the Senate did not consider the bill because of the short time remaining in the 89th Congress's legislative session. Congress did, however, insert into the Defense appropriation bill authority through 30 June 1968 for the president to call to active duty individual reservists from paid-drill units. This authority was never used.

On the first day of the 90th Congress, in January 1967, Representative Hébert, a longtime McNamara critic, re-introduced the essentially unchanged legislation except for the already-enacted proviso allowing the president to recall reservists to active duty. OSD continued its opposition to the proposed assistant secretary positions. To mollify criticism, in June 1967 it announced a revised Army Reserve force structure that eliminated 93 units but continued to authorize the 260,000 personnel for the Army Reserve that Congress wanted instead of the OSD-proposed 240,000. Concurrently OSD reorganized the Selected Reserve Force by adding new units to replace those scheduled for elimination in December 1967, giving the reorganized Selected Reserve Force II a total of 623 National Guard and 501 Army Reserve units with a combined authorized strength of 137,000 personnel. These concessions persuaded the Senate to shape a compromise and amend the House bill to redesignate the ASD (Manpower) as ASD (Manpower and Reserve Affairs). A deputy assistant secretary of defense for reserve affairs would coordinate all matters affecting the reserves. On 1 December 1967, Johnson signed the Reserve Forces Bill of Rights and Vitalization Act of 1967 into law.[10]

One other aspect of the Reserve and National Guard demanded attention: their racial composition. In a nation where African-Americans in 1964 comprised approximately 11 percent of the population and nine percent of the total active armed forces, they were dramatically underrepresented in the reserves, particularly the National Guard. As of 31 December 1966 the Army National Guard totaled just under 405,000 officers and enlisted personnel of whom 4,638 (1.15 percent) were African-American. The Air National Guard counted only 475 black Americans among its nearly 81,000 personnel, a mere six-tenths of a percent.[11] The inequity in the Guard and Reserve units was only one aspect of the racial troubles that the military faced continuously during the Vietnam War.

Conscripts and Volunteers: Lower Standards, Greater Inequality

Even before U.S. involvement in Vietnam had created unsustainable manpower pressures, personnel issues were a serious concern. In April 1964 the president announced a comprehensive study of the Selective Service System* to assess the feasibility of an all-volunteer force. Analysis of responses from thousands of soldiers on active duty and in the ready reserve as well as a Bureau of the Census sampling of 35,000 veterans and non-veterans, however, led to the conclusion that the draft was essential not only as a source of manpower but as an inducement to encourage voluntary enlistments.[12] Of first-tour voluntary enlistments, 38 percent were draft-motivated, with percentages running higher in the Army and Air Force (both about 43 percent). Significantly higher percentages of older (20–25 years old) and better educated enlistees would not have volunteered without the pressure of the draft. The same pressure motivated more than 40 percent of all newly commissioned officers, especially those from Officer Candidate Schools (51.4 percent) and the Reserve Officer Training Corps (ROTC) (45.4 percent). More than 70 percent of initial enlistments in the reserves or National Guard were draft-induced. DoD estimates of increased payroll costs for an all-volunteer force ranged from a low of $3.67 billion during bad economic conditions, when volunteers would be plentiful, to a high of $16.66 billion in boom times when they would be scarce. In sum, without the coercive effect of a draft, voluntary enlistments would drop precipitously, and the cost of maintaining an all-volunteer force would be prohibitive.

The same survey also determined that many young men rejected by Selective Service wanted to serve in the military and that many of the rejected would have been classified 1-Y, or acceptable for military duty during wartime or national emergencies.[13] This finding meshed with an idea McNamara had come up with during 1964 for a voluntary enlistment program designed to enroll 20,000 otherwise unqualified men for military service. As he and the president saw it, the Army would give these disadvantaged young men jobs, vocational training, and discipline that they could carry with them on returning to civilian life.[14]

---

* The final report remained classified, although OSD issued a lengthy summary of it in July 1966 when equality of military service had become a hot-button issue. See *New York Times*, 1 Jul 66; Flynn, *The Draft, 1940–1973*, 189.

McNamara's concept evolved into the Special Training and Enlistment Program or STEP. Under STEP the Army would provide six months of special instruction and "remedial therapy" to correct educational and physical shortcomings among a target group of volunteers. They would receive four hours of general educational instruction per day during 14 weeks of basic combat training and 8 weeks of advanced individual training. During this period, the Army would evaluate which trainees might prove effective soldiers to serve out the balance of a three-year enlistment while the others would be discharged without bias. McNamara wanted a minimum of 60,000 STEP enlistees trained at Fort Leonard Wood, Missouri, between April 1965 and March 1969 at an estimated cost of approximately $135 million.[15]

McNamara knew that Pentagon officers derided his plans for "moron camps," but, more importantly, he also encountered congressional resistance. In particular, Senator Russell strongly opposed STEP because he was unwilling to see large numbers of African-Americans from the deep South inducted under the program.[*] Congress ultimately refused to fund STEP, regarding it as a nonmilitary function that would overburden army training facilities involved in the Vietnam buildup. To ensure compliance, Congress specifically forbade the use of any money from DoD's FY 1966 and 1967 budgets to fund the program, thus dooming it.[16] Yet the Vietnam war demanded more and more American troops.

As in previous 20th century American conflicts, the early high physical and mental requirements for entry into the military could not be sustained. A tight labor market, wholesale exemptions from conscription, reserve units competing for recruits, and the lack of sufficient volunteers left the military short of men to meet the Vietnam War's voracious appetite for more and more troops. The need for a host of recruits to fill the rapidly expanding military led to revised draft policies designed both to expand the potential pool of draftees and induce far greater numbers of young men to volunteer for military service. Manpower specialists in OSD advised McNamara that the demands of the war made it undesirable as well as impractical to justify lowering induction standards in order to provide jobs or upgrade the skills of men currently rejected from military service. On the other hand, seeking a way to accomplish McNamara's purpose, they recommended that any new guidelines for military service be presented as implementing the president's stated aim to meet increased manpower needs to the maximum extent possible with volunteers.[17] More to the point, reducing standards would enable otherwise disqualified volunteers to enlist.

---

[*] By the time of the March 1965 decisions to dispatch marines to Vietnam, Russell had changed his mind and told Johnson there was need to lower induction standards to prevent "damn dumb bunnies" escaping the draft (telcon Pres and Russell, 6 Mar 65, WH 6503.03 Program No. 2, LBJL; see also Beschloss, *Reaching for Glory*, 212).

In late August 1965 a White House executive order eliminated deferments for married men. On 24 September McNamara informed the president of his intention to substitute civilians for military personnel in noncombat positions wherever possible to conserve servicemen for duty in Vietnam. He also proposed to further lower medical and "mental" standards to conscript or enlist inductees from a larger pool of young men, particularly the 100,000 volunteers turned away during the last year for fitness reasons. In November DoD lowered mental standards for induction to enlarge the draft pool, with the expectation of stimulating more voluntary enlistments.[18]

The Armed Forces Qualification Test (AFQT) determined mental ability by measuring a potential soldier's standing relative to the national youth population. The test results had five categories that were further divided into subcategories. A percentile score of 50 (Category IIIA), for example, signified that the person scored "as well as or better than half of the 'normative' population."[19] Existing regulations mandated that men in the lower range of AFQT had to pass supplemental aptitude tests for admission to the service. OSD's September 1965 revision, effective that November, qualified high school graduates with AFQT scores of 16 to 30 for military service without benefit of further testing, an adjustment that was expected to make approximately 50,000 otherwise disqualified young men eligible for military service by 30 June 1966.

Spurred by the relentless need for more manpower, OSD yet again revised mental aptitude standards downward effective April 1966. This latest change waived the requirement for a high score on arithmetic and verbal tests for non-high-school graduates with AFQT scores of 16–30. McNamara informed the president that this move alone was expected to bring in at least 12,000 additional men during the next 12 months. Taken together these decisions reduced the percentage of potential inductees rejected from 50 percent in FY 1965 to approximately 40 percent during FY 1966.[20]

Because proportionately more African-Americans suffered rejection on mental deficiency grounds (62 percent versus 22.7 overall), and because of the noticeably higher rejection rates throughout the Southern states, at the time of the first changes in September 1965 OSD Manpower advised McNamara to "expect proportionately many more negroes to make up the additional enlistment in all Services using the lower enlistment standards." McNamara accepted this condition because it squared with one of the original purposes of his STEP program—to "uplift" the African-American living in the rural South through military training. Such paternalism was not confined to the defense secretary. Writing for the New Republic in late 1966, Harvard sociologist Daniel P. Moynihan, who had authored a pioneering and sympathetic study on The Negro Family and was well aware of disproportionate losses among blacks in Vietnam, still argued that military service had "much to offer men with the limited current options of, say, Southern Negroes," hence African-Americans were "entitled to a larger share of employment in the armed forces and might well be demanding one."[21] A new OSD program made Moynihan's entitlement a reality.

Project 100,000

While no congressional approval was required for lowering minimum standards for induction, the legislation that killed STEP left McNamara unable to fund the remedial training that he considered essential for disadvantaged men. Then in July 1966 McNamara and his top aides heard a briefing about a Marine Corps program of "repetition of training and special remedial efforts" that turned low-aptitude inductees considered unsuitable for service into effective marines. Moreover the Marines operated their Special Training Branch within their normal training budget and needed no additional funding from Congress.[22]

Following hasty staff studies by OSD Manpower analysts, McNamara, as a way around congressional refusal to fund STEP, "ordered the services to ensure that all recruit training facilities included some special training units." Shortly afterward, on 22 August 1966, McNamara alerted Russell and Representative Mahon to OSD's plans to modify enlistment standards to permit the armed forces to draft or enlist men previously rejected for military service. Unlike the proposed STEP program, the men would be trained in regular training centers, not a single separate facility, and, in compliance with congressional bidding, no additional funds in the FY 1967 budget were allocated for the new program.[23]

The following day at the Veterans of Foreign Wars annual convention, McNamara publicly announced what came to be known as Project 100,000—the induction or enlistment of many previously rejected men into the military services. Citing statistics of the appalling and tragic poverty that existed in the United States, McNamara stated his conviction that at least 100,000 young men a year who did not qualify under DoD's fitness standards could be accepted into the services. He believed the application of advanced educational and medical techniques could "salvage" thousands of men each year for successful military careers and later for productive roles in society. For the remainder of FY 1967, he announced, the services would accept 40,000 men currently disqualified for mental or physical reasons; thereafter DoD planned to accept 100,000 annually from this category.[24]

The "New Standards Men"* of Project 100,000 were primarily from Category IV: those who scored 10–15 on the AFQT and those who achieved a score of 16–20 but did poorly in the verbal and mathematics portions of the test. A percentile score of 10 was the equivalent of a fifth grade education; while DoD insisted the AFQT was not an IQ test, a rough approximation was that Category IV personnel possessed an IQ in the 80s with some borderline or even mildly retarded. Generally such individuals needed intensive supervision and guidance during training,[25] but the mass of other draftees, volunteers, and junior officers headed for Vietnam also required extensive training.

---

* The term "New Standards Men" was the official label given to recruits entering the military under the reduced standards. ASD (Manpower) Thomas Morris requested use of the new nomenclature in January 1967; until then, such recruits were called "Below the Line Accessions." See Laurence and Ramsberger, *Low-Aptitude Men in the Military*, 154, n 15.

Nowhere in this connection did McNamara mention the need for additional manpower to fight the war in Vietnam. Rather he portrayed military service as a gateway to future success in a civilian career. Yet the true purpose of Project 100,000 remained unclear. While ostensibly first and foremost an anti-poverty program to uplift disadvantaged young men, inarguably it was also a way to enlarge the manpower pool at a time when Selective Service Boards were finding it difficult to meet high monthly draft calls of 35,000 men from the prime draft pool (that is, single men aged 19 to 25). Would it have been done without the wartime manpower crunch? It stemmed seemingly from a combination of motives—an idealistic intent to improve the competence and skills of disadvantaged youth through military service and an opportunity to meet a pressing demand for additional soldiers in wartime. In any case, by 1969 the project would be cited in official documents both for benefiting the disadvantaged and boosting voluntary enlistment.[26]

In characteristic fashion McNamara announced Project 100,000 without internal DoD coordination, telling the services to pay for the ambitious program from currently budgeted funds. In his haste to get started, McNamara overruled one of his best manpower experts who initially wanted a much smaller 3,000-man, low-key program that would have better odds of success in converting congressional skeptics.[27] His own strong belief that the program's success would vindicate his judgment impelled McNamara to implement it without delay.

Some 246,000 New Standards Men were accepted for military service during the first three years of the program, 92 percent as a result of lowered mental standards. Altogether they accounted for 10.7 percent of the total accessions to the enlisted ranks between October 1966 and September 1969. Fifty-three percent (130,000) of the 246,000 volunteered; their enlistments did lead to lower draft calls. About half of the volunteers (63,000) entered the Army or Marine Corps.[28]

A "typical" Project 100,000 serviceman was a Caucasian, slightly more than 20 years old, and a high school dropout with sixth grade reading and mathematics abilities. This profile belied the fact that minorities were vastly overrepresented in Project 100,000—more than 40 percent were African-American as compared to 9.1 percent African-Americans among all other newly accessioned recruits or inductees. Almost half of the New Standards Men, 65 percent of them African-American, hailed from the southern United States. Their most common military assignments were as infantrymen, artillerymen, cooks, clerks, and truck drivers. The overwhelming specialty was combat—41.2 percent in the Army and 55.8 percent in the Marine Corps—not a marketable skill in the civilian economy. Adding to the disparity, 44.5 percent of the Army's African-American New Standards Men received combat specialties as opposed to 38.8 percent of whites. Because the number of African-Americans in the program was high to begin with, they were overrepresented in the most dangerous military occupations. In the Marine Corps 54 percent of whites and 58.3 percent of blacks from Project 100,000 had combat arms assignments.[29]

The secretary of defense had also mandated that 25 percent of Army accessions were to be Category IV. Because the Army had the largest manpower requirements it took more than three-fourths of the total number of men inducted into all the services under Project 100,000. Thus, for Phase I (October 1966–September 1967) quotas, of the 40,000 New Standards Men to be inducted, 30,400 were allocated to the Army, 3,400 to the Navy, 3,600 to the Air Force, and 2,600 to the Marines. By late July 1967, 21,000 of them had entered basic training and of those, four percent failed to complete the course compared to two percent for all other men. McNamara declared this satisfactory and a failure rate "far less than expected."[30]

Yet the failure rate was deceptively low, skewed because most New Standards Men went into the Army, which was less demanding than the other services. From the Phase I group the Army eliminated about three percent of its Project 100,000 volunteers, the Air Force washed out about 9.5 percent, the Navy dropped 6.5 percent, and the Marine Corps 7.2 percent. Furthermore, to graduate, 13 percent of the Phase I New Standards graduates required extra help and time during basic training compared to five percent of all other men; this further strained the already overburdened training system. They had an even lower graduation rate in advanced skill training—87 percent compared to 95 percent of other trainees. Later more comprehensive statistics compiled in September 1969 showed the overall basic training discharge rate for New Standards Men at 5.4 percent, more than double a control group's numbers. Again the Army's size skewed the outcome because it dropped only 3.7 percent while the other services had much higher percentages of washouts.[31]

Since very few volunteer enlistees chose infantry, this left draftees, including those inducted as New Standards Men, to fill the ranks, with many ending up in line combat units in Vietnam. On 30 June 1966, for example, of roughly 133,000 Army enlisted personnel in Vietnam about one-third (44,654) were draftees. A year later, slightly more than half of the 258,000 soldiers were draftees (129,856), and on 30 June 1968 of about 310,000 troops, 43 percent or 133,400 were draftees. Of the 43,500 American servicemen killed as a result of hostile action through mid-August 1970, draftees accounted for 32 percent. In the Army the percentage of draftees among enlisted men killed in action reached 55 percent.* Such statistics bore out the grim fact that a draftee had a much greater chance of being killed than did an Army volunteer, reservist, or National Guardsman.[32]

---

* "Killed" meant soldiers slain in combat and did not include those who later died of wounds, died while missing or captured, or died in combat-related aircraft/helicopter incidents, a total of 6,052 Army personnel as of 1 April 1970. Furthermore, the Army listed an additional 4,992 soldiers dead from noncombat causes for the same period. (DIO, OSD, "Number of Casualties Incurred by U.S. Military Personnel in Connection with the Conflict in Viet-Nam: Cumulative from January 1, 1961 through March 28, 1970," fldr Casualties-Statistics 1970, box 286, Subj files, OSD Hist.)

By March 1971, the Pentagon was phasing out Project 100,000 as part of a larger effort to reach or approach a "zero draft." Despite McNamara's high hopes for their post-military careers, in 1986–1987 a small sampling of 311 veterans from Project 100,000 revealed the men either no better off or actually worse off than their civilian counterparts who had never served in the military. Still, nearly half of these veterans felt their military experience had had a positive effect on their later lives. Most of the others noticed no effect, although 14 percent believed their service had adversely affected their lives.[33] No one spoke for the dead.

Race and Casualties

On 31 December 1965 African-Americans constituted 9.5 percent of the active duty military force, an increase from 9.0 in 1964 and 8.2 in 1962. Yet they suffered disproportionately heavy casualties in Vietnam—16 percent of all battle deaths between 1961 and 1966 and 12.7 percent of the 9,300-plus Americans killed in action in 1967. As might be expected, battle deaths were highest in the Army where in late 1966 African-Americans were most heavily represented in the infantry units that bore the brunt of the ground fighting and its inevitable casualties.[34]

By early 1967, the Army had 20 percent African-Americans; in Vietnam they comprised about 13 percent of the 272,000 Army personnel but had suffered 21 percent of the Army's battlefield dead. At this time also, seven percent of the 74,000 Marines in Vietnam were African-Americans, but they had sustained 10.5 percent of the Marine battlefield dead.[35]

The Army attributed its disproportionate black fatalities to having the highest percentage of African-American enlisted personnel assigned either by choice or by skill level to ground combat units, especially the airborne divisions and brigades. Through December 1966, for example, blacks accounted for more than 20 percent of the strength of the two airborne units fighting in Vietnam and for 24.5 and 27.8 percent of the killed-in-action in those units, a trend that continued into late 1968. They volunteered for these elite units, according to the Army, for the challenge, prestige, rapid promotions, and extra pay paratroopers received. The lack of economic and educational opportunities in a segregated society had deprived many African-Americans of the skills needed for technical military specialties, leaving open to most of them only service in combat arms.[36] This was a key factor that McNamara and the designers of Project 100,000 had overlooked.

Thus, from the outset of the war African-Americans were disproportionately represented in the Army's frontline combat units that bore the brunt of the fighting. No matter how well intentioned, McNamara's Project 100,000 reinforced that disparity by drafting more and more young men from the black community to fight a war that fewer and fewer whites seemed willing to support. As public and media criticism of the inequity of conscription mounted, organized draft protests continued to grow, drawing increasing resonance from African-American civil rights leaders. While the administration could dismiss as young rabble-rousers such black radicals as Stokely Carmichael and H. Rap Brown, it could not disregard the concern and dismay among more mainstream African-American leaders, powerfully expressed in Martin Luther King's April 1966 appeal "to end a war that has played havoc with our domestic destinies."[37]

In response to growing African-American denunciation of conscription the administration released a summary of the still classified 1964 DoD study on the draft that pointed out the "class and race biases of the deferment system." The administration promised to address the issue and institute Selective Service reform. In a speech in Montreal, Canada, on 18 May 1966 McNamara acknowledged the inequities of the Selective Service System that inducted "only a minority of eligible young men." On 2 July President Johnson created the National Advisory Commission on Selective Service. The commission's report in February 1967 recommended, among other things, continuation of the Selective Service System, tightening of student or occupational deferments, and greater opportunities for women to serve in the military; it left those classified I-A with no prior service who enlisted in the Reserve and National Guard forces still eligible to be drafted.[38] But reports and promises could not change the perception of inequality in military service; they only added to the smoldering grievances of African-Americans that erupted with a terrible fury across the land.

Burning Cities: Rising Protest

During the first nine months of 1967 more than 150 cities witnessed varying degrees of lawlessness, ranging from minor disturbances to major race riots and accompanying destruction in Newark, New Jersey, and Detroit, Michigan. During the course of actual and feared outbreaks, state governors mobilized about 70,000 National Guardsmen to suppress urban riots and civil disturbances in their respective states.[39] For the Guard or its predecessors in state militias, this was a traditional mission. For federal troops in 1967 it was an extraordinary one.

Primary responsibility for providing military assistance to local authorities during civil disturbances fell to the secretary of the Army as DoD executive agent, reporting directly to the secretary of defense and/or the president. Initial Army civil disturbance planning began in 1963 in response to continuing disruptions and violence growing out of civil rights activities in the southern United States during the late 1950s and early 1960s. That July, Strike Command, at the instruction of the JCS, prepared an operations plan named "Steep Hill" to employ 21,000 troops organized in seven brigades for riot duty. Units assigned to Steep Hill deployed to Selma, Alabama, in March 1965 to maintain civil order and force local authorities to comply with a federal court order.[40]

Major civil disturbances and urban riots, however, signified a heightened level of unrest and alarm. Because of the stigma of failure associated with inability to maintain local security with their own resources, state officials were usually reluctant to call for federal forces. Governors relied instead on their state National

Guards to maintain or restore local order. They had requested federal troop assistance only 14 times since 1789, receiving full and immediate responses about
half the time. The two standard reasons for federal rejection of assistance were that
the state had not demonstrated its inability to quell the disturbance and that the
governor's request was incorrectly drawn.[41]

No federal troops participated in riot control duty during the large-scale August 1965 disorders in the Watts district of Los Angeles. Federal military forces did
provide logistic support, airlifting mobilized guardsmen from northern California
to Los Angeles. During a three-day period Army units and associated Air Force
troop-carrying aircraft remained in readiness for possible deployment to the riot
area. This airlift effort, coming as it did with upward of 10,000 U.S. troops still in
the Dominican Republic and thousands more en route to South Vietnam as part
of the initial buildup of U.S. forces there, consumed initially all available Military
Air Transport Service aircraft. If federal troops had had to intervene in Watts, they
could have deployed only at the expense of other pressing airlift requirements.[42]
The Los Angeles riots exposed how thinly stretched were federal military forces in
the United States as early as midsummer 1965. Unfortunately, Watts proved to be
the fire bell in the night that tolled for three long years.

Simmering African-American grievances against a white-dominated Newark,
New Jersey, political, municipal, and police infrastructure exploded into violence
following the arrest and injury of a black cab driver on 12 July 1967. Rumors
quickly spread that police had beaten the cabbie to death. Protests followed; next
evening arson and looting broke out in the city. During the early morning hours
of 14 July, the mayor of Newark requested New Jersey Gov. Richard Hughes to
send the state police and National Guard to restore order. At midday President
Johnson phoned Hughes, a Democrat and an especially strong supporter, to offer
assistance. Much to the president's relief, Hughes was determined to handle the
situation locally and did not ask for federal troops.[43] Instead the governor relied on
the National Guard and state troopers to restore order by 17 July.

A different political subtext came into play during the Detroit rioting that
erupted less than two weeks later. The president never spoke to Michigan Gov.
George Romney, a Republican presidential hopeful and possible rival in the 1968
election. Far from promises of help, the administration demanded a precisely
worded written request from Romney for federal troops and sent a senior official
to make an on-the-spot determination of Detroit's need for these forces. Although
Romney's waffling about an outright request for the troops likely delayed their deployment, Johnson's conduct throughout the emergency seemed highly partisan.

Meeting with Governor Romney just before midnight on Sunday 23 July, Jerome P. Cavanagh, mayor of Detroit, the nation's fifth largest city with a population
of almost 1.7 million, phoned U.S. Attorney General Ramsey Clark at his home to
alert him that a "very dangerous situation" existed in the city. Clark promptly notified Secretary of the Army Stanley Resor of the potential emergency. Romney also
phoned Clark in the early morning hours on Monday to say he might need federal

troops "to quell the rioting." There followed a confusing series of early morning phone calls between the Michigan authorities and administration officials. Despite Romney's apparent preference for federal troops, the assistant commander of the 46th Infantry Division (Michigan National Guard) assured the secretary of the Army that the Guard could handle the situation, an appraisal seconded by the division commander, Maj. Gen. Cecil L. Simmons, and the Detroit police department. There were about 2,000 guardsmen in Detroit by 5:00 a.m. on 24 July and another 3,000 were expected by noon.[44]

At 5:15 a.m. Clark phoned Romney to relay the news that the local authorities believed the situation under control. The governor, however, thought that total Guard strength was only 4,000 personnel, less than half of the actual number. Not wishing to take any chances, Romney felt he should get additional help, adding that "he had just told the press that federal troops were requested." Clark then informed the governor that a written request for troops was "desirable" and further advised him that he would have to say that there existed a state of insurrection or domestic violence that he could not suppress. Before making such a grave decision, however, the governor wanted to consult with state officials. Romney's indecision, nourished by contradictory early morning wire-service reports that the president had already ordered federal troops to Detroit, aroused Johnson's suspicions that political opponents were setting him up to take the fall for the riots.[45]

As looting and arson continued after dawn on the 24th, Romney again called Clark shortly before 9:00 a.m. recommending the use of federal troops to quell the disturbances. At the president's direction, Clark once more informed Romney that the Constitution and other laws made it necessary for the governor to request the use of such forces in writing and state unequivocally that local forces were unable to control the insurrection. Over the next two hours, Romney drafted a telegram to the president to request federal troops, and dispatched it to the president. In spite of coordinating the wording with Clark, the Michigan governor failed to certify that there existed an insurrection or state of violence beyond local control. To cover himself and avoid any onus for using federal troops, Johnson insisted on a strict interpretation of pertinent statutes before he committed federal troops to Detroit. Meanwhile, the president ordered troops of the 82nd Airborne Division at Fort Bragg, North Carolina, and of the 101st Airborne Division at Fort Campbell, Kentucky, to deploy as soon as possible to Selfridge Air Force Base, about 25 miles from Detroit.[46]

Johnson's sensitive political instincts convinced him that Republicans were laying a trap for him. In the words of a senior adviser, the president wanted "his own eyes and ears on the scene" as a precaution. For this purpose, around 11:00 a.m. on the 24th, McNamara contacted his former deputy, Cyrus Vance, at home to ask if he could go to Detroit in connection with the riots. Vance readily agreed, but before leaving for Detroit he set off for the White House. With Vance on his way, the president convened a meeting with Clark, McNamara, and others where he announced Vance's appointment as a special assistant to McNamara. Clark objected to sending Vance to Detroit because "it appeared that current executive personnel were unable to handle the situation" and that "the President was trying to disassociate himself from the crisis." To counter Clark's objections, McNamara cited his former deputy's solid record on civil rights enforcement and previous work during similar incidents. Vance's selection also accorded with Johnson's desire "to play down the military role and play up the civilian role of Federal involvement in Detroit." Images of federal troops shooting women and children clearly worried the president; he feared that his critics would charge that "we cannot kill enough people in Vietnam, so we go out and shoot civilians in Detroit." All eventually concurred that the president should wait until federal troops and Vance arrived in Detroit before federalizing Michigan National Guard units. Johnson's worry that federalizing state units would make him responsible for their actions complemented Romney's concern that federalization would deprive him of state forces to control disturbances reported elsewhere across Michigan.[47]

Vance departed Washington for Detroit with the clear understanding that the president had delegated to him all possible legal responsibility and that he should take such action as he deemed necessary after evaluating conditions there. In Detroit, Vance conferred with Romney, Cavanagh, Major General Simmons, and others. By the time Vance arrived, about 2,000 National Guard troops were already in the city, but he learned that local authorities had not yet deployed an additional 3,000 guardsmen pending the arrival of federal officials. He advised Simmons to order the deployments immediately and the general complied. Vance found Romney still unwilling to declare a condition of insurrection or domestic violence that state and local authorities could not manage.[*] The governor did admit, however, "there was reasonable doubt" whether state authorities could control the situation. This concession did not fulfill the preconditions for the commitment of federal troops, particularly given the president's insistence on holding to the exact letter of the law.[48]

While Vance and Romney conferred, at the weekly congressional leadership meeting at the White House the president responded to Republican charges that the big city rioting constituted "a national crisis" approaching "a state of anarchy" for which his administration was responsible. Despite a bold public face, the president privately worried that serious tensions developing in the District of Columbia might lead to "a very bad situation" there also. Yet the FBI could find no evidence of outside intervention or communist participation in the disorders. Johnson remained reluctant to commit federal troops to restore local order in Detroit, and in the course of his meeting with the congressional leadership he pushed for enactment of his domestic legislative agenda which, he argued, sought to alleviate some of the inner city unrest.[49]

---

[*] Having been advised that a declaration of insurrection might void insurance policies, Romney was unwilling to issue such a proclamation (Vance Final Report, 10, cited in n 44 above).

Meanwhile, Vance's initial impression after a drive in and around strife-ridden Detroit was somewhat encouraging. But as the night wore on, conditions worsened—rioting, vandalism, and looting increased to alarming levels, more than 230 incidents* per hour at 11:00 p.m. Faced with the steady deterioration, just before 11:00 p.m. Vance and Lt. Gen. John L. Throckmorton, Commander, XVIII Airborne Corps and the Army's Task Force Detroit, determined that local law enforcement officials could no longer control the violence. Shortly after, Vance phoned the White House to urge Johnson to order federal troops into Detroit and to federalize the Michigan National Guard.[50]

The president remained apprehensive about federalizing the National Guard. Only five days earlier Vice President Humphrey had cautioned McNamara about something Johnson knew full well: that the Guard forces deployed to Newark "were, for all practical purposes, white, segregated Guard units" that lacked training in both riot control and human relations. A reluctant Johnson concurred with Vance's recommendations but told him to make a final public appeal to the people of Detroit "to cease and desist and obey the law." Just before 10:30 p.m., FBI Director J. Edgar Hoover had warned the president, "They have lost all control in Detroit—Harlem† will break loose within thirty minutes." Johnson then signed the necessary documents to commit federal troops to Detroit. Shortly after, he approved Vance's proposed public statement about the situation. Just before midnight he addressed the nation on the crisis in a live radio and television broadcast that a close aide suggested "read like a partisan attack" on Romney.[51]

Coincident with the executive order, McNamara notified the service secretaries that he had delegated to the secretary of the Army authority to call into active federal service "any and all of the units or members" of the Michigan Army and Air National Guards. The Army secretary also received authority to use these forces and regular Army units as he deemed necessary.[52]

By 4:00 a.m. on 25 July, almost 15,000 Guard and Regular Army troops from the two airborne divisions had arrived in the Detroit area. More than 7,700 were committed to the city. To that time the riot toll stood at 21 dead, more than 1,000 wounded or injured, and property damage in excess of $150 million. By the next morning (the 26th) the tally had risen to 29 dead, including one policeman and one firefighter. By late afternoon on 28 July, 37 civilians had been killed, bad enough by any standard, but still a remarkably low total given the promiscuous firing by National Guard troops who had expended more than 155,000 rounds of ammunition as against only 202 rounds for both airborne divisions. Conditions improved, beginning 26 July; federal troops withdrew between 28 and 30 July. State troops remained until 6 August when Romney ended the state of emergency.[53]

---

* An incident was defined as "an event requiring police action" (Vance Final Report, 17, n 2).
† His reference was to an estimated 2,000 rioters in the Spanish Harlem district of New York City.

In his official report on the Detroit riot, Vance stated that he expected "other cities will suffer from riots, looting, and burning." It was essential therefore to improve the poor discipline, lack of proper training, and inadequate command and control of the National Guard units that, according to Vance, fell far below the Regular Army in "appearance, bearing, courtesy, and general behavior." Echoing Vice President Humphrey's earlier observation about Newark, Vance recommended immediate action to increase recruitment of African-Americans into National Guard units. Johnson reacted with instructions to review National Guard training; McNamara assured the president that reform along the lines suggested by Vance was already under way. Even before the Detroit riots ended, the president on 29 July created the 11-member National Advisory Commission on Civil Disorders, headed by Illinois Gov. Otto Kerner, to determine causes of the riots and what should be done to prevent recurrences.*[54]

Concurrent with the Detroit riot OSD prepared a number of less publicized policy revisions. On 27 July McNamara appointed Under Secretary of the Army David E. McGiffert to head a special task force to review planning for control of civil disturbances in the Washington area and make recommendations to OSD for improvements. The task force met the same day and quickly prepared a temporary plan of operations and responsibility. It looked to the police as "the first line of defense." Thereafter reliance would shift to the federalized District of Columbia National Guard and designated Army and Marine units from nearby military bases under a plan codenamed Cabin Guard. Subsequently, on 6 August the task force provided McNamara with a more formal plan that called for "maximum application of manpower and minimum application of force" that would "avoid a 'shoot-to-kill' approach while at the same time snuffing out the riot." Initial response to a civil disturbance would be handled by local police (D.C., Maryland, and Virginia), followed, if necessary, by the simultaneous commitment of federalized National Guard and the nearby designated federal units.[55]

Several of the local and state police forces in the first line of defense requested federal military equipment—arms and ammunition, chemical agents, gas masks, and helmets—in anticipation of future civil disorders. Existing policy called for either McNamara or his deputy secretary to approve personally such requests, a cumbersome, over-centralized arrangement. In a new less restrictive policy statement, issued 28 July, McNamara limited authorization to lend offensive equipment to himself, his deputy, and the JCS chairman; for "protective" equipment, however, service secretaries could delegate authority to local commanders or installations within the 50 states, the District of Columbia, and U.S. territories to lend such materials. A 30 September revision added emergency firefighting equipment to the list and established a weekly reporting system to the JCS for all civil disorder assistance requests and the action taken.[56]

---

* The "Report of the National Advisory Commission on Civil Disorders," usually referred to as the Kerner Report, was issued on 1 March 1968.

To avoid repetition of the Romney-Clark-Johnson contretemps that had marked the call for federal troops for the Detroit riots, on 7 August Clark informed all state governors of the rationale and written procedures for seeking federal intervention in future civil disturbances. He emphasized that the governors would normally have time to dispatch a telegram to the White House fulfilling the protocol for a written communication. Only in an "extreme emergency" would a verbal request suffice. His letter also impressed on the governors that to ask for federal troops represented "a most serious departure from our traditions of local responsibility for law enforcement," an action to be taken only as a last resort to restore law and order.[57]

As a result of the Detroit episode and the concurrent creation of a temporary civil disturbance task force for the Washington, D.C., area, in mid-January 1968 the Department of the Army established a Civil Disturbance Committee to oversee recommended improvements and to function as a planning group in times of actual civil turmoil. Instructions sent to state governors updated August 1967 guidelines. At Deputy Secretary Nitze's suggestion, the Army instituted an evaluation system for National Guard units; Army inspection teams began providing intense riot control training to units assigned to civil disturbance missions. And in line with a Kerner Commission proposal, efforts were accelerated to increase the number of African-Americans in reserve units; for example, the New Jersey Adjutant General was authorized a five percent overstrength solely to recruit more blacks.[58] All of these policy initiatives were undertaken in expectation of still another summer of violence in 1968.

The March on the Pentagon

Rioting in the urban ghettos contributed to a culture of violence that saw growing antiwar sentiment in the United States degenerate into a greater willingness on the part of demonstrators to resort to agitation to get attention. The attempt of an increasingly radical leadership to inject confrontation and disorder into the movement climaxed on 21 October 1967 with the March on the Pentagon organized by The National Mobilization Committee (NMC) to End the War in Vietnam. NMC organizers initially estimated five million people would participate in the Pentagon demonstrations, but later scaled back that number to one million, and finally to 100,000.[59]

March organizers made no secret of their intentions. By late August the press abounded with reports of the impending large antiwar protest in Washington, D.C., designed to "shut down the Pentagon" and other government buildings. Inflammatory rhetoric of leftist militants and vows by hippies to level the Pentagon in order to exorcise its demons created headlines, marginalized more moderate elements of the antiwar movement, and stirred concern among government officials in Washington about exactly what was in store. At the very time the antiwar movement was gaining momentum and headlines, Johnson sought to minimize domestic opposition to his Vietnam policies. As the president's focus shifted from fear of hawks to concern about doves as the major threat to his programs, he considered the impending march a personal affront and exclaimed that he intended to stay in Washington and not be run out of town by protesters.[60]

McNamara's personal experiences with the antiwar movement ranged from watching a Quaker immolate himself within 40 feet of his Pentagon office window in November 1965 through college commencements in 1966 where students protested the secretary's presence by wearing black armbands. To his "consternation" McNamara found that the number of protesters seemed to increase with the level of their academic standing. He also faced the ugly threat of physical harm when speaking at Harvard University in the fall of 1966, and more than once arsonists attempted to burn down his second home near Aspen, Colorado.[61]

Engrossed in the Pennsylvania negotiating initiative,[*] McNamara left it to his deputy, Nitze, to cope with the planned demonstration. On 12 September Nitze received a Justice Department briefing about proposed responses to the march, including the possibility of a court injunction to keep marchers off the 280-acre Pentagon reservation. The following day Nitze directed Army Secretary Resor to prepare contingency plans to ensure building security and continuity of day-to-day operations at the Pentagon. From its own intelligence sources the Army, responsible for security in the Military District of Washington (MDW), had already determined by 5 September that the MDW commander could provide security around the Pentagon but lacked sufficient forces to deal with simultaneous demonstrations elsewhere in the metropolitan area. Armed with Nitze's instructions to Resor to keep government buildings operating during any demonstrations, the Army staff, directed by McGiffert, commenced coordinated, detailed planning to neutralize the protests. Facilitated by the groundwork laid by McGiffert's special task force, preparations moved ahead, guided particularly by the admonition to rely on maximum manpower and minimum force.[62]

Army authorities originally predicated their planning on demonstrations ranging in size from 1,000 to as many as 100,000 protesters engaging in sporadic acts of violence beyond the ability of General Services Administration (GSA) police at the Pentagon to control. At the lowest level (up to 2,000 demonstrators), a prepositioned battalion of 600 military police drawn from outside the Washington area would deploy inside the Pentagon to repel attempts to enter the massive building. Thereafter, depending on the size of the demonstration, upwards of 26,000 additional troops from a number of Army bases would be employed. From the outset the Army emphasized maximum use of "passive defense measures . . . with escalation of effort as required by the situation."[63]

---

[*] Pennsylvania was a United States peace initiative to North Vietnam overseen by McNamara that occurred during the summer and early fall of 1967. See Chapter VII for details.

On 20 September, with the Pennsylvania negotiations ending in failure, McNamara became more actively involved in the preparations to control the march; along with other DoD, Justice, State, and GSA officials he met for 15 minutes with the president to discuss the FBI assessment that 40,000 to 50,000 demonstrators might move against such major government buildings as the Capitol, White House, and Pentagon. McNamara assured Johnson "that troops would be able to move in and handle those things determined necessary" at the Pentagon. He spoke of ringing the building with armed troops and positioning U.S. marshals between the soldiers and the protesters. Backup units inside the spacious Pentagon courtyard would stand ready to seal any breach in the troop line. McNamara told the president that he, General Wheeler, and Deputy Attorney General Warren Christopher, who served as Ramsey Clark's representative with military authorities, would personally monitor the operation from his office and the Pentagon roof. Two weeks later, on 3 October, after congressional leaders made plain to the president their displeasure over any large-scale demonstration, Johnson reemphasized to McNamara the need "to get going on plans to protect the White House, the Pentagon, and the Capitol." For his part, the defense secretary reminded the president of ongoing preparations and the possibility that there might be thousands of arrests during the demonstrations.[64]

Meanwhile, on 21 September OSD and Army authorities accelerated their preparations after receiving intelligence reports indicating that the Pentagon would be the primary target of the demonstrators. Two days later, after discussing alternative responses to an NMC request for a march permit, OSD principals and the secretary of the Army recommended that McNamara initially deny the demonstrators access to the Pentagon grounds. If NMC leaders assured GSA that any demonstration would be orderly, they could then hold a rally in the Pentagon's North Parking area, a location that afforded the most practical means of crowd control. Once McNamara approved this approach it became GSA's basic position during negotiations for a parade permit. Extended permit discussions with NMC leaders also enabled government agencies to learn more about their intentions, simultaneously stringing out the negotiations to make it difficult for organizers to set definite plans. David Dellinger and other NMC leaders appeared so anxious to obtain the permit that they reconciled themselves to using only the North Parking area for their Pentagon rally.[65]

On 26 September McNamara further defined the Army's role, assigning it responsibility for developing the overall plan to deal with any contingency in the Washington Metropolitan Area that might arise from the planned demonstrations. Because of the multiple jurisdictions involved, the Army effort would include possible military support to other affected federal, state, District, and local authorities. Assistant Secretary of Defense (Administration) Solis Horwitz had oversight for all of these plans and operations; he later recalled having little to do because McNamara took such an active part.[66]

The resulting Army plan, codenamed Cabinet Maker, aimed to prevent disruption of operation of the Pentagon and quell any civil disturbances elsewhere in the metropolitan area. Since the protest march was scheduled, not spontaneous, and it was concentrated at one site rather than dispersed, the Army had the luxury of conducting extensive advance planning that included concentrating and prepositioning troops. The Department of Justice exercised overall coordinating responsibility for federal, state, and District of Columbia agencies, while the Army chief of staff took direct control of all military forces employed in the operation. Meetings over the next month, including a war game, refined broadly drawn plans, assigning specific responsibilities including handling of those detained or arrested and determining the extent of government medical and sanitary support for the demonstration. At a 2 October meeting Nitze, McGiffert, Clark, and others agreed on four points: the administration would not actively block the demonstration if it had a proper permit; no demonstrators could enter any federal building; Pentagon demonstrators would be confined to North Parking; and the government would offer no medical or sanitary amenities but would be prepared to supply them at the last minute.[67]

Eleven days later the Attorney General's office issued guidelines for the permit that restricted the beginning of the rally to the Lincoln Memorial, routed the march over the Memorial Bridge, and confined the demonstration at the Pentagon to North Parking. The plan was intended to conserve military manpower. Attempting to halt marchers at the periphery of the Pentagon reservation would require more than four times as many troops and might possibly precipitate an early confrontation with the marchers.[*] Avoiding scenes of commotion and violence was the objective. As Army Chief of Staff General Johnson put it, McNamara and other senior members of the administration viewed the March on the Pentagon as a public relations problem.[68]

Cosmetic appearances loomed large to an image-conscious White House. Barriers around the Pentagon were kept to a minimum and barbed wire was intentionally not used because of the damaging impression it would convey to the world. In keeping with a low-key approach, military police reinforcements brought to the Pentagon beforehand remained in the inner courtyard hidden from outside view. Military police stationed outside the Pentagon wore their formal green dress uniforms and plastic helmet liners, while those concealed inside the building wore full battle dress and steel helmets. If the demonstration turned ugly, three battalions of troops armed with M-14 rifles and bayonets would respond from positions inside the Pentagon. An additional five battalions of military police were on standby at Fort Myer, Fort Meade, and the Anacostia Naval Station. A total of 236 U.S. marshals from the Justice Department stood ready, but basic policy prescribed avoiding mass arrests. Furthermore, a brigade of the 82nd Airborne Division from Fort

---

[*] In the event, 800 military police deployed outside the Pentagon in North Parking. It would have taken 3,600 men to surround the building.

Bragg deployed to Andrews Air Force Base, Maryland, to function as a reserve if major rioting erupted in the Washington environs.[69] These extensive preparations were designed to minimize disruption and spare the administration the adverse publicity that widespread violence and disorder would bring.

Beyond image, there existed a genuine concern about individual liberties. As McNamara announced at his 20 October staff meeting, he wanted to keep the Pentagon running while dealing with the protesters in a civilized manner. A checklist of actions prepared for the secretary by McGiffert the following day identified as a key goal ensuring the right of Americans to peaceful assembly and free speech in a demonstration that few other governments would dare tolerate. Once the various jurisdictions issued a permit on 19 October to the NMC for the march and rally on 21–22 October, McGiffert reiterated the steady approach he wanted federal troops to employ: to avoid "either overreacting or underreacting" and behave "with dignity and firmness" during the protests. On the morning of the demonstrations, McGiffert instructed General Johnson to consult with him before ordering any use of weapons or movement of troops against the marchers.[70]

At 8:00 a.m. the day of the march McNamara arrived at the Pentagon as he usually did for another Saturday of work. He wanted to maintain a business-as-usual atmosphere, something that General Johnson told his assembled commanders the previous day he regarded as highly unlikely. The general also reemphasized minimum force and respect for individual rights as the order of the day. Finally, he cautioned that the official answer to any reporter's questions was "no comment." True to his promise to the president, McNamara watched the protesters from his office window and later from the Pentagon roof, made certain nothing was done without his permission, and updated the president directly "on almost every move he took." McNamara was appalled at the demonstrators' unruliness; years later he insisted that he could have organized a peaceful, orderly protest that would have shut down the Pentagon.[71] He missed the point that for a radical minority of the demonstrators the intended purpose of the march was to foment disorder and get arrested.

Crowds variously estimated at from 22,000 to 35,000 gathered at the Pentagon during mid-afternoon on the warm, sunny day. Around 4:00 p.m. about 200 militants rushed the River entrance, creating a free-for-all that emboldened radicals. About an hour later troops from inside the Pentagon, carrying rifles with fixed, sheathed bayonets, reinforced the outer defensive cordon. Next about 30 members of the Students for a Democratic Society's Revolutionary Contingent charged through an open door into the Pentagon only to be met by troops waiting inside. After a brief, one-sided melee, scores of arrests followed. Toward midnight soldiers again pushed demonstrators back, after which only several hundred remained; most of them trickled away during the night. Next day the crowds had greatly diminished. When the parade permit expired at midnight U.S. marshals arrested the remaining 150 hard-core demonstrators. Maintenance crews quickly moved in to haul away debris and trash, so that when Pentagon employees reported for work Monday morning little sign of the weekend's tumult remained.[72]

Both sides claimed victory. Army officials concluded that despite higher estimates fewer than 20,000 protesters had demonstrated at the Pentagon. The president and McNamara commended the troops and U.S. marshals for acting with restraint throughout a potentially explosive event. Conversely, the very use of federal troops and U.S. marshals encouraged Dellinger to proclaim the march a "tremendous victory" that disrupted Pentagon activities and clearly demonstrated that the American people wanted the war ended. Certainly the march on the Pentagon ranked as the largest antiwar rally held in the nation's capital to date. Yet the violence and unseemly behavior of some of the demonstrators offended many Americans who saw such actions as encouraging the communists and betraying American soldiers in Vietnam. To others, it seemed the country was fraying at the seams.[73] But there was still more to come.

The 1968 Riots

Tumultuous national and international occurrences seemed almost commonplace during early 1968. The powerful and well-publicized North Vietnamese Tet offensive and North Korea's seizure of the USS *Pueblo* caused the mobilization of selected reserve units involving 24,500 men along with a draft call for an additional 48,000 in April, the second highest of the war. Johnson's decision not to seek reelection reverberated throughout the nation. Antiwar protesters continued to seek and gain notoriety. Racial tensions remained razor-sharp. In early February in Orangeburg, South Carolina, police fired into a crowd of black college student demonstrators, killing 3 and wounding 37. No one had any illusions about what the summer might bring. Even during the darkest days of Tet, the president and McNamara worried about "our summer situation," especially if the 82nd Airborne Division, two of whose brigades were assigned to civil disturbance missions, had to deploy to Vietnam.[74]

In the wake of the 1967 Detroit riot, the U.S. Army had developed an omnibus Civil Disturbance Plan, issued in February 1968, that earmarked 13 Army brigades or brigade equivalents (between 1,800 and 2,400 soldiers each) plus elements from armored and artillery units for use in civil disturbance missions in the summer of 1968. Detailed preparations for their employment, promulgation of civil disturbance doctrine, and improved training for the new mission were well advanced. As for National Guard forces, the adjutant general of each state had prepared a civil disturbance plan, Guard units had trained for civil disturbance missions, and liaison between Regular Army and state, local, and Guard officials had greatly improved. By late spring 1968 the forces would be ready to respond as needed to civil disorders expected that summer. In anticipation of such violence, police throughout the nation were stockpiling weapons, recruiting auxiliaries, and storing military equipment on loan from DoD.[75]

On 1 April 1968, McGiffert provided the attorney general's office with a status report on Army planning to control civil disturbances. Improved training, readiness, command and control, and equipment now typified both Regular and National Guard units. Seven active Army brigades and supporting units stationed in the United States stood available on special-alert status in case of disorders. As part of an interagency task force, the Army had also made extensive preparations to deal with possible rioting and violence in the nation's capital, where two task forces numbering approximately 28,000 men would be immediately available to respond to incidents. In addition to the overall planning, the Military District of Washington had focused specifically on the impending Poor People's March on Washington.[76] No one, however, anticipated what happened in Memphis, Tennessee, on 4 April 1968.

Martin Luther King, Jr., leader of the Southern Christian Leadership Conference, regarded as the most influential African-American in the country, had come to Memphis to support a lengthy and acrimonious strike by predominantly black sanitation workers against the city. Early in the evening of 4 April a sniper shot and killed King. The assassination became a lightning rod for nationwide civil disturbances. Initial shock and dismay in African-American communities over King's murder gave way to rioting and violence that raged across the United States. Major disturbances rocked Cincinnati, Detroit, Kansas City, Oakland, and Pittsburgh; the most serious outbreaks occurred in Baltimore, Chicago, and Washington, D.C.

On learning of King's death, the president cancelled a scheduled trip to Hawaii to confer with General Westmoreland and instead asked the general to come to Washington. Even before the president issued any executive orders, the Army, according to approved plans, activated key emergency operations centers and alerted selected Army units in the United States for deployment to troubled cities. Clark Clifford, newly on board as secretary of defense and engaged in preparations for talks with the Hanoi government, did not participate prominently in the activity. Instead OSD relied on the Army chief of staff to oversee the movement of federal troops to riot-torn cities.[77] The administration turned for assistance also to Vance and Ramsey Clark who had been deeply involved in managing the response to earlier civil disturbances.

Within hours after news of King's death, wild rumors abounded as to the circumstances; African-American crowds in Washington, D.C., began roaming the streets, breaking store windows, looting, and setting fires. At least 185 fires burned in widely scattered areas and smoke could be seen miles to the south of Washington. Firemen and local police were stoned and attacked. Against this backdrop, shortly before noon on 5 April and again shortly after, Deputy Attorney General Christopher met with White House officials, including the president, McGiffert, and senior Washington, D.C., police officers. About 2:00 p.m., the president phoned Christopher to relay D.C. Mayor Walter E. Washington's concern that conditions were again getting out of control in the city. Johnson told Christopher to tour the riot-stricken areas and determine whether federal and National Guard troops should be ordered into the District. Accompanied by the Army vice chief of staff, General Ralph E. Haines, Jr., Christopher drove through the riot areas in the D.C. police chief's car, radio-equipped for rapid communication. The radio promptly failed, leaving Christopher unable to call either the waiting mayor or the anxious president. About 4:00 p.m. Christopher finally resorted to a pay phone at a neighborhood gas station to call the White House. He recommended to a "very upset" president the immediate use of federal troops and Guard personnel to restore order. Johnson preferred that federal troops deploy first because of their earlier availability (National Guard units would take time to arrive at their assembly areas) and better training.[78] It is likely that the better training was the chief determinant.

Following Christopher's call, the president authorized federal troops to move to preassigned areas in the nation's capital. He instructed General Johnson to keep the movements "low key," which meant feeding units gradually into the District starting about an hour later. According to Clifford, the troops had "absolutely hard and fast" orders not to shoot at rioters because he feared that such confrontations would only make the already volatile situation in Washington "infinitely worse."[79]

Vance, summoned from his law office in New York City, arrived in Washington in the late afternoon of 5 April to assist Mayor Washington in restoring calm. Assuming command of Task Force Washington, Vance drew on his Detroit experience, emphasizing maximum restraint and minimal use of lethal weapons. General Johnson reported to Vance and Presidential Special Assistant Califano, who authorized his requests to move troops within the metropolitan area. An overall policy determination committee, operating from the White House with representatives from OSD and Justice, kept Clifford and Nitze informed about the fast-changing situation so that OSD might implement high-level decisions. More than 11,600 federal troops augmented by nearly 1,900 federalized National Guardsmen soon occupied the nation's capital. Approximately 2,000 additional Regular troops deployed to nearby Andrews Air Force Base as a reserve. Local authorities reported 350 civilians injured, 8 dead, and more than 1,570 arrested as of 2:00 a.m. on 6 April. Police and Justice Department officials felt that the troops should have arrived sooner or been prepositioned before the president's official call for military forces. Nonetheless, the overwhelming show of force returned the city to normal by the evening of 7 April, but given the tense atmosphere authorities decided to retain the troops for several more days. By mid-afternoon on 16 April all federal forces had departed the capital's streets.[80]

The commitment of federal troops to restore order in Baltimore was an equally tense affair. At first the Maryland city remained calm, but disturbances on 5 April proved serious enough for the governor to send Maryland National Guard troops there. Widespread lawless rampages persisted, however, and early on 7 April the Army operations center alerted the XVIII Airborne Corps commanding general,

Lt. Gen. Robert H. York, of the possible need to commit federal troops to the area. York flew to Baltimore to coordinate with National Guard officers. According to a late afternoon bulletin broadcast by a local radio station, the president had ordered federal troops to the city. The report was false, but believing it accurate York and the Army staff spent the next three hours devising deployment tactics. Only around 8:00 p.m. did General Johnson inform York that the president had not signed such an order. Soon afterward York and Presidential Representative Fred M. Vinson, Jr., reported to General Johnson that they saw no need for federal troops. Just an hour later the situation had worsened appreciably, leading York to recommend commitment of federal troops after all.

The president then signed an executive order authorizing the deployment; the first federal troops moved into Baltimore neighborhoods around midnight of 7–8 April. York ordered bayonets removed from rifles, forbade indiscriminate shooting, and emphasized soldierly appearance and good conduct on the part of all troops involved in the operation. Just after noon the following day, the Army ordered an infantry brigade in reserve at Andrews AFB to proceed to Baltimore to help control large crowds and prevent further looting. The heavy military presence in the central downtown section intimidated crowds and caused them to disperse; violence subsided. Federal and federalized Guard troops patrolled the city for the next several days; on 12 April Gov. Spiro T. Agnew recommended to the president that the federal forces withdraw.[81]

As in Washington and Baltimore, violence, arson, and looting also spread out of local control in Chicago. Through 5 April rioting in Chicago increased in tempo; by early evening extensive fires were reported burning at various locations in the city despite the presence of thousands of National Guardsmen. Widespread disorder continued into the following day; expecting even worse to follow, that afternoon the acting Illinois governor, at the request of Chicago Mayor Richard J. Daley, asked for the dispatch of 5,000 federal troops to suppress "this insurrection." The president promptly ordered federal troops to Chicago, called General Johnson to confirm the authorization, and instructed the general not to exceed the requested figure.[82]

Troops from Fort Hood, Texas, already on standby, received orders to move to Chicago. The roughly 6,800 National Guardsman then on duty in Chicago were federalized on 7 April and placed under Task Force III command. In the early morning hours of 7 April, federal troops relieved elements of National Guard units in Chicago, began patrolling streets, and shortly before noon dispersed two unruly mobs. Additional federal troops arrived during the day and fanned out through the city. Once again the presence of thousands of troops dampened the rioters' fervor, and by the evening of 9 April relative calm had returned to Chicago. Two days later federal troops began to return to Fort Hood.[83] Unlike the resort to indiscreet gunfire that had characterized the Newark and Detroit riots the previous year, troops relied on overwhelming numbers and the appearance of force, not firepower, to restore order in Washington, Baltimore, and Chicago.

In the ruins of the riots Clifford concluded that the lack of a centralized DoD agency had slowed the dispatch of troops to the affected cities. Within days, on 13 April, a steering group of high-level military and civilian officials began to plan creation of an interservice organization, the Directorate for Civil Disturbance Planning and Operations. An Army lieutenant general with an Air Force major general as deputy, together with some 180 multiservice support personnel, would man the directorate, serve as "a nerve center," and supervise the use of federal troops in civil disorders. An early test of the new organization came in May when the Poor Peoples Campaign brought a few thousand demonstrators to Washington for a stay of several weeks. The local police coped with the protests and such violence as occurred. The Army remained in the background providing logistical support and surveillance. On 8 June, in a 15-page DoD directive, Nitze formally spelled out in detail DoD's role in civil disturbances, including background, mission, funding, and organizational relationships.[84]

The nationwide violence following King's murder seemed to release much of the pent-up frustration and rage in the African-American communities; for all the foreboding, the summer of 1968 witnessed a "clear and significant decline" in riots and disorders. The disturbances declined but did not end. Major riots occurred in May in Salisbury, Maryland; in July in Akron, Ohio, Gary, Indiana, and Peoria, Illinois; in August in St. Paul, Minnesota; and in September in Newport News, Virginia. A shootout between armed black militants and Cleveland police in late July left seven dead and led to widespread rioting in that city.[85] Yet the worst racial strife was behind the nation, and the only other episode in 1968 involving federal troops and urban disorders was unrelated to racial tensions.

In this instance, Clifford feared that antiwar supporters of Sen. Eugene J. McCarthy's (D-Minn.) quest for the presidential nomination might provoke a major disturbance during the Democratic National Convention scheduled in Chicago from 26 to 29 August. In response to the secretary's precautionary directive to have federal troops on a high state of alert ready to move to the city at the first sign of trouble, the Army prepared detailed contingency plans. Although the extent of the threat in Chicago was extremely difficult to judge because of the diversity of the potential protesters—hippies, yippies, black militants, peace groups, antiwar radicals, McCarthy supporters—McGiffert proposed prepositioning federal troops in Chicago, making them readily available if needed; their very presence might lessen the likelihood of rioting. As convention week neared, Chicago Mayor Daley placed the entire city's police force on 12-hour shifts; at his request, the governor called about 5,000 National Guardsmen to duty on 20 August.[86]

On 22 August at a White House evening meeting, Clifford, Califano, Clark, and McGiffert argued the pros and cons of prepositioning federal troops in the Chicago area. Clark "unalterably opposed" the idea, but when the participants met with the president later that evening they learned that Johnson had already decided on prepositioning. Clifford then directed Secretary Resor to deploy federal forces to Chicago for the duration of the convention. Airlift of more than 6,000 troops from Fort Hood, Fort Sill, Oklahoma, and Fort Carson, Colorado began on 25 August, concluding during the early morning hours the next day. Troops assembled outside the city at nearby Glenview Naval Air Station and at the Great Lakes Naval Training Center. A week of intermittent protests in Chicago finally degenerated into full-scale violence on 28 August in what a special study panel later criticized as a "police riot"; the assembled federal troops nearby did not become involved.[87] The greatly increased demands of this and earlier civil disturbances deprived some military units in the United States of significant training time and added another major mission to the already overextended active forces.

The war in Vietnam intersected with the great civil rights revolution of the 1960s and became a catalyst for protests against both a perceived misguided military intervention and social and economic injustice at home. Inequities in the Selective Service System and dissenting attitudes in American society toward the war found expression in criticism over who served and with the military generally as an institution. For perhaps too many young white males the Reserves or National Guard offered a sanctuary denied their black and poorer white contemporaries who faced conscription. One might argue that the draft could never be totally equitable or universal.[88] During the Vietnam buildup conscription became blatantly unbalanced because the Defense Department administered it ineptly, failing to make the fundamental reform that could bring about a fairer system of selection. OSD's continual lowering of entry standards to meet the constantly expanding manpower need placed a heavier and heavier burden of military service on those less able to cope in a wartime military. Project 100,000 exemplified the contradiction between trying to meet military personnel needs and simultaneously seeking to resolve larger socioeconomic inequality that had created an ill-educated underclass available to fill the ranks.

The curse of Vietnam was that it forced the president to defer or limit uplifting social programs as it surfaced and exacerbated historic stresses and tensions in the society. The war created a wedge between those who took to the streets to protest and a government that employed federal troops in unprecedented numbers against its own citizens to get them to desist. Over the course of the decade OSD, the Army, and the National Guard improved in handling civil disorders. From a shaky and bloody beginning, both active and reserve forces developed and refined doctrine and practice to deal with urban uprisings; by 1969 they had successfully weathered the worst domestic disturbances since the Civil War. At the height of the 1967 Detroit rioting, Sen. John L. McClellan (D-Ark.) told the president that "we have sown the seeds, and now we are reaping them."[89] McClellan referred, of course, to the pervasive racial discrimination that still afflicted America, but he could just as well have been thinking about an ill-conceived and executed foreign war that begot its own racial controversy, domestic violence, and divisiveness.

Chapter XI

Another Cuba?

Even as urban unrest threatened to erupt in the spring of 1965, and a fateful decision about Vietnam impended, the Johnson administration found itself confronted by a perceived threat much closer to home than Vietnam—in the Caribbean. Overthrow of the government in the Dominican Republic and ensuing civil strife caused U.S. national security officials to fear that another Castro-style Cuba was in the making. To prevent what he viewed as a possible communist takeover of a neighboring country, President Johnson intervened with powerful military forces, even as he sought a political solution, to effect an outcome satisfactory to the United States. McNamara and OSD, through the JCS, directed the indispensable military aspect of the intervention, always subject to the overriding political concern of the president and the State Department.

Intervention in the Dominican Republic

U.S. military intervention in the Dominican Republic in April 1965 briefly eclipsed Vietnam, aroused strong national and international passions, and involved U.S. forces in a bloody civil war. The Caribbean island of Hispaniola is shared by the Dominican Republic and Haiti, two small nations whose histories have been marked by political corruption, economic instability, violence, and foreign intervention. In the early years of the 20th century, the United States intervened with military forces in both to restore order, thus averting intervention by European powers. In the 1960s, as the island once again descended into chaos, the Kennedy and then Johnson administrations worried about Soviet influence in the Caribbean and the spread of Cuban-style communism to the area.

Beginning in 1930, the Dominican Republic suffered for more than 30 years under the ruthless dictator Rafael Leonidas Trujillo y Molina, who ruled by fear and intimidation. His assassination on 30 May 1961 came as a welcome relief in Washington. Many years of Trujillo's mismanagement, corruption, and terror left

289

THE DOMINICAN REPUBLIC

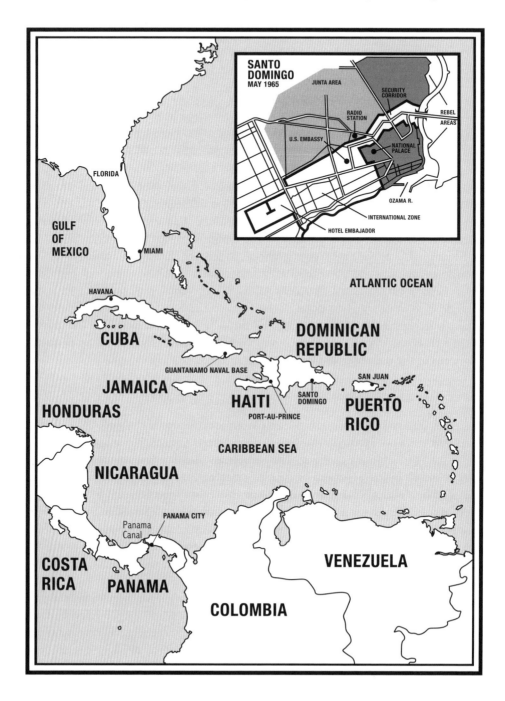

little on which to build a new political system, but in elections held in December 1962 Juan Bosch, an idealistic intellectual and reformer, easily won the presidency. Bosch, however, proved to be an inept administrator ill-suited to cope with the Byzantine political reality of the Dominican Republic.

Archconservatives in the Dominican military overthrew Bosch in September 1963 and suspended the constitution. Donald Reid Cabral, a member of a powerful Dominican family, ultimately emerged as the central political figure of a three-man civilian junta. Reid's ambitions alienated his military supporters while an eroding economy diminished his popular support. The combination united his enemies across the political spectrum into a pragmatic and temporary coalition with no overriding aim other than to get rid of Reid.[1] By this time the roots of U.S. intervention were following a familiar pattern.

In early 1965 Reid's power seemed on the verge of collapse; on 12 April the CIA reported the imminence of a coup led by Bosch and Dominican military officials to regain power. Expecting trouble, the State Department called the U.S. ambassador to the Dominican Republic, W. Tapley Bennett, Jr., home for consultations. Bennett's departure from Santo Domingo on 23 April left recently arrived Deputy Chief of Mission William B. Connett, Jr., in charge.[2]

One day later Reid tried to oust four officers accused of conspiring to overthrow the government, but they refused to resign, seized the chief of staff sent to dismiss them, and precipitated an armed uprising. Radio broadcasts of the overthrow of the government "spread like wildfire," and large crowds spilled into the streets of the capital city of 460,000 persons. At first the U.S. embassy believed the government was still in control and the coup attempt contained, but soon afterward it reported that troops were passing out weapons to civilians on the streets of the capital. Initial uncertainty and incomplete and often contradictory information was further compounded by undependable communications between Santo Domingo and Washington, military communications in particular. Unfortunately, these conditions persisted for weeks, often causing U.S. policymakers to assume the worst and act accordingly.[3]

Amidst rioting and demonstrations in Santo Domingo, on 25 April the coup leaders deposed Reid, largely because the air force and navy chiefs of staff turned against him. The rebel leadership then proclaimed Jose Molina Urena,* a leading Bosch supporter, provisional president; they demanded also the return of ex-president Bosch and reestablishment of the 1963 constitution. Thereafter they called themselves the "Constitutionalists," a mixture of rebel officers and civilian members of Bosch's Dominican Revolutionary Party (PRD) who wanted a return to the 1963 constitution. The same day the chaos in the Dominican capital prompted the State Department's director of Caribbean affairs to ask the Defense Depart-

---

* As last president of the Chamber of Deputies, dissolved after the 1963 coup, Molina was constitutionally in the line of succession to the presidency (Slater, *Intervention and Negotiation*, 23).

ment "on a 'contingency basis'—that is, without notifying the president but in accordance with established procedures"—to send ships to Dominican waters to evacuate U.S. citizens if necessary. JCS Chairman General Wheeler approved the request, as did Deputy Secretary Vance in McNamara's absence. Shortly afterward, the JCS requested the commander in chief, Atlantic Command (CINCLANT) to dispatch to the vicinity of Santo Domingo the minimum number of vessels suitable for embarkation of up to 1,200 U.S. citizens and await further orders.[4]

Meeting with his civilian advisers in the White House late that afternoon, the president heard an alarming update on conditions in Santo Domingo—anarchy and mob rule seemed prevalent, and the Dominican air force had attacked Constitutionalists in the presidential palace. From the outset, fear of a communist takeover tilted Washington's support to the Dominican armed forces, notwithstanding the administration's public pronouncements of neutrality. State, which assumed the lead departmental role in the crisis, initially told Connett to urge the Dominican military to unite in a provisional government that could restore order and prevent communist control.[5]

After a briefing from senior officials, including McNamara, around midday on 26 April, Johnson ordered Bennett back to Santo Domingo and asked for constant updates on the unfolding crisis. White House staffers in turn directed the National Military Command Center (NMCC) in the Pentagon to expedite all information to the president "if and when the ships go into DomRep." Johnson not only remained in close touch with Dominican events but also became so personally involved in policymaking that Rusk later described him as "the desk officer for the Dominican Republic."[6]

In Santo Domingo Connett reported that only major U.S. involvement— diplomacy followed by a military show of force if necessary—could forestall a communist victory. Yet he feared the deployment of U.S. combat troops would spark serious reactions throughout Latin America and was unsure that Washington could make a case "that this is [a] communist controlled movement at present time." Although personally believing that a communist takeover of the Dominican Republic posed a serious threat to U.S. interests, Connett recommended delaying a decision to use military force while pursuing further diplomatic action.[7]

Pending Bennett's return to Santo Domingo, State instructed Connett to contact the military leaders with the suggestion that they take steps to establish a military junta as a provisional government. U.S. primary objectives were: (1) restoring law and order, (2) preventing a possible communist takeover, and (3) protecting American lives. By this time the CIA was reporting the "prominent involvement of many Communists" and other radical leftists in the revolt and predicting that the Dominican Republic appeared "headed for [a] take-over by forces committed, indebted to or very sympathetic to the extreme left."[8]

On 27 April the Dominican capital became even more inflamed. During the early morning hours, an armed Constitutionalist mob burst into the Embajador Hotel, the location established by the U.S. embassy for processing American evacuees. Searching for a pro-government radio and television announcer, they lined American citizens against a wall and fired automatic weapons into the air. No one was injured, but reports of the terrifying experience helped convince Johnson that the breakdown of law and order directly endangered American lives. He ordered prompt evacuation of U.S. citizens. The operation proceeded smoothly; 1,176 Americans and other foreign nationals left that day through the port of Haina 10 miles west of the capital city.[9]

Meanwhile, with the formation of a Dominican military junta it appeared that a government offensive would crush the Constitutionalists, or rebels, as U.S. officials now labeled them. Fearing the Constitutionalist cause lost, Provisional President Molina approached the recently returned Bennett to broker a deal.* When the ambassador refused to negotiate a settlement, Molina promptly sought asylum at the Colombian Embassy. But his cause was not lost. For lack of strong leadership the government drive stalled, leaving the now reinvigorated Constitutionalists in control of downtown Santo Domingo.[10]

This sudden and unexpected reversal of fortune put the rebels on top, shattered White House expectations, and intensified Washington's fears of a communist takeover. Greatly influenced by Bennett's grim reports from Santo Domingo, the administration saw the government forces in disarray and the communists moving quickly to fill the vacuum by assuming the political leadership of the uprising. Johnson made plain to his top confidants that he did not want the rebels to win because he had "just about lived down the Bay of Pigs" and did not want to get "involved in another spot like that."[11]

Justifying Intervention

Concurrent with the U.S. naval squadron's arrival off Santo Domingo around mid-afternoon of 26 April, the JCS placed two battalions of the 82nd Airborne Division and their aircraft on a higher alert status. This routine precautionary measure stirred no special concern among the secretary of defense, the JCS, and 82nd Airborne commanders. After all, the 82nd claimed to have "been alerted nineteen times in three years to go to the Dominican Republic." Moreover, the Joint Chiefs were not kept informed of specific administration intentions regarding the crisis because the White House had not sought their military advice and would not include them in high-level policy deliberations until 29 April.[12]

---

* Bennett returned on 27 April, flown in by a U.S. helicopter. He resumed charge of the embassy at 1:00 p.m.

Bennett's cables resonated with shrill warnings of an imminent communist takeover mixed with pleas to Washington to consider U.S. military intervention. The State Department rejected armed intervention "unless outcome in doubt"— still believing that government forces could turn the tide. Bennett dispatched a series of cables on 28 April, each more alarming than the previous one, that described the discouragement among government forces and the likelihood of the communists prevailing, emphasized the danger to American lives, and recommended an immediate landing of U.S. Marines.[13]

McNamara and Rusk along with McGeorge Bundy and the president happened to be in a late afternoon meeting on 28 April at the White House discussing Vietnam when Bennett's request for troops reached the president at 5:30 p.m. They all agreed that the Marines should land immediately. Unwilling "to risk the slaughter of [remaining] American citizens," Johnson ordered the troops put ashore straightaway to provide the protection that the local authorities could not. He then invited congressional leaders to the White House so he could inform them of his decision.[14]

At the early evening meeting in the Cabinet Room, Rusk and McNamara briefed the legislators on the unfolding events in Santo Domingo and U.S. military contingency precautions to date. Admiral William Raborn, appointed director of CIA at noon that very day, revealed the "positive identification" of three top rebel leaders as Castro-trained agents. But Johnson ran the show. He read Bennett's most recent cables to the assembled congressmen, reviewed repeated U.S. requests to both sides to end the fighting, and announced that helicopters and other supporting equipment stood in position ready to act if needed. Within the hour Marine units would land to protect and escort American citizens to safety. The president concluded by asking for congressional support. The members present displayed no opposition to the decision. In effect, Johnson had used them to rehearse point-by-point his proposed public remarks on the crisis and received their approval, subject to minor changes. As the president addressed the nation later that evening of 28 April, the Joint Chiefs alerted four additional airborne battalions and their airlift for possible deployment to the Dominican Republic.[15]

Following his 8:40 p.m. television address Johnson reviewed Bennett's two latest cables that warned of a communist takeover and urged Washington to seriously consider armed intervention to reestablish law and order in the country. Concerned over this latest assessment, the president spoke by phone directly with Bennett. During their conversation, gunfire was audible in the background, and Johnson got the impression that the embassy was under heavy fire.* "We could hear bullets firing right by the American Embassy," he told Abe Fortas the next

---

* Asked three-and-one-half years later to reconstruct the event, State participants assumed the president referred to an incident that occurred on 30 April (memo George E. Brown for Amb Bowdler, 22 Oct 68, fldr Bowdler to Rostow Memo, box 8, NSC History Dominican Crisis 1965, NSF, LBJL). Johnson likely conflated the 28 and 30 April 1965 episodes in his June 1965 press conference.

day. The story grew with each telling, and when the president in mid-June related the incident to the press he had the ambassador under his desk with bullets flying through the windows as they spoke to him. However unsettling the impression, Johnson still remained reluctant to make the irreversible decision to intervene with large numbers of troops.[16]

On the morning of 29 April, Raborn told the president that a handful of communists had taken control of the Bosch forces. Amidst pessimistic messages from Bennett and confusion over who was winning or losing in the streets of Santo Domingo, at noon on 29 April the president met with McNamara and a fellow Texan, Under Secretary of State for Economic Affairs Thomas Mann. Deeming the Marine units ashore inadequate to perform their assigned mission against rebel opposition, Johnson directed the landing of another 500 Marines to protect American citizens. As a further precaution, McNamara got approval to deploy two battalions of the 82nd Airborne Division to a staging area at Ramey Air Force Base in nearby Puerto Rico. By 3:15 p.m. the JCS had ordered the landing of the 500 additional Marines and deployment of the two paratroop battalions to Ramey AFB for staging before an airdrop near San Isidro, Santo Domingo's airfield, the next morning. About one hour later the Chiefs instructed CINCLANT to land all remaining elements of the 6th Marine Expeditionary Unit (MEU) at once. The first echelon of two paratroop battalions, known as Power Pack I,* departed Fort Bragg, North Carolina, four hours later, around 8:00 p.m. More than 140 military transports formed a vast stream of aircraft that stretched across hundreds of miles in the night sky.[17]

As the day wore on Johnson became increasingly apprehensive over the possibility of a preemptive communist takeover of the Dominican Republic. According to Wheeler, the president feared that "the whole thing was going to fold up unless we could get some troops in. If we were to wait until dawn, we might not have anything to support." Presidential concern had already led Vance to ask the NMCC about notification time if it were decided to land the aircraft at San Isidro rather than at Ramey. Vance had also phoned the USS *Boxer* offshore Santo Domingo to find out if San Isidro had the facilities to handle more than 100 C-130 night landings. For his part, Wheeler had previously notified the naval task force commander that the United States wanted not only to protect Americans but also to prevent a communist seizure of the island.[18] All of this activity occurred before a scheduled White House conference call to Bennett for his latest assessment.

The discussion between the president's civilian and military advisers and Bennett preceded a White House meeting on the Dominican crisis scheduled for 7:30 p.m.† Concurring with the administration's analysis that a rebel victory would

---

* On the evening of 29 April the JCS assigned the unclassified code name Power Pack to U.S. military operations in the Dominican Republic.

† On the Washington end of the line were Ball, McNamara, Raborn, Rusk, and Wheeler.

probably lead to a pro-communist government, Bennett vividly described exhausted junta forces in danger of being defeated by "forces of [the] left" whom he characterized as "mad dogs." He agreed with creating a *cordon sanitaire* that night to seal off rebel strongholds in the downtown section, allegedly the location of the heaviest communist concentrations. Such a move could lead to establishment of a cease-fire and enable the Organization of American States (OAS) to negotiate a settlement. Since too few Marines were ashore to establish such a zone, it became imperative to commit substantial reinforcements within the next 12 hours "to do [the] job here rapidly and effectively."[19]

At the subsequent meeting, the president determined that communist control of the Dominican Republic would threaten hemispheric stability, that American citizens were still in danger, and that Washington would seek a cease-fire, an interim government, and free elections. To achieve these ends before the communists emerged victorious, participants agreed to land 2,500 paratroops in San Isidro. Shortly after the meeting concluded, Wheeler notified CINCLANT, who at around 9:30 p.m. diverted the aircraft for a landing at San Isidro. About an hour earlier, the JCS had ordered the 82nd Airborne Division to load two more battalions for an air landing at the field.[20]

Rusk then cabled Bennett to expect approximately 2,000 airborne troops at San Isidro beginning late on the night of 29 April with a stated mission to protect U.S. citizens and officials in the Dominican Republic. In strictest confidence, he alerted the ambassador that, pending OAS action, Washington was considering interposing U.S. military forces between the loyalist and rebel forces to effect a cease-fire. U.S. action might also serve to deter the spread of communist-controlled governments elsewhere in the hemisphere. Rusk expected that the emergency OAS meeting scheduled for 10:00 p.m. EDT would call for a cease-fire and establish a committee to proceed to Santo Domingo to enforce a truce and a return to constitutional government.[21]

The Dominican ambassador to the OAS had not requested OAS assistance on the assumption that, contrary to Bennett's dire prognosis, his government's forces would be able to defeat the Constitutionalists. Consequently, Johnson's announcement on the evening of 28 April of U.S. landings in the Dominican Republic took Latin members of the OAS by surprise. Attempting to preserve a chance for the OAS to function and to provide legitimacy for the U.S. intervention, the administration requested the convocation of a special meeting of the Council of the Organization of American States (COAS) for the next morning. COAS members gathered on 29 April, deliberated, recessed, and then reconvened that night.*

---

* At 11:21 p.m. the president met with his advisers for about a half hour to await in vain the OAS announcement (Historical Office, Dept of State, "The Response of the Department of State to the Dominican Crisis of April–May 1965," Jul 68, 27, fldr Dominican Crisis 1965—State-DoD-OAS Chronologies & Narratives (3 of 4), box 7, NSC History Dominican Crisis 1965, NSF, LBJL; "Dominican Crisis: Presidential Decisions," nd, fldr Bowdler to Rostow, box 8, ibid).

Contrary to the president's expectations, the special session dragged on into the early morning hours of 30 April, forcing the administration to defer immediate action on a cordon pending the outcome of the OAS deliberations.[22] Nevertheless Washington's policy was clear, if not yet public: the United States would intervene with armed force to prevent a communist takeover of the Dominican Republic.

The Council of the OAS finally adopted early on 30 April a U.S. resolution reiterating the call for a cease-fire together with the establishment of an international zone of safe haven in Santo Domingo. OAS resolution in hand, the State Department authorized U.S. forces in the Dominican Republic to establish an international security zone (ISZ) that could be enlarged if the ambassador and military commander deemed it "feasible and desirable."[23]

By this time, the president's fear of a communist takeover outweighed the risks of adverse hemispheric reaction and its consequences. At a morning meeting on 30 April when his advisers counseled awaiting further OAS action, Johnson's frustration boiled over. "I am not willing," he told them, "to let this island go to Castro." He remained convinced of the Cuban communist leader's involvement in the revolt and told McNamara "to get ready so that Castro cannot take over." Bundy and Rusk urged delay so the OAS could give U.S. intervention some legitimate cover. "We have done little in the past several days," Johnson retorted. Johnson also linked events in the Dominican Republic with recent policy decisions to increase U.S. troop strength in South Vietnam. "How can we," he asked, "send troops 10,000 miles away and let commies take over right under our noses?" He tasked McNamara to "find out what we need to take that island" and Rusk to "determine what it takes to make this take on the right color." McNamara estimated one or two divisions could "clean up the island"; one division could be on the island in 30 hours.[24]

Insisting on swift action—"We cannot stand with our hand in our pocket and let Castro win"—the president approved committing the 4th Marine Expeditionary Brigade (MEB) along with the entire 82nd Airborne Division. The 101st Airborne Division stayed in reserve ready to follow if needed. No final decision concerning deployment of the alerted forces came until the following morning. McNamara informed the Joint Chiefs at their regularly scheduled 2:00 p.m. meeting on 30 April of the decision and named the forces alerted for the Dominican Republic. Wheeler later explained to his colleagues that the president had made up his mind; regardless of appearances, he would do anything necessary to prevent another Cuba in the Caribbean.[25]

The president fretted impatiently throughout the rest of the day. He no doubt shared aide Jack Valenti's intuitive reaction that a Castro takeover in the Dominican Republic would constitute "the worst domestic political disaster any Administration could suffer." Johnson wanted the OAS to act, but he refused "to sit here and let [the] streets run red with human blood while they sit on their ditty boxes." He also remained firmly convinced, notwithstanding his top advisers' disclaimers to the contrary, that Fidel Castro's Cuba was supporting the rebels. Later in the afternoon he told McNamara his feeling that "if we don't take over that island within the next 24 hours or before the last man folds we never will."[26]

For a firsthand appraisal, Johnson also dispatched former U.S. ambassador to the Dominican Republic John Bartlow Martin to Santo Domingo. Martin, who had attended the 30 April White House meeting, officially was to open contact with noncommunist rebels, help the OAS and Papal Nuncio obtain a cease-fire, and report on the state of the country. To aid Bennett in dividing the insurgents and isolating extremists Martin would confidentially identify rebel strengths and weaknesses.[27]

On 1 May the foreign ministers of the American Republics in a formal meeting established a five-nation Special Committee and dispatched OAS Secretary General José A. Mora to the Dominican Republic to prepare for the formal arrival of the OAS Committee. They then adjourned to await further instructions from their respective governments. Johnson had fumed at OAS procrastination, declaring the organization "a phantom—they are taking a siesta while this is on fire." Criticism of U.S. intervention from some OAS members only fueled his ire.[28] If Johnson was upset with the OAS, that body no doubt reciprocated over Washington's unilateral intervention executed without consulting member nations that had legitimate concerns about the legality and appropriateness of their North American ally's actions.

During the day of 1 May, Marines established the ISZ in an area of about three square miles in the southwestern part of Santo Domingo that contained the U.S. embassy and Embajador Hotel. Paratroopers simultaneously occupied San Isidro airfield, about nine miles to the east of the ISZ, then moved along the highway to the capital where that afternoon they secured the Duarte Bridge spanning the Ozama River, formed a screening force on the river's east bank, and deployed small forces in a bridgehead on the west bank. McNamara favored a combination of Marine and paratroop units to secure the safe zone.[29]

To establish the communist link, Johnson turned to Admiral Raborn, at whose order CIA produced two lists identifying 58 communists or communist supporters within the rebel movement. When the names were released, the press quickly spotted duplications within each list, names of noncommunists, and even two or three dead persons. Such gross discrepancies soon discredited the administration's attempt to use the media to create a communist bogey. State notified U.S. embassies that the administration did not see the revolutionary movement as communist-led, but did discern "a clear and present danger" that a small group of well-trained, doctrinaire Dominican communists could capitalize on the chaos to lay the basis for a Castro-style communist domination in that country.[30]

By their own admission, on the afternoon of 24 April members of Dominican communist groups, whose ideology ranged from Soviet Marxism to Castro-style communism to Maoism, had roamed the streets inciting pro-Bosch crowds, staging rallies, and perhaps distributing weapons. They organized rank-and-file civilians, who soon outnumbered the original military participants, into disciplined units under student and communist leaders. But the spontaneity of the popular revolt took even the Dominican communists by surprise, so that they did not take full advantage of the opportunities that became available. Whether or not their superior organization and training managed to win for "a modest number" of them considerable influence in the revolt within the first few days remains uncertain, but Washington, and especially Johnson, did take their appearance seriously.[31] And to eliminate this specter, thousands of U.S. troops were pouring into the Dominican Republic.

United States Information Agency Director Carl T. Rowan pointed out the impossibility of justifying a massive military intervention solely on the grounds of protecting Americans and other foreigners. Rowan felt the administration "must exploit as shrewdly as possible, without overdoing it, . . . the fear that the Dominican Republic might become another Cuba." Johnson had been wanting to say the same thing from the outset of the crisis; he promptly adopted the theme during a national radio and television announcement of the dispatch of more U.S. troops. With knowing hyperbole, he told the American people on 2 May that he would not allow the communist conspirators who had seized control of "a popular domestic revolution" to prevail.[32]

On landing at San Isidro Ambassador Martin "forcibly and privately" told the loyalist junta leader that the United States would not let the Dominican Republic fall to communism. He soon found evidence of extremist domination of the rebels by elements including some members of the Dominican military and "hard core Castro-Communists," evidence that he provided early on the morning of 2 May for the "highest levels" as requested. Later that day by phone he privately received the president's approval to announce that the United States proposed to prevent a Castro-like communist takeover, after which he publicly told reporters at a press conference that in his personal opinion U.S. troops would remain to block such an attempt. Bennett heartily endorsed Martin's remarks, swore to their accuracy, and concluded that the United States could no longer negotiate with rebel leaders.[33] Amidst assertions of neutrality, Washington made it clear that it had taken sides.

Operational Plans and Planning Operations

U.S. operational plans prescribed that military intervention would occur whenever the political situation in the Dominican Republic endangered the interests of the United States or the OAS. Options ranged from a show of force to intervention by ground combat forces. No specific planning existed, however, for what U.S. forces would do after entry.[34] With thousands of U.S. combat troops on hand in the Dominican Republic and thousands more on the way, it became vital that the administration define the mission and purpose. Johnson, however, could not announce a definite military objective simply because no one had determined the overall mission.

At the same time he dispatched Martin to the Dominican Republic, the president ordered Wheeler to send "the best general in the Pentagon" to command U.S. forces in the Dominican Republic. Wheeler informed Lt. Gen. Bruce Palmer, Jr., deputy chief of staff for operations on the Army Staff, that the president had decided to intervene in force in the Dominican Republic to prevent a communist takeover. He then told Palmer: "Your announced mission is to save US lives. Your unstated mission is to prevent the Dominican Republic from going communist. The President has stated that he will not allow another Cuba—you are to take all necessary measures required to accomplish this mission. You will be given sufficient forces to do the job." Consistent with the administration's tight control of the intervention, Palmer never received written orders definitively spelling out his mission. He later described a "mealy-mouthed" cable from Wheeler instructing him to conduct the official mission of protecting the lives of Americans and others, but if a communist takeover appeared imminent to expect a broader mission designed to prevent such an outcome. To Palmer it was self-evident, as he later conceded, that "in the beginning we really weren't neutral. We were trying to contain the rebellion."[35] Still, the White House persisted in proclaiming U.S. neutrality even as restoring order in the streets of the Dominican capital obviously meant preventing a loyalist defeat.

U.S. strategy was to allow the junta to take advantage of any lull in the fighting to rebuild its armed strength in order to regain control of the country. During Palmer's travel from Washington to Santo Domingo via Fort Bragg, Juan Bosch, the symbolic leader of the revolt, then living in exile in Puerto Rico, agreed to a cease-fire. Both State and the JCS instructed their respective representatives in Santo Domingo, Bennett and Maj. Gen. Robert York, commander, 82nd Airborne Division, to pressure the loyalists to accept a cease-fire.[36]

As for the rebels, the Joint Chiefs directed CINCLANT to commence planning to cordon off Constitutionalist-held neighborhoods of the city, following OAS approval and then only in a manner that would not endanger U.S. forces. While the casualties were minor, the repercussions in Washington were major. Press reports of Marine losses reached Johnson late that afternoon. He later phoned McNamara for further information only to learn that his secretary of defense had no details yet. Throughout the Dominican intervention communications difficulties between Santo Domingo and Washington continually hampered accurate and timely reporting.* Radio communications equipment did not perform effectively; messages were grossly misrouted; frequent disruptions in phone conversations became the rule. Discrepancies between State and CIA accounts of events in the Dominican capital further confounded the White House and DoD.[37]

---

* The same communication failures were persistent features of the Six Day Arab-Israeli War and the *Pueblo* incident, severely affecting management of the crises. Failure to overcome these deficiencies reflected adversely on DoD.

Poor communications and misinformation during the first days of the crisis left McNamara inadequately informed prior to high-level discussions. Embarrassed at White House meetings when he could not answer the president's questions regarding DoD deployments and the numbers of Marines ashore, on occasion he had to depend on Rusk to share information and intelligence with him. Dissatisfied with the NMCC's inability to keep him apprised of fast-breaking developments in Santo Domingo, McNamara approved a Defense Intelligence Agency recommendation to establish a Dominican Task Force directly responsible to him in the NMCC. The new system took effect the evening of 30 April and served as McNamara's chief source of information for the remainder of the crisis. The ad hoc arrangement, however, did not resolve the chronic communications problem, which continued to bedevil the president's crisis management system. Without timely and accurate information from the field, it was impossible for the president and McNamara to exercise firm control over the developing military situation.[38]

After much haggling, during the late afternoon of 30 April the warring Dominican factions finally agreed to a cease-fire worked out by the OAS Special Committee. Bennett, the Papal Nuncio, and York also signed the agreement as an indication of their good offices in the settlement. When Palmer landed at San Isidro several hours later he learned from York that the rebels had soundly defeated the junta forces. More troubling to Palmer, the cease-fire kept U.S. forces widely separated, allowing the rebels to hold downtown Santo Domingo with its administrative, commercial, and communications facilities. Palmer notified Wheeler of his arrival and asked for two more battalions of the 82nd Airborne. Meanwhile the JCS had told CINCLANT that the president and his senior advisers would convene at 9:00 a.m. on 1 May to discuss the crisis and not to expect a decision about a cordon until early afternoon.[39]

Palmer could not accept the terms of the cease-fire. York then told Palmer that he had signed merely as a witness, not as a signatory, providing Palmer with the grounds to reject the agreement and follow his own military instincts. Without seeking permission from the JCS, Palmer ordered York to mount a reconnaissance-in-force at first light to determine rebel strength and locate a feasible route for a corridor to link the U.S. units. When Palmer called the NMCC at 4:45 a.m. on 1 May to request guidance, he was instructed to await further clarification and not to take "any offensive action" in the meantime that might invalidate the cease-fire. Evidently the general did not consider his reconnaissance-in-force an "offensive action"; it would merely establish an international line of communication or passageway to the ISZ that would allow overland access to and evacuation from San Isidro.[40]

About 10:00 a.m. on 1 May when paratroopers began moving westward into the city, Palmer arrived by helicopter at the U.S. embassy, which he found "blacked out, in a state of siege, [and] just scared to death," a scene that left him with an impression of "complete disorganization bordering on utter confusion." Bennett disclosed to Palmer that Martin had just concluded negotiations for the formal establishment of an ISZ. In his haste Martin had not consulted with the military before agreeing to sketchy and inaccurate boundaries that left the U.S. embassy isolated and exposed to the rebel front lines. If Martin did not consult with the military, neither apparently did Palmer inform Bennett of the reconnaissance operation. Only after the paratroopers began to move into the city did Palmer officially notify his military superiors that he had directed a "probe" to determine the situation in the gap and to link up with the Marines in the city. He acted because the "exact status of [the] cease fire was not rpt not clear," and it might not have been accepted by "communist-dominated rebel leaders." Palmer again requested thousands more troops, asserting that "we should not send a boy to do a man's job."[41]

While Palmer acted, top presidential advisers met at 8:40 a.m., 1 May, to formulate recommendations for the president. McGeorge Bundy wanted to slow the deployment of U.S. forces until OAS troop units arrived on the island. McNamara and Wheeler, with Rusk's support, argued for the immediate deployment of three more battalions, two airborne plus one Marine, to enable Palmer to execute any assigned mission. An hour later, the president joined the meeting where he received an update on OAS and U.S. military activities.[42]

Johnson approved the reinforcements McNamara had recommended, plus additional unannounced deployments over the next several days that would bring the total number of U.S. troops to more than 22,000. Responding to McNamara's advice, he pushed for Latin nations to provide military forces; he also ordered special messages be sent to U.S. embassies in Latin America explaining the administration's position. These moves, he hoped, would help curb criticism and demonstrations against the intervention in various Latin capitals and lend legitimacy to U.S. actions. The president also directed McGeorge Bundy to chair an interdepartmental Dominican crisis coordinating group that held its first meeting that same day.[43]

Johnson's decision to deploy overwhelming military force signified his determination to allow neither a communist nor a rebel victory. He told his senior advisers of the need "to be ready to hold that island under any circumstances." The additional forces sent just that day to the Dominican Republic seemed impressive enough—two Marine Battalion Landing Teams (BLTs), one by sea and one by air, the remainder of the Marine 4th MEB, and Power Pack II (two airborne battalions plus supporting units), some 7,180 troops. Furthermore a tactical fighter squadron (18 F-100 aircraft) and a tactical reconnaissance squadron (6 RF-101 and 3 RB-66 aircraft) simultaneously deployed to Ramey AFB.[44]

With these reinforcements en route, paratroopers opened a corridor into the city; around 1:00 p.m. they linked up with the Marines advancing from the ISZ. The joint force patrolled the immediate neighborhood for almost three hours before Palmer ordered them back to their original positions "to avoid further charges of breaking cease-fire." Confusion reigned in Washington about what was happening on the streets of Santo Domingo. As of the previous evening the Joint Chiefs, believing no cease-fire existed, thought the meeting of airborne troops with Dominican units at the Ozama River Bridge had achieved Palmer's initial operational goal.[45]

Knowing little of Palmer's doings, the Chiefs were mystified when the Constitutionalist military leader, Col. Francisco Caamano Deno, complained on 1 May about U.S. troops moving west into the city and sparking firefights that violated the cease-fire. Unaware of Palmer's reconnaissance-in-force, State officials, assuming that U.S. troops were maintaining but not expanding their established perimeter, phoned the Santo Domingo embassy for clarification. The line went dead in mid-conversation. Under Secretary Mann then dispatched a flash cable explaining that DoD stated all U.S. patrols were east of the Duarte Bridge and questioning exactly who was doing all the maneuvering and firing on the west side of the river. Bennett did not know but was checking Caamano's allegations that U.S. troops were moving west into the city.[46]

OSD was just as confused. When news reached the president that paratroopers advancing west from the bridge had sustained four casualties, two killed and two wounded, McNamara had heard nothing about it, and personally doubted wire-service accounts of the action. Around 6:00 p.m. he called Wheeler, who likewise had heard nothing about the reports. By the early evening, the embassy conceded "some confusion here this afternoon" about movement west of the river by 82nd Airborne forces, admitting that it could not "determine exactly what truth here is" beyond the U.S. patrols moving across the corridor. Around the same time, Wheeler acknowledged Palmer's "proposed patrol actions" in the gap and expressed his belief that the field commander, while "maintaining close touch with the situation," would report as appropriate any incidents, especially rebel noncompliance with the cease-fire. According to Palmer, Wheeler told him he thought the corridor a good idea, but he would have to get authorization from the OAS commission before Washington would approve it.[47] The ongoing debate over what to do next in Santo Domingo centered on the risks and rewards of sealing off not fully contained Constitutionalist enclaves.

In Washington, principals were pondering whether to close off the rebel-held sections of Santo Domingo by linking the U.S. forces in the ISZ with those along the Ozama River. For consideration at a high-level conference scheduled later that day, Wheeler requested the senior field commanders to provide by 8:00 a.m. on 2 May alternative courses of action to achieve this objective. Planners were told to assume that no effective cease-fire existed and to look at establishing three possible perimeters—"in close," sealing off the main rebel stronghold in downtown Santo Domingo; the current perimeter; or one further removed from the city. Wheeler particularly wanted Palmer's estimate of the forces, risks, and costs involved in such an operation. His message to Palmer, however, got misrouted, reaching Santo Domingo hours after a decision had been made.[48]

Admiral Thomas Moorer, who became CINCLANT on 1 May, did receive Wheeler's cable. He projected it would take 12 infantry battalions 48 hours to seal off completely the rebel stronghold in the city. Moorer anticipated relatively high casualties in street fighting, with accompanying destruction that would expose the United States to damaging political and military consequences throughout the hemisphere. Just to preserve the status quo, requiring eight battalions and a time frame of 24 hours, suffered the disadvantage of prolonging the stalemate and allowing the rebels more time to gather reinforcements from outside the city. The third alternative, involving a greatly extended perimeter, called for 16 battalions, would take three to five days, and possessed no significant advantages. Vance presented the scenarios at a 2 May meeting of senior administration officials and reported that Wheeler favored the second alternative. After considerable discussion, the group agreed. The specter of high casualties made the first course unpalatable, and the third handed the city to rebels, further strengthening their cause.[49]

Still unaware either of Wheeler's message or Washington's deliberations, Palmer had independently concluded that he could open a passageway with his available troops by pushing three battalions through the city streets under cover of darkness. Wheeler understandably expressed skepticism of the plan, having in hand Moorer's estimate that four times the force would be needed. Though nervous about the hazards of a complicated night operation in a densely populated city, Wheeler finally accepted Palmer's proposal and asked for presidential approval. Johnson then phoned Palmer in the early morning hours to voice his concern about possible U.S. casualties in the operation. The general apparently allayed the worries of the president, who approved the plan late on 2 May, subject to the caveat that the advance not begin before midnight. This injunction apparently reflected McNamara's counsel to approve the establishment of an "airtight corridor," but to delay launching the operation on a Sunday (2 May). Besides deferring to religious sensibilities, an extra day might also convince the OAS to act, but, regardless, the operation would begin on 3 May.[50]

Shortly after 2:00 p.m. on 2 May, the JCS alerted Palmer to be ready at daybreak on 3 May to form a perimeter linking the Marines and the paratroops. A few minutes before 9:00 p.m. the president told Bennett by phone to go ahead with the cordon operation. The formal JCS order, transmitted about two hours later, directed Palmer to start the operation "any time after midnight 2/3 May." To deflect criticism, the president purposely avoided discussion of the decision in his meeting with congressional leaders earlier that evening. Johnson insisted that the administration was "not supporting either side. We are trying to stop murder." He concluded his remarks by agonizing, "if I send in Marines I can't live in the Hemisphere—if I don't I can't live at home." McNamara explained the appearance of large numbers of U.S. troops on the island by the need "to do the security job."[51]

To preserve operational security, Rusk instructed Bennett to have the OAS Commission notify the Dominican people of the operation "not more than fifteen minutes" before U.S. forces advanced from the Duarte Bridge toward the safety zone. The "line of communication," the route scouted the previous day by an 82nd Airborne Division patrol, would be maintained whatever the attitude of the commission, although the advantages of the commission providing the United States political legitimacy and possibly reducing the dimensions of the fighting appeared obvious.[52]

By this time, the United States had almost 9,000 Marines and paratroops in the Dominican Republic, another 4,000 en route, and still another 20,000 alerted for possible deployment. Next afternoon, 3 May, at presidential direction, 2,000 more airborne troops and 1,200 Marines had arrived, and 8,000 more troops were en route. They were superfluous. Palmer launched his operation at one minute after midnight on 3 May. Paratroopers skirted the main Constitutionalist forces and linked up with advancing Marine units in just over one hour without a single loss. The textbook maneuver trapped 80 percent of the rebels in the southern part of the city, and the establishment of the military "line of communication" put Washington in the driver's seat.[53]

The Perils of Peacekeeping

In spite of Palmer's successful maneuver, the rebels established a Constitutionalist government headed by Col. Caamano Deno on 4 May.* Three days later the loyalists followed suit, creating a five-man junta with Brig. Gen. Antonio Imbert Barrera as the head of a new Government of National Reconstruction (GNR). Unable to find "a responsible, competent civilian leader" and with no one else willing to take the high-risk position, Martin and Bennett settled on Imbert. Although Martin favored Imbert over the other generals, Palmer dismissed him as "better than nothing"; the CIA described him as ineffectual. The two governments functioned independently throughout the crisis and beyond,[†] forcing the United States to negotiate with both, each side, like a "Chinese warlord" in McGeorge Bundy's apt phrase, well-armed and willing to use military force to disrupt U.S.-driven negotiations or gain temporary advantage.[54]

Around this same time presidential assistant Bill Moyers, worried about public support for the intervention, asked McNamara to tell Johnson that he should "not kid himself" into thinking that the administration's Dominican policy enjoyed "overwhelming" popular approval. Americans felt uneasy about "butting into other people's affairs," and those who approved the intervention did so because they believed it was necessary to stop Castro and communism.[55] Redeployment of some U.S. troops from the island would dramatically allay such fears.

At a meeting of Bundy's interdepartmental committee on 6 May, McNamara suggested withdrawing some U.S. forces to shore up the administration's public relations efforts. Without endangering ability to control the situation, one battalion could be removed immediately and a second as soon as some Latin American forces arrived on the scene. All present "heartily endorsed" the idea. McNamara also advocated further military contingency planning in the event OAS efforts towards a political resolution faltered. More cautious about redeployments, the Joint

* Caamano later went to Cuba, but returned in 1973 to the Dominican Republic where, at the head of a small band of guerrillas, he died fighting Dominican soldiers (Poole, *JCS and National Policy, 1965–68*, pt 2:483, n 49).

† Both continued until 3 September 1965 when a provisional government was established.

Chiefs queried CINCLANT about the prudent timing and sequence of withdrawals; they also anticipated a substantial residual force would have to remain in the Dominican Republic for some time to keep order. Further, they recommended consultations with U.S. civilian and military officials on the spot in Santo Domingo before any pullout; warned that a large-scale withdrawal would prove "militarily and psychologically harmful" to U.S. interests; and counseled against any redeployment until OAS forces were fully in place. Johnson ruled against even a token reduction of the roughly 20,000 U.S. military in the Dominican Republic for two reasons: (1) the danger of criticism that the United States had sent too many troops in the first place, and (2) any U.S. withdrawal might encourage rebel forces.[56]

In fact the cease-fire proved tenuous. With hatred from the brief but bloody civil uprising still deeply dividing rival Dominican factions, the resulting political and military stalemate paralyzed economic life in the capital. While the administration wanted the capital to return to its daily routine, rebel strongholds in the northern sector, home to most of the city's businesses, prevented any semblance of life as usual. Rebel-controlled Radio Santo Domingo also effectively encouraged defiance as its announcers used the airwaves to organize antigovernment demonstrations, incite anti-Americanism, and promote Constitutionalism, which they linked to food and jobs.[57]

As chances for a political solution waned, proposals for unilateral military action gained a fresh hearing. In reply to a 10 May JCS request for the field commanders' estimate of the situation, Palmer proposed that U.S. forces take the offensive to clear the city of armed rebels and restore law and order. To minimize destruction, the general would first isolate the rebel zones and then conduct search and clear operations to eliminate strongholds, using firepower commensurate only with enemy resistance. Moorer not only endorsed Palmer's plan, but to reduce U.S. casualties during the operation he recommended to the Joint Chiefs employment of "all available US forces," including tanks, air support, air reconnaissance, and naval gunfire. The "clear covert aim" should be to eliminate "the hard core communist rebel resistance."[58]

Still worried about a Castro takeover, the president wanted assurances from McNamara that the plan covered all military contingencies. The Bundy Committee relegated such large-scale military action to a last resort, should all diplomatic efforts fail, but it was anxious to restore normal life in the Dominican capital. On 12 May a joint State-Defense message instructed the U.S. embassy to prepare a contingency plan for clearing armed rebels from the industrial sector in the northern part of the city so that factories might reopen. It also requested information on Dominican political reaction, projected casualties, and required reinforcements for such an operation.[59]

Talks had almost collapsed the previous afternoon (11 May) when Colonel Caamano alleged that U.S. troops were killing or wounding rebels east of the river while on the west bank allowing loyalist troops to pass through roadblocks to attack rebel strongholds. With a political solution appearing remote, Moorer wanted to extend the corridor separating the rebel forces and completely isolate them in the capital. Palmer differed; with Bennett's blessing he announced that the time had come to seize Radio Santo Domingo as the first step of a contingency plan to secure the industrial heart of the capital. At the very moment on 13 May that Palmer's staff was preparing plans to seize the radio station, with the general himself on the phone to the OAS protesting Radio Santo Domingo's latest broadcast, loyalist planes suddenly flew at low level over the U.S. embassy on their way to strafe and rocket the station. The attack, executed without prior knowledge by Palmer or Bennett, temporarily knocked the station off the air. It also derailed Bennett's support for Palmer's operation to capture the radio station, causing Acting JCS Chairman Admiral McDonald to phone Palmer and verbally disapprove the plan as well. When discussing the incident the following day with the president, Mann observed that control of northern Santo Domingo was an essential part of any contingency plan. Johnson offered encouragement, remarking that "he wanted all the contingency plans he could get."[60]

In their reply to the earlier 12 May joint State-Defense inquiry, Bennett and Palmer judged it "virtually certain" that the rebel leaders would refuse to agree to an expanded safety zone that reduced rebel strongpoints in Santo Domingo. Once the Constitutionalists rejected the proposal, they continued, State should obtain OAS authorization for U.S. military operations to clear rebel strongholds and enlarge the ISZ into the northern sector of the capital, including the area occupied by Radio Santo Domingo. Capturing the station, Palmer felt, would provoke the most severe fighting. After the radio station came into U.S. hands, American troops would seize the industrial complexes and then isolate the city to cut off rebel escape routes. In reply to JCS concerns about the proposed operation, CINCLANT cautioned that street fighting might degenerate into a costly house-to-house battle with "lots of people, both theirs and ours, getting hurt"; nevertheless it had to be done, not only to prevent the loss of the Dominican Republic to communists, but also to keep the country safe from communism for a generation.[61]

The Joint Chiefs forwarded their endorsement of Palmer's plan to McNamara along with a rationale for it: unilateral U.S. military action to clear selected areas of Santo Domingo of armed rebels would allow life in the city to return to normal. They requested that the secretary authorize Bennett and Palmer to execute the contingency operation "immediately following Caamaño's refusal to agree" to a new zone, preferably with, but if necessary without, OAS approval. Palmer pushed the same line from Santo Domingo. Again questioning the viability of the shaky cease-fire, he requested a decision from the Chiefs on his plans for clearing the city. He warned that with the OAS unable to control the situation and the rebels stalling for time, "this country could slip away from us while we dance on the point of the needle."[62] American ability to control events in Santo Domingo was indeed slipping away, although not for the reasons Palmer feared.

General Imbert lacked popular support and repeatedly sought to attack the Constitutionalists, expecting that a military solution would assure his grasp on power. His loyalists launched an offensive on 15 May that slowly pushed back rebel outposts in the northern sector of the capital. Surprised when the operation showed signs of succeeding, the United States acquiesced in Imbert's latest ground offensive. Nevertheless, Washington was not about to let the Dominican general win a military victory, even to the point of having U.S. paratroopers block the runways at San Isidro with jeeps on 16 May to prevent pilots loyal to Imbert from taking off. Without the air force's added firepower, loyalist troops could not overwhelm their rebel opponents. This pragmatic neutrality signified Johnson's determination to seek a political solution to the crisis in the form of a coalition government.[63] But with neither warring faction capable of militarily dominating the other, neither felt compelled to negotiate seriously.

On 14 May the president selected Cyrus Vance and McGeorge Bundy as his emissaries to convey his policy to Santo Domingo. The move took the Joint Chiefs, still advocating a military resolution, by complete surprise. Wheeler admitted to his colleagues that he did not know "what goes" with the high-powered delegation and concluded, "I'm sort of a rump member of a rump organization—rather far back in this problem." This came as the second unexpected diplomatic initiative sprung on the Chiefs within a week. On 11 May, the JCS had received two days' notice, though not a complete explanation, of a pause in the bombing of North Vietnam.[64]

Bundy and Vance flew first to Puerto Rico on 15 May to meet with Bosch and Sylvestre Antonio Guzman, one of Bosch's former cabinet ministers and his choice for the post of constitutional president. The two Dominicans agreed on a Guzman-led cabinet, including an armed forces minister acceptable to the loyalists and Constitutionalists, and removal of the communists and Trujillistas, either by internment or deportation. McNamara had insisted that control of the armed forces post was crucial because it neutralized any communist presence in a new Dominican government. "Moderately encouraged" by their talks with Bosch, the two Americans continued on to Santo Domingo where they teamed with State's Mann and Assistant Secretary Jack Vaughn. Intending to produce a quick settlement, Vance and Mann negotiated with Imbert and the military while Bundy talked with rebel leaders. Bundy and Vance had in mind creating a strong role for Guzman in the interim government. Mann, however, objected to Guzman because of his Bosch connections, demanding categorical assurances to keep communists out of any new government. Johnson sided with Mann, a valued and highly trusted confidant.[65]

Neither Guzman nor Imbert cooperated with the Bundy mission. Imbert denounced the coalition as a "double cross," accused Guzman of being a Bosch puppet sympathetic to the communists, and claimed that his revitalized forces could crush the rebellion in four days. Guzman, equally obdurate, insisted the armed forces minister come from rebel ranks. He remained absolutely uncompromising about reestablishing the constitution. Guzman's stock fell even lower after Johnson polled his advisers by phone in the early morning hours of 17 May. Palmer evinced skepticism about Guzman's ability to control the Dominican military, suggesting that the country might slide under communist domination. Palmer already had devised contingency plans for U.S. paratroops to seize rebel-held neighborhoods should negotiations fail, first reducing Constitutionalist strongholds. Next, by denying water and electricity to the rebel-held parts of the city, they would weaken morale and resistance to a point that with "judicious use of CS [tear gas]" U.S. forces could clear the entire Constitutionalist area without inflicting heavy damage.[66]

The Joint Chiefs quickly approved Palmer's latest proposal. They recommended to McNamara that the United States act unilaterally because of the very unsettled political situation, the rebels' exposure of the impotence of the OAS, and the vague language of the U.N. Security Council resolution of 14 May that extended implicit recognition to the Constitutionalist cause, thus boosting insurgent morale. Acting before Latin forces arrived would consolidate loyalist gains, help restore stability in the capital, and confine the rebels in a small area, all steps that would enable the OAS units to take over with the rebel forces seriously weakened. McNamara acknowledged the JCS recommendations but informed the Chiefs that nothing would be done for the time being. ISA's John McNaughton likewise advocated delay to give the Bundy mission more time to forge a political agreement. McNaughton's recommendation effectively eliminated the military option; Palmer heard no more of his proposal.[67] The Bundy mission fared no better.

Bundy had expected to wrap up negotiations quickly, but he found the Dominican Republic a "cockpit of senseless hate." Deep-seated divisions, particularly over the appointment of the next minister of the armed forces, would not permit a political compromise between government and rebel forces. Steady loyalist military gains in the northern industrial part of the capital only hardened Imbert's position. For their part, the Constitutionalists, who still controlled large areas of downtown Santo Domingo, were unwilling to bargain from a position of weakness. To break this cycle of fighting and improve the chances for negotiations, on 18 May the senior U.S. civilian officials in the Dominican Republic, along with Palmer and the Bundy mission, recommended interposing U.S. military forces between the contending sides to stop the fighting on the north side of the city. U.S. paratroops would first capture heavily defended Radio Santo Domingo to deny both sides an outlet for their propaganda. Paratroops would next force open a new corridor to separate the combatants as well as isolate the Constitutionalists holding out in the northern district.[68] All the while, Imbert pressed his offensive.

On 19 May loyalist troops seized Radio Santo Domingo. Flushed with success, they threatened to drive all the way to the Ozama River, crushing rebel resistance in the northern part of the city. With loyalist military success imperiling negotiations, Bundy, Vance, Palmer, and Bennett proposed executing the military option. Then Imbert's drive faltered as it predictably encountered the stiffer resistance of hard-core rebel fighters barricaded behind strong positions in heavily built-up neighborhoods. In bloody fashion Imbert had unintentionally accomplished U.S. goals. Radio Santo Domingo was silenced; the Constitutionalists in the city were isolated, but not defeated. This state of affairs seemed to offer the equilibrium between the opposing factions seen as a prerequisite for meaningful negotiations. The standoff enabled Palmer to notify the Joint Chiefs that he no longer saw reason to interpose U.S. troops between the combatants. Nor was there any need for an immediate political settlement. Neither Dominican side could overwhelm the other militarily; the nation no longer lay in danger of falling under communist domination. A truce went into effect on 21 May, and by the end of the month the Bundy-Vance mission had returned home. [69]

Withdrawal

In early May, responding to U.S. requests that OAS member states send troops to the Dominican Republic, the ministers of foreign affairs of the American republics authorized the establishment of an Inter-American Force (IAF) to restore security and promote democratic institutions in the country. The Joint Chiefs wanted the small, lightly equipped Latin units under U.S. military control but, if politically necessary, would accept a Latin commander, provided Palmer served as his deputy. On 22 May the OAS asked the Government of Brazil (the largest non-U.S. contributor to the force) to designate the commander of the IAF. The precise relationship between the titular commander and the one who would hold real military power was not delineated. Military forces from Brazil, Costa Rica, Honduras, and Nicaragua arrived in the Dominican Republic in May, and in mid-June a small unit from Paraguay rounded out the Latin units. Formally established in Santo Domingo on 23 May, the IAF was redesignated the Inter-American Peace Force (IAPF) on 2 June. Its mission remained the same throughout its existence.[70]

When dispatching the Bundy-Vance mission in mid-May, Johnson had in mind withdrawal of U.S. forces from the Dominican Republic at the earliest possible date. Consequently, on 23 May Vance and Palmer agreed that one battalion of Marines now afloat could depart while another battalion could withdraw to ships offshore once the Brazilian contingent arrived. The president wanted to pull out as many as 10,000 U.S. troops by early June. Such substantial withdrawals, about half the total force, would place responsibility for reestablishing governmental control squarely in the hands of the OAS, relieving Washington of much of the international opprobrium associated with a military occupation.[71] A rapid departure might also add to the public image of reasonableness that Johnson sought to project even as he endured great pressure to expand the ground war in South Vietnam.

Vance and Palmer were already recommending the prompt withdrawal of 5,000 Marines and soldiers provided the political situation in the Dominican Republic remained stable. Palmer proposed to the JCS a progressive reduction, leaving only units from the 82nd Airborne Division in the country. More than 5,200 troops would depart immediately, all the remaining Marine units (another 4,500 troops) by 1 June, and 2,000 more soldiers by 8 June. For political reasons, the OAS made the official announcement of U.S. withdrawal, based on McNamara's conditions that (1) General Hugo Panasco Alvim, commander of the Inter-American Force, be consulted and agree to U.S. withdrawals, and (2) Alvim state the need to maintain a U.S. reserve force capable of rapid redeployment to the Dominican Republic if required. Withdrawals began on 26 May when Vance verbally relayed McNamara's instructions to remove 1,600 U.S. troops. The next day the Joint Chiefs endorsed Palmer's overall withdrawal concept, directed extra shipping be prepositioned to support an accelerated schedule of redeployments if ordered, and recommended using U.S. aircraft carrying the Brazilian force to the Dominican Republic to bring another 1,600 Army and Air Force personnel back to the United States.[72] By 30 May, Phase I of the withdrawal was completed.

Withdrawals agreed to and under way, Johnson turned to McNamara to justify the deployment of more than 20,000 U.S. troops[*] to the Dominican Republic in the first place. As he often did, Johnson desired written confirmation of his actions so that he might justify his conduct to present and future critics. The secretary of defense's explanation highlighted the changing missions of U.S. forces—from initially evacuating U.S. citizens to eventually maintaining the International Safety Zone—that created a constant demand for more troops. Operations after the initial landings left U.S. military contingents widely separated in a densely crowded area whose topography necessitated extra troops to secure lines of communication. Lastly, the explosive Dominican political situation required keeping units in ready reserve should fighting reignite and shatter the fragile cease-fire agreement. Not surprisingly Vance relied on the same script in his testimony before the Senate Foreign Relations Committee in mid-July.[73] The official reasons cited all had validity, but they also represented ex post facto justifications for public consumption that glossed over the administration's primary political reasons for intervening.

On 1 June Generals Alvim and Palmer recommended the phased withdrawal of the remaining 4,100 Marines in two increments by 6 June. After the JCS and OSD concurred, Vance hand-carried the decision to the president along with the caveat that he delay the prepared statement on the subject of the second withdrawal until 4 June so as not to preempt Johnson's own announcement of the pullout to Democratic Party stalwarts in Chicago on the evening of 3 June.[74] These latest redeployments represented tangible progress toward Johnson's goal of withdrawing about 10,000 troops in less than two weeks.

---

[*] According to an official study, peak U.S. strength was reached on 17 May with 23,889 U.S. service personnel deployed to the Dominican Republic. One Marine battalion, however, remained offshore as a floating reserve, so the actual number of troops on the ground was around 21,000 (WSEG, "Dominican Republic," 224, box 456, Subj files, OSD Hist).

Despite the unsettled and still volatile conditions in Santo Domingo, McNamara approved Palmer's discussions with Alvim and the OAS Commission between 9 and 12 June regarding the withdrawal of 1,500 more U.S. troops of the roughly 13,000 still remaining in the country. Alvim, though, was "somewhat reluctant" to approve further U.S. force reductions until the political situation in the country became more certain. Instead the Brazilian suggested a temporary redeployment of two airborne battalions to nearby Puerto Rico where they would remain as a readily available reserve if disorders erupted anew.[75]

Heavy demands for manpower for Vietnam lent urgency to a Dominican pullout. The 82nd Airborne constituted an essential element of the U.S. strategic reserve, rapidly being depleted by the quickening tempo of units deploying from the United States to Vietnam. Anxious to maintain the CONUS strategic reserve, the Joint Chiefs wanted the two battalions redeployed to Fort Bragg, not Puerto Rico. But some of the heaviest fighting of the intervention involving U.S. troops had erupted, so Palmer opted not to raise the issue with Alvim for the moment.[76]

The Constitutionalists made one last attempt on 15 June to break out of their downtown enclave, likely more for political capital (because they were greatly outnumbered) than for military victory. Two days of fighting left several Americans dead and a larger number wounded. Palmer believed the rebels had deliberately staged the outbreak to influence the U.N. Security Council to champion their cause. If so, the Constitutionalists paid heavily, suffering far greater casualties than the IAPF. Now seriously weakened and with the most dedicated rebel fighters gone, Colonel Caamano could have had only faint hope of further military action. Nor did Caamano's call for a general strike on 22 June generate much popular enthusiasm. As life settled back to an uneasy truce, Palmer received permission to renew discussions with Alvim about additional U.S. withdrawals.[77]

The recent fighting had interfered with the timetable to pull out the two airborne battalions, so McNamara and Vance approved a JCS alternative calling for the immediate redeployment of a few hundred support troops as well as small numbers of excess personnel. On 22 June Vance and the Joint Chiefs sought Palmer's views on further troop reductions. Palmer recommended withdrawal of two paratroop battalions by early July, and, following a political agreement, rapid reduction of the IAPF to his residual force requirement of three U.S. airborne battalions (nine were then in the Dominican Republic), with the Latin American brigade remaining in the country. McNamara approved and, with Washington's authorization, Palmer and Alvim agreed that conditions in Santo Domingo permitted the withdrawal of the two battalions of paratroopers. President Johnson announced the decision on 3 July. The latest withdrawal reduced authorized U.S. military strength to about 11,000, or less than half the 23,889 peak strength of mid-May.[78]

Diplomacy thenceforth predominated as U.S. Ambassador to the OAS Ellsworth Bunker patiently brokered a provisional government under President Hector Garcia Godoy. On 31 August, loyalist and Constitutionalist leaders accepted an "Act of Dominican Reconciliation" that installed a provisional government, granted general amnesty, and disarmed civilians, with the promise of presidential elections within nine months. Upon taking office on 3 September, the provisional government opened negotiations with the OAS over the timing of the IAPF withdrawal. Bunker's diplomatic successes enabled Palmer to reduce the 82nd Airborne Division forces to his desired three-battalion residual force. In early September the JCS, in accordance with Palmer's proposal, requested that McNamara provide for maintenance of an IAPF force of about 9,000 on the island, including 7,000 U.S. troops. A premature withdrawal, they cautioned, entailed "serious adverse effects" because once all IAPF units departed it would prove exceedingly difficult politically to redeploy any back to the Dominican Republic. Vance, with State concurrence, approved the recommendation. It was further proposed that an infantry brigade trained and equipped for peacekeeping duties would replace the paratroop units as soon as possible.[79]

McNamara had conceded the possibility if not probability after the mid-June fighting that U.S. troops would have to remain in the Dominican Republic for an indefinite period. At the time he questioned the secretary of the Army about the possibility of using special non-divisional units tailored for a peacekeeping role to replace the 82nd Airborne units that were needed for the strategic reserve. Secretary Resor proposed the 196th Infantry Brigade, the first of three new separate brigades formed under the 1965 Army buildup plan to support operations in South Vietnam, expected to reach acceptable readiness status by 15 May 1966. In April 1966, Bunker asked McNamara to allow the paratroops to remain in the Dominican Republic until sometime in July. With presidential elections set for 1 June, State may have worried that the Dominican people might construe troop rotations as a form of heavy-handed intimidation that could cast suspicion on the fairness of the election. McNamara approved the State request; the JCS, having no strong reasons to remove the few 82nd Airborne units, agreed to a July 1966 rotation.[*80]

Much to Washington's surprise, the closely monitored June 1966 election witnessed the defeat of candidate Juan Bosch in favor of Joaquin Balaguer. Provisional President Garcia had previously insisted that all foreign troops depart before the advent of the new administration on 1 July, but he ultimately agreed to an OAS foreign ministers' resolution calling for withdrawal over a 90-day period beginning in late June. Vance directed the Joint Chiefs to implement the resolution; the last echelon of U.S. troops along with the rest of the IAPF departed the Dominican Republic by late September 1966, 17 months after the first Marines had gone ashore, ostensibly to protect the U.S. embassy. The human toll of intervention for the United States was 25 military killed and 156 wounded. Two U.S. civilians were also wounded.[81]

---

[*] In mid-June the 196th found itself on immediate orders to Vietnam and departed Boston, Massachusetts, on 15 July 1966 (HQ US Continental Army Command, USCONARC/USARSTRIKE Annual Historical Summary, 1 Jul 66–30 Jun 67, 17 Jun 68, 97-98).

During the multiple crises that punctuated Johnson's tenure between 1965 and 1968 the president invariably sought the advice of his highest civilian counselors both in and out of government, relied on a few key senior advisers, usually civilians, in decisionmaking sessions, created a high-level ad hoc committee composed of trusted civilians to coordinate issues, retained tight control of information within the administration, and dispatched special envoys to the scene to expedite a solution. As decisions emerged, the president announced them, often with a spin that omitted significant details in favor of exaggerated unanimity. By contrast with his hesitancy during the long agony of Vietnam, in the relatively brief period of the Dominican intervention Johnson provided strong consistent leadership in policy and action.

"We want nothing," Lyndon Johnson told his top civilian advisers on 26 May 1965, except a broadly based Dominican government to rebuild the country.[82] By that time, U.S. military intervention had prevented the communist takeover of the Dominican Republic that the president had feared was imminent. Washington conveyed this mission clearly if secretly to U.S. diplomats and military commanders in the Dominican Republic. Early in the crisis the president's determination to intervene promptly ruled out alternatives and no doubt affected the influence and advice of senior confidants. McNamara played a less visible and influential role in policy formulation than usual. Through the Joint Chiefs he had a more significant role in implementing policy. For OSD the intervention demonstrated that successful application of military force could effect a desired political outcome. The Dominican venture may have also influenced the critical decisions made soon afterwards that committed the country to full-scale intervention in Vietnam.

With hindsight the 1965–1966 Dominican experience offered the Johnson administration abundant cautions on the complexities of military intervention. The chronic confusion of U.S. officials in Santo Domingo together with the unpardonable U.S. communications failures that resulted in delayed and misrouted messages affected the timing and the implementation of decisions. In mid-1965, however, one could view the experience as vindication—U.S. armed force had prevented the spread of communism to another nation. Military force backed a political and diplomatic effort that restored law and order as well as crafting a viable government.[83]

Thus, intervention either prevented "another Cuba" in the Caribbean and reestablished a democratically elected government or illegally suppressed a popular revolt against a corrupt government. In the near term, informed critics faulted the intervention as a violation of Good Neighbor Policy whose harmful effects on U.S.-Latin relations and the OAS seemed incalculable. Although some like Senator Fulbright grudgingly conceded that a "degree of order and stability" was restored to the Dominican Republic more quickly than they imagined possible in May of 1965, it did not follow that intervention was "necessary, justified, and wise."[84] Later critics, viewing the event from a longer perspective, reinforced this view and cast doubt on the likelihood of a communist takeover. Beyond question, the intervention demonstrated forcefully Washington's unwillingness to tolerate either communist regimes or dangerously unstable governments in the Caribbean region. The Dominican model of using overwhelming military force to effect a political solution satisfactory to the United States would have application later in military interventions in Grenada (1983), Panama (1989), and Haiti (1993–94).

CHAPTER XII

ARMS CONTROL: AN ELUSIVE GOAL

The urgent issues posed by nuclear proliferation and arms control impelled the Johnson administration to seek nuclear disarmament agreements with the Soviet Union even as the two superpowers engaged in unremitting clashes and arms competition in other arenas around the globe. Such initiatives had the strong support of Secretary McNamara, although he consistently favored retention of nuclear testing capabilities and inspection guarantees that made agreement difficult. His was a delicate balancing act between the advocates of a nuclear accord with the Soviets and those, principally military, who doubted the possibility of reaching an understanding that would not disadvantage the United States.

On 1 November 1964, two days before the presidential election, apparently prompted by Communist China's first atomic test conducted on 16 October, President Johnson appointed a special task force under former Deputy Secretary of Defense Roswell Gilpatric to study means of preventing the spread of nuclear weapons. The previous January Johnson had made known to Soviet Chairman Nikita Khrushchev his desire to ban tests of nuclear weapons, curtail their spread, and limit existing systems. There followed a high-level exchange of secret diplomatic correspondence (part of the Pen Pal messages that had originated in 1961 under President Kennedy) averaging about one letter per month. After Khrushchev's political demise in mid-October 1964, the new Soviet prime minister, Alexei Kosygin, notified Johnson on 3 November of his government's continuing interest in arms limitations. In December 1964 Soviet Foreign Minister Andrei Gromyko elaborated on Kosygin's position, informing Johnson and Rusk at a White House meeting that disarmament and nonproliferation were a high priority for the new regime.[1]

The president reaffirmed his sentiments in his 1965 New Year's greetings to the Soviet leaders and in a follow-up 14 January letter to Kosygin extolling the advantages of cooperative efforts to prevent nuclear proliferation. The Soviet chairman's reply, delivered 1 February, expressed doubts about meaningful nonproliferation so long as Washington remained intent on creating a NATO nuclear component in the form of a multilateral force (MLF), or any variation thereof. The administration chose not to respond to this message. Later, when asked the reason, William C. Foster, director of the Arms Control and Disarmament Agency (ACDA),[*] informed the Soviet ambassador to the United States, Anatoly Dobrynin, that unspecified "conditions in the world" made it inappropriate to reply, evidently a reference to the deteriorating situation in South Vietnam. Actually, by late February ACDA had prepared a suggested reply to Kosygin. The Joint Chiefs, however, questioned the appropriateness of responding, citing the Soviets' increasing lack of interest in talks and the threat of Chinese or Soviet intervention in Vietnam. Pen Pal exchanges then lapsed for almost two years, inhibited by the escalation of the Vietnam War and the institutional and routine tone of Soviet messages. Nevertheless, U.S. pursuit of nonproliferation and arms control agreements would continue, thanks largely to ACDA's efforts and NSC support.[2]

The Johnson administration sought to end the nuclear arms race by preventing further nuclear proliferation, enacting a comprehensive test ban treaty, and promoting strategic nuclear arms control agreements, on the theory that by limiting their own armaments the nuclear powers would encourage nonnuclear powers to forego the nuclear option. ACDA, a consistent and vigorous proponent of these aims, initiated multiple proposals; the JCS, OSD, State, the Atomic Energy Commission (AEC), and other interested agencies reviewed them, and the Committee of Principals,[†] the senior coordination and decision group for arms control matters, rendered final assessment and recommendation. The president decided on the committee's proposals based on the advice of his most trusted counselors—the national security adviser, the secretary of state, and the secretary of defense.[3]

McNamara was a strong supporter of holding the spread of nuclear weapons to an absolute minimum through a nonproliferation agreement, a test ban treaty, and military security guarantees to nonnuclear states opting not to acquire nuclear weapons. To realize these goals, McNamara deemed Soviet support and even collaboration essential and best secured at an early date. The Joint Chiefs of Staff were also on record favoring a test ban; their chairman, General Wheeler, believed a nonproliferation treaty desirable with the exception of what he regarded as the unnecessarily risky task of providing a security umbrella for the nonnuclear world in exchange for its support of nonproliferation. DoD senior civilians differed with their military counterparts over the requirements for any nonproliferation or arms control agreements with the Soviet Union.[4]

---

[*] ACDA was a separate agency housed in the State Department whose director was the principal adviser on arms control to the president and the secretary of state.

[†] The Committee of Principals, established by President Eisenhower and expanded under President Kennedy to coordinate the executive branch's review of arms control policy, consisted of the secretary of state, who served as chairman; the secretary of defense; the directors of CIA, ACDA, and the U.S. Information Agency; the chairmen of the AEC and the JCS; the administrator of NASA; and the president's national security and science advisers (Seaborg, *Stemming the Tide*, 8).

On 21 January 1965 the Committee on Nuclear Proliferation presented its report, generally called the Gilpatric Report, to President Johnson at a formal White House meeting. It concluded that proliferation in any form posed a grave threat to the security of the United States and was inimical to a broad range of U.S. interests. Options to check the spread of nuclear weapons included nonproliferation agreements, a comprehensive test ban, and the establishment of nuclear-free zones. The committee advanced new initiatives—strategic arms reductions and a halt in construction of new ABM or ICBM launchers—to gain Soviet cooperation in preventing the spread of nuclear weapons. Declaring it riddled with "major deficiencies and gaps in the analysis," Wheeler recommended the report be referred to the Joint Chiefs for comment before any decision was made on its proposals. Rusk thought that the Gilpatric Committee had in general underestimated the effects its recommendations would have on vital elements of U.S. foreign policy; in particular it subordinated the NATO alliance to the goal of a nonproliferation agreement with the Soviet Union. Together with a lengthy 13-page draft National Security Action Memorandum (NSAM), the report was distributed to the Committee of Principals on 23 January along with the president's admonition that any further dissemination of the documents required his express approval.[5]

McGeorge Bundy quickly advised against any public discussion of the Gilpatric findings, counseling the president to reserve his position pending further study of the matter. NSC staffer Spurgeon Keeny, a specialist on nuclear matters, feared that if the Gilpatric report disappeared "without a trace," the administration's disarmament community would be confused and demoralized. He proposed the Committee of Principals review the report, a brief NSAM setting forth U.S. nonproliferation policy be drafted, the president concisely restate the U.S. position on nonproliferation in a major speech, and the Pen Pal correspondence be resumed. Agreeing with Keeny, in late March Bundy recommended to McNamara and Rusk that after receiving the president's guidance they convene a meeting of the Committee of Principals to reaffirm support for the principles of nonproliferation and a comprehensive test ban treaty.[6] Although the Pen Pal exchanges stopped and the Gilpatric report went unpublicized, Keeny's other proposals stayed alive.

The president originally planned to announce ways to reduce proliferation based on the Gilpatric report in his speech at the twentieth anniversary commemoration of the United Nations in San Francisco on 25 June. Not wishing to appear to be following behind Robert Kennedy, who spoke in the U.S. Senate on the same subject two days earlier, Johnson deleted all references from his speech and instead alluded briefly to the urgency of controlling world armaments and his hope that other nations would join with the United States in the endeavor. Building on the statement, on 28 June Bundy issued a three-paragraph NSAM charging ACDA with responsibility for preparing a new program for arms control and disarmament that would prevent the spread of nuclear weapons. But little progress ensued on nonproliferation during 1965 because of limited presidential involvement on the American side and Soviet insistence that the possibility of an MLF or a British-proposed Atlantic Nuclear Force (ANF)* made a nonproliferation agreement impossible.[7]

The Multilateral Force

To persuade nonnuclear NATO states to forego nuclear weapons and particularly to satisfy German demands for an equal role in the alliance, the Eisenhower administration had advanced the idea of a multilateral nuclear force.† This would have involved transferring possession but not control of nuclear weapons to certain NATO nations, principally West Germany. It would have allowed for U.S. control of the alliance's nuclear warheads as well as a veto over their use by the allies. If kept on the proposed schedule, by 1963 the MLF would have consisted of 25 surface ships, each carrying eight Polaris A-3 nuclear-tipped missiles and each manned by multinational crews, with the nuclear warheads under joint custody and ownership.[8]

Events of the early 1960s undermined the MLF's prospects. France developed an independent nuclear weapon capability, the *force de frappe*, and Britain, disillusioned with the MLF, proposed the ANF, in which it would play the predominant role. Because DoD and State could not resolve their differences, interest in an MLF or ANF gradually diminished. According to Dean Rusk, there was never a direct presidential decision to kill the MLF, but rather an understanding that the United States would not press the matter and instead leave the MLF "on the table and let it die there."[9] That became a problem— without being laid to rest, the MLF's ghost frustrated progress in U.S.-USSR nonproliferation discussions.

Neither the West Germans nor the Soviets clearly understood the orphaned status of the MLF. Always enthusiastic about the MLF, the Germans alone among the major NATO partners continued to push for it, confirming Soviet suspicions that it was a "blatant attempt to give the West Germans access to nuclear weapons." Whether as a pretext to stall talks or as a genuine source of concern, Moscow repeatedly returned to the MLF issue during 1965. As the administration probed the Soviets for a nonproliferation accord, its dilemma lay in having to resolve the conflicting demands of stopping the spread of nuclear weapons while meeting existing NATO nuclear commitments to the allies and shaping future plans for a nuclear-sharing agreement. ACDA's Foster identified the MLF/ANF discussions as the chief impediment to a nonproliferation treaty. He suggested on 12 April 1965 that Washington inform Moscow privately that it would not press the NATO allies to agree on either the MLF or ANF, in effect killing the proposals.[10]

---

* The ANF would place British nuclear submarines and bombers into a mix-manned and jointly owned force in which the nuclear powers could participate (Kaplan, *Long Entanglement*, 125).

† For the origins of the MLF, see Kaplan et al, *McNamara Ascendancy*, ch XV.

Ten days later, meeting to discuss Foster's recommendation, the Committee of Principals, led by Rusk, McNamara, and Bundy, concluded that a nonproliferation treaty was impossible because Moscow's stipulations would limit U.S. options to equip NATO's proposed MLF with nuclear missiles. The committee sought an agreement that prohibited the transfer of control of nuclear arms to a nonnuclear power but implicitly permitted the transfer of control to a group of states, that is, the NATO alliance. In mid-May, the Joint Chiefs, less Air Force Chief of Staff John P. McConnell, agreed that the United States should seek to impede the spread of an independent nuclear weapon capability to additional nations but insisted that continued dispersal of U.S. nuclear weapons abroad and inter-allied nuclear arrangements remained essential for U.S. security. McConnell dissented, arguing that the security implications of a nonproliferation treaty needed further study before reaching a decision.[11]

Convinced the MLF had no future, Bundy, with presidential approval, had previously asked Rusk and McNamara to consider other possibilities for nuclear coordination within NATO. McNamara proposed in May 1965 a Select Committee of NATO defense ministers (which later became the Nuclear Planning Group) to improve and extend allied participation in nuclear planning, including use of strategic nuclear weapons.[12] The unclear status of the MLF remained an obstacle to U.S.-Soviet nonproliferation talks.

On 17 August the U.S. delegation to the UN Eighteen Nation Disarmament Committee (ENDC)* conference submitted a carefully phrased draft nonproliferation treaty that left open the possibility of a MLF/ANF or a future European nuclear force, commonly known as the European option, organized around a European federation. The Soviets promptly refused to consider the proposal unless it explicitly banned direct or indirect German access to nuclear weapons. The following month the Soviets submitted to the UN General Assembly their counter nonproliferation concept, which closed off every imaginable method of nuclear sharing in Europe or elsewhere in the world and raised questions about existing U.S.-NATO nuclear arrangements as well as joint nuclear planning. Meanwhile, Washington deferred to the Federal Republic of Germany (FRG), which did not want to push the nuclear issue before its September 1965 elections. Accepting the impasse, President Johnson remained content to leave the Germans and British to their respective MLF and ANF positions. Clearly, in October 1965 Washington felt that the MLF had no political or popular base of support in either Europe or the United States; there seemed no urgent need for an MLF.[13]

---

* ENDC was the main international forum for negotiating arms control measures. Its membership included five NATO countries (U.S., United Kingdom, Canada, France, and Italy); five Warsaw Pact nations (USSR, Bulgaria, Czechoslovakia, Poland, and Romania); and eight nonaligned states (Brazil, Burma, Ethiopia, India, Mexico, Nigeria, Sweden, and the United Arab Republic).

In early November ACDA again suggested that the president privately notify the Soviet leadership that the United States stood ready to negotiate a nonproliferation treaty based on an implicit understanding that no MLF/ANF force would come into existence. Since no one wanted the MLF, Bundy concluded, "we may well be able to make some money with Moscow if we tell them privately before we sink it publicly." Yet Washington could not unilaterally drop the MLF without risking grave damage to its role as a guarantor of NATO and its valued relationship with the FRG. During talks in Washington in December 1965, Johnson and West German Chancellor Ludwig Erhard agreed that the Federal Republic did not want national control of nuclear weapons and that no new weapon system was necessary. All signs pointed toward the end of the MLF. By this time, however, Vietnam had caused additional American-Soviet friction, leaving Johnson in late 1965 privately doubting that much could be accomplished in the way of nonproliferation.[14]

Test Ban and Nonproliferation

Despite the deadlock and the cessation of privately written exchanges between Washington and Moscow after February 1965, Soviet leaders used intermittent high-level discussions with U.S. allies or such senior American officials as Ambassador at Large Averell Harriman to make clear their continuing interest in discussing test bans and nonproliferation. Following up the June NSAM, ACDA concluded that curtailing nuclear testing would help prevent the spread of nuclear weapons. Foster believed that internationally available seismic systems and national intelligence assets could verify Soviet adherence to any test ban agreement. In mid-July he offered proposals for a threshold treaty, without on-site inspections, extending the 1963 Limited Nuclear Test Ban Treaty to include high-yield underground tests. A follow-on comprehensive test ban treaty would include limited on-site inspections, relating particularly to threats by one side or the other to withdraw over suspected treaty violations. Without on-site inspections the Joint Chiefs had little confidence that Washington could verify Soviet compliance with any treaty. They also feared that a threshold test ban would impair U.S. progress on an antiballistic missile warhead design and have the effect of conceding Moscow's suspected technological edge in high-yield nuclear experiments. Lastly, because the Chinese could continue to test while the United States could not, U.S. nuclear superiority would decline.[15]

McNamara, in contrast, supported ACDA's proposed threshold test ban treaty at a level that offered neither superpower a significant advantage in nuclear technology. Convinced that improved U.S. monitoring capabilities would detect any Soviet cheating, he believed that an agreement could be monitored with confidence. With or without further testing, U.S. nuclear superiority over China was bound to decline. Nevertheless, McNamara remained reluctant to endorse a comprehensive test ban, feeling that ACDA's analysis was too narrowly focused on the military capabilities of the United States, the USSR, and China to the neglect of potential nuclear states whose support was crucial to the success of any agreement.[16]

In mid-July the Committee of Principals discussed the president's message and Foster's statement to the ENDC meeting scheduled to convene in Geneva on 27 July. Accepting AEC Chairman Glenn Seaborg's position that on-site inspections of underground test sites were still needed despite technological advances in detection capability, members authorized Foster to express Washington's desire for a nonproliferation treaty and a comprehensive test ban treaty in a way that did not limit future U.S. nuclear tests.[17]

Since the opening of the ENDC session coincided with the administration's planned announcement of deploying large numbers of combat troops to South Vietnam, Rusk dryly observed that it was "a hell of a day to make a speech on disarmament."* Foster read the president's brief salutation that identified the three objectives of American policy as (1) nuclear nonproliferation; (2) nuclear arms control; and (3) a comprehensive test ban treaty. Some states that aspired to nuclear status, such as India, objected to a nonproliferation treaty because it imposed restrictions only on nonnuclear countries while reaffirming the "privileged status" of nuclear powers to expand their arsenals. Thus the eight nonaligned nations of ENDC, seeking linkage between nonproliferation and arms control, on 15 September proposed a threshold test ban treaty extending the Limited Nuclear Test Ban Treaty to cover underground testing generating signals greater than 4.75 on the Richter scale, the level thought verifiable without on-site inspections, roughly corresponding to a 30–40-kiloton explosion or one-and-one-half to two times more powerful than the Hiroshima bomb. DoD remained divided over the merits of extending the 1963 ban on nuclear weapon tests in the atmosphere, in outer space, and underwater, and whether to ban some or all underground testing. In opposition to the Chiefs, McNamara endorsed a threshold (or low-yield) test ban treaty and reliance on improved monitoring technology to verify Soviet compliance. He also favored reducing the number of on-site inspection requirements for a comprehensive test ban treaty but did not want to identify a fresh position on verification policy until the new technology proved its worth.[18]

Against this background ACDA developed nuclear test ban proposals as possible initiatives during the final three weeks of the ENDC session, expected to end about 9 September. The agency recommended four alternatives: (1) a comprehensive ban with no inspections; (2) an uninspected partial ban with a threshold at magnitude 4.5; (3) a comprehensive ban with a reduced number of inspections; or (4) an uninspected threshold ban that would become comprehensive if enough states agreed to it. As he had earlier informed Foster, McNamara supported options 2 or 3, but not 1. The JCS, and perhaps more importantly the Atomic Energy Commission, shared serious doubts that a comprehensive ban would be to the military advantage of the United States. The Chiefs reinforced their standing objections to verification procedures by declaring that suspected Soviet advances in

---

* The president addressed the nation on Vietnam on 28 July, one day after the ENDC opening ceremony.

ABM technology could diminish the overall effectiveness of U.S. offensive missile forces. This ominous development would require further high-yield underground testing to improve U.S. strategic offensive missile warheads by making them impervious to the high-energy X-rays emitted by ABMs that could, in theory, destroy larger numbers of incoming U.S. missiles.[19]

ACDA's efforts to develop new disarmament and nonproliferation proposals met determined opposition at the 25 August Committee of Principals meeting. McNamara doubted the timing was propitious for a new U.S. initiative. Concurring with Ambassador at Large Llewellyn Thompson, he believed the Soviets had no interest in any agreement because of Vietnam. Wheeler and Seaborg questioned ACDA's optimistic assessment of seismic verification capabilities, and Rusk concluded that any likely benefits were not worth the major effort of modifying the current U.S. position. The consensus held that the Soviets had displayed no interest in resolving the verification problem; Vietnam likely put them off an agreement of any kind. Members resolved not to change the basic U.S. position on a comprehensive test ban treaty lacking adequate inspection; they ended the meeting unable to agree on any of the ACDA proposals.[20]

Concerned over McNamara's support for a threshold test ban, Wheeler was also convinced that certain principals were sympathetic to a comprehensive test ban treaty that he felt would jeopardize U.S. national security. On 27 August he requested the Joint Staff prepare an in-depth study on the compatibility between a test ban treaty and U.S. security interests. A preliminary Joint Staff assessment, coincidentally forwarded to Wheeler the next day, concluded that effective monitoring under either type of nuclear test ban lay beyond U.S. capabilities. Extending the test ban would not only fail to prevent nuclear proliferation, it would give the Soviets significant advantages at the expense of the United States.[21]

At the 7 September ENDC session, the Soviets accepted a United Arab Republic-sponsored threshold test ban treaty. The U.S. representative rejected the proposal because it contained no provisions for on-site inspections. By the end of the summer of 1965 the test ban initiatives had faltered, nonproliferation talks were at a standstill, and Soviet negotiators in Geneva had countered recent U.S. arms control proposals by demanding explicit prohibitions on the transfer or control of nuclear weapons to nonnuclear allies. The Kremlin's "real and deep" concern over the possibility of the Federal Republic of Germany acquiring nuclear weapons through the MLF remained the major stumbling block to a nonproliferation treaty. Scrapping the MLF, Bundy advised the president in late November, opened the way "for a real Johnson break-through" toward a nonproliferation treaty.[22] After a year of preliminary discussions, for the Soviets the issue still rested chiefly on German possession of nuclear weapons, and for the Americans, on verification and additional testing for nuclear weapons development.

The Threshold Test Ban Treaty Debate

The new year brought the same old message from Kosygin, who declared on 11 January 1966 that there could be no nonproliferation agreement so long as the United States continued to attempt to arm Germany with nuclear weapons. On 24 January, Johnson replied to Kosygin by describing "Soviet concern over possible NATO defense arrangements" as unwarranted and indeed unrelated to the question of nuclear proliferation. From this position, the president accepted Kosygin's offer that their representatives to the ninth ENDC session, set to begin on 27 January,* exchange views regarding a nonproliferation treaty.[23]

Earlier, in mid-December 1965 ACDA's Foster proposed that the United States seek to negotiate a comprehensive test ban treaty (CTBT) when the ENDC representatives reconvened. Should the Soviets prove unresponsive, Washington would offer instead a threshold test ban treaty (TTBT). On 15 January 1966 in a memorandum to McNamara, the Joint Chiefs, echoing Seaborg's opinion that a comprehensive test ban would result in a "significant decline" in the AEC's weapons research and testing, again opposed a CTBT on the usual grounds of inadequate verification and the necessity for higher-yield tests related to the design of warheads to counter Soviet advances in the ABM field. They likewise rejected a threshold test ban treaty because verification of Soviet compliance depended entirely on U.S. intelligence capabilities that the JCS found inadequate to the task. Moreover, underground nuclear testing at ranges beyond those permitted by the proposed threshold test ban language was essential for the U.S. development of an ABM warhead and production of multiple independent reentry vehicle (MIRV) warheads for U.S. intercontinental ballistic missiles (ICBMs).[24]

Two days before the 21 January 1966 Committee of Principals meeting, Foster sent members a far-reaching draft presidential message to ENDC that emphasized among other proposals U.S. willingness to sign immediately a sweeping nonproliferation treaty, establish International Atomic Energy Agency controls on transfers of nuclear material to nonnuclear nations, implement a limited underground test ban treaty, and freeze the numbers of offensive and defensive strategic bombers and missiles. Meantime, the Joint Staff study on the implications of test ban proposals requested by Wheeler the previous August appeared in mid-January and bolstered JCS contentions that neither a comprehensive nor a threshold test ban treaty would prevent the Soviets from acquiring needed nuclear weapons technology, leaving the United States without any gain from such agreements. Furthermore, lack of testing would not inhibit the development of "primitive but effective fission weapons." As a consequence, on 21 January the Joint Chiefs informed McNamara of their opposition to the test ban initiatives because of inadequate verification, possible Soviet nuclear weapons technology superiority in certain areas, and the need for continued U.S. nuclear testing in light of the Soviet ABM

---

* The ninth session met from 27 January to 10 May 1966, and the tenth from 14 June to 25 August 1966.

deployment.[25] The AEC again expressed concern, especially objecting to a threshold test ban treaty.

Because of JCS and AEC objections, Foster opened the 21 January meeting of the Committee of Principals by announcing deferral of a threshold test ban treaty. As discussion moved to the president's proposed message to the ENDC, Lieutenant General Goodpaster, representing the JCS, requested removal of all reference to a comprehensive test ban treaty. Rusk and others rejected the JCS line as a reversal of U.S. policy; a nod to the comprehensive test ban proposal—however slight—remained in the president's message. McNamara, who did not attend the meeting, sided with the JCS and AEC, informing Foster the next day that a threshold test ban raised issues of verification, of impact on the military balance, and of influence on nuclear proliferation, all of which needed additional study prior to any policy decision.[26]

In late May Foster resurrected the TTBT with two premises. First, dramatically improved seismic detection capabilities made on-site verification of a treaty unnecessary. Second, the absence of nuclear test data that scientists needed for ABM warhead development could be offset by the redesign of the ABM, albeit at higher cost, by improving radars, and by deploying additional missiles.[27] By this time, however, there was little support for a threshold test ban.

Earlier, in mid-March, the Joint Chiefs had communicated their concerns to McNamara and the Committee of Principals about the "grave security implications" of a comprehensive test ban treaty, including a threshold ban, basically restating the requirements for verification, uneasiness over Soviet ABM advances, and the need for U.S. nuclear tests to develop an ABM to counter the Soviet threat. Two months later the CIA concluded that a threshold test ban treaty would neither inhibit Soviet underground testing nor halt Soviet ABM progress, although it would preclude development of new warheads. Verification remained a major problem, especially for tests of magnitudes registering less than 4.75 on the Richter scale. The agency anticipated Soviet cheating on an agreement; without on-site inspection it would be impossible to demonstrate the violations convincingly.[28]

As for the other contentious issue—nuclear weapon design—beyond building improved ABMs, U.S. underground nuclear testing concentrated on producing small, hardened (X-ray resistant) MIRV warheads for ICBMs and SLBMs. Uncertain knowledge of the Soviet nuclear weapon programs and the complexities of advanced weapon design made it imperative that the United States continue underground testing at more than double the Soviet rate. To maintain technological advantage in nuclear weapons, fully 87.5 percent of the 128 U.S. underground nuclear tests conducted between January 1965 and late December 1967 were weapon-related. Lastly, without "a strong Presidential push," prospects for a threshold test ban seemed very slim because the Joint Chiefs opposed it and McNamara, whose support was indispensable given the military's objections, was unenthusiastic over the latest ACDA proposals.[29]

ACDA's latest TTBT initiative predictably found few supporters at the 17 June 1966 meeting of the Committee of Principals. The CIA still insisted that the possibility of Soviet cheating on an agreement remained "very good." McNamara summarized the AEC's objections that a TTBT would not inhibit nuclear proliferation but would reduce U.S. ABM capability and defy verification. Seaborg insisted that a warhead for an ABM could not be produced under the restrictions of a threshold test ban treaty. Keeny felt that much of what Seaborg and the CIA said "was either incorrect or misleading," but they went unchallenged. He ascribed McNamara's reticence during the session to the secretary's decision to let the actions of the AEC and CIA representatives demonstrate "the problems he would have if he had to support such a treaty." The Chiefs provided an example of those problems with their summary rejection on 18 June of ACDA's latest threshold test ban proposals for the standard reasons—lack of sufficient verification and the effect on U.S. ABM development.[30]

Undaunted, ACDA pressed State to inform the president of the limited test ban issue. On 26 July Rusk sent a memorandum for the president to Walt Rostow, who forwarded it to Johnson a week later explaining that no clear recommendation appeared in sight. According to Rostow, the Chiefs objected to the treaty because of its consequences for underground nuclear tests while McNamara opposed it "because the battle with JCS and the Hill would use up more capital than the Treaty is worth." Given the lack of consensus regarding a TTBT, Rusk suggested that Johnson speak personally to the principals.[31]

On 29 July AEC requested presidential approval of plans for underground tests with yields up to 6–7 megatons (that is, beyond the proposed TTBT limits) at various supplemental testing sites. On 8 August Johnson approved initial surveys at some but not all possible additional test sites. As for the TTBT, apparently neither the president nor his chief advisers followed up. The issue was not seriously discussed again during his administration.[32] The Joint Chiefs remained the most vocal opponents of a threshold test ban, but AEC's requirements for additional testing, supported implicitly by OSD, were the decisive factor in the demise of the TTB initiative.

Comprehensive Test Ban Treaty

The proposed Comprehensive Test Ban Treaty met a fate similar to that of the TTB, perhaps, as one senior participant observed, because the president's heart never really seemed to be in it. Among the Gilpatric Committee's recommendations of January 1965 appeared a CTBT to be negotiated on the basis of the minimum number of on-site inspections consistent with verification of treaty compliance. When chances for a nonproliferation treaty seemed remote during 1965, increasing emphasis focused on obtaining a CTBT as a means of preventing proliferation. Toward this goal, at its August 1965 meeting the Committee of Principals discussed the possibility of reducing the number of on-site inspections, but they finally decided not to alter the on-site proviso, a fundamental principle of U.S. arms control policy.[33]

Foster's December 1965 proposal of a CTBT as an alternative, should the Soviets reject a threshold agreement, encountered strong opposition, especially from the JCS. On 15 January 1966, citing serious gaps in U.S. intelligence vis-à-vis Soviet weapon developments, the Chiefs warned against a CTBT and claimed that "vigorous nuclear testing . . . within LTBT [limited test ban treaty] restrictions" was needed to match Soviet development of an ABM system. A CTBT would make such measures impossible. The president's 27 January message to the ninth ENDC session did not explicitly mention a comprehensive test ban. It did endorse an extension of the Limited Test Ban Treaty to cover underground tests with verification provided as necessary by remote scientific instruments, as opposed to the JCS-favored on-site method.[34]

Although its concern for a CTBT was "sporadic," the administration remained sensitive to charges that it had lost interest in concluding a treaty because such a perception might jeopardize the U.S. position at the ongoing nonproliferation negotiations. To rebut such allegations, in mid-July 1967 Foster stated that the United States was willing to accept a comprehensive test ban, given adequate inspection controls. Seaborg disagreed, because current development of a new generation of nuclear weapons for the strategic offensive forces and for the Spartan ABM warhead required testing at least through 1970, and made it ill-advised to push for an immediate comprehensive test ban.[35]

More fruitful negotiations for a nonproliferation treaty plus the administration's decision in September 1967 to proceed with an ABM system further diminished interest in a comprehensive test ban treaty. In early July 1968, ACDA sought to resurrect the CTBT issue by recommending that the president advocate such an agreement in his message to the ENDC when it reconvened during the week of 15 July. Reaction within the administration underscored the continuing complexity of the issue. AEC again protested that such a statement was out of the question given the presidentially authorized continuing series of underground tests to produce advanced nuclear warheads. The Joint Chiefs argued as usual that continuation of nuclear testing without further restrictions remained critical to the U.S. strategic deterrent capability. OSD agreed the treaty was undesirable but preferred a mild, general statement of U.S. support for such initiatives. Although State and ACDA favored a CTBT offer, the difficulty of resolving the conflicting opinions within the short deadline available forced Rusk to advise the president to omit any reference to a comprehensive test ban in his 16 July statement to the ENDC.[36]

At a 24 July 1968 White House meeting, Rusk admitted that "while the Administration could not disavow earlier statements supporting a CTB," he wanted "merely to discuss the subject rather than cling to it as policy." With presidential approval, the comprehensive test ban was left by the wayside as the administration savored the recently signed Nonproliferation Treaty and the allure of imminent strategic arms reduction talks.[37]

The Nuclear Nonproliferation Treaty

During 1965, a year that saw the administration chiefly preoccupied with its deepening involvement in Vietnam, the MLF issue continued to be an obstacle to U.S. nonproliferation initiatives. Building on an ACDA idea to refocus attention on preventing the spread of nuclear weapons, Sen. John O. Pastore (D-R.I.), chairman of the Joint Committee on Atomic Energy, introduced a resolution on 18 January 1966 commending the president for his efforts to limit proliferation and supporting additional efforts in this field. McNamara quickly endorsed the Pastore resolution and warned of the danger to U.S. national security unless nuclear proliferation was immediately checked. During follow-up hearings held by the senator, both Rusk and McNamara reaffirmed that no contradiction existed between the nonproliferation treaty and possible nuclear arrangements proposed for the NATO alliance.[38] These statements appeared at odds with alliance politics and nuclear realities.

French withdrawal from NATO's military organization, formally announced in March 1966, directed attention to the unresolved problem of nuclear sharing for alliance defense and its implications for nonproliferation. Rusk soon after proposed to the president that he (Rusk) and McNamara confer with the West German and British foreign ministers about the proliferation issue and simultaneously discuss "some form of ANF" as well as McNamara's proposed special NATO nuclear committee. McNamara supported Rusk; with formation of a nuclear force such as the MLF unlikely, he sought establishment of a "more permanent nuclear planning group." The president responded with a late April call for recommendations from Rusk and McNamara on how to enlarge allied political and military participation in nuclear planning with or without the creation of a NATO nuclear force.[*] The secretaries' joint reply, delivered 28 May, recommended trilateral talks among the United States, UK, and FRG defense and foreign ministers to determine a nuclear program for NATO that "each will support." Meanwhile McNaughton and Keeny, working through presidential assistant Bill Moyers, convinced Johnson that the favorable publicity resulting from a nonproliferation treaty (NPT) might offset growing criticism of his Vietnam War policies.[39]

Because of the growing pressure for nuclear devices in India, on 7 June McNamara notified Rusk that they should reconsider the U.S. position on the NPT by tightening the draft language of Article I to prohibit the transfer of nuclear weapons to any nonnuclear states or association of such states. The following day Dobrynin indicated to Foster that the Soviets were "not concerned" with current U.S. weapons in Germany or greater consultation among NATO allies about the use of nuclear weapons. His message was consistent with the Soviet pronouncements at the ninth ENDC session that specified the Federal Republic of Germany's

---

[*] Departing from the MLF concept, the president's directive excluded mixed-manning of submarines or surface ships capable of firing nuclear weapons to ensure that nonnuclear powers did not get access to nuclear weapons.

"physical access" to nuclear weapons as the main impediment to a nonproliferation treaty. These events led Rusk to conclude the 17 June Committee of Principals meeting by suggesting that new, simplified language outlawing "physical access" to nuclear weapons might allay Soviet fears about German control of nuclear weapons, opening the way to an NPT agreement.[40]

On reviewing Rusk's subsequent draft in late June the Joint Chiefs objected to the term "physical access" because it brought into question and possibly jeopardized all existing NATO nuclear and consultative arrangements. ACDA also pointed out that "physical access" created more problems about existing nuclear arrangements than it resolved. The wording was subsequently dropped in favor of a simple "no transfer" formula. On 5 July McNamara concurred with Rusk's revised language with the understanding that it did not change existing nuclear-sharing arrangements or nuclear planning consultations in NATO. Several days later Johnson indicated renewed interest in a revised nonproliferation treaty agreeable to the Soviets.[41]

Frustrated with the stalemate over nonproliferation, twice during the summer of 1966 the president publicly addressed the need for an NPT and his willingness to conclude an agreement. Walt Rostow, aware of the president's commitment, assumed a dual role of policymaker and policybroker. On 12 August Johnson received Rostow's complex package linking nonproliferation, arms reduction, and nuclear organization in the NATO alliance. This new approach to an NPT emphasized that the president's absolute veto power over the firing of nuclear weapons prevented proliferation. If Moscow was serious about an agreement, Rostow reasoned, the Kremlin leaders would accept the guarantee. If not, the probe would reveal the Soviet intention of merely using the NPT as a means to undermine the NATO alliance in general and the FRG in particular.[42]

Rostow next discussed his ideas with McNamara, an unwavering advocate of centralized control of nuclear weapons, who agreed that the United States should never surrender its veto power over the firing of nuclear weapons in Europe. Although McNamara did not wish to raise this point directly with Rusk, possibly because Rusk's views on the matter differed,[*] he concurred with Rostow's assessment that such a guarantee might provide the basis for an agreement with Moscow. Furthermore, Foster explained to Rostow in mid-September that his private discussions with the Soviets at Geneva had convinced him that a nonproliferation agreement would not interfere with McNamara's NATO Nuclear Planning Group, provided Washington made clear to Moscow that joint ownership of nuclear weapons by the Federal Republic of Germany was not a U.S. option by reason of law as well as the attitude of both the administration and Congress.[43]

---

[*] To avoid any misunderstanding or undermining of Rusk's forthcoming talks with Gromyko at the United Nations, Rostow suggested the topic be placed on the Tuesday Lunch agenda. No record of that lunch has been found. See *FRUS 1964–68*, 11: 354, n1.

Rostow then apprised Rusk of his initiative as the secretary of state prepared for his late September meeting with Soviet Foreign Minister Gromyko in New York City on the occasion of the opening of the 21st session of the United Nations General Assembly. To minimize any unforeseen incident that might scuttle the high-level discussions, McNamara, with presidential approval, ordered Wheeler to defer strikes against politically sensitive targets in North Vietnam unless related to a specific emergency.[44]

During two meetings held 22 and 24 September, Gromyko disclosed to Rusk Moscow's willingness to sign a treaty banning direct and indirect proliferation. In the Soviet lexicon, indirect proliferation equated to the transfer of nuclear weapons through an alliance. Rusk responded that the United States would neither transfer nuclear weapons nor assist in their development for nonnuclear states; the president would retain control over all firings of U.S. nuclear weapons. The Soviets departed feeling "considerable progress" had been made on the substantive draft treaty, although they remained "not really satisfied." Washington felt more optimistic because Rusk's "no transfer" formula would eliminate any MLF/ANF question, resolve the issue of dual control over the firing of U.S. nuclear weapons, and permit consultation on nuclear matters in the NATO alliance, thus clearing the way for the realization of McNamara's nuclear planning committee concept.[45]

On the heels of the Gromyko talks, Johnson, Rusk, and McNamara met with Chancellor Erhard and his foreign minister in Washington to discuss nuclear sharing and nonproliferation. Under pressure, the Germans again indicated that they would not press for a hardware solution (that is, possession of nuclear weapons), and agreed in the communiqué on the need to prevent spread of nuclear weapons into the control of nonnuclear states. These positive developments led Johnson to gather his senior advisers at Camp David on 1 October 1966 to review the progress to date. He shared Rusk's approach of moving cautiously, consulting with major allies, and pushing for a nonproliferation treaty, but not at the expense of the NATO alliance. The president faced a critical decision: should he seek a compromise NPT agreement with Moscow that would not permit the MLF/ANF but would leave open possibility of future change? By deciding at Camp David to approve the concept of "no transfer" of nuclear weapons to nonnuclear nations he shut the door on a near-term establishment of an MLF for NATO and made agreement possible. With the MLF finally disposed of, a Soviet-American working group drafted the first two articles of a draft nonproliferation agreement with language prohibiting the MLF, but leaving open the question of future change.[46]

Following up, a State Department draft highlighted the signatories' agreement neither to transfer nuclear weapons nor to assist in their development by nonnuclear states and further not to relinquish control over such weapons to individual nonnuclear nations or to an alliance. McNaughton recommended McNamara support the State formulation because it did not disturb the existing arrangements, kept control of nuclear warheads in U.S. hands, left open the establishment of the nuclear planning committee in NATO, and allowed for American deployment of additional Polaris or other U.S. weapons to the alliance. On the evening of 16 October 1966 the defense secretary advised the president that he thought he saw a reasonable chance the Soviets would accept the draft even though the wording was not the precise language Gromyko had suggested. Rusk, by contrast, remained skeptical, believing there was "not one chance in a hundred that the Soviets will buy it." A few days later, however, a "confidential source" reported that Gromyko intended to "do his utmost" to convince Soviet leaders to conclude a nonproliferation agreement within the next few months.[47]

Over the next six weeks U.S. and Soviet negotiators did fashion an understanding on Articles I and II of a nonproliferation treaty that, by early December, contained mutually acceptable language pertaining to prohibition of nuclear weapons and agreement of nonnuclear states not to acquire such weapons. By year's end, both sides had reached a "large measure of agreement on a nonproliferation treaty" and consented to resuming ENDC meetings to further consider an NPT. Furthermore the West German elections had produced a coalition government whose new foreign minister, Willy Brandt, an advocate of improved relations with the Soviets, "opposed holding up a nonproliferation treaty for a sometime allied nuclear force."[48]

With the West Germans aboard, additional months of painstaking negotiations with the Soviets ensued. During this period ACDA, State, and DoD officials consulted extensively with the NATO allies on the implications that a nonproliferation treaty held for the alliance. They also worked to allay any second thoughts Moscow might have about the agreement. In April 1967, for instance, McNamara personally reassured Dobrynin that the seven-member NATO Nuclear Planning Group, which met for the first time on 6–7 April, was not an attempt to circumvent the legal restrictions on presidential authority over the control or release of nuclear weapons.[49]

At the 13th session of the ENDC, opening on 18 January 1968, the United States and the Soviet Union placed before the committee separate but identical drafts of a complete nonproliferation treaty. In mid-March ENDC submitted a revised final draft to the UN General Assembly.[50] After minimal debate, the Nonproliferation Treaty signing took place on 1 July 1968 at simultaneous ceremonies held in Washington, London, and Moscow.* This agreement barred nuclear powers from supplying atomic weapons to nonnuclear states, which in turn pledged not to build or acquire such arms. It was the high-water mark of the administration's efforts to limit the spread of nuclear weapons as well as the basis for future

---

* On 9 July, President Johnson sent the signed nonproliferation treaty to the Senate for ratification, but left office before the Senate actually approved the treaty on 13 March 1969. The NPT became effective on 5 March 1970, having been ratified by the requisite number of nations (the Big Three plus 40). (Ed note, *FRUS 1964–68*, 11:625-26.)

U.S.-Soviet arms control, nuclear prohibition, and test ban agreements. Considering the points of friction between the two superpowers—Vietnam, Korea, Eastern Europe, the Middle East, and the ABM issue—it provided a testament to the willingness of both parties to cooperate and compromise to achieve the treaty. On the negative side, China, already in possession of nuclear weapons, and several potential nuclear powers such as India, Israel, and Pakistan abstained from signing the treaty, leaving Johnson's accomplishment less than complete.

Arms Control–Through 1967

Test bans and nonproliferation were only two parts of the nuclear equation. Without some viable arms control agreement between the preeminent nuclear powers, the world remained a more dangerous place than Johnson and McNamara wished to tolerate.

ACDA pursued its mission of advocating arms control measures, most of which generally proved controversial. The Joint Chiefs, ever distrustful of the Soviets, were by far the chief opponents of ACDA initiatives. McNamara, usually sympathetic to ACDA's proposals, found it necessary to side with the JCS on some important issues. Johnson, eager to achieve an arms control agreement, had to endure drawn-out debates within the administration and intermittent frustrating negotiations with the Soviets.

Two concepts formed the bedrock of Secretary McNamara's approach to arms control. First, he had determined to his satisfaction that the U.S. strategic nuclear force structure sufficed for assured destruction of the enemy; any further increase would not be cost-effective. Second, his calculations had convinced him that not only would an enormously expensive arms race be destabilizing, it might actually provoke a suicidal conflict by upsetting the existing nuclear balance. These judgments made McNamara receptive to ACDA proposals for a freeze on nuclear weapons and reduction of existing nuclear stockpiles, positions that often left him at odds with the Joint Chiefs of Staff.

On several occasions during 1965 ACDA proposed major reductions in strategic nuclear delivery vehicles (SNDVs), missiles, and bombers, as well as a moratorium on the construction of land-based missile launchers. In April 1965 the JCS reacted to such recommendations by warning that a growing Chinese nuclear potential plus Soviet advantages in missile payload and ABM development threatened U.S. nuclear superiority, making both a freeze and reduction of missiles and launchers dangerous concessions to untrustworthy adversaries. The Committee of Principals, at its 22 April meeting, deferred action on ACDA's policy initiatives by requesting the agency to study further the implications of delivery vehicle reductions and relate the findings to previous discussions concerning a freeze and possible moratorium on the construction of land-based offensive and defensive missile launchers.[51]

The president's address to the United Nations on 25 June 1965 and dissemination of NSAM No. 335 three days later led to new ACDA proposals. After freezing the number and characteristics of SNDVs, the U.S. would reduce nuclear forces by 700 aircraft and missiles over a three-year period provided the Soviets made commensurate reductions, and would institute an 18-month ICBM launcher construction moratorium while attempting to implement the plan. The JCS again resisted these proposals, reiterating their requirement for on-site inspection to verify Soviet compliance and cautioning that the proposed limitations would severely curtail the development of the nation's ABM system. Faced with the expanding involvement in South Vietnam, the Chiefs further argued that the inappropriate timing of these proposals might lead Beijing and Moscow to conclude that Washington was negotiating arms agreements from a position of weakness, not strength.[52]

Still seeking an acceptable initiative, in late December 1965 ACDA proposed that the president announce in his annual State of the Union message an 18-month freeze on the construction of fixed, land-based ICBM and ABM missile launchers. Such an overture, according to Foster, would take "the warlike edge off" the annual address and reassure Moscow and presumably critics of the administration's policies that "the necessities of Vietnam have not reduced our interests in negotiations." McNaughton advised McNamara that a moratorium would affect the USSR more than the United States and give the "net security advantage" to the United States. He shared McNamara's belief that unilateral verification (by means of satellite imagery and signals intelligence) could detect any major increase in the Soviet strategic force structure. Minor covert violations "could alter but not upset the strategic balance." He counseled McNamara to approve ACDA's proposed moratorium and even extend it to include mobile missiles. The ACDA initiative, McNaughton believed, would freeze in midstream a major Soviet effort to harden their missile silos and deploy ABMs. On the other hand, there were 190 Minuteman II launchers still under construction; a proposed mid-1966 cessation could affect completion of 50 of them. For that reason and the impossibility of verifying Soviet compliance, the JCS opposed including the initiative in the president's address. With the contentious issue between OSD and the JCS unresolved, and the latter also chafing against the extended bombing halt over North Vietnam, the president made no mention of a moratorium in his 12 January 1966 State of the Union message and only a passing reference to arms limitation.[53]

In mid-March ACDA proposed in the Committee of Principals that it be authorized to open quiet discussions with the Soviets at Geneva to determine their interest in the freeze and in future SNDV reductions. The JCS insisted such an approach was contrary to U.S. national security interests and went well beyond established policy. Without a freeze on strategic systems, nothing could prevent a massive buildup of replacements or alternate systems. Furthermore, without a verifiable freeze (that is, one subject to on-site inspection) the United States could not be certain if an accelerated Soviet strategic program was shifting the strategic balance. Agreeing with the JCS, McNamara informed Foster on 31 March that the administration should not give the Soviets the impression that it would discuss reductions without a freeze.[54]

Rusk did inform Dobrynin in March that the U.S. government would be glad to discuss limitations on ICBMs and ABMs with the Soviet Union on a discreet, bilateral basis. Nothing more came of this initiative until December 1966 when, in accord with McNamara's attempt to delay deployment of an American ABM, Ambassador Thompson sounded out Dobrynin on the possibilities of reaching an understanding to limit antimissile defense systems. Thompson was taken aback by the Soviet diplomat's reply that the United States had never responded to his positive statement of the preceding March. Apparently after the Rusk-Dobrynin March conversations both sides incorrectly believed the initiative lay with the other. Thompson was not aware of the earlier March exchanges, Rusk did not recall them, and Foster had received no instructions on proceeding.[55] DoD also seemed unaware of Rusk's initiative.

There had been some follow-up in May 1966 when ACDA Deputy Director Adrian Fisher had suggested that President Johnson write to Premier Kosygin to offer an 18-month uninspected halt in the construction of strategic as well as antiballistic missile launchers. Although so weighted to preserve the existing U.S. military advantage, senior officials anticipated no Soviet interest, but hoped the initiative might prove useful for its propaganda effect. At McNaughton's 5 May urging, McNamara agreed to discuss Fisher's program with the president. The Joint Chiefs, raising their usual objections, including verification, dismissed the draft letter as a reprise of ACDA's failed attempt to include a moratorium in the 1966 State of the Union message. In spite of ISA's vigorous rebuttal of the JCS views and its anticipation of imminent White House discussions on the freeze, no progress occurred. On 8 July in Geneva the Soviets indicated that they had no interest in a freeze on offensive missiles. Although Rusk and McNamara agreed by August that the president should meet on the subject with the chief principals, such a meeting never took place nor was the proposed letter to Kosygin ever sent.[56]

Arms control issues wilted over the months that followed. In late September, ISA recommended and McNamara, over the objections of the Joint Chiefs, agreed to support ACDA's proposed offensive missile and ABM moratorium. Based on analysis of trends from a series of war games, however, the Chiefs feared that symmetrical force reductions could prevent the United States from achieving assured destruction of the Soviet Union. McNaughton persevered in the push for a moratorium; in early November he informed McNamara that Rusk, hitherto preoccupied with the Nonproliferation Treaty, now supported Foster's efforts to initiate arms control talks with the Soviets.[57]

ACDA subsequently dropped the 18-month moratorium, believing it would be unacceptable to the Soviets, who were in the midst of deploying an ABM system and offensive missiles. ACDA also felt the Soviets had to "get nearer to equality" with the United States before fruitful negotiations could occur. In December

McNaughton suggested "private, closely-held discussions" to determine whether the Soviets were interested in a moratorium on strategic weapons and ABMs, and advised an approach to the Soviets immediately through a letter from the president to Kosygin or a quiet discussion.[58] By that time, breakthroughs in ABM warhead technology had increased the pressure on McNamara from the Joint Chiefs for a decision to deploy the costly weapon system.

The pressure to deploy an ABM system that he opposed further impelled McNamara to seek negotiations with the Soviets on strategic arms limitations.[*] The Joint Chiefs voiced no objections to the negotiating probes, but along with their demand for on-site inspection they rejected any link between an arms control agreement and U.S. fielding of an ABM system. At the 23 January 1967 meeting of the deputy principals, Vance stated that he and McNamara agreed on the desirability of a strategic freeze that Vance believed could be unilaterally verified and should include offensive missiles as well as ABMs. Keeny, like the Joint Chiefs, wanted clarification that the Soviet Tallinn[†] network, then under construction, was not an ABM installation; unlike ACDA he was unwilling to ignore the potential system. In March a revised ACDA position on a freeze also ran afoul of the JCS because it could foreclose an ABM option for the United States, could degrade "programmed qualitative improvements" to U.S. strategic forces, and lacked appropriate verification safeguards.[59]

This latest ACDA initiative engaged the Committee of Principals at a meeting held 14 March 1967, where Wheeler restated the JCS concerns. Committee members, however, decided to go forward with a proposal to the Soviet Union contingent upon unilateral verification. In deference to McNamara's wishes, the overture would not be put in writing but instead would be made in the form of an oral statement. Following the meeting, the State Department cabled instructions on 18 March to Ambassador Thompson in Moscow who five days later outlined for Gromyko an approach to strategic weapons talks to begin 12 April. Thompson offered to "level-off" strategic offensive and defensive forces as a step toward longer-term strategic arms reductions. Verification of the agreed on limitations of ICBM launchers, ABM launchers, and associated radars would reside in unilateral means (overhead satellites), not in on-site inspections.[60]

Much to the administration's surprise, nothing had come from the Soviet side by 11 April, the eve of the proposed discussions. After McNamara voiced his concern to Dobrynin, the Soviet diplomat informed him that he would report the conversation on his arrival in Moscow on 13 April. While in Moscow Dobrynin informed Thompson on 24 April that Vietnam was affecting the Soviet government's consideration of arms control issues, presumably a reference to the possible loss of prestige it might suffer in the communist world if it engaged in private,

---

[*] See Chapter XIII.
[†] See Chapter XIII.

bilateral negotiations while Washington was still escalating the Indochina war. Besides Vietnam, the sudden rise in Mideast tension that culminated in the June 1967 Arab-Israeli War and the disappointing attempts to initiate arms control talks at Glassboro in late June deterred arms control progress. McNamara's mid-September public announcement of the decision to deploy an ABM further dampened possibilities for immediate talks, although he was still striving to produce a DoD consensus on the issue.[61]

On 4 October McNamara requested JCS views on recent NSC and State proposals to freeze the number of offensive strategic missile launchers, to deploy no more than an agreed upon number of antimissile launchers, and to rely on unilateral compliance verification. Predictably, the Chiefs replied that such a freeze would preserve Soviet advantages in ICBM throw weight and ABM systems and allow completion of launchers already under construction that would place the United States at a "significant disadvantage" within two years.[62] Critical events overtook arms limitation during 1967, with McNamara absorbed in drafting his final plea to end the bombing of North Vietnam and stabilize the fighting in the South and Rusk involved with the NPT. Hard budget deliberations in December consumed more time, and January 1968 witnessed one emergency after another.[*]

Arms Control 1968

The impasse that arms control talks reached at the end of 1967 persisted through the rest of the Johnson administration but not for want of trying by Johnson and his aides. DoD continued to play a highly visible role in arms control endeavors even though McNamara's successor, Clark Clifford, gave it limited time and attention.

Preoccupied with his Vietnam review, on taking office on 1 March 1968 Clifford may best be described as a caretaker for the strategic arms policies of his predecessor whose staff he inherited. Unlike McNamara, Clifford never fancied himself a strategist, and relied heavily for advice on Deputy Secretary Paul Nitze and ISA's Paul Warnke, McNaughton's successor. Clifford figured in the administration's attempts to present a concrete proposal on strategic arms control to the Soviets, but in a supporting, not dominating, role.

Amidst simultaneous crises—the siege of Khe Sanh, the *Pueblo* incident, and the Tet offensive—Johnson still searched for ways to jump-start arms control talks. Following a February 1968 NSC meeting, the president asked Rusk to consider steps "to prod the Soviets into accepting talks on offensive and defensive missile systems." The response, prepared without JCS input, attempted to meet the military's standing objections by among other things limiting the agreement to weapon systems that could be verified unilaterally and treating the Tallinn defenses as an

---

[*] See Chapter XVIII.

ABM network. Contrary to the Chiefs' desires, the authors would allow the Soviets to complete ICBM sites already under construction. Nitze tabled the recommendations for the time being, apparently in deference to Clifford's imminent arrival. Even so, the initiative was considered so sensitive that only after Clifford and Rusk agreed on the draft would Clifford and Nitze talk directly with General Wheeler, in effect presenting the Chiefs with a fait accompli.[63]

When in mid-April the Chiefs finally saw the State-ACDA draft negotiating proposal, Wheeler insisted that the offer exposed the nation to unacceptable risks solely "to entice the Soviets into commencing negotiations." The military leaders specifically objected to language pertaining to nuclear parity at the expense of U.S. superiority, unilateral verification, force modernization, and limitations on offensive and defensive missile site construction. Wheeler wanted the offending paragraphs, or roughly half the text, stricken from the message. Warnke dismissed these objections and derided the Chiefs for attempting to make the administration do what they "would like us to do, rather than what we intend to do." Clifford kept his views on the recommendations to himself, although Walt Rostow believed the defense secretary supported the proposal in principle. Three days after preliminary discussions at the 23 April Tuesday luncheon, Rusk recommended that the president approve the specific draft proposals despite JCS objections. Alternatives included dispatching either a lengthy or an abbreviated letter to Kosygin proposing an early announcement of bilateral negotiations to limit strategic offensive and defensive missiles. The president opted for the shorter version of a prepared letter that eliminated the specifics that so concerned the JCS. In that letter of 2 May to Kosygin he coupled the proposal with a request that the Soviets help defuse the volatile situation in the Middle East.[64]

The resulting hybrid correspondence appears to have diluted the force of the president's arms control overture. Kosygin replied at length on 12 May regarding the danger of the Middle East situation but his message said nothing about arms control. However, during the interval hints from high-ranking Soviet officials suggested a new willingness to discuss arms control issues, possibly because the president's announced shift away from a military solution in Vietnam allowed Moscow to justify negotiations to its communist allies.[65]

Kosygin finally replied to Johnson's May proposal for arms control talks on 21 June 1968, expressing his government's expectation that it might be possible "before long" to exchange views on limiting offensive and defensive strategic weapons. The president answered the next day stating his hope that the two sides might announce an agreement to hold talks on 1 July, when the signing of the Nonproliferation Treaty was scheduled. Kosygin responded promptly in a 27 June letter that expressed willingness to commit publicly to talks on limitation of both offensive and defensive systems. Speaking to the Supreme Soviet the same day, Gromyko announced that the USSR was ready to open such discussions. Clifford attributed the Soviet decision to the Senate's rejection of the Hart-Cooper amendment three days earlier. The defeat of this rider, which would have deferred funds earmarked for deployment of the Sentinel (ABM) system for one year, demonstrated to Moscow that Washington was serious about spending more on strategic arms, if necessary.[66]

Anxious to get bilateral talks under way during the remaining days of his presidency, Johnson agreed to the offer with alacrity. In statements issued simultaneously in Moscow and Washington and timed to coincide with the 1 July signing of the Nonproliferation Treaty, both leaders used identical language to announce an agreement to begin arms control talks "in the nearest future." Despite the administration's emphasis on arms control there was no real agreement among top U.S. officials on policy content for such discussions.[67] Divisive internal controversies over the complex, esoteric, and contentious issue made a quick consensus appear most unlikely.

Relations between ACDA and the JCS, never close, had deteriorated sharply following the November 1967 UN General Assembly resolution to establish an ad hoc committee to study the peaceful uses of the seabed (defined as the 12-mile offshore limit) and ocean floor. ACDA offered a proposal to sponsor a resolution to ban emplanting or emplacing nuclear weapons on the ocean floor; the Chiefs, with support from OSD, disagreed for reasons of technology, strategy, and lack of verification procedures. A contentious 3 June 1968 Committee of Principals meeting pitted Nitze and Wheeler against Foster, who expressed astonishment at the "astronomical" costs to deploy a military system on the seabed. Although the proposed seabed treaty went no further during the Johnson years,* debate over it underscored the need for some mechanism to overcome the JCS institutional and personal differences with the ACDA staff, whom the military regarded as "ritual disarmers."[68]

These tensions threatened to interfere with preparations for announced arms control talks. Warnke, for instance, cautioned Clifford and Wheeler to be noncommittal at the upcoming July meeting of the Committee of Principals, merely stating the need for study of any recommendations. Since the draft would likely "satisfy neither those who crave prompter steps toward disarmament nor those who fear any rapprochement with the Soviets," procrastination would also allow time for a more thorough evaluation of the complicated issues at stake.[69]

On 8 July, the Committee of Principals assembled to prepare the language for the U.S. negotiating position. Johnson's strong desire for an arms control agreement before he left office added to the pressure to move quickly toward a summit. Impatient with the military's apparent unwillingness to take any risks to halt the strategic arms competition, Rusk pushed the president's agenda to avoid a spiraling arms race that would only add to an already swollen Defense budget without improving

---

* On 7 December 1970 the UN General Assembly approved a draft seabed treaty prohibiting nuclear weapons on the seabed and ocean floor. The treaty became effective 19 May 1972, one day after its ratification by the United States, United Kingdom, and Soviet Union.

national security. It seemed obvious to him that after 18 months of preliminaries the Soviets would expect specific proposals from Washington. Clifford, however, following Warnke's lead, refused to commit OSD to a substantive position until general discussions in opening talks had tested Soviet sincerity.[70]

To bridge the divide between ACDA and the JCS, at its 8 July meeting the executive committee of the Committee of Principals formally established an interagency working group to prepare the U.S. proposals for the negotiations for consideration of the committee. ACDA's Adrian Fisher chaired the group, consisting of senior representatives from DoD, State, and ACDA. Within DoD, a recently formed ad hoc, informal working group directed by Morton Halperin, ISA deputy assistant secretary for policy planning and arms control, took the lead. To facilitate policy development and serve as an intermediary between the JCS and ISA, Wheeler designated Maj. Gen. Royal B. Allison, USAF, as assistant to the chairman for strategic arms negotiations. Although an exact date for the summit had not yet been set, Halperin's group worked to prepare a basic position paper and opening statement for the U.S. representative to the talks.[71]

For planning purposes, on 10 July the Interagency Working Group established a 15 August deadline for readying a U.S. arms control position. Throughout July the interagency team labored 12 to 14 hours a day to produce a "simple, clear proposal." The team benefited both from internal flexibility and its ability to coordinate issues rapidlyacross the range of interested government agencies. Both the mid-August deadline and the *modus operandi* of the group proved fortuitous; in late July Kosygin proposed to Johnson that the two sides meet at Geneva "within one month or a month and a half" to discuss an overarching reduction and mutually satisfactory limitation on offensive strategic delivery systems and ABMs. Quickly agreeing with the timing and locale, the president declared that the United States stood ready to initiate discussions at the level of heads of government, foreign ministers, or heads of special delegations. By this time, the interagency team had drafted its recommendations. It proposed to freeze construction of all land-based ICBM launchers except those already under way (but neither side could deploy more than 1,200 launchers); prohibit the construction of additional land-based IRBM/MRBM launchers; ban deployment of all land-based mobile and inland waterway-based ICBMs, IRBMs, and MRBMs; forbid construction of additional missile-launching submarines; and restrict ABM defenses to one set of fixed, land-based launchers and radars. There would be no mobile systems. All of these limitations would be verified by "national means."[72]

OSD requested JCS comments on Clifford's 2 August DPM stating DoD's position on the ACDA proposal for strategic talks. The DPM endorsed the interagency proposals in slightly modified form, and concluded that such an agreement would maintain the U.S. strategic deterrent against the USSR and, by implication, Communist China for the next 10 years (the proposed term for any agreement). To help allay JCS concerns, the DPM carried caveats, including the promise to make every effort to secure on-site inspection for verification purposes and a commitment to use national intelligence data to document publicly any Soviet violations. It also required assurances from Moscow that the Tallinn air defense system was not and would not become an ABM system.[73]

The Joint Chiefs agreed that the draft proposal, with "essential modification," offered a framework for a workable arms limitation agreement. While Systems Analysis, a strong proponent of arms limitations, asserted that the United States had the technology to detect and counter possible treaty violations, the military leaders still balked at State's and ACDA's proposed unilateral verification. To compensate for possible verification failures, the Chiefs called for an aggressive R&D and modernization program to incorporate the latest technology, including MIRVs, into strategic offensive and defensive weapon systems.[74]

Potentially more serious objections arose from the chief of naval operations and the commandant of the Marine Corps, who maintained that separate freeze agreements on land- and sea-based missiles would sacrifice the U.S. strategic maritime advantage and compromise the nation's qualitative edge in sea-based strategic missile technology. To capitalize on superior American submarine-launched ballistic missiles and anti-submarine warfare capabilities, both wanted the freedom to mix land-based and sea-based offensive and defensive launchers within the overall ceiling. Wheeler thought this approach would merely encourage the Soviets to shift to sea-based launchers and offset U.S. advantages in maritime forces. On 9 August the Chiefs forwarded a rare split reply to Clifford, but in a separate memorandum Wheeler, with Army and Air Force support, "strongly" recommended the secretary support the majority position, which Clifford ultimately did.[75]

The amended draft approved by the executive committee of the Committee of Principals on 14 August incorporated the JCS comments on the State-ACDA proposal verbatim. As for the DPM, major alterations to the final 13 August version accorded primacy to stringent verification measures and spelled out exemptions for advanced research as well as development and deployment of new-generation aircraft, civil defense installations (excepting ABMs), and anti-submarine warfare (ASW) technology. The revised language emphasized the right of either side to abrogate the treaty in the event that its national security was imperiled or its deterrent capability was threatened, if substantial concealment of weapon systems became detected, or if either party interfered with the verification process. In short, limitations were quantitative and dealt with weapon systems that could be unilaterally verified. Reduction of strategic arsenals was not a feature of the initial arms control offers, which aimed not at disarmament, "but merely [to] set limits to overarmament." To the contrary, exempting technological enhancements from the proposals made it possible to increase numbers of MIRV warheads significantly.[76]

While the U.S. side fine-tuned its position on strategic arms limitations, indications of a growing crisis between the USSR and Czechoslovakia became increasingly evident. On 24 July Rusk reported that the Soviet leaders, presumably preoccupied with events in eastern Europe, particularly Czechoslovakia, had not yet informed him about a date to begin arms talks. He considered it plain that if the Soviets intervened militarily in Czechoslovakia, Washington would have to reconsider the timing of any bilateral talks. Following Kosygin's 25 July proposal, Dobrynin took every opportunity to reassure senior American officials that if both sides approached the negotiations on an equal basis, results could be achieved. The Soviet ambassador singled out Wheeler at a 5 August reception to convey the message; the general's account of their conversation reached the president three days later. On 15 August Dobrynin informally mentioned to Rusk that Moscow's reply on an exact date for the opening of talks would likely arrive within a few days and reiterated seriousness of purpose. Nor, the Soviet ambassador disclosed, was the USSR overly concerned about the initial Minuteman III and Poseidon missile flight tests scheduled almost simultaneously with the announcement of the opening of the Strategic Arms Limitation Talks (SALT) talks. In fact, the next day the Air Force and Navy, respectively, test-fired the Minuteman III and Poseidon, largely so that Congress and the Soviets would not misread a unilateral moratorium on tests as a sign of weakness and thus hinder chances for a meaningful agreement.[77]

A few days later, on 19 August, while Warsaw Pact forces awaited final orders to invade Czechoslovakia, Dobrynin handed Rusk a note expressing Moscow's willingness to host a summit visit by Johnson to Leningrad early in October to discuss matters of mutual interest. On the following day Kosygin informed Johnson of the Soviet Union's agreement on a joint announcement for initiation of strategic arms limitation talks at the end of September in Geneva by special delegations from the two countries. Encouraged by these positive developments, the White House in turn prepared a background briefing concerning the breakthrough meeting, and ACDA finalized an initial recommended position on SALT. Then on the evening of 20–21 August the Soviet Union and several of its satellite nations invaded Czechoslovakia. At an emergency NSC meeting that same evening the president decided to place the not yet released summit announcement on hold indefinitely.[78]

Notwithstanding the shelving of the announcement and American denunciations of the Soviet invasion, study continued on the basic policy premises for use during the still anticipated SALT negotiations. Within OSD for example, ISA continued to modify the U.S. proposal; Warnke, though accepting the setback to U.S.-Soviet relations, argued against abandoning efforts to cooperate with the Russians on arms control talks and urged agreement at a future date to the proposed announcement that talks would begin on 30 September.[79]

For differing reasons, neither side wished to extinguish the possibilities for talks. Washington wanted to avoid the additional burden of a costly strategic arms race while maintaining the nation's assured destruction capability and conducting an expensive war in Southeast Asia. Defense budgets mattered to Moscow as well, and the Soviet leaders may have seen negotiations as a means to restore their badly tarnished reputation by drawing attention away from Czechoslovakia. Finally, the NATO allies still favored arms control talks between the superpowers. Even before the end of August, Dobrynin sounded out Thompson on the possibility of talks at the highest levels and signaled Moscow's willingness to locate the discussions at a venue of President Johnson's choice. This initiative was quickly relayed to the president, then in Texas.[80]

Worried about blame for overreaction in cancelling all initiatives with the Russians notwithstanding the Soviet aggression, at a 4 September NSC gathering Johnson remained interested in strategic arms negotiations. As directed, that evening Walt Rostow drafted a statement for him outlining ways to prepare the nation for talks. Abandoning efforts to limit the arms race, Rostow rationalized, would not help the Czechs while success in arms limitations would benefit all mankind.[81] Such an approach would enable the administration to protect its political flanks at home and in Western Europe against charges of caving in to Soviet military pressure.

Still considering a summit meeting, the president instructed Thompson to sound out the Soviets about holding talks at the highest level. By 7 September Johnson, growing more impatient to meet Kosygin, wanted talks to begin during 1–10 October, given "some chance—a modicum of hope—of agreement." Around the same time the president approved the Committee of Principals' strategic arms proposal, basic position paper, and initial presentation. At the president's instruction, Rostow invited Dobrynin to his home on 9 September to discuss a prospective summit meeting that would include "missile talks" and give the Soviet ambassador Johnson's conditions and proposals.[82]

The Joint Chiefs now opposed any talks because others might interpret bilateral discussions as approval for Soviet actions in Czechoslovakia and the meeting itself might further constrain U.S. military flexibility at a time of heightened world tension. They objected also to a draft State Department message instructing the U.S. Mission to NATO to inform the European allies that strategic arms reduction talks were the exception to the agreed upon policy of disapproval of Soviet actions. Following Warnke's advice, Clifford concurred that no message be sent "for the next week or two," but if the president decided to move forward on arms control the cable be sent "authorizing the discussion of this question with our NATO Allies."[83] Johnson did in fact continue to advance his arms control agenda.

In mid-September Dobrynin and Rostow exchanged notes outlining the general objectives for a summit, emphasizing their respective leaders' desire to curb strategic arms by limiting and reducing offensive and defensive missiles. Around the same time, Clifford explained to his aides that so long as Czechoslovakia stayed quiet, the administration planned to follow up the formal government-to-government memorandum with a personal message from Johnson to Kosygin in an effort to bring about a meeting. In exchange for the summit, Kosygin would assure Johnson that if the United States stopped bombing North Vietnam, Hanoi would respond in kind by deescalating the war in South Vietnam. Nitze was incensed by the scenario for tacitly approving Soviet conduct in Czechoslovakia. Warnke also opposed the initiative because he felt the Russians had to be more involved in the process. Ever focused on extricating the United States from Vietnam, Clifford claimed to favor anything that would get the president to end the bombing as a step forward to disengagement.[84] In reality, OSD had little role in the president's last-ditch effort to conclude an arms agreement.

The Soviet reply, delivered to Rusk by Gromyko on 2 October, endorsed Johnson's general provisions and affirmed the principle of limitation and subsequent reduction of both offensive and defensive weapons systems; it also expressed the opinion that an agreement based on such guidelines was possible. Rostow interpreted this response as Moscow's guarantee before the event that strategic weapon talks would enjoy a modestly successful outcome. With the Soviets engaged, Warnke apparently thought the timing appropriate for a Johnson-Kosygin summit, a position unanimously rejected by Clifford and members of his staff who thought it a bad idea likely to split NATO apart. They attributed the effort to Johnson's restlessness during his final days in office and the president's need for the "acclaim he thinks he'd get" from a summit. Clifford came to believe that Johnson's "passion" to talk with Kosygin in Moscow had "totally affected" U.S. policy. The secretary thought the whole idea of a summit "foolish"; he hesitated to broach arms talks with the president until the Saigon government's participation in the announced Paris talks was settled.[85] First to last, the Vietnam War remained Clifford's top priority.

Another strong Soviet signal of interest in arms reduction came through former defense secretary McNamara during an unscheduled meeting with Kosygin while on a personal visit to Moscow in November 1968. McNamara reported that the Soviet leader displayed much more interest in strategic arms control than he had evinced at Glassboro, attributing the change to the deleterious effects of the escalating cost of the arms race on other sectors of Soviet society. Meantime, at the president's urging, Rostow was working up a plan to start missile limitation talks at the highest level. The chief obstacles to such discussions were the Czechoslovakia crisis and president-elect Nixon. The former could be overcome by recycling Rostow's greater-good argument. Nixon proved more intractable. Unless Nixon assented to the talks, he could simply disavow anything accomplished by them. Johnson's failed attempt to co-opt the next president by including the Republican leader in any negotiations spelled the end to arms control talks during the Johnson presidency. By late November, politics overtook diplomacy. For his part, Nixon participated in slowing down Senate ratification of the Nonproliferation Treaty. Through intermediaries, he made known to Soviet leaders that he could not be bound by strategic arms agreements reached at any pre-inauguration summit meeting.[86]

On 25 November, Rusk raised with Dobrynin a series of questions that President Johnson agreed could be discussed if he met with the Soviet leaders. Shortly afterwards, Gromyko informed Thompson that the Russians were prepared to review the stated considerations concerning limitations on strategic arms as the basis to achieve an initial agreement on the subject. He could not, however, comment on a U.S. proposal for a mid-December summit in Geneva.[87]

Belatedly, in early December and into January 1969 Clifford expressed a desire to push ahead to clarify the U.S. governmental position on SALT for military as well as political reasons. Militarily, the United States could negotiate from a position of strength because it still maintained its strategic nuclear advantage over the Soviet Union, a condition subject to future change. Moreover the timing was auspicious because, after years of internal administration struggle to shape strategic arms policy, the JCS, whose support was essential to offset defense hawks' criticism of any arms control agreements, had finally concurred on the negotiating agenda. On the domestic political side, Clifford held, it was "unlikely" that a new administration would "call off the negotiations" if formal talks with the Soviets were begun. Reports that the Soviets wanted talks to succeed opened a possibility to "create a momentum towards world peace that would last for years to come." With the administration's time slipping away and Rusk and Johnson cooling on the idea of a high-level meeting, on 11 December Rostow urged the president to give the idea of a summit one last try or risk leaving the job to Nixon, "a decision we shall regret more than any other in the years ahead." Perhaps stirred by learning earlier that day that the Soviets completely understood if the president decided not to go ahead with the summit, Johnson noted: "I'm ready—are they?" By that time, however, what Clifford described as "a good deal of foot dragging"—not on Johnson's part—hindered any impetus for talks.[88]

There would be no further progress on strategic arms control during the remaining days of Johnson's tenure. On 21 December the president decided against Clifford's recommendation to develop a joint statement with the Soviets as the basis for future negotiations, instead deciding that the Nixon administration could handle the matter.[89]

The Johnson years were a time of great international turmoil that did not bode well for efforts to limit armaments. In particular the unpopular foreign adventures of the United States and the Soviet Union—Vietnam and Czechoslovakia, respectively—presented huge obstacles that could not be overcome by 1969. Compounding the difficulties were the deep-seated suspicion and distrust with which the two major powers continued to view each other. This was especially apparent in the consistent resistance of the Joint Chiefs of Staff to negotiations with the Soviets proposed by ACDA, OSD, and the State Department. No doubt the Soviet leaders encountered the same naysaying from their military.

In spite of the daunting prospect he faced, President Johnson remained constant in seeking to rein in the runaway nuclear competition by bringing about a historic breakthrough in U.S.-Soviet relations. The Limited Test Ban Treaty of 1963 had demonstrated that talks could lead to mutually acceptable agreements. Increasingly burdened by the enormous cost of huge war machines and the uncertainties of creating successful defense against attack, the adversaries searched for ways to avert the danger of nuclear conflict. The failure to reach a broader arms control agreement was a great disappointment to Johnson, McNamara, and Clifford, but the groundwork laid by them made it possible for the successor Nixon administration to get there. The Johnson years showed the way, albeit difficult and painstaking, to what could be accomplished.

CHAPTER XIII

ABM: Centerpiece of Strategic Defense

Even as he supported policies relating to all aspects of arms control, Secretary McNamara made certain that the United States would maintain strategic offensive forces fully capable of carrying out their mission. At the same time he viewed strategic defensive weapons, particularly the antiballistic missile defense system (ABM), as ineffective and too costly. Tenaciously opposed to fielding an ABM system, he found himself in persistent disagreement with the JCS and Congress. The ABM became a major source of contention between the United States and the Soviet Union, greatly complicating U.S. endeavors to bring about arms control. It was an obstacle that McNamara could not overcome for all of his powers of analysis and persuasion.

U.S. strategic nuclear forces had reached a plateau by early 1965, and the projected share of future Defense budgets allotted to them declined in the wake of the FY 1962–1964 buildup.[1] Abstruse computations by Systems Analysis that calculated the most cost-effective mixture to maintain U.S. offensive and defensive superiority provided McNamara the ammunition needed to oppose as unnecessary and wasteful the development, production, or deployment of an antiballistic missile defense system, the Advanced Manned Strategic Aircraft (AMSA), and a new manned interceptor aircraft. To maintain affordable and predominant strategic forces, he endorsed high-tech research to field more accurate ICBMs, Poseidon SLBMs, and ICBM-mounted multiple independently targeted reentry vehicles (MIRVs). In short, he intended to substitute quality for quantity in a missile force designed to ensure America's strategic nuclear preeminence.

Deterrence, the primary objective of U.S. strategic nuclear policy, required offensive forces capable of inflicting "assured destruction" on the Soviet Union. The original criteria for assured destruction consisted of a capability to retaliate after a Soviet first strike and to destroy 30 percent of the USSR's population, 50 percent of its industrial capacity, and 150 of its cities.* Damage beyond these levels was simply gratuitous and not cost-effective. To inflict this deadly level of devastation, Systems Analysis calculated in late 1964 that at least 400 U.S. one-megaton weapons had to survive an initial Soviet nuclear onslaught; McNamara's approved strategic force structure far exceeded this minimum. Projections in November 1965 anticipated that U.S. forces would have more than 1,700 missile-delivered and 2,770 bomber-delivered nuclear weapons in the 1970s. Analysts conjectured that more than 1,000 of the former and almost 1,400 of the latter could survive a Soviet first strike. Of these surviving weapons, 70 to 80 percent could be counted on to hit their targets.[2]

McNamara tended to assume that the Soviet Union, like the United States, had an aversion to nuclear warfare and accepted the doctrine of assured destruction together with the concept of deterrence. He also believed that in the absence of further quantitative increases in U.S. forces, Soviet strategic military power would remain relatively modest. This overlooked the destabilizing effect on the arms race exerted by the technological advances that OSD promoted to guarantee long-term U.S. nuclear superiority. The illogic of asking the Soviets to accept permanent strategic second place, to swallow OSD's chosen strategy of assured destruction, and to bank on the good intentions of the United States not to exploit its nuclear superiority also seemed to escape him.[3] What McNamara did grasp was that the ABM posed a destabilizing threat to the nuclear arms environment because its potential to limit damage from a nuclear attack undermined the foundation of the doctrine of assured destruction.

The secretary and his civilian staff, particularly those in Systems Analysis, assumed that Washington's decisions influenced Moscow's behavior and vice versa. This created a tendency toward mirror-imaging that underlay McNamara's conviction that he could reliably forecast the Kremlin's reaction to U.S. increases in offensive striking power or improved defenses to limit damage from a nuclear attack. Certainly the Air Force doubted the existence of any clear pattern of Soviet reactive decisions on weapon system acquisition and discerned no way of predicting Soviet responses to U.S. decisions.[4] These divergent views made for a heated debate over the ABM.

McNamara had come to believe that the U.S. deterrent capability, the nation's strategic offensive forces, not the damage-limiting strategic defensive forces, protected American society. OSD-directed studies confirmed his analysis of ABM's dubious cost-effectiveness. Even pouring a prohibitive $35 billion into an ABM network would preserve no more than 75 percent of the U.S. population, calling into question its value. To attain McNamara's objective of 90 percent would ex-

---

* The numbers varied somewhat in later iterations.

ceed $60 billion (or $10 billion more than the entire FY 1965 Defense budget). Also discouraging, the Soviets could offset the U.S. defensive improvements at increasingly less relative cost because ICBMs were easier to build and cheaper than ABMs. The additional ICBMs could overwhelm the expensive ABM network, whose more complicated construction could not keep pace with the offensive buildup. This reality made reliance on any ABM system to limit damage seem a dangerous illusion.[5]

Led by Alain Enthoven, Systems Analysis provided the statistical underpinnings of McNamara's strategic logic. Yet many questioned the premises of the complex studies produced under Enthoven's direction. No one, for instance, could explain why inflicting approximately 30 percent casualties on the Soviet population became a primary criterion for strategic effectiveness. Others suspected Enthoven responded to criticism by changing "the rationale of the DoD figures without changing the figures." McNamara also used numbers loosely to promote his agenda. He once testified that missiles had a higher dependability than manned bombers but neglected to mention that a bomber on alert was more survivable, carried more nuclear warheads than a missile, and had better accuracy than an ICBM. When informed by the Joint Chiefs of his error, the defense secretary simply changed his definition of dependability—from destroying a target to merely reaching it—but stuck to his original statement.[6]

Criteria for assured destruction of the Soviet Union changed five times in as many annual DPMs.[7] While critics decried the revisions as mendacious distortions, the changes responded to radical advances in weapon technology, the unexpectedly rapid Soviet buildup of ICBMs and ABMs, and an increasingly volatile international environment during the second Johnson administration. These changing circumstances prompted greater attention to alleged deficiencies in OSD's nuclear strategy and exacerbated the stormy relationship between military and civilian leaders.

Disagreements between OSD and the JCS over estimates of the reliability of missiles, reducing the number of bombers, deferring the development of interceptors, and developing AMSA figured prominently in the debate over defense during the bitterly fought 1964 presidential election. Johnson's landslide victory failed to silence critics in Congress and elsewhere who judged the administration too soft on defense. By late 1964 the controversy over preproduction funding for an ABM system joined the list of major JCS-OSD disagreements.[8] Policy decisions required by the Joint Chiefs' proposals to develop and deploy new strategic weapons and McNamara's intention to reduce or limit existing weapon systems spurred both parties to appeal to the president for support.

Strategic Forces, 1965

The secretary presented OSD's annual posture statement to the House Armed Services Committee in early February 1965. The lengthy document, drawn from the DPMs related to 10 mission areas of the budget, explained OSD's policy and the rationale for its decisions and set the scene for the secretary's testimony in their support. The posture statement combined for the first time strategic offensive forces, the continental air and missile defense forces, and civil defense because of the close interrelationship and interaction of those three components of the general nuclear war posture.[9]

Following the 1962–64 buildup, budget outlays for strategic weapons and civil defense had decreased from a 1962 high of $11.3 billion (TOA) to a proposed $6.3 billion (TOA) for 1966. Enhanced offensive technology such as improved ICBM guidance systems, MIRVs, penetration aids for missile warheads, and a new Poseidon SLBM, McNamara assured congressional committees in February 1965, would improve the missile force capability by 30 to 40 percent, the equivalent of 300–400 additional ICBMs. These qualitative advances enabled McNamara to hold the line on the 1,000-ICBM limit, phase out older model B-52 heavy bombers, and reject as cost-inefficient Air Force recommendations to develop AMSA.[10] They also served to counter charges of being soft on national defense.

The outlook for strategic defensive forces was more ambiguous. In late 1964 U.S. continental defenses remained oriented against a Soviet heavy bomber attack, an eventuality McNamara regarded as unlikely. To rectify this deficiency, he proposed to convert the existing early-warning radar networks stretching across Canada and the United States into a ballistic missile warning system. Nor in the missile age was there any requirement for obsolete Air National Guard interceptors or for that matter a new advanced manned interceptor.[11] But common sense suggested a possible future need for an ABM system to protect the United States from enemy missile attacks.

The technology of destroying an incoming ICBM in flight with an ABM was extremely complex, enormously expensive, and, for McNamara as well as many scientists, still unproven. During preliminary discussions about ABM deployment, Systems Analysis advanced the standard OSD argument that the extra cost to the Russians of increasing their offensive missile forces to offset increases in U.S. ABM defenses was substantially less than the additional cost to Washington to improve defenses. Among OSD civilian officials there existed concern that the United States would bear responsibility for starting a new arms race by deploying even a limited ABM system.[12]

In early March 1965 congressional testimony McNamara downplayed the need to deploy a yet untested ABM system at a time when the Soviets were not increasing their offensive strategic forces as rapidly as the administration had previously anticipated. Aware of the gradual strengthening of USSR strategic missile forces, McNamara remained skeptical of mid-1964 CIA estimates that foretold a "dynamic expansion" of Soviet strategic forces; he reminded Congress that over the years estimates of Soviet ballistic missile strength had erred consistently on the high side.[13]

Civil Defense

After years of neglect, civil defense as a component of the general nuclear war posture received greatly increased attention for several years beginning in 1960–61. Mounting public concern over the expanding Soviet missile threat, the Bay of Pigs fiasco, and nuclear saber-rattling over Berlin led President Kennedy to place civil defense under DoD in July 1961[*] with the intention of giving it greater emphasis and integrating it more closely into the overall military structure. McNamara embraced the change energetically, taking charge of a proposed large-scale public shelter program; he promised to develop improved fallout protection for 50 million Americans. Congress quickly provided initial supplemental funding for public shelter identification and stockage. When concern about attack diminished, intense interest in and debate about civil defense and fallout shelters waned, as did congressional funding. In March 1964 McNamara transferred responsibility for civil defense to the Army, signifying its diminished status.[14]

In early 1965, as part of his anti-ABM position, McNamara found it expedient to stress the merits of civil defense as preferable to the deployment of an expensive and imperfect antimissile defense to protect the public from the growing Soviet missile threat. Although once again trumpeting civil defense, he recognized that prohibitively expensive blast shelter construction—estimated by OSD at $20 billion—offered little protection against accurate nuclear explosions powerful enough to destroy any known hardened structure. It was possible, though, to protect most citizens against radioactive debris, and this McNamara proposed to accomplish by identifying potential fallout shelter spaces in existing or planned structures. There was a need for some new shelters, but Congress had thus far refused to enact legislation to fund the federal part of a proposed federal-state-local-private program over a five-year period. Nor, with one exception in FY 1962, had Congress appropriated more than a fraction of the DoD request for overall civil defense funding.[15]

In late 1964 McNamara's FY 1966 budget submission had requested $193.9 million (TOA) to pay for identifying and stocking public shelters, an amount previously submitted but disapproved by Congress, plus routine requests for minor modifications to proposed shelters and limited new construction. Final congressional action, however, appropriated only $106.8 million, despite McNamara's appeals. Thereafter McNamara dropped requests for federal matching funds to encourage state and local civil defense programs and submitted minimal budgets for stockage and upkeep. As the program languished, McNamara accused Congress of failing to fund his fallout shelter plans; interested congressmen criticized him for not doing enough on the program's behalf.[16]

The criticism contained some truth. The search for savings in non-Vietnam-related spending made McNamara content to submit minimal budgets for civil defense. Congress reduced even these small requests. By early 1967 the secretary

---

[*] Previously the Office of Civil and Defense Mobilization had responsibility for civil defense.

dropped his usual urgings of the importance of the damage limitation role of civil defense as the ABM controversy monopolized that subject. Civil defense budgets continued to decline, and what promised in 1961 to be a dynamic program had withered by 1968 to a system on life support.

The Soviet Buildup

Although stymied on civil defense as a substitute for the ABM, in 1965 McNamara could defer a decision on production and deployment of an ABM because the proposed system's still unproven technology and unfavorable cost-benefit numbers together with the thaw in U.S.-Soviet relations early in the year allowed him to do so with minimum risk of serious second-guessing by the Joint Chiefs or administration critics. But the reverse was also true. Significant improvements in ABM technology, acceleration of Soviet ICBM deployment, or worsening of U.S.-Soviet relations would make it more difficult to prevent the fielding of an ABM network.

Perhaps the most puzzling and disturbing question in early 1965 was whether the Soviets were fielding an ABM network. Initial evidence pointed to construction of ABM sites around Moscow, but a defensive belt of missile sites that U.S. intelligence originally identified as an ABM system protecting Leningrad was now judged to be targeted against aircraft. Armed with calculations that showed that 84 percent of U.S. bombers could penetrate current Soviet defenses, McNamara derided the Leningrad effort as "the greatest single military error in the world, today."[17] The dismissive remark nevertheless masked a deepening concern over Soviet intentions.

On 27 January 1965 McNamara launched a follow-up to a September 1964 study on the allocation of resources for damage limiting purposes. To determine a proper force structure, he required the Joint Chiefs and the services to analyze four different but not necessarily exclusive combinations of assured destruction and damage limitation. As the respective studies progressed, so too did an unexpectedly large expansion of Soviet strategic forces. Beginning in March, U.S. intelligence detected construction at an unprecedented rate of at least two types of single-silo ICBM launchers in the Soviet Union, a sizable growth in ICBM testing facilities, public displays of both a new intermediate and a long-range missile, development of a next-generation interceptor aircraft, and the anticipated deployment in 1967–68 of at least a limited ballistic missile area defense. The speed of the latest buildup caught U.S. intelligence off guard because trendline extrapolations had underestimated the ambitious scope of the Soviet's strategic weapons program.[18]

The November 1964 National Intelligence Estimate (NIE) had forecast 400 to 700 Soviet ICBMs deployed by mid-1970 against 1,000 U.S. ICBMs; the actual count of Russian missiles in 1970 was 1,292. The 1966 forecast estimated between 800 and 1,120 for mid-1972; the count was 1,527. Also unpredicted, there appeared in 1967 the first Soviet Y-class nuclear submarine, a vessel capable of launching nuclear missiles from underwater; 21 were operational by 1971, more than double the 1966 U.S. estimate of 10.[19] The errors occurred because of the complexity and uncertainty of intelligence-gathering, verification difficulties, and the Soviet success at secrecy.

This expansion, regarded as exceeding the Soviets' basic deterrence requirements, seemed to confirm a deep-seated image of the Soviet Union as an aggressive, revolutionary nation intent on expanding its power and influence. The surge, after all, occurred while the Soviets were proposing arms control. It also coincided with the deepening U.S. military involvement in Southeast Asia that could only add to the tension between Moscow and Washington. A manifestation of the increased tension came in mid-July 1965 when Premier Kosygin charged that President Johnson had broken his promise to reduce defense spending because his May supplemental request for $700 million for Vietnam raised the U.S. Defense budget beyond the previous year's.[20]

As Soviet-American relations deteriorated and prospects for arms control dimmed, weapon development took on added importance, particularly the ABM system. In early July, Army representatives presented a briefing on the Nike-X to McNamara, who in turn directed them to prepare by 1 October a recommended deployment of the Nike-X antimissile system against a small, that is Chinese, ICBM threat, followed by one against Soviet missiles by the end of December.[21]

The Army DEPEX (Nike-X Deployment) Study of 30 September recommended a combination area and point defense against a Chinese ICBM attack that would be capable of growth to meet larger threats from any quarter.* The study proposed to field by 1970 a light ABM system providing area antiballistic missile coverage of the continental United States and Hawaii plus point or terminal protection for 25 American cities. Designated Phases I and II, with an estimated cost of $9.4 billion, this part of the system had a completion date of June 1975. Expansion during Phases III and IV would provide point defense for another 26 cities and improved defenses at all 51 cities. To meet the Phase I schedule, the Army requested initial preproduction funding of $188 million for FY 1967 as well as authorization of the Nike-X deployment for planning purposes. Following a briefing by Army leaders on 8 October, McNamara directed continued Nike-X development but deferred any expenditure for its production or deployment.[22]

The Army's plan had potentially momentous military, economic, and political consequences. Building a U.S. ABM system, McNamara believed, would force the Soviets to react in order to maintain their nuclear deterrent, thus touching off a costly arms race. The Strategic Military Panel of the President's Scientific Advisory Committee (PSAC) worried that even authorizing preproduction funds for the

---

* An area defense relied on destroying enemy missiles or bombers en route to targets but before they reached the target itself. A terminal or point defense destroyed enemy weapons within the target area before impact.

ABM project would make it difficult to reject deployment during the following budget year. Nevertheless, on 29 October PSAC supported McNamara's decision to continue R&D work on Nike-X and withhold preproduction funds. Less certain that the administration could safely defer Nike-X decisions, DDR&E John Foster* maintained that limited preproduction funding of $70-$80 million was essential to preserve the Nike-X's initial operational date of 1970. The following month the Joint Chiefs sharply criticized the PSAC for drawing conclusions from an "undue emphasis upon the limited threat" of Chinese attack based on "incomplete military and political considerations." Delaying an operational Nike-X, they declared, jeopardized U.S. ballistic missile defense, particularly against the Soviet threat.[23]

In an attempt to resolve the swirling controversy, Systems Analysis developed a worst-case scenario premised on the Soviets simultaneously deploying highly accurate MIRV-equipped ICBMs together with a massive and sophisticated ABM network. The offensive punch could destroy a large portion of the U.S. force before launch, and the Soviet defensive screen could intercept surviving U.S. ICBMs. Even in this extreme contingency, the study contended, enough nuclear weapons would survive to retaliate against Soviet cities with at least 400 one-megaton warheads, the standard measure of assured destruction. As a hedge against the unlikely scenario, Enthoven proposed advancing the operational date for the Poseidon missile to August 1970, hardening Minuteman silos to diminish the Soviet offensive threat, and equipping warheads with penetration aids to offset any USSR ABM systems. McNamara's 1 November 1965 DPM on strategic forces incorporated the Systems Analysis "greater-than-expected-threat" model to justify strategic offensive weapon system augmentation in the FY 1967 budget submission.[24]

McNamara wanted to maintain the Minuteman force at 1,000 missiles but improve it qualitatively by retrofitting Minuteman IIs with a more powerful and accurate reentry capability. He also planned to replace the aging Minuteman I with Minuteman II and the new, MIRV-equipped Minuteman III.[†] The advanced Minuteman III and the oncoming Poseidon SLBM, also equipped with multiple warheads, were expected to overwhelm an antiballistic missile defense either by forcing it to shoot at every acquired target and so exhaust the defender's supply of missiles, or by saturating the system's acquisition radars with so many reentry vehicles that accurate tracking became impossible. MIRV allowed McNamara to resist JCS recommendations for more ICBMs because multiple warheads per missile increased the striking power of the land-based missiles. But these expensive technological improvements (around $2.9 billion for replacing Minuteman I with Minuteman II and III during FY 1967–71)[25] came at a time when the administration was trying to hold down non-Vietnam military spending.

---

* Foster became DDR&E on 1 October 1965.
† MIRV-equipped Minutemen III became operational during FY 1969, with the complete conversion occurring by the end of June 1972.

At the annual BoB-DoD meeting on 9 November 1965 to finalize the proposed FY 1967 military budget, DoD officials contended that if the Soviets decided to deploy ABM defense systems the United States had to add more MIRV-equipped missiles to its land and sea-based forces to maintain its assured destruction capability. BoB questioned this contention and rejected DoD's assertion that because the submarine-launched Polaris missile would be unable to penetrate a heavy Soviet ABM defense, Poseidon development had to be accelerated at a cost of $210 million in FY 1967 alone.[26]

Old Bombers, New Bombers, Advanced Bombers

With improved strategic missiles costing far more than anticipated, savings had to come from other strategic weapons, particularly the manned bomber force. This accorded with McNamara's assertions of higher confidence in the improving reliability and survivability of missile systems than in manned bombers. He adamantly opposed full funding for AMSA, viewing it as the most expensive strategic offensive weapon system, far more costly than land-based Minuteman, Polaris, or an upgraded B-52 force launching short-range attack missiles (SRAM). McNamara allowed research, preliminary avionics development, and advanced engine propulsion efforts for AMSA to continue during FY 1966 while suggesting that a strategic bomber version of the F-111, the FB-111, might be a suitable replacement for the aging B-52 fleet.

McNamara's thinking on AMSA and the FB-111 crystallized during 1965; by November he saw no need for full-scale development of the former. Instead, he endorsed Air Force recommendations to replace 345 older model B-52s and all 80 B-58 bombers with 210 FB-111s during the FY 1966–71 period. The cost would be $1.9 billion; not only would this provide commonality in a dual-purpose aircraft—strategic and tactical bomber—it would also offer cumulative savings of $3 billion on the high maintenance B-58s and aging B-52s through FY 1975.[27]

By pronouncing the FB-111 the new—not interim—strategic bomber, he could also put off full-scale development of AMSA and reap additional savings. With only the Air Force pushing AMSA in the FY 1967 budget, the absence of a unified military position made McNamara's decision easier.[28]

The expensive FB-111 procurement raised eyebrows in BoB at a time when the administration was looking for ways to save money in a tight budget situation brought about by the mushrooming costs of the war in Vietnam. To make an FB-111 decision more attractive financially, McNamara proposed to reduce costs by delaying the purchase of spare parts, avionics, and so forth, and procuring only 10 instead of 33 aircraft during FY 1967. To mollify the Joint Chiefs, he approved their recommendation to retain 555 B-52s during FY 1967 as opposed to the 465 OSD had originally proposed. The decision only temporarily slowed the B-52 phaseout schedule; OSD still wanted to trim to 255 by FY 1971.[29]

On 8 December 1965 McNamara revealed the phaseout of the B-58s and aging B-52s as part of a more comprehensive base closure action announced two days earlier. When congressional critics reacted predictably to the proposed bomber reductions, McNamara twitted them at a press conference on the 10th as he disclosed plans to build and deploy a new dual-purpose bomber, the FB-111.[30] He did not mention that the previous month he had already agreed to slip production funding for the FB-111 to accommodate the president's desire for an austere defense budget.

The cost, questionable effectiveness, and vulnerability of the manned bomber force to enemy attack caused McNamara to favor the intercontinental ballistic missile as the primary weapon of assured destruction. He acknowledged that bombers compelled the Soviets to waste resources by splitting their air defenses to protect targets against aircraft as well as missile attack, but since only a few hundred bombers were needed for such a role he could drastically cut the heavy bomber force.[31] On the other hand, leading members of Congress questioned the wisdom of decreasing the number of strategic bombers at a time when the Soviet Union was augmenting its strategic nuclear power.

On 11 January 1966, the chairman of the House Committee on Armed Services delegated Representative Hebert's subcommittee to conduct an inquiry into the decision to reduce the number of B-52 and B-58 bombers and replace them with FB-111s. The following day Rep. Craig Hosmer (R-Calif.) denounced McNamara, claiming that he had ignored military advice in his bomber decision, had exercised questionable judgment on numerous earlier defense issues, and had seriously weakened U.S. national security.[32] This constituted the opening salvo of a six-month running battle between McNamara and the Hébert subcommittee over the future of manned bombers.

The dispute escalated later that month when McNamara testified in favor of completely phasing out older model B-52 and B-58 bombers by FY 1971. Insisting that the replacement FB-111 was a strategic bomber, he also declared that at the moment there was no need to decide on the development and production of a follow-on bomber. AMSA's fate promptly became the lightning rod of the hearings. Witness after witness, including McConnell flanked by three other Air Force general officers and retired General Curtis E. LeMay, came before the committee to testify on behalf of a new strategic bomber. Hebert's report, released on 24 April 1966, impugned McNamara's motives for dismissing the military advice of the JCS (who had not actually called for the AMSA development in the FY 1967 budget), challenged the defense secretary's plans to reduce the bomber force, and questioned his refusal to order a follow-on manned bomber. McNamara immediately denounced the report as "a shockingly distorted picture of the true situation"; just as promptly Hébert accused the secretary of misrepresenting the record and challenged McNamara to release the JCS position on a new bomber.[33] Continued open bickering and selective leaks to the news media kept the issue in the public eye.

On 12 May, during a particularly bewildering press conference, repeatedly interrupted by reporters' laughter, McNamara insisted that he was right all along, but that "a badly drafted" OSD memorandum had confused the Joint Chiefs. Hébert quickly claimed victory, expressing his gratification at McNamara's concession that "the confusion in the public's mind over the Joint Chiefs of Staff position was caused by misleading documents emanating from his office."[34]

McNamara anticipated serial production of the FB-111 by late 1968 and completion of the buildup by June 1971. The first production model rolled off the line in mid-July 1968; the first delivery to an Air Force bomber wing did not occur until 25 September 1969.[35]

The April 1966 AMSA hearings, coming as they did on the heels of OSD's unexpectedly large annual and supplemental budget requests, further chipped away at McNamara's reputation for infallibility. The unfortunate experience eroded confidence in his credibility on the eve of the high-profile, politically charged debate over the ABM, one of the two (the TFX was the other) most contentious strategic weapon system issues of his tenure.

The ABM Debate

A rapidly expanding Soviet offensive nuclear arsenal, cooling of U.S.-USSR relations, and Soviet ABM developments pushed the ballistic missile defense system to the front of the U.S. political stage. The Army, main proponent and budget beneficiary of the Nike-X project, predictably asserted in December 1965 that the United States had no effective defense against "a powerful and growing Soviet ICBM threat." It contended that if production of the Nike-X system began during FY 1966, by late 1970 the United States could protect its principal population centers against such a missile attack. The Army envisaged an expansible deployment, initially to defend against the Chinese ICBM threat, and subsequently as a "building block for larger defenses." Declaring the risk involved too great and the future uncertainties too numerous to ignore, the Army wanted $9.4 billion over four years (FY 1967–70) to produce and deploy minimum defensive coverage of the continental United States; a total system could cost as much as $20 billion.[36]

Neither McNamara nor Vance thought Nike-X justified the investment, now estimated for the five-year period (FY 1967–71) at $12.7 billion; they so informed the president on 9 December. To meet the Chinese threat, both OSD officials thought an ABM might be desirable, but given the slow progress and relative primitiveness of the Chinese missile the president could safely defer a deployment decision for another year. Instead of deployment money, McNamara requested more than $400 million for FY 1967 to expand Nike-X development, testing, and evaluation. This decision ignored BoB objections that the development program seemed to place more emphasis on future growth toward a heavy system than on a light system to counter a near-term threat.[37]

In late 1965 an operationally effective ABM system seemed a long way off. Although the Army was making advances with exoatmospheric interceptions (above 300,000-foot altitude) as well as interceptions at lower altitudes, many unanswered questions persisted about design and performance of the system; warhead testing was still ongoing. In March 1966 McNamara testified to a joint congressional committee that the initially planned Nike-X would not protect the nation from a large-scale Soviet attack that could saturate or confuse it, but it might successfully fend off a "nonsophisticated" attack of perhaps 100 Chinese ICBMs. His clinching argument remained that the inevitable Soviet reaction—increasing its offensive missile forces—to any ABM deployment meant that Nike-X could provide neither stability to the arms race nor security to the nation.[38] So long as McNamara's propositions seemed plausible, few could argue strongly with his decision.

The year 1966 witnessed significant changes in the Soviet offensive and defensive strategic arsenal. Moscow continued building hardened ICBM silos at a faster than expected rate, apparently to shelter the SS-11, a new, smaller, and presumably more accurate missile. The Soviets deployed far more ICBM launchers during 1966 than U.S. intelligence had estimated the previous year.[*] And, while direct evidence was lacking, analysts presumed Soviet development of MIRVs for their SS-9 missiles.[39]

As for strategic defensive weapons, by early 1966 the Soviets were building a massive defensive network across the northwest approaches to the Soviet Union—the so-called Tallinn system—whose purpose was a subject of dispute in Washington but was believed to defend against aircraft. More significant, the appearance around Moscow of six confirmed ABM complexes under construction, employing the advanced Galosh missile, set off alarm bells. Though telemetry and test data were lacking on Galosh, the very size of the newly observed Soviet missile suggested a greater range and a larger-yield warhead than heretofore, and consequently a greater capability of knocking down incoming U.S. missiles.[40]

Assessing the Soviet buildup, Chinese belligerency, and emerging technology, by early spring 1966 ABM advocates in the Pentagon, specifically the JCS and DDR&E, Congress, and some of the media began campaigning for the immediate deployment of an ABM system. A fervent strain of anticommunism on Capitol Hill, especially prevalent among long-time, conservative Southern Democrats holding sway on the key armed services and appropriations committees, predisposed many to favor Nike-X deployment at any cost. Representative Rivers would later remark in March 1967 that he "would rather be a live American with an empty pocketbook than a dead one with a full one." Others in the House and Senate looked for opportunities to embarrass the administration. If McNamara did not plan to deploy the ABM, Representative Lipscomb inquired at a 15 February 1966 hearing, why bother to spend any money to develop it?[41]

---

[*] Compared to its 1965 estimate of between 514 and 582 Soviet operational launchers in FY 1968, U.S. intelligence in November 1966 believed that there would be between 670 and 765.

Meantime another pillar of McNamara's opposition to Nike-X was giving way. He conceded during House hearings in early 1966 that technological improvements in warhead design had reached a stage where there was a possibility that an ABM system could prevent substantial damage to the United States from a Chinese attack. The breakthrough had occurred with the planned addition of long-range, exoatmospheric antimissile missiles to the system. Attacking large numbers of objects at altitudes well above the atmosphere with improved nuclear warheads could increase the ABM's radii of destruction from a few thousand feet to as much as 10 miles for hardened incoming reentry vehicles and 10 to 100 miles for unhardened ones.[42]

The dramatic enlargement of Nike-X's kill zone seemed to make possible a feasible and cost-effective ABM area defense. Whereas the initial ABM network would have required dozens of sites and thousands of short-range missiles for point defense, later computer-aided studies showed that a system of 4 long-range acquisition radars, 16 missile site radars, and 400 interceptor missiles at a relatively cheap price tag of $3 billion could theoretically offer a thin defense over the entire United States against a Chinese nuclear attack.[43]

As if to reinforce the need to protect against large-scale attack, in May 1966 China exploded a device containing thermonuclear material, further diminishing the force of McNamara's argument that China presented no immediate threat. By October 1966 the Chinese had tested a nuclear-tipped intermediate-range ballistic missile (IRBM). The Soviets simultaneously appeared intent on constructing a Galosh-equipped ABM ring around Moscow and perhaps elsewhere. How, proponents wondered, could Washington not field an ABM defense when the Soviets were now building one as well as numerous ICBM missile launchers? The JCS proposal for ABM preproduction funding found growing support in Congress as Nike-X became a hot political issue that isolated McNamara and left President Johnson with the unhappy prospect of campaigning for reelection in 1968 open to charges of an "ABM Gap."[44]

On 30 September 1966, DDR&E John Foster voiced his concern that the Soviets could destroy the Minuteman force if they modified their SS-9 and SS-11 missile forces, using basic technology they already possessed. To counter this possibility, Foster suggested deployment of ABMs to protect Minuteman sites. Critical of Foster's "imbalanced analysis" and lack of hard evidence for his contentions, McNamara relied on the more benign assessment of Systems Analysis that no recent evidence confirmed any Soviet attempt either to improve missile accuracy or develop MIRVs. Consequently, the likely effectiveness of Soviet ICBMs against U.S. strategic offensive forces remained unchanged and made the requirement for a potentially destabilizing ABM system less attractive. Foster agreed with the defense secretary that the deployment of a U.S. ABM system "would cause a fundamental change in the strategic situation," but he contended that Sino-Soviet technological advances would continue whether or not the United States fielded an ABM.[45]

Response to new technology that might permit "a blanket of protection" for the entire nation against a relatively small number of incoming missiles and ultimately against heavier attacks on 25 major cities came in mid-October 1966 when Congress earmarked $153.5 million exclusively for preproduction funding of the Nike-X system and added $14.4 million to McNamara's request of more than $400 million for its RDT&E. The congressional intent was to fund the eventual manufacture of the Nike-X system at least one year earlier than the secretary had indicated as a possible starting date. McNamara initially refused to obligate the additional $167.9 million appropriation, a bureaucratic tactic he had resorted to in 1962 to deny appropriated funds for the RS-70 bomber.* Because of that experience, however, Congress shortly afterward changed the law to compel the executive branch to spend appropriated funds. OSD eventually would either have to fund the ABM or risk a constitutional confrontation, hardly one the increasingly beleaguered administration sought.[46]

The tide was running against McNamara. The bitter fight over AMSA with his nemesis Hébert left the secretary looking ill-advised at a time when his differences with the Joint Chiefs and Congress over Nike-X deployment had attracted public attention. Friction between the secretary and the military over Vietnam was well-known; McNamara's relations with Congress, which had never been cordial, deteriorated even further because of contention over the conduct of the war.

Within DoD the secretary of the Army and DDR&E favored deployment of a light, area defense version of the Nike-X system. The defense secretary's 9 November 1966 DPM on Strategic Forces, originally prepared by Systems Analysis and revised by McNamara, rejected categorically the JCS recommendations for a light deployment against the USSR's offensive forces. His longstanding reasons endured—the uncertainty of the Soviet response and the high cost and limited effectiveness of the ABM.[47]

At a press conference the next day at the president's Texas ranch,† McNamara declared it still premature to deploy an ABM network against a Chinese threat. He sought to reassure the country that the United States retained unquestioned nuclear superiority by announcing the administration's intention to produce and deploy the Poseidon missile. But this news also kindled popular demand for a better defense. The effect of McNamara's announcement on the Soviets also concerned the administration, especially in light of the spate of articles in the U.S. press about the ominous shift in the strategic balance. State Department analysts judged in early 1967 that the Russians were somewhat perplexed and showed less concern about the ABM issue than about what they perceived as McNamara's accelerated offensive strategic arms program that threatened to wipe out Moscow's recent gains in its attempt to redress the strategic balance.[48]

---

* See Kaplan et al, *McNamara Ascendancy*, 100-06.
† McNamara went to Texas to attend a meeting with General Wheeler and the president. Wheeler had just returned from a trip to South Vietnam to update the president on the Vietnam situation, MACV's request for additional reinforcements, and strategic issues.

McNamara had reaffirmed his opposition to the Nike-X on 17 November when he circulated OSD's proposed FY 1968 budget recommendations for internal DoD comment. Citing his "fixed belief" that the United States and the Soviet Union both shared the "fundamental objective" of assured destruction, he told Wheeler that Moscow would "undertake at any cost" a buildup to overcome a U.S. ABM network. Nevertheless, in a strongly worded response on 25 November the JCS declared that the lack of an ABM imperiled the survival of the nation's population, industry, and a portion of its assured destruction force. Meantime, within OSD opponents and proponents of the ABM were marshaling their arguments, which in turn became the raw material for McNamara's extraordinary DPM on Nike-X. After several major revisions, the contentious draft was finally rewritten in McNamara's office because Systems Analysis and DDR&E could not reconcile their respective views on the effectiveness of the proposed ABM system.[49]

On 29 November 1966, about a week before the annual budget meeting with the president, McNamara circulated a revised draft on the ABM program to the JCS and service secretaries for comment. He enumerated the circumstances that brought to a head longstanding ABM issues: accelerated Soviet deployment of hardened ICBM launchers; Soviet deployment of an ABM system; Chinese testing of an MRBM and evidence of work on an ICBM; the technological progress that made Nike-X deployment feasible; JCS pressure; and congressional appropriations mandated for an ABM defense. Though he still objected to fielding an ABM system, the congressional FY 1967 appropriation that specifically funded it forced him to hold open the option to deploy a light version to defend against a Chinese threat or accidental launch of an enemy ICBM and to protect Minuteman installations.[50]

The service chiefs and the secretary of the Army disagreed with McNamara's "informal memorandum," feeling it understated damage-limitation benefits to the United States and overstated probable Soviet reaction by assuming the Russians had unlimited resources and the technical capability to counter an American ABM system. Although the Joint Chiefs individually differed among themselves on Nike-X's capabilities, in Admiral McDonald's words, they were convinced that "the time has come for us to effect deployment of this system." Their proposed revisions displayed a unanimity and determination to obtain a presidential decision on the issue.[51]

McNamara and Vance discussed the ABM at length with the Joint Chiefs during their 2 December budget meeting. McNamara admitted that the president was "95 percent for ABM," but the secretary still remained strongly against deployment. Vance expressed concern about how to suggest a light ABM version to Congress instead of a comprehensive defensive system, but Wheeler countered that it could be proposed as the first step toward a more thorough defensive network.[52]

McNamara incorporated several of the JCS comments into his 2 December DPM for the president but rejected their main contention that "the lack of an ABM defense directly endangers the security of the United States." Because of its importance, the revised DPM went to the president attached to McNamara's annual budget DPM that further buttressed his case against ABM deployment for economic reasons. But the old arguments were no longer unassailable. Technological breakthroughs now made Nike-X appear feasible and affordable, and evidence of a Soviet buildup of ICBMs and ABMs made its deployment seem judicious. Some earlier skeptics became supporters.[53]

On 6 December McNamara and the Joint Chiefs met with the president at the Federal Building in Austin, Texas, to finalize the FY 1968 Defense budget requests. The defense secretary had warned the president in his budget DPM of 3 December that cost overruns, engineering changes to eliminate defects, and inevitable redesign to overcome Soviet countermeasures could double the military's estimated $20 billion cost to deploy a full Nike-X system between FY 1967 and FY 1976. Beyond the prohibitive expense, McNamara insisted the Soviets would take countermeasures to overcome this system just as the United States was at work countering the Soviet defensive network. The Joint Chiefs reaffirmed their previous position supporting their damage-limiting argument and challenging OSD's assumptions that a Soviet reaction to Nike-X deployment would be "equal, opposite, feasible and possible." Even the Air Force chief of staff, never a strong advocate of Nike-X, now favored deployment to protect Minuteman sites, apparently because of the effect the Soviet ABM would exert on U.S. targeting and planning.[54]

Surprised by the JCS united front, McNamara argued vigorously against deploying a Nike-X on a scale capable of defending 25 major American cities. He appealed for rational deliberation on an "inherently emotional" issue. But he believed the Soviet nuclear defense policy had been wrongheaded for a decade, allowing spending of vast sums on defenses "not worth a damn." He insisted the Soviets would have to react to an American ABM, touching off an even costlier arms race that would leave neither nation better off than at present. Recognizing the "terrible dilemma" the president faced, McNamara then suggested a fallback position. He would ask for initial Nike-X deployment money in the January budget submission, announcing at the same time that DoD would not use the money if the Soviets indicated willingness to consider talks on ABM limitations.[55]

During the meeting the president consistently sought a "middle ground," finally wondering aloud if moving ahead with the ABM on a limited basis and, as McNamara proposed, seeing what could be negotiated with the Soviets, might be the best course. The next day, through McNamara, Johnson directed State and DoD to inform Soviet Ambassador Dobrynin that he wanted to initiate discussions with the USSR on the ABM issue. Still, Johnson imposed no deadline on his defense secretary to produce results.[56] Budget pressures, however, lent a sense of urgency to getting negotiations under way with Moscow and to show progress.

Acting without delay, Ambassador at Large Thompson raised with Dobrynin the idea of an exchange of views on limiting ICBM and ABM production and deployment; he stressed the urgency of a Soviet response before McNamara presented the Defense budget request to Congress in January 1967.[57] Soviet interest in negotiations would also allow the president breathing room to deflect criticism from Nike-X advocates and postpone a decision by arguing that deploying the system might jeopardize a possible new round of talks to avoid an arms race.

As was his custom when confronted with policy disagreements, Johnson canvassed other opinions within the executive branch about ABM deployment. On 10 December he received their replies. Deputy Under Secretary of State Foy Kohler expected the Soviets to react to a U.S. ABM system by improving both their offensive and defensive strategic forces. The staggering financial burden of such an effort, though, might make Moscow receptive to proposals for a freeze on both ICBMs and ABMs. Acting Secretary of State Katzenbach and Ambassador Thompson believed the Soviets would respond with qualitative improvements to their strategic forces, but thought the time appropriate to approach them about a freeze. CIA Director Helms warned that a new arms race "would at the very least retard what movement we thought might be developing toward moderation in the Soviet outlook. . . ."[58]

Donald F. Hornig, the president's special assistant for science and technology, favored continued diplomatic efforts to achieve arms control and opposed any ABM deployment until solid intelligence showed unambiguously that (1) a new threat existed from a Soviet antimissile system; (2) the deployment would give the United States a meaningful military advantage; and (3) it could be accomplished without provoking a new arms race. Walt Rostow also felt that Moscow would have to respond to a U.S. ABM deployment if only to reestablish the credibility of its assured destruction capability. The Soviets might seek to do this in the cheapest possible way, either negotiating to achieve arms control or producing ICBMs carrying very large warheads.[59] On the other hand, a substantial majority in Congress, led by Senator Russell, Johnson's close friend and adviser, favored deployment of an ABM.

McNamara well knew that a decision against fielding an ABM system risked the displeasure of Congress (which had appropriated an unused $168 million in FY 1967 funds for that purpose). From the public could come both a backlash in favor of such a system just because the Soviets had one and denunciation of the president for not properly defending the country. On 10 December Vance presented the possible alternatives to Johnson: take no action, which given the Soviet ABM deployment would be unpopular with Congress and the American public; deploy a "thin" or light ABM system which, if selected, would be coupled with talks with the Soviet Union on arms limitation; or deploy the "thick" and enormously expensive system recommended by the JCS.[60]

Concurrently on the 10th, four days after the Austin meeting, in line with the president's guidance, McNamara revised his DPM to make use of the previously appropriated funds to begin the production and deployment of the light ABM system to protect Minuteman sites as well as counter a future Chinese threat, an accidental attack, or nuclear blackmail. He further requested that the president formally authorize him and Rusk to start negotiations with the Soviets to limit

ABM systems. On 22 December McNamara asked the Joint Chiefs to comment on this latest DPM. Their response, delivered a week later, supported the light deployment as a first step toward the comprehensive version but expressed reservations about including ABM systems as bargaining chips in arms control negotiations. Any decision to delay deployment pending progress in arms talks, they felt, would fritter away U.S. military and diplomatic bargaining leverage on Moscow.[61]

To counter what seemed a rush to deploy the ABM, at the president's direction McNamara arranged for a White House meeting on 4 January 1967 with current and former PSAC heads and DDR&Es to discuss ABM policy with the JCS and the president. Several days before the session, McNamara met individually with some of the scientists and provided all of them with the revised DPM that recommended limited deployment. Just before the meeting, the advisers met in White House science adviser Hornig's office and found they all opposed any deployment. They then decided to state their own individual views to the president.[62]

The Joint Chiefs believed that the president had already made up his mind or, more likely, McNamara had made it up for him, but they expected the scientific advisers to support the ABM or, at the very least, acquiesce in a limited deployment. Speaking for the Joint Chiefs, Wheeler opened the session with the case for a heavy ABM deployment protecting 25 U.S. cities from Soviet attack. George B. Kistiakowsky, special assistant for science and technology under Eisenhower, declared that such action would accelerate the arms race and doom any prospects of arms control agreements. Kistiakowsky recommended postponing any decision pending the outcome of the administration's diplomatic efforts. Even deploying a light system was dangerous, he insisted, because it created an irresistible pressure to expand. Reinforcing the point, McNamara remarked that once you started an ABM deployment, "you are pregnant. It will be virtually impossible to stop." All five scientists present opposed a heavy deployment; four opposed any deployment as destabilizing; only Hornig halfheartedly accepted the thin version, in part for negotiating flexibility. As he summarized the meeting, McNamara stated that the rationale for the thin system was "marginal"; he wanted to withhold judgment and present his views to the president later.* That evening he explained to Johnson that he had offered no recommendation at the meeting to avoid a potential difference of opinion with the president. McNamara added that he personally doubted the worth of any system, but he recognized that political pressures might force the president to go ahead with a thin version.[63]

Immediately after the meeting, McNamara redrafted his DPM, recommending against deployment of any ABM system but continuing vigorous development and testing. Again he proposed negotiations with the Soviets and, if talks proved unsuccessful, reconsideration of the deployment decision. He also recommended

---

* After McNamara publicly announced in September 1967 the deployment start of a light ABM system, several of the outside scientists denounced the decision, claiming that he had misrepresented their position expressed at the White House.

that the forthcoming FY 1968 budget contain a request of $375 million for Nike-X production, should that become necessary. On 10 January 1967 in his annual State of the Union message to Congress, the president spoke of the mutual responsibility of the United States and Soviet Union "to slow down the arms race between us."[64] He made no mention of the ABM, still awaiting a response from Moscow to the administration's recent overtures.

On 14 January Kohler asked Dobrynin for a Soviet response to Ambassador Thompson's earlier proposals for ABM talks. Pointing to the president's low-key treatment of the ABM in his State of the Union address, Kohler observed that Johnson would have to be more explicit in his forthcoming budget message. If the Soviets agreed to discussions on the ABM freeze, this would affect requests for funding in the message. Dobrynin commented that he had not understood the urgency but admitted to the absence of a consensus within the Soviet government on the issue.[65]

Four days later, on 18 January, Dobrynin notified Rusk that the Soviet government accepted in principle the U.S. proposal for talks on limiting ABMs with the understanding that these discussions would also cover offensive missile systems; no mention was made of time, place, or level of participation. Despite its vagueness, the answer was good enough for Johnson, still predisposed against deployment. Using language that reflected McNamara's DPM of 4 January, the president stated in his budget message of 24 January that he would not deploy an ABM system pending the initiation and progress of talks with Moscow. Should the discussions prove unsuccessful, he would reconsider his decision. To cover such an eventuality the president requested $375 million in production funds, thus indicating "a contingent U.S. decision to deploy an ABM defense."[66]

To Glassboro

On 21 January, three days after Dobrynin's reply, Johnson informed Kosygin that the first priority of Llewellyn Thompson, newly appointed U.S. ambassador to the Soviet Union, was to discuss with Soviet leaders an understanding to curb the strategic arms race. Kosygin, however, appeared preoccupied with the ABM issue, believing as he did that ABM systems were designed to save lives, "and no negotiations were needed to prove it." During his early February meeting with British leaders in London, for example, the Soviet premier, seeking to appropriate the higher moral ground, castigated the American position as one that preferred cheaper offensive weapons to more expensive defensive ones. Which was more conducive to peace, he asked rhetorically, a country that based itself on offensive or defensive systems? Kosygin reassured Thompson in mid-February that Moscow's delay in replying to Johnson's letter was "due to [the] Soviet desire to give [a] constructive reply." He also emphasized that any discussions had to consider both offensive and defensive weapon systems because, as he had stated publicly in London, the Soviet Union would not talk in a context of how it was cheaper to kill people.[67]

Taken aback by Moscow's hard line, McNamara expressed "some doubts" that the Russians really understood the magnitude of the U.S. offensive buildup planned to counter their ABM. Kohler assured him that the latest statements were perfectly consistent with Soviet policy and served notice that Moscow intended to maintain its ABM forces, increase its ICBMs, and perhaps accept U.S. deployment of some ABMs. Anxious to jump-start negotiations, McNamara proposed to meet in Geneva, Switzerland, with the Soviet disarmament representative, but Kohler explained that the man to see was Dobrynin, a vastly more influential Soviet official with far better contacts than the Geneva representative. Pronouncing the Soviet leader's remarks "not unpromising," Rostow counseled the president to adopt a wait-and-see attitude for the formal Soviet reply.[68]

Kosygin's official response politely emphasized that disarmament, not a freeze on some "balance of power," was essential. When presenting the reply to Thompson on 28 February, Gromyko in his amplifying remarks decried the U.S. "buildup of the means of nuclear attack" for contributing to the "armaments race spiral." In his eagerness to show diplomatic results that would make ABM deployment unnecessary, Johnson seemed to read more into Kosygin's letter than the contents justified; at a 2 March press conference he announced the Soviet willingness to begin talks.[69]

McNamara viewed the possible negotiations as similar to his NATO Nuclear Planning Group (NPG)* meetings, that is, didactic sessions where both sides would learn about the use of strategic nuclear weapons and each other. For this reason, he favored a loosely structured agenda to open a dialogue with the Soviets. State officials on the other hand contended that it was necessary to offer specific proposals to the Russians for the talks to go anywhere. As a compromise, the initial call for discussions to begin on 12 April used a modified McNamara approach. It omitted a detailed proposal pending a dialogue to identify issues that would enable the United States to settle on a specific course but left the door open to Soviet initiatives by indicating a willingness to discuss particular proposals.[70]

McNamara had to produce progress in arms control talks within a reasonable time. Although the Soviets had indicated interest in discussing limits on or elimination of defensive and offensive strategic weapons, the start of such talks remained unscheduled.[71] Mid-April found Washington still awaiting Moscow's agreement to a date, a delay attributed to differences within the Soviet government about how to proceed with negotiations.

To break the impasse, McNamara personally intervened, inviting Dobrynin on 11 April to a private meeting and lunch at his home. He explained to the ambassador his philosophy of assured destruction and its inexorable conclusion that if either side deployed an ABM system, the other would have to offset it by adding more missiles to its offensive arsenal. The resulting nuclear instability, enormous

---

* See Chapter XIV for a discussion of the Nuclear Planning Group.

cost, and greater strategic uncertainty would only diminish, not add to national security. In sum, McNamara proposed lowering the military risks and costs without reducing the deterrent capability of either nation. Despite all these efforts, Moscow still declined to name a time and place to open substantive negotiations on the arms race. On 19 May, the president again wrote a wide-ranging letter to Kosygin expressing his hope that the Soviet government would respond favorably to U.S. proposals to begin discussions on the ABM and ICBM as well as negotiation of a nuclear nonproliferation treaty.[72]

The disruptive effect of the Six-Day War in the Middle East (5–10 June), the first explosion of a Chinese hydrogen bomb (17 June), and behind-the-scenes diplomatic maneuvering finally drew Johnson and Kosygin to the small college town of Glassboro, New Jersey, on 23 June. McNamara favored a summit because the potential drawbacks of the talks were small, the possible gains large. If nothing else the two leaders could size each other up, thereby improving future understanding. There was always a chance, admittedly less than 50 percent, that discussions might lead to progress on Vietnam, strategic arms limitations, and control of arms deliveries to the Middle East.[73]

The president selected the meeting site at the last possible moment, but preparations for a summit with the Soviet leader had been under way since Kosygin let it be known in early June that he would welcome a meeting with Johnson during his forthcoming visit to the United Nations. While Vietnam dominated the Glassboro agenda, the need for a Middle East settlement and the administration's desire for strategic arms talks with Moscow were also priority issues.[74] For all the forewarning, the preparation of position papers, and the stakes involved, McNamara's presentation of arms reductions arguments at Glassboro had the overtones of an *opéra bouffe*.

According to Dobrynin's version of events, he had led Kosygin to expect a substantive and formal presentation by McNamara on the arms race and the ABM. Instead, at the president's direction the Soviet leader received an impromptu discourse during lunch. McNamara laid out the administration's desire for inclusive talks designed to limit offensive and defensive weapons. Sensitive to Soviet concerns, he insisted the issue was not that offensive weapons were cheaper to build than defensive ones, but rather the prevention of a costly and ultimately destabilizing arms race. Aware of the secretary's numerous public statements on cost-effectiveness of weapon systems, an emotional Kosygin declared this "commercial approach" immoral. As the weekend summit progressed, the president could not draw Kosygin out on strategic arms discussions; Soviet positions only hardened. During subsequent private meetings with Johnson, Kosygin repeatedly implied that the Americans were only interested in limiting defensive weapons like ABMs.[75]

The president and his defense secretary left Glassboro disappointed. McNamara reported little gain from the summit but thought it helpful that both leaders at least had the chance to gauge each other. His own exchange with Kosygin had exposed "the tremendous philosophical gap" between U.S. and Soviet thinking on nuclear strategy. McNamara and Rusk blamed the breakdown on Kosygin who, they believed, had not been fully briefed on the subject of arms control, had no instructions from the Politburo about it, and was thus unable to react to the dialogue. Soviet participants later recalled their grave disappointment with McNamara's ABM presentation, describing it as little more than a rehash of the secretary's previous public statements. The two sides had separate agendas that had them talking past each other: Washington pressed for a Vietnam solution and arms control talks, Moscow for a Mideast settlement favorable to the Arab nations. Within 10 days of the lackluster summit, McNamara decided to recommend deployment of a thin ABM system, instructing his staff to prepare estimates for its initial components, lead times, and costs.[76]

Announcing the Deployment of the ABM

Well before the disappointing Glassboro meetings a sea change toward the ABM had occurred within DoD. By May 1967 each of the service secretaries, the DDR&E, and the director of DoD's Advanced Research Projects Agency (ARPA) favored deployment of a light, area-defense version of the Nike-X system absent genuine negotiations with the Soviet Union. On 4 July Enthoven joined their ranks, conceding the prudence of deploying a thin ABM defense for Minuteman sites. He reasoned that it would be politically difficult to do nothing; a thin (anti-Chinese) system, though not absolutely necessary, could be useful and also strengthen OSD's case to reject the more expensive, less effective, and unnecessary heavy anti-Soviet antimissile defense. On 27 July, the Joint Chiefs formally appealed to McNamara to deploy Nike-X either to move Moscow to negotiate or expose the Soviets' lack of genuine interest in such talks.[77]

By 2 August McNamara had completed the first draft of a speech to be delivered in mid-September at the United Press International editors' convention, announcing deployment of a Chinese-oriented thin ABM system. Simultaneously, he circulated a tentative strategic offensive and defensive force DPM for FY 1969–73 calling for a light ballistic missile defense against a Chinese threat but rejecting the more costly system against a Russian threat. On 28 August, the Joint Chiefs, though disagreeing sharply with the DPM, endorsed this proposal as the first step toward the expanded ABM defense that they deemed essential for U.S. national survival in the early 1970s. As Assistant Secretary of Defense for Public Affairs Phil Goulding recalled, "Our choice in the Pentagon in the late summer and fall of 1967 was not a small ABM versus none at all, but rather a small ABM versus a big one."[78]

On 19 August McNamara had forwarded a draft of his intended speech to the president for approval and distributed copies to senior civilian officials for comment. A number had reservations or were opposed. The Arms Control and Disarmament Agency expected the announcement would complicate the ongoing nonproliferation talks. White House special assistants Walt Rostow and Joseph Califano thought the secretary should include cost estimates in his talk and indicate that ABM deployment was financially affordable and would not drain funds excessively from domestic programs. Califano thought the speech was "fine," but unless Mc-Namara defused potential criticism he expected that "all hell is likely to break loose from the liberals and the urbanists." The sharpest criticism came from NSC's Spurgeon Keeny who opposed the timing and likely negative domestic and international impact of a speech that satisfied no constituency and sent a message that would be interpreted as a major step-up in the arms race. Keeny also contended that McNamara's emphasis on U.S. nuclear superiority was ill-advised; it would only antagonize OSD's congressional critics and complicate discussions with the Soviets. Following the internal review, the secretary informed the Joint Chiefs in early September of his impending announcement.[79]

As Rusk had instructed, Ambassador Thompson advised Gromyko on 12 September of the substance of McNamara's forthcoming statement, taking care to stress that Washington still desired talks with Moscow to mutually limit and rein in the strategic arms race. Over the next two days McNamara personally alerted his NATO defense minister counterparts on the Nuclear Planning Group, and Washington notified NATO's North Atlantic Council (NAC) of the impending dramatic announcement. The last-minute disclosure became an embarrassment because at the April 1967 NPG meeting McNamara had pledged to the defense ministers that the United States would not act on ABMs without first consulting them.[80] Despite the administration's efforts to downplay the issue, McNamara's speech on 18 September to the UPI editors stirred controversy at home and abroad because, as Keeny had foreseen, it persuaded no one.

The speech—beginning with an impassioned call for arms restraint and ending with the announced deployment of a significant new strategic weapon system—the ABM—seemed to muddle the strategic arms issue even more. The disconnect in the speech was intended for Soviet leaders, who knew its contents beforehand, not UPI editors. It was a deliberate effort on McNamara's part not to surprise the Soviets but to alert them; not to start an arms race but to begin arms reduction talks. The basic problem, however, was that McNamara had so identified himself with the anti-ABM camp that his volte-face left him open to the increasingly familiar charges of duplicity, expediency, and doing the politically convenient thing, not the right thing. The defense secretary only reinforced such perceptions by cavalierly brushing aside criticism. At the September 1967 NPG meeting in Ankara, Turkey, British Defense Minister Denis Healey denounced the ABM decision, claiming that the U.S. secretary had promised to consult initially with the NATO allies. McNamara countered that there was no evidence the allies wanted to be consulted on matters related to a Chinese threat.*[81]

During the Pentagon media blitz immediately preceding his talk, McNamara met individually with leading columnists and representatives of the most influen-

---

* McNamara had provided Healey a copy of his speech several days before its delivery. Healey, however, felt the announcement was unfortunate for it had not been discussed in meaningful fashion by the NATO ministers. (Msg 2071 London to State, 19 Sep 67; note McNamara for Healey, 16 Sep 67: Cable files, OSD Hist.)

tial news organizations to explain the purpose of his announcement. Nevertheless his speech drew fire from the liberal press for playing politics to appease Republican critics.[82] If McNamara crafted his speech to reassure Soviet leaders, OSD's media campaign to reassure the American public about U.S. strategic superiority did not help serve that purpose.

In his exclusive interview with a *Life* magazine reporter timed to coincide with the ABM announcement, McNamara revealed that Minuteman and Poseidon missiles were being equipped with MIRV warheads. He proclaimed that the United States enjoyed three- to fourfold superiority in strategic nuclear weapons over the USSR. These revelations and the ABM decision made it difficult for Russian proponents of arms control talks to advance their case. Dobrynin told William Foster in early October that the delay in a Soviet response to U.S. initiatives on arms control resulted from Moscow's institutional difficulty in coordinating differing points of view on the proposal within the Foreign Ministry and the Defense Ministry.[83] By appealing to everyone, McNamara satisfied no one, least of all the Joint Chiefs.

McNamara's early October version of the DPM on strategic forces endorsed procurement of a Chinese-oriented ABM system that could also protect Minuteman sites, but it disapproved the JCS recommendation to deploy Nike-X to defend American cities from a Soviet attack. Twice in November, on the eve of his annual budget meeting with BoB representatives, McNamara and the Chiefs discussed the outstanding issues raised in the DPM on strategic forces and in the FY 1969 Defense budget. To the president, Wheeler characterized the sessions as "the most far-reaching and most extensive exchange of views [by] the JCS . . . in the four years he [had] participated." But no minds were changed on the ABM question. The JCS still wanted a heavy, anti-Soviet ABM system as well as AMSA and, with McNamara still unmoved by their arguments, they proposed to discuss the outstanding issues with the president. At a 4 December White House meeting, the president urged both sides to reconcile their differences before testifying to Congress. Otherwise the media and administration critics would distort minor disagreements into "deep divisions between the civilian and military leadership" as they had done the previous August with the Stennis hearings on the air war against North Vietnam.* But Johnson also emphasized the need for a $4 billion budget reduction, with half coming from DoD.[84]

In line with presidential guidance BoB proposed in mid-November that OSD save $500 million in the FY 1969 budget by postponing the operational date of Minuteman III by one year instead of the five-month delay proposed in the secretary's DPM. Besides the much needed savings, BoB judged the Soviet ABM threat insufficient to require so rapid a deployment of the latest ICBM and felt that the additional time gained by slipping production could be used to correct flaws in the missile's guidance system. Slowing construction of the thin ABM system, as BoB also proposed, could reap $800 million in short-term savings. McNamara had given this

---

* See Chapter VIII.

system the name of Sentinel* to distinguish it from the Nike-X, which continued as a separate research and development effort with the bigger objective of protecting most large American cities from a Soviet attack.[85]

Following his 18 November meeting with BoB Director Schultze, McNamara agreed to slip the Minuteman III's operational date another six months and initially procure only Spartan missiles for area defense. His finalized DPM sent to the White House in early 1968 contained these decisions along with his usual rejection of JCS recommendations to deploy the Soviet-oriented Nike-X system. Still unconvinced of the ABM's efficacy and fearful of its consequences, during his final days in office McNamara retained procurement of 480 Spartan missiles but decreased the number of Sprint missiles from 456 to 192 by deleting those intended for Minuteman protection; he also deferred decisions on missile site defense until the next budget cycle. The initial Sentinel deployment, too, it turned out, could be delayed until October 1972 because Chinese ICBM development had not progressed as rapidly as anticipated.[86] Unable in a strong pro-ABM political environment to prevent the decision to field a thin ABM system, McNamara resorted to budgetary legerdemain to minimize its size and delay its initial operational date.

Overall, McNamara reshaped U.S. strategic forces significantly. ICBMs became the backbone of national defense. Strategic bombers declined in numbers and importance, particularly after McNamara rejected development of AMSA. Qualitative technological advances that he sponsored greatly enhanced the power of U.S. offensive weapons, but they also created paradoxes. OSD might limit the number of ICBMs to stabilize the arms competition but MIRV technology multiplied the effectiveness of each missile and destabilized the strategic equation. While McNamara could reject many JCS demands for even more strategic weapons, he felt compelled to deploy a light ABM system that he thought unnecessary and too costly. His evolving concept of assured destruction altered the debate over strategic nuclear weapons. He advanced arms control talks to a new level, but his single-minded certitude that assured destruction was the only nuclear strategy that made sense alienated the Soviet leaders, whom he could not convince of its validity. Although his mechanistic worldview assumed that the logic of assured destruction motivated both Washington and Moscow to react in predictable ways, this expectation of like responses to perceived threats did not come about. As with other areas he touched as secretary of defense, McNamara did not get as much as he hoped in strategic arms matters, but perhaps more than he had a right to expect. Even so, he left much unfinished business for his successors.

---

* The Sentinel system had four components: long-range acquisition radars; interceptor-controlling radars; a long-range, exoatmospheric interceptor missile, the Spartan, for area defense; and a high-acceleration atmospheric interceptor missile, the Sprint, for terminal defense. The Spartan defended against a small attack of the kind China might launch; the Sprint protected American ICBMs from a larger Soviet attack. If completed by 1975, the planned Sentinel network would include 6 acquisition radars, 17 controlling radars, 480 Spartans, and 192 Sprints. (SecDef Ste before House Subcte on DoD Appropriations on the FY 1969–73 Defense Program and 1969 Defense Budget, 16 Feb 68, 90-91; *Life*, 29 Sep 67, 28A.)

Clifford's Approach to Strategic Arms

Like McNamara, Clark Clifford opposed the Nike-X, doubting that it could protect cities against large-scale Soviet ICBM attacks. Unlike his predecessor, however, Clifford proved a hard-line advocate of Sentinel deployment during heated 1968 congressional debates. In mid-April Sen. John Sherman Cooper (R-Ky.) proposed in an amendment to a FY 1969 authorization bill that Sentinel not be deployed pending certification of its practicability and verification of its expected cost. His effort failed, but only by the narrow margin of three votes.[87]

Encouraged by a "curious coalition" of liberal senators who opposed the ABM and conservative ones who wanted a larger version than Sentinel, anti-ABM forces in the Senate persisted in challenging the Sentinel deployment. Opponents within OSD now sensed an opportunity to reverse the Sentinel decision. In mid-May, Systems Analysis, supported by ISA, pointed to delays in China's ICBM effort, an apparent slackening of Soviet ICBM and ABM development, and rising costs as reasons to slip Sentinel deployment one year.[88]

DDR&E John Foster viewed the Systems Analysis memo as an attempt by Enthoven to take control of Sentinel development from him. According to Foster, Systems Analysis had oversimplified complicated deployment issues by slighting the uncertainties involved in projecting Chinese or Soviet strategic capabilities. It was true that Sentinel costs were rising, but the increases fell within the range anticipated when McNamara had opted to deploy the ABM system. Clifford sided with Foster because he believed Sentinel necessary to protect the United States against a Chinese or an accidental ballistic missile attack, defend Minuteman silos, improve the bargaining leverage in arms talks with the Soviets, and gain valuable experience from the construction itself.[89] OSD also employed these arguments to ward off continued congressional challenges.

In mid-June Cooper again offered an amendment, co-sponsored by Sen. Philip Hart (D-Mich.), to strike the $227.3 million ABM construction authorization from the proposed budget. After what Clifford later described as "quite a donnybrook in the Senate," on 24 June the latest attempt failed by a 52 to 34 vote; the next day the authorization bill easily passed, 78 to 13. Convinced that any ABM postponement would affect future U.S.-USSR arms negotiations unfavorably, Clifford had personally lobbied the administration's case with Senator Russell. When passage of the Cooper-Hart amendment still appeared possible, it took the personal intervention of the president, then engaged in an exchange of correspondence with Kosygin, to swing the vote decisively against the rider.[90]

On 21 June, Kosygin had replied to Johnson's May appeal for arms control talks by suggesting negotiations in the not distant future. The next day the president proposed—and the Soviet leader quickly agreed—that they jointly announce the agreement on 1 July (to coincide with the signing of the Nonproliferation Treaty).[*] On 27 June, three days after the Senate rejected the Cooper-Hart resolution, Gromyko announced Moscow's readiness to discuss strategic weapon reductions. In Clifford's mind, this completely torpedoed Senate arguments that Sentinel deployment would endanger such negotiations.[91]

Sentinel deployment did not proceed smoothly. The Army vacillated over site selection, anticipating the program would suffer from the president's mandated reductions in Defense spending. In early September, Clifford insisted deployment adhere "as closely as possible" to the approved milestones; later he resisted White House attempts to slip the system schedule by several months to save $250 million. Unexpected public resistance also slowed site selection. Of 17 sites planned for Sentinel, construction at only one—Boston, Massachusetts—was under way by early December. Official announcement of site selections in some of the Chicago and Seattle metropolitan areas encountered local political opposition. According to Foster, congressmen from the affected districts had "to fight parochial battles" on behalf of their constituents, who feared that proximity of sites to their cities would be dangerous.[92]

Also keeping the ABM issue in the headlines, at least as a regional issue, were objections to scheduled underground nuclear tests deemed necessary for Sentinel warhead design. Residents in California, Nevada, and other western states voiced concern that such tests might possibly trigger earthquakes. In early December, Clifford argued strongly and successfully against any testing delays because they would only increase costs, retard ABM deployment, and induce congressional foes once again to attempt to kill the program. Keeny concurred that postponement would "focus greater public concern" on the issue, making it more difficult for the new administration to continue the system. The one-megaton test went off at the Nevada test site on the morning of 19 December in what turned out to be the climax of the short-lived Sentinel project. In early February 1969 Secretary of Defense Laird, who succeeded Clifford on 22 January, suspended Sentinel deployment pending a comprehensive review.[†93]

Clifford carried McNamara's other strategic weapons priorities forward with one other important exception. He sharply reduced the planned size of the controversial FB-111 force from 210 to 90 aircraft and instead retained the B-58 along with a number of older B-52s for continued service.[94] The stated reason was to save money, but cutting the FB-111 buy was an easy way for Clifford to mend fences with such powerful legislators as Senator Symington and Representative Hébert, both big-bomber advocates, as well as the array of critics who regarded the F-111 program as a prime example of a McNamara inspired and dominated attempt to force the unneeded and unsuitable plane on the services.

---

[*] The Johnson-Kosygin exchange of letters is discussed more fully in Chapter XII.
[†] Signing of the SALT I agreement by the United States and the USSR in 1972 effectively disposed of the ABM issue. Both nations were allowed only two ABM complexes, one to protect national capitals and the other to defend a field of ICBMs.

The United States continued to develop and buy Minuteman IIIs with MIRVs for its land-based ICBM force. Development of Poseidon proceeded apace as did conversion of 31 Polaris submarines to accommodate the new missile. Plans for ABM deployment progressed. Defense outlays for strategic arms swelled to more than $15.6 billion in FY 1969 to purchase advanced strategic weapons, notably ABM, Poseidon, and MIRV technology. In November 1965 McNamara had forecast a leveling off of spending to around $4.9 billion (TOA) on strategic arms by FY 1970. In January 1969 Clifford recommended Congress authorize $12.2 billion (TOA) for strategic forces for FY 1970. For the five-year FY 1970–74 plan more than $50 billion (TOA) was ticketed for strategic weapons' procurement and development.[95] As the United States and the Soviet Union scrambled for technological improvements to counter real or imagined deficiencies, sophisticated strategic weapons became increasingly expensive, contributing to defense imbalances, economic stress, and rising inflation. Assured destruction was working, but in a way McNamara had not anticipated.

CHAPTER XIV

NATO READJUSTMENT

Ever present as an essential component of U.S. international security policy, the North Atlantic Treaty Organization (NATO) had to be taken into account in decisions relating to strategic policy, international nuclear negotiations, and development and deployment of weapons. In pursuing U.S. policy interests President Johnson and Secretary McNamara had to look across the Atlantic and ask themselves what would be the effect on NATO and what would be the reaction of NATO countries. McNamara's chief concerns after 1965 included de Gaulle's decision to withdraw France from the military alliance; how Vietnam was affecting NATO; and how to convince the European allies that a strategy of flexible response would bring about a better balance between nuclear and conventional forces.

McNamara had succeeded in getting NATO to pay lip service to flexible response in MC 14/3,[*] but it was already clear by then that the European partners would not be willing or able to provide the forces necessary to make a reality of the new strategy. This was no great difference from the past experience of the alliance—forces-in-being had never met force goals. The United States had always demanded the highest goals and imposed them on reluctant allies who knew that they could not and would not meet them. Although the European nations had gone a long way toward restoring their economies after the devastation of World War II, as with the United States their domestic economic concerns often exercised greater influence than their international concerns.

Since 1962 America's NATO allies had listened repeatedly to McNamara's lectures emphasizing the central role of conventional forces in his strategy of flexible response. This complex strategy had multiple and interconnected goals: adapting NATO to meet the challenge of an evolving Soviet military threat by placing

---

[*] For the earlier evolution of the flexible response doctrine, see Kaplan et al, *McNamara Ascendancy*, ch XII.

greater reliance on conventional forces and less on nuclear weapons; making the allies share more of the burden of men and money; and providing the allies with greater information about and insight into the U.S. strategic and tactical nuclear arsenals while retaining control of nuclear weapons in U.S. hands.

Despite McNamara's injunctions, redefining NATO strategy and revamping its force structure proceeded at a glacial pace until early 1966 when France's announced withdrawal from NATO's integrated military command arrangements signaled removal of a major obstacle to decisionmaking by the remaining 14 members regarding alliance military strategy and nuclear weapons policies. By that time, however, the competing and growing demands of Vietnam for troops and money had cast doubt on the American commitment to NATO, complicating the U.S. position. Furthermore, reconciling the tangle of NATO issues—a revised military strategy, nuclear sharing, force structure, and burden sharing—was problematic under any circumstances. Adding to this combustible mix, the ever cost-conscious McNamara wanted to reduce U.S. forces and military expenses in Europe. Paradoxically, French withdrawal from the military alliance offered the secretary further opportunity to move in that direction.

France Secedes

On 21 February 1966 President Charles de Gaulle publicly announced his decision to withdraw French armed forces from NATO control. In March, he officially notified President Johnson and NATO that France intended to leave the alliance's military organization and expected the removal of NATO forces from French soil by 1 April 1967. For several years de Gaulle had been openly charting an independent course for France—the nuclear *force de frappe* was the outstanding change. The French president had also withdrawn his Mediterranean fleet from NATO command and forced the redeployment from France of nuclear-capable aircraft. Washington and Paris also differed over the control of nuclear weapons; U.S. insistence on final say over use was anathema to de Gaulle, who wanted an independent nuclear force.[1]

With de Gaulle's words and actions signaling his intent, as early as May 1964 McNamara, keenly aware of the serious effects of a French withdrawal, had asked the Joint Chiefs of Staff to consider the implications for NATO. Their late June response warned that without the line of communication (LOC) running across central France, NATO's forward defense strategy seemed infeasible. McNamara did not officially reply to the memorandum, but he let it be known that the Chiefs' views would get consideration in ongoing studies.[2]

As de Gaulle stepped up his criticism of U.S. policies, in May 1965 McNamara tasked the Joint Chiefs to prepare emergency plans for an evacuation of France and provide estimated costs and military personnel requirements involved in transferring U.S. forces from French installations. In their 19 May answer the

JCS anticipated moving 7,000 military personnel assigned to LOC duties in western France to similar duties in Germany rather than reducing U.S. forces in Europe. They expected American troops would continue to operate depots in eastern France as well as POL facilities and Air Force installations throughout the country. This partial withdrawal and establishment of a new LOC would cost roughly $170 million and take between 18 and 36 months. For a complete redeployment from France, the Chiefs proposed various combinations of support bases located outside of France over an 18–36 month period at a projected cost of $1 billion. Leaving France, they warned, would have major consequences for NATO plans and force structure. A subsequent JCS appraisal, submitted in mid-August, found no acceptable substitute for the French bases, adding that an alternative line of communication through the Low Countries entailed substantial risk, higher costs, and possibly increased NATO reliance on nuclear weapons.[3]

Meantime, in early July, General Wheeler proposed a State-Defense Steering Committee to coordinate and centralize policy guidance on the French situation. Deputy Secretary Vance endorsed the proposal; he, George Ball, and Wheeler would head the committee, supported by a designated working group. The senior officials met first on 26 August to lay out an agenda for future discussions. At a session involving high officials from State, OSD, the JCS, and the White House in early October 1965, Ball, speaking for Rusk and with McNamara's support, advocated a tough line with Paris. A draft National Security Action Memorandum prepared for the meeting and coordinated in advance with OSD proposed that the president reexamine the U.S. security commitment to France should the French end their participation in alliance activities. Johnson, however, wanted from the outset "to control what is said to the French and when"; he did not approve the draft.[4]

In February 1966, de Gaulle's public pronouncements and reports from the U.S. embassy in Paris presaged imminent French action on withdrawal. On 6 March, Rusk, Ball, McNamara, and Vance, drawing on their October discussions, tentatively agreed to treat whatever move de Gaulle made as a France-NATO issue rather than a bilateral one between France and the United States. They further agreed to "move everything out of France" if necessary and seek no wartime reentry rights. Although considering contingencies for relocating from France, Washington anticipated having more time because de Gaulle's public and private remarks and those of high French officials had implied that France would lay down conditions for discussion, not present the alliance with a fait accompli. The suddenness of the French president's 7 March letter to Johnson terminating participation in NATO's command structure, followed on 29 March by the notice establishing the 1 April 1967 deadline for all NATO forces to depart France, came as a surprise.[5]

Johnson responded succinctly, expressing grave concern about the consequences of de Gaulle's action for the alliance. Rather than haggle with the French over basing rights in exchange for allied cooperation in air defense, intelligence, early warning, and overflight rights as some suggested, Johnson acceded to French demands in order to avoid an unseemly, and what he believed ultimately fruitless, attempt to change de Gaulle's mind. Johnson focused on rebuilding NATO with initiatives such as nuclear planning that could bind the alliance more closely together. Throughout the relocation Johnson, apparently relying on the advice of Deputy Special Assistant for National Security Affairs Francis Bator, pursued a restrained and patient course, bowing to the inevitable; he instructed his secretaries of state and defense to do the same.[6]

During the interval between de Gaulle's 7 March letter and his clarifying memorandum of 29 March, Vance instructed the Joint Chiefs on 18 March to prepare alternatives for relocating U.S. and NATO activities from France and to appraise possible adjustments in NATO's military structure. Wheeler favored a reorganization of NATO and U.S. military structures while simultaneously reconstituting the line of communication in Europe. In particular he wanted to elevate SACEUR to a new command level, Supreme Allied Commander, NATO, with authority over European, Atlantic, and Channel Commands, although he realized Congress would be reluctant to fund costly reorganization initiatives.[7]

OSD defined withdrawal of U.S. forces from France in economic terms— the cost of building new facilities as well as relocating equipment, headquarters, troops, and supplies. The central issue within DoD swirled around the differing relocation plans of OSD and JCS and their effect on NATO force structure. Stated briefly, the JCS wanted to move an intact force structure from one European location to another; OSD wanted to reduce the American force structure in Europe.

In 1966 there were 20 major U.S. military bases (440 separate facilities total) on French soil. Systems Analysis considered needlessly expensive the replication of the U.S. French facilities and functions elsewhere in Europe. Aside from the 550-mile oil pipeline that ran through France, other parts of the logistics infrastructure might better be returned to the United States or entirely eliminated. The "efficient solution" was to reduce the vulnerability of existing facilities "rather than adding more vulnerable bases."[8]

The U.S. 12 April reply to the French memorandum of 29 March challenged the 1 April 1967 deadline but stated the U.S. intention "to remove its facilities . . . as promptly as possible." Both McNamara and Rusk had already agreed on moving the North Atlantic Council (NAC) from Paris and relocating NATO military headquarters with the NAC. DoD assumed responsibility for planning the relocation of NATO and U.S. elements from France and reorganizing the command structure. At a White House luncheon on 5 April McNamara advocated getting out of France "as quickly as possible," even removing some air units "right away." Shaking his head, a skeptical president questioned the European reaction to such a "quick" move, leaving McNamara to remark that he intended to consult with U.S. allies to give them "a couple of months of notice" on any withdrawals.[9]

On 13 April the Joint Chiefs formally proposed establishing a Supreme Allied Commander, NATO (SACNATO), relocating Supreme Headquarters Allied Powers Europe (SHAPE) near Brussels along with U.S. European Command Headquarters (EUCOM), and shifting Headquarters, Allied Forces, Central Europe to

Trier, Germany or Luxembourg. Until new storage facilities could be built in Germany the JCS wanted to maintain stocks for the existing force structure by temporarily storing vital materiel in the United Kingdom or afloat. Because they opposed dual-basing* for fear that any withdrawals of American forces would lend credence to de Gaulle's allegations about U.S. unreliability, the Chiefs recommended retention of six U.S. aircraft squadrons redeploying from nine French air bases to nine comparable air bases in Europe. U.S. forces and their 40,000 dependents in France would be relocated elsewhere in Europe; over the next five years DoD would construct a permanent infrastructure to house the relocated personnel and materiel at a cost of $600 million. Another $200 million needed to cover short-term costs brought the total to $800 million for the relocation, down 20 percent from mid-1965 estimates.[10]

A week earlier OSD had already decided to withdraw the U.S. aircraft in France from continental Europe by sending two squadrons to the United Kingdom to replace two others deploying to Vietnam and returning the four remaining units to the United States. JCS discussions with OSD representatives in mid-April revealed OSD's intention to remove the squadrons, its reluctance to co-locate SHAPE and EUCOM, and its resistance to building the requested new supply depots.[11]

These positions appeared in McNamara's 21 April DPM as an effort to reduce war reserve stockages, storage facilities, and support personnel in Europe because the European allies' war material could support operations for only 15 to 30 days. The memorandum also endorsed dual-basing and questioned the need to replace the air bases in France one-on-one elsewhere in Europe. The Chiefs rejoined on 3 May that the savings entailed disproportionate military risks and created the appearance among the allies of a fundamental shift in U.S. policy toward NATO.[12]

The defense secretary rebutted the Joint Chiefs' objections to his DPM in a 17 May memorandum that branded building and maintaining new storage depots for ammunition and other war material as wasteful and inefficient. Hewing closely to the Systems Analysis line, he proposed culling depots to obviate the need for new storage areas in Germany. Dual-basing air squadrons would eliminate the requirement for new air bases at a savings between $205 million and $240 million over JCS-projected costs. Merging headquarters would eliminate another 2,000 to 3,000 personnel slots and save $40 million in relocation costs.

OSD rejected JCS proposals for a new command structure headed by a Supreme Allied Commander, NATO. As for locating SHAPE and EUCOM headquarters in Belgium, McNamara pronounced it cheaper to move EUCOM to Germany than to build expanded facilities in Belgium to house the two headquarters. He moved EUCOM headquarters from France to existing facilities in Stuttgart, West Germany, because of "the substantial budgetary and gold savings" of $40

---

* Dual-basing meant that units redeployed to facilities in the United States maintained alternate bases in Europe where they would deploy periodically.

million.* He ultimately approved the Chiefs' proposal to move SHAPE from Roc-quencourt, France, to Casteau, Belgium, about 25 miles southwest of Brussels. Personnel adjustments required the movement of large numbers during 1966–67. Altogether, 16,000 military and civilian personnel plus 19,000 U.S. dependents stayed in Europe, mostly in Germany and the United Kingdom. Nearly 39,000 others in all three categories returned to the United States from France, saving more than $100 million in balance of payments.[13]

Removing six U.S. reconnaissance squadrons from France saved more money and helped with the balance of payments deficit and gold flow problems. Besides, if required, the aircraft could be redeployed to Europe "within a few days." The same logic applied to replacing French air bases on a one-to-one basis, which McNamara thought unnecessary. He proposed further study of overall air base requirements in Europe to achieve an optimum result. Nevertheless, the secretary insisted that his proposals did not signal "a fundamental change" in the U.S. commitment to NATO but only his desire to eliminate wasteful practices. All told, he estimated these measures would save more than $200 million in defense costs at a time when OSD was intent on holding down non-Vietnam spending.[14]

Despite McNamara's disclaimers, the Joint Chiefs did regard the secretary's proposals as fundamental changes to the alliance driven by the principle that fi-nancial savings overrode military risks. Their continued objections led to a 20 May 1966 meeting with McNamara and Vance where the former tabled his 21 April NATO DPM in favor of further study of the relocation issue. Participants agreed that the JCS would be responsible for the study on relocation from France; the EUCOM commander for the study to consolidate European headquarters; and the Air Force secretary and chief of staff for alternative relocation plans for the air units in France.[15]

Five days later McNamara notified the president that the U.S. military would leave France "as promptly as practicable" at an estimated cost "somewhere in the tens of millions of dollars." The operation was codenamed FRELOC (Fast Reloca-tion). While most U.S. stocks in France would move to Germany, relocation of the remainder and the disposition of American support personnel needed further study. So did OSD and JCS differences over the relocation of EUCOM headquar-ters and redeployment of reconnaissance aircraft from France to either U.S. or European bases. McNamara would work with Rusk to resolve other outstanding issues, particularly the status of the lengthy POL pipeline running across France to Germany.[16] Additional study did not necessarily mean additional funding.

What stores to retain and at what level and where proved difficult to resolve because of continuing differences between OSD and JCS. To get a head start on relocation, McNamara authorized General Lyman L. Lemnitzer, Supreme Allied

---

* This was accomplished by consolidating Headquarters, U.S. Seventh Army and Headquarters U.S. Army, Europe, at Heidelberg.

Commander, Europe, and U.S. Commander in Chief, Europe, and other American commanders to begin moving excess stocks from U.S. facilities in Germany and Italy back to the United States and replacing them with stores from U.S. depots in France. In June McNamara further authorized the movement from French to German facilities of stocks required to support 60 combat days for U.S. forces; he rejected Wheeler's 10 June request to build two new storage depots for the materiel.[17]

The Chiefs argued on 1 August that concentrating so much materiel at so few depots in Germany left it more vulnerable to "ground attack, sabotage, and infiltration." In a subsequent memorandum of 19 August they contended that war reserves stocks must remain at a "reasonable safety margin" of 90 combat days; to achieve that level they recommended building new depots in Britain. McNamara questioned the wisdom of a British base and requested the Chiefs provide him with further analysis of their position before he reached a final decision.[18]

McNamara's plan to reduce American ammunition stockages officially signaled OSD's retreat from its long-held position that the NATO allies had to build their supply levels to U.S. criteria. It acknowledged that American logistics standards exceeded European capabilities to such an extent that the allies' entire stockpile of conventional bombs amounted to less than the United States dropped in 10 days in Vietnam. From the European perspective, however, it made no sense to stock ammunition and supplies for a large conventional war because they believed any conflict would go nuclear within a few days.[19]

During June and July the Chiefs and McNamara continued to debate the redeployment of aerial units from France. The military wanted four air squadrons to remain in Europe while McNamara favored three, all stationed in Great Britain. A late July revision of McNamara's April DPM by Systems Analysis specifically incorporated the defense secretary's emphasis on dual-basing of tactical aircraft though it toned down the recurring and more controversial debate between Enthoven and the Joint Chiefs over exactly how many U.S. aircraft were needed in NATO. While the Joint Chiefs had expected to maintain air bases in France, perhaps as dual-basing installations, the French foreign minister made clear in early August 1966 that France would grant the U.S. reentry rights only in the event of a war in which his country was a participant. Because the United States could no longer depend on French bases in support of NATO operations, McNamara instructed the Joint Chiefs and appropriate European commanders to plan for the withdrawal of all Air Force personnel and salvageable property from France. By this time only a few dozen U.S. tactical reconnaissance aircraft remained in France, the rest—77 aircraft—having been redeployed to Vietnam or CONUS by late spring 1966.[20] Most of the tactical and transport aircraft still in France relocated to 10 British bases and one German airfield.

McNamara's finalized 21 September 1966 DPM reaffirmed his April proposals. He recommended 60 combat-day levels for stockages in Europe and redeployment of American support troops from France to the United States. Furthermore, he alerted Johnson that OSD was considering "substantial reductions" of U.S. ground forces in Europe, dual-basing of air units, and a reexamination of the assumptions behind the Strategic Army Forces (STRAF) commitment to NATO to determine the optimum reinforcing capability. These measures had become possible because overestimates of the capability of Soviet and Warsaw Pact forces had led to grossly exaggerated requirements for NATO forces. Lastly, the secretary doubted that the loss of the French rear base significantly degraded NATO capabilities, but it did render U.S. support troops in France superfluous.[21]

In early October the Chiefs produced a specific proposal for British bases as McNamara had previously requested. They argued the British option was cost-effective and cheaper in relocation and operating costs than comparable facilities in the United States. Moreover, it had the added advantages of depth and dispersion that reduced risking loss of critical war materiel in forward areas of Germany. McNamara wanted to return the war stocks to the United States but, concerned over the Chiefs' estimates for resupplying forces in Europe from U.S. bases, he requested further study of the issue. By early November, however, 156,000 short-tons of war reserve and stocks had to leave France; the Joint Chiefs noted it was cheaper to place them in Britain than the United States, pending study completion and high-level discussions on future NATO policy then in progress. On 12 December 1966 the defense secretary approved the JCS recommendation to stock the materiel in the United Kingdom, subject to limitations on one-time relocation costs governing construction and rehabilitation of facilities and personnel.[22]

Understandings on the alliance's use of the oil pipeline and its access to French airspace had to be hammered out. The JCS had earlier specified POL resupply as a major difficulty; the existing pipeline could barely meet wartime requirements. McNamara had approved their recommendation to build storage tanks in the Benelux countries and/or Germany. However, hidden costs greatly exceeding the original estimate caused the Chiefs to propose a halt to the storage tank project, leaving the alliance dependent on the French-controlled pipeline. Fortunately de Gaulle proved flexible, assuring NATO in March 1967 of the continued use of the pipeline in peacetime, although not guaranteeing wartime utilization. Also, in mid-March 1967 the French government extended U.S. overflight rights beyond the 1 April deadline for withdrawal with the stipulation that Paris would approve such flights on a month-to-month not an annual basis as formerly. In early August 1967, Paris informed Washington that as of January 1968 it would resume permitting overflights on an annual basis.[23]

The French withdrawal offered DoD the opportunity to achieve its long discussed and much debated changes in U.S. force structure in NATO and to do so without extended negotiations with alliance members. Withdrawals involved large-scale reductions in U.S. NATO forces. Combat and support units plus military and civilian personnel departed Europe as the base infrastructure was dismantled. Dual-basing of USAF aircraft, previously considered by OSD as still another way to economize on U.S. defense spending for NATO, became a reality. While withdrawing forces, OSD also promoted a new strategy that emphasized conventional forces, a contradiction not lost on the Europeans.

The consequences of French withdrawal from NATO military commitments, less dire than doomsayers predicted, nevertheless brought fundamental change to the alliance. For McNamara the French departure opened the way to address urgent economic, military, and strategic issues facing the alliance. OSD, carefully calculating the costs of relocating American forces from France, gave less attention to the purely military implications of the French defection. Decisions about relocation further strained relations between OSD and the Joint Chiefs. McNamara's preference for cost-effective and money-saving solutions seemed to the military to ignore or misrepresent the serious military threat NATO faced. The JCS argued that new facilities and retention of all U.S. forces elsewhere in Europe could preserve the status quo ante, while McNamara sought to establish a precedent for future unilateral U.S. troop withdrawals.

The Nuclear Planning Group

McNamara's instinctual aversion to reliance on nuclear weapons to deter, and if necessary, defend against Soviet attack spurred him on in his efforts to persuade both the NATO allies and the Soviet Union to forego or at least severely limit the use of the nuclear option. With France no longer present to obstruct U.S. initiatives, it became possible to give serious thought to changing NATO policies and strategy.

The defense secretary's efforts at the Athens meeting in 1962[*] to moderate the nuclear views of the other NATO countries met with little success. NATO ministerial guidance issued there called for a nuclear response to a Soviet nuclear attack against the alliance and, if necessary, the use of nuclear weapons against a Soviet full-scale conventional attack. Otherwise, use of nuclear weapons by the alliance would be subject to prior consultation with the North Atlantic Council. Although the so-called Athens Guidelines had implicitly acknowledged that the alliance might not necessarily use nuclear weapons against a Warsaw Pact conventional attack, NATO's strategy and force structure remained fashioned to wage a general nuclear war. For the European allies this seemed a cheaper alternative than maintaining large conventional forces, more so because before 1966 most NATO nuclear planning was done by the United States, which did not inform its European partners, with the exception of the United Kingdom, of nuclear weapon plans.[24]

This imposed ignorance left the nonnuclear European allies on the outside unable to plan seriously for the consequences of Soviet retaliation in kind, the possibility of escalation into general war, or the devastation likely from the use of tactical nuclear weapons. Believing that once the allies more fully understood the futility

[*] See Kaplan et al, *McNamara Ascendancy*, 305ff.

of use of nuclear weapons they would endorse flexible response, McNamara determined to give them a greater voice in alliance nuclear planning and consultation as a means of raising their awareness of the complex and perhaps insoluble consequences of nuclear warfare. By convincing the allies that they did not need nuclear hardware he hoped to "end talk of the Multilateral Force," a policy originally conceived as a means for alliance members to share nuclear weapons. In particular McNamara believed that giving Germany a substantially greater voice in alliance nuclear planning, consultation, and responsibility would relieve German pressure for nuclear weapon sharing and ensure the Bonn government's support for nuclear nonproliferation talks between the United States and USSR then in progress.*[25]

McNamara's vehicle of enlightenment eventually grew out of his suggestion at the NATO defense ministers meeting in Paris in late May 1965 that the formation of a "Select Committee," composed of four or five NATO defense ministers, would enable the allies to participate in nuclear planning. He wanted a limited membership, perceiving "a very direct inverse relationship between the number of participants and the degree or extent of accomplishment." By insisting further that only defense ministers could participate in deliberations he expected to avoid the ritualized sessions typical of international meetings. After much work, including changes that increased the committee's membership, the NATO defense ministers meeting in Paris in November 1965 established a Special Committee to provide further allied participation in nuclear planning and improve the consultation process among alliance members.[26]

Following France's withdrawal from NATO's military structure, the NAC gave the Defense Planning Committee (DPC), established in 1963 to oversee NATO force planning, responsibility for all defense matters in which France no longer participated. For political reasons, the Special Committee included 10 of the 14 Defense Planning Committee members.† McNamara acceded to the larger committee membership because he expected the United States, Great Britain, and West Germany would "coordinate and run it behind the scenes." He was not completely successful, as Italy and Germany had their own agendas. The Italians insisted on inclusion in any nuclear planning arrangement and the Germans, dubious about mere consultation, still desired common ownership and management of nuclear weapons.[27]

At the last minute, the Dutch representative, ignoring the defense ministers' informal consensus on organization and assignments reached beforehand, insisted on five- rather than four-member working groups. Thus the Special Committee, now including representatives of all NATO member countries, organized itself into three five-member working groups to conduct its business. The most important by design, Working Group III, also known as the Nuclear Planning Working Group (NPWG), included defense ministers from the United States, United Kingdom,

---

* See Chapter XII.
† Portugal and Norway were not considering candidacy for the nuclear planning group at this time. Iceland and Luxembourg were non-joiners.

West Germany, Italy, and Turkey (selected by lot as the fifth member). It had the responsibility to recommend ways to improve and expand participation in planning for the use of nuclear weapons to defend NATO.

Between February and September 1966 the NPWG held four meetings to consider nuclear policy matters and the creation of a permanent organizational structure to deal with NATO nuclear matters. The ministers dealt with a variety of nuclear issues, including first use of nuclear weapons and the role of tactical nuclear weapons in defense of NATO.[28]

At its fourth and final meeting in Rome, on 23 September 1966, the NPWG recommended to the Special Committee the formation of a permanent organization within NATO to deal with nuclear policy. The Special Committee in turn proposed that the NAC's ministerial meeting in December establish a plenary body, the Nuclear Defense Affairs Committee (NDAC), and a subordinate working group called the Nuclear Planning Group (NPG). The former would propose general policy for the nuclear defense of Europe and advise the DPC on nuclear affairs of the alliance. The latter, composed of five NATO defense ministers and chaired by the NATO secretary general, would perform the detailed work involved in nuclear planning and prepare specific proposals for the NDAC. In mid-December 1966, the NATO ministerial meeting in Paris approved the Rome report, but committee memberships and length of tenure on the permanent committees required additional compromises by McNamara.[29]

McNamara's strong preference for a small group of ministers to comprise the NPG was thwarted by the insistence of nations other than the United Kingdom and Germany that they be included in the NPG. The defense secretary acquiesced to Italian demands for a seven-member NPG in lieu of the five he felt was the maximum number to conduct affairs candidly and efficiently, resulting in four permanent NPG members—the United States, the United Kingdom, Germany, and Italy—and three rotating ones, although they were not referred to as such. McNamara also gave way on his preference for a one-year appointment when the Dutch representative wanted a two-year term. A "gentleman's agreement" split the difference by approving 18-month tenures. Compromises made and bargaining completed, in mid-December 1966 at the NATO ministerial meeting in Paris, the DPC officially created NDAC and the NPG.[30]

McNamara's design for a limited, and therefore manageable and efficient, committee had to yield to the allies' demands for inclusiveness and greater say. Still he rightly praised the NPWG "for the very great progress" of the past two years in nuclear planning. At an April 1967 press conference, he passed on without attribution British Defense Minister Denis Healey's recent remark "that there had been more progress in NATO nuclear matters in the past 12 months than in the preceding 17 years."[31]

As formally constituted, NATO's nuclear planning organization had a three-tiered arrangement. The Defense Planning Committee represented all NATO members except France which had left the DPC. Within the DPC, a Nuclear Defense Affairs Committee included 12 of the 14 DPC member nations* and within NDAC came the Nuclear Planning Group. The NPG consisted of NATO defense ministers while the NDAC could meet with both defense and foreign ministers present or at the NATO Permanent Representative level. For ministers to achieve the expertise and sophistication demanded for such active involvement, however, required thorough and extensive preparations by their staffs, a condition that, according to Paul Warnke, encouraged later "ballooning attendance and excess of paper." By April 1968 the NPG meetings routinely saw each of seven ministers bring four advisers and the NATO Secretary General bring three staff members, which together with the presence of the chairman of the NATO Military Committee and SACEUR made for a minimum of 41 attendees per session.[32]

The NPG's creation was a tribute to McNamara's determination and flexibility. After initial skepticism among the Europeans, his personal involvement and willingness to speak candidly about strategic and tactical nuclear weapons planning led the NPG to deal "frankly with mutual doubts and common problems."[33] His commitment helped convince doubters of the merit of his proposals. McNamara now had a structure within NATO to inform the Europeans further about the complexities of nuclear war and the two-edged use of tactical nuclear weapons for deterrence and defense on the continent.

The first meeting of the NPG defense ministers, held in Washington on 6–7 April 1967, endorsed the adequacy of NATO's nuclear forces to deter a large-scale Soviet attack but reaffirmed that the alliance's use of nuclear weapons could not prevent unacceptable damage to NATO countries. Further confirming the earlier NPWG's April 1966 assessments, the ministers also accepted the adequacy of tactical nuclear weapons available to the alliance. They concurred on the importance of developing plans for NATO's first-use of tactical nuclear weapons, if necessary, "in response to an aggression less than general war." Although the Athens Guidelines approved that possibility, uncertainty lingered over the military advantage, if any, the alliance might gain from such action. The conundrum was apparent. If using only a handful of the 7,000 tactical nuclear weapons in Europe resulted in national suicide, particularly for Germany, how could NATO expect to fight a war with them? Could tactical nuclear weapons even serve as an effective deterrent? Was it possible to employ low-yield weapons and avoid mass casualties and destruction? These were the basic questions and complex issues related to overall NATO strategy and force structure that the NPG had to address.[34]

McNamara's actions between the April meeting and the September 1967 session in Ankara undermined his stated principle of consultation among allies about nuclear weapons. At the April meeting, he had forcefully argued against ABM

---

* NDAC member countries were: Belgium, Canada, Denmark, Germany, Greece, Italy, Netherlands, Norway, Portugal, Turkey, the United Kingdom, and the United States. Iceland and Luxembourg were not represented.

deployment and for greater consultation. NPG ministers in turn had endorsed his stand against any ABM system.* On 18 September 1967, when McNamara publicly announced that the United States would deploy a limited ABM system, he stunned the NPG ministers because he had not consulted with them in advance, merely informing them of the decision a few days beforehand.[35]

At the 28–29 September 1967 Ankara meeting McNamara's rationale that the American ABM was directed against China, making it unnecessary to consult the NPG, only aggravated the European defense ministers' displeasure. Healey denounced the lack of promised prior consultation, but McNamara countered that he had no evidence the allies wanted consultations on matters related to a Chinese threat. The sting felt especially painful because McNamara's actions nullified his words and threatened the concept of the NPG as a meaningful forum for consultation.[36]

Although rancor over the ABM decision highlighted the Ankara meeting, the ministers found time to discuss a wide variety of nuclear policy issues on the agenda, including the possibility of a European-based ABM system that they determined merited further study. Preliminary conversations about tactical employment of nuclear weapons in NATO's Central Region, led by the Germans, convinced members that the German government should complete its analysis on tactical use of nuclear weapons for the next meeting. In doing so they should follow the Athens Guidelines and the newly issued DPC guidance of 9 May 1967 that defined tactical nuclear weapons as "an essential component" of NATO's deterrent.[37]

Meeting for the first time at the ministerial level in Brussels on 12 December 1967, the NDAC, after receiving a status report from the NPG, encouraged it to continue its studies and submit recommendations as soon as it could do so; it agreed also that consultation on the use of nuclear weapons would remain permanently on its agenda. At its 10 May 1968 meeting, the NDAC endorsed NPG recommendations to increase national participation in nuclear planning.[38]

In November 1967, Karl Carstens, first state secretary in the West German Ministry of Defense, proposed to Deputy Secretary Nitze a greater role for Germany in NATO nuclear planning and in consultations on the use of nuclear weapons on German soil. In March 1968 Clifford and Rusk recommended, and the president approved, a confidential arrangement allowing prior consultation before selective release of nuclear weapons in Germany with an understanding that the United States would not release the weapons to German units without confirmation by the German government. OSD supported as "desirable goals" the German position that an expression of general principles would resolve the release issue at the upcoming NPG meeting and satisfy the other members without getting into the specifics of the confidential U.S.-German negotiations on the matter.[39]

---

* See Chapter XIV.

At the 18–19 April 1968 NPG meeting in The Hague, ministers approved as a general principle the German desire that nuclear consultations give "special weight" to the views of NATO countries directly affected. They also discussed several studies, notably the German tactical nuclear report, as they developed political guidelines and military doctrine governing the use of tactical nuclear weapons.[40]

To allay suspicion that the United States was either not serious about using tactical nuclear weapons or had stacked the deck to prove such weapons could not be used and could "therefore be withdrawn," Clifford followed Ambassador Cleveland's advice and reassured his European colleagues that their work to date was valuable. Participating in his first NPG meeting, Clifford, like McNamara, would dwell on the "grave dilemmas" involved in the use of tactical nuclear weapons, insist that "dogmatic conclusions" be avoided, and encourage the ministers to formulate fundamental principles or doctrine to overcome the generalizations about tactical nuclear weapons that characterized their studies to date. He pursued the theme of continuity in nuclear planning policy—between himself and McNamara and between the United States and the European allies. At his suggestion, the ministers responded by approving continued work on four guideline papers* for the next meeting.[41]

The 10–11 October NPG meeting in Bonn convened under the shadow of the recent Soviet invasion of Czechoslovakia. The defense ministers exchanged ideas about employing tactical nuclear weapons for purposes of a demonstration, for self-defense, against battlefield targets, and for a war at sea. The familiar points of contention arose. Europeans regarded nuclear weapons primarily as deterrent against any level of aggression, while the U.S. side expressed greater concern about the risk of escalation and damage limitation in a nuclear war. The Bonn meeting did not resolve the issue, but NPG members did decide that the British and Germans should continue to refine their position papers on initial use of tactical nuclear weapons on land and at sea for the May 1969 meeting in London. This meant that for the first time European nations, including nonnuclear Germany, held responsibility for developing guidelines for the initial use of nuclear weapons. These studies in fact became the basis for NATO's provisional guidelines governing the initial defensive use of tactical nuclear weapons adopted by the NPG in November and by NATO in December 1969.[42]

Creation of the NPG thus gave the European allies a larger role in alliance nuclear planning and provided a forum for high-level discussion of fundamental, longstanding questions about the nature of nuclear war in Europe. As McNamara anticipated, by sharing in the nuclear planning process the allies underwent a learning experience that forced them to reconsider the consequences of nuclear

---

* The United States examined the use of nuclear weapons for demonstration purposes, West Germany for battlefield use, Great Britain for maritime use, and Italy for defensive use (atomic mines and nuclear air defense). See Daalder, *The Nature and Practice of Flexible Response*, 72.

warfare. Nevertheless, despite his deep-felt personal involvement, including formal NATO ministerial meetings and active leadership in the NPG, McNamara could never completely overcome the European notion that security ultimately depended on nuclear weapons. His clumsy handling of the ABM decision only reinforced the European perception that the United States looked out for its interests first, not Europe's. Even the allies' embrace of flexible response remained conditional on the NPG continually reviewing and updating NATO's nuclear needs and the continued presence of U.S. tactical nuclear weapons at SACEUR's disposal.[43]

Flexible Response

Flexible response posited that sole reliance on nuclear weapons to deter or meet communist aggression was unrealistic, that it was essential to be able to respond selectively and proportionately to various levels of attack—from localized hostilities to all-out nuclear war. This approach required that greater emphasis be placed on the use of conventional forces to meet most contingencies and relegated nuclear forces from first-choice response to last resort. The ability to respond to attack at any level would strengthen the overall allied deterrent.[44] This was the essence of McNamara's concept of flexible response.*

Evolving conditions in Eastern Europe, the continuing growth of the Soviet nuclear threat, and the booming prosperity of Western Europe's postwar recovery shaped OSD's analysis of the appropriate NATO strategy for the 1960s and beyond. By mid-1964, the CIA had detected a loosening of Moscow's influence in Eastern Europe, a trend that continued to gain momentum in 1965 as rising nationalism in the satellite states gradually "whittled away" Soviet control. This "transformation of the Communist Bloc," concluded McNamara, made an all-out Soviet attack on NATO unlikely in the foreseeable future. The intelligence community's assessments meshed nicely with the secretary's assessment that NATO's existing strategy was unsatisfactory because of its overemphasis on general nuclear war.[45]

NATO Military Committee Document MC 14/2 (Revised) of April 1957, the alliance's strategic military directive, anticipated fighting a general nuclear war, including first use of nuclear weapons, if necessary. There was no "NATO concept of limited war with the Soviets." So long as the West had enjoyed an absolute and then a relative nuclear advantage against the USSR, the threat of tactical nuclear weapons wreaking disproportionate damage on Soviet forces and territory had deterred conventional aggression, in effect compensating for NATO's weaker conventional forces. As that advantage diminished, the specter emerged of a theater nuclear exchange in a thickly populated region inflicting unacceptable damage on both adversaries

---

* Heuser, *NATO, Britain, France and the FRG*, 53, offers an alternative term of "flexible escalation." While agreeing with her analysis, I retained "flexible response" for its familiarity to American readers.

and possibly escalating to general nuclear war.[46] To avoid this catastrophe, McNamara's new approach of flexible response proposed an expansion and improvement of the alliance's conventional forces that would enable them to withstand a major Soviet nonnuclear assault in Central Europe without recourse to nuclear weapons.

The export version of the U.S. doctrine of flexible response met a cool reception or outright rejection across the Atlantic. Determined to free France from an American-dominated NATO, President de Gaulle emerged as the outspoken opponent of a shift away from massive retaliation and a vociferous proponent of the need for an independent nuclear force, his *force de frappe*. The French attitude doomed any attempt to alter NATO's MC 14/2 (Revised) strategy during the early 1960s. The British and West Germans, although more willing to discuss flexible response, entertained serious doubts that conventional forces alone could stop a Soviet attack against Western Europe. They expected early use of nuclear weapons in any conflict; the Germans worried greatly that the Americans would not authorize the use of nuclear weapons in time to prevent large areas of their country from being overrun.[47] Other NATO allies generally agreed that they could never afford to build conventional forces capable of matching those of the Eastern Bloc. Consequently they preferred to rely on strategic or tactical nuclear weapons as the cheapest and most effective means of defense. OSD's policies in the mid-1960s of increasing tactical nuclear weapons in Europe while decreasing U.S. conventional forces only reaffirmed the allies' belief that conventional forces of the scale McNamara proposed were unnecessary so long as the Europeans remained under the American nuclear umbrella.

McNamara justified the deployment of tactical nuclear weapons to Western Europe on political, not military grounds. As he told President Johnson, the weapons were there. To remove them would only create European concerns about an imminent U.S. withdrawal or arouse fears that Washington intended to restrict future wars to Europe, leaving the United States and Soviet Union unscathed. Nor could McNamara renege on commitments made during the Eisenhower administration to increase NATO's tactical nuclear stockpiles. The secretary grudgingly acknowledged that the tactical nuclear arsenal deterred first-use of nuclear weapons by the Soviets, likely had some conventional deterrent value, and was a last-ditch hedge against the collapse of NATO's conventional forces. But for McNamara the presence of tactical nuclear weapons in Europe remained a sop—it reassured the allies of U.S. willingness to use all necessary weapons in their defense; it avoided a bitter confrontation with his military service chiefs; and it still permitted him to pursue his advocacy of conventional force structures.[48] Yet the presence of so many tactical nuclear weapons in Europe could easily lead to misunderstanding or deliberate misinterpretation of America's revised nuclear policy for NATO.

Despite the substantial accomplishments of the NPWG in fostering a reconsideration of nuclear warfare, by the end of 1966 McNamara complained that the allies still refused to increase conventional defense outlays to the levels he deemed adequate. Indeed, the trend was running the other way. On the other hand, French withdrawal from NATO military arrangements during 1966 had freed the alliance to press ahead with recasting military strategy. Here too McNamara did not get all he expected.[49]

During the first half of 1966, Wheeler and his German military counterpart narrowed points of disagreement over a new strategy, but the Germans, still dubious about the efficacy of conventional defense, were unwilling to forego nuclear options. Building on this limited progress, on 7 October an informal meeting of the Military Committee (MC) reviewed NATO's military strategy and recommended a more flexible approach to meet varying contingencies. Shortly afterward at a 10 November trilateral meeting,* representatives from Germany, Great Britain, and the United States agreed that the alliance needed "a full spectrum of military capabilities" including nuclear and conventional forces. John J. McCloy, the U.S. representative to the talks, informed the president that he viewed a NATO strategy of flexible response as "essential for US security." Given the consensus among the three major military members of the alliance, the other allies, after initial complaints about the "self-appointed group,"[50] agreed to review NATO's military strategy. Meaningful participation in deliberations likely made the other allies receptive to a strategic reappraisal by reassuring them that they would retain a voice in the formulation of alliance military policy.

At the 12–13 December 1966 meeting the MC chiefs of staff approved the proposal to prepare a new directive to replace MC 14/2. The following February the International Military Staff (IMS), the executive agent for the Military Committee, circulated a draft concept for a new military strategy. The JCS and Vance identified problems with the draft—notably the concept of warning time as well as exaggerated estimates of Soviet conventional and strategic nuclear capabilities—but accepted it for planning purposes. At its 9 May 1967 meeting in Brussels the Defense Planning Committee gave approval to the military authorities to continue work toward a possible revision of military strategy to encompass nuclear and conventional capabilities. Military planners were also tasked to correct imbalances in conventional forces, taking into account the important proviso that the alliance would likely receive sufficient warning of Soviet aggression in time to mobilize and deploy its forces to meet the threat. The aim was to reaffirm reliance on nuclear weapons while seeking to strike a compromise between the Europeans' preference for modest conventional forces and Washington's goal of strong conventional forces that could check Soviet aggression without resorting to nuclear weapons.[51]

Responding to the DPC's guidance, the International Military Staff circulated a draft MC 14/3 redefining NATO's "defense concept" in terms of flexible response. In June the European allies reached a "general consensus" on the new strategy; on 1 July 1967 the Joint Chiefs advised McNamara that the draft was

---

* See Chapter XV section on the Tripartite Talks.

generally satisfactory. Harboring misgivings about differences between military and ministerial guidance over nuclear weapons policy, in mid-August McNamara insisted that ministerial wording prevail before authorizing the U.S. representative to the MC to help finalize MC 14/3.[52]

The resulting defense concept, approved by the NATO chiefs of staff in mid-September and adopted by the DPC on 12 December 1967, formally articulated a version of McNamara's flexible response strategy in MC 14/3 of January 1968. To gain approval the United States had accepted a compromise "that committed NATO to respond at whatever level of force—conventional or nuclear—was chosen by the aggressor." At the time McNamara admitted to the president that "after years of effort" NATO's strategic objectives still fell short of "providing for a capability to deal successfully with any kind of nonnuclear attack without using nuclear weapons ourselves."[53] He no doubt had in mind the continuing failure of the European members to provide conventional forces adequate to make a reality of MC 14/3.

Neither the formation of the NPG nor the revision of NATO's military strategy fully achieved McNamara's intended goals, although certainly not from lack of effort on his part. The secretary threw himself wholeheartedly into NATO planning perhaps, as a former aide has suggested, because it "distracted him from his agonies over Vietnam."[54] The linkage between NATO and Vietnam, however, was inescapable.

NATO and Vietnam

Besides distracting Washington's attention from Europe, the demands of Vietnam strained the U.S. forces committed to NATO far beyond what anyone in OSD had imagined in the summer of 1965. McNamara's credibility with Europeans suffered as he encouraged the allies to modernize and strengthen their national forces while he simultaneously deferred modernization and weakened U.S. conventional forces committed to NATO. As U.S. involvement in Vietnam deepened, the withdrawals undercut OSD's exhortations to NATO for strong conventional capabilities.[55]

Alliance members formally committed and identified forces available to NATO when responding to the annual Defense Planning Review Questionnaire (DPQ). Protocols dating from 1955 mandated that substantive changes to prospective force contributions or withdrawals to meet an emergency elsewhere be immediately reported to NATO military authorities and the NAC. When the attack carrier *Independence* left for Vietnam waters in June 1965, OSD, as required, informed the NAC that the warship's status changed from Category A (available to NATO within 48 hours after M-Day) to Category B (available from 48 hours to M+30 days). Beginning in the fall of 1965 OSD similarly reported the recurring withdrawals of U.S. Air Force tactical fighter and reconnaissance squadrons from Europe to Vietnam. In mid-September 1965 General Lemnitzer cautioned that shipments of ammunition and other combat equipment bound for Vietnam from French ports might prove embarrassing to Washington, especially given McNamara's previous insistence that no U.S. troops or material would move from Europe to Vietnam.[56] As redeployments of units and shipments of war supplies continued, the administration worried about the political fallout in NATO from further withdrawals.

To meet increased air support requirements in Vietnam, on 31 March 1966 the JCS proposed that the attack carrier *Franklin D. Roosevelt*, then assigned to Atlantic Command, be temporarily deployed to Pacific Command for nine months commencing in July. With an endorsement by Enthoven, on 11 June Vance approved the recommendation. Emphasis on temporary deployments would allay fears among the allies that the United States was permanently withdrawing committed forces at a time when "disruptive influences were at work within the NATO structure."[57] By mid-1966 the growing demands of the Vietnam fighting had put the squeeze on numerous U.S. naval and air units assigned to Europe. Warships, however, operated tens or hundreds of miles off European shores and were rarely seen except during port calls. Similarly aircraft were always coming or going so the average European would hardly notice their absence. But the many thousands of American GIs and airmen and their families stationed in Europe would quickly be missed if they departed.

The most visible and politically sensitive evidence of U.S. support to NATO was the five-plus Army divisions stationed in Germany backed by U.S. commitment of six additional reinforcing divisions from the Strategic Army Forces available in an emergency. These conventional forces were the centerpiece of McNamara's flexible response strategy. During the initial Vietnam buildup in the summer of 1965, McNamara insisted the U.S. Army had to maintain its strength in Europe as programmed. Without an imminent Soviet threat, however, he saw no need in the near future to reinforce Europe from the STRAF. This assessment allowed him to draw heavily on STRAF units to support the Vietnam deployments, a necessity occasioned by President Johnson's July 1965 decisions neither to call up reserve units nor to degrade the U.S. commitment to NATO. During the last half of 1965, the Army tapped about 130,000 STRAF personnel to expand its training base or to deploy to Vietnam. In late November when more troops were needed for Vietnam, McNamara turned to Europe. He proposed units there be made available for Vietnam service despite the fears of others that the decision would "maybe tear hell out of Europe."[58]

By January 1966 the magnitude of the Vietnam deployments caused the JCS to inform McNamara of the dangers of diverting NATO-reinforcing STRAF units to Vietnam. In starkest terms, the fewer the conventional forces available to defend Europe the more likely the need to resort to nuclear weapons earlier than anticipated. Yet Vietnam demanded still more troops. To fulfill Westmoreland's troop requirements identified at the February 1966 Honolulu Conference, McNamara ordered the Chiefs to meet the even larger Vietnam Phase IIa deployment schedule, once again without benefit of reserve mobilization or tour-of-service extensions.[59] By this time U.S. forces in NATO were the only sizable units relatively unscathed by the buildup, but even they could not accommodate MACV's ambitious reinforcement timetable.

The Army would have to draw down at least 58,800 servicemen from Europe, including those highly skilled in aviation maintenance, construction, and signal specialties. The Air Force would have to withdraw four tactical reconnaissance and six tactical fighter squadrons comprising 7,000 personnel. The Navy's share would amount to a Marine Corps battalion landing team from the Sixth Fleet as well as 6,500 personnel from the Atlantic Command, thereby reducing 38 combatant ships to a one-third manning level. Repeating their warning that such drawdowns would necessitate even greater reliance on the early employment of nuclear weapons in a war, on 1 March 1966 the JCS proposed spreading the latest Vietnam reinforcements over 16 months into mid-1967 instead of cramming them into the remaining 10 months of 1966.[60]

McNamara agreed to stretch out deployments to Vietnam, but the cost to U.S. forces in Europe still remained high. Reductions claimed approximately half to two-thirds of the USAF reconnaissance aircraft immediately available to NATO. Besides having earlier transferred 10,000 enlisted men possessing critical skills to Vietnam, the Department of the Army exacted another 20,000 European-based troops for Southeast Asia service. For the first time the strength of U.S. Army, Europe fell eight percent below authorization, which, when combined with the loss of officers and enlisted specialists, reduced combat effectiveness for "several months." Ultimately Vietnam requirements claimed more than 1,000 Army aviators and nearly 30,000 Army skilled enlisted personnel from NATO assignments, almost all between January and July 1966. McNamara spoke in terms of a temporary drawdown of 15,000 troops to be replaced by the end of 1966; actually 55,000 U.S. servicemen based in West Germany went to Vietnam and were replaced by 40,000 newly trained recruits. The extent of the withdrawals was kept secret from the American public, who were informed only of the 15,000-man reduction.[61]

To make matters worse, leaks within the administration led to informed press speculation about these troop withdrawals before the government could officially notify NATO or even informally tell German authorities. McNamara compounded that slight and added to German confusion by failing to contact his German counterpart about the decisions after the story broke.[62] McNamara could protest to his European counterparts that the drawdowns were temporary and would be made good by year's end, but they could plainly see that Vietnam now had top priority on U.S. troops and equipment.

This diversion of units from their NATO role, together with using four of the six CONUS-based active divisions for training and processing new recruits, eroded U.S. capability for prompt dispatch of reinforcements to Europe. Indicative of this turmoil, in April 1966 the CONUS-based strategic reserve was changed from a tank-heavy, European-oriented configuration of one mechanized and two armored divisions to a weaker, more generally oriented force of one mechanized, one infantry, and one airborne division.[63] Even as STRAF's stateside readiness declined, McNamara was considering further reductions to U.S. general purpose forces in Europe.

OSD-directed studies conducted during 1966 had convinced McNamara that NATO far overrated the size and capabilities of Warsaw Pact armies. Systems Analysis accordingly proposed to replace the current U.S. 11-division commitment to NATO with an 8-division force (5 divisions in Europe and 3 from the STRAF). Enthoven expected that the change would compel the military to rethink and justify their recommendations for large Europe-oriented forces. As he anticipated, his radical proposals reignited controversy between McNamara and the JCS over the suitable U.S. force structure for Europe.[64]

McNamara's 1 August preliminary DPM on NATO strategy and force structure incorporated the Systems Analysis projections. The JCS reacted sharply, pronouncing the DPM flawed militarily because it underestimated the capabilities of the Warsaw Pact, overestimated available warning time of impending attack, and overlooked the possible absence of French support during wartime operations. Rejecting any reduction in U.S. military strength in Europe and warning of the consequences of U.S. "withdrawals and restructuring" on NATO, they concluded that the document "cannot be supported on military grounds." Since the British had already declared their intention to reduce forces in Germany, any U.S. withdrawals might spark a chain reaction as other members followed France out of the alliance or cut their forces, thereby further reducing NATO's military capabilities.[65]

This development, Sen. Mike Mansfield's call in late August 1966 for a substantial reduction of U.S. forces in Europe, and White House statements on troop reductions made around the same time convinced Wheeler by early September that the tentative, as yet unannounced, decision to withdraw larger numbers of troops from Europe was in the works. As Wheeler anticipated, McNamara overrode JCS objections and advised the president that unless the European allies did more for their own defense, an outcome he regarded as improbable, a major reorganization of U.S. forces in Europe to reduce overhead along with additional redeployments from Europe were inevitable.[66]

McNamara's 21 September 1966 DPM proposal formally endorsed Enthoven's recommendation for reducing support personnel in Europe, judging the commitment of 11 U.S. divisions to NATO excessive in light of the recent reassessment of Soviet and Warsaw Pact capabilities. McNamara believed an eight-division force (a combination of the three committed M-Day divisions in the United States plus the five divisions stationed in Europe) offered a rough parity with Warsaw Pact ground forces, a contention hotly disputed by the JCS. Lastly, and once again contrary to JCS advice, McNamara reduced from 90 to 60 days the authorized war reserve stocks for U.S. forces in Europe and cut total procurement for the forces in Europe from 180 to 90 days stockage.[67] OSD had previously maintained a fully supported force structure for Europeans to emulate. By late 1966, in an effort to hold down his ballooning Defense budget, McNamara dictated lower supply levels in Europe. This left U.S. forces in NATO to gradually live off their existing stockpiles while he reprogrammed funds otherwise earmarked for European procurement into Vietnam requirements. This also left fewer troops with less equipment to meet still formidable Western European military requirements.

In early October 1966, responding to CINCPAC's latest requests for Southeast Asia reinforcements, the JCS advised McNamara that, if the services complied, the resulting personnel and equipment shortages would leave the Army until mid-1968 with only two airborne brigades to reinforce NATO. CONUS-based tactical air forces would be entirely committed to a training role by late 1967, leaving them 32 squadrons short of their NATO requirements. Redeploying naval vessels from the Mediterranean to reinforce Seventh Fleet's requirements would diminish CINCLANT's capability to respond to contingencies between 20 and 50 percent throughout 1967. Significant withdrawals of equipment from reserve formations to support new units in the active forces had so hampered reserve training that mobilization would only marginally accelerate Army deployments to Southeast Asia. The Chiefs concluded the services could not meet CINCPAC's adjusted requirements; doing so even on a delayed basis would only further impair U.S. worldwide military readiness.[68]

A subsequent DPM on redeployment of U.S. forces from Europe, issued 19 January 1967, recommended pulling out two U.S. divisions from Europe in a rotation arrangement and dual-basing more than 400 U.S. aircraft previously deployed at Western European bases. This arrangement accorded with McNamara's longer-term objective, expressed during policy formulation for the tripartite talks, to reduce U.S. forces in Europe because their excessive numbers exacerbated the balance of payments deficit, created unnecessary expenses, and discouraged the European allies from doing more for their own defense. The Joint Chiefs reiterated their judgment that they perceived no military justification to reduce U.S. forces in Europe. Their arguments reappeared in a vigorous rebuttal of McNamara's January 1967 proposals for redeployments prepared for McCloy's use at the tripartite negotiations.[69]

Nonetheless, McNamara's 29 May 1967 DPM on General Purpose Forces justified the eight-division force, this time because NATO's logistical systems would not be able to sustain the mobilized American divisions on their arrival in Europe. His proposal almost halving U.S. Air Force aircraft in Europe from 1,100 to 576 planes drew fire from the secretary of the Air Force and General McConnell, who characterized it as methodologically flawed with its exclusive focus on close air support and without a strategy useful for force planning. Contending the defense secretary had overstated NATO's capabilities and understated the Warsaw Pact's, the Chiefs again insisted there was no military justification for a reduction of U.S. or allied troops committed to NATO; they wanted the DPM "revised in its entirety." OSD's recommendations entailed "an excessive degree of risk." Citing intelligence estimates and strategic objectives, the JCS called for a 10-division force for NATO. McNamara subsequently approved an 11-division Army force (8 active, 3 reserve), but retained his caveat on the allies lamentable state of logistics.[70]

The strains on NATO created by Vietnam involved much more than shifting, deploying, or reducing military forces in Europe. Paying for the war, which in October 1966 McNamara had concluded would be a long one, stoked inflation at home and worsened the U.S. balance of payments deficit. Congressional leaders and ordinary Americans alike questioned the value of European partners who seemed willing neither to pay for their own defense nor to contribute to the struggle against communism in Vietnam. Demands for wholesale troop reductions in Europe soon reached the White House. The State Department had neatly summed up the problem: the United States needed "to reduce its force levels in Europe in order to meet budgetary and BOP (balance of payments) constraints as well as military requirements elsewhere."[71]

Demands from MACV in March 1967 for another 200,000 men added to pressures to dismantle the U.S. military presence in Europe. The Joint Chiefs now voiced concern that current force ceilings would not allow the United States to prosecute the war in Vietnam decisively and still meet other worldwide military commitments. It was time, they argued, to reconstitute the strategic reserve as well as the NATO-deployed or -committed forces and replenish pre-positioned stocks because, as matters now stood, the much depleted STRAF could not reinforce Europe in a timely manner.[72] The Chiefs' plea for mobilization came in the midst of a high-level review of Vietnam policy and the effect on the economy and federal budget of sending additional large numbers of reinforcements to Southeast Asia. Resolution of the amount of the proposed tax surcharge to help pay for the war, perhaps key to the policy review, also hinged on the mobilization question.

On 5 July 1967, Systems Analysis, contrary to the Joint Chiefs, explained to McNamara that improved personnel management could deploy three and two-thirds division equivalents to MACV by 31 December 1968 without changing tours of duty, calling reserves, or deploying entire units from the strategic reserve forces earmarked for NATO. Nine days later McNamara approved a modified version of these recommendations, rejecting Army requests for increased personnel end strength and actually decreasing personnel by 50,000 soldiers. The tradeoff, however, drew heavily on individual soldiers with critical skills as well as equipment from NATO-committed units, thus temporarily reducing their readiness. With more than 40,000 additional men approved for departure to Vietnam, the strategic reserve received no replacements, greatly reducing the STRAF's ability to reinforce NATO. In place of one mechanized and two armored divisions previously listed as available by M+30, the JCS had to substitute one and one-third airborne divisions.[73]

When the Joint Chiefs proposed notifying the NATO Military Committee that the demands from Saigon rendered three U.S. Army NATO-oriented divisions unable to meet alliance deployment commitments anytime before 1969, OSD staffers "softened or deleted" their language. The Chiefs' "compensating actions" to restore U.S. capability to reinforce NATO involved an "expansion of the active Army structure" that would help to restore normal reinforcing capability.[74] McNamara approved their milder tone in his notification to the NAC. No matter what the wording, at the end of 1967 only one and one-third airborne divisions were available to NATO by M+30. U.S. conventional forces were stretched far too thin to conduct the multiple contingency missions flexible response doctrine assigned them.

McNamara's NATO swan song of December 1967, delivered in his absence by Deputy Secretary Nitze, sounded upbeat about NATO's pending approval of MC 14/3 strategy and the value of alliance discussions in shaping future policy. He pointed to the existence of a state of mutual deterrence in Europe, dismissing military naysayers, who regarded the growing Soviet nuclear arsenal as a destabilizing force. McNamara's words also reminded the high-level audience of his six-year effort to create a balanced, cost-effective, NATO force capable of meeting a Soviet military force "*of any kind or at any level.*" Despite evident gains, the alliance still lacked a well-balanced force structure and the Europeans had yet to take still greater responsibility for their defense. Only near the end of the address did he mention Vietnam, and then only to reassure the Europeans that they retained first claim on U.S. military resources. At the same time he was urging the allies to improve the quality of their forces, the departing secretary was finalizing plans, after some 18 months of tough negotiations within NATO, to withdraw more than 33,000 troops from Germany during 1968. And, in keeping with his revised downward estimate of Warsaw Pact capabilities, McNamara was still proposing to redeploy 524 Air Force aircraft from Europe.[75] By January 1968 when McNamara agreed to the 11-division force for NATO, such issues were moot.

McNamara left the NATO alliance a new strategy, the concept for a new force structure and a greater understanding of nuclear weapons and their use. Simultaneously, he created the perception among the allies of a weakening U.S. commitment to Europe: U.S. air, ground, and naval units in Europe stripped to support Vietnam operations; all U.S. services in Europe lacking adequate logistic support for wartime missions; shortages of trained and experienced personnel; badly diminished quality of the officer and noncommissioned officer corps; and inability of the CONUS strategic reserve in April 1968 to muster a single combat-ready division.[76] In seeking to reduce U.S. forces in Europe and getting the other NATO countries to share more of the burden of troops and money, he had little choice but to subjugate the commitment to the European partners to the dictates of public and congressional opinion at home and the insatiable demands of the Vietnam War.

CHAPTER XV

NATO: BURDEN-SHARING AND U.S. TROOP REDUCTION

Getting the European NATO countries to respond favorably to U.S. initiatives on flexible response and nuclear weapons was closely linked with efforts to persuade them to share a larger part of the cost borne by the United States. During 1965–69 U.S. insistence on greater burden-sharing by the European partners was probably the most charged issue within NATO. The U.S. demands met with resistance and limited success. Efforts to strike a balance between competing priorities resulted in compromises not wholly satisfying to either side. Spurred on by the money requirements of Vietnam and the Great Society, McNamara continually pressed for more resources from European NATO. Given the nature of alliances requiring consensus, especially one with as many diverse members as NATO, negotiations dealing with changes in policy and contributions of men and money were bound to be slow and protracted. McNamara, despite his dynamism as a catalytic agent, could not overcome the European inertia.

Framing the Issue

"Bob McNamara is sometimes torn between his very sound political assessments and his obligations as a salesman of dollar-earning hardware," wrote McGeorge Bundy. "One of our jobs," Bundy informed the president, "is to introduce McNamara the statesman to McNamara the merchant and make sure they do not get in each other's way."[1] By 1965 McNamara's plan to reorganize NATO conventional forces and arm the allies with U.S.-made weapons and equipment united the thinking of statesman and merchant as he attempted to readjust the burden of the defense of Western Europe.

McNamara sought to reduce the more than $4 billion in annual costs to station U.S. forces in Europe. For 1965–67 the average annual deficit between Defense expenditures and receipts on the continent amounted to $500 million, a substantial source of America's balance of payments problem.[2] In the dual role of statesman and merchant, McNamara introduced a flexible response doctrine that emphasized upgrading NATO's conventional ground and air forces to U.S. standards, including arming them with American-made and -bought equipment. If NATO allies shouldered a larger share of their defense, Washington could withdraw major U.S. forces from the continent, saving money and reducing the red ink in the balance of payments ledgers.

European defense ministers, insisting that NATO conventional forces could pose no credible deterrent unless they matched the Warsaw Pact one-to-one, at the same time contended that they could never afford the enormous expense of fielding the 50 to 60 divisions thought needed to counterbalance the Soviet forces. With that option unaffordable, nuclear weapons became all the more necessary to defend Europe. Senior OSD civilian officials, however, felt increasingly certain that overstating the Soviet conventional threat to Europe had skewed NATO's force structure, resulting in overreliance on the nuclear deterrent at the expense of conventional forces.

For McNamara, the quintessential "numbers-cruncher," the figures used to calculate the size and strength of the opposition did not add up. How, the secretary wondered, could two million Soviet servicemen support a combat-ready 175-division force structure when the U.S. Army could squeeze just 16 divisions from half as many men? He set his OSD "whiz kids" to work rechecking the numbers and applying systems analysis methodology to the issue. Assuming that nonviability for the United States meant the same for the USSR, their reevaluation of intelligence data and "more careful analysis" concluded that only 60 to 75 of the newly estimated 120 to 140 Soviet divisions were near full strength and combat ready. Furthermore, Soviet units deployed from the Chinese border to the Berlin Wall obviously could not mass 140 divisions on the NATO front. In January 1965, U.S. intelligence counted 22 first-line Soviet divisions stationed in East Germany and Poland. Reinforced by 23 second-echelon divisions in the western USSR and 5 to 15 satellite divisions, the Warsaw Pact could array between 50 to 60 total divisions against NATO. The numbers and the effectiveness of those divisions remained a contentious issue within NATO because, as McNamara acknowledged early in 1965, "the whole question of the feasibility of a nonnuclear defense turns on this issue." Subsequent refinements completed by October 1965 estimated a maximum of 65 Soviet divisions could be supported in combat. This appeared to show the Pact forces as less overwhelming than believed, so conventional NATO forces could match the Soviets "within approximately current defense budgets and manpower levels."[3]

McNamara had consistently intoned that Western Europe's vulnerability to nonnuclear attack lay in an unbalanced force structure and inefficient allocation of resources. Chronic shortages of equipment, personnel, combat supplies, and support units necessary for sustained combat by active forces, organizational and training deficiencies of reserve formations, and untimely deployment of mobilization units rendered NATO's European armies unready for conventional operations. Furthermore, by continually overrating the Soviet threat Europeans had created exaggerated and thus unattainable conventional force structure goals for NATO members. McNamara determined to break the vicious cycle and implement his strategy of flexible response by creating strong conventional forces that offered NATO affordable options to respond to Soviet aggression at any level. The key lay in more efficient management and proper allocation of available resources.[4]

Force Structures

What were NATO's conventional force requirements? Previous force planning exercises conducted by NATO's Defense Planning Committee became the basis for two sets of proposals for tentative 1970 force goals submitted to the DPC in August 1964 by the major NATO commanders. The first, or "optimum" goal, called ALPHA, required sizable, fully manned and equipped conventional forces of 29 1/3 active and 8 reserve divisions deployed on NATO's Central Front, roughly from the Baltic Sea to the Austrian border. The second, or "acceptable" goal, labeled BRAVO, identified fewer available forces (28 2/3 active and 2 reserve divisions) if members held defense spending to the 1964 level. Bravo and Alpha required respectively gradual NATO military budget increases of 20 to 30 percent to reach a 1970 budget level sufficient to bring forces to full strength with 100 percent weapons and equipment by mobilization day. Based on the OSD comptroller's contentions that the scenarios overinflated prices, required excessive equipment, and ignored otherwise available but non-NATO committed forces, McNamara's 13 October 1965 DPM dismissed both targets as unrealistic financially and in direct conflict with his hypothesis that a credible conventional force structure was available within NATO's current resources.[5] Convincing the European nations of this proposition was a herculean task.

Another study, this one completed by Supreme Headquarters Allied Powers, Europe on 30 April 1965, concluded pessimistically that at most the allies could hold their forward positions against a conventional Soviet attack between just one and three days. If correct, there was little need for NATO to invest in a forlorn hope. The Joint Chiefs criticized the report for overestimating Soviet bloc capabilities, underestimating NATO's, and ignoring U.S. land and air reinforcements. They recommended to both McNamara and the Military Committee that the study be used to revise neither strategic concepts nor force structures. Nonetheless, NATO's Military Committee forwarded the appraisals, without incorporating the

U.S. reservations, to the DPC in June 1965. Undercutting McNamara's precepts for conventional augmentation and modernization, the SHAPE study only hardened the European conviction that conventional defense was "totally infeasible."[6] Refuting the strongly held judgment that conventional defense was either a hopeless endeavor or impossibly expensive was, of course, critical to OSD's commitment to flexible response, which mandated restructuring and expanding NATO's conventional forces.

Although the Joint Chiefs of Staff supported a rejuvenation of NATO's conventional forces, they too remained skeptical that a conventional defense of Western Europe unsupported by tactical nuclear weapons could succeed against a powerful Soviet assault. Unlike McNamara, they viewed conventional and nuclear capabilities as "interrelated options," not as mutually exclusive choices. They also contested his revised threat estimates which, they felt, underestimated Soviet strength arrayed against NATO. While expressing their reservations, on 15 October 1965 the Chiefs, with the exception of Army Chief of Staff General Johnson, nonetheless endorsed the BRAVO goals, terming the ALPHA targets unacceptable, "politically and economically, to the NATO nations." In a separate memo sent the same day, Wheeler informed the secretary that approval of BRAVO goals was about the most that Washington could currently expect. He also criticized General Johnson's approach of ALPHA or nothing because it risked any progress toward a substantial conventional force and carried the added political and psychological implications of portraying a dysfunctional alliance "unable to get on with the business to which it is dedicated."[7]

McNamara and McNaughton, however, favored only a tentative acceptance of modified BRAVO force levels, conditional on the NATO allies submitting detailed plans, including cost analyses, to realize a flexible response capability. They further insisted on an annual appraisal within NATO to measure progress toward the five-year force goals. At the NATO ministerial meeting held in Paris on 15 December, McNamara urged his counterparts to examine their force structure goals in order to correct serious deficiencies in NATO's military forces, military plans, and defense budgets. He warned of the ever-growing difficulty of explaining to the American people why they should support NATO when the allies were contributing less and planning further reductions. Countries did submit annual plans that proved useful in establishing the alliance's FY 1969–1973 force goals that ultimately replaced the ALPHA and BRAVO recommendations, but predictably they failed to meet McNamara's expectations. ISA termed the August 1967 allied proposals "mixed blessings" that continued to exaggerate the Soviet threat; it reported that the JCS pronounced the documents lacking in "real programming and costing capability."[8]

McNamara's conviction that NATO could have an affordable, but still credible conventional defense continued to hinge on his belief that order of battle comparisons matching only numbers of divisions were overly simplistic. OSD analysts provided support for his position. In 1965 U.S. Army war games based on revised "cost-equivalency" factors had concluded that in a defensive scenario one U.S. division force equaled two such Soviet units. Additional analysis revealed that active U.S. divisions also enjoyed greater firepower, twice as much manpower, and cost twice as much to field as their Soviet counterparts. Relying on such cost-effective reasoning, McNamara "proved" that by costing twice as much to field, one U.S. division, if efficiently organized, was the equivalent of two Soviet ones. The Joint Chiefs doubted the validity of McNamara's force matching concept and by extension his proposed force structure that depended so heavily on quantification techniques; they also faulted OSD's methodology for underestimating Soviet conventional strength and consequently the danger posed to NATO. Reevaluations of the Soviet nonnuclear threat by OSD and the intelligence community, however, strengthened McNamara's analysis that fewer NATO divisions than previously estimated could defend Western Europe. Instead of the unaffordable and thus unattainable 50- to 60-division force structure to match the Pact, the alliance needed half that number and, just as important, could afford them "within approximately current Defense budgets and manpower levels."[9] Such a solution might mute both American urgings for alliance members to do more on their own behalf and European objections that they could do no more than their present effort. McNamara next had to convince the NATO allies to implement the latest guidance.

In a memorandum to the president on 13 October 1965 the secretary of defense deftly wove the compelling rationale for a smaller, better, and affordable force structure. As OSD's yardstick to measure forces he used the so-called division slice, a planning figure obtained by dividing the total strength and total materiel by the number of divisions in theater. One full-strength NATO division slice amounted to 33,600 men and $330 million in equipment.[*] Relying on computer-generated data and the promise of technology doubling U.S. strategic lift capability, McNamara's calculations demonstrated not only that the allies could field the required 21 division slices needed for conventional defense of NATO's Central Front, but that, with the exception of Belgium, they could do it for far less money and, aside from Germany, with fewer troops. Based on the division-slice concept, the 21 European divisions should have totaled 705,600 men with $6.9 billion in equipment. McNamara, however, qualified requirements by assigning a European division lesser logistics capabilities, lower levels of equipment stockpiles and ammunition, and fewer troops than a U.S. division-slice. This enabled him to compute a total of 608,000 active Army men at under $3 billion per year for the European allies on the Central Front.[10] Efficient management and cost-effective purchases of U.S. military equipment could transform the alliance, though a cynic might regard the latter condition as a thinly disguised version of McNamara's unabashed "Buy-American" campaign.

---

[*] In May 1965 ASD Comptroller Hitch computed full-support division slices at 34,000 for U.S. divisions and 23,800 for NATO divisions in the Central Region.

As much as McNamara later insisted that the buildup of conventional forces was financially and politically practical, his policies mismatched strategy and force structure. The European allies continued to hang on to the belief that the NATO threat to use nuclear weapons sufficed to blunt Soviet ambitions by keeping the potential risk far out of proportion to any anticipated gain. Conventional forces, no matter how strong, never offered that same degree of security. McNamara's figures to the contrary, skeptical Europeans remained unwilling to embark on what they thought would be a very expensive dual-strategy of flexible response that might end up bankrupting them. As for arguments about the potential devastation of nuclear warfare, the historical experience and geography of Europe decreed that even a successful conventional defense would still leave large areas of the continent in ruin. Lastly Europeans were increasingly concerned that McNamara's calls for them to upgrade their conventional forces presaged U.S. troop withdrawals, more so given the growing involvement in Vietnam.[11]

Reduction of U.S. Forces in Europe

Europeans were not mistaken in their apprehension of U.S. withdrawals. During 1966 OSD indeed looked for ways to substantially reduce U.S. forces in Europe, chiefly for financial reasons. As summarized in McNamara's 21 September 1966 DPM, one proposal would cut Army and Air Force manning levels to alleviate worsening balance of payments problems, especially with Germany hedging on its agreed upon payments to offset the cost of stationing U.S. troops there and other NATO nations scrimping on their defense commitments. He proposed also to capitalize on the impending French withdrawal from NATO military operations by decreasing U.S. support troops assigned in France and streamlining, with attendant cost savings, NATO's defenses. A third proposal, also originating in OSD, would withdraw some support forces, limit combat stocks to 60- rather than 90- day levels, and halve the CONUS-based reinforcement commitment to NATO from six to three active divisions. This last appeared possible because the weak NATO logistical systems would not be able to support all six U.S. reinforcing divisions when they arrived in Europe. Thus it made more sense both in strategic and financial terms to fill out the five U.S. divisions already in Europe and augment them with three more from the United States. McNamara also forecast withdrawals of American combat troops from Europe, suggesting that unless the Europeans improved their capabilities the time had come for a probing reevaluation of NATO commitments. It may be argued that with Vietnam deployments rapidly depleting the strategic reserve the secretary was making a virtue of necessity, but McNamara continually insisted that political considerations, among which congressional pressure was not the least, not military strategy, prevented redeploying U.S. troops from Europe and elsewhere.[12]

From the European perspective, however, it made no sense to stock what they regarded as excess ammunition and supplies for large conventional forces when they believed any fighting would quickly escalate to nuclear conflict. Moreover, intelligence assessments of Moscow's diminishing control over its Eastern Europe satellites and McNamara's own view of European stability convincingly argued against the possibility of imminent Soviet aggression. Although he understood that the political climate of détente embodied in the Harmel study* on the future of NATO, under way since November 1966, might lead to changes in the alliance, McNamara failed to grasp that the easing of East-West tensions also made the Europeans still more reluctant to pay more, as they saw it, for a conventional defense.[13] This standoff eventually forced the United States, Britain, and West Germany to redefine the concept of burden-sharing in the NATO alliance.

If NATO in September 1966 was "a tired and sick beast of burden," as Timothy Stanley, defense adviser to the U.S. NATO mission, suggested, surely carrying multiple heavy loads contributed to the alliance's malaise. Besides French defection and its attendant relocation costs and disruptions, the alliance faced a host of problems: possible British troop reductions; U.S. congressional pressure to reevaluate the American commitment; JCS opposition to leaving inadequately supported forces in Germany; and a worsening balance of payments issue.[14] The "tired beast" still faced a long journey.

Assessing Germany's Share of the Load

From the very beginning of his presidency, President Johnson faced pressing political and fiscal difficulties caused by the maintenance of U.S. military forces in Europe. Funding considerations constantly interacted with domestic political tensions surrounding the U.S. role in Europe and the future of the Atlantic alliance.[15] McNamara's post-1965 adaptations to a conventional force structure that aimed to resolve the balance of payments deficit, growing economic woes at home, and increasing demands of Vietnam for more troops—all augured basic changes to the NATO alliance.

Seeking to overcome allied reluctance to equip and supply forces to U.S. flexible response standards, by the mid-1960s McNamara singled out the unsatisfactory West German force structure and its inadequate defense budget for his harshest criticism. Unless the Germans improved their ground forces, he doubted whether the United States and Britain could continue their heavy financial and military contributions to the defense of Europe. In some measure, the secretary's enthusiasm for permanent U.S. withdrawals from Europe was not necessarily a product of Vietnam—though perhaps stimulated by the demands of the war—but

---

* Belgian Foreign Minister Pierre Harmel chaired the NATO study on the future of the alliance. The resulting report, issued in mid-December 1967, recommended a "two pillar doctrine" based on military security and détente.

a task he thought long overdue. As McNamara told German Chancellor Ludwig Erhard in mid-December 1965, the American involvement in Southeast Asia would lead Congress and the American people to question why the United States bore a proportionately heavier "burden in men, money, and blood" than the European allies.[16]

In 1965, with French participation in NATO uncertain, Germany more than ever became the linchpin of the alliance; in McNamara's mind it had to bear a larger share of defense costs. Agreements concluded in May 1964 had obligated the German government to purchase $1.35 billion in U.S. military goods during 1965 and 1966 to offset that portion of the U.S. troop costs in Germany that involved the international balance of payments. Even after its paced buildup during the early 1960s, the German government remained well short of recruiting the 500,000 men planned for its 12 divisions.[17] The resulting division slice of almost 42,000 men would be well above McNamara's 33,600 slice.

McNamara's insistence on a reinvigorated conventional defense irritated German leaders who had difficulty finding a justification, much less a need, to buy expensive equipment for units that existed only on paper. When senior German advisers informed McNamara in early November 1965 that Germany would meet just slightly more than 50 percent of its offset procurement, he insisted that specific requirements in the form of orders placed by 31 December 1966 meet the full $1.35 billion offset target. He also counseled Johnson to be hard-nosed about the obligation during the upcoming talks with Chancellor Erhard, a view supported by the U.S. ambassador to Bonn.[18]

At his 20 December 1965 meeting with the German leader Johnson linked the financial strains of the Vietnam fighting to the overall U.S. balance of payments deficit. To avoid further unsettling of U.S. international accounts, he expected the Federal Republic to meet its offset payments. Facing budget troubles of his own, Erhard agreed to honor the offset agreement, but pending further discussions, he refused to commit the FRG to specific payment schedules. Buried near the end of the joint statement issued after the Johnson-Erhard meeting of 21 December, a passage endorsed the great value of full execution of the offset arrangements. The two leaders had in fact agreed that their respective defense and finance ministers should ensure that future offset arrangements would produce German military orders and payments to fulfill the conditions for the years 1965 and 1966 as well as develop additional proposals for requirements through 1970.[19]

McNamara's follow-up meeting on 21 December with FRG Defense Minister von Hassel, who had accompanied the chancellor, concluded that Germany and the United States had to maintain an equally high level of combat capability. Accordingly, while keeping pace with McNamara's plans for major force improvements, the Germans would still meet the offset requirements and alleviate U.S. balance of payments shortfalls. The officially approved minutes restated the Johnson-Erhard agreement while omitting specifics of the defense ministers' discussions.[20]

By early 1966, however, McNamara saw "many signs" of the FRG backing off its offset agreements with the United States and Britain. Besides the difficulties this created for the administration, the British had indicated that without offset payments they would have to cut their ground forces in Germany to save on foreign exchange. Such a development might in turn lead other allies to reduce their military commitments to NATO. British Defense Secretary Healey's warning of late January 1966 encouraged McNamara to pressure the Germans into paying more for their defense.[21]

Joint military reviews held since the December 1965 agreement had identified German interest in buying almost $400 million worth of medium helicopter and transport aircraft. During his May 1966 meeting in Washington with von Hassel to discuss these purchases, McNamara remained adamant that his German counterpart fulfill the offset and provide him in writing with specific items and dollar amounts of ordered materiel. He discounted von Hassel's remarks about the increasing difficulties of identifying enough military materiel for procurement as well as his assertion that France's intention to withdraw from the NATO command structure would likely place greater burdens on the German defense budget. As in previous meetings, McNamara told von Hassel that unless the Germans met the full offset, the United States would have to reduce its forces.[22]

Leaked versions of McNamara's statement made their way into the German press, embarrassing the already hard-pressed Erhard cabinet for succumbing to "McNamara's heavy hand." Reviled for "penny pinching and unreasonable" demands, McNamara became the lightning rod for German outbursts against overbearing American pressure on the Erhard government to increase defense outlays. The secretary's June 1966 congressional testimony, implying reductions in support personnel and spending but not combat capabilities, sowed further uncertainties among the West Germans about the imminence of future troop withdrawals.[23]

Meantime, as the German economy slowed, Erhard's government had increased social welfare spending and correspondingly reduced its defense outlays for 1964–1966, leaving it without money to pay for additional purchases of U.S. military equipment. Erhard's notification to Johnson on 5 July 1966 of his desire to amend the offset arrangement preceded by a few days Senator Mansfield's letter serving notice to President Johnson of the Democratic Policy Committee's concern over economic problems occasioned by the gold outflow and balance of payments deficit in Europe. Committee members wanted the president to know that they favored a "substantial" reduction of U.S. forces stationed in Western Europe. Should the president fail to act on this advice, the Senate planned to introduce a resolution to that effect.[*]

---

[*] On 31 August 1966 Mansfield offered a nonbinding resolution, endorsed by 32 senators, declaring substantial reductions in U.S. forces in Europe would not affect adversely resolve or ability to meet NATO commitments; it did not pass. The senator reintroduced his resolution again in January 1967.

Using Mansfield's letter as a thinly veiled threat to force Germany into buying more American equipment, ISA drafted a strongly worded presidential reply that explained the economic facts of life to Erhard: either the Bonn government paid for equipment or the United States could not afford to keep its existing forces in Germany. McNamara was to hand-carry the president's tough message to Bonn when he met with von Hassel later that month. Keenly aware of growing opposition in Congress to a business as usual approach to NATO, but with his senior advisers divided, Johnson tabled the draft, preferring to wait on the results of Erhard's forthcoming defense budget and a gauging of the chancellor's political fortunes. In early August the president opted against ISA's tough letter, instead convening his advisers to hear their conflicting viewpoints before making any decision.[24]

Nevertheless, during the interim McNamara pressed his hard line, ignoring a warning from the U.S. ambassador to Bonn who viewed the offset as the "single greatest source of friction" between the two governments. He notified the Joint Chiefs on 18 July that the American public would no longer permit disproportionate U.S. participation in NATO, so the Germans had to carry their fair share of the defense buildup and do more on their own. McNamara was acting on behalf of both Washington and London. The British cabinet imposed deflationary policies to redress Britain's balance of payments deficit and indicated that unless the full German offset was forthcoming Britain would significantly reduce its units in Germany, an outcome McNamara thought disastrous for the alliance. Consequently at the July 1966 ministers meeting of the Nuclear Planning Working Group in Paris he pressed his West German counterpart to increase all forms of defense spending.[25]

McNamara showed no sensitivity to Germany's problems of unemployment, Common Market competition, and inflation created by heavy spending on social welfare and defense. Even von Hassel's promises to raise the defense budget only elicited McNamara's rejoinder that the whole of the offset had to be covered. Although the U.S.-FRG joint statement of 24 July announced that the offset agreements for 1965–1966 would be fully met, German insistence on new terms after the accord expired in mid-1967 left the long-term offset question unresolved. It was in this context, and with his key advisers still split over possible solutions, that the president had postponed his reply to Erhard, understanding that if he decided against a tough response he then needed an alternative strategy for talks among the three allies.[26]

The imminent collapse of Anglo-German offset negotiations led to the 19 August 1966 British announcement of troop withdrawals from Germany, providing the catalyst for tripartite negotiations. Four days later U.S. Assistant Secretary of State for European Affairs John Leddy suggested a trilateral approach to resolve outstanding offset, force structure, and nuclear issues in the alliance. The following evening, 24 August, Johnson met with his senior foreign policy advisers to discuss the offset and U.S. force levels in Germany. At that time he apparently determined that McNamara's full-offset-or-withdrawal policy seemed too extreme; if interpreted as proof the alliance was unraveling, it might bring down the already weakened Erhard cabinet. Deputy Special Assistant for National Security Affairs Francis Bator's proposal to resolve the problem through trilateral discussions rather than by fiat seems to have appealed to Johnson's preferred method of dealing with thorny issues. Concerned about possible British withdrawals from Germany, his own problems with the offset and Congress, and de Gaulle's "antics," the president agreed to negotiations. Within two days he dispatched letters to Erhard and to British Prime Minister Wilson suggesting the three allies meet soon in a "tripartite exploration" of ways to resolve in an equitable manner "the problem of forces, deployments—and the sharing of the foreign exchange burden."[27]

Despite the president's overture, McNamara, especially upset over the admission by Erhard on 9 September that his government could not meet the current offset arrangement and his accompanying request for a payment moratorium, continued to insist that Germany had to honor its financial obligations. Consistent with his July advice, McNamara prepped Johnson on the likelihood that Erhard would try to settle the offset matter in Germany's favor when the two met in September. In contrast to McNamara's tough approach, State favored greater accommodation, deeming the German financial crisis so serious that Erhard deserved some relief.[28]

Treasury Secretary Fowler sided with McNamara; together they pushed for a tough stance to force the Germans to pay the current offset goal, if necessary by borrowing against future orders. Both insisted the Bonn government commit to purchase the full amount of $1.4 billion in weaponry, although they recommended stretching out by 6–12 months the requirement that the Germans place these orders by the end of 1966. Fully recognizing the risks and implications of substantial U.S. troop withdrawals, McNamara, contrary to JCS advice, counseled the president in mid-September 1966 to reduce Army strength in Europe by 50,000 support personnel and dual-base about half of the 700 reconnaissance and fighter aircraft deployed there. The inadequate German military budget left the United States two means to close the balance of payments gap: cut its military expenditures in Germany, or absorb the amount by which U.S. spending exceeded the German offset.[29]

This frame of reference accounted for the rough treatment McNamara meted out to von Hassel in late September 1966. Supremely confident of his facts and figures, McNamara even spoke of the U.S. moral right to offset payments, leaving von Hassel, who had come seeking more lenient terms, "increasingly embarrassed" and appearing to give up. Washington's blunt message amounted to pay up or tell us to get our troops out of Germany. McNamara justified controversial force reductions to the president by pointing to improvements in U.S. strategic airlift capability that would allow Washington to return the units to Europe "easily in 2 weeks," thereby retaining the same level of military effectiveness with reduced forces in Germany.[30]

Shortly before the president's 26 September meeting with Erhard, Johnson received recommendations from Rusk, McNamara, and Ball that he recognize that Erhard's budgetary difficulties made it impossible for Germany to meet the full offset, but that he inform the chancellor the resulting balance of payments deficit was unacceptable to the United States. While a short-term solution might be possible, a tripartite military and financial review that Johnson hoped Erhard would join seemed the only long-term solution. The Erhard government had shown no enthusiasm about trilateral talks for fear Britain and America would gang up on Germany.[31]

The president, building on ground prepared by McNamara's treatment of von Hassel, initially took a hard line in his private meeting with Erhard, pushing the chancellor into a corner by questioning Germany's sincerity and loyalty. Then Johnson suggested referral of the offset and U.S. troop level issues to economic and military experts. The resulting joint statement proposed a "searching reappraisal" of alliance military strategy and force levels as well as a review of equitable sharing of defense burdens. At a later, larger meeting of the delegations, Johnson recounted the discussion in more conciliatory terms, reassuring Erhard that he did not want to add to the chancellor's problems.[32] The president's proposal was neither as spontaneous nor as generous as it appeared, but rather the culmination of a carefully calculated, thoroughly discussed design to make Germany pay more of NATO's defense costs.

OSD, the JCS, and Troop Reductions in Germany

The appropriate size of the U.S. withdrawal from Europe remained the other major NATO issue under consideration in Washington during the summer of 1966. In mid-June, anticipating a possible initiative from the Soviet Union, Secretary of State Rusk had asked McNamara for a fresh assessment of the purely military implications of proposals for mutual force reductions of U.S. and Soviet troops in Europe. McNamara turned to the JCS for their views. The Chiefs estimated that mutual troop reductions would only compound the dangers of instability threatening the alliance. France had already announced its intention to leave the military organization and the remaining European members had not fully met their commitment to build dual-purpose forces. Citing allied perception of ongoing U.S. withdrawals as "an indication of a major shift in strategic posture from Europe to Asia," the Chiefs on 8 July recommended against further reductions.[33]

After examining their input, McNamara asked the JCS on 23 August to provide him with the military implications of a pullout of two divisions plus appropriate air and support forces; a reduction of four divisions plus appropriate air and support forces; or the retention of major ground forces at reduced strength with some decrease and thinning out of air and support units. General Lemnitzer responded from Europe that given the recent substantial withdrawals to meet Vietnam requirements, de Gaulle's pullout, and the likelihood of British force reductions, no military justification existed for cutting U.S. or allied forces any deeper. Incorporating Lemnitzer's comments, the JCS replied to McNamara in mid-September that with fewer ground forces the greater reliance on airpower precluded the withdrawal of any air forces. The loss of two divisions would greatly weaken the Central Front and "jeopardize the integrity of the entire defense and probably require earlier use of nuclear weapons. . . ." A two-division reinforcement flown directly from the United States could not close rapidly enough to meet Washington's commitment to NATO. This contradicted McNamara's positive view of reinforcement from CONUS. Withdrawing four U.S. divisions from Europe would negate the concept of forward defense and likely necessitate the immediate use of nuclear weapons in case of Soviet aggression. The third option would degrade combat capability and exert a crippling effect on the alliance.[34]

While endorsing trilateral discussions as a means to close the foreign exchange gap incurred by U.S. military deployments to Germany, in mid-September McNamara reminded Johnson that additional cuts to military expenditures in Europe were still needed. As of 1 September, the Germans had ordered only half of their obligated $1.35 billion of military equipment and made only 20 percent of the promised payments. Although the JCS did not concur with his recommendation, McNamara believed that reducing 50,000 support personnel from Europe would result in significant savings. Neither the president nor his secretary of defense kept the Joint Chiefs fully informed, leaving them to infer from public statements by administration officials that OSD and the White House had already cut a deal for substantial cutbacks of U.S. troops in Europe. According to Wheeler, the scenario would most likely take the guise of pulling out support units to preserve "the facade of the magic 5 divisions . . . until the political ground has been more thoroughly plowed for further reductions."[35]

Only on 4 October did the secretary officially request the Chiefs' views on how best to reduce U.S. Army forces in Europe by 50,000 military personnel and on alternative methods of dual-basing U.S. Air Force squadrons in Europe and the continental United States. Although they did not believe that the military situation in Europe justified any reduction of NATO forces, the Joint Chiefs, bowing to political and economic pressures, on 27 October grudgingly allowed that the least undesirable alternative was to return the 24th Infantry Division (Mechanized) plus one brigade intact to the United States. Since that division, stationed in southern Bavaria, lay outside the U.S. Seventh Army defense sector, its removal would not appreciably worsen the status of the Seventh Army, which was already left dangerously exposed on its northern flank from having to rely on the FRG's "paper army." The division's entire complex could be closed with savings of $120 million. Dual-basing 12 or 15 air squadrons in the United States would save $30 million or $41 million, respectively, but at the price of reduced conventional combat capability and substantial loss of the Air Force's nuclear strike capability in Europe.[36]

An OSD-commissioned RAND study completed in November challenged the JCS conclusions by asserting that a minimum of 50,000 troops could be withdrawn to meet the personnel cutback while still retaining a balanced force structure capable of resisting a conventional surprise attack. The RAND study closely paralleled a Systems Analysis effort that also called for a similar reduction. While the studies were under way, in mid-September 1966, DoD NATO adviser Stanley recommended "for political and military reasons" that one division return home and dual-basing of aircraft begin in order to meet balance of payments requirements.[37]

With OSD anxious to trim forces in Europe and the administration concerned with the balance of payments deficit, the trilateral forum appeared to offer an expeditious solution to both issues. Yet the Erhard government hesitated to participate in talks. The British, for their part, preferred a bilateral agreement with Washington before negotiations began in order to prevent the Germans from playing the Americans and British against each other. The British, despite Johnson's pleading, also appeared determined to announce further troop withdrawals from Germany, perhaps as early as mid-October, to reduce their foreign exchange drain. For its part, the Johnson administration still lacked a unified position on a desired outcome of any talks; the president felt deep concern about the repercussions that could result from further British troop withdrawals from the continent.[38]

The Tripartite Talks

In late September Erhard met with the president in Washington, and an agreement was soon reached to begin tripartite talks promptly. Two weeks later Johnson officially announced his selection of John McCloy, former United States high commissioner to Germany, as the U.S. representative to the talks. McCloy had figured prominently in the rebuilding of postwar West Germany and staunchly championed NATO. He vigorously opposed any withdrawals on the grounds that such action would weaken the U.S. conventional military options in Europe; if other allies followed, the alliance might unravel. McCloy's initial instructions were to appraise Soviet and NATO military capabilities, propose equitable foreign exchange burdens for stationing troops in Germany, and recommend reasonable burden-sharing of defense among alliance members.[39] The first session of the talks was held in Bonn on 20–21 October; negotiations were barely under way when the Erhard government fell in late October.

Two tripartite sessions took place in November, but given the protracted transition to Chancellor Kurt Kiesinger's new government little progress occurred for the next three months. At the 9 November working group sessions, McCloy offered a wide-ranging review of U.S. NATO policy that concluded by endorsing the strategy of flexible response with existing conventional forces. In a 21 November letter to Johnson, contradicting McNamara's earlier assertions, McCloy warned that any significant withdrawal of U.S. forces from Europe would likely trigger comparable allied force cuts, threatening the integrity of the alliance. He also questioned McNamara's position that withdrawing U.S. troops would not affect military effectiveness because they could quickly return to Germany.[40]

The impasse at the talks had serious repercussions because each passing day added to the grave financial and political problems facing the British cabinet, already under strong domestic pressure to cut forces in Germany if an acceptable offset arrangement proved impossible. In late November Prime Minister Wilson stressed to Johnson the necessity of reaching an early agreement on the offset. Should this prove impossible by 30 June 1967, London would take whatever measures it saw fit to resolve the foreign exchange costs of stationing British troops in Germany. To keep the talks alive, Johnson, who had already broached the idea to Wilson on 15 November, quickly agreed that the United States would shore up Britain's foreign exchange by purchasing $35 million of British military equipment in exchange for London's pledge to keep troops on the Rhine through June 1967.[41] At the same time in Washington, State, OSD, the JCS, White House, and McCloy engaged in fierce political argument over how much to reduce U.S. forces in Germany.

On 25 October Wheeler offered McCloy a candid and unflattering portrait of the NATO allies, concluding that he saw no military justification for withdrawing U.S. troops from Europe. Deficiencies in Western European mobilization policies, reserves, funding, manning, and logistics, plus the thaw with the Soviet Union, left alliance nations predisposed to reduce their military forces, a tendency only strengthened by the proposed British redeployment. Because withdrawing troops "[would] have an adverse impact" on U.S. Seventh Army's capability, Wheeler advocated maintaining U.S. forces in Europe at their present levels. If withdrawal proved inevitable, it ought to be made clear that it was for political and economic reasons, not military. Furthermore, any withdrawn forces should remain earmarked for NATO's use, and the administration should ensure that the pullouts did not cause the alliance to unravel.

The CIA estimated that troop reductions per se would not encourage Soviet aggression, downplaying the likelihood of immediate disastrous consequences. In the long term, however, withdrawal risked setting in motion the deterioration of an alliance that might slowly wither away as its members lost sight of the original reasons that brought them together. In short, the political risks outweighed any short-term marginal advantages in the balance of payments calculus.[42]

With these cautions from the JCS and CIA in mind, McCloy worried that any substantial troop withdrawals would touch off a chain reaction by the allies to cut their NATO forces, thereby jeopardizing the alliance. He instead proposed to "squeeze as much offset money as possible out of the Germans," with the United States prepared to make up any shortfalls, likely including the amount involved in the British-German offset dispute. With talks on resolving the offset issue deadlocked, McNamara informed the president that a relocation of U.S. and U.K. forces was necessary for political, financial, and military reasons. He anticipated saving $200 million by withdrawing at least one-plus division from Germany and believed that domestic political pressure made a "no-cut" position impossible. Unless the administration brought sufficient forces home from Europe, he feared that Congress would make far deeper reductions "than any of us think safe." Rather than force a confrontation with McCloy in front of the president, however, McNamara counseled delay because the final decision would depend on McCloy's determining how much the Germans would pay, a position supported by Bator and Rostow. The two White House aides advised the president to postpone any decision on troop withdrawals pending "time to probe, explore, and find out" what might constitute a basis for compromise.[43]

Talks on resolving the offset issue remained deadlocked as the German approach to calculating the offset differed from the analysis used by the U.S. and British delegates. Germany requested postponement of the scheduled 12 January 1967 session on balance of payments issues until mid-February, but McNamara had already informed the president in mid-December that a relocation of U.S. and U.K. forces had to take place. The defense secretary continued his push for substantial reductions, this time focusing on how troop reductions would affect military effectiveness. His mid-January 1967 DPM argued that available political warning time and the speed with which improved strategic air mobility could deploy U.S. reinforcements to Europe enabled the United States to maintain its military effectiveness while reducing its forces in Germany. Rotating two divisions and dual-basing 432 of 676 tactical aircraft then stationed in Europe would realize $200 million in balance of payments savings. McNamara suggested a decision on redeployments by 15 February 1967, private notification to the British and Germans one week after the scheduled 21 February trilateral session, and official notification by 15 March.[44]

According to custom, McNamara had circulated the DPM for comment. The Joint Chiefs reacted by reaffirming that they saw no military justification for reducing U.S. forces in Europe, noting inconsistencies in OSD's cost analysis. State also questioned OSD's cost projections and estimated savings from redeployments. Pointing out that DoD's figures differed widely from its own, State estimated that at most about half of OSD's anticipated $200 million balance of payments savings might materialize.* Rusk and McNamara also differed sharply over the latter's proposal to pressure the Germans by suggesting additional U.S. troop reductions. On this point McNamara was relentless, insisting the Germans had brought the difficulties on themselves because they refused to budge on the offset issue.[45]

---

* After one-time costs of relocation, the annual balance of payments savings was expected to amount to $75 million and budgetary savings to $43 million (Insert for pages 697 following line 3, fldr House Approp Cmte Hearings-P.M. FY 69 Budget, 2/16/68, box 74, ASD(C) files, OSD Hist).

Throughout the tripartite negotiations the Joint Chiefs insisted they would not support "a phoney military rationale" that downplayed the effect on military readiness or reevaluated the Soviet threat to justify reductions of U.S. forces from NATO. Instead they wanted a straightforward presentation to NATO members of the economic and political decisions driving the withdrawals. By mid-February, when withdrawals appeared inevitable, the Joint Chiefs voiced concern that a persistent dwindling of NATO forces would transform the U.S. commitment to defend Western Europe into a liability. They judged the breaking point would occur when Central Front forces shrank to about 16 (including 3 U.S.) divisions.[46]

Disagreement between Rusk, McNamara, Treasury Secretary Fowler, and McCloy over the extent of cuts resulted on 23 February in the three secretaries submitting a joint memorandum for the president, and McCloy a separate one. McCloy contested any current withdrawal and strongly opposed McNamara's proposed dual-basing of two divisions and six air wings. Rusk favored dual-basing of two-thirds of one U.S. Army division and 162 of 216 aircraft in three air wings in West Germany and the United States. McNamara believed dual-basing should involve two-thirds of two divisions and 324 of the 432 aircraft in six air wings. He favored such heavy reductions in aircraft because they "did not contribute much militarily" and were expensive to maintain abroad in terms of gold flow.[47]

At a 24 February meeting with Rusk and various subcabinet level officials from Defense, State, Treasury, and the White House, McNamara again argued that the United States could withdraw 1 1/3 divisions and 4 1/2 air wings from Europe without reducing military effectiveness. Rusk favored smaller cuts, and then only if absolutely necessary because the Soviet threat had not receded and reductions might foreshadow NATO disintegration, with major consequences for U.S. prestige. McNamara countered that only deep cuts would satisfy the Senate, but he was willing to await German offset proposals and British reaction before acting. The president, fearful that large troop withdrawals would encourage Moscow to start trouble, preferred to move slowly and let the British and Germans resolve their offset issues themselves. He favored minimum force reductions along with minimum spending to keep the British from reducing their military commitment in Germany. He also rejected McNamara's argument that units returned to the United States could prove as effective as those in Europe.[48]

At a follow-up meeting the next day, McNamara agreed to a 35,000-man reduction, but he still believed that Congress would oppose such a small cut. Johnson instructed Rusk and McNamara to canvass congressional leaders and explain the reasoning behind the withdrawals. A few days later, the president adopted a hard line, one more arbitrary than he preferred, as he explained his policy to a divided congressional leadership, senators in general favoring the cuts, representatives opposing them. Johnson announced that despite his reluctance to make any cuts to U.S. forces in Europe, pressure from Congress left him considering a troop rotation plan involving relatively small numbers of men. Washington would simultaneously pressure London not to cut British forces in Germany and Bonn to do more on the offset.[49]

On 1 March the president significantly modified the U.S. negotiating position, apparently heeding Bator's (and Rusk's) counsel to avoid any reductions or else risk leaving himself open to charges that he had "helped pull the Alliance down around our ears," damaging chances for a real money deal with the Germans and reducing American chips for a mutual withdrawal agreement with the Russians. Meeting with McCloy that day, Johnson reviewed his written instructions and emphasized that with Congress determined to reduce U.S. forces in Europe the administration would "be very lucky if we do not have to go to cut 2 divisions." Stressing the importance of financing the British offset situation, he dismissed McCloy's fears that the alliance verged on collapse and instructed him to work with Britain and Germany to determine NATO force levels on the basis of security considerations. The Germans had to realize the gravity of the financial situation and recognize that growing congressional and American public resentment was directed toward them as the source of the U.S. overseas deficit. Johnson approved allowing the Germans to determine how much military equipment they needed to purchase from the United States and Britain rather than insisting on fulfilling military sales orders by 30 June 1967 as McNamara preferred. He also acceded to earlier German proposals and determined that German purchase of U.S. government bonds or other financial steps, in addition to buying military equipment, might serve to settle the balance of payments deficit. McCloy had to make clear to the Germans the issues at stake, pressure them "to pay the bill," and, most important, "find out what they will do."[50] McCloy returned to London for the fourth session of the trilateral negotiations to present the new instructions to the tripartite representatives and hold private discussions with the delegation leaders and later with the British and German prime ministers.

Back in Washington for an 8 March meeting, McCloy reported to the president and his senior advisers that the major remaining problem centered on the $40 million shortfall between the British offset demand and the German offer.* After considering various options the president decided on a combination of credits, accelerated purchases, and extra American procurement in Britain to make up the difference provided the Germans raised their offset purchase offer.[51]

Heeding the advice of the German ambassador to the United States that a letter from Johnson would sway the chancellor to do more, on 11 March 1967 Johnson wrote to Kiesinger. In response the German leader increased the German government's offset purchases in Britain, leaving it to the talks to work out final details of the bargain. At the trilateral plenary session on March 20–2 Bonn agreed to purchase more British-manufactured military equipment. In return London announced it would withdraw one brigade from Germany in early 1968. McCloy reported that the increased German offset offer to Britain coupled with a number of purchases and credits from the United States would help cover most of London's foreign exchange

---

* The British demanded $154 million; the Germans initially offered $86 million and later under U.S. pressure upped that to $114 million, leaving the $40 million gap.

costs. In a private meeting McCloy informed the other two representatives that the United States might withdraw as many as 35,000 men. Washington would provide Bonn with details as soon as possible.[52]

With that issue resolved, it remained to inform the Germans of the specifics of the U.S. troop rotation plan. Reluctant to do so in detail, McNamara worried, according to Bator, "that a full blueprint will get him into a war with the Chiefs—he would much prefer to remove the veils one at a time." Siding with McCloy in favoring a full presentation of redeployment plans, on 23 March Bator urged Johnson to "give Bob a gentle signal that you are impressed by the McCloy judgment." The same day McNamara informed the JCS of his decision to implement a rotation plan involving one division—the 24th Infantry—and three air wings. As agreed with McNamara, McCloy had told the Germans that 35,000 U.S. troops would redeploy to the United States; the secretary requested the Joint Chiefs to adjust plans so that no more than that number would return home. The Chiefs responded a week later by restating their professional judgment that no military justification existed for the withdrawals and proposed an alternative Army plan to "retain the division base element . . . on a permanent basis" and rotate all three brigades on a six-month cycle that would demonstrate both U.S. commitment to NATO and ability to reinforce the alliance.[53]

On 5 April the director of the Joint Staff officially informed the inspector general of the FRG Armed Forces of the forthcoming withdrawal of 35,000 U.S. troops from Germany. Three days later McNamara instructed his OSD staff to work out details of redeploying at least 28,000 Army and 6,100 Air Force personnel and their dependents, with planning scheduled for completion by mid-May. The proposal, drafted in ISA, called for the redeployment of two-thirds of a division plus various support forces amounting to as many as 30,000 troops along with three tactical fighter wings totaling 216 aircraft. The redeployment (the word "withdrawal" was to be avoided) involved a rotation of U.S. forces with part of the ground and air units remaining in Germany at all times.[54]

The rotation plan became the last hurdle. After studying the details, the Germans became anxious over the scale of the air withdrawal and proposed the U.S. redeploy only 72 aircraft instead of the finally proposed 144. McNamara agreed, contingent on withdrawal of another 10,000 U.S. servicemen from Europe. Feeling that his original redeployment figures had been whittled down by the president's advisers, he opposed further reductions to redeployment. As Bator informed the president, the defense secretary was not fully aware of some other issues between Washington and Bonn. Acting on Bator's advice, Johnson got McNamara to agree to McCloy's proposed compromise of 96 aircraft to satisfy the Germans. With that presidential determination made during the last tripartite session in London, the negotiations concluded successfully on 28 April 1967. The final report of the trilateral talks issued in late April encompassed these provisions. At McNamara's direction, the United States would redeploy 35,000 military personnel from the 24th Infantry Division and three tactical fighter wings. The units would remain committed to NATO and redeploy once a year to Germany for exercises involving the entire division.[55] This was the beginning of the U.S. Army's annual REFORGER (REturn of FORces to GERmany) exercise and the USAF's CRESTED CAP deployment.

McNamara's May 1967 DPM reflecting these reductions drew harsh criticisms from the Joint Chiefs who recommended the memorandum "be revised in its entirety." Still holding to the no-military-justification line for any further troop reductions, the Chiefs insisted that OSD overstated NATO capabilities while it understated the Warsaw Pact's. In early June the uniformed leaders dismissed the assumptions that a state of mutual deterrence existed between conventional forces and that an adequate period of "political warning" would precede any military confrontation.[56] But McNamara had already justified to himself the necessity for major withdrawals.

Attempts to resolve NATO's conventional force structure imbalances had brought together McNamara the statesman and McNamara the merchant. The statesman believed that withdrawals of U.S. troops from Europe had strategic merit, would not degrade military effectiveness, and would force the Europeans to do more for their own defense. The merchant believed that reducing troops and increasing military sales to NATO countries would significantly improve the balance of payments deficit as well as reduce congressional and public frustration over what was seen as Europe's free ride on defense at U.S. expense. Yet just as the statesman's large-scale withdrawals proved too drastic for the president, the merchant's demanding salesmanship could alienate the best potential customers for American-made arms and military equipment.

European suspicions that Washington was retreating on its NATO commitments provoked greater European interest in peaceful coexistence with the Soviet Union. The way was opened for NATO's European members to nudge the alliance toward a policy of détente, expounded in the Harmel Report.[57] Ironically, the extended contretemps had created an effect the opposite of what McNamara intended—it reinforced the conviction among European allies that their security depended ultimately on nuclear weapons, possibly on a rapprochement with Moscow, but certainly not on strong conventional forces.

Clark Clifford and NATO

In taking over the NATO portfolio from McNamara, Clark Clifford may have differed from his predecessor in style, but both felt strongly that the European allies had to share more of the burden of their defense since the United States could not indefinitely continue its current level of support to NATO. However tempting the concept of cutting U.S. troops in Europe to achieve budgetary savings, any further trimming of conventional forces on the heels of the tripartite reductions looked extremely difficult. During the March 1968 review of DoD policy,* for example, Systems Analysis chief Alain Enthoven advocated maintaining the existing level of military forces backing NATO. Relying solely on "the real or threatened use of nuclear weapons" to deter the Soviets would invalidate the strategic concept of flexible response, the very scenario that OSD had been trying to avoid since 1961.[58]

Defense reviews then in progress in Great Britain and the Federal Republic of Germany, both experiencing severe financial pressures, suggested an overall decrease in NATO defense spending. Dollars, marks, and pounds remained scarce at the exact time NATO's newly adopted flexible response strategy required modifications to existing force plans. General Lemnitzer argued for five air mobile brigades, but the Major NATO Commanders' (MNCs) force proposals recommended further study of the costs and utility of air mobile units in Europe. Lemnitzer also proposed reorienting strike aircraft from a primarily nuclear to a dual-capable role, but the JCS questioned the expense of such conversions during times of fiscal belt-tightening. The Joint Chiefs also thought that the MNC recommendations to implement MC 14/3 failed to authorize sufficient military strength for the full range of options envisioned for flexible response. Accepting the proposed force levels entailed risks, but the Chiefs seemed resigned to further reductions in NATO forces given the political and financial restraints operating throughout the alliance.[59]

Since the early days of his administration, the president had pursued a number of initiatives aimed at improving relations with the Soviet Union—ranging from cultural exchanges to overtures about strategic arms limitations. Genuinely interested in easing tensions between the superpowers, Johnson also dreamed of capping his presidency with a dramatic summit meeting with the Soviets to launch arms control negotiations. In favor of mutual force reductions in Europe, he thought that by maintaining NATO's existing forces he could negotiate from a position of strength. Thus Clifford had to proceed cautiously with any further reductions to U.S. forces in Europe. He intended to resolve the balance of payments issue without sacrificing combat strength in Europe by eliminating overhead and support functions there. Launched in March 1968 as the REDCOSTE (REDuced COSTs in Europe) program, this became one of Clifford's major initiatives.†[60]

During the March 1968 policy review, the president's advisers worried that troop levels in Europe might come into question should large numbers of reserves get called to active duty for the Vietnam and Korean emergencies. Once Johnson decided in late March to activate a minimum number of reservists the affair seemed settled. Apparently responding to congressional concerns, Johnson told Wheeler that he was thinking of announcing a follow-on reserve call-up to improve the strategic reserve in the continental United States. Clifford discussed the issue in a more wide-ranging context with the president in early May; in mid-June he recom-

---

* See Chapter VII.
† For details of REDCOSTE see Chapter XVIII.

mended against calling additional reserves because of measures already under way to bring the STRAF (Strategic Army Forces) back to full strength. He proposed instead consolidating units to concentrate resources on fewer ready divisions rather than spread them thinly over less ready units.[61]

Meanwhile renewed congressional pressure for major cuts in defense spending had led the president to ask McNamara where the administration could reduce the DoD budget. The former defense secretary recommended $3 billion in savings that included withdrawing a division from Germany. Clifford rejected that solution in favor of rebuilding the strategic reserve. More and more members of Congress thought otherwise, and pressure increased from Capitol Hill to reduce NATO-committed forces. Earlier OSD studies had revealed that only by eliminating a NATO-deployed division completely from the force structure and not merely returning it to the United States could DoD realize large ($400–500 million) savings. A better option, according to the cost accountants, involved cutting force structure in CONUS. Aside from a balance of payments deficit, it was about as expensive to maintain a division in the United States committed to NATO as to keep one in Europe. This paradox arose because DoD would have to stock and maintain extra equipment in Germany for use by the returning unit. Bringing a division home but still obligating it to Europe merely shifted a unit from one continent to another. It neither strengthened the strategic reserve nor helped meet manpower demands from Vietnam. Finally, if the unit was dedicated to go back to Europe anyway, better to leave it there in the first place.[62]

These considerations and Clifford's determination to concentrate resources in order to strengthen the STRAF led him in mid-June, over JCS protests, to deactivate the partly built 6th Infantry Division in the United States, apportioning its personnel and equipment to other active units. Although Clifford satisfied himself that the nation ran no unacceptable risks in a period of reduced capabilities, the Joint Chiefs sharply disagreed by pointing out that the military was left with such an "extremely limited range of response options" that any emergency in Europe or Korea would demand immediate mobilization and/or the redeployment of U.S. units from Southeast Asia. Army Chief of Staff General Johnson went so far as to assert that DoD either had to retain the 6th Division to augment STRAF forces or reduce its worldwide security commitments, especially in Southeast Asia and Korea.[63]

Clifford, still contending that NATO forces remained a reasonable match for Warsaw Pact forces, further declared that the USSR could not reinforce its frontline formations quickly enough to gain a decisive strategic advantage. Ominous signs from Eastern Europe such as recent Soviet troop maneuvers near the Polish-Czech border and Moscow's unresponsiveness to proposals for mutual force reductions were disquieting but for Clifford secondary to restoring the nation's economic well being. Thus in early June 1968 OSD directed the services to propose significant reductions in DoD personnel and facilities in Europe to meet an anticipated $300–500 million balance of payments NATO deficit for FY 1969.[64]

General Lemnitzer's personal reply declared that he perceived no military justification for any reduction of U.S. forces in Europe at a time when the Warsaw Pact was increasing its combat capability. Looming political ramifications of such actions were even more serious. Any further reduction of U.S. troops threatened to undo the years of effort it had taken to convince NATO ministers to accept the new strategy of flexible response with its emphasis on conventional operations. The most recent withdrawals had triggered a downward spiral of allied conventional capability at the very time NATO had placed increased emphasis on conventional forces. A new redeployment initiative from Washington would only accelerate the process and might well cause a disintegration of the alliance.[65]

In early August the Chiefs, weary of piecemeal force reductions for what they considered financial reasons, sought a long-term solution to the balance of payments dilemma based on maintaining a well-balanced three-division force in Germany. By then their appeals to military judgments lacked clout in deliberations about reducing U.S. forces assigned to NATO. Earlier, on 19 April, Senator Symington had announced his intention to introduce an amendment to the FY 1969 DoD appropriations bill calling for a cutoff of funding after 31 December 1968 for all but 50,000 of the 337,000 U.S. troops in Europe. Clifford hoped to water down Symington's amendment through bureaucratic delaying tactics or, in the worst case, to stretch out reductions over five years. In no mood to preside over the dismantling of NATO during the closing days of his administration, the president vigorously lobbied against the initiative. The State Department, still hopeful of mutual force reductions despite current Soviet uninterest, adamantly rejected any reductions.[66]

Clifford had already sent an alarming appraisal of the consequences of Symington's proposed legislative directive to key Senate leaders. He saw NATO as vital to preserving security in Europe and to "letting Germany contribute to European defense without arousing fear among its neighbors." The secretary's polemic warned that massive troop cuts would upset the conventional balance of forces in Europe, convince the Germans that the United States had abandoned them, and still not resolve the balance of payments problem. Instead his REDCOSTE plan would achieve better results and "preserve the cohesiveness and strength of NATO."[67]

Years of congressional frustration over NATO, however, were building to a momentum that seemed strong enough to pass the Symington amendment. Having testified only a few weeks earlier that a congressionally mandated unilateral U.S. withdrawal from Europe might break up the alliance, Clifford on 1 July said he had to come up with a plan to reduce U.S. forces in NATO well beyond the 34,000 troops scheduled for redeployment or watch the Senate pass the amendment. In an effort to sway Senator Russell, regarded by the administration as the key to the success or failure of the Symington amendment, Nitze proposed to Clifford a combination of withdrawals of U.S. ground and air units and new offset agreements with the allies.[68]

ISA believed that withdrawal of 100,000 of the 330,000 military personnel in Europe "within the next year or two" was essential to convince Congress that the administration was serious and the Symington amendment unnecessary. The withdrawals, joint basing, and shared facilities in Germany, largely paid for by the Germans, would also alleviate the $300 million balance of payments deficit and further appeal to a Congress determined to slash defense expenditures. Proposed reductions of such magnitude left the Joint Chiefs privately considering a total withdrawal from Western Europe. Their official alternative, however, recommended retention of bases and quick reaction forces in Europe, a view shared by State. To compensate, they suggested deactivating six air defense battalions and transferring their equipment to the Germans.[69]

Three years of complicated Defense budget and force structure decisions left OSD no attractive solution except to withdraw as many as 40,000 additional troops over and above the 18,000 already eliminated in the relocation from France and the 33,000 scheduled for REFORGER/CRESTED CAP redeployments by September 1968. Otherwise the specter of the Symington amendment threatened to weaken U.S. military forces to a degree that the European members could not possibly compensate for; it would negate the consultation process within the alliance and wreak havoc with U.S. policies and goals in NATO and Western Europe.[70]

The Aftermath of Czechoslovakia

The Czechoslovakian crisis of August 1968[*] put a quick end to the possibility of passing the Symington amendment. In answering the Joint Chiefs' ambitious and expensive proposed responses to the crisis Clifford demonstrated anew the primacy he attached to restoring the nation's economic health. Even as he addressed their concerns, the secretary reminded the Chiefs that the likelihood of still greater economic problems in FY 1970 meant that readiness had to improve within available resources. When Nitze proposed a $50 million package to strengthen NATO forces, the Chiefs judged the figure inadequate. Now that Soviet aggression had called into question Washington's preconceptions about Moscow's willingness to resort to naked force, they believed that the United States had to demonstrate its commitment to NATO by immediate and visible military actions "despite the serious weakness of its military force posture." Besides advocating conducting several large field exercises, they wanted a moratorium on further NATO reductions as well as cancellation or reconsideration of numerous REDCOSTE and other economy initiatives.[71]

Clifford opted instead for ISA's more austere combination of smaller exercises and limited construction of aircraft shelter and storage facilities in Europe. Though the Joint Chiefs approved the proposal, for them it fell short of conveying to the

---

[*] See Chapter XVIII.

Soviets Washington's determination and leadership role in strengthening NATO. A compromise with OSD incorporated several JCS recommendations—keeping a brigade of the 24th Division permanently in Germany, retaining a maritime patrol squadron, and improving electronic warfare capabilities in Europe. In exchange the Chiefs dropped plans to deploy a brigade from Korea to Europe and accepted the $50 million ceiling on a response "package." Clifford implemented DoD's $50 million package response, highlighted by REFORGER/CRESTED CAP exercises in January-February 1969 that demonstrated U.S. ability to redeploy units rapidly to Europe. Provision was made for permanent retention of one brigade of the 24th Infantry Division in Germany. Other measures—construction of aircraft shelters and munitions storage facilities—were made conditional on the European allies also undertaking significant improvements to their forces.[72]

The dismal U.S. reply to the Defense Planning Questionnaire (DPQ) delivered to NATO on 10 September 1968 acknowledged several realities: Vietnam commitments left the U.S. Army dependent on redeploying some forces from Southeast Asia to reinforce NATO rapidly; readiness levels of SACLANT's naval forces had dropped between 9 and 25 percent depending on the type of warship; and the Air Force could muster only four dual-based tactical squadrons for NATO during 1968. As of the final day of October, none of the three Army divisions committed to deploy to Europe within 30 days of M-Day would be able to accomplish that mission, the best time being 63 days, the worst 119 days. Mid-November's proposed changes to the DPQ described the enhanced readiness of the U.S. Army strategic reserve and promised further improvements in deployment capability. By 31 December, the 5th Infantry Division (Mechanized) would be able to deploy in 7 days, and the two armored divisions in between 77 and 84 days. This would mark the first time in approximately three years that DoD could show improvements in the availability of the NATO-oriented STRAF divisions.[73]

The litany of all too familiar American complaints—deficiencies in the NATO allies' conventional force structure, domestic pressure in the United States to reduce the NATO defense burden, offset issues, and balance of payments deficits—were as valid in 1968 as in 1962. If the United States still bore what it believed an unfair burden, at least OSD conceded that there were financial limits to conventional defense. As Clifford informed the president, the risk of surprise attack was so low and the cost of sufficient conventional forces to preclude resort to nuclear weapons so high that no reason existed to set higher objectives for conventional forces.[74]

Yet despite the dissatisfaction, the NATO alliance had adjusted to major changes in strategy, force structure, nuclear planning, and burden-sharing between 1965 and 1968. The "tired and sick beast" had carried its burden—the defense of Western Europe—despite the French withdrawal from the alliance, substantial troop reductions by the United States, the unseemly, often harsh, disputes among allies about sharing defense costs, and strains exerted by fundamental and potentially far-reaching changes in Eastern and Western Europe. More to the point, despite the upheavals, the alliance had endured and accomplished its primary goal—preserving the integrity of Western Europe by deterring Soviet aggression. Perhaps part of the credit for NATO's success during these years belongs to the Soviet Union which, burdened by its own domestic problems and having to deal with unrest in its East European satellites, may have had no intention of attacking NATO.

CHAPTER XVI

CRISIS IN THE MIDDLE EAST

In May 1967, deeply engaged in fighting a war in Vietnam and seeking to deter a war in Europe, the Johnson administration at the same time found itself confronted with an impending conflict in the Middle East. The longstanding enmity between Israel and its Arab neighbors exploded into a brief but intense war in early June 1967 that also precipitated a dramatic and dangerous confrontation between the United States and the Soviet Union. In the long term the conflict's aftermath radically altered U.S. policy in the Middle East and accelerated the prewar trend of the United States becoming Israel's main arms supplier. For the Department of Defense, concerned about the military balance in the area, this required reluctant changes in attitude and conduct toward the region and particularly toward Israel.

Genesis of the Crisis

Since the founding of the state of Israel in 1948 the United States had supported the territorial integrity of all nations in the Middle East.* Though not bound by any treaty commitment, along with France and Great Britain the United States had signed the 1950 Tripartite Declaration, which promised to oppose any effort to change by force the national borders in the region. During the 1956 war between Israel and Egypt, enlarged by British and French military intervention, Israeli units occupied the Sinai Peninsula, including the Egyptian military base at Sharm el Sheikh that dominated the Straits of Tiran, entrance to the Gulf of Aqaba. Israeli troops withdrew only after United Nations emergency forces were positioned along the armistice line dividing Israel and Egypt and at Sharm el Sheikh. Washington assured Tel Aviv that the Gulf of Aqaba, Israel's sole outlet to the Red

---

* For the purposes of this chapter, the Middle East includes Egypt and all the Arab states, Israel, and Iran. At the time, Near East and Middle East were used interchangeably.

THE MIDDLE EAST

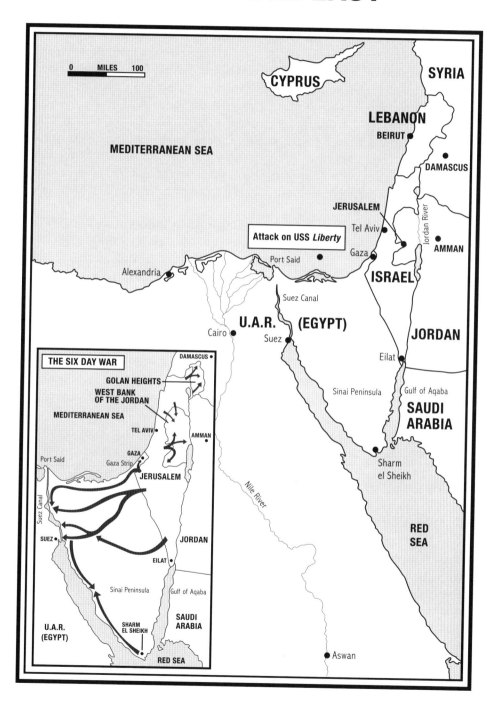

CYPRUS

SYRIA

LEBANON

BEIRUT

DAMASCUS

MEDITERRANEAN SEA

JERUSALEM

Tel Aviv

Attack on USS *Liberty*

Port Said

Gaza

ISRAEL

AMMAN

Jordan River

Alexandria

Suez Canal

U.A.R.   (EGYPT)

JORDAN

Cairo

Suez

Eilat

Sinai Peninsula

Gulf of Aqaba

SAUDI ARABIA

Sharm el Sheikh

RED SEA

Nile River

Aswan

THE SIX DAY WAR

DAMASCUS

GOLAN HEIGHTS
WEST BANK OF THE JORDAN

MEDITERRANEAN SEA

TEL AVIV

AMMAN

Port Said

GAZA
Gaza Strip

JERUSALEM

Suez Canal

SUEZ

JORDAN

EILAT

Sinai Peninsula   Gulf of Aqaba

U.A.R. (EGYPT)

SHARM EL SHEIKH

SAUDI ARABIA

RED SEA

0   MILES   100

Sea and the Indian Ocean, would remain open as an international waterway.[1] Although successive American presidents had reaffirmed these guarantees, Congress never approved such commitments. The hastily drawn 1957 armistice agreements were susceptible to a variety of interpretations.

In March 1958, Egypt and Syria, two of the four Arab states sharing a border with Israel (Lebanon and Jordan the others) combined as the United Arab Republic (UAR) under the leadership of Egyptian President Gamal Abdul Nasser.* Border disputes, sporadic terrorism, and bellicose rhetoric characterized relations between Israel and its Arab neighbors during the early 1960s. For its part, the United States attempted to avoid appearing overly favorable to Israel in order not to alienate less vitriolic countries such as Jordan and Iran. Complicating Washington's balancing act, the Soviets expanded their influence in the region by championing the UAR and providing economic and military assistance. Rearmed and backed by a super-power, the UAR under Nasser exerted considerable pressure on other Arab states, especially Jordan.

During 1964 Washington tried to counter Soviet influence and maintain a military balance in the region by direct arms sales to Jordan. To avoid antagonizing the Muslim states, the United States used West German channels to supply tanks to Israel surreptitiously. After public exposure uncovered this stratagem by early 1965, President Johnson, in part to mollify Israel over Washington's sale of military equipment to Jordan, on 21 February 1965 authorized direct sales to Israel. Shortly afterwards U.S. representatives offered to make good the tank deal in the now com-promised German agreement and to find "a few" aircraft for Israel.[2]

The Joint Chiefs, leery of any arms policy that supported either side, opposed any action that would serve to identify the United States with Israel and the Soviet Union with the Arab world, fearing that such polarization would only strengthen anti-U.S. feeling. On 6 May the Chiefs endorsed the status quo—the United States should not sell aircraft to Israel but continue to rely on Western European nations to meet Israel's needs. In late October, however, after completing negotiations for the rest of its tank requirements, Israel complicated matters by asking the United States for 210 new fighter bombers, almost nine times the earlier proposed "few" aircraft, on the grounds that neither Britain nor France could supply its requirements.[3]

After months of foot-dragging, DoD and State supported the sale of 36 fight-ers to Jordan and as many as 48 fighter-bombers to Israel. In early February 1966 Johnson instructed McNamara to make a hard-nosed deal for the aircraft on Tel Aviv's promise to "sew up everyone in Congress to keep quiet about our Jordan and Israeli sales." In exchange for 48 aircraft sold on lenient credit terms, McNamara pressured Israeli Foreign Minister Abba Eban, who had little choice, to accept U.S. arms sales to Jordan and maintain full secrecy about the deal until Washington pub-licized it. On 31 March, McNaughton reported to McNamara that "negotiations

---

* Syria withdrew from the union in September 1961, but Nasser retained the name for Egypt.

are . . . successfully behind us" with both countries. On 2 April State announced the Jordanian sale and followed on 20 May with a statement on the Israeli purchase but emphasized that there was "no connection between the sale to Israel and the sales of equipment to Jordan."[4]

Meanwhile regional tensions were rising as Arab confidence grew, reflecting a combination of circumstances: plans to divert Jordan River waters at Israel's expense, newfound cooperation among Arab states, the creation of a multinational military command structure (the United Arab Command), and greater availability of conventional arms in the region. Terrorist activity against Israel also surged as sophisticated raids by Palestinian guerrillas became a major security problem for Israelis. By late December 1965 Tel Aviv felt concern that Washington did not fully understand its defense needs, especially in light of the Arab military buildup. From February 1966 the radical leftist regime that took power in Syria promptly encouraged more infiltration and terrorist operations against Israel, some originating from Jordanian soil.[5]

Plagued by persistent Syrian-sponsored terrorist attacks, on 13 November 1966 the Israeli army retaliated with a major counterblow against suspected guerrilla strongholds in Jordan's West Bank. Walt Rostow felt the disproportionate Israeli reaction, "aimed at the wrong target," had undermined pro-Western King Hussein, Washington's hope as a stabilizing factor along Israel's longest border.[6] To defuse the latest crisis, the administration issued public and private warnings to Israel and bolstered the Jordanian king with additional military assistance.

Another upsurge in Syrian-initiated terrorist attacks during early January 1967 prompted the Israeli government to ask Washington for additional military assistance, including 200 armored personnel carriers (APCs) and $2 million in M-48 tank spares provided on a grant basis plus $14 million in liberal credits to purchase Hawk missiles and M-48 tanks. The United States had never before given Israel grant military aid and refused to break the precedent. McNamara and the Joint Chiefs also consistently opposed the sale of APCs, believing that Israel had no "serious military requirement" for them.[7] Despite the tension along Israel's borders with Jordan and Syria, in the late spring of 1967 a full-scale conflict seemed remote.

Onset of an Emergency

On the eve of Israel's Independence Day celebration of 15 May, belligerent rhetoric from leading Israeli officials, further distorted by press reports, threatened Syria with retaliation for the growing number of terrorist attacks. Convinced by past Israeli reactions that some form of retribution was imminent, Syrian leaders readily accepted a Soviet report of 13 May that Israel was massing its forces to invade Syria, likely between 17 and 21 May. No evidence has appeared that the Israelis were concentrating large military forces for an invasion; retired officials and scholars in Moscow later admitted the report resulted from "improperly evaluated intelligence." Nasser nevertheless accepted the Soviet report as valid and mobilized Egyptian forces on 14 May. Two days later Israel responded cautiously by calling up a reserve armor regiment and some artillery units.[8]

As the crisis evolved, the highest levels of the Johnson administration were preoccupied with a major, and divisive, reassessment of Vietnam policy. Vietnam strained the nation's military and financial resources and soured the administration's relations with Congress. Johnson certainly did not need another international crisis, but if one arose he absolutely needed congressional support for his policies. And congressional caution ruled out unilateral American military action.[9]

Though focused on Vietnam, the administration had not lost interest in the Middle East. Much time and effort went into making decisions on military aid for Israel and Jordan that would preserve the traditional U.S. Middle East policy of evenhandedness thought necessary to keep moderate Arab states in the Western camp. The sad truth was that hardly anyone—Arab, Israeli, Russian, American— even in May 1967 foresaw the possibility of war in the Middle East.[10]

In response to the simmering Middle East situation Johnson formed a number of ad hoc task forces. The earliest, organized on 14 May and headed by Eugene V. Rostow, under secretary of state for political affairs, monitored all interdepartmental activities related to the unfolding emergency. Two weeks later, as the crisis intensified, Rostow also took the chair of the Control Group, which primarily analyzed long-range diplomatic and military aspects and made recommendations to the secretary of state to assist decisionmaking at the highest level. Membership of the Control Group was intentionally kept small to facilitate policy formulation.[*] Deputy ASD(ISA) Townsend Hoopes attended meetings as an OSD representative; a senior officer from the Joint Staff's Plans and Policy Directorate (J-5) also attended, when invited. Subordinate to the Control Group, a task force chaired by State's Lucius Battle and supported by several subcommittees was formed. The subcommittees were organized functionally to deal with issues such as contingency military planning, economic vulnerabilities, legal matters, evacuation of U.S. citizens, political settlement, and so forth. A reorganization dropped the JCS's visitation rights before the Control Group; State contended that Vance's permanent status allowed him to bring anyone he wanted to the meetings. As the crisis worsened, however, the Joint Chiefs, deprived of a regular representative, felt the change adversely affected their feedback from the Control Group.[†11]

On 16 May Nasser demanded partial removal of the United Nations Emergency Force (UNEF) patrolling the Egyptian side of the Israeli-Egyptian 1957 armistice line; two days later he sought UNEF's complete withdrawal, including

---

[*] Members included Chairman Eugene Rostow, Walt Rostow (White House), Cyrus Vance (DoD), Foy Kohler (deputy under secretary of state for political affairs), and Lucius Battle (assistant secretary of state for Near Eastern and South Asian affairs).

[†] This situation was remedied on 7 June, after the outbreak of hostilities, when the newly-established Special Committee included the CJCS.

the unit stationed at Sharm el Sheikh, which controlled access to the Gulf of Aqaba. This prompted a high-level policy review at the White House where Johnson decided, as part of a broader U.S.-USSR rapprochement, to enlist Kosygin's cooperation to defuse the growing tension in the Middle East. Following ISA's recommendations, on 19 May McNamara and Wheeler shifted major U.S. Sixth Fleet units from the Italian coast to the eastern Mediterranean. The next day the ships were ordered to positions off Crete and Rhodes, within one to two days steaming time from the critical area.[12]

On the 19th, reacting to Nasser's ouster of the UNEF and the Egyptian military buildup in the Sinai, the Israeli defense minister directed a large-scale mobilization. On the same day, the Israeli Foreign Office assured the U.S. ambassador the call-ups were purely precautionary, "nowhere near mobilization," and portended no military initiatives. Israel also secretly requested—unsuccessfully—that a U.S. destroyer then exiting the Gulf of Aqaba turn back and visit Eilat, its port on the gulf. Tel Aviv further asked Washington to decide favorably on Israel's still pending arms request, but the president continued to pigeonhole it.[13]

Then, on 22 May, Egyptian forces occupied Sharm el Sheikh, and Nasser promptly announced the closure of the Straits of Tiran, which separated the Gulf of Arabia from the Red Sea, denying access to Eilat-bound ships and thus severing commerce to the Indian Ocean. Since only one Israeli-registered merchantman had passed through the heavily traveled straits in the past two and one-half years, Nasser's decision transformed a regional crisis into an international one involving innocent passage of the ships of many nations in the Gulf of Aqaba. The following day Johnson approved the long-pending Israeli military assistance requests that only 48 hours earlier he had deferred. Secret terms included the cash sale of 100 APCs, preferably Italian-built on U.S. license, a $2 million cash sale of tank spare parts, a $14 million credit at five percent interest for Hawk and tank spare parts, and other cash and loan sales.[14] Delivery had not yet begun when war erupted on 5 June 1967.

While the president relied on personal diplomacy, sending messages to Israeli Prime Minister Levi Eshkol, Nasser, and Kosygin urging restraint, the Middle East Control Group recommended dispatching a second carrier task force to the eastern Mediterranean along with a U.S. Marine battalion landing team from Naples. McNamara objected that such actions would only inflame the volatile situation. On 24 May British Minister of State for Foreign Affairs George Thomson arrived in Washington to share with Eugene Rostow and Rusk his government's concern that an Egyptian attempt to close the Gulf of Aqaba might provoke a bloodier war than had occurred in 1956. Thomson informally proposed an international declaration reaffirming free passage through the gulf, combined planning for Anglo-American warships to escort merchant vessels during their passage, and a show of force in the Mediterranean.[15]

In afternoon discussions with U.S. and British defense officials, a British admiral fleshed out a plan for a small UK-U.S. probing force to escort merchant vessels through the Straits, later known informally as the Red Sea Regatta. As part of the plan, a covering force (off Aden some 1,250 miles distant) would distract the Egyptians while a deterrent force consisting of the Sixth Fleet, a British carrier, and British bombers on Cyprus was prepared to strike UAR air bases or military targets near the entrance to the Gulf of Aqaba, if required. For ISA, Hoopes expressed concern that the British proposal might draw the United States into fighting in the Middle East, a reversal of historic American policy, with enormous political implications. Eugene Rostow, who seemed favorably disposed toward the British plan, thought that two or three weeks might remain to formulate plans and put them into effect.[16]

At a follow-on meeting on the military merits of the British proposal, U.S. senior officers reacted negatively to the British plan, finding it carelessly drawn and employing but a single British frigate for the most dangerous operation, the probe force. Both the Joint Staff director and Wheeler expressed alarm at London's willingness to force the Straits without air cover or ASW and minesweeper protection. They suspected that the British intended to create a pretext to strike Egypt with a punishing blow and saw no need to sacrifice a U.S. destroyer and crew for the purpose.[17] From the outset of the crisis, then, top officials in OSD and the JCS expressed serious reservations about using American military forces to intervene directly in the region.

Johnson had heard the gist of Thomson's plan at a midday NSC meeting on 24 May. Clearly skeptical (later that day he reportedly said the idea was "idiotic"), he pressed his advisers on what the United States could do if the international effort failed.[18] Rusk found things "serious but not yet desperate," while McNamara assured the president that, despite opinion to the contrary as voiced by Senators Fulbright and Symington, the United States could manage both Vietnam and the Middle East contingencies at the same time. Taking his cue from the defense secretary, Wheeler described the powerful U.S. naval force in the Mediterranean but acknowledged a paucity of ground forces—one understrength Marine BLT—and the lack of a readily available anti-submarine warfare unit needed to neutralize two Egyptian submarines operating in the Red Sea.

If worse came to worst, Wheeler advised backing long-term Israeli military operations to the hilt. Later, if the United States had to intervene to preserve Israel's security, he believed "the USSR might just cut its losses and back out." A more apprehensive McNamara foresaw any war starting with a fierce battle to achieve air superiority. As both sides suffered heavy losses, they would demand the United States and USSR intervene with air support, thus escalating a regional war to a dangerous threshold. Wheeler, though, was confident the Israelis could hold their own. Although CIA Director Richard Helms thought the recent Israeli performance against Syrian MIGs* boded well for its air capability in any conflict, the agency was not overly sanguine on the subject.[19]

---

* During a major border clash on 7 April Israeli warplanes shot down six Syrian MIGs in dogfights that carried as far as the skies over Damascus (Poole, *JCS and National Policy, 1965–1968*, pt 2:543).

Personal Diplomacy

On 25 May, after talks in Paris and London, Israeli Foreign Minister Abba Eban arrived in Washington to explore the feasibility of American support for the British proposal that a group of maritime nations undertake to keep the Straits of Tiran open on behalf of the international community and to learn the degree of U.S. commitment to the plan. During Eban's travels, Tel Aviv's concern had expanded from the Aqaba blockade to an Egyptian military buildup in the Sinai. The Israeli government now asserted that a surprise attack by Egypt and Syria could occur at any moment and wanted Washington to announce publicly that an attack on Israel would be considered an attack on the United States.[20]

Such a guarantee, Rusk informed Eban during their 25 May discussion, was beyond the scope of presidential authority; it required congressional approval. Besides, U.S. intelligence assessed the deployment of an Egyptian armored division into the Sinai as a defensive move. The Israeli-furnished selective intelligence data about an offensive threat was regarded by U.S. officials as a gambit to get Washington to put more pressure on Nasser and provide more military supplies, a public statement of support, and approval of Israeli military initiatives.* The CIA did conclude that Israel felt fighting was unavoidable since the move of the armored division showed that the UAR was seeking war. Eban did not press the issue further with Rusk, who assured him that Johnson would fulfill American commitments. To do so, however, the president required congressional and public support; preemptive action by Israel would endanger the consensus he was trying to build.[21]

After speaking with Eban, Rusk advised in writing that the president had two options for his scheduled meeting with the Israeli diplomat on 26 May. Johnson could "unleash" the Israelis and let them decide how best to protect their national interests. This Rusk found unacceptable and instead recommended a "positive position, but not a final commitment" on the British proposal, namely to use the United Nations Security Council to avert war, publicly declare along with other maritime nations the right of free passage through the Straits of Tiran, and formulate a contingency plan for an international naval presence in the area of the Gulf of Aqaba. Although the UN would probably prove ineffective, the United States had to make the attempt if only to demonstrate that the international organization was unable to act in the situation.[†22]

---

* According to Egyptian sources, the UAR air force had decided to launch air strikes the morning of 27 May, but Nasser countermanded the order on 26 May (Quandt, "Lyndon Johnson and the June 1967 War," 209, n 29).

† Oren, *Six Days of War*, 111, asserts without documentation that Johnson cabled Israel's warning of an imminent Arab attack to Moscow, apparently on the night of 25 May. The only evidence found is a 19 May message to Kosygin that offers a general statement of concern over rising tensions in the region; see ltr Johnson to Kosygin, 19 May 67, *FRUS 1964–68*, 14:486.

Eban next consulted with McNamara, Wheeler, and other OSD officials at the Pentagon during mid-morning on 26 May, emphasizing the immediate danger of the Gulf of Aqaba closure that threatened to isolate Israel from half the world "and leave it crippled." He appealed to a February 1957 aide-memoire that Israel interpreted as a binding U.S. commitment to use force to keep the Straits open. Without definite American assurances, Eban continued, "the balloon would go up" the following week. McNamara remained unmoved, dubious that a few U.S. Navy escort ships would cause Nasser to change his mind, and convinced such an action would leave the United States with an open-ended commitment. The defense secretary also warned Eban that Washington could not support Israel if it launched a preemptive attack. Halfway through the discussion Eban received a note reconfirming the message a day earlier that a UAR-Syrian attack against his country was imminent. Wheeler restated the American view that Israel would win any war no matter who fired the first shot. Eban agreed but insisted he had to know what the United States would do if Israel were attacked. McNamara indicated, as Rusk had earlier, that the president would respond when Eban met with him.[23]

A few hours later at a White House meeting McNamara told the president of his warning that Israel would "stand alone" if it initiated an attack. The defense secretary also took issue with Eban's assertion of an unconditional and unilateral U.S. commitment to keep the Straits open. OSD's review of the pertinent 1957 documents had revealed that then Secretary of State John Foster Dulles had qualified any such assistance by stating that without congressional action the president did not have the right to use force to protect vessels flying other flags.[24]

Wheeler outlined the status of the Israeli military mobilization, allowing that it could be sustained for two months without serious economic dislocation. Regardless of the deployment of 50,000 Egyptian troops to the Sinai, no signs indicated that the UAR intended to attack Israel. McNamara questioned whether Thomson's proposal had full British military support. In any event, a U.S. naval probe of the Straits remained out of the question until the UN had played itself out or until Congress had endorsed the administration's proposal. Realizing it might take two or three weeks to marshal legislative support, McNamara suggested there was "no 'perishability'" in the situation (that is, the Israelis would win a war regardless of timing, so there was no pressure for them to act). The critical factor was Israel's inability to sustain a prolonged mobilization without enduring tremendous economic costs. He suggested the president inform Eban that if Israel initiated an attack it would stand alone, and that if the UN failed, the president, subject to congressional approval, would work with other nations to ensure keeping the Straits open. At the end of the meeting Rusk drafted a position paper that the president could use that evening when he met with the foreign minister.[25]

At this meeting Eban insisted that without access to the Gulf of Aqaba Israel was cut off from half the world—Asia and East Africa—and his country had "either to surrender or to stand." The president and the others disagreed, suggesting a third possibility—an international solution. They also differed with Tel Aviv's assessment of an impending Arab attack. Johnson took pains to point out that he was "of no value to Israel" without the support of Congress and the American people. Noting that he had to follow constitutional processes, the president stressed that Israel should not initiate hostilities, reiterating, "Israel will not be alone unless it decides to go it alone." He picked up on McNamara's assertion that U.S. intelligence agencies were unanimous that an attack was not imminent, adding that if the UAR did attack, "you will whip hell out of them."[26]

The president concluded the meeting by handing Eban an aide-memoire listing the constitutional restrictions on his war powers, the ongoing United Nations process, his own public commitments on the Straits, and a warning that a first strike would isolate Israel internationally. Although four successive presidents had made commitments, they had never received congressional sanction; that lack limited what Johnson alone could promise Israel. Without solid congressional backing, Johnson had earlier told Israeli Minister Ephraim Evron, "I'm just a six-foot-four Texan friend of Israel."[27]

Meantime OSD set several actions in motion. Because of concern that Israel, by itself, might not be able to maintain mobilization or wage a protracted war, on 26 May ISA requested information on Israeli 30-day requirements and what needs could be filled by U.S. sources. ASD(I&L) replied that Israel could continue its current state of readiness indefinitely without foreign help, although full and prolonged mobilization would harm the civilian economy. Israeli stockpiles were judged adequate for 30 days of sustained combat, but beyond that period, logistic support to Israel would require the United States to dip into NATO or Southeast Asia stocks and increase munitions production on a continuing basis.[28]

Affected American unified commands affirmed their readiness, within limits, to intervene militarily if required. USCINCEUR pointed out that political restrictions on U.S. military overflights and use of staging and operating bases would hamper operations by land-based American tactical air units in Europe. This placed the burden for initial military support on the Sixth Fleet, whose two aircraft carriers had fortuitously been reinforced by the aircraft carrier *Intrepid*, then awaiting orders to transit the Suez Canal en route to Southeast Asia.* Sixth Fleet pronounced itself ready to execute contingency plans as necessary even though its amphibious task force was understrength and its Marine BLT had no helicopters. If the Marines went ashore, an airborne brigade from the United States would land simultaneously as planned. U.S. forces in Europe would not be used to avoid giving the Soviets an opportunity to increase pressure against a depleted NATO Central Front.[29]

---

* *Intrepid* was scheduled to transit the canal on 24 May, but fear of the warship being trapped in the confines of the canal by Israeli action to close the waterway and concern that the UAR could interpret the move as an imperialist plot to deploy U.S. military capability in the Red Sea led to a decision to hold the carrier southwest of Crete awaiting further developments.

CINCLANT reported such significant shortfalls that, barring mobilization, available ground forces had only limited capability to conduct operations in any Mideast conflict. Sixth Fleet aircraft, however, could ensure air superiority and freedom of maneuver for Israeli ground units. Citing the larger Cold War context, CINCSTRIKE saw no reason for engaging in a regional affair likely to enhance Soviet influence at U.S. expense. He strongly endorsed complete impartiality, opposed open support of Israel, and concluded that unilateral American military action should be undertaken as a last resort and then only to end the fighting.[30] Clearly, the field commanders urged caution on military intervention because of political and operational uncertainties.

On 27 May, Kosygin, dissatisfied with the president's 22 May letter, wrote Johnson that the Soviet government had information that Israel was preparing to attack its Arab neighbors. Referring to the president's correspondence that called for restraint on both sides, Kosygin insisted Israel would "not dare step over the line" without American encouragement. If Israel did attack, the USSR would aid those countries "subjected to aggression." The president promptly cabled Eshkol the gist of the Soviet statement and warned Israel against a preemptive strike that would brand it the aggressor. This letter and the president's remarks to Eban in Washington no doubt influenced the Israeli cabinet's decision on the afternoon of 28 May to postpone military action pending a possible diplomatic solution. In an attempt to make diplomacy work, the president informed Kosygin the same day of his "maximum effort" to counsel moderation on Israel and stressed the need for Soviet cooperation in seeking a prompt resolution of the Straits of Tiran issue.[31]

Meanwhile, on 27 May Thomson informed Eugene Rostow that by 30 May a British naval force would be in position in the eastern Mediterranean and another the following day in the Gulf of Aden. But the JCS had earlier faulted the British concept for its implicit assumption that the probe force could accomplish its mission without provoking a hostile reaction from the UAR. There was no fallback position. If the Egyptians did respond militarily, the British proposed to retaliate in force against a wide variety of targets throughout the UAR. The Chiefs found this willingness to expand the fighting "astonishingly reckless." Furthermore the British plan failed to provide adequate protection for the probe force—air cover, air defense, ASW, and minesweeping capabilities were all dangerously limited or nonexistent.[32]

The Chiefs offered a scenario confining any hostilities to the immediate international waters under dispute or, if no hostilities erupted during the naval probe, testing Egyptian resolve by progressively running merchant vessels and warships through the Tiran Straits to ensure the blockade was lifted. They considered four courses of action. Courses I and II used U.S. naval units east of Suez, unilaterally in I and in combination with British forces in II. Courses III and IV required reinforcements from the Mediterranean to pass through the Suez Canal to the Red Sea and would take until 20 June to assemble. Besides the issue of timing, the Chiefs rejected III and IV because of the possibility that blockage of the canal could jeopardize the warships in transit, a reluctance to use carriers in the restricted waters of the Red Sea, and uncertain Egyptian or Israeli reaction to such a deployment.[33]

At the urging of Admiral McDonald, and then only reluctantly, the Joint Chiefs endorsed Course II. They did so out of political considerations—to restrain Israel from attacking by taking action against the blockade in a timely fashion. To have any effect, the British assumed that a probe had to be executed between 28 May and 1 June. Although Course II, for combined Anglo-American action by forces east of Suez, could not meet this timetable because they would take about eight days to assemble, it still offered the best chance of success with the fewest risks. But the Joint Chiefs refused to minimize the danger. With only two U.S. destroyers then available east of Suez, both a unilateral and a combined naval challenge to the blockade faced the same "serious risks" from Egyptian shore batteries and UAR aircraft. They warned McNamara on 27 May that all proposed courses involved the risk of war or a U.S.-UAR armed confrontation, and that Washington should not take any action unless the administration was prepared to accept the consequences.[34]

ISA declared the JCS proposal "unduly pessimistic" for overestimating the probe force's vulnerability and discounting air support available from Cyprus or Sixth Fleet carriers. Since the United States had restrained an Israeli attack for the moment, Townsend Hoopes recommended to McNamara further consultation with Wheeler to develop more detailed plans for an augmented naval force that could be in position in two or three weeks. McNamara agreed. Yet harboring doubts about the British initiative, he recommended against further combined planning until the UN Security Council process had been exhausted. Henceforth political and diplomatic initiatives would take precedence over Anglo-American naval conversations.[35]

Continuing with contingency planning, on 28 May the Control Group prepared a draft presidential memorandum that described a multinational maritime declaration upholding free passage of the Straits, a scenario to test it, and a supporting congressional resolution. McNamara demurred because the draft congressional resolution did not clearly provide for the possibility of military action. Without such a provision in the resolution, he saw little sense in joint military planning or any declaration since neither could be backed up in a showdown.[36]

McNamara expressed his doubts when he and Rusk reworked the memorandum. They outlined a three-step scenario: (1) take action in and outside the UN to avert hostilities; (2) elicit from maritime nations formal and public affirmation of the principle that the Straits of Tiran and Gulf of Aqaba were international waterways; and (3) induce continued Israeli restraint by completing contingency planning to test the UAR blockade with merchant shipping within two weeks. As the two prepared their recommendation, the prospect of a drawn-out UN debate increased; only the Dutch and possibly the Canadians seemed interested in a multinational naval task force to support the principle of open access to international waterways.*[37]

---

*On 1 June Australian Prime Minister Harold Holt personally promised President Johnson two cruisers for the expedition (Johnson, *Vantage Point*, 295).

Their formal memorandum, sent to the president on 30 May, incorporated these points and their version of a naval contingency plan to reopen the Straits. They envisioned a protective force in the Red Sea, albeit devoid of adequate air cover and ASW protection, to escort merchantmen transiting the Straits. Another force composed of U.S. and British warships in the eastern Mediterranean would attack major UAR air bases and other military installations if the UAR fired on the merchantmen or their escorts. The willingness of both secretaries to expand the potential area of hostilities reflected the earlier British position, ignoring the Joint Chiefs' recommendations to limit military action to the immediate Straits vicinity. Finally, they counseled Johnson to seek a joint congressional resolution authorizing him to use military force but warned him to consider carefully the request's timing. "While it is true that many Congressional doves may be in the process of conversion to hawks," they wrote, "the problem of 'Tonkin Gulfitis'* remains serious." In short, the resolution might get "bogged down in acrimonious debate" in Congress, a recurring Johnson worry. On 31 May, an unenthusiastic president met with McNamara and Rusk about the proposed naval probe. He did agree to a maritime declaration whose draft text State sent to all posts on 31 May.[38] The recommendations, however, quickly unraveled.

The unwillingness of non-U.S. flagged tankers to test the blockade meant no ship would immediately enter the Straits. Moreover, it would take one to two weeks either to charter non-U.S. flags or to requisition tankers of U.S. registry for the trial run; there was doubt that the Israelis would or could sit still for that long. More alarming, Israel decided that it could not permit even a peaceful refusal of transit to an Israeli-flagged ship without immediate recourse to military action. Combined naval planning was also coming apart given the growing reservations on the British side over the consequences of armed force. The cabinet in London hedged its commitment to force once ministers fully realized the course Thomson was proposing.[39]

Other imponderables included uncertain Egyptian and Soviet reactions. Contrary to Wheeler's belief that Nasser would fold, American diplomats in Cairo warned that unless confronted by overwhelming military might Nasser would fight to maintain the blockade. If that happened, "U.S. use of force would hardly fail to involve USSR on a serious level." Rusk, with McNamara at his side, assured the Senate Foreign Relations Committee on 1 June that the administration would make any final decision on the use of force only after UN remedies were exhausted and congressional support was obtained.[40]

---

* Reference to the Tonkin Gulf Resolution of 1964.

To the Breaking Point

On 29 May Nasser announced that the USSR would back his blockade, which State took to mean Moscow would support the Egyptian move politically. The following day, 10 Soviet warships sailed as previously scheduled into the Mediterranean and Jordan signed a mutual defense pact with the UAR, conjuring up in Israeli minds the image of unified Arab armies launching multifront offensives against Israel's borders. Faced with this latest threat, Eshkol, replying to the president's 28 May letter, informed Johnson on 30 May that "the possibility of a concerted Arab assault" made it out of the question for Israel to continue to stand by "for any considerable time" before acting on its own to break the Egyptian blockade. While U.S. guarantees were welcomed, it was crucial that the international naval escort move through the Straits "within a week or two." Officials in Washington knew that just to assemble a tanker fleet for a test run would require about 15 days, and by this time it was questionable whether the British would participate in an escort force.[41]

Both McNamara and Rusk believed it would be useful also to test Egyptian resolve by sending the U.S. carrier *Intrepid* from the Mediterranean through the Suez Canal. Although scheduled for Vietnam service, once the carrier reached the Red Sea it would become available for contingency operations in the Gulf and Straits. Even with the augmentation of the carrier and its escorts, the Red Sea Regatta, likely to consist only of U.S. and UK ships, would still lack sufficient air cover and ASW protection, making any probe politically and militarily dangerous. Possibly for these reasons, on the morning of 31 May the president urgently requested other options than the regatta.[42]

Late that day, Vance and McNamara discussed a request from the president for recommendations on the Sixth Fleet's role in countering possible Soviet moves into the troubled area. Vance thought any riposte was fraught with danger and likely to increase tensions even further. McNamara considered the possibility of holding the *Intrepid* in the Red Sea, announcing the fact, and implying a naval buildup in lieu of shifting the Sixth Fleet from point to point. The two forwarded this recommendation to Walt Rostow at the White House.[43]

In Israel the imminent peril of a combined Arab attack added to the urgency of resolving the Straits issue. Convinced his nation was in mortal danger, Eshkol dispatched the head of Israel's intelligence service, Maj. Gen. Meir Amit, to Washington to learn the Americans' "real intentions" and make them aware of the "seriousness of the situation." During his brief day-and-a-half stay, Amit met with McNamara on 1 June; Amit told him that Israel could not continue indefinitely on a war footing because the economy, already in a recession, had reached a standstill, an estimate the CIA shared. On his return to Israel, Amit would recommend going to war. McNamara's official version had Amit trying to portray Israel's problem as a U.S. problem in an effort to secure American support. McNamara, noncommittal, asked only two questions: how long would the war last and how many casualties did Israel expect? Amit replied: seven days and "in the neighborhood of 4,000 casualties." The Israeli intelligence chief conveyed a similar sense of Tel Aviv's imminent decision for war to CIA Director Helms, assuring him that Israel could "then handle its own case" quickly and with minimal losses so long as the United States continued to supply already ordered weapons, offered diplomatic support, and kept "the USSR out of the ring."[44]

On 1 June Eshkol withdrew his opposition to military action; the same day Amit's report from Washington arrived stating that the Red Sea Regatta was "running into heavier water every hour." On 4 June, in view of the imminent threat to the country's existence, the Israeli cabinet voted to launch an immediate preemptive attack. The same day Walt Rostow informed the president that the Israelis would only wait about another week but wanted Nasser to fire the first shot.[45] Rostow's assessment was, of course, erroneous but indicative of how from 1 June onward the administration's continuing focus on the blockade as the fundamental policy consideration caused it to misread Israeli fears and intentions.

On 2 June, in response to ISA's 28 May recommendation, the Joint Chiefs produced a longer-range scenario for naval action. It would take 31 days to assemble a balanced U.S. naval force in the Red Sea. Should a decision be made to conduct a probe before that, the warships then available would have to be used even though they stood little chance of survival from UAR air and sea attacks. Even with the stronger option, the Chiefs agreed that it was operationally unsound to position carriers in restricted waters and divide naval units between the Red and Mediterranean seas. They wanted to concentrate a naval force off the Straits of Tiran while deploying American and British carrier forces in the eastern Mediterranean within striking distance of UAR targets. Then, to test the blockade, they would dispatch merchant ships through the Straits ad seriatim: (1) non-Israeli; (2) Israeli owned, but non-Israeli flagged; (3) Israeli owned and flagged. If the Egyptians militarily challenged the Anglo-American attempt to ensure the right of free passage, the United States had to be prepared to conduct strikes ranging from "discriminating air and naval attacks against selected military targets to full-scale airstrikes against all UAR military targets."[46]

Prospects for broad international participation in a naval force and a maritime declaration continued to wane as the Western nations believed such measures would present serious threats to their Middle East interests. The Canadians clearly stated that they would not participate in a naval force; furthermore, their approval of a declaration would depend entirely on adherence to a peaceful resolution of the crisis. Prime Minister Lester Pearson later informed Johnson of his personal concern that naval force would be counterproductive. The British cabinet, keenly aware of its economic vulnerabilities in the region (the effect on oil revenues, access to the Suez Canal, and Saudi and Kuwaiti sterling deposits in London), was likewise softening its position. With the United States lacking strong international support, on 2 June ISA suggested working toward a compromise political settlement rather than a strong maritime declaration or show of naval force.[47]

Israeli statements created the impression that the administration still had time to find a diplomatic solution to the crisis. On 2 June, for instance, Evron had told Walt Rostow that his government would "hold steady for about two weeks" but added this was not an "ironclad" figure. Later that day, considering the possible lengthening of the crisis, the Joint Chiefs permitted Sixth Fleet to make port calls for upkeep but warned they might be curtailed on short notice. Indicative of a lowering of tension, at least in official Washington, the National Military Command Center (NMCC) in the Pentagon reduced the size of its morning Middle East situation report.[48]

Also on 2 June a high-level British delegation composed of foreign and defense office heads plus representatives of the prime minister met with McNamara and Rusk and other senior administration officials for an overall review. Both secretaries emphasized that any use of military force required congressional support; given the "passionate aversion on the Hill to any unilateral action by the US," such backing was not available. McNamara noted the Israelis' belief that their military capabilities deteriorated over time, but he insisted they could even delay another two to four weeks and still defeat the Arabs in a week to 10 days. Continuing mobilization, however, was hurting the Israeli economy, and McNamara expected that political considerations would force a decision within two weeks. While he judged unlikely the worst-case scenario—American armed intervention to prevent Israeli defeat—the defense secretary expressed concern that "we would have a real problem if the Soviets came in to save Egypt." The British indicated hesitancy to move too fast militarily; both sides agreed on no further combined naval force planning.[49]

By 3 June Rusk had grown pessimistic about the chances of averting conflict because the "Holy War" psychology of the Arabs, matching the apocalyptic vision of the Israelis, fed a crisis atmosphere in which both antagonists felt confident of battlefield victory. The CIA reported a growing belief in Israel that time was running out; a corresponding bandwagon of momentum was building in Arab capitals sensing the possibility of success against Tel Aviv. For its part, the United States could not abandon commitments made in 1957 guaranteeing transit through the Straits of Tiran. But the administration could not risk unilateral action to open the straits because Congress had made plain its disapproval of any course of action that did not rely on multinational forces preferably acting under UN auspices. Unwilling to "throw up our hands and . . . let them fight while we try to remain neutral," Rusk canvassed his ambassadors for their suggestions on alternative diplomatic approaches to the crisis.[50]

The president replied to Eshkol's 30 May letter on 3 June, reviewing the constitutional processes he had to follow on matters involving war and peace. Once again Johnson counseled restraint and stressed that Israel must not isolate itself by starting hostilities. He reiterated his admonition to Eban that "Israel will not be alone unless it decides to go alone," adding that his administration found such a decision unimaginable. Johnson noted that a complete and full exchange of views with General Amit had occurred. Since Amit had told McNamara and Helms that war was likely, Israeli leaders may have taken this statement to mean that Johnson understood time had run out and that Israel was going to act on its own. Intentionally or otherwise, they were mistaken. According to Under Secretary of State Katzenbach, "We tried to get the Israelis to cool it. I think the President thought that he had an assurance from the Israelis that there would be no war. He certainly felt he had one, but they nonetheless went ahead. . . ." Johnson was blunter. "I had a firm commitment from Eshkol and he blew it. Now he says he did it all himself. That old coot isn't going to pay any attention to any imperialist pressures."[51]

U.S. military and political assessments accepted Israeli battlefield success as a foregone conclusion but feared the consequences of a Mideast war. In late May the JCS operations staff projected that Israel would win a regional war lasting 10 days to two weeks, but at heavy cost. The Israelis would also seize major portions of Egyptian territory for postwar bargaining leverage. To maintain U.S. influence in the region, Washington had several objectives: prevent Soviet military participation in the conflict and limit Moscow's role in any postwar settlement; sustain such pro-West Arab regimes as Jordan and Saudi Arabia; preserve territorial integrity of all nations in the area; keep American forces out of the fighting; reduce Nasser's regional influence; ensure free passage of the Straits; and "lay some basis for resolution of outstanding Arab-Israeli issues."[52]

Walt Rostow sought to avoid polarization in the region, that is, the destruction of Israel or the cementing of a radical Arab bloc unified by anti-Israeli hostility. He proposed that Johnson offer a compromise to Nasser: Washington would honor its 1957 commitments coupled with a willingness to move forward on issues of concern to the Egyptian president. The administration would then approach Congress for a resolution supporting the 1957 agreements and thereby hold off Israeli military action for another week or so. The extra time would enable Washington to push Moscow to pressure Egypt for a diplomatic solution and to organize a force to test the blockade. The Control Group deliberated from late morning of 4 June into the evening, including a meeting with Rusk and McNamara. The group drafted, among other documents, messages for the president to transmit to the several involved heads of state urging restraint.[53] Unfortunately time ran out.

The Six-Day War

The opening of hostilities, reported shortly before 3:00 a.m. Eastern Daylight Time on 5 June, took official Washington by surprise. As the president stated two days later, "We thought we had a commitment from those governments, but it went up in smoke very quickly." Cables from the U.S. defense attaché in Tel Aviv and U.S. ambassadors serving in the belligerent nations soon confirmed media

Above: An antiballistic missile (ABM) on parade in Moscow, May 1965.
Below: The Joint Chiefs, top science advisors, and Secretary McNamara meet at the White House to discuss ABM policy, 4 Jan 1967.

Above: Secretary McNamara, Prime Minister Nguyen Cao Ky, President Johnson, and President Nguyen Van Thieu meet in Honolulu, 8 Feb 1966.
Below: At the Glassboro Summit, Secretary McNamara speaks to Soviet Premier Aleksei Kosygin while President Johnson observes.

Above: Secretary McNamara and President Johnson confer during a meeting with West German Chancellor Ludwig Erhard (seated under portrait), 21 Dec 1965.
Below: A lighter moment during policy discussions concerning the tripartite talks on forces stationed in West Germany, 5 Mar 1967.

Above: Secretary McNamara, President Johnson, Secretary Rusk and Walt Rostow discuss the Soviet nuclear nonproliferation offer at Camp David, Maryland, 2 Oct 1966.
Below: The first meeting of the NATO Nuclear Planning Group, originated by Secretary McNamara, 6 Apr 1967.   He is flanked by British defense minister Denis Healey (left) and the secretary general of NATO, Manlio Brosio (right).

Above: USS *Liberty* after Israeli air and naval attacks on 8 Jun 1967 that killed 34 crew members and wounded another 171.
Below: An Israeli Army command post looks out over Jerusalem just before launching an attack into the Old City, Jun 1967.

Above: American personnel clean up following the crash in Greenland of a B-52 bomber carrying nuclear weapons, Jan 1968.
Below: Secretary McNamara speaks on the phone while President Johnson and other senior advisors discuss the conflict in the Middle East, 8 Jun 1967.

Above: The USS *Pueblo*. The North Koreans precipitated a crisis when they seized this intelligence gathering ship in January 1968.
Below: Soviet tanks in Prague, Aug 1968. The Warsaw Pact occupation of Czechoslovakia was another in a series of crises that bedeviled U.S. policymakers that year.

Above: A Tuesday luncheon, 23 Jan 1968. Clockwise from President Johnson (back to camera): Secretary McNamara, General Wheeler, Clark Clifford, Walt Rostow, Tom Johnson, George Christian, CIA Director Richard Helms, Secretary Rusk. It was at this meeting that Clifford responded to a joking McNamara: "May I leave now?"

Below: USS *Enterprise*, USS *Long Beach*, and USS *Bainbridge*, the first nuclear-powered task force, 31 Jul 1964. The Navy's goal to build more nuclear-powered ships conflicted with McNamara's budget reduction plans.

bove: A Marine cleans his M-16 rifle during the battle in Hue City, Feb 1968. The weapon was *rone to malfunction, and critics blamed McNamara for rushing it into service.
elow: The F-111A swing-wing in action. Originally conceived as the TFX, it was supposed to save *ioney by serving both the Air Force and the Navy, but it proved to be expensive and ineffective for *iis dual role.

Above: The B-52 was a workhorse of the aerial campaign in Vietnam even as Secretary McNamara sough[t] to retire the aircraft. Congress stuck by it.

Below: Secretary McNamara briefs the press on his cost reduction program.

COST CUTTING SOUND EFFECT

WILL THE REAL JULIUS M'NAMARA PLEASE STAND UP?

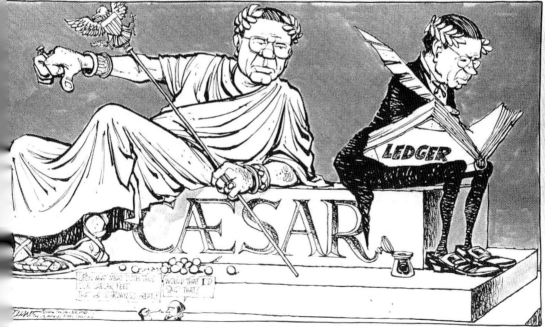

Above: Drifting Apart: President Johnson and Secretary McNamara, 5 Dec 1967.
Below: A meeting of the Wise Men, 2 Nov 1967. Seated clockwise from left (far side of table): Robert Murphy, Ambassador Averell Harriman, Dean Acheson, General Omar Bradley, General Maxwell Taylor, Justice Abe Fortas, Clark Clifford, Secretary Dean Rusk, President Johnson, Secretary McNamara, Douglas Dillon, McGeorge Bundy.

Above: Secretary McNamara departs Pentagon at the end of his tenure, 29 Feb 1968
Below: Secretary Clifford (far left) and his "8:30 Group"—the trusted advisors he met with daily.
From left to right: Colonel Robert Pursley, George Elsey, Phil Goulding, Paul Warnke, and Paul Nitze.

Above: Secretary Clifford, Secretary of State Dean Rusk and President Johnson in the Oval Office, 26 Mar 1968.
Below: Secretary Clifford and General Earle Wheeler in the Cabinet Room at the White House, 5 Dec 1968.

Above: The Joint Chiefs meet with Secretary Clifford (far right) and President Johnson about FY 1970 budget shortages, 26 Dec 1968.
Below: President Johnson (leaning over) meets with Generals Wheeler and Creighton Abrams, 26 Mar 1968.

Above: President Johnson reads a banner headline announcing his decision to halt all bombing of North Vietnam, 31 Oct 1968.

stories that fighting had erupted. Shortly after 5:00 a.m. intelligence reached the White House indicating numerous Egyptian airfields were unserviceable.* Within minutes the president authorized a State Department message to the Soviet foreign minister expressing U.S. dismay and surprise at the outbreak of the conflict as well as Washington's determination to work with the UN Security Council to bring the fighting to an end as quickly as possible. In the cable Rusk told the outraged Soviets that the outbreak of hostilities had surprised the United States as much as it had the USSR. After all, the administration had earlier told Moscow of Israeli affirmations that Tel Aviv would not initiate hostilities. The Soviet leadership found Rusk's reassurances "in no way credible," but, unable to extend decisive assistance to its Arab clients, silently accepted the American message.[54]

Shortly before 0800 McNamara informed the president that the NMCC Hot Line, the so-called MOLINK, a teletype line connecting Moscow and Washington established in 1963, clattered to life operationally for the first time (previously it had only undergone periodic testing). The NMCC duty officer promptly notified McNamara, who learned to his surprise that the teletype line terminal was in the basement of the Pentagon. The secretary told the duty officer to "get that damned line patched over to the White House," as much to facilitate communication with the president (its intended purpose) as to comply with the Soviet operator's insistence that Johnson be physically present at the American end of the hot line before he would transmit Kosygin's message. McNamara notified the president and then joined him and Rusk in the White House Situation Room to await the transmission.[†][55]

The Soviet premier called on the United States to cooperate with the Soviet Union to end the fighting and hoped Washington would "exert appropriate influence on the Government of Israel." Later that afternoon Wheeler described the message as "hard line," but it was more terse and stylized than intimidating. Within an hour of getting Kosygin's message, the president replied over the hot line that the United States would use its influence to bring hostilities to an end and was pleased that the Soviets planned to do the same. There were no further exchanges that day.[56]

About the time of the president's reply to Kosygin, a message arrived from Eshkol explaining that Israel had gone to war in self-defense. Appealing to Johnson's friendship, fidelity, and leadership, he hoped the United States would prevent the Soviet Union from "exploiting and enlarging the conflict." A few hours later, Eugene Rostow told British Ambassador Patrick Dean that the Israelis had assured the administration that they had no territorial ambitions; by localizing the conflict they sought to restore peace within existing boundaries.[57]

---

* Later in the day, the Israeli air commander announced that 374 Egyptian, Jordanian, Syrian, and Iraqi warplanes had been destroyed or damaged. By war's end, this figure had grown to approximately 440, most of them attacked on 25 bases but with about 60 destroyed in air-to-air combat.
† All told, the two leaders exchanged 19 messages over the hot line between 5 and 10 June 1967 (Washington-Moscow "Hot Line" Exchange, nd, vol 7, Appx G, #6, box 19, NSF NSC History of Mideast Crisis, LBJL). A twentieth MOLINK message was a duplicate of Rusk's 5 June message sent earlier by cable to Foreign Minister Gromyko.

At the highest levels in Washington, the first inclination was to try to identify who fired the first shot. Rusk instinctively felt the Israelis "probably kicked this off," but could not be certain. Walt Rostow asked Clark Clifford to make that determination. McNamara also repeatedly tried to pin down an answer, but by the afternoon of 5 June available U.S. intelligence was still silent on the matter. Although unable to prove it, the Joint Chiefs believed Israel had launched a preemptive attack; the CIA also indicated that Israel had probably fired the first shot. At midday the president convened a meeting in the Cabinet Room of his secretaries of state and defense as well as other senior advisers including Clifford. According to Rostow, Clifford was emphatic that the Israelis had attacked with "minimum provocation" to gain air superiority and then go after the UAR ground forces in the Sinai.[58]

As the day wore on the question of who fired the first shot diminished in importance. In the late afternoon Walt Rostow notified the president of an Associated Press eyewitness account that confirmed Eshkol's claims that an Egyptian artillery bombardment preceded the Israeli strike across the borders. "Whatever the truth of the matter," Rostow wrote, "this dispatch gives them a better propaganda case." The stunning Israeli military success relieved the administration of need to mobilize U.S. public support for possible military aid or support to Israel and having to justify a preemptive strike to the American people. As press reports and official channels confirmed "the first day's turkey shoot," Rusk expressed the administration's relief "that we didn't have to get [the] military involved." Walt Rostow later explained that the rapid Israeli victory freed the United States from the predicament "of having to make a choice of engaging ourselves or seeing Israel thrown into the sea or defeated."[59]

But Israeli battlefield successes complicated American efforts to gain a cease-fire. Washington favored having one in place until other issues such as free navigation of the Straits of Tiran could be settled. The Soviets argued for a return to the status quo ante, and the Israelis wanted a simple cease-fire that would de facto leave them in charge of the occupied territories. Unwilling to endorse U.S. conditions, but with Israeli forces steadily advancing into the Sinai and Jordan, the Russians finally agreed on 7 June to a simple cease-fire resolution, in effect temporarily accepting the Israeli position.[60]

A day earlier the Joint Chiefs had supplied McNamara with their appraisal of the strategic situation. They favored reversing Nasser's rising prominence in the Arab world without damaging U.S. interests in the region or allowing the Soviets any opportunity to increase their influence among the Middle East nations. To accomplish these goals the Chiefs recommended a policy promoting territorial integrity and the restoration of political and economic stability in the region. They proposed noninvolvement of the United States in any military action that would imply partiality for one side or the other, continuation of efforts to end the fighting, and suspension of logistic support to all belligerents.[61] In brief, the Chiefs reaffirmed a longstanding position, but events in the Middle East would soon challenge traditional American policy.

The Arab Reaction

Despite a DoD press release of denial on 5 June, early the next morning Radio Cairo broadcast an official report that warplanes flying from British and American carriers had participated in the Israeli air strikes against the UAR and Jordan. Queried by the Joint Chiefs, Sixth Fleet reconfirmed that no direct or indirect communications had occurred between the fleet and any Israeli source. In the West, Arab fabrications quickly collapsed when the Israelis released transcriptions of an intercepted radio telephone conversation between Nasser and King Hussein apparently agreeing to trump up charges that British and American warplanes had aided Israel.* Tel Aviv explained the deception as the Egyptian president's attempt to rescue his dwindling prestige by claiming his forces retreated not before the Israeli onslaught but because of the massive intervention of foreign forces. But the Arab world presumed Western complicity in the attacks; the damage was done. Despite prompt denials by London and Washington, anti-American riots erupted throughout the Middle East, nowhere more alarming than in Libya where crowds demonstrated around Wheelus Air Base and a mob sacked the U.S. embassy in Tripoli. As Arab rage against the West mounted, Muslim states from Mauritania to Iraq broke diplomatic relations with the United States;† Kuwait, Iraq, and others suspended oil shipments as well. This newfound unity directed against Israel and the United States had neither been foreseen nor considered likely.[62]

What *had* been taken into account was the dependence of the United States, the industrial West, and Japan on Arab oil. One-third of the industrial nations' oil came from Middle Eastern states, accounting for 70 percent of Western European and 80 percent of Japanese oil imports. Saudi Arabia and Bahrain supplied almost all the aviation fuel used by the U.S. military in Vietnam. Recognizing U.S. dependence on Arab oil, especially for jet fuel, in early February 1967 Deputy Assistant Secretary of Defense (Supply and Services) Paul Riley had proposed reviewing and/or preparing contingency plans to deal with an interruption of oil flow from the Persian Gulf.[63]

The Pacific theater required 6.5 million barrels of oil products monthly. Should distribution suffer disruption, sources in the United States and Caribbean could fill the slack in about 30 days by shifting some four percent of their refining capacity. Reliance on Western Hemisphere oil would, however, double the transportation time to Southeast Asia, from 30–35 days to about 60–70 days, a development that would necessitate an increase in oil tankers to move the POL products.[64]

---

* The voices on the tapes were judged genuine, but ISA remained suspicious that the Israelis might have doctored the recordings. The key passage was ambiguous, stating either "Did you say" (a request for information) or "Shall we say" (collusion on a false statement). See ltr Dir, Office of Research & Analysis, NESA to DepAsstSecISA(NESA), 8 Sep 67, fldr A/I/S 3-12-3 1967 Crisis Settlement #3, box 1, ISA Regional files, Acc 330-76-140.

† Algeria, Egypt, Iraq, Mauritania, Syria, Sudan, and Yemen severed diplomatic relations.

Even as fighting erupted in the Middle East, ASD(I&L) instructed the Defense Supply Agency to negotiate contingency contracts by 9 June with oil companies operating in the United States and the Caribbean area for 6.5 million barrels of oil monthly through 31 December 1967. McNamara informed the president and the public of the revised procurement to ensure an uninterrupted flow of oil to Vietnam. By 9 June, the Defense Fuel Supply Center had arranged to buy or reallocate a one-month supply of POL and would decide within 3 days whether or not to order the next month's requirement from the new sources established by the contingency contracts. DoD chartered 35 additional tankers, but with the easing of tensions delivery schedules from Western Hemisphere sources were reduced to 5.4 million barrels for July and to only 0.8 million for August.[65] The effects of the oil disruption proved negligible for the United States, but the expanding anti-Israeli reaction among Islamic nations provided the cement for a united front directed against Israel and its presumed allies.

Unexpected Muslim unity coupled with Israeli intransigence over withdrawal from newly conquered lands without security guarantees made any postwar settlement difficult. By 7 June Israel's battlefield dominance was obvious to all. The issue in Washington became whether or not Tel Aviv could translate overwhelming military success into an enduring Middle East settlement. A stable and definitive peace, however, required concessions by all nations in the region, and none of the belligerents seemed willing to oblige.[66]

At the NSC meeting held on 7 June, Rusk focused on postwar issues and the U.S. role in maintaining peace in the troubled region. Certainly Israel's lightning victories made the situation "more manageable than five days or three days ago." But those same triumphs made it likely that Israel would no longer accept the territorial status quo that had formed the bedrock of U.S. policy toward the Middle East. Rusk doubted Israel would accept a "puny settlement." Johnson worried that the Soviet Union would not accept such a stunning reversal to its ambitions in the Middle East and lamented "by the time we get through with all the festering problems we are going to wish the war had not happened.[67] His apprehension was justified.

The previous day, 6 June, the president had decided to create a separate committee to coordinate U.S. activities aimed at ending hostilities and finding a peaceful solution for the Middle East. On the 7th, he publicly announced its establishment as the Special Committee of the NSC and the recall of McGeorge Bundy to serve as its executive secretary. The committee* met daily in the White House. Bundy's appointment also allowed the shifting of some of the burden from Walt Rostow, who was heavily engaged in shaping Vietnam policy and handling other national security matters.[68]

---

* The committee consisted of the secretaries of state (Rusk), defense (McNamara), and treasury (Fowler); the CIA director (Helms); the JCS chairman (Wheeler); the Foreign Intelligence Advisory Board chairman (Clifford); and Special Assistant Walt Rostow. The president stated that he, Vice President Humphrey, and UN Ambassador Goldberg would meet with the committee as necessary.

Because the Arab-Israeli War of 1967 raised a spectrum of questions about oil supply, economic sanctions, currency fluctuation, military planning, and diplomatic initiatives, the committee proved ideal as a daily forum for coordinating the efforts of the principal decisionmakers. Bundy's ability to give undivided attention to the fast-breaking developments greatly helped the committee formulate U.S. policy in response to the crisis, and, when the president attended, make on-the-spot decisions. Beyond its immediate emergency management role, the Special Committee also developed a postwar U.S. position. At its inaugural 7 June meeting, the president announced that the committee had top priority "ahead of anything else."[69]

Within the administration, ISA and State differed sharply over reaching a political settlement. Hoopes regarded State's approach of negotiating early peace treaties under UN auspices as overly optimistic. He also faulted State's analysis for not comprehending the incompatibility of Israel's objectives with Arab aspirations and U.S. interests. An Israeli government seeking a "Carthaginian peace" and unwilling to compromise on legitimate Muslim interests was as much of a problem as a radical, anti-Zionist Arab state. Likewise, Hoopes maintained, if Israel did accept a compromise, the United States had to be willing to support traditional Israeli objectives, among them: recognition of Israel's existence by the Arab states; freedom of access to the Gulf of Aqaba; freedom from terrorist attacks; and an expanded presence in Old Jerusalem.[70]

Then there was Moscow's attempt to make good military equipment lost by its Mideast clients during the fighting. In late May the United States had decided not to cut off military supplies to Israel nor, in an effort to retain influence among pro-Western Arab states, to Jordan and Saudi Arabia. Military shipments would continue, but no new commitments would be undertaken. After fighting erupted, McNamara issued instructions on 8 June to control deliveries of military equipment to Middle East states. He immediately suspended the release of additional military materiel to any Middle East nation either in the form of a Military Assistance Program or a DoD-controlled sale unless approved by a representative of the secretary of defense or the secretary of state.* Military equipment destined for states that had broken relations with Washington was being repossessed to the extent it remained under U.S. control. While licenses for existing munitions shipments to Israel and Arab countries that had not broken relations continued in effect, no new licenses were being approved for Israel or those nations at war with Israel. McNamara anticipated requests from the Israelis for "substantial quantities" of ammunition, replacement equipment, and spare parts. Vance and Katzenbach were to review such requests personally and submit their recommendations to the Special Committee.[71]

Frequent Soviet resupply flights to Arab capitals aroused American suspicions. At a Special Committee meeting on 8 June, Rusk speculated that the Soviet call for a cease-fire was a pretext to buy time for Moscow to reequip the Arab air forces for a

---

*This action suspended grant and sales aid to Algeria, Egypt, Iraq, Mauritania, Syria, Sudan, and Yemen.

surprise attack against Israel. Alarmed by the magnitude of Soviet logistics support, Israel wanted 48 A-4 aircraft as well as additional tanks and ammunition from the United States. McNamara felt the domestic pressure on the administration to meet those requests would be intolerable. The solution, as he saw it, was to approach Moscow and suggest that both sides stop the arms flow into the Mideast. Johnson preferred either to freeze arms shipments to all parties or stall on a decision for a day until the situation became clearer.[72]

The Control Group expressed concern that a total cutoff of military supply to Muslim states would be dangerous and counterproductive to U.S. interests because it would risk American lives in the area, jeopardize U.S. oil and other commercial interests, and forfeit any chance to negotiate meaningful agreements with the Soviets to limit the supply of conventional arms to the region. At a meeting on 9 June the Special Committee agreed to continue shipments already in the pipeline to Saudi Arabia as well as Israel. The White House, however, extended the embargo to Jordan and Lebanon. Neither had broken diplomatic relations with Washington, but apparently for domestic political reasons the president wanted to say privately that he had stopped military consignments to all nations contiguous to Israel.[73] It would prove much more difficult to restart shipments of arms and military equipment to Middle East nations than it had been to embargo them.

The Attack on the Liberty and the U.S.-Soviet Crisis

The war struck home on 8 June when the USS *Liberty*, a communications intelligence vessel under control of the National Security Agency and Sixth Fleet, was attacked and two-thirds of its crew killed or wounded. *Liberty's* original 23 May orders directed the ship to proceed from the Ivory Coast to the eastern Mediterranean. On 1 June new orders authorized the *Liberty* to proceed to within 12 1/2 nautical miles of the UAR coast. Then on 7 June the ship was ordered to stay at least 20 nautical miles from the coastline; a later JCS message, transmitted several hours before the attack the next day, instructed the *Liberty* to withdraw 100 nautical miles off the coast. Because of clerical misrouting, the last two messages did not reach the *Liberty*. On the morning of 8 June, Washington time, Israeli warplanes and gunboats attacked the vessel, then 13 nautical miles off the Sinai coast, killing 34 Americans and wounding 171.[74]

Learning of the attack from a *Liberty* radio message, the Sixth Fleet commander directed one carrier task force to proceed toward the scene and informed CINCEUR that within the hour he would launch armed aircraft to defend the embattled ship. CINCEUR in turn notified the NMCC, which relayed word of the attack to the president shortly before 10:00 a.m. Since *Liberty's* flash report had not identified her attackers, immediate suspicion in Washington fell on the Soviet Union or UAR. Amidst this confusion, McNamara authorized the use of whatever force necessary to defend the stricken ship. For 70 anxious minutes the White

House had no idea who was responsible for the assault, but by 11:00 a.m. had learned from the U.S. Defense attaché in Tel Aviv that Israeli planes and torpedo boats had carried out the attacks in error.[75]

To avoid any misunderstandings about the sudden upsurge in U.S. naval air and sea operations that followed, State officials initially notified the Soviet embassy and subsequently the president explained to Kosygin over the hot line that the sole purpose of launching aircraft was to investigate the condition of the *Liberty*, "apparently . . . torpedoed by Israeli forces in error." Upon receiving the dispatch from the attaché office in Tel Aviv, the Sixth Fleet commander immediately recalled all aircraft, and the Joint Chiefs directed discontinuance of any use of force. Clifford, particularly incensed by the Israeli attack and finding it inconceivable that it was an accident, argued for the administration to take as tough a stand as it would have against an Arab or Soviet attack on the ship.[76] Washington instead adopted a low-key approach by accepting a bland Israeli apology and solatium payments to casualties or their survivors.

By the time of the attack on the *Liberty*, the overwhelming extent of the Israeli victory had become apparent, to the dismay and frustration of the Soviet leadership. Defeated, Egypt, Syria, and Jordan had been forced by 8 June to accept a humiliating cease-fire. On 9 June, however, Israel charged Syria with violating the truce; Israeli armor and infantry, supported by massive air strikes, invaded Syria and advanced toward Damascus. The Soviet Union now found itself smarting from a major diplomatic defeat brought about by underestimating Israel, overestimating Egypt, and miscalculating the U.S. response to the fighting. Accusing Israel of ignoring Security Council resolutions, on 10 June the Soviet leaders notified Johnson via the hot line that, unless fighting stopped "in the next few hours," they were ready to take independent action, including military, even though it might "bring us into a clash, which will lead to a grave catastrophe."[77]

The president, in the Situation Room with his senior staff, responded with celerity, informing Kosygin that Washington was pressuring Tel Aviv to honor a cease-fire. Indeed Israel had assured the United States more than six hours previously of its intention to stop the fighting. Within five minutes Kosygin answered that the fighting had not stopped, that the Israelis were advancing toward Damascus, and that "the matter cannot be postponed." After the president briefly left the room McNamara asked whether the Sixth Fleet should deploy eastward. All agreed it should, aware that Soviet submarines shadowing the fleet would immediately report the change to Moscow along with the self-evident message "that the United States was prepared to resist Soviet intrusion in the Middle East." On his return, in a "deathly still" room, Johnson approved the recommendation; McNamara issued the order over a nearby secure telephone.[78]

The Joint Chiefs alerted CINCEUR just after 10:00 a.m. of the impending orders, sent about 90 minutes later. At Wheeler's direction, the orders explained that the continued fighting had caused the Soviet Union to warn that it might intercede militarily against Israel. As a precaution, the two U.S. carrier task forces were to move east at moderate speed to about 100 miles off the coast, placing themselves within range to cover both Israel and the Sinai area while awaiting further instructions. Amphibious units were held south of Crete. A message for the Strategic Air Command to initiate an airborne alert and commence generating sorties was drafted, but as the emergency dissipated during the late morning hours it did not go out.[79]

At 10:58 a.m. the president replied on the hot line to Kosygin's threat, stating that Washington had been pressing Israel to end the fighting and that he had received categorical assurances from the Israelis that they were not advancing on Damascus. Kosygin responded at 11:31 a.m. that fighting was continuing on the strategic Golan Heights and proposed that if military action ended that day, the next step was a return to the status quo ante. Johnson's noncommittal reply, dispatched at 11:58 a.m., stated that the fighting seemed to be concluding; he hoped that all future efforts could be devoted to a "lasting peace throughout the world."[80] Shortly afterward Israel and Syria agreed to a cease-fire and the Soviet-American crisis subsided. By that time the Israeli troops had occupied the Golan Heights.

Although CIA Director Helms recalled the atmosphere as tense and apprehensive and Ambassador Thompson characterized the morning of 10 June as "a time of great concern and utmost gravity," McGeorge Bundy remembered no such air, primarily because of his conviction that Israel would not seize Damascus. Besides, underneath the harsh rhetoric, Bundy estimated "the Russians' possibilities were not really that impressive." At the time, Johnson downplayed the hot line as more a gimmick than a useful crisis management tool. On further reflection, he praised the system because it forced leaders and their top advisers to come to grips immediately with major issues.[81]

Aftermath

Defeated and humiliated, the Arab states received strong support from the Soviet Union. A flow of Soviet arms into the region and an accompanying rise in Soviet influence that continued after the cease-fire worried the president. By 12 June, 140 Soviet transport aircraft may have arrived in the UAR or other parts of the area, as many as 78 Soviet jet fighters had arrived in the UAR or Iraq, and a merchant ship carrying a cargo of arms originally destined for Cuba had been re-routed toward Algiers. The CIA regarded these shipments as routine; the Control Group was less certain.[82]

As McNamara had foreseen, Israeli pressure to fulfill the president's 23 May arms decision intensified in the wake of the June war. Early in July he and Bundy concluded that the United States should abide by the terms because the amount of equipment was small, it would help future negotiations, and, most important, it would show Tel Aviv that the president kept his word. McNamara expected that by supplying Israel and permitting previously approved arms sales to moderate Arab states Washington could reestablish its diplomatic balancing act to maintain influence in the region. With the exception of a $3 million cash sale to Israel authorized in early August, however, congressional resistance prevented further arms sales in the region until mid-October.[83] Meantime, Moscow's rearmament of radical Arab and Muslim states and offers of cheap and plentiful military equipment to moderate ones like Jordan and Morocco enhanced Soviet prestige in the Middle East.

On 16 June McNamara asked for a JCS assessment of the impact of Mideast polarization on the U.S. military's regional contingency plans, communications, logistic capabilities, and military posture in North Africa, the Mediterranean, and the Indian Ocean. The military leaders foresaw "almost certain" renewal of fighting, forcing Washington to either abandon or directly support Israel. Moscow's influence would wax, Washington's would wane with attendant loss of U.S. base rights, communications facilities, and intelligence collection sites, lengthened sea lines of communication, and possible disruption of oil supplies.[84]

Israeli victories and the territorial aggrandizement that accompanied them had reversed the strategic equation in the Middle East. Israeli cities and industry were safely behind the existing front lines while the capitals of its enemies were within easy striking range of Israeli air and ground forces. But the corollary also held. By advancing their frontiers far beyond what the JCS thought militarily necessary, the Israelis badly overextended their forces, particularly those deployed in forward positions along the Suez Canal. In doing so they overturned the administration's cardinal principle of preservation of national borders of all states in the region. In McNamara's words, this left Washington "in a heck of a jam on territorial integrity."[85]

Seeking to encourage Israeli withdrawal from occupied territory and fearful that Moscow would soon "get fed up with Israel's braggadocio," Johnson wanted to paint as black a picture as possible of Soviet arms shipments into the region. Tell the Israelis, he said, "It wasn't Dayan* that kept Kosygin out." While it was well and good to agree that Israel had to give up territory, no one believed the president would force Israel to withdraw without prospect of a reasonable settlement.[86]

Eshkol's public rejection on 12 June of a return to the prewar status quo forced a reevaluation of U.S. Middle East policy if for no other reason than to prepare a rigorously defined position to replace what McNamara had previously termed "some pretty bad language" in the 1957 commitments. Without some form of agreement, McNamara feared the bellicose attitudes would predominate. Yet a resolution of the territorial question likely required a U.S. guarantee to all parties, which Bundy doubted Congress would approve. After the Special Committee agreed that a statement by the president of U.S. policy appropriate to the postwar conditions was essential, Bundy suggested that Johnson state the problems and ask the parties involved in the dispute to propose specific solutions.[87]

---

* Moshe Dayan, Israeli defense minister from June 1967.

The president adopted this approach; on 19 June he publicly enunciated five fundamental principles for a settlement: (1) acceptance of the right of all nations to live; (2) justice for refugees; (3) guaranteed maritime rights; (4) prevention of a new arms race; (5) respect for political independence and territorial integrity of all states. Troops must be withdrawn, he continued, but in the context of the five principles. While the United States would cooperate with others to promote negotiations, he stressed that "the parties to the conflict must be the parties to the peace." Johnson's efforts had no immediate effect. As the summer lengthened, administration policy became one of "watchful waiting" as the cease-fire lines hardened into a de facto settlement.[88]

By late summer the Muslim states had regained sufficient confidence to agree not to recognize Israel, not to negotiate with Israel, and not to make peace with Israel. Faced with the uncompromising hard-line policy, Tel Aviv adamantly refused to withdraw to its prewar boundaries which, after all, "had produced war instead of peace." In late October Eban told Rusk of Israel's need for "security frontiers." Reminded that Eshkol had stated earlier that Israel had no territorial ambitions, Eban replied, "That was before Syria and Jordan entered the war."[89]

The issue went to the UN Security Council where all parties accepted an ambiguously worded British compromise; on 22 November the Security Council adopted Resolution 242 modeled on Johnson's five principles and calling specifically for Israeli withdrawal and respect for the sovereign integrity of nations in the area. Further progress, however, proved elusive. Israel's occupation of territory nurtured revenge in Arab capitals, fostered a far more radical Palestinian guerrilla movement, and in combination with Arab enmity nullified efforts to obtain peace. Yitzhak Rabin, chief of staff of the Israeli Defense Forces, admitted in mid-December 1967 that the Israelis were in a less favorable position than before the outbreak of the war when they had a formal armistice, "whereas they now find themselves with, at best, an armed truce."[90]

Arab hostility targeted the United States, which fairly or unfairly became identified as Israel's main arms supplier and chief ally. The shift in French policy under President de Gaulle to a pro-Arab stance pushed the United States into assuming that supply role. But the timing and circumstances of real and imagined American actions during and after the war embittered many Arab states.[91] Anti-American demonstrations flared throughout the region in manifestations of the new and enduring attitude.

Rearming Israel

The USSR's decision to replace military equipment lost by the Arabs during the fighting threatened to precipitate a regional arms race that would upset the military balance. To offset Soviet arms deliveries and expanding influence, on 15 August Rusk and McNamara requested the president to approve arms supplies to

Israel and pro-Western Arab nations subject to congressional consultation after the vote on the administration's foreign assistance package. When the House of Representatives just 10 days later not only reduced the administration's $3.4 billion foreign aid request by $600 million but also eliminated DoD's revolving credit fund program, it was judged fruitless for the moment to consult further with Congress. Only in mid-October could Johnson release limited quantities of military material for Israel and selected Arab states, most of it through the Foreign Military Sales program or by direct commercial purchase.[92] It was too little too late.

By November 1967 Israel was asking for 27 A-4Hs to replace combat losses, in addition to the 48 already contracted for but not yet delivered and, more significantly, 50 advanced F-4 Phantom aircraft that would tip the military balance overwhelmingly in Israel's favor. State and Defense agreed that it was in the U.S. national interest for Israel to have a conventional military capability to defend itself; otherwise Tel Aviv might resort to surface-to-surface missiles or even nuclear weapons. The Joint Chiefs insisted that the A-4 deliveries alone would maintain the prewar Israeli edge through 1969, while acquisition of F-4s would likely force the Soviets to step up their arms shipments to their Arab clients. State wanted to provide the additional 27 A-4s and defer decision on the F-4s "for the better part of a year."[93]

Agreeing to the additional A-4s, McNamara and Rusk advised withholding action on the F-4s. On 13 December Johnson postponed a decision on both since the delay would not affect delivery dates. In preparation for the president's forthcoming meeting with Eshkol, on 5 January 1968 Walt Rostow proposed a "*secret-go ahead*" on the additional A-4s but postponement of any decision on the F-4s until events crystallized in the Middle East. McNamara still opposed the sale of F-4s and maintained that the additional A-4s without accelerated deliveries sufficed for Israel's security. Introducing F-4s into the region might spark an arms race inimical to announced administration policy, jeopardizing the UN mission then seeking a comprehensive Arab-Israeli settlement.[94]

When Johnson met Eshkol and other Israeli leaders at his ranch on 8 January he was emphatic that, contrary to Israeli wishes, he would not now make a decision on the F-4s. He did, however, instruct McNamara to ascertain the deadline for a decision if the F-4s were to reach Israel by 1 January 1970. Lastly, to assuage Eshkol, Johnson offered to add more A-4s to the current sale and, if necessary, to start accelerated training for Israeli F-4 air and ground crews to eliminate any lag between delivery and operational deployment.[95]

The U.S. Navy, itself short of aircraft, had objected to supplying Israel with either additional A-4s or any F-4s unless hostilities ended in Southeast Asia. Four days after the president's decision, however, McNamara overrode these concerns and directed the accelerated delivery of A-4 aircraft beginning in January 1969. On 30 January 1968, Israel signed a purchase agreement to buy 40 additional A-4Hs for $60 million. As for the F-4s, after OSD and the Air Force reviewed the timing of pilot training and manufacture, McNamara informed the president in early February that 31 December 1968 would be the latest date for a decision to assure the beginning of delivery in January 1970. On 3 March 1968, Nitze instructed the secretary of the Air Force to make preparations, contingent on a presidential decision, to sell 50 F-4s to Israel; in mid-July Air Force officials issued procurement authorization for $14.1 million in FY 1969 funds for parts and training equipment.[96]

Meantime State grew increasingly apprehensive about Israel's plans for the short- and medium-range surface-to-surface missiles being built under contract in France. Over the next several months OSD and State tried to link the F-4 sale with Israel's strategic programs, fearing that if Israel received the F-4s and then deployed surface-to-surface missiles, the impact on the Middle East arms balance would be "grave." The Israelis, however, seeking to pressure administration officials for a decision on the F-4s, pointed to the growing Soviet presence in the Arab air defense system and reports that more aircraft were en route from the USSR to replace Arab losses. These arguments failed to impress the Joint Chiefs. In early May Wheeler believed that Israeli qualitative advantages in training, morale, motivation, intelligence, logistics, and leadership more than compensated for any quantitative advantages the Arabs might enjoy. Even Israeli fears that France would renege on its delivery of 50 Mirage V fighters failed to sway Wheeler's position.[97]

On 18 June Wheeler informed Clifford that the Soviets appeared to be concentrating on improved training to develop Arab military skills in lieu of supplying additional arms. This development, coupled with improved air defense capabilities, might enable Arab nations to fight an aerial war of attrition against a numerically inferior Israeli air force. Although Tel Aviv could now make a better case for the F-4 aircraft, political factors—Arab reactions, probable Soviet escalation of arms deliveries, lessening of chances for peace and arms control in the region—also had to be weighed.[98]

As possibilities for a comprehensive Middle East settlement dimmed, Eshkol wrote Johnson in early August reminding him of their discussion in Texas and encouraging him to decide promptly on the F-4 sale. Clifford concurred in a noncommittal draft response prepared by the State Department that apparently was never sent. Faced with a politically sensitive issue, the president characteristically shifted responsibility for the F-4 sale to Congress, which responded in Section 651 of the Foreign Assistance Act of 1968, passed 8 October, expressing support for an agreement with Israel for the sale of as many supersonic aircraft as necessary for its defense. With this justification, Johnson authorized negotiations on the F-4 sales to begin.[99]

ISA expected to use the discussions to extract a sought-after quid pro quo from Tel Aviv for the Phantoms, namely Israel's signature on the Non-Proliferation Treaty, a commitment not to deploy surface-to-surface missiles, and termination of Israel's domestic strategic missile development. At Warnke's urging, Clifford proposed a presidential statement requiring that Israel meet these conditions in exchange for receiving 50 F-4s. On 22 October, Johnson informed Eban that while Israel's signature on the nonproliferation treaty was not a formal condition, he had strong feelings about it; he read Clifford's comments to the Israeli foreign minister. Subsequently, however, the president shifted and strongly opposed linking the sale to the concessions. Accordingly, on 1 November Rusk requested Clifford to inform the Israeli ambassador that there now was "agreement in principle" on the sale.[100]

Clifford and Warnke deemed the failure to establish a linkage as a "road to disaster." Consequently, regardless of White House intentions, Warnke persisted in pressing his demands on now Ambassador Rabin[*] during a series of meetings in early November. The Israeli brushed them aside, but soon became even less cordial and rejected any concessions in exchange for the F-4s. Meeting with the president on 7 November Rusk and Clifford insisted that "nuclear weapons in the Middle East were extremely dangerous for the national security of the United States." Johnson maintained that he had promised the F-4s without conditions and that remained his position. A meeting the next day between Warnke and Rabin degenerated into testy exchanges; Rabin, obviously aware of the president's position, "flatly and rather brutally" dismissed DoD's proposals regarding strategic missiles. With the White House siding with Rabin, on 12 November Warnke agreed that an earlier Israel promise incorporated in the A-4 sale not to use American aircraft to carry nuclear weapons and not to be the first to introduce nuclear weapons into the region (Tel Aviv's original ambiguous position) sufficed to conclude the transaction. Ten days later Rabin formally requested that the United States sell Israel the 50 Phantoms and included the protocols of the 12 November meeting; on 27 November Warnke formally agreed to the sale.[101]

Shortly afterward, citing the need for an apparent deterrent to the growing Arab air threat, the Israelis proposed to Wheeler that delivery of F-4s, even though not yet combat ready, begin in April 1969 rather than the agreed January 1970 date. After studying the probable status of the opposing air forces through June 1970, the effect of early delivery on the U.S. Air Force, and the political implications stemming from an accelerated schedule, on 11 December Wheeler recommended to Clifford that F-4 deliveries begin in September 1969. On 20 December Warnke told the Israeli delegation that the decision lay with the White House. The next day Clifford informed the president that the United States could technically deliver the F-4s by April, but the Israelis would be unable to maintain the aircraft in operational status. The Israeli air commander acknowledged as much but reiterated that the mere presence of the advanced aircraft would exercise a deterrent. Nevertheless Clifford, with Rusk's concurrence, recommended and the president approved Wheeler's proposed delivery date of September 1969. The actual agreement was signed on 27 December 1968.[102]

---

[*] Rabin became Israel's ambassador to the United States in February 1968.

The F-4 sale likely helped to destabilize the region, encourage Soviet military aid to the Arabs, fuel a regional arms race, and transform the United States into the main arms purveyor to Israel. It demonstrated the extent to which U.S. aims for the area, however firm and farsighted on paper, were subject to the shifting sands of Middle East politics as well as domestic political pressures. The complex aircraft transaction, at the mercy of circumstances the administration could not control, produced short-term results that conflicted with long-term goals and presaged the formidable obstacles ahead for an evolving U.S. policy in the Middle East.

The Six-Day War had profound consequences for both U.S. and Soviet policy that went far beyond the 9 June crisis and affected relations between the superpowers beyond the Middle East. On the day (19 June) the president in Washington announced his five principles for a Mideast accord, in New York Kosygin called on the UN General Assembly to brand Israel an aggressor, demanding its immediate withdrawal from occupied Arab territory and payment of reparations for war damages. A few days later at the Glassboro Summit, Kosygin made the resolution of the Middle East fracas his highest priority. Preoccupied with obtaining a rapid Israeli withdrawal, the Soviet premier remained unreceptive to the American proposals for strategic arms limitations.[103] The lack of a U.S.-USSR understanding on the Middle East impeded arms negotiations in the larger arena and prolonged the arms race.

The administration's prewar effort to prevent war failed as did its postwar attempts to lay the foundation for a lasting peace settlement. During and after the crisis, DoD was hampered by a lack of immediately available forces, absence of congressional support, and inability to influence Israel decisively, much less the radical Arab states that seemed prepared to accept the prospect of a major war. Washington's failure to restrain Israel stemmed from Tel Aviv's unreasonable requests for absolute (and unconstitutional) U.S. guarantees of Israel's security and from the Israelis' penchant to read into American responses the nuances they needed to legitimize a preemptive attack.

By checkmating possible Soviet military moves during the conflict Washington managed to confine the fighting to the region, the chief accomplishment of its crisis management. But that success did not contain the flow of Soviet arms and influence into the region or enhance the prospect for an enduring peace. So long as the United States supported Israel's right to exist, it was impossible to prevent the USSR from exploiting grievances among Arab nations that rejected Washington's most fundamental policy principle—a commitment to the political independence and territorial integrity of all nations in the area. Voicing the dilemma that all subsequent administrations would face, McGeorge Bundy conceded, "we can't tell the Israelis to give things away to people who won't even bargain with them."[104] The Six-Day War and its aftermath left an already fragile U.S. Middle East policy in shambles, compelling DoD to readjust its policies and plans to accommodate the radically altered political, strategic, economic, and geographic landscape that appeared after June 1967.

CHAPTER XVII

THE BATTLE OVER
MILITARY ASSISTANCE

By 1965 the United States had been providing economic and military assistance to selected foreign countries for almost all of the two decades since World War II. In particular, nations in danger of communist takeover from without or within were accorded top priority for assistance by successive U.S. administrations. Further, to contain communist expansion the United States also assisted in promoting the development of other free and independent states.

Despite the overwhelming support the military aid program enjoyed within DoD, outside the Pentagon the program encountered significant opposition not only to the cost but to the very idea. Objections to military assistance by the public and by congressional members persisted and grew stronger and more contentious as U.S. involvement in Vietnam grew, particularly after 1965. Caught between the demands of the military for continuing substantial foreign military assistance and increasing doubt and opposition in Congress, McNamara and Clifford struggled to find viable compromises, with decreasing success. They found themselves having to make almost continuous adjustment of the finances and organization of the program. The administration's constant efforts to control the federal budget usually centered on holding down the DoD share, requiring the Pentagon in turn to make frequent and unwanted adjustments across the board. The juggling act could not always succeed—many balls were dropped, and many constituencies, including military assistance interests, were disappointed and unhappy. Still, DoD found ways to offset the worst consequences of fund cuts and other restrictions.

The original statutory sanction for military assistance came in the Mutual Defense Assistance Act of 1949, which provided for both reimbursable and grant aid. In practice most of the aid in the 1950s and into the 1960s was grant aid. In 1961 the Foreign Assistance Act replaced previous assistance legislation; it sought to shift military assistance from a grant system to a sales program to get allied countries to pay for a greater share of their defense. Subsequent amendments to the 1961 act broadened the president's authority to sell military equipment to friendly nations on liberal credit terms and established a revolving account to finance additional sales until the reserve was exhausted. Appropriated Military Assistance Program (MAP) funds could also directly finance credit sales of arms; to further promote military sales, in mid-1964 Congress agreed to greater participation by private credit agencies and the Export-Import Bank (Ex-Im Bank) in commercial financing of military sales to developed countries. The amended Foreign Assistance Act of 1964 permitted DoD to use MAP funds (either appropriated or revolving accounts) to guarantee repayment in cases of default to U.S. citizens or U.S. firms selling arms to foreign countries or international organizations.[1]

The secretary of state provided supervision and general direction of all assistance programs including determination of a country's eligibility and the amount of military assistance it might receive. The secretary of defense had responsibility for MAP logistics and for supervising use of the military equipment by recipient countries. Within OSD, the assistant secretary of defense for international security affairs (ISA) furnished general direction, interagency coordination, and administration of Military Assistance Programs.[2]

Under McNamara the MAP Planning-Programming-Budgeting system involved three alternative, often competitive, approaches: (1) ISA-approved dollar guidelines based on the secretary's instructions, (2) estimates from military attachés presented during the annual fall review of country plans, and (3) JCS objectives, found in Annex J, Joint Strategic Operations Plan, that set levels of military assistance, amounts of equipment, and priorities. The JCS were uneasy about the OSD's dollar guidelines, ISA regarded Annex J as a "highly generalized and dubiously costed program," and the attachés were often dismissed as advocates for their particular country. OSD and State's Agency for International Development* reviewed the military's submissions and forwarded their recommendations to the president, via the Bureau of the Budget.[3]

To receive appropriations DoD had to request annual authorization for military assistance funding from the Senate Foreign Relations and House Foreign Affairs Committees and then justify the authorization to the Senate and House appropriations committees.[4] The cumbersome, reiterative legislative process folded economic and military assistance into a single appropriation bill. After long effort the yearly appropriation came in the form of an amendment to the 1961 act that specified not only the amount of funding but provided a vehicle for whatever legislative changes to the 1961 law individual members of Congress might seek.

---

* AID was the point of contact with State until January 1968 when Rusk redelegated responsibility to the under secretary and deputy under secretary of state for political affairs.

The FY 1966 MAP Request

In the early 1960s, Congress had routinely slashed desired MAP funding levels. In 1964 McNamara reacted by setting a $1 billion[*] ceiling for the FY 1966 military assistance request. Toward the close of that year, however, South Vietnam's requirements for additional arms, ammunition, and military equipment forced OSD to shift FY 1965 MAP funds earmarked for other nations to offset Vietnam costs, including a $50 million transfer out of the AID contingency fund.[†] With MAP expenditures for Vietnam and Laos running about $300 million annually, the $1 billion ceiling for FY 1966 became impracticable.[5] Redistributing MAP allocations to meet Vietnam expenses became commonplace.

By early January 1965 McNamara needed another $50 million for Vietnam and proposed to meet the extra costs by cutting back approved FY 1965 MAP funding for Korea, Turkey, Greece, and Taiwan—the so-called forward defense countries, that is, those adjacent or proximate to the borders of the Soviet Union and the People's Republic of China (PRC). The State Department opposed such a course, believing it "unthinkable," according to Dean Rusk, to reduce military assistance to those four nations. State and AID preferred that DoD draw on its own stocks to cover any differences, permissible under Section 510 of the Foreign Assistance Act so long as the withdrawals were replaced with appropriations in the next fiscal year. McNamara agreed to use Section 510 legislation to make up an additional $75 million in military assistance for Vietnam.[6]

For FY 1966, in November 1964, following McNamara's guidance, ISA prepared a $1 billion "normal" MAP budget submission and then added $191 million extra for "special" expenses associated with Vietnam and Laos, a total of $1.191 billion. As part of the overall effort to hold down the total federal budget, however, OSD requested $1.17 billion for the FY 1966 MAP by reducing the "abnormal element" for Vietnam and Laos to $170 million.[7]

Along with its budget proposal, OSD submitted a legislative package to streamline the MAP process by separating MAP legislation from the Foreign Assistance Act, which included economic aid. Transferring MAP to the DoD budget and securing multi-year authorizations would, McNamara thought, facilitate approval of funding, avoid the duplication involved in testifying before several congressional committees for MAP appropriations, simplify the internal DoD administrative transfer of funds to meet emergencies, and promote military sales through commercial channels. With the notable exception of Senate Foreign Relations Committee Chairman Fulbright, committee members generally opposed sweeping changes on the order suggested. The State Department also objected vigorously to

---

[*] All figures represent New Obligational Authority (NOA) unless otherwise noted.
[†] With two exceptions, the president could authorize transfer of ten percent of each AID appropriation account to MAP, provided the total did not increase MAP by more than 20 percent. For an account of early preparation of the FY 1966 request, see Kaplan et al, *McNamara Ascendancy*, 443-46.

McNamara's proposal, believing that the DoD language effectively wrote out State control "over foreign policy aspects of military assistance." AID Administrator David Bell suggested that the president propose multi-year authorizations that would ease Fulbright's legislative burden.[8]

Congressional hearings on the FY 1966 MAP funding request began on 9 March 1965; unlike the acrimonious sessions of the past few years, they proceeded smoothly. The recent commitment of U.S. ground forces to South Vietnam and the bombing campaign against North Vietnam likely softened congressional attitudes regarding military assistance. McNamara's numbers, though, puzzled the legislators. It made no sense to Rep. Peter Frelinghuysen (R-N.J.) for the secretary to ask for $230 million for South Vietnam in FY 1966 when that amount was less than the $268 million already spent during FY 1965. McNamara agreed the request was an approximation but expected that large expenditures of 1965 for aircraft and ammunition would not be duplicated in 1966. Besides, as he argued elsewhere, the situation was so fluid in Vietnam that one could not possibly predict exact financial requirements 15 months in advance.[9]

As for the proposed legislative changes, the Senate Foreign Relations Committee questioned transferring MAP to the DoD budget, but Fulbright looked favorably on the two-year authorization for the overall foreign aid program and the separation of economic from military aid. Even McNamara's old nemesis, Louisiana Rep. Otto Passman, a longtime, outspoken opponent of foreign aid, told the secretary, "Just give me a break and I will help you out." Passman concluded his hearings by offering to speed MAP legislation through his Subcommittee on Foreign Operations and Related Agencies Appropriations once OSD received authorization for its FY 1966 program.[10]

By 28 April the Senate Foreign Relations Committee had reported out a bill recommending two-year authorization, but that subsequently withered in the House. By 30 August, however, Passman's subcommittee had delivered a bill to the full House Appropriations Committee and the Senate Appropriations Committee quickly followed suit. As anticipated, Congress passed the Foreign Assistance Act on 6 September, authorizing $1.170 billion for MAP, approving a revolving fund, and extending Section 510 authority for one year. On 20 October, Congress appropriated the full MAP authorization.[11]

Before MAP legislation began to work its way through congressional committees, the administration pushed initiatives to improve its foreign assistance programs. As early as December 1964, State's Policy Planning Council had distributed an assessment of the future of military assistance. The report saw the program at a "major turning point," with requested funds falling while MAP requirements were rising. To remedy this condition, the council proposed the administration maintain MAP at least at the $1 billion level and obtain congressional approval to incorporate military assistance into the regular DoD budget. Ideally, members advocated an increased MAP appropriation and the transfer of Vietnam and Laos expenses as well as NATO infrastructure costs to the regular DoD budget. To retain its paramount position in foreign aid, State would closely coordinate with OSD to craft the military sales program and work with the Joint Staff to formulate the "political-military judgments which underlie the force goals."[12]

Also in December 1964, McNamara, apparently at the urging of NSC staffer Robert Komer, instructed ISA to reappraise the major Military Assistance Programs for purposes of recommending a comprehensive MAP plan for the FY 1967–1971 period. ISA Deputy Assistant Secretary Townsend Hoopes took charge of the study.[13]

In his June 1965 draft report Hoopes proposed to shift the basis for MAP from regional alliances to local forces tailored to meet local threats. The United States would remain responsible for deterring the major threats. As a consequence, Taiwan and Korea would reduce their ground forces, with corresponding reductions in MAP. Thailand's army, supported by additional MAP, would expand but restructure for "lower-scale conventional warfare," while Philippine forces would realign themselves into constabulary units. As for Greece and Turkey, they too would receive fewer MAP dollars, much to the distress of the Joint Chiefs who insisted conditions in the eastern Mediterranean made it "a particularly inopportune time to reduce military aid levels." Despite Komer's encomium that the work was "the first genuinely fresh new look at MAP to emerge from the Defense Department in years," serious oversights in the planning assumptions undercut the overall assessment.[14]

Hoopes believed that developments in Vietnam did not invalidate his basic proposals, so his report did not address the ripple effect Vietnam might have on recommendations to reduce military assistance elsewhere. During a July review of these conclusions, William Bundy hit the nail on the head: how could Washington urge reduction of South Korean forces while simultaneously asking Seoul to dispatch Korean troops to Vietnam,[15] a question to which there was no satisfactory answer.

In early 1965, over State's objections, OSD had wanted to withdraw substantial U.S. forces from South Korea and gradually reduce military assistance by reorganizing and modernizing the ROK army force structure from 18 to 15 active divisions. President Johnson, however, encouraged South Korean President Park Chung Hee in mid-May to send a Korean infantry division to South Vietnam, with assurances that the United States would extend all aid possible to South Korea and maintain U.S. troop strength on the peninsula. McNamara still wanted to impose his notions of a cost-effective defense on the South Koreans, but concessions in mid-July to the Korean government in exchange for troops forced him to divert funds from other MAP recipients or to cover costs by asking Congress for more money. The existing force structure that McNamara had wanted to reduce would instead be preserved and expanded.[16]

In effect, the July 1965 agreement amounted to the first installment of Washington's incentives to Seoul for dispatching troops to faraway Vietnam.* South Korea not only absorbed more MAP dollars in an era of shrinking MAP budgets, it had its

---

* On 13 August 1965, the Korean National Assembly authorized sending a division of combat troops to Vietnam.

substantial and mounting Vietnam costs completely underwritten by a combination of small amounts of additional MAP and large amounts from the regular or supplemental DoD budgets.

Vietnam Assistance and FY 1966 MAP

Skyrocketing demands for arms, ammunition, and equipment for South Vietnam soon pierced OSD's carefully crafted FY 1966 military assistance budget ceiling. By the end of July 1965, just one month into the new FY 1966 budget cycle, it became apparent that the costs of military assistance to Vietnam for FY 1966, even with favorable congressional action on the pending MAP request, would exceed the $300 million limitation of Section 510 authority. Unable to go to Congress for additional money because of the president's insistence on limiting any supplemental request, McNaughton tried to broker a transfer of AID funds to MAP. Earlier that month AID's Bell had rejected Deputy Secretary Vance's plea for funding to support operations in the Dominican Republic; in mid-August he informed McNaughton that available AID appropriations were "more than fully committed."[17]

Despite apportioning $230 million of the $1.17 billion MAP request to Vietnam, by late 1965 OSD needed an additional $565 million for Vietnam. McNamara financed the deficit by using $300 million of inventories under Section 510 authority and transferring $61 million from other country programs. The remainder came with passage of the FY 1966 DoD supplemental budget request on 25 March 1966. This provided $204 million for the support of South Vietnamese and other free world military assistance forces in South Vietnam,* plus money to reimburse the military departments for the Section 510 drawdowns of $75 million for FY 1965 and $300 million for FY 1966.[18]

In early November 1965 McNamara had proposed to Johnson the transfer of funding requirements for the support of allied forces in Vietnam from the MAP budget to the regular Defense budget. South Vietnam and Laos, both actually fighting communist aggression, clearly fell into a different category that the Military Assistance Program was not designed to support. The Korean War had established a precedent for separate funding when the U.S. Army's consolidated supply system for U.S., Korean, and United Nations forces had funded allied operations with appropriations from service budgets. Other advantages of applying a similar system in Vietnam included improved logistics support by elimination of parallel supply pipelines and stockages—one for MAP, one for DoD—consolidated administration, reduced paperwork, and greater flexibility and responsiveness to immediate needs. More important, removing Vietnam and Laos funding from MAP would appeal to Congress by substantially reducing the FY 1967 MAP request.[19]

---

* This amount would carry only through June 1966.

Thus by early 1966 Vietnam had already significantly altered the military assistance landscape. During FY 1966, MAP requests were submitted and received in increments. The March 1966 supplemental marked the inception of service-funded military assistance for South Vietnam, whose military aid thereafter would be financed from regular DoD budget appropriations rather than from military assistance funds. OSD would eventually rely on this practice to fund military assistance for Laos, Thailand, the Philippines, and South Korea; DoD-funded military assistance doubled between FY 1967 and FY 1970.[20]

TABLE 9

DoD-Funded Assistance, FY 1967–1970
(In thousands of dollars)*

	FY 1967	FY 1968	FY 1969	FY 1970
South Vietnam	$ 1,100	$ 903.6	$ 1,447.7**	$ 1,578.3
Laos		$ 97.0	$ 84.9	$ 94.4
Thailand		$ 61.3	$ 177.7	$ 165.2
Korea		$ 366.3		$ 382.6
Philippines		$ 13.9		$ 6.0
TOTAL	**$ 1,110**	**$ 1,422.1**	**$ 1,710.3**	**$ 2,226.5**

* Estimates
** Includes Korea and Philippines.

Sources: Transc McNamara test, 23 Jan 67, SCAS and SCA hearings on Suppl Authorization and Appros for FY 1967 (Excerpts), 23–25 Jan 67, 60, box 34, SecDef Bio files, OSD Hist; transc McNamara test, 20 Feb 67, HCA hearings on Suppl Authorization and Appros for FY 1967 (Excerpts), 20 and 21 Jan 67, insert 503-04, fldr Vietnam 1967, box 35, ibid; Military Assistance Program FY 1969 Estimates,137, box 72, Subj files, OSD Hist; Military Assistance Program Congressional Presentation FY 1970 Program Justification, 115, box 73, ibid.

The FY 1967 MAP

Following OSD guidance of $1.15 billion for the FY 1967 MAP, in June 1965 McNaughton asked the Joint Chiefs to evaluate the military risks if the current MAP dollar guidelines were followed through FY 1967–1971 and, excluding Southeast Asia, to propose adjustments, including increased funding, to offset the dangers. The JCS mid-August reply found that existing dollar guidelines for MAP left "serious quantitative and qualitative deficiencies" in providing for the activation and equipment of allied forces. Their major concern, however, centered on nations engaged in "open hostilities," such as those in Southeast Asia where requirements far exceeded FY 1966 MAP appropriations. Either MAP strategy, objectives, and force guidelines had to be curtailed, with the resulting adverse foreign political reaction, or the FY 1967 MAP had to have more money.[21] Increased funding stood little chance because McNamara was slashing non-Vietnam related defense expenditures, including MAP, as he attempted to hold down the overall FY 1967 Defense budget.

On 26 October 1965 the defense secretary circulated for review a DPM on Military Assistance for FY 1967–1971, his first ever on the subject. Woven into the document were key sections of Hoopes's reappraisal of MAP, such as the emphasis on properly equipped indigenous forces to defeat insurgencies. McNamara's proposal to specialize these forces to capitalize on comparative military advantages placed greater emphasis on local ground forces as opposed to the traditional balanced air-land-sea assistance programs. The MAP request, reduced to $897 million, did not include Laos and Vietnam. Separating them was necessary because financing an "ever-growing Vietnam effort out of a finite MAP . . . appropriation" would, if continued, "endanger U.S. interests in other parts of the world."[22]

Reaction ranged from critical to hostile. Komer praised the spirit of the DPM but damned the contents "which . . . do not measure up to the bold words at the outset." In early November the Joint Chiefs voiced "deep concern," especially over the reductions of indigenous ground troops in South Korea and Taiwan and the proposed withdrawal of a U.S. division from Korea. These actions and the reduced MAP funding request led to the JCS conclusion that the OSD program "involves substantial risks to US security interests" and the recommendation that it not go forward to the president. Bureau of the Budget analysts favored only $867 million for MAP but offered to compromise around $900 million. They noted that the DPM postponed reductions in military assistance to the levels in the Hoopes report until after FY 1967. Although accepting the difficulty of reducing forces in Korea, they questioned increasing MAP grant aid to that country. BoB did support McNamara's proposal to merge the MAP appropriation into the regular DoD budget; like the Chiefs, it suggested OSD seek a MAP supplemental to pay for additional Vietnam requirements.[23]

The same day that McNamara circulated his DPM on military assistance, ISA issued revised financial guidance for preparation of the FY 1967 MAP request. The standard $1 billion ceiling remained in effect, including an assumed "normal" (non-wartime) level of assistance totaling $103 million for South Vietnam and Laos. This left $897 million to sustain the integrity of small country programs, maintain forward defense countries, and support MAP requirements for other countries fighting communist-backed insurgencies. At the 13 November budget meeting to review DoD's submission, BoB, anxious to hold down the total budget, recommended a $100 million reduction in the overall FY 1967 MAP request and suggested FY 1966 recoupments might be used instead of a supplemental appropriation for Vietnam.[24]

On 3 December, McNamara addressed the Chiefs' concern that reductions of Korean or Taiwan forces might cast doubt on the ability of free world forces to meet Soviet or Chinese Communist challenges elsewhere in Asia, presenting serious consequences for U.S. foreign policy. He agreed to postpone drawdowns of Korean army strength so long as the war in Vietnam continued to require the presence of major U.S. and ROK combat units.[25]

The secretary's revised 29 December DPM incorporated these changes and also alerted Johnson to the Joint Chiefs' grave reservations that reducing MAP below their "essential military assistance figure" of $1.3 billion might require larger U.S. forces and overseas deployments and entail increased military risks. Under pressure from State and BoB, McNamara finally proposed a MAP budget of $847 million for FY 1967 and $897 million a year for FY 1968–1971, exclusive of Vietnam and Laos assistance. His austere program, he insisted, focused military aid on the forward defense countries, which needed it most. He posited Red China as the greater of the two communist superpower threats, thereby shifting the center of gravity of the U.S. defense problem perceptibly eastward, according greater strategic importance to countries along an arc from India to Japan than to the west—Pakistan, Iran, Turkey, and Greece. Acting on the assumption that military assistance to Greece and Turkey might be prudently reduced without undue risk would allow reprogrammed MAP funds to flow eastward.[26]

To vest all MAP authority in OSD with appropriations made directly to DoD, the secretary continued to advocate separate legislation for military and economic aid programs. On 19 October 1965, however, he had acceded to earlier State and AID objections to such a sweeping reorganization, approving a separate MAP bill under the existing statutory arrangements, by which appropriations were made to the president. This initiative, the transfer of Vietnam MAP to the DoD budget, and a multi-year authorization were subsequently endorsed by the Cabinet Committee on AID and became part of the preliminary legislative proposals for the FY 1967 AID program. BoB concurred with the merger of Vietnam MAP into the regular Defense budget in FY 1967 and raised no objections to separate authorizing bills for economic and military assistance for FY 1967. Rusk's 31 January 1966 recommendation, approved by the president, modified preliminary proposals. The FY 1967 foreign aid proposal would separate the military and economic aid programs as well as seek approval for a five-year authorization for military and economic assistance, assuming that the secretaries of state and defense retained policy oversight of the Military Assistance Program.[27]

After some further changes, on 1 February 1966 the president requested $917 million for non-Vietnam military assistance under a proposed new Military Assistance and Sales Act of 1966. His message included major revisions—submitting military assistance separately from economic aid, a five-year authorization with annual requests for appropriations, a shift from grant aid to military sales where possible, and the exclusion of South Vietnam from the MAP program.[28]

Compared to the previous year, the mood in Congress over MAP had soured. Traditional foes of military assistance found new allies among their liberal colleagues, chiefly because of growing congressional frustration and disillusionment over Vietnam that made doubters of previous supporters. During congressional committee hearings in March and April, Fulbright and others contended that the unintended consequences of MAP were dragging the United States into situations like Vietnam that it could not control. Besides his usual complaints about foreign aid giveaways, Passman described military assistance as a "guns and not butter" approach that only encouraged military coups.[29]

Critics also questioned whether MAP stymied economic progress in developing nations by forcing them to divert scarce funds to buy weapons. Sen. Allen Ellender (D-La.) professed to be "dumbfounded" to learn that the Export-Import Bank financed "the sales of military hardware to countries all over the world," while Passman was "somewhat shocked" to learn of the extent of the Bank's involvement in arms sales. Others wondered about the propriety of a Military Assistance Program that enabled MAP recipients India and Pakistan to fight a border war with U.S.-supplied arms. Finally there was the issue of the administration's credibility. Opposing the multi-year authorization, Rep. Frances P. Bolton (R-Ohio) pointedly told McNamara there were too many issues "that we don't quite trust you people on."[30]

Reflecting growing misgivings, House and Senate committees rejected the five-year authorization in favor of an annual review and imposed numerous restrictions on proposed FY 1967 MAP legislation. Despite pressure from the president to reconsider multi-year authorizations, with the exception of moving Vietnam military assistance from MAP to the regular Defense budget, congressional committees voted down executive branch amendments, reduced the requested MAP authorization to $875 million, limited to 40 the number of countries able to receive grant military assistance, restricted sales and grants of military equipment to Latin America to $85 million, and mandated that the administration manage military sales in ways to discourage regional arms races. The president signed the authorization bill into law on 19 September 1966, expressing his concern over the numerous limitations and restrictions that Congress had imposed.[31]

The next day the Joint Chiefs interpreted the 40-country restriction as further evidence of the "accelerating downward trend of the Military Assistance Program," declaring that it reduced flexibility and precluded responding to contingencies in other countries that might need military assistance during the year. The military leaders advocated that OSD work with Congress to ease the restrictions on MAP, effect the transfer to AID of technical and civic action programs currently funded by MAP, and oppose similar restrictive legislation in the future. In reply, McNamara informed the Joint Chiefs in early November that DoD had maintained close liaison with Congress throughout the MAP legislative process but concluded it was "the sense of Congress" to restrict the number of countries receiving grant aid. Worse yet, the secretary predicted that more stringent restrictions might occur in the future.[32]

McNamara's pessimism stemmed from the latest congressional attack on MAP, in the Foreign Assistance Appropriation Act for Fiscal Year 1967. The 15 October legislation reduced the appropriation for non-Vietnam-related military assistance to just $792 million, down from the requested $917 million and the previously authorized $875 million, as both chambers compromised on the amounts of several foreign assistance appropriations. Overall the FY 1967 foreign aid appropriation of $2,936 million was the lowest since FY 1958, but the president blamed the defeat less on Congress than on the AID staff's weak effort to sway House conferees during conference meetings.[33]

More Is Needed

Unanticipated demands for military assistance added to the woes following the congressional reduction of $125 million from the FY 1967 MAP request. President Johnson, exuberant after his October 1966 trip to Bangkok, raised Thailand's MAP from $35 million to $60 million in recognition of the country's role in supporting the Vietnam War effort. Laos required an additional $36.6 million, mainly to replace ammunition and aircraft expended in heavier fighting; NATO Headquarters needed $7 million extra because of its relocation from France; and the president approved $3 million in additional MAP costs to pay for the deployment of a second ROK division to Vietnam.[34]

The administration's decision in November 1965 to double the size of U.S. forces in South Vietnam had again led Washington to Seoul's door. "There's no question but what the Koreans will come," McNamara remarked to the president in mid-January 1966. "It's just a matter of price." Park's asking price—"about $600–700 million worth of cumshaw"—both State and Defense considered outrageous, countering with offers of about $70 million in extra economic and military assistance. Even McNaughton's modest military package, approved reluctantly by McNamara on 28 January, contained lucrative concessions and sweetened the already favorable military and economic credit terms for Korean businesses. The extra FY 1967 costs for Korea amounted to $51.4 million.*[35]

To defray these latest MAP deficits, on the advice of the JCS and ISA McNamara drew on other sources, chiefly India-Pakistan money. To create a fund desired by State to cover unanticipated contingencies McNamara had to reduce Greek and Turkish military assistance by several million dollars. Reapportionments provided a FY 1967 MAP budget of $951.6 million in total obligational authority,[36] but mortgaged the MAP future to meet short-term financial exigencies.

McNamara revealed a radical shift in his thinking on MAP in midsummer 1966 when he proposed to eliminate all MAP to Latin American and African nations, excepting training, base rentals, and credit sales. He wanted to know "when and under what circumstances" grant military aid to the forward defense countries—Greece, Turkey, Taiwan, and Korea—might be terminated. And he wanted to consider reshaping MAP completely by aiding only those countries facing a serious threat of external aggression, blending all other assistance—training, base rentals, infrastructure payments, and credit sales—into the DoD budget.[37] McNamara wanted DoD to take greater control of military assistance.

Assuming removal of MAP funding for Laos, Thailand, and NATO infrastructure and headquarters, the secretary planned to request $606 million from Congress for FY 1968. This low figure was made possible by McNamara's sweeping proposals to phase out grant assistance to many countries by the end of FY 1967. Exempt from cuts were Portugal and Spain, where the United States had base rights, and Greece and Turkey, whose economies were unable to support the full defense burden. Spared, too, were the African nations of Libya and Ethiopia, where the United States had bases; Tunisia and Morocco, where assistance might offset Soviet influence; and Liberia and Congo, where aid might promote democratic regimes. As for Asia, OSD would reduce assistance to Taiwan, offer steady support for the Koreans "so long as their participation in Vietnam continues," and assist the Philippines while shifting Filipino emphasis from external defense to internal security requirements.[38]

Responding to McNamara's DPM of 5 November, the Joint Chiefs endorsed the transfer of MAP for Thailand and Laos to the DoD budget, but little else. They disagreed with "some of the rationale, conclusions, and recommendations" contained in the DPM; phasing out grant aid to Latin America, they felt, would weaken hemispheric security, lessen U.S. influence, and invite Latin American nations to purchase military equipment from other countries. Instead of acquiescing to congressional pressure to reduce appropriations and restrict MAP, the military men recommended basing future planning on requirements for military assistance. Again they proposed that OSD make efforts to convince Congress of the necessity

---

* Following intense and sometimes bitter debate, on 20 March the Korean Assembly approved the reinforcements; on 1 June the Korean defense minister officially announced that the additional forces would be sent to Vietnam.

THE KOREAN PENINSULA

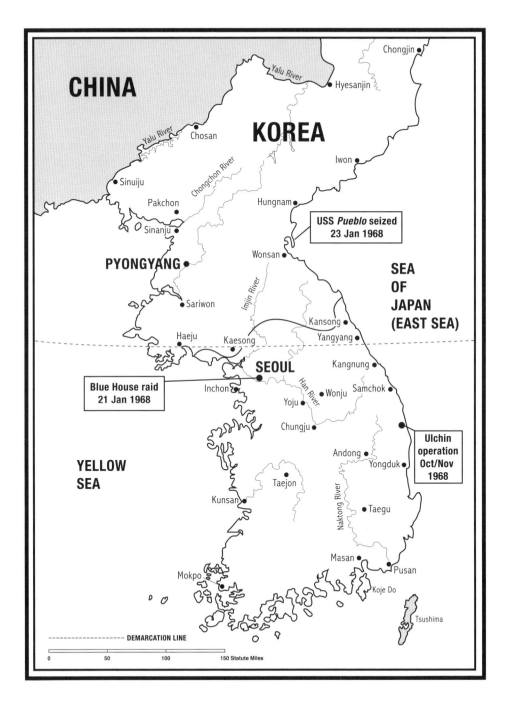

CHINA

KOREA

Yalu River

Chongjin

Hyesanjin

Yalu River

Chosan

Iwon

Sinuiju

Chongchon River

Pakchon

Hungnam

Sinanju

USS *Pueblo* seized
23 Jan 1968

PYONGYANG

Wonsan

Imjin River

Sariwon

SEA
OF
JAPAN
(EAST SEA)

Haeju

Kaesong

Kansong

Yangyang

Blue House raid
21 Jan 1968

SEOUL

Kangnung

Inchon

Han River

Wonju

Samchok

Yoju

YELLOW
SEA

Chungju

Andong

Ulchin
operation
Oct/Nov
1968

Yongduk

Taejon

Naktong River

Kunsan

Taegu

Masan

Mokpo

Pusan

Koje Do

Tsushima

- - - - - - - - - - - DEMARCATION LINE

0   50   100   150 Statute Miles

for additional MAP funding. AID did not respond directly to the DPM, although Acting Secretary of State Katzenbach wrote to McNamara on 9 December providing State's views on the FY 1968 funding levels. State and AID opposed the phased elimination of grant aid to Latin America and argued for $51 million more to increase grant aid to that region as well as to Taiwan, the Philippines, and Thailand. McNamara agreed to State's proposals provided that any future congressional cuts to the MAP would come first from those four accounts.[39]

DoD and State differed over specifics of increased MAP for Thailand. State favored more grant assistance as the best means to ensure Thai cooperation in Vietnam operations and improve Bangkok's counterinsurgency effort. DoD felt that the $60 million proposal contained too much conventional heavy equipment, such as fighter planes and helicopters, which would divert Thai military forces from counterinsurgency operations. Unable to resolve the issue, the secretaries submitted their conflicting proposals to the president on 13 October 1966. The president—besieged on his budget—rejected the recommended increases for Latin America, Taiwan, and the Philippines but approved additional MAP for Thailand. Following the decision, McNamara in turn asked AID Administrator William S. Gaud* on 7 January 1967 to request an FY 1968 MAP of only $596 million.[40]

The figure, which appeared in McNamara's finalized January 1967 DPM, was lower than that desired by State or the JCS. As in the past, the forward-deployed nations—Greece, Turkey, Taiwan, and Korea—received the bulk of the funding, Korea chiefly because of the administration's expectations of getting more Korean troops for South Vietnam. Contrary to State and JCS advice the secretary continued efforts to phase out military aid to Latin America. He considered MAP necessary only for countries unable to afford military forces to combat serious threats of armed insurgency. Thirteen Latin American countries had heavily armed military establishments capable of meeting any insurrection, yet these same nations accounted for 80 percent of U.S. military aid to the region. Even the three "special cases"—Bolivia, Colombia, and the Dominican Republic—would be strong enough to do without MAP by FY 1971.[41]

Meanwhile BoB and OSD wrangled over the MAP budget. Confronting another huge budget deficit by November 1966, the administration looked to the Military Assistance Program for savings to trim FY 1967 expenditures. BoB accordingly asked OSD to consider $50 million worth of deferrals, stretchouts, and cutbacks, but McNamara responded that "further downward adjustments" were unacceptable. Congressional appropriation of $792 million was $83 million less than FY 1967 MAP authorization. The austere MAP budget forecast for FY 1968, the result of McNamara's restructuring of the program, made it impossible to transfer FY 1967 deferrals into the new fiscal year.[42]

---

* Gaud replaced Bell on 1 August 1966.

BoB also contested McNamara's plan to transfer FY 1968 MAP funding for Laos and Thailand to the Defense budget. OSD argued that Laos was engaged in open hostilities related to the Vietnam fighting and needed more money for light aircraft and ammunition. Thailand's case rested on the air and logistics bases it provided for U.S. operations in Southeast Asia and the Thai government's promise of ground troops for Vietnam. Despite BoB's caution that the plans might embarrass the president by playing into the hands of congressmen who contended the administration was seeking to expand the war and conceal its costs by scattering military assistance throughout the Defense budget, McNamara persisted. State and AID agreed to the transfer with the understanding they would be able to review "MAP-type" programs for both countries and participate in decisions about them. On 17 January 1967 the president approved the shift of fund sites effective 1 July 1967; McNamara promptly alerted Senator Fulbright to the president's intent and the reasons for the transfers in his FY 1968 MAP submission.[43]

The Export-Import Bank Credit Controversy

With hindsight these interdepartmental disagreements proved to be minor irritants compared with the buzz saw of congressional criticism directed at the FY 1968 MAP submission. Hearings the previous year on the FY 1967 MAP had revealed deep-rooted opposition not only to military grant aid but especially to military sales. At the April 1966 hearings McNamara had testified that DoD, supplemented by private commercial and Export-Import Bank capital, projected $1.5 billion worth of military export credit sales during FY 1967. He regarded this as good business that created American jobs, made profits for U.S. corporations, and reduced the balance of payments deficit. The Senate's 7 July 1966 report on military assistance and sales, however, expressed "considerable uneasiness" about a program that provided arms to too many countries that could not—or should not—support large military forces. Casting the United States as the arms salesman to the world and using rhetoric reminiscent of the merchants of death polemics of the 1930s, senators berated the administration for "taking blood money from poorer countries" to redress the unfavorable U.S. balance of payments.[44]

A follow-up January 1967 study commissioned by the Senate Committee on Foreign Relations voiced concern over the Export-Import Bank's role in such credit transactions and the use of the Military Assistance Credit Account, the so-called revolving fund, whose $300 million capitalization could support $1.2 billion in credit for arms sales.* The report concluded correctly that the "sale of arms has

---

* The Mutual Security Act of 1957 provided $15 million to DoD to arrange credit terms for arms sales. The FAA of 1961 (sec. 508) authorized that repayments from such sales be available until expended solely for the purpose of furnishing military assistance on cash or credit terms. Through a combination of repayments and yearly appropriations ranging from $21 million to $83 million, the fund grew to $300 million. In 1964 Congress allowed DoD to fund 100 percent of credits extended by U.S. banks for military assistance while obligating 25 percent of the amount in the credit reserve. See SCFR, *Arms Sales and Foreign Policy*, S Staff Study, 25 Jan 67, 5-6.

now replaced the giving of arms as the predominant form of U.S. military assistance." In FY 1961 military sales amounted to slightly more than one-third of the $1.97 billion total for military assistance. Four years later, potential sales orders accounted for more than $2 billion of the $2.94 billion in projected military aid. In mid-November 1966 McNamara proclaimed foreign military sales a "magnificent program," one "imaginatively conceived" and one he intended to defend against those whom he termed irresponsible critics.[45]

McNamara's 25 January 1967 statement in support of FY 1968 MAP funding enumerated three governing principles for the foreign military sales program: (1) the United States would not sell military equipment to foreign countries that it believed could not afford it or should not have it; (2) it would never ask potential customers to buy anything not truly needed by their armed forces; and (3) it would not ask a foreign country to buy anything that it could buy elsewhere more cheaply or easily. Senator Ellender continued to challenge OSD's use of the Export-Import Bank to underwrite arms sales; McNamara again defended the practice as good business. "We should not kill the goose that has laid these golden eggs, and these are eggs that help us militarily, and eggs that help us commercially. We have been paid $5 billion in cash in this period [FY 1962 through FY 1966]." Ellender's verdict was more succinct: "it just smells." He vowed to try to prohibit the Ex-Im Bank from extending credits for the sale of military hardware.[46]

Representative Passman's 20 March 1967 grilling of Harold F. Linder, president and chairman of the Board of Directors, Export-Import Bank, on the institution's financing of sales of military equipment for DoD set the trend. During the hearings, congress charged that DoD's military sales program was promoted to redress an unfavorable balance of payments and that it lacked effective political control, contributed to a worldwide conventional arms race, and followed dubious financial practices. In rebuttal, McNamara pointed out that every sale passed review by the Department of State, AID, and other relevant agencies. Almost 90 percent of the credit sales (chiefly aircraft) went to developed countries—NATO, Australia, and Japan—and conformed to national objectives. "Although we sell arms abroad," he concluded, "we do so in a very responsible manner."[47]

After listening to McNamara's prepared statement on 4 April, Passman pronounced himself "not . . . any less confused this year than I have been in previous years." As committee members questioned the secretary on the military sales program, particularly the increasingly controversial role of the Ex-Im Bank in the transactions, Passman made it plain he would also oppose OSD's proposal to shift military assistance for Laos, Thailand, and NATO Military Headquarters to the DoD budget.[48]

In mid-July 1967 the arms export credit business hit the newspapers when the House Banking and Currency Committee released data on the Ex-Im Bank's "secret arms loans." More than one-third of the Bank's loan business involved purchases of U.S. military hardware by foreign governments. Worse still, in the course of the contentious hearings Rep. William B. Widnall (R-N.J.) charged that the administration had deliberately attempted to conceal the magnitude of such loans—some $1.59 billion to 17 countries over the past five years. Some involved "Country X" loans by which the Bank provided credit loans without knowing the identity of the borrower.[49]

For all the sensationalism and headlines, the "Country X" loans were legal. As permitted by the Foreign Assistance Act of 1965, DoD awarded "Country X" loans and guaranteed repayment to protect the Ex-Im Bank against default. On 20 September 1965 McNamara had informed Linder, who accepted the terms, that unless otherwise agreed to in writing by DoD and the Ex-Im Bank, neither the foreign governments nor the military equipment being sold to them would be identified in purchase documents. DoD thus awarded "Country X" loans and the Export-Import Bank provided the credit arrangements with an unconditional DoD guarantee of repayment. To its displeasure, the House Committee on Banking and Currency had been generally unaware of the arrangement whereas the Senate and House armed services committees knew of the practice but not all the specifics.[50]

Through the Ex-Im Bank OSD had financed foreign military credit sales totaling almost $2.4 billion between FY 1962 and FY 1966. Of this total the Bank directly financed arms sales of $771 million; slightly over $480 million went to industrialized countries, primarily Australia ($134 million), Italy ($205 million), and Great Britain ($110 million). In addition, with DoD guaranty the Bank had indirectly financed another $290 million in loans to "Country X" nations, including $68 million to Latin America to buy military equipment and $222 million to Asia and the Middle East, of which oil-rich Iran and Saudi Arabia accounted for almost half the total.[51] But it was the secretive nature of the "Country X" transactions that became the source of much contention in July 1967 and led to sweeping revisions to DoD's credits sales programs.

OSD particularly feared that Ellender would take advantage of the controversy to terminate the bank's authority to lend money for military sales to underdeveloped countries and perhaps even eliminate entirely Ex-Im Bank cooperation with DoD. With financing from the Ex-Im Bank or private banks no longer available, DoD would have to underwrite sales directly; this would require an increase of $232.5 million in FY 1968 MAP—from $60 million to $292.5 million—plus another $200 million annually thereafter to defray estimated outstanding credit arrangements.[52]

When McNamara testified before the Senate Foreign Relations Committee on 26 July 1967, feeling in Congress was "running very high" against arms sales. He tried to "set the record straight because of our failure to make clear to the committee the manner in which these sales were processed." While senators agreed that neither DoD nor McNamara had engaged "in any kind of flimflam," they did question whether the Export-Import Bank was chartered to finance arms sales. To counter unfavorable news reports, OSD Public Affairs released a list of McNamara's statements before Congress on the Ex-Im Bank dating back to April 1964. The handout emphasized that while the bank's primary charter did not include extending credit for military sales, this did not preclude it from doing so.[53] Nonetheless Congress remained upset, the public angry, and the administration yet again on the defensive trying to salvage its dwindling credibility.

The day after McNamara's appearance, the Senate Foreign Relations Committee report on the foreign aid bill cut MAP by over $200 million, abolished the revolving fund, and revoked the authority of the Ex-Im Bank to finance arms sales. The committee's 9 August report explained that given the mounting costs of the Vietnam war, unprecedented budget deficits, domestic unrest, a ten percent "war tax," and balance of payments difficulties there was a "strong consensus . . . for cutting back on the foreign aid program." Even the president's Texas colleague, George Mahon, chairman of the House Appropriations Committee, in late October adhered to a $1 billion reduction in the $3.2 billion overall economic and military assistance foreign aid package.[54]

Actual cuts, though less than $1 billion, nonetheless proved severe. According to advance reports, the House-Senate Conference Committee intended to authorize $2.86 billion for economic and military assistance against the administration's requested $3.25 billion. MAP authorization was reduced by $110 million to $510 million, the revolving fund eliminated after 30 June 1968, and credit sales guarantees limited to $190 million. On 14 November 1967, the president signed the Foreign Assistance Act of 1967, which retained the 40-country limitation for military assistance and lowered ceilings on military grants, sales, and services for Latin America and Africa.[55]

Meanwhile, on 6 November, the House Committee on Appropriations approved a recommendation from Passman's subcommittee to appropriate just $365 million for MAP. McNamara appealed to the Senate Appropriations Committee 10 days later for restoration of the House cuts. Senators agreed that a reduction of such magnitude would have serious consequences for U.S. security objectives and appropriated $510 million for MAP.[56]

McNamara's victory was short-lived as a subsequent Senate compromise with the House Appropriations Committee resulted in a drastically reduced MAP appropriation of $400 million. Besides reducing appropriations, the Foreign Assistance Appropriation Act of 2 January 1968 imposed still more limitations on MAP—notably that the revolving fund could not finance directly or indirectly the purchase of sophisticated weapons by underdeveloped countries unless the president determined such purchases were vital to the national security of the United States. The law also permitted the president to withhold economic assistance in the amount equivalent to that spent by any underdeveloped country, other than Greece, Turkey, Iran, Taiwan, the Philippines, South Korea, and Israel, for the purchase of sophisticated weapons. Especially hard hit by the diminished funding were the other so-called forward defense countries, suffering a 27 percent reduction; the "Base Rights" grant aid nations lost 25 percent; and Latin American countries went down 40 percent.[57] Only South Korea emerged with its planned grant military aid intact.

North Korea had stepped up infiltration during 1967 against the Park regime, causing a significant upsurge in gun battles and casualties along the Korean DMZ. Seoul's military leaders believed one of Pyongyang's motives was to prevent ROK forces from deploying to Vietnam. To secure more Korean troops for Vietnam, in September 1967 recently appointed Ambassador William J. Porter proposed offering Park additional military equipment to improve ROK border security plus an enhanced counter-infiltration capability. McNamara and the new ASD(ISA), Paul Warnke, opposed the deal, fearing that impending large-scale congressional cuts to OSD's MAP request might oblige the military services to pay for any extra Korea expenditures (estimated at $45.5 million for FY 1968–1969) from their own budgets. In mid-November, McNamara suggested substituting anti-infiltration equipment for other items already programmed under Korean MAP because congressional cuts made any increase in MAP funding for Korea impossible.[58]

The president's insistence on more ROK soldiers in Vietnam again undid the secretary of defense's plans. When Park agreed in early December 1967 to send another division to Vietnam, McNamara, following the president's direction, approved increases for 1968 to pay for a U.S. military-recommended $20 million counter-infiltration package for South Korea plus another $10 million for the now obligatory replacement of the units deployed to Vietnam. Estimated overall DoD costs for MAP support to Korea for FY 1969 were almost double the 1968 figures.[59] Even at a time of dire economic distress in the United States, with the president demanding substantial reductions in the Defense budget, the administration was still willing to pay large sums to get more Korean troops to Vietnam.

The Blue House[*] raid and the *Pueblo* incident of January 1968 ended the reinforcement plan, but increased tensions on the Korean peninsula persuaded the United States to provide the ROK government with additional ammunition, weapons, and equipment to bring the 18 Korean divisions to their full authorized strength. OSD asked for and received from Congress on 2 July 1968 a $100 million supplemental appropriation to cover this emergency outlay. Since Congress had previously authorized $510 million in military assistance but appropriated only $400 million for FY 1968, holding the additional request under $110 million meant that OSD required no special authorizing legislation (with the inevitable accompanying policy debate) for the latest funding. This appropriation, however, marked the end of the line for open-ended funding of ROK military forces. As the pace of Vietnamization quickened, in late 1968 the U.S. military began shifting to South Vietnam equipment originally intended for the third Korean division. Moreover, OSD reduced

---

[*] On 21 January 1968 North Korean commandos attacked the Blue House, the official residence of the president of South Korea.

planned FY 1969 military aid for Korea by almost $21 million as the ROK military contribution in South Vietnam had become dispensable.[60]

The FY 1969 MAP

McNamara's January 1967 DPM on military assistance for the period FY 1968–1972 forecast a FY 1969 MAP request of $630 million. In March 1967 the Joint Chiefs warned that the current guidance fell $1.2 billion short of meeting their MAP force objectives for FY 1969–1973. Given the huge discrepancy, McNamara later questioned whether such objectives were "in actuality reasonably attainable"; in early June he instructed the Chiefs to test their MAP priorities by applying them against those of the field commanders, who based their estimates on ISA-derived dollar and policy guidelines. The JCS response of 13 September contended that OSD's projected funding levels would continue and even accelerate obsolescence of equipment in allied hands throughout the FY 1969–1973 period. Such deficiencies would encourage communist leaders to see the United States as unwilling to stand behind its commitments. A subsequent November JCS memorandum justified projected force levels that still exceeded OSD's targets; the Chiefs pressed for additional grant aid for eight countries, half of them in Latin America. Although the "application of dollars does not mathematically guarantee a corresponding reduction in risk," they reasoned, equivalent dollars for U.S. forces would not produce the same results as those for allied forces.[61]

McNamara's FY 1969 military assistance DPM, circulated for comment during December 1967, proposed an appropriation of $540 million—$420 million for grant assistance and a $120 million credit authorization to support a $280 million credit sales program, well below the Chiefs' recommended $794 million. The original draft incorporated all forward defense, base rights, and training country programs into the regular DoD budget while shifting civic action and internal security programs to the AID budget. It also proposed separate legislation and appropriations for the military sales program as a key ingredient in restructuring MAP for the future. McNamara hoped to make the program more attractive to Congress by offsetting reduced grant aid through cash and credit sales. The Joint Chiefs still believed the amount insufficient to achieve U.S. national objectives.[62]

State officials recoiled at the DPM and accused DoD of clinging to an "outmoded thesis" that MAP existed to advance U.S. military as opposed to political interests. Such an approach would only provoke further congressional opposition to military assistance as too expensive, too entangled with unwanted foreign commitments, too conducive to local arms races and wars, and increasingly unnecessary given the improved strategic mobility of U.S. forces. State's Policy Planning Council recommended the secretary of state, not AID, take primary responsibility for the entire program and develop a military assistance coordinating staff within the State Department. State would take over the MAP program and justify the MAP budget to Congress. DoD naturally dissented and asserted just the opposite—keeping MAP in the Foreign Aid Assistance legislation "leads to extended Congressional hearings, conference stalemates and excessive attention to foreign aid costs."[63]

A task force including representatives from State, AID, DoD(ISA), JCS, and BoB considered the congressional and administrative pros and cons of legislation to restructure MAP and foreign aid. The report, submitted to Under Secretary of State Katzenbach in mid-November 1967, considered 1968 "a bad year to propose major legislative changes." To avoid a repetition of the "foreign aid fight" with Congress, Katzenbach, in his capacity as chairman of the Senior Interdepartmental Group (SIG),* forwarded to the White House on 11 December the task force's recommendations on the future course of the foreign aid program. Although the report was silent on military assistance, several of its initiatives, such as encouraging the Ex-Im Bank to increase lending to qualified developing countries of greatest foreign policy interest, presenting a military sales bill to Congress as a separate piece of legislation, and shifting most of MAP out of the Foreign Assistance Act, would affect DoD's administration of military assistance.[64]

During December 1967 McNamara scheduled meetings with Senator Fulbright and House Foreign Affairs Committee Chairman Thomas E. Morgan (D-Pa.) to smooth troubled relations. He wanted to convince them that credit arms sales should go into a separate bill and MAP should be restructured as part of the regular Defense budget. Time mattered because ISA had to complete all changes to the MAP submission by 10 December, the date the DoD budget closed. OSD had to choose either to retain MAP in its present form for the FY 1969 budget submission or delay the DoD budget until McNamara decided on restructuring. On 6 December, however, McNamara opted to submit the FY 1969 plan according to standard MAP procedures, choosing not to approach congressional leaders until they completed action on the FY 1968 Foreign Assistance Appropriation Act. Nevertheless, he had not given up hope of restructuring MAP and directed ISA to continue work on such a plan.[65]

Next day McNamara met with Morgan to discuss separate sales legislation and the shift of MAP to the DoD budget. As expressed in his December DPM, McNamara wanted to transfer to the DoD budget grant assistance to the forward defense and base rights countries; all expenses related to training and the NATO Military Headquarters; and the cost of Military Assistance Advisory Group support and administrative overhead. State would pick up MAP programs for Latin America, Africa, the Middle East, and Asia. Integrating MAP into the budget accounts of the military services would obviate the need for OSD to seek autho-

---

* To bring order and unity to the administration's conduct of foreign affairs, the president established the Senior Interdepartmental Group (SIG) in 1966. Its high-level, inter-agency members would, among other tasks, coordinate foreign policy matters, deal with interdepartmental issues that might arise, and ensure U.S. government resources went to properly selected areas or issues. See NSAM No. 341, 2 Mar 66, fldr 040 SIG Jan–May 1966, box 30, SecDef Subject Decimal files, Acc 70A-4443.

rization from the Senate Foreign Affairs and House Foreign Relations committees, but DoD would keep the committees informed of the intended value of military assistance to be delivered.[66]

Though not objecting to McNamara's proposals, Morgan remained noncommittal, preferring to canvas his committee members and give the secretary their reaction in January. No meeting with Fulbright occurred. While aware that the Senate Foreign Relations Committee and the Armed Services Committee might contest jurisdiction over MAP, McNamara still thought that a compromise might salvage most of his proposals. More realistic review within ISA questioned the reorganization plan's acceptability to Congress, much less to State and AID, and raised fundamental issues about State's role in internal security affairs and military training.[67]

The Joint Chiefs vigorously contested the reorganization scheme. They opposed the division of the MAP budget between the various military service budgets, the inclusion of forward defense and base rights countries in DoD/Service program packages, and the transfer of internal security programs to AID. In early December the Chiefs suggested instead the transfer of MAP to DoD in its entirety as an identifiable and separate budget program. McNamara approved the original restructuring plan over their objections. State also feared fragmentation of supervision and general program guidance should McNamara's reorganization plan succeed. The Policy Planning Council believed the secretary of state should retain responsibility and authority for MAP but recommended that Rusk withhold any comment until he reviewed the proposed legislation.[68]

In a familiar refrain, on 4 January 1968 the Joint Chiefs informed McNamara that the small amount of MAP grant aid requested for FY 1969 might damage U.S. credibility and entailed "serious risks to collective security arrangements." The magnitude of the reductions was such that the cutbacks, rather than "substantially delay" programs, would actually prevent achievement of U.S. objectives in many parts of the world. The Chiefs continued to oppose restructuring of MAP for the same reasons enunciated previously. State again sided with the military leaders; Rusk contended in an 11 January 1968 letter to his DoD counterpart that the political impact abroad of the reductions recommended in the DPM could be "considerably sharper" than OSD estimated. A MAP increase, according to the secretary of state, was necessary to meet the "political security requirements" in the forward defense countries of the Middle East and Far East. Latin America, a continuing sore point between the two departments, also needed additional funds to oppose insurgency movements. Concluding that the mood in Congress made restructuring unlikely, Rusk suggested retention of existing arrangements for MAP, excepting the sales program, through FY 1969.[69]

Still persisting, McNamara instructed Warnke to draft a memorandum for the president that summarized the restructuring proposal. From BoB, Schultze tried "to head off McNamara"; his concerns led the NSC staff to enlist Walt Rostow in opposition to the proposal. Rostow cautioned the president that McNamara's approach would subject the administration to charges that it was trying to "hide MAP in the face of last session's criticism." On 18 January, the defense secretary decided against submitting the restructuring issues to the White House pending a meeting with Johnson on 23 January, but he directed ISA to continue planning as "if the restructuring were approved by the president." Otherwise the only modification to his earlier position was a concession to the Joint Chiefs directing that aid for internal security programs involving 16 countries should remain in the Foreign Assistance Act as a DoD responsibility.[70]

On 19 January, with McNamara's appearance before the House Foreign Affairs Committee only days away, it became evident that Morgan and other members of his committee, although willing to hear McNamara out, stood "firmly against transferring any MAP from the Foreign Assistance Act." Republican members of the committee were almost unanimous in keeping MAP as part of foreign aid, the only dissenter being H. R. Gross (R-Iowa), who commented that "it would be easier to kill economic aid if MAP was out of the bill." McNamara still expected to discuss a transfer in his posture statement set for delivery on 29 January, but he backtracked by agreeing, should a transfer take place, to keep MAP within the overall Defense budget rather than dispersing the appropriation into the accounts of the various services. He also sounded out Morgan on transferring Korean MAP out of the DoD budget into a military service account, a move administration insiders believed would still leave him open to charges that he was hiding MAP from its critics. As events unfolded, the North Korean seizure of the *Pueblo* caused a postponement of the planned discussion and the hearings.[71]

Faced with opposition from Congress, BoB, the State Department, and the Joint Chiefs, McNamara gave in. His diluted MAP DPM of 1 February 1968, pessimistic in tone, dwelt on the ramifications of congressional unwillingness to provide much more in the way of MAP funding than it had in the lean FY 1968 budget. Gone were plans to integrate MAP into the DoD budget. Absent too were proposals to shift internal security programs to AID. The defense secretary still called for separating grant assistance from military sales legislation; his restructuring program aimed to avoid the "considerable confusion" created by a combined economic and military assistance bill, the mixture of grant MAP and foreign military sales, and the complexity of credit sales arrangements.

His recommended $540 million for MAP appeared to be a healthy increase over the $400 million appropriated the previous year, but it was symptomatic of a program in disarray. With $420 million going for grant assistance and with little prospect for more funding, McNamara acknowledged that many of the goals OSD had sought were now beyond reach. His much heralded military sales program, now hamstrung by congressionally imposed restrictions, required an extra $120 million to support a credit sales program, largely to compensate for congressional elimination of the revolving fund account and restrictions on the Export-Import Bank's activities.[72]

Efforts to restructure foreign aid and military assistance did not end with McNamara's departure from office on 29 February 1968. Although President Johnson in late January 1968 had demurred on a "full-dress critique" of the foreign assistance program, State persevered in attempts to reorganize foreign aid. On 28 February Rusk proposed to Congress a FY 1969 MAP funding program that would separate grant aid under the Foreign Assistance Act from military sales under a newly conceived Foreign Military Sales Act. State's announced purpose was to enable the United States to sell military equipment to countries that had previously received grant assistance but could now finance their own defense. To allay concerns in Congress and the public about the volume and nature of foreign military sales, particularly those to economically less developed countries, the proposal barred the Export-Import Bank from any involvement in financing military sales to underdeveloped countries but allowed the Bank to finance military sales to developed, noncommunist countries.[73]

Newly installed Secretary of Defense Clifford did not want to testify on behalf of MAP before the Senate Foreign Relations Committee in March 1968 because he suspected that the committee intended to pillory him and military assistance policy. Convinced that communication between the State Department and the Senate committee was "almost impossible," Clifford worked behind the scenes to regain congressional support for DoD's policies on Capitol Hill. By meeting privately with key senators Clifford hoped to avoid an angry public debate over Vietnam such as had marred Rusk's 11 March testimony before the committee. In early April Clifford sent Deputy Secretary Nitze to testify on behalf of MAP before Passman's subcommittee. Besides defending the MAP request, Nitze explained that the newly revised foreign military sales program would require an appropriation of $296 million, not the $120 million in McNamara's calculations. DoD required the extra funding to finance outstanding long-term credit agreements from appropriations instead of a combination of appropriated funds and Export-Import Bank loans as originally requested.[74]

Clifford initially testified on MAP and military sales before the Senate Foreign Relations Committee on 17 May. He reported to his staff that he had come through "practically unscathed," an outcome he ascribed to the major change in congressional attitudes following the president's 31 March speech and the beginning of negotiations with Hanoi. Senator Fulbright's absence from the hearings* certainly aided Clifford's cause as did Warnke's reassuring presence at Clifford's side to answer questions. Yet such questions as withdrawal of American forces from NATO, pullout of U.S. troops in Korea, and military aid to Latin America pointed up enduring and fundamental problems about MAP and military sales that Clifford could not easily dismiss.[75]

Congressional opposition to the worldwide U.S. military burden, evidenced by the widespread support for the Symington Amendment to reduce U.S. forces in NATO, criticism of the unwillingness of U.S. allies to spend more on their own

---

* Fulbright was in his home state of Arkansas, which had recently suffered severe tornado damage.

defense, and doubts about the utility of foreign aid in general threatened the administration's FY 1969 foreign aid package. The bickering between congressional leaders and the president over a tax bill added to the tension; as a result a total of six separate aid-related bills languished in committee. By mid-May the foreign aid packages were in serious trouble in Congress amidst widespread talk of a one-year moratorium on all foreign assistance authorizations. Any moratorium, in ISA's estimation, would signal other nations that the United States was withdrawing from the world arena. Moreover, elimination of FY 1969 military assistance would force the U.S. military to shoulder more responsibility around the globe as the operational readiness of America's allies declined.[76]

Within the administration some officials gave thought to a bargain on foreign aid after the passage of the tax bill. In exchange for the tax increase, the administration would offer House Appropriations Committee Chairman Mahon a compromise FY 1969 foreign aid package entailing about $1 billion in reductions. MAP would incur a reduction from $420 million to $340 million in grant assistance and from $296 million to $200 million for credit sales. Even proponents thought the complex package deal had little chance of success. The impasse between the president and Congress over the administration's proposed surtax and Morgan's decision on 25 May to reconvene the House Foreign Affairs Committee to mark up the foreign aid request added to the pessimism.[77]

The House committee report of 19 June proved less severe than anticipated. It recommended an authorization of $390 million for MAP grant aid, a $30 million reduction from the president's request. Testifying a week later, Clifford urged Morgan's committee to support the full $296 million appropriation requested in the separate arms sales legislation package. The secretary affirmed the U.S. role as the source of weapons and military equipment for treaty allies and countries sharing common security interests. He also endorsed State's position that the controls and limitations incorporated into the proposed legislation ought to alleviate fears in Congress and the public about the basis for arms sales and the policy governing such transactions.[78]

Nevertheless, foreign aid and MAP legislation remained entangled in the dispute over the tax surcharge. By signing the Revenue and Expenditure Control Act of 1968 on 28 June, Johnson got his tax increase at the cost of agreeing to an overall $6 billion reduction in federal spending, with Defense responsible for half that amount. Pursuant to the legislation, OSD reduced FY 1969 MAP obligations by $45 million and expenditures by $9 million. Of the $50 million eventually realized in savings, nearly $21 million came from programmed military assistance for Korea and about $15 million from Greek and Turkish MAP accounts.[79]

Congressional committee action on foreign assistance legislation saw further attempts to reduce U.S. commitments overseas to lessen the strain on U.S. resources. The lawmakers eventually compromised because a "substantial minority" believed the bill attempted too much while a smaller group felt it did not do enough.

Thus the Foreign Assistance Act of 1968, signed on 9 October, authorized $375 million for military assistance. Although OSD had requested $420 million, the lower figure came as no surprise. Clifford had expected roughly that amount and in midsummer had remarked that given "today's climate we have really done quite well on military assistance." Amendments tacked on to the legislation continued the prohibition against furnishing sophisticated weapons—absent a presidential determination—to less developed countries, lowered ceilings on grant military assistance to Latin America and Africa, declared congressional support for sales of supersonic aircraft to Israel, and requested the president to reappraise foreign assistance with an interim report to Congress by 1 July 1969.[80]

Meantime, in a surprise vote, the separate Foreign Military Sales bill easily passed the House on 10 September. The legislation then languished in the Senate Foreign Relations Committee where, by boycotting sessions, Republican members tried to prevent a quorum vote on the Nonproliferation Treaty. Although the GOP's tactics successfully delayed passage of the NPT until the next administration, Congress enacted the Foreign Military Sales Act on 22 October 1968, authorizing $296 million for military sales credits during FY 1969. The Supplemental Appropriation Act of 1969, passed the previous day, had already appropriated that amount. As for military assistance, on 17 October Congress had appropriated the full $375 million authorization.[81]

The Final MAP Proposal

In mid-August 1968 BoB director Zwick notified Clifford of the planning figures for the FY 1970 MAP budget—$330 million for grant military assistance and $200 million for foreign military sales credits. Estimated operations and maintenance costs for MAP equipment alone would run $264 million; the remaining $66 million was insufficient for "any modernization of significance" of MAP-supported forces. With these financial restrictions in mind, Warnke in mid-October circulated for comment a DPM on Military Assistance and Arms Transfers (the latter term a euphemism for what was formerly called arms sales) offering a new approach to MAP planning. Conceding that congressional sentiment was running so strongly against MAP grant aid that it threatened to "degrade our influence in underdeveloped countries and debase some of our existing security ties," the DPM suggested sales, transfer of DoD assets, or service-funded assistance to offset the reductions in grant aid.[82]

As a new feature the DPM recommended release of some 800,000 excess stock items valued at $10 billion, so-called "long supply" assets, on a nonreimbursable basis to meet MAP and Foreign Military Sales requirements. This procedure would enable DoD to meet MAP requirements without an increase in military assistance funding. Other initiatives called for the secretary of defense to set approved force goals for MAP in order to anticipate what ISA considered the unrealistic JCS requirements for military assistance. To enhance the DPM as a decisionmaking tool, Warnke further recommended the joint signatures of the secretaries of state and defense on the document when it went to the president.[83]

Rather than examining military assistance and arms transfers as separate entities, Warnke's holistic approach calculated their relationship and interdependence with U.S. economic assistance programs provided by AID, service-funded transfers of military equipment, AID-financed military assistance including budget support, long supply and other assets not chargeable to MAP, as well as commercial cash and credit sales outside the MAP budget. The price tag for MAP in FY 1970 was $400 million in grant assistance and $325 million for arms sales credits. Both figures fell well below State and JCS wishes, but exceeded BoB's targets. The transfer from MAP to service programs of funding for NATO Military Headquarters and base rentals also drew the Chiefs' opposition.[84]

In their mid-November critique the JCS faulted the DPM for leaving the forward defense countries without a credible military deterrent against communist expansion. Lacking adequate MAP funding those allies would be unable to modernize their military forces, thus requiring increases in U.S. forces to offset those deficiencies. Such a development, they warned, would mean a greater probability of early U.S. military involvement in local crises, something the DPM specifically hoped to avoid. The State Department recommended more money for MAP and proposed redistributing accounts to increase grant assistance at the expense of foreign military sales. State also wished to review any OSD studies related to force goal guidance for forward defense countries, cautioning that there might be "serious difficulties" in persuading Congress to transfer additional MAP programs to service funding.[85]

Meanwhile, on 25 October the President's General Advisory Committee on Foreign Assistance Programs, formally convened by Johnson in March 1965, recommended the separation of military assistance from economic development assistance by transferring MAP to the DoD budget. The entire AID program would, however, remain under the policy guidance of the secretary of state. Otherwise the focus of a reorganized and streamlined successor to AID would be economic assistance concentrating on improving food production, expanding family planning, and promoting education. Asked by Walt Rostow to comment on the findings Nitze, responding for OSD, advised that attempts to separate MAP legislation from economic assistance would likely provoke strong congressional opposition. He instead suggested transferring certain programs into the service budgets, including the funding of MAP for countries "engaged in ongoing military operations," such as South Vietnam, Laos, Thailand, and South Korea.[86]

The revised DPM, issued 29 November, integrated JCS and State comments, added a lengthy analysis of world trends, and, in light of recent congressional reductions of MAP grant appropriations to $375 million, requested that same diminished amount for grant assistance and $275 million to support a sales credit program for FY 1970. State, DoD, and BoB agreed on the $375 million so that State and Defense could send the jointly signed document to the president during the week of 13 January 1969. Six months later, the new administration requested the amount proposed by its predecessors, describing the appropriation as "rock-bottom" austerity for MAP. The same was true of the foreign military sales request for $275 million.[87]

The precipitous decline in MAP funding between 1965 and 1969 was real, yet not as drastic as might appear. Military Assistance Program appropriations fell throughout the period, but the transfer of all MAP funding for Vietnam, Laos, and Thailand as well as partial costs for Korea and the Philippines to the DoD budget created the perception of large reductions, whereas total costs were simply split between two different budgets. Even so, paying the price for Vietnam caused a reduction in MAP grant assistance to other recipient nations, indicating the waning of MAP as a useful foreign policy tool.

Table 10

Military Assistance and Military Sales, 1965–1968
(All figures in millions of dollars)

	1965	1966	1967	1968
Military Assistance	$ 1,055	$ 1,170	$ 792	$ 400
Military Sales	$ 1,248	$ 1,777	$ 1,182	$ 1,003

Source: OASD(ISA), Military Assistance and Foreign Military Sales Facts, March 1970, 9 and 23, fldr Military Assistance 1970, box 63, Subj files, OSD Hist.

Contrary to original expectations, military sales failed to exceed the decline in grant military aid funds caused by congressional restrictions and reduced authorizations; ironically, these were provoked in part by McNamara's aggressive military sales policies. In an atmosphere of suspicion, recrimination, and mistrust, the Military Assistance Program suffered from serious underfunding, skewed grant aid distribution, and a shackled military sales program. By January 1969 MAP had been restructured and reformed, not by OSD, but by an unsympathetic Congress.

Chapter XVIII

Year of Crises

Lyndon Johnson spoke of his final year in office—1968, an election year—as "living in a continuous nightmare," a perception that aptly described a succession of international military incidents and emergencies that required quick reactions from the Department of Defense. Although overshadowed by the demands following the dramatic upsurge in fighting in Vietnam commencing with the Tet offensive in February, the unforeseen military requirements growing from these contingencies placed further burdens on an already strained DoD. Violent unrest at home and a Congress hostile to many of the government's policies—Vietnam, NATO, foreign assistance, taxes—added to the troubles of the administration in its closing year.[1]

The year began with three major aircraft crashes in January, inaugurating a time of seemingly unending disasters. After a U.S. Marine transport plane crashed on 11 January 1968 in Nevada killing all 19 aboard and a high-speed, high-altitude SR-71 crashed in California the next day, on 21 January a B-52 carrying four hydrogen bombs crashed in Greenland. On that same date North Korean commandos boldly attacked the Blue House, the official residence of the South Korean president. Two days later, North Koreans seized the USS *Pueblo*, an intelligence collection vessel, on the high seas, beginning a procession of Navy misfortunes. Three ships ran aground in a single week; one in the Persian Gulf, one off Rhode Island, and one in the Aegean Sea. On 11 February a jet trainer crashed into the Oakland Bay Bridge in California. The worst naval disaster of the year occurred in late May when the nuclear submarine *Scorpion* with 99 men aboard was reported overdue and presumed lost at sea. In the meantime, federal troops were called on to suppress rioting that erupted across the United States during early April following the assassination of Martin Luther King. Growing disillusionment over the administration's Vietnam policies fomented antiwar sentiment that crystallized in larger, more violent protests in the aftermath of the Tet offensive. On 30 June a

U.S. charter aircraft carrying 214 U.S. Army replacements to Vietnam violated Soviet airspace and was forced to land in the Kuril Islands by Soviet fighters. In August the administration's hopes for an arms limitation agreement with the USSR vanished when Soviet and Warsaw Pact forces invaded Czechoslovakia. Nor had much progress been made toward a Vietnam settlement, despite the president's 31 March decision not to seek reelection and to suspend the bombing of much of North Vietnam.

Losing H-Bombs

At 3:30 p.m. EST on 21 January 1968, a B-52 bomber on a routine airborne alert mission crashed on the ice of North Star Bay, about seven miles southwest of Thule Air Base, Greenland. No one knew what happened to the four nuclear weapons on board the doomed aircraft. This marked the second air disaster involving the loss of nuclear weapons in just over two years. Two years earlier, on 17 January 1966, a B-52 flying a nuclear alert mission collided in midair with a KC-135 tanker aircraft over the village of Palomares in southeastern Spain. Of the four nuclear devices carried by the B-52, one weapon remained intact after the crash of the two aircraft, one fell into the sea, and the nonnuclear high explosive in the other two detonated on impact. The explosions scattered plutonium over a wide area and created the possibility of a radiation hazard.[2]

Although OSD and other government agencies had prepared a public affairs plan to handle just such a contingency, they envisaged the loss of a nuclear device on U.S., not foreign, soil. To further complicate reporting and recovery efforts, at the request of the Spanish government the United States agreed not to disclose that the B-52 lost in the crash had been carrying nuclear weapons. Madrid's acute sensitivity to public statements about the accident resulted in a public relations blackout that, together with rumors of a still missing nuclear bomb, only whetted media interest in the story. After four days of silence, a U.S. Air Force spokesman officially announced on 21 January that the bomber involved in the accident was carrying "unarmed nuclear armament." No official announcement about the missing fourth bomb came until more than six weeks after the crash. By that time an intensive search for the missing bomb, involving several thousand American military and civilian personnel, was under way; on 15 March the U.S. Navy located the missing weapon five miles offshore under 2,550 feet of water. Twenty U.S. Navy ships and three submersibles participated in the undersea recovery operation that ended on 7 April with the retrieval of the nuclear device. Meanwhile, to decontaminate Spanish farmland exposed to possible plutonium hazards, teams plowed, scraped, and removed 385 acres of topsoil, sealed the dirt in 55-gallon barrels, and shipped the radioactive residue to the United States for disposal. Harvested crops were also burned. As a result of the mishap, the administration suspended U.S. nuclear overflights of Spain.[3]

Profiting from the Spanish experience, OSD handled the Greenland accident differently. The day after the Greenland crash, 22 January 1968, DoD's public announcement of the accident explained that the bomber had carried unarmed nuclear weapons so there was no danger of a nuclear explosion. The remote crash site, continuous darkness, deep snow, and subzero temperatures hampered recovery efforts, and, unlike the Spanish incident, limited press coverage of the salvage operation. By 29 January Air Force teams had located parts of all four weapons; further searches concluded that the tremendous explosion and fire accompanying the aircraft's impact had completely destroyed the weapons and contaminated a large area around the crash site.[4]

Meanwhile the State Department and the Danish ambassador to the United States had agreed on the contents and timing of a press release describing the incident. The Copenhagen government favored as early an announcement as possible because it wanted news of low-level radioactivity found at the crash scene to precede the departure of four Danish nuclear experts to the site. Washington took the position that no environmental hazard would exist if the impact areas were left untouched after debris cleanup. The Danes, understandably concerned by the ecological consequences of the crash on their territory, eventually reached a "gentleman's agreement" with the United States. The mid-February accord required a limited ecological study and the removal of the blackened crust from the burn area to reduce the amount of radioactivity present by half.[5] More significant were the political repercussions of the accident.

On 22 January, coincidentally while the United States was acknowledging the nuclear accident, the Danish government announced that its policy prohibited overflights of Greenland by U.S. planes carrying nuclear weapons. Washington did not share this understanding, and it would take four months of negotiations to produce a new agreement between the two countries on nuclear matters. General elections in Denmark on 23 January had led to the formation of a new government that, like its predecessor, wanted detailed information from Washington about the crash site. The incoming cabinet further asked for issuance of a U.S. statement that B-52s in Greenland both before and after the crash had a nonnuclear purpose. Lacking a U.S. answer, the Danes would consider "taking very serious steps."[6] During the lengthy discussions that followed, State coordinated with DoD to find language acceptable to both the Danish cabinet and ISA.

ISA objected to parts of State's original position, especially statements that overflights with nuclear weapons had stopped and that the United States saw no need in peacetime to renew such flights. Although State would urge the Danish government to say nothing publicly about the U.S. guarantees, ISA considered it "highly improbable" that the Danes would not go public with the information. ISA particularly worried that if a pledge not to overfly Danish territory became public knowledge, it would put pressure on other countries either to secure a similar promise or to deny overflight rights to U.S. aircraft carrying nuclear weapons.

Nor would OSD want to confirm that as of 26 January all overflights of Danish territory had stopped. Instead ISA offered a bland, general statement saying that there were now no overflights of Greenland by strategic aircraft but omitting any mention of requirements for such flights in peacetime. State concurred, and informed the Danish ambassador on 27 January that no nuclear weapons were stored in Greenland nor were there any overflights of the island by U.S. aircraft carrying nuclear weapons.[7]

Copenhagen, however, sought discussions with Washington to clarify the April 1951 agreement between the two nations concerning the defense of Greenland. In particular, the Danes proposed to make the large island a nuclear-free zone by precluding the storage of nuclear weapons there as well as denying overflight rights to aircraft carrying nuclear weapons. Washington in turn pointed to its previous attempts in November 1957 to clarify the April 1951 agreement. At that time the Danish prime minister's "informal, personal, highly secret and limited" statement took note of U.S. views; he also decided on no further comment or publicity; apparently, preferring to remain uninformed. During the 1968 negotiations, the State Department's proposed response followed a similar path, seeking secret exchanges that would make storage and overflights subject to consultation between the two parties.[8]

By late April, ISA provisionally agreed to a State draft, revised at Danish suggestion, that omitted reference to overflights with nuclear weapons during a serious crisis without advance notification to or approval of the Danish government. ISA's final approval hinged on State's furnishing the Danish ambassador with a written memorandum of conversation to the effect that requirements for unannounced storage or overflights might exist in time of crisis. DoD continued to resist any joint public statement with the Danish government on the subject of nuclear storage or overflights. On the final day of May 1968, the Danes did release a statement that confirmed their nuclear policy; no nuclear arms were stocked in Greenland, and no overflights with such weapons took place. They lauded recent discussions with Washington that ensured the policy was respected in Greenland. No public mention was made of agreed upon actions during crisis situations. The Danish foreign office, however, orally "noted" a verbally delivered U.S. reservation, recorded in a memorandum of conversation that was a formal part of the negotiating record, that "under circumstances of a grave and sudden threat" the United States might not be able to consult with the Danes before conducting overflights by aircraft bearing nuclear weapons.[9] By that time, renewed heavy fighting in Vietnam and other events had relegated Greenland to the back pages.

Pueblo and the Blue House

For a time in the first month of 1968 Northeast Asia displaced Southeast Asia as the primary international concern of the U.S. government. The *Pueblo* and Blue House incidents created a crisis that enveloped North Korea, South Korea, and the United States. Efforts to resolve the potentially explosive situation had to take into account factors other than the two incidents, rendering matters even more complex and difficult. Exercising a direct effect on decisions and negotiations was how much military assistance the United States would provide Korea for its defense and as compensation for the services of additional troops in Vietnam. Unraveling this tangled web of circumstance taxed the nerves and patience of the American negotiators and decisionmakers.

Shortly after midnight, Washington time, on 23 January 1968, North Korean gunboats, supported by MIG fighter jets, surrounded the USS *Pueblo*, a U.S. Navy electronic intelligence collection ship operating in international waters. An armed party boarded the ship. The seizure of a naval vessel on the high seas off the port of Wonsan caught the administration by complete surprise, "flat on our ass with[out] any reaction plan" as McNamara put it a few days later. No one in authority could offer a plausible explanation for the motives behind Pyongyang's action. Johnson's initial and natural reaction was to see the capture of the *Pueblo* as part of a coordinated, worldwide communist design to divert U.S. military forces from Vietnam and pressure South Korea to withdraw its forces from that country. He also feared another blow, perhaps in Berlin, as the communists continued to test a seemingly overcommitted U.S. military establishment. Such analysis left Johnson cautious; he never seriously considered using military force to resolve the Korean crisis. Rather, he concluded that "our enemies" judged the United States to be weak and divided at home, overstretched militarily abroad, and so anxious to end the Vietnam War that the nation would accept "if not defeat, at least a degree of humiliation."[10]

McNamara agreed with Johnson's assessment that Moscow knew ahead of time of Pyongyang's intentions, relying on the impressions of Ambassador Llewellyn Thompson in Moscow that the Soviets had decided in advance of the seizure to reject the president's official request that they secure the immediate release of the ship and crew from North Korea. Going beyond the president, the defense secretary believed that the North Koreans had a broader purpose in mind than to reduce the level of South Korean forces serving in South Vietnam—namely to curtail U.S. military strength in all of Southeast Asia by tying down American forces elsewhere.[11]

McNamara came to share Johnson's conviction that the North Koreans had coordinated their action with the impending Tet offensive in South Vietnam; he further believed that if the United States showed weakness in dealing with the *Pueblo* crisis it would "prolong the Vietnam war substantially." To avoid such an

---

* See the map on p. 467.

outcome, on 24 January he advocated a general military deployment into the Korean area as a show of force to signal U.S. intentions and indicate "things to come." McNamara would couple that move with a presidential call-up of military reserves and a request to Congress to authorize involuntary extension of terms of active-duty servicemen.[12]

Later that same evening he pushed his design at a meeting of senior State, OSD, and JCS officials, suggesting sending substantial air reinforcements (100 to 300 aircraft) to the region. Such a deployment would be easy, relatively riskless, and "should be done." More circumspect, defense secretary-designee Clifford favored a cooling-off period of several days, viewing the incident as too ambiguous to serve as grounds for major military actions. The source of doubt lay in Washington's uncertainty that throughout its entire covert mission, beginning 10 January 1968, the *Pueblo* had remained outside of North Korean territorial waters. As for military moves, McNamara and Rusk favored dispatching another intelligence collector, the USS *Banner*, to the North Korean coast, this time protected by heavy air cover, a "demonstration" that appealed to the defense secretary. McNamara also supported a Black Shield (strategic reconnaissance overflight) mission over North Korea along with efforts to restrain South Korean leaders from any inflammatory actions.[13]

At a subsequent meeting on 24 January, this time including the president, McNamara recommended deploying to Korea and Japan about 250 Air Force and Marine jet fighters and bombers plus the aircraft carrier USS *Enterprise*. These deployments would buy time for possible diplomatic pressure on the Pyongyang regime. A selective call-up of Air Force and Marine reserve air units would replace the aircraft deployed to Korea. Johnson approved McNamara's advice, further urging him to dispatch 300 aircraft immediately following the meeting. The president also accepted McNamara's recommendation to resume shipboard intelligence collection by sending the USS *Banner* to the Korean coast; additionally, he authorized a Black Shield overflight of North Korea for the following day. Finally, Johnson agreed to send a personal message to Kosygin requesting Soviet assistance in securing the release of the *Pueblo* and its crew.*[14]

By next morning, 25 January, McNamara had in hand detailed information on moving 303 aircraft to the Korean area, diverting to South Korea 10,000 tons of bombs bound for South Vietnam, and calling up 332 aircraft from reserve units. In the face of the president's questioning he insisted that the reinforcements were necessary to offset North Korean air superiority in the region. Johnson concurred and further approved deploying a second carrier, the USS *Kitty Hawk*, to Korean waters.

---

* The cable from Johnson to Kosygin was sent at 1627Z 25 January 1968. The president's appeal to Kosygin to intercede in obtaining the release of the American ship and its crew met a prompt and negative response from the Kremlin that fixed blame for the incident on repeated U.S. military provocations. The Soviets did, however, inform the North Koreans of the U.S. message. See msg 104325 State to Moscow, 25 Jan 68, and msg 2604 Moscow to State, 27 Jan 68, *FRUS 1964–68*, 29, pt 1:504-05, 533-34.

After the meeting, McNamara convened his senior military and civilian staffs and made clear the primary objective—the return of the crew. "Excessive military pressure," he explained, might lessen chances for achieving that goal. General Wheeler, in turn, advised CINCPAC later that day of the president's wish to avoid the appearance of confronting either Pyongyang or Moscow with an ultimatum, adding that Johnson had to take into account the domestic divisions spawned by Vietnam. While no "overt action" to reinforce Korea and Japan would occur as yet, McNamara did authorize the Air Force and Navy to issue warning orders alerting designated units to the possibility of an imminent deployment. The *Kitty Hawk*, then in Southeast Asian waters, would move to Korea. Although the secretary insisted that adequate bomb stocks be made available in the Korean theater, he emphasized that the military should move nothing out of Southeast Asia or Europe without written approval from him or Deputy Secretary Nitze. Furthermore, following Systems Analysis recommendations, he deferred JCS requests to increase U.S. Eighth Army in Korea by 8,500 men in order to raise the command from 79 to 90 percent of authorized strength.[15]

At a White House working lunch on the 25th, McNamara favored giving the president the authority to summon as many as 150,000 reservists. He reacted sharply to a suggestion that critics would accuse the administration of using the crisis "to plug up all the loopholes . . . in our current military posture," insisting that there were no gaps in U.S. forces. Because no one had a plan to get the ship and crew returned safely, McNamara could not answer the president's question about the purpose of deploying men and planes and extending tours of duty. Nonetheless Johnson approved moving 15 B-52 heavy bombers to Okinawa and 11 to Guam, disavowing any intent to use them to attack North Korea. Clifford continued to urge caution about mobilization and a military buildup in order to avoid a spiraling escalation and the appearance of empty threats.[16]

At the final 25 January meeting, held that evening, Wheeler explained to Johnson that the aircraft deployments were first for defense and second for reprisal attacks against North Korea, if the administration so decided. McNamara added the aircraft were needed to provide air support to the *Banner* should that mission be approved. The president finally decided to space out the movement of aircraft to South Korea over an eight-day period to avoid the appearance of needless provocation. Clifford, ever careful, proposed diplomatic approaches through the UN and Kosygin to accompany the start of a "*quiet* build up." Lastly, the president approved the mobilization of 28 Air Force and Navy reserve units, amounting to 14,787 men and 372 aircraft.[17]

On the same busy day, Johnson also directed U.S. Ambassador to the UN Arthur Goldberg to request an urgent meeting of the Security Council to consider the *Pueblo* crisis. The Security Council convened the next day, 26 January; two days of debate left Goldberg convinced that the Council was not going to do a "damn thing" but "fiddle around." State then opted to open direct negotiations with Pyongyang on the *Pueblo* issue using the machinery of the Military Armistice Commission in Panmunjom. Rusk, with McNamara and the president, believed that the North Koreans, fully realizing the possible consequences of their rash act, might "talk tough and try to humiliate us and [the] ROK." All three agreed that a "velvet glove" approach, ignoring the ranting from Pyongyang, which knew the glove contained a "steel fist," would prove best. Indeed they initially expected the first round of talks would produce the early release of the crew.[18] Such optimism proved misplaced.

While these diplomatic initiatives got under way, DoD was implementing presidential decisions to put steel in the fist. At the 26 January White House meeting, McNamara provided Johnson with a schedule for aircraft movements beginning Sunday, 28 January, and closing the following Thursday. Altogether 347 aircraft, including 26 B-52s, would deploy within striking distance of North Korea. The defense secretary further requested that the president ask Congress to authorize extension of current military enlistments and mobilize individual reservists to fill gaps in units on active duty. Lastly he proposed to increase South Korean MAP by $100 million during 1968.[19] Johnson made no decision.

A high-level advisory group, composed of former senior State and Defense officials, including George Ball, Maxwell Taylor, and Cyrus Vance, met on 29 January to review operational alternatives. They agreed unanimously: taking no diplomatic or military actions until the United States could determine whether or not the Panmunjom channel might be useful. Accordingly, they recommended against deploying the *Banner* on station and effectively eliminated recourse to other military measures—mining North Korean ports, air attacks, blockade—then under consideration. Their report to the president later that day apparently convinced him of the unattractiveness of the contemplated military alternatives except for the ongoing buildup of aircraft in Korea to support the U.S. diplomatic effort.[20]

Johnson, McNamara, Rusk, and Wheeler met with the congressional leadership the following day, 30 January. After Wheeler's opening presentation, McNamara and Wheeler responded to questions about the *Pueblo's* mission, its lack of escort, and the inability of nearby U.S. military forces to aid the ship; Rusk then reviewed the diplomatic initiatives under way. McNamara explained that the administration had yet to make its final decisions on military actions but "might be considering with the Congress" the idea of extending enlistments, retaining in Korea some of the reinforcements already sent there, and substantially increasing military aid to South Korea. Although the United States was keeping its military options open should diplomacy fail, the probability of use of armed force was negligible.[21]

That reality became even clearer in early February when Kosygin indicated to Johnson that if the United States reduced its naval forces in Korean waters the Soviet Union would attempt to influence North Korea to resolve the incident. The Soviet premier, however, made no guarantee of success. Around the same time, Soviet Ambassador Dobrynin reemphasized the Kremlin's concern that the U.S. threat of force against North Korea made mediation difficult, adding that if Washington resorted to force Moscow would have to react. Johnson informed Kosygin on the evening of 5 February that there would be no further buildup of U.S. military forces in northeast Asia. Furthermore, one carrier battle group would soon move southward from the area. The naval redeployment suited CINCPAC Admiral Sharp, who agreed that military force would likely not secure the release of the *Pueblo* crew and expressed a strong need to maintain all available naval airpower in the Tonkin Gulf. During his final days in office, McNamara notified Rusk that DoD "desired no role in coordinating the diplomatic initiatives" regarding the *Pueblo*. It would continue to prepare information on the incident for Congress and, in coordination with State and the Joint Chiefs, draft some general military contingency papers.[22]

Negotiations with Pyongyang got off to a rocky start. During meetings in mid-February, the North Koreans demanded an admission of wrongdoing and an apology from the United States for the *Pueblo's* alleged illegal violation of the North's territorial waters. Rusk, Clifford, and Walt Rostow promptly rejected that demand, but the issue of an apology emerged as the major obstacle to a settlement. In early March, Warnke suggested that the United States apologize to North Korea provided Pyongyang agreed in advance that the apology would result in the release of the *Pueblo* crew. Debriefings of the returned crewmen could then confirm that the *Pueblo* never violated North Korean territorial waters, allowing Washington to retract an apology extracted by use of erroneous information supplied by the North Koreans. This convoluted scenario in fact became the model for the resolution of the incident, although its final shape required months of often frustrating negotiations. Warnke continued to push his idea with Nitze and later with Clifford. Nitze and ISA Deputy Assistant Secretary for East Asia and Pacific Affairs, Richard C. Steadman, the latter in charge of *Pueblo* negotiations for DoD, worked closely with State Department officials to secure the release of the crew. Finally on 23 December 1968, 11 months after the incident, the U.S. representative at Panmunjom signed an apology, prepared by Pyongyang's negotiators, for violating North Korea's territorial waters. Before signing, however, he repudiated its contents, as previously agreed to by the North Koreans, and stated that he was signing "only to free the crew."[23] The strange ceremony ended a bizarre incident whose repercussions roiled U.S.-South Korean relations throughout 1968.

U.S. negotiations with the South Koreans during the drawn-out *Pueblo* bargaining demanded as much tact and patience as those conducted at Panmunjom with the North Koreans. The seizure of the *Pueblo*, two days after the North Korean attack on the Blue House, produced a crisis in confidence between the United States and the Republic of Korea further exacerbated by the sometimes extraordinary, and often belligerent, conduct of ROK President Park Chung Hee.

On 21 January 1968, about 30 North Korean commandos attacked the Blue House in downtown Seoul during an unsuccessful attempt to assassinate Park. Several North Koreans were killed in the streets, and the fleeing survivors became the object of a nationwide manhunt. It was during this Korean national emergency that Pyongyang seized the *Pueblo*, sparking an immediate American reaction. Park was furious with Washington's suggestions that his government avoid reprisals for the raid, but the deeper issue became the radically different U.S. response to the two events. An "emotionally irate" ROK minister of national defense berated General Charles H. Bonesteel, III, chief of staff of the United Nations Command/U.S. Forces, Korea (UNC/USFK), for merely calling a meeting at Panmunjom after the attempt on Park's life, while the U.S. government deployed F-105 fighter-bombers* to Osan Air Base outside Seoul without consulting ROK officials, sent the carrier *Enterprise* to Korean waters, and seemed to be willing to risk war because of the *Pueblo*. The ROK joint chiefs spoke bluntly to Bonesteel of the "strong feeling at all levels of the republic" that the United States had not acted forcefully enough after the Blue House raid.[24]

As early as 23 January, the State Department had instructed the U.S. representative at Panmunjom to treat both incidents with equal attention to avoid giving the ROK government the impression that the United States attached more importance to the *Pueblo* than to the attempt on Park's life.[25] In a 25 January telegram Rusk instructed U.S. Ambassador to Korea William J. Porter to tell Park that Johnson was "considering an immediate decision to send promptly" some 250–300 land- and carrier-based aircraft to Korea and immediate adjacent areas. Porter was to ask Park if the deployment created any major political problems for him.

As Park saw it, North Korea was attempting to split the U.S.-ROK alliance. He insisted, along with hardliners in his ministries, party, and army that the North Koreans had to be hit, and hit hard, or they would continue to "kill his people." Although he assured Porter in early February that he would take no ROK military action for the time being, Park was increasingly obsessed with the desire to strike back at the North Koreans across the DMZ. Seoul interpreted Washington's advice against unilateral ROK action to mean that the United States only wanted to protect its negotiating position at Panmunjom while it ignored Seoul's legitimate security concerns.[26]

In a 7 February letter to Park, the president sought to convince the ROK leader that the Blue House and *Pueblo* issues, while part of one overall problem, had to be dealt with by different measures: improvement of the ROK's military posture in the former case, private negotiations in the latter. Johnson explained why the United States was meeting in private with North Korean representatives at Panmunjom, his appreciation of the political and public relations problems this approach caused Park's government, and U.S. determination to provide "tangible and continuing measures to strengthen the Republic of Korea militarily." To back up his words, he

---

* The Commander, U.S. Fifth Air Force in Japan ordered 12 F-105s stationed on Okinawa to deploy to Osan Air Base on the afternoon of 23 January. (Transc McNamara test, 1 Feb 68, for Hearings Senate Cte on Armed Forces, Military Procurement FY 1969, 1 Feb 68 p.m. session, 163, fldr Hearings Snte Armd Svcs Cmte—2/1/68/aftn—FY 69 Budget, box 72, ASD(C) files, OSD Hist).

offered Park a $32 million package of military equipment including barrier fencing, searchlights, night vision devices, and communications gear for ROK counterinfiltration operations, along with two additional destroyers for the ROK navy, equipment for a self-propelled artillery battalion, helicopters for a Korean army company, plus $100 million in increased FY 1968 MAP funding.[27]

Park was not about to spurn the infusion of military aid with which he could bolster counterguerrilla operations, but he chafed at U.S. policy that kept his country passive in the face of what he considered continual North Korean provocations. He denounced Washington's decision to move the *Enterprise* southward and insisted that deploying the carrier northward would achieve better results. Direct negotiations, he asserted, actually encouraged reckless behavior by North Korean leader Kim Il-Sung, who only understood military force. The ROK Air Force chief of staff confided in General Bonesteel his fear that Park might order him to launch unilateral air strikes against the North.[28]

Park demanded assurances from Johnson that if North Korea failed to apologize for the Blue House attack and to pledge no repetitions in the future, ROK and U.S. forces would automatically take "an immediate retaliatory action." The South Korean government also pressed for a revision of the Mutual Defense Treaty to authorize a guaranteed U.S. response to any further North Korean raids.[29]

To calm the volatile situation, Prime Minister Chong Il-kwon suggested to Porter that sending a distinguished presidential special envoy to Korea would defuse resentment over U.S. private talks with North Korea. Johnson selected Vance for the sensitive assignment, to explain why private meetings with North Koreans offered the only prospect for a speedy release of the *Pueblo* crew. Otherwise the incident threatened to become a major issue in the United States during an election year. Armed with a broad delegation of authority from State and the White House, Vance decided he would seek to persuade Park of firm U.S. support, in return getting assurances from Park that his government would refrain from military action against the North, dampen domestic propaganda for such retaliation, and consent to the U.S.-North Korean discussions at Panmunjom. Following this agenda, Vance quickly rejected Park's demands for revision of the security treaty and automatic reprisals.[30]

In exchange for his commitments to restraint, Park wanted roughly $1.5 billion in U.S. military assistance (chiefly for airfield renovation or construction) and weapons (principally six squadrons of F-4s),* and a commitment not to redeploy U.S. aircraft from South Korea until the ones he requested were in place. Though outrageous, Park's demands reflected South Korea's fixation on the threat from

---

* The ROK MOD had been pressuring OSD since March 1967 for a squadron of F-4s to offset MIG-21 deliveries to North Korea (memcon, Visit of Korean Defense Minister Kim, 20 Mar 67, fldr Korea 091.112-1967, box 62, SecDef Subject Decimal files, Acc 72A-2468).

the North, concern about its ability to contain North Korean infiltration teams, and fears of an attack against a major economic facility in the South. Indicative of this mindset, Park eventually used the $100 million extra U.S. military aid package to reorganize mobilization planning and reequip militia reserves to counter Pyongyang's guerrilla warfare. His decision displeased the Korean joint chiefs and minister of defense, who had anticipated using the funds to modernize the regular armed forces. Displeased, too, was Johnson, who had expected the money would go for a combination of modernization (F-4 aircraft) and counterguerrilla operations. Vance ultimately recommended $100 million for 1968 (but nothing more beyond), and about $200 million for 1969, along with some F-4s, the latter primarily to enable the ROK government to show the South Korean people that the United States was providing up-to-date aircraft to meet the communist threat.[31]

After rejecting demands for retaliation against the North, Vance came away from his meeting with Park with a short-term commitment to avoid retaliation and a personal impression that Park's mercurial personality helped make the situation "acutely dangerous to our national interest and to peace in that area." Park remained upset and angry over the U.S. failure to permit retaliatory action for the Blue House raid and over Washington's continued inaction on the *Pueblo*. "[M]oody, volatile, and . . . drinking heavily," Park, according to Vance, was "a danger and rather unsafe." Worse still, the minister of defense was "an absolute menace" who had his own elite commando unit that had been conducting raids across the DMZ into North Korea, 11 in all, from October 1966 through November 1967.[32]

The ROK prime minister and chiefs of staff apparently depended on Washington to restrain Park from taking retaliatory action; Bonesteel had made it clear to the ROK uniformed military leaders that if they moved against the North he would recommend the United States withdraw its troops from South Korea. Warnke advised Clifford to continue urging caution during the visit of the new Korean minister of national defense to Washington in late May. By that time tensions had eased somewhat. The CIA, in fact, concluded that Pyongyang did not intend to invade the South; for the next year or so it would refrain from high-risk actions that might provoke another war.[33]

During this period of emergency in Korea the use of South Korean troops in Vietnam became an important factor in the involved negotiations with the United States. Since 1965 the administration, and in particular President Johnson, had been seeking assistance from allied countries. South Korea had been the largest contributor of forces and continued to be the ally most likely to provide future assistance.

During August 1967 when Clifford and Taylor were soliciting U.S. allies in Asia for additional troops for Vietnam, Park had remained noncommittal, citing domestic political problems. Under continual U.S. pressure, in early December 1967 Park agreed to send a light division, pending approval by the National Assembly. Meeting in Canberra, Australia, on December 21, Johnson and Park sealed the deal.[34]

In exchange for the additional Korean troop contributions to Vietnam, in December McNamara approved a counterinfiltration package for South Korea recommended by military commanders, as well as additional self-propelled artillery, helicopters, and, in principle, one U.S. Navy destroyer. This appears to have been the basis for Johnson's offer to Park in February 1968. At Park's insistence, the South Korean government in January offered to send additional troops to South Vietnam as early as 1 March 1968. A week after the Blue House raid and the *Pueblo* incident, the Koreans dropped the reinforcement plan as being overtaken by events. Perhaps Washington's only immediate consolation was that Seoul had not withdrawn its forces already serving in Vietnam in anticipation of renewed hostilities on the Korean peninsula.[35]

When Johnson reminded Park at their mid-April 1968 meeting in Honolulu that the United States had lived up to its part of the Canberra agreements, the South Korean leader said it would be "impossible" to send regular troops to South Vietnam given circumstances in South Korea. Park left Honolulu "deeply disappointed" and critical of Johnson who, in Park's estimation, waffled on military assistance to Korea and a formal revision of the ROK-U.S. Mutual Defense Treaty.[36]

The January incidents loomed large in U.S.-Republic of Korea relations. The volatile and dangerous situation along the Demilitarized Zone convinced Seoul that it could not afford to send additional combat troops to South Vietnam. Second, Park's reaction to what he saw as unequal U.S. responses to Blue House and the *Pueblo* badly strained military ties between Seoul and Washington. Third, continued North Korean aggression that culminated in a major seaborne infiltration by 120 North Korean commandos—the so-called Ulchin operation—in November kept tensions high on the Korean peninsula for the rest of 1968.[37] Finally, the crisis caused a dramatic turnaround in U.S. military aid to the Seoul regime.*

Prague Spring: Moscow Summer

While coping with upheavals in Vietnam and Korea, the administration had Europe ever in mind. Periodically, beginning with the Berlin airlift in 1948, the Soviets had precipitated crises in Europe that challenged the United States and its allies. In the spring and summer of 1968 another climactic event, this time in Czechoslovakia, threatened the peace of the continent.

On 22 March 1968, the Czechoslovak president bowed to popular pressure and resigned, an unprecedented event in the history of a communist government. A reform-oriented cabinet that took power in early April instituted a program that restored human rights, granted greater political autonomy, and proposed economic reforms. The swiftness of these developments caught Moscow unprepared, but Soviet leaders soon began to exert political and psychological pressures on the new regime to slow the momentum of reforms known as Prague Spring.[38]

---

* See Chapter XVII.

The first overt Soviet military pressure against the reformers occurred in May when Russian troops stationed in Poland conducted field exercises near the Czechoslovak border. Upon conclusion of the maneuvers, Moscow prevailed on Prague to announce that Warsaw Pact military exercises would commence in Czechoslovakia and Poland in June. Despite concern in some quarters of the State Department about Soviet military intervention, throughout the unfolding events U.S. intelligence analysts presumed that the Pact troop deployments and Soviet mobilizations were for the purpose of maneuvers, not a prelude to invasion.[39]

High-ranking State officials pondered whether a "deterrent signal" might discourage Soviet adventurism in Czechoslovakia. State favored a low-key approach that emphasized the exercise of "great prudence." Following State's lead, in mid-May OSD agreed on a policy of non-action. The Warsaw Pact exercises announced in May took place in Czechoslovakia and other eastern European states between 19 and 30 June, but Soviet troops remained in Czechoslovakia afterward. Caution remained the watchword for NATO as SACEUR Commander General Lemnitzer assured OSD that U.S. forces would take no actions that might provide the Soviets with a pretext for delaying the withdrawal of their forces. The West German foreign office indicated it would pass on similar word to its military units and border police commands.[40]

Izvestia's 23 July edition carried a front-page story about the mobilization of thousands of reservists for a new exercise of rear-area services in the western USSR scheduled to last until 10 August. Yet no intelligence indicators pointed to an invasion of Czechoslovakia. Soviet announcements of additional military maneuvers, though unusual, were regarded as a form of political, not direct military pressure on the Czechs. From Moscow, Ambassador Thompson advised a continuation of restraint, believing that any U.S. appeal to Moscow would only reveal Washington's weakness to influence events.[41]

On 24 July, Rusk told the president of his conviction that the "real crisis has subsided"; Walt Rostow likewise continued to doubt that the Soviets would move militarily against Czechoslovakia. The NATO allies shared this view. German defense minister Gerhard Schroeder, for example, assured Clifford that the Soviets, fearing foreign and especially domestic reaction, would not intervene militarily. The next day Schroeder told Johnson he believed the Russians would try to deescalate the crisis and achieve a diplomatic settlement.[42]

Although differing on the odds of Soviet military action, State and CIA doubted the USSR would resort to military force, even while Rusk admitted that "nobody knows what they will do." Meantime, by the end of July units from 10 Soviet divisions had moved to southern East Germany adjacent to the Czechoslovak border in a display of Moscow's military muscle on the eve of talks between Czechoslovak and Soviet leaders.[43]

These air and ground reinforcements, air defense exercises, large-scale rear service exercises in the western USSR, and an increased state of readiness in certain Pact forces provided, in Lemnitzer's words, "an ideal cover for preparatory actions against the Central Region" of NATO. In early August the SACEUR requested Washington's political guidance on the Czech situation due to the "increasing political tension" of the past month that could be a forewarning. On 5 August, though, a relieved Clifford thought the crisis past as the Soviets seemed to pull back from the brink of military action. Wheeler, less sanguine, observed with alarm that the Soviets had moved large numbers of men and equipment undetected by U.S. intelligence and declared that those same Soviet forces could have overrun Czechoslovakia in 48 hours. The implications of allied inability to detect the Soviet troop movements were serious because the failure cast doubt on the presumption of strategic early warning that underpinned U.S. NATO strategy. By 10 August, the CIA estimated that the crisis had eased but not ended; the tense situation continued. U.S. policy remained low-key to avoid giving Moscow any pretext for military action.[44]

As tension waxed and waned, the president tried to finalize plans for his long sought-after summit meeting with Kosygin to discuss strategic arms limitations. Continuing Soviet military activity, however, including the movement of two or three divisions south from Berlin towards the border with Czechoslovakia, Soviet press rhetoric, and continuing mobilizations kept the crisis simmering sufficiently for Clifford to counsel Johnson against meeting with Kosygin "during the time that Czechoslovakia is still hot." The president agreed, but he still seemed to believe that perhaps in a few weeks the crisis might resolve itself peacefully. He also felt strongly that merely waiting for the next Soviet move on arms talks might well incline the United States simply to accept whatever offer Moscow put on the table. Johnson's hopes seemed realized when on 19 August Ambassador Dobrynin notified Rusk that the Soviets were prepared to engage in discussions on peaceful uses of nuclear power. The ambassador suggested that talks begin in Moscow on 15 October, "or any other date close to that time"; a joint news release was planned for 21 August to announce the impending summit.[45] Within the next 24 hours, the world changed.

During the early evening hours of 20 August, Dobrynin informed the president that Soviet and Warsaw Pact forces had moved into Czechoslovak territory. On 20–21 August, 17 Soviet and 4 Polish divisions (supported by contingents from Bulgarian, Hungarian, and East German divisions) occupied the country. The ambassador assured Johnson that Soviet military action in Czechoslovakia threatened neither U.S. national interests nor peace in Europe; he hoped it would not interfere with U.S.-Soviet relations. After dismissing Dobrynin, the president quickly convened an emergency meeting of the NSC at which Secretaries Clifford and Rusk expressed their surprise at the Soviet invasion. Wheeler lamented that the United States could take no military action because it lacked the forces to do so. Only a single U.S. brigade along with two French and two German divisions stood immediately available for possible intervention. To employ additional military units required NATO to mobilize; estimates suggested it would take six months to achieve planned force levels.[46]

Besides the immediate international crisis precipitated by the invasion, Johnson faced the questions of whether summit talks should go forward with the Soviets and whether such meetings would appear to condone Soviet aggression. He instructed Rusk to call Dobrynin that same night and tell him there would be no announcement as previously agreed of a presidential visit to the Soviet Union or of the strategic arms talks. Clifford endorsed the president's position on delaying the announcement and counseled a wait-and-see approach. Wheeler speculated that the Soviet deployments could be no more than the maneuvers seen three weeks earlier, and perhaps Kosygin and Brezhnev had acted in good faith but found themselves overruled by hardliners in the Kremlin.[47] In any event, Johnson had foreclosed only the 20 August announcement of a summit, leaving open the possibility of arms limitation talks with Moscow in the near future.

As for the Soviet leaders, they had apparently decided only on 16–17 August to move militarily against Czechoslovakia. They chose the 20 August date because it coincided with the final meeting of the Czechoslovak Presidium, an occasion that presented the last opportunity for a pro-Soviet coup by diehard Czech communists. Any further delay would allow the Slovak Party Congress to convene on 23 August; in Moscow's eyes, the Congress was the first step toward a "counterrevolutionary coup." According to Ambassador Thompson, the last-minute decision for the invasion took "all friendly diplomats" in Moscow by surprise. For general consumption within the administration, the president, Rusk, and Clifford put the best face on U.S. puzzlement over the timing and the reason for the Soviet invasion. Johnson assured a 22 August meeting of the cabinet that "we did not assume there would be no military intervention." Rusk informed the same group that a U.S. decision not to act was made Monday (19 August) because military intervention would have resulted in a world war. This decision appeared all the more prudent in light of a Soviet strategic missile alert on the day of the invasion. At a meeting in the Cabinet Room the following day, Clifford related the Soviet invasion to Moscow's October 1967 announcement of increased military spending and the Kremlin leaders' intention to find ways to translate their increased military power into greater political influence.[48]

Rumors abounded concerning Romania as the next Soviet target. At Nitze's request, the Joint Chiefs analyzed possible U.S. countermoves to such an eventuality. Besides diminishing the effectiveness of U.S. ground forces in Europe,* McNamara had deployed active tactical squadrons based in the United States as part of

---

* See Chapters XII, XIII, and XV for various aspects of the U.S. military decline in Europe.

the strategic air reserve to Korea in January 1968, where the planes and their crews remained. Their replacements, drawn from reserve units in the continental United States, often flew older-model aircraft, rendering them less capable than previously U.S.-based air units committed to NATO's defense in mid-1968. Available U.S. forces, the JCS reasoned, precluded any major contingency operations. Furthermore, because of military weakness, the United States should act with "extreme caution" in the situation.[49]

To discourage possible Soviet designs on Romania, State proposed redeploying to Europe 35,000 troops and four squadrons of aircraft withdrawn earlier in the year, reinforcing Berlin with a battalion from the United States, deploying two tactical air squadrons to Spain, asking Britain to redeploy its withdrawn forces to NATO, and suggesting that West Germany mobilize 20,000 territorials for assignment to NATO. Warnke counseled nonintervention because it would take too long to redeploy the U.S. units, be too expensive, bring into question the rationale for withdrawing American troops in the first place, and skew the balance of payments issue. Finally, Warnke insisted that redeployments besides being irrelevant "would be a bluff we are not prepared to support."[50]

As events developed, after speaking to Thompson and Rusk on 30 August, Dobrynin called at Rusk's home the following evening to assure the Americans that "fears and rumors" of Soviet military action against Romania were completely unfounded and that there would be no moves by the Warsaw Pact against Berlin. At an NSC meeting on 4 September Rusk somewhat allayed concerns about Romania's fate. He attributed Soviet caution to the president's 30 August speech warning a "would-be aggressor" not to misjudge the resolve of the administration or the American people.[51]

Most troubling to OSD was that the Soviet transition from an exercise scenario directly to vigorous operations took NATO by surprise. After all, by successfully concealing, or at least plausibly misrepresenting, a sizable mobilization preceding major operations, the Soviets and the East European allies had managed to deploy as many as 250,000 troops and quickly overrun Czechoslovakia in a sophisticated and efficient military operation. The Soviet military planning and airlift capabilities during the invasion impressed both U.S. military leaders and the CIA, leading them to question the strategic concept of "political warning time" underpinning NATO's reinforcement scenarios—that allied intelligence detection of such deployments in advance would provide NATO members sufficient warning time to react.[52]

Sharing that concern, State recommended a reexamination of the concept of "political warning time." From ISA Warnke vigorously dissented, contending that political warning related to an attack on NATO, not Czechoslovakia; besides there had been indications since January 1968 of increasing Soviet aggressiveness. He appeared to be in a minority. Walt Rostow's military assistant, Brig. Gen. Robert Ginsburgh, argued that the Soviet invasion raised serious doubts about the concept of strategic warning, a "key element in the posture of our NATO forces." General Lemnitzer, concerned that NATO appeared "helpless, hopeless and harmless," advised "close scrutiny" of the notion of political warning.[53]

The Joint Chiefs supported Lemnitzer's recommendations; in early September they requested a reevaluation of NATO and U.S. readiness to respond to contingencies. They questioned OSD views that Europe was achieving stability, that the Soviets desired détente to reach arms control and mutual force reduction agreements, and the idea that the Soviets "think and act like us." More significantly for OSD's long-term NATO policy, they questioned also the "assumption that a surprise attack in Europe is unlikely."[54]

State's analysis concluded that the Soviet invasion had not altered NATO's strategic concepts of flexible response and forward defense fundamentally but conceded that the doctrine of political warning time required reexamination. During Senate Appropriation Committee hearings in mid-September, Sen. Henry Jackson asked Clifford whether the assumption that NATO would have political warning time was still valid. The defense secretary replied that intelligence had kept up with the Soviet military exercises preceding the invasion but they did not constitute a threat against NATO; hence political warning remained valid. Distinguishing between "ample knowledge" of Soviet capabilities to invade Czechoslovakia and the inability to perceive the Kremlin's intent, Wheeler concluded that "actual usable warning time" was reduced.[55]

Later, OSD cited statements by SHAPE and the NATO Military Committee that distinguished between political warning and strategic warning.[*] The invasion had been preceded by a three-month period of political warning (Czech-Soviet tension) and strategic military warning (Warsaw Pact military buildup and deployment) before actually occurring. Had the Soviet military action been directed against NATO members, the alliance would have used this time to mobilize and deploy its forces against the aggressor. Without doubt the speed of the Soviet movement into Czechoslovakia appeared to raise doubts in Clifford's mind about warning time, the cardinal premise of McNamara's NATO strategy. In a marked departure from previous years, the defense secretary informed the president in early 1969 that without resort to nuclear weapons even a somewhat improved NATO force structure probably could not stop a full-scale conventional Soviet attack preceded by a "successfully concealed mobilization." As for the alliance members, the invasion of Czechoslovakia confirmed their fears that only a nuclear deterrent could protect them from attack by overpowering Soviet conventional military strength.[56]

Although Ambassador Harlan Cleveland, the permanent U.S. Representative to NATO, described the crisis in Czechoslovakia as a "momentous event" sending "shivers" through Europe, and the JCS termed it a "turning point in NATO's his-

---

[*] Political and strategic warning were often used interchangeably.

tory," the Soviet invasion of a fellow socialist state did not spur NATO's European members to greater defense efforts. After their initial reaction to the Soviet invasion, none of the NATO allies abandoned their frugal attitude toward defense spending or rushed to endorse the strategy of flexible response. The NATO ministerial meeting did hear pledges by alliance members not to implement planned reductions (Belgium, FRG, Netherlands) or to ask for, but not commit to, higher defense budgets (FRG, Greece, Netherlands, Norway). Belgium and Italy had increased their defense budgets before the storm broke, and Italy promised to bring its forces up to NATO standards. Neither the United Kingdom nor Canada promised major improvements; both remained tight-lipped about any increases. Nor did European efforts toward détente entirely wither. The overall result was "far more promise than performance" from the Europeans.[57]

The Soviet invasion of Czechoslovakia brought to a halt promising preliminary arms control conversations between the United States and the Soviet Union. Opposition from within the administration, particularly from Clifford and Nitze, and among the European allies restrained Johnson from moving ahead, as he would have liked, during the closing months of his administration. The Czech effect lasted until the Nixon administration came to office and resumed arms control negotiation.[*]

REDCOSTE and the Czech Effect

A long-term crisis of a different nature confronting DoD required urgent attention and a stern attempt at resolution in 1968. The large cost of maintaining strong U.S. forces in Europe adversely affected the economy because of the growing negative balance of payments (BoP) and the gold outflow. The huge expenditures for Vietnam greatly increased the pressure to cut U.S. costs in Europe. Through most of his tenure McNamara had worked assiduously to lower the cost of maintaining U.S. troops in Europe.

Facing mounting demands from within the administration and from Congress, in March 1968 Clifford initiated REDCOSTE (Reduction of Costs in Europe). He believed that reducing overhead and support costs in Europe would resolve the balance of payments deficiency without detracting from the combat forces. OSD expected that over a five-year period REDCOSTE would streamline and consolidate headquarters as well as support activities, thereby eliminating 43,000 of the 337,000 DoD personnel in the European Command area, with accompanying BoP savings of $150 million and annual budget savings of about $400 million. On 6 June, Clifford forwarded draft proposals to the JCS and the military services for review and comment.[58]

Harlan Cleveland questioned the wisdom of eliminating several small but politically sensitive U.S. units in NATO—two Hawk air defense battalions in West Germany, U.S. ground troops in Italy, and an aerial reconnaissance squadron—to

---

[*] For an account of arms control efforts in 1968 see Chapter XII.

achieve minimal BoP and budgetary savings. The Joint Chiefs went on record that force reductions in Europe could not be justified on military grounds, but they accepted that current domestic economic and financial considerations might override military strategy. They opposed the REDCOSTE package because its consolidations would hamper command and control arrangements, degrade SACEUR's nuclear strike plan, and, by pulling troops out of Italy, weaken NATO's southern flank.[59] During June and July, discussions between OSD, the JCS, the military services, and State modified the original REDCOSTE proposals.

Meantime, in early June OSD directed SACEUR to find ways to offset the anticipated DoD $300–500 million BoP deficit in Europe during FY 1969 and to propose major reductions in DoD personnel and facilities there to help realize that savings. Lemnitzer's personal reply reaffirmed the JCS position that reduction of U.S. forces in Europe could not be justified at a time of increasing Warsaw Pact combat capability. Even more serious, the political ramifications of such actions, Lemnitzer contended, threatened to undermine acceptance by NATO countries of the U.S.-sponsored strategy of flexible response. Recent U.S. withdrawals, contrary to the assurances of proponents, had set off a decline in allied conventional forces at the very time such forces were greatly needed. A new initiative from Washington might cause an unraveling of the alliance. In an effort to find a long-range solution to the gold flow problem, the Joint Staff also solicited EUCOM's views on the feasibility of a "well-balanced, three-division force in Germany," aiming to provide maximum combat power with minimum support structure. Despite opposition by State, the Joint Chiefs, and SACEUR, ISA insisted that OSD had to "bite [the] bullet" on large-scale troop reductions in Europe.[60]

That military concerns were no longer paramount when discussing reductions to U.S. forces in NATO was brought home to DoD in April 1968 when Senator Symington proposed to introduce an amendment to cut funding for all but 50,000 of the U.S. troops in Europe after 31 December 1968. Clifford told the German defense minister that he hoped to find ways to avoid the worst effects of Symington's amendment. He doubted that massive cuts would solve the balance of payments problem and believed that REDCOSTE would achieve better results and "preserve the cohesiveness and strength of NATO." Nitze proposed withdrawals of approximately 100,000 U.S. troops and new offset agreements with the allies.[61]

DoD had already pulled out more than half that total—18,000 in 1967 during the relocation from France and 33,000 in 1968 for REFORGER/CRESTED CAP*—and further proposed that REDCOSTE eliminate another 43,000 military spaces, or 94,000 military slots in all. An incremental reduction of another 6,000 troops could be implemented if Congress insisted on a symbolic 100,000-man withdrawal. Such huge reductions led the Joint Chiefs privately to consider a total withdrawal from Western Europe. Officially, however, they recommended re-

---

* See Chapter XV.

taining bases and quick reaction forces. Moreover, unanticipated expenses to cover costs associated with the Tet offensive and *Pueblo* deployments had left DoD short of funds for NATO. On 17 August, Nitze approved an Army request to delete FY 1969 funds for REFORGER I, and four days later the JCS, again because of a lack of money, requested that Clifford postpone the exercise until October 1969. Three years of manipulative Defense budget and force structure decisions seemed to leave OSD little choice but to withdraw tens of thousands more U.S. troops from Europe. Otherwise the Symington Amendment threatened devastating consequences: a weakening of U.S. military forces that the European members could not possibly compensate for; the negation of the consultation process within the alliance; and a crippling of U.S. policies and goals for NATO and Western Europe.[62]

The Czechoslovakia crisis of August 1968 killed the Symington amendment by laying to rest, in Warnke's words, the belief "that the Soviet leadership was now so transformed that Soviet military action in Europe was impossible." The ruthlessness of the Soviet action, he believed, showed what a grave mistake it would be for the United States to withdraw large forces from Europe.[63] But the Soviet willingness to resort to armed force did not halt REDCOSTE.

State officials devised an ambitious set of responses in the event the USSR invaded Romania. Although Rusk did not press OSD to implement all of these proposals, he did believe it "politically imperative" after the Soviet invasion for OSD to conduct REFORGER in January 1969 as originally scheduled in order to bolster allied confidence in the U.S. commitment to NATO. He further recommended to Clifford dropping key elements of REDCOSTE, such as reduction of the Southern European Task Force (SETAF) in Italy and withdrawals of air defense and combat support units in Germany, until NATO had time to assess the full implications of Soviet actions. Clifford's brief and bland reply assured Rusk that there would be "little difficulty" in meeting most of State's suggestions; he would keep the secretary of state informed about the REDCOSTE studies.[64] Tension between OSD and State over REDCOSTE decisions persisted throughout the waning days of the Johnson administration.

The Czech crisis served to reinvigorate the military's objections to OSD's REDCOSTE plans. Wheeler asked the top U.S. commanders in Europe in late August to recommend whether NATO should respond to the Soviet invasion, and if so, with what actions and when. Respondents recommended a cessation of troop withdrawals and a series of military exercises in Europe. The Joint Chiefs in turn urged Clifford to reinstate the January 1969 REFORGER I exercise as well as suspend selected REDCOSTE and other reductions that would adversely affect the readiness of U.S. forces in NATO. This would demonstrate American leadership and "the will and cohesiveness of NATO."[65]

After reviewing the arguments and considering the impact of the Soviet invasion of Czechoslovakia, Clifford issued a revised REDCOSTE plan on 18 September. He made plain that the services were to comment on the merits of the specific proposals, not the timing, because DoD would withdraw no U.S. troops so long as Soviet troops remained in Czechoslovakia. As redrawn, REDCOSTE planned to pull more than 35,000 U.S. military out of Europe, saving $178 million annually in BoP and $424 million in budget expenditures. Conceding State's concerns about reducing combat forces after the Czechoslovak crisis, OSD dropped plans to remove three air units from Spain and an aerial reconnaissance squadron from Germany, and to retire the flagship cruiser from the Sixth Fleet. Withdrawals from SETAF and the turnover to the Germans or elimination of two Hawk battalions would continue, regardless of JCS and State objections.[66]

Another contentious issue between OSD and State involved Nitze's proposal in early October to cancel the U.S. commitment to rotate the brigades of the 24th Infantry Division (Mechanized) in and out of Germany every six months. The previous May, ISA had recommended dropping the rotation feature of REFORGER, not to save money (only $2–3 million in budget savings) but to reduce unit personnel turbulence and relieve pressure on the Army rotation base already strained by the demands of Vietnam. Reminding Clifford that the rotation concept was a central feature of the U.S. proposals that culminated in the Tripartite Agreement* of April 1967, Rusk stressed the "political imperatives" of the rotation and wondered what "countervailing positive steps" OSD was considering in lieu of the unit exchanges. Lemnitzer supported the cancellation of the planned rotation and advocated instead the permanent retention of one brigade of the division in Germany to improve overall combat readiness. Clifford's reply to Rusk relied on Lemnitzer's arguments, and concluded that it would not be too difficult to convince the NATO allies of the benefits of the intended cancellation. Rusk objected to raising the matter of cancellation with German political leaders for the present, suggesting that Lemnitzer sound out his FRG military counterpart on rotation preferences before any policy decisions.[67] Having fenced with State, Clifford next dueled with the JCS.

To the Joint Chiefs' ambitious and expensive proposed responses to the Czech crisis, Clifford demonstrated anew the primacy he attached to restoring the nation's economic health. The military leaders consistently advocated conducting several large field exercises in Europe and wanted a moratorium on further NATO reductions as well as cancellation or reconsideration of numerous REDCOSTE and other economy initiatives. Even as Clifford addressed JCS concern, he reminded them that the likelihood of greater economic problems in FY 1970 than in FY 1969 meant that any improvements to military readiness had to come from available resources. Since Soviet aggression had called into question Washington's preconceptions about Moscow's willingness to resort to naked force, the Chiefs believed that, "despite the serious weakness of its military force posture," the United States had to demonstrate its commitment to NATO by immediate and visible military actions.

---

* See Chapter XV.

In early October, when Nitze offered a $50 million package to improve NATO forces, the Chiefs responded that the figure was inadequate. The Chiefs again proposed a moratorium on force level reductions, relief from REDCOSTE, and other reductions; they wanted additional money to demonstrate the "leadership/prestige and economic capacity of the United States" during the crisis.[68]

Clifford, ever mindful of the fragile national economy and under intense White House pressure to hold the line on defense spending, rejected the elaborate JCS proposals and instead opted for ISA's more austere combination of smaller exercises and limited construction of aircraft shelter and storage facilities in Europe. While approving the proposal, the Joint Chiefs believed that it fell far short of conveying to the Soviet Union Washington's determination and leadership role in strengthening NATO. A compromise with OSD did incorporate several JCS recommendations, notably rescheduling the REFORGER exercise; in exchange for the concessions the Chiefs dropped plans to deploy a brigade from Korea to Europe and accepted the $50 million ceiling on a response package. REFORGER/CRESTED CAP exercises rescheduled for January-February 1969 showcased U.S. ability to redeploy units rapidly to Europe. Other lesser exercises, construction of aircraft shelters and munitions storage facilities, and permanent retention of one brigade of the 24th Infantry Division in Germany were made subject to the European allies also undertaking significant improvements to their forces.[69]

Meanwhile the State Department cabled all NATO capitals announcing the U.S. decision to call a meeting of the NATO foreign, finance, and defense ministers for 18 through 20 November as a substitute for the regular December meeting of the Defense Planning Committee. Treasury Secretary Fowler learned of the meeting, which he was supposed to attend, only by reading an account of it in the *Washington Post*. OSD found out about it through routine cable traffic. State's maneuvering incensed Warnke who had previously counseled against moving the annual meeting forward out of concern that the American November elections would overshadow the conference and thus diminish its importance.[70]

Clifford made the best of State's fait accompli, telling the assembled defense ministers that the November meeting had been rescheduled from its usual December date to demonstrate the deep concern of all NATO countries over the Soviet action in Czechoslovakia. If his concern was surely genuine, his prescription was all too familiar—NATO must do more militarily to respond to the Soviet invasion because member nations could afford to do more. He announced that withdrawals of U.S. support and headquarters forces would continue and that the allies had to cooperate to find a lasting solution to the problem of inequities in the contributions of NATO members relative to that of the United States.[71]

Since June 1968, the administration had been telling the NATO allies in very broad terms of U.S. efforts to reduce costs without decreasing overall combat capability, but had not revealed any specifics of REDCOSTE. During that time, REDCOSTE had gone through a series of four formal detailed reviews lasting into November as proposals got "modified, dropped, or replaced." After months of bargaining, four main proposals still remained unsettled: relocation of USAF headquarters from Wiesbaden to Ramstein in Germany; reduction of two Hawk battalions in Germany; withdrawal of the Southern European Task Force from Italy; and reduction at Aviano Air Base in Italy. Taken together these outstanding actions involved just over 12,000 personnel, almost $100 million in budget savings, and $40 million in balance of payments' economies, or roughly 25 percent of the anticipated REDCOSTE benefits.[72]

On 10 December, Clifford issued OSD's approved REDCOSTE plan, a close-hold document whose public release was banned; he directed that implementation planning begin. The final amended version relocated almost 34,000 military from Europe at a saving of $158.4 million in the balance of payments and $428.8 million in budget funds. In his cover letter to Rusk, Clifford explained that his decisions relocated about 10,000 fewer personnel than originally estimated, and, per Rusk's 2 September letter, involved no combat or combat support units, with the exception of the one Sergeant missile battalion taken from Italy. The removal of two Hawk battalions from Germany involved no reduction in combat strength because they would be replaced with different U.S. air defense systems. Clifford included a lengthy exposition on how to present these withdrawals in the proper light to European allies.[73] As events transpired, this was wishful thinking on Clifford's part.

The Bonn government still hesitated to accept the operation and maintenance of two Hawk battalions, four Nike-Hawk battalions, and three air control and warning sites. Lemnitzer was outspoken about the dire implications REDCOSTE posed for NATO. He warned that further U.S. withdrawals of support and service units would dangerously reduce American combat capability, create a force structure vacuum the Europeans would not fill, and likely lead to another round of reductions by the NATO allies. The Joint Chiefs, protesting that the cutbacks would seriously impair overall U.S. combat capability in Europe, endorsed Lemnitzer's concerns about sparking a new round of force reductions by other NATO members. Then State deferred over half the REDCOSTE plan pending further study by the incoming administration. The deferrals included troop withdrawals from southern Europe, Turkey, and North Africa as well as minor redeployments from Germany, the relocation of USAF headquarters in Europe, withdrawal of two Hawk battalions, and reductions of U.S. forces in Italy. These postponements affected significant percentages of the military personnel withdrawals and the projected BoP savings. No final decisions on REDCOSTE were made during the last days of the Johnson years. By default the issue carried over to the Nixon administration, where the differences between OSD and State over NATO force levels persisted. The new secretary of state favored further delay pending completion of a presidentially mandated NSC study on NATO; the new secretary of defense pressed for expeditious action on the reductions.[74] In the end, REDCOSTE's demise owed more to bureaucratic infighting in Washington than to the Soviet invasion of Czechoslovakia.

The other crises of 1968 were not mere sideshows that distracted the administration's attention from Vietnam, although they may have seemed so. The nuclear accident in Greenland soon vanished from the press. In South Korea little seemed to change. The *Pueblo* crew was returned, the ship was not. U.S. reinforcements were withdrawn, but friction between the two Koreas continued to ignite DMZ incidents and climaxed in the large-scale North Korean infiltration by sea into the South. As for Czechoslovakia, to outward appearances little changed in NATO. Reductions of U.S. troops were postponed, the European allies settled back into their pre-Czechoslovakia NATO habits, efforts at détente slowly reemerged, and the U.S. balance of payments continued in the red. But each of the incidents of 1968 had significant long-term consequences for U.S. national security policy.

The Greenland accident forced alterations to U.S. strategic war plans resulting from rerouting B-52s away from the island. It also raised fundamental questions about suspension of nuclear and overflight rights and cancellation of certain strategic bomber routes that DoD did not officially wish to address. The *Pueblo* incident bound the United States more closely to South Korea and its mercurial leader Park Chung Hee than Washington preferred. Aside from the humiliation of losing a U.S. Navy ship to a lesser communist country, the response imposed on DoD's already tight Defense budget the extra burdens of deployment and reserve mobilization costs. The Czechoslovak crisis ended the possibility of meaningful strategic arms limitations talks between Washington and Moscow during the Johnson administration despite the president's best efforts to keep negotiations alive. It also aided REDCOSTE opponents in their efforts to derail plans for military reductions, thereby contributing significantly to continued balance of payments deficits and scuttling efforts to cut swollen Defense budgets.

Efforts to deal with one emergency after another disclosed that U.S. conventional forces were stretched to their limits, if not beyond, as exemplified by the extraordinary number of training and operational accidents that occurred during the year. Early in 1968 Johnson perceived that enemies saw the United States as weakened and disorganized by the Vietnam War. He opted to assuage the domestic discord by withdrawing from the presidential race. Unfortunately, he took no meaningful steps to rebuild a weakened military because to do so would demand domestic sacrifices—higher taxes, reserve mobilization, larger Defense budgets, abandonment of his Great Society dream—that he knew were unacceptable to the majority of Americans. Domestic priorities triumphed even when Johnson faced his year of international crises.

Chapter XIX

Strategy and Cost-Effectiveness

Strategy has deep roots in the complex support structure of military forces. Under McNamara, DoD was made acutely aware that all meaningful activities of the military serve as tools for the fashioning of strategy, beginning with the budget, from which all else flows. His search for greater efficiency extended to areas that had a profound effect on U.S. strategy in Vietnam and elsewhere in the world. The concept of cost-effectiveness he espoused encompassed the whole range of human and material resources for the military—weapon system development and use, procurement contracting and administration, cost reduction, force reduction, and flexible allocation of resources. The last had to do with the especially difficult and troublesome drawdown of men and materiel from other parts of the world on behalf of the forces fighting in Vietnam.

A Cost-Efficient War?

As a principal architect and manager of the Vietnam War McNamara directed key elements of its prosecution—the air war, the barrier system, enemy casualty accounting, logistical support, and military unit readiness. In all of these particulars he demanded maximum effectiveness at minimum cost. Fulfillment of this ideal proved difficult, often not possible.

Repeated disappointments of the air war[*] against the North led McNamara to a costly strategic decision that represented his one direct intrusion into ground operations in the South. In mid-1966, he concluded that the way to minimize the bombing of North Vietnam was to construct a barrier across South Vietnam's northernmost province, a project he ramrodded through over the objections of General Westmoreland and the JCS. He was willing to spend huge sums of money

---

[*] For the air war see Chapters III and VIII.

on the project, but money and technology failed him. According to the understated congressional testimony of Defense Secretary Melvin R. Laird in 1969, the original plan for the barrier "did not work out as expected." The continuous strong point/obstacle line was never completed; by March 1969 it had been indefinitely deferred. Most strong points had been abandoned. A second subsystem of sensors covering the main foot trails used for infiltration never was implemented, although a third sensor system, covering main truck routes through Laos, came into operation and proved quite successful in monitoring North Vietnamese vehicle traffic. The failure of various special munitions associated with the barrier led DoD to terminate production of most of them.[*1]

Lavish spending on the barrier that emphasized firepower and technology seemed to contradict McNamara's cost-effectiveness policies. Yet carping by critics that it cost $400,000 to kill a single Viet Cong did not deter him. Established policy, the defense secretary reminded such critics, by substituting firepower and mobility for manpower lessened the loss of U.S. lives "no matter what the cost."[2]

Always in search of ways to measure progress in the war, DoD resorted to the "body count," the tabulation of enemy dead as a strategic tool, to determine, as McNamara later put it, "what we should be doing in Vietnam to win the war while putting our troops at the least risk." After the 1965 U.S. buildup CINCPAC and MACV used enemy casualty statistics as an index to estimate communist capabilities as well as for intelligence purposes. Both commands attempted to centralize the reporting of communist casualties, standardize reporting criteria and terminology to avoid duplication, and ensure accurate data on enemy losses. This allowed, again in McNamara's words, "some means of deciding whether you were moving forward or not moving forward." Nevertheless, the resulting statistics depended on raw data from U.S. field units, whose level of detail and accuracy varied, and on Vietnamese forces that used different but probably no more accurate methods to compute communist losses.[3]

In a study of 77 U.S. operations conducted from January through October 1966 Systems Analysis found that the mandatory after-action reports had sufficient data to permit classification of only 38 percent of claimed casualties (3,600 out of 9,458) as enemy losses from enemy initiatives or active willingness to engage. The remaining communist losses went unexplained in the reports or were described in terms too vague to be interpreted. As the war dragged on, increasing skepticism from the media and even within the administration, including McNamara himself, greeted MACV's "body count," convincing the Saigon command to de-emphasize the statistics. Rather than a measure of success much needed by the Johnson administration, the "body count" eventually became synonymous with exaggeration, duplication, and inflation of enemy casualties, as well as a notorious shorthand accounting system that dehumanized Vietnamese losses.[4]

---

[*] For an account of the barrier system see Chapters V and VII.

On another statistical front—his never ending attempts to control the financial cost—McNamara applied analysis and business management techniques to identify the least expensive and most productive material resources with which to fight the war. Initially, by use of existing supply inventories, and later by careful monitoring of production he sought to avoid the waste typical in most American wars. As a result, there occurred "shortages of key items, including ammunition, and bitter complaints from a military forced to fight on short rations in an age of abundance."[5]

McNamara relied on a "hot line" concept that provided built-in flexibility to increase or decrease production at relatively short notice without a sudden production spurt followed by complete close down of production. Within 90 days of a request, production could be increased to meet the order. During the interim, shipments from the worldwide inventory would cover the difference. This procedure presumably would avoid the "very loose financial control" that led to $30 billion overfunding for the Korean War and left the huge residue of excess stockpiles characteristic of the post-1953 era.[6]

Yet McNamara's practice of "buying only what we need" often failed to meet urgent military needs. For instance, DoD procured artillery ammunition based on the level of actual usage rather than on forecast consumption. Remorseless escalation that invariably outstripped previous usage did not permit production to catch up with consumption for a full 24 months after Washington began deploying major U.S. forces to Vietnam. At first McNamara met shortfalls by drawing on ammunition stockpiles in DoD's worldwide inventory, but these stocks became depleted seven months before production caught up with consumption. By that time, he faced a shortage of 3.5 million rounds of artillery ammunition in the worldwide inventory. Premium costs for production stops and starts as well as stretchouts and telescoping of procurement orders added $1.7 million to the total cost of 105-mm. artillery ammunition.[7]

The air war also underwent unexpectedly rapid escalation, requiring staggering expenditures of bombs, rockets, and 20-mm. ammunition over North and South Vietnam as well as Laos. Shifting aerial attacks from South to North Vietnam increased aircraft losses; early October 1966 found McNamara asking Congress for permission to reprogram funds to purchase 196 additional fighter bombers.[8] As the war in Vietnam continually expanded at a faster tempo than McNamara anticipated, and as each passing month produced higher casualties and unexpectedly greater costs, shortages of troops, equipment, and supplies became commonplace throughout U.S. military units.

Allegations about the lack of equipment and material for U.S. units fighting in Vietnam in early 1966 stoked congressional unease with OSD's handling of the war, bringing McNamara some of his most uncomfortable days in office. Hardly a week passed without some sensational new charge of shortages appearing in the press, in congressional committees, or on television. Scarcities were inevitable in so rapid and vast a military buildup, but McNamara doggedly insisted that there were no shortages, only problems of distribution, a distinction lost on those who needed something and did not have it. His rigidity and determination on the issue left him appearing either doctrinaire, or foolish, or untruthful.

Much of the trouble was attributed to McNamara's cost-effectiveness policies. In July 1965, Mendel Rivers, Chairman of the House Committee on Armed Services, requested Porter Hardy, Jr. (D-Va.), Chairman of the Special Investigations Subcommittee, Committee on Armed Services, to "conduct an immediate inquiry" into the secretary of defense's third annual cost reduction program report to determine, among other things, if McNamara's management policies adversely affected combat readiness and logistic support to the forces in Vietnam.[9] As the committee proceeded with its broad-based investigation, damaging leaks about shortages of ammunition, equipment, and overall military readiness made their way to McNamara's critics.

On 11 February 1966, a CBS News broadcast reported that a critical ammunition shortage had left some U.S. warplanes in Vietnam unable to fly missions with full bomb loads and had reduced the United States to scouring Europe for leftover World War II-era bombs. Ten days later the *New York Times* featured military writer Hanson Baldwin's scathing indictment of the Johnson administration's mismanagement of the armed services. Citing unnamed military officers, Baldwin blasted the cost-effectiveness program as "too rigidly applied" to "allow a sufficient 'cushion' of supplies and equipment for emergencies"; he disparaged OSD's centralized control procedures as "too inflexible or too slow" to respond to service needs. A lack of field grade officers, uniforms, clothing, and munitions all hampered the war effort. Specific shortages identified in the *Times* included ammunition for the M-16 rifle, 2.75-inch rockets, illuminating shells, and 750-pound bombs. Baldwin also alleged that the United States had almost exhausted its trained and ready military units. The active forces, spread thin in Vietnam and elsewhere, had no new units available for several months to meet other contingencies.[10]

Testifying before Senate committees just four days after Baldwin's story appeared, McNamara dismissed all the charges. He denied an ammunition shortage, insisting that never had U.S. conventional forces been stronger, with abundant reserves available to meet any emergency. He conceded only that "appearance of a 'strain'" in the armed forces resulted from the decision to meet Vietnam requirements without resort to emergency measures such as calling up reserves or involuntarily extending tours of duty. Actually OSD had reduced the Army's planned ammunition production by $156 million (from $589 million to $433 million) and $161 million (from $569 million to $408 million) in FYs 1964 and 1965 respectively, in part because projected combat consumption rates were considered inflated.[11]

Behind his reasonable demeanor, McNamara was seething. "Utterly enraged" by Baldwin's allegations—"practically crawling up the curtains" wrote Marine Corps Commandant General Greene—McNamara lambasted "irresponsible gripers." He lamented that disunity was the "biggest danger facing the country at the present time." McNamara instructed the service secretaries and military chiefs to work through the weekend on point-by-point rebuttals of Baldwin's allegations for his use at a press conference. He also made the service secretaries individually initial each page of the rebuttal with the admonition that he would hold them responsible for any disparities or inaccuracies.[12]

At the hastily arranged 2 March press conference, McNamara insisted that recent newspaper allegations of U.S. military overextension were not true. Reiterating his recent congressional testimony, McNamara maintained that the administration's success in strengthening the conventional forces over the past five years had enabled the military to fight the war in Vietnam without resort to mobilization or controls on the civilian economy. Of course spot shortages existed, as expected in an army operating across the globe, but he depicted them as stemming from distribution problems, not lack of production. Expansion of the active forces, strengthening of the reserve components, and the vast increase in production and logistics capability meant that "far from overextending ourselves we have actually strengthened our military position."[13]

During the ensuing contentious question-and-answer period, one reporter asked whether the Vietnam buildup was accomplished by stripping units in Europe and the United States of manpower and equipment. McNamara avoided a direct answer by rattling off an array of figures on forces deployed, units available, ammunition consumed, and so forth. When the correspondent rejoined that the numbers did not "get to the point at all," McNamara angrily insisted that U.S. forces were combat ready. "These figures demonstrate it. Next question."[14] The numbers, though, did not add up.

Even as McNamara heatedly denied in public that U.S. ground forces appeared overstretched in support of the Vietnam buildup, the Army in private agreed that Baldwin's assertion that virtually all the combat ready units in the United States had been committed to Vietnam was "substantially true." The Marine Corps faced similar readiness issues. The 2nd Marine Division, for example, although listed as combat ready could not deploy 30 percent of its officers and men because of administrative restrictions* on Vietnam service. The Marine Corps also had shortages of certain critical military skills that it expected to remedy by September 1966.[15] Conditions at Army and Marine training centers substantiated Baldwin's contention that several months would pass before any new units became available for combat.

. In early March 1966, this time before the Senate Foreign Relations Committee, McNamara again denied that a lack of equipment hampered U.S. troops in Vietnam. Around the same time, he angrily berated a West German reporter for suggesting that U.S. strategic mobility had suffered, proclaiming that he was "sick and tired" of implications that the administration had drawn down U.S. forces in

---

* Sole surviving son, expiration of enlistment, 17 years old, returned from overseas less than 6 months.

Europe to meet Vietnam requirements. Just six weeks later in a background briefing, McNamara announced the temporary withdrawal of 15,000 U.S. Army specialists from Germany by the end of June.[16] Such flip-flops steadily eroded OSD's credibility with the press, Congress, and ultimately the American public. By early April, McNamara found himself constantly on the defensive as more allegations of DoD mismanagement and shortages among field units surfaced.

On 12 April 1966, DoD acknowledged curtailment of U.S. air strikes in Southeast Asia as a result of civil turmoil in South Vietnam. Assistant Secretary of Defense for Public Affairs Arthur Sylvester further described a "temporary problem in the distribution of bombs" because Vietnamese dockworkers at Da Nang were staying away from their jobs. The press then quoted "other reliable Pentagon sources" who claimed that local and worldwide bomb shortages, particularly of the 750-pound bomb, also hampered the air campaign. According to these same sources, OSD was repurchasing 750-pound bombs from West Germany and other allies. Two days later Rep. Gerald Ford (R-Mich.) accused the administration of "shocking mismanagement" in its handling of the Vietnam War; he blamed McNamara's policies for scarcities of bombs "despite all the billions we have voted for defense."[17]

McNamara's tendency to obfuscate, to volley statistics in lieu of direct answers, came on full display during a hurried press conference called the same day to refute Ford's remarks. The defense secretary denied any bomb shortage. DoD had repurchased 750-pound bombs from the West Germans, but the amounts represented a tiny fraction of the total 600,000 tons of bombs to be dropped on Vietnam in 1966. Repurchasing bombs from the Germans hardly indicated a shortage because drawing on abundant inventories would carry DoD through until July 1966 when production of 750-pound bombs caught up with consumption.[18]

McNamara damaged his cause during his 20 April and 11 May testimony before the Senate Foreign Relations Committee. First he explained to the senators that production lines for 750-pound bombs had been shut down between 1955 and 1965, so the Air Force bought back 5,500 bombs that it previously had disposed of as surplus to the Germans. It turned out that OSD paid $21.00 per bomb to buy back the surplus sold in 1964 for $1.70 each to a German firm for use as scrap and fertilizer. Still McNamara later stubbornly defended the decision. "In retrospect, it was wise to sell them and wise to buy them back," because the cost of producing a new weapon was $300 to $400. An incredulous Sen. Karl E. Mundt (R-S.Dak.) responded: "You are not trying to tell us that is a good bargain. . . . It had a very bad psychological effect." It created the impression that the United States was "getting desperately short of the right kind of bomb."[19] More awkward disclosures followed.

A copy of a letter written on 31 March by McNaughton to Rep. Durward G. Hall (R-Mo.), made available after McNamara testified on 20 April, stated that the Pentagon was considering buying back bombs, ammunition, and other equipment—"reacquisition" according to McNaughton—on the principle that recovery would amount to no more than the original cost. In an effort to forestall further criticism, on 21 April assistant secretary Sylvester announced DoD's decision against reacquiring previously sold surplus ordnance because the bombs were no longer needed. The entire contretemps left the defense secretary appearing foolish for telling anyone still willing to listen that shortages did not exist. Two days later a *New York Times* editorial remarked, "McNamara does himself no credit by trying to deny the obvious."[20] Was there a bomb shortage or was it simply a distribution problem exaggerated far out of proportion by administration opponents?

According to a 1970 study conducted by the Joint Logistics Review Board, a "critical shortage of air munitions in early 1966" halted the rise in use of bombs for the first four months of 1966. Contracts let in July 1965 called for an initial delivery of 750-pound bombs in June 1966, but the production rate reached the forecast expenditure rate only in February 1967—nineteen months from the initiation of the contract. During the interval, the services hoarded 750-pound bombs for use against targets in North Vietnam because those weapons offered the best combination of maximum destruction and minimum disruption of the strike aircraft.[21]

Air Force spokesmen insisted during the buildup that by careful allocation and some substitution of 500-pound bombs for 750-pounders they had prevented cancellation of any airstrikes in Vietnam. When McNamara questioned an "underexpenditure" of bombs versus projections during June 1966, he learned that while the gross tonnage of bombs available in Southeast Asia sufficed, there were imbalances between the most used ordnance (750-pounders) and the least used that limited overall consumption.[22]

In the midst of McNamara's clashes with the media over scarcities, Congressman Hardy's investigating subcommittee issued a classified report identifying shortages in 20-mm. ammunition, 2.75-inch rockets, flares, and missiles, as well as 500- and 750-pound bombs that directly hampered combat capabilities in Vietnam. Committee members zeroed in on the worldwide lack of spare parts, blaming shortages on McNamara's "apparent overzealous dedication to economy" at the expense of combat troops. After all, the secretary had boasted that his cost-effectiveness programs had achieved major savings by purchasing fewer spare parts. This false economy, according to the committee, created "the single most crippling shortage" the U.S. armed forces faced—a lack of spare parts. Rivers forwarded Hardy's report to McNamara with the injunction not to treat the findings lightly or brush them aside with a simple response that no shortages existed.[23]

McNamara replied about three weeks later with his now standard arguments. He cited the inevitable effect on strategy of delay in providing necessary support to field units—a delay attributable to "budget cycles and the lead time required for procurement, production, . . . and distribution." Overall, conventional ammunition inventories for the Army and Marine Corps were excellent, those for the Navy and Air Force adequate; shortages were primarily local rather than worldwide. McNamara just as adamantly maintained that the Cost Reduction Program had no relationship to the alleged supply deficiencies. Indeed, he maintained, his buildup of inventories during peacetime had allowed the services to live temporarily off their war reserve stocks until they received deliveries from new production.[24] As the war went on, McNamara had to deal with continuing criticism of his handling of logistical support for Vietnam and its limiting effect on strategic decisions.

Strategic Forces

Further contributing to McNamara's financial and logistical problems was the need to balance costs between U.S. strategic and conventional forces while trying to restrain an already swollen Defense budget. The huge cost of major weapon systems, particularly strategic weapons not required for Vietnam use, offered large potential savings if reduced in numbers. By way of justification, in several instances McNamara successfully cited emerging technology as a reason to reduce or forestall major weapon projects. One such advance, MIRV technology, allowed McNamara to argue that its qualitative improvements made it possible to strike more targets in the Soviet Union and to overcome any Soviet ABM defenses without adding missile launchers. The additional warheads on each strategic missile, in fact, justified cuts in planned Minuteman deployment from 1,200 to 1,000 launchers.[25] Thus, MIRV technological innovation enabled the defense secretary to hold down overall costs of strategic weapons procurement without political damage. The opposite happened with the ABM system.

McNamara vigorously opposed constructing an ABM system, believing it incorporated the worst features of a new weapon—it was unworkable, expensive, and destabilizing. He repeatedly contended that state-of-the-art technology was not sufficiently advanced to design a foolproof missile defense. His embrace of assured destruction strategy caused him to see the ABM as a wrong solution. For political reasons—he was unwilling to force a showdown with the Joint Chiefs and their powerful supporters in Congress—McNamara never killed the ABM program, instead keeping it on life support by small annual appropriations for advanced research. Ironically, breakthrough technology that seemed to make the system feasible and affordable belied McNamara's reasons for opposing it. As domestic political considerations and Soviet hesitation to enter meaningful arms control talks further overrode the defense secretary's opposition, Johnson announced his decision to build an ABM system.[*]

Another instance where political maneuvering, though of a different sort, proved decisive came in OSD's decision on nuclear aircraft carriers. During the early 1960s, McNamara had consistently opposed as too costly construction of larger nuclear-powered aircraft carriers using four reactors and carrying more expensive planes. Instead he favored utilizing improved technology in the form of a more compact and efficient two-reactor propulsion system that lowered over-

---

[*] For the ABM see Chapter XIII.

all costs. This breakthrough justified McNamara's September 1965 proposal for a nuclear carrier in the FY 1967 budget, but he soon deferred its construction in response to a White House effort to hold down overall defense spending in order to meet the spiraling financial demands of the Vietnam War. His attitude toward carriers was consistent with his strategic preference for missiles—land- and sea-based—over bombers and carriers. Nevertheless, primarily to appease the Joint Chiefs the defense secretary eventually approved the nuclear carrier construction in January 1966; he told Congress that technological improvements warranted a two-reactor nuclear carrier in the FY 1967 budget. Two additional nuclear carriers were slated for construction beginning in FY 1969 and FY 1971 respectively.[*26]

McNamara reduced overall carrier costs still further by thinning out naval carrier air wings, which accounted for roughly half the total cost of a carrier task group. Rather than equipping each carrier with its full complement of aircraft, three Carrier Reserve Air Wings (land-based naval aircraft capable of rapid augmentation of carrier-based warplanes) would reinforce the carrier-based air wings during emergencies.[27] OSD expected that this decision, plus planned modernization of two attack carriers, would produce a 15-carrier force structure (4 nuclear-powered) at a reasonable price by 1973.

Modernization proved more difficult and costly than anticipated. The USS *Midway's* overhaul, originally projected to take 24 months and cost $88 million, ended up taking twice as long and costing twice as much, resulting in a January 1969 decision to cancel further modernization. Meantime, the price tag for the nuclear carrier USS *Nimitz* rose from the initially approved $427.5 million in September 1965 to $544.2 million in March 1969. In December 1967 McNamara had endorsed Navy recommendations for another $116.7 million, most of which ($103.4 million) went to pay for increased shipyard expenses, that is, basic construction plus nuclear fuel and machinery costs. Besides the *Nimitz*, significant delays hindered construction of other ships as the Navy's shipbuilding program encountered major cost overruns.[28]

Changes in priorities also affected many other types of Navy vessels. Priority accorded to the reactivation of more than 520 ships, boats, and small craft for Southeast Asia service, begun during FY 1965, also delayed or lengthened previously programmed new construction and conversion of vessels. DoD cancelled conversion of seven destroyers and one guided missile cruiser and extended the conversion of eight other destroyers. It sought further economies by pushing fleet modernization into the future. The near doubling of reports of breakdowns, from 5,250 in 1965 to 10,320 in 1968, gave clear indication of general decline in the condition of Navy ships.[29] The Navy's experience provided further evidence of the troubles involved in the procurement and operation of complicated, technologically sophisticated weapon systems.

---

[*] See Chapter VI.

Procurement Contracting Impact

Procurement costs represented a huge part of DoD's expenditures. The details of procurement contracts, their priorities, and their administration by DoD greatly affected the availability of weapon systems and other materiel for combat use. Because he felt that Cost-Plus-Fixed-Fee (CPFF) contracts gave contractors little incentive to hold down project costs, McNamara introduced major changes in procurement contracting. A CPFF contract set a target cost that included the contractor's fee, but the cost was not binding because the government agreed to reimburse the contractor for all costs incurred in fulfilling the contract.[30] In effect, the government committed itself to underwrite the risks involved in the uncertainties of developing new weapons by guaranteeing contractors a profit no matter how much the project cost.

McNamara determined to shift the risk and reward to the contractor through the use of the Fixed-Price-Incentive-Fee contract (FPIF). Once negotiated, the price of a weapon system remained fixed at an upper limit set by the government, usually 30 percent above the target cost. This system in theory made costs and profits inversely related because by spending more the contractor reduced the potential amount of profit built into the contract. The converse held true, so the contractor had an incentive, written into every contract, to keep costs low. According to McNamara, converting CPFF arrangements to fixed-price or incentive contracts resulted in estimated savings of 10 to 15 percent; no one could demonstrate this contention with quantitative data. Furthermore incentive contracts usually involved fulfilling multiple targets established by DoD and the contractors, placing a premium on system performance over delivery time and cost.[31]

Statistical analysis of 427 Air Force contracts in a Rand study of September 1966 challenged OSD's conventional wisdom that incentive contracts provided substantial motivation for increased contractor efficiency and tighter control resulting in major cost reductions. Instead, the cost underruns associated with incentive contracts might have resulted, according to the sampling, because contractors initially overstated prices and later inflated costs of supplemental changes. This was possible because technical competence, design, and sole source solicitations were the primary criteria in selecting a contractor. Since DoD awarded few contracts on the basis of price alone competition did not necessarily hold down costs. A later study concluded that more performance incentive fees were earned than were lost. Incentives were earned regardless of cost outcomes (that is, of 34 contracts analyzed, 26 received performance incentives—9 involved cost underruns, 10 overruns, and 7 came in on target).[32]

Still another flaw was the revision of the original contract by writing engineering change proposals. Working with known technology and specifications, engineering changes would be few, for such alterations might be anticipated and included in the initial statement of work. But enormously complex weapon designs, such as the TFX, ABM, and the Vietnam barrier, that demanded not only the application of new technology but often the creation of new technology, opened the way for many engineering change proposals. Moreover, the myriad changes derived from new information or operational experience added more to the enormous difficulty of identifying all the desirable variables and outcomes in advance.[33]

Because contracts were not "definitized" until a contractor had completed a major portion of the work, there often were thousands of changes to incentive contracts that dramatically drove up costs. For example, during the RDT&E phase of its F-111 contract General Dynamics incurred significant cost overruns resulting in a ten percent or $9.6 million penalty. Yet higher development costs led to renegotiated contracts whose higher profits, an estimated $557 million versus an original $326 million, more than offset any penalties. Thus "contract incentives . . . [had] little meaning," DoD's Comptroller told McNamara, because the contractor knew he could recover overruns through change orders. Only a portion of the work, moreover, was put in the original contract. Of the proposed $3.9 billion to build the F-111, for instance, only $480 million found its way into the initial contract for airframe development. Project changes increased costs to $8.8 billion negotiated in a sole source context.[34]

McNamara also expected that multi-year procurement and total package contracting—a single contract for development, production, and system support—would enable bidders to offer the government lower prices for bulk quantities; longer production runs usually lowered unit costs. Few firms, however, had the skilled personnel, physical plant, technology, or expertise to undertake the whole research, development, and production cycle involved in fielding major weapon systems. In 1968, DOD awarded almost 46 percent of $38.8 billion in contract awards to 25 corporations; General Dynamics, prime contractor for the F-111, accounted for 5.8 percent of the total. Furthermore, lowest competitive bids from qualified firms, that is, companies inspected and evaluated by DOD as capable of performing the contract, automatically received contract awards.[35]

The C-5A transport aircraft procurement process suffered from several of these often knotty problems. The contract, a Fixed-Price-Incentive-Fee type for the entire package from drawing board to runway, entailed total costs that rose from the October 1965 estimate of $3.087 billion to $4.348 billion by 31 March 1969. After tabulating overruns for inflation at $500 million projected through 1973 and the contractor's original underestimate of $379 million, disputed by Lockheed the prime contractor, DoD found that there still remained technical overruns (engineering changes) amounting to $382 million. To force the contractor in such multibillion dollar programs to absorb the overruns might well put the specialized and arguably essential corporation out of business and leave the government with nothing to show for all the money spent.[36]

With a theoretically more efficient contracting process in place, McNamara also expected to realize economies of scale during production through commonality—the use of common, interchangeable weapons and parts by two or more services. The TFX (Tactical Fighter Experimental), redesignated the F-111 in 1963, was the jewel in his cost-effectiveness crown. Its joint development for both Navy and Air Force use, he claimed, would save $1 billion by developing one common, not two separate, aircraft.[37] Those words came back to haunt him.

Told by experts that no engineer understood enough about certain technological aspects of the project even to write its specifications, McNamara insisted that no contractor should sign a contract until he knew that the risks were manageable; moreover, profits should be related to risks. Yet how exactly did one estimate how much it would cost to build a variable geometry wing for an aircraft from scratch? How did one prepare specifications for avionics equipment using technology that did not exist in 1961? While a contractor could control efficiency, it was exactly such uncertainties that reduced his possibilities of controlling costs. Since before World War II the military had consistently underestimated the costs of weapons, largely because of the changes to the overall price caused by the unpredictability of fast changing, cutting edge technology.[38] McNamara and his staff fared no better. Perhaps the TFX provided the best known example of this shortsightedness.[*]

Problems plagued TFX development from the start for a host of reasons: the aircraft's demanding specifications; its revolutionary design; the U.S. Navy's antipathy to the plane; political pressure; and major differences in weight, mission, range, and armament desired by the Air Force and the Navy. Permitting many changes to the respective service versions of the aircraft would of course undermine cost savings achieved by the commonality aspects of a joint fighter. Nevertheless, it became apparent that many airframe, structural, and equipment items had to be peculiar to the specific service model. By December 1966 the overall amount of commonality slipped, most glaringly in the avionics systems. By that time, McNamara had already declared the aircraft as developed to date to be "unsatisfactory"— with a "disgraceful cost position," total expenses having almost doubled despite reducing overall procurement. Flight tests revealed further problems, especially with the plane's engines and, in the Navy version, with cockpit visibility. Commonality in airframe and structure in the Navy version, nearly 98 percent in June 1967, dropped to 74 percent that December and to 67 percent by March 1968.[39] All the while costs mounted.

The plan eventually adopted for the F-111A called for delivery of 739 tactical fighter aircraft at a cost of $3.96 billion, later revised to $5.097 billion for 591 units that were heavier, with shorter range, and a lower combat ceiling than original specifications. Changes between February 1966 and March 1969 totaled $149.3 million for RDT&E. For production changes to design and capability, mainly avionics and engine modifications, the added cost was $494.2 million. Within five months of McNamara's departure, the Navy cancelled its version (the F-111B) after having built only five test and two operational aircraft. Production

---

[*] For TFX development, see Kaplan et al, *The McNamara Ascendancy*.

of the USAF strategic bomber version (FB-111) eventually fell from 263 to 76 aircraft. The March 1970 estimate of the total expenditures at the completion of the F-111 program came to $8.5 billion against the original estimate of $5.5 billion, or a cost overrun of $3 billion for far fewer aircraft having much less commonality, a far cry from the $1 billion in savings that McNamara had promised the taxpayer.[40] The failure of the F-111 to meet either financial goals or performance expectations was a prime instance of McNamara's stubborn insistence on discounting evidence that contradicted his approach to an issue or his conclusions.

Besides the financial investment in the F-111 models, controversy surrounded the F-111A's initial combat operations. By June 1967 McNamara concurred with Air Force requests to accelerate preparations of the plane for possible deployment to Southeast Asia. Aware that the Air Force wanted the aircraft to meet the need for accurate night, all-weather bombing of North Vietnam and might sacrifice quality to get early acceptance for the deployment, Air Force Secretary Brown closely monitored the testing process, including refinements to avionics and the delivery schedules for aircraft and engines.

The first 11 production fighters underwent tests appropriate to their planned combat missions, but not total structural testing. Brown, worried that testing standards and requirements might be set too low, along with DDR&E Foster insisted that sufficient time be allowed for tactical testing. The need for further modifications led to a decision around 20 December 1967 to postpone deployment from mid-January 1968 to mid-March or later. By the time the first F-111As arrived in Thailand on 25 March, McNamara had left office. On 28 March, only three days after their entry into combat operations, an F-111A crashed. Two days later another crashed, and within a month a third. The aircraft's initially poor showing in combat along with six accidents during testing caused the Air Force to quickly withdraw it from combat.* Critics like Senator McClellan believed that the planes were rushed into combat primarily "to get some publicity."[41]

The U.S. Army also experienced an instance of McNamara's attempt to achieve commonality and cost-efficiency, this time with the West German allies. In August 1963 the United States and the Federal Republic of Germany signed an agreement to develop a new weapon system—the Main Battle Tank (MBT)—that would incorporate significant improvements in mobility, firepower, and endurance, an admittedly vague series of specifications. "It was easy enough to make the tank's *requirement* all things to all people, but quite another thing to develop an *actual* tank for all interested parties."[42] Technology and differing performance requirements by the two armies soon defeated commonality and efficiency by creating duplication and increased costs.

---

* Only after extensive modifications were the F-111As returned to Southeast Asia in 1972.

Respective armor doctrine further complicated overall design. The U.S. Army expected its new Shillelagh missile to extend the range of tank engagements to 2,000–3,000 meters. Mobility at such long ranges was less important than heavier armor; additional tank weight required a larger and heavier engine. The Germans, in contrast, preferred using a main gun for close-in engagements, 1,000 meters or less, that placed a premium on mobility for survival. They also wanted a lighter tank capable of crossing the 50-ton limit bridges found on most of West Germany's secondary roads.[43]

Diverging requirements drove up development costs and extended the anticipated cost and date of the first production model from an initial $80–$100 million in August 1963 to $200 million by December 1966, leading Systems Analysis in July 1967 to recommend cancellation because the program "has clearly gotten out of hand." Faced with rising costs, in September 1967 the German government proposed eliminating the MBT-70 program, but McNamara wanted to complete the development and testing phase to prove that a combined development program could work. Whether or not the Germans actually built any tanks, he told his counterpart, was their decision.[44]

In March 1968 the two countries agreed to continue development of a single tank with a maximum weight of 48.5 metric tons that met previous specifications of "firepower, mobility, and protection." The target date for series production was January 1973; to reach that goal the partners increased funding for the project from $138 million to $303 million, the United States bearing $173 million of the new cost.[45]

By mid-1968 research and development had produced the prototypes, but series production costs reached nearly double the existing M-60 tank cost of $300,000 to $330,000 per vehicle; meanwhile Washington and Bonn were still bickering about the weight of the new tank. The pilot model weighed 50.6 metric tons, but the Germans insisted it not exceed 48.5 metric tons because it would otherwise be too heavy for German bridges. Major technological components, such as the German-developed automatic ammunition loading system, likewise encountered problems that drove up costs. DDR&E and Systems Analysis questioned continuing the program; Bureau of the Budget analysts wanted to cancel it, but the U.S. Army thought the problems of weight and cost capable of solution. Increasing congressional criticism of the program and a new administration led to the formal cancellation of the MBT-70 joint program in FY 1972, by which time the United States had spent slightly more than $300 million on the failure.[46]

By contrast with the F-111 and MBT, the development and fielding of the Polaris and Poseidon nuclear-equipped ballistic missile submarine (SSBN) fleets, both generally regarded as well managed and cost-effective, if expensive, programs, highlighted the effectiveness of decentralized management and firm fixed-price contracts. The SSBN program benefited from high priority, special management attention, and liberal funding. Conversely, the nuclear attack submarine (SSN) program suffered as the Navy diverted equipment, manpower, and management to the SSBN effort.[47]

By the time McNamara reached office the Polaris program, which had begun in 1956, required 41 submarines, each carrying 16 missiles, to destroy 656 targets in the Soviet Union; four spare submarines provided backup. Influenced by a Navy analysis that 656 Polaris missiles could destroy all Soviet targets, the McNamara standard for assured destruction, the number of submarines and missiles had such strong political support that the only way left for McNamara to save money was to eliminate the four extra submarines. Strangely there appears to have been little or no consideration given to the large Air Force nuclear weapon capacity that had theretofore constituted the U.S. strategic assault force.[48]

The rush to deploy early versions of strategic offensive missiles—such as Minuteman and Polaris—also forced the competing managers of these major programs, under accelerated production schedules, to accept significant design compromises in range, payload, and accuracy for the sake of operational deployment. Work on Polaris had begun with letter contracts, not the specific statements of work and detailed cost estimates that McNamara later introduced in the incentive type contract.[49] Subsequent changes meant increased costs, and OSD accepted legitimate overruns in the interests of national security.

Even for the improved Poseidon, developed during McNamara's tenure, incentive contracts came into play only in the production phase, after the prototypes had been produced and priced according to Cost-Plus-Fixed-Fee arrangements. RDT&E costs for Poseidon rose appreciably from the original October 1966 estimate of $1.38 billion to $1.81 billion in March 1969. Production costs increased from $1.75 billion to $2.29 billion for the same period. Total program costs, including submarine conversions to carry the new missile, grew from $5.15 billion to $6.99 billion because of requirements for greater accuracy, a new, improved guidance system, a re-entry warhead, penetration aids, and the propulsion system. Moreover, OSD did not require the Naval Special Projects Office, which ran the fleet ballistic missile program, to reopen the entire Poseidon development to competition. Only one contract was awarded on the basis of competition; all the others were sole-source awards. This suggests that different types of contracts were appropriate to different types of weapon development and circumstances. Poseidon's enhanced technology validated McNamara's original judgment that it would be worth the extra expense because it was so much more effective per dollar than Polaris.[50]

The land-based Minuteman II underwent a similar pattern of rushed development and fielding and increased costs. In mid-1967 mechanical problems with the Minuteman II's computerized guidance and control components reportedly put 40 percent of the 250 strategic weapons out of commission. Air Force Secretary Harold Brown, who had a month earlier asked McNamara for an additional $18 million to remedy Minuteman II program shortcomings, admitted that the sensitive components did require more maintenance than earlier predicted, but he insisted reliability would improve "as the system matures." Modifying and buying spare guidance kits for Minuteman II to correct its failure rate cost $100 million while another $73 million went to improve the guidance system's survivability with improved shielding and hardening of its electronic parts. Critics complained that the Air Force had known for years about the flaws in the missile's guidance system and general mismanagement of the project yet kept quiet and poured more money into the sole source supplier.[51] Technology's rapid growth in the world of semi-conductors and computers during the 1960s made such problems inherent in any large-scale project that incorporated the latest innovations. No doubt mismanagement and inflated profits occurred, but these were likely not as systemic as McNamara's harshest critics claimed.

McNamara left a mixed contracting and procurement legacy. Melvin Laird, McNamara's longtime congressional opponent and Richard Nixon's defense secretary, testified that many of the serious problems encountered in the deployment of major weapon systems (delays, cost overruns and failure to meet performance specifications) could probably have been avoided if more time had been taken to complete development, test, and evaluation of the critical subsystems and components. "The tendency to rush into large scale production before development has been completed," Laird said, "may well cost more time and money over the long run than a more systematic and orderly approach."[52] Strategic imperatives forced McNamara to rush some weapons, such as Minuteman and Polaris, into production. For other weapon systems, such as the F-111, he had to accept responsibility for persisting in producing a faulty weapon.

In sum, McNamara's procurement contracting and contract management were less effective in practice than in theory. It was not possible to foresee all of the contingencies that inevitably arose in huge and complex weapon programs during a period of rapid technological change and unstable domestic (especially economic) and international conditions. It was beyond the capacity of the secretary of defense.

Cost Reduction

Efforts to reduce costs, ranging across the whole spectrum of DoD functions, constituted a significant element in the constant struggle for cost-effectiveness. McNamara's mantra during his years as secretary of defense, cost reduction, meant: (1) buying only what was needed; (2) buying at the lowest sound price; and (3) reducing operating costs through integration and standardization.[53] The program did achieve financial efficiencies, save the government money, and impose improved management techniques on DoD. As often in support of his own initiatives, however, it appears that McNamara uncritically accepted every reported cost reduction when compiling his annual posture statement.

In July 1966, for instance, McNamara informed the president that the DoD Cost Reduction Program had realized cumulative savings of more than $14 billion since January 1961. The defense secretary implied that economy and efficiency stimulated by the program made possible the Vietnam buildup without resort to economic controls or reserve mobilization. Base closures, reduced workforces, elimination of a number of different items in DoD inventories, competitive contracts, redesign of equipment to avoid "goldplating" (extraneous and unnecessary components), and reduced operating costs had saved taxpayers billions of dollars. Innovative contracting procedures for development, production, and system support enabled bidders to offer the government cheaper prices for bulk quantities and lower individual unit costs through longer production runs.[54] How much of this cost-effectiveness, McNamara's congressional opponents wondered, reflected reality and how much bookkeeping smoke and mirrors?

A bit of both, concluded the Subcommittee for Special Investigations of the House Committee on Armed Services. For example, during FYs 1964 and 1965, DoD claimed savings of $2.8 and $4.8 billion respectively under the Cost Reduction Program. A selective and random examination of these claims by Government Accounting Office (GAO) employees on loan to the subcommittee resulted in 43 case studies of 53 savings actions involving approximately $1.25 billion. In 19 of these cases, savings of $132 million did result; in 6 cases involving $109 million, no savings were apparent; as for the remaining 18 involving slightly over $1 billion, $297 million qualified, while $339 million, as well as "some undeterminable part of the balance of $415.4 million," did not.[55]

The subcommittee's report, dated 12 September 1966, criticized DoD's "inadequate criteria and befogging policy guidance" which made it impossible to measure actual savings. Among other procedures, DoD criteria mandated that savings reported for one year be reported for each succeeding year so long as the practice remained in effect. As a hypothetical example, substituting a plastic grommet for a metal one might have saved $50,000 during FY 1965. For each year thereafter that the plastic grommet remained in use, DoD could report a saving of $50,000. In an actual instance, DoD claimed that by modernizing its M-48 model tanks instead of buying newer M-60 models the Marine Corps saved almost $150 million. Although the Marine Corps never intended to buy the new tanks, the action nevertheless still qualified as a reportable savings.[56]

DoD also took credit for savings realized by defense contractors who adjusted pricing as they reevaluated projects. In other instances where evolving technology had rendered an existing developmental project obsolete, cancellations were claimed as savings. Some transactions seemed to involve paper transfers. The Air Force cancelled procurement of Bullpup A missiles and claimed a savings of $50 million although half of the "savings" went for the newer Bullpup B missile. Likewise McNamara's decision in FY 1965 to purchase fewer F-4s for the Navy resulted in claimed savings of $32.5 million, but attrition in Vietnam and revised tactical air considerations forced DoD to spend more than the "savings" to buy additional F-4s to replace losses. Finally, under DoD criteria once an item was removed from inventory, a savings of $100 per item could be claimed each year thereafter. In FY 1966, this practice of built-in, accumulated savings amounted to $83.5 million.[57]

OSD was "pleased to know that the Subcommittee found that its cost reduction program" had saved significant money, but it rejected contentions that it had degraded combat potential or fallen considerably short of the results claimed. Beginning with FY 1967, however, McNamara limited reported savings from a particular action to the year in which the savings occurred and the next two years, even though the recurring effects of the action might continue for another 5 or 10 years. Furthermore, during FY 1967 and thereafter DoD would take no credit for savings accrued before 1 July 1966.[58]

The Cost Reduction Program featured prominently in McNamara's first Five-Year Defense Program launched in 1961. In January 1967, he announced to Congress that the program had met its goals and that he intended to broaden the effort by establishing annual targets for savings in each future year. Acknowledging that the more than $14 billion in claimed savings during the initial five-year plan could not likely be duplicated over the succeeding five years, the defense secretary still expected DOD to realize significant savings, especially in costs attributable to the rapid military buildup for Vietnam.[59]

McNamara's successor, Clark Clifford, endorsed the Cost Reduction Program and encouraged DoD senior officials to emphasize cost reduction as they had in the past. Although Clifford adopted a more bureaucratically benign title of "Logistics Management Improvement," the program's goals remained the same. In early October 1968, Clifford reported new savings during FY 1968 of $1.2 billion plus economies in excess of $500 million in Vietnam under a program sponsored by MACV known as "MACONOMY." Still for every legitimate savings McNamara or Clifford would name, critics would counter with "horror" stories of the Defense Supply Agency buying a "handle, spare, synchronizing" for $312.50 when the same item, a knob for a gas range, was available commercially for $1.62. Apprised that a 50 cent rod became "precision shafting" costing DoD $25.55, Representative Pike caustically remarked, "For once the American taxpayer got precisely what he paid for."[60] Whether the view was as critical as Pike's or as uncritical as McNamara's, the cost-effectiveness programs saved money and generally prevented egregious waste, but to quantify the amount of savings with any certainty did not seem possible.

The Global Drawdown

Of direct strategic consequence was the need for DoD to maintain an adequate, yet cost-effective, strategic reserve, particularly to fulfill NATO treaty commitments, while fighting the war in Southeast Asia. To offset the spiraling costs of the expanding Southeast Asian war, OSD determined to hold down costs associated with conventional units not committed to Vietnam. Johnson's decision in July 1965 not to mobilize Guard and Reserve forces for the Vietnam buildup left the active Army ground forces—16 divisions and 7 separate brigades—to bear the burden of training for, deploying to, and fighting a war, all the while maintaining worldwide U.S. treaty and alliance commitments. To sustain the efficiency of the Strategic Army Forces (STRAF) in the United States during the buildup for Vietnam, in October McNamara recommended increasing the force structure by one active division and three separate brigades, plus augmenting the six reserve divisions in the priority Army reserve with two National Guard divisions brought to a higher level of readiness.[61] The difficulties involved in force adjustments of such a magnitude were further complicated by the STRAF's dependence on reserve units for its combat service support.

Without mobilized reservists, the Army had to levy on active units to support Vietnam operations; to hold down expenditures, OSD drew freely on non-SEA committed active forces for personnel and materiel for the Vietnam fighting. This served to reduce the non-Vietnam committed Army forces to 90 percent or less of authorized manning. By the fall of 1965 the Army reported its six U.S.-based divisions could implement some, but not all, of their contingency plans. The 1st Armored Division, for instance, had an authorization of 14,821 troops, but as of 30 September 1965 had only 8,915 assigned. Three other divisions were in similar straits. Still McNamara insisted during a testy exchange with Sen. Strom Thurmond (R-S.C.) on 28 February 1966 that the units were not understrength "in relation to our military program today" which had put large numbers of troops into Vietnam, had the capability to put even greater forces there by the end of 1966, and had the ability to field nine divisions within 90 days to meet contingencies, provided reserves were called.[62] Indeed by February 1966, increased draft calls and enlistments had refilled the ranks of the active divisions, though with green recruits, not well trained soldiers. Meantime the influx of recruits for the expanded Army Reserve and National Guard created unprecedented personnel disruptions in those formations.

Besides the manpower turmoil, the Army Reserve reported shortages of light helicopters, self-propelled 155-mm. howitzers, truck tractors, and recoilless rifles into mid-1968 despite an infusion of money for modern equipment. By the fall of 1966, significant withdrawals of equipment from reserve formations to support new units in the active forces had so hampered reserve training that the JCS felt mobilization would only marginally accelerate Army deployments to Southeast Asia. Although McNamara's Selected Reserve Force (SRF) units had received priority in personnel and equipment in the Army Reserve, they too suffered from shortages of modern equipment, forcing them to rely on worn or obsolete items which in turn demanded increased maintenance to keep them functional. Furthermore, domestic unrest required that specified units involving more than 200,000 reservists shift their training regimens to focus on civil disturbance operations. Overall, the Reserve decreased training exercises during FY 1968 and limited field training to battalion echelon. As a consequence, during 1968 reserve divisions needed between 21 and 35 weeks to achieve suitable readiness levels, a far cry from their M+30 day commitment to reinforce NATO. Early in 1969 Nitze acknowledged that through 1970 reserve divisions probably would need 14 weeks to deploy under existing reserve readiness standards; he felt uncertain that DoD could improve on that schedule.[63]

The role of the reserves became interwoven with mobilization issues in force structure decisions made between 1965 and 1969. In early November 1965 the JCS proposed measures to restore the strategic military posture because the demands of Phase I deployments to Vietnam had rendered Army divisions in the United States unready for combat until sometime between March 1966 and March 1967. The Navy and Marines suffered from an inadequate training and rotation base, and the Air Force had only three to five tactical fighter squadrons and two tactical reconnaissance squadrons deployable from CONUS. The larger Phase II deployments to Vietnam then under consideration, if ordered, would leave strategic forces at home unable to execute the current strategic concept unless they were reconstituted by a combination of more active duty units and selected reserve mobilization. As defined by the Joint Chiefs, that concept included maintaining the NATO-committed STRAF, countering Chinese Communist intervention in either SEA or Korea, and handling a minor contingency in the Western Hemisphere.[64]

At the time, according to General Greene, McNamara professed indifference to ripping apart the Army, including its European-based units, to fulfill Westmoreland's requirements to the letter. Only a few months later, in early February 1966, he revealed to then Navy Secretary Paul Nitze his feeling that many of the contingency plans of the unified commands no longer reflected logistical reality. Nitze relayed the remark to Chief of Naval Operations Admiral McDonald who admitted he did not know what was being done to align capabilities with current responsibilities. McDonald in turn advised Wheeler that existing plans should get a "new look," whereupon Wheeler directed the Joint Staff to prepare for him position papers assessing the effect of deficiencies in equipment, logistical support, and strategic lift on existing contingency plans for use in his discussions with the Joint Chiefs.[65]

These served as the basis for the Chiefs' response to McNamara on 1 March 1966 explaining the inability of the services to meet Westmoreland's requirements in full and on time without "an extremely harmful effect on EUCOM and LANTCOM capabilities." Not one of the five and one-third Army divisions stationed in the United States was ready for deployment. Two airborne divisions would be available in May and July 1966 respectively, and the remaining three divisions would reach acceptable readiness standards between October 1966 and January 1967. None would have appropriate combat or logistical support for sustained operations. The Air Force would have no readily deployable tactical fighter or reconnaissance squadrons in Strike Command available in the United States. The Navy would need additional carriers, air squadrons, and warships as well as support units to meet its Vietnam requirements. Stretching out the Phase II reinforcements would lessen the risk of further degrading the U.S. worldwide military posture. McNamara decided that all the JCS proposals needed further study, but in the meantime plans for Phase II deployment would be met.[66]

The shortages that the services were experiencing in early 1966 simply did not vanish. Instead their debilitating effect grew cumulatively over time and corroded the ability of U.S. armed forces elsewhere than Vietnam to conduct their assigned missions. In the spring of 1966, the House Special Investigations Subcommittee reported that the U.S. 7th Infantry Division in Korea lacked almost one-third of its basic equipment and was not combat ready. Shortages of trained mechanics and helicopter pilots hindered unit training in Korea and Europe. Drawdowns of experienced enlisted sailors and petty officers degraded fleet readiness; high personnel turnover buffeted the Atlantic Fleet. U.S. Army, Europe (USAREUR)* suffered most from a shortage of captains, majors, and maintenance warrant officers—the skilled and experienced mid-level leaders of any units—as well as a lack of enlisted personnel possessing critical military skill specialties.[67]

Even before the escalation in Vietnam, McNamara had been whittling away at the Army's logistic infrastructure in Europe to reduce balance of payments deficits and, he hoped, spur the allies to do more for their own defense. When he asserted that between June 1964 and December 1965 U.S. Seventh Army actually added 1,000 logistical personnel, he neglected to mention to the press that during the same period two reorganizations of USAREUR's logistical structure decreased supply and support units by 10,900 troops or 19 percent and phased out three of the five U.S. Army depot complexes in Europe. The defense secretary insisted that the decrease was offset by the greater efficiency of reorganized supply and support units; the JCS thought otherwise. The relocation of U.S. forces from France further disrupted logistic capability in Europe and left the Alliance dependent on "malpositioned commercially leased" POL facilities. By late 1968 mergers of units and headquarters, closure of bases and facilities, and reduction of support units, the Chiefs claimed, had steadily eroded USEUCOM's logistic capabilities. As deleterious as cutbacks were, the manner of reducing the force structure to meet Vietnam requirements was more debilitating. According to SACEUR, the "piecemeal and unbalanced reductions" of US forces in Europe had left the military with "little or no control of the tactical disposition of forces or the . . . personnel . . . to perform the assigned military mission."[68]

During the Vietnam buildup, U.S. military units stationed around the world had to redistribute their war reserve stocks to support the forces in Southeast Asia, thereby impairing their own readiness. The Air Force had shipped almost all available 500 pound bombs from units stationed in Europe and Japan to Southeast Asia, leaving Headquarters, USAF Europe, with no 500-pound bombs against a 32,864

---

* USAREUR was the U.S. Army component of the unified U.S. European Command. The Seventh Army was USAREUR's major element.

bomb requirement and Fifth Air Force in Japan and Okinawa with just 1,260 of its required 19,635 bombs. Higher priorities for Vietnam left the Atlantic Fleet chronically short of bombs, aerial missiles, spare parts, and modern aircraft. Aging equipment and deactivations to save money forced the Navy to transfer some 50 ships from the Atlantic to the Pacific Fleet between mid-1965 and mid-1968. In Korea by early 1966 general ammunition levels were nearly exhausted, some units having only enough ammunition for three days of fighting. Simultaneously, U.S. Army units were sending ammunition and helicopters to Southeast Asia. So much 20-mm. ammunition from West Germany and the United States was shipped to Vietnam that war readiness material (WRM) stockages almost became depleted—something potentially embarrassing to DoD because McNamara's Cost Reduction program for FY 1965 had highlighted savings of more than $26 million achieved by using excess 20-mm. ammunition from stocks in lieu of new procurement.[69]

The problems of understrength and underequipped units that surfaced in early 1966 worsened over time. To equip Southeast Asia squadrons in 1966 with the latest F-4D aircraft, units in Japan retained the older model F-4C. Two years later at the time of the *Pueblo* Incident, no Japan-based U.S. Air Force units were rated combat ready because the pilots were undergoing their long-delayed upgrading to F-4Ds and had yet to have their proficiency evaluated. When the USS *Enterprise* entered Korean waters in late January 1968 its aircraft had no Shrike radar-seeking air-ground missiles, no improved Sidewinder air-to-air missiles, and only 55 of the radar-guided, long range Sparrow air-to-air missiles. Its shortages typified those plaguing the Pacific Fleet. Only after the seizure of the *Pueblo* did OSD approve rebuilding a 45-day stockage of air munitions in Northeast Asia to include reconstituted pre-positioned war reserve stocks and naval ordnance, but this buildup encountered delays because of huge demands for ammunition in Vietnam for the Tet and Spring offensives.[70]

The seven U.S. Army divisions stationed overseas, except in Vietnam, were kept deliberately understrength to conserve manpower, materiel, and money for the Vietnam forces. The actual number of division troops averaged 60–70 percent of assigned strength with personnel turnover rates averaging 150–200 percent per year. These huge shortages of trained personnel and the severe "personnel turbulence" due to Southeast Asia rotation requirements contributed greatly to lower overall readiness.[71]

The demands of Vietnam reinforced congressional, budgetary, and strategic pressures to reduce the number of U.S. troops in Western Europe. In October 1968 USAREUR remained long on inexperienced draftees and still short of experienced NCOs, captains, and majors. Obsolete equipment, a lack of sufficient maintenance facilities, and shortages of spare parts further diminished unit readiness. Despite efforts to retain skilled enlisted soldiers, readiness in USAREUR had steadily declined since 1965 because of the demands placed on the command by the war in Southeast Asia.[72]

As for Korea, in mid-December 1966 U.S. Ambassador Winthrop G. Brown commented that the problem ran deeper than personnel shortages because "we did not have people with the right qualifications and experience." This resulted in a lower combat effectiveness than mere numbers would suggest. By mid-summer 1968 both U.S. infantry divisions stationed in Korea were evaluated as "Not Combat Ready," for lack of personnel and spare parts.[73]

Living off inventories and drawing on personnel, equipment, and stocks of units not slated for Vietnam deployment steadily eroded the readiness of the diminished commands. Furthermore, given McNamara's decision to avoid a buildup of large excesses at the end of the Vietnam conflict, OSD either delayed replacement of withdrawn stocks or never filled the shortages, a decision that affected future military readiness. Yet to reconstitute the non-Southeast Asia force would require the administration to mobilize the reserves, activate additional new units, and spend even more dollars on defense. Johnson rejected these options and continued to rely on McNamara to make the Vietnam deployments as painless as possible for the American public. In mid-1968 the Joint Chiefs asserted that requirements for Vietnam had so reduced the combat readiness of the M-Day Strategic Reserve divisions that the United States could not meet its NATO commitments to deploy these forces by M+30.[74] The disruption to the readiness of U.S. military forces worldwide was the price paid for Johnson's political calculations and McNamara's faithful adherence to the president's wishes.

On 8 February 1968, Wheeler reiterated for Special Presidential Consultant Maxwell Taylor the JCS concern about a "restrictive worldwide military posture vis-à-vis our commitments." True, the "highly ready" Air Force reserve units were rapidly deployable as they were demonstrating in response to the *Pueblo* crisis. Reserve formations of all services fell generally short in quantity and quality of equipment. The scale of the Tet Offensive demanded U.S. reinforcements for Vietnam, but maintaining even minimum essential deployable units to NATO and the Western Pacific left U.S. military forces spread so thin that any contingency involving significant forces would require redeploying units from Southeast Asia or mobilizing the reserves.[75]

In April 1968, the six active divisions in the United States fell to their lowest readiness condition in several years because of the U.S. response to the Tet Offensive and the *Pueblo* crisis. No Army divisions in the United States were immediately deployable to NATO. On paper two airborne divisions were available as substitutes by M+30, but the entire 101st Airborne and a brigade of the 82d Airborne were fighting in Vietnam. Of the 37 USAF tactical fighter squadrons listed for NATO contingencies, only 6 Air National Guard squadrons were immediately available, with 4 of those scheduled to meet future Vietnam requirements. As for the Navy, with its ships fully committed to sustaining worldwide deployments, any reinforcement of NATO would necessitate substantial redeployments from SEA. Of 2 Marine division/wing teams listed to reach Europe by M+60 only 1 and 1/3 could actually do so without redeployments from Vietnam. In mid-May the Joint Chiefs again warned Clifford that the nation was "running high risks" because of the decreased readiness of U.S. forces worldwide and the limited capability of the strategic reserve.[76]

In June Clifford reported the JCS assessment to the president along with their estimate that another incident demanding significant U.S. forces would require immediate mobilization and/or redeployment from Southeast Asia. Clifford had already begun the rehabilitation of the conventional force in early April when he approved the mobilization of almost 23,000 reservists and began to reconstitute the STRAF, then at 4 divisions, none immediately deployable. He received an alarming message from General Lemnitzer in May reporting that serious shortages of equipment and lack of spare parts relegated 96 percent of USAREUR units to a "marginally ready" or "not ready" status. At Nitze's behest, the secretary of the Army investigated EUCOM readiness, and attributed deficiencies in Europe to priorities that assigned people and distributed equipment to Southeast Asia. Shortages of qualified personnel left the Army's logistics structure barely adequate to maintain peacetime rates of activities much less support wartime operations on a sustained basis.[77]

Atlantic Fleet endured similar declines in readiness as OSD shifted the fleet's resources to Southeast Asia. With fewer attack carriers available in the Atlantic, deployments to the Mediterranean became more frequent and of longer duration. By mid-1968 overextended deployments, coupled with shortened turnaround time in port, adversely affected training, morale, maintenance, and carrier readiness. Personnel shortages, wear and tear on ships, lack of sophisticated electronic equipment, shortages of new attack aircraft, and "serious deficiencies of new generation conventional weapons" hampered the Atlantic Fleet. In mid-October 1968 the Navy reported 43 percent of its ships and 25 percent of its aircraft assigned to Europe not combat ready by virtue of shortages of personnel or skilled petty officers.[78] While Sixth Fleet was deteriorating, Soviet naval activity in the Mediterranean was on the rise.

U.S. Air Force, Europe, reported insufficient storage facilities that taxed maintenance and security, severe shortages of conventional munitions, and insufficient numbers of aircrews. Not a single Air Force squadron in Europe was rated "Fully Combat Ready" as of June 1968, whereas two years earlier 22 squadrons had achieved that status. In late September 1968, Lemnitzer outlined for visiting Wheeler the gradual erosion of manpower, facilities, and materiel readiness in EUCOM since 1961 that accounted for the command's steady decline as its NATO commitments remained unchanged. He attributed priorities given to Southeast Asia requirements as largely accountable for the drop in combat capabilities. Commenting in December 1968 on a General Accounting Office draft report on the state of U.S. forces in Europe, the Joint Chiefs described the shortcomings as cumulative in nature and attributed them to the practice of "living off US worldwide inventories in order to meet combat requirements in Southeast Asia, without adequate compensatory funding and procurement, . . . [which] resulted in equipment and ammunition shortages in USEUCOM (and throughout the entire US military structure)."[79]

As forecast, the next big international crisis after Vietnam faced by the Johnson administration exposed the weakened state of U.S. forces. In the month after Soviet Union-led Warsaw Pact forces invaded Czechoslovakia in August 1968, combat ready strategic reserves in the United States amounted to one Army brigade available for deployment in three weeks and three other brigades ready in four. The Navy could augment Sixth Fleet with one attack carrier from the Atlantic plus antisubmarine warfare carriers and destroyers from both Atlantic and Pacific within one week. Two Marine battalions, one in the Caribbean and one in the Mediterranean, were immediately available, while the Air Force could deploy three tactical fighter squadrons from the United States to Europe in one to seven days followed by three more squadrons four to six weeks later. With 10 of 22 active Army and Marine* divisions committed to Vietnam, with materiel and personnel shortages rampant in forces everywhere except in Southeast Asia, and with reserve air units deployed to Northeast Asia, precious little military strength existed to react to the Czech emergency.[80]

Clifford's reconstitution plan eventually did show progress; by early November 1968 the 82nd Airborne and the 5th Mechanized divisions plus two separate Army brigades had reached acceptable readiness levels. The 2d Armored Division was scheduled to complete its training by 31 March 1969 and the 1st Armored by 30 June of that year. Only then, and then only for the first time in three years, would the United States show improvement in the availability of its NATO-oriented STRAF divisions. In his first posture statement, incoming Secretary of Defense Melvin Laird observed that "the overriding priority given to the needs of our forces in Southeast Asia during the last 3 1/2 years has apparently caused some significant distortions in the over-all balance of our General Purpose Forces"; it was "highly unlikely" that these could be rectified until the war ended.[81]

McNamara's short-term expediencies that met Vietnam demands by gutting active units in the United States and Europe carried long-term consequences for the armed forces and the nation. When he left office in February 1968, the seriously weakened conventional forces in the strategic reserve that he had earlier spent so many years and so much money rebuilding stood at about the same substandard levels of readiness as in 1961 when he arrived in Washington. International perceptions of a weak and divided United States left the nation at greater risk, as the *Pueblo* incident and Czechoslovakia notably demonstrated.

---

* Statements of numbers of Army and Marine divisions from different sources varied over time chiefly because of inclusion or exclusion of brigades from the computations; thus, three brigades might be included as a division.

As for minimal costs, many of McNamara's measures contributed genuine and substantial savings, but the inflated results of other initiatives could not stand close scrutiny. It proved impossible for him to control the developmental costs of strategic weapons, but by limiting the quantities of such weapons he achieved significant economies. His procurement and contracting policies were open to question but overall may have saved the taxpayer significant money. Yet McNamara also wasted tax dollars by single-mindedly pursuing expensive projects that seemed attractive in theory but proved unworkable in practice, notably the F-111 tactical fighter and the Vietnam barrier. However laudable McNamara's efforts, they could not compensate for the extraordinary escalating costs of the Vietnam War that would skew the national economy for years to come.

Long after he left office McNamara summarized his goals for DoD: defend the nation at minimum risk and minimum cost and, in time of war, with minimum loss of life. His prolonged and increasingly agonized effort to achieve these goals in years of great domestic and international turmoil tragically demonstrated that big wars do not lend themselves to cost-effectiveness, McNamara's ultimate measurement tool. The strategic direction of the Vietnam War by the Johnson administration—hesitant, uncertain, vacillating, baffled by an unyielding enemy—made impossible the most efficient use of available resources.

McNamara failed to achieve his stated goals for defense of the nation. Most painful to him of all the failures must have been the high human toll—more than 30,000 killed in action between 1961 and 1968. Inability to extricate the United States from the military stalemate in Vietnam yielded an ever growing number of American military killed in action—1,369 in 1965; 5,008 in 1966; 9,378 in 1967; and 14,592 in 1968.[82]

When McNamara left office with the nation engaged in a seemingly endless war, he had come to have grave misgivings about the conflict and his role in it. No doubt he fully realized that for all of his managerial genius he had not achieved the balance between strategy and cost-effectiveness needed to bring the Vietnam War to an acceptable conclusion.

Chapter XX

Conclusion

Between March 1965 and January 1969, Vietnam preoccupied both secretaries of defense and the defense establishment, but the tumultuous period also witnessed a series of national and international crises cascading onto the nation during four of the most momentous years in U.S. history. Besides Vietnam, the administration handled a major war in the Middle East in 1967 and a series of volatile incidents in Korea during 1968 with a combination of skillful diplomacy backed by military shows of force. It responded to lesser threats in the Dominican Republic in 1965 with overwhelming military might and sought to reinvigorate NATO's European members after the Soviets entered Czechoslovakia in August 1968. By January 1969, after a year of the bloodiest fighting in Vietnam, prospects for a negotiated settlement to the conflict, so great the previous April, were diminished, in part because the United States was still unwilling to abandon South Vietnam.

Robert McNamara's last day, 29 February 1968, seemed to epitomize the secretary's struggles to escape the trap of the Vietnam War. Along with the president and his entourage, he got stuck in a Pentagon elevator. While the elevator operator sought assistance, McNamara, trying to help, began pushing buttons, remarking, "let me see if I can't get this to work." The elevator lurched upward, but stopped between floors. Maintenance workers opened an elevator door on the floor above and helped the presidential party climb out.[1] Pushing buttons on a stalled elevator was an apt metaphor for McNamara's futile, increasingly desperate efforts to escape a war he had ceased to believe in.

McNamara's theories of limited war and escalation failed in Vietnam. After recognizing the futility of the war, he publicly continued to support administration policy, some would insist too enthusiastically, while privately he tried to end or at least cap the violence. To his credit, he realized this by early 1966 and unsuccessfully sought ways to end the fighting or to reduce Westmoreland's, Sharp's, and the JCS' incessant requests for more troops and planes and a wider war. To his discredit, he officially went along with the administration's expansion of the conflict, providing a constant stream of reinforcements for the ground war in the South and adapting the air war against the North to conform to Johnson's political requirements.

McNamara's bombing policy alienated the Joint Chiefs, military commanders, and congressional hawks without accruing any benefits for the administration. His controversial strategy originally hinged on fashionable escalation theory to intimidate the enemy. Like everyone else, he underestimated the North Vietnamese resilience and tenacity—the on-again, off-again bombing campaign never accomplished its goals. McNamara later insisted that it never could have succeeded and his critics just as vocally retorted it never was given a chance. North Vietnamese accounts have revealed occasions of near helplessness during the heightened bombing campaigns; unaware of their duress McNamara supported bombing halts at critical junctures in hope of opening the way to negotiations.

McNamara's management of the air war relied on secrecy, wishful thinking, and the exclusion of contradictory evidence. He went from one extreme to another—initially a hawk in early 1965 who advocated massive air strikes—by 1967 he had become a dove who proposed first to restrict the bombing to southern North Vietnam and then to stop it entirely. In between he imposed restrictions on the bombing campaign to limit expanding the war and supported the gradualism policy of bombing pauses invariably followed by heavier bombing and renewed pauses. The POL attacks in mid-1966 and the strikes against Hanoi and Haiphong in late 1966 come to mind. Despite his growing doubts, he generally supported these shifting strategies with his usual certainty and enthusiasm.

McNamara never accepted that his single-minded determination to manipulate Rolling Thunder operations contributed to the dysfunctional air campaign. As he saw it, every JCS war-winning scheme advanced during 1965 and 1966 came to naught—the initial Rolling Thunder operations, the interdiction campaign, and most of all the POL attacks—and left the secretary and his coterie more convinced than ever that Rolling Thunder had outlived its usefulness. Conversely, McNamara and McNaughton prided themselves on their sophisticated ability to transmit and receive nuanced "signals" from adversaries and manage conflict, but they displayed repeated ineptitude, failing to coordinate overtures for negotiations with stepped-up bombing operations, not keeping U.S. military commanders informed, and agonizing over what Hanoi's statements really meant.

If JCS bombing projections did not produce the promised results, the same was true of McNamara's barrier strategy. It pinned U.S. troops near the DMZ and initially concentrated airpower in the southern half of North Vietnam and Laos. Despite the investment of lives, technology, and money, the barrier did not lead to the eventual cessation of the bombing of North Vietnam as McNamara hoped, while its interdiction value remained contentious. The war acquired a momentum of its own that McNamara feared but was unable to check. Clifford's willingness to end the bombing of the north unconditionally also angered the military, but the communist Tet offensive and subsequent heavy fighting during the first six months of 1968 soured the public on the war and the military leadership making it easier for Clifford to overcome their resistance.

Vietnam was McNamara's conundrum because the cost of winning was as morally prohibitive as was the price of losing. Powerful domestic restraints—competing money demanded by the Great Society, growing opposition to the war, civil unrest, instability in the economy—greatly influenced the judgment and decisions of the president and the secretary of defense in waging the war. So, too, did the near-universal condemnation of the international community to which McNamara professed to pay little heed. The presence of Communist China and the Soviet Union as close supporters of North Vietnam could not help but give Johnson and McNamara pause and inhibit how far they could go in attacking North Vietnam. The cost of the war in blood and money could not be borne indefinitely. It was a faraway conflict fought with a conscript army under unfavorable circumstances, lacking the public support needed to sustain it. The war became a stalemate, witnessing heavier bombing, more American reinforcements, and correspondingly higher casualties on all sides.

With McNamara worn down after seven years by a grueling work pace overseeing and controlling the OSD bureaucracy and handling wars, interventions, and crises, Johnson turned to Clifford to support his Vietnam agenda only to be surprised when Clifford brought his own plans to the table. Clifford also quickly discovered that political restrictions left the Chiefs without a formula to win or end the war, and he relied on his own staff to craft a withdrawal strategy. He bluntly asserted control over the MACV commander's conduct of the ground war, something McNamara did, and rejected JCS and MACV appeals to broaden the war. To the very end, Clifford was storming about the "garbage" from Abrams proposing an invasion of Cambodia: "They keep sending accounts of new offensives and other crap none of which are accurate or mean anything." As far as Clifford was concerned, Abrams' schemes were "all stuff and fluff."[2] Clifford concentrated on convincing Johnson to seek a political settlement to the war without preconditions.

While both McNamara and Clifford ultimately concluded that Vietnam was not worth the price in American lives and treasure, Clifford aimed to reduce the U.S. combat role and even withdraw American troops. For all his cogent memoranda against further expansion, McNamara never reached that point. To the end of his tenure, the argument with the Joint Chiefs was always over how many more troops to deploy. Clifford broke that pattern, first by persistently and outspokenly counseling Johnson to end the bombing of much of North Vietnam and then by encouraging a sometimes faltering president to cap the number of U.S. troops in South Vietnam. Clifford insisted that Vietnam could not continue as before and continually clashed with Johnson, Abrams, Rusk, and Westmoreland by challenging their more-of-the-same approach. Finally McNamara seemed oblivious to the political implications of his advice, while Clifford considered every piece of counsel in terms of the domestic political influence on national security policy. Clifford, however, became so enmeshed in getting the United States out of the war that he ignored the consequences for South Vietnam. The toll for Vietnam extended far beyond the battlefield. Consistently sharp increases in defense spending for the war added almost $80 billion to DoD expenditures by mid-FY 1969. Efforts to hold down spiraling costs merely postponed a full accounting of the wartime budgets on the military's force structure and the civilian economy. By 1968, even before the Tet offensive, the extra costs associated with Vietnam had seriously weakened the national economy, helped to undercut the strength of the U.S. dollar, disrupted domestic social welfare spending, created undreamed of federal deficits, and unloosed inflationary surges that would plague the economy for the next decade.

TABLE 11

INCREMENTAL COSTS OF VIETNAM WAR
($ BILLIONS)

Expenditure	FY 66	FY 67	FY 68	FY 69	TOTAL
Military Personnel	$ 1.6	$ 4.4	$ 5.5	$ 6.2	**$ 17.7**
Operating Costs	$ 3.0	$ 6.6	$ 7.3	$ 8.5	**$25.4**
Ammunition	$ 2.0	$ 3.7	$ 5.3	$ 6.3	**$ 17.3**
Aircraft Attrition	$ 0.9	$ 1.2	$ 1.7	$ 1.9	**$ 5.7**
Equipment/Spares	$ 1.2	$ 2.4	$ 3.1	$ 3.6	**$ 10.3**
Construction	$ 0.6	$ 0.9	$ 0.8	$ 0.3	**$ 2.6**
R&D	$ 0.1	$ 0.2	$ 0.3	$ 0.2	**$ 0.8**
TOTAL	**$ 9.4**	**$ 19.4**	**$ 24**	**$ 27**	**$ 79.8**

Source: Ltr Nitze to Goodpaster, 26 Apr 68 w/encl 1, fldr SEA Costs, box 326, Subject Files, OSD Hist.

McNamara's strong suits were budget preparation and management, but he was at the mercy of an unpredictable war and a volatile international arena. Presiding over an increasingly unpopular war, McNamara tried to manage the Department of Defense in a peacetime fashion, searching for economies here and there but never acknowledging the true cost of Vietnam. Since budget formulation was supposedly what McNamara did best, critics charged that he misrepresented war costs in a deliberate effort to conceal them from the American people. After all, only McNamara knew the president's wishes; only McNamara knew the dimensions of the Vietnam buildup; and only McNamara, it was reputed, understood the Defense budget. Still, he kept Congress informed in general terms of the mounting cost of the war, and most members willingly appropriated money for the effort until the Tet offensive of 1968 forced a reexamination of the administration's claims.

McNamara had promised an efficient and affordable defense. Vietnam ruined those goals. Instead of economy and lower Defense budgets, Vietnam brought expanded forces, enormous Defense budgets, and gargantuan supplemental requests. The war forced McNamara to increase conventional military strength far in excess of any plan. Military manpower rose about 20 percent, from 2.85 million in 1965 to 3.4 million in 1968. The marked expansion of the Army and Marine Corps by nearly 500,000 additional personnel testified to their predominant role in Vietnam.[3]

The one area he should have controlled, he did not. His use of ad hoc financing schemes only robbed Peter to pay Paul and left the service programs in disarray. Although McNamara understood the potential penalties for overspending, he always made certain that the Pentagon met the Vietnam portion of the Defense budget. That priority spared President Johnson hard choices until late in his tenure, by which time the president had wagered too much in Vietnam to throw in his hand. Clifford, too, feared for the national economy, but unlike McNamara, he made across-the-board spending reductions, including Vietnam expenditures, in his attempt to restore the nation's financial health and force the president to make painful decisions.

Despite all of McNamara's ingenuity and his insistence that the United States could afford both a war and major social programs, it was not so. He held the non-Vietnam portion of the Defense budget to an artificial minimum by postponing modernization, delaying needed infrastructure improvements, and deferring procurement and payments. He only succeeded in mortgaging DoD's future. His advice to raise taxes to pay the costs of the war was overwhelmed by domestic political concerns and eventually became a test of wills between Johnson and Congress. But here, too, McNamara's public expressions belied his private concerns.

Johnson force-fed the national economy by serving up guns and butter. Along with McNamara, he tried and failed to contain defense costs. McNamara usually recommended larger Defense budgets than the president desired, but in the end followed Johnson's lead and modified (critics would say manipulated) the numbers to stay within tolerable ranges.

TABLE 12

NEW OBLIGATIONAL AUTHORITY
($ BILLIONS)

Fiscal Year	Normal Budget	Southeast Asia Budget	TOTAL
1965	$ 46.070	$ 0.103	**$ 46.173**
1966	$ 48.597	$ 5.812	**$ 54.409**
1967	$ 47.333	$ 20.133	**$ 67.466**
1968	$ 50.826	$ 26.547	**$ 77.373**
1969	$ 48.978	$ 28.812	**$ 77.790**

Source: *The Budget of the United States Government: Fiscal Year 1970*, 74.

They failed, abetted by economic advisers who believed they had unlocked the secret to economic prosperity. Minimizing the financial cost of the Vietnam War ultimately ruined Johnson's social agenda and created large federal deficits that brought on a ruinous inflation. McNamara and Clifford worked closely with the Bureau of the Budget to finalize a Defense budget acceptable to the White House, but McNamara received preferential treatment and usually found ways to meet presidential targets. Clifford's one experience was harsher, and he refused to accept presidentially imposed limitations.

On the international scene, President Johnson often appeared frustrated by the world situation, perhaps because it detracted from his ambitious domestic agenda. Still, Johnson acted decisively during the Middle East War of June 1967 and displayed statesmanship of a high caliber. He set the tone for relations with de Gaulle's France and proved a determined negotiator with West German and British leaders. He may have acted rashly during the Dominican crisis of 1965, but his fear about the effects on domestic opinion of another communist triumph close to home motivated him. On the other extreme, the president moved with painstaking deliberateness in making major military decisions about Vietnam when perhaps more decisiveness was needed. Committed to a domestic policy of social and economic advancement, Johnson also handled well a myriad of foreign issues and crises. But Vietnam tormented him, and all his political skills were of no avail against an enemy who wanted nothing the United States had to offer.

In Western Europe, the North Atlantic Treaty Organization was in turmoil. Relations between the United States and other NATO members grew strained, chiefly by differing views about Vietnam, but also because of unilateral U.S. decisions on alliance issues such as ABM deployment and more importantly U.S. pressure to build up and reorganize their conventional forces to comport with McNamara's flexible response strategy. Chronically under-funded defense budgets left West European governments unable to meet agreed-upon force goals. Try as he did, McNamara was never able to wean the West Europeans from their dependence on the U.S. nuclear deterrent. To compensate for the substandard West European militaries, the United States had to maintain disproportionately large conventional forces in Western Europe, undermining McNamara's effort to save money by withdrawing U.S. troops from Western Europe. Complaints that NATO allies were not bearing their fair share of defense costs as determined by McNamara fell on deaf ears; the West Europeans complained that the Americans did not comprehend the forces of détente at work on the continent. Unwillingness or inability to recognize any weakness in his position rendered McNamara insensitive to the West Europeans and dismissive of their legitimate concerns; for example, his heavy-handed approach to the offset issues alienated many West German leaders.

The continental Europeans, especially West Germany, did not enjoy a free ride on defense. In offset arrangements negotiated and renegotiated as the Tripartite Agreement of 1967, the West Germans spent huge sums of money for U.S. manufactured weapons and military equipment; the minor allies purchased lesser amounts. Furthermore, concessions to the British and compromises with the West Germans formulated in the agreement, accomplished over McNamara's objections by State Department officials, somewhat lessened the NATO burden borne by the United States. Still, by 1969 the defense of Western Europe rested primarily on the nuclear deterrent of the United States and stationing of U.S. troops in Germany, in spite of McNamara's vigorous efforts to implement the burden sharing necessary to adopt his flexible response strategy.

France's President de Gaulle was in a class by himself—impervious, aloof, quick to criticize the United States, and always hoping to reassert French influence in Europe and beyond. France's departure from the military alliance created new demands on members. Yet OSD, working with the French, handled the relocation from France expeditiously and, following presidential guidance, without rancor. More than de Gaulle, the Vietnam War increasingly alienated the NATO allies, particularly the Canadian and British prime ministers. The war also undercut U.S. support for NATO. While demanding that the West Europeans do more in their own defense, McNamara pulled experienced U.S. troops and units from Western Europe for Vietnam duty, replacing them with recruits fresh from basic training. He stripped the U.S. strategic reserves to meet Vietnam reinforcement timetables, leaving units without the personnel and equipment to augment NATO in time of crisis, as happened during the Czechoslovak crisis of August 1968.

The insatiable demands of the Vietnam War exercised a telling effect on the Military Assistance Program that McNamara considered essential for national security. In revamping the program, he wanted to prop up anticommunist or neutral regimes by selling them arms and military equipment and in turn use the resulting profits to ease the U.S. balance of payments deficit. McNamara's encouragement of the export and sale of conventional weapons was the centerpiece of his effort to revamp the Military Assistance Program and quietly shift it from a predominately grant aid system to a massive, worldwide military sales program. He aimed to wean allies from grant aid and make MAP a self-sustaining and self-sufficient program. While he did not deliberately mislead Congress about his intentions, there was sufficient ambiguity about the Export-Import Bank's role in financing the arms sales programs to confuse even the most experienced eye. Congress brought McNamara up short on this idea, more as a reaction to Vietnam than to the wisdom or ethics of arming the world from stockpiles of American weapons.

Vietnam also skewed military assistance and often left McNamara working at cross-purposes. In early 1965 he looked forward to reducing military assistance to South Korea, but the need for allies in Vietnam eventually led to increased military and economic aid to the Seoul government. Following the *Pueblo* incident in early 1968, OSD used military assistance funds to underwrite exactly the type of conventional military buildup of South Korean forces that McNamara wanted to avoid and committed large numbers of American troops to the peninsula for the foreseeable future. Sales of advanced warplanes to Israel after the Middle East War complicated U.S. relations with Israel and its Arab neighbors. Clifford's staff, especially Paul Warnke, opposed the initiative and bore the brunt of confrontations with tough-minded Israeli negotiators. The president ultimately decided the matter.

In the Western Hemisphere, the Dominican Republic became an overnight crisis, perhaps due more to Johnson's vivid imagination and fears of communist subversion than anything else. Still the administration believed that the United States could not risk another communist takeover so close to home, and McNamara played an important, if secondary, role in policymaking throughout the crisis. DoD's response with overwhelming military force ensured a relatively stable, pro-U.S. Dominican government for the next two decades. It also made clear that President Johnson would act immediately to protect U.S. interests in the Caribbean and Latin America and seemed to validate military intervention.

If the administration focused on the stalemate in Vietnam, a growing number of Americans questioned the nation's course and priorities. The war served as a catalyst for the civil rights movement, radical student activism, and antiwar sentiment to explode into a major force of protest against government policies. Massive antiwar demonstrations, major disruptions on college and university campuses, race riots across the country, and large-scale political disorder in Chicago in 1968 marked the end of unquestioning public acceptance of government policies. The sentiment spread, in John McNaughton's words, that "'the Establishment' is out of its mind."[4]

Indeed with rioters setting America's cities on fire and U.S. troops guarding the Capitol, it seemed the country had lost its bearings; the rage in the ghettos that erupted into nationwide rioting saw the military in the streets suppressing civil insurrection. OSD performed well in containing riots, restoring order, and, in the case of the march on the Pentagon, handling large-scale antiwar protest with minimum force. On the home front McNamara fared less well. His decisions regarding the augmentation of the reserves and National Guard turned those institutions into havens for young men who did not wish to be drafted or go to Vietnam.

McNamara continued his efforts started under President Kennedy to ensure civil rights and equitable race relations and acted to eliminate injustice and prejudice. He saw the military services as a means to resolve racial and economic inequality and promote skills transferable to the civilian economy, much as the GI Bill of World War II had lifted up his generation. He was sensitive to the condition of African-Americans and sincerely believed that giving more of the disadvantaged a chance to serve in the military would uplift them and the nation. His conviction was misplaced. Project 100,000 filled the draftee and enlistment quotas and probably ended up sending more African-Americans to Vietnam than would otherwise have been the case. Race mattered, and McNamara's attempts to recast the National Guard and reserve forces had limited success. It almost seemed that despite McNamara's good intentions, his programs generated greater disharmony and estrangement.

Under McNamara OSD energetically pursued arms control and arms limitations initiatives with the Soviet Union and repeatedly sought to enlist Moscow's assistance as an intermediary to jump start negotiations with the Hanoi government. Even the Soviet invasion of Czechoslovakia in August 1968 did not completely dash those hopes. Rather than a lost opportunity because of Vietnam or the Czech crisis, the deep-seated suspicion on both sides of the superpower divide, made progress on arms control agonizingly slow but still possible.

Restrictions on the spread of nuclear weapons were important to Johnson, although he dithered on an initiative in 1965 for domestic political reasons. McNamara and other strong proponents of nuclear arms limitations shared the president's enthusiasm for a nuclear arms agreement, but the secretary generally supported JCS reservations about ACDA's more radical proposals and always endorsed the Chiefs' demands for verification as part of any nuclear arms control package. Building on the Limited Test Ban Treaty of 1963, the Johnson administration concluded the Nuclear Nonproliferation Treaty in June 1968, the high point of its arms control efforts. Johnson continued to press seriously for further arms reductions talks with Moscow. McNamara's notable efforts included his determined struggle to block deployment of an ABM system, his impassioned plea to Soviet Premier Kosygin at Glassboro for a renunciation of strategic defensive systems, his personal diplomacy with various Soviet senior officials, and his public statements on nuclear weapons.

By the mid-1960s McNamara had fashioned a strategic nuclear arsenal of ICBMS, SLBMs, and B-52 bombers. In related programs he had little success in having his way. Attempts to secure funding for civil defense shelters failed, an ABM system he did not want could not be avoided, proposed reductions of heavy bombers met congressional and popular opposition, and the pursuit of the F-111B as a replacement strategic bomber became an albatross around McNamara's neck. Nevertheless, McNamara maintained U.S. nuclear superiority over the Soviet Union, although he was realistic enough to grasp that any advantage was relative and ephemeral. Rethinking the role of nuclear weapons was surely one of his premier contributions as secretary; his concept of nuclear strategy was bold, visionary, and extreme. He could take justifiable pride in the adoption of his strategy of flexible response, a more realistic reckoning of the use of military forces.

The first secretary of defense to grapple with the strategic implications of nuclear warfare, McNamara exported his concept of flexible response to the West European allies through the Nuclear Planning Group sessions. This institution gave West European defense leaders greater authority in nuclear planning and arrangements while keeping control of nuclear weapons firmly in U.S. hands. McNamara worked with NATO's Nuclear Planning Group to make the allies aware of the consequences of mutual atomic devastation in Central Europe, yet paradoxically deployed thousands of tactical nuclear warheads to double the number available in Western Europe.[5] He likewise sought accommodation of nuclear weapons with the Soviet Union, but on his terms and on his understanding of nuclear weapons systems.

McNamara had to adjust to rapid technological advances in strategic weapons with far-reaching implications for military strategy and national policy. The spiral of nuclear and missile technology during the mid-1960s—smaller, improved warheads, multiple reentry vehicles, area ABM capability, and Polaris SLBMs—led to a new generation of very expensive strategic arms that still could only guarantee assured destruction. His comprehension of the paradoxical nature of nuclear weapons, complemented by numerous studies, reports, and assessments, convinced him of the futility of an antiballistic missile defense. He improved the U.S. strategic offensive nuclear capability qualitatively, making it more destructive with fewer strategic weapons, but more nuclear warheads. After his overtures to the Soviets failed, he reluctantly agreed to the construction of a light ABM system, a compromise disliked by West Europeans. Unlike his predecessor, Clifford had only a limited understanding of nuclear weapons and strategy. He devoted his efforts to ensuring deployment of the Sentinel ABM for reasons that had less to do with nuclear strategy than with his attempts to short-circuit congressional attempts to pull massive numbers of U.S. troops out of NATO.

McNamara's decisions and recommendations on defense matters, including Vietnam, were little influenced by public opinion. He was not swayed by what he regarded as an emotional military, and he sought to shape public opinion, not follow it. He paid less attention to criticism than he did to his intellectual comprehension of issues.

McNamara was a central figure in a small group of policymakers surrounding the president. Johnson preferred this informal, ad hoc arrangement to ensure secrecy, keep his options open, and maneuver freely. McNamara took advantage of the system to exert his influence, often unilaterally, to sway the president's judgment in his direction. McGeorge Bundy, who interacted frequently with McNamara and observed him closely, told the president that McNamara was prone to make "the case his way without checking with everybody else."[6] He was determined to pursue his decided course and demonstrate its wisdom to doubters. His self-certitude made him many enemies, usually with long memories.

Already by 1965 McNamara's style was wearing thin in Congress. He could still dazzle congressional committees with his brilliance, self-confidence, and the thoroughness of his knowledge of the workings of DoD. The secretary lost much of his luster as a series of battles with Congressmen over Vietnam, military assistance, budgets, weapons systems, and military strategy tarnished his reputation; there was a growing perception that he was not always honest with them.)

As his direction of the war came under increasing criticism from hawks and doves alike, he stubbornly insisted that he was right and blamed Congress for not doing its job or reminded members that they had previously approved his course of action. His assertions often backfired, especially when he denied the obvious shortages of equipment, bombs, and ammunition in Vietnam or differences between himself and the Joint Chiefs. On budget matters, where he was supposedly infallible, he repeatedly had to ask for enormous supplements yet insisted there was no need to raise the annual budget submission. As his prestige waned, his opponents in Congress, the media, and the public sector criticized him more and more openly, refusing to implement his programs, mocking his statements, and denouncing him as a warmonger. McNamara might have been smoother, might have cultivated congressional members, but that was not his style. Right to the end, he refused to concede anything to his critics in Congress. It was left to Clifford to repair the damage with Congress and patch things over with the Joint Chiefs.

Throughout his tenure McNamara and Secretary of State Dean Rusk worked together with mutual respect. Both initially supported Vietnam escalation, although McNamara was more hawkish. Both consulted on major policy issues, but McNamara was prone to approach the president unilaterally with his recommendations. As McNamara's enthusiasm for the war waned, Rusk's remained constant. Some in State felt McNamara dominated Rusk and used ISA as a "little State Department" to formulate foreign policy. State did respond to policies McNamara drafted on Vietnam, including negotiating initiatives and bombing pauses, and McNamara more or less ran the Pennsylvania overture in 1967 from his office. But State had the lead in nuclear nonproliferation talks, played the dominant role in the Dominican Republic crisis of 1965, oversaw arms control talks, and through Rusk had a great say in target selection during the bombing of North Vietnam. State also successfully resisted McNamara's more extreme proposals for reorganizing military assistance and withdrawing U.S. troops from NATO. Conversely Rusk and Clifford clashed over Vietnam, NATO policy, the Czechoslovakia crisis, and bombing of North Vietnam.

McNamara did not ignore the Joint Chiefs, but he often sidestepped them by making direct recommendations to the president. Besides the bombing campaign, McNamara and the Chiefs disagreed on a host of issues: deployment of the ABM, reduction in numbers of manned bombers, advanced bombers and new generation aircraft, the TFX or F-111 development, numbers of nuclear submarines, aircraft carriers, and major fleet escorts, troop reductions in NATO, reserve mobilization, troop ceilings in Vietnam, and the barrier strategy in Vietnam. Almost all involved funding, but the JCS also questioned McNamara's ideas about strategic nuclear deterrence. Frustrated by the secretary, the Joint Chiefs drew closer together, minimized their inter-service differences, and slowly and steadily eroded McNamara's dominance of them. Clifford challenged the JCS on Vietnam policy, but otherwise was more sympathetic to their viewpoints on redeployment from NATO, deployment of the ABM, the Navy's cancellation of the F-111B, as well as personnel and strategic reserve issues.

McNamara's success in rebuilding conventional forces between 1961 and 1965 enabled him to handle the Vietnam buildup expeditiously. As he enjoyed reminding reporters and skeptics, never before in history had so many troops been moved so far so fast. His statistics, while accurate, betrayed him. Units deployed, but in piecemeal fashion that dissipated their overall value. Moreover his original plan involved mobilizing the reserves to expedite reinforcements to Vietnam. When Johnson rejected this course, McNamara still moved the troops but only by dismantling the active forces. His approach seriously diminished U.S. conventional forces for years to come.

Weaknesses in U.S. forces outside of Vietnam appeared in NATO as early as January 1966 and were pronounced during the Middle East crisis of mid-1967 when sufficient aircraft, ground troops, and ships were unavailable to offer policymakers a range of options. The situation recurred in January 1968 with the *Pueblo* incident when shortages of aircraft and ships made an immediate response to North Korea's challenge impossible and conditioned a diplomatic solution. American forces assigned to NATO were likewise unable to do much when the Soviets invaded Czechoslovakia in August 1968. Nor indeed could the United States afford the vast reinforcement for Vietnam proposed in 1968 by Westmoreland and Wheeler.

McGeorge Bundy best encapsulated McNamara's personality when he wrote to the president in September 1964 that "Bob McNamara is the ablest man in the government, but when he makes a basic decision and gets up a head of steam, he does not always keep the sharpest eye out for new evidence. Others of us could have been more alert than we were to help guard against this one weakness of an extraordinary man."[7] This "one weakness" recurred with regularity throughout his tenure.

McNamara made decisions quickly acting on rational steel-trap logic. But once he made a commitment he left no option except to carry it through to fruition. Convinced of his correctness, he pushed ahead, ignoring naysayers on such issues as the

Vietnam barrier, Project 100,000, offsets and troop reductions in NATO, and de-velopment of the TFX aircraft and main battle tank. McNamara was strong willed, resolute, often arrogant, dismissive of criticism, and convinced of his correctness, but such attitudes hardly differentiate him from other of top-level executives. To the Office of the Secretary of Defense he brought an intense determination to provide the leadership to get the job done. He entertained little self-doubt, except on Vietnam, and even there he often seemed to pursue new changes in policy with the same self-certainty and enthusiasm as he had earlier policies. Soviet or North Vietnamese dismissal of what he considered compelling logic left him at a loss that permitted no effective response.

Having earned a justified reputation as a man of efficiency and cost-effec-tiveness, McNamara contradicted that persona with his single-minded pursuit of certain programs. Stubbornly insisting there were no shortages of military person-nel or equipment while pulling troops from Europe for Vietnam service made him appear foolish. His insistence that he could make the Soviet leaders understand his brand of nuclear policy was presumptuous. His conviction that the TFX aircraft and main battle tank justified his approach to commonalty and savings led him to condone cost overruns and continue procurement programs that wasted tax dol-lars. His determination to accomplish things and reap favorable outcomes ignored the human and material costs of many of his undertakings.

McNamara believed it his duty to loyally execute the policy of the president. In public McNamara supported the administration's Vietnam policy, although in private he tried to change it. He clashed with his military advisers, in general over Vietnam and in particular when he axed specific service programs. As time passes, tales of McNamara's duplicity or gullibility have gained prominence, but he did what he believed was correct, and that included shielding from criticism a presi-dent with whom he increasingly differed on the conduct of the war. Clifford was much more pragmatic and willing to make concessions to accomplish his goal. He never wavered from his conviction that the United States had to get out of Viet-nam and subordinated everything to that end. He risked his relationship with the president to force the issue, alienated Rusk during the process of opening negotia-tions, and often flummoxed the Joint Chiefs.

McNamara left office with much undone. Vietnam was the most obvious, but the Middle East was still seething and arms sales fueled more ire. North Korea had humiliated the United States by seizing a U.S. Navy vessel and its crew on the high seas. Great strides had been made in nuclear nonproliferation and would culmi-nate with the treaty in June 1968, but arms control efforts with the Soviets had floundered over the issue of defensive strategic nuclear weapons. Thus one must ask whether McNamara made the United States more secure.

Communism was contained in the Western Hemisphere by decisive inter-vention in the Dominican Republic, but Castro's Cuba remained an irritant as it proselytized communist revolution to Latin and Central American neighbors.

The United States was locked in a military technology race with the Soviet Union, trying to maintain or gain an advantage in strategic nuclear weapons with state-of-the-art innovations. NATO was frayed, but managed to stand together during the Soviet invasion of Czechoslovakia. U.S. conventional military forces were over-stretched and overcommitted, dangerously understrength in relation to their assigned missions, especially to defend northwest Europe. The stalemate in Vietnam, the Soviet's expanding presence in the Middle East, the Czechoslovakian situation, and the rapid Soviet and Chinese Communist advances in nuclear weaponry left many Americans convinced that the world was far more dangerous than in early 1965. McNamara had analyzed the risks, made his decisions, and enforced them. In some cases his judgment was vindicated, in others not, and in still others unknowable. Who, for instance, really knew if his restrictions on strategic nuclear arms imperiled national security or not? He left his successor a large-scale conventional war entering its bloodiest phase, a homefront deeply divided over Vietnam policies, and a keystone alliance in search of itself.

Although McNamara departed office at the end of February 1968, this book is primarily his story. His dominance of the Department of Defense far surpassed Clifford's. McNamara realized his intention to bring managerial and organizational changes that resulted in greater centralization of control of the Department of Defense in the office of the secretary—an office that grew and exercised closer direction of the military departments than ever before. A brilliant and original thinker, McNamara's surpassing intellectual gifts often made him impatient or dismissive of lesser men. He grasped minutia and possessed an almost inexhaustible amount of energy to get things done. He did the vital, demanding day-to-day work for more than seven years and no one has since approached his mastery of the enormity and complexity of the Pentagon. Daring, inventive, dominating, he could not surmount the intractable obstacle that came to define his career—coping with the Vietnam War. And for all his luminous achievements, his choices that led to the Vietnam disaster will forever remain McNamara's enduring legacy.

List of Abbreviations

AAA	Anti-Aircraft Artillery
AASD	Acting Assistant Secretary of Defense
Acc	Accession
ABM	Antiballistic Missile
ACDA	Arms Control and Disarmament Agency
ACMC	Assistant Commandant of the Marine Corps
ACS	Acting Chief of Staff
AEC	Atomic Energy Commission
AFB	Air Force Base
AFPC	Armed Forces Policy Council
AFP, CD	American Foreign Policy, Current Documents
AFQT	Armed Forces Qualification Test
AGC	Acting General Counsel
AID	Agency for International Development
AMSA	Advanced Manned Strategic Aircraft
ANF	Atlantic Nuclear Force
APC	Armored Personnel Carrier
ARPA	Advance Research Projects Agency
ARVN	Army of the Republic of Vietnam
ASD	Assistant Secretary of Defense
ASD(C)	Assistant Secretary of Defense, Comptroller
ASD(ISA)	Assistant Secretary of Defense, International Security Affairs
ASD(I&L)	Assistant Secretary of Defense, Installations And Logistics
ASD(M)	Assistant Secretary of Defense, Manpower
ASD(SA)	Assistant Secretary of Defense, Systems Analysis

ASW	Anti-Submarine Warfare
BMD	Ballistic Missile Defense
BLT	Battalion Landing Team
BoB	Bureau of the Budget
BOP	Balance Of Payments
C	Comptroller
CA	Circular Airgram
CEA	Council of Economic Advisors
CF	Country File
CIA	Central Intelligence Agency
CINCEUR	Commander in Chief, Europe
CINCLANT	Commander in Chief, Atlantic Command
CINCPAC	Commander in Chief, Pacific
CINCSTRIKE	Commander in Chief, U.S. Strike Force
CINCUNC	Commander in Chief, United Nations Command
CINCUNC/USFK	Commander in Chief, United Nations Command/ U.S. Forces, Korea
CJCS	Chairman of the Joint Chiefs of Staff
CM	Chairman of the Joint Chiefs of Staff Memorandum
CMAAG	Chief, Military Assistance Advisory Group
CMC	Commandant of the Marine Corps
CMDR	Commander
CMH	U.S. Army Center of Military History
COAS	Council of Organization of American States
CONUS	Continental United States
CNO	Chief of Naval Operations
COMUSKOREA	Commander, U.S. Forces, Korea
COMUSMACV	Commander, U.S. Military Assistance Command, Vietnam
Conf	Conference
Cong Rec	Congressional Record
CPFF	Cost-Plus-Fixed-Fee Contract
CRS	Congressional Research Service
CSA	Chief of Staff of the Army
CSAF	Chief of Staff of the Air Force
CTBT	Comprehensive Test Ban Treaty
Cte	Committee
CY	Calendar Year
DA	Department of the Army
DASD	Deputy Assistant Secretary of Defense
DCPG	Defense Communications Planning Group
DCI	Director of Central Intelligence

DDCI	Deputy Director of Central Intelligence
DDG	Guided Missile Destroyer
DDR&E	Director of Defense Research & Evaluation
DEPEX	Nike-X Deployment
DepSecDef	Deputy Secretary of Defense
DIA	Defense Intelligence Agency
DIRNSA	Director, National Security Agency
DJSM	Director Joint Staff Memorandum
DLGN	Frigate (Nuclear Powered)
DMA	Director, Military Assistance
DMZ	Demilitarized Zone
DoD	Department of Defense
DPC	Defense Planning Committee (NATO)
DPM	Draft Presidential Memo
DPQ	Defense Planning Questionnaire
DR&E	Defense Research and Engineering
DRV	Democratic Republic of Vietnam
DSA	Defense Supply Agency
DXGN	Guided Missile Destroyer (Nuclear Powered)
EAPR	East Asia and Pacific Region
Emb	Embassy
ENDC	United Nations Eighteen Nation Disarmament Committee
EUCOM	European Command
EUR	Bureau of European Affairs, Department of State
Ex-Im Bank	Export-Import Bank
FAA	Foreign Assistance Act
FBI	Federal Bureau of Investigation
FPIF	Fixed-Price-Incentive-Fee Contract
FRELOC	Fast Relocation (from France)
FRG	Federal Republic of Germany
FRUS	Foreign Relations of the United States
FY	Fiscal Year
FYDP	Five-Year Defense Program
FYFS&FP	Five-Year Force Structure and Financial Program
GAO	Government Accounting Office
GNP	Gross National Product
GNR	Government of National Reconstruction
G/PM	Office of Politico-Military Affairs, Department of State
GSA	General Services Administration
H	House of Representatives
HCA	House Committee on Appropriations
HCAS	House Committee on Armed Services

HCFA	House Committee on Foreign Affairs
HQDA	Headquarters, Department of the Army
HQUSAF	Headquarters, United States Air Force
HSCA	House Subcommittee on Appropriations
I&L	Installations and Logistics
IAF	Inter-American Force
IAPF	Inter-American Peace Force
ICBM	Intercontinental Ballistic Missile
IDA	Institute for Defense Analysis
IMS	International Military Staff (NATO)
INR	Bureau of Intelligence and Research, Department of State
Interv	Interview
IRBM	Intermediate-Range Ballistic Missile
ISA	International Security Affairs
ISZ	International Security Zone
JCAE	Joint Committee on Atomic Energy
JCS	Joint Chiefs of Staff
JCSM	Joint Chiefs of Staff memorandum
JLRB	Joint Logistics Review Board
JSOP	Joint Strategic Objectives Plan
LANTCOM	Atlantic Command
LBJL	Lyndon B. Johnson Presidential Library
LC	Library of Congress
LOC	Line of Communication
LTBT	Limited Test Ban Treaty
Ltr	Letter
M	Manpower
M&RA	Office of the Assistant Secretary of Defense for Manpower and Reserve Affairs
MAAG	Military Assistance Advisory Group
MACV	Military Assistance Command, Vietnam
MAP	Military Assistance Program
MBT	Main Battle Tank
MC	Military Committee (NATO)
MDW	Military District of Washington
MEB	Marine Expeditionary Brigade
Memrcd	Memorandum for the Record
MEU	Marine Expeditionary Unit
MLF	Multilateral Force
MHC	Marine Corps Historical Center
MHI	Military History Institute, United States Army
Mins	Minutes

MIRV	Multiple Independently Targetable Reentry Vehicles
MNC	Major NATO Commander
MOD	Ministry of Defense
MOLINK	Moscow-Washington Direct Communication Link
MRBM	Medium-Range Ballistic Missile
Msg	Message
Mtg	Meeting
NAC	North Atlantic Council
NASA	National Aeronautics and Space Administration
NATO	North Atlantic Treaty Organization
NDAC	Nuclear Defense Affairs Committee
NDU	National Defense University
NESA	Near East and South Asia
NIE	National Intelligence Estimate
NHC	U.S. Navy Historical Center
NMC	National Mobilization Committee
NMCC	National Military Command Center
NOA	New Obligational Authority
NPG	Nuclear Planning Group
NPWG	Nuclear Planning Working Group (NATO)
NSAM	National Security Action Memorandum
NPT	Nuclear Nonproliferation Treaty
NSC	National Security Council
NSF CF	National Security File Country File
NVA	North Vietnamese Army
O&M	Operations and Maintenance
OAS	Organization of American States
OASD	Office of the Assistant Secretary of Defense
OCI	Office of Current Intelligence, Central Intelligence Agency
OCMH	Office of the Chief of Military History
ODMA	Office of the Director, Military Assistance
OMB	Office of Management and Budget
OSD	Office of the Secretary of Defense
OST	Office of Science and Technology
PA	Public Affairs
PACOM	Pacific Command
PAVN	People's Army of Vietnam
PCD	Program Change Decision
PCP	Program Change Proposal
PDD	President's Daily Diary
PEMA	Procurement of Equipment and Munitions, Army
PPBS	Planning, Programming, Budgeting System

PL	Public Law
POL	Petroleum, Oil, and Lubricants
PRC	People's Republic of China
PRD	Dominican Revolutionary Party
Pres	President
PSAC	President's Scientific Advisory Committee
R&D	Research and Development
RDT&E	Research Development Testing & Evaluation
REDCOSTE	Reduction of Costs in Europe
REFORGER	Return of Forces to Germany
REP	Reserve Enlistment Program
RG	Record Group
ROK	Republic of Korea
S	U.S Senate
S&L	Supply and Logistics
SA	Systems Analysis
SAC	Strategic Air Command
SACEUR	Supreme Allied Commander, Europe
SACLANT	Supreme Allied Commander, Atlantic
SACNATO	Supreme Allied Commander, NATO
SALT	Strategic Arms Limitation Talks
SAM	Surface-to-Air Missile
SASC	Senate Armed Services Committee
SCAF	Sub-Committee on Administrative and Financial Matters
SCA	Senate Committee on Appropriations
SCAN	Office of Scandinavian Affairs, Department of State
SCAS	Senate Committee on Armed Services
SCF	Senate Committee on Finance
SCFR	Senate Committee on Foreign Relations
SEA	Southeast Asia
SEAPRO	Southeast Asia Programs Office
SEATO	Southeast Asia Treaty Organization
SecA	Secretary of the Army
SecAF	Secretary of the Air Force
SecDef	Secretary of Defense
SecN	Secretary of the Navy
SFRC	Senate Foreign Relations Committee
SHAPE	Supreme Headquarters Allied Powers, Europe
SIG	Senior Interdepartmental Group
SLBM	Submarine-Launched Ballistic Missile
SNDV	Strategic Nuclear Delivery Vehicle
SNIE	Special National Intelligence Estimate

S/P	Policy Planning Council, Department of State
SRAM	Short-Range Attack Missile
SRF	Selected Reserve Force
SSBN	Ballistic Missile Submarine (Nuclear Powered)
SSC	Senate Subcommittee
SSCA	Senate Subcommittee on Appropriations
SSN	Attack Submarine (Nuclear Powered)
STEP	Special Training and Enlistment Program
STRAF	Strategic Army Forces
Svc Secs	Service Secretaries
Telcon	Telephone Conversation
Test	Testimony
TFX	Tactical Fighter Experimental
Transc	Transcript
TOA	Total Obligational Authority
TTBT	Threshold Test Ban Treaty
UAR	United Arab Republic
UK	United Kingdom
UNC/USFK	United Nations Command/ U.S. Forces, Korea
UNEF	United Nations Emergency Force
UNSC	United Nations Security Council
UPI	United Press International
USAREUR	U.S. Army, Europe
USAMHI	U.S. Army Military History Institute
USCINCEUR	U.S. Commander in Chief European Command
USCINCMEAFSA	U.S. Commander in Chief Middle East, Africa South of the Sahara, and Southern Asia.
USCONARC	U.S. Continental Army Command
USEUCOM	U.S. European Command
USFK	U.S. Forces, Korea
USIB	United States Intelligence Board
USNMR	United States National Military Representatives
USUN	United States Mission at the United Nations
VC	Viet Cong
WH	White House
WHCF	White House Central Files
WRM	War Readiness Material
WSEG	Weapons Study and Evaluation Group

NOTES

Where no record group is specified in the citation, archival accessions are part of the Record Group (RG 330), retired records of the Office of the Secrtary of Defense. At the time they were consulted, these records were stored at the Washington National Records Center, Suitland, Maryland. Where record group numbers are given in the notes, it should be understood that the records are at the National Archives, College Park, Maryland. Files identified as "OSD Hist" are in the custody of the OSD Historical Office. Readers should consult the bibliography for complete information regarding the publisher and date of publication of printed works.

I. MOVERS AND SHAKERS

1. *DoD Annual Report for Fiscal Year 1965*, Tables 1, 382, 17, 400, 18, 401, 2, 383 and 3, 384; *DoD Annual Report for Fiscal Year 1968*, Tables 1, 498, 23, 522, 24, 523, 2, 499, and 10, 506.
2. *DoD Annual Report for Fiscal Year 1965*, 103 and Tables 19 and 20, 402-03; *DoD Annual Report for Fiscal Year 1968*, Table 26, 525.
3. Interv Robert E. Pursley by Alfred Goldberg and Roger Trask, 6 Sep 95, pt 1:18, OSD Hist.
4. White, "Revolution in the Pentagon," *Look*, 23 Apr 63, 31.
5. Interv Robert S. McNamara by Alfred Goldberg and Maurice Matloff, 3 Apr 86, 17, OSD Hist.
6. Interv Cyrus Vance by Paige E. Mulhollan, 3 Nov 69, 9-11, 13, Internet copy, LBJL.
7. McNamara interv, 3 Apr 86, 21 (quote); DoD Directive 5132.2, 20 May 61.
8. Halberstam, *Best and Brightest*, 364, 488; McMaster, *Dereliction of Duty*, 74; Shapley, *Promise and Power*, 303; Hughes, "Experiencing McNamara," *Foreign Policy*, Fall 95, 165 (quote).
9. DoD Directive 5118.3, 22 Mar 61.
10. DoD News Release 450-65, 7 Jul 65; memo DepSecDef for SvcSecs et al, 17 Sep 65, fldr Systems Analysis 1965-1969, box 614, Subj files, OSD Hist; DoD Directive 5141.1, 17 Sep 65; Cole et al, eds, *Department of Defense: Documents*, 239; Fuller, "Congress and the Defense Budget," Ph.D. diss., 72 (quote); Shapley, *Promise and Power*, 13; interv Henry Glass by Alfred Goldberg, Lawrence Kaplan, Robert Watson, and Maurice Matloff, 4 Nov 87, pt 4:10 (quote), OSD Hist.
11. Interv Alain Enthoven by Maurice Matloff, 3 Feb 86, 3, OSD Hist. In the interview, Enthoven described his organization as providing "independent, quantitative, systematic analyses of the costs versus effectiveness of alternative strategies and forces." Interv Paul H. Nitze by Roger Trask and Maurice Matloff, 9 Oct 84, 49 (quote), OSD Hist; George Elsey, notes of SecDef morning staff conf, 15 Nov 68 (quote), fldr VanDeMark Transcripts, box 1, Elsey Papers, LBJL.
12. Interv Harold Brown by Alfred Goldberg and Maurice Matloff, 20 Apr 90, 22-23, OSD Hist; Cole et al, eds, *Department of Defense: Documents*, 204-05.

13. Hewes, *From Root to McNamara*, 305; "Draft Administrative History of the Department of Defense, 1963-1969," 4:1361-62, OSD Hist; *New York Times*, 16 Jul 64; DoD News Release 518-64, 15 Jul 64; DoD Directive 5110.1, 11 Jul 64; interv Alfred Goldberg by Diane Putney, 14 Apr 03, 2-3, fldr Asst SecDef Admin 1961-69, box 609, Subj files, OSD Hist.

14. DoD Directive 5126.22, 30 Jan 61; Cole, et al, eds, *Department of Defense: Documents*, 239.

15. DoD Directives 5120.27, 31 Jan 61, 5120.27, 7 Jun 63, and 5120.36, 26 Jul 63; interv Thomas D. Morris by Alfred Goldberg and Maurice Matloff, 4 Jun 87, 25-26, OSD Hist; Ignatius, *On Board*, 82-83.

16. DoD Directive, 5122.5, 10 Jul 61; memo SecDef for SvcSecs, 21 Feb 64, fldr Public Affairs Organization 1961-68, box 613, Subj files, OSD Hist.

17. Interv Leonard Niederlehner by Alfred Goldberg and Maurice Matloff, 6 May 87, 1, 14.

18. DoD Directive 5148.5, 13 Nov 61.

19. DoD Directive 5148.2, 7 Jan 59.

20. Position Description, 2 Apr 64; OSD Historian, Office of Special Asst, 6 Jul 84, 8-9: fldr OSD Inner Office/Special Asst, 1961-69, box 606, Subj files, OSD Hist.

21. Interv Robert Pursley by Alfred Goldberg and Roger Trask, 6 Nov 97, 1, OSD Hist.

22. McNamara interv, 3 Apr 86, 10, 19.

23. *Baltimore Sun*, 7 Jul 65; Nitze interv, 9 Oct 84, 15, 18-20 (quote, 20); interv Harold Brown by Alfred Goldberg and Roger Trask, 4 Dec 81, 3 (quote), OSD Hist; interv Harold Brown by Alfred Goldberg and Maurice Matloff, 20 Apr 90, 22.

24. Watson, *Into the Missile Age*, 17-18 (quote); Trask and Goldberg, *Department of Defense 1947-1997*, 28.

25. Interv Harold K. Johnson by Col George H. Gray, 1 Aug 74, 18; Halberstam, *Best and the Brightest*, 555-59; Sorley, *Honorable Warrior*, 270.

26. Thompson, *To Hanoi and Back*, 22-23; McMaster, *Dereliction of Duty*, 223-24; interv John P. McConnell by Dorothy Pierce McSweeny, 28 Aug 69, 5, AC 79-71, LBJL.

27. "Reminiscences of Adm McDonald," U.S. Naval Institute, Nov 76, 5:388-91; "Reminiscences of Adm Moorer," Aug 75, 1:478 (quote); Jan 76, 2: 810, 859-60 (quote): NHC; Kennedy, "David Lamar McDonald," in Love, ed, *The Chiefs of Naval Operations*, 334, 349.

28. Memrcd CMC, 26 Jun 65, Greene Papers, MHC (quote); memos CMC for SecN, 17 Aug 67, Nitze for Pres, 16 Sep 67, ltr Wheeler to McNamara, 5 Sep 67 w/McNamara's marginalia: fldr DoD Personnel 1967, box 3CL, Nitze Papers, LC; tel interv Benis Frank by Edward Drea, 26 Feb 03; interv Leonard F. Chapman, Jr, by Benis Frank, 6 Apr 83, 7:44, MHC.

29. See for example McConnell interv, 28 Aug 69, I-7; McConnell, "Some Reflections," 4. McMaster develops these themes in *Dereliction of Duty*.

30. Interv Stephen Ailes by Maurice Matloff, 6 Jun 86, 22-23, OSD Hist; interv Earle G. Wheeler by Dorothy Pierce McSweeny, 21 Aug 69, 1, 12, AC 78-87, LBJL; McNamara interv, 3 Apr 86, 18 (quote).

31. Interv Roswell L. Gilpatric by Maurice Matloff, 14 Nov 83, 11, OSD Hist; Lt Col H. J. Lewis, Statistics of the JCS Organization, nd but after 30 Sep 67, fldr Special Files 1967, box 145, Wheeler Papers; Palmer, "US Intelligence and Vietnam," 32-33; McConnell interv, 28 Aug 69, I-8/9; Herring, *LBJ and Vietnam*, 29-30; McMaster, *Dereliction of Duty*, 225.

32. Ltr Taylor to McNamara, 1 Jul 64, *FRUS 1964-68*, 10:97, 101.

33. Memrcd Maxwell Taylor, mtg of JCS w/ Pres, 4 Mar 64, fldr Presidential Meetings, box 1, McNamara files, Acc 71A-3470; memo Bowman for M. Bundy, 6 Oct 64 (quote), fldr JCS (2 of 2), box 30, NSF Agency File, LBJL; memo Valenti for Pres, 14 Nov 64 (quotes), fldr FG 115-4 JCS, box 21, Confidential File FC 115 (1966), LBJL. See also McMaster, *Dereliction of Duty*, ch 9 on the JCS role and their dissatisfaction and exclusion from high-level councils. Memrcd James Thomson, White House mtg, 19 Nov 64, *FRUS 1964-68*, 1:916 (quote); memrcd CMC, special mtg of JCS, 7 Feb 65, Greene Papers.

34. Greene Diary, 230940 Aug 67, Greene Papers; McNamara interv, 3 Apr 86, 18 (quote).

35. Califano, *Triumph & Tragedy*, 10.

36. Clifford, *Counsel*, 386.

37. Humphrey, "Tuesday Lunch at the Johnson White House," 100 (quote); Trewhitt, *McNamara*, 17; Herring, *LBJ and Vietnam*, 45 (quote).

38. Johnson, *Vantage Point*, 366.

39. Humphrey, "NSC Meetings during the Johnson Presidency," 35-36, 40-41, 43 (quote); Smith, *Organizational History of NSC*, 57.

40. CMC notes of regular mtg of JCS at 1400, 15 Sep 65 (quote), Greene Papers; memrcd Gen Creighton W. Abrams, 20 Sep 65, *FRUS 1964-68*, 3:398; CM-2519-67 for JCS, 19 Jul 67, fldr 337 SecDef/JCS Meetings, box 102, Wheeler Papers.

41. These topics and dates are identified in SecDef Staff Meetings, fldrs Staff Meeting January-June and July-December 1965, box 12 and January-March 1966, box 13: Armed Forces Policy Council, Acc 77-0062.

42. Memrcd LtGen A. J. Goodpaster, 14 Dec 65, fldr Goodpaster Chron Files (Jan 65), Tab 105, box 141, Wheeler Papers.

43. Rearden, "Secretary of Defense and Foreign Affairs," Dec 95, V-14, Rearden files, OSD Hist.

44. Humphrey, "Tuesday Lunch," 88-89; Schoenbaum, *Waging Peace and War*, 414; Sharp, *Strategy for Defeat*, 86-87 (quote).

45. Interv Bromley Smith by Paige E. Mulhollan, 25 Sep 69, 1, 15-16, Internet copy, LBJL. Rusk believed the "sterile" minutes of the meeting lost the intensity of the times "we fought like dogs with each other." Interv Dean Rusk by Henry Brandon, 21 Feb 86, 6, fldr 3, box 20, Brandon Papers, LC; interv Robert McNamara by Walt Rostow, 8 Jan 75, 18 (quotes); interv Dean Rusk by Paige E. Mulhollan, 1, 28 Jul 69, 1:17-18, Internet copy, LBJL describes the Tuesday lunch; Dean Rusk, "A modest note to future archivists, historians, and other scholars:" 13 Jan 75 (quotes), transc Dean Rusk Oral History, 1, Internet copy, LBJL. Rusk's subsequent note accompanies the 28 July 1969 interview.

46. Bundy's remarks are cited in Humphrey, "Tuesday Lunch," 92; interv Benjamin H. Read by Paige E. Mulhollan, 13 Jan 69, 1:6, Internet copy, LBJL.

47. McDonald, "Reminiscences," 364, 387.

48. Interv Paul Warnke by Maurice Matloff and Roger Trask, 10 Sep 84, 12 (quote), OSD Hist; Hughes, "Experiencing McNamara," 171 (quote).

49. Interv Robert S. McNamara by Roger Trask and Maurice Matloff, 22 May 86, pt 2:20 (quote), OSD Hist; interv Robert S. McNamara by Alfred Goldberg, Lawrence Kaplan, and Maurice Matloff, 24 Jul 86, pt 3:19 (quotes), OSD Hist.

50. Memo LtGen Mock for CSA, 3 Jul 1966, w/atchmt Exercise of Power in the U.S. Government, 9 (quote), Demma Papers, CMH; Goulding, *Confirm or Deny*, 175-76.

51. Interv Lyndon Johnson by William Jorden, 12 Aug 69, 21 (quotes), AC 66-1, LBJL; Hughes, "Experiencing McNamara," 165 (quote); Ailes interv, 6 Jun 86, 15-16.

52. Interv Henry Glass by Alfred Goldberg, Lawrence Kaplan, Robert Watson, and Maurice Matloff, 28 Oct 87, pt 3:7, OSD Hist; interv David Packard by Alfred Goldberg and Maurice Matloff, 9 Nov 87, 5, ibid; Nitze interv, 9 Oct 84, 40.

53. Memo Keeny for M. Bundy, 5 Dec 64 (quote), fldr 1964, Strategic Arms, Johnson Library Papers, OSD Hist; Goulding, *Confirm or Deny*, 222. I base my description of the DPM on my paraphrasing and supplementing of Newhouse, *Cold Dawn*, 82 (quote). See also "Putting Together the Defense Department's Budget," nd, likely 1968, fldr #3, box 11, Enthoven Papers, LBJL.

II. VIETNAM: ESCALATION WITHOUT MOBILIZATION

1. Draft memo McNaughton for McNamara, 27 Jan 65, Gravel ed, *Pentagon Papers*, 3:686-87; memo Bundy for Pres, 27 Jan 65, memo Bundy for Pres, 7 Feb 65: *FRUS 1964-68*, 2:95-97, 175; *JCS and the War in Vietnam*, pt 2:17/17-19. On the Pleiku attack see Kaplan et al, *McNamara Ascendancy*, 529.

2. CMC notes on JCS mtg, No 28, 8 Feb 65, Greene Papers, MHC; *JCS and the War in Vietnam*, pt 2:18/6-8; ed note and JCSM-100-65 for SecDef, 11 Feb 65, *FRUS 1964-68*, 2:212, 240-42.

3. ACMC notes on SecDef staff mtg, 15 Feb 65, Greene Papers; *JCS and the War in Vietnam*, pt 2:19/2.

4. McNamara, *In Retrospect*, 172; Herring, *LBJ and Vietnam*, 47-48; notes on cong leadership mtg, 10 Feb 65, memo Bundy for Pres, 16 Feb 65, memo Goodpaster, mtg w/Pres, 17 Feb 65, *FRUS 1964-68*, 2:225-26, 283, 298-308.

5. Msg 473 Taylor to JCS, 22 Feb 65, msg MAC JOO 5633 MACV to CINCPAC, 23 Feb 65, msg JCS 736-65 CJCS to CINCPAC, 27 Feb 65, msg DEF 6181 OSD to Saigon, 2 Mar 65: *FRUS 1964-68*, 2:347-49 (quote), 351, 380-81, 395.

6. Van Staaveren, *Gradual Failure*, 80-83; msg DEF 6181 OSD to Saigon, 2 Mar 65, msg JCS 736-65 CJCS to CINCPAC, 27 Feb 65, memo Bundy for Pres, 6 Mar 65, msg MAC 1190 MACV to CJCS, 6 Mar 65: *FRUS 1964-68*, 2:395 (quote), 380, 402, 400-01; memo SecDef to CJCS et al, 1 Mar 65, memo SecDef to SvcSecs and JCS, 1 Mar 65: fldr Official Correspondence Army Chief of Staff, Close Hold, box 76, H. K. Johnson Papers, MHI; Janicik, "Southeast Asia Force Deployments Buildup" (hereafter "Buildup"), pt 1, 1965, Critical Incident No. 13, IDA Report R-137, Mar 68, 37, box 246, Subj files, OSD Hist.

7. Memo Bundy for Pres, 6 Mar 65, *FRUS 1964-68*, 2:402-05 (quote); telcon McNamara and Pres, 1 Mar 65, Tape WH6503.01, # 3, LBJL; memrcd CMC, special mtg of JCS, No 27, 7 Feb 65, Greene Papers.

8. McNamara, *In Retrospect*, 173-74; Berman, *Planning a Tragedy*, 146. A succinct summary of the world view of senior U.S. leaders may be found in Dallek, "Presidential Address," 148-49.

9. Telcon McNamara and Pres, 6 Mar 65, Tape WH6503.03, # 3, LBJL; see also Beschloss, *Reaching for Glory*, 213-16 for another version of the conversation.

10. For McNaughton's pre-visit assessment see dft memo, 2 Mar 65, *FRUS 1964-68*, 2:390-92; for his post-visit views see ASD(ISA) paper, 10 Mar 65, ibid, 2:427; Bundy mtg notes, 9 Mar 65 (quotes), box 3, McGeorge Bundy Papers, LBJL.

11. Bundy mtg notes, 10 Mar 65, box 3, Bundy Papers. McNamara's interpretation appears in transc McNamara classified test, 11 Mar 65, HCFA, *Hearings on Foreign Assistance Act of 1965* (Excerpts), fldr Vietnam 1965, 311 (quotes), 319-20, box 31, SecDef Bio files, OSD Hist.

12. Bundy, mtg notes, 10 Mar 65, cited in note 11 (quote); memo CSA for SecDef et al, 14 Mar 65 (quote), fldr Viet 333 Johnson 65, box 6, SecDef Subject Decimal files, Acc 70A-1265; Johnson Report Outline, 14 Mar 65, *FRUS 1964-68*, 2:438-39.

13. The president had used this turn of phrase earlier in telcon McNamara and Pres, 26 Feb 65, in Beschloss, *Reaching for Glory*, 194 (quote); memrcd CMC, mtg JCS w/Pres at White House on South Vietnam, 15 Mar 65, 19 Mar 65, Greene Papers (quote).

14. Memrcd CMC, 15 Mar 65 (quote), cited in note 13; CMC notes on regular JCS mtg, No 40, 15 Mar 65, msg JCS 0936-65 Wheeler to Sharp and Westmoreland, 16 Mar 65: Greene Papers; Bundy mtg notes, 16 Mar 65, box 3, Bundy Papers.

15. *JCS and the War in Vietnam*, pt 2:18/21, 19/10-14; CMC work notes, JCS mtg, No 41, 17 Mar 65 (quotes), msgs JCS 0936 Wheeler to Sharp and Westmoreland, 16 Mar 65, 180840Z CINCPAC to JCS, 18 Mar 65, 171825Z Westmoreland to Wheeler, 17 Mar 65: Greene Papers; Janicik, "Buildup," 45-47; Schlight, *Years of the Offensive*, 23; JCSM-204-65 for SecDef, 20 Mar 65, *FRUS 1964-68*, 2:466-67.

16. Ed note, *FRUS 1964-68*, 2:473.

17. Smith summary notes of 550th NSC mtg, 26 Mar 65, ibid, 482-86 (quote, 484).

18. Msg 2131 State to Saigon, 30 Mar 65, memrcd McCone, disc w/AmbTaylor, 31 Mar 65, ibid, 2:492-93, 498; Heath Bottomly note to Control Div, mtg of JCS and SecDef w/Amb Taylor, 29 Mar 65, fldr Vietnam 091 March 1965, box 44, Wheeler Papers (quote, 6); comments on the state of logistic support are found in *JCS and the War in Vietnam*, pt 2:ch 20; memo Goodpaster for Wheeler, 3 Apr 65, fldr Goodpaster Chron files (Jan 1965) TAB 137, box 141, Wheeler Papers. On North Vietnamese troops see Moyar, *Triumph Foresaken*, 370; USIB Watch Rpt, 7 Apr 65 and DIA Intel Bull, 68-65, 8 Apr 65, both fldr Vietnam INSS Jan-Jun 1965, box 329, Subj files, OSD Hist. A CIA-DIA joint memorandum dated 21 April 1965 confirmed the presence of the 325th People's Army of Vietnam (PAVN) Division in South Vietnam's central highlands; see *Pentagon Papers*, bk 4, IV.C.5, 46-47.

19. Memos Bundy for Pres, 31 Mar 65, 1 Apr 65, *FRUS 1964-68*, 2:500, 509. The 1 April memo noted McNamara's recommendation to defer the three-division decision pending further review after 60 days. Bundy personal notes of a mtg w/Pres, 1 Apr 65, ibid, 2:511-12 (quote).

20. Memo DirCIA for DepDir, 1 Apr 65, *FRUS 1964-68*, 2:513-14 is McCone's account of the above meeting with the president. The JCS version of the 1 April meeting is available in msg JCS 1181-65 to COMUSMACV and CINCPAC, 3 Apr 65, Eyes Only Message File 1 Apr-30 Jun 65, Westmoreland Papers, CMH; McNamara, *In Retrospect*, 179; Cooper summary notes of 551st NSC mtg, 2 Apr 1965, memrcd DirCIA, 2 Apr 65, NSAM No 328, 6 Apr 65: *FRUS 1964-68*, 2:514-16, 517-18, 539, (quote).

21. Kim, "The Making of Tigers," 159-62; Kim, "The U.S.-Korean Alliance in the Vietnam War," 156-59; msg 2131 State to Saigon, 30 Mar 65 and NSAM No 328, 6 Apr 65: *FRUS, 1964-68*, 2:493, 538; memcon mtg Brown and Park, 19 Dec 64 and memcon mtg Johnson and Park, 17 May 65: ibid, 29:53-54, 97-98.

22. *Johnson Public Papers*, 1965, 1:394-97; Westmoreland, *Soldier Reports*, 135-36.

23. Trewhitt, *McNamara*, 202 (quote); Hilsman, *To Move a Nation*, 43 (quote); Herring, *LBJ and Vietnam*, 37-38; McNamara, *In Retrospect*, 182; Jack Raymond in *New York Times*, 11 Apr 65; memo Moyers for Pres, 30 Sep 66, *FRUS 1964-68*, 4:677-78 (quote).

24. Msg JCS 1181-65 to COMUSMACV, 3 Apr 65, cited in note 20; Janicik, "Buildup," 59, 61; msg 3384 Saigon to State, 14 Apr 65, *FRUS 1964-68*, 2:554-55; msg JCS 008528 to CINCPAC, 6 Apr 65, Cable files, OSD Hist; memo SecDef for CJCS, 5 Apr 65 (quote), fldr Vietnam 370 (Apr-Jun 65), box 6, SecDef Subject Decimal files; *JCS and the War in Vietnam*, pt 2: 21/3-4; William P. Bundy, "History of Vietnam," ms (hereafter Bundy ms), ch 25/2, OSD Hist. On the DRV's negative response to the president's 7 April speech, see *Washington Post*, 12 Apr 65.

25. Commander's Estimate of Military Situation in South Vietnam, 26 Mar 65, 6, fldr MACV Cmdrs Estimate, box 7, SecDef Subject Decimal files, Acc 70A-1265; msg 121530Z COMUSMACV to CINCPAC, 12 Apr 65, Eyes Only files 1 Apr-30 Jun 65, Westmoreland Papers; memrcd CMC, conf w/Pres, 8 Apr 65, Greene Papers (quotes).

26. Memrcd CMC, JCS conf w/Pres, 13 Apr 65, Greene Papers; Janicik, "Buildup," 67-68.

27. Ed note, *FRUS 1964-68*, 2:553-54.

28. Jt State-Def msg DEF 9164 DoD to Saigon, CINCPAC, COMUSMACV, 15 Apr 65, ibid, 561-62.

29. VanDeMark, *Quagmire*, 125; msg 3421 Saigon to State (quote), msg 3423 Saigon to State, msg 3424 Saigon to State, msg 3432 Saigon to State, msg CAP 65120 White House to Saigon, all 17 Apr 65: *FRUS, 1964-68*, 2:563-71 and 571, n 2 (quote).

30. *JCS and the War in Vietnam*, pt 2:21/6, 8-9, 16; msg JCS 00913 to CINCPAC et al, 17 Apr 65, SecDef Cable files; Janicik, "Buildup," 73.

31. VanDeMark, *Quagmire*, 125-27; diary entry by Taylor, 20 Apr 65, memo SecDef for Pres, 21 Apr 65: *FRUS 1964-68*, 2:573, 574-76; *JCS and the War in Vietnam*, pt 2:21/16. Taylor believed it would take months, not years, to achieve a favorable settlement: see msg 3504 Saigon to State (Eyes only for McNamara), 24 Apr 65, *FRUS 1964-68*, 2:605-06; Janicik, "Buildup," 74.

32. Memrcds McCone, 21, 22 Apr 65, Board of National Estimates, Intelligence Memorandum, 21 Apr 65, memo Ball for Pres, nd: *FRUS 1964-68*, 2:578-81 (quote, 580), 597-600, 595 (quote, emphasis in original), 583. Ball's memo was attached to a covering memo Ball for Pres, 21 Apr 65, ibid, 582. A copy of the intelligence memo was sent to the White House on the morning of 22 April for study before the afternoon gathering. Colby, *Lost Victory*, 182.

33. Memrcd McCone, 22 Apr 65, msg 2397 State to Saigon, 22 Apr 65 (quotes): *FRUS 1964-68*, 2:599, 602-03; VanDeMark, *Quagmire*, 130; Janicik, "Buildup," 74-75; Dallek, *Flawed Giant*, 268-69.

34. SecDef news conf, 26 Apr 65, *McNamara Public Statements, 1965*, 4:1505-09; excerpts from memrcd Mc-Giffert, SecDef conv w/Cong Rivers et al, 28 Apr 65, SecDef brf on SVN and Dom Rep for SCAS, 29 Apr 65, 449, 451, 456: fldr Vietnam 1965, box 31, SecDef Bio files, OSD Hist.

35. Msg 2397 State to Saigon, 22 Apr 65, msgs 3552 and 3559 Saigon to State, 27, 28 Apr 65: *FRUS 1964-68*, 2:602, 609-13; McNaughton, Possible 'Pause' Scenario, 25 Apr 65 (2d draft), fldr Memos 4/21-30/65, vol 33, box 16, NSF, CF Vietnam, LBJL; McMaster, *Dereliction of Duty*, 283. A bombing pause code-named Mayflower did begin on 12 May, Washington time. JCSM-321-65 for SecDef, 30 Apr 65, fldr VN 370 (Jun-Sep 65), box 6, SecDef Subject Decimal files, Acc 70A-1265; *JCS and the War in Vietnam*, pt 2:21/17-18; Janicik, "Buildup," 75.

36. Memos ISA for SecDef, 13 May 65, SecDef for CJCS, 15 May 65 (quote), fldr VN 370 (Jun-Sep 65), box 6, SecDef Subject Decimal files, Acc 70A-1265; jt State-Def msg DEF 1097, DoD to Saigon, 30 Apr 65, *FRUS 1964-68*, 2:615-16; *JCS and the War in Vietnam*, 2:21/18-19.

37. Bundy ms, ch 25/18-19; *Johnson Presidential Papers, 1965*, 1:494-95; *AFP, CD, 1965*, 868.

38. Gravel ed, *Pentagon Papers*, 3:438-39; msg 4074 Saigon to State, 5 Jun 65, memo Bundy for Pres, 5 Jun 65, msg MAC JOO 19118 COMUSMACV to JCS 7 Jun 65: *FRUS 1964-68*, 2:722-24, 724-25, 735. The troop strength figures appear in Smith summary notes of 552d NSC mtg, 11 Jun 65, ibid, 758; VanDe-Mark, *Quagmire*, 151; McNamara, *In Retrospect*, 187-88 (quotes).

39. Bundy personal notes of mtg w/Pres, 10 Jun 65, memrcd Helms, Cabinet Room mtg on Vietnam, 8 Jun 65: *FRUS 1964-68*, 2:745-49 (quote, 746, emphasis in original), 739-41; Janicik, "Buildup," 87, 90; Van Staaveren, *Gradual Failure*, 150; McNamara's account is found in *In Retrospect*, 188-89; Bundy ms, ch 26/10-15; telcon McNamara and Pres, 10 Jun 65, Beschloss, *Reaching for Glory*, 348-50.

40. JCSM-457-65 for SecDef, 11 Jun 65, *FRUS 1964-68*, 2:754-56. The appendix is in fldr Deployment of Major U.S. Forces to Vietnam, July 1965, vol 6, box 42, NSF, NSC History, LBJL; Janicik, "Buildup," 91; Smith summary notes of the 552d NSC mtg, 11 Jun 65, diary entry Taylor, 7-12 Jun 65, Bundy personal notes of mtg w/Pres, 10 Jun 65: *FRUS 1964-68*, 2:758-59, 737, 746.

41. SecDef press conf, 16 Jun 65, *McNamara Public Statements, 1965*, 5:1793-94; telcon McNamara and Pres, 16 Jun 65, Beschloss, *Reaching for Glory*, 357-58; *Johnson Public Papers*, 1965, 2:680.

42. Smith summary notes of 552d NSC mtg, cited in n 38; VanDeMark, *Quagmire*, 162; Bundy ms, ch 26/ 9 and 15A; telcon Pres and McNamara, 21 Jun 65, Beschloss, *Reaching for Glory*, 365 (quote).

43. Msg MAC JOO 20055 COMUSMACV to CINCPAC 13 Jun 65, memo Bundy for Pres, 24 Jul 65 w/ encl: *FRUS 1964-68*, 3:1-5, 233, 235; *AFP, CD, 1965*, 880, n 59; *Washington Post*, 14, 15 Jun 65; Janicik, "Buildup," 95-96; Deployments to Viet Nam Since 1 Jan 1965, 26 Jul 65, fldr Southeast Asia Deployments-FY 1966, box 96, ASD(C) files, OSD Hist; Bundy, draft NSAM, 19 Jun 65, fldr Defense, Dept. of, vol 3 6/65, box 11, NSF Agency File, LBJL; Gravel ed, *Pentagon Papers*, 3:476.

44. VanDeMark, *Quagmire*, 163-64; memo Bundy for Pres, 30 Jun 65, *FRUS 1964-68*, 3:84; mins of Cabinet mtg, 18 Jun 65, 43, 52-53, box 3, Cabinet Papers File, LBJL; excerpts from McNamara test, 28 Jan 66, HCA on suppl approp for FY 66, fldr Vietnam 1966, 390, box 32, SecDef Bio files, OSD Hist.

45. Joseph Alsop in *Washington Post*, 18 Jun 65 (quote); Neil Swanson in *Baltimore News-American*, 20 Jun 65 (quotes); Bundy, draft NSAM, 19 Jun 65, cited in note 43; Dallek, *Flawed Giant*, 271.

46. Memo Ball for Pres, 18 Jun 65, memrcd Helms, mtg in the Cabinet Room, 23 Jun 65, ed note: *FRUS 1964-68*, 3:16-21, 39-40, 40-41; Bundy ms, ch 26/22-25.

47. CMC notes on regular mtg of JCS, No 62, 25 Jun 65, Greene Papers (quote); memrcd CMC, "Observations," 26 Jun 65, Greene Papers (quotes); Van Staaveren, *Gradual Failure*, 153 (quotes).

48. McNamara, *In Retrospect*, 193-94; McNaughton, 6-Month Program of Expanded Military and Political Moves with Respect to Vietnam, 3d draft, 24 Jun 65, fldr June 1965, box 6, Gibbons Papers, LBJL; memo SecDef for Pres, 1 Jul 65, *FRUS 1964-68*, 3:97-104. On 24 June Westmoreland informed Wheeler "the struggle has become a war of attrition" that he saw no likelihood of ending quickly; see msg MAC 3240 Westmoreland to Wheeler, 24 Jun 65, ibid, 3:42; Westmoreland, *Soldier Reports*, 140-41.

49. Memo Bundy for Pres, 30 Jun 65, msg 4422 Saigon to State, 29 Jun 65: *FRUS 1964-68*, 3:90 (quote), 71 (quote); McNamara, *In Retrospect*, 194; Bundy mtg notes, 29 Jun 65, box 3, Bundy Papers; *New York Times*, 2 Jul 65.

50. CMC notes on regular mtg of JCS, No 63, 28 Jun 65 (quote), CMC notes on regular mtg of JCS, No 64, 2 Jul 65: Greene Papers; Janicik, "Buildup," 101; JCSM-515-65 for SecDef, 2 Jul 65, fldr VN 370 Jul-Sep 65, box 6, SecDef Subject Decimal files, Acc 70A-1265; Cosmas, *MACV: Years of Escalation*, 310.

51. Memo SecDef for Pres, 1 Jul 65, *FRUS 1964-68*, 3:97-104 (quote, 102); Janicik, "Evolution of Missions for US Land Forces (March 1965-July 1966)," Dec 68, 13, IDA Document TS/HQ 68-235, box 4, ISA General files, Acc 72A-1499.

52. Two memos Bundy for Pres, 1 Jul 65, *FRUS 1964-68*, 3:115-16, 117-18; telcon Pres and McNamara, 2 Jul 65, Beschloss, *Reaching for Glory*, 381-82 (quote). McNamara, *In Retrospect*, 200-01 errs in dating this phone conversation 14 July. He relied on the date as 7/14/65 listed on the tape, but archivists at the Johnson Library determined the actual date and time as 7/2/65, 8:41 a.m.

53. McNamara, *In Retrospect*, 195 (quote); Rusk, Vietnam, 1 Jul 65, Ball, A Compromise Solution for South Viet-Nam, nd, W. Bundy, A 'Middle Way' Course of Action in South Vietnam, 1 Jul 65, ed note, msg CAP 65799 Bundy to Pres, 3 Dec 65: *FRUS 1964-68*, 3:104-115, 118-19, 594-97 (quote, 596); Bundy ms, ch 27/13. The president's priorities are noted in Beschloss, *Reaching for Glory*, 384, n 2.

54. McNamara, *In Retrospect*, 202; JCSM-515-65 for SecDef, 2 Jul 65, cited in n 50; msgs JCS 2400-65 Wheeler to Sharp and Westmoreland, 29 Jun 65, 300100Z Sharp to Westmoreland and Emrick, 30 Jun 65: Westmoreland Papers; msg MAC 3320 Westmoreland to Wheeler, 30 Jun 65, *FRUS 1964-68*, 3:76; quote cited in CRS, *U.S. Government and the Vietnam War*, pt 3:357.

55. Memo McNaughton for Goodpaster, 2 Jul 65 (quote), fldr Vietnam July 1965, box 45, Wheeler Papers (also in *Pentagon Papers*, bk 5, IV.C.6, 1-4); memrcd CMC, mtg w/SecDef, 10 Jul 65, Greene Papers; see also McMaster, *Dereliction of Duty*, 306-07.

56. Memo Friedman for Vance, 5 Jul 1965 w/atchmt, 29 Jun 65, fldr Vietnam Buildup Mat'l to SecDef, Phase I, 22 Jul 1965, box 94, ASD(C) files, OSD Hist. This synthesis of the intelligence appreciations was prepared for Vance as a background paper for the July Foreign Policy Advisors' meeting.

57. Msg Def 5319 DoD to Saigon, 7 Jul 65, *FRUS 1964-68*, 3:134-37; memrcd McNaughton, SecDef mtg, 9 Jul 65, fldr Jun-Aug 1965, Vietnam Buildup, box 94, ASD(C) files, OSD Hist; CMC notes on regular mtg of JCS, No 67, 9 Jul 65, CMC notes on JCS/SecDef mtg, No 68, 10 Jul 65: Greene Papers.

58. Memrcd McNaughton, 9 Jul 65, CMC notes, 10 Jul 65: both cited in note 57.

59. Interv Henry Glass by Alfred Goldberg et al, 4 Nov 87, pt 4:12 (quote), OSD Hist; CMC, notes, 10 Jul 65 (quotes), cited in note 57.

60. Memrcds Sylvester, SecDef mtg, 12 Jul 65, and 63 Battalion Plan, 12 Jul 65: fldr Jan-Aug 1965, Vietnam Buildup, box 94, ASD(C) files, OSD Hist; memrcd DepSecDef, 13 Jul 65, fldr Vance (Jul 65) box 1, Vance Papers, Acc 69A 2317; ltr SecDef to Stennis, 14 Jul 65, fldr Vietnam 1965, 637-38, box 31, SecDef Bio files, OSD Hist.

61. McNaughton, Analysis and Options for South Vietnam, 1st draft, 13 Jul 65, Notebook, Compilation of Data assembled by Sec McNamara for and during his July 1965 Trip to Vietnam, box 7, SecDef Subject Decimal files, Acc 70A-1265.

62. CM-744-65 for JCS, 14 Jul 65 w/atchd Report of the Ad Hoc Study Group, "Intensification of the Military Operations in Vietnam: Concept and Appraisal," ii, iv, vii, G-3, H-6, I-1, fldr Vietnam Buildup Material to SecDef, Phase I, 22 Jul 1965, box 94, ASD(C) files, OSD Hist; CRS, *U.S. Government and the Vietnam War*, pt 3:364 (quote). McMaster, *Dereliction of Duty*, 307-08; memo Bowman for Bundy, 21 Jul 65 w/ atchmt, 14 Jul 65, *FRUS 1964-68*, 3:181-87(quote, 185).

63. Memrcd Greenleaf, SVN mtg, 15 Jul 65, memrcd Greenleaf, SVN follow-on mtg #2, 16 Jul 65, memo Goulding, ActASD(PA) for DirInfoServices, 16 Jul 65, memo DepSecDef for SecA, 16 Jul 65: fldr Jul-Aug 1965, Vietnam Buildup, box 94, ASD(C) files, OSD Hist. Vance issued similar appropriate guidance to the

other service secretaries. The draft statement was cabled to Saigon in msg 180001Z Vance to McNamara, 18 Jul 65, fldr Viet 350.00 1965, box 6, SecDef Subject Decimal files, Acc 70A-1265; tab A to JCSM-515-65, 2 Jul 65, cited in note 50.

64. Msg 172042Z Vance to McNamara in Saigon, 17 Jul 65, *FRUS 1964-68*, 3:162-63.

65. Memrcds Greenleaf, SVN follow-on mtg #3, 17 Jul 65, Part I:0935-1025 Hours, Part 2: 1025-1050 Hours, SVN follow-on mtg #4, 19 Jul 65: fldr Jul-Aug 1965, Vietnam Buildup, box 94, ASD(C) files, OSD Hist.

66. Memrcd Greenleaf, SVN follow-on mtg #5, 19 Jul 65 (quote), memo McGiffert for Vance, 20 Jul 65: ibid.

67. Memo Hitch for SecDef, 20 Jul 65 w/atchmt FY 1966 Suppl Estimates, Plan I, nd, memo ActGenCoun for DepSecDef, 20 Jul 65: fldr Vietnam Buildup Material to SecDef, 21 Jul 1965: ibid. Information on the Army's projected share of the call-up is found in Adds-ons to Army Force Structure, 15 Jul 1965, fldr Vietnam Buildup Material to SecDef, 23 July Phase II, ibid; Glass, The President's Report to the Nation on the Situation in Southeast Asia, 2d draft, 15 Jul 65, fldr Jul-Aug 1965, Vietnam Buildup, ibid.

68. Ltr Vance to W. Bundy, 15 Jul 65 w/atchmt draft memo for DirCIA, nd, fldr Vance Jul 65, box 1, Vance files, Acc 69A 2317; memo SecState for DirCIA, 16 Jul 65, CIA, SNIE 10-9-65, Communist and Free World Reactions to a Possible US Course of Action, 20 Jul 65 (quote, 12): fldr Deployment of Major U.S. Forces to Vietnam, July 1965, vol 6, box 43, NSF, NSC History, LBJL.

69. McNamara, *In Retrospect*, 201 (quote), 203; McNamara Questions-Taylor Answers, Tab A (quote), fldr McNamara Vietnam Trip 16-20 Jul 65, box 246, Subj files, OSD Hist; Comparative Casualties Southeast Asia, fldr Vietnam Statistics-Casualties, 6 Feb 74, box 327, ibid.

70. McNamara Questions-Taylor Answers, cited in note 69.

71. Memcon, mtg w/GVN on 16 Jul 65, *FRUS 1964-68*, 3:153-62. The account was drafted on 24 July and subsequently transmitted to State on 27 July.

72. Memo Krulak for Greene, 2 Aug 65 w/atchmt MACV ACS J-3 briefing for SecDef and Party, 16-17 Jul 65, Greene Papers; *JCS and the War in Vietnam*, pt 2:22/6-7; Janicik, "Buildup," 112-13; memo Westmoreland for SecDef, 20 Jul 65 (quote), fldr McNamara Vietnam Trip 16-20 Jul 65, box 246, Subj files, OSD Hist.

73. Memo SecDef for Pres, 20 Jul 65, *FRUS 1964-68*, 3:171-79; McNamara, *In Retrospect*, 204.

74. Memo Bundy for Pres, 19 Jul 65, *FRUS 1964-68*, 3:166 (quote); Johnson, *Vantage Point*, 146-48.

75. Accounts of the meetings are available in Valenti notes of mtg, 21 Jul 65 and memrcd Cooper, mtgs on Vietnam, 21 Jul 65: *FRUS 1964-68*, 3:189-97, 197-204.

76. Valenti notes of mtg, 22 Jul 65, noon-2:15 p.m., ibid (quotes, 212, 215).

77. Valenti notes of mtg, 22 Jul 65, 3-4:20 p.m., ibid, 218; memrcd CMC, Conf on SEA at White House, 22 Jul 65, Greene Papers; CRS, *U.S. Government and the Vietnam War*, pt 3:414; memrcds Glass, 23 Jul 65, Glass (?), Projects assigned by Secretary via Hitch (Glass), nd but after 24 Jul 65; memos Comptr for SecA, 22 Jul 65, Comptr for SecN, 22 Jul 65: fldr Projects for SecDef-Vietnam Buildup, and memo SecA for SecDef, Army Alternative Plan for Buildup, w/encl 1 to Tab A, 23 Jul 65, fldr Vietnam Buildup Material to SecDef, 23 Jul Phase II: box 94, ASD(C) files, OSD Hist.

78. CRS, *U.S. Government and the Vietnam War*, pt 3:414-15; memrcd CMC, 24 Jul 65, w/atchmt, McNamara, Plan 3, 24 Jul 65, Greene Papers; memo Bundy for Pres, 24 Jul 65 w/encl, *FRUS 1964-68*, 3:236.

79. Msg Vance to McNamara in Vietnam, 17 Jul 65, *FRUS 1964-68*, 3:162-63 (quote); Johnson, *Vantage Point*, 149, (quote as stated by the president at the 27 July NSC meeting). Smith summary notes of 553d NSC mtg, 27 Jul 65, *FRUS 1964-68*, 3:260-63; Bundy ms, 30/9-10; McNamara interv, 22 May 86, pt 2:19-20, OSD Hist (quotes); interv Stephen Ailes by Maurice Matloff, 2 Jul 86, pt 2:17 (quotes); telcon Pres and Russell, 26 Jul 65, in Beschloss, *Reaching for Glory*, 409-10 (quotes).

80. Johnson, *Vantage Point*, 146-47; Shapley, *Promise and Power*, 346; McNamara, *In Retrospect*, 205. McGeorge Bundy, at presidential direction, had rewritten his memo on July 23; memo Bundy for Pres, 19 Jul 65, *FRUS 1964-68*, 3:165 and n1; Berman, *Planning a Tragedy*, 147-48.

81. Memo Comptr for SvcSecs, 23 Jul 65, fldr Projects for SecDef-Vietnam Buildup, memos SecA for SecDef 24 Jul 65, CMC for SecN, nd: fldr Vietnam Buildup Material to SecDef, 23 July Phase II: box 94, ASD(C) files, OSD Hist; memrcd Glass (?), nd but after 24 Jul 65, cited in note 77; memrcd CMC, mtg w/SecN 1930 on 23 Jul 65, Greene Papers (quotes).

82. Memrcd CMC, JCS mtg w/SecDef, 24 Jul 65, Greene Papers (quotes); interv Harold K. Johnson by Col George H. Gray, 1 Aug 74, 12-13 (quote), Senior Officer Oral History Program, MHI.

83. Two memos Paul for SecDef, 26 Jul 65 and Increased Readiness for Selected Reserve Component Units, nd: fldr Vietnam Buildup Material to SecDef, 24 July Phase 3, box 94, ASD(C) files, OSD Hist.

84. Ltr Clifford to Pres, 17 May 65, *FRUS 1964-68*, 2:672 (quote); Valenti notes of mtg, 25 Jul 65, ibid, 3:238; Beschloss, *Reaching for Glory*, 406; Clifford, *Counsel*, 420.

85. Smith summary notes, 27 Jul 65, cited in n 79, 262 (quote); Johnson, *Vantage Point*, 149 (quotes); McMaster, *Dereliction of Duty*, 318-19.

86. Memo Bundy, mtg w/jt cong leadership, 27 Jul 65, *FRUS 1964-68*, 3:264-69.

87. Smith summary notes, cited in note 79, 261; memo Bundy, cited in note 86, 266; memo Blouin, DirFarEastProgram(ISA) for McNaughton, 24 Jul 65 w/atchmt Additional Deployment Requirements from MACV Shopping List, 24 Jul 65, fldr Vietnam 381, box 63, Pentagon Papers Backup, Acc 330-75-062; DPM SecDef for Pres, Recommended FY 1966 SEA Supplemental Appropriation, 11 Dec 65, fldr Memos for Pres CY 1965 Budget FY 1967, box 119, ASD(C) files, OSD Hist; Janicik, "Buildup," 115; memrcd CMC, mtg w/SecN on 23 Jul 65, cited in note 81.

88. *Johnson Public Papers, 1965*, 2:794-97.

89. JCSM-590-65 for SecDef, 30 Jul 65, fldr Vietnam 381, box 63, Pentagon Papers Backup, Acc 330-75-062; *JCS and the War in Vietnam*, pt 2:22/8-9; JCSM-643-65 for SecDef, 23 Aug 65 as excerpted in US Deployments and Force Levels, RVN, 26 Aug 65, memo ISA for SecDef, 20 Aug 65: fldr VN 370 Jul-Sep 65, box 6, SecDef Subject Decimal files, Acc 70A-1265; memo SecDef for Pres, 1 Sep 65, *FRUS 1964-68*, 3:366.

90. Memos SecDef for Pres, 22 Sep 65, Smith for Bundy, 24 Sep 65, memrcd Califano, luncheon mtg w/Pres, 29 Sep 65, *FRUS 1964-68*, 3:411-12 (quote, 412), 417, 419-20 (quote, 419).

91. Draft memo Bundy for Pres, 25 May 64, *FRUS 1964-68*, 1:377 (quote); McMaster, *Dereliction of Duty*, 327; Herring, *LBJ and Vietnam*, 4-6, 34.

92. Interv Eugene M. Zuckert by Alfred Goldberg and Maurice Matloff, 10 Oct 84, 36, OSD Hist (quote); on protecting the president, see Shapley, *Promise and Power*, 234.

93. See for example memo Mansfield for Pres, 27 Jul 65, *FRUS 1964-68*, 3:270-72; memo SecDef for Pres, 28 Jul 65, McNamara background briefing for Pres, 28 Jul 65: fldr Vietnam 1965, 668, box 31, SecDef Bio files, OSD Hist; Trewhitt, *McNamara*, 237-38.

94. McNamara, *In Retrospect*, 198.

95. In press conferences and interviews during the second half of 1965, McNamara readily reported the number of troops deployed in Vietnam. For example, on 16 September he said there were 120,000 there; on 30 September, he reported 130,000; on 13 October, 140,000; and in mid-November, 160,000 on the ground and 50,000 in the Navy offshore. See *McNamara Public Statements, 1965*, 5:2062, 2076, 2101, 2149, 2194.

III. THE AIR WAR AGAINST NORTH VIETNAM, 1965–1966

1. Ford, *CIA and Vietnam Policymakers*, 68; ed note, paper prepared by NSC working grp, 21 Nov 64, McNaughton notes on mtg, 1 Dec 64, paper prepared by ExCom, 2 Dec 64, msg CAP 64375 Pres for Taylor, 30 Dec 64: *FRUS 1963-68*, 1:866-88, 920, 968, 970, 1057-58; summary notes of 547th NSC mtg, 8 Feb 65, ibid, 2:189; Gravel ed, *Pentagon Papers*, 3:239.

2. Herring, *LBJ and Vietnam*, 5, 39; McNamara, *In Retrospect*, 160; memo McNaughton for SecDef, 23 Jan 66, doc #73, fldr McNTN II—Drafts 1966(3), John McNaughton Files, box 1, Warnke Papers, LBJL; CIA intell memo, 21 Apr 65, *FRUS 1964-68*, 2:596-97.

3. Kearns, *Lyndon Johnson*, 264; Shapley, *Promise and Power*, 323; msg CAP 64375 cited in n 1; interv Robert S. McNamara by Alfred Goldberg, Lawrence Kaplan, and Edward Drea, 8 Jan 98, 33, OSD Hist; interv Robert S. McNamara by Walt W. Rostow, 8 Jan 75, 31, interv Lyndon B. Johnson by William J. Jorden, 12 Aug 69, 18: both LBJL.

4. Moyers, "One Thing We Learned," 662; CRS, *U.S. Government and the Vietnam War*, pt 3:119; Trewhitt, *McNamara*, 225; Clodfelter, *Limits of Air Power*, 65; Tilford, *Setup*, 92-93, 104; memrcd Goodpaster, mtg w/Pres, 17 Feb 65, *FRUS 1964-68*, 2:298, 303.

5. SecDef Background Briefing for Industry, 10 May 65, 569, fldr Vietnam 1965, box 31, SecDef Bio files, OSD Hist.

6. Palmer, *The 25-Year War*, 34-35 (quote); Herring, *LBJ and Vietnam*, 30-31; McMaster, *Dereliction of Duty*, 225; Palmer, "US Intelligence and Vietnam," 32-33.

7. Cosmas, *MACV: Years of Escalation*, 37-38.

8. For the evolution of the complex Air Force command relations in the SEA conflict, an excellent source is Momyer, *Air Power in Three Wars*.

9. Clodfelter, *Limits of Air Power*, 84-88; transc Wheeler test, 28 Jan 66, for HSCA Hearings on Supplemental Defense Appropriations, 1966, 363-66, fldr Sec'y McNamara and Gen. Wheeler testimony before House Appropriations Cte, Supple, Appro, '66 -1/28/66, box 46, ASD(C) files, OSD Hist; interv Benjamin H. Read by Paige E. Mulhollan, 13 Jan 69, 1:5-6, Internet copy, LBJL; Sharp, *Strategy for Defeat*, 86-87.

10. Burke and Greenstein, *How Presidents Test Reality*, 138, 184 (quotes); interv Bromley Smith by Paige E. Mulhollan, 25 Sep 69, 1:15-16, Internet copy, LBJL; McNamara interv, 8 Jan 75, 36.

11. Ted Gittinger, ed, "The Johnson Years," 79; Clodfelter, *Limits of Air Power*, 88.

12. Memos McNaughton for SecDef, 18 Jun 65, SecDef for CJCS, 22 Jun 65 (quote): both fldr Viet 381 (20-30 Jun 65), box 7, SecDef Subject Decimal files, 70-A-1265.

13. Memo McNaughton for SecDef, 22 Jun 65, ibid; *JCS and the War in Vietnam*, pt 2: 25/11-12; Bundy, Agenda prepared for mtg w/Pres, 23 Jun 65, Tab 1, *FRUS 1964-1968*, 3:38.

14. Memo ASD(ISA) for SecDef, 5 Mar 68, fldr SEA Memoranda, box 3, item #15, NSF, Clark Clifford Papers, LBJL.

15. Memo Bundy for Pres, 27 Jan 65, Smith summary notes of 545th NSC mtg, 6 Feb 65, memrcd Vance, 7 Feb 65, msg 2420 Saigon to State, 7 Feb 65, ed note, memo Bundy for Pres, 7 Feb 65, Annex A: *FRUS 1964-68*, 2:96-97, 157, 164, 165, 173, 181; Van Staaveren, *Gradual Failure*, 9, 17-18, 20-24; McNamara, *In Retrospect*, 170; Ford, *CIA and Vietnam Policymakers*, 72.

16. Memcon, SecDef w/Amb Dobrynin, 11 Apr 67, fldr Reading File Apr 1967, box 128, McNamara Records; Dobrynin, *In Confidence*, 136; ed note and Smith summary notes of 545th NSC mtg, 6 Feb 65: *FRUS 1964-68*, 2:436, 156-57; transc McNamara test, 22 Feb 65 for HCAS Hearings on the Authorization Bill for FY 1966 (Excerpts), 62-63, fldr Vietnam 1965, box 31, SecDef Bio files, OSD Hist; *Pentagon Papers*, bk 4, IV.C.3, 64 (quote); *JCS and the War in Vietnam*, pt 2:17/19, 22.

17. Msg Pres to Taylor, 8 Feb 65, memo of mtg and memrcd McCone, both 8 Feb 65: *FRUS 1964-68*, 2:202, 187, 197; CMC notes of JCS mtg (Major Policy Decisions Indicated), 8 Feb 65, No 28, vol 3, Greene Papers, MHC; *JCS and the War in Vietnam*, pt 2:18/5. On the sensitivity of Phuc Yen see memrcd Matthews, General Points of Interest from Ambassador's Consultations in Washington, Apr 65, fldr "D" Amb to Vietnam—1965 Cables, item #2c, box 52, Taylor Papers, NDU.

18. JCSM-100-65 for SecDef, 11 Feb 65 (quote), CIA, SNIE 10-3/1-65, Communist Reactions to Possible US Courses of Action Against North Vietnam, 18 Feb 65, paper by Rusk, Vietnam, 23 Feb 65: *FRUS 1964-68*, 2:240-41, 322-23, 357; msg JCS 005349 to CINCPAC, 16 Feb 65, msg JCS-IN 44176 CINCPAC to JCS, 27 Feb 65 (quote), Cable files, OSD Hist; msg 2888 Saigon to State, 8 Mar 65, fldr 157-69E (VN-Cables-1964-65 Etc.) item #33, box 51, Taylor Papers, NDU.

19. Bruce diary entry, 13 Feb 65, msg 1718 State to Saigon, 13 Feb 65, msg 5147 State to London, 16 Feb 65: *FRUS, 1964-68*, 2:262, 263, 294; McNamara, *In Retrospect*, 173; Dallek, *Flawed Giant*, 249. On McNamara's views of loyalty to superiors see Goulding, *Confirm or Deny*, 176; Herring, *LBJ and Vietnam*, 48. On charges of lying see Shapley, *Promise and Power*, 359-60. McNamara's alleged deceptions and lies are the thesis of McMaster's *Dereliction of Duty*, an explanation for the Americanization of the war in Vietnam.

20. Msg JCS 739-65 Wheeler to Westmoreland, 1 Mar 65, *FRUS 1964-68*, 2:388-89; *JCS and the War in Vietnam*, pt 2:18/12; Herring, *LBJ and Vietnam*, 31.

21. McNamara test, 2 Mar 65, HSCA, Hearings: *Department of Defense Appropriations Act 1966*, pt 3:3; *JCS and the War in Vietnam*, pt 2:18/16-19; ed note, memo Bundy for Pres, 6 Mar 65, memo DDCI for Bundy, 8 Mar 65, w/atchmt: *FRUS 1964-68*, 2:390, 402, 421-22.

22. Msg 2889 Saigon to State, 8 Mar 65 (quote), two memrcds McCone, 18 Mar 65 (quote), ed note, msg DEF 006181, OSD to Taylor, 2 Mar 65: *FRUS 1964-68*, 2:412, 457-60, 473, 395; memo Johnson for SecDef et al, "Report on Survey of the Military Situation in Vietnam," 14 Mar 65, fldr Vietnam 333 Johnson 1965, box 6, SecDef Subject Decimal files, Acc 70A-1265; memrcd CMC, JCS mtg w/Pres on 15 Mar 65, 19 Mar 65, vol 3, Greene Papers; *JCS and the War in Vietnam*, pt 2:18/20-22 (quote); msg JCS 007484 to CINCPAC, 20 Mar 65, Cable files, OSD Hist; Hist Div, Jt Secretariat, JCS, Chron of Development of Restraints & Objectives in Air Campaign Vietnam, 1961-1966, 23 Dec 66, 28 (hereafter JCS Chron Air Campaign).

23. *JCS and the War in Vietnam*, pt 2:18/22; JCSM 221-65 for SecDef, 27 Mar 65, fldr VN 381 (27-31 Mar 65), box 7, SecDef Subject Decimal files, Acc 70A-1265. The Joint Staff had presented a conceptual briefing of this air campaign to McNamara, the Joint Chiefs, and visiting Admiral Sharp on 22 March. Subsequently the JCS revised their views as evidenced by their 27 March memo.

24. Note to Control Division, mtg of JCS and SecDef w/Amb Taylor, 29 Mar 65, fldr Vietnam 091 March 1965, box 44, Wheeler Papers.

25. Atchmt A, Rolling Thunder Chron, 2, TAB XYZ, fldr #20, McNtn Bombing of NVN, box 2, OSD Records from SecDef Vault (Mr. Laird), Acc 330-74-142; msg JCS 1182-65 Wheeler to Sharp, 3 Apr 65 (quote), fldr Chron-Apr 65, box 116, Wheeler Papers; memo SecDef for CJCS, 3 Apr 65, fldr 091 Vietnam Apr 65, box 44, ibid; CM-534-65 for SecDef, 6 Apr 65, CM-616-65 for SecDef, 17 May 65, memo W. Bundy for SecState, 13 Apr 65: *FRUS 1964-68*, 2:535-37, 670-71, 551-52; *JCS and the War in Vietnam*, pt 2:18/25.

26. Msg CAP 65120 Bundy to Taylor, 17 Apr 65, memo SecDef for Pres, 21 Apr 65, and memrcd Matthews, 4 Apr 65: *FRUS 1964-68*, 2:571, 574-77, 533; *JCS and the War in Vietnam*, pt 2:21/15; Janicik, "Buildup," 72-73, box 246, Subj files, OSD Hist; CRS, *U.S. Government and the Vietnam War*, pt 3:230; Sharp, *Strategy for Defeat*, 79-80; McNamara, *In Retrospect*, 182-83; msg DEF 009653 OSD to Saigon, 23 Apr 65, Cable files, OSD Hist. McNamara based his memo almost entirely on memo McNaughton for SecDef et al, Minutes of the April 20, 1965, Honolulu Meeting, 23 Apr 65, fldr Demma Files, CMH; msg JCS 005349, 16 Feb 65 and msg JCS-IN 44176, 27 Feb 65: both cited in note 17.

27. Memo SecDef for Pres, 21 Apr 65, *FRUS 1964-68*, 2:574. The accounts of Taylor and William Bundy, both also present at the meeting, seem closer to McNamara's version; see diary entry by Taylor, 20 Apr 65, ibid, 573-74 and Bundy ms, ch 25/4-5. HQ CINCPAC, Record of Proceedings Secretary of Defense Conference, 20 Apr 65, fldr 337 Honolulu Conf 19-21 Apr 65, box 91, Wheeler Papers; msg JCS 1433-65 Wheeler to Sharp, 22 Apr 65, fldr Chron-Apr 65, box 116, ibid; msg DEF 009653 OSD to Saigon, 23 Apr 65, msg 230421Z CINCPAC to COMUSMACV, 23 Apr 65: Cable files, OSD Hist. See also memo SecDef for CJCS, 14 Apr 66 and CM-1347-66 for Gen Johnson et al, 15 Apr 66: fldr 091 SEAsia Jul 65-Apr 66, box 35, Wheeler Papers.

28. Memrcd McCone, 21 Apr 65, *FRUS 1964-68*, 2:578 and 580, n 8.

29. Ltr McCone to Pres, nd, memrcd McCone, 28 Apr 65, ltr McCone to Pres, 28 Apr 65, ltr Raborn to Pres, 8 May 65: ibid, 521-22, 613-15, 622-23; McNamara, *In Retrospect*, 185; McNaughton, Possible 'Pause' Scenario, 25 Apr 65 (2d draft), vol 33, Memos 4/21-30/65, box 16, NSF, CF, Vietnam, LBJL.

30. Herring, ed, *Secret Diplomacy*, 45-46; memo Bundy for Pres, 23 Apr 65, *FRUS 1964-68*, 2:604; msg CAP 65799 Bundy to Pres, 2 Dec 65, ibid, 3:596 (quote); Johnson, *Vantage Point*, 136-37; McNamara, *In Retrospect*, 184-85; McNamara, *Argument Without End*, 262-63; Herring, *LBJ and Vietnam*, 40.

31. Herring, *LBJ and Vietnam*, 97; *Pentagon Papers*, bk 4, IV.C.3, 110-17 (quote, 112); msg 55813 Sharp to JCS, 11 May 65, *FRUS 1964-68*, 2:641-42; JCS Chron Air Campaign, 38.

32. McNamara, *Argument Without End*, 263-65; Valenti notes of mtg, 16 May 65, msg 2600 State to Saigon, 17 May 65: *FRUS 1964-68*, 2:666 (quote), 669.

33. *JCS and the War in Vietnam*, pt 2:25/9-10; CM-667-65 for SecDef, 11 Jun 65, fldr Correspondence and Misc Documents 1965, box 63, Pentagon Papers Backup, Acc 330-75-062.

34. JCSM-457-65 for SecDef, 11 Jun 65, *FRUS 1964-68*, 2:756 (quote); ed note, memo SecDef for Pres, 1 Jul 65: ibid, 3:41, 99-100.

35. CIA memo, 30 Jun 65, memo Bundy for SecDef, 30 Jun 65, ed note: ibid, 3:88 (quote), 90, 118-19; McNamara, *In Retrospect*, 194; McMaster, *Dereliction of Duty*, 302; memo Bundy for Pres, 1 Jul 65, *FRUS 1964-68*, 3:117; Question 9, TAB A-McNamara Questions-Taylor Answers (quote), fldr McNamara Vietnam Trip, box 246, Subj files, OSD Hist.

36. Memo SecDef for Pres, 20 Jul 65, *FRUS 1964-68*, 3:176.

37. Memo SecDef for Pres, 30 Jul 65, ibid, 280-84.

38. Memo Bundy for Pres, 5 Aug 65, msg 240030Z Sharp to JCS, 23 Aug 65, JCSM-652-65 for SecDef, 27 Aug 65 w/app, memo McNaughton for SecDef, 8 Sep 65, memo Bundy for Pres, 12 Sep 65, ltr W. Bundy to McNaughton, 1 Oct 65: ibid, 304, 341-42, 357, 361-62, 377-78, 384, 429-30; JCSM-613-65 for SecDef, 27 Aug 65, fldr Vietnam 2EE, box 75, NSF, CF, Vietnam, LBJL; memo W. Bundy for McNaughton, 16 Sep 65, memo McNaughton for CJCS, 22 Sep 65, CM-876-65 for ASD(ISA), 24 Sep 65: fldr 091 Vietnam Sep 65, box 45, Wheeler Papers.

39. JCSM-670-65 for SecDef, 2 Sep 65 (quote), item #5, Tab D, fldr 326-69B (Joint Staff Papers) 1965-1966, box 54, Taylor Papers; *JCS and the War in Vietnam*, pt 2:26/9; memo Bundy for Pres, 12 Sep 65, memrcd Califano, mtg w/Pres et al, 13 Sep 65, memo SecDef for CJCS, 15 Sep 65: *FRUS 1964-68*, 3:383, 385-86, 389-90; CM-2501-67 for SecDef, 13 Jul 67, encl B, fldr Viet 385.1 (July-Dec) 1967, box 6, SecDef Subject Decimal files, Acc 72A-2467.

40. Bundy ms, ch 25/5 (quote); ed note, *FRUS 1964-68*, 2:700-01 (quote); memo Bundy for Pres, 4 Jun 65, ibid, 30:173-74.

41. Chen Jian, "China's Involvement," 366-67; Qiang Zhai, *China and the Vietnam Wars*, 132-33; USIB Watch Rpt, #772, 9 Jun 65, TSC-372-65, fldr VN Class Jan-Jun 1965, box 329, Subj files, OSD Hist; ed note, *FRUS 1964-68*, 2:700-01.

42. Whiting, *The Chinese Calculus of Deterrence*, 176-77, 186, argues the Chinese were confident reports of this activity would reach Washington and act as a deterrent. If so, the Chinese message was received, if not properly interpreted. See USIB Watch Rpt, #744, 25 Nov 64, TSC-918-64 and USIB Watch Rpt, #766, 28 Apr 65, TSC-285-65, fldr VN Class Jan-Jun 1965, and NNMC Opsum 220-65, 21 Sep 65, CIA OCI Weekly Summary 8 Oct 65, fldr Vietnam classified Jun-Dec 65: box 329, Subj files, OSD Hist; Chen,

"China's Involvement," 377; Gardner, *Pay Any Price*, 269; Hershberg and Chen, "Reading and Warning the Likely Enemy," 58-60, 76-77; Gittinger, ed, *The Johnson Years*, 93 (quote); Schoenbaum, *Waging Peace and War*, 424. Rusk had been assistant secretary of state for Far Eastern affairs when China crossed the Yalu River into North Korea in 1950, and he still bore the scars of that experience.

43. McNamara, *In Retrospect*, 213; *JCS and the War in Vietnam*, pt 2:26/14; JCS Chron Air Campaign, 52.

44. CIA, SNIE 10-11-65, 22 Sep 65, *FRUS 1964-68*, 3:403, 406-07. State's objections are found at 407-11; memrcd Califano, mtg w/Pres et al, 29 Sep 65, ibid, 421 (quotes).

45. Paper by Thompson, 11 Oct 65, Bundy draft paper, Elements of Second Pause Scenario, 22 Oct 65 (quote), W. Bundy paper, Policy Choices and Decision-Making Procedures on Vietnam, 23 Oct 65: *FRUS 1964-68*, 3:443-45, 475, 486-91; CRS, *U.S. Government and the Vietnam War*, pt 4:77-79; Bundy ms, ch 31/32-33; memo McNaughton for Vance, 22 Oct 65, fldr Vietnam 380 "Tet Truce," box 6, SecDef Subject Decimal files, Acc 70A-1265.

46. CM-844-65 for DirJtStaff, 14 Sep 65, fldr 091 Vietnam Sep 65, box 45, Wheeler Papers; draft memo SecDef for Pres, 3 Nov 65, Bundy personal notes of mtg, 6 Dec 65: *FRUS 1964-68*, 3:521 (quote), 605.

47. CIA/DIA intell memo, An Appraisal of the Bombing of North Vietnam, No. 2391/65, 27 Oct 65, *FRUS 1964-68*, 3:500, 503; *JCS and the War in Vietnam*, pt 2:26/15-16 citing memo DirDIA for CJCS, 22 Oct 65.

48. Draft memo SecDef for Pres, 3 Nov 65, *FRUS 1964-68*, 3:514-28 (quotes, 528). A copy went to the president in Texas on 7 November (see ibid, 514, n 1); McNamara, *In Retrospect*, 218-20.

49. Van Staaveren, *Gradual Failure*, 153-54; CRS, *U.S. Government and the Vietnam War*, pt 3:376-77; CM-844-65 CJCS for DirJtStaff, 14 Sep 65, DJSM-1087-65 for CJCS, 17 Sep 65: fldr 091 Vietnam Sep 65, box 45, Wheeler Papers; transc McNamara test, 26 Jan 66 for HCA Hearings on Proposed Supplemental Appropriation for DoD, 97-98, fldr House Appropriations Hearings 1966 Supplemental (unpub classified exec sess), box 44, ASD(C) files, OSD Hist; transc McNamara test, 26 Jan 66 for HCA Hearings on Supplemental Appropriation of $12.3 Billion for FY 66 (Excerpts), 279-80, fldr 1966, box 32, SecDef Bio files, OSD Hist; transc McNamara test, 25 Aug 67 for Preparedness Investigating Subcte of SCAS Hearings on Air War against North Vietnam (Excerpts), 1097, 1125, fldr 1967, box 36, ibid.

50. Msg CAP 65799 Bundy to Pres, 2 Dec 65, memo SecDef for Pres, 30 Nov 65: *FRUS 1964-68*, 3:594-95.

51. Memo Taylor for McNamara, 6 Dec 65, fldr T-32469E Phase II (1965-68), item #2, box 53, Taylor Papers; CMC notes on special SecDef conf w/SvcSecs and Chiefs of Staff, 30 Nov 65, CMC work notes on regular JCS mtg, 15 Nov 65: vol 7A, Greene Papers; memrcd CMC, summary of conv w/SecN, 17 Nov 65, vol 7, ibid; Van Staaveren, *Gradual Failure*, 202-03 (quote).

52. Telcon McNamara and Johnson, 2 Dec 65, 12:15 p.m., WH6512.01, PNO 9305, LBJL; telcon SecDef and Pres, 2 Dec 65 cited in McNamara, *In Retrospect*, 223-24; memrcd McNamara, telcon w/Pres, 2 Dec 65, fldr MFRS, box 1, McNamara papers, Acc 71A-3470 (quote); Bundy notes on mtgs, 3 Dec 65, fldr Dec 3, 1965, box 1, McGeorge Bundy Papers, LBJL (quote).

53. Valenti notes of mtg, 17 Dec 65, *FRUS 1964-68*, 3:644-47 (quotes, 646, 647) and 672, n 3; Johnson, *Vantage Point*, 235; Goodpaster mtg notes, 17 Dec 65, fldr 3, South Vietnam, box 90, Goodpaster Papers, NDU.

54. Johnson, *Vantage Point*, 236-37; Valenti notes of mtg, 18 Dec 65, ed note: *FRUS 1964-68*, 3:658-59, 691; *Baltimore Sun*, 18 Dec 65; msg Goodpaster to Wheeler (in Tokyo), 18 Dec 65, msg SecDef to Wheeler (in Tokyo), 19 Dec 65, msg Goodpaster to Rosson (in Saigon), 19 Dec 65: fldr 3, South Vietnam, box 90, Goodpaster Papers; msg Wheeler to McNamara, 21 Dec 65, vol 9, bk 1, Greene Papers; memrcd CMC, resume of JCS mtg 5 Jan 66, memrcd CMC, debrief of remarks made by CJCS at Chiefs mtg of 5 Jan 1966, both dtd 6 Jan 66: vol 9, bk 5, ibid; Greene, "The Bombing 'Pause': Formula for Failure," 37 (quote).

55. Memrcd CMC, 29 Dec 65, memrcd CMC, summary of spec conf called by SecDef, 29 Dec 65: vol 9, bk 1, Greene Papers; Greene, "The Bombing Pause," 37; msg MAC 6569 Wheeler (in Saigon) to McNamara, 21 Dec 65, *FRUS 1964-68*, 3:673-74; msg JCS 9332 to CINCPAC et al (from DepSecDef), 25 Dec 65, fldr Vietnam 380 "Tet Truce," box 6, SecDef Subject Decimal files, Acc 70A-1265.

56. JCSM-907-65 for SecDef, 27 Dec 65, fldr Vietnam 380 "Tet Truce," box 6, SecDef Subject Decimal files, 70A-1265; Greene, "The Bombing Pause," 38; msg 45265, COMUSMACV to CINCPAC, 27 Dec 65, forwarded by msg CAP 65917, Bundy for Pres, 27 Dec 65, msg CAP 65918, 27 Dec 65, draft msg Bundy for Pres, 27 Dec 65: *FRUS 1964-68*, 3:702-03 (quote), 703, n 3 (quote), 715; McNamara, *In Retrospect*, 225-26; telcon McNamara and Johnson, 22 Dec 65, 10:10 a.m., Tape WH 6512.04 Side A, PNO 9327, LBJL.

57. Herring, *LBJ and Vietnam*, 42; msg SecDef 5038-65 McNamara to Westmoreland et al, 28 Dec 65 (quotes), msg SecDef 5041-65 McNamara to Wheeler et al, 29 Dec 65: Eyes Only Message File 1 Oct-31 Dec 65, Westmoreland Papers, CMH; memrcd CMC, summary of spec conf 29 Dec 1965, cited in note 54; Greene, "The Bombing Pause," 38. Wheeler was still on his Asian trip at the time.

58. McNamara, *Argument Without End*, 274-76; Herring, *LBJ and Vietnam*, 100; msg 315 Rangoon to State, 29 Dec 65, FRUS 1964-68, 3:736; summary notes of 555th NSC mtg, 5 Jan 66, ibid, 4:19-20.

59. Valenti notes of mtg, 3 Jan 66, JCSM-16-66 for SecDef, 8 Jan 66: *FRUS 1964-68*, 4:7-11 (quote, 8), 35-36; *JCS and the War in Vietnam*, pt 2:30/2; JCS Chron Air Campaign, 58.

60. Valenti notes of mtg, 10 Jan 66, *FRUS 1964-68*, 4:37-40 (quote, 39); CSAF memo, 12 Jan 66, encl to JCS 2343/744-2, 13 Jan 66, Suppl 1, *Chronology of Events Concerning the Christmas Truce and Tet Stand-Down, 1965-66*, 27 (quote), JCS Hist Div.

61. Telcon Pres and SecDef, 17 Jan 66, *FRUS 1964-68*, 4:74; CMC notes of regular SecDef staff mtg, 24 Jan 66, vol 8, Greene Papers; JCSM-56-66 for SecDef, 25 Jan 66 (quote), fldr 326-69B (Joint Staff Papers) 1965-1966 item #11, TAB J, box 54, Taylor Papers; see also ISA, Expectations Prior to Initiation of Attacks, 29 Jun 66, dtd 16 Aug 67, TAB P, fldr #20, McN on Bombing of NVN, box 2, OSD Records from SecDef Vault (Mr. Laird), Acc 330-74-142; memo SecDef for CJCS, 15 Feb 66, fldr Reading File Feb 1966, box 124, McNamara Records.

62. Johnson, *Vantage Point*, 239-40 (quote); series of Valenti prepared mtg notes in *FRUS 1964-68*, 4, for 24 Jan 66 (126-28), 25 Jan 66 (141-45), 26 Jan 66 (153-55), 27 Jan 66 (164-70), and 28 Jan 66 (174-81). (Quote, 181).

63. Clark Clifford, Points, 28 Jan 66 (quote), fldr Mr. Clifford's Pencilled Notes Vietnam, box 1, Clifford Papers, LBJL. An abbreviated version of Clifford's remarks is also available in Valenti notes of mtg, 28 Jan 66, *FRUS 1964-68*, 4:180-81. Clifford at this time served as an unofficial adviser to Johnson. Valenti notes of mtg, 29 Jan 66, and Smith summary notes of 556th NSC mtg, 29 Jan 66: *FRUS 1964-68*, 4:182-85, 185-86, 187 (quote); *Johnson Public Papers, 1966*, 1:114-16; Johnson, *Vantage Point*, 240.

64. *Pentagon Papers*, bk 6, IV.C.7.(a), 74-75; *JCS and the War in Vietnam*, pt 2:30/14 and pt 2:31/9-10; Sharp, *Strategy for Defeat*, 110-11.

65. *JCS and the War in Vietnam*, pt 2:26/16-17; JCSM-810-65 for SecDef, 10 Nov 65, fldr Vietnam JCS Memos vol 1 [1 of 2], box 193, NSF, CF, Vietnam, LBJL (quote); JCSM-811-65 for SecDef, 10 Nov 65, fldr 326-69B (Joint Staff Papers) 1965-1966 item #7, TAB F, box 54, Taylor Papers (quote).

66. Diary entry for 19 Nov 65, fldr Private Diary General Wheeler (1965), box 201, Wheeler Papers; memo telcon, ActgSecState and SecDef, 23 Nov 65, *FRUS 1964-68*, 3:579-80 (quote, 579).

67. Memo SecDef for DCI, 24 Nov 65, fldr Viet 385 Reactions (Sen), box 6, SecDef Sensitive Files 1949-1969, Acc 330-91-007; memo Kent for DCI, 27 Nov 65, fldr Vietnam 091 December/65, box 46, Wheeler Papers (quote, 1); memo Kent for DCI, 2 Dec 65, fldr T 324-69E Phase II (1965-68) item #6, box 53, Taylor Papers.

68. CM-1006-65 for SecDef, 2 Dec 65, fldr Vietnam 091 December/65, box 46, Wheeler Papers; *Pentagon Papers*, bk 6, IV.C.7.(a), 70-73; JCSM-914-65 for SecDef, 30 Dec 65, fldr 326-69B (Joint Staff Papers) 1965-1966 item #8, TAB G, box 54, Taylor Papers; ISA paper, cited in note 60.

69. Memo McNaughton for SecDef, A Barrier Strategy, 30 Jan 66, fldr McNTN II—Drafts 1966(3), John McNaughton Files, box 1, Warnke Papers, LBJL; McNaughton, Summary of Some Paragraphs on Vietnam, 20 Jan 66 (quote), doc no. CK3100263201, Declassified Documents Reference System, http://galenet.galegroup.com; Valenti notes of mtg, 18 Dec 65, *FRUS 1964-68*, 3:663.

70. Valenti notes of mtg, 28 Jan 66, *FRUS 1964-68*, 4:175-76; *JCS and the War in Vietnam*, pt 2:31/8-9.

71. Memo Hand for McNamara, 28 Feb 66, w/atchmt CIA, Preliminary Report, TS No.190080, 28 Feb 66 (quotes), fldr Vietnam 000.1-373.5, box 11, ISA General files, Acc 70A-6649; Gravel ed, *Pentagon Papers*, 4:71-73 (quote); memo DirDIA for CJCS, 22 Mar 66, fldr Vietnam 091 Mar 66, box 47, Wheeler Papers.

72. Hammond, *Military and the Media*, 227-28; Moyers, "One Thing," 660; Herring, *LBJ and Vietnam*, 135; James Reston in *New York Times*, 17 Nov 65 (quote).

73. Hanson Baldwin in *New York Times*, 27 Dec 65; transc McNamara test, 25 Feb 66 for SCAS and SSCA Hearings on Military Authorizations and Defense Appropriations for FY 1967, vol 2, pt 4 of 9:225 (quote), 227, fldr Sec McNamara testimony-Senate Armed Services and Appro Ctes-Feb 25, 1966, Afternoon-only, box 52, ASD(C) files, OSD Hist.

74. *JCS and the War in Vietnam*, pt 2:31/11, 14; JCSM-153-66 for SecDef, 10 Mar 66, fldr Vietnam JCS Memos, vol II, box 193, NSF, CF, Vietnam, LBJL; memo Smith for Pres, 19 Mar 66, note by Pres for Smith, 19 Mar 66: *FRUS 1964-68*, 4:290-91; msg JCS 1508-66, Wheeler to Sharp, 22 Mar 66 (quotes), fldr Vietnam 091 (March 1966), box 47, Wheeler Papers; JCS Chron Air Campaign, 62.

75. *JCS and the War in Vietnam*, pt 2:31/15, 24; action memo DepAsstSecState Unger for SecState, 30 Mar 66, JCSM-189-66 for SecDef, 26 Mar 66: *FRUS 1964-68*, 4:310-11, 299-301.

76. Memo McNamara for Pres, nd, fldr McNTN II, John McNaughton Files, box 1, Warnke Papers, LBJL (quote); memo Smith for Pres, 31 Mar 66, fldr Vietnam 2EE, box 75, NSF, CF, Vietnam, LBJL; CMC notes

of regular JCS mtg, 1 Apr 66, No 119, vol 11, Greene Papers (quote); *Pentagon Papers*, bk 6, IV.C.7.(a), 88-89; Sharp, *Strategy for Defeat*, 116-17.

77. *JCS and the War in Vietnam*, pt 2:31/16; JCS Chron Air Campaign, 65; memo Whiting for Unger, 4 Apr 66, fldr April 1966, box 14, Gibbons Papers, LBJL; action memo DepAsstSecState Unger for SecState, 30 Mar 66, *FRUS 1964-68*, 4:312.

78. *JCS and the War in Vietnam*, pt 2:38/1-12; *Pentagon Papers*, bk 6, IV.C.7.(a), 109.

79. Herring, *Secret Diplomacy*, 159-61 (quote); Preston, "Missions Impossible," 130-33. Ronning's socialist politics, pro-Chinese communist position, and outspoken criticism of U.S. foreign policy also affected his credibility with the administration.

80. Memrcd CMC, JCS mtg w/Pres, 2 May 66, fldr vol 12, Greene Papers; *JCS and the War in Vietnam*, pt 2:31/22; President's daily diary, 2 May 66, box 6, Daily Diary, LBJL; memrcd Wheeler, 9 May 66, fldr Assessment of Attacks on Selected Targets in NVN (Prepared by JCS & CIA), box 96, McNamara Records.

81. Memo Ball for Rusk, 5 May 66, memo Rostow for Pres, 6 May 66 w/atchd memo Rostow for SecState and SecDef, 6 May 66: fldr May 1966, box 15, Gibbons Papers, LBJL; memo Rostow for Pres, 10 May 66, memcon Harriman and SecDef, 14 May 66, msg Pres to Prime Minister Wilson, 14 Jun 66: *FRUS 1964-68*, 4:378, 385, 426.

82. Msg JCS 2897 Wheeler to Westmoreland, 24 May 66, Westmoreland Papers, CMH; *JCS and the War in Vietnam*, pt 2:31/25-26; telcon McNamara and Ball, 27 May 66, memo Rostow for Pres, 30 May 66 (quote): fldr May 1966, box 15, Gibbons Papers, LBJL.

83. Msg JCS 3086-66 Wheeler to Sharp and Westmoreland 2 Jun 66 (quote), Westmoreland Papers, CMH; msg COMUSMACV to CINCPAC, 5 Jun 66, in 29 June 66 ISA paper, cited in note 60 (quote); *JCS and the War in Vietnam*, pt 2:31/27.

84. Johnson interv, 12 Aug 69, 19; *Pentagon Papers*, bk 6, pt IV.C.7.(a), 120-24; telcon McNamara and Ball, 6 Jun 66, memo Rostow for Pres, 8 Jun 66, 10:20 a.m.; fldr June 1966, box 16, Gibbons Papers, LBJL; ed note, *FRUS 1964-68*, 4:411-12; memo Rostow for Pres, 8 Jun 66, 9 a.m., fldr Vietnam 2EE, box 75, NSF, CF, Vietnam, LBJL; msg 3395-66 SecDef to CINCPAC, 15 Jun 66, fldr Reading File June 20-1, 1966, Tab 23, box 125, McNamara Records.

85. Smith summary notes of 559th NSC mtg, 17 Jun 66, *FRUS 1964-68*, 4:437-44; Dallek, *Flawed Giant*, 373.

86. Christian notes of Pres mtg w/NSC, 22 Jun 66, *FRUS 1964-68*, 4:448-51 (quote, 449); memo Rostow for Pres, 16 Jun 66, telcon McNamara and Ball, 22 Jun 66: fldr June 1966, box 16, Gibbons Papers, LBJL; msg JCS 5003 to CINCPAC, 22 Jun 66, fldr 110. POL, box 370, Subj files, OSD Hist.

87. Memo Rostow for Pres, 22 Jun 66, fldr June 1966, box 16, Gibbons Papers, LBJL; note W. Bundy to Vance, 23 Jun 66 (quote) w/atchd Points to be Made, nd, paper OSD Public Affairs, Possible Press Questions (and Answers) on POL Storage Facilities Strikes, nd (quote): fldr 110. POL, box 370, Subj files, OSD Hist.

88. Memrcd DepDirOps, NMCC, 24 Jun 66, Philip Geyelin in *Wall Street Journal*, 24 Jun 66: fldr 110. POL, box 370, Subj files, OSD Hist; telcon McNamara and Ball, 25 Jun 66, fldr June 1966, box 16, Gibbons Papers, LBJL; ed note, *FRUS 1964-68*, 4:458 and 452, n4; CMC notes on interrogation by FBI, 26 Jun 66, vol 12, Greene Papers.

89. Telcons McNamara and Pres, 28 Jun 66, 7:59 a.m., 2:40 p.m., 5:33 p.m., WH6606.6 PNO 10266, 10270, and 10273, LBJL; memrcd CMC, NSC mtg 22 Jun 66, memrcd Buse, mtg 29 Jun 66: vol 12, Greene Papers.

90. Pribbenow, "The -Ology War," 179 (Pribbenow relies on Vietnamese official military histories for his account); *JCS and the War in Vietnam*, pt 2:31/29, 31; ed note, *FRUS 1964-68*, 4:460; msg CTG 77.4 to AIG 914, 29 Jun 66, fldr 110. POL, box 370, Subj files, OSD Hist; SecDef news conf, 29 Jun 66, *McNamara Public Statements, 1966*, 7:2422; Van Staaveren, *Gradual Failure*, 289-90.

91. Memrcd Brown, 8 Jul 66, Demma File, CMH; memrcd McDonald, 11 Jul 66 (quote), fldr TS Sensitive Memos org by 00-1966, box 88, Double Zero-1967, NHC; CMC notes on regular JCS mtg, 11 Jul 66, No 137, vol 13, Greene Papers.

92. Msg 101945Z CINCPAC to COMUSMACV, 10 Jul 66, msg CJCS 4277-66 Wheeler for Sharp, 21 Jul 66 (quote): fldr Vietnam 091 Jul 66, box 48, Wheeler Papers; CM-1638-66 for SecDef, 23 Jul 66, fldr 1966 CMs 1600-55-1649-66, box 2, ibid; CM-1697-66 for SecDef, 24 Aug 66, fldr Vietnam 000.1-373.5, box 11, ISA General files, Acc 70A-6649.

93. Dallek, *Flawed Giant*, 376; *JCS and the War in Vietnam*, pt 2:36/1.

94. CIA intell memo, 23 Jul 66, No. 1683/66, CIA intell rpt, S-3690/AP-2F, Aug 66: *FRUS 1964-68*, 4:517, 615; OP-50-A, Daily Situation Report, 26 Aug 66, item #2, box 202, NSF, CF, Vietnam, LBJL.

95. CM-1697-66 for SecDef, 24 Aug 66, cited in n 91; memo SecDef for Pres, 14 Oct 66, w/app, *FRUS 1964-68*, 4:736; CM-1730-66 for SecDef, 7 Sep 66, fldr Southeast Asia Jul 66-Oct 66, box 35, Wheeler Papers (McNamara's marginalia on this document describe the decision); msg 090730Z CINCPAC to JCS, 9 Sep 66 (quotes), Cable files, OSD Hist; *Pentagon Papers*, bk 6, IV.C.7.(a), 141.

96. CMC work notes on JCS mtg, 12 Sep 66 (quote), No 144, vol 14, Greene Papers; *Pentagon Papers*, bk 6, IV.C.7.(a), 144 (quote); McNamara test, 23 Jan 67, SCAS and SSCA, Hearings: *Supplemental Military Procurement and Construction Authorizations, FY 1967*, 71 (quote); McNamara, *In Retrospect*, 246.

97. *JCS and the War in Vietnam*, pt 2:36/3-4; *FRUS 1964-68*, 4:599, n2; ed notes, ibid, 617-18, 649; memo Hughes (INR) for ActgSecState, 17 Aug 66, fldr August 1966, box 18, Gibbons Papers, LBJL; msg JCS 2105 Wheeler to Sharp and Westmoreland, 8 Sep 66, Westmoreland Papers; msg 042008Z CINCPAC to JCS, 4 Sep 66, msg JCS 5333-66 to CINCPAC and COMUSMACV, 8 Sep 66 (quote): Cable files, OSD Hist.

98. Memcon Harriman and McNamara, 28 May 66, Harriman further notes on conv w/McNamara on 28 May, dtd 27 Jun 66, fldr McNamara, Robert S. file Special Files Public Service JFK-LBJ, box 486, Harriman Papers, LC; memo SecDef for Pres, 14 Oct 66, JCSM-672-66 for SecDef, 14 Oct 66: *FRUS 1964-68*, 4:727-34, 740-42.

99. Msg JCS 6313-66 Wheeler to Westmoreland and Sharp, 15 Oct 66 (quote), Westmoreland Papers; Smith summary notes of 565th NSC mtg, 15 Oct 66, msg JCS 6399-66 Wheeler to Westmoreland, 17 Oct 66: *FRUS 1964-68*, 4:752, 758; *JCS and the War in Vietnam*, pt 2:36/14.

100. Ed note, memo Westmoreland for Rostow, 24 Oct 66, msg 91125 Sharp to JCS, 26 Oct 66, rpt by Jt Staff, JCS, Oct 66, CM-1906-66 for SecDef, 8 Nov 66: ibid, 4:579, 777-79, 780-82, 791, 809-12. McNamara transmitted CM-1906-66 to Johnson by memo SecDef for Pres, 8 Nov 66, fldr Vietnam 2EE, box 75, NSF, CF, Vietnam, LBJL; *JCS and the War in Vietnam*, pt 2:36/17-18.

101. CIA intell memo, Nov 66, *FRUS 1964-68*, 4:802-04; memo Ginsburgh for Rostow, 14 Dec 66, fldr Ginsburgh Memo's TAB 53, box 141, Wheeler Papers.

102. CM-1906-66 for SecDef, 8 Nov 66, msg CAP 66932 Rostow to Pres, 9 Nov 66, ed note: *FRUS 1964-68*, 4:809, 812-13, 816, and 818, n 4; memrcd Harriman, 26 Nov 66, fldr McNamara, Robert S. file Special Files Public Service JFK-LBJ, box 486, Harriman Papers, LC.

103. Msg JCS 6926-66 Wheeler to Westmoreland and Sharp, 11 Nov 66, Westmoreland Papers.

104. Herring, ed, *Secret Diplomacy*, 211-12.

105. DPM for Pres, 17 Nov 66, DPMs FY 1968-72 Programs 1966, FY 68, bk 6, 13-15, box 120, ASD(C) files, OSD Hist; *JCS and the War in Vietnam*, pt 3:40/6, pt 2: 36/19; msg 83718 Jt State/Defense to Saigon, 13 Nov 66, Cable files, OSD Hist.

106. DIA Intelligence Bulletin, 5 Dec 66, A-1 fldr Vietnam Classified Oct-Dec 66, box 329, Subj files, OSD Hist; Pribbenow, "The -Ology War," 180; msg 12247 Saigon to State, 1 Dec 66, *FRUS 1964-68*, 4:893.

107. Ed notes, *FRUS 1964-68*, 4:916, 897; msg JCS 7591-66 Wheeler to Sharp and Westmoreland, 10 Dec 66 (quote), Westmoreland Papers; CM-1994-66 for McDonald et al, 10 Dec 66, vol 15, Greene Papers, remarks cryptically that the president deferred Rolling Thunder 52 because of "sensitive activities in train of which you are aware." Dallek, *Flawed Giant*, 389; DIA Intelligence Bulletin, 5 Dec 66, A-1 DIA Intelligence Bulletin, Supplement: Summary of Air Strikes Against Special Targets 22 Nov-14 Dec 66, 16 Dec 66: both fldr Vietnam Classified Oct-Dec 66, box 329, Subj files, OSD Hist; CRS, *U.S. Government and the Vietnam War*, pt 4:496.

108. *JCS and the War in Vietnam*, pt 2:36/20, pt 3:40/7; msg 1471 Warsaw to State, 15 Dec 66, *FRUS 1964-68*, 4:936-38; CRS, *U.S. Government and the Vietnam War*, pt 4:495-96; McNamara, *In Retrospect*, 249-50 (quote); memo Ginsburgh for Wheeler, 16 Dec 66 (quote), fldr Ginsburgh Memo's Tab 52, box 141, Wheeler Papers; msg JCS 1471 to CINCPAC, 15 Dec 66, Cable files, OSD Hist.

109. Memo SecDef for Pres, 9 Mar 67, fldr Sen Robert Kennedy's Posture on Vietnam-Analysis of, box 8, NSF, Files of Walt W. Rostow, LBJL (the secretary did not identify the North Vietnamese members seeking negotiations); memcon SecDef w/Amb Dobrynin, 11 Apr 67, fldr Reading File Apr 1967, box 128, McNamara Records.

110. Herring, *LBJ and Vietnam*, 106-07; *JCS and the War in Vietnam*, pt 2:36/21, pt 3:40/8; McNamara, *Argument Without End*, 228-29; Read interv, 13 Jan 69, 1:9-10, Internet copy, LBJL; msg 107911 State to Warsaw, 23 Dec 66, msg Sharp to CJCS, 24 Dec 66: *FRUS 1964-68*, 4:969-70 (quote).

111. Ed note, *FRUS 1964-68*, 4:973; Hammond, *Military and the Media*, 274-79; Goulding, *Confirm or Deny*, 52-53, 92; *JCS and the War in Vietnam*, pt 2:36/24-26.

112. Rosen, "Vietnam and American Theory," 96; interv Bromley Smith by Paige E. Mulhollan, Interview II, 25 Sep 69, Internet copy, 2-3, LBJL.

113. "Southeast Asia Weather," DIA *Special Intelligence Supplement*, 18 Jun 65, box 320, Subj files, OSD Hist; memo Hughes for SecState, 1 Nov 67, fldr Vietnam 3F 3/67-10/68 Memos on Bombing in Vietnam, box 83, item #43, NSF, CF, Vietnam, LBJL; Thompson, *To Hanoi and Back*, 28.

IV. PAYING FOR A WAR: BUDGETS, SUPPLEMENTS, AND ESTIMATES, 1965–1967

1. Memo SecDef for SvcSecs et al w/atchmt, 13 Dec 63, fldr FY 1966 Budget, box 41, ASD(C) files, OSD Hist. This draft was the basis for McNamara's 21 December 1963 memo establishing the schedule for program submissions and reviews; Poole, *JCS and National Policy, 1965-1968*, 9, pt 1:14-16. For a negative assessment of PPBS refer to Palmer, *McNamara Strategy and the Vietnam War*, 120, 127-29.
2. Memo SecDef for SvcSecs et al, 6 Jun 64, memo Enthoven for SA staff, 15 Jan 64: both in fldr FY 66 Budget, box 41, ASD(C) files, OSD Hist.
3. Enthoven, "Putting Together the Defense Department's Budget," nd but likely late 1968, 2, fldr #3, box 11, Enthoven Papers, LBJL; interv Paul H. Nitze by Maurice Matloff and Roger Trask, 9 Oct 84, 39-40, OSD Hist; interv David L. McDonald by John T. Mason, Jr., #5, 24 Jan 76, 359, NHC; Kanter, *Defense Politics*, 61; memo Hitch for SecDef, 10 Oct 64, w/atchmt, fldr 110.01 (9 Jan 64) Projects, cy 64 Aug-Oct 1964, box 37, SecDef Subject Decimal files, Acc 69-A-7425; Enthoven, "Putting Together," 3-4; interv David Packard by Alfred Goldberg and Maurice Matloff, 9 Nov 87, 5, OSD Hist.
4. On PPBS see Kaplan et al, *McNamara Ascendancy*, 72-95; Enthoven, "Putting Together," 7, 11.
5. Sec McNamara's Appearances Before Congressional Committees, 1966, nd, fldr North Vietnam 1966, box 32, SecDef Bio files, OSD Hist; interv Robert S. McNamara by Alfred Goldberg, 27 Aug 86, 17, OSD Hist.
6. SecDef statement before HCAS on FY 1966-70 Defense Program and 1966 Defense Budget, 2 Feb 65, FY 1966, box 4, SecDef Statements 1965-66, OSD Hist; *DoD Annual Report, FY 1966*, 441; msg Secto 7 USUN to State, 2 Dec 64, fldr FY 1966 Budget, box 41, ASD(C) files, OSD Hist.
7. Transc McNamara test, 2 Mar 65, HCA Hearings on DoD Appropriations for FY 1966, 2128, fldr SecDef Transcript—House Approp Cte, March 2, 1965, box 38, ASD(C) files, OSD Hist; excerpts from Hearings on DoD Appropriations for 1966 before DoD Subcte of HCA, 4 Mar 65, TAB V, Backup Book FY 1966 SEA Emergency Fund, vol III, box 45, ibid.
8. McNamara test, 25 Feb 65, SSC on DoD of SCA and SCAS, *Hearings: Department of Defense Appropriations, 1966*, pt 1:294; McNamara test, 5 Mar 65, HSCA, *Hearings: Department of Defense Appropriations for 1966*, pt 3:372-75; memo McGiffert for SecDef, 26 Jul 65, fldr FY 1966 Reclama Backup, box 37, ASD(C) files, OSD Hist; HCA, *Department of Defense Appropriation Bill, 1966*, H Rpt 528, 17 Jun 65, 24-25, 66; PL 89-213, 29 Sep 65 (79 Stat 880); McNamara test, 1 Mar 65, Preparedness Investigating Subcte of SCAS, *Hearings: Proposal to Realine the Army National Guard and the Army Reserve Forces*, pt 1:36 (quote), 45.
9. McNamara test, 25 Feb 65, cited in note 8, 302; ltr Vance to Russell, 23 Jul 65, fldr FY 1966 Budget, box 37, ASD(C) files, OSD Hist; memo Harper for Roderick, 31 Mar 65, ltr McNamara to Russell, 25 Mar 65: both fldr F 1966 Budget, box 41, ibid; telcon McNamara and Pres, 17 Jun 65, Beschloss, *Reaching for Glory*, 358.
10. DoD Appropriation Act, 1966, Reclama, 16 Jul 65, fldr FY 1966 Budget, box 41, ASD(C) files, OSD Hist; memo McGiffert for SecDef, 26 Jul 65, cited in note 8; SecDef statement before Subcte on DoD Appropriations of SCA, 4 Aug 65, fldr FY 1966 Budget Reclama, box 37, ibid.
11. OASD(C), FAD-523(2), 6 Jun 66, Budget Data FY 1966-68, III, OSD Hist; *DoD Annual Report, FY 1966*, 47.
12. Memo SecDef for SvcSecs and JCS, 1 Mar 65 (quote), fldr Official Correspondence: Army Chief of Staff, Close Hold, box 76, H. K. Johnson Papers, MHI; Taylor, *Financial Management of the Vietnam Conflict*, 17-18; Bottomly, Note to Control Division, Mtg of JCS and SecDef w/Amb Taylor, 29 Mar 65 (quote), fldr Vietnam 091 March 1965, box 44, Wheeler Papers.
13. Memo Glass for SecDef, 3 Oct 66, fldr Vietnam Background, box 95, ASD(C) files, OSD Hist; service expectations are well spelled out in memo Comptr of Army for CSA, 24 Mar 65, fldr CS 091 Vietnam (24 Mar 65), Westmoreland Papers, CMH.
14. Sens. Mike Mansfield (D-Mont.) and George Aiken (R-Vt.) were calling for international negotiations to end the fighting; Frank Church (D-Idaho) and William Fulbright (D-Ark.) were advocating direct and unconditional discussions with Hanoi; and Jacob Javits (R-N.Y.) and Joseph Clark (D-Pa.) were suggesting that the president seek congressional support for his Vietnam policies. See CRS, *U.S. Government and the Vietnam War*, pt 3:238-39; interv Arthur Okun by David G. McComb, III, 15 Apr 69, 7-8, LBJL.

15. Pres remarks, 4 May 65, *Johnson Public Papers, 1965*, 1:485, 488 (quote), 492; Pres Spec Msg to Cong, 4 May 65, ibid, 1:494; ed note, *FRUS 1964-68*, 2:617-18. Both McNamara and Rusk were present during the White House session.

16. Transc McNamara test, 5 May 65, Jt SCA and SCAS Exec Sess Hearings on Additional Appros to Finance Certain Mil Operations, 64 (quote), fldr SecDef Transcripts SAC & SASC FY 65 Supplemental, box 33, ASD(C) files, OSD Hist. For the administration's authority to spend beyond authorizations see transc McNamara test, 4 May 65, HCAS Hearings regarding $700 Million SEA Supplemental Appropriation for FY 65 (excerpts from Exec Sess, not subsequently published), 476, 511 (quote), fldr Vietnam 1965, box 31, SecDef Bio files, ibid.

17. Transc McNamara test, 4 May 65, cited in note 16, 490, 493; Summary Comparison of Service Requests and President's Budgets FY 1963-FY 1967, fldr Comparison Service Requests and President's Budget, FY 1963 on, box 113, ASD(C) files, OSD Hist.

18. On construction funding see transc McNamara test, 4 May 65, cited in note 16, 495-96. On ammunition procurement refer to transc McNamara test, 5 May 65, SCAS and SCA Hearings regarding $700 Million SEA Supplemental Appropriation for FY 65 (Excerpts), 5 May 65, 528, fldr Vietnam 1965, box 31, SecDef Bio files, OSD Hist; memo SecDef for SvcSecs, 14 May 65, fldr Southeast Asia Supplemental FY 1965, box 35, ASD(C) files, ibid.

19. Transc McNamara test, 5 May 65, cited in note 16, 22; trans McNamara test, 5 May 65, cited in note 18, 535.

20. Bundy ms, ch 25/18-19; statement by Pres, 18 May 65, *Johnson Public Papers, 1965*, 1:559 (quote); Kearns, *Lyndon Johnson*, 298 (quote).

21. Bundy ms, ch 25/18-29 (quote). An early (1972) indictment is in Halberstam, "How the Economy Went Haywire," 56-60. Later criticisms include Campagna, *The Economic Consequences of the Vietnam War*, 32-35 and Buzzanco, *Masters of War*, 238-40.

22. Ltr Mahon to SecDef, 4 June 1965, fldr FY 1966 Budget, box 41, ASD(C) files, OSD Hist; ltr SecDef to Mahon, 9 Jun 65 (quote), fldr Vietnam 1965, 607-09, box 31, SecDef Bio files, OSD Hist. On 25 June 1965, describing its contents as "in response to a Congressional inquiry," OASD(PA) released McNamara's letter to the press; see *McNamara Public Statements, 1965*, 5:1808-09.

23. McNamara, *In Retrospect*, 198.

24. Draft memo for DCI, nd, fldr (July 1965), box 1, Vance Files, Acc 69-A-2317. A covering note conveying the draft from Vance to William Bundy for review, dated 15 July 1965, said the memo should go out over Dean Rusk's signature.

25. Msg 172042Z Vance to McNamara in Vietnam, 17 Jul 65, *FRUS 1964-68*, 3:162-63.

26. Memo Bundy for Pres, 19 Jul 65, ibid, 165 and n 1; *Baltimore Sun*, 15 Jul 65; Kearns, *Lyndon Johnson*, 295 (quote); Johnson, *Vantage Point*, 325-26. The president told Bundy to revise his July 19 memo omitting a reference to the guns and butter debate hurting the domestic legislative program. The revised memo is dated July 23.

27. Memo Hitch for SecDef, 20 Jul 65 w/atchmt, fldr Vietnam Buildup Material provided to the Secretary of Defense 21 Jul 65, box 94, ASD(C) files, OSD Hist. The procedure of financing personnel and O&M costs under Section 512 was similar to that used to finance the mobilization during the Berlin Crisis of 1961; see Palmer, *McNamara Strategy and Vietnam War*, 125.

28. Memo SecDef for Pres, 20 Jul 65, *FRUS 1964-68*, 3:175. The "X" figure also was used during the preparatory meeting without the president held in the Cabinet Room on 21 July 1965; see memrcd Cooper, 22 Jul 65, ibid, 198. McNamara's version is found in Shapley, *Promise and Power*, 346-47 (quote).

29. Memo Bundy for Pres, 21 Jul 65, *FRUS 1964-68*, 3:207; Valenti notes of mtg, 22 Jul 65, noon-2:15 p.m., ibid, 212; Valenti notes of mtg, 22 Jul 65, 3-4:20 p.m., ibid, 219; memo Bundy for Pres, 21 Jul 65, ibid, 206-07.

30. Interv Robert McNamara by Walt W. Rostow, 8 Jan 75, 27, 29-30, LBJL. The phrase "trying to pull a fast one," attributed to McNamara, is found in memo Bundy for Pres, 21 Jul 65, cited in note 29. McNamara, *In Retrospect*, 205 (quote), and Shapley, *Promise and Power*, 346, recount the president's reaction to McNamara's tax proposal.

31. Memo Bundy, 27 Jul 65, *FRUS 1964-68*, 3:264-65, 267 (quote). Bundy actually prepared this memo in December 1968 based on his meeting notes (ibid, 264, n 1); Califano, *Triumph & Tragedy*, 44 (quote); Helsing, *Johnson's War*, 184, n 69; *New York Herald Tribune*, 2 Aug 65; *Cong Rec*, 25 Aug 65, 21709.

32. Ltr McNamara to Schultze, 30 Jul 65, fldr Budget Development FY 1966 Budget, box 41, ASD(C) files, OSD Hist; *DoD Annual Report, FY 1966*, 46; SecDef Classified Statement before HCAS, 6 Aug 65, 12,

fldr FY 66 Amendment-Stat of SecDef-HASC-8/6/65, box 43, ASD(C) files, OSD Hist; transc McNamara test, 4 Aug 65, SCA and SCAS Hearings regarding $1.7 Billion Amendment to FY 66 Defense Budget (Excerpts), 726-27, fldr Vietnam 1965, box 31, SecDef Bio files, ibid.

33. Transc McNamara test, 4 Aug 65, cited in note 32, 723-24. See classified testimony with the redacted responses in McNamara test, 4 Aug 65, SSCA, *Hearings: Department of Defense Appropriations for 1966*, pt 2:805-06, 816.

34. Compare SecDef statement before SSCA, 2d draft, 29 Jul 65, 20b, 21, and Table 2, where all specific financial data was excised and replaced with the quoted statement and the final classified version of the secretary's statement before HCAS (Amendment to the FY 1966 Defense Budget), 6 Aug 65, 11, which reads, "None of these personnel and operation and maintenance costs can be estimated with any degree of precision at the present time." Both are in fldr SecDef FY 66 Amendment House Armed Svcs Cte 8/6/65, box 43, ASD(C) files, OSD Hist; SCA, *Department of Defense Appropriation Bill, 1966*, S Rpt 625, 18 Aug 65, 7; PL 89-213, 29 Sep 65 (79 Stat 872).

35. Califano, *Triumph & Tragedy*, 106-07; memo Ackley for Pres, 30 Jul 65, *FRUS 1964-68*, 3:286-88 (quote).

36. SEA Cost Escalation (DoD Estimate, FY 66 and FY 67), 9 Dec 65, fldr FY 67 Budget Summaries by OASD(P&FC), box 5, Comptroller files, Acc 73-A-1389; interv Charles L. Schultze by David G. McComb, III, 10 Apr 69, 2:9, LBJL (quote); Smith summary notes of 554th NSC mtg, 5 Aug 65, *FRUS 1964-68*, 3:308 (quote).

37. Memo Ackley for Pres, 30 Jul 65 (quote), cited in note 35; Califano, *Triumph & Tragedy*, 111 (quotes).

38. Memo DepSecDef for SvcSecs, et al, 19 Jul 65, fldr Jul-Aug Vietnam Buildup—SecDef Meetings, box 94, ASD(C) files, OSD Hist.

39. Memo SecDef for SvcSecs et al, 27 Aug 65, fldr Budget Development FY 67, box 54, ibid; memo ASD(C) for SecDef, 24 Sep 65, memo SecDef for SvcSecs, 28 Sep 65 (quote): both in fldr 110.01 (9 Jan-Dec 65), box 10, SecDef Subject Decimal files, Acc 70-A-1265.

40. Memo SecDef for SvcSecs et al, 5 Oct 65 (quote), fldr 110.01 (9 Jan-Dec 65), box 10, SecDef Subject Decimal files, Acc 70-A-1265; memo SecDef for SvcSecs et al, 11 Oct 65, fldr FY 67 Budget & FY 66 Supplemental, box 49, ASD(C) files, OSD Hist.

41. Memo Glass for SecDef, 3 Oct 66, fldr Vietnam Background, box 95, ASD(C) files, OSD Hist; memrcd Spark, 4 Oct 65, fldr 7100/3 1967 Budget, box 22, Double Zero 1965, Subject files 7100/3 thru 7300, NHC.

42. Halberstam, "How the Economy Went Haywire," especially 56, 60, subsequently retold in Halberstam, *The Best and the Brightest*, 604-05; Califano, *Triumph & Tragedy*, 111; SecDef background briefing for the Press, 20 Aug 1965, fldr Vietnam 1965, box 31, SecDef Bio files, OSD Hist; SecDef remarks to the press, 26 Oct 65, *McNamara Public Statements, 1965*, 5:2113; Bundy ms, ch 31/11 (quote); McNamara, *In Retrospect*, 209; msg 753 State to Saigon, 14 Sep 65, *FRUS 1964-68*, 3:386. Operation Starlite trapped two VC battalions along the coast at Chu Lai about 50 miles south of Da Nang and killed more than 600 of the enemy compared with the loss of 45 Marines; Shulimson and Johnson, *U.S. Marines in Vietnam: The Landing and the Buildup 1965*, 69-83; transc McNamara test, 6 Aug 65, HCAS Hearings regarding Appropriations for South Vietnam (Exec Sess, not subsequently published), 796, fldr Vietnam 1965, box 31, SecDef Bio files, OSD Hist.

43. Memo Ackley for Pres, 2 Sep 65 (quote), fldr FI II Taxation 6/29/65-3/16/66, box 55, WHCF, GEN FI 9 3/21/68, LBJL; Evans and Novak in *Washington Post*, 2 Sep 65; Edwin L. Dale, Jr., in *New York Times*, 10 Sep 65; Shapley, *Promise and Power*, 370.

44. McNamara, *In Retrospect*, 212-13; *Johnson Public Papers, 1965*, 2:1043; Bundy ms, ch 31/31.

45. On the success of the briefing see msg JCS 3912-65 to Sharp/Westmoreland, 18 Oct 65, Westmoreland Msg file, 1 Oct-31-Dec 65, CMH; summary of DePuy briefing for SecDef, 18 Oct 65, Westmoreland History file, Oct 65, ibid; Bundy paper, 23 Oct 65, *FRUS 1964-68*, 3:486. Bundy ms, ch 31/31-32, remarks that DePuy's briefing was "a familiar and hardly surprising change." Nonetheless the briefing also became the catalyst for Secretary McNamara's 3 November 1965 DPM recommending a stepped-up war effort. Memrcd Hawkins, 18 Oct 65, Westmoreland Papers, CMH. McNamara wanted the input by Friday as DePuy was scheduled to return to Saigon that Saturday (23 October).

46. Memo SecA for SecDef, 22 Oct 65, fldr VN 370 (Oct 65), box 6, SecDef Subject Decimal files, Acc-70-A-1265; J-3, talking paper for JCS for mtg on 23 Oct 65, ibid; SEA Phase II, 22 Oct 65, fldr 110.01 (9 Jan-Dec 65), box 10, ibid; DPM SecDef for Pres, 3 Nov 65, *FRUS 1964-68*, 3:522, 528.

47. See, for example, msg 43202 COMUSMACV to CINCPAC, 9 Dec 65, fldr VN 370 (Nov-Dec 65), box 6, SecDef Subject Decimal files, Acc 70-A-1265; ed note, 11 Nov 65, *FRUS 1964-68*, 3:561-62; *McNa-*

mara Public Statements, 1965, 5:2148-49; memrcd Glass, 12 Nov 65, draft memrcd Enthoven, 12 Nov 65 (quote), memo ASD(C) for Glass, 13 Nov 65: all in fldr Record of Meeting on Vietnam Phase II Deployments, box 96, ASD(C) files, OSD Hist.

48. Memo SecDef for SvcSecs and CJCS, 17 Nov 65, fldr FY 67 Budget Development and FY 66 Supplemental, box 54, ASD(C) files, OSD Hist; SEA Phase II, 22 Oct 65, cited in note 46. The description of the secretary's discussion with the president is based on McNamara's debrief of his meeting to the JCS on 16 November; see msg JCS 4431-65 to CINCPAC and COMUSMACV, 17 Nov 65, Westmoreland Msg file, CMH.

49. Msg 41485 COMUSMACV to CINCPAC, 23 Nov 65, fldr Vol 43, box 24, NSF, CF, Vietnam, LBJL; memrcd CMC, JCS mtg, 24 Nov 65 (quote), vol 7, Greene Papers, MHC; McNamara, *In Retrospect*, 221-23; msg JCS 4542-65 to CINCPAC and COMUSMACV, 23 Nov 65, Westmoreland Msg file, CMH.

50. Msg JCS 4658-65 to CINCPAC, 1 Dec 65, Westmoreland Msg file, CMH; memo Thomas D. Morris, ASD(M) for SvcSecs et al, 1 Dec 65 w/atchmt McNamara, South Vietnam Action List, 30 Nov 65, fldr staff Meeting Jul-Dec 1965, box 12, AFPC files, Acc 330-77-0062; memcon McNamara, telcon SecDef and Pres, 2 Dec 65, fldr MFRS, box 1, McNamara Papers, Acc 71A-3470; telcon McNamara and Johnson, 2 Dec 65, 12:15 p.m. (quote), No. 9305, PNO 5, WH6512.01, LBJL; memo Office of Budget Review for DirBoB, 8 Nov 65, fldr 1966 Budget Review, box 37, OMB Records, RG 51, Series G1.15; memo Hoover for Anthony, 15 Dec 65, fldr 1967 Budget Estimates, box 5, Comptroller files, Acc 73A-1389. Johnson's displeasure with the budget estimates appears in Sylvester notes, mtg w/SvcSecs et al, 11 Dec 65, Oct 65-Feb 66, OSD Hist (LtCol George H. Sylvester was McNamara's Air Force military aide); see also McNamara test, 26 Jan 66, HCA, *Hearings: Supplemental Defense Appropriations for 1966*, 24; memo SecDef for Pres, 9 Dec 65, JCSM-867-65 for SecDef, 8 Dec 65: fldr Budget Development FY 1967, box 54, ASD(C) files, OSD Hist; memos SvcSecs for SecDef, 7 Dec 65, JCSM-866-65 for SecDef, 8 Dec 65: all in fldr 110.01 (9 Jan-Dec 65), box 10, SecDef Subject Decimal files, Acc 70-A-1265.

51. Memrcd McNamara, telcons w/members of Cong, 8-9 Dec 1965, 9 Dec 65, fldr Memos for the Record, box 1, McNamara Papers, Acc 71-A-3470; DPM SecDef for Pres, 11 Dec 65, fldr 031.1 WH PDM, box 9, SecDef Subject Decimal files, Acc 70-A-1265; McNamara estimated ground combat costing $300 million a month or $1.8 billion for six months; air operations ran $375 million per month, or $2.25 billion for six months. See memo SecDef for Pres, 9 Dec 65, cited in note 50; msg 8419 SecDef to Saigon, 11 Dec 65, Vietnam 370 (Nov-Dec) 65, box 6, SecDef Subject Decimal files, Acc 70-A-1265.

52. *McNamara Public Statements, 1966*, 1:3; *New York Times*, 18 Jan 66, 7; McNamara test, 14 Feb 66, HSCA, *Hearings: Department of Defense Appropriations for 1967*, pt 1:6.

53. *Johnson Public Papers, 1966*, 1:32-33; SecDef test, 20 Jan 66, SCA and SCAS hearings re Suppl App of $12.3 Billion for FY 66 (Excerpts), 20 Jan 66, 38, fldr Vietnam 1966, box 32, SecDef Bio files, OSD Hist. See also the redacted testimony in McNamara test, 20 Jan 66, SCA and SCAS, *Hearings: Supplemental Defense Appropriations for Fiscal Year 1966*, 4, 9, 45-46; SCA, *Supplemental Defense Appropriation Bill, 1966*, S Rpt 1074, 17 Mar 66, 3.

54. Bowen, "The Vietnam War: A Cost Accounting," 119-21; interv Henry E. Glass by Edward Drea, 22 Oct 97, 9-10, OSD Hist; Sloan, "President Johnson, the Council of Economic Advisers, and the Failure to Raise Taxes," 92; Helsing, *Johnson's War*, 193.

55. Helsing, *Johnson's War*, 8, 121, 230; Anderson and Hazleton, *Managing Macroeconomic Policy*, 6 (quote), 31, 33; Sloan, "President Johnson," 89, 92.

56. McNamara test, 20 Jan 66, SCA and SCAS, *Hearings*, cited in note 53, 46; paper, Reasons for the Additional Funds Required for the Support of the Vietnam Effort, 20 Jun 66, fldr FY 1967 Budget & FY 66 Supp, box 49, ASD(C) files, OSD Hist; Kettl, "The Economic Education of Lyndon Johnson," in Divine, ed, *The Johnson Years*, 2:60.

57. Bundy notes of mtg, 3 Dec 65, box 1, Papers of McGeorge Bundy, LBJL; memo Schultze for Pres, 4 Dec 65, fldr Bureau of Budget, vol 1, box 7, NSF Agency file, LBJL.

58. Califano, *Triumph & Tragedy*, 107 (quote). See, for example, McNamara test, 8 Mar 66, HCAS, *Hearings on Military Posture and H.R. 13456*, 7289; Bundy ms, ch 33-22/23.

59. Helsing, *Johnson's War*, 216; memo Ackley for Pres, 25 Nov 65, fldr Vol II, Doc. Supplement, pt 1 [2 of 2], box 1, Admin History of CEA, LBJL; memo Fowler, Ackley, and Schultze for Pres, 1 Dec 65, fldr Dec 1, 1965 Memo to Pres, box 9, Federal Records, CEA, LBJL; msg CAP 65799 Bundy, Califano, and Moyers to Pres, 2 Dec 65 (quote), fldr Messages to President at the Ranch, 6 Sep-12 Dec 65, box 55, NSF Situation Room file, LBJL; memo Ackley for Pres, 2 Dec 65, fldr Council of Economic Advisors, box 10, NSF Agency file, LBJL; draft memo SecDef et al for Pres, 12 Dec 65, fldr 031.1 WH PDM Dec 65, box 9, SecDef Subject Decimal files, Acc 70-A-1265.

60. Memo Califano for Pres, 17 Dec 65 w/atchd memo Ackley for Pres, 17 Dec 65, fldr FI 11 Taxation 6/29/65-3/16/66, box 55, WHCF GEN FI 9 3/21/68, LBJL.

61. Hargrove and Morley, eds, *The President and the Council of Economic Advisors*, 248 (quote); interv Gardner Ackley by Joe B. Frantz, 7 Mar 74, 2:2, LBJL.

62. Johnson, *Vantage Point*, 325; CRS, *U.S. Government and the Vietnam War*, pt 4:215-16; see Anderson and Hazleton, *Managing Macroeconomic Policy*, 12, on Johnson's attitudes toward economic policy; McNamara interv, 8 Jan 75, 30, analyzes Johnson's concern about taxes and the Great Society. CRS, *U.S. Government and the Vietnam War*, pt 4:214, relates the president's concern in mid-November 1965 over a proposed speech to a business group by Treasury Secretary Fowler; see also memo Schultze for Pres, 4 Dec 65, fldr Bureau of Budget, vol 1, #11, NSF Agency file, LBJL.

63. Ltr Schultze to McNamara, 8 Nov 65, fldr 110.01 (9 Jan-Dec 65), box 10, SecDef Subject Decimal files, Acc 70-A-1265; memo Keeny for Bundy, 9 Nov 65, fldr DoD FY 1967 Budget Book (2 of 2), box 17, NSF Agency file, LBJL; memrcd Glass, 10 Nov 65, fldr 110.01 (9 Jan-Dec 65), box 10, SecDef Subject Decimal files, Acc 70-A-1265; memrcd Glass, 15 Nov 65, fldr DoD FY 1967 Budget Book (2 of 2), box 17, NSF Agency file, LBJL; paper, FY 1967 Defense Budget, nd, ibid; memo SecDef for Pres, 9 Dec 65, cited in note 50; interv McGeorge Bundy by Maurice Matloff and Alfred Goldberg, 15 Apr 91, 16, OSD Hist (quote).

64. McNamara test, 16 Feb 66, HSCA, *Hearings: Department of Defense Appropriations for 1967*, pt 1:280; Gen Johnson test, 21 Feb 66, ibid, 368-69; Brown test, 23 Feb 66, ibid, 510-12; Nitze test, 28 Feb 66, ibid, 657; McDonald test, 28 Feb 66, ibid, 660-66, 674-75; paper, Summary Comparison Svc Requests and Pres Budget FY 1963-67, fldr Comparison Service Requests & President's Budget FY 1963-on, box 113, ASD(C) files, OSD Hist; memrcd Hoover, 9 Dec 65, fldr 1967 Budget Estimates, box 5, Comptroller files, Acc 73-A-1389; DPM SecDef for Pres, 11 Dec 65, fldr 031.1 WH PDM Dec 65, box 9, SecDef Subject Decimal files, Acc 70-A-1265.

65. Telcon McNamara and Johnson, 20 Dec 65, 9:12 a.m., Tape WH6512.03, PNO 10, LBJL.

66. Gen Johnson test, 16 Feb 66, HSCA, *Hearings*, cited in note 64, 368-69; Brown test, 23 Feb 66, ibid, 510-12; Nitze test, 23 Feb 66, ibid, 657; McDonald test, 23 Feb 66, ibid, 675; memo SecDef for Pres, 9 Dec 65, cited in note 50 (quote). The amounts eliminated for construction were Army, $422 million; Navy, $282 million; Air Force, $548 million.

67. Memo SecDef for Pres, 9 Dec 65, fldr Budget Development-FY 1967, box 54, ASD(C) files, OSD Hist; JCSM-856-65 for SecDef, 3 Dec 65, JCSM-867-65 for SecDef, 8 Dec 65: both fldr 110.01 (9 Jan-Dec 65), box 10, SecDef Subject Decimal files, Acc 70-A-1265.

68. JCSM-856-65 for SecDef, 3 Dec 65 w/app with McNamara's emendations, cited in note 67.

69. Msg CAP 65744 Califano to Pres, 30 Nov 65, fldr Messages Sent to President at Ranch, 6 Sep-12 Dec 65, box 55, NSF Situation Room Reports, LBJL (quote); CMC notes of special JCS mtg w/SecDef, 8 Dec 65, vol 8, Greene Papers, MHC; memo SecDef for Pres, 9 Dec 65, cited in note 67; memo McDonald for SecDef, 9 Dec 65, fldr 110-01 (9 Jan-Dec 65), box 10, SecDef Subject Decimal files, Acc 70-A-1265; memo SecDef for Pres, 9 Dec 65, cited in note 50.

70. Memrcd CMC, mtg w/Pres 10 Dec 65, and memrcd CMC, Visit to LBJ Ranch, 10 Dec 65 (quote): vol 8, Greene Papers, MHC; interv McDonald, 24 Jan 76, 390, NHC; memrcd Beach, 29 Nov 65, fldr FY 67-Texas meeting, box 22, Double Zero 1965, Subject files 7100/3 thru 7300, NHC.

71. Memo Califano for Pres, 18 Dec 65, doc no 3100314575, Declassified Documents Reference Service, http://gealnet.galegroup.com; telcon McNamara and Johnson, 22 Dec 65, 10:10 a.m., WH 6512.04, Side A, PNO 9327, LBJL; msg CAP 50645 Califano to Pres, 23 Dec 65 (quote), fldr FG 110 Department of the Treasury 12/4/65-1/26/66, box 150, EX FG 110, 12/4/65, LBJL; Annual Budget Msg to Cong, FY 1967, 24 Jan 66, *Johnson Public Papers, 1966*, 1:54, 57; Anthony test, 17 Feb 66, HSCA, *Hearings: Department of Defense Appropriations for 1967*, pt 1:321. The administrative budget required congressional authorizations for $106.3 billion and $15.6 billion from permanent authorizations.

72. Memo Heller for Pres, 22 Dec 65, fldr Telegrams Sent to Ranch, 27 Dec 65-2 Jan 66, box 55, NSF Situation Room File, LBJL; memo Ackley for Pres, 27 Dec 65 (quote), ibid; memo Schultze for Pres, 27 Dec 65 (quote), ibid; CRS, *U.S. Government and the Vietnam War*, pt 4:215-17.

73. Thomas E. Mullaney in the *New York Times*, 17 Jan 66 (quotes); McNamara test, 14 Feb 66, HSCA, *Hearings*, cited in note 71, pt 1:4; news conf, 17 Jan 67, *McNamara Public Statements, 1966*, 1:3.

74. McNamara test, 14 Feb 66, HSCA, *Hearings*, cited in note 71, pt 1:6; Weidenbaum, *Economic Impact of the Vietnam War*, 28-29.

75. Holtz, "The War Budget," 9, makes the argument for deliberate underestimates.

76. Bowen, "The Vietnam War: A Cost Accounting," 259 (emphasis in the quote is in the original).

77. Kettl, "Economic Education," 61; Anderson and Hazelton, *Managing Macroeconomic Policy*, 6, 31-33 (quote); Weidenbaum, *Economic Impact*, 19; Stevens, *Vain Hopes, Grim Realities*, 11.

78. For a discussion see Campagna, *Economic Consequences of the Vietnam War*, 19-20; Weidenbaum, *Economic Impact*, viii, ix, 17.

79. Kettl, "Economic Education," 72.

80. Kearns, *Lyndon Johnson*, 259-260, 298.

V. VIETNAM: ESCALATING A GROUND WAR, JULY 1965–JULY 1967

1. Pres news conf, 28 Jul 65, *Johnson Public Papers, 1965*, 2:795; memrcd Califano, 29 Sep 65, *FRUS 1964-68*, 3:419.

2. Herring, *LBJ and Vietnam*, 35, 37; U.S. District Court, Southern District of New York, Deposition of Robert S. McNamara, 26 Mar 84, 10 (I am indebted to Deborah Shapley for sharing this document with me). McNamara, *In Retrospect*, 218-21; interv Paul C. Warnke by Maurice Matloff and Roger Trask, 10 Sep 84, 12, OSD Hist (quote); Goulding, *Confirm or Deny*, 175-76. As has been noted elsewhere, McNamara's memoranda and confidential comments for the president bore little resemblance to his public remarks; see Karnow, *Vietnam*, 425, 500. On Westmoreland's optimism, see interv Robert S. McNamara by Edward Drea, Alfred Goldberg, and Lawrence Kaplan, 8 Jan 98, 37-38, OSD Hist.

3. Deposition of Robert S. McNamara, 26 Mar 84, 175.

4. On Westmoreland's later recollections, see *Soldier Reports*, 153. On his 1965 recommendations, refer to msg MAC 3240 Westmoreland to Wheeler, 24 Jun 65, *FRUS 1964-68*, 3:42; McNamara interv, 8 Jan 98, 34; interv William C. Westmoreland by Dorothy Pierce McSweeny, 8 Feb 69, 12-13, AC 77-32, LBJL; transc McNamara and Wheeler test, 4 Aug 65, SSCA, *Hearings: DoD Appropriations for FY 1966*, 1455-57, fldr Transcript-SecDef before Stennis Aug 4 Morn, box 42, ASD(C) files, OSD Hist; transc Wheeler test, 20 Feb 67, HCA, *Hearings: DoD Appropriations for FY 1967 Supplemental for Southeast Asia*, 47, fldr Mahon Cte-Supplemental for SEA-Feb 20, 1967, McNamara-Gen Wheeler, box 53, ibid; Bundy ms, ch 27/28 (quote). On the reluctance of anyone to challenge Westmoreland's strategy, see Herring, *LBJ and Vietnam*, 43.

5. Hammond, *Military and the Media, 1962-1968*, 170; memo Vance for Pres, 21 Aug 65, fldr August 1965, box 1, Vance files, Acc 69A-2317; JCSM-652-65 for SecDef, 27 Aug 65, w/app, *FRUS 1964-68*, 3:356-63 (quote, 356).

6. JCSM-652-65 for SecDef, cited in note 5 (quote, 358); memo McNaughton for SecDef, 8 Sep 65, *FRUS 1964-68*, 3:377-78 (quote).

7. Memos Bundy for Pres, 12 Sep, 23 Sep 65, ibid, 384-85, 414; msg 753 State to Saigon, 14 Sep 65 and msg 953 Saigon to State, 18 Sep 65, ibid, 386-87, 394-95; Westmoreland's reaction is found in Westmoreland History files, entry for 18 Sep 65 (quote), fldr 29 Aug 65-24 Oct 65, CMH, and, in somewhat muted form, in *Soldier Reports*, 161; memrcd Califano, 29 Sep 65, *FRUS 1964-68*, 3:419.

8. Westmoreland History files, entry for 18 Sep 65; msg 161914Z Wheeler to Sharp and Westmoreland, 16 Sep 65, fldr Westmoreland Eyes Only Msg file, 1 Jul-30 Sep 65, CMH, quoted the pertinent parts of State msg 753 cited in note 7; Westmoreland, *Soldier Reports*, 161; MACV Directive 525-4, 17 Sep 65, in Carland, "Winning the Vietnam War," 557-70; Clarke, *Advice and Support: The Final Years*, 106-07; MACV Briefing on Phase 2 Concepts and Forces, 18 Oct 65, slide 49, fldr FY 1967-MACV J-3 Briefing, 18 Oct 65 in NMCC, box 56, ASD(C) files, OSD Hist.

9. Summary of DePuy briefing for SecDef, 18 Oct 65, encl to MACV J-3 October Historical Summary, 29 Nov 65, fldr Oct 65, Westmoreland Papers, CMH; paper by the Ambassador at Large (Thompson), 11 Oct 65, *FRUS 1964-68*, 3:442-43, 445.

10. Summary of DePuy briefing for SecDef, 18 Oct 65, cited in note 9.

11. MACV briefing on Phase 2 Concept and Forces, 18 Oct 65, cited in note 8, 6, 29.

12. Summary of DePuy briefing for SecDef, 18 Oct 65, cited in note 9; msg JCS 4827 CJCS to CINCPAC/CO-MUSMACV, 22 Oct 65, Cable files, OSD Hist. On Taylor's views, see msg JCS 4500-65 Wheeler to Sharp and Westmoreland, 20 Nov 65, fldr Westmoreland Eyes Only Msg file, 1 Oct-31 Dec 65, CMH. Similar reservations were echoed in draft msg Bundy to Saigon, 26 Oct 65, *FRUS 1964-68*, 3:498-99; msg WDC 9154 DePuy to Westmoreland, 22 Oct 65, fldr Westmoreland Eyes Only Msg file, 1 Oct-31 Dec 65, CMH; CM-929-65 for DirJtStaff, 27 Oct 65 (quote) and DJSM 1341-65 for CJCS, 15 Nov 65: fldr Vietnam 091 Oct 1965 and fldr Vietnam 091 Nov 65, box 46, Wheeler Papers, RG 218.

13. Memrcd ActgSecA, 18 Oct 65, fldr Oct 1965, Westmoreland History files, CMH; Cosmas, *MACV: Years of Escalation*, 252-54.

14. Bundy ms, ch 31/31 (quote); msg 1377 Saigon to State, 21 Oct 65, *FRUS 1964-68*, 3:470.

15. Draft memo SecDef for Pres, 3 Nov 65, *FRUS 1964-68*, 3:514-28 (quote, 528). It was delivered to the Texas ranch on 7 November.

16. Johnson, *Vantage Point*, 233-34. No record of the meeting is available; see *FRUS 1964-68*, 3:514, n1 and ed note, 561-62. CMC work notes on regular JCS mtg, 15 Nov 65; memrcd CMC, summary of conv w/SecN, 17 Nov 65: Greene Papers, MHC; JCSM-811-65 for SecDef, 10 Nov 65, fldr Correspondence and Misc Documents, 1965, box 63, Pentagon Papers Backup, Acc 75-062; *JCS and the War in Vietnam*, pt 2:22/10.

17. Memo Taylor for McNamara and Wheeler, 19 Nov 65, fldr Vietnam 091 Nov 65, box 46, Wheeler Papers, RG 218; *JCS and the War in Vietnam*, pt 2:22/11.

18. Msg 1677 Saigon to State, 11 Nov 65, *FRUS 1964-68*, 3:563-68.

19. Carland, *Stemming the Tide*, 133, 145, 150; Special DIA Intell Suppl, SIS-1811-65, 18 Nov 65, Cable files, OSD Hist; McNamara, *In Retrospect*, 221 (quote); msg 231104Z COMUSMACV to CINCPAC, 23 Nov 65, which replied to questions posed in msg 200429Z CINCPAC to COMUSMACV, 20 Nov 65, vol 43, box 24, NSF, CF, Vietnam, LBJL; memo telcon ActgSecState (Ball) and SecDef, 23 Nov 65, *FRUS 1964-68*, 3:580.

20. Msgs JCS 4431-65, 17 Nov 65, and JCS 4542-65, 23 Nov 65, both Wheeler to Westmoreland and Sharp: fldr Westmoreland Eyes Only Msg file, 1 Oct-31 Dec 65, CMH; msg 200429Z CINCPAC to COMUS-MACV, 20 Nov 65, cited in note 19 (quote).

21. McNamara, *In Retrospect*, 221-22; msg 4539-65 SecDef to Lodge and Westmoreland, 23 Nov 65, fldr West-moreland Eyes Only Msg file, 1 Oct-31 Dec 65, CMH.

22. Westmoreland's History Notes, entries for 28 and 29 Nov 65, fldr Westmoreland History files, #2, 25 Oct-20 Dec 65, CMH; COMUSMACV briefing for SecDef, vol 1, 28 Nov 65 (quote), fldr Notebook, box 6, SecDef Subject Decimal files, Acc 70A-1265. On McNamara's request for DePuy see msg JCS 4542-65, 23 Nov 65, cited in note 20.

23. SecDef press conf 29 Nov 65, *McNamara Public Statements, 1965*, 5:2180; McNamara interv, 8 Jan 98, 29 (quote); McNamara, *In Retrospect*, 222 (quote). Stanley Karnow, present at the press conference, remarked that McNamara's attitude had altered perceptibly during his brief Saigon trip (Karnow, *Vietnam*, 480). Syl-vester, "A Think Piece," nd, and impressions from SVN Trip, nd (quote), Notes on SVN trip—Nov 65, OSD Hist.

24. Memo SecDef for Pres, 30 Nov 65, *FRUS 1964-68*, 3:591-94; CMC notes on special SecDef conf w/SvcSecs and JCS, 30 Nov 65 and Nov trip of RSM to SVN, nd (quotes), Greene Papers.

25. Msg JCS 7787 to CINCPAC, 3 Dec 65, fldr Correspondence and Misc Documents, 1965, box 63, Pentagon Papers Backup, Acc 75-062; msg JCS 4758-65 Wheeler to Sharp, 1 Dec 65, fldr Westmoreland Eyes Only Msg file, 1 Oct-31 Dec 65, CMH; msg WDC 10453 Johnson to Westmoreland, 1 Dec 65, ibid; CMC notes of SecDef staff mtg, 6 Dec 65, Greene Papers; McNamara, *In Retrospect*, 223-24; telcon McNamara and Johnson, 2 Dec 65, 12:15 p.m. PNO 9305, WH 6512.01, LBJL; McNaughton 2d dft, Some Observations about Bombing NVN, 18 Jan 66, doc no. CK 3100260202, Declassified Documents Reference System, *http://galenet.galegroup.com.* and 3d dft, Some Paragraphs on Vietnam, 19 Jan 66, excerpted in *Pentagon Papers*, bk 6, IV.C.7.(a), 41-44.

26. Bundy personal notes of mtg, 6 Dec 65 and memo Bundy for Pres, w/atchmt memo for SecDef, 9 Dec 65, *FRUS 1964-68*, 3:604-05, 631-35; memos SecDef for Pres, 30 Nov, 7 Dec 65, ibid, 591-94, 615-19.

27. Valenti notes of mtg, 17 Dec 65; Bundy personal notes of mtg w/Pres, 7 Dec 65; Valenti notes of mtg, 18 Dec 65: ibid, 645-47 (quote, 645), 620, 662-63; telcon McNamara and Johnson, 2 Dec 65, 12:15 p.m., cited in note 25.

28. McNamara describes his emotions in *In Retrospect*, 207 (quote); see also Clifford, *Counsel*, 434-35 (quote); CMC notes on spcl JCS mtg w/SecDef and UnderSecDef, 8 Dec 65, Greene Papers.

29. CMC notes of SecDef staff mtg, 6 Dec 65, cited in note 25; msg 954 State to Bangkok and other posts, 3 Dec 65, Cable files, OSD Hist.

30. Memrcd CMC, mtg w/Pres, 10 Dec 65, memrcd CMC, personal notes covering CMC visit to LBJ Ranch 10 December 1965, 12 Dec 65 (quotes), CMC notes on regular JCS mtg, 1 Dec 65 (quote): all Greene Papers.

31. Valenti notes of mtg, 20 Jan 66, *FRUS 1964-68*, 4:98-100 (quote); memo SecDef for Pres, 24 Jan 66, ibid, 112-17.

32. Johnson, *Vantage Point*, 246. The president's comments appear in telcon Pres and SecDef, 7 Mar 66, *FRUS 1964-68*, 4:273; ed note, ibid, 691.

33. McNamara made these remarks to the service secretaries, JCS, and key OSD members. See Steadman, draft Summary for Record, 9 Feb 66, *Pentagon Papers*, bk 5, IV.C.6.(a), 29-33. On Taylor's observation, see draft msg Taylor to Sharp, 28 Dec 65, *FRUS 1964-68*, 3:728-29.

34. JCSM-76-66 for SecDef, 3 Feb 66, *FRUS 1964-68*, 4:198-201 (quote); msg CJCS 2837-66 Wheeler to Westmoreland, 20 May 66, ibid, 394-95 (quotes).

35. *JCS and the War in Vietnam*, pt 2:32/1-2; U.S. Army Mil Assist Command, Vietnam, "MACV Command History, 1966," ch 3:66, fldr Vietnam, box 63, Pentagon Papers Backup, Acc 75-062; Carland, *Stemming the Tide*, 155-57; memo ASD(SA) for SecDef, 14 Jan 66, excerpted in *Pentagon Papers*, bk 5, IV.C.6.(a), 26-27; msg JCS 1838 JCS to CINCPAC, 17 Jan 66, Cable files, OSD Hist.

36. CMC, debrief by SecDef of his mtg in Honolulu w/Pres and Vietnamese ldrs, 9 Feb 66, Greene Papers; Westmoreland History files, #4, 30 Jan-13 Mar 1966, 10-11; Westmoreland History Notes, 2 Jan-8 Jan 1966, 54, CMH; paper by McNamara and McNaughton, 10 Feb 66, *FRUS 1964-68*, 4:216, n2; Herring, *LBJ and Vietnam*, 68, 135; Carland, *Stemming the Tide*, 155-56.

37. Steadman, draft Summary for Record, 9 Feb 66, cited in note 33; CMC, debrief, 9 Feb 66, cited in note 36; memo SecDef for SvcSecs and CJCS, 10 Mar 66, fldr Southeast Asia Area, 000.1-320.2, box 8, ISA General files, Acc 70A-6649.

38. *JCS and the War in Vietnam*, pt 2:32/4-5; JCSM-130-66 for SecDef, 1 Mar 66, fldr 320.2 Southeast Asia 1 Mar 66, fldr Southeast Asia Area, 000.1 320.2, box 8, ISA General files, Acc 70A-6649; memos SecDef to SvcSecs and JCS w/encl, 10 Mar 66, SecDef for SvcSecs et al, SEA Deployment Plan, 11 Apr 66: fldr SEA Deployments—CY 1966, box 324, Subj files, OSD Hist; memo SecDef for SvcSecs, CJCS, ASDs, 2 Jul 66, fldr Correspondence and Misc Documents, 1966, box 63, Pentagon Papers Backup, Acc 75-062; memo SecDef for Pres, Sched of Deployments to SVN, w/atchmt, 15 Jul 66, fldr SEA Deployments—CY 1966, box 324, Subj files, OSD Hist.

39. Poole, *JCS and National Policy, 1965-68*, 9, pt 1:317-18; Carland, *Stemming the Tide*, 158; Cosmas, *MACV: Years of Escalation*, 259, 397.

40. Msg JCS 1838 JCS to CINCPAC, 17 Jan 66, cited in note 35; Enthoven and Smith, *How Much is Enough?*, 274; Steadman, draft Summary for Record, 9 Feb 66, cited in note 33; CMC, debrief, 9 Feb 66, cited in note 36 (quote); DoD News Release 453-68, 15 May 68.

41. Memo SecState for Pres, 24 Apr 66, w/atchmt, Basic Choices in Vietnam, 25 Apr 66, *FRUS 1964-68*, 4:360-65; Smith summary notes of 557th NSC mtg, 10 May 66, ibid, 382 (quote); memcons Harriman w/ SecDef, 14 May, 28 May, 30 May 66, ibid, 385, 404-05; Clarke, *The Final Years*, 127-29, 141.

42. Ltr CINCPAC to JCS, 18 Jun 66, fldr Correspondence and Misc Documents, 1966, box 63, Pentagon Papers Backup, Acc 75-062; *JCS and the War in Vietnam*, pt 2:32/7-8; "MACV History, 1966," ch 3:70; memo Pres for SecDef, 28 Jun 66, *Pentagon Papers*, bk 5, IV.C.6.(a), 49.

43. News confs, 7 and 11 Jul 66, *McNamara Public Statements, 1966*, 7:2441, 2450; NIE 14.3-66, 7 Jul 66, *FRUS 1964-68*, 4:488-89; paper by McNamara and McNaughton, 10 Feb 66, ibid, 217-18; Westmoreland, *Soldier Reports*, 160-61; ltr CINCPAC to JCS, 4 Aug 66 w/encl CINCPAC briefing for SecDef, 8 Jul 66, fldr SEA Deployments—CY 1966, box 324, Subj files, OSD Hist.

44. JCSM-450-66 for SecDef, 8 Jul 66, w/app (quote), memo ASD(SA) for SecDef, 13 Jul 66: fldr Correspondence and Misc Documents, 1966, box 63, Pentagon Papers Backup, Acc 75-062; memos SecDef for Pres, Schedule of Deployments to SVN, 15 Jul 66 (quote) and SecDef for Pres, Approval for Additional Deployments to South Vietnam, 15 Jul 66: fldr Vietnam 1966 1223-24, box 34, SecDef Bio files, OSD Hist.

45. Msg 032207Z Emrick (Hawaii) to Westmoreland, 3 Aug 66 (quote), fldr Westmoreland Eyes Only Msg file, 1 Jul-30 Sep 66, CMH; *JCS and the War in Vietnam*, pt 2:32/8 (quote); memo SecDef for JCS, 5 Aug 66 (quotes), fldr SEA Deployments—CY 1966, box 324, Subj files, OSD Hist.

46. Msg MAC 6814 COMUSMACV to CINCPAC, 7 Aug 66, *FRUS 1964-68*, 4:564-65; msg 29797 COMUSMACV to CINCPAC, 26 Aug 66, ibid, 603-06; memo Taylor for Pres, 30 Aug 66, memo Rostow for Pres, 31 Aug 66: ibid, 608, 613.

47. Memcon Harriman w/SecDef, 14 May 66, ibid, 385; McNamara, *In Retrospect*, 262; memo SecDef for DCI, 2 Sep 66 (quote), fldr Vietnam, 1309, box 34, SecDef Bio files, OSD Hist; Hunt, *Pacification*, 73, 76-78; DPM SecDef for Pres, 22 Sep 66, *FRUS 1964-68*, 4:659; memo SecA for SecDef, 2 Jun 66, Livesay mins, SecDef staff mtg, 13 Jun 66 w/atchmt, PROVN Briefing, nd: fldr Staff Meetings, Apr-June 1966, box 12, AFPC and SecDef Staff Meeting files, Acc 330-77-0062; memo SecDef for Starbird, 14 Sep 66, *FRUS 1964-68*, 4:635-37 (quotes).

48. Rpt of Ad Hoc Study Group, "Intensification of the Military Operations in Vietnam—Concept and Appraisal," 14 Jul 65, H6 thru 8, fldr Vietnam Buildup Mat'l to SecDef, Phase I, 22 Jul 1965, box 94, ASD(C) files, OSD Hist; November 1965 Saigon Conf w/SecDef, nd, tab 5b, fldr Notebook, box 97, ibid; *JCS and the War in Vietnam*, pt 3:35/21-22; memo McNaughton for SecDef, 30 Jan 66, fldr McNTN 2-Drafts 1966 (3) box 1, Warnke Papers, John McNaughton files, LBJL; CRS, *U.S. Government and the Vietnam War*, pt 4:454; Shapley, *Promise and Power*, 362-63.

49. McNamara, *In Retrospect*, 246; ltr Kistiakowsky to SecDef, 23 Jun 66, *FRUS 1964-68*, 4:455-57; IDA, JASON Division, "Air-Supported Anti-Infiltration Barrier," Study S-255, Aug 66, 11, 12, 27, 33, fldr JTF 728, box 4, ISA General files, Acc 70A-6649 (quotes). The group presented their conclusions to McNamara and McNaughton on 30 August 1966 in Washington; see *Pentagon Papers*, bk 6, IV.C.7.(a), 160 and Naulty, *The War against Trucks*, 8-10.

50. Memo SecDef for CJCS, w/atchmt, 3 Sep 66, fldr 381-1966 Jan, box 4, ISA General files, Acc 70A-6649; memrcd Foster, 7 Sep 66 (quote), fldr 381 JTF 728 Jan 66, ibid; memo SecDef for CJCS, 10 Sep 66, w/ atchmt memo SecDef for Starbird, 10 Sep 66 (draft), fldr Reading File Sep 12-1, 1966, box 126, McNamara Records, RG 200; CM-1732-66 for SecDef, 8 Sep 66, fldr 091 SEA-Barrier thru 30 Dec 66, box 36, Wheeler Papers, RG 218; memo SecDef for DirDCA, 15 Sep 66, *FRUS 1964-68*, 4:635-37; msg 130705Z CINCPAC to JCS, 13 Oct 66, Cable files, OSD Hist; JCSM-594-66 for SecDef, 17 Sep 66, *FRUS 1964-68*, 4:639-40; CMC notes on JCS mtg, 15 Sep 66, Greene Papers. Greene later argued that McNamara's memo to the president stating the JCS concurred with the barrier concept had misrepresented their position; see memrcd CMC, 24 Nov 66, Greene Papers.

51. Memcon mtg McNaughton w/Sullivan, 28 Jun 66, *FRUS 1964-68*, 28:473-74; msgs ASD(ISA) to Vientiane, 7 Oct 66, 2108 Vientiane to Saigon, 9 Oct 66: fldr JTF 728, box 4, ISA General files, Acc 70A-6649; ltr Sullivan to W. Bundy, 17 Oct 66, *FRUS 1964-68*, 28:517-18 (quote).

52. Memo SecDef for Pres, 14 Oct 66, *FRUS 1964-68*, 4:729 (quote); msg Jt Def-State 6070 SecDef to Vientiane, 21 Oct 66, fldr JTF 728, box 4, ISA General files, Acc 70-6649; msg 182005Z Defense Communications Planning Grp to MACV, 18 Oct 66, Cable files, OSD Hist; memo SecDef for Pres, 14 Nov 66, *FRUS 1964-68*, 4:842; transc Wheeler test, 23 May 68, SSCA DoD FY 1969 Appropriations hearing, fldr—Clifford/Nitze—23 May 68, 1808, box 71, ASD(C) files, OSD Hist. See also memo SecDef for Pres, 11 Sep 67, fldr Vietnam 1967, 1250-52, box 36, SecDef Bio files, OSD Hist.

53. Answer to Question No. 127, fldr Symington Questions 1-304, Re FY 69 Posture Statement – Office Master, box 75, ASD(C) files, OSD Hist; JCSM-652-66 for SecDef, 10 Oct 66, fldr JTF 728, box 4, ISA General files, Acc 70A-6649; msgs 46500 COMUSMACV to CJCS, 21 Oct 66, JCS 8228 JCS to CINCPAC, 18 Nov 66, JCS 8390 JCS to CINCPAC, 19 Nov 66, 230410Z CINCPAC to JCS, 23 Nov 66: Cable files, OSD Hist. On the $1.5 billion in construction costs, see Wheeler test, 23 May 68, SSCA, *Hearings: DoD Appropriations for FY 1969*, 2489; CMC work notes on JCS mtg No 150, 5 Oct 66, Greene Papers; memo SecDef for Pres, 11 Sep 67, fldr Vietnam 1967, box 36, SecDef Bio files, OSD Hist; msgs JCS 7166-66 Wheeler to Sharp and Westmoreland, 23 Nov 66 and MAC 10295 Westmoreland to Sharp, 24 Nov 66: fldr 091 SEA Barrier thru 30 Dec 66, box 36, Wheeler Papers, RG 218; JCSM-740-66 for SecDef, 1 Dec 66, fldr JTF 728, box 4, ISA General files, Acc 70A-6649 noted the availability in Vietnam of only 1,800 or so troops of the more than 45,000 JTF 728 required; *JCS and the War in Vietnam*, pt 3:45/22.

54. Cover for 12/12 Meeting on Project 728, 9 Dec 66, fldr JTF 728, box 4, ISA General files, Acc 70A-6649; Cosmas, *MACV: Years of Escalation*, 424. McNaughton's handwritten marginalia on the cover sheet describe McNamara's 12 December decision. MACV's lengthy, four-part cable questioning the Defense Communications Planning Group's (DCPG) assumptions was apparently the catalyst for the meeting; see msg MAC J321 COMUSMACV to DCPG, 8 Dec 66, Cable files, OSD Hist; telcon McNamara and Pres, 12 Dec 66, in ed note, *FRUS 1964-68*, 4:932 (quotes); *JCS and the War in Vietnam*, pt 3:45/18.

55. *JCS and the War in Vietnam*, pt 2:32/7-8; telcon SecDef and Pres, 19 Sep 66, *FRUS 1964-68*, 4:649; JCSM-646-66 for SecDef, 7 Oct 66, fldr JCSMs 603-66 to 699-66, box 183, Wheeler Papers, RG 218.

56. SecDef remarks to press, 8 Oct 66, *McNamara Public Statements, 1966*, 2:2702; msg 4244 SecDef to Saigon, 2 Oct 66, *FRUS 1964-68*, 4:684-85; Jt Logistics Rev Bd, *Logistic Support in the Vietnam Era*, monograph 14, "Military Personnel in Operational Logistics," A/6-7; msg 7332 Saigon to State and DoD for McNamara, 1 Oct 66, fldr Cables 1966-1967, box 65, Pentagon Papers Backup, Acc 75-062; Cosmas, *MACV: Years of Escalation*, 412-14; msg 44378 COMUSMACV to CINCPAC, 5 Oct 66, Cable files, OSD Hist; CRS, *U.S. Government and the Vietnam War*, 4:457. The savings were made by computing an average (not year-end) total strength of 430,000 troops. That meant if 300,000 servicemen were in Vietnam on 1 January 1966 and 463,000 by 31 December 1966, the lower average strength, 381,500, not the higher end-strength figure of 463,000, would be used to compute piaster costs.

57. On Lodge's remark see CRS, *U.S. Government and the Vietnam War*, pt 4:452-53, but see also McNamara, *In Retrospect*, 262-63.

58. Memo SecDef for Pres, 14 Oct 66, *FRUS 1964-68*, 4:727-35.

59. JCSM-672-66 for SecDef, 14 Oct 66 (quotes), Smith summary notes of 565th NSC mtg, 15 Oct 66, msg JCS 6339-66 to COMUSMACV, 17 Oct 66: *FRUS 1964-68*, 4:738-42, 752, 756-57; *Pentagon Papers*, bk 5, IV.C.6.(a), 96-97; memo McNaughton for SecDef, 26 Oct 66, msg MAC 9451 Westmoreland to

Wheeler, 27 Oct 66, Rostow notes of mtg, 23 Oct 66: *FRUS 1964-68*, 4:784, 787, 773; msg 48649 CO-MUSMACV to CINCPAC, 7 Nov 66, Cable files, OSD Hist; see also Cosmas, *MACV: Years of Escalation*, 378-79.

60. JCSM 702-66 for SecDef, 4 Nov 66, *Pentagon Papers*, bk 5, IV.C.C.6.(a), 100-01; *JCS and the War in Vietnam*, pt 2:32/9; SecDef remarks at news conf, 5 Nov 66, *McNamara Public Statements, 1966*, 2:2728-29 (quote, 2729).

61. *Pentagon Papers*, bk 5, IV.C.6.(a), 101-03 (quote, 103); memo SecDef for CJCS, 11 Nov 66, *FRUS 1964-68*, 4:826-27; *JCS and the War in Vietnam*, pt 2:32/10-11.

62. Memo SecDef for Pres, 17 Nov 66 (quote), excerpted in ed note, *FRUS 1964-68*, 4:850-52; memrcd Harriman, Addition to McNamara Conv, 26 Nov 66, fldr McNamara, Robert S. file, Special files, Public Service JFK-LBJ, box 486, Harriman Papers, LC.

63. CRS, *U.S. Government and the Vietnam War*, pt 4:479-81; memo Moyers for Pres, 30 Sep 66, *FRUS 1964-68*, 4:677-78.

64. Draft NSAM, 10 Dec 66, memo Rostow for Pres, 30 Nov 66, w/atchmt "A Strategy for Viet Nam, 1967," 28 Nov 66: *FRUS 1964-68*, 4:922-24, 873-82; msg JCS 1663 to CINCPAC, 14 Dec 66, Cable files, OSD Hist.

65. Msg 200805Z CINCPAC to JCS, 20 Dec 66, Cable files, OSD Hist; *Pentagon Papers*, bk 5, IV.C.6.(a), 9-11.

66. Taylor paper, 1 Jan 67, memo Komer for Pres, 23 Jan 67, msg MACJOO-00160 COMUSMACV to CJCS and CINCPAC, 2 Jan 67: *FRUS 1964-68*, 5:1-2, 56, 7-8; McNamara, Blight, and Brigham, *Argument Without End*, 307-08.

67. Msg JCS 1284-67 Wheeler to Sharp and Westmoreland, 17 Feb 67, Westmoreland History files, #13, CMH.

68. Msg MAC 1658 Westmoreland to Wheeler, 17 Feb 67, msg 191602Z Wheeler to Sharp and Westmoreland, 18 Feb 67: Westmoreland Eyes Only Msg file, 1 Jan-31 Mar 67, CMH; notes of mtg w/Pres, 17 Feb 67, *FRUS 1964-68*, 5:184-85 (quotes).

69. The original JCS proposals, prepared for Deputy Secretary Vance, included three programs with a category of risk assessment for each; see memo Vance for Katzenbach, 21 Feb 67, *Pentagon Papers*, bk 5, IV.C.6.(b), 49-51. The final version, prepared by McNaughton and distributed to the president and others at the meeting, evaluated in narrative form the benefits and dangers of the various proposals; see CRS, *U.S. Government and the Vietnam War*, pt 4:563-66 (quote); msg JCS 1422-67 Wheeler to Sharp and Westmoreland, 22 Feb 67, fldr February 1967, box 22, Gibbons Papers, LBJL; McNaughton, Military Program Against North Vietnam, 2d redraft, 13 Feb 67, fldr Viet 320 1967, box 5, SecDef Subject Decimal files, Acc 72A-2467.

70. MACV's insufficiency of forces is acknowledged in msg MACV 09101 COMUSMACV to CINCPAC, 18 Mar 67, *FRUS 1964-68*, 5:253-55; *JCS and the War in Vietnam*, pt 3:42/12. On marine operations see Telfer, Rogers, and Fleming, *Fighting the North Vietnamese 1967*, chs 1-5; msg MACJ321 COMUSMACV to CINCPAC, 19 Apr 67 (quote), fldr Cables 1966-1967, box 65, Pentagon Papers Backup, Acc 75-062.

71. *JCS and the War in Vietnam*, pt 3:42/13; msg MACV 09101 COMUSMACV to CINCPAC, 18 Mar 67, cited in note 70; Westmoreland, *Soldier Reports*, 214 (quotes); notes of General Westmoreland's report in Mar 67 to Pres et al at Guam Conference in Barrett, ed, *LBJ's Vietnam Papers*, 404 (quote); memcon Carver, 21 Mar 67, *FRUS 1964-68*, 5:277; *Background Briefings of Secretary of Defense McNamara, 1967*, 29, 31; msg 9619 SecDef to CSA et al, 23 Mar 67, Cable files, OSD Hist.

72. Memo Rostow for Pres, 10 Mar 67, *FRUS 1964-68*, 5:241-42 (quote); msg JCS 59881 JCS to CINCPAC, 24 Mar 67, fldr Cables 1966-1967, box 65, Pentagon Papers Backup, Acc 75-062; msg MACJ 312 CO-MUSMACV to JCS, 28 Mar 67, Cable files, OSD Hist; Johnson, *Vantage Point*, 369; Westmoreland, *Soldier Reports*, 227-28 (quotes). On 13 April 1967, the J-3 recommended approval of MACV optimum force requirements with reserve call-up and involuntary extensions; see *JCS and the War in Vietnam*, pt 3:43/2.

73. Gard notes, staff mtg, 24 Apr 67 (quote), Gard Notebook, OSD Hist; Palmer, *The 25-Year War*, 48.

74. Thompson, *To Hanoi and Back*, 67-68; *JCS and the War in Vietnam*, pt 3:43/2-3; JCSM 218-67 for SecDef, 20 Apr 67, fldr Viet 370, 1967, box 5, SecDef Subject Decimal files, Acc 72A-2467; ed note, *FRUS 1964-68*, 5:336-37.

75. Memo ActgSecState Katzenbach for McNaughton, 24 Apr 67, excerpted in *Pentagon Papers*, bk 5, IV.C.6.(b), 77-78; memo Komer for SecDef and DepSecDef, 24 Apr 67, *FRUS 1964-68*, 5:345-47; memo Rostow for Pres, 27 Apr 67, in Barrett, ed, *LBJ's Vietnam Papers*, 411-12.

76. Christian notes on discus w/Pres, 27 Apr 67, *FRUS 1964-68*, 5:349-51; McNamara, *In Retrospect*, 265; Westmoreland History Notes, 27 Mar-30 Apr 67, Westmoreland History files, #15, CMH. Christian's notes state that Westmoreland said with the maximum force the war could be ended in two years. The

discrepancy may result from Westmoreland basing his estimate from the time the units actually deployed to Vietnam.

77. Memo W. Bundy for Katzenbach, 1 May 67, *FRUS 1964-68*, 5:361-66; Philip Odeen et al, COMUS-MACV's Minimum Force Requirements – An Analysis, nd [likely late Apr 67], dft memo Enthoven for SecDef, 28 Apr 67: fldr Misc Documents, 1967, box 65, Pentagon Papers Backup, Acc 75-062; memo Enthoven for SecDef, 1 May 67, ibid; ed note, *FRUS 1964-68*, 5:366-67.

78. Memo McNaughton for SecDef, 6 May 67, *FRUS 1964-68*, 5:381-83.

79. McNamara, *In Retrospect*, 269 (quote); SecDef DPM for Pres, 19 May 67, *FRUS 1964-68*, 5:423-38; Shapley, *Promise and Power*, 421 (quote, emphasis in original).

80. On the proposed visit see msg JCS 3332 Wheeler to Westmoreland, 5 May 67, *FRUS 1964-68*, 5:381; Johnson, *Vantage Point*, 366 (quote), 370.

81. JCSM-286-67 for SecDef, 20 May 67, fldr Viet 385 (Jan-May) 1967, box 5, SecDef Subject Decimal files, Acc 72A-2467; JCSM-288-67 for SecDef, 20 May 67, fldr McNTN Memoranda 1967 (2), box 5, Warnke Papers, John McNaughton files, LBJL; ed note, *FRUS 1964-68*, 5:458-59.

82. Msg JCS 3891 Wheeler to Sharp, 25 May 67 (quote), fldr May 1967, box 25, Gibbons Papers, LBJL; JCSM-307-67 for SecDef, 1 Jun 67 (quotes), fldr Misc Documents, 1967, box 65, Pentagon Papers Backup, Acc 75-062; ed note, *FRUS 1964-68*, 5:458-59; msg 130013Z Sharp to Westmoreland, 13 June 67, Westmoreland Eyes Only Msg file, 1 Apr-30 Jun 1967, CMH.

83. Memo Rostow for Pres, 20 May 67, fldr Vietnam 2EE 1965-1967, box 75 NSF, CF Vietnam, LBJL; msg JCS 4476 Wheeler to Sharp and Westmoreland, 15 Jun 67 (quote), Westmoreland Eyes Only Msg file, 1 Apr-30 Jun 1967, CMH; ed note, *FRUS 1964-68*, 5:583-84.

84. Memo ASD(SA) for SecDef et al, 25 Jul 67, w/atchmt Briefings Given SecDef, Saigon, South Vietnam, July 7-8, 1967, 3, 9, 14-16, 59, 128, fldr Notebook, Secretary of Defense Vietnam Trip (Briefings), 25 Jul 67, box 97, ASD(C) files, OSD Hist; SecDef Briefings, 7-8 Jul 67, fldr July 1967, box 27, Gibbons Papers, LBJL; memo Kerwin for Westmoreland w/atchmt, SecDef Briefing, 6 Jul 67, Westmoreland History files, #19, CMH.

85. Briefings Given SecDef, cited in note 84, 129, 133, 138; Westmoreland History Notes, 7-9 Jul 67, fldr Westmoreland History files, #19, CMH.

86. Msg JCS 1473 JCS to CINCPAC, 15 Jul 67 and Westmoreland History Notes, 7-9 Jul 67, fldr Westmoreland History files, #19, CMH; msg 893 Saigon to State, 12 Jul 67, *FRUS 1964-68*, 5:593.

87. CMC notes of JCS mtg, 19 Jul 67 (quote), Greene Papers; memo Enthoven for SecDef, 5 Jul 67, fldr Misc Documents, 1967, box 65, Pentagon Papers Backup, Acc 75-062.

88. On McNamara's mood see McNamara, *In Retrospect*, 283 (quote). Tom Johnson notes of mtg, 12 Jul 67, *FRUS 1964-68*, 5:601-02 (quote), 607 (quote), 609; memrcd Taylor, mtg w/Pres, 12 Jul 67, fldr 621-A-71H VN Policy 1967, item #20, box 55, Taylor Papers, NDU.

89. Westmoreland History Notes, 12 Jul 67 (quote), fldr Westmoreland History files, #19, CMH; Tom Johnson notes of mtgs, 13 Jul 67, 12:40-1:02 p.m. and 1:25-2:45 p.m., *FRUS 1964-68*, 5:610-11.

90. Memrcd Brehm, SEA Deployments, 14 Jul 67, fldr Misc Documents, 1967, box 65, Pentagon Papers Backup, Acc 75-062; Nitze notes, 3:15 p.m. mtg, 13 Jul 67, fldr DoD Deputy Secretary Defense Notes 1967 (1 of 3), box 85, Nitze Papers, LC; Tom Johnson notes of mtg, 14 Jul 67, *FRUS 1964-68*, 5:619-21; memrcd Taylor, Disc of Clifford-Taylor Mission w/McNamara, July 15, 1967, 17 Jul 67, fldr 621-C A Clifford-Taylor Mission to SEA-Jul-Aug, 67 (67-69), item #1, box 58, Taylor Papers, NDU. President Johnson had broached the possibility a few days earlier; see Tom Johnson notes of mtg, 12 Jul 67, *FRUS 1964-68*, 5:609.

VI. MORE THAN EXPECTED: SUPPLEMENTALS AND BUDGETS, 1966–1968

1. "Draft Administrative History of the Department of Defense, 1963-1969" (hereafter "DoD Admin History"), 6:2071, OSD Hist.

2. King, "The President & Fiscal Policy in 1966," 688.

3. Memrcd McNamara, 9 Dec 65, telcons w/members Congress re South Vietnam, 8-9 Dec 65, fldr Memos for the Record, box 1, McNamara Papers, Acc 71A-3470.

4. Memcon Vance and Sikes, 10 Jan 66, fldr 101 Interviews with Members of Congress, box 4, ibid.

5. Memrcd Vance, 12 Jan 66, box 49, McNamara Records, RG 200.

6. SecDef statement before HSCA, 26 Jan 66, Supplemental for Southeast Asia, FY 1966, 3, 5-7, 15, Table 4, fldr House Appropriations Hearings 1966 Supplemental, January 26, 1966, box 44, ASD(C) files, OSD Hist.

7. Transc McNamara test, 26 Jan 66, HSCA, Hearings regarding Proposed Supplemental Appropriation for DoD, 4, 17-18, 20, 21, ibid.

8. McNamara test, 26 Jan 66, HSCA, *Hearings: Supplemental Defense Appropriations for 1966*, 21.

9. Transc McNamara test, 28 Jan 66, HSCA, Hearings regarding Proposed Supplemental Appropriation for DoD, FY 1966, 399 (quote), 419-20, fldr Sec'y McNamara and Gen. Wheeler testimony before House Appropriations Cte, Suppl Appro, 66-1/28/66, box 46, ASD(C) files, OSD Hist. These "off-the-record" remarks were deleted from the published version cited in note 8, 155, 160.

10. HCA, *Supplemental Defense Appropriation Bill, 1966*, H Rpt 1316, 11 Mar 66, 19.

11. *Hearings*, cited in note 8, 160.

12. PL 89-374, 25 Mar 66 (80 Stat 79); Livesay mins SecDef staff mtg, 10 Jan 66, fldr Staff Meeting Jan-Mar 1966, box 12, AFPC, Acc 330-77-0062.

13. McNamara test, 14 Feb 66, HSCA, *Hearings: Department of Defense Appropriations for 1967*, pt 1:1, 78-79.

14. FY 1966 Budget Amendment and Planned Supplemental for SEA, 24 Jul 65, fldr vol II FY 66 Budget Supplemental Supporting Data, box 1, McNamara Papers, Acc 71A-3470.

15. McNamara test, 10 Mar 66, HCAS, *Hearings: Military Posture and H.R. 13456*, 7586-87.

16. Ibid, 7589-90.

17. Memo Schultze for Pres, 17 Jan 66, fldr New Legislative Programs and the 1968 Budget, box 9, Federal Records, CEA, LBJL; memo Schultze for Pres, 18 Feb 66, fldr Bureau of Budget, vol 1, box 7, NSF Agency file, LBJL; memo Ackley for Pres, 4 Mar 66, in msg CAP 66075, fldr Sent Ranch 3/53/6 66, box 55, NSF Situation Room files, LBJL; Califano, *Triumph & Tragedy*, 140-41.

18. Memo Leventhal for Pres, 4 Mar 66, fldr FI 11 Taxation 6/29/65-3/16/66, box 55, WHCF GEN FI 9 3/21/68, LBJL; memo Califano for Pres, 5 Mar 66, fldr LA 2 2/16/65-4/4/66, box 7, WHCF LABOR EX LA 2 9/3/65-7/11/67, LBJL; memo Pres for Heads of Exec Depts and Agencies, 15 Mar 66, fldr Budget Development-FY 1967, box 54, ASD(C) files, OSD Hist.

19. Memrcd Glass, mtg on DoD FY 67 Budget, (13 Nov 65), 15 Nov 65, fldr DoD FY 67 Budget Book (2 of 2), box 17, NSF Agency file, LBJL; memo Nitze for SecDef, 26 Feb 66, fldr 110.01 Jan-Mar 1966, box 34, SecDef Subject Decimal files, Acc 70A-4443. At a 10 January staff meeting, McNamara stated the supplemental funds were needed by 1 March. See Livesay mins, SecDef staff mtg, 10 Jan 66, cited in note 12.

20. Memo ASD(C) for SecDef, 25 Feb 66, fldr 110.01 Jan-Mar 1966, box 34, SecDef Subject Decimal files, Acc 70A-4443.

21. Memo DepSecDef for SvcSecs et al, 2 Mar 66, fldr Compt Mangt CY 66, box 785, Subj files, OSD Hist.

22. Memo DepSecDef for SvcSecs et al, 19 Mar 66, fldr 110.01 Jan-Mar 1966, box 34, SecDef Subject Decimal files, Acc 70A-4443.

23. Memo SecDef for SvcSecs et al, 11 Apr 66, fldr 110.01 Apr 1-15 1966, ibid. Service budget estimates are found as memos SecAF for SecDef, 4 Apr 66, SecA for SecDef, 4 Apr 66, and SecN for SecDef, 4 Apr 66, ibid.

24. Memos ASD(C) for SecDef, 21, 22 Apr 66, 5 May 66, fldr 110.01 1-15 Nov 1966, box 33, ibid; memrcd McNamara, conv between Mahon, McNamara and Vance on 4 May 1966, fldr Memos for the Record, box 1, McNamara Papers, Acc 71A-3470.

25. McNamara test, 8 Mar 66, HCAS, *Hearings*, cited in note 15, 7289.

26. McNamara test, 14 Feb 66, cited in note 13, 4.

27. Transc McNamara test, 3 Mar 66 at SCFR hearings regarding amendments to the Foreign Assistance Act (Excerpts) (Exec Sess, not subsequently published), 828-29, fldr Vietnam 1966 II, box 33, SecDef Bio files, OSD Hist.

28. Hargrove and Morley, eds, *The President and the Council of Economic Advisers*, 252.

29. McNamara test, 9 Mar 66, HCAS, *Hearings*, cited in note 15, 7432-33.

30. Memo ASD(C) for SecDef, 17 Jan 66, fldr 110.01 Jan-Mar 1966, box 34, SecDef Subject Decimal files, Acc 70A-4443.

31. Memo ASD(C) for SecDef, 21 Apr 66, cited in note 24.

32. Memrcd McNamara, conv between Mahon, McNamara and Vance on 4 May 1966, cited in note 24.

33. Memo SecDef for SvcSecs et al, 22 Jun 66, fldr Budget Development-FY 1967, box 54, ASD(C) files, OSD Hist.

34. Transc McNamara test, 5 Oct 66, for HCAS Regarding Reprogramming Actions, FY 1967 (Excerpts), 1372, fldr Vietnam, 1966 III, 1967 I, box 34, SecDef Bio files, OSD Hist.

35. Memo SecDef for SvcSecs et al, 22 Jun 66, cited in note 33.

36. CMC notes of regular JCS meeting, 23 May 66 (quotes), No 130, vol 11, Greene Papers, MHC; memrcd Kalen, mtg SecDef and SecN, 30 May 66, fldr 5050/2 #2, Trip Reports, box 20, Double Zero-1966 Subject files 5050/2 thru 5060, NHC.

37. Memos Rath for ASD(C), 26 May 66, ASD(C) for SecDef, 9 Jun 66, fldr 110.01 1-15 Nov 1966, box 33, SecDef Subject Decimal files, Acc 70A-4443.

38. Hargrove and Morley, eds, *President and the Council of Economic Advisers*, 226, 250.

39. Ibid, 254-55; interv Gardner Ackley by Joe B. Frantz, 13 Apr 73, 1:32, LBJL.

40. King, "The President & Fiscal Policy," 687.

41. Memo Califano for Pres, 5 Mar 66, fldr LA 2 2/16/66-4/4/66, box 7, WHCF Labor EX LA 2 9/3/65-7/11/67, LBJL.

42. Memo Ackley for Pres, 4 Mar 66, in msg CAP 66075, fldr Sent Ranch 3/5-3/6 66, box 55, NSF Situation Room files, LBJL; memo Ackley et al for Pres, 12 Mar 66, fldr FI 11 Taxation, box 44, White House Confidential file FI 9, LBJL; memo Califano for Pres, 25 Mar 66, fldr 11-3 CEA 2/18/66-3/26/66, box 58, WHCF EX FG 11-3 9/11/65, LBJL; King, "The President & Fiscal Policy," 694-95. Compare with the president's version in Johnson, *Vantage Point*, 444.

43. Johnson, *Vantage Point*, 444; King, "The President & Fiscal Policy," 694-95 (quote).

44. Economic Report of the President, 26 Jan 67, *Johnson Public Papers, 1967*, 1:78; *Annual Report of the Council of Economic Advisers*, 19 Jan 67, H Doc 28, 49-50.

45. Memos Ackley for Pres, 10 May 66, Schultze for Pres, 11 May 66: fldr FI 11 3/17/66-8/20/66, box 56, WHCF EX FI 11 3/17/68, LBJL; Anderson and Hazleton, *Managing Macroeconomic Policy*, 36-37; King, "The President & Fiscal Policy," 696-97.

46. King, "The President & Fiscal Policy," 697 (quote); memo Ackley for Pres, 4 Jun 66, fldr Council of Economic Advisors, box 10, NSF Agency file, LBJL; "Business Roundup," *Fortune*, Jul 66, 15; "Business Roundup," ibid, Aug 66, 19. The July assessment was also read into the *Cong Rec*, 28 Jul 66, 16626.

47. Memo Schultze for Ackley, 10 Jun 66, fldr 110.01 1-15 Nov 1966, box 33, SecDef Subject Decimal files, Acc 70A-4443.

48. Memo Mansfield for Pres w/atchmt, 29 Jun 66, *FRUS 1964-68*, 4:464-67; memo Schultze for Pres, 21 Jun 66, fldr Bureau of the Budget, vol I (1 of 2), box 7, NSF Agency file, LBJL.

49. Memos Tom Johnson for Pres, 18, 19 July (quote), mtgs w/Cong leaders, box 1, Tom Johnson Notes of Meetings, LBJL.

50. Kearns, *Lyndon Johnson and the American Dream*, 123.

51. Califano, *Triumph & Tragedy*, 174.

52. News conf, 11 Jul 66, *McNamara Public Statements, 1966*, 7:2448.

53. McNamara test, 1 Aug 66, SSCA, *Hearings: Department of Defense Appropriations for FY 1967*, pt 2:682-83.

54. Richard Wilson in *Washington Evening Star*, 3 Aug 66.

55. McNamara test, 1 Aug 66, SSCA, *Hearings*, cited in note 53, pt 2:671-72, 737.

56. Russell made his statement on 18 August 66 and Mahon a week later; Anthony test, 24 Apr 67, Jt Econ Cte, *Hearings: Economic Effects of Vietnam Spending (1967)*, 1:6.

57. George C. Wilson in *Washington Post*, 6 Oct 66 (quote); McNamara's classified exchanges with Pike are found in transc McNamara test, 5 Oct 66, cited in note 34.

58. Memo SecDef for Pres, 24 Jan 66, paper by McNamara and McNaughton, 10 Feb 66: *FRUS 1964-68*, 4:113, 216. On the cost of B-52 operations see McNamara test, 4 Aug 65, SSCA, *Hearings: Department of Defense Appropriations for 1966*, pt 2:824.

59. McNamara test, 16 Feb 66, HSCA, *Hearings*, cited in note 13, pt 1:135.

60. DPM SecDef for Pres, 25 Oct 66, fldr SEA 1966 000.1-320.2, box 8, ISA General files, Acc 70A-6649; "DoD Admin History," 5:1721.

61. During budget discussions in late 1967, McNamara emphasized the need for better forecasts and his concern about repeating the FY 1967 experience "when we concealed expenditures." Gard notes, staff mtg, 18 Dec 67, Notebook, OSD Hist. Gard was a military assistant to McNamara.

62. Memo SecDef for Pres, 26 Oct 66, *FRUS 1964-68*, 4:786. On the December 1965 projections see ASD(C), Southeast Asia Cost Escalation (DoD Estimates, FY 66 and FY 67), 9 Dec 65, fldr FY 67 Budget Summaries, box 5, Comptroller files, Acc 73A-1389.

63. Anthony test, 24 Apr 67, Jt Econ Cte, *Hearings*, cited in note 56, 1:11-13.

64. Memo ASD(C) for SecDef, 9 Aug 66, fldr FY 1968 Budget Information, box 5, Comptroller files, Acc 73A-1389.

65. McNamara test, 1 Aug 66, SSCA, *Hearings*, cited in note 53, pt 2:672.

66. Memos UnderSecN for SecDef, 21 Jul, 5 Aug 66: fldr 110.01 1-15 Nov 1966, box 33, SecDef Subject Decimal files, Acc 70A-4443; memo SecN for SecDef, 21 Jul 66, fldr 7100/2-1966 Budget, box 27, Double Zero-1966 5860/6 thru 7100/3, NHC; PL88-213, 29 Sep 65 (79 Stat 870); PL 89-687, 15 Oct 66 (80 Stat 987).

67. Tom Johnson notes of mtg, Pres w/Sen Cte Chairmen, 25 Jul 67, box 1, Tom Johnson Notes of Meetings, LBJL.

68. Annual Budget Msg to Congress, FY 1967, 24 Jan 66, *Johnson Public Papers, 1966*, 1:49; *Annual Report of the Council of Economic Advisers*, 19 Jan 67, cited in note 44, 48-49.

69. Statement by Pres, 29 Aug 66, *Johnson Public Papers, 1966*, 2:933-34 (quote); Califano, *Triumph & Tragedy*, 146-47.

70. Memo Ackley for Pres, 9 Aug 66, fldr FI 11 3/17/66-8/20/66, box 56,WHCF EX FI 11 3/17/18, LBJL; memo Schultze for Ackley, 19 Aug 66, ibid; King, "The President & Fiscal Policy," 698-99.

71. Memo Heller for Pres, 20 Aug 66, fldr Tax 1965, box 1, Legislative Background Tax Increase, LBJL; Hargrove and Morley, eds, *The President and the Council*, 254-55.

72. Memo Ackley for Pres, 26 Aug 66, fldr FI 6/17/66-16/10/66, box 1,WHCF EX FI 11/22/63, LBJL; Califano, *Triumph & Tragedy*, 147-48. Rising interest rates meant government-guaranteed federal bonds paid substantially higher interest than corporate dividends; see Bernstein, *Guns or Butter*, 365.

73. Memo Fowler et al for Pres, 2 Sep 66, fldr 11-3 Council of Economic Advisors 8/3/66-9/19/66, box 59, WHCF EX FG 11-3, 8/3/66, LBJL (quotes); Pres special msg to Cong on fiscal policy, 8 Sep 66, *Johnson Public Papers, 1966*, 2:985, 988; *Washington Post*, 9 Nov 66; Califano, *Triumph & Tragedy*, 148.

74. Tel Califano to Johnson, 22 Nov 66, fldr 11-4 10/11/66-12/15/66, box 60, WHCF EX 11-4, LBJL.

75. King, "The President & Fiscal Policy," 702-03.

76. Ibid, 703; Kettl, "Economic Education," 66; Califano, *Triumph & Tragedy*, 148, 181; memo SecDef for Pres, 13 Dec 66, fldr Reading File, Dec 29-9, 1966, box 127, McNamara Records, RG 200; memos Ackley for Pres, Martin for Pres, 13 Dec 66, fldr 11-4 10/11/66-12/15/66, box 60, WHCF EX FI 11-4 7/7/66, LBJL; memo Ackley, Schultze, and Fowler for Pres, 31 Dec 66, fldr FI 11 8/21/66-1/2/67, box 56, WHCF EX FI 11 3/17/68, ibid.

77. HCA, *Department of Defense Appropriation Bill, 1967*, H Rpt 1652, 24 Jun 66, 2-3. The Senate reduced the House markup by almost $427 million. SCA, *Department of Defense Appropriation Bill, 1967*, S Rpt 1458, 12 Aug 66, 1; PL 89-687, 15 Oct 66 (80 Stat 980); *Washington Post*, 17 Oct 66; ASD(C), Cong Action on FY 67 Budget Requests, Section A, 7 Jun 67, vol III, Budget Data, FY 1966-68, ASD(C) files, OSD Hist.

78. *Business Week*, 29 Oct 66, 182; interv Henry Glass by Edward Drea, 22 Oct 97, 8, 12, 17, OSD Hist.

79. Memo ASD(C) for SvcSecs et al, 30 Aug 66 w/encl, fldr FY 1968 Budget Information, box 5, Comptroller files, Acc 73A-1389.

80. McNamara test, 24 Jan 67, SCAS and Subcte on DoD of SCA, *Hearings: Supplemental Defense Appropriations and Authorizations, FY 1967*, 121-25; ASD(C), FY 1967 Supplemental Budget Review: Summary of SecDef Review Adjustments by DoD Component, 18 Jan 67, Tab 1A, SecDef FY-67 Backup Book, bk 1, vol 1 & 2, box 48, ASD(C) files, OSD Hist; SCA, *Supplemental Defense Appropriation Bill, 1967*, S Rpt 74, 17 Mar 67, 2.

81. DPM SecDef for Pres, 17 Nov 66, fldr DPMs FY 1968-72 Programs, 1966, FY 68, box 120, ASD(C) files, OSD Hist. In his classified congressional testimony, McNamara estimated total losses at slightly more than 1,500 aircraft; see transc McNamara test, 3 Feb 67, HCAS hearings on Supplemental Authorization Bill for FY 1967 (Excerpts), 386, 2 & 3 Feb 67, 386, fldr Vietnam 1967, II, box 35, SecDef Bio files, OSD Hist. Normal procurement during peacetime replaced 300 aircraft annually, accounting for the difference.

82. Special msg to Cong on fiscal policy, 8 Sep 66, *Johnson Public Papers,1966*, 2:987-88; Pres news confs, 22 Sep, 29 Nov 66, ibid, 2:1056, 1406; ltr Johnson to McNamara, 2 Dec 66, fldr 110.01 (December 1966), box 33, SecDef Subject Decimal files, Acc 70A-4443; see also "Most Cutbacks Are Delays," in *New York Times*, 1 Dec 66.

83. News conf, Johnson and McNamara, 6 Dec 66, *McNamara Public Statements, 1966*, 7:2764 (quote); draft notes on mtg in Austin, Texas, 6 Dec 66, Pres, McNamara, and JCS, 10 Dec 66, *FRUS 1964-68*, 10:459.

84. For examples of press reaction see *New York Times*, 7, 8 Dec 66; *Washington Post*, 9 Dec 65; *New York Post*, 8 Dec 65; *Wall Street Journal*, 9 Dec 66.

85. Memo Heller for Pres, 14 Dec 66, fldr 110.01 (December 1966), box 33, SecDef Subject Decimal files, Acc 70A-4443.

86. Memo Glass for Michaels, 17 Jan 67, fldr Material for House Appro Cte 1967(1968 Budget), box 59, ASD(C) files, OSD Hist.

87. Ltr Pres to Speaker of the House, 24 Jan 67, *Johnson Public Papers, 1967*, 1:61-62.

88. McNamara test, 20 Feb 67, HSCA, *Hearings: Supplemental Defense Appropriations for 1967*, 62.

89. McNamara test, 3 Feb 67, HCAS, *Hearings: FY 1967 Supplemental Authorization for Southeast Asia*, 151-54.

90. McNamara test, 2 Feb 67, ibid, 81; McNamara test, 23, 24 Jan 67, SCAS and SubCte on DoD of SCA, *Hearings*, cited in note 80, 34, 53 (quote). For classified testimony identifying the troop levels see transc

McNamara test, 23 Jan 67, SCAS and SCA hearings on Supplemental Authorization and Appropriation for FY 67 (Excerpts) 23, 24, 25 Jan 67, 55, fldr, Vietnam 1966 III - 1967 I, box 34, SecDef Bio files, OSD Hist.

91. PL 90-8, 4 Apr 67 (81 Stat 8); SCA, *Supplemental Defense Appropriation Bill, 1967*, S Rpt 74, 17 Mar 67, 1-2.

92. Memo SecDef for SvcSecs et al, 12 Mar 66, fldr Compt Mgmt CY 66, box 785, Subj files, OSD Hist.

93. Memo SecDef for SvcSecs et al, 8 Apr 66, fldr FY 1968 Budget Information, box 5, Comptroller files, Acc 73A-1389; memo ASD(C) for SvcSecs et al, 6 Jan 66 (quote), memo McKinsey & Company, Inc for ASD(C), nd [c Jan 66], fldr PBBS, box 26, ISA General files, Acc 71A-2701; Gard notes, staff mtg, 18 Dec 67, cited in note 61.

94. ASD(C), Sketch of Budgetary Guidance, 18 Jul 66, fldr FY 1968 Budget Information, box 5, Comptroller files, Acc 73A-1389.

95. Memo ASD(C) for SvcSecs et al, 5 Aug 66, fldr Budget Development - FY 1968, box 59, ASD(C) files, OSD Hist. Subsequent memoranda revised the original schedule slightly. See, for example, memo ASD(C) for SvcSecs et al, 3 Nov 66, ibid.

96. Memo ASD(C) for SvcSecs et al, 30 Aug 66, cited in note 79.

97. Memo ASD(C) for SecA et al, 19 Nov 66 w/encl 1, "Guidance for Review of Budget Estimates," nd, fldr FY 1968 Budget Information, box 5, Comptroller files, Acc 73A-1389; DPM SecDef for Pres, 17 Nov 66, DPM SecDef for Pres, 27 Dec 66, 14 (quote): fldr DPMs FY 1968-1972 Program 1966, FY 68, box 120, ASD(C) files, OSD Hist. Logistics guidance was issued 12 September 1966, but the record of decision superseding the 12 September 1966 memo appeared in the 27 December DPM.

98. McNamara test, 20 Feb 67, HSCA, *Hearings*, cited in note 88, 10-11. McNamara read the same material during Senate and House hearings on the 1967 supplemental request and FY 1968 budget submission.

99. McNamara test, 23 Jan 67, SCAS and Subcte on DoD of SCA, *Hearings*, cited in note 80, 54.

100. DoD Background Briefing on FY 1968 Defense Budget, 23 Jan 67, 3, fldr DoD Budget General CY 67, box 785, Subj files, OSD Hist (quote). See the classified version in transc McNamara test, 23 Jan 67, SCAS and Subcte on DoD of SCA hearings on FY 1968 Budget and FY 1967 Supplemental, 178, fldr SecDef Transcript Senate Armed Svcs and Appropriations 1/23/67 (Glass Master copy), box 61, ASD(C) files, OSD Hist. His remark was excised from the published proceedings; SCAS and Subcte on DoD of SCA, *Hearings*, cited in note 80, 79. ASD(C) Robert Anthony in later congressional testimony elaborated on the connection between a stabilized level of operations and a supplemental; see Anthony test, 24 Apr 67, Jt Econ Cte, *Hearings*, cited in note 56, 1:7.

101. FY 1968 Logistics Guidance with Secretary's Certificates, 12 Jan 67, TAB 3D2, fldr SecDef Backup Book FY 1968, bk 2, v 3, 4 & 5, box 60, ASD(C) files, OSD Hist.

102. Memo ASD(C) for SecDef, 25 Oct 66, fldr 110.01 (Oct 11-31) 1966, box 33, SecDef Subject Decimal files, Acc 70A-4443.

103. Telcon McNamara and Pres, 16 Oct 66, cited in ed note, *FRUS 1964-68*, 10:438.

104. Memo ASD(C) for SecDef, 1 Nov 66, fldr 110.01 (1-15 Nov) 1966, box 33, SecDef Subject Decimal files, Acc 70A-4443.

105. ASD(C), FY 1968 Budget Review, 18 Jan 67 (rev), TAB 1D and FY 1967 Supplemental Request for Stock Funds, TAB 1C: SecDef Backup Book FY 1968, bk 1, vol 1 & 2, box 60, ASD(C) files, OSD Hist.

106. ASD(C), Program/Budget Decisions Reviewed FY 1968 Budget, 9 Jan 67, Tab 1 G, ibid. The FY 1968 budget review administrative procedures differed from those of the preceding fiscal year in two ways. First, "Subject/Issues" were replaced by "Program/Budget Decisions" (P/BDs). Second, P/BDs were required for the total budget request, not just the individual areas or specific programs where issues were developed for the secretary's decision.

107. H. K. Johnson and Resor test, 9 Mar 67, HSCA, *Hearings: Department of Defense Appropriations for 1968*, pt 2:580-82.

108. Brown test, 13 Mar 67, ibid, 737-38.

109. Nitze test, 15 Mar 67, ibid, 887, 896.

110. ASD(C), FY 1968 Budget Review, 18 Jan 67 (rev), TAB 1 D, fldr SecDef Backup Book FY 1968, bk 1, v 1 & 2, box 60, ASD(C) files, OSD Hist; memo SecDef for SvcSecs, 17 Nov 66, TAB A, fldr 110.01 01 (16 -30 Nov 66) 1966, box 33, SecDef Subject Decimal files, Acc 70A-4443; DPM SecDef for Pres, 9 Nov 66, DPMs FY 1968-72 Program 1966, FY 68, box 120, ASD(C) files, OSD Hist.

111. CM-2055-67 for SecDef, 14 Jan 67 w/Tab B, fldr 1968 Budget-SecDef Supplemental-Service Comments, box 63, ASD(C) files, OSD Hist; McNamara test, 23 Jan 67, Subcte on DoD of SCA and SCAS, *Hearings*, cited in note 80, 10-11.

112. McDonald test, 15 Mar 67, HSCA, *Hearings*, cited in note 107, pt 2:870, 933-35.

113. JCSM-734-66 for SecDef, 26 Nov 66, fldr Top Secret Budget Memos, 1965-1969 (1 of 2), box 10, Enthoven Papers, LBJL; DPM SecDef for Pres, Summary of JCS Recommendations on Draft Presidential Memoranda and Related SecDef Actions, 5 Dec 66, TAB M, DPMs FY 1968-72 Program 1966, bk 6, box 120, ASD(C) files, OSD Hist; Secretary, JCS, Issues Where JCS were Unanimous and Overruled by SecDef, 23 Dec 66, TAB 1E, SecDef Backup Book FY 1968, bk 1, vol 1 & 2, box 60, ASD(C) files, OSD Hist. Cp w/memo SecDef for SvcSecs et al, 8 Apr 66, fldr FY 1968 Budget Information, box 5, Comptroller files, Acc 73A-1389.

114. ASD(C), Major Unresolved Issues, 10 Dec 66, fldr 110.01 1 Dec 66, box 33, SecDef Subject Decimal files, Acc 70A-4443.

115. Memo ASD(C) for DDR&E et al, 16 Nov 66, fldr Budget-FY 1968, box 64, ASD(C) files, OSD Hist; ASD(SA), Budget Issue: Minuteman II/III, 19 Nov 66 and SSN Procurement Fact Sheet, 19 Nov 66, ibid; DASD(C), FY 1968 Budget Review Summary of Adjustments to Service FY 1968 Requests, 16 Jan 67, fldr SecDef Backup Book FY 1968, TAB D, bk 1, vol 1 & 2, box 60, ibid.

116. Memo SecDef for Pres, 5 Dec 66, DPM SecDef for Pres, 3 Dec 66 w/atchmts: fldr Budget for FY 1968 and Supplemental Appropriation for FY 1967, box 12, NSF, LBJL.

117. Draft notes of mtg, 6 Dec 66, *FRUS, 1964-68*, 10:459-60 (quote); memrec, 6 Dec 66, ibid, 468.

118. Memo MilAsst (I&L) to CJCS for Glass, 1 Feb 67, fldr SecDef Transcript-Sen. Armed Serv & Sen Appro SubCte Supplemental-67, 25 Jan 67-Glass master, box 64, ASD(C) files, OSD Hist; DPM DepSecDef for Pres, 10 Dec 66, fldr 103 ABM Memo & JCS View, box 4, McNamara Papers, Acc 71A-3470; DASD(C), FY 1968 Budget Review Summary, 16 Jan 67, cited in note 115.

119. Telcon McNamara and Pres, *FRUS 1964-68*, 10:459, n2.

120. Annual budget msg to Cong, FY 1968, *Johnson Public Papers*, 1967, 1:44-46; Estimated Expenditures FY 1966-1968 and FY 1968 Defense Review Summary, fldr Backup Book FY 1968, bk 1, vols 1 & 2, box 60, ASD(C) files, OSD Hist.

121. McNamara test, 6 Mar 67, HSCA, *Hearings*, cited in note 107, 180-81.

122. ASD(C), Cong Action on FY 1968 Budget Requests, 9 Jun 67, fldr Material for House Appro Cte 1967(68 Budget), box 59, ASD(C) files, OSD Hist; HCA, *Department of Defense Appropriation Bill, 1968*, H Rpt 349, 9 Jun 67, 1-4.

123. *Wall Street Journal*, 8, 22, 28 Jun 67; CMC, JCS and Secs mtg w/Pres on National Debt Ceiling, 7 Jun 67, Greene Papers, MHC (quote); SCF, *Public Debt Limit*, S Rpt 357, 26 Jun 67, 6, 8.

124. Ltr McNamara to Russell, 22 Jul 67, fldr Budget FY 1968, box 64, ASD(C) files, OSD Hist.

125. Memo ASD(C) for ASD(Admin), 16 Aug 67, ibid.

126. Transc Nitze test, 10 Aug 67, Subcte of HCA hearing on Current Status of FY 68 Defense Budget, 10 Aug 67, 10-11, fldr House Appropriations SubCte on Senate Action on DoD FY 1968 Budget Request, box 63, ibid.

127. Transc Nitze test, 14 Jul 67, Subcte on DoD Appros SCA hearings on Appeals on House Action on the FY 68 Defense Budget, fldr Reclama FY 1968, box 62, ibid; ASD(C), Congressional Action on FY 1968 Budget Requests, FAD 581, 4 Dec 67, Notebook Budget Data FY 1966-68, OSD Hist; H Rpt 349, 9 Jun 67, cited in note 122, 4; HCA, *Appropriations for the Department of Defense for 1968*, H Rpt 595, 23 Aug 67, 6; Department of Defense Appropriation Act, 1968, 29 Sep 67 (PL 90-96; 81 Stat 231).

128. *New York Times*, 2 Oct 67; *Johnson Public Papers, 1967*, 2:881; ltr DepSecDef to DirBoB, 10 Sep 67, w/ encl, fldr Budget-FY 1968, box 64, ASD(C) files, OSD Hist.

129. Memo Pres for Heads of Exec Depts and Agencies, 4 Oct 67 (quote); memo McNamara for SvcSecs, 5 Oct 67; memo DirBoB for Heads of Depts and Agencies, 6 Oct 67: fldr Budget-FY 1968, box 64, ASD(C) files, OSD Hist.

130. Cong Action on Military Budget Construction Request, 1 Dec 67, TAB FY 1968, Notebook Budget Data FY 1966-1968, OSD Hist.

VII. AN ENDLESS WAR: 1967–1968

1.   Tom Johnson notes of Pres mtg with McNamara, Wheeler, Westmoreland, and Christian, 13 Jul 67, *FRUS 1964-68*, 5:613; Tom Johnson notes of mtg, 14 Jul 67, ibid, 5:619-21; Clifford, *Counsel*, 448-51; Taylor, *Swords and Plowshares*, 376; Clifford-Taylor Report to the President, 5 Aug 67, 4-7, fldr Vietnam (Jul & Aug 67), box 2, McNamara files, Acc 77-0075; Tom Johnson notes of mtg, 5 Aug 67, *FRUS 1964-68*, 5:674; Paul Nitze mtg notes, 5 Aug 67, fldr DoD Deputy Secretary of Defense Notes 1967 (2 of 3), box 85, Nitze Papers, LC. For a different view of the trip see memo Taylor for Kissinger, 26 Jun 69, fldr 621-C A (Clifford-Taylor Mission to SEA - Jul-Aug 67 [67-69]), box 58, Taylor Papers, NDU.

2. Tom Johnson notes of Pres mtg w/Democratic Congressmen, 9 Aug 67, Tom Johnson Personal Papers, LBJL; Jones notes of mtg, 18 Aug 67, *FRUS 1964-68*, 5:710.

3. Shapley, *Promise and Power*, 302, 425-26; interv Cyrus Vance by Paige E. Mulhollan, 9 Mar 70, 3:13, electronic copy, LBJL; McNamara, *In Retrospect*, 280; memcon Harriman and McNamara, 1 Jul 67, fldr McNamara, Robert S. file, Special Files Public Service JFK-LBJ, box 486, Harriman Papers, LC. See also Gelb, "The Pentagon Papers and *The Vantage Point*," 25-41. Gelb, then a member of the ISA staff, served as editor of the project. McNamara originally assigned the project to ISA director John McNaughton and envisioned the assembly of a compendium of documents as the "raw materials" for a retrospective look by future political scientists and military experts. After McNaughton's death, the project passed to Gelb who produced an analytical narrative based on the documents. Interv Robert S. McNamara by Maurice Matloff and Alfred Goldberg, 24 Jul 86, 23, 26, OSD Hist (quote).

4. Shapley, *Promise and Power*, 426-27; McNamara, *In Retrospect*, 313; memrcd, mtg w/Robert McNamara, 29 Apr 94, 29, OSD Hist; Califano, *Triumph & Tragedy*, 249; DirInfoOps, OSD, Southeast Asia Military Casualties, 19 Dec 69, fldr Vietnam Statistics-Casualties, box 327, Subj files, OSD.

5. Special msg to Cong, 3 Aug 67, *Johnson Public Papers, 1967*, 2:736; Hammond, *Military and the Media, 1962-1968*, 297; memos Jones for Pres, 5, 12 Sep 67, *FRUS 1964-68*, 5:754, 779; DirJ-3, talking paper, 8 Sep 67, fldr Miscellaneous 1967, box 65, Pentagon Papers Backup, Acc 75-062.

6. DirJ-3, talking paper, 8 Sep 67, cited in note 5; memo DO, DCSMO for DO, JS, 8 Sep 67; DJSM 1118-67 for ActgCJCS, 9 Sep 67; memos SecA for SecDef, 16 Sep 67, SecDef for SecA, 22 Sep 67: fldr Miscellaneous 1967, box 65, Pentagon Papers Backup, Acc 75-062.

7. *JCS and the War in Vietnam*, pt 3:45/6, 10; msg 31998 COMUSMACV to CINCPAC, 28 Sep 67, fldr Cables 66-67-68, CM-2668-67 for DepSecDef, 28 Sep 67, fldr Miscellaneous 1967: box 65, Pentagon Papers Backup, Acc 75-062; msg Johnson to Westmoreland, 021201Z Oct 67, Westmoreland Eyes Only msg files, Oct 67, CMH.

8. Tom Johnson notes of mtg, 3 Oct 67, *FRUS 1964-68*, 5:841; memo SecA for SecDef, 3 Oct 67, memo SecDef for SecA, 6 Nov 67: fldr Miscellaneous 1967, box 65, Pentagon Papers Backup, Acc 75-062; memo SecDef for Pres, 4 Oct 67, msg JCS 8356 H.K. Johnson to Sharp, Westmoreland, 5 Oct 67: fldr 031.1 President Jul 64-Oct 67, box 10, Wheeler files, RG 218-92-0015.

9. *JCS and the War in Vietnam*, pt 3:4/13-14; Hammond, *Military and the Media, 1962-1968*, 315-16.

10. DPM SecDef for Pres, 1 Nov 67, *FRUS 1964-68*, 5:943-50; memo McNamara for Pres, 18 Oct 67, w/ atchmt, JCSM-555-67 for SecDef, 17 Oct 67, fldr Viet 370, 1967, box 5, SecDef Subject Decimal files, Acc 72A-2467; memo Warnke for SecDef, 21 Oct 67, fldr Viet 383 (Sensitive Jun-Oct) 1967, box 3, SecDef Sensitive files, 1949-1969, Acc 71-0017; memo M. Bundy for Pres, 17 Oct 67, *FRUS 1964-68*, 5:882; Tom Johnson notes of mtg, 3 Oct 67, ibid, 844; Johnson, *Vantage Point*, 372.

11. DPM SecDef for Pres, 1 Nov 67, cited in note 10; Johnson, *Vantage Point*, 372.

12. Memo Helms for Pres, 12 Sep 67, w/atchmt, Implications of an Unfavorable Outcome in Vietnam, 11 Sep 67, Doc. No. CK3100019865, Declassified Documents Reference System, *http://galenet.galegroup.com* (quote, 33); memo Jones for Pres, 2 Nov 67, ed note, *FRUS 1964-68*, 5:955-70, 777; McNamara, *In Retrospect*, 306-09.

13. Johnson, *Vantage Point*, 373-77; memos Rostow for Pres, 2 Nov 67, Taylor for Pres, 3 Nov 67, Fortas for Pres, 5 Nov 67, Clifford for Pres, 7 Nov 67, Rusk for Pres, 20 Nov 67, and Rostow for Pres, 20 Nov 67, *FRUS 1964-68*, 5:971-73, 978-80, 991-92, 992-94 (quote), 1037-40, 1040-42.

14. Memo for file by Pres, 18 Dec 67, *FRUS 1964-68*, 5:1118-20.

15. Hammond, *Military and the Media, 1962-1968*, 333-34; memrcd Westmoreland, breakfast mtg at White House, 22 Nov 67, Westmoreland History Files, CMH, describes reporting of the war and ways to improve the administration's image; msg JCS 9298 Wheeler to Westmoreland, 31 Oct 67, msg JCS 9449 Wheeler to Westmoreland, 3 Nov 67, msg JCS 9465 Wheeler to Westmoreland, 4 Nov 67, msg JCS 9573 Wheeler to Sharp and Westmoreland, 9 Nov 67: Westmoreland Eyes Only msg files, Oct and Nov 67, CMH; msg HWA 3445 Westmoreland to Abrams, 25 Nov 67, *FRUS 1964-68*, 5:1071-72.

16. Tom Johnson notes of mtg, 21 Nov 67, *FRUS 1964-68*, 5:1050-59 (quote, 1058); Hammond, *Military and the Media, 1962-1968*, 338.

17. Westmoreland History Notes, 21 Aug - 26 Dec 67, Westmoreland History File, #8, 21 Aug-26 Dec 67, CMH.

18. CM-2743-67 for DirJtStaff, 7 Nov 67, JCSM-663-67 for SecDef, 27 Nov 67: fldr Miscellaneous 1967, box 65, Pentagon Papers Backup, Acc 75-062; Tom Johnson notes of mtg, 21 Nov 67, *FRUS 1964-68*, 5:1054; msg MAC 9616 Westmoreland to Sharp, 13 Oct 67, Westmoreland Eyes Only msg files, Oct 67, CMH; memo DirINR for SecState, Estimated North Vietnamese Reaction to Limited US Ground Attacks North of DMZ, 7 Oct 67, Cable files, OSD Hist.

19. Hammond, *Military and the Media, 1962-1968*, 338-39. On 29 November the World Bank confirmed Mc-Namara's nomination for the presidency of that institution. White House spokesmen denied the secretary was being forced out, and the State Department emphasized: 1) he had not yet formally resigned, and 2) in any case there was no implication of a change in U.S. policy towards Vietnam; cir msg 76976 State to dipl posts, 30 Nov 67, Cable files, OSD Hist.

20. Msg COMUSMACV to CINCPAC, 260255Z Jan 68, Cable files, OSD Hist; msg CINCPAC to JCS, 010156Z Jan 68, box 66, Pentagon Papers Backup, Acc 75-062.

21. Msg MAC 11956 Westmoreland to Wheeler, 10 Dec 67, Westmoreland Eyes Only msg files, Dec 67, CMH; Shulimson et al, *U.S. Marines in Vietnam, 1968*, 18.

22. Memo Westmoreland for Wheeler, 12 Feb 67, w/atchmt, memrcd Tillson, LtGen Starbird's Exit Interview with COMUSMACV, 5 Feb 67, fldr 091 SEA Barrier, Jan 67-Jul 67, box 36, Wheeler files, RG 218-92-0015; paper, Khe Sanh, nd but c Mar 68, fldr Miscellaneous #1, Documents and Correspondence, box 66, Pentagon Papers Backup, Acc 75-06; CM-2908-68 for SecDef, 13 Jan 68, *FRUS 1964-68*, 6:30-32.

23. CM-2134-67 for SecDef, 22 Feb 67, fldr Split File (1967), box 145, Wheeler files, RG 218-92-0015; msg 23274 Saigon to State, 17 Apr 67, Cable files, OSD Hist; *JCS and the War in Vietnam*, pt 3:45/18-25; JCSM-162-67 for SecDef, 23 Mar 67, CM-2195-67 for SecDef, 23 Mar 67: fldr Viet Barrier 385 (Jan-Jul) 1967, box 7, SecDef Subject Decimal files, Acc 72A-2467. Westmoreland assigned that task to the Marines because their familiarity with the area permitted construction to begin immediately; msg COMUSMACV to CINCPAC 191125Z Apr 67, fldr Cables 66-67-68, box 65, Pentagon Papers Backup, Acc 75-062.

24. Msg 30673 COMUSMACV to CINCPAC, 16 Sep 67, msg CINCPAC to JCS 180740Z Sep 67, Cable files, OSD Hist; memo Warnke for SecDef, 20 Sep 67 w/atchmt A, fldr Viet Barrier 385 (Aug-Sep) 1967, box 7, SecDef Subject Decimal files, Acc 72A-2467. McNamara's quoted comments are in a marginal note on Warnke's memo.

25. SecDef briefings, 7-8 Jul 67, 12-13, fldr July 1967, box 27, Gibbons Papers July 1967, LBJL; memo Jones for Pres, 2 Nov 67, *FRUS 1964-68*, 5:969 (quote).

26. Shapley, *Promise and Power*, 450, 457; McNamara, *In Retrospect*, 246 (quote). Clifford later offered qualified support for some parts of the barrier, believing the sensors in particular helpful to the military; Clifford test, 23 May 68, HSCA, *Hearings: DoD Appropriations for Fiscal Year 1969*, 2488. Wheeler, in later testimony, defended the system, but admitted it had not yet proved cost-effective; transc Wheeler test for SSCA Hearings on DoD Appropriations for FY 1969, 17 Sep 67, 2745, fldr Transcript-Hearings before Senate Approp Cte for FY 1967, September 17, 1968 (a.m. & p.m.), box 77, ASD(C) files, OSD Hist. A redacted version is available in Wheeler test, 17 Sep 67, SSCA, *Hearings: DoD Appropriations for Fiscal Year 1969*, pt 5:2621; memo DCPG for DDR&E and CJCS, 15 Oct 68, w/atchmt, Evaluation of an Anti-Infiltration System, 15 Oct 68 (quote), fldr 091 (SEA Barrier) Sep 68-Dec 69 Bulky, box 37, Wheeler Papers, RG 218-92-0015.

27. CIA Weekly Summary, 26 Jan 68, #4/68, box 331, Subj files, OSD Hist; ed note, *FRUS 1964-68*, 5:1123; msg MAC 10931 Abrams to Westmoreland, 15 Nov 67, Westmoreland Eyes Only msg files, Nov 67, CMH. For an evaluation of the intelligence process before the Tet offensive see Ford, *CIA and the Vietnam Policymakers*, 104-18; msg MAC 992 Westmoreland to Sharp, 21 Jan 68, msg MAC 1165 Westmoreland to Sharp and Wheeler, 24 Jan 68, Westmoreland Eyes Only msg files, Jan 68, CMH.

28. Shulimson et al, *U.S. Marines in Vietnam, 1968*, 72, 258-59, 264, 269.

29. CM-2908-68 for SecDef, 13 Jan 68, *FRUS 1964-68*, 6:30-32; msg JCS 343 Wheeler to Westmoreland, 11 Jan 68, msgs MAC 547 Westmoreland to Wheeler, 12 Jan 68, Sharp to Wheeler, 142146Z Jan 68 (quote), Westmoreland Eyes Only msg files, Jan 68, CMH.

30. Herring, *LBJ and Vietnam*, 152; memo DePuy for DirJtStaff, 31 Jan 68, fldr Miscellaneous 1968, box 65, Pentagon Papers Backup, Acc 75-062; Clifford, *Counsel*, 466; Tom Johnson notes of mtgs, 24, 29 Jan 68, JCSM-63-68 for Pres, 29 Jan 69, *FRUS 1964-68*, 6:65-67, 71-72, 69-70; memrcd Taylor, mtg Pres w/JCS, 29 Jan 68, fldr 312-69-A (Khe Sanh) fldr #2, box 56, Taylor Papers, NDU; *JCS and the War in Vietnam*, pt 3:48/22-23; see Wheeler's explanation in Wheeler test, 15 Feb 68, HSCA, *Hearings: DoD Appropriations for 1969*, pt 1:81. Wheeler told the press that as usual he signed the JCS memorandum for the president stating Khe Sanh could and should be defended; SecDef/CJCS press interview, 5 Feb 68, *McNamara Public Statements, 1968*, 1:443; Johnson, *Vantage Point*, 385.

31. Tom Johnson notes of mtg, 23 Jan 68, *FRUS 1964-68*, 29:460-63 (quote, 460).

32. White House conv w/Gen Westmoreland, 30 Jan 68, Cable files, OSD Hist; Tom Johnson notes of mtg, 30 Jan 68, *FRUS 1964-68*, 6:79-82 (quote).

33. Ed note, *FRUS 1964-68*, 6:74; ibid, 120, n5. Westmoreland's remarks on the imminent offensive were made during conversations by telephone on 1 and 2 February 1968 with Wheeler who quoted the comments to a congressional committee. Transc Wheeler test, 1 Feb 68 for SCAS Hearings, Military Procure-

ment FY 1969, 1 Feb 68, Morning, 17-18 (quote), fldr FY 69 Budget -Hearings Senate Armed Svcs Cte - 2/1/68 -morning, box 72, ASD(C) files, OSD Hist; msg JCS 1147 Wheeler to Westmoreland 1 Feb 68, Westmoreland Eyes Only msg files, Feb 68, CMH; msg Sharp to Wheeler, 020208Z Feb 68, tab T, fldr March 31st Speech, vol 2, box 47, NSC Histories, NSF, LBJL (quotes).

34. Msg JCS 1272 Wheeler to Westmoreland, 3 Feb 68, Westmoreland Eyes Only msg files, Feb 68, CMH; CM-2944-68 for Pres, 3 Feb 68, *FRUS 1964-68*, 6:117-20; Wheeler test, 2 Feb 68, SCAS, *Hearings: Authorization for Military Procurement, Research, and Development Fiscal Year 1969, and Reserve Strength*, 73; memrcd Taylor, Khe Sanh, 5 Feb 68, fldr 312-69-A (Khe Sanh) fldr #2, box 56, Taylor Papers, NDU (quotes).

35. Msg JCS 1529 Wheeler to Westmoreland, 8 Feb 68,Westmoreland Eyes Only msg files, Feb 1968, CMH; msg JCS 1590 Wheeler to Westmoreland, 8 Feb 68, Cable files, OSD Hist; interv Earle G. Wheeler by Dorothy Pierce McSweeny, 7 May 70, 2, 7-8, fldr AC 78-88, LBJL; Herring, *LBJ and Vietnam*, 155; Tom Johnson notes of mtg, 7 Feb 68, *FRUS 1964-68*, 6:141-44.

36. Msg MAC 1586 Westmoreland to Wheeler, 3 Feb 68, Westmoreland Eyes Only msg files, Feb 68, CMH; excerpt of Westmoreland's 4 Feb 68 message cited in William C. Westmoreland, "The Origins of the Post-Tet 1968 Plans for Additional American Forces in RVN," 9 Nov 70, 4, Westmoreland Papers, CMH; msg MAC 1858 Westmoreland to Wheeler, 9 Feb 68, *FRUS 1964-68*, 6:153-58; msg MAC 1924 Westmoreland to Wheeler, 11 Feb 68, fldr Miscellaneous #2, box 66, Pentagon Papers Backup, Acc 75-062; msg MAC 1975 Westmoreland to Wheeler, 12 Feb 68, *FRUS 1964-68*, 6:183-85; msg MAC 2018 Westmoreland to Wheeler, 12 Feb 68, Westmoreland Eyes Only msg files, Feb 68, CMH, msg Westmoreland to Wheeler and Sharp, 081440Z Feb 68, fldr Official Correspondence-Army Chief of Staff, Backchannel Messages Jan 1968, box 88, H.K. Johnson Papers, MHI.

37. Msg 1529 Wheeler to Westmoreland 8 Feb 68, msg JCS 1590 Wheeler to Westmoreland 9 Feb 68: both cited in note 35; Brower, "Strategic Reassessment in Vietnam," 36-40.

38. Cosmas, *MACV: Years of Withdrawal*, 88-104.

39. Tom Johnson notes of mtg, 9 Feb 68, *FRUS 1964-68*, 6:162, 167; msg JCS 18582 Saigon to State, 8 Feb 68, ibid, 148; msg JCS 1529 Wheeler to Westmoreland, 8 Feb 68, msg JCS 1590 Wheeler to Westmoreland, 9 Feb 68: both cited in note 35.

40. *JCS and the War in Vietnam*, pt 3:49/4; Tom Johnson notes of mtg, 10 Feb 68, *FRUS 1964-68*, 6:168-72.

41. Msg MAC 1858 Westmoreland to Wheeler, 9 Feb 68; Tom Johnson notes of mtg, 11 Feb 68, *FRUS 1964-68*, 6:153-58, 175-82.

42. Msg MAC 1975 Westmoreland to Wheeler, 12 Feb 68, telcon McNamara and Pres, 12 Feb 68, Tom Johnson notes of mtg, 12 Feb 68: *FRUS 1964-68*, 6:183-85 (quote), 186-88, 188-89; memo Taylor for Pres, 12 Feb 68, fldr A-1 Clifford Study Group - Tet 1968, box 59, Taylor Papers, NDU; *JCS and the War in Vietnam*, pt 3:49/6-8.

43. Tom Johnson notes of mtg, 12 Feb 68, *FRUS 1964-68*, 6:188-96 (quote, 193)), also 207, n2; Clifford, *Counsel*, 478; Cosmas, *MACV: Years of Withdrawal*, 92; *JCS and the War in Vietnam*, pt 3:49/8.

44. JCSM-91-68 for SecDef, 12 Feb 68, w/annex A, 17, fldr Miscellaneous 1968, box 65, Pentagon Papers Backup, Acc 75-062; Tom Johnson notes of mtg, 13 Feb 68, *FRUS 1964-68*, 6:207-10; JCSM-96-68 for SecDef, 13 Feb 68, fldr 312-383.4 (Sensitive), box 1, SecDef Sensitive files, Acc 91-0017.

45. Memrec Westmoreland, 16 Feb 68, fldr William C. Westmoreland-Top Secret #29 History File 1-29 Feb 1968 TS-0101-80, Westmoreland Papers, MHI (quote); memo Carver for Rostow, 17 Feb 68, Cable files, OSD Hist (quote); Johnson, *Vantage Point*, 388; msg JCS 1974 Wheeler to Westmoreland, 17 Feb 68, Westmoreland Eyes Only msg files, Feb 1968, CMH; memo Taylor for Pres, 14 Feb 68, fldr 312-69-A G (Khe Sanh) fldr #2, box 56, Taylor Papers, NDU; Tom Johnson notes of mtg, 11 Feb 68, FRUS 1964-68, 6:176-77.

46. Memo Wheeler for Pres, 27 Feb 68, *FRUS 1964-68*, 6:263-66 (quotes); Cosmas, *MACV: Years of Withdrawal*, 93-96. Clifford in a 1972 interview described Wheeler returning "with a story that was frightening" (quoted in Schandler, *Unmaking of a President*, 118-19).

47. Westmoreland, *Soldier Reports*, 356-57; ltr Westmoreland to Taylor, 7 Apr 69, w/atchmt, Chron of Summarized Communications Relative to Troop Augmentations February, March 1968, fldr 11-71C Cables Post Tet 1968, box 57, Taylor Papers, NDU; msg OSD 2175 Rostow to Wheeler/Westmoreland, 23 Feb 68, Westmoreland Eyes Only msg files, Feb 1968, CMH; msg CAP 80542 Rostow to Pres, 24 Feb 68, *FRUS 1964-68*, 6:242-44.

48. Memrcd Westmoreland telcon w/Rostow, 31 Mar 69, William C. Westmoreland Close Hold communications, Jul 68 – Mar 69, MHI. One of Westmoreland's marginal comments on msg JCS 2848 Wheeler to Westmoreland, 12 Mar 68, read: "Wheeler wanted a requirement that would permit the deployment of a

substantial reserve for worldwide use." See Barrett, ed, *Johnson's Vietnam Papers*, 668. Westmoreland, "The Origins of the Post-Tet 1968 Plans for Additional American Forces in RVN," 22-28, nd, Westmoreland Papers, CMH; interv Wheeler by McSweeny, 7 May 70, 2:5-8, AC 78-88, LBJL; memo Wheeler for Pres, 27 Feb 68, *FRUS 1964-68*, 6:263-66; Schandler, *Unmaking of a President*, 109-11. Taylor's recollection was that Westmoreland asked for 30,000 reinforcements immediately and indicated that he might need another division in September and a second division by the end of the year; memrcd Taylor disc w/Wheeler re events of February-March, 1968, etc, 27 Mar 70, fldr 12-71E Vietnam Alternatives 1968, box 57, Taylor Papers, NDU; Hoopes, *Limits of Intervention*, 159-65; memo SecA for SecDef, 27 Feb 68, fldr Miscellaneous 1968, box 65, Pentagon Papers Backup, Acc 75-062.

49. McPherson notes of mtg, 27 Feb 68, *FRUS 1964-68*, 6:260-62 (quote). The account of McNamara's outburst is a composite of Shapley, *Promise and Power*, 444; Clifford, *Counsel*, 485 (quote); and Califano, *Triumph & Tragedy*, 263.

50. Tom Johnson notes of mtg, 28 Feb 68, *FRUS 1964-68*, 6:267-75; Johnson, *Vantage Point*, 392; Clifford, *Counsel*, 486.

51. Clifford, *Counsel*, 486-87; McNamara, *In Retrospect*, 316-17; Shapley, *Promise and Power*, 458.

52. Hedrick Smith in *New York Times*, 6 Mar 69; Phil Goulding, *Confirm or Deny*, 306-10. For the retrospective assessment, see Califano, *Triumph & Tragedy*, 264n; Clifford, *Counsel*, 465; interv Clifford by Mulhollan, 14 Jul 69, 3:9, Internet copy, LBJL.

53. Nitze, From *Hiroshima to Glasnost*, 274; interv John P. McConnell by Dorothy Pierce McSweeny, 28 Aug 69, 1:38, fldr AC 79-71, LBJL; intervs Robert Pursley by Alfred Goldberg and Roger Trask, 6 Sep 95, 36-37; 7 May 96, 3-7; 15 Aug 97, 2, 19, 39: OSD Hist. On the 0830 staff meetings see memo Gard for SecDef, staff mtg, Monday 13 May, 12 May 68, fldr Staff Meeting Memos, TAB J, box 1, Pursley files, Acc 73A-1934. Pursley and Gard prepared the meeting agenda.

54. Memo Rostow for Pres, 28 Feb 68, w/atchmt, draft memo from Pres to Rusk and McNamara, 28 Feb 68, *FRUS 1964-68*, 6:276-78. Schandler, *Unmaking of a President*, 133-176, relying on extensive interviews with participants, has the most detailed study of the review group. Clifford, "Viet-Nam Reappraisal," 609-10; Clifford, *Counsel*, 492-93. No transcript was kept of the proceedings. William Bundy (?), Outline for Subjects and Division of Labor on Viet Nam Staff Study, nd, but likely 29 Feb 68, Misc Clifford Working Papers, Westmoreland Papers, CMH. For a discussion of and excerpts from these documents, see Gravel, ed, *Pentagon Papers*, 4:549-584.

55. Paper, Heyman, OASD(SA), Viet-Nam, nd, Misc Clifford Working Papers, Westmoreland Papers, CMH; ISA draft paper, nd, fldr 627-71A (Clifford Task Force, Review of VN Policy [March 1968], box 59, Taylor Papers, NDU; paper, Taylor, nd, Misc Clifford Working Papers, Westmoreland Papers, CMH. *Pentagon Papers*, bk 5, IV.C.6.(c), 22, states the paper went to the president before the Clifford group's report of 4 Mar 68. Nitze memo, 3 Mar 68, fldr Miscellaneous 1968, box 65, Pentagon Papers Backup, Acc 75-062; McPherson notes of mtg, 27 Feb 68, *FRUS 1964-68*, 6:260-62; Plans and Policy Dir, Short Range Branch, J-5, JCS, Analysis of COMUSMACV Force Requirements and Alternatives, 1 Mar 68, ibid, 292-97.

56. Clifford interv, 14 Jul 69, 3:3, 9-10; interv Clifford by Mulhollan, 2 Jul 69, 2:16-17, Internet copy, LBJL; Clifford, *Counsel*, 493-94; Gard staff mtg notes, 6 Mar 68, Gard Notebook, OSD Hist.

57. Clifford, *Counsel*, 494; DPM SecDef for Pres, 4 Mar 68, *FRUS 1964-68*, 6:314-16. On the president's wishes, see CM-3069-68 for CSA, 1 Mar 68 and memo DepSecDef for CJCS, 1 Mar 68: fldr Miscellaneous 1968, box 65, Pentagon Papers Backup, Acc 75-062.

58. Tom Johnson notes of mtg, 4 Mar 68 (quote), ed note: both *FRUS 1964-68*, 6:316-27, 307; Gard staff mtg notes, 6 Mar 68, cited in note 56.

59. Msg JCS 2590 Wheeler to Westmoreland, 5 Mar 68, Westmoreland Eyes Only msg files, Mar 68, CMH (quote); Tom Johnson notes of mtg, 5 Mar 68, *FRUS 1964-68*, 6:328-31; telcon Johnson and Russell, 7 Mar 68, ibid, 6:346-47; Clifford, *Counsel*, 498.

60. CM-3098-68 for SecDef, 8 Mar 68, *FRUS 1964-68*, 6:355-56; Johnson, *Vantage Point*, 402; Clifford, *Counsel*, 499; msg JCS 2767 Wheeler to Westmoreland, 9 Mar 68, ed note, *FRUS 1964-68*, 6:355-56, 357-58 (quote), 354-55.

61. *New York Times*, 10 Mar 68; William Bundy (?), Extracts from Notes Concerning the President's Decisions of March 31, 1968, Prepared by former Assistant Secretary of State in January 1969, nd, fldr A-1 Clifford Study Group-Tet 1968, box 59, Taylor Papers, NDU; Tom Johnson notes of mtg, 11 Mar 68, msg JCS 2858 Wheeler to Westmoreland, 12 Mar 68, *FRUS 1964-68*, 6:369-70, 372-73.

62. *Pentagon Papers*, bk 5, IV.C.6.(c), 71-72; memo DepSecDef for CJCS, 14 Mar 68, memo SecDef for Pres, nd, ed note, *FRUS 1964-68*, 6:381-83, 384-85, 385-90.

63. Clifford notes, 18 Mar 68, fldr Notes Taken at Meetings [1], box 1, Clifford Papers, LBJL; memo Warnke for SecDef, 18 Mar 68, w/atchmt fldr Memos to Read [2], ibid.

64. Tom Johnson notes of mtg, 19 Mar 68, *FRUS 1964-68*, 6:416-17; Christian notes luncheon mtg, 22 Mar 68, fldr Closed Material-#4, box 1, Meeting Notes File, LBJL; Westmoreland, "Origins of Post-Tet 1968 Plans," cited in note 48; ltr Westmoreland to Taylor, 7 Apr 69 w/atchmt, cited in note 47; Tom Johnson notes of mtg, 26 Mar 68, *FRUS 1964-68*, 6:462.

65. Tom Johnson notes of mtg, 19 Mar 68, *FRUS 1964-68*, 6:413-15; ed note, ibid, 457-58; Clifford, *Counsel*, 512-13 (quotes). On Carver's presentation see Ford, *CIA and Vietnam Policymakers*, 134-35. Interv Cyrus R. Vance by Paige E. Mulhollan, 9 Mar 70, 3:14, AC 74-260, LBJL.

66. Tom Johnson notes of mtg, 26 Mar 68, 10:30 a.m.-12:15 p.m., *FRUS 1964-68*, 6:459-65.

67. Tom Johnson notes of mtgs, 26 Mar 68, 1:15 p.m-3:05 p.m. and 3:15 p.m.-4:32 p.m., ibid, 6:466-70; 471-74; memrcd Taylor, 27 Mar 70, disc w/Wheeler re events of February-March, 1968, etc., fldr 12-71E Vietnam Alternatives 1968, box 57, Taylor Papers, NDU (quote); Johnson, *Vantage Point*, 416-18.

68. Ed note, *FRUS 1964-68*, 6:475-76; memo DCSMO for CSA, 27 Mar 68, fldr Miscellaneous 1968, box 65, Pentagon Papers Backup, Acc 75-062; *Johnson Public Papers, 1968-69*, 1:472; msg 138438 State to Saigon, 29 Mar 68, *FRUS 1964-68*, 6:486.

69. Memrcd Nitze, re 29 March, *FRUS 1964-68*, 6:488-90; memo ASD(SA) for SecDef, 3 Apr 68, memo SecDef for SvcSecs, CJCS, 4 Apr 68: fldr FY 1968-SEA Supplemental-April 68-File #1, box 67, ASD(C) files, OSD Hist; JCSM-215-68 for SecDef, 6 Apr 68, CM-3187-68 for SecDef, 6 Apr 68: fldr [STRAF 1 of 2], box 18, Enthoven Papers, LBJL.

70. Paper, Vietnam Programs, nd but c 20 May 68; paper, Spiller, 12 Apr 68; paper, OASD(SA)SEA Programs, 26 Apr 68: fldr Miscellaneous, box 65, Pentagon Papers Backup, Acc 75-062.

71. During the first six months of 1968, 9,532 Americans had been killed and 59,682 wounded, 30,835 of whom required hospitalization. NMCC Op Sum 156-68, 3 Jul 68, Vietnam - CINCPAC Weekly Rpts, Statistics, Casualties 1968-1972, box 335, Subj files, OSD Hist; Spector, *After Tet*, 24-25. In early March Clifford questioned Westmoreland's denigrating the enemy and predicting victory and advocated a more conservative, low-key approach to "benefit . . . our public image" and not create false hopes of imminent victory; msg JCS 2721 Wheeler to Westmoreland, 8 Mar 68, *FRUS 1964-68*, 6:351-53. On the renewed emphasis on what became known as Vietnamization, see memos ISA for SecDef, 12 Apr 68 and SecDef for CJCS, 16 Apr 68: fldr Miscellaneous 1968, box 65, Pentagon Papers Backup, Acc 75-032. See also Spector, *After Tet*, 25.

72. Transc Clifford test, 23 May 68, for SSCA Hearings on DoD Appropriations for FY 1969, 1650, 1653-54, fldr Transcripts-Hearings before Senate SubCte on Defense Appropriations – Clifford/Nitze 23 May 68, box 71, ASD(C) Files, OSD Hist; transc Clifford test, 23 May 68, for HSCA Hearings on DoD Appros, Supp Appros for 1968, 112, fldr hearings SecDef before House Sub Cte on DoD Appropriations 5/28/68 A.M. & P.M. Sessions (Master), box 69, ASD(C) files, OSD Hist; Clifford, *Counsel*, 528; Elsey, staff mtg notes, 4 May 68, fldr VanDeMark Transcripts, box 1, Elsey Papers, LBJL.

73. *Clifford Public Statements, 1968*, 1:309, 311; transc of SSCA Hearings, 23 May 68, cited in note 72, 1798.

74. H.K. Johnson notes, SecDef mtg w/JCS, 29 Apr 68, fldr Official Papers – Army Chief of Staff, HKJ's Meeting Notes President and Secretary of Defense (4 Dec 67-1 Jul 68), box 115, H.K. Johnson Papers, USAMHI; Tom Johnson notes of mtg, 4 May 68, *FRUS 1964-68*, 6:634-36.

75. Msg 27134 Saigon (Komer) to State, 13 May 68, Cable files, OSD Hist. Between 27 Jan-24 Feb 68, 1,829 Americans died in action compared to 1,920 killed during the period 28 Apr-25 May 68; memrcd NMCC, Casualty Figures in SVN, atchmt 2, 9 Jun 68, Cable files, OSD Hist. The memorandum was prepared in response to a White House request. NMCC Op Summ, 156-68, 3 Jul 68, Vietnam – CINCPAC Weekly Reports, Statistics, Casualties, 1968-1972, box 335, Subj files, OSD Hist; msg 26928 Saigon to State, 10 May 68, msg 24497 Saigon to State, 18 May 68: *FRUS 1964-68*, 6:654-57, 673-76; Clifford, *Counsel*, 539; Elsey, staff mtg notes, 18 May 68, fldr VanDeMark Transcripts, box 1, Elsey Papers, LBJL (quotes); Pursley interv, 15 Aug 97, 4-5, OSD Hist.

76. Dft memo ISA (Warnke) for SecDef, nd, fldr Memos to Read (1), box 1, Clifford Papers, LBJL (I am indebted to John D. Wilson for providing me with a copy of this document); Clifford, *Counsel*, 539; Tom Johnson notes of mtg, 21 May 68, *FRUS 1964-68*, 6:690-97.

77. Ltr Taylor to Pres, 6 May 68, fldr 167-69H (VN Policy 1968), box 57, Taylor Papers, NDU.

78. Memo SecDef for CJCS, 13 May 68, fldr Miscellaneous 1968, box 65, Pentagon Papers Backup, Acc 75-062; JCSM-315-68 for SecDef, w/app, 21 May 68, *FRUS 1964-68*, 6:682-88; JCSM-221-68 for SecDef, 10 Apr 68, fldr 167-69H (VN Policy 1968), box 57, Taylor Papers, NDU.

79. Note Rostow to Pres, 20 May 68, w/atchmt CM-3333-68 for Rostow, 20 May 68, fldr Meetings with the President, May-June 1968 (2), box 2, Walt Rostow Papers, LBJL; memo SecDef for CJCS, 24 May 68, box 3, Pursley files, Acc 73A-1934.

80. JCSM-343-68 for SecDef, 29 May 68, ibid. Nitze's marginalia contesting the JCS assessment are found on the cited document. The text of the memo is also printed in *FRUS 1964-68*, 6:735-39; memo Warnke for SecDef, nd, w/atchmt draft memo SecDef for Pres, nd, box 3, Pursley files, Acc 73A-1934.

81. Msg 26928 Saigon to State, 10 May 68, *FRUS 1964-68*, 6:654-57; msg 28267 Saigon to State, 25 May 68, Westmoreland History Notes, MHI; Westmoreland notes, 30 May 68, fldr Policy/Strategy 21-30 May 68, box 3, Paul L Miles Papers, USAMHI; msg 15971 COMUSMACV to JCS, 3 Jun 68, Cable files, OSD Hist.

82. Memo Rostow for Pres, 5 Jun 68, w/atchmt, ltr Kosygin to Johnson, 5 Jun 68, Tom Johnson notes of mtg, 9 Jun 68, *FRUS 1964-68*, 6:753-55, 767-77; memrcd Harriman, 14 Dec 68, fldr Vietnam General April 1968-1969, Special Files Public Service JFK-LBJ, box 521, Harriman Papers, LC (quote); Elsey staff mtg notes, 7 Jun 68, fldr VanDeMark Transcripts, box 1, Elsey Papers, LBJL; Clifford, *Counsel*, 547-48.

83. Notes of Pres mtg w/Adm Sharp, 9 Apr 68, box 2, Meeting Notes file, NSF, LBJL.

84. Personnel Assignments Which Should Be Decided by February 1, 1968, 19 Jan 68, fldr FG 115 1/20/68-2/15/68, box 165, FX FG 115 3/23/67, LBJL (quote). McNamara told the press on 5 February 1968 that he knew of no plans to replace Westmoreland; SecDef press interv, 5 Feb 68, 182, fldr McNamara and Vietnam, 1968, box 36, SecDef Bio files, OSD Hist; telcon Johnson and Russell, 22 Mar 68, ed note, Christian notes of mtg, 8 Apr 68, *FRUS 1964-68*, 6:447-51, 451-53, 550-51 (quote), also 720, n2; Westmoreland History Notes, 1 January-30 April 1968, CMH; Spector, *After Tet*, 10; memo Taylor for Pres , 27 Mar 68, fldr 167-69H (VN Policy 1968 - Memos to Pres), box 57, Taylor Papers, NDU (quote); Pres news conf, 10 Apr 68, *Johnson Public Papers, 1968-69*, 1:505; *Washington Star*, 10 Jun 68.

85. Msg 27121 Saigon to State, 13 May 68, doc. no. CK3100542140, Declassified Documents Reference System *http://galenet.galegroup.com*; Tom Johnson notes of mtg, 14 May 68, *FRUS 1964-68*, 6:663-66; memo Lansdale for Bunker, 12 May 68 w/atchmt, memo Sweet for Lansdale, 12 May 68, doc. no. CD3100101904, Declassified Documents Reference System *http://galenet.galegroup.com*; extracted in Barrett, ed, *Johnson's Vietnam Papers*, 744-45; msg JCS 6117 Wheeler to Abrams, 5 Jun 68, fldr 1, General Abrams's EO'S, box 10, Misc Abrams msgs, CMH.

86. Msg MACV 7404 Abrams to Wheeler, 5 Jun 68, Abrams Backchannels, June 1968, CMH (quote); dft memo Warnke for SecDef, nd, cited in note 80; interv Pursley, 7 May 96, 24-25, OSD Hist (quote); Elsey staff mtg notes, 7 Jun 68, fldr VanDeMark Transcripts, box 1, Elsey Papers, LBJL; memo SecDef for CJCS, 8 Jun 68, quoted in msg JCS 6312 Wheeler to Abrams, 8 Jun 68, msg JCS 6293 Wheeler to Abrams, 7 Jun 68, msg MAC 7600 Abrams to Wheeler, 9 Jun 68 (quote), msg JCS 6361 Wheeler to Abrams, 10 Jun 68: Abrams Backchannels, June 1968, CMH; Clifford, *Counsel*, 542-44 (quote).

87. Transc of Hearings before SSCA, 23 May 68, 1798, cited in note 72.

88. Msg 30199 Saigon to State, 17 Jun 68, Cable files, OSD Hist; Elsey staff mtg notes, 20 Jun 68, fldr VanDeMark Transcripts, box 1, Elsey Papers, LBJL; Spector, *After Tet*, 230-31 (quotes); Hammond, *Military and the Media, 1968-1973*, 34-37; *JCS and the War in Vietnam*, pt 3:52/15-16; Shulimson et al, *U.S. Marines in Vietnam, 1968*, 324-27.

89. Tom Johnson notes of mtg, 9 Jun 68, *FRUS 1964-68*, 6:770, 776; CM-3423-68 for Pres, 24 Jun 68, fldr Statistics, box 3, Pursley files, Acc 73A-1934.

90. Memo Pres for SecDef, 10 Jul 68, msg CAP 81609 White House to Clifford in Saigon, 15 Jul 68: fldr Notes, box 3, Pursley files, Acc 73A-1934.

91. Memo ASD(ISA) for SecDef et al, 7 Aug 68, w/encl MACV Briefing for SecDef, 15 Jul 68, 4, 6, 9 16, General Correspondence, ibid; memo SecDef for Pres, 18 Jul 68, *FRUS 1964-68*, 6:875; *JCS and the War in Vietnam*, pt 3:52/21-22; CM-3489-68 for Pres, 19 Jul 68, fldr TS 170/80-192/80, Westmoreland Papers, MHI; Clarke, *Advice and Support: Final Years*, 298.

92. Memrcd Clifford, 16 Jul 68, fldr Memos on Troop Strength Increases and Other Subjects, box 1, Clifford Papers, LBJL; Elsey staff mtg notes, 22 Jul 68, fldr VanDeMark Transcripts, box 1, Elsey Papers, LBJL.

93. Memo SecDef for Pres, 18 Jul 68, *FRUS 1964-68*, 6:875-82; Elsey staff mtg notes, 22 Jul 68, cited in note 92; Clifford, "Annals of Government-III," 70-71; Clifford, *Counsel*, 552.

94. *JCS and the War in Vietnam*, pt 3:52/23; news conf, 31 Jul 68, *Johnson Public Papers, 1968-69*, 2:860; Elsey staff mtg notes, 1 Aug 68, fldr VanDeMark Transcripts, box 1, Elsey Papers, LBJL.

95. *JCS and the War in Vietnam*, pt 3:52/24-25; Smith summary notes of 590th NSC mtg, 4 Sep 68, *FRUS 1964-68*, 7:10-12; msg CAP 82361 Rostow for Pres, 3 Sep 68, box 2, Meeting Notes file, NSF, LBJL; Spector, *After Tet*, 240-41; msg MAC 11819 Abrams to Wheeler, 1 Sep 68, Abrams Backchannels, CMH.

96. Tom Johnson notes of Emergency NSC mtg, 20 Aug 68, *FRUS 1964-68*, 17:242-45; Gardner, *Pay Any Price*, 481; transc Clifford briefing, 10 Sep 68, before HSCA, 77, fldr Transcript of SecDef Briefing before Hse SubCte on DoD Appros, 10 Sep 68, box 76, ASD(C) files, OSD Hist.

97. Msg Abrams to Wheeler in msg CAP 82361, 3 Sep 68, cited in note 95; summary notes of 590th NSC mtg, 4 Sep 68, *FRUS 1964-68*, 7:10-12; ASD(A) Cable Branch, Vietnam: Synopsis of Msg, w/atchmt, msg 20872 Paris to State, 15 Sep 68, fldr Senate Appropriations Cte, Sec Clifford, 1968, Tab D "Negotiations," box 1, Pursley files, Acc 73A-1934.

98. Tom Johnson notes of mtg, 17 Sep 68, *FRUS 1964-68*, 7:54-55; msg 38599 Saigon to State, 24 Sep 68, unmarked fldr, box 3, Pursley files, Acc 73A-1934. Clifford regarded Bunker as a detriment in any progress toward a political solution; see Clifford, *Counsel*, 532-33. Msg 22253 Paris to State, 11 Oct 68, msg 40117 Saigon to State, 12 Oct 68: *FRUS 1964-68*, 7:155-58, 162-64; Rostow dft notes of mtg, 14 Oct 68, 9:40 a.m., Tom Johnson notes of mtgs, 14 Oct 68, 10 a.m.-12:07 p.m., 1:38 p.m.-3:40 p.m., ibid, 7:175-77, 177-84, 185-196; Johnson, *Vantage Point*, 516.

99. Tom Johnson notes of mtg, 22 Oct 68, msg 260480 State to Paris, 23 Oct 68, msg 22993 Paris to State: *FRUS 1964-68*, 7:282-85, 316-18, 362-64; *JCS and the War in Vietnam*, pt 3:54/5-8; telcons Johnson and Wheeler, 28 Oct 68 and Johnson, Rostow and Rusk, 28 Oct 68: *FRUS 1964-68*, 7:380-82, 382.

100. Tom Johnson notes of mtgs, 29 Oct 68, 2:20 a.m.-7:35 a.m., ibid, 399-416; Herring, *LBJ and Vietnam*, 173.

101. Tom Johnson notes of mtgs, 29 Oct 68, 6:17 a.m., 1-2:20 p.m.: *FRUS 1964-68*, 7:413-16 (quote), 428-33 (quote); msg JCS 12492 Wheeler to Abrams, 30 Oct 68, fldr 5, box 70, Goodpaster Papers, NDU.

102. Tom Johnson notes of mtgs, 29 Oct 68, 6:17 a.m., 6:28-7:40 p.m.: *FRUS 1964-68*, 7:416, 437-41 (quotes); Elsey staff mtg notes, 31 Oct 68, fldr VanDeMark transcripts, box 1, Elsey Papers, LBJL; msg JCS 12492 Wheeler to Abrams, 30 Oct 68, cited in note 101; Johnson, *Vantage Point*, 517; *JCS and the War in Vietnam*, pt 3:54/12-13; Tom Johnson notes of mtg, 29 Oct 68, 1-2:20 p.m., *FRUS 1964-68*, 7:429 (quote).

103. Smith summary notes of 593rd NSC mtg, 31 Oct 68, *FRUS 1964-68*, 7:483-85; memrcd Westmoreland, mtgs w/Pres, 14, 31 Oct 68, 22 Mar 71, fldr TS 0191-80, box TS 171/80-192/80, Westmoreland Papers MHI (quote); *Johnson Public Papers, 1968-69*, 2:1100-02.

104. Ed notes, *FRUS 1964-68*, 7:571, 618; press conf, 12 Nov 68, *Clifford Public Statements, 1968*, 4:988-991; CIA memo, 26 Nov 68, *FRUS 1964-68*, 7:699-700; Spector, *After Tet*, 305 (quote).

105. Spector, *After Tet*, 240; *JCS and the War in Vietnam*, pt 3:52/36-37.

106. Tom Johnson notes of mtgs, 3, 5 Dec 68: *FRUS 1964-68*, 7:722-25, 733-36; memo Rostow for Pres, 12 Dec 68, ibid, 751-53.

107. Elsey staff mtg notes, 15 Nov 68, fldr VanDeMark Transcripts, box 1, Elsey Papers, LBJL (quote); memo ActgASD(SA) for SecDef, 5 Feb 69, fldr Notebook, box 80, ASD(C) files, OSD Hist; SecDef statement, The FY 1970-74 Defense Program and 1970 Defense Budget, 13 Jan 69, 155, fldr Final FY 1970 Posture Statement, box 6, SecDef Statements 1968-70 FYs 1969-71, ASD(C) files, OSD Hist; Clifford, *Counsel*, 600; Herring, *LBJ and Vietnam*, 176.

108. Elsey, staff mtg notes, 13 Dec 68, fldr VanDeMark Transcripts, box 1, Elsey Papers, LBJL; memrcd Taylor, disc w/Wheeler re events of February-March, 1968, etc., 21 Mar 70, fldr 12-71E Vietnam Alternatives 1968, box 57, Taylor Papers, NDU; Elsey staff mtg notes, 15 Nov 68, cited in note 107.

VIII. THE AIR WAR AGAINST NORTH VIETNAM:
ESCALATION TO CESSATION, 1967–1968

1. "Joint Chiefs wear a different hat," *Business Week*, 30 Jul 66, 68, 70 (quotes, 68); Background Briefing, 23 Dec 66, *Background Briefings of Secretary of Defense McNamara, 1966*, 405-06. See also, for example, Smith summary notes of 568th NSC mtg, 8 Feb 67, *FRUS 1964-68*, 5:98; McNamara, *Argument Without End*, 407-08.

2. For example, "Building the 'Credibility Gap,'" *Washington Star*, 3 Jan 67; "Johnson's Credibility Gap," *Baltimore Sun*, 16 Jan 67; "Wheeler Hits U.S. Policy on ABM," *Washington Post*, 23 Feb 67.

3. McNamara test, 23 Jan 67, Subcte on DoD of SCA and SCAS, *Hearings: Supplemental Defense Appropriations and Authorizations, FY 1967*, 62 (quote); transc McNamara test, 23 Jan 67, Senate Subcte on DoD of SCA and SCAS Hearings on Military Authorizations and Defense Appropriations FY 1968 and FY 1967 Supplemental for Southeast Asia, 141-43, 154-56, 161-62, fldr SecDef Transcript-Senate Armed Services and Appropriations - 1/23/67 (Glass Master), box 61, ASD(C) files, OSD Hist. Press reports of the failure of the bombing include "Confusion on Vietnam," *New York Times*, 21 Feb 67; *Washington Post*, 21 Feb 67; *Washington Star*, 20 Feb 67.

4. Msg CINCPAC to JCS, 040334Z Jan 67, fldr Viet 385.1 (July-Dec) 1967, box 6, SecDef Subject Decimal files, Acc 72A-2467; msgs CINCPAC to JCS, 142140Z Jan 67, CINCPAC to JCS, 182210Z Jan 67: Cable

files, OSD Hist; memo Rostow for Pres, 23 Jan 67, *FRUS 1964-68*, 5:58-59; Herring, *LBJ and Vietnam*, 107-08.

5. Schoenbaum, *Waging Peace and War*, 456-58; Johnson, *Vantage Point*, 253-54; McNamara, *In Retrospect*, 251; *JCS and the War in Vietnam*, pt 3:40/11-12; memo Rostow for Pres, 7 Feb 67, telcon Johnson and Rostow, 11 Feb 67, *FRUS 1964-68*, 5:94, 122-24; ltr Johnson to Ho Chi Minh, [8 Feb 67], ibid, 5:91-93.

6. DIA Intelligence Bulletin 30-67, 13 Feb 67, box 330, Subj files, OSD Hist; Johnson, *Vantage Point*, 252-55 (quote, 253); CM-2111-67 for SecDef, 11 Feb 67, *FRUS 1964-68*, 5:134-35; msg 1156-67 Wheeler to Westmoreland and Sharp, 11 Feb 67, Westmoreland Eyes Only msg files, 1 Jan-31 Mar 67, CMH; telcons Johnson and Rostow, 11 Feb 67, 9:15 a.m. and 9:49 a.m., *FRUS 1964-68*, 5:122-24, 126-28.

7. Tom Johnson notes of mtg, 13 Feb 67, Personal Papers Tom Johnson, LBJL (also in ed note, *FRUS 1964-68*, 5:164-65); see also msg 3562 Moscow to State, 18 Feb 67, *FRUS 1964-68*, 5:186-91; msg JCS 6129 CJCS to CINCPAC, 11 Feb 67, Cable files, OSD Hist; Johnson, *Vantage Point*, 254-55; McNamara, *In Retrospect*, 251.

8. Tom Johnson notes of mtg, 13 Feb 67, LBJL (quote); ed note, ltr Ho Chi Minh to Lyndon B. Johnson, 15 Feb 67, *FRUS 1964-68*, 5:164-65, 173-74; McNamara, *In Retrospect*, 251; CMC notes of JCS mtg, 13 Feb 67, vol 16, Greene Papers, MHC (quote); *JCS and the War in Vietnam*, pt 3:41/1; Thompson, *To Hanoi and Back*, 56; msg JCS 1284-67 Wheeler to Sharp and Westmoreland, 17 Feb 67, Westmoreland Eyes Only msg file, 1 Jan-31 Mar 67, CMH.

9. McNaughton, Military Program Against North Vietnam, 2d redraft, 13 Feb 67, 14, 23, fldr Viet 320 1967, box 5, SecDef Subject Decimal files, Acc 72A-2467; memo Rostow for Pres, 17 Feb 67, fldr February 1967, box 22, Gibbons Papers, LBJL; msg JCS 1337-67 Wheeler to Sharp and Westmoreland, 18 Feb 67, Westmoreland Eyes Only msg file, 1 Jan -31 Mar 67, CMH (quote); Rostow notes of mtg w/Pres Johnson, 17 Feb 67, *FRUS 1964-68*, 5:182-85.

10. *Pentagon Papers*, bk 5, IV.C.6(b), 49-51; Rostow notes of mtg w/Pres, 17 Feb 67, cited in note 9; Gravel ed, *Pentagon Papers*, 4:148; msg JCS 1422-67 Wheeler to Sharp and Westmoreland, 22 Feb 67, fldr February 1967, box 22, Gibbons Papers, LBJL; circ msg 144313, State to All US Dipl Missions, 27 Feb 67, Cable files, OSD Hist .

11. *JCS and the War in Vietnam*, pt 3:41/4; msgs JCS 6955 CJCS to CINCPAC, 23 Feb 67 and JCS 6972 JCS to CINCPAC, 23 Feb 67: Cable files, OSD Hist; Pres news conf, 27 Feb 67, *Johnson Public Papers, 1967*, 1:219 (quote).

12. Msg JCS 1691-67 Wheeler to Sharp and Westmoreland, 6 Mar 67, fldr March 1967, box 23, Gibbons Papers, LBJL.

13. Memos Taylor for Pres, 9 Mar 67, Rostow for Pres, 9 Mar 67, SecState for Pres, 10 Mar 67, and SecDef for Pres, 9 Mar 67: fldr Sen Robert Kennedy's Position on Vietnam - Analysis of, box 8, NSF, Rostow Files, LBJL.

14. Memo Rostow for Pres, 10 Mar 67, *FRUS 1964-68*, 5:241-43.

15. Msg JCS 1883-67 Wheeler to Sharp, 14 Mar 67 (quotes); CM-2201-67 for Svc Chs, 29 Mar 67 (quote): fldr 337 Guam Conf/Gen Brown Msn to Saigon - Mar 67, box 91, Wheeler Papers, RG 218; msg JCS 9614 CJCS to CINCPAC, 22 Mar 67, Cable files, OSD Hist.

16. *JCS and the War in Vietnam*, pt 3:41/4-5; msg CINCPAC to JCS, 120205Z Apr 67, Cable files, OSD Hist; memo W. Bundy for Katzenbach, 22 Apr 67, note Read to SecState, 15 Apr 67 w/atchd msg JCS 2766-67 Wheeler to Sharp, 15 Apr 67: fldr April 1967, box 24, Gibbons Papers, LBJL.

17. *JCS and the War in Vietnam*, pt 3:41/5; memo Rostow for Pres, 22 Apr 67, fldr Meetings with the President, box 1&2, NSF, Rostow Files, LBJL; CIA D/I Wkly Summary, 28 Apr 67, #0287/67, fldr VN April 1 - June 30, 67, box 331, Subj files, OSD Hist.

18. Gard notes, SecDef Staff mtg, 24 Apr 67 (quote), Gard Notebook, OSD Hist.

19. Christian notes on disc w/Pres, 27 Apr 67, memo W. Bundy for Rusk, 2 May 67 (quote), memo Rostow for Pres, 9 May 67 (quote): *FRUS 1964-68*, 5:349-52, 367-68, 399-401; memo Rostow, lunch mtg w/Pres, 2 May 67 (quote), fldr Walt Rostow - May 1-15, 1967, 2 of 2 (volume 27), box 16, NSF, Memos to the President, Walt Rostow, LBJL.

20. Memo Bundy for Pres, 3 May 67, memo Rostow for Pres, 9 May 67: *FRUS 1964-68*, 5:370-77, 399-400 (quote); CM-2318-67 CJCS for Pres, 5 May 67, fldr McNTN XIII-Memoranda 1967 (2), box 5, Warnke Papers, McNaughton files, LBJL. Walt Rostow forwarded the response to the president; msg CAP 67398 Rostow to Pres, 6 May 67, fldr Walt Rostow - May 1-15, 1967, 1 of 2 (volume 27), box 16, NSF, Memos to the President, Walt Rostow, LBJL.

21. DPM McNaughton for Pres, 5 May 67, box 2, Warnke Papers, McNaughton files, LBJL; memo Rostow for Pres, 6 May 67, memo SecDef and DepSecDef for Pres, 9 May 67: *FRUS 1964-68*, 5:383-88, 401-03.

22. Memo W. Bundy, Bombing Strategy Options for the Rest of 1967, 9 May 67 (quote, 10), fldr Vietnam 2EE, box 75, NSF, CF Vietnam, LBJL. The first portion of the memo is in *FRUS 1964-68*, 5:404-05; memo Rostow for Pres, 9 May 67, 7:30 p.m. (quotes), fldr Walt Rostow - May 1-15, 1967, 1 of 2 (volume 27), box 16, NSF, Memos to the President, Walt Rostow, LBJL.

23. Memo Rostow for Pres, 15 May 67 (quote), memo Taylor for Pres, 11 May 67: *FRUS 1964-1968*, 5:412-13, 410-11; Wheeler memrcd, mtg at White House, 16 May 67, vol 16, Greene Papers (quote); memo Rostow for Pres, 10 May 67, fldr Walt Rostow - May 1-15, 1967, 1 of 2 (volume 27), box 16, NSF, Memos to the President, Walt Rostow, LBJL.

24. *JCS and the War in Vietnam*, pt 3:41/9-10; Thompson, *To Hanoi and Back*, 65-66.

25. DPM SecDef for Pres, 19 May 67, fldr Vietnam 2EE, box 75, item # 18a, NSF, CF Vietnam, LBJL. An excerpted version is in *FRUS 1964-68*, 5:423-38.

26. Memo Rostow for Pres, 19 May 67, *FRUS 1964-68*, 5:420-22.

27. Herring, *LBJ and Vietnam*, 54; Karnow, *Vietnam*, 503 (quote), 505.

28. Msg JCS 3891 Wheeler to Sharp, 25 May 67 (quote), fldr May 1967, box 25, Gibbons Papers, LBJL; Herring, *LBJ and Vietnam*, 53; McNamara, *In Retrospect*, 277; msg JCS 4476 Wheeler to Sharp 15 Jun 67, Westmoreland Papers, CMH.

29. CM-2381-67 for SecDef, 29 May 67, fldr Viet 370, 1967, box 5, SecDef Subject Decimal files, Acc 72A-2467; JCSM-307-67 for SecDef, 1 Jun 67, fldr Miscellaneous 1967, box 65, Pentagon Papers Backup, Acc 330-75-062; ed note, *FRUS 1964-68*, 5:458-59.

30. Memo Rostow for Pres, 20 May 67 (quotes), fldr Vietnam 2EE, box 75, NSF, CF Vietnam, LBJL; ltr Helms to McNamara w/atchmt, 1 Jun 67 (quote, 7), fldr Viet 370 1967, box 5, SecDef Subject Decimal files, Acc 72A-2467.

31. Johnson, *Vantage Point*, 368-69; msgs CINCPAC to JCS, 290506Z May 67 (quote) and CINCPAC to JCS, 210430Z Jun 67: Cable files, OSD Hist.

32. JCSM-286-67 for SecDef, 20 May 67, CM-2377-67 for SecDef, 24 May 67: fldr Viet 385 (Jan-May) 1967, box 5, SecDef Subject Decimal files, Acc 72A-2467; memo SecDef for CJCS et al, 20 May 67, fldr McNTN XIII - Memoranda 1967 (2), box 5, Warnke Papers, McNaughton Files, LBJL.

33. JCSM-312-67 for SecDef, 2 Jun 67, fldr Viet 370 1967, box 5, SecDef Subject Decimal files, Acc 72A-2467.

34. DPM SecDef for Pres, Summary, 12 Jun 67 draft w/atchd DPM SecDef for Pres, Alternative Military Actions Against North Vietnam, 12 Jun 67 draft, fldr Vietnam 2EE, box 74, NSF, CF, Vietnam, LBJL. An excerpted version is in *FRUS 1964-68*, 5:474-81.

35. Msg 198583 State to Moscow, 19 May 67, *FRUS 1964-68*, 5:485-87 transmitted the text of the letter to be forwarded to Kosygin; memo Rostow for Pres, 9 Jun 67 w/atchd draft ltr, fldr June 1967, box 26, Gibbons Papers, LBJL; memos Rostow for Pres, 11 Jun 67, 15 Jun 67, 10:45 a.m.: *FRUS 1964-68*, 5:472-73, 515; *Washington Post*, 14 Jun 67; Johnson, *Vantage Point*, 481; Gaiduk, *The Soviet Union and the Vietnam War*, 123-24; memo Rostow for Pres, mtg w/Pres on Vietnam, 15 Jun 67, 11:30 a.m., AGENDA, fldr Meetings with the President, box 1 & 2, NSF, Rostow Files, LBJL.

36. Memcon Johnson and Kosygin, 23 Jun 67, 11:30 a.m.-1:30 p.m., *FRUS 1964-68*, 14:522-23; memcon Johnson and Kosygin, 23 Jun 67, 3:44 p.m. to 4:35 p.m., ed note, 25 Jun 67, *FRUS 1964-1968*, 5:531-32, 551; CRS, *The U.S. Government and the Vietnam War*, pt 4:723; Johnson, *Vantage Point*, 256-57.

37. The Military History Institute of Vietnam, *Victory in Vietnam*, trans Merle L. Pribbenow, 207; McNamara, *Argument Without End*, 282; Ang Cheng Guan, "Decision-making Leading to the Tet Offensive (1968)," 345-47. The Soviets also noted that after April 1967 Hanoi was inflexible in its refusal to maintain contacts with the United States; Gaiduk, *Soviet Union and the Vietnam War*, 128.

38. Notebook, Air Campaign North Vietnam: July 1967: Secretary McNamara: Rolling Thunder, TAB A, SecDef VN Trip, 25 Jul 67, CINCPAC Appraisal (quote, 146), fldr Viet 385.1 Rolling Thunder 8 Jul 67, box 6, SecDef Subject Decimal files, Acc 72A-2467; Sharp, *Strategy for Defeat*, 184.

39. Tom Johnson notes of mtg, 12 Jul 67, *FRUS 1964-68*, 5:600-09.

40. Memo Stempler OATSD(LA) for DepSecDef, Interim Trip Report - Preparedness Investigating Subcommittee, Senate Committee on Armed Services, 10 Jul 67, fldr Viet 385.1 (July-Dec) 1967, box 6, SecDef Subject Decimal files, Acc 72A-2467; *JCS and the War in Vietnam*, pt 3:47/4-5.

41. Tom Johnson notes of mtg, 18 Jul 67, *FRUS 1964-68*, 5:623-24 (quotes); msg JCS 1859 CJCS to CINCPAC, 20 Jul 67, Cable files, OSD Hist; Sharp, *Strategy for Defeat*, 185 (quote).

42. Msg MAC 6978 Westmoreland to Sharp, 25 Jul 67, Westmoreland Eyes Only msg files, 1 Jul-30 Sep 67, CMH; The Air War, 5 Aug 67 (quote), fldr 328-69 B Clifford-Taylor Mission Report to the President, item #2, box 58, Taylor Papers, NDU; memo Habib for Rusk, 5 Aug 67, *FRUS 1964-68*, 5:669.

43. Herring, *LBJ and Vietnam*, 116; McNamara, *In Retrospect*, 295-98; Tom Johnson notes of mtg, 26 Sep 67, *FRUS 1964-68*, 5:824; Tom Johnson notes of mtg, 8 Aug 67, LBJL.

44. McNamara, *In Retrospect*, 298-99 (quote); memo for Kissinger, nd, *FRUS 1964-68*, 5:687; Johnson, *Vantage Point*, 266 (quote); msg JCS 4343 CJCS to CINCPAC, 19 Aug 67, Cable files, OSD Hist; Sharp, *Strategy for Defeat*, 199-200.

45. Tom Johnson notes of mtg, 8 Aug 67 (quote), cited in note 43; Herring, *LBJ and Vietnam*, 57; msg JCS 3365 CJCS to CINCPAC, 9 Aug 67, Cable files, OSD Hist.

46. Sharp, *Strategy for Defeat*, 194 (quote); memo Rostow for Pres, 9 Aug 67 (quotes), fldr August 1967, box 27, Gibbons Papers, LBJL.

47. Memo SecDef for Pres, 11 Aug 67, fldr Vietnam 2EE, box 75, NSF, CF Vietnam, LBJL; Tom Johnson notes of mtg, 16 Aug 67, *FRUS 1964-68*, 5:697-99 (quotes).

48. Jim Jones notes of mtg, 18 Aug 67, *FRUS 1964-68*, 5:703-04 (quote, 703); Tom Johnson notes of mtg, 8 Aug 67 (quote), cited in note 43; McNamara, *In Retrospect*, 284.

49. Memo Helms for McNamara, 22 Aug 67, TAB F, fldr #20, McN on Bombing NVN, box 2, OSD Records from SecDef Vault (Mr Laird) Acc 74-142; CIA, Intelligence Memos: Effects of the Rolling Thunder Program, 16 Aug 67, and Reactions To A Certain US Course of Action, 18 Aug 67: fldr McNamara on bombing of NVN, box 7, McNamara Papers, Acc 71A-3470.

50. Ltr Stennis to McNamara, 10 Aug 67; CM-2583-67 for SecDef, 12 Aug 67; memo Pursley for SecDef, 15 Aug 67 w/cover note 16 Aug 67, ltr McNamara to Stennis, 16 Aug 67: all in fldr Viet 385.1 (July-Dec) 1967, box 6, SecDef Subject Decimal files, Acc 72A-2467.

51. Sharp test, 9 Aug 67, Preparedness Investigating Subcte of SCAS, *Hearings: Air War Against North Vietnam*, pt 1:8, 10, 15, 40, 53, 73; Wheeler and Momyer test, 16 Aug 67, ibid, pt 2:127, 132, 162; McConnell test, 22 Aug 67, ibid, pt 3:212-14; Johnson and Greene test, 28-29 Aug 67, ibid, pt 5:389-91, 397-98, 401-15, 441, 461; McNamara, *In Retrospect*, 285-86. Generals Johnson and Greene testified on 28 and 29 August respectively, that is after McNamara's testimony.

52. Jim Jones notes of mtg, Rusk, McNamara et al, 18 Aug 67, *FRUS 1964-68*, 5:708; CM-2595-67 for SecDef, 17 Aug 67, fldr Viet 385.1 (July-Dec) 1967, box 6, SecDef Subject Decimal files, Acc 72A-2467; McNamara, *In Retrospect*, 284 (quote); U.S. District Court, Southern District of New York, Testimony Robert S. McNamara, General William C. Westmoreland v. CBS, Inc., et al, 6 Dec 84, 4958 (quote).

53. McNamara test, 25 Aug 67, *Hearings*, cited in note 51, pt 4:278-81 (quote, 278), 286, 318, 357; transc McNamara test, 25 Aug 67, Preparedness Investigating Subcte of the SCAF on the Air War against North Vietnam (Excerpts) 25 Aug 67, 1096, fldr Vietnam 1967, box 36, Bio Files, OSD Hist.

54. McNamara test, *Hearings*, cited in note 53, 304-05, 357-58 (quotes).

55. Ibid, 334-35.

56. Dallek, *Flawed Giant*, 478; CRS, *The U.S. Government and the Vietnam War*, pt 4:750-52; President's Daily Diary, 25 Aug 67, box 2, Daily Diary, LBJL (I am indebted to John Wilson for providing this information); Wheeler Private Diary, 25 Aug 67, fldr 1967, box 201, Wheeler Papers, RG 218.

57. *New York Times*, 29 Nov 67, 3 Dec 67 (quote); Herring, *LBJ and Vietnam*, 56-57 (quote, 57); Mark Perry, *Four Stars*, 162-66; CMC work notes, JCS mtg, 29 Nov 67, vol 17, Greene Papers, MHC; James Reston in *New York Times*, 29 Nov 67; Tom Johnson notes of NSC mtg on 29 Nov dated 1 Dec 67 (quote, 10), LBJL.

58. *New York Times*, 11 Oct 67; Pres news conf, 1 Sep 67, *Johnson Public Papers, 1967*, 2:816-17 (quote, 817); Herring, *LBJ and Vietnam*, 57; memo Jones for Pres, 5 Sep 67, *FRUS 1964-68*, 5:752.

59. Jones notes of mtg, 18 Aug 67, *FRUS 1964-68*, 5:703-04; ibid, 716, n2, 722, n3.

60. Memrcd NNMC, 23 Aug 67 0900 EDT; NNMC Sitrep for Pres, 23 Aug 67, 1:00 p.m. EDT; memrcd NMCC for SecDef, 28 Aug 67; memrcd NMCC, 30 Aug 67: all Cable files, OSD Hist; CIA D/I Wkly Summary, #0304/67, 25 Aug 67, fldr VN Jul-Dec 1967, box 331, Subj files, OSD Hist; memo CSAF for DepSecDef, 24 Aug 67, box 6, SecDef Subject Decimal files, Acc 72A-2467.

61. Tom Johnson notes of mtg, 24 Aug 67, *FRUS 1964-68*, 5:723-25 (quote, 725); McNamara, *In Retrospect*, 299; *JCS and the War in Vietnam*, pt 3:44/11.

62. *New York Times*, 8 Oct 67 (quote); memo Helms for Pres, 29 Aug 67, *FRUS 1964-68*, 5:733-34.

63. *New York Times*, 3, 8 Oct 67; memo Jones for Pres, 12 Sep 67, *FRUS 1964-68*, 5:777-84 (quotes, 779).

64. Memo SecDef for CJCS, 8 Sep 67, fldr Reading File Sept 15-1, 1967, box 130, McNamara Records, RG-200; memo Rostow for Pres, 11 Sep 67, *FRUS 1964-68*, 5:767-69; msg CINCPAC to JCS, 210028Z Sep 67, Cable files, OSD Hist; CM-2660-67 for SecDef, 22 Sep 67, fldr Viet 385.1 Rolling Thunder 22 Sep 67, box 6, SecDef Subject Decimal files, Acc 72A-2467; Tom Johnson notes of mtg, 26 Sep 67, *FRUS 1964-68*, 5:822-27 (quote, 825).

65. *JCS and the War in Vietnam*, pt 3:47/6; address on Vietnam, 29 Sep 67, *Johnson Public Papers, 1967*, 2:878-

79 (quote): Max Frankel in *New York Times*, 2 Oct 67, 2; Herring, *LBJ and Vietnam*, 118-19; *New York Times*, 4 Oct 67 (quotes).

66. Ed note and Tom Johnson notes of mtg, 3 Oct 67, *FRUS 1964-68*, 5:837-46.

67. *JCS and the War in Vietnam*, pt 3:47/15; Tom Johnson notes of Pres mtg w/McNamara et al, 4 Oct 67, *FRUS 1964-68*, 5:856-60 (quote, 857); note McNamara to Pres, 18 Oct 67 w/atchd JCSM-555-67 for SecDef, 17 Oct 67, fldr Viet 370 1967, box 5, SecDef Subject Decimal files, Acc 72-A-2467. See also *FRUS 1964-68*, 5:903, n12.

68. Ed note and Tom Johnson notes of mtgs, 5, 18 Oct 67: *FRUS 1964-68*, 5:870-72, 865-70 (quote, 866), 893-905. McNamara had continued to push Pennsylvania following Hanoi's 4 October statement; see his instructions for Kissinger dated 7 October 1967, fldr 2, Peace Negotiations w/Vietnam-Memos for Dr. Kissinger, box 92, Goodpaster Papers, NDU.

69. Pribbenow, *Victory in Vietnam*, 214; McNamara, *Argument Without End*, 296, 300; Johnson, *Vantage Point*, 268; msg from Kissinger in Paris to State, 26 Oct 67, *FRUS 1964-68*, 5:912-13.

70. Tom Johnson notes of mtgs, 17, 23 Oct 67, *FRUS 1964-68*, 5:887-90, 915-17 (quotes, 915, 916); *New York Times*, 23 Oct 67; Thompson, *To Hanoi and Back*, 90.

71. *JCS and the War in Vietnam*, pt 3:47/8; CM-2701-67 for Goodpaster, 19 Oct 67, CM-2700-67 for Goodpaster, 19 Oct 67: fldr 4, Sea Cabin, box 101, Goodpaster Papers; CMC work notes, JCS mtg 20 Oct 67, vol 17, Greene Papers.

72. Memo Helms for Rostow, 24 Oct 67, fldr Vietnam 3H (2) 1967, box 84, NSF, CF, Vietnam, LBJL; memo Carver for SecDef, 23 Oct 67 (quote) w/atchmt, fldr An Alternative Fifteen-Month Program for Vietnam, Oct 67, box 97, McNamara Records, RG 200; memo McPherson for Pres, 27 Oct 67, fldr Vietnam 3F 3/67-10/68 - Memos on Bombing in Vietnam, box 83, NSF, CF, Vietnam, LBJL.

73. Memo SecDef for Pres, 1 Nov 67 w/atchd DPM SecDef for Pres, A Fifteen Month Program for Military Operations in Southeast Asia, 1 Nov 67, *FRUS 1964-68*, 5:943-50. On the president's reaction see his memo, 18 Dec 67, ibid, 1118-20.

74. "Sec. McNamara's draft recommendations of Nov. 1, 1967 and the views of others on the issues raised," nd, fldr McNamara Robert S. - Vietnam, box 3, NSF, Rostow Files, LBJL. The nine were McGeorge Bundy, Bunker, Clifford, Fortas, Katzenbach, Rostow, Rusk, Taylor, and Westmoreland. Memos Katzenbach for Pres, 16 Nov 67, Rostow for Pres, 2 Nov 67, Rusk for Pres, 20 Nov 67, Rostow for Pres, 20 Nov 67: *FRUS 1964-68*, 5:1032-35, 971-73, 1037-40, 1040-42.

75. Memos Clifford for Pres, 7 Nov 67, Taylor for Pres, 3 Nov 67: *FRUS 1964-68*, 5:992-93, 978-79 (quote).

76. Memo Havens for Warnke, CIA Analysis of the 1967 Campaign Against LOCs, nd, likely early Nov 67, fldr Miscellaneous 1967, box 65, Pentagon Papers Backup, Acc 330-75-062; Clifford, *Counsel to the President*, 455; memos Jim Jones for Pres, 2 Nov 67, Rostow for Pres, 2 Nov 67: *FRUS 1964-68*, 5:954-70, 951-53; McNamara, *In Retrospect*, 309.

77. JCSM-663-67 for SecDef, 27 Nov 67, memo Warnke for SecDef, 5 Dec 67: fldr Miscellaneous 1967, box 65, Pentagon Papers Backup, Acc 75-062; Tom Johnson notes of mtg, 21 Nov 67, FRUS 1964-68, 5:1050-59; CIA/DIA, An Appraisal of the Bombing of North Vietnam (through 16 November 1967), Nov 67, fldr 3H (2) 1967, box 84, NSF, CF, Vietnam, LBJL.

78. Institute for Defense Analysis, JASON, The Bombing of North Vietnam, vol 1, Summary, 16 Dec 67 (quote, 3), fldr Viet 385.1 (16 Dec 67) TS Con 3711, box 6, SecDef Subject Decimal files, Acc 72A-2467; ed note, *FRUS 1964-68*, 5:1116-17.

79. Memo Warnke for SecDef, 3 Jan 68, fldr Miscellaneous 1968, box 65, Pentagon Papers Backup, Acc 33075-062; Sharp, *Strategy for Defeat*, 207.

80. Sharp, *Strategy for Defeat*, 206; memo Warnke for SecDef, 22 Dec 67, fldr Southeast Asia 000.1-1968, box 10, ISA General files, Acc 72A-1499; memo Seignious for Goodpaster, 22 Nov 67 w/encl, fldr SEA CABIN Study Group/JCS - Study of Political-Military Implications in SE Asia of Cessation of Aerial Bombardment, 22 Nov 67 (quote, 2-8), box 97, McNamara Records, RG 200.

81. JCSM-78-68 for SecDef, 3 Feb 68, fldr Miscellaneous 1968, box 65, Pentagon Papers Backup, Acc 75-062; Tom Johnson notes of mtg, 6 Feb 68, *FRUS 1964-68*, 6:138-40.

82. Tom Johnson notes of mtg, 13 Feb 68, McPherson notes of mtg, 27 Feb 68: *FRUS 1964-68*, 6:206-10, 260-62 (quote); Johnson, *Vantage Point*, 387; Califano, *Triumph & Tragedy*, 263-64 (quote); Clifford, *Counsel*, 485; Shapley, *Promise and Power*, 444.

83. Memo Rostow for Pres, 4 Mar 68, *FRUS 1964-68*, 6:311-13 (quote); DPM SecDef for Pres, 4 Mar 68, TAB F-1, The Air Campaign Against North Vietnam, fldr 627-71A (Clifford Task Force, Review of VN Policy March 1968) item #5, box 59, Taylor Papers. Excerpts of the 4 March DPM appear in Gravel ed, *Pentagon Papers*, 4:575-83. See also DPM for Pres Johnson, 4 Mar 68, *FRUS 1964-68*, 6:314-16; DPM, 4

Mar 68, TAB F, Significance of Bombing Campaign in North to our Objectives in Vietnam, 3 Mar 68, fldr March 31st Speech, vol 7, box 49, NSF, NSC History, LBJL.

84. Tom Johnson notes of mtg, 4 Mar 68, *FRUS 1964-68*, 6:326-27 (quote); interv Dean Rusk by Paige E. Mulhollan, 26 Sep 69, 2:9, Internet Copy, LBJL; Johnson, *Vantage Point*, 399, 410-11; memo Clifford for Wheeler, 5 Mar 68 w/atchd Rusk draft, Comments on the Attached Draft, nd, fldr Memos on Vietnam Feb-Mar 68, box 2, NSF, Clifford Papers, LBJL.

85. Memo Hoopes for SecDef, 14 Mar 68, *FRUS 1964-68*, 6:379-81; Hoopes, *The Limits of Intervention*, 186-96; memo ASD(ISA) for SecDef, DPM on Vietnam, 2d draft, 18 Mar 68, fldr Memos to Read (2), box 1, NSF, Clifford Papers, LBJL; Clifford notes, 18 Mar 68, fldr Notes Taken at Meetings (1), ibid; Clifford, "A Vietnam Reappraisal," 610-11; interv Clark M. Clifford by Paige E. Mulhollan, 14 Aug 69, 3:9-10, Internet Copy, LBJL.

86. Tom Johnson notes of mtg, 19 Mar 68, *FRUS 1964-68*, 6:412-15; McPherson notes of mtg, 20 Mar 68 (quote), NSF, Meeting Notes File, LBJL. On dating the McPherson document see *FRUS 1964-68*, 6:432, n1.

87. CM-3129-69 for SecDef, 20 Mar 68, *FRUS 1964-68*, 6:422-23 (quote); telcon Clifford and Pres, 20 Mar 68, ibid, 6:428-31 (quotes).

88. Christian notes of mtg, 22 Mar 68, memos McPherson for Pres, 23 Mar 68, Rusk for Pres, 25 Mar 68 w/ atchmt, Rostow for Pres, 25 Mar 68: *FRUS 1964-68*, 6:444-46, 453-54, 454-55 (quote), 454, n4.

89. Tom Johnson summary of notes, 26 Mar 68, Nitze memrcd, 29 Mar 68: *FRUS 1964-68*, 6:471-74, 488-90; Johnson, *Vantage Point*, 418; interv Cyrus Vance by Paige E. Mulhollan, 29 Dec 69, 3:14, AC 74-260, LBJL; interv Clifford by Mulhollan, 14 Jul 69, 3:2; Clifford, *Counsel*, 518 (quote).

90. Pres address, 31 Mar 68, *Johnson Public Papers, 1968*, 1:470, 476; ed notes, *FRUS 1964-68*, 6:483-84, 494-95; *JCS and the War in Vietnam*, pt 3:50/2-3 (quote).

91. *JCS and the War in Vietnam*, pt 3:50/5; Johnson, *Vantage Point*, 420n; memo Harriman for Pres, 2 Apr 68, fldr Vietnam General April 1968-1969, Special Files Public Service JFK-LBJ, box 521, Harriman Papers, LC; Tom Johnson notes of mtg, 2 Apr 68, telcon Pres, Clifford, and Mansfield, 2 Apr 68: *FRUS 1964-68*, 6:501-04.

92. Ed note, *FRUS 1964-68*, 6:510; Clifford, *Counsel*, 529; records of conv, Zhou Enlai and Pham Van Dong, Beijing, 13 Apr 68 and 19 Apr 68 (quote), Cold War International History Project, Internet Copy. The announcement also caught Ho Chi Minh, then in Beijing for medical treatment, off guard. Quiang Zhai, "Beijing's Position on the Vietnam Peace Talks, 1965-1968," Internet Copy; *JCS and the War in Vietnam*, pt 3:50/11.

93. Msg JCS 3668 Wheeler to Sharp, 3 Apr 68, Westmoreland Eyes Only msg file, 1 Apr-30 Apr 1968, CMH; Johnson, *Vantage Point*, 494; CM-3263-68 for SecDef, 29 Apr 68, fldr Vietnam 3F 3/67-10/68, box 83, Memos on Bombing in Vietnam, NSF, CF Vietnam, LBJL.

94. Tom Johnson notes of mtg, 4 May 68, *FRUS 1964-68*, 6:634-36; Elsey notes of SecDef Morning Staff Confs, 6 May 68, fldr VanDeMark Transcripts, box 1, Elsey Papers, LBJ Library (quotes); memos Rostow for Pres, 9, 10 May 68, CM-3282-68 for SecDef, 8 May 67: fldr Vietnam 3G 5/67-8/68, box 83, NSF, CF, Vietnam, LBJL.

95. Tom Johnson notes of mtgs, 14, 15 May 68, *FRUS 1964-68*, 6:663-66, 667-70; memo Warnke for SecDef, Operational Authorities in NVN Between 19 and 20 N Latitude (CM-3282-68), 14 May 68; memo Warnke for SecDef, Reasons Against Moving the Bombing from the 19th to the 20th Parallel, 14 May 68 (quote, emphasis in the original): fldr #16, Expanded Bombing, box 2, OSD Records from SecDef Vault (Mr. Laird), Acc 74-142.

96. Elsey notes of SecDef Morning Staff Confs, 18, 22 May 68 (quotes), fldr VanDeMark Transcripts, box 1, Elsey Papers, LBJL; *JCS and the War in Vietnam*, pt 3:53/12; Tom Johnson notes of mtg, 21 May 68, *FRUS 1964-68*, 6:690-97; Clifford, *Counsel*, 541.

97. These characterizations are found in Johnson, *Vantage Point*, 509; Schoenbaum, *Waging Peace*, 486; Herring, *LBJ and Vietnam*, 165 (quote); Elsey notes of SecDef Morning Staff Confs, 30 Aug 68 (quote), fldr VanDe-Mark Transcripts, box 1, Elsey Papers, LBJL; Cooper, *The Lost Crusade*, 415; memrcd Harriman, General Review of Last Six Months, 14 Dec 68, fldr Vietnam General April 1968-1969, Special Files Public Service JFK-LBJ, box 521, Harriman Papers, LC.

98. Msg 202032 State to Paris and Saigon, 13 Jul 68, *FRUS 1964-68*, 6:855; Elsey notes of SecDef Morning Staff Confs, 22 Jul 68, fldr VanDeMark Transcripts, box 1, Elsey Papers, LBJL.

99. Clifford, *Counsel*, 539-40; Elsey notes of SecDef Morning Staff Confs, 18 May 68, fldr VanDeMark Transcripts, box 1, Elsey Papers, LBJL; interv LtGen Robert Pursley by Alfred Goldberg and Roger Trask, 15 Aug 97, 3:4-5, OSD Hist; memo Warnke for SecDef, How Can We Best Achieve Our Objective in South Vietnam, nd, fldr Memos to Read (1), box 1, Clifford Papers, LBJL.

100. *JCS and the War in Vietnam*, pt 3:53/13; JCSM-343-68 for SecDef, 29 May 68, JCSM-354-68 for SecDef, 4 Jun 68: *FRUS 1964-68*, 6:735-39, 747-49.

101. Memo Warnke for SecDef, 28 May 68, fldr Warnke Notebook on Vietnam 1968 (4), box 9, Warnke Papers, McNaughton Files, LBJL. Nitze's annotations appear on a copy of JCSM-343-68, 29 May 68 (cited in note 100), no fldr, box 3, Pursley Files, Acc 73A-1934; DPM SecDef for Pres, Negotiating and Bombing Alternatives, nd but early Jun 68, ibid. An earlier second draft of the document dated 5 June 1968 is available in fldr Warnke Notebook on Vietnam 1968 (1), box 9, Warnke Papers, McNaughton Files, LBJL

102. Msg CAP 81241 Rostow to Pres, 3 Jun 68, w/atchd msg 15436 Paris to State, 3 Jun 68, memo Rostow for Pres, 5 Jun 68 w/atchd ltr Kosygin to Johnson, 5 Jun 68: *FRUS 1964-68*, 6:746-47 (quote), 753-55.

103. Tom Johnson notes of mtg, 9 Jun 68, *FRUS 1964-68*, 6:767-77 (quote, 770); Clifford, *Counsel*, 547; memrcd Harriman, cited in note 97; Johnson, *Vantage Point*, 510.

104. Ltr Johnson to Kosygin, 11 Jun 68, memcon Bohlen, 12 Jun 68: *FRUS 1964-68*, 6:782-84 (quote), 788-89 (quote); Herring, *LBJ and Vietnam*, 171.

105. CM-3423-68 for Pres, 24 Jun 68, box 3, Pursley Files, Acc 73A-1934; JCSM-406-68 for SecDef, 26 Jun 68, Tab A, fldr #16, Expanded Bombing, box 2, OSD Records from SecDef Vault (Mr Laird), Acc 74-142.

106. Memrcd Nitze, 17 Jul 68; msg WDC 10622 Nitze to Clifford and Wheeler (in Hawaii), 18 Jul 68: fldr 337 (Saigon Trip) July 67 Bulky, box 102, Wheeler Papers, RG 218; memo Warnke for Clifford, 1 Jul 68, fldr Vietnam 3 May 68-9 Jul 68, box 26, NSF, Clifford Papers, LBJL.

107. CM-3526-68, 31 Jul 68, TAB I, fldr #16, Expanded Bombing, box 2, OSD Records from SecDef Vault (Mr Laird), Acc 74-142; CM-3531-68 for Pres, 31 Jul 68, fldr SEA Memoranda, box 3, NSF, Clifford Papers, LBJL; Tom Johnson notes of mtg, 30 Jul 68, *FRUS 1964-68*, 6:920-23 (quote); Elsey notes of SecDef Morning Staff Confs, 1 [?] Aug 68, fldr VanDeMark Transcripts, box 1, Elsey Papers, LBJL (quote).

108. Tom Johnson notes, 30 Jul (quote) and Elsey notes, 1[?] Aug: both cited in note 107; memrcd Taylor, Tuesday Luncheon, 30 Jul 68 (quote), fldr T 315-69 Project Lull, box 59, Taylor Papers, NDU; "Hanoi Shows Restraint," *New York Times*, 29 Jul 68.

109. Memo Taylor for Pres, 30 Jul 68, fldr 167-69H (VN Policy 1968 Memos to Pres), item #19, box 57, Taylor Papers, NDU; memo Smith for Pres, 1 Aug 67, *FRUS 1964-68*, 6:924-26; CM-3532-68 for Pres, 1 Aug 68, memo SecState for Pres, 31 Jul 68: fldr 167-69H (VN Policy 1968 Memos to Pres), items #21 and #22, box 57, Taylor Papers, NDU.

110. Memo SecDef for Pres, 1 Aug 68 (quotes), TAB J, fldr #16, Expanded Bombing, box 2, OSD Records from SecDef Vault (Mr. Laird), Acc 74-142; Elsey notes of SecDef Morning Staff Confs, 1 [?] Aug 68 (quotes), cited in note 107.

111. Clifford talks w/LBJ, 4 Aug 68, fldr Mr. Clifford's Penciled Notes Vietnam, box 1, NSF, Clifford Papers, LBJL; Elsey notes of mtgs, 5 Aug 68, *FRUS 1964-68*, 6:939-41 (quote); Clifford, *Counsel*, 568.

112. Smith summary notes of 590th NSC mtg, 4 Sep 68; Elsey notes of SecDef Morning Staff Confs, 16 Sep 68: *FRUS 1964-68*, 7:11 (quote), 37-38 (quote); Synopsis, OASD(Admin) Cable Branch, Vietnam w/atchd msg 20872 Paris to State, 15 Sep 68, fldr Senate Appropriations Cte, Sec Clifford, 1968, TAB D "Negotiations," box 1, Pursley Files, Acc 73A-1934.

113. Elsey notes 16 Sep 68, cited in note 112; Johnson notes of 591st NSC mtg, 25 Sep 68, notes of Pres mtg w/JCS on Vietnam, 14 Oct 68: *FRUS 1964-68*, 7:86-91, 185.

114. Spector, *After Tet*, 295-97; memo McPherson for Pres, 9 Oct 68, Tom Johnson notes of Pres mtg w/SecDef et al, 14 Oct 68, Tom Johnson notes of Pres mtg w/Sec Rusk et al, 29 Oct 68: *FRUS 1964-68*, 7:153, 186, 400-01; Smith summary notes of Pres mtg w/JCS, 14 Oct 68, msg CAP 82361, Rostow to Pres, 3 Sep 67: box 2, NSF, NSC Meetings, LBJL.

115. Smith summary notes of Pres mtg w/JCS, 14 Oct 68, cited in note 114; memrcd Westmoreland, mtgs w/ Pres, 14, 31 Oct 68, 22 Mar 71 (quote), fldr TS-0191-80-192/80, file TS 0191-80, Westmoreland Papers, USAMHI; *JCS and the War in Vietnam*, pt 3:54/7.

116. Msg 254719/Todel 1263 State to Paris, 14 Oct 68, *FRUS 1964-68*, 7:170-74; memrcd Rostow, mtg w/ Pres, 23 Oct 68, 2:45 p.m., ibid, 309-12.

117. Tom Johnson notes of Pres mtg w/Sec Rusk et al, 29 Oct 68 (quote), cited in note 114; record of conv Chen Yi and Le Duc Tho, Beijing, 17 Oct 68 (quote), Cold War International History Project, Internet Copy.

118. Elsey notes of SecDef Morning Staff Confs, 17 Oct 68, Tom Johnson notes of Pres mtg with Sec Rusk et al, 29 Oct 68: *FRUS 1964-68*, 7:229-32, 402, 407; Clifford, *Counsel*, 585-86. Abrams's trip was unknown even to his military superior General Westmoreland whom the president told about it after the NSC meeting on 31 October. Smith summary notes of 593d NSC mtg, 31 Oct 68, *FRUS 1964-68*, 7:485.

119. Elsey notes of SecDef Morning Staff Confs, 31 Oct 68, Smith, summary notes of 593d NSC mtg, 31 Oct 68: *FRUS 1964-68*, 7:464-69 (quote, 464), 483-85; Pres address to the nation, 31 Oct 68, *Johnson Public Papers*, 1968, 2:1100.

IX. BILLS COME DUE: THE BUDGETS AND SUPPLEMENTALS, 1968–1970

1. Califano, *Triumph & Tragedy*, 182 (quote). The signatories were Treasury Secretary Fowler, BoB Director Schultze, CEA Chairman Ackley, Labor Secretary Wirtz, Commerce Secretary Connor, Clifford, McNamara, and Califano. Among them only Wirtz opposed a tax increase. State of the Union msg, 10 Jan 67, *Johnson Public Papers, 1967*, 1:8; Pierce, *Politics of Fiscal Policy Formulation*, 149; Kettl, "Economic Education of Lyndon Johnson," 66.

2. Notes from mtg on Post-Vietnam Planning, 11 Mar 67, 24 Mar 67, fldr Vietnam, box 63, microfilm CEA, LBJL (quote). Preliminary planning for the study commenced in early February, and on 1 March the president issued a directive to accelerate and integrate executive office planning for the post-Vietnam era. See memo Pres for Secs Fowler, McNamara, Rusk, and Wirtz, Dir Schultze, ActgSec Trowbridge; Chm Ackley, 1 Mar 68, ibid; Anthony and Schultze test, 24 Apr 67, Jt Econ Cte, *Hearings: Economic Effects of Vietnam Spending*, pt 1:8-9, 31.

3. King, "The President & Fiscal Policy in 1966," 706; memo Fowler, Schultze, and Ackley for Pres, 29 Mar 67, fldr Vol II, Doc. Supplement, pt 1 (1 of 2), box 1, Administrative History of CEA, LBJL.

4. Anthony test, 24 Apr 67, Jt Econ Cte, *Hearings*, cited in note 2, pt 1:1, 20; *Cong Rec*, 13 Jun 67, 15539.

5. CEA, *Economic Report to the President Together With The Annual Report of the Council of Economic Advisors*, 25 Jan 68, 43, 54.

6. Ibid, 105-06; Bernstein, *Guns or Butter*, 367; *Wall Street Journal*, 8 Jun 67 (quote); memo Ackley for Califano, 9 Jun 67, fldr Vol II Doc. Supplement pt 1 (1 of 2), box 1, Administrative History of CEA, LBJL.

7. Memo Califano for Pres, 12 Jun 67, fldr FI 11-4 6/11/67-7/15/67, box 60, EX FI 11-4, 7/7/66, LBJL; memo Ackley for Pres, 19 Jun 67, fldr vol II Doc. Supplement pt 1 (1 of 2), box 1, Administrative History of CEA, LBJL (quote); memo Ackley for Pres, 11 Jul 67, ibid; memo Schultze for Pres, 11 Jul 67, fldr Decisionmaking on the 10% - Jun-Jul 67, box 1, Legislative Background Tax Increase, LBJL; memo Califano for Pres, 12 Jul 67, w/atchmt, draft memo Fowler, Schultze, and Ackley for Pres, 12 Jul 67, fldr FI 11-4 6/11/67-7/15/67, box 60, EX FI 11-4 7/7/66, LBJL; memo Califano for Pres, 10 Jul 67, w/atchmt, msg Califano for McNamara, 7 Jul 67, fldr FI 11-4, Income Tax 1967, box 44, WHCF, LBJL; draft memo Zwick et al for Fowler et al, 12 Jul 67, fldr vol II, Doc. Supplement, pt 1 (1 of 2), box 1, Administrative History of CEA, LBJL.

8. Msg CIA to the White House (McNamara 9094 to Califano), 10 Jul 67, fldr FI 11-4, Income Tax 1967, box 44, WHCF, LBJL; memo Enthoven for SecDef, 5 Jul 67, fldr Miscellaneous Documents -67, box 65, Pentagon Papers Backup, Acc 75-062; memo SecDef for SecA, 7 Sep 67, fldr Items for FY 69 Posture Statement, box 72, ASD(C) files, OSD Hist.

9. Califano, *Triumph & Tragedy*, 244; memo Fowler et al for Pres, 22 Jul 67, fldr Tax Materials (xerox), box 4, Legislative Background Tax Increase, LBJL; memo Califano for Pres, 21 Jul 67, fldr Decisionmaking on the 10% - Jun-Jul 67, box 1, Legislative Background Tax Increase, LBJL for details of meeting of advisers on the tax hike.

10. Tom Johnson notes from Pres mtg w/Cong Leadership, 24 Jul 67, notes on mtg of Pres w/Senate Cte Chairmen, 25 Jul 67: Tom Johnson Personal Papers, LBJL; Califano, *Triumph & Tragedy*, 244; Tom Johnson notes of Pres mtg w/Democratic Cong Leadership, 31 Jul 67, Tom Johnson Personal Papers, LBJL; Pres news conf, 3 Aug 67, *Johnson Public Papers, 1967*, 2:740-46.

11. Gard staff mtg notes, 7 Jun 67, Gard Notebook, OSD Hist; memo SecDef for Pres, 8 Jun 67, fldr Reading File June 15-1, 1967, box 128, McNamara Records, RG-200; memo ASD(C) for SvcSecs et al, 16 Jun 67, Hoover for Program/Budget Staff, 2 Nov 67: fldr FY 1969 Budget Memos, box 6, Comptroller files, Acc 73A-1389.

12. Pres special msg to Cong, 3 Aug 67, *Johnson Public Papers, 1967*, 2:734, 736 (quote); Pres news conf, 3 Aug 67, ibid, 2:744; HCA, *Department of Defense Appropriation Bill, 1968*, H Rpt 349, 9 Jun 67, 4-5; SCA, *Department of Defense Appropriation Bill, 1968*, S Rpt 494, 4 Aug 67, 4; memo Anthony for SecDef, 31 Aug 67, fldr Old, box 327, Subj files, OSD Hist.

13. Memo ASD(C) for SvcSecs et al, 30 Aug 67, fldr FY 1969 Budget Memos, box 6, Comptroller files, Acc 73A-1389; Current Status of FY 1968 Defense Budget, 10 Aug 67, (Glass Master), table insert between 114-15, fldr House Appropriations Subcte on Senate Action on DoD FY 1968 Budget Request, box 63, ASD(C) files, OSD Hist; McNamara's handwritten comment of 8 Sep 67 appears on memo Anthony for SecDef, 31 Aug 67, cited in note 12.

14. Current Status, 10 Aug 67, cited in note 13, 3, 7, 10-14.

15. HCA, H Rpt 349, 9 Jun 67, cited in note 12, 4; HCA, SCA, SRpt 494, 4 Aug 67, 1; *Appropriations for the Department of Defense for 1968*, H Rpt 595, 23 Aug 67, 1-7; Pres statement, 30 Sep 67, *Johnson Public Papers, 1967*, 1:881 (quote).

16. Memo Ackley for Pres, 3 Aug 67, Vol II, Doc. Supplement, pt 1 (1 of 2), box 1, Administrative History of CEA, LBJL; Gard staff mtg notes, 20 Nov 67, Gard Notebook, OSD Hist; McNamara test, 14 Feb 68, HSCA, *Hearings: Department of Defense Appropriations for 1969*, pt 1:92 (quote); Johnson, *Vantage Point*, 443. Conservative sentiment is expressed in Tom Johnson notes of Pres mtg w/Democratic Congressmen, 8 Aug 67, Tom Johnson Personal Papers, LBJL.

17. Tom Johnson notes, 31 Jul 67, cited in note 10; notes 8 Aug 67, cited in note 16; notes of Pres mtg w/ Democratic Congressmen, 9 Aug 67, notes of Pres mtg w/House GOP Freshmen, 17 Aug 67: Tom Johnson Personal Papers, LBJL; memo Sanders for Pres, 13 Sep 67, fldr FI 11-4 8/15/67-9/21/67, box 61, EX FI 11-4 7/16/67, LBJL; memo Jones for Pres, mtg w/Secs Rusk and McNamara, Unger and Rostow, 15 Sep 67, box 1, NSF Meeting Notes File, NSF, LBJL; Johnson, *Vantage Point*, 450-51; memo SecDef for Pres, 7 Oct 67, fldr Reading File Oct 10-2, 1967, box 131, McNamara Records, RG 200.

18. Tom Johnson notes of Pres mtg w/Cong Leaders, 17 Oct 67, Tom Johnson Personal Papers, LBJL.

19. Memo SecDef for Califano, 16 Oct 67, fldr Reading File, Oct 31-11, 1967, box 130, McNamara Records, RG-200 (quote); memo Schultze and Ackley for Pres, 13 Oct 67, fldr Vol II, Doc. Supplement, pt 1 (1 of 2), box 1, Administrative History CEA, LBJL; Tom Johnson notes of Pres mtg w/Bipartisan Leadership, 20 Nov 67, Tom Johnson Personal Papers, LBJL (quote).

20. Collins, "The Economic Crisis of 1968," 399-411; Kaufman, "Foreign Aid and the Balance-of-Payments Problem," in Divine, ed, *The Johnson Years*, 2:93-94; Johnson, *Vantage Point*, 316-17; Hargrove and Morley, eds, *The President and the Council*, 220.

21. Kaufman, "Foreign Aid," 91; Gard staff mtg notes, 18 Dec 67, Gard Notebook, OSD Hist; memo OASD (Economics & Resource Analysis) for SecDef, 10 Jul 68, tab U, fldr #11, box 1, OSD Records for SecDef Vault (Mr. Laird), Acc 74-0142; Johnson, *Vantage Point*, 317; Petty mins of mtg, 21 Dec 67, ed note: *FRUS 1964-68*, 8:456, 460, 478-81.

22. Rostow notes on Pres mtg w/Leadership, 18 Nov 67, *FRUS 1964-68*, 8:441-42; Tom Johnson notes of Pres mtg w/Bipartisan Leadership, 20 Nov 67, Tom Johnson Personal Papers, LBJL; memo SecDef for SvcSecs et al, 2 Nov 67, fldr Budget - FY 1968, box 64, ASD(C) files, OSD Hist; Gard staff mtg notes, 18 Dec 67, Gard Notebook, OSD Hist; Pierce, *Politics of Fiscal Policy Formulation*, 159-60; Johnson, *Vantage Point*, 449.

23. Memo Ackley for Pres, 12 Dec 67, fldr Vol II, Doc. Supplement, pt 1 (1 of 2), box 1, Administrative History of CEA, LBJL.

24. Memo ASD(C) for SvcSecs et al, FY 1969 Budget Estimates, 16 Jun 67, fldr FY 1969 Budget Memos, box 6, Comptroller files, Acc 73A-1389.

25. Gard staff mtg notes, 20 Nov, 27 Nov, 11 Dec 67, Gard Notebook, OSD Hist; CMC work notes, JCS mtg, 22 Nov 67, Greene Papers, MHC (quote); McNamara test, 16 Feb 68, HSCA, *Hearings: Department of Defense Appropriations for 1969*, pt 1:119.

26. FY 1969 Budget Review, Summary of SecDef Budget Review Adjustments by DoD Component, fldr Hearings - Snte Armd Svcs Cte - FY 69 Budget 2/2/68 Aftn, box 73, ASD(C) files, OSD Hist; McNamara test, 16 Feb 68, HSCA, Hearings, cited in note 25, pt 1:119; Comparisons of Departments of Army, Navy, and Air Force Requests to OSD with President's Budget for FY 1969, fldr Hearings - Snte Armd Svcs Cte - FY 69 Budget 2/2/68 Aftn, box 73, ASD(C) files, OSD Hist; Gard staff mtg notes, 20 Nov 67, cited in note 25.

27. FY 1969 Budget Review, SecDef Adjustments to Service Requests Classified by Primary Rationale, fldr Hearings - Snte Armd Svcs Cte - FY 69 Budget 2/2/68 Aftn, box 73, ASD(C) files, OSD Hist.

28. Remaining Significant FY 69 Budget Disagreements between JCS and SecDef, 8 Nov 67, fldr Final Memo to the President, 1 Dec 67, box 7, McNamara files, Acc 71A-3470; memo SecDef for CJCS, 9 Nov 67, JCSM-638-67 for SecDef, 16 Nov 67, App B: fldr FY 1969 Budget Development, box 75, ASD(C) files, OSD Hist; Shapley, *Promise and Power*, 390-91.

29. Gard staff mtg notes, 27 Nov 67, cited in note 25

30. CM-2767-67 for SecDef, 18 Nov 67, CM-2779-67 for SecDef, 22 Nov 67: fldr FY 1969 Budget, box 71, ASD(C) files, OSD Hist; McNamara notes, 17, 24 Nov 67, fldr Final Memo to President, box 75, McNamara Records, RG-200; paper, Fowler, "What subjects did the JCS discuss with the SecDef on the FY 1969 Defense Budget Recommendations," 8 Jan 68, fldr FY 1969 Budget Hearings - Pueblo, box 75, ASD(C) files, OSD Hist; memo Keeny for Rostow, 17 Nov 67, w/atchmt, fldr Johnson Library Papers, OSD Hist

31. DPM SecDef for Pres, 1 Dec 67, *FRUS 1964-68*, 10:622-25.

32. Memo Keeny for Rostow, 17 Nov 67, cited in note 30.

33. Ibid; BoB-DoD Meeting on the FY 1969 Defense Budget, nd, fldr 1969 Budget, box 71, ASD(C) files, OSD Hist.

34. DPM SecDef for Pres, 1 Dec 67, w/TAB B "Summary of Recommendations by the SecDef and Related Recommendations by the JCS with FY 69 Budget Implications," 28 Nov 67, *FRUS 1964-68*, 10:622-41.
35. Clifford notes, 1/17/67[sic], fldr "1968" (2), box 14, Clifford Papers, LBJL.
36. Tom Johnson notes of Pres mtg w/McNamara et al, 4 Dec 67, *FRUS 1964-68*, 10:642-46 (quote, 646). The contretemps over the conflicting congressional testimony of McNamara and the JCS during August 1967 hearings is treated in Chapter VII. See CM-2920-68 for SecDef, 18 Jan 68, fldr FY 1969 Budget, box 71, ASD(C) files, OSD Hist.
37. PL 90-218, 18 Dec 67 (81 Stat 662); Pres statement, 19 Dec 67, *Johnson Public Papers, 1967*, 2:1174-75.
38. Memo ASD(A) for DDRE et al, 30 Nov 67, fldr Compt Mangt 1967, box 786, Subj files, OSD Hist; Anthony test, 19 Feb 68, HSCA, *Hearings*, cited in note 25, 480-81; *DoD Annual Report for FY 1968*, 60.
39. Ltr Zwick to Pres, 12 Feb 68, in *Revision of Department of Defense Appropriations, 1968*, H Doc 255, 12 Feb 68, 2.
40. McNamara test, 5 Feb 68, SCAS, *Hearings: Authorization for Military Procurement, Research and Development, Fiscal Year 1969, and Reserve Strength*, 280-82 (quote); McNamara test, 16 Feb 68, HSCA, *Hearings*, cited in note 25, 274; the classified version is in DoD Appropriations for 1969, 16 Feb 68, 561, fldr House Appropriations Cmte - FY 1969 Budget Hearings -A.M. 2/16/68, box 74, ASD(C) files, OSD Hist; ASD(C), FY 1968 Budget Revision-NOA: Summary of Rationale, rev 1 Feb 68, fldr SecDef Statement - Adjustments to FY 1968 Budget, box 64, ASD(C) files, OSD Hist (quote).
41. McNamara test, 16 Feb 68, HSCA, *Hearings*, cited in note 25, 273-75.
42. BrigGen L.B. Taylor test, 21 Feb 68, ibid, 633; MajGen D.L. Crow test, 28 Feb 68, ibid, 846-51; Ignatius test, 28 Feb 68, ibid, 887; ASD(C), FY 1968 Revision-NOA Summary of Rationale, rev 1 Feb 68, cited in note 40.
43. McNamara test, 5 Feb 68, SCAS, *Hearings*, cited in note 40, 279; Crow test, 28 Feb 68, HSCA, *Hearings*, cited in note 25, 852-53.
44. Tom Johnson notes of Pres mtg w/Natl Alliance of Businessmen, 27 Jan 68, Tom Johnson Personal Papers, LBJL; ltr McNamara to Schultze, 27 Jan 68, fldr FY 1969 Budget Memos, OASD(P&FC) Budget Estimates 1968-1970, box 6, Comptroller files, Acc 73A-1389; Pres msg to Cong, 29 Jan 68, *Johnson Public Papers, 1968*, 1:83-84, 87, 89-91, 94.
45. Tom Johnson notes of Pres mtg w/McNamara et al, 13 Feb 68, *FRUS 1964-68*, 6:209, n7; Dallek, *Flawed Giant*, 509. The cost figures appear in McPherson notes of mtg, McNamara, Rusk, Clifford et al, 27 Feb 68, box 1, NSF Meeting Notes file, NSF, LBJL; Tom Johnson notes of Pres mtg w/Clifford, Fowler et al, 4 Mar 68, *FRUS 1964-68*, 6:324-25.
46. Memo Zwick for Pres, 2 Mar 68, fldr Memos to Read [1], box 1, Clifford Papers, LBJL; Memo Zwick for Clifford, 6 Mar 68, ibid.
47. Note ASD(C) for SecDef, 20 Mar 68, w/encl, memo Benson for ASD(C), 20 Mar 68, fldr FY 1969 Budget Development, box 75, ASD(C) files, OSD Hist; draft memo ASD(C) for SecDef, 13 Mar 68, ibid (quote).
48. Jones notes on Pres mtg w/Cong Democratic Leaders, 19 Mar 68, box 2, Meeting Notes file, NSF, LBJL; Tom Johnson notes of Pres mtg w/Fiscal Advisers, 20 Mar 68, Tom Johnson Personal Papers, LBJL.
49. Memo Enthoven for SecDef, 3 Apr 68; memo Enthoven for SvcSecs et al, 3 Apr 68; memo SecDef for SvcSecs and CJCS, 4 Apr 68: fldr FY 1968 SEA Supplemental, Apr 68 - File #1, box 67, ASD(C) files, OSD Hist; Gard staff mtg notes, 18 Mar 68, Gard Notebook, OSD Hist; Pierce, *Politics of Fiscal Policy Formulation*, 162-64.
50. Note Rostow to Pres, 6 Mar 68 w/atchd memo Nitze for Pres, 6 Mar 68, fldr Defense, Dept of, vol V Aug 67 (1 of 2), box 12/13, NSF Agency file, LBJL (quote); interv Paul H. Nitze by Maurice Matloff and Roger Trask, 9 Oct 84, 42, OSD Hist.
51. Livesay mins, SecDef staff mtg, 11 Mar 68, fldr Minutes of SecDef Staff Mtgs - Mar-Sep 68, box 18, Clifford Papers, LBJL; memo Rostow for Pres, 16 Mar 68, fldr Defense, Dept of, vol V Aug 67 (1 of 2), box 12/13, NSF Agency file, NSF, LBJL.
52. Memo DepSecDef for DDRE and AsstSecDefs, 9 Mar 68, ltr Nitze to Zwick, 13 Mar 68: fldr FY 1969 Budget, box 71, ASD(C) files, OSD Hist; memo ASD(C) for SvcSecs et al, 11 Mar 68, fldr FY 1969 Budget Memos, box 6, Comptroller files, Acc 73A-1389.
53. Ltr DepSecDef to DirBoB, 9 Apr 68, fldr FY 1968 SEA Supplemental, Apr 68 - File #1, box 67, ASD(C) files, OSD Hist; memo SecDef for Pres, 10 Apr 68, ibid.
54. Johnson, *Vantage Point*, 453. On the timing of the request see Gard staff mtg notes, 15 Apr 68, Gard Notebook, OSD Hist.
55. Nitze test, 14 Jun 68, SCA, *Hearings: Second Supplemental Appropriations for Fiscal Year 1968*, 186-87, 211-12, 216.

56. Nitze test, 28 May 68, HCAS, *Hearings: Second Supplemental Appropriation Bill, 1968*, 745-46; Clifford test, 23 May 68, SSCA, *Hearings: Department of Defense Appropriations for Fiscal Year 1969*, 2410. Five days later he read identical remarks in testimony before the House Subcommittee on DoD Appropriations.

57. PL 90-392, 9 Jul 68 (82 Stat 307); SCA, *Second Supplemental Appropriation Bill, 1968*, S Rpt 1269, 19 Jun 68, 11; HCA, *Second Supplemental Appropriation Bill, 1968*, H Rpt 1531, 7 Jun 68, 12.

58. Memo Zwick for Pres, 16 Mar 68, fldr Bureau of the Budget vol 2, box 7, NSF Agency file, NSF, LBJL; Jones notes, Pres breakfast mtg w/Cong Leadership, 2 Apr 68, box 2, Meeting Notes file, LBJL.

59. Memo Zwick for Pres, 27 Apr 68, fldr Tax Material (xerox), box 4, Legislative Background file, Tax Increase 1968, LBJL; Livesay mins, SecDef staff mtg, 6 May 68, fldr Minutes of SecDef Staff Mtgs - Mar-Sep 68, box 18, Clifford Papers, LBJL.

60. Johnson, *Vantage Point*, 452-54; Tom Johnson notes of Pres mtg w/Cabinet, 14 May 68, Tom Johnson Personal Papers, LBJL; Clifford notes, 14 May 68, fldr Notes Taken at Meetings [1], box 1, Clifford Papers, LBJL; ltr Nitze to Rivers w/encl, 14 May 68, fldr FY 1969 Budget, box 71, ASD(C) files, OSD Hist. Identical letters were sent to 10 other members of Congress.

61. Johnson, *Vantage Point*, 456-57; Gard staff mtg notes, 6 May 68, Gard Notebook, OSD Hist. Gard also records Congress demanding more than a $4 billion reduction in federal spending. Elsey notes, Clifford's staff conf, 13 May 68, fldr Personal Papers of George M. Elsey, box 1, Elsey Papers, LBJL.

62. Note Okun to Pres, 9 May 68 w/atchd memo Okun for Pres, fldr Legislative Struggle - vol vii, 2 May - 27 May 68, box 6, Legislative Background file, Tax Increase 1968, LBJL; Tom Johnson notes of Pres mtg w/ Cabinet, 14 May 68, cited in note 60; Johnson, *Vantage Point*, 454-56; memo Fowler, Okun, Zwick for Pres, 20 May 68, fldr Tax Material (xerox), box 4, Legislative Background file, Tax Increase 1968, LBJL (quote); memo Okun for Pres, 21 May 68, ibid; Califano, *Triumph & Tragedy*, 286.

63. Memo Okun for Pres, 27 May 68, fldr Council of Economic Advisors, box 10, Agency file, NSF, LBJL; Jones notes, Pres mtg w/Democratic Congressmen, 27 May 68, box 3, Meeting Notes file, LBJL; Maguire mins, Cabinet mtg of May 29, 1968, fldr Cabinet Meeting 2/29/68 [1 of 3], box 13, Cabinet Papers, LBJL; Johnson, *Vantage Point*, 458-59; Livesay mins, SecDef staff mtgs, 10, 17 Jun 68, fldr Minutes of SecDef Staff Mtgs-Mar-Sep 68, box 18, Clifford Papers, LBJL.

64. PL 90-364, 28 Jun 68 (82 Stat 270); memo Johnson for Heads of Depts and Agencies, 28 Jun 68, fldr FY 1969 Budget, box 71, ASD(C) files, OSD Hist; Johnson, *Vantage Point*, 460; Tom Johnson notes, 14 May 68, cited in note 60; memo DirBoB for Heads of Exec Depts and Establishments, "Limitations on budget authority and outlays for fiscal year 1969," *BoB Bulletin* No. 68-16, 28 Jun 68, fldr FY 1969 Budget, box 71, ASD(C) files, OSD Hist; Nitze's Backup Book, Tab 1, Revenue and Expenditure Control Act of 1968, fldr SecDef Clifford Talking Papers before Policy Cte of House Armed Svcs Cte - FY 69 Expenditure Reductions - 8/1/68, box 76, ibid.

65. Tom Johnson notes of Pres mtg w/Cabinet, 14 May 68, cited in note 60. See also Elsey notes, Clifford's staff conf, 20 Jun 68, box 1, Elsey Papers, LBJL, for Clifford's favorable attitude toward deploying the Sentinel system.

66. Memo DepSecDef for SvcSecs et al, 25 Jul 68 w/encl, fldr FY 1970 T-Day Planning (Pre 1/20/69), box 79, ASD(C) files, OSD Hist; ltr Nitze to Okun, 4 Dec 68, ibid; *Washington Post*, 26 Jun 68.

67. DoD News Release 617-68, 2 Jul 68, *Clifford Public Statements, 1968*, 2:602; DoD News Releases 800-68, 27 Aug 68, 776-68, 20 Aug 68, 764-68, 16 Aug 68: all fldr DoD Expd Adj'mts, box 787, Subj files, OSD; ltr Rivers to Clifford, 4 Sep 68, fldr FY 1969 Budget, box 71, ASD(C) files, OSD Hist; ltrs Sikes to Clifford, 29 Jul 68, Clifford to Sikes, 9 Aug 68: ibid; ltr Rivers to Clifford, 29 Jul 68, fldr SecDef Clifford Talking Papers before Policy Cte of House Armed Svcs Cte - FY 69 Expenditure Reductions - 8/1/68, box 76, ibid.

68. Elsey notes, Clifford's staff conf, 5 Jul 68, box 1, Elsey Papers, LBJL.

69. Memo Greenleaf for SvcSecs et al, 5 Jul 68 w/atchd papers, Possible non-SEA Reductions to FY 1969 Program, (NOA), 10 Jul 68, Detail Possible Non- SEA Reductions to FY 1969 Program, (NOA), nd: all fldr SecDef Clifford Talking Papers before Policy Cte of House Armed Svcs Cte - FY 69 Expenditure Reductions - 8/1/68, box 76, ASD(C) files, OSD Hist; Nitze test, 17 Sep 68, SSCA, *Hearings: Department of Defense Appropriations for Fiscal Year 1969*, pt 5: 2573-74; Classified Statement of DepSecDef Nitze before Senate SubCte of the Cte on DoD Appropriations Appeals on House Action on the FY 69 Defense Budget, 17 Sep 68, 3, fldr Transcript-Hearings Before Senate Approp. Cte for FY 1969-September 17, 1968 (a.m. & p.m.), box 77, ASD(C) files, OSD Hist.

70. *Washington Post*, 19 Jul 68; ASD(C), Congressional and Project 693 Actions on FY 1969 Defense Budget and Authorization Requests, 12 Sep 68, fldr Snte Apprp Cte, Sec Clifford 1968, TAB K - FY 68 Supplemental, Pursley files, box 1, Acc 73A-1934; Ltr Mahon to Staats, 6 Aug 68, fldr FY 1969 Budget, memo SecN for SecDef, 26 Mar 68, fldr Statement on FY 1969 Authorization Changes, box 76: ASD(C) files, OSD Hist.

71. ASD(C), Cong and Project 693 Actions cited in note 70; HCA, *Department of Defense Appropriation Bill, 1969*, H Rpt 1735, 18 Jul 68, 64-68; ltr Nitze to Russell, 24 Jul 68, fldr FY 1969 Budget, box 71, ASD(C) files, OSD Hist.

72. Transc Clifford test, 10 Sep 68, for House Subcte hearings on DoD Appropriations, 71-72, box 76, ibid: Clifford reaffirmed these views in less sensational fashion during his Senate testimony the following week. SSCA, *Hearings*, cited in note 69, 2603. Classified insert for line 2, Page 2699 Senate Appropriations Cte Hearings, 17 Sep 68, fldr Transcript - Hearings Before Senate Approp. Cte for FY 1969 - September 17, 1968 (a.m. & p.m.), box 77, ASD(C) files, OSD Hist.

73. Nitze test, 17 Sep 68, SSCA, *Hearings*, cited in note 66, 2574; ltr Nitze to Russell, 13 Sep 68, fldr Transcript - Hearings Before Senate Approp. Cte for FY 1969 - September 17, 1968 (a.m. & p.m.), box 77, ASD(C) files, OSD Hist; Tom Johnson notes of Pres mtg w/Tuesday Luncheon Group, 17 Sep 68, Tom Johnson Personal Papers, LBJL.

74. SCA, *Department of Defense Appropriation Bill, 1969*, S Rpt 1576, 19 Sep 68, 34-35.

75. Elsey notes, Clifford's staff conf, 21 Sep 68, box 1, Elsey Papers, LBJL. OSD ultimately developed a new schedule for conversions of two in FY 68, two in FY 69, six in FY 70, seven in FY 71, six in FY 72, five in FY 73 and three in FY 74 to permit the completion of the program in FY 75 as previously planned. Clifford statement, 15 Jan 69, *Clifford Public Statements, 1968*, 4:1166; ltr Clifford to Mahon, 7 Oct 68, fldr FY 1969 Reclama, box 1, Comptroller files, Acc 73A-496.

76. HCA, *Department of Defense Appropriations, 1969*, H Rpt 1970, 10 Oct 68, 4-5; Cong Action on FY 1969 Budget Request by Appropriation Title and Item, 25 Oct 68, Notebook: Budget Data FY 1966-68, ASD(C) files, OSD Hist; Hargrove and Morley, *President and the Council*, 303 (quote); PL 90-580, 17 Oct 68 (82 Stat 1120).

77. Memo SecDef for SvcSecs et al, 2 Feb 68, fldr FY 1970 Budget (Pre -1/20/69), box 79, ASD(C) files, OSD Hist.

78. Memo DepSecDef for SvcSecs et al, 6 Mar 68, ibid.

79. Tom Johnson notes of Pres mtg w/Foreign Policy Advisors, 24 Jul 68, *FRUS 1964-68*, 4:890; memo ASD(C) for SvcSecs et al, 21 Jun 68, fldr FY 1970 Budget, box 6, Comptroller files, Acc 73A-1389; Tom Johnson notes on Pres mtg w/Tuesday Luncheon Group, 20 Nov 68, Tom Johnson Personal Papers, LBJL; Elsey notes, Clifford's staff conf, 3 Dec 68, box 1, Elsey Papers, LBJL; memo ASD(SA) for SecDef, 5 Feb 69, fldr SA Fact Sheets (FY 70) Feb 1969, box 80, ASD(C) files, OSD Hist.

80. Livesay mins, SecDef staff mtgs, 1 Jul, 13 May 68 (quote), fldr Minutes of SecDef Staff Mtgs-Mar-Sep 68, box 18, Clifford Papers, LBJL; memo ASD(C) for SvcSecs et al, 13 Aug 68, fldr FY 1970 Budget, box 6, Comptroller files, Acc 73A-1389.

81. Livesay mins, SecDef staff mtgs, 7, 21 Oct 68 (quotes), fldr Minutes of SecDef Staff Mtgs-Mar-Sep 68, box 18, Clifford Papers, LBJL; memo SecN for SecDef, 30 Sep 68, fldr Initial FY 1970 Budget Requests, box 15, Comptroller files, Acc 73A-1389.

82. Memo SecAF for SecDef, 30 Sep 68, fldr AF FY 1969 Rev Budget & FY 1970 Budget Estimates (Pre-1/20/69), box 80, ASD(C) files, OSD Hist.

83. Memo SecA for SecDef, 3 Oct 68, fldr Initial FY 1970 Budget Requests, box 15, Comptroller files, Acc 73A-1389.

84. DASD(C), FY 1970 Budget Review Summary of SecDef Budget Review Adjustments by DoD Component, 28 Jan 69, fldr FY 1970 Budget, box 6, ibid; DASD(C), Comparison of Department of Army, Navy, Air Force, and Defense Agency Requests to OSD w/Pres Budget for FY 1970, 28 Jan 69, ibid; memo ActgASD(SA) for SecDef, 5 Feb 69, fldr SA Fact Sheets Feb 1969 (FY 70), box 80, ASD(C) files, OSD Hist; Clifford statement, 19 Jan 69, *Clifford Public Statements, 1968*, 4:71-72.

85. Memo Califano for Pres, 12 Nov 68, fldr Budget-Appropriations (1967), box 42, CF FI 2 (1966-68), LBJL; ASD(C), briefing paper, 30 Nov 68, fldr Press Conferences, box 7, Clifford Papers, LBJL.

86. JCSM-701-68 for SecDef, 26 Nov 68, fldr FY 1970 Budget, box 81, ASD(C) files, OSD Hist (quote); CM-3811-68 for SecDef, 19 Dec 68, w/encl A, CM-3943-68 for Rostow, 26 Dec 68: *FRUS 1964-68*, 10:771-73, 785-86; *Washington Post*, 27 Dec 68.

87. DPM SecDef for Pres, 2 Dec 68, fldr Interagency Memoranda 1961-68, box 9, Enthoven Papers, LBJL.

88. Ibid.

89. Memo Fowler, Zwick, and Okun for Pres, 10 Dec 68, fldr Budget-Appropriations (1967), box 42, CF FI 2 (1966-68), LBJL. A memo from the same trio on 27 March 1968 (fldr Tax Material (xerox), box 4, Legislative Background Tax Increase, LBJL) had advised that the economy would cool off during the second half of 1968. Memo Barr, Zwick, and Okun for Pres, 27 Dec 68, fldr Budget-Appropriations (1967), box 42, CF FI 2 (1966-68), LBJL.

90. Elsey notes, Clifford's staff conf, 13 Dec 68, box 1, Elsey Papers, LBJL.

91. Memo Zwick for Pres, 16 Dec 68, fldr Budget DoD, box 14, Clifford Papers, LBJL; memrcd Clifford, telcon w/Zwick, 30 Dec 68, fldr Bureau of the Budget, box 14, Clifford Papers, LBJL.

92. Ltr DepSecDef to DirBoB, 17 Jan 69, fldr FY 1970 Budget (pre-1/20/69), box 79, ASD(C) files, OSD Hist; Clifford statement, 15 Jan 69, *Clifford Public Statements, 1968*, 4:1. During the 1961 transition from the Eisenhower to the Kennedy administration, outgoing Secretary of Defense Thomas Gates had prepared a general statement on the philosophy underpinning the FY 1962 budget at the behest of Chairman Mahon; see Watson, *Into the Missile Age*, 760, 958.

93. ASD(C), Incremental Cost of SEA Conflict, 3 Jul 68, fldr Sec Clifford's Trip to Vietnam Jul 68, Vietnam Buildup Papers, TAB N, box 3, Pursley Correspondence file, Acc 73A-1934.

X. THE HOME FRONT

1. Smith Summary Notes of 553d NSC mtg, 27 Jul 65, *FRUS 1964-68*, 3:261; DPM SecDef for Pres, 20 Oct 65, fldr Memos for Pres, CY 1965, Budget FY 1967, box 119, ASD(C) files, OSD Hist; Background Briefing for the Press, 6 Aug 65, *McNamara Background Briefings, 1965*:217, 226; SecDef Statement before SSCA (Amendment to FY 1966 Defense Budget), 4 Aug 65, 14-15, fldr Vietnam Buildup-Sec/Def Speech before Senate Cmte on Approps, FY 1966 Amendment-August 1965, box 44, ASD(C) files, OSD Hist; DPM SecDef for Pres, 11 Dec 65, fldr Memos for Pres, Cy 1965, Budget FY 1967, box 119, ibid.

2. Report of The National Advisory Commission on Selective Service, "In Pursuit of Equity: Who Serves When Not All Serve?," Feb 1967, 4 (hereafter "Who Serves"); OASD(M), Rejection Rates for Military Service, 28 Dec 66, TAB 5S vol 5, SecDef Backup Book, FY 1968, bk II (vols 3, 4, 5), FY 1968 Budget, box 60, ASD(C) files, OSD Hist.

3. Glass, "Draftees Shoulder Burden of Fighting and Dying in Vietnam," 1753; DoD News Releases Apr 64 - May 65, fldr Draft Calls 1961-68, box 1072, Subj files, OSD Hist.

4. OASD(M), Inductions and Draft Calls, nd (likely Jan 67), Tab 5R, Vol 5, SecDef Backup Book, FY 1968, bk II (vols 3, 4, 5), FY 1968 Budget, box 60, ASD(C) files, OSD Hist. Although the Marine Corps dropped its two-year enlistment option in October 1966, a shortage of volunteers required its reinstitution in May 1967; Shulimson, et al, *U.S. Marines in Vietnam, 1968*, 557-58; memo Actg ASD (M) for SecDef, 1 Sep 65, fldr Notebook, Mental & Physical Standards (July 1965-October 1965), TAB M, box 1, M & RA files, Acc 73A-1954 (quote); ASD(M), Enlistments, 17 Dec 65, Tab H3, vol 5, fldr SecDef Backup Book, FY 1967 Budget, box 48, ASD(C) files, OSD Hist (quote).

5. DPM SecDef for Pres, 11 Dec 65, cited in note 1; News conf, 30 Sep 65, *McNamara Public Statements, 1965*, 5:2074-77; ASD(M), Selected Reserve Force, 10 Jan 66, Tab F2, vol 4, SecDef Backup Book 1967, FY 1967 Budget, box 48, ASD(C) files, OSD Hist; Paper, "Is the U.S. Militarily Overextended," nd but c Feb 66, fldr Baldwin/Lippman Articles – Feb 21,22 1966, Vietnam, 1965-1967, box 96, ibid.

6. Gerhardt, *The Draft and Public Policy*, 282.

7. DSS, ASD (C), Reserves in Paid Status, 6 Jan 66, TAB A; ASD(M), Reserve Enlistment Program – Army Reserve Components, 20 Dec 65, TAB B2: vol 4, SecDef Backup Book 1967, FY 1967 Budget, box 48, ASD(C) files, OSD Hist; *DoD Annual Report for FY 1965*, table 23, 406.

8. ISA, Draft SecDef Statement before SubCte on DoD Appros of SCA, Amendment to FY 1966 Defense Budget August 3, 1965, Second Draft 29 Jul 65, 20, fldr FY 66 Amendment, Statement SecDef-House Armed Svcs Cte –8/6/65, FY 1966 Budget, box 43, ASD(C) files, OSD Hist; Gerhardt, *Draft and Public Policy*, 273; ASD, Reserve Enlistment Program: Army Reserve Components, 1 Dec 66, fldr vol IV General Purpose Forces, 1966-1967, TAB Z, box 92, McNamara Records, RG 200.

9. ASD(M), Reserve Enlistment Program-Army Reserve Components, 20 Dec 65, cited in note 7; ASD(M), Reserve Enlistment Program: Army Reserve Components, 1 Dec 66, cited in note 8; *Washington Post*, 5 Oct 66; McNamara test, 16 Feb 66, HSCA, *Hearings: Department of Defense Appropriations for 1967*, pt 1:271-72.

10. McNamara test, 28 Feb 66, SCAS and SSCA, *Hearings: Military Procurement Authorizations for Fiscal Year 1967*, 362-63, 376-77; HCAS, *Reserve Bill of Rights*, H Rpt No 13, 13 Feb 67, 1-3, 7-9, 13-19; Background Briefing for the Press, 25 Aug 66, *McNamara Background Briefings, 1966*:272; Gerhardt, *Draft and Public Policy*, 283; PL 89-687, 15 Oct 66 (80 Stat 981); *DoD Annual Report for FY 1968*, 40-44; Cole et al, eds, *Department of Defense: Documents on Establishment and Organization*, 246-48; PL 90-168, 1 Dec 67 (81 Stat 521).

11. ASD(M), Negro Participation in the Armed Forces, Nov 66, Tab 5 R2, Vol 5, bk II, FY 1968 Backup Book, FY 1968 Budget, box 60, ASD(C) files, OSD Hist; "Who Serves," 22; Scheips and Stark, "Use of Troops in Civil Disturbances," Supplement 2 (1967), Apr 1969, 102, CMH.

12. *New York Times*, 1 Jul 66.

13. ASD(M), *Reference Materials from the DoD Study of the Draft*, Jul 66, TAB G, Manpower Recruitment Capability Without a Draft, Table 2, 18.6, Table 3, 18.7, Table 4, 18.8, and Table 8, 18.17.

14. Telcon McNamara and Johnson, 14 Nov 64, WH 6411.20, LBJL. An abridged version appears in Beschloss, *Reaching for Glory*, 140-41.

15. ASD(M), Special Training and Enlistment Program (STEP), and TAB A, Estimated Cost of STEP, 21 Dec 64, TAB C, Vol 4, SecDef Backup Book, FY 1966 Budget, box 36, ASD(C) files, OSD Hist.

16. Telcon McNamara and Johnson, 14 Nov 64, cited in note 14 (quote); Beschloss, *Reaching for Glory*, 141; memrcd Vance, 13 Jul 65, fldr July 1965, box 1, Vance files, Acc 69A-2317; ASD(M), *Reference Materials*, cited in note 13; TAB F, Programs to Assist Rejectees for Military Service, STEP Program, 17.a.

17. Memo Actg ASD(M) for SecDef, 1 Sep 65, fldr Notebook, Mental & Physical Standards (July 1965-October 1965), TAB M, box 1, M & RA files, Acc 73A-1954.

18. Memo SecDef for Pres, 24 Sep 65, ibid; E.O. 112411, 26 Aug 65 (30 *Fed Reg* 11129); Gerhardt, *Draft and Public Policy*, 279; memo SecDef for Pres, 2 Mar 66, fldr Reading File Mar 66, box 124, McNamara Records, RG 200.

19. Laurence and Ramsberger, *Low-Aptitude Men in the Military*, 7. AFQT categories and equivalent percentile ranges were:

AFQT Category	Percentile Range
I	93-99
II	65-92
IIIA	50-64
IIIB	31-49
IVA	21-30
IVB	16-20
IVC	10-15
V	1-9.

20. Memo SecDef for Pres, 2 Mar 66, memo SecDef for SvcSecs, 2 Mar 66: fldr Reading File Mar 1966, box 124, McNamara Records, RG 200; ASD(M), Chronology of Recent Changes in Mental Standards for Induction, 5 Jan 67, TAB O, fldr Vol 5, R&D/Gen Support/Personnel/Misc 1966-67, box 91, ibid; ASD(M), Rejection Rates at Preinduction Examinations, By Cause, 28 Dec 66, Tab 5S, Vol 5, bk II, FY 1968 Backup Book, box 60, ASD(C), OSD Hist.

21. Memo Paul for SecDef, 13 Aug 65; Disqualification Rates of 18-Year Old Out of School Youth by State and Race, nd; memo Actg ASD(M) for SecDef, 1 Sep 65, Tab M (quote): fldr Notebook, Mental & Physical Standards (July 1965-October 1965), Tab B, box 1, M & RA files, Acc 73A-1954 (quote); Moynihan, "Who Gets in the Army?" 22 (quote).

22. Dawson, "Impact of Project 100,000 on the Marine Corps," 79; Laurence and Ramsberger, *Low-Aptitude Men*, 18 (quote); Livesay notes, SecDef Staff Mtg, 18 Jul 66, fldr Staff Meeting Jul-Sep 1966, box 12, AFPC files, Acc 77-0062.

23. Dawson, "The Impact of Project 100,000," 79-80 (quote) 169, based on an interview with Robert S. McNamara; ltr McNamara to Russell, 22 Aug 66, fldr Material Sent to Senate Armed Svcs Cte 1967, Files re Senate and House Ctes 1965-69, box 91, ASD(C) files, OSD Hist.

24. *McNamara Public Statements, 1966*, 7:2588, 2592 (quote).

25. ASD (M&RA), Project One Hundred Thousand: Characteristics and Performance of "New Standards" Men, 8, fldr Project 100,000, Selective Service System, 1969-1976, box 1089, Subj files, OSD Hist, hereafter Project One Hundred Thousand; OASD(M), Reference Materials from the DoD Study of the Draft, July 66, TAB E, "Mental Standards," 12.a.1; Laurence and Ramsberger, *Low-Aptitude Men*, 8.

26. For a variety of views, see Sticht, et al, *Cast-off Youth*, 9; *New York Times*, 16 Oct 66; and Laurence and Ramsberger, *Low-Aptitude Men*, 20-21; Project One Hundred Thousand, xxvii.

27. Shapley, *Promise and Power*, 385.

28. The program accounted for 7 percent of total accessions between October 1966 and September 1967; 11.2 percent between October 1967 and September 1968; and 13.3 percent between October 1968 and September 1969. Project One Hundred Thousand, x, 4.

29. Ibid, xiii, xiv, 13, xvii, 29, 32.

30. *New York Times*, 16 Oct 66; "DoD Admin History," 4:1512-16; memo SecDef for Pres, Project One Hundred Thousand, 25 Jul 67, fldr Reading File July 28-15, 1967, box 129, McNamara Records, RG 200 (quote).

31. *Air Force Times*, 25 Oct 67; "DoD Admin History," 4:1516-17; Project One Hundred Thousand, 23. The control group consisted of men selected by each service as representative of accessions under previous mental standards. It thus included men with above average, average, and slightly below average scores on the Armed Forces Qualification Test. Project One Hundred Thousand, 12.

32. Glass, "Draftees," 1748, 1752. The study relied on Army statistics that 23,890 Army personnel were killed as of 31 March 1970. OSD compilations placed the number killed for that period at 22,063.

33. *Washington Star*, 25 Mar 71; Laurence and Ramsberger, *Low-Aptitude Men*, 122-23.

34. ASD(M), Negro Participation in the Armed Forces, Nov 66, Tab 5 R2, Vol 5, bk II, FY 1968 Backup Book, box 60, ASD(C) files, OSD Hist; *Washington Post*, 12 Oct 68; memo Dir Mil Personnel Policy for CSA, Evaluation of the Marshall Report Pertaining to Negro Distribution and Casualties, 10 Apr 67, TAB F, fldr II, Vietnam Race Relations, CMH.

35. *National Review*, 18 Apr 67. The percentage of black personnel in divisions, regiments, and brigades on 31 October 1968 was 13.4 percent, and the percentage of African-American deaths in those units through 31 December 1968 was 15.4 percent. Army Casualties in South Vietnam by Race: Army Strength by Race as of 31 October 1968, nd, fldr II, Vietnam Race Relations, CMH.

36. Fact Sheet, Negro Participation in the Armed Forces and in Vietnam, rev 18 Jan 67, fldr II, Vietnam Race Relations, CMH; memo Dir Mil Personnel Policy for CJCS, Vietnam Strength and Casualty Statistics by Race, 18 Feb 67 and TAB A, Statement re Vietnam Strength and Casualty Statistics by Race (Army), ibid. As late as October 1968, blacks were still overrepresented in airborne units and their percentage of battle deaths continued to outstrip their proportional strength in those forces. Army Casualties in South Vietnam by Race, cited in note 35; "Who Serves," 26; Dir Mil Personnel Policy, White House Fact Sheet, Percentage of Negro Army Casualties in Vietnam, 2 Mar 67, fldr II, Vietnam Race Relations, CMH; Moskos, "Minority Groups and Military Organization," in Ambrose and Barber, eds, *The Military in American Society*, 195.

37. Jeffreys-Jones, *Peace Now!*, 113-17; *New York Times*, 14 Apr 66, (quote); Lawson, "Civil Rights," in Divine, ed, *The Johnson Years*, 1:108-09. In 1964 and 1965 many African-American leaders either supported the president's Vietnam policies or at least muted their opposition. Helsing, *Johnson's War/Johnson's Great Society*, 111. In July 1965, for example, King had told a rally the Vietnam war must be stopped. Five days later, however, he phoned Johnson to say the press lifted his remarks out of context. Telcon King and Johnson, 7 Jul 65, 8:05 p.m. in Beschloss, *Reaching for Glory*, 388. King did not emerge as a major antiwar figure until February 1967. Woods, "Politics of Idealism," 13.

38. Flynn, *The Draft*, 1940-1973, 190 (quote); *McNamara Public Statements, 1966*, 7:2306 (quote); E. O. 11289, 2 Jul 66, reproduced in "Who Serves," 66-67; "Who Serves," 4, 7; memo Vance for Califano, 10 Feb 67, fldr February 1967, box 2, Vance files, ACC 69A-2317.

39. Scheips and Stark, "Use of Troops in Civil Disturbances," Supplement 2: (1967), 5, 201.

40. AR 500-50, 25 Feb 64, 1; DoD Dir 3025.1 18 Nov 65; DDRE, WSEG, "Joint Command and Control Problems Attending Military Support Operations in Domestic Emergencies: Steep Hill-14 and Tempest Rapid 'Betsy,' 1965," 8 Jun 66, 1, fldr IDA Crisis Studies for JCS, Command and Control Problems in Domestic Emergencies, 1965, box 694, Subj files, OSD Hist; OCMH, "Use of Troops in Civil Disturbances, 1963-1968," in "DoD Admin History," 7:annex 6, 2305-06, OSD Hist; msg BG Graham to DA War Room, 220148Z Mar 65, fldr Cable files, OSD Hist.

41. Interv Ramsey Clark by Harri Baker, 16 Apr 69, 4: 5, Electronic Copy, LBJL; Scheips and Stark, "Use of Troops in Civil Disturbances," 88-89.

42. DDRE, WSEG, "Joint Command and Control Problems," 8 Jun 66, 4, 22-23, cited in note 40; memo SecA for DepSecDef, 17 Aug 65 and memo DepSecDef for SecA, 17 Aug 65: fldr Gemini 1965, box 4, SecDef Subject Decimal files, Acc 70A-1266.

43. Califano, *Triumph & Tragedy*, 209; Army Ops Ctr, Information Brief #4, 16 Jul 67, Cable files, OSD Hist.

44. Final Report of Cyrus R. Vance, Spec Asst to SecDef, Concerning the Detroit Riots, July 23 through August 2, 1967, nd but c 11 Sep 67, 1-3, file HU2/St22, #4, box 56, Confidential File, HU2 (1964-1966), LBJL. Hereafter Vance Final Report.

45. Vance Final Report, 3 (quotes); Califano, *Triumph & Tragedy*, 214; Scheips, *Role of Federal Military Forces in Domestic Disorders*, 180-81; "Report of the National Advisory Commission on Civil Disorders," 1 Mar 68, 53.

46. Vance Final Report, 4-5. (Emphases in original); Johnson, *Vantage Point*, 168; Califano, *Triumph & Tragedy*, 214-15; Scheips, *Role of Federal Military Forces in Domestic Disorders*, 180-84, 190; Scheips and Stark, "Use of Troops in Civil Disturbances," Supplement 2 (1967), 83.

47. Califano, *Triumph & Tragedy*, 214-17 (quote); Vance Final Report, 6; Tom Johnson notes of Pres mtg w/ Attorney General, Secretary McNamara et al, 11:15 a.m.-12:20 p.m.," 24 Jul 67 (quotes); Tom Johnson notes of Pres Activities During the Detroit Crisis, 24 Jul 67, 10 p.m. to 12:30 a.m. [25 Jul] (quote): box 1, Meeting Notes File, LBJL; Johnson, *Vantage Point*, 170; Scheips and Stark, "Use of Troops in Civil Disturbances," Supplement 2 (1967), 92.

48. Vance Final Report, 2-3, 7, 10-11.

49. Tom Johnson notes from Pres Mtg w/ Cong Leaders, 24 Jul 67, box 1, Meeting Notes File, LBJL.

50. Tom Johnson, Mtg of Pres w/ Vance, 29 Jul 67, ibid; Johnson, Vantage Point, 169-70; Msg DASITREP No. 1/250600, DA to JCS DLVD, 25 Jul 67, Cable files, OSD Hist; Vance Final Report, 17-18.

51. Memo Vice Pres for SecDef, 19 Jul 67, fldr 370.61 Civil Disturbances 1967, box 38, SecDef Subject Decimal files, 72A-2468 (quote); Califano, *Triumph & Tragedy*, 217; (quote); Tom Johnson notes of Pres Activities during the Detroit Crisis, cited in note 47 (quote); Pres Remarks to the Nation, 24 Jul 67, *Johnson Public Papers, 1967*, 2:715-17.

52. Memo SecDef for SvcSecs, Implementation of Executive Order, 24 Jul 67, fldr Reading File July 28-15, 1967, box 129, McNamara Records, RG 200.

53. Scheips and Stark, "Use of Troops in Civil Disturbances," Supplement II (1967), 91; msg DASITREP No. 1/250600, DA to JCS DLVD, 25 Jul 67; msg DASITREP No. 3/260600, DA to JCS, 26 Jul 67: msg DASITREP No. 8/281800, DA to JCS, 29 Jul 67: Cable files, OSD Hist; Scheips, *Role of Federal Military Forces in Domestic Disorders*, 196.

54. Vance Final Report, 48 (quote), 51 (quote), 52; Tom Johnson Notes from Pres Mtg w/ National Advisory Commission on Civil Disorders, July 29, 1967, box 1, Meeting Notes File, LBJL; Tom Johnson notes of Pres Mtg w/ Sec McNamara et al, 8 Aug 67, ibid.

55. Memrcd McCafferty, 27 Jul 67, fldr chron file Jan 1, 1967 [3 of 4], box 1, Files of Art McCafferty, NSF Name File, National Security File, LBJL; memrcd McGiffert, Mins of mtg of Civil Disturbance Task Force, 27 Jul 67, memo Under SecA for SecDef, 6 Aug 67, w/atchmt (quotes): fldr 370.61 ALPHA 1967, box 38, SecDef Subject Decimal files, Acc 72A-2468.

56. Memo Spec Counsel for SecN, 27 Jul 67, memo DepSecDef for CJCS and SvcSecs, 27 Jun 64, memo SecDef for CJCS and SvcSecs, 9 Jul 64: fldr 370.61 Civil Disturbances 1967, box 38, SecDef Subject Decimal files, 72A-2468; memo DepSecDef for CJCS, SvcSecs et al, 28 Jul 67, memo DepSecDef for CJCS, SvcSecs et al, 30 Sep 67 (quote): ibid.

57. Ltr Atty Gen to State Govs, 7 Aug 67, App O to Vance Final Report.

58. Nitze paper, Summer Riot Preparation, 10 Jan 68, fldr DoD DepSecDef Notes 1968 (1 of 6), box 85, (fldr 4) Nitze Papers, LC; ltr McGiffert to Christopher, 1 Apr 68 w/ atchmt, Status of DA Civil Disturbance Planning, nd, fldr Civil Disturbances 1968, #1 (1 of 2) box 11, Papers of Warren Christopher, LBJL; interv Solis Horwitz by Paige E. Mulhollan, 9 Jan 69, 1:44-45, LBJL; msg DA 828252, SecA to CS New Jersey NG, 16 Aug 67, Cable files, OSD Hist.

59. Memo CMDR MDW for CSA, 13 Nov 67, w/ atchmt, fldr AAR Operation Cabinet Maker 21-22 Oct 1967, box 4, Anti-War Demonstrations-March on the Pentagon, Oct 1967, CMH.

60. DeBenedetti, "Lyndon Johnson and the Antiwar Opposition," in Divine, ed, *The Johnson Years*, 2: 29; DeBenedetti, *An American Ordeal*, 196-97; memo Dir Ops Army for SecA, 12 Sep 67, fldr Anti Vietnam War Demonstrations at the Pentagon 21-22 October 1967, Chronological File, box 2, Anti-War Demonstrations – March on the Pentagon, October 1967, CMH (quote); memo Jones for Pres, Notes on mtg, 5 Sep 67, Tom Johnson notes of Pres Mtg w/ Sec Rusk, Sec McNamara, et al, 3 Oct 67: box 2, Meeting Notes Files, LBJL. On the shift in Johnson's thinking see Herring, *America's Longest War*, 181-82.

61. McNamara, *In Retrospect*, 216, 253-54 (quote); 297; Shapley, *Promise and Power*, 435-36.

62. Nitze, Notes, 12 Sep 67, fldr DoD DepSecDef Notes 1967 (2 of 3), box 85, Nitze Papers, LC; memo DepSecDef for SvcSecs, 13 Sep 67, fldr 370.61 ALPHA 1967, box 38, SecDef Subject Decimal files, Acc 72A-2468; memo CMDR MDW for CSA, 13 Nov 67, cited in note 59; memo Dir Ops Army for SecA, 12 Sep 67, cited in note 60.

63. Memo DepSecDef for SvcSecs, 13 Sep 67, cited in note 62; memo ASD(A) for SecDef, The October 21, 1967 Demonstration, 19 Sep 67, w/atchmt TAB C, Tentative Concept for Countering Anti-Vietnam Demonstration at the Pentagon on 21-22 October 1967, fldr 370.61 Pentagon (Jan-Sep) 1967, box 38, SecDef Subject Decimal files, Acc 72A-2468; Scheips, *Role of Federal Military Forces in Domestic Disorders*, 246-47; memo DirOpsArmy for SecA, 12 Sep 67, cited in note 60 (quote).

64. McNamara, *In Retrospect*, 303; Tom Johnson notes of Pres mtg w/ Sec McNamara et al, 20 Sep 67, Meeting Notes File, box 2, LBJL (quote);Tom Johnson notes of the Pres mtg w/ Sec Rusk et al, 3 Oct 67, *FRUS 1964-68*, 5:839-40 (quote).

65. Memo ASD (A) for SecDef, 21 Sep 67, fldr 370.61 Pentagon (Jan-Sep) 1967, box 38, SecDef Subject Decimal files, Acc 72A-2468; memo ASD(A) for SecDef, 23 Sep 67, ibid; OCMH, "Use of Troops in Civil Disturbances, 1963-1968," Aug 68, in "DoD Admin History," 7:annex 6, 2358, OSD Hist; Van Cleve memrcds No. 3 and No. 5, 30 Sep, 11 Oct 67, fldr 370.61 Pentagon (1 thru 15 Oct) 1967, box 38, SecDef Subject Decimal files, Acc 72A-2468; Scheips, *Role of Federal Military Forces in Domestic Disorders*, 242-44.

66. Memo SecDef for SecA, 26 Sep 67, fldr Reading File Sept 29-22, 1967, box 130, McNamara Records, RG 200; Horwitz interv, 9 Jan 69, 1:44.

67. Memo CMDR MDW for CSA, 13 Nov 67, cited in note 59; memrcd McGiffert, 2 Oct 67, fldr Anti Vietnam War Demonstration at the Pentagon 21 & 22 October 1967, Chronological File, vol I, box 2, Anti War Demonstrations- March on the Pentagon, Oct 1967, CMH.

68. Memo DASD(A) for DepSecDef, 14 Oct 67, fldr 370.61 Pentagon (1 thru 15 Oct) 1967, box 38, SecDef Subject Decimal files, Acc 72A-2468; memo UnderSecA for ASD(A), 19 Sep 67, fldr Anti Vietnam War Demonstration at the Pentagon 21-22 October 1967, Chronological File, Vol 1, 12 Sep to 6 Oct 67, box 2, Anti-War Demonstrations – March on the Pentagon, October 1967, CMH; Orientation of Military Commanders by the Chief of Staff Army, 20 Oct 67, fldr Anti Vietnam War Demonstration at the Pentagon, 21 & 22 October 1967, Chronological File, Vol 3, 17 Oct to 20 Oct 67, box 3, ibid.

69. Memo UnderSecA for ASD(A), 19 Sep 67, cited in note 68; memo CMDR MDW for CSA, 13 Nov 67, cited in note 59; memo Civil Disturbance Office for DirOps, ODCSOPS, 19 Oct 67, Synopsis and Cable Book for AOC Team Chief, 21-22 Oct 67 Synopsis, 1 thru 100, box 1, Anti-war Demonstrations March on Pentagon, October 1967, CMH; memo Under SecA for SecDef, 21 Oct 67, box 5, Anti-war Demonstrations March on Pentagon, October 1967, CMH; OCMH, "Use of Troops in Civil Disturbances, 1963-1968," Aug 68, in "DoD Admin History," 7:Annex 6:2360-61, OSD Hist.

70. Livesay, SecDef Staff mtg notes, 20 Oct 67, fldr Staff Meetings, Oct-Dec 1967, box 13, AFPC, Acc 77-0067; memo Under SecA for SecDef, 21 Oct 67, cited in note 69; ltr National Park Service et al to NMC, 19 Oct 67, memo Under SecA for CSA, 20 Oct 67: fldr 370.61 Pentagon (16 Oct –30 Oct) 1967, box 38, SecDef Subject Decimal files, Acc 72A-2468 (quote); memo UnderSecA for CSA, 21 Oct 67, ibid.

71. Orientation of Military Commanders by the Chief of Staff Army, 20 Oct 67, cited in note 68 (quote); Horwitz interv, 9 Jan 69, 1:44, LBJL (quote); McNamara, *In Retrospect*, 305; Shapley, *Promise and Power*, 435-6; see also Hendrickson, "McNamara, Specter of Vietnam," *Washington Post*, 10 May 84.

72. This account is based on George C. Wilson, Chronology of Pentagon's Siege, *Washington Post*, 23 Oct 67; memrcd NMCC, 21-22 October Demonstration, 23 Oct 67, fldr 370.61 Pentagon (16 Oct-30 Oct) 1967, box 38, SecDef Subject Decimal files, Acc 72A-2468; Scheips, *Role of Federal Military Forces in Domestic Disorders, 1945-1992*, 254-63; and Vogel, *The Pentagon*, 374-77.

73. Memo CMDR MDW for CSA, 13 Nov 67, cited in note 59; Garfinkle, *Telltale Hearts*, 153; *Washington Post*, 23 Oct 67 (quote); *New York Times*, 23 Oct 67; DeBenedetti, *An American Ordeal*, 197-99; memo Pres for SecDef and Atty Gen, 23 Oct 67, memo SecDef for SvcSecs et al, 28 Oct 67: *McNamara Public Statements, 1967*, 7:2617-18.

74. DOD News Release 186-68, 23 Feb 68; *Washington Post*, 24 Feb 68; *DOD Annual Report for FY 1968*, 205; Tom Johnson notes of Pres Mtg w/Senior Foreign Policy Advisors, 9 Feb 68, Meeting Notes File, LBJL (quote). On the status of the 82d Airborne Division's civil disturbance mission, see DCS MilOps, After Action Report, 4-17 April Civil Disturbances, nd, notebook, Draft After-Action Report, April 1968, 3, CMH.

75. DCS MilOps, After Action Report, cited in note 74, 3-4. The number of Army brigades increased to 18 by April 1968; Scheips, *Role of Federal Military Forces in Domestic Disorders*, 225; Parker, ed, *Violence in the U.S.*, 1968-71, 2:7-8.

76. Ltr McGiffert to Christopher, 1 Apr 68 w/atchmt, Status of DA Civil Disturbance Planning, nd, fldr Civil Disturbances 1968, #1 (1 of 2) box 11, Papers of Warren Christopher, LBJL.

77. OTAG, HQDA, After Action Report – TF CHICAGO, HQ, III Corps, 4-13 April 1968, 14 May 68, 1-5, fldr After Action Report Chicago Riots 1968, Scheips files, CMH; Johnson, *Vantage Point*, 174, 538; intervs Clark Clifford by Joe B. Frantz, 15 Dec 69, 4: 11, and 24 Apr 70, 7: 1, both Electronic Copies, LBJL.

78. DCS MilOps, After Action Report, cited in note 74, 2;memrcd DepDirOps, NMCC, 6 Apr 68, Cable files, OSD Hist; memo for the files Christopher, nd, fldr April 1968 Civil Disturbances, box 14, Papers of Warren Christopher, LBJL (quote); President's Daily Diary, 5 Apr 68, 7, Electronic Copy, LBJL.

79. TF Washington, After Action Report, 4-16 Apr 68, 30 Jul 68, 4 and Appx D, 38 (quote); Clifford interv, 24 Apr 70, 7:1-2, 6 (quotes).

80. DCS MilOps, After Action Report, cited in note 74, 6, and Annex A; memo Christopher, cited in note 78; Clifford interv, 24 Apr 70, 7:5; memrcd DepDirOps, NMCC, 6 Apr 68, cited in note 78; Nitze mtg notes, 6 Apr 68, fldr DoD, DepSecDef Notes 1968 (3 of 6), box 85, (fldr 6) Nitze Papers, LC; *Washington Star*, 17 Apr 68.

81. HQ XVIII Airborne Corps, After Action Report of Task Force BALTIMORE (RCS CSFOR-65), 7 May 68, I/1-7, fldr Baltimore Riots, 1968, AAR, Scheips files, CMH.

82. Scheips, *The Role of Federal Military Forces in Domestic Disorders*, 299-303 (quote, 303).

83. OTAG, HQDA, After Action Report, cited in note 77, 5-11.

84. Clifford interv, 24 Apr 70, 7:2-6; memo UnderSecA for CSA, 13 Apr 68, fldr Civil Disturbances Steering Cite, box 14, Papers of Warren Christopher, LBJL (quote); "Use of Troops," cited in note 69, annex 6:2312; Livesay notes of SecDef Staff mtg, 6 May 68, 5, box 18, NSF-Papers of Clark Clifford, LBJL; DoDD 3025.12, Employment of Military Resources in the Event of Civil Disturbances, 8 Jun 68, DoDD & DoDI 3000.2-.3305.6, OSD Hist; SecA, Terms of Reference for the Directorate for Civil Disturbance Planning and Operations, 26 Aug 68, memo DepSecDef for SecA, Terms of Reference for DoD Steering Cte and the DCDPO, 18 Sep 68: both fldr Civil Disturbances Steering Cte, OSD, Scheips files, CMH.

85. Parker, ed, *Violence in the U.S.*, 2:45-49, 51 (quote).

86. Elsey notes of SecDef Staff Conf, 12 Aug 68, fldr Personal Papers of George M. Elsey, box 1, Papers of George M. Elsey, LBJL; Tom Johnson notes of Pres mtg w/Tuesday Luncheon Grp, 20 Aug 68, Meeting Notes Files, box 3, LBJL; memo UnderSecA for SecDef, 20 Aug 68, fldr Nat'l Dem. Conv Chicago, 1 of 2, box 14, Papers of Warren Christopher, LBJL.

87. Elsey notes of SecDef Staff Conf, 23 Aug 68, fldr Personal Papers of George M. Elsey, box 1, Papers of George M. Elsey, LBJL (quote); Observations of the Disturbance During the Democratic National Convention, 20 Sep 68, fldr Chicago Convention, Scheips files, CMH; Parker, ed, *Violence in the U.S.*, 2:43 (quote).

88. Flynn, *The Draft*, 167, 194.

89. Tom Johnson notes, Mtg of Pres w/ Senate Cte Chairmen, 25 Jul 67, Tom Johnson Meeting Notes, box 1, LBJL.

XI. ANOTHER CUBA?

1. Yates, "Power Pack," *Leavenworth Papers*, 15:7, 14-15, 19; Johnson, *Vantage Point*, 189; Lowenthal, *Dominican Intervention*, 48, 54.

2. Msg TDCS-314/04798-65 (Santo Domingo) CIA to White House Sit Room, 12 Apr 65, fldr Dominican Republic 350.001 (2 May 65), box 3, SecDef Subject Decimal files, Acc 70A-1266; memo Martin for Rusk, 26 May 65 w/atchmt, fldr 1965 Background Documents [1 of 4], box 7, NSC History Dominican Crisis 1965, NSF, LBJL; Yates," Power Pack," 24.

3. Johnson, *Vantage Point*, 189-90; msg Critic One SantoDomingo to DIRNSA et al, 24 Apr 65 (quote), msg Critic Two SantoDomingo to DIRNSA et al, 24 Apr 65: fldr Dominican Republic 350.001 (2 May 65), box 3, SecDef Subject Decimal files, Acc 70A-1266; msg 1043 SantoDomingo to State, 25 Apr 65, fldr Incoming State Cables, Apr 24 – May 4, 1965 (Closed) box 4-11 [box 1 of 2 closed boxes], NSC History Dominican Crisis 1965, NSF, LBJL; Yates, "Power Pack," 39, 86, 174-75; WSEG, "The Dominican Republic Crisis of 1965," 16 Aug 66, 68, fldr The Dominican Republic Crisis of 1965, box 456, Subj files, OSD Hist.

4. Sequence of Events, nd but c 1 May 65, fldr Dominican Republic 350.001 (2 May 65), box 3, SecDef Subject Decimal files, Acc 70A-1266; Military Operations in the Dominican Republic—An Overview, 1, nd but c 12 Jul 65, Notebook Background Book for Fulbright Hearings on Dominican Republic, TAB A, box 3, SecDef Subject Decimal files, Acc 70A-1266; Yates, "Power Pack," 37 (quote); Johnson, *Vantage Point*, 190; msg JCS 9731 to CINCLANT, 25 Apr 65, fldr Dominican Republic 381 (26 Apr 65) dtd 24 June 65, TAB III, Section B, box 2, SecDef Subject Decimal files, Acc 70A-1265; WSEG, "Dominican Crisis," 21-22.

5. Johnson, *Vantage Point*, 190-91; msg 633 State to SantoDomingo, 25 Apr 65, fldr Outgoing State Cables [A-1] Apr 25-May 14,1965, box 5, NSC History Dominican Crisis 1965, NSF, LBJL.

6. Msg 1071 SantoDomingo to State, 26 Apr 65, Cable files, OSD Hist; memo Martin to Rusk, 26 May 65 w/atchmt, fldr 1965 Background Documents [1 of 4], box 7, NSC History Dominican Crisis 1965, NSF, LBJL. A list of attendees is found in note to Pres, 12 May 65, fldr Valenti File, re: Dom Rep 1 of 2, box 8, Name File, NSF, LBJL; WSEG, "Dominican Crisis," 34 (quote); interv Dean Rusk by Paige E. Mulhollan, 2 Jan 70, 3, Tape 2, 19, electronic copy, LBJL (quote).

7. Msg 1071 SantoDomingo to State, 26 Apr 65, cited in note 6.

8. Msg 644 State to SantoDomingo, 27 Apr 65, *FRUS 1964-68*, 32:66-67; Doc atchmts to text of Pres Speech on the Dominican Situation, 2 May 65, fldr Dominican Republic 350.001 (2 May 65), box 3, SecDef Subject Decimal files, Acc 70A-1266 (quotes).

9. Johnson, *Vantage Point*, 191-92; Greenberg, *Unilateral and Coalition Operations*, 32-33; msg 645 State to SantoDomingo, JCS et al, 27 Apr 65, fldr Outgoing State Cables April 25-May 14, 1965 [A-1], box 5, NSC History Dominican Republic Crisis 1965, NSF, LBJL; msg JCS 9840 to CINCLANT, 27 Apr 65, fldr Dominican Republic 381 (26 Apr 65) dtd 24 Jun 65, TAB III, Section B, box 2, SecDef Subject Decimal files, Acc 70A-1265; memo SecDef for Pres, 26 May 65, fldr Dom Rep May 23-30, 1965, box 454, Subj files, OSD Hist.

10. Johnson, *Vantage Point*, 191-93.

11. WSEG, "Dominican Crisis," 53, 55; Military Operations in the Dominican Republic—An Overview, 2, cited in note 4; CIA Memo, No. 1120/65, 7 May 65, *FRUS 1964-68*, 32:139; ed note, ibid, 74 (quotes).

12. Msg JCS 9802 to CINCLANT et al, 26 Apr 65, fldr Dom Rep Jan - 30 Apr 65, box 453, Subj files, OSD Hist; Yates, "Power Pack," 55; WSEG, "Dominican Crisis," 36, citing NMCC Emergency Action Tapes 26 Apr 65. On McNamara's attitude, ibid, 37; interv Bruce Palmer by Ted Gittinger, 28 May 82, 1:4, AC 92-49, LBJL (quote); Palmer, *Intervention in Caribbean*, 3.

13. See for example msgs 1071 SantoDomingo to State, 26 Apr 65, cited in note 6, and 1155 SantoDomingo to State, 28 Apr 65: *FRUS 1964-68*, 32:84-85; 1132 SantoDomingo to State, 28 Apr 65, fldr Dominican Republic 350.001, box 3, SecDef Subject Decimal files, Acc 70A-1266; Critic 4 SantoDomingo to State, 28 Apr, *FRUS 1964-68*, 32:73-74; msg 657 State to SantoDomingo, 28 Apr 65, fldr Outgoing State Cables April 25-May 14, 1965 [A-1], box 5, NSC History Dominican Crisis 1965, NSF, LBJL (quote); msgs 1146 SantoDomingo to State, 28 Apr 65, Critic 5 SantoDomingo to DIRNSA, 28 Apr 65: *FRUS 1964-68*, 32:71-77.

14. Johnson, *Vantage Point*, 194-95 (quote); transc McNamara test, 16 Feb 66, for HSCA hearing on Defense Appropriations, 501-02, fldr Mahon Cte Transcript of 1967 Posture Ste, 2/16/66, box 50, ASD(C) files, OSD Hist; Rusk interv, 2 Jan 70, 13; Presidential Daily Diary, 28 Apr 65, fldr Daily Diary Apr 65, box 3 PDD, LBJL; Beschloss, *Reaching for Glory*, 289.

15. Mins mtg w/Cong Leadership on Dominican Republic, 28 Apr 65, *FRUS 1964-68*, 32:81-84 (quote); Rusk interv, 2 Jan 70, 13; statement by Pres Upon Ordering Troops Into the Dominican Republic, 28 Apr 65, *Johnson Public Papers, 1965*, 1:461; msg JCS 9988 to CINCLANT, 28 Apr 65, Cable files, OSD Hist.

16. Msg 1155 SantoDomingo to State, 28 Apr 65, cited in note 13; Johnson, *Vantage Point*, 197-98; telcon Johnson and Fortas, 29 Apr 65, 4:45 p.m., WH 6504.07 PNO 5 7388, LBJL (quote); WSEG, "Dominican Crisis," 57; News conf, 17 Jun 65, *Johnson Public Papers, 1965*, 2:678. Bennett later contradicted the president's statement that he had been forced to take cover under his desk during the early stages of the Dominican revolution. Before the Senate Foreign Relations Committee on 3 May 1966, Bennett could not recall any bullet holes in his office. Dan Kurzman in *Washington Post*, 4 May 66, 1; SCFR, vol 1, Report of Proceedings, 89 Cong, 2 sess, 3 May 66, 28-29, Congressional Information Service, unpublished U.S. Senate Cte Hearings, Cte on Foreign Relations, 1965-1966 (89) Sfo-T.21, card 1 of 2.

17. Telcon Raborn and Pres, 29 Apr 65, *FRUS 1964-68*, 32:89; Dominican Crisis: Presidential Decisions, nd, fldr Bowder to Rostow, box 8, NSC History of Dominican Crisis 1965, NSF, LBJL; msg 1173 SantoDomingo to State, 29 Apr 65, fldr Incoming State Cables Apr 24-May 4, 1965 "A" 2 of 2, box 4, ibid; telcon McNamara and Johnson, 29 Apr 65, 8:42 a.m., WH 6504.06 PNO 8 7374, LBJL; Johnson, *Vantage Point*, 199; telcons McNamara and Johnson, 29 Apr 65, 1:04 p.m., WH 6504.06 PNO 13 7379, Johnson and Ball, 29 Apr 65, 2:22 p.m., WH 6504.06, PNO 14 7380, LBJL; Beschloss, *Reaching for Glory*, 293 has excerpts of the 1:04 p.m. phone conversation. Msg 681 State to SantoDomingo, 29 Apr 65, fldr Outgoing State Cable [A-1] Apr 25-May 14, 1965, box 5, NSC History Dominican Crisis 1965, NSF, LBJL; Alerting, Movement, and Execution Orders Directed by JCS, nd but after 30 Jun 65, Notebook Background Book for Fulbright Hearings on Dominican Republic, Deployment Chronology, box 3, SecDef Subject Decimal files, Acc 70A-1266; msg JCS 1023 to CINCLANT et al, 29 Apr 65, Cable files, OSD Hist; Yates, "Power Pack," 68.

18. WSEG, "Dominican Crisis," 89-90; Poole, *JCS and National Policy, 1965-68*, pt 2:458 (quote). The WSEG study places Wheeler's quotation to the Vice J-3 at 7:36 p.m. Msg CJCS to CINCLANT, 291707Z Apr 65, fldr Dominican Republic May 20, 1965, box 33, Papers of Bromley K. Smith, LBJL.

19. Transc of telcon between State and SantoDomingo, 29 Apr 65, *FRUS 1964-68*, 32:94-99, (quotes 95, 99, 98).

20. Johnson, *Vantage Point*, 201; Valenti notes, Mtg in Cabinet Room, 29 Apr 65, 7:15 p.m., fldr Meeting Notes (Handwritten) 4/30-5/15/65, box 1, Office of the President File, RAC Material (Closed), LBJL;

msg CINCLANT to CJTF 122, 300230Z Apr 65, fldr DoD Messages April 25-May 5, 1965 (1 of 3), box 6, NSC History Dominican Crisis 1965, NSF, LBJL; msg JCS 1089 to CINCLANT, 30 Apr 65, Data Concerning Roles and Actions of the Department of Defense in the Dominican Republic, fldr HRC 091 Dominican Republic, box HRC 091 Dom Rep, CMH.

21. Msg 2562 State to USUN et al, 30 Apr 65, fldr Dom Rep Jan-30 Apr, box 453, Subj files, OSD Hist.

22. DeptState, "Action of the Organization of American States in the Dominican Republic," 24 Jun 65, 2-4, Notebook Background Book for Fulbright Hearings on Dominican Republic, TAB OAS Involvement, box 3, SecDef Subject Decimal files, Acc 70-A-1266; msg JCS 1092 to CJTF 122/CINCLANT, 30 Apr 65, fldr Santo Domingo thru 30 April, box 453, Subj files, OSD Hist.

23. Msg 693 State to SantoDomingo, 30 Apr 65 fldr Outgoing State Cables, April 25-May 4, 1965 [A-1], box 5, NSC History Dominican Crisis 1965, NSF, LBJL (quote); msg 695 State to SantoDomingo, 30 Apr 65, *FRUS 1964-68*, 32:106-07.

24. Valenti notes, Mtg in Cabinet Room, 30 Apr 65, 8:30 a.m., fldr Meeting Notes (Handwritten) 4/30-5/15/65, box 1, RAC Material (Closed), Office of the President File, LBJL (quotes). Sections of this lengthy document are available in ed note, *FRUS 1964-68*, 32:100-01. Interv McGeorge Bundy by Alfred Goldberg and Maurice Matloff, 15 Apr 91, 32, OSD Hist; Rusk, *As I Saw It*, 373.

25. Valenti notes, 30 Apr 65, 8:30 a.m., cited in note 24 (quote); Poole, *JCS and National Policy, 1965-68*, pt 2:460; msgs JCS 1095 to CINCLANT, 30 Apr 65, JCS 1113 to CINCLANT, 30 Apr 65, fldr Data Concerning Roles and Actions of the Department of Defense in the Dominican Republic 24 Apr - 22 Jun 65, box HRC 091 Dom Rep, CMH; msg JCS 1205 to CINCLANT, 1 May 65, fldr 228.01 HRC 091 Dom Rep, ibid; CMC notes of 30 April 1965 mtg at 1400 in Pentagon, 30 Apr 65, No 51, fldr vol 4, Greene Papers, MHC.

26. Memo Valenti for Pres, 30 Apr 65, fldr ND 19/CO 62 1/1/65-5/5/65, box 201, National Security-Defense (Gen ND 19/CO 57), LBJL (quote); telcon Johnson and McNamara, 30 Apr 65, 12:52 p.m., WH 6504.8 PNO 7416, LBJL (quote); see also Beschloss, *Reaching for Glory*, 301; telcon Johnson and McNamara, 30 Apr 65, 5:40 p.m., WH 6504.09 PNO 11 7429, LBJL (quote); see also Beschloss, *Reaching for Glory*, 303.

27. Martin, *Overtaken by Events*, 661; msg 703 State to SantoDomingo, 30 Apr 65, fldr Outgoing State Cables, April 25-May 4, 1965 [A-1], box 5, NSC History Dominican Crisis 1965, NSF, LBJL.

28. "Action of the Organization of American States in the Dominican Republic," 24 Jun 65, 5, cited in note 22; Resolution Adopted by the Tenth Mtg of Consultation of Ministers of Foreign Affairs of the American Republics, 1 May 65, *AFP, CD 1965*, 959-60; Valenti notes, Mtg in Cabinet Room, 30 Apr 65, 8:30 a.m., cited in note 24 (quote); Johnson, *Vantage Point*, 198; telcon Johnson and Mansfield, 30 Apr 65, 11:51 a.m., Beschloss, *Reaching for Glory*, 300; Lowenthal, *Dominican Intervention*,116.

29. Military Operations in the Dominican Republic, 5, cited in note 4; Valenti notes, Mtg in Cabinet Room, 30 Apr 65, 8:30 a.m., cited in note 24.

30. Greenberg, *Unilateral Coalition Operations*, 25; Palmer, *Intervention*, 144; CIA memo, OCI No 1116/65, Communist Participation in Dominican Republic Rebellion, 30 Apr 65, fldr Dominican Republic 381 (26 Apr 65) Jan-10 May 1965, box 4, SecDef Subject Decimal files, Acc 70A-1266 listed 65 names; msg Circ 2085 State to various posts, 30 Apr 65, fldr DomRep Jan-30 Apr 65, box 453, Subj files, OSD Hist (quote).

31. WSEG, "Dominican Crisis," 27; Slater, *Intervention and Negotiation*, 36-37; Quello and Isa Conde, "Revolutionary Struggle in the Dominican Republic," pt 1:97 and pt 2:53; CIA memo, OCI No 1120/65, The Communist Role in the Dominican Republic, 7 May 65, *FRUS 1964-68*, 32:139 (quote); Slater, *Intervention and Negotiation*, 37.

32. Memo Rowan for Pres, 1 May 65, fldr Dominican Republic 381 (26 Apr 65) Jan-10 May 1965, box 4, SecDef Subject Decimal files, Acc 70A-1266 (quote); Pres Radio and TV Report, 2 May 65, *Johnson Public Papers, 1965*, 1:471 (quote); Yates, "Power Pack," 93.

33. Martin, *Overtaken by Events*, 662; msg 1224 SantoDomingo to State, 1 May 65, fldr Dom Rep May 1-2, 1965, box 453, Subj files, OSD Hist (quote); msgs 736 State to SantoDomingo, 2 May 65 (quote), and 1258 SantoDomingo to State, 2 May 65 (quote), ibid; telcon Johnson and Martin, 2 May 65, 3:42 p.m., WH 6505.22 PNO 1 7519, LBJL; *Washington Post*, 3 May 65; Martin, *Overtaken by Events*, 676; msg 1334 SantoDomingo to State, 4 May 65, Cable files, OSD Hist.

34. WSEG, "Dominican Crisis," 9; Palmer, *Intervention*, 31.

35. Lowenthal, *Dominican Intervention*, 116 (quote); Palmer, *Intervention*, 4-5. Palmer attributed his selection less to the president's criterion, which he did not believe anyway, than to Wheeler's desire to remove Palmer in order to open up the DCSOPS position for a crony. Interv Bruce Palmer by Ted Gittinger, 28 May 82, AC 92-49, 1:2, 9 (quote), LBJL; G-2, XVIII Airborne Corps, Stability Operations Report Dominican Republic, 31 Aug 65, 1, pt 1, ch 2, 1, fldr HRC 319.1, box HRC 319.1 Dominican Republic Rpt, CMH

(quote); msg CJCS 1596-65 to CINCLANT et al, 30 Apr 65, fldr Dominican Republic May 20, 1965, box 33, Papers of Bromley K. Smith, LBJL; interv Bruce Palmer by Shelton and Smith, 23 Apr 71, 173, Senior Officers Debriefing Program, Carlisle Barracks, Pa, 1976 (quote).

36. List of Assignments, 1 May 65, fldr Meeting on the Dom Rep –Planning Group, box 2, Files of Gordon Chase, LBJL; msg JCS to CINCLANT, 301712Z Apr 65, fldr 228.01, HRC 091 Dom Rep, box HRC 091 Dominican Republic, CMH.

37. Msg JCS 1088 to CINCLANT, 30 Apr 65, fldr DoD Messages April 25-May 5, 1965 [1 of 3], box 6, NSC History Dominican Crisis 1965, NSF, LBJL: msgs CJTF 122 to CINCLANT, 301904Z Apr 65, and CJTF 122 to CINCLANT 010545Z May 65: fldr DoD Messages April 25-May 5, 1965 [2 of 3], box 6, ibid; Yates, "Power Pack," 79, 82; Poole, *JCS and National Policy, 1965-68*, pt 2:461-63; telcon M. Bundy and Johnson, 30 Apr 65, 5:00 p.m. Tape WH6504.09 PNO 6 7424, LBJL; see also Beschloss, *Reaching for Glory*, 301-02; telcon Johnson and McNamara, 30 Apr 65, 5:40 p.m. Tape WH6504.09 PNO 11 7429, LBJL; see also Beschloss, *Reaching for Glory*, 303; memo telcon Raborn and Ball, 28 Apr 65, 1:45 p.m., fldr Dominican Republic 4-28-65-6-26-65, box 3, Papers of George W. Ball, LBJL; WSEG, "Dominican Crisis," 266, 276, 283.

38. WSEG, "Dominican Crisis," 292-93; Yates, "Power Pack," 52.

39. Military Operations in the Dominican Republic, 4, cited in note 4; Palmer, *Intervention*, 36-37; Stability Operations Report Dominican Republic, 1, pt 1, ch 2:7, cited in note 35; msg COMLAN [Palmer] to JCS, 010720Z May 65, fldr Dom Rep May 1-2, 1965, box 453, Subj files, OSD Hist; msg JCS to CINCLANT, 010026Z May 65, fldr 228.01 HRC 091 Dom Rep, box HRC 091 Dominican Republic, CMH.

40. Yates, "Power Pack," 87 and 200, n20; Palmer interv, 28 May 82, 7; Stability Operations Report Dominican Republic,1, pt 1, ch 2: 7, 9, cited in note 35; msg 1217 SantoDomingo to State, 1 May 65, fldr Incoming State Cables Apr 24-May 4, 1965 "A" 1 of 2, box 4, NSC History Dominican Crisis 1965, NSF, LBJL; msg CINCLANT to CINCLANFLT 010806Z May 65, fldr DoD Messages April 25, 1965 (2 of 3), box 6, ibid. Both these messages state that York signed the cease-fire. WSEG, "Dominican Crisis," 133 (quote).

41. Palmer interv, 28 May 82, 11 (quote); WSEG, "Dominican Crisis," 134 (quote); Yates, "Power Pack," 85, 88; Stability Operations Report Dominican Republic, 1, pt 1, ch 2: 7, cited in note 35; msg JTF 120 San Isidro DR to JCS, 011455Z May 65, fldr Dom Rep May 1-2, 1965, box 453, Subj files, OSD Hist (quotes).

42. Valenti notes, Mtg in Cabinet Room, 1 May 65, 8:40 a.m., fldr Meeting Notes (Handwritten) 4/30-5/15/65, box 13, Valenti Notes of Meetings during 1965 and 1966, Office of the President File, LBJL.

43. Ibid; List of Assignments, 1 May 65, cited in note 36; see also *FRUS 1964-68*, 32:113, n9.

44. Valenti notes, Mtg in Cabinet Room, 1 May 65, 8:40 a.m., cited in note 42 (quote, emphasis in the source); Alerting, Movement, and Execution Orders Directed by JCS, cited in note 17; WSEG, "Dominican Crisis," 271-72.

45. Ringler and Shaw, "U.S. Marine Corps Operations in the Dominican Republic, April-June 1965," 37; msg COMJTF 120 to COMJTF 122, 012245Z May 65, fldr DoD Messages April 25-May 5, 1965 (3 of 3), box 6, NSC History Dominican Crisis, 1965, NSF, LBJL (quote); telcon Johnson and McNamara, 1 May 65, 2:45 p.m., WH 6505.01 PNO 8 7508, LBJL; msg JCS 1195 to AIG 936 et al, 30 Apr 65, fldr Dom Rep Jan-30 Apr 65, box 453, Subj files, OSD Hist; WSEG, "Dominican Crisis," 171.

46. Msgs 1242 SantoDomingo, 1 May 65, 1245 SantoDomingo, 1 May 65, 718 State to SantoDomingo, 1 May 65, 675 State to SantoDomingo, 29 Apr 65: fldr Dom Rep Jan-30 Apr 65, box 453, Subj files, OSD Hist; Yates, "Power Pack," 88-90.

47. Ringler and Shaw, "U.S. Marine Corps Operations," 37; telcon McNamara and Johnson, 1 May 65, 5:31 p.m., WH 6505.01 PNO 11 7511, LBJL; WSEG, "Dominican Crisis," 171; msg 1245 SantoDomingo to State, 1 May 65, cited in note 46 (quotes); msg JCS 1236 to CINCLANT/CJTF 122, 1 May 65 (quotes), fldr Dom Rep May 1-2, 1965, box 453, Subj files, OSD Hist; Palmer interv, 23 Apr 71, 167.

48. Msg JCS 1237 to CINCLANT et al, 1 May 65, fldr DR May 1-2, Cable files, OSD Hist (quote); Poole, *JCS and National Policy, 1965-68*, pt 2:463-64.

49. Talking Paper for CJCS, Alternative Courses of Action in the Dominican Republic, 2 May 65, fldr Dominican Republic 381 (26 Apr 65) Jan-10 May 65, box 2, SecDef Subject Decimal files, Acc 70A-1265; msg CJTF 122 to JCS, 020714Z May 65, fldr 228.01, box HRC 091, Dom Rep, CMH; memrcd Chase, Mtg on Dominican Republic—May 2, 1965, 4 May 65, *FRUS 1964-68*, 32:117-19.

50. Presidential Daily Diary, 2 May 65, fldr Daily Diary May 65, box 3, PDD, LBJL sets the time at 4:32 a.m., 2 May; Palmer, *Intervention*, 47; Stability Operations Report Dominican Republic, 1, pt 1, ch 2:8-9, cited in note 35; memo Bundy for Pres, 2 May 65, w/atchmt, SecDef Notes, nd but likely 2 May 65, fldr Dominican Republic 381 (26 Apr 65) Jan-10 May 1965, box 4, SecDef Subject Decimal files, Acc 70A-1266 (quote).

51. Msg JCS 1251 to CINCLANT, 2 May 65, fldr Dominican Republic 381 (26 Apr 65) dtd 24 Jun 65, TAB III, box 2, SecDef Subject Decimal files, Acc 70A-1265; Chronology Continued, 23, fldr Chronology April 19-May 3, 1965 (Tabs 111-141), box 9, NSC History Dominican Crisis 1965, Chronology, April 24-Sep 21, 1965, NSF, LBJL; msg JCS 1261 to CINCLANT/CTF 120, 3 May 65, fldr Dominican Republic 381 (26 Apr 65) dtd 24 Jun 65, TAB III, 1, box 2, SecDef Subject Decimal files, Acc 70A-1265 (quote); memo Bundy for Pres, 2 May 65, cited in note 50; Valenti notes, Briefing, 2 May 65, 6:45 p.m., fldr Meeting Notes (Handwritten) 4/30-5/15/65, box 13, Valenti Notes of Meetings During 1965 and 1966, Office of the President File, LBJL (quotes, emphasis in the source).

52. Msg 742 State to SantoDomingo, 2 May 65, *FRUS 1964-68*, 32:119-20.

53. Msg JCS 1260 to AIG 936, et al, 030052Z May 65, Cable files, OSD Hist; memrcd Chase, Meeting on the Dominican Republic—May 2, 1965, cited in note 49; NMCC, Situation Summ US Forces Involved in Dominican Republic Operations as of 032000Z May 1965, No. 9, 3 May 65, Cable files, OSD Hist; Stability Operations Report Dominican Republic, 1, pt 1, ch 2:10, cited in note 35.

54. Stability Operations Report Dominican Republic, 1, pt 1, ch 2, 12 (quote), cited in note 35; CIA, OCI Weekly Summ, 14 May 65, fldr Dom Rep 10-15 May 65, Subj files, OSD Hist; msg 1776 Santo-Domingo to State, 18 May 65, *FRUS 1964-68*, 32:196-97 (quote).

55. Memo Moyers for McNamara w/atchmt, 5 May 65, fldr Dominican Republic 381 (26 Apr 65) Jan – 10 May 1965, box 4, SecDef Subject Decimal files, Acc 70A-1266.

56. Action memo, Bundy Cte Mtg, 6 May 65, fldr Dom Rep 5-9 May, box 453, Subj files, OSD Hist; Poole, *JCS and National Policy, 1965-68*, pt 2:469-70 (quote); memrcd Chase, Dominican Republic Task Force Mtg-6 May 65, 7 May 65, *FRUS 1964-68*, 32:133-36 (quote); msg JCS 1547 to CINCLANT, 6 May 65, fldr Dominican Republic 381 (26 Apr 65) dtd 24 Jun 65, TAB III, 1, box 2, SecDef Subject Decimal files, Acc 70A-1265; memo Vaughn for Rusk, McNamara et al, White House mtg of 6 May - 3:00 p.m., fldr Dominican Republic 381 (26 Apr 65) Jan –10 May 1965, box 4, SecDef Subject Decimal files, Acc 70A-1266; msg JCS 1521 to AIG 936 et al, 5 May 65, Cable files, OSD Hist.

57. Msg 1558 SantoDomingo to State, 10 May 65, *FRUS 1964-68*, 32:142-45; action memo, Bundy Cte mtg, 12 May 65, fldr Dom Rep 10-15 May, box 453, Subj files, OSD Hist; *AFP, CD, 1965*, 980, n83; Poole, *JCS and National Policy, 1965-68*, pt 2:471.

58. Msg USCOMDOMREP to CINCLANT, 110450Z May 65, fldr Dom Rep May 10 - 15, 1965, box 453, Subj files, OSD Hist; msg CINCLANT to JCS, 111258Z May 65, ibid (quotes).

59. Action memo, Bundy Cte mtg, 12 May 65, cited in note 57; msg 979 State-Defense to SantoDomingo, 12 May 65, fldr Outgoing State Cables April 25-May 14, 1965 [B-2], box 5, NSC History Dominican Crisis 1965, NSF, LBJL.

60. Msg 1612 SantoDomingo to State, 12 May 65, fldr Dom Rep May 10 -15, 1965, box 453, Subj files, OSD Hist; msg CINCLANT to CJCS 131622Z May 65, msg Palmer to CINCLANT, 131759Z May 65:ibid; msg 1674 SantoDomingo to State, 13 May 65, ibid; msg Palmer to CINCLANT, 140127Z May 65, ibid; msg 1690 SantoDomingo to State, 14 May 65, fldr Incoming State Cables, May 5-14, 1965, "B" [2 of 2], box 4, NSC History Dominican Crisis 1965, NSF, LBJL; memo telcon Mann and Johnson, 14 May 65, 12:55 p.m., fldr Telephone Conversations with LBJ Jan 14,1964-April 30, 1965, box 1, Mann Papers, Gordon Chase Files, LBJL (quote).

61. Msg 1682 SantoDomingo to State, 14 May 65, fldr Dom Rep May 10 - 15, 1965, box 453, Subj files, OSD Hist (quote); msg CINCLANT to JCS, 142016Z May 65, ibid (quote).

62. JCSM-372-65 for SecDef, 15 May 65, ibid (quote); msg USFDR-CG6293 USCOMDOMREP to CIN-CLANT, 14 May 65, ibid (quote).

63. Msgs 1576 SantoDomingo to State, 10 May 65, fldr Dom Rep 10 - 15 May 65, NMCC to White House, 160931Z May 65, fldr Dom Rep May 16 - 22, 1965: box 454, ibid; msg 1746 SantoDomingo to State, 16 May 65, ibid; Stability Operations Report Dominican Republic, 1, pt 1:14, cited in note 35; Poole, *Joint Chiefs of Staff and National Policy, 1965-68*, pt 2:473-74; Yates, "Power Pack," 116; Johnson, *Vantage Point*, 202-03; Yates, "Power Pack," 116; Rusk interv, 2 Jan 70, 18.

64. CMC notes of 17 May 1965 Special mtg of JCS No 53, fldr vol 4, Greene Papers, MHC (quotes); Domini-can Crisis: Presidential Decisions, nd, cited in note 17; memo Bundy to Rusk, 11 May 65, *FRUS 1964-68*, 2:634-35.

65. Poole, *JCS and National Policy, 1965-68*, pt 2:473; msgs 1824 Bundy to SecState, 19 May 65, *FRUS 1964-68,* 32:207-10, 1153 SecState to Bundy, 20 May 65: fldr Bundy's Mission on the Dominican Problem, box 23, Files of Gordon Chase, NSF, LBJL; msg 1798 SantoDomingo to State (Bundy for Pres) and McNa-mara's marginalia on the cable, 19 May 65, Cable files, OSD Hist; msg 69 Bundy and Vance to Pres, 16 May 65, *FRUS 1964-68*, 32:182-83 (quote); interv Thomas C. Mann by Joe B. Frantz, 4 Nov 68, 1, 15,

electronic copy, LBJL; Palmer, *Intervention*, 57; Rusk, As I Saw It, 375. Johnson professed greater confidence in Mann's judgment than in Bundy's, and during the Dominican crisis told Abe Fortas that he had not found Mann wrong. Telcon Johnson and Fortas, 19 May 65, 11:40 a.m., Side B, #7910, Tape SR 6505.01, LBJL. See also Beschloss, *Reaching for Glory*, 332-33.

66. Msg 1756 SantoDomingo to State, 17 May 65, fldr "Davidson," box 51, CF, Dominican Republic, NSF, LBJL (quote); Palmer, *Intervention*, 58; Stability Operations Report Dominican Republic, 1, pt 1, ch 2: 13-14, cited in note 35; msg USFDR-CG 6350 USCOMDOMREP to CINCLANT, 16 May 65, fldr Dominican Republic #381 (26 Apr 64) 11 May-31 Jul, box 3, SecDef Subject Decimal files, Acc 70A-1266 (quote).

67. JCSM-377-65 for SecDef, 17 May 65, fldr Dom Rep May 16-25, 1965, box 454, Subj files, OSD Hist; UNSC Res 203, 14 May 65, *AFP, CD 1965*, 979-80; memos ISA for SecDef, 19 May 65, SecDef for CJCS, 21 May 65: fldr Dominican Republic #381 (26 Apr 65) 11 May-31 July, box 3, SecDef Subject Decimal files, Acc 70A-1266; Stability Operations Report Dominican Republic, 1, pt 1, ch 2:14, cited in note 35.

68. Msg 1752 SantoDomingo to State, (Bundy for Pres), 17 May 65, *FRUS 1964-68*, 32:185-87 (quote); msg 1776 SantoDomingo to State, 18 May 65, ibid, 196-97.

69. Msg 1805 SantoDomingo to State, 19 May 65, ibid, 206; see also telcon Rusk and Moyers, 20 May 65, Tape WH SR6505.05, #8015, LBJL; DIA Intelligence Bulletin, 96-65, 18 May 65, msg USFOR-J1 6400 USCOMDOMREP to CINCLANT, 18 May 65: fldr Dom Rep 16-22 May 1965, box 454, Subj files, OSD Hist; msg USFDR-CG 6449 USCOMDOMREP to CINCLANT, 20 May 65, ibid; msg Pres to SantoDomingo, 25 May 65, fldr Dom Rep 23 - 30 May, 1965, ibid.

70. DeptState, "Action of the Organization of American States in the Dominican Republic," 24 Jun 65, 5-7, 10-11, cited in note 22; *AFP, CD 1965*, 974-75, 991; JCSM-344-65 for SecDef, 8 May 65, JCSM-363-65 for SecDef, 14 May 65, JCSM-393-65 for SecDef, 20 May 65: fldrs Dom Rep 5 - 9 May and May 14 - 22, box 454, Subj files, OSD Hist; Poole, *JCS and National Policy, 1965-68*, pt 2:468-69.

71. Msg 1824 SantoDomingo to State, 19 May 65, cited in note 65; msg 1916 SantoDomingo to State, 23 May 65, fldr Dom Rep May 23-30, 1965, box 454, Subj files, OSD Hist; msg JCS 2703 to CINCLANT, 24 May 65, ibid.

72. Msg USFDR-CG 6582 Vance and Palmer (DomRep) to SecDef, 24 May 65, ibid; msg USFDR-CG 6599 USCOMDOMREP to CINCLANT, 25 May 65, ibid; msgs USFDR-CG 6638 USCOMDOMREP to CINCLANT, 26 May 65, JCS 2780 to CINCLANT/COMDOMREP, 25 May 65, ibid; JCSM-414-65 for SecDef, 27 May 65, ibid.

73. Memo McNamara for Califano, 24 May 65, ibid; memo SecDef for Pres, 26 May 65, *FRUS 1964-68*, 32:247-51; Statement DepSecDef before SFRC, 14 Jul 65, 6-8, fldr Dom Rep July, box 454, Subj files, OSD Hist.

74. Memo Vance for Pres, 1 Jun 65, JCSM-423-65 for SecDef, 1 Jun 65: fldr Dom Rep Jun 1 - 15, box 454, Subj files, OSD Hist; Pres remarks, 3 Jun 65, *Johnson Public Papers, 1965*, 2:633-34.

75. JCSM-443-65 for SecDef, 8 Jun 65, fldr Dom Rep June 1 - 5, 1965, box 454, Subj files, OSD Hist; JCSM-476-65 for SecDef, 18 Jun 65, fldr Dom Rep June 16 - 30, 1965, ibid; Poole, *JCS and National Policy, 1965-68*, pt 2:481; msg USFDR-CG 7012 USCOMDOMREP to JCS, 10 Jun 65, fldr Dom Rep June 1 - 15, 1965, Cable files, OSD Hist (quote).

76. JCSM-476-55 for SecDef, 18 Jun 65, cited in note 75.

77. Palmer, *Intervention*, 82; memo NMCC for SecDef, 15 Jun 65, fldr Dom Rep June 1 - 15, 1965, box 454, Subj files, OSD Hist; msg 2443 SantoDomingo to State, 16 Jun 65, fldr DR June, Cable files, OSD Hist; Poole, *JCS and National Policy, 1965-68*, pt 2:483.

78. JCSM-476-65 for SecDef, 18 Jun 65, cited in note 75; A marginal note on the document states Vance's approval came on 25 June. Memo SecDef for CJCS, 23 Jun 65, fldr Dom Rep Jun 16 - 30, 1965, box 454, Subj files, OSD Hist; msgs JCS 4381 to CINCLANT/USCOMDOMREP, 22 Jun 65, USFDR-CG 7247 USCOMDOMREP to CINCLANT/JCS, 23 Jun 65, ibid; msgs JCS 4526 to CINCLANT, 24 Jun 65, JCS 4502 to CINCLANT, 24 Jun 65, USFDR-CG 7289 USCOMDOMREP to CINCLANT/JCS, 25 Jun 65: all ibid; msg DEF 5082 OSD to USCOMDOMREP, 2 Jul 65, ibid; Pres Statement, 3 Jul 65, *Johnson Public Papers, 1965*, 2:721; Status of US Forces in Dominican Republic at Peak Deployment and on Other Dates, 15 Jul 65 and Military Operations in the Dominican Republic, nd but c 12 Jul 65, cited in note 4.

79. *AFP, CD 1965*, 999-1001; *FRUS 1964-68*, 32:294, n3; Poole, *JCS and National Policy, 1965-68*, pt 2:485; JCSM-674-65 for SecDef, 4 Sep 65, fldr Dom Rep September 1965, box 455, Subj files, OSD Hist (quote); memo DASD(A) for CJCS, 25 Sep 65, ibid; msg USFDR-JO 7966 USCOMDOMREP to CINCLANT, 31 Aug 65, fldr Dom Rep Aug 1965, box 454, ibid.

80. Memo SecDef for SecA, 22 Jun 65, fldr Dom Rep Jun 16-30, 1965, ibid; memo SecA for SecDef, 1 Jul 65, fldr Dom Rep July 1965, ibid; Poole, *JCS and National Policy, 1965-68*, pt 2:486-87; memo SecDef to

CJCS, 4 Apr 66, CM-1299-65 for SecDef, 9 Apr 66: fldr Dominican Republic 1966-1972, box 455, Subj files, OSD Hist.

81. Memo Yarmolinsky for Vance, 24 Jun 66, ibid; memo DepSecDef for CJCS, 27 Jun 66, ibid; Status of US Forces in Dominican Republic at Peak Deployment and on Other Dates, 15 Jul 65, and Military Operations in the Dominican Republic, nd but c 12 Jul 65, cited in note 4; *AFP, CD 1966*, 265-66 and n65.

82. Smith notes of mtg, 26 May 65, fldr Dom Rep May 26, 1965, box 83, Papers of Bromley K. Smith, LBJL.

83. For a different interpretation see Slater, "The Dominican Republic, 1961-1966," in Blechman and Kaplan eds, *Force Without War*, 340-41.

XII. ARMS CONTROL: AN ELUSIVE GOAL

1. Ed note, NSAM 320, 25 Nov 64, *FRUS 1964 -68*, 11:120-21, 126; ltr Johnson to Khrushchev, 20 Jan 64, *Johnson Public Papers, 1963-1964*, 1:153-54; msg Soviet Govt to Pres, 3 Nov 64, *FRUS 1964-68*, 14:165; memcon Johnson w/Gromyko, 9 Dec 64, ibid, 137-39. On the Pen Pal exchanges see ibid, *1961-63*, 6:x and ibid, *1964-68*, 11:431, n3.

2. Ltr Johnson to Soviet Leaders, 30 Dec 64, *Johnson Public Papers,1963-64*, 2:1673; ltr Johnson to Kosygin, 14 Jan 65, *FRUS 1964-68*, 11:168-69; msg Kosygin to Johnson, 1 Feb 65, ibid, 186-87; memcon Foster w/Dobrynin, 30 Mar 65, ibid, 198 (quote); JCSM-269-65 for SecDef, 13 Apr 65 and Annex to App B, ACDA msg, 24 Feb 65: both fldr 1965, Strategic Arms 1, Backup Material, "History of Strategic Arms Competition, 1945-1972," OSD Hist; Chron of Exchanges with the Soviet Government, 9 Feb 65 and 15 Feb 65 entries, fldr Strategic Arms 2, ibid; memos Klein for Bundy, 3 Mar 65 and Thompson for Rusk, 25 Oct 66, *FRUS 1964-68*, 14:249-50 and 432. The flow of messages resumed only after the U.S. initiative in January 1967 to seek a formal limitation on ABM deployments, see "Strategic Arms Competition, 1945-1972," pt 2:740-42.

3. U.S. ACDA, The U.S. Arms Control and Disarmament Agency During the Johnson Administration, 9 Dec 1970 draft, 16, fldr 9, box 1268, Subj files, OSD Hist (hereafter ACDA History); Poole, *JCS and National Policy, 1965-68*, pt 1:200; Seaborg, *Stemming the Tide*, 184.

4. Murray, mins of Briefing by Sec McNamara on Issues Related to Proliferation, January 7, 1965, 15 Jan 65, fldr Strategic Arms 2, as cited in note 2.

5. Ed note and Rpt to Pres by Cte on Nuclear Proliferation, 21 Jan 65, *FRUS 1964-68*, 11:172-76, 180; CM-450-65 for Bundy, 24 Feb 65, fldr Strategic Arms 2, as cited in note 2 (quote); draft memo Rusk for Pres, nd, ibid; Rpt by Cte on Nuclear Proliferation, 21 Jan 65, *FRUS 1964-68*, 11:173, n 1.

6. Memo Bundy for Pres, 21 Jan 65, fldr Strategic Arms 2, as cited in note 2; ed note, *FRUS 1964-68*, 11:172; see also Seaborg, *Stemming the Tide*, 143, 148-49; memos Keeny for Bundy, 26 Mar 65 (quote) and Bundy for SecState/SecDef, 27 Mar 65, fldr National Security files, box 6, Keeny Papers, LBJL.

7. Telcon Johnson and Bundy, 24 Jun 65, 10:00 a.m., Beschloss, *Reaching for Glory*, 369: telcon Johnson and Gerald Griffin, 24 Jun 65, 4:55 p.m., ibid, 371; Journal of Glenn T. Seaborg, 1 Jan 65-30 Jun 65, 10, January 1989, 630, 662, 674, fldr Diary, box 2, Seaborg Papers, LBJL; *Johnson Public Papers, 1965*, 2:704-05; NSAM 335, 28 Jun 65, *FRUS 1964-68*, 11:216-17; Hal Brands, "Progress Unseen," 268-69; memcon Rusk w/Stewart, 22 Mar 65, *FRUS 1964-1968*, 68, 11:195.

8. Kaplan, "The INF Treaty and the Future of NATO," 146; Potter, *Nuclear Power and Nonproliferation*, 41.

9. Keeny, The Non-Proliferation Treaty, 3, 24 Dec 68, fldr NPT Vol 1 (1 of 3), box 55/56, NSC History Non-Proliferation Treaty, NSF, LBJL (hereafter Keeny, The Non-Proliferation Treaty); Kaplan et al, *McNamara Ascendancy*, 393; interv Dean Rusk by Paige E. Mulhollan, 8 Mar 70, 4:11, Electronic Copy, LBJL (quote).

10. Potter, *Nuclear Power and Nonproliferation*, 41 (quote); Keeny, The Non-Proliferation Treaty, 1-2; memo Foster for Cte of Principals, 12 Apr 65 w/atchmt, U.S. Position on a Program to Inhibit, and Hopefully Stop, Nuclear Proliferation, fldr Strategic Arms 2, as cited in note 2; "Draft Administrative History of the DoD, 1963-1969," 1:45.

11. Poole, *JCS and National Policy, 1965-68*, pt 1:240. mtg of Cte of Principals, 22 Apr 65, fldr Cte of Principals, Vol 2 (2 of 2), box 14, Subject File, NSF, LBJL; JCSM-375-65 for SecDef, 17 May 65, fldr 471.6 29 May 1965, box 8, ISA General files, Acc 70A-5127; CM-621-65 for SecDef, 17 May 65, fldr 1965 CMs (583-65-645-65), box 1, Wheeler Papers, RG 218.

12. Memo Bundy for Rusk, 4 Mar 65, *FRUS 1964-68*, 13:188; circ msg 2412 State to NATO Capitals, 2 Jun 65, ibid, 212-13; Seaborg, *Stemming the Tide*, 172-73.

13. Seaborg, *Stemming the Tide*, 164-66; *New York Times*, 18 Aug 65; Keeny, The Non-Proliferation Treaty, 2-3; memo Bundy for Rusk, 4 Mar 65, msg Secto 19 Rusk in London to State, 14 May 65: *FRUS 1964-68*,

13:187-88, 209; Cte on Nuclear Proliferation(?), The Case for a Fresh Start on Atlantic Nuclear Defense (with no Mixed Manned Forces or Plans for Such Forces), 18 Oct 65, fldr Mr. Bundy for 6 o'clock mtg, box 26, Subject File, Multinational Force, NSF, LBJL.

14. Memo Foster for Pres, 10 Nov 65, fldr Treaty-Nonproliferation I 1965, box 8, Keeny Papers, NSF, LBJL; memcon Bundy w/Dobrynin, 24 Nov 65, *FRUS 1964-68*, 13:273 (quote); Bunn, *Arms Control by Committee*, 68; memo Bundy for Pres, 25 Nov 65, Backup Material as cited in note 2; memcon McNamara, Johnson, and Erhard, 20 Dec 65, *FRUS 1964 -68*, 15:349; ltr Johnson to Wilson, 23 Dec 65, ibid, 13:296; Jt Statement, 21 Dec 65, *Johnson Public Papers, 1965*, 2:1165; memcon Johnson w/Erhard, 20 Dec 65, *FRUS 1964-68*, 13:291.

15. Msg 216 Moscow to State, 21 Jul 65, *FRUS 1964-68*, 14:310-11; memcon Rusk w/Stewart, 22 Mar 65, ibid, 11:195; USACDA, Proposed Disarmament Measures Paper on a Comprehensive Test Ban Treaty, 14 Jul 65, USACDA, Proposed Disarmament Measures Paper for Seismic Threshold Test Ban, nd but c 14 Jul 65: fldr ACDA, vol II [2 of 2], box 6, Agency File, NSF, LBJL; Poole, *JCS and National Policy, 1965-68*, pt 1:204-06; ACDA History, 34-36.

16. Ltr McNamara to Fisher, 7 Aug 65, fldr 1, box 89, Goodpaster Papers, Special Collections Library, NDU.

17. Record of mtg of Cte of Principals, nd but 22 Jul 65, *FRUS 1964-68*, 11:224-28.

18. Ibid, 225 (quote); Johnson msg to ENDC, 27 Jul 65, *Johnson Public Papers, 1965*, 2:790; ed note, *FRUS 1964-68*, 11:232; Seaborg, *Stemming the Tide*, 217-18 (quote); JCSM-602-65 for SecDef, 5 Aug 65, fldr Disarmament (ENDC) Vol 1, box 13, Subject File: Disarmament, NSF, LBJL; ltr McNamara to Fisher, 7 Aug 65, cited in note 16.

19. Memo Keeny for Bundy and Hornig, 24 Aug 65, fldr Cte of Principals, Vol 2, box 14, Subject File: Disarmament, NSF, LBJL; mins of mtg of Cte of Principals, 25 Aug 65, *FRUS 1964-68*, 11:242; JCSM-645-65 for SecDef, 21 Aug 65, fldr 388.3 (2 Feb 65) (Dec-July), box 14, SecDef Subject Decimal files, Acc 70A-1265.

20. Mins of mtg of the Cte of Principals and Summary of Actions, 25 Aug 65, *FRUS 1964-68*, 11:237-43; ACDA History, 36.

21. CM-812-65 for Dir Jt Staff, 27 Aug 65, DJSM-999-65 for CJCS, 28 Aug 65: both fldr 1965 CMs (783-817-65), box 1, Wheeler Papers, RG 218.

22. Seaborg, *Stemming the Tide*, 221; *New York Times*, 8 Sep 65; Poole, *JCS and National Policy, 1965-68*, pt 1:243; memcon Bundy w/Dobrynin, 24 Nov 65, *FRUS 1964-68*, 11:266 (quote); memo Bundy for Pres, 25 Nov 65, ibid, 264 (quote).

23. Msg Kosygin to Johnson, 11 Jan 66, *FRUS 1964-68*, 11:278-80; ltr Johnson to Kosygin, 24 Jan 66, ibid, 297-300, n1 (quote, 299).

24. Ltr Wheeler to Seaborg, 25 Oct 65 w/encl Technical Questions, "Seaborg Journal," 1 Jul 65-31 Dec 65, vol 11, Jan 89, fldr AC 90-1, box 2, Seaborg Papers, LBJL (quote); JCSM-28-66 for SecDef, 13 Jan 66, JCSM-37-66 for SecDef, 15 Jan 66: *FRUS 1964-68*, 11:283-84, 287-88; ltr McNamara to Foster, 22 Jan 66, fldr 388.3 Jan 1966, box 7, ISA General files, Acc 70A-6649; Seaborg, *Stemming the Tide*, 230-31.

25. Memo Foster for Cte of Principals, 19 Jan 66 w/encl, Dft Presidential Msg for Opening of the ENDC, fldr 388.3 Jan 1966, box 7, ISA General files, Acc 70A-6649; JCSM-77-66 for SecDef, 3 Feb 66 w/atchmt, Report of the Ad Hoc Panel to the JCS through the CSAF, 14 Jan 66, fldr 388.3 3 Feb 66, ibid (quote); JCSM-49-66 for SecDef, 21 Jan 66, fldr 388.3 Jan 1966, ibid; SAACM-119-66, Spec Asst to JCS, Arms Control, for DepAsstSec, ISA, 15 Apr 66 w/atchmt, ltr Goldberger and Long to McConnell, 9 Mar 66, fldr 388.3, ibid.

26. Seaborg, *Stemming the Tide*, 231; Summary of Action, mtg of the Cte of Principals, 21 Jan 66, *FRUS 1964-1968*, 11:293-94; Pres msg to the ENDC, 27 Jan 66, *Johnson Public Papers, 1966*, 1: 93; ACDA History, 54; ltr McNamara to Foster, 22 Jan 66, cited in note 24.

27. Poole, *JCS and National Policy, 1965-68*, pt 1:213-14; memo DDRE for SecDef, 28 Oct 66, fldr 471.94 ABM, box 16, SecDef Subject Decimal files, Acc 70A-4662.

28. JCSM-163-66 for SecDef, 16 Mar 66 w/atchmt, fldr 388.3 16 March 1966, box 7, ISA General files, Acc 70A-6649 (quote); CIA, NIE 11-11-66, 25 May 66, *FRUS 1964-68*, 11:321-22.

29. Memo DDRE for DepSecDef, 20 Nov 67, Info Paper ATSD(AE), 21 Dec 67: both fldr A400.112, 1967, box 14, SecDef Subject Decimal files, Acc 72A-2467; memo Keeny for Rostow, 8 Jun 66, fldr 1966, fldr Strategic Arms 1, as cited in note 2 (quote).

30. Record of mtg of Cte of Principals, 17 Jun 66, *FRUS 1964-68*, 11:337 (quote); Seaborg, *Stemming the Tide*, 231; "Seaborg Journal," 1 Jan 66-30 Jun 66, 614-15, cited in note 24; memo Keeny for Moyers, 17 Jun 66, fldr Cte of Prins Mtg – 6/17/66 & follow-up Correspondence – Threshold Test Ban Treaty, box 3, Keeny Papers, NSF, LBJL (quotes); JCSM-379-66 for SecDef, 18 Jun 66, fldr 388.3 Jan 1966, box 7, ISA General files, Acc 70A-6649.

31. Memo Rostow for Pres, 3 Aug 66, fldr Test Ban Treaty, box 11, NSF Intelligence File, LBJL (quote); memo Rusk for Pres, 26 Jul 66, *FRUS 1964-68*, 11:342.

32. Ed note, *FRUS 1964-68*, 11:346; Seaborg, *Stemming the Tide*, 232.

33. Seaborg, *Stemming the Tide*, 214, 220-21; Rpt to Pres by Cte on Nuclear Proliferation, 21 Jan 65, *FRUS 1964-68*, 11:176; Summary of Actions, mtg of Cte of Principals, 25 Aug 65, *FRUS 1964-68*, 11:243.

34. Abstract of rpt of Ad Hoc Panel on Technical Aspects of Nuclear Test Ban Proposals, 14 Jan 66, *FRUS 1964-68*, 11:285-86; JCSM-37-66 for SecDef, 15 Jan 66, ibid, 286-88 (quote); Seaborg, *Stemming the Tide*, 229; Summary of Action, mtg of Cte of Principals, 21 Jan 66, *FRUS 1964-68*, 11:293-94. See para. 4, Pres msg to ENDC, 27 Jan 66, *Johnson Public Papers, 1966*, 1:93.

35. *FRUS 1964-68*, 11:492, n 2; Seaborg, *Stemming the Tide*, 235 (quote); Statement Foster to ENDC, 11 Jul 67, USACDA, *Documents on Disarmament 1967*, 294; ltr Seaborg to Rusk, 4 Aug 67, *FRUS 1964-68*, 11:492-93.

36. Ltr Seaborg to Pres, 13 Jul 68, *FRUS 1964-68*, 11:644-45; DJSM-859-68 for SecDef, 12 Jul 68, fldr Disarmament (ENDC) Vol III, box 13, Subject File: Disarmament, NSF, LBJL. The joint staff submitted the recommendation on behalf of the JCS because the time allotted for review was minimal; Poole, *JCS and National Policy, 1965-68*, pt 1:217-18; ed note, *FRUS 1964-68*, 11:645-46; *Johnson Public Papers, 1968-69*, 2:815-17.

37. Poole, *JCS and National Policy, 1965-68*, pt 1:218.

38. Bunn, *Arms Control by Committee*, 73; Seaborg, *Stemming the Tide*, 180; Rusk test, 23 Feb 66, McNamara test, 7 Mar 66, JCAE, *Hearings: S. Res. 179 Nonproliferation of Nuclear Weapons*, 5, 74, 76.

39. Memo Rusk for Pres, 11 Apr 66, *FRUS 1964-68*, 13:364-65 (quote); memrcd NATO Special Committee, 19 Apr 66, fldr NATO General, Vol III (1 of 2), box 36, Agency file, NSF, LBJL (quote); NSAM 345, 22 Apr 66, *FRUS 1964-68*, 13:374; memo SecState and SecDef for Pres, 28 May 66, ibid, 402-03 (quote); Bunn, *Arms Control by Committee*, 74.

40. Ltr McNamara to Rusk, 7 Jun 66, w/encl, *FRUS 1964-68*, 11:329-30; USACDA, *International Negotiations on the Treaty on the Nonproliferation of Nuclear Weapons*, 30 Dec 68, 33, 37; memo Keeny for Rostow, Dobrynin-Foster Meeting, 9 Jun 66, *FRUS 1964-68*, 11:333 (quote, emphasis in original); Poole, *JCS and National Policy, 1965-68*, pt 1:245-46 (quote); Record of mtg of Cte of Principals, 17 Jun 66, *FRUS 1964-68*, 11:339 (quote); JCSM-437-66 for SecDef, 29 Jun 66, fldr Treaty-Nonproliferation II – 1966a, box 8, Keeny Papers, NSF, LBJL; memo Keeny for Moyers, 17 Jun 66, fldr Cmte of Prins Mtg – 6/17/66 & follow-up Correspondence – Threshold Test Ban Treaty, box 3, ibid.

41. JCSM-437-66 for SecDef, 29 Jun 66, cited in note 40; Keeny, The Non-Proliferation Treaty, 4 (quote); Poole, *JCS and National Policy, 1965-68*, pt 1:246-47; ltr McNamara to Rusk, 5 Jul 66, fldr The Non Proliferation Treaty, vol II [#1-30], box 56, NSC History Non-Proliferation Treaty, NSF, LBJL; memo Foster for Moyers, 20 Jul 66, fldr Treaty Non-Proliferation II 1966a, box 8, Keeny Papers, NSF, LBJL.

42. For examples of the president's interest see News Conf, 5 Jul 66 and Remarks, 26 Aug 65, *Johnson Public Papers, 1966*, 2:710, 902. Two contemporary senior officials, Spurgeon Keeny and Glenn Seaborg, both credit Johnson's commitment to obtaining a treaty for its success. Keeny, The Non-Proliferation Treaty, 5; Seaborg, *Stemming the Tide*, 197; memos Rostow for Pres, 12 Aug 66 and 12 Aug 66, 6:00 p.m.: both Backup Materials as cited in note 2; Keeny, The Non-Proliferation Treaty, 3.

43. Memo Rostow for Pres, 2 Sep 66, *FRUS 1964-68*, 11:354-55; memo Foster for Rostow, 15 Sep 66 w/atchmt, memo Foster for Pres, 15 Sep 66, fldr The Non Proliferation Treaty, vol II [#61-80], box 56, NSC, NSF, LBJL.

44. Memo Rostow for Rusk, 3 Sep 66, Backup Material, as cited in note 2; see McNamara's marginalia on CM-1730-66 for SecDef, 7 Sep 66, fldr Southeast Asia Jul 66-Oct 66, box 35, Wheeler Papers, RG 218.

45. Memcons Rusk w/Gromyko, 22 and 24 Sep 66: *FRUS 1964-68*, 11:371-73 and 382, n 3(quotes); Keeny, The Non-Proliferation Treaty, 4-5 (quote).

46. Keeny, The Non-Proliferation Treaty, 1, 5; Joint Statement, Johnson and Erhard, 27 Sep 66, *Johnson Public Papers, 1966*, 2:1079; Johnson, *Vantage Point*, 478-79; Seaborg, *Stemming the Tide*, 192-93; Rostow, *Diffusion of Power*, 378; memrcd Rusk, Note on Pres Views on Non-proliferation, 3 Oct 66, fldr The Non-Proliferation Treaty, Vol II [#81-110], box 56, NSC History Non-Proliferation Treaty, NSF, LBJL; interv Eugene Rostow by Paige E. Mulhollan, 2 Dec 68, 1:15, AC 74-72, LBJL; "Control of Nuclear Proliferation," in Barton and Weiler, eds, *International Arms Control*, 299.

47. Memo McNaughton for SecDef, 15 Oct 66 and TAB A, Draft Article I of a Non-Proliferation Treaty, *FRUS 1964-68*, 11:395-96, and n 4 (quote); ltr J. Edgar Hoover to McNamara, 20 Oct 66 w/encl Soviet Personnel Intelligence Activities, 20 Oct 66, fldr Russia 1966 000.1, box 11, ISA Country Files, Acc 70A-6649 (quotes).

48. Seaborg, *Stemming the Tide*, 194-95; Bunn, *Arms Control by Committee*, 78-79; Johnson, *Vantage Point*, 479; ISA, Status of Arms Control Negotiations, 3 Jan 67, fldr Vol II NATO/MAP/Arms Control 1966-67, TAB C, box 91, McNamara Records, RG 200 (quote); Bunn, *Arms Control by Committee*, 79-80 (quote).

49. Msg CAP 67291, Rostow to Pres in Texas, 15 Apr 67, *FRUS 1964-68*, 11:475.

50. Memrcd 584th NSC mtg, 27 Mar 68, ibid, 558-59; Poole, *JCS and National Policy, 1965-68*, pt 1:250.

51. JCSM-269-65 for SecDef, 13 Apr 65, memo Bowman for Bundy, 16 Apr 65: fldr 1965, Strategic Arms 1, as cited in note 2; memo Foster for Cte of Principals, 12 Apr 65 w/atchmt, fldr Strategic Arms 2, ibid; Summary of Action, mtg of Cte of Principals, 22 Apr 65, fldr Cte of Principals, Vol 2 (2 of 2), box 14, Subject File, NSF, LBJL. The committee had discussed such a proposal the previous July, but had not as yet prepared a specific U.S. policy for a freeze; mtg of Cte of Principals, 23 Jul 64, *FRUS 1964-68*, 11:88-89.

52. ACDA History, 38; JCSM-633-65 for SecDef, 14 Aug 65, fldr 388.3 (2 Feb 65) (Dec-July), box 14, SecDef Subject Decimal files, Acc 70A-1265.

53. Draft memo Foster for Pres, 28 Dec 65, fldr 388.3 Jan 1966, box 7, ISA General files, Acc 70A-6649 quotes). The formal proposal sent to the president was dated 4 January 1966. Ltr Foster to McNamara, 3 Jan 66 w/atchmt, draft memo Foster for Pres, ibid; ltr McNaughton to Califano, 7 Jan 66, memo McNaughton for SecDef, 8(?) Jan 66, fldr Strategic Arms 2, as cited in note 2 (quotes); JCSM-14-66 for SecDef, 7 Jan 66, fldr 388.3 Jan 1966, box 7, ISA General Files, Acc 70A-6649. *Johnson Public Papers, 1966*, 1:8.

54. CM-1270-66 for SecDef, 17 Mar 66, fldr 1966 CM's 1227-66-1308-66, box 2 Wheeler Papers, RG 218; Poole, *JCS and National Policy, 1965-68*, pt 1:263; ACDA History, 58.

55. Strategic Delivery Systems Talks: Chronology, entries for 18 Mar 66 and 6 Dec 66, Backup Material as cited in note 2; memcon Thompson w/Dobrynin, 6 Dec 66, *FRUS 1964-68*, 11:405-06; Garthoff, "BMD and East-West Relations," in Carter and Schwartz, eds, *Ballistic Missile Defense*, 294-95.

56. Memo Keeny for Rostow, 2 May 66, Backup Material, as cited in note 2; memo Fisher for Pres, 2 May 66; *FRUS 1964-68*, 11:314-16; ACDA, Draft U.S. Proposal, ACDA-2595, 2 May 66; memos McNaughton for SecDef, 5 May 66; JCSM-311-66 for SecDef, 9 May 66; memo McNaughton for SecDef, 23 Jan 67 w/ atchd Chronology: fldr 388.3 (Sensitive), box 1, SecDef Sensitive files 1949-1969, Acc 330-91-001; ACDA History, 58-59.

57. JCSM-574-66 for SecDef, 10 Sep 66, fldr 388.3 Jan 1966, box 7, ISA General files, Acc 70A-6649; memo McNaughton for SecDef, 21 Sep 66, fldr 388.3 (Sensitive), box 1, SecDef Sensitive files, 1949-1969, Acc 330-91-0017. McNamara approved the ISA recommendation on 28 September. Memo McNaughton for SecDef, 2 Nov 66, fldr 471.6 TS Eyes Only 1966 Jan, box 8, ISA General files, Acc 70A-6649.

58. Memo McNaughton for SecDef, 16 Dec 66, fldr 388.3 (Sensitive) box 1, SecDef Sensitive files 1949-1969, Acc 330-91-0017.

59. JCSM-30-67 for SecDef, 19 Jan 67, *FRUS 1964 -68*, 11:427-28; memo Keeny for Rostow, 27 Jan 67, fldr Cmte of Principals Mtg 3/14/67 w/backup and follow-up on correspondence Freeze, box 2, Keeny Papers, NSF, LBJL; ltr Wheeler to Rostow, 14 Mar 67 w/atchmt, Talking Paper for CJCS, SAAC-T-3-67, 13 Mar 67, fldr Joint Chiefs of Staff, box 30, Agency Files: JCS, NSF, LBJL (quote).

60. Notes of mtg of Cte of Principals, 14 Mar 67, *FRUS 1964-68*, 11:466-67; Strategic Delivery System Talks Chronology, entry for 23 Mar 67, Backup Material as cited in note 2; msg 158191 State to Moscow, 18 Mar 67, *FRUS 1964-68*, 11, 468-69 (quote).

61. Memcon McNamara w/Dobrynin, 11 Apr 67, *FRUS 1964-68*, 11, 476; Strategic Delivery System Talks Chronology, entry for 24 Apr 67, Backup Material, as cited in note 2; Barton and Weiler, *International Arms Control*, 174; memo Warnke for SecDef, 26 Sep 67, fldr 388.3 (Sensitive), box 1, SecDef Sensitive files 1949-1969, Acc 330-91-0017.

62. Memo Garthoff for Keeny, 8 Sep 67, fldr 1967, Strategic Arms #1, Backup Material as cited in note 2; memo Keeny for Rostow, 6 Sep 67, *FRUS 1964-68*, 11:510-11; memo SecDef for CJCS, w/encl, 4 Oct 67, fldr Reading File Oct 10-2, 1967, box 131, McNamara Records, RG 200; JCSM-596-67 for SecDef, 2 Nov 67, fldr 091 Soviet Union (22 Aug 68), box 39, Wheeler Papers, RG 218 (quote).

63. Memo Warnke for SecDef, 27 Feb 68, fldr Kosygin-Talks with Soviet Union (3), box 22, Clifford Papers, LBJL (quote). In disapproving the memo on 14 March Nitze through whom the memo was routed wrote: "Hold for time being." Note Keeny to Rostow, 4 Mar 68, fldr 1968, Strategic Arms 1, as cited in note 2.

64. Memo Bohlen for Rusk, 5 Apr 68, Tab A, *FRUS 1964 -68*, 11:568-71; CM-3227-68 for SecDef, 22 Apr 68, fldr 091 Soviet Union (22 Apr 68), box 39, Wheeler Papers, RG 218 (quote); memo Warnke for SecDef, nd but likely 22 Apr 68, fldr Kosygin-talks with Soviet Union (1), box 22, Clifford Papers, LBJL (quote); memo Rostow for Pres, 23 Apr 68, *FRUS 1964 -68*, 11:584; memo Rusk for Pres, 26 Apr 68, fldr 1968, Strategic Arms 1, as cited in note 2; ltr Johnson for Kosygin, 2 May 68, fldr Kosygin (3), box 10, Files of Walt W. Rostow, NSF, LBJL. The option papers appear in *FRUS 1964 -68*, 11:568-71. The excerpt from Johnson's letter dealing with arms control appears ibid, 590-92. When forwarding Rusk's memo Rostow

recommended the president meet with both secretaries and General Wheeler before making any decision. It is unclear whether or not Mr. Johnson heeded his advice. Memo Rostow for Pres, 27 Apr 68, Backup Material, as cited in note 2.

65. Ltr Kosygin to Johnson, 12 May 68, fldr Strategic Arms 2, as cited in note 2; memo Rostow for Pres, 4 May 68 w/atchmt, Bundy memcon, 30 Apr 68, memo Rostow for Pres, 24 May 68 w/atchmt, Kissinger memcon, 17 May 68, Warnke memcon, 28 Jun 68: all fldr 1968, Strategic Arms 1, as cited in note 2; Barton and Weiler, *International Arms Control*, 174.

66. Ltr Kosygin to Johnson, 21 Jun 68, *FRUS 1964-68*, 11:623 (quote); ltr Johnson to Kosygin, 22 Jun 68, ibid, 623-24; ltr Kosygin to Johnson, 27 Jun 68, ibid, 624; *New York Times*, 28 Jun 68; mins of SecDef Staff mtg, 1 Jul 68, fldr Minutes of SecDef Staff Mtgs Mar-Dec 68, box 18, Clifford Papers, LBJL.

67. Ltr Kosygin to Johnson, 27 Jun 68 and ed note, *FRUS 1964-68*, 11:624-25 (quote); memo Rostow for Pres, 27 Jun 68, fldr 1968, Strategic Arms 1, as cited in note 2; Nitze, *From Hiroshima to Glasnost*, 290-91.

68. Seaborg, *Stemming the Tide*, 407, 436 (quote); JCSM-272-68 for SecDef, 27 Apr 68, App; record of mtg of the Cte of Principals, 14 May 68:*FRUS 1964-68*, 11:588-89, 593-94; record of mtg of the Cte of Principals, 3 Jun 68, ibid, 609-10 (quote).

69. Memo Warnke for SecDef, 4 Jul 68, fldr Kosygin-Talks with Soviet Union (1), box 22, Clifford Papers, LBJL.

70. Seaborg, *Stemming the Tide*, 432-35; record of mtg of Exec Cte of the Cte of Principals, 8 Jul 68, *FRUS 1964 -68*, 11:633-37.

71. Newhouse, *Cold Dawn*, 112-19 has a detailed description of the committee's work. Poole, *JCS and National Policy, 1965-68*, pt 1:275.

72. Summary of mtg of Working Grp on Strategic Missile Talks, 10 Jul 68, *FRUS 1964-68*, 11:638; Newhouse, *Cold Dawn*, 119 (quote), 121; ltr Kosygin to Johnson, 25 Jul 68, *FRUS 1964-68*, 11:652 (quote); ltr Johnson to Kosygin, 30 Jul 68, ibid, 658; paper prepared by Interagency Working Group, 31 Jul 68, ibid, 659-61(quote); ACDA History, 173-74.

73. Memo DepSecDef for CJCS, 2 Aug 68 w/encl DPM, Proposal for Limiting Strategic Offensive and Defensive Systems, nd, fldr Kosygin-Talks with Soviet Union (3), box 22, Clifford Papers, LBJL.

74. JCSM-498-68 for SecDef, 9 Aug 68, fldr Kosygin – Talks with Soviet Union (2), ibid (quote); memo Halprin for SecDef, 6 Aug 68 (?), w/atchmt, Systems Analysis, Analysis of State/ACDA Proposal, fldr USSR 338.3, Misc Source Materials, 1945-1970, box 26 Strategic Arms Competition, OSD Hist; notes of mtgs, 7 Aug 68, *FRUS 1964-68*, 11:663-64.

75. JCSM-498-68 for SecDef, 9 Aug 68, cited in note 74; CM-3572-68 for SecDef, 9 Aug 68, fldr Kosygin-talks with Soviet Union (2), box 22, Clifford Papers, LBJL (quote); Poole, *JCS and National Policy, 1965-68*, pt 1:278-79.

76. JCSM-498-68 for SecDef, 9 Aug 68, cited in note 74; Paper Approved by the Exec Cte of Cte of Principals, 14 Aug 68, *FRUS 1964-68*, 11:675-76; see also Newhouse, *Cold Dawn*, 128-29; memo Clifford for Pres, 13 Aug 68, *FRUS 1964-68*, 11:669; paper prepared by the Interagency Working Group, 31 Jul 68, ibid, 659-61; memo Keeny for Rostow, ibid, 666-67; memo DepSecDef for CJCS, 2 Aug 68, cited in note 73; Seaborg, *Stemming the Tide*, 436-37 (quote).

77. Memo Rostow for Pres, 24 Jul 68, *FRUS 1964-68*, 11:651; CM-3549-68, memrcd Wheeler conv w/Dobrynin, 5 Aug 68, ibid, 662; memo Smith for Pres, 8 Aug 68, fldr 1968, Strategic Arms 1, as cited in note 2; memcon Rusk w/Dobrynin, 15 Aug 68, *FRUS 1964-68*, 11:686-87; memo Keeny for Rostow, 12 Aug 68, ibid, 667; *Baltimore Sun*, 17 Aug 68.

78. Msg CAP 82080 Rostow to Pres in Texas, 19 Aug 68, *FRUS 1964-68*, 11:681; msg Kosygin to Johnson, 20 Aug 68, ibid, 682; memos Rostow for Pres, 20 Aug 68 and Rostow for Rusk w/atchd briefing notes, 20 Aug 68, Backup Material as cited in note 2; ACDA 2951/Rev 3, Strategic Missile Talks, 20 Aug 68, fldr Cte of Principals, vol 4 (1 of 2), box 14, Subject File: Disarmament, NSF, LBJL; ed note, *FRUS 1964-68*, 11:690; Tom Johnson, Notes of Emergency NSC mtg, 20 Aug 68, ibid, 17:244; see also Mastny, "Was 1968 a Strategic Watershed,"166.

79. Elsey notes of SecDef Morning Staff Conf, 23 Aug 68, fldr VanDeMark Transcripts, box 1, Elsey Papers, LBJL; memo Rostow for Pres, 29 Aug 68, *FRUS 1964-68*, 11:699-700; memo Warnke for SecDef, 21 Aug 68, fldr USSR (Sensitive) 1968, box 5, SecDef Sensitive files 1949-1969, Acc 330-91-0017.

80. Smith summary notes of 594th NSC mtg, 25 Nov 68, *FRUS 1964-68*, 11:739-42; msg CAP 82219 Smith to Pres in Texas, 28 Aug 68, ibid, 14:690.

81. Summary notes of 590th NSC mtg, 4 Sep 68, ibid, 17:273, 277; memo Rostow for Pres, 4 Sep 68, fldr 1968, Strategic Arms 1, as cited in note 2.

82. Instr for Thompson, 5 Sep 68, *FRUS 1964-68*, 14:691(quote); ed note, ibid, 11:716 (quote); memo Rostow for Pres, 9 Sep 68, w/atchmt, Six Points paper, ibid, 14:694-95; memo SecDef for CJCS, 10 Sep 68, fldr 388.3 Sensitive 1968, box 5, SecDef Sensitive files, 1949-1969, Acc 330-91-0017.

83. Draft msg State to US NATO, 6 Sep 68, CM-3642-68 for SecDef, 10 Sep 68, memo ISA for SecDef, 12 Sep 68, memo SecDef for CJCS, 12 Sep 68 (quotes): all fldr USSR 388.3, box 26, Misc Source Materials 1945-1970, Strategic Arms Competition, OSD Hist.

84. Memo Rostow for Pres, 13 Sep 68 w/atchmt, Copy of Dobrynin's handwritten paper, Backup Material as cited in note 2. A copy of Dobrynin's note is also available in *FRUS 1964-68*, 11:717-18. Memo Govt of U.S. to Govt of USSR, 16 Sep 68, ibid, 718-19; memo Rostow for Pres, 16 Sep 68, 8:10 p.m., ibid, 14:711-14; Elsey notes of SecDef Morning Staff Conf, 16 Sep 68, fldr VanDeMark Transcripts, box 1, Elsey Papers, LBJL. Emphasis in original.

85. Msg Govt of USSR to Govt of U.S., nd, *FRUS 1964-68*, 11:725-26; memo Rostow for Pres, 4 Oct 68, ibid, 14:735; Elsey notes of SecDef Morning Staff Conf, 2 Oct 68 (quote), 4 Oct 68 (quote) and 9 Nov 68, as cited in note 84.

86. Memo Rostow for Pres, 12 Nov 68 w/atchmt, msg 6409 Moscow to State, 11 Nov 68, fldr 1968, Strategic Arms #1, as cited in note 2; see also Newhouse, *Cold Dawn*, 135-36; Seaborg, *Stemming the Tide*, 439-40; memo Rostow for Pres, 20 Nov 68, FRUS 1964-68, 14:757-58; Johnson, Vantage Point, 489-90.

87. Memo telcon Thompson and Rusk, 29 Nov 68, *FRUS 1964-1968*, 11:742-43; Johnson, *Vantage Point*, 490.

88. Elsey notes of SecDef Morning Staff Conf, 3 Dec 68, as cited in note 84; SecDef Statement, The FY 1970-74 Defense Program and 1970 Defense Budget, 15 Jan 69, *Clifford Public Statements, 1968*, 4:1112; memo SecDef for Pres, 2 Dec 68, *FRUS 1964-68*, 11:744-47 (quotes). See also Clifford's remarks in Notes of Foreign Policy mtg, 26 Nov 68, ibid, 14:764-65; memo Rostow for Pres, 11 Dec 68, ibid, 11:757 (quote); memo Rostow for Pres, 11 Dec 68, 9:55 a.m., ibid, 14:780, note 2 (quote); Johnson, *Vantage Point*, 490; interv SecDef on "Face the Nation," 15 Dec 68, *Clifford Public Statements, 1968*, 4:1056 (quote).

89. Memrcd Clarke, 7 Feb 69 w/atchmt, draft memo Clifford for Pres, Strategic Missile Discussions with the Soviet Union, 21 Dec 68, fldr USSR 388.3 Sensitive 1968, box 5, SecDef Sensitive files 1949-1969, Acc 330-91-0017.

XIII. ABM: CENTERPIECE OF STRATEGIC DEFENSE

1. SecDef Statement before HCAS on the FY 1966-70 Defense Program and 1966 Defense Budget, 2 Feb 65, 93, box 4, SecDef Statements 1965-66 for FYs 1966-67, OSD Hist.

2. "History of the Strategic Arms Competition 1945-1972," pt 2:521, Mar 81, OSD Hist, (hereafter "Strategic Arms," pt 2); USAF, ACS, Studies and Analysis, "A Review of Draft Presidential Memoranda on Strategic Offensive and Defensive Forces 1961-1968," 1 May 69, 15-16, fldr Miscellaneous Memoranda and Reports, box 870, Subj files, OSD Hist; DPM SecDef for Pres, Recommended FY 1966-1970 Programs for Strategic Offensive Forces, Continental Air and Missile Defense Force, and Civil Defense, 5 Nov 64, fldr D Memo to Pres - SUBJ: Recom FY 66-70 Programs for Strategic Retaliatory Forces, Cont. Air & Miss Def Forces & Civ Def, 3 Nov 64, box 118, ASD(C) files, OSD Hist; DPM SecDef for Pres, Recommended FY 1967-71 Strategic Offensive and Defensive Forces, 1 Nov 65, fldr Memos for Pres. CY 1965 Budget FY 1967, box 119, ibid.

3. "Strategic Arms," pt, 2:630; Holloway, *The Soviet Union and the Arms Race*, 44.

4. Enthoven and Smith, *How Much Is Enough*, 175-76 has a concise description of this phenomenon. HQ, USAF, "Air Force Project *Blue Lance*—Interrelationships Between Strategic Offensive and Defensive Forces," 15 Dec 65, 197-98, box 679, Subj files, OSD Hist. Hereafter cited as *Blue Lance*.

5. Enthoven and Smith, *How Much Is Enough*, 184; DDRE, A Summary Study of Strategic Offensive and Defensive Forces of the U.S. and USSR, 8 Sep 64, 120-21, box 39, Strategic Arms Competition, OSD Hist; "Strategic Arms," pt 2:522, 552-53; Worden, *SDI and the Alternatives*, 47-48.

6. *Blue Lance*, 203; ltr Kaysen to Bundy, 25 Oct 63, Backup Material, Strategic Arms, OSD Hist (quote). Kaysen served as Deputy Special Assistant to President Kennedy under McGeorge Bundy, the Special Assistant to the President. Memo Smith for Bundy, 6 Feb 64, ibid.

7. USAF, Review of Draft Presidential Memoranda, 1 May 69, 18, cited in note 2.

8. Hanson W. Baldwin in *New York Times*, 12 Oct 64; memo DepSecDef for Pres, 14 Dec 64, fldr 1964, fldr Strategic Arms I, Backup Material, Strategic Arms, OSD Hist.

9. SecDef Statement, 2 Feb, 65, 43, cited in note 1.

10. Ibid, 70-75, 93; DPM, 5 Nov 64, cited in note 2.

11. SecDef Statement, 2 Feb 65, 76-80, cited in note 1.

12. Ibid, 83-86; memrcd Bowman, mtg on 27 May 1965, 2 Jun 65, fldr Goodpaster Chron Files (Jan 65), box 141, Wheeler Papers, RG 218.

13. Transc McNamara test, for HSCA, 4 Mar 65, 2462-66, fldr SecDef Transcript, box 39, ASD(C) files, OSD Hist; McNamara test, 5 Mar 65, HSCA, *Hearings: Department of Defense Appropriations for 1966*, pt 3:355; memcon Beam, 12 Aug 64, *FRUS 1964-68*, 11:93-94, (quote).

14. Kaplan et al, *McNamara Ascendancy*, 29-35.

15. *Hearings*, cited in note 13, 359; SecDef statement, 2 Feb 65, 87, cited in note 1; "Draft Administrative History of the Department of Defense, 1963-1969," 1:321, OSD Hist.

16. McNamara test, 24 Feb 65, SCAS and Subcte on DoD of SCA, *Hearings: Military Procurement Authorizations, Fiscal Year 1966*, Table 2, 207; McNamara test, 14 Feb 66, HSCA, *Hearings: Department of Defense Appropriations, 1967*, pt 1:122-23; Yoshpe, "Our Missing Shield," FEMA, 1981, 380-89.

17. SecDef statement, 2 Feb, 65, 52, cited in note 1; transc McNamara test, 3 Mar 65, 2368, cited in note 13 (quote).

18. DDRE, Summary Study, 8 Sep 64, cited in note 5; memo SecDef for SecA et al, 27 Jan 65 in *Blue Lance*, atchmt 2, 215-17; ibid, 15; "Strategic Arms," pt 2:830; Taylor, "Wohlstetter, Soviet Strategic Forces, and National Intelligence Estimates,"1-8.

19. Taylor, "Wohlstetter," 1, 7; NIE 11-8-65, 7 Oct 65; NIE-11-8-66, 20 Oct 66, *FRUS 1964-68*, 10:264, 440.

20. "Strategic Arms," pt 2:660; memcon Harriman w/Kosygin, 21 Jul 65, *FRUS 1964-68*, 11:222-23.

21. Memo SecDef for SecA, 9 July 65; memo SecA for SecDef, 21 Jul 65, w/encl: fldr 381 SRF (19 Jan 65) July thru 1965, box 14, SecDef Subject Decimal files, Acc 70A-1265.

22. Memo SecA for SecDef, 30 Sep 65 w/encl DEPEX Study, 1 Oct 65, fldr SRF (9 Jan 65) X-5669 DEPEX Study, ibid; memo SecDef for DDRE, 22 Oct 65, *FRUS 1964-68*, 10:272-73; memo SecDef for SecA, 14 Jan 66, fldr Reading File Jan 66, box 124, McNamara Records, RG-200.

23. Strategic Military Panel of Pres Science Adv Cte, Report on the Proposed Army-BTL BMD System, 29 Oct 65, *FRUS 1964-68*, 10:273-82; memo Foster for SecDef, 25 Oct 65, fldr 381 SRF (9 Jun 65) thru 1965, box 14, SecDef Subject Decimal files, Acc 70A-1265; JCSM-807-65 for SecDef, 6 Nov 65, *FRUS 1964-68*, 10:322-24 (quotes).

24. OASD, Systems Analysis, A Review of the Adequacy of the Approved Forces for Assured Destruction, nd likely Oct 65, fldr DPM to Pres. Subject. Recom FY 67-71 Prgms F. Strategic Ret Frcs, Cont Air & Miss Def Forces & Civil Defense, FY 1967 Budget, box 49, ASD(C) files, OSD Hist; DPM SecDef for Pres, Recommended FY 1967-71 Strategic Offensive and Defensive Forces, 1 Nov 65, *FRUS 1964-68*, 10:284-85.

25. *FRUS 1964-68*, 10:285, 317; "Strategic Arms," pt 2:584; York, *Making Weapons, Talking Peace*, 224; Greenwood, Making the *MIRV*, 1.

26. Memo Keeny for Bundy, 9 Nov 65, Backup Material, Strategic Arms, OSD Hist; memo Enthoven for Hoffman and Murray, 9 Nov 65, fldr DoD/BoB FY 1967 Budget Meetings, FY 1967 Budget, box 49, ASD(C) files, OSD Hist; DPM, 1 Nov 65, *FRUS 1964-68*, 10:285.

27. DPM SecDef for Pres, 5 Nov 64, cited in note 2; DPM SecDef for Pres, 1 Nov 65, *FRUS 1964-68*, 10:285, 298, 317.

28. Memo SecDef for Pres, Defense Department Budget Issues for FY 1967 and Supplemental Appropriation for FY 1966, 9 Dec 65, fldr 1965, Strategic Arms 1, Backup Material, OSD Hist; DPM, 1 Nov 65, *FRUS 1964-68*, 10:285, 296.

29. BoB Agenda, mtg w/SecDef, 9 Dec 65, fldr DoD/BoB FY 1967 Budget Meetings, box 49 ASD(C) files, OSD Hist; memo SecDef for Pres, 9 Dec 65, cited in note 28.

30. DoD News Release 887-65, 8 Dec 65, *McNamara Public Statements, 1965*, 5:2210; SecDef News Conf, 10 Dec 65, ibid, 2233-35.

31. McNamara test, 25 Jan 66, House Subcte No 2, HCAS, *Hearing: Department of Defense Decision to Reduce the Number and Types of Manned Bombers in the Strategic Air Command*, 6084.

32. Transc McNamara test 25 Jan 66 for HCAS, SubCte No. 2, Exec Sess, *Hearings*, 25 Jan 66, 2, fldr McNamara Statement Before Hébert Cte on AMSA Jan 25, 1966, FY 1967 Budget, box 56, ASD(C) files, OSD Hist; *Cong Rec*, 12 Jan 66, 112-14.

33. *Hearing*, cited in note 31, 6090-91; memo Glass for SecDef, 10 Mar 66, fldr Hébert Subcommittee - Jan 25, 1966 - AMSA, FY 1967 Budget, box 56, ASD(C) files, OSD Hist; press release, Hébert, 26 Apr 66, ibid; *New York Times*, 24 and 25 Apr 66; News conf, 25 Apr 66, *McNamara Public Statements, 1966*, 6:2231(quote).

34. Ltr Wheeler to Hébert, 9 May 66, fldr Hébert Subcommittee, as cited in note 33; press release, Hébert, 12 May 66, ibid; SecDef press conf, 12 May 66, *McNamara Public Statements, 1966*, 6:2271-73, 2275 (quote); *Washington Post*, 15 May 66 (quote).

35. Gunston, *F-111*, 88; *Washington Post*, 20 Mar 69. In 1969 FB-111 production was cut to 76 aircraft, the new Republican defense secretary Melvin Laird justifying the cut on the grounds that the expensive FB-111 did not meet the requirements for an intercontinental bomber. To complete the circle, Laird declared that

because rising per unit cost of the FB-111 made an AMSA again feasible, he intended to use the FB-111 savings to help pay for a reinvigorated advanced bomber program.

36. Holston, Talking Paper: Nike-X, 8 Dec 65, box 10, fldr Tab 37, file 031.1 President Jul 64-Oct 67, Wheeler Papers, RG 218.

37. Memo SecDef for Pres, 9 Dec 65, cited in note 28; SecDef statement Before HCA on the FY 1967-71 Defense Program and the 1967 Budget, (Classified Version), 14 Feb 66, 93, box 4, SecDef Statements 1965-1966 FYs 1966-67, OSD Hist; DPM SecDef for Pres, 1 Nov 65, *FRUS 1964-1968*, 10:318; BoB Agenda mtg w/SecDef, 9 Dec 65, cited in note 29.

38. SecDef Statement, 14 Feb 66, 70, 92, cited in n 37; Poole, *JCS and National Policy, 1965-68*, 9, pt 1:213-14; McNamara test, 7 Mar 66, JCAE, *Hearings: S. Res. 179 Nonproliferation of Nuclear Weapons*, 99-100 (quote).

39. DPM SecDef for Pres, 9 Nov 66, fldr FY 1968 DPMs, box 120, ASD(C) files, OSD Hist.

40. SecDef Statement Before Jt Sess of SCAS and Senate Subcte on DoD Appros on the FY 1968-72 Defense Program and the 1968 Defense Budget, (Classified Version), 23 Jan 67, 44, 46, 49-51, box 5, SecDef Statements 1966-67 FYs 1967-68, OSD Hist; NIE 11-3-65, 18 Nov 65, NIE 11-3-66, 17 Nov 66, memo Rostow for Pres, 22 Dec 66: *FRUS 1964-68*, 10:331, 447-49, 509; SecDef statement, 14 Feb 66, 59-60, cited in note 37; memo Keeny for Rostow, 31 May 66, *FRUS 1964-68*, 10:402-03.

41. Transc Foster test, 3 Mar 67, for HCAS, Hearings on FY 1968 Antiballistic Missile, Exec Sess, 121, fldr Sec'y McNamara-Gen Wheeler - House Armed Services 3/3/67, FY 1968 Budget, box 65, ASD(C) files, OSD Hist; transc McNamara test, 25 Feb 66, for SCAS and SSCA, Hearings on Military Authorizations and Defense Appros for FY 1967, 25 Feb 66, insert to page 187, fldr Sec McNamara testimony Sen Armed Serv & Sen Appro Ctes - Feb 25, 1966 Morning Session, FY 1967 Budget, box 51, ibid. It was only on 9 August 1968 that the United States obtained the first telemetry from a Galosh in powered flight; Tauss, "An Endangered Intelligence Tool," 7. An example of media hyperbole appears in the headline "70 Million Lives at Stake: Developing Issue in Defense," *U.S. News and World Report*, 23 May 66, 48-52; McNamara test, 3 Mar 67, HCAS, *Hearings: Military Posture and A Bill (H.R. 9240)*, 430 (quote); McNamara test, 15 Feb 66, HSCA, *Hearings: Department of Defense Appropriations for 1967*, pt 1:115. McNamara in turn had previously criticized Congress and the public for rejecting what he termed a more important and cheaper defensive measure—to build a national fallout shelter system. McNamara test, 14 Feb 66, ibid, 87.

42. McNamara test, 8 Mar 66, HCAS, *Hearings: Military Posture and H.R. 13456*, 7327; McNamara test, 14 Feb 66, cited in note 41, 61-62; Jayne, "The ABM Debate," Ph.D. diss. MIT, 1969, 279-80; DPM SecDef for Pres, 22 Dec 66, *FRUS 1964-68*, 10:484, 491-92.

43. DPM SecDef for Pres, 9 Nov 66, 20, cited in note 39; Foster test, 6 Apr 66, HSCA, *Hearings: DoD Appropriations for 1967*, pt 5:32-33, 37, 40.

44. Seaborg, *Stemming the Tide*, 414-15; Strategic Arms, 2:563-64 (quote); Newhouse, *Cold Dawn*, 84-85; Greenwood, *Making the MIRV*, 76; Halperin, "The Decision to Deploy the ABM," 75-76; PRC Statements, 9 May 66 and 27 Oct 66, *AFP, CD, 1966*, 666, 676.

45. Memo DDRE for SecDef, 30 Sep 66 w/atchmt, memo Dir Systems Analysis for SecDef, 30 Dec 66: fldr Russia 0-800, box 5, SecDef Subject Decimal files, Acc 70-A-4662. The quote is from McNamara's notations on Foster's memo. OAD/DS/DDR&E, Ballistic Missile Defense - 1966, 19 Nov 66, fldr ABM Memo (McNamara Markup) (TS) 1/12/67, box 103, ASD(C) files, OSD Hist (quote).

46. SCAS, *Authorizing Appropriations During Fiscal Year 1967 for Procurement of Aircraft, Missiles, Naval Vessels, and Tracked Combat Vehicles, and Research Development, Test, and Evaluation for the Armed Forces*, S Rpt No 1136, 25 Apr 66, 4-5 (quote); PL 89-687, 15 Oct 66, (80 Stat 986); HCAS, *Authorizing Defense Procurement and Research and Development, and Military Pay*, H Rpt No 1536, 16 May 66, 18-19; SCAS, *Authorizing Appropriations During Fiscal Year 1968 for Procurement of Aircraft, Missiles, Naval Vessels, and Tracked Combat Vehicles, and Research Development, Test, and Evaluation for the Armed Forces*, S Rpt No 76, 20 Mar 67, 4; Shapley, *Promise and Power*, 107; tel interv Robert S. McNamara by Edward J. Drea, 6 Mar 2000, OSD Hist.

47. DPM SecDef for Pres, 9 Nov 66, 20-21, cited in note 39.

48. News conf, 10 Nov 66, *McNamara Public Statements, 1966*, 7:2751; *Washington Star*, 11 Nov 66; memos Hughes for SecState, 10 Jan, 1 Mar 67: fldr Strategic Arms 2, Backup Material, Strategic Arms, OSD Hist.

49. Memo Meier for Glass, 1 Feb 67, fldr SecDef Transcripts - Senate Armed Serv & Senate Cte on Appro - 1968 Budget - 1/27/67, Glass Master, box 66, ASD(C) files, OSD Hist; memcon, Wheeler and SecDef, 21 Nov 66, fldr 091 Soviet Union (thru 31 Dec 68), box 39, Wheeler Papers, RG 218 (quotes); "Strategic Arms," pt 2:564, n; DDR&E Comments on Systems Analysis Nike-X Paper, nd but after 18 Nov 66, fldr ABM 1967, box 104, ASD(C) files, OSD Hist; OASD Systems Analysis, Objectives/Should We Decide

Now to Deploy ABM?, 18 Nov 66, draft, fldr Memo for the Pres. Production & Deployment of Nike-X (ABM) Dec 66 - File #2, box 103, ibid; OAD/DS/DDR&E, Ballistic Missile Defense - 1966, 19 Nov 66, draft, fldr 471.94 ABM (Nov & Dec) 1966, box 16, SecDef Subject Decimal files, Acc 70-A-4662.

50.   Memo SecDef for Pres, 28 Nov 66 Draft, fldr Memo for the Pres. Production & Deployment of Nike-X (ABM) Dec. 1966 - File #1, box 103, ASD(C) files, OSD Hist; McNamara tel interv, 6 Mar 2000; DPM SecDef for Pres, 3 Dec 66, DoD Budget for FY 1968 and Supplemental Appropriation for FY 1967, w/ atch Summary of JCS Recommendations, fldr LBJ-Arms Control, box 6, Rearden Study files, OSD Hist.

51.   Memo SecA for SecDef, 1 Dec 66, JCSM-742-66 for SecDef, 2 Dec 66 (quote): fldr 471.94 ABM, box 16, SecDef Subject Decimal files, 70-A-4662; memo CNO for SecN, 30 Nov 66, fldr TS Sensitive memos org by 00-1966, box 86, Double Zero-1967 TS/Sensitive 1963-1968, NHC (quote).

52.   Memrcd CMC, Special SecDef/JCS Meeting at 1130 re Budget, 2 Dec 66, Greene Papers, MHC (quote); Shapley, *Promise and Power*, 390.

53.   JCSM-742-66 for SecDef, 2 Dec 66, cited in note 51 (quote); DPM SecDef for Pres, 2 Dec 66 Draft, fldr Memo for the Pres, Production & Deployment of Nike-X (ABM) Dec. 1966 - File #1, box 103, ASD(C) files, OSD Hist; memo SecDef for Pres, 5 Dec 66, fldr LBJ-Arms Control, box 6, Rearden Study files, OSD Hist; ltr AsstSecA to DepSecDef, 2 Dec 66, fldr 471.94 ABM, box 16, SecDef Subject Decimal files, Acc 70-A-4662.

54.   DPM SecDef for Pres, 3 Dec 66, cited in note 50; JCS(?) Paper, 10 Dec 66 (?), fldr 471.94 ABM, box 16, SecDef Subject Decimal files, Acc 70-A-4662 (quote); JCSM-791-66 for SecDef, 29 Dec 66, fldr 471.6, 29 Dec 1966, box 8, ISA General files, Acc 70-A-4649; McNamara tel interv, 6 Mar 2000.

55.   There are multiple versions of the meeting. I have relied primarily on Draft Notes on mtg w/Pres in Austin, Texas, 6 Dec 66 w/Sec McNamara and JCS, 10 Dec 66, *FRUS 1964-68*, 10:459-464 (quotes) and supplemented that record with interv Robert S. McNamara by Walt W. Rostow, 8 Jan 75, 70-72, LBJL; McNamara tel interv, 6 Mar 2000, OSD Hist; Halperin, "The Decision to Deploy the ABM," 84-85; and Shapley, *Promise and Power*, 391.

56.   Draft Notes on mtg, 6 Dec 66, cited in note 55 (quote); *FRUS 1964-68*, 11:406, n 4; McNamara tel interv 6 Mar 2000.

57.   Strategic Delivery System Talks: Chronology, nd but after Feb 1968, entry for 6 Dec 66, Backup Material, Strategic Arms, OSD Hist; memcon Thompson and Dobrynin, 7 Dec 66, *FRUS 1964-68*, 11:405-07.

58.   Statement by DepUnderSecState Kohler re Possible Soviet Reaction to U.S. Deployment of ABM'S, 10 Dec 66, fldr 471.94 ABM, box 16, SecDef Subject Decimal files, Acc 70-A-4662; Rostow, *The Diffusion of Power*, 387; memos Katzenbach for Rostow, 10 Dec 66, Thompson for Rostow, 10 Dec 66, Helms to Rostow, 10 Dec 66 w/atchmt, Sherman Kent, Soviet Reactions to a US Decision to Deploy ABM Defenses, 10 Dec 66, *FRUS 1964-68*, 11:407-17 (quote, 411).

59.   Memo Hornig for W. Rostow, 10 Dec 66, *FRUS 1964-68*, 10:476-78; memrcd Rostow, 10 Dec 66, ibid, 10:479.

60.   Memo Vance for Pres, 10 Dec 66, ibid, 10:474-76.

61.   McNamara tel interv, 6 Mar 2000; DPM SecDef for Pres, 10 Dec 66 Draft, fldr Memo for the Pres. Production & Deployment of Nike-X (ABM) Dec. 1966 - File #1, box 103, ASD(C) files, OSD Hist; DPM SecDef for Pres, Production and Deployment of the Nike-X, 22 Dec 66, JCSM-804-66 for SecDef, 29 Dec 66: *FRUS 1964-68*, 10:508-11.

62.   York, *Making Weapons*, 225; CMC Work Notes on Special JCS Meeting No 164, 22 Dec 66, Greene Papers, MHC; Cahn, "Scientists and the ABM," Ph. D. diss. MIT, 1971, 37; McNamara tel interv, 6 Mar 2000; OSD paper, Distribution of ABM Memo to President Dated December 22, 1966, nd, fldr Reading File Dec 29-9, 1966, box 127, McNamara Records, RG-200.

63.   CMC Work Notes, 22 Dec 66, cited in note 62; memrcd ACMC, mtg of JCS w/Pres on 4 Jan 67, 10 Jan 67, Greene Papers, MHC; Rostow, rcd of mtg w/Pres on 4 Jan 67, 6 Jan 67, *FRUS 1964-68*, 10:526-31(quotes); McNamara notes, 4 Jan 67, fldr ABM Memo of JCS View, box 68, McNamara Records, RG-200; Poole, *JCS and National Policy, 1965-68*, pt 1:95-96; telcon McNamara and Johnson, 4 Jan 67, ed note, *FRUS 1964-68*, 10:531-32.

64.   DPM SecDef for Pres, 4 Jan 67 Draft (revised 17 Jan 67), fldr Memo for the Pres, Production & Deployment of Nike-X (ABM) Dec. 1966 - File #1, box 103, ASD(C) files, OSD Hist; *Johnson Public Papers, 1967*, 1:11 (quote).

65.   Msg 118864 State to Moscow, 14 Jan 67, fldr Strategic Arms 2, Backup Material, Strategic Arms, OSD Hist; Strategic Delivery System Talks, entry for 14 Jan 67, ibid.

66.   Memcon Rusk and Dobrynin, 18 Jan 67, *FRUS 1964-68*, 11:424-25; msg 121549 State to Moscow, 19 Jan 67, fldr USSR Cables, vol XIV 1/67-3/67, box 223, NSF, Russia, LBJL; Dobrynin, *In Confidence*,

150; memo Moose for Rostow, 11 Jan 67, fldr 1967, Strategic Arms 1, Backup Material, Strategic Arms, OSD Hist; *Johnson Public Papers, 1967,* 1:48; Garthoff, "BMD and East-West Relations," in Carter and Schwartz, eds, *Ballistic Missile Defense*, 281 (quote).

67. Ltr Johnson to Kosygin, 21 Jan 67, *FRUS 1964-68*, 11:431; Johnson, *Vantage Point*, 479-80; ltr Kohler for Rostow, 1 Mar 67, fldr Strategic Arms 2, Backup Material, Strategic Arms, OSD Hist; Dobrynin, *In Confidence*, 150 (quote); msg 3560 Moscow to State, 18 Feb 67, *FRUS 1964-68*, 11:443 (quote).

68. Memo Kohler for Acting SecState, 15 Feb 67, fldr 1967, Strategic Arms 1, Backup Material, Strategic Arms, OSD Hist (quote); memo Rostow for Pres, 18 Feb 67, ibid (quote).

69. Ltr Kosygin to Johnson, 27 Feb 67, Oral Statement Delivered to Thompson, 28 Feb 67, *FRUS 1964-68*, 11:450-52 (quotes); msg 3674 Moscow to State, 28 Feb 67, fldr Strategic Arms 2, Backup Material, Strategic Arms, OSD Hist; Seaborg, *Stemming the Tide*, 417.

70. Rostow, *Diffusion of Power*, 389; notes on mtg of Principals, 14 Mar 67, *FRUS 1964-68*, 11:467. See also memo Keeny for Rostow, 10 Mar 67, fldr Cte of Principals, vol 4, box 14, NSF Subject File: Disarmament, LBJL; memo Rostow for Pres, 17 Mar 67, Backup Material, Strategic Arms, OSD Hist; msg 158191 State to Moscow, 18 Mar 67, *FRUS 1964-68*, 11:468-70.

71. Transc McNamara test, 3 Mar 67, for HCAS Hearings on Posture (Antiballistic Missile) Hearings, Exec Sess, 133-34, fldr Sec'y McNamara-Gen Wheeler - House Armed Services 3/3/67, box 65, ASD(C) files, OSD Hist.

72. Msg CAP 67291, Rostow to Pres, 15 Apr 67, *FRUS 1964-68*, 11:476; Dobrynin, *In Confidence*, 151; Johnson, *Vantage Point*, 480; ltr Johnson to Kosygin, 19 May 67, *FRUS 1964-68*, 14:485-87. The letter was forwarded to Kosygin on 22 May.

73. Memo SecDef for Pres, 21 Jun 67, *FRUS 1964-68*, 14:497-98.

74. Memo Rostow for Pres, 21 Jun 67, ibid, 500-02.

75. Dobrynin, *In Confidence*, 165-66; Shapley, *Promise and Power*, 393; memcon Bundy and Dobrynin, 26 Apr 68, *FRUS 1964-68*, 14:645-46; President's Daily Diary, 23 Jun 67, 9-12, Electronic Copy, LBJL; memcon Johnson and Kosygin, Glassboro, N.J., 23 Jun 67, 1:30-3:10 p.m., *FRUS 1964-68*, 14:529(quote); Dobrynin, *In Confidence*, 165; Johnson, *Vantage Point*, 484-85; debriefing by Pres on his talks w/Kosygin, morning of June 23, 1967, at Hollybush, Glassboro State College, Glassboro, New Jersey, nd, doc. no. CK3100066713, Declassified Documents Reference System, *http://galenet.galegroup.com*; Gard notes, SecDef Monday A.M. Staff mtg, 26 Jun 67, Gard Notebook, OSD Hist.

76. Johnson, *Vantage Point*, 485; Shapley, *Promise and Power*, 393-94; Gard notes, 26 Jun 67, cited in note 75; Herken, *Counsels of War*, 197 (quote); Seaborg, *Stemming the Tide*, 430. Recent scholarship tends to confirm Rusk's and McNamara's impression; see Brands, "Progress Unseen," 279; memcon Bundy and Dobrynin, 26 Apr 68, cited in note 75; Gard, SecDef staff mtg, 5 Jul 67, Gard Notebook, OSD Hist; McNamara, Points for Inclusion in San Francisco Speech on Strategic Nuclear Arms, 4 Jul 67, fldr Strategic Nuclear Balance and Backup to S.F. ABM Speech, Sept 18, 1967, TAB A, box 95, McNamara Records, RG-200.

77. Yanarella, *Missile Defense Controversy*, 131; memo ASD(SA) for SecDef, Nike-X Deployment, 4 Jul 67 w/ encl, Systems Analysis, Deployment of Nike-X, fldr 471.94 ABM 1967, box 14, SecDef Subject Decimal files, Acc 72-A-2467; Halperin, "Decision to Deploy the ABM," 71; Poole, *JCS and National Policy, 1965-68*, pt 1:99-100; JCSM-425-67 for SecDef, 27 Jul 67, *FRUS 1964-68*, 10:563-64.

78. Memo Rostow for Pres, 2 Aug 67, *FRUS 1964-68*, 10:564-65;memo SecDef for CJCS, 2 Aug 67 w/atchmt, DPM Strategic Offensive and Defensive Forces, 1 Aug 67, fldr Reading File, Aug 21-12,1967, box 130, McNamara Papers, RG-200; Point Paper, JCSM-481-67, 26 Aug 67, fldr Congressional Testimony, box 79, McNamara Records, RG-200; Poole, *JCS and National Policy, 1965-68*, pt 1:101; Goulding, *Confirm or Deny*, 233 (quote).

79. Memo SecDef for Pres, 19 Aug 67 w/atchmt, Draft Remarks by Robert S. McNamara Before UPI Editors and Publishers, 9 Aug 67, fldr 1967, Strategic Arms 1, Backup Material, Strategic Arms, OSD Hist; ltr Actng DirACDA to USRep to ENDC, 1 Sep 67, *FRUS 1964-68*, 11:501-02; memos Califano for Rostow, 27 Aug 67 (quotes) and Rostow for Pres, 28 Aug 67: fldr 1967, Strategic Arms 1, Backup Material, Strategic Arms, OSD Hist; memo Keeny for Rostow, 29 Aug 67, *FRUS 1964-68*, 11:499-501; memo Keeny for Rostow, 28 Aug 67, Backup Material, Strategic Arms, OSD Hist; CMC, Work Notes on JCS mtg, 11 Sep 67, Greene Papers, MHC.

80. Msg 32089 State to Moscow, 5 Sep 67, fldr 1967, Strategic Arms 1, Backup Material, Strategic Arms, OSD Hist; Strategic Delivery System Talks Chronology, entry for 12 Sep 67, ibid; Newhouse, *Cold Dawn*, 95-97; msg 37035 State to USMission to NATO, 14 Sep 67, *FRUS 1964-68*, 11:512-15; msg 5460 Paris to State, 14 Sep 67, doc. no. CK3100243115, Declassified Documents Reference System, *http://galenet.galegroup. com*; ltr McNamara to Healey, 13 Sep 67, fldr Nuclear Planning Group-Backup, Ankara, Sep 1967, TAB

K-2, box 95, McNamara Records, RG-200. An annotation on the Healey letter notes that similar versions were sent to the Canadian, Dutch, German, Italian, and Turkish defense ministers. Memo ASD(ISA) for SecDef, 20 Sep 67 and Tab B, Excerpt from memcon of 6 Apr 67: fldr 471.94 ABM 1967, box 14, SecDef Subject Decimal files, Acc 72-A-2467.

81.   McNamara address, 18 Sep 67, *McNamara Public Statements, 1967*, 7:2546-70 (especially 2567); ed note, *FRUS 1964-68*, 10:614-18; msg 5913 Ankara to State, 29 Sep 67, fldr Strategic Arms 2, Backup Material, Strategic Arms, OSD Hist.

82.   Goulding, *Confirm or Deny*, 217-19; James Reston in *New York Times*, 22 Sep 67.

83.   Interv Robert McNamara by Richard Stolley on 16 Sep 67 in *Life*, 29 Sep 67; Goulding, *Confirm or Deny*, 239; memcon Foster and Dobrynin, 4 Oct 67, *FRUS 1964-68*, 11:518.

84.   DPM SecDef for Pres, 4 Oct 67, fldr 1967, Strategic Arms 1, Backup Material, Strategic Arms, OSD Hist; Fowler, Strategic Forces and Analysis Branch, USA, Paper, 8 Jan 68, fldr FY 69 Budget Hearings - Pueblo, box 75, ASD(C) files, OSD Hist; CM-2724-67 for SecDef, 4 Nov 67, CM-2764-67 for SecDef, 15 Nov 67, and CM-2789-67 for SecDef, 27 Nov 67: fldr Notes of mtg with JCS, box 75, McNamara Records, RG-200; Tom Johnson notes of mtg w/Pres, 4 Dec 67, *FRUS 1964-68*, 10:642-46 (quote).

85.   Memo Keeny for Rostow, 17 Nov 67, Backup Material, Strategic Arms, OSD Hist.; Goulding, *Confirm or Deny*, 244; SecDef Statement before the House Subcte on DoD of HCA on the FY 1969-73 Defense Program and 1969 Defense Budget, 16 Feb 68, 90-91, fldr FY 69, box 5, SecDef Statements 1968-70 FYs 1969-71, OSD Hist. McNamara, Notes of Actions Required on the ABM Project, 19 Sep 67, fldr Strategic Nuclear Balance and Backup to S.F. Speech, Sept 18, 1967, TAB C, box 95, McNamara Records, RG-200 has McNamara's decision for a new name to differentiate it clearly from Nike-X and a Soviet-oriented system.

86.   Summary of Recommendations by SecDef and related Recommendations by the JCS With FY 69 Budget Implications, 28 Nov 67, fldr Hearings - Snte Armed Svcs. Cte - 2/2/68 Aftn - FY 69 Budget, box 73, ASD(C) files, OSD Hist; DPM SecDef for Pres, 15 Jan 68, *FRUS 1964-68*, 10:655-57; insert to page 539 of transc House DoD Appropriations SubCte, nd, fldr House Approp. Cte - Hearings - A.M. 2/16/68 FY 1969 Bgt, box 74, ASD(C) files, OSD Hist.

87.   Yanarella, *Missile Defense Controversy*, 150.

88.   *Washington Post*, 19 Apr 68 and 17 Jun 68 (quote); memos ASD(SA) for DepSecDef, 14 May 68 and ASD(ISA) for DepSecDef, 24 May 68: fldr Sentinel ABM, #38, box 25, Clifford Papers, LBJL.

89.   Memo DDRE for Mil Asst to DepSecDef, 14 May 68, fldr Sentinel ABM, box 25, Clifford Papers, LBJL; Elsey notes of SecDef morning staff mtg, 20 Jun 68, fldr VanDeMark Transcripts, box 1, Elsey Papers, LBJL; ltr Warnke to Hart, 11 Jun 68, fldr Cont'l Defense - 1968, box 696, Subj files, OSD Hist. Warnke's letter responded to seven questions posed by Senator Hart on the ABM.

90.   *Washington Post*, 17 Jun 68; Defense Briefing, 10 Sep 68, 80, fldr Transcript of SecDef Briefing before Hse Subcte on DoD Appropriations,10 September 1968, box 76, ASD(C) files, OSD Hist (quote); *Washington Post*, 25 and 26 Jun 68; ltr Clifford to Russell, 18 Jun 68, fldr Strategic Arms 2, Backup Material, Strategic Arms, OSD Hist; Livesay notes, SecDef staff mtg, 1 Jul 68, fldr Minutes of SecDef Staff Meetings, Mar-Sep 1968, box 18, Clifford Papers, LBJL.

91.   Livesay notes, 1 Jul 68, cited in note 90; ltrs Kosygin to Johnson, 21 Jun 68, Johnson to Kosygin, 22 Jun 68, and Kosygin to Johnson, 27 Jun 68, *FRUS 1964-68*, 10:623-24.

92.   Memo SecA for SecDef, 10 Sep 68, fldr Sentinel/ABM, box 25, Clifford Papers, LBJL (quote); memcon Clifford and Zwick, 30 Dec 68, fldr Bureau of the Budget, #2, box 14, ibid; memos SecA for SecDef, 10 Dec 68 and 13 Dec 68: fldr Sentinel/ABM, box 25, ibid; Livesay notes, SecDef Staff mtg, 2 Dec 68, fldr Minutes of SecDef Staff Meetings, Oct 6-Jan 69, box 18, Clifford Papers, LBJL (quote).

93.   Livesay notes, SecDef Staff mtg, 9 Dec 68, as cited in note 92; memo Rostow for Pres, 7 Dec 68, fldr Meeting with President (1) Jul-Dec 68, box 1/2, NSF, Files of Walt Rostow (Closed), LBJL (quote); *Washington Post*, 20 Dec 68; Schwartz, "Past and Present, in Carter and Schwartz, eds, *Ballistic Missile Defense*, 341; Baucom, *Origins of SDI*, 39-40; *Washington News*, 28 May 72.

94.   SecDef Statement on FY 1970-74 Defense Program and 1970 Defense Budget, 15 Jan 69, 114, fldr Final FY 1970 Posture Statement, box 6, SecDef Statements 1965-70, FYs 1969-71, OSD Hist.

95.   Ibid, 118-19; DPM Clifford for Pres, 9 Jan 69, fldr FY 1970 DPMs & TS, box 122, ASD(C) files, OSD Hist; DPM SecDef for Pres, 1 Nov 65, *FRUS 1964-68*, X:284; "Strategic Arms," pt 2, Table 31.

XIV. NATO READJUSTMENT

1.   Kaplan, "The U.S. and NATO," in Divine, ed, The Johnson Years, 3:127; ltr de Gaulle to Johnson, 7 Mar 66, *FRUS 1964-68*, 13:325-26; de Gaulle news conf, 21 Feb 66, French memo to 14 NATO govts, 29 and 30 Mar 66: *AFP: CD, 1966*, 316-17, 324-26; Wells, "Charles de Gaulle and the French Withdrawal," in Kaplan, ed, *American Historians and the Atlantic Alliance*, 85, 87; msg 51 Paris to State, 2 Jul 65, SecDef Cable files, OSD Hist.

2.   Memos SecDef for CJCS, 2 May 64 and Roche for Sec, JCS, 7 Jul 64: fldr France 092 NATO (64-65 Papers), box 4, SecDef Subject Decimal files, Acc 70A-4443: Poole, *JCS and National Policy, 1965-1968*, pt 1:290-91.

3.   Poole, *JCS and National Policy, 1965-1968*, pt 1:291-93; JCSM-373-65 for SecDef, 19 May 65, fldr NATO 381 1965 (16 Jan thru 22 Oct 65), box 4, SecDef Subject Decimal files, Acc 70A-1265.

4.   CM-730-65 for SecDef, 6 Jul 65; memo Lang for Vance, 12 Jul 65; ltr Vance to Ball, 19 Jul 65; ltr Ball to Vance, 21 Jul 65; memo McNaughton for Vance, 25 Aug 65; ltr Ball to McNamara, 4 Oct 65 w/atchmt, Draft NSAM: all fldr France 092 NATO (64-65 Papers), box 4, SecDef Subject Decimal files, Acc 70A-4443; memcon, France and NATO, 8 Oct 65 and Draft NASM, nd: both *FRUS 1964-68*, 13:253-54 (quote), 258 and 253, n 2.

5.   Msg 4058 State to Paris, 21 Feb 66, *FRUS 1964-1968*, 13:108-09; de Gaulle news conf, 21 Feb 66, cited in note 1; memcon, France-NATO, 6 Mar 66, doc no. CK3100488730, Declassified Documents Reference System, *http://galenet.galegroup.com* (quote); msg 533 Rome to State, 1 Sep 65, *FRUS 1964-68*, 13:239-43; msg 2182 Paris to State, 21 Oct 65, Cable files, OSD Hist; msg 2484 State to NATO Posts, 10 Jun 65, memcon, France and NATO, 16 Jun 65, *FRUS 1964-68*, 13:215-20; msg 5247 Paris to State, 25 Feb 66, ibid, 12:110-11; ltr de Gaulle to Johnson, 7 Mar 66, French Memo to 14 NATO Governments, 29 and 30 Mar 66: both cited in note 1.

6.   Ltr Johnson to de Gaulle, 7 Mar 66, *FRUS 1964-68*, 13:326, n 2; msg 6300 Paris to State, 28 Mar 66, doc no CK3100064140, Declassified Documents Reference System, *http://galenet.galegroup.com*; memo Johnson for Rusk and McNamara, 4 May 66, NASM 345, 22 Apr 66: *FRUS 1964-68*, 13:376-77, 374-75; memo Bator for Pres, 16 Mar 66, fldr France-NATO Dispute, vol I, Memos [1 of 2] 2/66-3/66, box 177, Country File, NSF, LBJL; Johnson, *Vantage Point*, 305; memo Pres for SecState and SecDef, 4 May 66, *FRUS 1964-68*, 13:376. See Johnson's later equanimity in Smith, Summary notes of 566th NSC mtg, 13 Dec 66, *FRUS 1964-68*, 13:512-13.

7.   Memo DepSecDef for CJCS, 18 Mar 66, fldr France 370.02 Jan-May 1966, box 4, SecDef Subject Decimal files, Acc 70A-4443; Poole, *JCS and National Policy, 1965-1968*, pt 1:299-300.

8.   OASD(SA)SP, Status of Relocation from France, nd but Jan 67, Back-up Book FY 1968-Bk I (vols 1&2) Tab 2Q, box 60, ASD(C) files, OSD Hist; memo Enthoven for McNaughton, 9 Apr 66 w/atchmt, Relocation of U.S. Facilities in France, 7 Apr 66, fldr 381 Jan 1966, box 4, ISA General files, Acc 70A-6649 (quotes).

9.   Aide-Memoire From U.S. Government to French Government, 12 Apr 66, *FRUS 1964-68*, 13:362; memcon, France-NATO, 4 Apr 66, ibid, 13:353-54; memrcd McDonald, White House Luncheon 5 April 1966, fldr TS-Sensitive Memos Originated by 00 Jan 66 thru Jun, box 86, Double Zero-1967, TS-Sensitive 1963-1966, NHC (quotes).

10. JCSM-234-66 for SecDef, 13 Apr 66, fldr France 370.02 (13 Apr 66), box 4, SecDef Subject Decimal files, Acc 70A-4443.

11. Memo Enthoven for McNaughton, 9 Apr 66, cited in note 8; msg JCS 2105-66 to SSO EUCOM, 19 Apr 66, fldr 031 Vietnam Apr 66, box 47, Wheeler Papers, RG 218; memo Wyle for Bator, 18 Apr 66, doc no CK3100060053, Declassified Documents Reference System, *http://galenet.galegroup.com*.

12. Note Wheeler to McNamara, 3 May 66 w/atchmt, JCSM-291-66 for SecDef, 3 May 66, fldr France 370.02 Jan-May 1966, box 4, SecDef Subject Decimal files, Acc 70A-4443.

13. Memo SecDef for CJCS, 17 May 66, fldr France 320.02 1966, box 3, SecDef Subject Decimal files, Acc 70A-4462 (quote); memo SecDef for Pres, 3 Apr 67, fldr NATO 1967, box 99, ASD(C) files, OSD Hist. The exact numbers vary. See, for example, ASD(SA)SP, Status of Relocation from France, nd but c Jan 67, Back-up Book FY 1968-Bk I (vols 1&2) Tab 2Q, box 60, ASD(C) files, OSD Hist. See also *Department of Defense Annual Report for FY 1967*, 46.

14. Memo SecDef for CJCS, 17 May 66, cited in note 13.

15. Memo DepSecDef for CJCS, 20 May 66, doc no CK3100037822, Declassified Documents Reference System, *http://galenet.galegroup.com*; Poole, *JCS and National Policy, 1965-1968*, pt 1:307.

16. Memo SecDef for Pres, 25 May 66, fldr France 370.02 FRELOC Decision Papers 20 May 66, box 3, SecDef Subject Decimal files, Acc 70A-4662 (quotes).

17. Memo DepSecDef for CJCS, 20 May 66, cited in note 15; msg JCS 3057 to USCINCEUR, 27 May 66, doc no CK3100385556: Declassified Documents Reference System, *http://galenet.galegroup.com*; CM-1532-66 for SecDef, 10 Jun 66, memo SecDef for CJCS, 16 Jun 66: fldr France 370.02 June 1966, box 4, SecDef Subject Decimal files, Acc 70A-4443.

18. Memo SecDef for CJCS, 17 May 66, cited in note 13; JCSM-497-66 for SecDef, 1 Aug 66, fldr France 370.2 July-Aug 1966, box 4, SecDef Subject Decimal files, Acc 70A-4443 (quote): JCSM-522-66 for SecDef, 19 Aug 66 (quote), memo SecDef to CJCS, 2 Sep 66: fldr NATO 400 1966, box 4, SecDef Subject Decimal files, Acc 70A-4662.

19. Memo SecDef for CJCS, 27 Aug 66, fldr 471.6 1966 July, box 8, ISA General files, Acc 70A-6649; memo SecDef for CJCS, 17 May 66 cited in note 13.

20. Poole, *JCS and National Policy, 1965-1968*, pt 1:308; JCSM-432-66 for SecDef, 28 Jun 66, fldr France 000.1, 1966, box 10 ISA General files, Acc 70A-6649; memo OSD (SA) for SecDef, 28 Jul 66, fldr NATO (ALPHA) 1966, box 4, SecDef Subject Decimal files, Acc 70A-4662; CM-1620-66, AF Spec Asst to CJCS for SecDef, 16 Jul 66 and memo of understanding Enthoven and Spivy, 14 Jul 66 w/atchmt, Comparison of NATO/Warsaw Pact Tactical Air Capabilities, fldr NATO 452 1966, ibid; memo SecDef for SecAF, 5 Aug 66, fldr France 370.02 1966, box 3, ibid. On French attitudes regarding reentry rights see "Draft Administrative History of the Department of Defense 1963-1969," 1:34-35 (hereafter "DoD Admin History"); US Recce A/C Situation in Europe, 25 May 66, fldr France 370.02 1966, ibid.

21. DPM SecDef for Pres, NATO Strategy and Force Structure, 21 Sep 66, fldr NATO (ALPHA) 1966, box 4, ibid.

22. JCSM-643-66 for SecDef, 7 Oct 66, memo Enthoven for SecDef, 26 Oct 66 w/McNamara's marginalia, memo SecDef to CJCS, 31 Oct 66, JCSM-703-66 for SecDef, 3 Nov 66: fldr NATO 400 1966, ibid; memo SecDef for CJCS, 12 Dec 66, fldr France 370.02 FRELOC Decision Papers 20 May 66, box 3, ibid.

23. JCSM-234-66 for SecDef, 13 Apr 66, fldr France 370.02 (13 Apr 66) 1966, box 4, SecDef Subject Decimal files, Acc 70A-4443; CM-1536-66 for SecDef, 11 Jun 66, fldr France 370.02 June 1966, box 4, ibid; "DoD Admin History," 1:33: ASD(ISA) European Region, Notes on French Issues Chairman Rivers May Raise, 21 Mar 67, fldr Misc, box 76, McNamara Records, RG 200: Harrison, *Reluctant Ally*, 151: Kaplan, *NATO and the United States, Updated Edition: The Enduring Alliance*, 102.

24. Athens Guidelines for NPG mtg, 18-19 Apr 68, fldr NATO NPG, SecDef Briefing Book - NPG Meeting, Bonn 10-11 Oct 68, TAB E and msg 2598 USMission NATO to SecDef, 11 Apr 68: fldr NATO 334 NPG 11 Apr 68, box 5, SecDef Subject Decimal files, Acc 73A-1304; Shapley, *Promise and Power*, 401.

25. Memo Warnke for SecDef, Nuclear Planning Group (NPG), 11 Apr 68, SecDef Briefing Book - NPG Meeting Bonn, 10-11 Oct 68 , TAB B, fldr NATO 334 NPG 11 Apr 68, box 5, SecDef Subject Decimal files, Acc 73A-1304; Background briefing for press, 23 Sep 66, *Background Briefings by Secretary of Defense McNamara, 1966*:317; Kaplan, "U.S. and NATO in Johnson Years," 135; Smith, Summary notes of 566th NSC mtg, 13 Dec 66, *FRUS 1964-68*, 13:511-13 (quote, 512); msg 2599 USMission NATO to SecDef, 11 Apr 68, fldr NATO Messages, vol II, (1 of 2), box 37, NATO General, NSF Agency File, LBJL.

26. Msg circ 2412 State to NATO Posts, 2 Jun 65, *FRUS 1964-68*, 13:212-13; memo Warnke for SecDef, 11 Apr 68, cited in note 25; Background briefing for press, 23 Sep 66, cited in note 25 (quote). See the mixed reaction of NATO Permanent Representatives to the proposal; msg Polto 1875 USMission NATO and Eur Reg Orgs to State, 29 Jun 65, *FRUS 1964-68*, 13:221-24: msg circ agm CA-4576 State to NATO Posts, 26 Oct 65, ibid, 250-51; Haftendorn, *NATO and the Nuclear Revolution*, 164-65.

27. Pedlow, ed, *NATO Strategy Documents 1949-1969*, xxiv; memcon, France and NATO, 8 Oct 65, memo Asst SecState Eur Affairs for SecState, 8 Nov 65: *FRUS 1964-68*, 13:257 (quote) and 262.

28. Msg Polto 19 USMission NATO and Eur Reg Orgs to State, 28 Nov 65, *FRUS 1964-68*, 13:276-77; memo Warnke for SecDef, 11 Apr 68, cited in note 25; ltr McNamara to Brosio, 12 Jul 66 w/atchmt, Special Cte of NATO Defense Ministers NPWG, Country Papers and Working Group Documents, Jul 66, I-1, fldr NATO 322 ACE, 1966, box 4, SecDef Subject Decimal files, Acc 70A-4662.

29. Ltr McNamara to Brosio, 23 Sep 66, ISA paper, Nuclear Defense Affairs Committee (NDAC) and Nuclear Planning Group (NPG), 24 Sep 68: fldr NATO 334 NPG 11 Apr 68, box 5, SecDef Decimal files, Acc 73A-1304; DepState Background Paper, The Special Committee, 14 Nov 66, doc no CK3100339726, Declassified Documents Reference System, *http://galenet.galegroup.com*.

30. Msg Def 1083 SecDef to Paris, 10 Dec 66, doc no CK3100240221, Declassified Documents Reference System, *http://galenet.galegroup.com*; memcon, 1 Dec 66, *FRUS 1964-68*, 13:503; msg 2598 USMission NATO to SecDef, 11 Apr 68, fldr NATO 334 NPG 11 Apr 68, box 5, SecDef Subject Decimal files, Acc

73-A-1304; msg 9132 Paris to State, 15 Dec 66, fldr NATO NPG, NPG Meeting, Bonn 10-11 Oct 68, ibid (quote); *AFP: CD, 1966*, 376-77.

31. News conf, 3 Apr 67, *McNamara Public Statements, 1967*, 6:1900 (quotes); DoD News Release 284-67, 3 Apr 67, ibid, 6:1914; Stromseth, *Origins of Flexible Response*, 183.

32. Msg 2598, 11 Apr 68, cited in note 30; memo Warnke for SecDef, 11 Apr 68, cited in note 25 (quote); ISA paper, 24 Sep 68; cited in note 29.

33. Msg 2598, 11 Apr 68, cited in note 30.

34. Minute of the NPG Ministers' mtg, 6-7 April 1967, nd, fldr NATO 334 NPG 11 Apr 68, box 5, SecDef Subject Decimal files, Acc 73A-1304 (quote); msg 170596 State to USMission NATO and Eur Reg Orgs, 7 Apr 66, *FRUS 1964-68*, 13:556-57.

35. Memo Warnke for SecDef, 11 Apr 68, cited in note 25.

36. Ibid; msg 1571 Ankara to State, 29 Sep 67, fldr Strategic Arms #2, Johnson Library Papers at OSD, OSD Hist: msg 2600 USMission NATO to SecDef, 11 Apr 68, fldr NATO 334 NPG 11 Apr 68, box 5, SecDef Subject Decimal files, Acc 73A-1304; msg 2599 USMission NATO to SecDef 11 Apr 68, fldr NATO Meetings Vol II 1 of 2, box 37, NATO General, NSF Agency File, LBJL; Haftendorn, *NATO and the Nuclear Revolution*, 170-71.

37. Agreed Minute, NPG Mtg of Ministers, 28-29 Sep 67, nd, fldr NATO 334 NPG 11 Apr 68, box 5, SecDef Subject Decimal files, Acc 73A-1304; note Brosio to DPC, 11 May 67 and Annex II to DPC/D(67)23, Guidance to the NATO Military Authorities, in Pedlow, ed, *NATO Strategy Documents*, 333, 341 (quote).

38. ISA paper, Nuclear Defense Affairs Committee (NDAC) and Nuclear Planning Group (NPG), 24 Sep 68, fldr NATO 334 NPG 11 Apr 68, box 5, SecDef Subject Decimal files, Acc 73A-1304.

39. Memo SecDef and SecState for Pres, 16 Mar 68, *FRUS 1964-68*, 13:679-80; memo Warnke for SecDef, 11 Apr 68, cited in note 25 (quote).

40. Msg 4939 The Hague to State, 19 Apr 68, *FRUS 1964-68*, 13:690.

41. Msg US Mission NATO to SecDef, 112225Z Apr 68, fldr NATO 334 NPG 11 Apr 68, box 5, SecDef Subject Decimal files, Acc 73A-1304 (quote); ISA paper, SecDef Remarks for NPG Meeting 18-19 April 1968, 15 Apr 68, ibid (quotes); ISA paper, 24 Sep 68, cited in note 38.

42. State, Background Paper, Progress in NDAC and NPG, 4 Nov 68, doc no CK3100489715, Declassified Documents Reference System, *http://galenet.galegroup.com*; Haftendorn, *NATO and the Nuclear Revolution*, 172; Stromseth, *Origins of Flexible Response*, 184-85.

43. Stromseth, *Origins of Flexible Response*, 184-85; Rearden, "The Secretary of Defense and Foreign Affairs," Dec 1995, IV-22, OSD Hist.

44. Watson, *Into the Missile Age*, 36-37; Address by SecDef McNamara at NAC Ministerial Mtg, 5 May 62, *FRUS 1961-1963*, 8:275-81.

45. Special Report by the CIA, 27 Mar 64; CIA, NIE 12-64, 22 Jul 64; CIA, Special Memorandum, 18 Feb 65, *FRUS 1964-1968*, 17:2-3 and 8, 21-22 and 29 (quote); Special Report by the CIA, OCI No. 0308/65B, 24 Sep 65, Cable files, OSD Hist; DPM SecDef for Pres, 15 Jan 65, fldr 320.2 1965 1-35086/65-15 Jan 1965, box 2, ISA General files, Acc 70A-5127 (quote).

46. MC 14/2 (Revised) 21 Feb 57 and Enclosure (revised 6 Apr 57) in Pedlow, ed., *NATO Strategy Documents*, 291 (quote). The implementing measures were approved by the NAC on 23 May 1957 as MC 48/2. SecDef Statement before the House Armed Svcs Cte on the FY 1966-70 Defense Program and 1966 Defense Budget, 2 Feb 65, 100-101, box 4, SecDef Statements, OSD Hist; memo SecDef for CJCS, The Role of Tactical Nuclear Forces in NATO Strategy, 26 Oct 64, V-109, fldr pt 1, sections V, VI, VII, box 3, ibid.

47. Stromseth, *Origins of Flexible Response*, 52-54, 102; msg 3887 Bonn to State, 7 Apr 65, msg 3289 State to Bonn, 30 Apr 65: Cable files, OSD Hist.

48. In his introduction to Stromseth, *Origins of Flexible Response*, ix, former British Defense Minister Denis Healey comments on the influx of weapons; see also ibid, 56, 91. DPM SecDef for Pres, 15 Jan 65, cited in note 45; Shapley, *Promise and Power*, 405-06 imputes sinister motives to the process.

49. Duffield, "Evolution of NATO's Conventional Force Posture," (Ph.D. diss), 408; interv Lyman L. Lemnitzer by Maurice Matloff, 24 Jan 84, 16, OSD Hist.

50. Poole, *JCS and National Policy, 1965-1968*, pt 1:352-54: Pedlow, ed, *NATO Strategy Documents*, xxiv; ltr McCloy to Pres, 21 Nov 66, *FRUS 1964-68*, 13:495 w/atchmt, NATO Strategy and Forces (quotes) in doc no CK3100211995, Declassified Documents Reference System, *http://galenet.galegroup.com*. See also McAuliffe, Trilateral Talks Reference Paper, 2 Dec 66 w/atchmt, fldr 092.2 NATO Relocation Nov 66-Nov 67, box 70, Wheeler Papers, RG-218; msg 6006 USMission NATO and Eur Reg Orgs to State, 22 Oct 66, *FRUS 1964-68*, 13:485-86 (quote).

51. Pedlow, ed, *NATO Strategy Documents*, xxiv; Annex I to DPC/D(67) 23, 9 May 67, ibid, 335; Poole, *JCS and National Policy, 1965-1968*, pt 1:355-59; Stromseth, *Origins of Flexible Response*, 176.

52. Poole, *JCS and National Policy, 1965-1968*, pt 1:359-61.

53. Report, MC to DPC, Military Decision on MC 14/3, 22 Sep 67 and Encl 1 Report, MC to DPC, Final Decision on MC 14/3, 16 Jan 68, in Pedlow, ed, *NATO Strategy Documents*, 345-48; Kaplan, "U.S. and NATO in Johnson Years," 135 (quote); DPM SecDef for Pres, 16 Jan 68, fldr Notebook DPMs FY 1969, box 123, ASD (C) files, OSD Hist (quotes).

54. Shapley, *Promise and Power*, 406, quoting Timothy Stanley, Harlan Cleveland's deputy.

55. Stromseth, *Origins of Flexible Response*, 4-5.

56. Memo DepDir, Regional and NATO Affairs, ISA for Barber, 26 Oct 65, fldr 320.2 October 1965, box 2, ISA General files, Acc 70A-5127; memo McNaughton for SecDef, 20 May 66, fldr 320.2 May Jun 1966, box 2, ISA General files, Acc 70A-6649; msg USCINCEUR to JCS 301455Z Aug 65 and msg USCINCEUR to CJCS 111113Z Sep 65, fldr 091 Vietnam Sep 65, box 45, Wheeler Papers, RG 218; Lemnitzer referred specifically to statements contained in SecDef Background Briefing for the Press, 28 Jul 65, *Background Briefings of Secretary of Defense McNamara, 1965*:204.

57. JCSM-199-66 for SecDef, 31 Mar 66, memo Enthoven for SecDef, 6 May 66, memo Vance for CJCS, 11 Jun 66: fldr 560 1966-Jan, box 8, ISA General files, Acc 70A-6649; memo UnderSecN for SecDef, 27 May 66, ibid (quote).

58. Memrcd Abrams, mtg w/SecDef, 21 Sep 65, fldr TS 0015-82-0024-82, Chief of Staff Collection, MHI; memo DepDirReg & NATO Affairs, ISA for Barber, 26 Oct 65, fldr 320.2 October 1965, box 2, ISA General Files, Acc 70A-5127; Sorley, *Honorable Warrior*, 260; CMC notes on Special SecDef Conf w/ SvcSecs and Chiefs of Staff, 30 Nov 65, November trip of RSM to SVN, nd: Greene Papers, MHC (quote).

59. JCSM-25-66 for SecDef, 15 Jan 66, fldr 320.2 Jan-Apr 1966, box 2, ISA General files, Acc 70A-6649; Debrief by SecDef of his mtg in Honolulu w/Pres and Vietnamese Leaders, 9 Feb 66, Greene Papers, MHC.

60. JCSM-130-66 for SecDef, 1 Mar 66, fldr 320.2, SEA 1 Mar 66, box 8, ISA General files, Acc 70A-6649; msg JCS 1002-66 Wheeler to Lemnitzer, 2 Mar 66, fldr #35, 1966, E.O. Messages IN - January-June TS," box 175, Lemnitzer Papers, NDU; Carland, *Stemming the Tide*, 156-57.

61. Memo Dougherty for McNaughton w/atchmt, 5 May 66, fldr 320.2 1966 May-June, box 2, ISA General files 1966, Acc 70A-6649 (quote); Joint Logistics Review Board, "Logistic Support in the Vietnam Era," 2: app A, "Impact of the Vietnam Conflict on Readiness in Other Areas of the World," A-19, box 321, Subj files, OSD Hist; Haftendorn, *NATO and the Nuclear Revolution*, 240; Background briefing, 7 Apr 66, *Background Briefings of Secretary of Defense McNamara, 1966*:111.

62. Memrcd McNamara-Von Hassel conversation, 29 Apr 66, fldr McNamara/von Hassel Meeting - 13 May 1966 - bk I, Doctrine & Strategy, Prep'd by Eur Reg, box 3, ISA Military Assistance files, Acc 72A-1494; msg 3245 Bonn to State, 12 Apr 66, msg 3402 Bonn to State, 22 Apr 66, and msg 6859 Paris to State, 15 Apr 66: Cable files, OSD Hist; msg 2012 Bonn to State, 17 Aug 66, *FRUS 1964-1968*, 15:391; Haftendorn, *NATO and the Nuclear Revolution*, 239.

63. Benjamin Welles in *New York Times*, 30 Mar 66, 2; JCSM-133-66 for SecDef, 2 Mar 66, fldr 319.1 Order of Battle 1966 Jan, box 2, ISA General files, Acc 70A-6649; Poole, *JCS and National Policy, 1965-1968*, pt 1:380; memo McNaughton for SecDef, 9 Apr 66, fldr NATO 381 1966, box 4, SecDef Subject Decimal files, Acc 70A-4662.

64. Memo OSD (SA) for SecDef, 28 Jul 66, fldr NATO (ALPHA) 1966, box 4, SecDef Subject Decimal files, Acc 70-A-4662.

65. JCSM-560-66 for SecDef, 1 Sep 66, ibid; Poole, *JCS and National Policy, 1965-1968*, pt 1:381-82.

66. Msg JCS 5279-66 Wheeler to Lemnitzer, 7 Sep 66, fldr #37 1966 EO Messages In July-December TS, box 175, Lemnitzer Papers, NDU; DPM SecDef for Pres, NATO Strategy and Force Structure, 21 Sep 66, fldr DPMs FY 1968-72, Programs 1966, box 120, ASD(C) files, OSD Hist.

67. DPM, 21 Sep 66, cited in note 66; memo Enthoven for SecDef, 17 Sep 66, fldr NATO (ALPHA) 1966, box 1, SecDef Subject Decimal files, Acc 70A-4662.

68. JCSM-648-66 for SecDef, 7 Oct 66, fldr JCSM's 603-66 to 699-66, box 183, Wheeler Papers, RG 218.

69. Msg JCS 0709-67 Spivy to Lemnitzer, 26 Jan 67, fldr #39 1967 EO Messages In July-December TS, box 175, Lemnitzer Papers, NDU; JCSM-46-67 for SecDef, 28 Jan 67, fldr Trilateral Negotiations and NATO 1966-67, bk 4, TAB 41, box 51, NSC History, NSF, LBJL; ltr Wheeler to McCloy w/encl, 3 Feb 67, fldr 1967 Ltrs Signed by Gen Wheeler 1 Jan 67-30 Jun 67, box 125, Wheeler Papers, RG 218.

70. Poole, *JCS and National Policy, 1965-1968*, pt 1:157-59 (quote); Precis of JCSM-313-67, 2 Jun 67, fldr JCS Comments on DPMs 1967, box 75, McNamara Records, RG 200 (quote); memo CSAF for SecAF, 5 Jun

67, memo SecAF for SecDef, 7 Jun 67: fldr NATO 381 OPM, box 4, SecDef Subject Decimal files, Acc 72A-2467; DPM SecDef for Pres, General Purpose Forces and Logistics Guidance, 9 Jan 68, fldr DPMs FY 69, box 121, ASD(C) files, OSD Hist.

71.   Ltr U. Alexis Johnson for McNaughton, 3 Sep 66 w/atchmt, Troop Withdrawals from Germany, fldr 320.2 1966 September, box 2, ISA General files, Acc 70A-6649.

72.   JCSM-288-67 for SecDef, 20 May 67, fldr McNtn-Memoranda 1967(2), box 5, Papers of Paul C. Warnke, John McNaughton files, LBJL; see also *JCS and the War in Vietnam*, pt 3:42/12-13.

73.   Memo OASD(SA) for SecDef, 5 Jul 67 w/atchmt, memrcd ASD(SA), SEA Deployments, 14 Jul 67: fldr Miscellaneous 1967, box 65, Pentagon Papers Backup, Acc 330-75-062; memo ASD(SA) for SecDef, 5 Jul 67, memo SecDef for CJCS, 10 Aug 67: ibid; msg ARV 1380 from Saigon, Wheeler to H.K. Johnson, 8 Jul 67, fldr 337 Saigon Trip July 1967, box 102, Wheeler Papers, RG 218; JCSM-522-67 for SecDef, 23 Sep 67, fldr NATO 320.2 DPQ (23 Sep 67), box 3, SecDef Subject Decimal files, Acc 72A-2467; Poole, *JCS and National Policy, 1965-1968*, pt 1:174.

74.   Cf JCSM-522-67 for SecDef, 23 Sep 67, App A (quote), memo ASD/ISA (Warnke) for SecDef, 2 Oct 67 (quotes): fldr NATO 320.2 DPQ (2 Oct 67), box 3, SecDef Subject Decimal files, Acc 72A-2467.

75.   Statement by McNamara to DPC of NATO, 8 Dec 67, 4, fldr Index-SecDef Statement -NATO 12/67, box 99, ASD(C) files, OSD Hist (quote, emphasis in the source); DPM SecDef for Pres, NATO Strategy and Force Structure, 16 Jan 1968, DPM, General Purpose Forces and Logistics Guidance, 9 Jan 68: fldr Notebook DPMs FY 1969, box 121, ibid.

76.   Msg JCS 6412 to USCINCEUR, 26 Nov 68, item #49, msg USCINCEUR to USNMR SHAPE, 100927Z Dec 68, item # 48: fldr 57, Logistics/Gold Flow, box 148, Lemnitzer Papers, NDU; Shapley, *Promise and Power*, 401; Sorley, *Honorable Warrior*, 273-74; Poole, *JCS and National Policy, 1965-1968*, pt 1:177.

XV. NATO: BURDEN-SHARING AND U.S. TROOP REDUCTION

1.   Memo Bundy for Pres, 8 Nov 64, *FRUS 1964-68*, 13:105.

2.   The NATO costs appear in DPM SecDef for Pres, NATO and the United States Five-Year Force Structure and Financial Program, 13 Oct 65, fldr FY 67 Memos for Pres, box 119, ASD(C) files, OSD Hist. The balance of payments figures are taken from "Draft Administrative History of the Department of Defense, 1963-1969," 1:29, OSD Hist (hereafter "DoD Admin History").

3.   Enthoven and Smith, *How Much Is Enough?*, 133-35; DPM SecDef for Pres, Recommended Army and Marine Corps General Purpose Forces, FY 1967-1971, 20 Oct 65, fldr FY 67 Memos for Pres, box 119, ASD(C) files, OSD Hist (quote); DPM SecDef for Pres, The Role of Tactical Nuclear Forces in NATO Strategy, 15 Jan 65, fldr Memos to Pres. FY 66-70 Programs, box 118, ibid (quote); DPM SecDef for Pres, NATO and the United States Five-Year Force Structure and Financial Program, 13 Oct 65, fldr Memos for Pres. Cy 1965, FY 1967, box 119, ibid (quote).

4.   DPM SecDef for Pres, Recommended FY 1964-68 General Purpose Forces, 4 Dec 62, fldr Notebook DPMs FY 64, box 116, ibid ; memo McNaughton for SvcSecs, CJCS, 12 Aug 66, encl 1, Remarks by Secretary McNamara, Defense Ministers' Meeting, Paris, France, 25 Jul 66, fldr NATO 1967, box 99, ibid; DPM SecDef for Pres, 13 Oct 65, cited in note 2; DPM SecDef for Pres, Recommended FY 1965-69 Army and Marine Corps General Purpose Forces, 19 Dec 63, fldr DoD DPMs Recommended FY 1965-FY 1969 Defense Programs, box 117, ASD(C) files, OSD Hist.

5.   NATO Branch J-5, Talking Paper for use by CJCS in discussions with the US Representative, NATO Standing Group (US Rep, SGN/MC), J-5 TP-77-65, 10 Aug 65, fldr 323.3 SAC/CINCEUR Jul 65-Oct 66, box 82, Wheeler Papers, RG 218; "DoD Admin History," 1:27-28, OSD Hist; DPM SecDef for Pres, 13 Oct 65, w/Annex B, cited in note 2. NATO's Central Front MC 26/4 goals were 29 2/3 division equivalents at full strength with 100 percent weapons and equipment on M-Day and 21 1/3 more divisions in reserve. Memo Hitch for SecDef w/encl NATO force goals and the U.S. Five-Year Force Structure and Financial Program, 27 May 65, fldr NATO 381 1965 (16 Jan thru 26 Oct 65), box 4, SecDef Subject Decimal files, Acc 70A-1265.

6.   CM-649-65 for SecDef, 4 Jun 65, Encl A, Current Conventional Capability Appraisal of ACE Forces - 1965: Summary of Conclusions, fldr NATO 471.61 (ALPHA), 1966, box 5, SecDef Subject Decimal files, Acc 70A-4662; memo McNaughton for SecDef, 30 Jun 65, fldr 353 Mountbatten 1965, box 12, SecDef Subject Decimal files, Acc 70A-1265; JCSM-454-65 for SecDef, 11 Jun 65, ibid; DPM SecDef for Pres, 13 Oct 65, cited in note 2 (quote).

7. DPM SecDef for Pres, 15 Jan 65, cited in note 3; JCSM-743-65 for SecDef, 9 Oct 65, JCSM-752-65 for SecDef, 15 Oct 65 (quote), CM-911-65 for SecDef, 15 Oct 65 (quote): fldr 320.2 October 1965, box 2, ISA General files, Acc 70A-5127; Poole, *JCS and National Policy, 1965-1968*, pt 1:115-116, 118; NATO Branch, J-5, Mtg Wheeler and Trettner, Paris, December 1965, fldr 092.2 (NATO) Bulky #2, box 72, Wheeler Papers, RG 218.

8. Memo McNaughton for SecDef, 18 Oct 65, fldr 320.2 October 1965, box 2, ISA General files, Acc 70A-5127; msg CA-6367 State to CINCLANT et al, 17 Dec 65, fldr NATO 0923 Min Mtg, box 4, SecDef Subject Decimal files, Acc 70A-1265; "DoD Admin History," 1:28: msg 1335 USMission NATO to State, 15 Jan 68, Cable files, OSD Hist; memo ISA for SecDef, 25 Jan 68, fldr 334 NATO 1968 Jan-, box 7, ISA General files, Acc 72A-1499 (quotes).

9. DPM SecDef for Pres, 20 Oct 65, cited in note 3; Enthoven and Smith, *How Much Is Enough?*, 137; DPM SecDef for Pres, 13 Oct 65, cited in note 2 (quote).

10. JCS, Comparison of Soviet Division Slice and US Division Force, 20 Dec 66, TAB 2K, SecDef 68 Backup Book, bk 1 (vols 1&2), box 60, ASD(C) files, OSD Hist. McNamara described his complex methodology in detail in DPM SecDef for Pres, 13 Oct 65, cited in note 2, 16-18 and Annex H, fldr FY 67 Memos for Pres, box 119, ASD(C) files, OSD Hist; memo Hitch for SecDef w/encl, 27 May 65, fldr NATO 381 1965 (16 Jan thru 26 Oct 65), box 4, SecDef Subject Decimal files, Acc 70A-1265.

11. McNamara, "The Military Role of Nuclear Weapons," 63-64; Park, "Defense, Deterrence, and the Central Front," in Kaplan et al eds., *NATO After Forty Years*, 225-26; Kaplan, "The U.S. and NATO in the Johnson Years," in Divine, ed., *The Johnson Years*, 3:120, 135.

12. DPM SecDef for Pres, NATO Strategy and Force Structure, 21 Sep 66, fldr DPMs FY 68-72 Program, 1966, box 120, ASD(C) files, OSD Hist; Kaplan, *NATO and the United States, Updated Edition*, 99; Poole, *JCS and National Policy, 1965-1968*, pt 1:157, 382; McNamara's remarks in Minutes of the Cabinet Committee on Balance of Payments, 21 Dec 67, fldr The 1968 Balance of Payments Program [Tabs 4-18], box 54, NSC Histories, NSF, LBJL.

13. Stromseth, *The Origins of Flexible Response*, 165-66; Special Report by the CIA, Nationalism in Eastern Europe, 27 Mar 64, CIA, National Intelligence Estimate, Changing Patterns in Eastern Europe, NIE 12-64, 22 Jul 64, CIA, Spec Memo, Prospects for Independence in Eastern Europe, 18 Feb 65: *FRUS 1964-1968*, 17:2-3, 8, 21-22, 29; Kaplan, *NATO, Updated Edition*, 103; McNamara's remarks on NATO's changing potential in his 1968 Posture Statement, SecDef Statement before Jt Session of SASC and Sen SubCte on DoD Appros on FY 1968-72 Defense Program and 1968 Defense budget, 23 Jan 67 (Secret Version), 28, fldr, FY 1967, box 4, SecDef Statements 1966-67 for FYs' 1967-68, OSD Hist. On the origins of the Harmel Report see msg 91669 State to EmbBrussels, 26 Nov 66, Cable files, OSD Hist.

14. Memo Spec Asst to SecDef for NATO Force Planning (Timothy W. Stanley) for SecDef, 16 Sep 66, fldr NATO (ALPHA) 1966, box 4, SecDef Subject Decimal files, Acc 70A-4662.

15. The Trilateral Negotiations and NATO, nd, fldr Trilateral Negotiations and NATO 1966-67, bk 1, Tab 1a, box 50, NSC Histories, NSF, LBJL.

16. Memcon, UK Defense Review - NATO Area, 27 Jan 66, *FRUS 1964-68*, 13:303; memcon, Vietnam, 20 Dec 65, ibid, 15:346 (quote).

17. Stromseth, *Origins of Flexible Response*, 124, 142. The initial (1955) goal of a 500,000 man Bundeswehr was modified to a target of 350,000 in 1958. By 1961 the Bundeswehr numbered 325,000; by 1962, 389,400; by 1963 403,000; and 454,800 in 1966. However, memcon, 27 Jan 66, cited in note 16, has a McNamara figure of 240,000. Trewhitt, *McNamara*, 186-87; unsigned memo SecDef for Pres, 11 Nov 65, fldr Johnson/Erhard Mtg 19-21 Dec (T) LBJ Ranch, box 3 ISA General files, Acc 72A-1494.

18. Msg 7175 SecDef to CMAAG Bonn, 24 Nov 65, Cable files, OSD Hist; unsigned memo SecDef for Pres, 11 Nov 65, msg 1379 Bonn to State, 13 Dec 65: fldr Johnson/Erhard Mtg 19-21 Dec (T) LBJ Ranch, box 3, ISA General files, Acc 72A-1494.

19. Memcon, Vietnam, 20 Dec 65 and memcon, Offset, 20 Dec 65: *FRUS 1964-1968*, 15:347, 348; memcon McNamara, Pres Johnson and Chancellor Erhard, 20 Dec 65, ibid, 349; *Johnson Public Papers, 1965*, 2:1167. Guidance on US/FRG Offset Arrangement, nd, fldr Johnson/Erhard Mtg 19-21 Dec (T) LBJ Ranch, box 3, ISA General files, Acc 72A-1494.

20. Draft Agreed Minute Sec McNamara/Minister Von Hassel Mtg on US/FRG Cooperative Logistics, Washington, D.C., December 1965, 23 Nov 65, fldr Johnson/Erhard Mtg 19-21 Dec (T) LBJ Ranch, box 3, ISA General files, Acc 72A-1494; Agreed Minute Sec McNamara/Minister Von Hassel Mtg on US/FRG Cooperative Logistics, Washington, D.C. 21 Dec 65, fldr McNamara Briefing-21 Apr 1966, ibid.

21. Memcon, 27 Jan 66, *FRUS 1964-1968*, 13:305.

22. OSD/ISA (ILN), Military Sales Program for Germany - Offset Agreement, 19 Apr 66, fldr McNamara Briefing-21 Apr 1966, box 3, ISA General files, Acc 72A-1494; Draft Agreed Minute Sec McNamara/Minister Von Hassel Mtg on US/FRG Logistics, 13 May 66 and Draft Agenda Item I - Report on Current Status of FRG Calendar Year 65/66 Procurement and FY 66-67 Payments, nd, but likely 13 May 66: fldr Final US/FRG Min Dirs' Mtg-Washington 10-11 May 1966, box 3, ISA General files, Acc 72A-1494. The latter was the basis for the official Agreed Minute Sec McNamara/Minister Von Hassel Mtg on US/FRG Logistics, fldr McNamara/von Hassel Meeting - 13 May 66 - bk I Doctrine & Strategy, Prep'd by Eur Reg, box 3, ibid.

23. Msg 1160 USMission Berlin to State, 14 Jun 66, *FRUS 1964-1968*, 15:371-72 (quote); msg 1834 Bonn to State, 12 Aug 66, ibid, 388 (quote); McNamara test, 21 Jun 66, SSC on Nat Security and Internal Opns of the Cte on Govt Opns, *Hearings: The Atlantic Alliance*, 21 Jun 66, pt 6:194, 216-17; msg 286 Bonn to State, 7 Jul 66, *FRUS 1964-1968*, 15:378.

24. Ltr Erhard to Johnson, 5 Jul 66, *FRUS 1964-68*, 15:375-76; OASD/ISA (PolPl), Sec McNamara/Minister Von Hassel Mtg, Bonn, July 1966: Bilateral Military Payments Offset Planning (Defense Position Brief, - 1st Draft), 30 Jun 66, fldr US/FRG Ministerial Director's Mtg Bonn-7-8 Jul 66, box 3, ISA 1966 General files, Acc 72A-1494; Johnson, *Vantage Point*, 307; DepState, Analysis of Major Decisions in Trilateral Talks, nd, fldr Trilateral Negotiations and NATO: 1966-67, bk 2, [2 of 2] Tabs 72-98, box 50, NSC Histories, NSF, LBJL; ltr Mansfield to the President, 14 Jul 66 (quote), draft ltr Johnson to Erhard, nd, but responding to Erhard's 5 July letter, draft ltr Johnson to Mansfield, nd but after 14 July: fldr McNamara/von Hassel July 1966 Meeting, Memcons & Records (v. II), box 3, ISA General files, Acc 72A-1494; memo Bator for Pres, 11 Aug 66, *FRUS 1964-1968*, 13:444-45, 447; Zimmermann, *Money and Security*, 197-98.

25. Msg 286 Bonn to State, 7 Jul 66, *FRUS 1964-1968*, 15:377 (quote); CMC Notes on JCS Meeting, #137, 18 Jul 66, Greene Papers, MHC; memrcd McNaughton, McNamara-Healey conversation in Paris, 25 July 66, item #21, fldr 29b, Secy of Defense, box 141, Lemnitzer Papers, NDU.

26. Memcon McNaughton, McNamara-von-Hassel Conversation No. 2 in Paris, 26 Jul 66, fldr McNamara/von Hassel July 1966 Meeting, Memcons & Records (v. ii), box 3, ISA General files, Acc 72A-1494; Jt Statement of Minister von Hassel and Sec McNamara, 24 Jul 66, TAB A, fldr Secretary McNamara's Visit to Bonn 23-24 Jul 1966 and memcon McNaughton, McNamara-von-Hassel Conversation No. 1 in Paris, 26 Jul 66, ibid; memo SecDef for Pres, 27 Jul 66, *FRUS 1964-1968*, 15:383-84.

27. Analysis of Major Decisions in Trilateral Talks, nd, fldr Trilateral Negotiations, bk 2, [2 of 2], box 50, NSC Histories, NSF, LBJL; memo Leddy to SecState, 23 Aug 66, fldr Trilateral Negotiations & NATO: 1966-67, bk 1, Tabs 1-9, ibid; memo Bator for Pres, 23 Aug 66, 4 PM, fldr NATO General, vol IV, 202, box 36, Agency File NATO, NSF, LBJL; memo Bator for Pres, 24 Aug 66, Box 17, Bator Papers, LBJL; memo Bator for Pres, 23 Aug 66, *FRUS 1964-68*, 13:453-55; Presidential Daily Diary, 24 Aug 66, fldr Daily Diary August 16-31, 1966, box 7, The President's Daily Diary, LBJL; Zimmermann, *Money and Security*, 198; msg Johnson to Wilson, nd, but sent 26 Aug 66, *FRUS 1964-1968*, 13:457 (quote); ltr Johnson to Erhard, 25 Aug 66, ibid, 15:392-93; (quotes).

28. Memo McNamara for Pres, 19 Sep 66, *FRUS 1964-1968*, 15:413-16; Zimmermann, *Money and Security*, 201; memo Bator for Pres, The Offset Problem, 13 Sep 66, fldr Tuesday Luncheon Suggested Agenda, box 2, NSF, Files of Walt W. Rostow, LBJL.

29. Memo Bator for Pres, 21 Sep 66, *FRUS 1964-1968*, 15:420-21; memo SecDef for Pres, 19 Sep 66, ibid, 416.

30. Shapley, *Promise and Power*, 399; McGhee, *At the Creation of a New Germany*, 191 (quote); telcon SecDef and Pres, 26 Sep 66, *FRUS 1964-1968*, 15:435 (quote).

31. Memo Rostow for Pres, 26 Sep 66, *FRUS 1964-1968*, 15:428-29; msg 42890 State to Bonn, 8 Sep 66, ibid 13:465-66.

32. Msg 3361 Bonn to State, 19 Sep 66, Cable files, OSD Hist; memcon, Offset and Troop Levels, 26 Sep 66, *FRUS 1964-1968*, 13:471-77; msg Johnson to Wilson, 1 Oct 66, ibid, 13:477-78; McGhee, *At the Creation*, 193; Jt Statement Following Discussions with Chancellor Erhard of Germany, 27 Sep 66, *Johnson Public Papers, 1966*, 2:1078-79 (quote); memcon, 26 Sep 66, 12:30 p.m., *FRUS 1964-1968*, 15:430.

33. Ltr Rusk to McNamara, 13 Jun 66, memo SecDef for CJCS, 27 Jun 66: both fldr 370.5 Jan 1966, box 4, ISA General files, Acc 70A-6649; JCSM-452-66 for SecDef, 8 Jul 66, fldr 370.5 Sensitive 1966 Jan --, ibid (quote).

34. Memo SecDef for CJCS, 23 Aug 66, ibid; msg ALO-329 CINCEUR for JCS, 1 Sep 66, item #49, fldr 30, Joint Chiefs of Staff, box 142, Lemnitzer Papers, NDU; JCSM-605-66 for SecDef, 22 Sep 66, fldr 370.5 1-36171/66 22 Oct 66, box 4, ISA General files, Acc 70A-6649 (quote).

35. Analysis of Major Decisions in Trilateral Talks, cited in note 24; memo SecDef for Pres, 19 Sep 66, *FRUS 1964-68*, 15:413-16; msg JCS 5279-66 Wheeler to Lemnitzer, 7 Sep 66, fldr 323.3 SAC/CINCEUR Jul 64-Oct 66, box 82, Wheeler Papers, RG 218 (quote).

36. Memo SecDef for CJCS, 4 Oct 66, fldr 334 NATO Sep-Oct 1966, box 13, ISA General files, Acc 70A-6648; JCSM-693-66 for SecDef, 27 Oct 66, fldr 370.5 I-36318/66 27 Oct 66, box 4, ISA General files, Acc 70A-6649.

37. Anderson, Holliday, and Rainey, "Alternative Force Structures for the U.S. Army in Europe," RAND Project 9489, 23 Nov 66, fldr 320.2 1966 Oct, box 2, ISA General files, Acc 70A-6649; memo Spec Asst to SecDef for NATO Force Planning (Stanley) for SecDef, 16 Sep 66, fldr NATO (ALPHA) 1966, box 4, SecDef Subject Decimal files, Acc 70A-4662.

38. Msg Johnson to Wilson, nd, but sent 26 Aug 66; msg Johnson to Wilson, nd, but sent 1 Sep 66; msg Johnson to Wilson, nd, but sent 1 Oct 66: *FRUS 1964-1968*, 13:457-58, 460-61, and 477; msg 42890 State to Bonn, 8 Sep 66, ibid, 465-66; memo Bator for Pres, 21 Sep 66, ibid, 15:421.

39. Memo Rostow and Bator for Pres, 22 Nov 66, fldr Trilateral Negotiations and NATO 1966-67, bk 1, Tab 39, box 50, NSC Histories, NSF, LBJL; Statement by Pres, 11 Oct 66, *Johnson Public Papers, 1966*, 2:1139; The Trilateral Negotiations and NATO, cited in note 15; Statement by Pres, 11 Oct 66, *Johnson Public Papers, 1966*, 2:1139.

40. Msg 82537 and msg 83112, State to Bonn, London, Paris, both 10 Nov 66: fldr McNamara/von Hassel Meeting 23-24 July 1966 (Kuss Book), box 3, ISA General files, Acc 72A-1494; ltr McCloy to Pres Johnson w/encl, 21 Nov 66, *FRUS 1964-1968*, 13:495, 497-98; memo Rostow and Bator for Pres, 22 Nov 66, fldr Trilateral Negotiations & NATO 1966-67, bk 1, Tab 39, box 50, NSC Histories, NSF, LBJL.

41. Msg Johnson for Wilson, 1 Sep 66, *FRUS 1964-1968*, 13:460-61; msg Johnson to Wilson, 1 Oct 66, ibid, 477-78; Johnson, *Vantage Point*, 307-08; msg 2349 Paris to OSD, 22 Aug 66, Cable files, OSD Hist; memo SecDef for CJCS, 12 Dec 66, fldr France 370.03 FRELOC Decision Papers 20 May 66, box 3, SecDef Subject Decimal files, Acc 70A-4662; msg Johnson to Wilson, 15 Nov 66, *FRUS 1964-1968*, 13:491-92; msg Wilson to Johnson, 291500Z Nov 66 and msg Johnson to Wilson, 051736Z Dec 66: fldr Trilateral Talks Oct-Dec 1966, box 13, Bator Papers, LBJL; Zimmermann, *Money and Security*, 214.

42. Memcon McAuliffe, Conv Wheeler and McCloy, Trilateral Talks, 25 Oct 66, fldr Trilateral Negotiations and NATO 1966-67, bk 3, TAB 13, box 51, NSC Histories, NSF, LBJL (quote); memo Helms for McCloy, 8 Nov 66, Tab 27, fldr 031.1 President Jul 65-Oct 67 and memo Helms for McCloy, 8 Nov 66: box 10, Wheeler Papers, RG 218.

43. Memo Rostow and Bator for Pres, 22 Nov 66, cited in note 39.

44. Memo Cooper for McCloy, Trilateral Financial Talks, Nov 21-25, 25 Nov 66, fldr McNamara/von Hassel Meeting 23-24 July 1966 (Kuss Book), box 3, ISA General files, Acc 72A-1494; Smith, Summary Notes of the 566th NSC mtg, 13 Dec 66, *FRUS 1964-1968*, 13:512; ISA Information Paper, Trilateral Talks, 3 Jan 67, fldr vol II NATO/MAP/Arms Control 1966-67, Tab M, box 91, McNamara Records, RG 200; DPM SecDef for Pres, Redeployment of Certain US Forces from Europe, (1st draft) 19 Jan 67, fldr Trilateral Memos to President & JCS, box 73, McNamara Records, RG 200.

45. JCSM-46-67 for SecDef, 28 Jan 67, fldr Trilateral Negotiations and NATO 1966-67, bk 4, TAB 41, box 51, NSC Histories, NSF, LBJL; JCSM-60-67 for SecDef, 2 Feb 67, fldr Trilateral Memos to President & JCS, box 73, McNamara Records, RG 200; ltr Wheeler to McCloy w/encl, 3 Feb 67, fldr 1967 Ltrs signed by Gen Wheeler, 1 Jan 67-30 Jun 67, box 125, Wheeler Papers, RG 218; memo E. Rostow et al for SecState, 30 Jan 67, fldr Trilateral Negotiations & NATO 1966-67, bk 4, Tabs 32-42, box 51, NSC Histories, NSF, LBJL; memo Bator for Pres, 25 Feb 67, fldr Trilateral Negotiations and NATO 1966-67, bk 1, TAB 50, box 50, NSC Histories, NSF, LBJL; memcon McNamara, Cleveland, et al on 3 Feb 67, dated 15 Feb 67, item #32, fldr 29b, Secy of Defense, box 141, Lemnitzer Papers, NDU.

46. Ltr Wheeler to McCloy w/encl, 3 Feb 67, cited in note 45; CM-2118-67 for DirJtStaff, 16 Feb 67, DJSM-641-67 for CJCS, Study on US Contribution to NATO (Short Title: CHECKPOINT), w/atchmt, Jt Staff Study on US Contribution to NATO (Focusing on Central Region, ACE), 23 May 67; Register of Personnel Handling Classified Document, Study of US Contribution to NATO, 2 Jun 67, fldr 092.2 NATO Oct 66-Jul 67, box 70, Wheeler Papers, RG 218; memcon Wheeler and Stanley, 23 Jan 67, ibid (quote).

47. Memo McCloy for Pres, 23 Feb 67, fldr Trilateral Negotiations and NATO 1966-67, bk 1, Tab 58c, box 50, NSC Histories, NSF, LBJL; The Trilateral Negotiations and NATO, cited in note 15; memo Bator for Pres, 23 Feb 67, *FRUS 1964-68*, 13:535; memcon McNamara, Cleveland, et al, 3 Feb 67, dated 15 Feb 67, item #32, fldr 29b, Secy of Defense, box 141, Lemnitzer Papers, NDU (quote).

48. Memcon McNaughton (?), Pre-lunch and Lunch w/Pres, 24 Feb 67, notes Francis M. Bator, Results of mtg w/Pres on 24 Feb 67; fldr Trilateral Negotiations and NATO 1966-67, bk 2, Tabs 45-52a, box 50, NSC Histories, NSF, LBJL.

49. McNaughton (?), Mtg notes, 25 Feb 67, ibid; memrcd Bator, Pres Conv w/McCloy et al on 1 Mar 67, 2 Mar 67, ibid; Bator, Record of Pres 27 Feb mtg w/Cong leadership, nd, bk 1, Tab 52g, ibid.

50. Memo Bator for Pres, 25 Feb 67, Tab 50, ibid (quote); memrcd Bator, Pres Conv w/McCloy et al on 1 Mar 67, 2 Mar 67, ibid (quotes); bk 2, Tabs 53-71, ibid (quotes); ltr Johnson to McCloy, 1 Mar 67, *FRUS 1964-68*, 13:536-37.

51. Record of mtg w/Pres, 8 Mar 67, *FRUS 1964-68*, 13:546; The Trilateral Negotiations and NATO, cited in note 15.

52. The Trilateral Negotiations and NATO, cited in note 15; msg 153411 State to Bonn, 11 Mar 67, rcd of mtg w/Pres, 8 Mar 67: *FRUS 1964-68*, 13:546-49; memrcd Halperin, Trilateral mtg 20-21 March 1967, 22 Mar 67, fldr Trilateral Negotiations & NATO 1966-67, box 51, NSC Histories, NSF, LBJL; ltr McCloy to Pres, 22 Mar 67, bk 1, Tab 75c, box 50, ibid.

53. Memo Bator for Pres, 23 Mar 67, fldr Trilateral Negotiations and NATO 1966-67, bk 1, Tab 75a, box 50, NSF, NSC Histories, LBJL (quotes); memo SecDef for CJCS, 23 Mar 67, bk 4, Tab 47, box 51, ibid; JCSM-180-67 for SecDef, 30 Mar 67 (quote); Tabs 47 and 49, ibid.

54. Memcon Spivey, Mtg 5 Apr on Proposed Redeployment of U.S. Forces from Germany, 6 Apr 67, bk 2, Tabs 72-98, ibid; McNaughton notes on mtg, Rotation Plan, 8 Apr 67, fldr Trilateral Negotiations and NATO: 1966-67, box 51, ibid; memo Halperin for SecDef, 30 Mar 67 w/atchmts, Proposed U.S. Rotation Plans and Talking Paper on U.S. Redeployments, 30 Mar 67, fldr Chron File, Jan-Jun, 1967 [2 of 2] box 1, Papers of Morton Halperin, LBJL.

55. Rostow Agenda, Mtg w/Pres, 22 Apr 67, fldr Meetings with the President, item #24, box 1 & 2, Files of Walt W. Rostow, NSF, LBJL; memo Bator for Pres, 27 Apr 67, fldr Trilateral Negotiations and NATO 1966-67, bk 1, Tab 90a, box 50, NSC Histories, NSF, LBJL; The Trilateral Negotiations and NATO, cited in note 15; memo SecDef for CJCS, SecA SecAF, 31 May 67, memo SecDef for SecAF, 31 May 67: fldr 323.3 SAC/CINCEUR Nov 66-31 Mar 68, box 82, Wheeler Papers, RG 218; Final Report on Trilateral Talks, nd, atchmts 2 and 4, *FRUS 1964-68*, 13:562-68; msg JCS 4631 to USCINCEUR, 23 Aug 67, Cable files, OSD Hist.

56. JCSM-313-67 for SecDef, 2 Jun 67, fldr JCS Comments on DPMs 1967, box 75, McNamara Records, RG 200.

57. Memo Counselor of Dept State for SecState, 16 Oct 67, *FRUS 1964-68*, 13:624.

58. Livesay mins, SecDef Staff mtg, 13 May 68, fldr Minutes of SecDef Staff Meetings March-September 1968, box 18, NSF-Papers of Clark Clifford, LBJL; Smith Summary notes of 586th NSC mtg, 22 May 68, *FRUS 1964-68*, 15:675; OASD(SA), Is the U.S. Doing Too Much for NATO [?], draft, 18 Mar 68, Tab 126, fldr 092.2 NATO Mar 68-Jul 68, box 71, Wheeler Papers, RG 218.

59. Msg 1335 USMission NATO to SecState/SecDef 15 Jan 68, Cable files, OSD Hist; memo ISA for SecDef, 25 Jan 68, fldr 334, NATO 1968 Jan - , box 7, ISA General files, Acc 72A-1499; JCSM-18-68 for SecDef, 13 Jan 68, fldr NATO 320.2 1968, box 3, 1968 SecDef Subject Decimal files, Acc 73A-1304.

60. Clifford, *Counsel*, 559: msg 119536 State to USMission NATO, 22 Feb 68, FRUS 1964-68, 13:670-71; transc Clifford test, 23 May 68 to SSCA hearings on DoD Appros for FY 1969, 23 May 68, 1818-19, fldr Transcripts - Hearings before Senate SubCte on Defense Appropriations - Clifford/Nitze 23 May 68, box 71, ASD(C) files, OSD Hist.

61. Memo Rostow for Pres, 22 Mar 68, *FRUS 1964-68*, 13:683; msg Wheeler to SecDef, 160415Z Apr 68, fldr STRAF (incl 6th Infantry Division), box 26, Clifford Papers, LBJL; memo SecDef for Pres, 21 Jun 68, fldr Memos on Troop Strength Increases and other Subjects, box 1, ibid.

62. Elsey notes SecDef Staff Conf, 13 May 68, fldr Personal Papers of George M. Elsey, box 1, Papers of George M. Elsey, LBJL; memo ASD(C) for SecDef, nd but likely Feb 68, fldr Memos to Read [1], box 1, Clifford Papers, LBJL.

63. Memo SecDef for Pres, 21 Jun 68, cited in note 61 (quote); memo CSA for SecA, 26 Jun 68, fldr STRAF (incl 6th Infantry Division), box 26, Clifford Papers, LBJL.

64. Memo SecDef for Pres, 21 Jun 68, cited in note 61; memo SecDef for SvcSecs and CJCS, 6 Jun 68, fldr Europe 123 DPM 1968, box 1, SecDef Subject Decimal files, Acc 73A-1304.

65. Msg ALO 581 SHAPE to JCS, 1 Aug 68, Cable files, OSD Hist.

66. Msg JCS/DJS 08661 to DepUSCINCEUR, 1 Aug 68, fldr 44, 1968 E.O. Messages IN Jul - 11 Sep, box 176, 1967-1968 General Lemnitzer Eyes Only Messages File 1955-1969, Lemnitzer Papers, NDU; memcon, 23 Jul 68, *FRUS 1964-68*, 15:723-24; msg 190741 State to Reykjavik (for Rusk), 26 Jun 68, ibid, 13:721; Livesay mins, SecDef Staff mtg, 1 Jul 68, fldr Minutes of SecDef Staff Meetings March-September 1968, box 18, Clifford Papers, LBJL. Sen Symington withdrew his amendment during the markup of the appropriations bill.

67. Memo Warnke for SvcSecs, CJCS, et al, 12 Jul 68 w/encl, fldr Europe 320.2 Jan 1968, box 11, ISA General files, Acc 72A-1498. Clifford sent the enclosure to Senators Russell, Jackson, and Stennis on 11 July. The enclosure is printed in *FRUS 1964-68*, 13:727-32 (quotes).

68. Livesay mins, SecDef Staff mtg, 1 Jul 68, fldr Minutes of SecDef Staff Meetings March-September 1968, box 18, Clifford Papers, LBJL; CM-3440-68, for H.K. Johnson et al, 26 Jun 68, fldr 323.3 SAC/CINCEUR Apr 68-Dec 68, box 82, Wheeler Papers, RG 218

69. Memo Warnke for SecDef, 8 Jul 68, fldr Troops in Europe and Balance-of-payment, box 17, Clifford Papers, LBJL (quotes); Poole, *JCS and National Policy, 1965-1968*, pt 1:400-01.

70. Talking Paper Prepared in DoD, nd, attached to 11 July memo Clifford for Rusk, *FRUS 1964-68*, 13:728-32.

71. Memo SecDef for CJCS, 8 Oct 68, fldr Staff, JCS, box 13, Clifford Papers, LBJL; Poole, *JCS and National Policy, 1965-1968*, pt 1:409-10 and 404; JCSM-547-68 for SecDef, 14 Sep 68 (quote), JCSM-538-68 for SecDef, 7 Sep 68: fldr 334 NATO 1968 Jan -, ISA General files, Acc 72A-1499.

72. Memo ISA for DepSecDef, 19 Oct 68, memo SecDef for CJCS et al, 23 Oct 68: fldr NATO 381, box 5, 1968 SecDef Subject Decimal files, Acc 73A-1304; JCSM-651-68 for SecDef, 31 Oct 68, fldr 334 NATO 1968 Jan - , box 7, ISA General files, Acc 72A-1499; Paper on Europe, Tab G-1, fldr #15 JCS Meeting 28 Dec 68, box 2, OSD Records from SecDef Vault (Mr. Laird), Acc 330-74-142; memo SecDef for SvcSecs et al, 7 Dec 68, Tab G-2, ibid.

73. DPQ[68] United States-D/1 1968 Defense Planning Review, United States of America, Memorandum, Item I, 10 Sep 68, memo SecA for SecDef, 12 Nov 68, fldr NATO 320.2 DPQ 1968, box 3, SecDef Subject Decimal files, Acc 73A-1304; HQDA, Agenda for Discussion with Secretary Clifford and Secretary Nitze, STRAF Readiness, 5 Nov 68, fldr STRAF (incl 6th Infantry Division), box 26, Clifford Papers, LBJL.

74. DPM SecDef for Pres, NATO Strategy and Force Structure, 7 Jan 69, fldr FY 1970 DPMs & TS, box 122, ASD(C) files, OSD Hist.

XVI. CRISIS IN THE MIDDLE EAST

1. Johnson, *Vantage Point*, 287-89; aide-memoire DeptState to IsraeliEmb, Washington, 11 Feb 57, FRUS 1955-57, 17:133.

2. Poole, *JCS and National Policy, 1965-68*, pt 2:525-27; msg 3005 Bonn to State, 11 Feb 65, Cable files, OSD Hist; memos SecState for Pres, 19 Feb 65, Pres for Harriman and Komer, 21 Feb 65, *FRUS 1964-68*, 18:340-41 and 343-46; msg 896 State to TelAviv, 8 Mar 65, ibid, 391-92 (quote).

3. JCSM-337-65 for SecDef, 6 May 65, *FRUS 1964-68*, 18:449-50; memo Komer for Pres, 25 Oct 65, ibid, 508.

4. Memo ISA for SecDef, 18 Jan 66, fldr Reading File Jan 66, box 124, McNamara Records, RG-200: draft memo SecState and SecDef for Pres, nd, memrcd Komer, Pres mtg on Israel/Jordan Matters, 11 Feb 66, *FRUS 1964-68*, 18:534-35, 551 (quote); memrcd Komer, 11 Feb 66, memcon, mtg McNamara w/Eban, 12 Feb 66, ibid, 550-51, 552-53; memcon Hoopes, 19 Feb 66, fldr 452.1 Jan 1966, box 7, ISA General files, Acc 70-A-6649; memo McNaughton for McNamara, 31 Mar 66, *FRUS 1964-68*, 18:571-73 (quote); Statement, DeptState, 2 Apr 66 and News conf, DeptState, 20 May 66 (quote), *AFP, CD, 1966*, 540-41.

5. NIE 30-65, 10 Mar 65, *FRUS 1964-68*, 18:402-03; msg 151 State to Amman, 8 Oct 65, ibid, 500; memcon, 29 Dec 65, ibid, 530-32; Parker, "The June 1967 War," 178.

6. Memo Rostow for Pres, 15 Nov 66, *FRUS 1964-68*, 18:658-60.

7. Msg 121337 State to TelAviv, 18 Jan 67, memo Rostow for Pres, 13 Feb 67, ibid, 748, 761 (quote); memo McNamara for Pres, 17 Apr 67, fldr Reading File Apr 1967, box 128, McNamara Records, RG 200.

8. Brown and Parker, "Introduction," in Parker, ed, *The Six Day War: A Retrospective*, 6-7; Saunders, Pres in Middle East Crisis, May 12-June 19, 1967, 19 Dec 68, vol 1, box 17, NSC History of Middle East Crisis, NSF, LBJL; memo for DCI, 9 Jun 67, *FRUS 1964-68*, 19:403; Parker, "June 1967 War," 179, 181(quote); Parker, *Politics of Miscalculation in the Middle East*, 3. For an extensive and multinational treatment of this still contentious report, see Brown, "Origins of the Crisis," in Parker, ed, *The Six Day War*, 28-43, 52-54, and 71-73. Golan, "Soviet Union and Outbreak of the June 1967 Six-Day War," 6; Brecher, *Decisions in Crisis: Israel, 1967* and 1973, 49.

9. Johnson, *Vantage Point*, 293; interv Dean Rusk by Paige E. Mulhollan, 8 Mar 70, 4: 3, LBJL.

10. Rusk interv, 8 Mar 70, 4: 1. For differing views see Cohen, "Lyndon Baines Johnson vs Gamel Abdul Nasser," in Cohen and Tucker, eds, *Lyndon Johnson Confronts the World*, 296 and Schoenbaum, *Waging Peace and War*, 461; memo Saunders for Rostow, 21 Mar 67, fldr Israel Cables & Memos, vol VI, box 140, CF, Israel, NSF, LBJL; Brown and Parker, "Introduction," in Parker, ed, *The Six Day War*, 3.

11. Seventh Control Group mtg, 1 Jun 67, fldr Middle East 334, box 63, SecDef Subject Decimal files, Acc 72A-2468; E. Rostow, Organization for the Middle East Crisis, 31 May 67, vol 3, box 18, NSC History of Middle East Crisis, NSF, LBJL; Wainstein, "Some Aspects of the U.S. Involvement in the Middle East

Crisis, May-June 1967," Critical Incident No. 14, February 1968, IDA Report R-132, 62-65, box 140, Subj files, OSD Hist.

12. Parker, "June 1967 War," 179-80; ltr Johnson to Kosygin in msg 198583 State to Moscow, 19 May 67, *FRUS 1964-68*, 14:485-87. The letter was forwarded to Kosgyin on 22 May. Spec Rpt of UN Secy Gen Thant, 18 May 67, *AFP, CD, 1967*, 480; memo Hoopes for SecDef, 19 May 67, w/atchmt, fldr Middle East 092 (Jan-May) 1967, box 62, SecDef Subject Decimal Files, Acc 72-A-2468. Hoopes memo without the atchmt is available in *FRUS 1964-68*, 19:33-34; Summary: Movements of the Sixth Fleet, nd, vol 7, App H, box 19, NSC History of Middle East Crisis, NSF, LBJL.

13. Brecher, *Decisions in Crisis*, 91; msg 3681 TelAviv to State, 21 May 67, fldr Vol 1, Memos and Misc.(2 of 2), box 105, CF, Middle East, NSF, LBJL (quote). Marginal annotations on the cable record the president's decision.

14. Sisco, Prospects for a Political Settlement, 2 Jun 67, fldr ME 092 (1 thru 12 June) 1967, box 62, SecDef Subject Decimal files, Acc 72A-2468. Poole, *JCS and National Policy, 1965-68*, pt 2:544-45; *FRUS 1964-68*, 18:819, n 6; memo Rostow for Pres, 23 May 67, ibid, 19:72-73 and 73.

15. Ltr Johnson to Eshkol in msg 198955 State to TelAviv, 21 May 67, ltr Johnson to Nasser in msg 199704 State to Cairo, 22 May 67, ltr Johnson to Kosygin in msg 199728 State to Moscow, 22 May 67, *FRUS 1964-68*, 19:46-47, 58-59, 68, n 3; Poole, *JCS and National Policy, 1965-68*, pt 2:546; memo Saunders to Rostow, 23 May 67, Memos and Misc, vol 1, box 105, NSC History of Middle East Crisis, NSF, LBJL; DeptState, Historical Office, RP No 879, "United States Policy and Diplomacy in the Middle East Crisis, May 15-June 10, 1967," Jan 69, 44-46, vol 9, app P, box 19, NSC History of Middle East Crisis, NSF, LBJL; DeptState Paper, 26 May 67, *FRUS 1964-68*, 19:116-17.

16. Memcon, UK/US Plenary Session on Near East Crisis, 24 May 67, Memos and Misc, vol 1, box 105, NSC History of Middle East Crisis, NSF, LBJL; memrcd Sibley, Mtg of Control Group/Middle East and UK Reprs, 24 May 67, fldr A/I/S 2-12-5, 1967 Crisis (Overall), box 1, ISA Regional files, Acc 330-76-140; "United States Policy and Diplomacy," 47-48; memo Hoopes for SecDef, 25 May 67, fldr Middle East 092 (Jan-May) 1967, box 62, SecDef Subject Decimal files, Acc 72A-2468; interv Nicholas DeB Katzenbach by Paige E. Mulhollan, 11 Dec 68, 3:7, LBJL.

17. Wainstein, "Some Aspects," 32.

18. Saunders, Pres in Middle East Crisis, cited in note 8; memrcd Hoopes, Control Group mtg, 25 May 67, 29 May 67, fldr A/I/S 2-12-6 (68) 1967 Crisis Special File, box 1, ISA Regional files, Acc 330-76-140 (quote).

19. Memrcd Saunders, Record of NSC Mtg, 24 May 67 (quotes), memo CIA, 23 May 67, *FRUS 1964 -68*, 19:87-91 and 73-74. On the concerns of Symington and others about the administration's ability to handle two conflicts simultaneously see *New York Times*, 24 May 67.

20. Circ msg 204952 State to All AmDip Posts, 31 May 67, Cable files, OSD Hist; Oren, *Six Days of War*, 107-08; Brecher, *Decisions in Crisis*, 131-32. Such a guarantee was written into the NATO treaty, but the elliptical language allowed each member to take actions it deemed necessary. Unsaid but understood was the requirement that only Congress could decide if armed force would be necessary; Kaplan, *Long Entanglement*, 5.

21. Memcon Rusk and Eban, 25 May 67, *FRUS 1964-68*, 19:109-12; memo CIA, Appraisal of an estimate of Arab-Israeli Crisis by the Israeli Intelligence Service, 25 May 67 and memo CIA, Israeli Intelligence Estimate of the Israeli-Arab Crisis, 25 May 67: vol 2, box 17, NSC History of Middle East Crisis, NSF, LBJL; memrcd Hoopes, 25 May 67, cited in note 18; memcon Rusk and Eban, 25 May 67, *FRUS 1964-68*, 19:110. On the implications of preemption see memo SecState for Pres, 26 May 67, ibid, 124, 126.

22. Memo SecState for Pres, 26 May 67, *FRUS 1964-68*, 19:123-25.

23. Memcon Eban w/McNamara et al, 26 May 67, ibid, 118-22 (quotes); memo Rostow for Pres, 26 May 67, vol 2, box 17, NSC History of Middle East Crisis, NSF, LBJL.

24. Memrcd Saunders, Mtg on Arab-Israeli Crisis on 26 May, 27 May 67, *FRUS 1964-68*, 19:127-36 (quote, 129); aide-memoire DeptState to IsraeliEmb, 11 Feb 57, SecState News conf, 19 Feb 57, *AFP, CD, 1957*, 908, 920-21.

25. Memrcd Saunders, 27 May 67, *FRUS 1964-68*, 19:127-36 (quote); Saunders, Pres in Middle East Crisis, cited in note 8.

26. Memcon Pres w/Eban, 26 May 67, *FRUS 1964-68*, 19:140-46; (quotes); Brecher, *Decisions in Israel's Foreign Policy*, 391-93.

27. The text is quoted in ltr Johnson to Eshkol, 3 Jun 67, *FRUS 1964-68*, 19:263; Saunders, Pres in Middle East Crisis, cited in note 8; quoted in Reich, "The Israeli Response," Parker, ed, *The Six Day War*, 133.

28. Memos DASD (ISA) for DirDIA, ASD(I&L), 26 May 67 and DASD(I&L) for ASD(ISA), 8 Jun 67: fldr A/I/S 2-12-5 1967 Crisis (General), box 1, ISA Regional files, Acc 330-76-140.

29. Msg USCINCEUR to CINCSTRIKE/ USCINCMEAFSA, 281655Z May 67, Cable files, OSD Hist.

30. Wainstein, "Some Aspects," 79-80.

31. Msg 874 UKEmbMoscow to Foreign Office, 24 May 67, fldr Middle East 092 (Jan-May) 1967, box 62, SecDef Subject Decimal files, Acc 72A-2468. Johnson's letter, sent to the U.S. Embassy on 19 May and delivered to Kosygin on 22 May, dealt primarily with Vietnam, ballistic missiles, and nonproliferation, and only incidentally with the Mid-East crisis, blaming it primarily on the Syrians. Msg 198583, State to Moscow, 19 May 67, *FRUS 1964-68*, 14:485-88; ltr Kosygin to Pres, 27 May 67, ibid, 19:159-60 (quotes); msg 203943 State to TelAviv, 27 May 67, ibid, 162-64. Johnson deleted this sentence from the State/OSD draft: "Preemptive actions by Israel would make it impossible for the friends of Israel to stand at your side." Ibid, 19:163 n 6; msg 3833 TelAviv to State, 28 May 67, vol 4, app S (May 28-31), box 22-23, NSC History of Middle East Crisis, NSF, LBJL; ltr Eshkol to Johnson, 30 May 67, *FRUS 1964-68*, 19:187-89. A meeting at the prime minister's home on 3 June reversed this decision. Ltr Johnson to Kosgyin in msg 203963 State to Moscow, 28 May 67, ibid, 167-68 (quote).

32. Memo Dean for E. Rostow, 27 May 67 w/atchmt, msg Thomson to E. Rostow; memrcd Sibley, J-5, Mtg of Control Group/Middle East and UK Reps, 24 May 67: fldr A/I/S 2-12-5 1967 Crisis (Overall), box 1, ISA Regional files, Acc 330-76-140; Wainstein, "Some Aspects," 41 (quote); JCSM-301-67 for SecDef, 27 May 67, Annex B, Review of the UK Proposal, fldr Middle East 381.3 1967, box 63, SecDef Subject Decimal files, Acc 72A-2468.

33. JCSM-301-67, 27 May 67, Annex A, Contingency Outline Plan, fldr Middle East 381.3 1967, box 63, SecDef Subject Decimal files, Acc 72A-2468.

34. Poole, *JCS and National Policy, 1965-68*, pt 2:553; JCSM-301-67 for SecDef, 27 May 67, and Annex A, cited in note 33 (quote).

35. Memo Hoopes for SecDef, 28 May 67, FRUS 1964-68, 19:171-72 (quote); Wainstein, "Some Aspects," 44; Poole, *JCS and National Policy, 1965-68*, pt 2:555.

36. Wainstein, "Some Aspects," 47-48; draft memo, SecState and SecDef for Pres, 28 May 67, fldr Middle East 381.3 1967, box 63, SecDef Subject Decimal files, Acc 72A-2468.

37. Memo SecState and SecDef for Pres, 30 May 67, *FRUS 1964-68*, 19:190-94.

38. Ibid (quotes); Wainstein, "Some Aspects," 51; ed note, msg 205690 and 205691 State to All Posts, 31 May 67, *FRUS 1964-68*, 19:196, 204-06, and 206-07.

39. Memo Hoopes for DirJtStaff, 30 May 67, fldr A/I/S 2-12-5 1967 Crisis (General) box 1, ISA Regional files, Acc 330-76-140; memo Hoopes for SecDef, 2 Jun 67, *FRUS 1964-68*, 19:259-62; memo Saunders for Rostow, Arab-Israeli Control Group mtg, 4:30 p.m., 1 Jun 67, vol 3, box 18, NSC History of Middle East Crisis, NSF, LBJL; Walsh, Agenda for Control Group Meeting, 4:30 p.m., June 1, 1 Jun 67 w/atchmt, draft memo Hoopes for Middle East Control Group, 1 Jun 67, fldr Middle East 334, box 63, SecDef Subject Decimal files, Acc 72A-2468; Wainstein, "Some Aspects," 44-45.

40. Poole, *JCS and National Policy, 1965-68*, pt 2:550 (quote); Rusk test, 1 Jun 67, SFRC Ex Sess, Briefing on the Middle East Situation, *Executive Sessions of the SFRC together with Joint Sessions with the SASC (Historical Series)*, Made Public 2007, XIX:602, 606-07, 613, 615, and 622; Hedrick Smith in *New York Times*, 5 Jun 67. Rusk previously explained the administration's position in Circ Msg 204952 State to All Posts, 31 May 67, cited in n 20.

41. *New York Times*, 31 May 67; DeptState INR, Intelligence Note #434, 2 Jun 67, fldr ME 092 (1 thru 12 June) 1967, box 62, SecDef Subject Decimal files, Acc 72A-2468; Brecher, *Decisions in Israel's Foreign Policy*, 412; DIA Int Bul, 107-67, 2 Jun 67, Cable files, OSD Hist; *AFP, CD, 1967*, 504; ltr Eshkol to Johnson, 30 May 67, *FRUS 1964-68*, 19:187-89 (quotes), Johnson, *Vantage Point*, 294; draft memo Hoopes, 1 Jun 67, cited in note 39.

42. Msg CAP 67478 Rostow to Pres, 29 May 67, *FRUS 1964-68*, 19:173; memo McNamara and Rusk for Pres, 30 May 67, ed note, ibid, 190-93, 196.

43. Wainstein, "Some Aspects," 89. The remarks are based on NMCC Emergency Actions Tapes recorded at 010101Z Jun 67.

44. Meir Amit quoted in Brecher, *Decisions in Crisis*, 153; memrcd Conv Amit w/McNamara, 1 June 1967, *FRUS 1964-68*, 19:223-25 (quote); Reich, "The Israeli Response," in Parker, ed, *The Six Day War*, 139-40; Oren, *Six Days of War*, 147; memo Kent for DCI, 26 May 1967, fldr Middle East 092 (Jan-May) 1967, box 62, SecDef Subject Decimal files, Acc 72A-2468. The Israeli ambassador to the United States later suggested that actual Israeli losses were approximately 750 killed and 2,500 wounded; OSD Transcript, "Arab-Israeli War Briefing," vol III, 12 Sep 67, 106, fldr A/I/S 2-12 1967 Arab-Israel War (General), box 1, ISA Regional files, Acc 330-76-140. Memo DCI for Pres, 2 Jun 67, (quote) w/atchmt, Views of General Meir Amit, 2 Jun 67 (quote), fldr Middle East Situation-1967- 4 of 6 Status Reports – Misc, box 1, ISA Regional files, Acc 73A-1345.

45. Amit's report is quoted in Brecher, *Decisions in Crisis*, 157; Oren, *Six Days of War*, 156-58; msg 3937 TelAviv to State, 5 Jun 67, Cable files, OSD Hist; memo Rostow for Pres, 4 Jun 67, *FRUS 1964-68*, 19:272.

46. JCSM-310-67 for SecDef, 2 Jun 67, vol 3, box 18, NSC History of Middle East Crisis, NSF, LBJL (quote); Poole, *JCS and National Policy, 1965-68*, pt 2:560.

47. Memo Hoopes for SecDef, 2 Jun 67, *FRUS 1964-68*, 19:261; msg 207920 State to Ottawa, 4 Jun 67, fldr Cable files, OSD Hist; memo Hoopes for Middle East Control Group, 4 Jun 67, fldr Middle East 381.3 1967, box 63, SecDef Subject Decimal files, Acc 72A-2468.

48. Memo Rostow for Pres, 2 Jun 67, *FRUS 1964-68*, 19:244-46 (quotes); Johnson, *Vantage Point*, 294; Summary: Movements of the Sixth Fleet, nd, vol 7, App H, box 19, NSC History of Middle East Crisis, NSF, LBJL; Wainstein, "Some Aspects," 91.

49. Memcon Leddy, 2 Jun 67, *FRUS 1964-68*, 19:239-244.

50. Circ msg 207956 State to Arab Capitals, 3 Jun 67, ibid, 266-68 (quotes); CIA memo, 3 Jun 67, ibid, 270; interv Rusk, 8 Mar 70, 4:3, LBJL.

51. Ltr Johnson to Eshkol, 3 Jun 67, *FRUS 1964-68*, 19:262-64 (quote); Bergus, "The View from Washington," in Parker, ed, *The Six Day War*, 210; interv Katzenbach, 11 Dec 68, 3: 6, LBJL (quote, emphasis in the source); see also Rusk, interv 8 Mar 70, 4:2, LBJL; NSC Special Comm mtg notes, 9 Jun 67, *FRUS 1964-68*, 19:400, n 11 (quote).

52. Contingency Paper, J-3, JCS, 28 May 67, Tab 5, Agenda for Control Group Meeting, 3 Jun 67, fldr ME 334, box 63, SecDef Subject Decimal files, Acc 72A-2468 (quote).

53. Memo Rostow for Pres, 4 Jun 67, *FRUS 1964-68*, 19:272-77; mins of 9th mtg of the Middle East Control Group, 4 Jun 67, ibid, 283-85.

54. Memrcd Saunders, NSC mtg on 7 Jun 67, dated 7 Jan 69, ibid, 347-48 (quote); Saunders notes, NSC Special Comm mtg, 7 Jun 67, ibid, 19:351-54; memrcd Saunders, Walt Rostow's Recollections of June 5, 1967, dated 17 Nov 68, ed note, ibid, 287-93; Circ msg 208032 State to White House, 5 Jun 67, Cable files, OSD Hist; see also Wainstein, "Some Aspects," 92-95, Smith Hempstone in *Washington Star*, 6 Jun 67; *Aviation Week*, 12 Jun 67; Johnson, *Vantage Point*, 297; msg from the White House to Kosygin, 5 Jun 67, *FRUS 1964-68*, 19:301; Rusk interv, 8 Mar 70, 4:6, LBJL. In this later interview Rusk referred to "the Israeli Attack." Georgiy Kornienko, *The Cold War: Testimony of a Participant*, cited in Brown, "Origins of the Crisis," in Parker, ed, *The Six Day War*, 70 (quote). Kornienko was chief of the American Department, Soviet Foreign Ministry, in 1967.

55. Ed note, *FRUS 1964-68*, 19:298-99; interv Robert McNamara by Walt W. Rostow, 8 Jan 75, 42-43, LBJL (quote); memcon Davis, The Hot Line Exchanges, 4 Nov 68, vol 7, App G, box 19, NSC History of Middle East Crisis, NSF, LBJL.

56. Hot Line Msg Kosygin to Johnson, recd 8:15 a.m., 5 Jun 67, *FRUS 1964-68*, 19:300 (quote); CMC Work Notes JCS Meeting (ME), 5 Jun 67, vol 16, Greene Papers, MHC (quote); Hot Line Msg Johnson to Kosygin, 8:57 a.m., 5 Jun 67, *FRUS 1964-68*, 19:304; Johnson, *Vantage Point*, 298; Washington-Moscow Hot Line Exchanges, fldr vol 7, App G, box 19, NSC History of Mideast Crisis, NSF, LBJL.

57. Ltr Eshkol to Johnson in msg 3935 TelAviv to State, 5 Jun 67, *FRUS 1964-68*, 19:302-03 (quote); msg 201840 State to London, 5 Jun 67, Cable files, OSD Hist.

58. Ed note, *FRUS 1964-68*, 19:293 (quote); memrcd Saunders, cited in note 54; Wainstein, "Some Aspects," 93-94; CMC Work Notes, 5 Jun 67, cited in note 56 (quote); CIA memo, 5 Jun 67, *FRUS 1964-68*, 19:318-19.

59. Note Rostow for Pres, 5 Jun 67, 4:40 p.m., w/atchmt (quote), msg 2851 TelAviv to State, 5 Jun 67, memo Rostow for Pres, 5 Jun 67, 9:05 p.m., w/atchmt (quote): all Cable files, OSD Hist; Saunders notes, 7 Jun 67, cited in note 54 (quote); memrcd Saunders, cited in note 54 (quote).

60. Msg USUN 5644 to State, 7 Jun 67, Cable files, OSD Hist; Saunders, Pres in Middle East Crisis, cited in note 8; Johnson, *Vantage Point*, 299.

61. JCSM-315-67 for SecDef, 6 Jun 67, fldr Middle East 381 1967, box 63, SecDef Subject Decimal files, Acc 72A-2468.

62. DoD News Release 525-67, 5 Jun 67, fldr Middle East June 1-10. 1967, box 139, Subj files, OSD Hist; msgs 8586 and 8597 Cairo to State, 6 Jun 67, Cable files, OSD Hist; msg COMSIXTHFLT to JCS, 070626Z Jun 67, ibid; *Washington Star*, 9 Jun 67, 11; Wainstein, "Some Aspects," 97-101; ltr Austin to Schwartz, 8 Sep 67, fldr A/I/S 2-12-3 1967 Crisis Settlement #3, box 1, ISA Regional files, Acc 330-76-140; Poole, *JCS and National Policy, 1965-68*, pt 2:565.

63. Memo Hoopes for Vance, 1 Jun 67 w/atchmts, memo Battle for SecState, SecDef, Control Group, 31 May 67, Tabs A and C, fldr Middle East 092 (1 thru 12 June) 1967, box 62, SecDef Subject Decimal files, Acc

72A-2468. Tab A is in *FRUS 1964-68*, 19: 211-13; memo Riley for DirDSA, 3 Feb 67, fldr Middle East 400.137 1967, box 63, SecDef Subject Decimal files, Acc 72A-2468.

64. JCSM-315-67 for SecDef, 6 Jun 67, Annex B, 11 and Paper, Contingency Contracts, nd, fldr Middle East 381 1967, ibid; memo ASD(I&L) for SecDef, 31 May 67, ibid.

65. Memo ASD(I&L) for DSA, 5 Jun 67, fldr Middle East 400.137 1967, ibid; memo SecDef for Pres, 7 Jun 67, ibid; DoD News Release 539-67, 7 Jun 67, *McNamara Public Statements, 1967*, 6:2173-74; memo ASD(I&L) for DepSecDef, 9 Jun 67, fldr Middle East 400.137 1967, box 63, SecDef Subject Decimal files, Acc 72A-2468; *DoD Annual Report for FY 1967*, 76.

66. Memo Rostow for Pres, 7 Jun 67, *FRUS 1964-68*, 19:339-41.

67. Memrcd Saunders, NSC mtg on June 7, 1967, dated 7 Jan 69, ibid, 347-48 (quotes); Saunders notes, 7 Jun 67, cited in note 54 (quote).

68. Pres Statement, 7 Jun 67, *Johnson Public Papers, 1967*, 1:599: Draft NSAM, 6 Jun 67, vol 7, App I (1-3), box 19, NSC History of Middle East Crisis, NSF, LBJL; Johnson, *Vantage Point*, 300; memrcd Saunders, cited in note 54.

69. Saunders paper, 16 Jul 68, fldr Intro to Files of SC, NSC Jun-Aug 67, box 1, Files of Special Cte of NSC, LBJL; Saunders notes, 7 Jun 67, cited in note 54 (quote).

70. Memo Hoopes for SecDef, 9 Jun 67 (quote), w/atchmt, DeptState, An Approach to Political Settlement in the Near East, 8 Jun 67, fldr Middle East 092 (1 thru 12 June) 1967, box 62, SecDef Subject Decimal files, Acc 72A-2468.

71. Draft memo Hoopes for Middle East Control Group, 1 Jun 67, fldr Middle East 334, box 63, ibid; memo SecDef for Bundy, 8 Jun 67, *FRUS 1964-68*, 19:382-83 (quote); memo SecDef to SecA et al, 8 Jun 67, fldr Middle East 400 (Jan-Sept) 1967, box 63, SecDef Subject Files, Acc 72-A-2468; memo SecDef for Pres, 8 Jun 67, fldr Reading File June 15-1, 1967, box 128 McNamara Records.

72. Notes NSC Spec Comm mtg, 8 Jun 67, vol 7, App I (1-3), box 19, NSC History of Middle East Crisis, NSF, LBJL.

73. Draft Memo Control Group for Bundy, 9 Jun 67, fldr Middle East 400 (Jan-Sept) 1967, box 63, SecDef Subject Decimal files, Acc 72A-2468; Saunders notes NSC Spec Comm mtg, 9 Jun 67, *FRUS 1964-68*, 19:399; memo Hoopes for SecDef, 10 Jun 67, fldr Middle East Settlement 1967 1 of 5 Memos & Directives on Arms Control, box 1, ISA General files, Acc 73A-1345.

74. Poole, *JCS and National Policy, 1965-68*, pt 2:570; ed note, *FRUS 1964-68*, 19:360-61; Wainstein, "Some Aspects," 106-07; ltr SecDef to Chairman, House Cte on Appros, 11 Aug 67 w/atchmt #2, Details of Significant Messages Sent to USS *Liberty*, fldr Middle East 301-380 1967, box 63, SecDef Subject Decimal files, Acc 72A-2468; Cristol, "The *Liberty* Incident," Ph.D. diss, 1997, 1. See also Cristol, *The Liberty Incident*, 85.

75. Msg COMSIXTHFLT to USCINCEUR, 081320Z Jun 67, *FRUS 1964-68*, 19:364. To allay any charge of active involvement in the war, the fleet's aircraft were not armed, thus the delay in getting them airborne; Wainstein, "Some Aspects," 108; Cristol, "The *Liberty* Incident," 409; memo Rostow for Pres, 8 Jun 67, *FRUS 1964-68*, 19:362; McNamara test, 1 Feb 68, SCAS, *Hearings: Authorization for Military Procurement, Research and Development, FY 1969, and Reserve Strength*, 47; msg JCS 7354 to USCINCEUR, 081416Z Jun 67, fldr Joint Chiefs of Staff Messages, *http://www.nsa.gov/liberty/jcs.cfm*; msg USCINCEUR ECJC-L 09060 to CINCUSNAVEUR, 081446Z Jun 67, fldr CINC Messages, *http://www.nsa.gov/liberty/jcs.cfm*; Johnson, *Vantage Point*, 300.

76. Hot Line msg Johnson to Kosygin, 8 Jun 67, 11:17 a.m., *FRUS 1964-68*, 19:368 (quote); Wainstein, "Some Aspects," 108-09; Saunders notes NSC Spec Comm mtg, 9 Jun 67, *FRUS 1964-68*, 19:398. For post-mortems on the event see memos Chairman President's Foreign Intelligence Advisory Board (Clifford) for Rostow, 18 Jul 67, DirINR for Acting SecState, 13 Jun 67, and CIA Intell memo, 13 Jun 67: *FRUS 1964-68*, 19: 678-82, 474-76, 469-71.

77. Brecher, *Decisions in Israel's Foreign Policy*, 432-33; OSD Transcript, "Arab-Israeli War Briefing," Vol I, 11 Sep 67, 48, fldr A/I/S 2-12 1967 Arab-Israel War (General), box 1, ISA Regional files, Acc 330-76-140; memcon Kohler w/Can Amb, w/atchmt, 8 Jun 67, fldr Middle East 092 (1 thru 12 June) 1967, box 62, SecDef Subject Decimal files, Acc72-A-2468; Hot Line msg Kosygin to Johnson, 10 Jun 67, 8:48 a.m., *FRUS 1964-68*, 19:409 (quotes).

78. Hot Line msg Johnson to Kosygin, 10 Jun 67, 9:39 a.m., *FRUS 1964-68*, 19:414. The president had approved the response at 9:30, less than thirty minutes after receipt of the Kosygin threat. Hot Line msg Kosygin to Johnson, 10 Jun 67, 9:44 a.m., ibid, 19:415 (quote); Johnson, *Vantage Point*, 302 (quotes); memrcd Saunders, Hot Line Meeting June 10, 1967, dated 22 Oct 68, *FRUS 1964-68*, 19:410.

79. Msg JCS 7628 to USCINCEUR, 10 Jun 67, *FRUS 1964-68*, 19:422; Wainstein, "Some Aspects," 123-26.

80. Hot Line msg Johnson to Kosygin, 10 Jun 67, 10:58 a.m., *FRUS 1964-68*, 19:421; Hot Line msg Kosygin to Johnson, 10 Jun 67, 11:31 a.m. and Hot Line msg Johnson to Kosygin, 10 Jun 67, 11:58 a.m., ibid, 19:422-23 and 423 (quote).

81. Memrcd Saunders, Hot Line Meeting June 10, 1967, dated 22 Oct 68 and memcon Davis, The Hot Line Exchanges, 4 Nov 68, ibid, 19:410 and 411-14 (quote); memrcd Davis, The Hot Line Meetings and the Middle East in New York, 7 Nov 68, vol 7, App G, box 19, NSC History of Middle East Crisis, NSF, LBJL (quote); McNamara, *In Retrospect*, 279; Johnson, *Vantage Point*, 302-03; Pres News conf, 13 Jun 67, *Johnson Public Papers, 1967*, 1:615-16.

82. CMC Work Notes, JCS mtg 188, 9 Jun 67, vol 16, Greene Papers, MHC; memo Hoopes for SecDef, 12 Jun 67, fldr Middle East 334, 14 Jun 67, box 63, SecDef Subject Decimal files, Acc 72A-2468.

83. Memo Bundy for Pres, 11 Jul 67, *FRUS 1964-68*, 19:630-33; memrcd Hoopes, 1 Aug 67, ibid, 745-46; memo Rostow for Pres, 3 Aug 67, ibid, 750-51; see McNamara's caveat and endorsement on memo Bundy for McNamara, 11 Jul 67, w/atchmt, Bundy's 11 Jul memo for Pres, fldr Middle East 092 (July-1967), box 63, SecDef Subject Decimal files, Acc 72A-2468.

84. Memo SecDef for CJCS, 16 Jun 67, fldr Middle East 092 (13 thru 30 June) 1967, box 62, SecDef Subject Decimal files, Acc 72A-2468; JCSM-374-67 for SecDef, 29 Jun 67, *FRUS 1964-68*, 19:589-90 (quote).

85. Brecher, *Decisions in Israel's Foreign Policy*, 433; memo SecDef for CJCS, 19 Jun 67 and JCSM-373-67 for SecDef, 29 Jun 67: fldr Middle East 092 (13 thru 30 June) 1967, box 62, SecDef Subject Decimal files, Acc 72A-2468; Saunders notes NSC Spec Comm mtg, 12 Jun 67, *FRUS 1964-68*, 19:447 (quote).

86. Saunders notes, 12 June 67, *FRUS 1964-68*, 19:446-47 (quotes); Saunders, Pres in Middle East Crisis: Preface, cited in note 8.

87. Memrcd Saunders, 26 May, *FRUS 1964-68*, 19:135 (quote); Eshkol statement in Knesset, 12 Jun 67, *AFP, CD 1967*, 524-25; Saunders notes informal NSC Spec Comm mtg, 13 Jun 67, *FRUS 1964-68*, 19:463.

88. Address at DeptState Foreign Policy Conf for Educators, 19 Jun 67, *Johnson Public Papers, 1967*, 1:632-33 (quote); memo Bundy for Pres, 31 Jul 67, *FRUS 1964-68*, 19:739-40 (quote).

89. Campbell, "American Efforts for Peace," in Kerr, ed, *Elusive Peace in the Middle East*, 283-84 (quote); cited in Poole, *JCS and National Policy, 1965-68*, pt 2:591 (quotes).

90. Campbell, "American Efforts for Peace," 284; UNSC Res 242, 22 Nov 67, *AFP, CD 1967*, 616-17; ed note, *FRUS 1964-68*, 19:1062-63; memrcd CM-2832-67, Middle East Situation as Seen by General Rabin, 16 Dec 67, fldr Middle East 092 (July -1967), box 63, SecDef Subject Decimal files, Acc 72A-2468 (quote).

91. The Special State-Defense Study Group, "Near East, North Africa and the Horn of Africa: Annexes to a Recommended American Strategy," vol II, Jul 67, C-7; "Draft Administrative History of the Department of Defense, 1963-1969," 1:106, 116-17, OSD Hist.

92. Memo SecState and SecDef for Pres, 15 Aug 67, *FRUS 1964-68*, 19:783-85; *Baltimore Sun*, 26 Aug 67; memo Kohler and Hoopes for SecState and SecDef, 29 Aug 67, fldr Middle East 400 (Jan-Sep) 1967, box 63, SecDef Subject Decimal files, Acc 72A-2468; memos SecState and SecDef for Pres, 13 Oct 1967 and ASD(ISA) for SvcSecs, 26 Oct 67: fldr Middle East 400 (Oct-Dec) 1967, ibid. A marginal note on the 13 Oct 67 document states that the president approved the recommendation the same day.

93. Saunders, Summary of State-Defense Positions on Israeli Aircraft Request, 22 Nov 67, fldr Israel Cables & Memos, vol III, box 140, Middle East, Israel (Classified), NSF CF, LBJL.

94. Memos Katzenbach for Pres, 11 Dec 67, Rostow for Pres, 13 Dec 67, *FRUS 1964-68*, 20:29-30, 38; memo Acting ASD/ISA for SecDef, 13 Dec 67, fldr Middle East 400 (Oct-Dec) 1967, box 63, SecDef Subject Decimal files, Acc 72A-2468; memo Rostow for Pres, 5 Jan 68, *FRUS 1964-68*, 20:65 (quote, emphasis in the source); msg CAP 80169 Rostow to Pres in Texas, 7 Jan 68, ibid, 77-79.

95. Memcon, U.S.-Israeli Talks, 8 Jan 68, sess III, *FRUS 1964-68*, 20:97; memrcd Wheeler, 8 Jan 68, fldr Israel 452.1 Jan-Jul 1968, box 10, ISA General files, Acc 72A-1499.

96. Memos Under SecN for ASD/ISA, 5 Jan 68, fldr Israel 000.1-333, 1968, box 10, ISA General files, Acc 72A-1499; Warnke for SecDef, 11 Jan 68 and Tab A; memo McNamara for Warnke, 12 Jan 68: all ibid; memo Rostow for Pres, 6 Feb 68, *FRUS 1964-68*, 20:142; memo SecDef for Pres, 6 Feb 68, ibid, 141; CM-3013-68 for SecDef, 14 Feb 68, fldr Israel 334-451 1968; Warnke for DepSecDef, 12 Aug 68 and Tab C, fldr Israel 000.1-333, 1968: all box 10, ISA General files, Acc 72A-1499; memos DepSecDef for SecAF, 3 Mar 68 and DepUnderSecAF for DepAsstSec (Near East and South Asian Affairs), OASD/ISA, 16 Jul 68: both fldr Israel 452.1 Jan-Jul 1968, ibid.

97. NIE 35-68, 11 Apr 68, memo Battle for Rusk, 20 Jun 68, *FRUS 1964-68*, 20:281-83 (quote); info memo Rostow for Pres, 29 Feb 68, action memo Rostow for Pres, 23 Apr 68, ibid, 194-95, 297; memrcd CM-2832-67, 16 Dec 67, fldr Middle East 092 (July - 1967), box 63, SecDef Subject Decimal files, Acc 72A-2468; CM-3275-68 for Pres, 3 May 68, *FRUS 1964-68*, 20:322-25.

98. CM-3411-68 for SecDef, 18 Jun 68, fldr Joint Chiefs of Staff, box 30, Agency File JCS, NSF, LBJL.

99. Ltr Eshkol to Pres, 5 Aug 68, draft memo SecState for Pres, 12 Aug 68, w/atchmt, memo Warnke for Clifford, 15 Aug 68: all fldr Israel 0001.-333, 1968, box 10, ISA General files, Acc 72A-1499; msg 252286 State to Selected Posts, 9 Oct 68, *FRUS 1964-68*, 20:548; Pres statement, 9 Oct 68, *Johnson Public Papers, 1968*, 2:1018.

100. Memo Acting ASD/ISA for Acting SecDef, 10 Oct 68, fldr Israel 452.1 Aug 1968, box 10, ISA General files, Acc 72-A-1499; memo Warnke for SecDef, ibid; memcon Rostow, 22 Oct 68, *FRUS 1964-68*, 20:563; memo Warnke for SecDef, 29 Oct 68, memo telcon, Rusk and Clifford, 1 Nov 68, 10:15 a.m.: *FRUS 1964-68*, 20:580, 582, 586; memo Warnke for SecDef, 2 Nov 68, fldr Israel 452.1 Aug 1968, box 10, ISA General files, Acc 72A-1499 (quote).

101. Memo telcon, Rusk and Clifford, 1 Nov 68, memcons Murray, 4, 5 Nov 68: *FRUS 1964-68*, 20:586(quote), 605-06, 611-12; memo Warnke for SecDef, 6 Nov 68 w/atchmt, Draft Memorandum of Agreement, nd, fldr Israel 000.1-333, 1968, box 10, ISA General files, Acc 72A-1499; memcon Murray, 8 Nov 66, draft memrcd Schwartz, 9 Nov 68, *FRUS 1964-68*, 20:614, 618 (quotes); ltrs Rabin to Warnke, 22 Nov 68, Warnke to Rabin, 27 Nov 68: fldr Israel 452.1 Aug 1968, box 10, ISA General files, Acc 72A-1499; memcon Murray, 12 Nov 68, *FRUS 1964-68*, 20:627-30 (quote).

102. CM-3824-68 for SecDef, 11 Dec 68, fldr 091 Israel (31 Dec 69), box 27, Wheeler Papers, RG 218; memcon Murray, 20 Dec 68, *FRUS 1964-68*, 20:705-06; memo SecDef for Pres, 21 Dec 68, fldr Israel 452.1 Aug 1968, box 10, ISA General files, Acc 72A-1499; *Baltimore Sun*, 28 Dec 68.

103. Drew Middleton and Max Frankel, *New York Times*, 20 Jun 67; memcon Johnson and Kosygin, 25 Jun 67, *FRUS 1964-68*, 19:545.

104. Memo Bundy for Pres, 31 Jul 67, *FRUS 1964-68*, 19:739.

XVII. THE BATTLE OVER MILITARY ASSISTANCE

1. PL 87-195, 4 Sep 61 (75 Stat 424); Yackiel and Menestrina, "A Study of Selected Legislative Restrictions," (MS thesis, Air Force Institute of Technology, 1970), 64-65; memo AsstGenCounsel, International Affairs, for ASD/ISA, 14 Oct 64, fldr Vietnam, box 3, Niederlehner Files, OSD Hist; DoD News Release 692-67, 27 Jul 67, *McNamara Public Statements, 1967*, 7:2388-90.

2. PL 87-195, 4 Sep 61, Sec 622(a) and 623 (75 Stat 446-47); "DoD Admin History," 6:1960-61.

3. Memo Shaw for Yarmolinsky, 24 Mar 66, fldr PBBS, box 26, ISA, Military Assistance & Sales files, Acc 71A-2701 (quote); "DoD Admin History," 6:1965-67.

4. Memo AsstGenCounsel, 14 Oct 64, cited in note 1.

5. Memo McNaughton for SecDef, 2 Oct 64, *FRUS 1964-68*, 9:25-26; memo Bell for Rusk, 11 Jan 65, ibid, 88; memo Komer for Bundy, 1 Dec 64, fldr MAP General-1964, 1965, 1966-Jan-Feb-Mar [2 of 2], box 40, Komer files, NSF, LBJL.

6. Memo Bell for Rusk, 11 Jan 65, *FRUS 1964-68*, 9:88-89; ltr Rusk to McNamara, 26 Mar 65, ibid, 92 (quote); ltr McNamara to Rusk, 8 Apr 65, fldr Vietnam 1965, box 31, Bio files, OSD Hist.

7. Memo ISA for SecDef, 19 Nov 64, fldr Defense Budget – FY 1966, box 16, Agency File, NSF, LBJL (quotes); JCSM-1046-64 for SecDef, 17 Dec 64, JCSM-888-64 for SecDef, 20 Oct 64: fldr 091.3 MAP FY 66 (19 Nov 64) 1964, box 34, SecDef Subject Decimal files, Acc 69A-7425; memrcd Wood, 25 Nov 64, fldr MAP General-1964, 1965,1966- Jan-Feb-Mar, box 40, Komer files, NSF, LBJL; transc McNamara test, 24 Mar 65, SCFR hearings on FAA of 1965 (Excerpts), 352, fldr Vietnam 1965, box 31, Bio files, OSD Hist (quote); Poole, *JCS and National Policy, 1965-68*, pt 2:428.

8. *FRUS 1964-68*, 9:39, n 2; ltr McNamara to Cannon, 13 Dec 63, fldr McNamara Reading File, Dec 63, box 55, McNamara Records, RG 200; memo Thompson for Rusk, 9 Nov 64, *FRUS 1964-68*, 9:39 (quote); memo AID (Bell) for Bundy, 21 Dec 64, ibid, 9:82-84.

9. Transc McNamara test, 11 Mar 65, HCFA hearings on FAA of 1965 (Excerpts), 308, fldr Vietnam 1965, box 31, Bio files, OSD Hist. The $268 million is from transc McNamara test, 24 Mar 65, SCFR hearings on the FAA of 1965 before SCFR (Excerpts), 361-62, ibid.

10. McNamara test, 24 Mar 65, SCFR, *Hearings: Foreign Assistance, 1965*, 463, 474, 483; McNamara test, 7 Apr 65, HSCA, *Hearings: Foreign Assistance and Related Agencies Appropriations for 1966*, 237 (quote), 260-62.

11. SCFR, *Foreign Assistance Act of 1965*, S Rpt 170, 28 Apr 65, 5-6; H Rpt 811, *Conference Report on Foreign Assistance Act of 1965*, 18 Aug 65, 26; memo Hamilton for Bundy, 30 Aug 65, fldr AID, Vol II (2), box 1, Agency File, NSF, LBJL; PL 89-171, 6 Sep 65 (79 Stat 653); PL 89-273, 20 Oct 65 (79 Stat 1002). See also *FRUS 1964-68*, 9:124, n 3.

12. Ed note, *FRUS 1964-68*, 9:93; DeptState, Policy Planning Council, "The Future of Military Assistance," 7 Dec 64, fldr MAP General-1964, 1965, 1966 Jan-Feb-Mar [1 of 2], box 40, Komer files, NSF, LBJL (quotes).

13. Memo Komer for Bundy, 1 Dec 64, ibid; ASD/ISA, "Military Assistance Reappraisal FY 1967-1971," vol 1, "Report," June 1965, I -1, fldr For Policy Mil Asst, box 71, Subj files, OSD Hist.

14. ASD/ISA, "Military Assistance Reappraisal," II/23-28; JCSM-742-65 for SecDef, 9 Oct 65, fldr 091.3 MAP 28 Sep 65, box 10, SecDef Subject Decimal files, Acc 70A-1265 (quote); memrcd HHS, 30 Jul 65, memo Komer for McNaughton, 29 Oct 65 (quote): fldr MAP General-1964, 1965, 1966 Jan-Feb-Mar [1 of 2], box 40, Komer files, NSF, LBJL.

15. Memrcd HHS, 30 Jul 65, cited in note 14.

16. ASD/ISA, "Military Assistance Reappraisal," IV/53, 62, 68; memcon, McNamara-Kim, 18 May 65, msg 1271 Seoul to State, 3 Jun 65, msg 1278 Seoul to State, 4 Jun 65, msg 40 Seoul to State, 10 Jul 65: *FRUS 1964-68*, 29:110-23; Porter test, 24 Feb 70, Subcte on US Security Agreements and Commitments Abroad, of SCFR, *Hearings: United States Security Agreements and Commitments Abroad, Republic of Korea*, pt 1: appx 1, 1708; ISA paper, 5 Jan 67, fldr Viet 0 thru 199 (Sensitive) 1967, box 3, SecDef Sensitive Files 1949-1969, Acc 91-0017; ed note, *FRUS 1964-68*, 29:125.

17. Ltr Bell to McNaughton, 17 Aug 65, *FRUS 1964-68*. 9:104.

18. Transc McNamara test, 30 Mar 66, HCA hearings regarding Military Assistance Appros (Excerpts), 978, fldr Vietnam 1966, box 33, Bio Files, OSD Hist; SCA, *Supplemental Defense Appropriation Bill, 1966*, S Rpt 1074, 17 Mar 66, 26; DPM SecDef for Pres, 11 Dec 65, fldr Memos for Pres, CY 1965 Budget FY 1967, box 119, ASD(C) files, OSD Hist.

19. DPM SecDef for Pres, 29 Dec 65, fldr Memos for Pres, CY 1965 FY 1967, box 119, ASD(C) files, OSD Hist; memo SecDef for Pres, 8 Nov 65, fldr 1965 II, box 32, Bio files, OSD Hist; memo General Counsel/DoD for SecDef, 9 Apr 65, fldr Vietnam, box 3, Niederlehner files, OSD Hist; DPM, 11 Dec 65, cited in note 18.

20. Transc McNamara test, 23 Jan 67, SCAS and SCA hearings on Suppl Authorization and Appro for FY 1967, (Excerpts), 60, fldr Vietnam 1967, box 34, Bio files, OSD Hist; transc McNamara test, 20 Feb 67, HCA hearings on Suppl Appros for FY 1967 (Excerpts), 503-04, fldr Vietnam 1967, box 35, ibid; DoD, Military Asst Prog FY 1969 Estimates, nd, but 1968, 137, box 72, Subject files, OSD Hist; DoD, "Military Assistance Program: Congressional Presentation Fiscal Year 1970 Program Justification," 26 May 69, 115, fldr MAP Est FY 1950-69, box 73, ibid.

21. JCSM-632-65 for SecDef, 14 Aug 65, fldr 091.3 MAP (Jun-Aug 65), box 26, SecDef Subject Decimal files, Acc 70A-1266 (quotes); Poole, *JCS and National Policy, 1965-68*, pt 2:430-31.

22. Poole, *JCS and National Policy, 1965-68*, pt 2:431; "DoD Admin History," 6:1980 (quotes). McNamara deleted this observation from his finalized 29 December 1965 DPM, cited in note 19.

23. Memo Komer for McNaughton, 29 Oct 65, fldr MAP General-1964, 1965, 1966 Jan-Feb-Mar [2 of 2], box 40, Komer files, NSF, LBJL (quote); JCSM-802-65 w/appx for SecDef, 3 Nov 65, fldr 091.3 28 Sep 65, box 10, SecDef Subject Decimal files, Acc 70A-1265 (quotes); memo IntlDiv for DirBoB, 10 Nov 65, fldr MAP General-1964, 1965, 1966 Jan-Feb-Mar [1 of 2], box 40, Komer files, NSF, LBJL.

24. Memo Pinkston for Komer et al, 26 Oct 65, fldr MAP General-1964, 1965. 1966 Jan-Feb-Mar [2 of 2], ibid; memo Hoover for Bundy et al, 26 Nov 65, fldr Defense, Department of, vol III 6/65, box 11, Agency File, NSF, LBJL.

25. Memo SecDef for CJCS, 3 Dec 65, memo McNaughton for SecDef, 2 Dec 65: fldr 091.3 MAP (28 Sep 65), box 10, SecDef Subject Decimal files 1965, Acc 70A-1265.

26. DPM SecDef for Pres, 29 Dec 65, cited in note 19.

27. Memo ASD/ISA for SecDef, 18 Oct 65, fldr 091.3 MAP (October 1965), box 26, SecDef Subject Decimal files, Acc 70A-1266. McNamara approved the recommendation on 19 October. Memo Bundy for Cab Comm on AID, 9 Nov 65; draft White House memo, 28 Dec 65: fldr 091.3 MAP Nov/Dec 1965, ibid; memo ISA Plans & Programs for ASD/ISA, 15 Nov 65, fldr FY 1967 MAP, box 18, ISA, Military Assistance & Sales files, Acc 71A-2701; memo SecState for Pres, 31 Jan 66, *FRUS 1964-68*, 9:138; memo Bator for SecTreasury et al, 3 Feb 66, fldr 091.3 MAP Jan-Mar 1966, box 31, SecDef Subject Decimal files 1966, Acc 70A-4443.

28. DPM SecDef for Pres, 29 Dec 65, cited in note 19; Pres Msg to Cong, 1 Feb 66, *Johnson Public Papers, 1966*, 1:123-24.

29. McNamara test, 20 Apr 66, SCFR, *Hearings: Foreign Assistance, 1966*, pt 1:166; McNamara test, 30 Mar 66, HSCA, *Hearings: Foreign Assistance and Related Agencies Appropriations for 1967*, pt 1:525 (quote).

30. McNamara test, 30 Mar 66, HSCA, *Hearings*, cited in note 29, 525 (quote), 567, 571-72, 577, 579, 581; McNamara test, 20 Apr 66, SCA, *Hearings: Foreign Assistance and Related Agencies Appropriations for FY 1967*, pt 1: 22 (quote); McNamara test, 30 Mar 66, HCFA, *Hearings: Foreign Assistance Act of 1966*, pt 2:279-80, 285, 321 (quote).

31. "DoD Admin History," 6:1974; memo Rostow for Pres, 1 Jun 66 w/atchmt, *FRUS 1964-68*, 9:141-43; SCFR, *Military Assistance and Sales Act*, S Rpt 1358, 7 Jul 66, 1-3, 5, 10; PL 89-583, 19 Sep 66 (80 Stat 795); memo DoD Office of General Counsel, 20 Sep 66, fldr Legislation 68, box 18, ISA, Military Assistance & Sales, Acc 71A-2701; Pres statement, 19 Sep 66, *Johnson Public Papers, 1966*, 2:1037.

32. JCSM-623-66 for SecDef, 30 Sep 66, fldr 091.3 MAP Apr-1966, box 31, SecDef Subject Decimal files, Acc 70A-4443 (quote); memo Hoopes for SecDef, 3 Nov 66, memo SecDef for CJCS, 4 Nov 66 (quote): both fldr 091.3 MAP (Oct 1966), box 30, ibid.

33. PL 89-691, 15 Oct 66 (80 Stat 1018); H Cte of Conference, *Foreign Assistance and Related Agencies Appropriations Bill, 1967*, H Rpt 2203, 6 Oct 66, 3; memo Gaud for Pres, 6 Oct 66, *FRUS 1964-68*, 9:160.

34. Poole, *JCS and National Policy, 1965-68*, 2:433; memo McNaughton for SecDef, 3 Nov 66, fldr 091.3 MAP (Oct 1966), box 30, SecDef Subject Decimal files, Acc 70A-4443.

35. Msg 713 Seoul to State, 10 Jan 66, *FRUS 1964-68*, 29:146-47; telcon Johnson and McNamara, 17 Jan 66, ibid, 4:79 (quotes); memo ASD/ISA for SecDef, 27 Jan 66, ibid, 29:155-56; msg 777 State to Seoul, 27 Jan 66, ibid, 158-59; ISA Paper, FY 67 and FY 68 Military Asst, w/atchmt, Tab A, 5 Jan 67, ISA paper, 27 Jan 67, ASD(C) paper, 25 Jan 67: fldr Viet 0 thru 199 (Sensitive) 1967, box 3, SecDef Sensitive Files 1949-1969, Acc 91-0017.

36. JCSM-690-66 for SecDef, 27 Oct 66, fldr 091.3 MAP (Oct 1966), box 30, SecDef Subject Decimal files, Acc 70A-4443; memo McNaughton for SecDef, 3 Nov 66, cited in note 34; Poole, *JCS and National Policy, 1965-68*, pt 2:434; memo SecDef for CJCS, 8 Nov 66, fldr Reading File Nov 16-2, 1966, box 126, McNamara Records, RG 200.

37. Memo SecDef for ASD/ISA, 28 Jul 66; memo SecDef for ASD/ISA, 2 Jun 66 (quote); memo SecDef for ASD/ISA, 28 Jul 66: fldr 091.3 MAP Apr-1966, box 31, SecDef Subject Decimal files, Acc 70A-4443.

38. Memo SecDef for CJCS, 5 Nov 66 w/atchmt, DPM on MAP FY 1968-1972, 4 Nov 66 (quote), fldr 091.3 MAP (DPM) 1966, ibid. McNamara sent an earlier, different draft to AID expressing his concurrence with congressional attempts to rein in MAP programs. Memo SecDef for Administrator, AID, 5 Nov 66, ibid.

39. JCSM-728-66 for SecDef, 25 Nov 66, fldr Memorandum for the President, box 23, ISA, Military Assistance & Sales files, Acc 71A-2701 (quote); ltr Katzenbach to McNamara, 9 Dec 66 fldr 091.3 MAP (DPM) 1966, box 31, SecDef Subject Decimal files, Acc 70A-4443; memo Acting Asst Sec/ISA for DepSecDef, 15 Dec 66, fldr 091.3 MAP (Oct 1966), box 30, ibid; ltr McNaughton to Gaud, 19 Dec 66, fldr Memo for President, box 18, ISA, Military Assistance & Sales files, Acc 71A-2701.

40. "DoD Admin History," 6:1999. The developments may be traced in ltr Rusk to McNamara, 6 Aug 66, memo W. Bundy for Rusk w/Tab A, 17 Sep 66, memo SecState for Pres, 13 Oct 66 w/atchmt, memo SecState and SecDef for Pres, 13 Oct 66, memo Rostow for Pres, 15 Oct 66, memo ASD/ISA for SecDef, 17 Oct 66, JCSM-632-66 for SecDef, 29 Sep 66, memo ASD/ISA for SecDef, 6 Oct 67, memcon, Pres and Thai FM Khoman, 6 Oct 67, memcon SecDef and Thai FM, 6 Oct 67, w/atchmt, DoD Paper: *FRUS 1964-68*, 27:694, 697-700, 718-25, 730-37 and 801-08. Ltr McNamara to Gaud, 7 Jan 67, Memoranda for the President, box 23, ISA Military Assistance & Sales files, Acc 71A-2701.

41. DPM SecDef for Pres, MAP FY 1968-1972, 6 Jan 67, notebook DPMs FY 68, bk 6, DPMs FY 1968-1969, box 120, ASD(C) files, OSD Hist.

42. Ltr SecDef to DirBoB, 11 Nov 66, fldr Reading File Nov 16-2, box 126, McNamara Records, RG 200.

43. DPM, 6 Jan 67, TAB P, cited in note 41; memo SecDef for Pres, 17 Dec 66, fldr Vietnam 1966, box 34, Bio files, OSD Hist; ODMA/ISA, Fact Sheet, 18 Nov 66 (quote), memo SecDef for SvcSecs, et al, 9 Jun 67: fldr Budget - FY 1968, Budget files FY 1968, box 64, ASD(C) files, OSD Hist; ltr McNamara to Fulbright, 18 Jan 67, fldr Vietnam 1967, box 34, Bio Files, OSD Hist; memo SecDef for Pres, 17 Dec 66; memo Rostow for Pres, 19 Dec 66: fldr Defense Department of, 6/66 vol IV [2 of 2], box 12, Agency File, NSF, LBJL. Johnson's approval is noted on the 19 December memo.

44. McNamara test, 20 Apr 66, SCA, *Hearings*, cited in note 30, 8, 20-23, 29; SCFR, *Military Assistance and Sales Act*, S Rpt 1358, 7 Jul 66, 3 (quotes).

45. SCFR, *Arms Sales and Foreign Policy*, S Staff Study, 25 Jan 67, 3, 12 (quote); ISA/ILN, Summary Comparison, 28 Dec 64, fldr SecDef Backup Book FY 1966 Budget vol I-III FY 1966 Budget, box 36, ASD(C) files, OSD Hist; Livesay notes, SecDef Staff mtg, 21 Nov 66, fldr Staff Mtg Oct-Dec 1966, box 12, AFPC files, Acc 77-0062 (quotes).

46. McNamara test, 25 Jan 67, SCAS and SSCA, *Hearings: Military Procurement Authorizations for Fiscal Year 1968*, 40; transc McNamara test, 25 Jan 67 for SCAS and SSCA on The FY 1968-72 Defense Program

and 1968 Budget, 32 (quote), fldr SecDef Transcript-Sen Armed Serv & Sen Approp Scte 1968 Budget, FY 1968 Budget, box 61, ASD(C) files, OSD Hist; Ellender quote, 26 Jan 67, 246, fldr SecDef Transcript-Sen Armed Serv & Sen Approp Scte 1968 Budget 1/26/67, box 66, ibid.

47. Linder test, 20 Mar 67, HSCA, *Hearings: Foreign Assistance and Related Agencies Appropriations for 1968*, pt 1:17-24; memo SecDef for Pres, 9 Feb 67, fldr 091.3 MAP Congressional Witness Book, vol 2, FY 1968, box 9, SecDef Subject Decimal files, Acc 72A-2468 (quote).

48. McNamara test, 4 Apr 67, HSCA, *Hearings*, cited in note 47, 461(quote), 476.

49. *St. Louis Post-Dispatch*, 23 Jul 67 (quotes); Linder test, 17 Jul 67, House Cte on Banking and Currency, *Hearings: Export-Import Bank and Credit Sales of Defense Articles*, 10.

50. PL 89-171, 6 Sep 65 (79 Stat 653); ltr McNamara to Linder, 20 Sep 65, fldr 091.3 Economic Conditions 1965, box 26, SecDef Subject Decimal files, Acc 70A-1266; interv Paul C. Warnke by Dorothy Pierce, 8 Jan 69, 27-28, AC 74-264, LBJL.

51. Foreign Military Sales Financed by Arrangement of the Export-Import Bank FY 1962-1966, nd, in SCAS and SSCA hearings on the FY 1968-72 Defense Program and 1968 Budget, 32 insert, fldr SecDef Transcript-Sen Armed Serv & Sen Approp Scte 1968 Budget, FY 1968 Budget, box 61, ASD(C) files, OSD Hist.

52. ISA/ILN, Export-Import Bank Legislative Issues, 25 Jul 67, fldr 091.3 (MAP) Jul 1967, box 9, SecDef Subject Decimal files, Acc 72A-2468; memo DepSecDef for Vice Pres, 22 Jul 67 w/Tab D, Credit Sales Account, 20 Jul 67, ibid.

53. Memo Asst to the Secretary (Leg Affairs) for SecDef, 25 Jul 67, ibid (quote); McNamara test, 26 Jul 67, SCFR, *Hearings: Foreign Assistance Act of 1967*, 275, 293 (quotes); DoD News Release 692-67, 27 Jul 67, cited in note 1.

54. Memo Rostow for Pres, 27 Jul 67, fldr AID, vol IV, [2], box 2, Agency File, NSF, LBJL; memo Gaud for Pres, 25 Oct 67, ibid; SCFR, *Foreign Assistance Act of 1967*, S Rpt 499, 9 Aug 67, 2-3, 6 (quotes).

55. Memo Gaud for Pres, 2 Nov 67, fldr AID, vol IV, [1], box 2, Agency Files, NSF, LBJL; *Conference Report on the Foreign Assistance Act of 1967*, H Rpt 892, 7 Nov 67, 31; PL 90-137, 14 Nov 67 (81 Stat 445); memo AsstGenCounsel, IA, 15 Dec 67, fldr Legislation 68, box 18, ISA, Military Assistance & Sales files, Acc 71A-2701.

56. HCA, *Foreign Assistance and Related Agencies Appropriations Bill, 1968*, H Rpt 891, 6 Nov 67, 20; McNamara test, 16 Nov 67, SCA, *Hearings: Foreign Assistance and Related Agencies Appropriations for Fiscal Year 1968*, 327-28; SCA, *Foreign Assistance and Related Agencies Appropriation Bill, 1968*, S Rpt 807, 28 Nov 67, 13; memo Gaud for Pres, 28 Nov 67, fldr AID, vol IV [1], box 2, Agency File, NSF, LBJL.

57. PL 90-249, 2 Jan 68 (81 Stat 936); DPM SecDef for Pres, The Military Assistance Program, FY 1969-1973, 1 Feb 68, Notebook DPMs FY 1969, DPMs FY 1969-1970, box 121, ASD(C) files, OSD Hist.

58. Msg KRA-1579 CINCUNC/USFK to CINCPAC, 21 Jul 67, FRUS 1964-68, 29:265; memcon Steadman, 20 Jul 67, fldr Korea 091.112 (Jul 1967), box 62, SecDef Subject Decimal files, Acc 72A-2468; memo Warnke for SecDef, 20 Sep 67, fldr Korea 370-1967, ibid; memo Warnke for SecDef, 3 Nov 67, memo SecDef to Warnke, 8 Nov 67; msg DEF 2566 SecDef to Seoul, 10 Nov 67: fldr Korea 0-349-1967, ibid; memcon Steadman, 16 Nov 67, fldr Korea 091-112 (Jul-1967), ibid.

59. Memo Steadman for ASD (C), 29 Dec 67, fldr Korea 370 1967, ibid; memo Rostow for Pres, 29 Dec 67, *FRUS 1964-68*, 29:305-06.

60. Msg JCS 9150 to CINCUNC/COMUSKOREA, 4 Feb 68, fldr Korea Pueblo Feb 1968, Cable files, OSD Hist; memo AASD/I&L for DepSecDef, 8 Feb 68 w/atchmt, fldr Korea 385 DMZ, 1968, box 2, SecDef Subject Decimal files, Acc 73A-1304; "DoD Admin History," 6:1977; Yi, "U.S.-Korea Alliance in the Vietnam War," in Gardner and Gittinger, eds, *International Perspectives on Vietnam*, 174; memo DirJtStaff for Smith, 7 Sep 68, fldr 5D(3) Allies: Troop Commitments; box 91, Vietnam Country File, NSF, LBJL; DOD, MAP Cong Presentation FY 1970 Prgm Justification, 26 May 69, 110, fldr MAP Cong Pres, FY 1970-1972, box 73, Subj files, OSD Hist.

61. DPM SecDef for Pres, 6 Jan 67, cited in note 41; memo SecDef for CJCS, 8 Jun 67, fldr Military Assistance Manual – 1968, box 24, ISA, Military Assistance & Sales, Acc 71A-2107 (quote); JCSM-503-67, DepDir-JtStaff for SecDef, 13 Sep 67, ibid; JCSM-618-67 for SecDef, 9 Nov 67, fldr 091.3 MAP (Aug-1967), box 9, SecDef Subject Decimal files, Acc 72A-2468 (quote); DPM SecDef for Pres, 1 Feb 68, Table II A and Table 700, cited in note 57.

62. Poole, *JCS and National Policy, 1965-68*, pt 2:439-440 cites the 18 Dec 67 DPM. The JCS figure of $794 million is in Table II A, cited in note 61.

63. DeptState, Policy Planning Council, U.S. Military Assistance, 20 Nov 67, fldr Policy Planning Council, box 25, ISA, Military Assistance & Sales, Acc 71A-2701 (quote); memo Warnke for Poats, 18 Nov 67 w/

atchmt, memo AdminAID for UnderSecState, nd, fldr Restructured Foreign Assistance Program, box 26, ibid (quote).

64. Report of the Task Force on Foreign Aid, nd, submitted 11 Dec 67, *FRUS 1964-68*, 9:196 (quote), 201-04; memo AdminAID forUnderSecState, nd, fldr Restructured Foreign Assistance Program, box 26, ISA, Military Assistance & Sales files, Acc 72A-2701.

65. Memrcd, DMA Staff Mtg, 27 Nov 67, fldr Miscellaneous, 1967, box 25, ibid; memo Heinz for Warnke, 29 Nov 67, fldr Restructuring Foreign Assistance Programs, box 26, ibid; memo Heinz for Lee, 6 Dec 67, fldr Restructuring of MAP, bk I, box 29, ibid.

66. Memo ASD/ISA for SecDef, 15 Dec 67, *FRUS 1964-68*, 9:207-08.

67. Memo ISA for SecDef, 12 Jan 68 w/atchmt and McNamara marginalia, fldr Restructuring of MAP, bk 1, box 29, ISA, Military Assistance & Sales, Acc-71A-2701; memrcd DirMilAsst, 7 Dec 67, fldr Restructuring Foreign Assistance Programs, box 26, ibid; memo Lee for Blick, 12 Dec 67, fldr Restructuring of MAP, bk I, box 29, ibid.

68. Memo JCS J-5 for ASD/ISA, 11 Dec 67, fldr Restructuring Foreign Assistance Program, box 26, ibid; memo ASD/ISA for SecDef, 15 Dec 67, *FRUS 1964-68*, 9:208-09; memo S/P for AID/PPC/MAD & G/PM, 26 Dec 67, fldr Restructuring of MAP, bk I, box 29, ISA, Military Assistance & Sales files, Acc 71A-2701.

69. JCSM-8-68 for SecDef, 4 Jan 68, fldr Memorandum for the President, box 23, ibid (quotes); ltr Rusk to McNamara, 11 Jan 68, ibid (quotes).

70. Memo Hamilton for Rostow, 18 Jan 68, *FRUS 1964-68*, 9:209-210 (quotes); memo Rostow for Pres, 19 Jan 68, fldr AID, vol IV, [1], box 2, Agency File, NSF, LBJL; memo Warnke for SecDef, 12 Jan 68; memo Warnke for SecDef w/atchmt, 16 Jan 68; memo AsstGenCounsel, IA for AGC(FM) and DMA/ISA, 18 Jan 68 (quote): fldr Restructuring of MAP, bk I, box 29, ISA, Military Assistance & Sales, Acc 71A-2701.

71. Memo Knaur for Heinz, 19 Jan 68, fldr Restructured Foreign Assistance Program, box 26, ISA, ibid (quotes); memo Schultze for Pres, 22 Jan 68; memo Hamilton for Rostow, 23 Jan 68: fldr AID, vol IV, [1], box 2, Agency File, NSF, LBJL; memo Hamilton for Rostow, 25 Jan 68, doc no. CK3100080922, Declassified Documents Reference System, *http://galenet.galegroup.com*.

72. DPM SecDef for Pres, 1 Feb 68, cited in note 61.

73. Ltr Chairman Pres Advisory Comm on For Asst Programs to Pres, 31 Jan 68, *FRUS 1964-68*, 9:215 (quote); DCS, S&L, HQUSAF, "Information and Guidance on Military Assistance Grant Aid and Foreign Military Sales," 11th ed., 1968, 16, fldr FY 1970 Military Assistance Program (Pre 1/20/69), FY 1970 Budget, box 79, ASD(C) files, OSD Hist; DoD, "Foreign Military Sales: Annual Report including FY 1969 Estimates," 1 Apr 1968, fldr For Pol Mil Asst, box 71, Subj files, OSD Hist. The bill appears in HCFA, *Hearings: Foreign Military Sales Act*, 26 Jun 68, 1-6.

74. Livesay mins, SecDef Staff mtg, 25 Mar 68, fldr Staff Mtgs Jan-Mar 1968, box 13, AFPC files, Acc 77-0062 (quote); Zeiler, *Dean Rusk*, 181; ltr Nitze to Zwick, 6 Jul 68, fldr FY 1969 Budget, box 71, ASD(C) files, OSD Hist; Nitze test, 8 Apr 68, HSCA, *Hearings: Foreign Assistance and Related Agencies Appropriations for 1969*, pt 1:429, 437.

75. Livesay mins, SecDef Staff Mtg, 20 May 68, fldr Staff Meeting Apr - June 1968, box 13, AFPC files, Acc 77-0062 (quote); Clifford test, 17 May 68, SCFR, *Hearings: The Foreign Assistance Act of 1968*, pt 2:431-32, 439-440, 444-46,454-57.

76. Draft memo SecState et al for Pres, 21 May 68, *FRUS 1964-68*, 9:216-21; ISA, Impact of a MAP Moratorium in FY 1969, 16 May 68, fldr Moratorium, box 25, ISA, Military Assistance & Sales files, Acc 71A-2701.

77. Draft memo SecState et al for Pres, 21 May 68, *FRUS 1964-68*, 9:218, 220-21; memo Hamilton for Rostow, 27 May 68, ibid, 9:221-24.

78. Memo Gaud for Pres, 19 Jun 68, fldr AID, vol IV [1], box 2, Agency File, NSF, LBJL; Clifford test, 26 Jun 68, HCFA, *Hearings*, cited in note 73, 6-7.

79. Defense Agencies Summary: DoD Project 693, nd, fldr FY 1969 Budget, box 71, ASD(C) files, OSD Hist.; DoD, MAP Cong Presentation FY 1970, nd but late May 1969, fldr MAP Cong Presentations FY 1970-72, box 73, Subj files, OSD Hist; Johnson, *Vantage Point*, 459-60.

80. Memo Gaud for Pres, 25 Jul 68, fldr AID, vol IV, [1], box 2, Agency File, NSF, LBJL; SCFR, *Foreign Assistance Act of 1968*, S Rpt 1479, 26 Jul 68, 3 (quote); Livesay notes, SecDef Staff mtg, 29 Jul 68, fldr Minutes of SecDef Staff Mtgs, Mar-Sep 68, box 18, Papers of Clark Clifford, LBJL (quote); PL 90-554, 8 Oct 68 (82 Stat 960).

81. ISA Fact Sheet, ISA, Foreign Military Sales Bill, 17 Sep 68, fldr 337 WH (Sens) 1968, box 1, SecDef Sensitive files, 1949-1969, Acc 91-0017; PL 90-629, 22 Oct 68 (82 Stat 1321); PL 90-608, 21 Oct 68 (82 Stat 1190); PL 90-581, 17 Oct 68 (82 Stat 1137).

82. Ltr Zwick to Clifford, 23 Aug 68, fldr MAP FY 70, box 25, ISA, Military Assistance & Sales files, Acc 71A-2701; memo Lee for Comptroller, ODMA et al, 3 Sep 68, w/atchmt (quote), fldr Miscellaneous-1968, ibid; DepSecDef, DPM on Mil Asst and Arms Transfers, (Draft for Comment), 18 Oct 68, 7, 18 (quote), fldr Memorandum for the President, 71-75, box 23, ibid.

83. DPM, 18 Oct 68, cited in note 82.

84. Ibid; memo DepAsstSecState for Politico-Military Affairs for DepAsstSecDef (Policy Planning and Arms Control), 14 Nov 68; JCSM-674-68 for SecDef, 9 Nov 68: fldr Memorandum for the President, 71-75, box 23, ISA, Military Assistance & Sales files, Acc 71A-2701.

85. JCSM-674-68, 9 Nov 68; memo DepAsstSecState, 14 Nov 68 (quote): both cited in note 84.

86. Report of Pres Genl Advis Cte, 25 Oct 68, *FRUS 1964-68*, 9:93 and 228-29 (excerpt); memo Rostow for Rusk et al, 4 Nov 68 w/atchmt, 25 Oct 68, fldr 091.3 (October 1968), box 44, SecDef Subject Decimal files, Acc 73A-1250; memo DepSecDef for Pres, 4 Dec 68, ibid (quote).

87. DPM on Military Asst and Arms Transfers, 29 Nov 68; memo ASD(ISA) for DepSecDef, 10 Jan 69: fldr Memorandum for the President, 71-75, box 23, ISA, Military Assistance & Sales files, Acc 71A-2701; ISA(ODMA), Status of MAP, 29 Nov 68, fldr Transition, box 27, ibid; Laird test, 24 Jun 69, HCFA, *Hearings: Foreign Assistance Act of 1969*, pt 3:515-19 (quote).

XVIII. YEAR OF CRISES

1. Johnson, *Vantage Point*, 533.

2. Memrcd NMCC, 21 Jan 68, Cable files, OSD Hist; memo WH Situation Room for Pres, 18 Jan 66, *FRUS 1964-68*, 12:383-84; "DoD Admin History," 7:2417.

3. Goulding, *Confirm or Deny*, 26-27, 40; msgs 855, 19 Jan 66, and 871, 22 Jan 66, both Madrid to State: *FRUS 1964-68*, 12:384-87; *Baltimore Sun*, 21 Jan 66 (quote); "Annual Report of the Secretary of the Air Force July 1, 1965 to June 30, 1965," in *DoD Annual Report for FY 1966*, 348; "DoD Admin History," 7:2417; memo ASD(ISA) for SecDef, 27 Jan 68, w/TAB C, U.S. Nuclear Overflights, fldr Denmark 1968, box 10, ISA General files, Acc 72-A-1499.

4. Memcon AsstSecState EUR and Danish Amb, 23 Jan 68, fldr Denmark 001-333 1968, box 11, ISA General files, Acc 72-A-1498; memrcds, NMCC, 29 Jan and 3 Feb 68, Cable files, OSD Hist; ed note, *FRUS 1964-68*, 12:1.

5. Memcon, AsstSecState EUR and Danish Amb, 23 Jan 68; msg 103631 State to Copenhagen, 24 Jan 68: fldr Denmark 001-333 1968, box 11, ISA General files, Acc 72-A-1498; "DoD Admin History," 7:2419 (quote).

6. Memo ASD(ISA) for SecDef, 27 Jan 68, w/Tab A, Statement by Danish Foreign Minister Tabor, 22 Jan 68, fldr Denmark 1968, box 10, ISA General files, Acc 72-A-1499; ed note, *FRUS 1964-68*, 12:1; msgs 2835 and 2837 Copenhagen to State, 22 Jan 68, Cable files, OSD Hist; memcon AsstSecState EUR and Danish Amb, 26 Jan 68, fldr Denmark 001-333 1968, box 11, ISA General files, Acc 72-A-1498 (quote).

7. Memo ASD(ISA) for SecDef, 27 Jan 68, fldr Denmark 1968, box 10, ISA General files, Acc 72-A-1499 (quote); note State EUR/SCAN to Deputy ASD(ISA) (European and NATO Affairs) 26 Jan 68, w/atchmt, Talking Paper for Appointment with Danish Ambassador, January 27, fldr Greenland 360.33 1968, box 2, SecDef Subject Decimal files, Acc 73-A-1304; informal rcd of Remarks, 27 Jan 68, *FRUS 1964-68*, 12:7; memo ASD(ISA) for SecDef, 27 Jan 68, fldr Denmark 1968, box 10, ISA General files, Acc 72-A-1499.

8. Note Danish Amb to SecState, 26 Feb 68, *FRUS 1964-68*, 12:19; msg 128993 State to Copenhagen, 13 Mar 68, ibid, 22; note State EUR/SCAN, 26 Jan 68, cited in note 7 (quote); action memo AsstSecState EurAffairs for UnderSecState, 28 Mar 68, *FRUS 1964-68*, 12:24.

9. Ltrs Leddy to Warnke, 17 Apr 68 and Warnke to Leddy, 26 Apr 68, *FRUS 1964-68*, 12:26-27; ed note, ibid, 36; memo Warnke for DepSecDef, 5 Jun 68, fldr Denmark 001-333 1968, box 11, ISA Country Files, Acc 72-A-1498 (quotes).

10. Msg 102940 State to Moscow, 23 Jan 68; Tom Johnson, notes of mtg, 23 Jan 68, telcon Johnson and McNamara, 29 Jan 68: *FRUS 1964-68*, 29, pt 1:459, 461-62, 554 (quote); Johnson, *Vantage Point*, 535; Tom Johnson notes of Pres Tuesday Natl Security Lunch, 23 Jan 68, *FRUS 1964-68*, 29, pt 1:462-63; Clifford, *Counsel*, 466; draft memo Pres for SecState, SecDef, and DirBoB, 31 Jan 68, fldr Pueblo, box 74, McNamara Records, RG 200 (quotes).

11. Johnson, *Vantage Point*, 535; msg 2550 Moscow to State, 23 Jan 68, fldr Korea Pueblo Jan 1968, Cable files, OSD Hist; Tom Johnson notes of Pres mtg w/NSC, 24 Jan 68, *FRUS 1964-68*, 29, pt 1:480. North Korea may have acted unilaterally without prior notification or approval from its allies; see Lerner, "A Dangerous

Miscalculation," 7, 10-12; McNamara notes on WH ExCom on Pueblo, 24 Jan 68, fldr Pueblo Incident 1968, box 75, McNamara Records, RG 200.

12. Tom Johnson notes of Pres Thursday night mtg on *Pueblo* Incident, 25 Jan 68, *FRUS 1964-68*, 29, pt 1:516 (quote), 518; summary Mins of Pueblo Group, 24 Jan 68, ibid, 469-70, 473 (quote).

13. Smith mins of mtg on Korean Crisis without Pres, 24 Jan 68, ibid, pt 1:483 (quote), 487, 490-91 (quote).

14. Tom Johnson notes of Pres mtg, 24 Jan 68, ibid, 493-95.

15. Tom Johnson notes of Pres Breakfast mtg, 25 Jan 68, ibid, 497-504; Poole, *JCS and National Policy, 1965-68*, pt 2:762-64; memo Acting ASD(SA) for SecDef, 25 Jan 68, fldr Pueblo Incident 1968, box 75, McNamara Records, RG 200 (quotes); Nitze notes, 25 Jan 68, fldr DoD DepSecDef Notes, 1968 (1 of 6), box 85 (fldr 4), Nitze Papers, LC; memo ASD(SA) for SecDef, 31 Jan 68, *FRUS 1964-68*, 29, pt 1:318-20; JCSM-53-68 for SecDef, 25 Jan 68; memos SecA for SecDef, 29 Jan 68, SecDef for CJCS, 1 Feb 68: all fldr Korea 370 1968, box 11, SecDef Subject Decimal files, Acc 73-A-1250.

16. Tom Johnson notes of Pres Luncheon mtg, 25 Jan 68, *FRUS 1964-68*, 29, pt 1:507-11 (quote, 508).

17. Tom Johnson notes of Pres Thursday night mtg on the *Pueblo* Incident, 25 Jan 68, ibid, 514-19 (quote, emphasis in the source); Poole, *JCS and National Policy, 1965-68*, pt 2:763.

18. Tom Johnson notes of Pres Luncheon mtg, 25 Jan 68, *FRUS 1964-68*, 29, pt 1:513; telcon Johnson and Goldberg, 28 Jan 68, ibid, 545 (quotes); DeptState, Historical Office, R.P. 939-C, "The USS *Pueblo* Incident," Oct 68, 9, fldr Pueblo Crisis, vol 1- Basic Study & Presidential Decisions, box 27, NSC Histories, *Pueblo* Crisis, 1968, NSF, LBJL (hereafter "The USS *Pueblo* Incident"); msg 3702 Seoul to State, 27 Jan 68; ed note: *FRUS 1964-68*, 29, pt 1:536-37, 570-71; msg 106085 State to Seoul, 28 Jan 68, ibid, 547 (quotes).

19. Tom Johnson notes of Pres Friday Morning mtg on *Pueblo* Incident, 26 Jan 68, *FRUS 1964-68*, 29, pt 1:525-26.

20. "The USS *Pueblo* Incident," 6; Rostow rpt on mtg of Advisory Group, 29 Jan 68, *FRUS 1964-68*, 29, pt 1:556-59; Tom Johnson notes of Pres Luncheon mtg w/Senior Advisors, 29 Jan 68, ibid, 565-68; also Tom Johnson notes of Pres Foreign Affairs Luncheon, 30 Jan 68, ibid, 572.

21. Rostow notes mtg w/Pres, 30 Jan 68, fldr Korea Pueblo Incident Ball Cte Briefing Book 2/68, box 264, CF, Korea Pueblo Incident (Closed), NSF, LBJL (quote); memo Rusk for Pres, nd circa 3 Feb 68, *FRUS 1964-68*, 29, pt 1:587-89.

22. "The USS *Pueblo* Incident," 15; Chronology of the *Pueblo* Case, nd (circa 5 Feb 68), fldr Pueblo, box 74, McNamara Records, RG 200; *FRUS 1964-68*, 29, pt 1:592, note 3; msg Johnson for Kosygin, 060003Z Feb 68, ibid, 610; msg Sharp to Wheeler, 310706Z Jan 68, fldr 091 Pueblo Incident (Jan 18), box 29, Wheeler Papers, RG 218; memo Warnke for SecDef, nd but before 5 Mar 68, *FRUS 1964-68*, 29, pt 1:655 (quote).

23. Memo Rostow for Pres, 19 Feb 68, msg CAP 80489 Rostow to Pres, 22 Feb 68: fldr Korea Pueblo Incident, vol Ib, pt A, box 258, CF Korea (Closed), NSF, LBJL; memo Warnke for SecDef, cited in note 22; memo Warnke for Nitze, 11 Mar 68, *FRUS 1964-68*, 29, pt 1:660, also ibid, 703, n 3; Clifford, *Counsel*, 466-67; ed note, *FRUS 1964-68*, 29, pt 1:740; State Dept Statement No 280, 22 Dec 68, fldr Pueblo March-December 1968, box 207, Subj files, OSD Hist (quote).

24. Ed note, msg 3598 Seoul to State, 24 Jan 68: *FRUS 1964-68*, 29, pt 1:309-11; msg CINCUNC/COMUS-KOREA to CINCPAC, 231405Z Jan 68, Cable files, OSD Hist (quote); msg CINCUNC/USFK to CJCS, 27 Jan 68, *FRUS 1964-68*, 29, pt 1:317 (quote).

25. "The USS *Pueblo* Incident," 2-3; msg 3706 Seoul to State, 28 Jan 68, *FRUS 1964-68*, 29, pt 1:541.

26. "The USS *Pueblo* Incident," 4, 17-18; msg 104293 State to Seoul, 25 Jan 68, and msg 3961 Seoul to State, 3 Feb 68: *FRUS 1964-68*, 29, pt 1:315-16 (quote), 321 (quote).

27. Msg 111263 State to Seoul, 7 Feb 68 and msg 111264 State to Seoul, 7 Feb 68: *FRUS 1964-68*, 29, pt 1:337-41 (quote); paper, $32 Million Counter-infiltration Package, nd, SecDef Briefing Book, 28 May 68, TAB I, fldr Korea 300-370.02 1968, box 11, SecDef Subject Decimal files, Acc 73-A-1250.

28. Msg 4083 Seoul to State, 8 Feb 68, *FRUS 1964-68*, 29, pt 1:343-44; Poole, *JCS and National Policy, 1965-68*, pt 2:771.

29. Msg 4131 Seoul to State, 10 Feb 68, *FRUS 1964-68*, 29, pt 1:364 (quote); msg 4142 Seoul to State, 10 Feb 68, ibid, 366-67.

30. Msg 4087 Seoul to State, 8 Feb 68, ibid, 346; memo Vance for Pres, 20 Feb 68, ibid, 384-91; "The USS *Pueblo* Incident," 21.

31. Tom Johnson notes of Pres mtg w/Vance, 15 Feb 68, *FRUS 1964-68*, 29, pt 1:376-83. Early in July, 72 F-4s returned to the United States, replaced by 50 F-100s from activated reserve units. No other U.S. planes redeployed from Korea during 1968; Poole, *JCS and National Policy, 1965-68*, pt 2: 780-81; "The USS *Pueblo* Incident," 20; msg KRA 742 COMUSKOREA to CINCPAC, 29 Feb 68, Cable files, OSD Hist; Tom Johnson notes, 15 Feb 68, *FRUS 1964-68*, 29, pt 1:381.

32. Memo Vance for Pres, 20 Feb 68, *FRUS 1964-68*, 29, pt 1:384-91, (quote 384); Tom Johnson notes, 15 Feb 68, ibid, 380, 377 (quotes); msg COMUSKOREA to CINCPAC 210951Z May 68, TAB J, fldr Korea 300-370.02 1968, box 11, SecDef Subject Decimal files, Acc 73-A-1250.

33. Tom Johnson notes, 15 Feb 68, *FRUS 1964-68*, 29, pt 1:377; memo ASD(ISA) for SecDef, 25 May 68, fldr Korea 300-370.02 1968, box 11, SecDef Subject Decimal files, Acc 73-A-1250; SNIE 14.2-68, 16 May 68, *FRUS 1964-68*, 29, pt 1:427.

34. Memo Warnke for SecDef, 12 Aug 67, fldr Korea 091.112-1967, box 62, SecDef Subject Decimal files, Acc 72-A-2468; msg 2769 Seoul to State, 6 Dec 67, *FRUS 1964-68*, 29, pt 1:297; msgs 77501 State to Seoul, 30 Nov 67; msg 2769 Seoul to State, 6 Dec 67; msg 2337 Canberra to State, 21 Dec 67, ibid, 296-297, 301; memo SecDef for SvcSecs et al, 16 Jan 68, fldr Reading File, Jan 1968, box 131, McNamara Records, RG-200.

35. Memos Warnke for JCS, 22 Dec 67, Warnke for DepSecDef, 28 Dec 67: fldr Korea 370-1967, box 62, SecDef Subject Decimal files, Acc 72-A-2468; msg JCS 9150 to CINCUNC/COMUSKOREA, 4 Feb 68, Cable files, OSD Hist; Nitze notes, 25 Jan 68, fldr DoD DepSecDef Notes, 1968 (1 of 6), box 85 (fldr 4), Nitze Papers, LC.

36. Summary of convs between Johnson and Park, 17 Apr 68 (quote); CIA, Intelligence Information Cable, 23 Apr 68: *FRUS 1964-68*, 29, pt 1:419, 421 (quote).

37. Note DirINR to SecState, 8 Nov 68, ibid, 445-47.

38. Msg 1667 Prague to State, 25 Mar 68, FRUS 1964-68, 17:188; also ibid, 185, n 2; Valenta, *Soviet Intervention in Czechoslovakia, 1968*, rev ed, 12-13.

39. Memo E. Rostow for Rusk, 10 May 68, *FRUS 1964-1968*, 17:193, n 3; Grabo, "Soviet Deception in the Czechoslovak Crisis," 81; see for example Smith, Summary notes of 587th NSC mtg, 5 Jun 68, box 2, NSC Meetings, NSF, LBJL; Tom Johnson notes of mtg, 24 Jul 68, *FRUS 1964-68*, 17:216; msg 2894 USMission NATO to SecState, SecDef, 3 Aug 68, item #7, fldr Soviet-Czechoslovakia Confrontation, box 160, Lemnitzer Papers, Special Collections Library, NDU; Tom Johnson notes of emergency NSC mtg, 20 Aug 68, *FRUS 1964-68*, 17:242.

40. Memo E. Rostow for Rusk, 10 May 68, *FRUS 1964-68*, 17:193-94 (quote); Grabo, "Soviet Deception," 82; msg 162669 State to USMission NATO, 11 May 68, *FRUS 1964-68*, 17:196 (quote); Elsey notes of SecDef's Morning Staff Conf, 13 May 68, fldr VanDeMark Transcripts 1 of 2, box 1, Elsey Papers, LBJL; Dept-State, Contingency Paper: UN and Czechoslovakia, 12 Jul 68, *FRUS 1964-68*, 17:204; memo ASD(ISA) for SecDef, 20 Jul 68, fldr Germany 091.112 1968, box 2, SecDef Subject Decimal files, Acc 73-A-1304.

41. Dawisha, *The Kremlin and the Prague Spring*, 249; memo Rostow for Pres, 23 Jul 68, fldr Czechoslovakia Memos, vol II, 1/68-8/68, box 179, CF, Europe & USSR Czechoslovakia, NSF, LBJL; msg 4751 Moscow to State, 22 Jul 68, *FRUS 1964-68*, 17:211-12.

42. Tom Johnson notes of mtg, 24 Jul 68, *FRUS 1964-68*, 17:216 (quote); Nitze notes, 23 Jul 68, fldr DoD DepSecDef Notes 1968 (4 of 6), box 86, fldr 1, Nitze Papers, LC; memcon, Schroeder and Clifford, 23 Jul 68 and memrcd, Pres mtg w/Schroeder, 24 Jul 68 *FRUS 1964-68*, 15:721-22 and 732.

43. Tom Johnson notes of Pres mtg w/Foreign Policy Advisors, 30 Jul 68, box 3, Tom Johnson Notes of Meetings, LBJL (quote); note Smith to Pres, 30 Jul 68, w/atchmt, CIA, The Situation in Czechoslovakia as of 4:00 p.m. EDT, 30 Jul 68, fldr Czechoslovakia Memos, vol II, 1/68-8/68, box 179, CF, Europe & USSR Czechoslovakia, NSF, LBJL.

44. Guidance to the NATO Military Authorities, 11 May 67, para 15, Annex II to DPC/D(67) 23 in Pedlow, ed, *NATO Strategy Documents 1949-1969*, 340; msg 2894 USMission NATO to SecState/SecDef, 3 Aug 68, item #7, fldr Soviet-Czechoslovakia Confrontation, box 160, Lemnitzer Papers, NDU (quotes); Elsey notes of SecDef's Morning Staff Conf, 5 Aug 68, Elsey Papers, LBJL; Nitze Staff mtg notes, 3 Aug 68, fldr DoD DepSecDef Notes, 1968 (5 of 6), box 86 (fldr 2), Nitze Papers, LC; Tom Johnson notes of mtg, 10 Aug 68, *FRUS 1964-68*, 17:234.

45. For details of the numerous contacts see Transcript of mtg w/Pres, 29 Jul 68, *FRUS 1964-68*, 17:225-26 (quote); memo DepUnderSecState for SecState, 26 Jul 68, ibid, 217; Johnson, *Vantage Point*, 487-89 (quote); ltrs Kosygin to Johnson, 21 Jun 68, Johnson to Kosygin, 22 Jun 68, Kosygin to Johnson, 27 Jun 68, and ed notes: *FRUS 1964-68*, 11:623-25, 689.

46. Summary of mtg w/Pres, Dobrynin, and Rostow, 20 Aug 68, *FRUS 1964-68*, 17:236-41; Poole, *JCS and National Policy, 1965-68*, pt 1:403; Tom Johnson notes of Emergency NSC mtg, 20 Aug 68, *FRUS 1964-68*, 17:242, 244. For a different assessment see Mastny, "Was 1968 a Strategic Watershed of the Cold War?"; memo Ginsburgh for Rostow, 23 Jul 68, *FRUS 1964-68*, 17:215; memo William Lemnitzer (NSC) for Rostow, 22 Jul 68, fldr Czechoslovakia Memos, vol II, 1/68-8/68, box 179, CF, Europe & USSR, Czechoslovakia, NSF, LBJL.

47. Tom Johnson notes of Emergency NCS mtg, 20 Aug 68, *FRUS 1964-68*, 17:242-45; Johnson, *Vantage Point*, 488; Nitze Staff mtg notes, 21 Aug 68, fldr DoD DepSecDef Notes, 1968 (5 of 6), box 86 (fldr 2), Nitze Papers, LC.

48. Valenta, *Soviet Intervention in Czechoslovakia, 1968*, 174 (quote); msg 5178 Moscow to State, 21 Aug 68, *FRUS 1964-68*, 17:246 (quote). For expressions of surprise by Rusk, Clifford, and the president, see Tom Johnson notes of Emergency NSC mtg, 20 Aug 68, ibid, 242-44; Tom Johnson notes of Cabinet mtg, 22 Aug 68, *ibid*, 248-49 (quote). A reference to the Soviet missile alert appears in Summary notes of 590th NSC mtg, 4 Sep 68, ibid, 277; summary of mtg, 23 Aug 68, ibid, 251.

49. Poole, *JCS and National Policy, 1965-68*, pt 1:407, n 75.

50. Memo Warnke for SecDef, 31 Aug 68, fldr Briefing and Other Press Materials, box 17, Clifford Papers, LBJL.

51. Memcon Rusk and Dobrynin, 30 Aug 68; msg CAP 82331 Rostow to Pres, 1 Sep 68: *FRUS 1964-68*, 17:451-54 (quote); summary notes of 590th NSC mtg , 4 Sep 68, ibid, 275-76; Pres remarks in San Antonio, 30 Aug 68, *Johnson Public Papers, 1968*, 2:919-20 (quote).

52. Grabo, "Soviet Deception," 19-21; Summary of mtg, 23 Aug 68, *FRUS 1964-68*, 17:250-51; CIA Intel Memo No. 2049/68, 4 Nov 68, ibid, 778-80 (quote).

53. DeptState paper, nd but circulated to NSC Council members on 3 Sep for 4 Sep 68 NSC meeting, *FRUS 1964-68*, 17:269 (quote); memo ASD(ISA) for SecDef, 4 Sep 68, fldr NATO 381, box 5, DoD OASD(C) SecDef Subject Decimal files, Acc 73-A-1304; memo Ginsburgh for Rostow, 22 Aug 68, fldr Johnson Library Papers, OSD Hist (quote); memo Acting Dir for Plans & Policy, JtStaff, for CJCS, 29 Aug 68, Tab 198, fldr 092.2 NATO Aug 68-Oct 68, box 71, Wheeler Papers, RG 218 (quotes).

54. JCSM-538-68 for SecDef, 7 Sep 68, fldr 334 NATO Jan 68, box 7, ISA General files, Acc 72-A-1499.

55. DeptState paper, cited in note 53; transc Clifford test, 17 Sep 68 SSCA hearings on DoD Appropriations for FY 1969, 2600-2605, fldr Transcript-Hearings before Senate Appropriation Cte for FY 1969 – September 18, 1968 (a.m. & p.m.), box 77, ASD(C) files, OSD Hist.

56. DPM SecDef for Pres, 7 Jan 69, fldr FY 1970 DPMs & TS, box 122, ASD(C) files, OSD Hist; Tom Johnson notes of Pres mtg w/House Leadership, 9 Sep 68, box 2, NSC Meetings, NSF, LBJL; DPM SecDef for Pres, 15 Jan 69, fldr FY 1970 DPMs & TS, box 122, ASD(C) Files, OSD Hist (quote); CIA memo, 4 Nov 68, cited in note 52.

57. Summary notes of 590th NSC mtg, 4 Sep 68, *FRUS 1964-68*, 17:750 (quote), 752; JCSM-651-68 for SecDef, 31 Oct 68, fldr 334 NATO 1968 Jan-, box 7, ISA General, Acc 72-A-1499 (quote); CIA memo, 4 Nov 68, cited in note 52 (quote); memo ASD(ISA) for SecDef, 2 Dec 68, TAB G, 3 fldr #15, JCS Meeting 28 Dec 68, box 2, OSD Records from SecDef Vault (Mr Laird), Acc 330-74-142.

58. OASD/SA, NATO Div, SecDef Briefing on REDCOSTE, 3 Feb 69, fldr NATO, box 1, Rearden Study Files, OSD Hist; ASD(SA) paper, 12 Mar 69, TAB L-27, fldr SecDef Congressional Briefing Book, vol 2, 91 Cong 1 sess, ASD(C) Files, OSD Hist; memo SecDef for SvcSecs and CJCS, 6 Jun 68, fldr Europe 123 DPM 1968, box 1, SecDef Subject Decimal files, Acc 73-A-1304.

59. Ltr Cleveland to Clifford, 24 Jun 68, fldr REDCOSTE 923 May-10 Jul 68), box 23, Clifford Papers, LBJL; JCSM-429-68 for SecDef, 5 Jul 68, ibid.

60. Msg ALO 581 USNMR SHAPE Belgium to JCS, 1 Aug 68, Cable files, OSD Hist; msg JCS/DJS 08661 to USEUCOM, 1Aug 68, fldr #44 1968 E.O. Messages IN July-11 Sep, box 176, 1967-1968, General Lemnitzer's Eyes Only Messages File 1965-1969, Lemnitzer Papers, Special Collections Library, NDU (quote); memo Warnke for SecDef, 8 Jul 68, w/atchmt, fldr Troops in Europe and Balance of Payments, box 17, Clifford Papers, LBJL (quote).

61. Memcon Schroeder and Clifford, 23 Jul 68, *FRUS 1964-68*, 15:723-24; memo Warnke for SvcSecs, et al, 12 Jul 68 w/encl, Talking Paper Prepared in DoD. Encl printed ibid, 13:727-33 (quote). Clifford sent the document to Senators Russell, Jackson, and Stennis on 11 July. CM-3440-68 for H.K. Johnson et al, 26 Jun 68, fldr 323.3 SAC/CINCEUR Apr 68-Dec 68, box 82, Wheeler Papers, RG 218.

62. Memo ASD(ISA) for SecDef, 9 Jul 68, fldr REDCOSTE (23 May-10 Jul 68), box 23, Clifford Papers, LBJL; Poole, *JCS and National Policy, 1965-68*, 9, pt 1:400-03; msg JCS 9554 to Lemnitzer, 23 Aug 68, fldr #44 1968 E.O. Messages IN July-11 Sep, box 176, 1967-1968, General Lemnitzer's Eyes Only Messages File 1965-1969, Lemnitzer Papers, Special Collections Library, NDU; Talking Paper, cited in note 61.

63. Memo Warnke for SecDef, 21 Aug 68, fldr USSR (Sensitive) 1968, box 5, SecDef Sensitive Files 1949-1969, Acc 330-91-0017.

64. Ltr Rusk to Clifford, 2 Sep 68; ltr Clifford to Rusk, 12 Sep 68: fldr Balance of Payments Cabinet Cte, box 7, Clifford Papers, LBJL.

65. Msg JCS 9796 to Lemnitzer, 28 Aug 68; msg BRU 868 USREPMILCOM NATO to Wheeler, 1 Sep 68; msg 2881 Burchinal to Lemnitzer 9 Sep 68: fldr #44, 1968 E.O. Messages IN Jul - 11 Sep, box 176, 1967-1968

General Lemnitzer Eyes Only Messages File 1955-1969, Lemnitzer Papers, Special Collections Library, NDU; msg Lemnitzer to Wheeler 022057Z Sep 68, fldr #47, ibid; JCSM-538-68 for SecDef, 7 Sep 68, cited in note 54 (quote).

66. Memos SecDef for SvcSecs et al, 18 and 20 Sep 68, w/annexes, fldr FY 1970 – REDCOSTE, box 83, ASD(C) Files, OSD Hist; memo OASD(SA) for SecDef, 18 Sep 68, fldr Balance of Payments Cabinet Cte, box 7, Clifford Papers, LBJL.

67. Memo OASD(ISA) for SecDef, 7 May 68, fldr REDCOSTE (23 May-10 Jul 68), box 23, ibid; ltr Rusk to Clifford, 24 Oct 68, fldr State Department, box 7, ibid, (quotes); memo SACEUR for CJCS, 30 Oct 68, ibid; ltr Clifford to Rusk, 4 Nov 68, ibid; ltr Rusk to Clifford, 9 Nov 68, fldr Germany 333 1968, box 11, ISA General files, Acc 72-A-1498.

68. JCSM-547-68 for SecDef, 14 Sep 68, fldr 334 NATO 1968 Jan -, box 7, ISA General files, Acc 72-A-1499 (quote); memo SecDef for CJCS, 8 Oct 68, fldr Staff, JCS, box 13, Clifford Papers, LBJL; memo ASD(ISA) for DepSecDef, 19 Oct 68, fldr NATO 381, box 5, SecDef Subject Decimal files, Acc 73-A-1304; JCSM-594-68 for SecDef, 8 Oct 68, fldr 334 NATO Jan 68, box 7, ISA General files, Acc 72-A-1499 (quote).

69. Memos ISA for DepSecDef, 19 Oct 68, SecDef for JCS et al, 23 Oct 68: fldr NATO 381, box 5, SecDef Subject Decimal files, Acc 73-A-1304; JCSM-651-68 for SecDef, 31 Oct 68, fldr 334 NATO 1968 Jan - , box 7, ISA General files, Acc 72-A-1499; Europe, Tab G, 1, fldr #15 JCS Meeting 28 Dec 68, box 2, OSD Records from SecDef Vault (Mr. Laird), Acc 330-74-142; Poole, *JCS and National Policy, 1965-68*, pt 1:411-12; memo SecDef for SvcSecs et al, 7 Dec 68, TAB G-2, fldr #15, JCS Meeting 28 Dec 68, box 2, OSD Records from SecDef Vault (Mr Laird), Acc 330-74-142.

70. Memo ASD(SA) for SecDef, 4 Sep 68, cited in note 53; memo Warnke for Clifford, 5 Oct 68, item #19, fldr State Department, box 7-8, Clifford Papers, LBJL. Clifford attributed the poor relations to his success in the March policy review, which made Rusk see OSD as a threat; Elsey notes of SecDef Morning Staff Conf, 30 Aug 68, Elsey Papers, LBJL.

71. Memo SecDef for SvcSecs et al, 7 Dec 68, TAB G-2, w/atchmt 1, 14 Nov 68, fldr #15, JCS Meeting 28 Dec 68, box 2, OSD Records from SecDef Vault (Mr Laird), Acc 330-74-142.

72. OASD(SA), NATO Div, SecDef Briefing, 3 Feb 69, cited in note 58 (quote); memos ASD(SA) for DepSecDef, 4 Dec 68 and SecDef for SvcSecs et al, 10 Dec 68, w/atchmt, REDCOSTE Plan Summary, 5 Dec 68, fldr FY 1970 -- REDCOSTE, box 83, ASD(C) Files, OSD Hist.

73. Memo SecDef for SvcSecs et al, 10 Dec 68 cited in note 72; ltr Clifford to Rusk, 10 Dec 68, fldr State Department, box 7, Clifford Papers, LBJL.

74. Msg ALO 687 USNMR SHAPE to JCS, 26 Dec 68, SecDef Cables, OSD Hist; OASD(SA) NATO Div, SecDef Briefing on REDCOSTE, 3 Feb 69, cited in note 58; JCSM-4-69, ACJCS for SecDef, 4 Jan 69, fldr REDCOSTE (3 Oct 68-20 Jan 69), box 24, Clifford Papers, LBJL; ltrs SecState to SecDef, 27 Jan 69 and SecDef to SecState, 31 Jan 69, fldr NATO, box 1, Rearden Study Files, OSD Hist.

XIX. STRATEGY AND COST-EFFECTIVENESS

1. SecDef Statement before SCAS, Amendments to the FY 1969 Supplemental and FY 1970 Defense Budget, 19 Mar 69, 41, fldr FY 69-70 Supplementals, FYs 1969-71, box 6, SecDef Statements 1968-70, OSD Hist.

2. McNamara test, 8 Mar 67, SubCte on DoD of HCA, *Hearings: Department of Defense Appropriations for 1968*, pt 2:405.

3. McNamara, *In Retrospect*, 237-38 (quotes); msg CINCPAC to COMUSMACV, 302105Z Oct 65, fldr Body Count, box 369, Subj files, OSD Hist; memo OASD(SA) SEA Programs Div for DepSecDef, ibid; interv Robert S. McNamara by Maurice Matloff and Alfred Goldberg, 24 Jul 86, 29, OSD Hist (quote).

4. OASD (SA) SEA Programs Div, *Southeast Asia Analysis Report*, May 1967, 14, fldr SEA Analysis Reports, box 315, Subj files, OSD Hist; Hammond, *Military and the Media, 1962-1968*, 318-20; Shapley, *Promise and Power*, 251, 350.

5. Herring, *LBJ and Vietnam*, 45.

6. McNamara test, 1 Aug 66, SSCA, *Hearings: Department of Defense Appropriations for Fiscal Year 1967*, pt 2:719-20 (quote); McNamara test, 5 Oct 66, for HCAS hearings on Reprogramming Actions FY 1967 (Excerpts) 1389, fldr Vietnam 1966, box 34, SecDef Bio files, OSD Hist (quote).

7. Report by Joint Logistics Review Board, 354-70, "Logistic Support in the Vietnam Era," Monograph 2, "Ammunition," Appx C through H, D-27 (1970), box 321, Subj files, OSD Hist. (Hereafter "Ammunition.")

8. McNamara test, 5 Oct 66, cited in note 6, 1371,1381.
9. Ltr Rivers to Hardy, 28 Jul 65, atchd to ltr Rivers to McNamara, 28 Apr 66, fldr 400 28 Apr 66, box 7, ISA General files, Acc 70A-6649.
10. McNamara test, 16 Feb 66, HSCA, *Hearings: Department of Defense Appropriations for 1967*, pt 1:281; *New York Times*, 21 Feb 66 (quotes).
11. McNamara test, 25 Feb 66, SCAS and SubCte on DoD of SCA, *Hearings: Military Procurement Authorizations for Fiscal Year 1967*, 283-84 (quote); memo Glass for McNamara, 21 Apr 66, fldr History of Ammunition Procurement Policies Prior to Vietnam Buildup (Jan 61-Jan 65), box 95, ASD(C) files, OSD Hist.
12. Memrcd Greene, Summary of SecDef Staff mtg, 21 Feb 1966, Greene Papers, MHC (quotes); McNamara test, 28 Feb 66, *Hearings*, cited in note 11, 374-75; memrcd Kidd, 1 Mar 66, fldr TS-Sensitive Memos originated by OO, Jan 1966 thru Jun, box 86, Double Zero 1967, T/S Sensitive 1963-1966, NHC.
13. McNamara News conf, 2 Mar 66, *McNamara Public Statements, 1966*, 5:1392-94.
14. Ibid, 1401.
15. OPS/OD/RE, Fact Sheet, 21 Feb 66, fldr Baldwin/Lippman articles – Feb 21,22, 1966, box 96, ASD(C) files, OSD Hist (quote); memo CMC for UnderSecN, 21 Feb 66, ibid.
16. SecDef Statement, 3 Mar 66, *McNamara Public Statements, 1966*, 5:1442-43; News conf, 2 Mar 66, ibid, 5:1396 (quote); Background Briefing, 14 Apr 66, *Background Briefings of Secretary of Defense McNamara, 1966*:125.
17. *Washington Post* and *Chicago Tribune*, both 12 Apr 66 (quotes); *Baltimore Sun*, 15 Apr 66 (quotes).
18. News conf, 14 Apr 66, *McNamara Public Statements, 1966*, 6:2051-56.
19. McNamara test, 20 Apr 66, SCFR, *Hearings: Foreign Assistance, 1966*, 203, 205; McNamara test, 11 May 66, ibid, 678-79 (quotes, 679).
20. Ltr McNaughton to Hall, 31 Mar 66, fldr FRG Excesses-General, box 23, ISA MAP files, Acc 71-A-2701 (quote); *Washington Star*, 21 Apr 66, *Baltimore Sun*, 22 Apr 66; *Baltimore Sun*, 22 Apr 66; *New York Times*, 25 Apr 66 (quote).
21. "Ammunition," D/7- 9.
22. Ltr Rivers to McNamara, 28 Apr 66 w/ encl, cited in note 9;Van Staaveren, *Gradual Failure*, 179, 264-65; CM-1724-66 for SecDef, 6 Sep 66, fldr 1966 CMs (1710-1798), box 2, Wheeler Papers, RG 218 (quote).
23. Ltr Hardy to Rivers, nd (Mar 66), fldr SubCte for Spec. Inv Rpt on Military Shortages, Etc (Comments on Letter from Hardy to Rivers) box, 90, ASD(C) files, OSD Hist (quotes); ltr Rivers to McNamara, 28 Apr 66, cited in note 9.
24. Ltr McNamara to Rivers, 17 May 66 w/ encls, fldr Subcte for Spec Inv Rpt on Military Shortages, Etc (Comments on Ltr from Hardy to Rivers), box 90, ASD(C) files, OSD Hist.
25. "History of Strategic Arms Competition 1945-1972," pt 2:581-84, OSD Hist.
26. McNamara test, 16 Feb 66, HSCA, *Hearings*, cited in note 10, 253. Also involved were questions of the cost-effectiveness of nuclear propulsion, carrier doctrine, and naval strategy; see Roherty, *Decisions of Robert S. McNamara*, 151-82; DPM SecDef for Pres, 28 Sep 65, 1, fldr Memos for Pres, DPMs FY 1967, box 119, ASD(C) files, OSD Hist.
27. DPM, cited in note 26, 28; memo SecDef for SecN and CJCS, 6 Oct 65, ibid.
28. SecDef Statement on FY 1970-74 Defense Program and 1970 Defense Budget, as prepared 13 Jan 69, 184, box 6, SecDef Statements 1968-70, FYs 1969-71, OSD Hist; CVAN (New) #68, Program Status Report as of 31 Mar 69, fldr Program Status Reports – 1969, FY 1969 Budget, box 77, ASD(C) files, OSD Hist; SecDef Guidance Memo, Shipbuilding, 13 Jan 69, fldr 020 SA 1968, box 42, SecDef Subject Decimal files, Acc 73A-1250.
29. JLRB Report, cited in note 7, appx A, A-57-60, box 321, Subj files, OSD Hist; SecDef Ste before SCAS, 19 Mar 69, 45, fldr FY 69-70 Supplementals, box 6, SecDef Statements 1968-70, FYs 1969-71, OSD Hist.
30. Art, *The TFX Decision*, 89.
31. Ibid, 89-93; ltr McNamara to Curtis, 18 Feb 66, fldr McNamara-Joint Economic Committee – Jan 24, 1966, box 87, ASD(C) files, OSD Hist; memo SecDef for Pres, DoD Cost Reduction Program, 5 Jul 62, *McNamara Public Statements 1962*, 4:1521; test Ruegg, Charles, and Moot, 18 Jul 66 and 20 Jul 66, House SubCte for Special Investigations of HCAS, *Hearings: Examination of Department of Defense Cost Reduction Program*, 195-96, 303; Sapolsky, *Polaris System Development*, 212-13.
32. Fisher, "Cost Incentive and Contract Outcomes," Rand Memorandum RM-5120-PR, Sep 66, v-vi, 5-6, 32-33, 45-46; Belden, "Defense Procurement Outcomes in the Incentive Contract Environment," Thesis, Stanford University, Department of Industrial Engineering Technical Report No. 69-2, May 1969, 92.
33. Sapolsky, *Polaris System Development*, 211. Sapolsky was speaking specifically about the Polaris program, but his point applies across the procurement board.

34. Memo ASD(C) for SecDef, 12 Oct 67 w/ atchmt, fldr McClellan, box 5, Niederlehner files, OSD Hist.

35. Memo SecDef for Pres, DoD Cost Reduction Program – Fourth Annual Progress report, 8 July 66, fldr Cost Reduction Memo Working File July 1966, box 52, ASD(C) files, OSD Hist; Belden, "Defense Procurement" 46; McNamara test, 24 Jan 66, Jt Ec Cte, SubCte on Fed Procurement and Reg, *Hearings: Economic Impact of Federal Procurement*, 16.

36. C-5A, Program Status Report as of 31 Mar 69, fldr Program Status Reports – 1969, box 77, ASD(C) files, OSD Hist; Sapolsky, *Polaris System Development*, 213-14.

37. Remarks by SecDef, 15 Oct 64, *McNamara Public Statements, 1964*, 4:1654-55.

38. Test Brick, 16 Apr 70, Senate, Perm SubCte on Invest of the Cte on Government Operations, *Hearings: TFX Contract Investigation*, (Second Series), pt 3:558; memcon Pursley, 30 Mar 67, fldr F-111 Folder #3, box 16, Pursley Papers, Acc 330-75-104; Poole, "An Overview of Acquisition, 1959-1968," 10 Sep 2001, np, 12-13, has a useful discussion of the phenomenon. I am indebted to Dr. Poole for providing me with a copy of his conference paper. Bradley and McCuistion, "Contractor Decision Making and Incentive Fee Contracts," 22 Dec 65, ii and vi'; McNaugher, *New Weapons Old Politics*, 60.

39. Office of History, HQ, AF Systems Command, "The TFX: Conceptual Phase to F-111B Termination 1958-1968," nd, 25, 46, 48, 51, box 879, Subj files, OSD Hist; Memcons Pursley, 25 Aug 66 (quote), 17 Nov 66 (quote): both fldr F-111 Folder #2, box 16, Pursley Papers, Acc 330-75-104.

40. FB-111 and F-111 A/E/D, Program Status reports as of 31 Mar 69, fldr Program Status Reports – 1969, box 77, ASD(C) files, OSD Hist; test O'Neill, 13 Oct 69, *Hearings*, cited in note 38, pt 1:168.

41. Test Nitze, 14 Jul 67, ibid, pt 1:127; test Brick, 16 Apr 70, ibid, pt 3:561; test Keating, 13 Oct 69, ibid, pt 1:175-76 (quote, 176); test O'Neill, 13 Oct 69, ibid, pt 1:177-78; memcons Pursley, 19 Aug 67, 21 Sep 67, 26 Oct 67, 1 Dec 67, 11 Jan 68, fldr F-111 Folder #3, box 16, Pursley Papers, Acc 330-75-104; AF Systems Command, "The TFX," 53.

42. McNaugher, "Collaborative Development of Main Battle Tanks," Rand Note N-1680-RC, August 1981, 19. Italics in original.

43. Ibid, 11-13.

44. Ibid, 21; memo Enthoven for SecDef, 12 Jul 67, fldr Weapons and Vehicles, box 874, Subj files, OSD Hist (quote); memcon Schmidt w/ McNamara, 21 Sep 67, fldr Germany 333 Aug-Sep 1968, box 11, ISA General files, Acc 72A-1498.

45. Agreed Minute, MBT-1970 Program, 7-8 Mar 68, Tab 7, encl B, Nuclear Planning Group Meeting Notebook, 18-19 Apr 68, fldr Germany 337, 1968, box 2, SecDef Subject Decimal files, Acc 73A-1304.

46. ODDR&E, Main Battle Tank – 1970, 18 Jul 68, fldr Germany 091.112 1968, ibid; McNaugher, "Collaborative Development," 20.

47. SecDef Guidance Memo, Shipbuilding, 13 Jan 69, fldr 020 SA 1968, box 42, SecDef Subject Decimal files, Acc 73A-1250.

48. Sapolsky, *Polaris System Development*, 160-61; Enthoven and Smith, *How Much Is Enough?*, 171.

49. "Strategic Arms Competition," pt 2:571; Sapolsky, *Polaris System Development*, 206.

50. UGM-73A, Program Status Report as of 31 Mar 69, fldr Program Status Reports – 1969, box 77, ASD(C) files, OSD Hist; Sapolsky, *Polaris System Development*, 206-07; DPM SecDef for Pres, 22 Sep 66, fldr 314A-69 Draft Presidential Memos (McNamara File), box 71, Taylor Papers, Special Collections Library, NDU.

51. *New York Times*, 28 Jul 67; *Baltimore Sun*, 29 Jul 67 (quote); Fitzgerald, *The High Priests of Waste*, 111-31; Answer to Senator Symington's Question No. 67 re SecDef Testimony before Senate Armed Services Cte, fldr Symington Questions, 1-103, RE FY 69 Posture Ste-Office Master, box 75, ASD(C) files, OSD Hist.

52. SecDef Statement before SCAS, Amendments to the FY 1969 Supplemental and FY 1970 Defense Budget, 19 Mar 69, 7, fldr FY 69-70 Supplementals, box 6, SecDef Statements 1968-70, OSD Hist.

53. Memo SecDef for Pres, 5 Jul 62, *McNamara Public Statements, 1962*, 4:1519; DoD Instruction 7720.6, 20 Jan 64, codified criteria to identify savings under the Cost Reduction Program.

54. Memo SecDef for Pres, 8 July 66, fldr Cost Reduction Memo Working File July 1966, box 52, ASD(C) files, OSD Hist.

55. Rubin test, 13 Jul 66, House, SubCte for Special Investigations of HCAS, *Hearings: Examination of DoD Cost Reduction Program*, 4- 5.

56. Subcte for Special Investigations of HCAS, *Report of the Examination of Defense Cost Reduction Program*, 12 Sep 66, 7 (quote), 9, 14-15.

57. Ibid, 2.

58. DoD News Release 795-66, 16 Sep 66, *McNamara Public Statements, 1966*, 7:2656 (quote); memo SecDef for Pres, 5 Jul 67, fldr Cost Reduction Program (7/5/67) First Drafts, box 58, ASD(C) files, OSD Hist.

59. Transc McNamara test, 23 Jan 67, Jt Sess of SCAS and Senate SubCte on DoD Appros on the FY 1968-72 Defense Program & 1968 Defense Budget, 23 Jan 67, 254, fldr FY 1967, box 5, SecDef Statements 1966-67, OSD Hist; memo SecDef for Pres, 5 Jul 67, cited in note 58.

60. Memo SecDef for SvcSecs et al, 3 May 68, fldr Cost Reduction Program (7/5/67) First Drafts, box 58, ASD(C) files, OSD Hist; memo SecDef for Pres, 3 Oct 68, *Clifford Public Statements, 1968*, 3:882-3; *Cong Rec*, 24 Aug 67, 23904 (quote); ibid, 9 Aug 67, 21938 (quotes).

61. DPM SecDef for Pres, 20 Oct 65, Notebook Memos for Pres, CY 1965 FY 1967, box 119, ASD(C) files, OSD Hist.

62. JLRB Report, A-46, cited in note 7; transc McNamara test, 28 Feb 66, SCAS and SubCte on DoD of SCA hearings on Military Authorizations and DoD Appropriations, 28 Feb 66, 437 and 439, fldr Joint Senate Armed Svcs & DoD Approp Committee Transcripts 28 Feb 1966, box 51, ASD(C) files, OSD Hist (quote).

63. Office of Chief, Army Reserve, Annual Historical Summary, 1 Jul 67-30 Jun 68, pt 3: 3-6, USARF-1968; DA, Office of Reserve Components, Annual Historical Summary, 1 Jul 66-30 Jun 67, 6, CO RC-1967: CMH; JCSM-646-66 for SecDef, 7 Oct 66, fldr JCSM's 603-66 to 699-66, box 183, Wheeler Papers, RG 218; HQ CONARC, USCONARC/USARSTRIKE Annual Historical Summary, 1 Jul 65 - 30 Jun 66, 16 Jun 67, 214; HQ CONARC, USCONARC/USARSTRIKE Annual Historical Summary, FY 1968, 7 May 69, 150-151, box 651, Subj files, OSD Hist; DPM SecDef for Pres, 11 Jan 69, 2, Notebook FY 1970 DPMs & TS, box 122, ASD(C) files, OSD Hist.

64. JCSM-814-65 for SecDef, 10 Nov 65, fldr 325-69A, 13 A (US & VN Military Forces), box 54, Taylor Papers, NDU; Poole, *JCS and National Policy, 1965-1968*, pt 1:119-20.

65. TAB [30 Nov 65] - November trip of RSM to SVN, Greene Papers, MHC; memo 0044-66 McDonald for Wheeler, 3 Feb 66, fldr 00 Memo's 001-66 to 00-0105, 1-105-1966, box 1, Double Zero 1966 Memos, 1-410, NHC (quote); CM-1184-66 for DirJtStaff, 15 Feb 66, fldr 1966 CM's 1142-66 - 1226-66, box 2, Wheeler Papers, RG 218.

66. JCSM-130-66 for SecDef, 1 Mar 66, fldr Southeast Asia 1 Mar 66, 320.2, box 8, ISA General files, Acc 70A-6649 (quote); memo SecDef for SvcSecs, CJCS, 10 Mar 66, ibid.

67. HCAS, Spec Invest Subcte Rpt, 23, 40, 45, nd but atchd to ltr Rivers to McNamara, 28 Apr 66, cited in note 9; JLRB Report, A/9-10, cited in note 7; OPS/OD/RE, Fact Sheet, 21 Feb 66, Tab II, 8: fldr Baldwin/Lippman articles – Feb 21, 22, 1966, box 96, ASD(C) files, OSD Hist.

68. Response II-8, (Classified); News Release No. 170-66, 2 Mar 66, Response II. 7: ibid; "Annual Report of the Secretary of the Army," in *DoD Annual Report for FY 1965*,120; "Annual Report of the Secretary of the Army," in *DoD Annual Report for FY 1966*,126-27; msg JCS 6412 to USCINCEUR, 26 Nov 68, fldr 57 Logistics/Gold Flow, box 148, Lemnitzer Papers, Special Collections Library, NDU (quote); JCSM-712-68 for SecDef, 3 Dec 68, fldr Europe 400. 1968, box 2, SecDef Subject Decimal files, Acc 73A-1304. The JCS recalled this memo on 6 December after Wheeler spoke to Nitze by phone about the issues. Msg ALO 581, USNMR SHAPE Belgium to JCS, 1 Aug 68, Cable files, OSD Hist (quotes).

69. HCAS, Rpt, cited in note 9, 18, 23, 76; JLRB Report, cited in note 7, 2: app A, A/8-9 and 54-55; "Ammunition," E/3-5.

70. JLRB Report, A/37; "Ammunition," G/5.

71. DPM SecDef for Pres, 15 Jan 69, 8 (quote), and DPM, 11 Jan 69, 6: both Notebook FY 1970 DPMs & TS, box 122, ASD(C) files, OSD Hist.

72. Memo Holmes for Pursley, 15 Oct 68 w/ atchmt, fldr Germany 333 Clifford 1968, box 2, SecDef Subject Decimal files, Acc 73A-1304; memo Acting SecA for DepSecDef, 5 Aug 68, fldr EUCOM 322 1968, box 1, ibid.

73. Ltr Brown to W. Bundy, 13 Dec 66 quoted in *FRUS 1964-1968*, 29:226, n3; JCSM-53-68 for SecDef, 25 Jan 68, memo SecA for SecDef, 29 Jan 68, memo SecDef for CJCS, 1 Feb 68: fldr Korea 370 1968, box 11, SecDef Subject Decimal files, Acc 73A-1250; OASD/ISA/EAPR, Combat Readiness of U.S. and ROK Forces in Korea, 12 Jun 68, fldr Korea 300-370.02 1968, ibid.

74. JLRB Report, A/48; JCSM-443-68 for SecDef, 12 Jul 68, fldr NATO 320.2 DPQ 1968, box 3, SecDef Subject Decimal files 1968, Acc 73A-1304.

75. CM-2969-68 for Taylor, 8 Feb 68, fldr A1 Clifford Study Group-Tet 1968, box 59, Taylor Papers, NDU Library.

76. JCSM-221-68 for SecDef, 10 Apr 68, *FRUS 1964-68*, 10:679-84; JCSM-315-68 for SecDef, 21 May 68, fldr Miscellaneous 1968, box 65, Pentagon Papers Background, Acc 330-75-062.

77. Memo SecDef for Pres, 21 Jun 68, fldr Defense, Department of April 1968 vol VI, box 12/13 (Classified), Agency File, NSF, LBJL; Poole, *JCS and National Policy 1965-68*, pt 1:177-78; DJSM-555-68 for SecDef, 8 May 68, fldr EUCOM 322, 1968, box 1, SecDef Subject Decimal files, Acc 73A-1304 (quotes); memo

DepSecDef for SvcSecs, 16 May 68, memo ActSecA for DepSecDef, 5 Aug 68: ibid.

78. JCSM-431-68 for SecDef, 5 Jul 68, fldr Mediterranean 560.1 1968, box 3, SecDef Subject Decimal files 1968, Acc 73A-1304; memo Office of SecN for SecDef, 20 Jul 68, fldr EUCOM 322, 1968, box 1, ibid (quote); note Holmes to Pursley, 15 Oct 68 w/ atchmt, fldr Germany 333 Clifford 1968, box 2, ibid; CM-3702-68 for SecDef, 4 Oct 68, fldr Europe 333 Jan 68, box 11, ISA Country Files, ACC 72A-1498.

79. Synopsis of Briefing to be Presented by General Wade, nd atchmt to CM-3702-68 for SecDef, 4 Oct 68, fldr Europe 333 Jan 1968, box 11, ISA General files, Acc 72A-1498; memo SecAF for SecDef, 4 Jun 68, fldr EUCOM 322 1968, box 1, SecDef Subject Decimal files, Acc 73A-1304; JCSM-712-68 for SecDef, cited in note 68 (quote). As noted there, the JCS recalled this memo.

80. Poole, *JCS and National Policy 1965-68*, pt 1:194 -95.

81. Agenda for Discussion with Sec Clifford and Sec Nitze, 5 Nov 68, fldr STRAF (incl 6th Infantry Division), box 26, Clifford Papers, LBJL; SecDef Statement before SCAS, 19 Mar 69, 6, cited in note 1 (quotes).

82. Untitled paper, 8 Apr 71, fldr Body Count, box 369, Subj files, OSD Hist.

XX. CONCLUSION

1. Memo Chief, Physical Security Branch for DASD(A), 1 Mar 68, fldr 020 SA 1968, box 42, DASD(C) 1968 SecDef Files, Acc 73-A-1250.

2. Elsey, Notes of SecDef Staff Mtg., 13 Jan 69, Elsey Papers, LBJL.

3. OSD, DSS, *Selected Manpower Statistics*, 15 Apr 69, 7, box 1127, Subject Files, OSD Hist.

4. Memo McNaughton for McNamara, 6 May 67, *FRUS 1964-68*, 5:382.

5. ISA, Key Issues and Accomplishments During the Past Seven Years and Issues and Ability to Deal with Problems During the Next Five Years, 12 Jan 68, fldr #79, box 7, Records of SecDef (Mr. Laird) 1969-72, Acc 330-74-142.

6. Memo Bundy for Pres, 2 Apr 64, *FRUS 1964-68*, 9:14.

7. Memo Bundy for Pres, 4 Sep 64, fldr 313.4, box 1, Acc 330-79-0050.

NOTE ON SOURCES
AND SELECTED BIBLIOGRAPHY

The basic source for this history has been the records of the Office of the Secretary of Defense and its components covering the years 1965 through January 1969. Beginning in 1970 and thereafter, the records for each year from 1965 through January 1969 were transferred to the National Archives. At the time of this writing, the National Archives and Records Administration, College Park, Maryland, has accessioned portions of the 1965 and 1966 records, but the bulk of the material remains under OSD control at the Washington National Records Center (WNRC), Suitland, Maryland. The chief finding aid for the Suitland materials is the Standard Form 135, "Records Transfer and Receipt," whose description of the retired records varies greatly. Thus it was necessary to go through each collection, folder by folder, to identify pertinent documents. The most important are the correspondence and records of the secretary of defense, especially for the McNamara years. Less complete are the deputy secretary of defense materials and the documentation for the Clifford era. Other significant collections are the records of the assistant secretary for international security affairs, which often duplicate the secretary's records, the assistant secretary (comptroller), and the assistant secretary for systems analysis. All of these files are part of Record Group 330, and where no Record Group (RG) number is indicated in note citations, RG 330 is to be understood.

Copies of the assistant secretary (comptroller) files for the period remain in the possession of the OSD Historical Office, and are the richest sources for following the course of defense budget development. The Historical Office maintains an extensive Subject File collection, and its Biographical Files of the Secretary of Defense accession is especially valuable for the McNamara period. The office also has a copy of the "Draft Administrative History of the Office of the Secretary of Defense, 1963–1969," (five volumes) covering the Johnson presidency, but this must be used with caution because of numerous errors and omissions.

The photocopier is the boon and bane of historians. It facilitates research, but the proliferation of photocopies often results in the same document being found in several different archival collections. As a rule, I have cited the document where I initially located it. The files of the Joint Chiefs of Staff offer an example. They constitute Record Group 218 at the National Archives, College Park, but copies of numerous JCS messages and memoranda are found in RG 330 as well as in the holdings of the Lyndon Baines Johnson Presidential Library, Austin, Texas, and other archival repositories. Furthermore the RG 218 materials for the period under discussion are not fully accessioned and much pertinent documentation remains closed to nonofficial researchers.

Collections at the Lyndon Baines Johnson Presidential Library proved indispensable for this volume. The National Security Council histories, National Security Files, Country Files, NSF Country Files, Vietnam, Subject Files, Agency Files, and Memos to the President from McGeorge Bundy and Walt W. Rostow enable one to trace the policymaking process in detail. Especially helpful are the 26 boxes of Clark Clifford material. The library's extensive oral history collection supplements the written documentation. Lastly, the taped telephone conversations between Johnson and his staff, personal advisers, and confidants offer a singular perspective on the president's decisionmaking process.

McNamara's personal papers in RG 200 at the National Archives form a mixed collection. Much of it duplicates documentation found elsewhere, especially the RG 330 files, but there are also unique items related to the ABM and the defense budget. His collection at the Library of Congress is mainly unofficial in nature. Clifford appears to have left no large collection of papers regarding his tenure as secretary of defense, but the papers of George Elsey and Paul Warnke, available at the Johnson Library, as well as those of Robert E. Pursley, located at the WNRC, fill gaps in the policy process under Clifford. Notes of staff meetings held by McNamara and Clifford compiled by Robert Gard, military assistant to both secretaries between March 1967 and June 1968, and R. Eugene Livesay, who served as recorder for such meetings throughout the period, provide insights into the defense secretaries' goals and attitudes. Gard's notebook is available at the OSD Historical Office, while Livesay's notes are found in the Armed Forces Policy Council (AFPC) files at the National Archives as well as the LBJ Library.

General Wheeler's papers in RG 218 are another mixed collection. While there is much pertinent information, a great deal of the collection consists of invitations, personal correspondence, and the like. The "Double-Zero" files at the U.S. Navy Historical Center have many useful records pertaining to Admiral David McDonald's tenure as Chief of Naval Operations and the admiral's multipart oral history is also available there. Among the Joint Chiefs, the papers of Marine Commandant General Wallace C. Greene, held at the Marine Corps History Office, are far and away the most useful. Greene's chronological compilation of documents, meeting notes, and memoranda related primarily to Vietnam decisionmaking between

1964 and 1967 is a candid and unique record of the interaction among the Joint Chiefs, OSD, and the president. General Maxwell Taylor's papers at the Special Collections Library, National Defense University, are especially valuable for the period. Taylor's role as special assistant to the president enabled him to suggest policy initiatives and to comment on OSD and JCS recommendations. General Lyman Lemintzer's papers, also at NDU, are fittingly more NATO-oriented, and General Andrew Goodpaster's records cover his service on the Army staff and as a member of the negotiating team in Paris during 1968. The papers of Paul Nitze and W. Averell Harriman, both at the Library of Congress, fill in details of the McNamara and Clifford tenures. The Henry Brandon Papers contain a helpful interview with Dean Rusk. General Westmoreland's papers and cables are available at the U.S. Army Center of Military History, Fort McNair, Washington, D.C., while the Abrams and Harold K. Johnson materials are found at the U.S. Army Military History Institute, Carlisle Barracks, Pennsylvania. The Westmoreland and Abrams cable files are especially valuable in delineating the military appreciation of Vietnam, and Westmoreland's history notes offer his interpretation of events.

The Department of State's *Foreign Relations of the United States* series includes 34 volumes for the period 1964-1968. If a document appears in the *Foreign Relations* series, as a rule it will be cited as that source in the narrative. Exceptions occur when the published document has been redacted or is otherwise incomplete, i.e., an attached appendix not printed. State's *American Foreign Policy: Current Documents*, an annual compilation from 1956 through 1967, contains unclassified official papers relevant to the foreign policy of the United States. Other published sources include the *Public Papers of the Presidents of the United States*, a collection of presidential speeches, press conferences, and statements issued by the White House. The OSD Historical Office has compiled the *Public Statements* of the secretaries and some deputy secretaries of defense. OSD also published the *Annual Reports of the Secretary of Defense* which covered the fiscal year (1 July-30 June). Activities of the Joint Chiefs of Staff are discussed in studies issued by the Joint History Office, namely the *Joint Chiefs of Staff and the War in Vietnam, part 2, 1964-1968* and *The Joint Chiefs of Staff and National Policy, 1965-1968*, volume 9.

The Internet is becoming a major source of documentation. Online archives such as the Cold War International History Project and the National Security Archive offer researchers a variety of scholarly reports and archival materials. The Declassified Documents Reference System provides quick access to numerous important documents of the period. Finally, the Johnson Library's online interviews are particularly helpful. The largest collection of such interviews is at the Johnson Library, and the OSD Historical Office has also assembled an extensive oral history collection, including numerous important interviews for this volume. Interviews with participants in the events described in this volume have supplemented the written record.

EXECUTIVE BRANCH: DOCUMENTS AND REPORTS

Cole, Alice C., Alfred Goldberg, Samuel A. Tucker, and Rudolph A. Winnacker, eds. *The Department of Defense: Documents on Establishment and Organization, 1944–1978.* Washington, DC: Historical Office, Office of the Secretary of Defense, 1978.

U.S. Department of Defense. *Annual Report for Fiscal Year 1965 Including the Reports of the Secretary of Defense, Secretary of the Army, Secretary of the Navy, Secretary of the Air Force.* 1967.

____. *Annual Report for Fiscal Year 1966 Including the Reports of the Secretary of Defense, Secretary of the Army, Secretary of the Navy, Secretary of the Air Force.* 1968.

____. *Annual Report for Fiscal Year 1967 Including the Reports of the Secretary of Defense, Secretary of the Army, Secretary of the Navy, Secretary of the Air Force.* 1969.

____. *Annual Report for Fiscal Year 1968 Including the Reports of the Secretary of Defense, Secretary of the Army, Secretary of the Navy, Secretary of the Air Force.* 1970.

____. *United States - Vietnam Relations 1945–1967.* 12 vols. 1971.

____. Directorate for Information Operations and Reports. Washington Headquarters Services. *Department of Defense Selected Manpower Statistics Fiscal Year 1993.* 1993.

____. Office of the Secretary of Defense. Office of the Assistant Secretary of Defense (Public Affairs). *Department of Defense Fact Book.* 1985.

____. ____. Historical Office. *Department of Defense Key Officials, 1947–2004.* 2004.

____. ____. ____, comp. *Background Briefings of Secretary of Defense Robert S. McNamara, 1965–1967.* 3 vols.

____. ____. ____, comp. *Public Statements of Deputy Secretary of Defense Cyrus R. Vance, 1964–1967.* 4 vols.

____. ____. ____, comp. *Public Statements of Deputy Secretary of Defense Paul H. Nitze, 1967–1969.* 3 vols.

____. ____. ____, comp. *Public Statements of Secretary of Defense Clark M. Clifford, 1968–1969.* 4 vols.

____. ____. ____, comp. *Public Statements of Secretary of Defense Robert S. McNamara, 1961–1968.* 38 vols.

Executive Office of the President. Council of Economic Advisors. *Economic Report of the President together with The Annual Report of the Council of Economic Advisers.* 1967.

____. ____. *Economic Report of the President together with The Annual Report of the Council of Economic Advisers.* 1968.

General Services Administration, National Archives and Records Service, Office of the Federal Register. *Public Papers of the Presidents of the United States: Lyndon Baines Johnson, 1963–1969.* 10 vols. 1965–70.

Haines, Gerald K. and Robert E. Leggett, eds. *CIA's Analysis of the Soviet Union, 1947–1991: A Documentary Collection.* Washington, DC: Center for the Study of Intelligence, Central Intelligence Agency, 2001.

Hutchings, Robert L., comp. *Tracking the Dragon: National Intelligence Estimates on China During the Era of Mao, 1948–1976.* Washington, DC: Center for the Study of Intelligence, Central Intelligence Agency, 2004.

National Intelligence Council. *Estimative Products on Vietnam, 1948–1975.* Washington: U.S. Government Printing Office, 2005.

Report of The National Advisory Commission on Civil Disorders. 1 March 1968.

Steury, Donald P., ed. *Intentions and Capabilities: Estimates of Soviet Strategic Forces, 1950–1983.* Washington, DC: History Staff, Center for the Study of Intelligence, Central Intelligence Agency, 1996.

The National Advisory Commission on Selective Service. *In Pursuit of Equity: Who Serves When Not all Serve?* Washington, D.C.: U.S. Government Printing Office, 1967.

U.S. Arms Control and Disarmament Agency. *Arms Control and Disarmament Agreements 1959–1972.* 1 June 1972.

____. *International Negotiations on the Treaty on the Nonproliferation of Nuclear Weapons.* 30 December 1968.

____. *Documents on Disarmament 1965.* 1966.

U.S. Department of State. *American Foreign Policy: Current Documents, 1965, 1966, 1967.* Washington, DC: U.S. Government Printing Office, 1968–1969.

____. *Foreign Relations of the United States, 1964-68.* 34 vols. to date, Washington, DC: U.S. Government Printing Office.

OTHER DOCUMENTS

Barrett, David M., ed. *Lyndon B. Johnson's Vietnam Papers: A Documentary Collection.* College Station, TX: Texas A&M University Press, 1997.

Beschloss, Michael, ed. *Reaching for Glory: Lyndon Johnson's Secret White House Tapes, 1964–1965.* New York: Simon & Schuster, 2001.

Pedlow, Gregory W., ed. *NATO Strategy Documents, 1949–1969*. Brussels: North Atlantic Treaty Organization,1997.
The Senator Gravel Edition of the Pentagon Papers. 4 vols. Boston: Beacon Press, 1971.

MEMOIRS

Ball, George W. *The Past Has Another Pattern: A Memoir*. New York: W.W. Norton, 1982.
Busby, Horace. *The Thirty-First of March: An Intimate Portrait of Lyndon Johnson's Final Days in Office*, New York: Farrar, Straus and Giroux, 2005.
Clifford, Clark M., with Richard Holbrooke. *Counsel to the President: A Memoir*. New York: Random House, 1991.
Colby, William, with James McCargar. *Lost Victory: A Firsthand Account of America's Sixteen-Year Involvement in Vietnam*. Chicago: Contemporary Books, 1989.
Cooper, Chester L. *The Lost Crusade: America in Vietnam*. New York: Dodd, Mead, 1970.
Dobrynin, Anatoly. *In Confidence*. New York: Times Books, 1995.
Goulding, Phil G. *Confirm or Deny: Informing the People on National Security*. New York: Harper & Row Publishers, 1970.
Hoopes, Townsend. *The Limits of Intervention*. New York: David McKay Co., 1969.
Ignatius, Paul R. *On Board: My Life in the Navy, Government, and Business*. Annapolis, MD: Naval Institute Press, 2006.
Johnson, Lyndon Baines. *The Vantage Point: Perspectives of the Presidency, 1963–1969*. New York: Holt, Rinehart and Winston, 1971.
Martin, John Bartlow. *Overtaken by Events: The Dominican Crisis from the Fall of Trujillo to the Civil War*. New York: Doubleday & Company, Inc., 1966.
McGhee, George. *At the Creation of a New Germany: From Adenauer to Brandt: An Ambassador's Account*. New Haven: Yale University Press, 1989.
McNamara, Robert S., with Brian VanDeMark. *In Retrospect: The Tragedy and Lessons of Vietnam*. New York: Times Books, 1995.
Nitze, Paul, with Ann M. Smith and Steven L. Rearden. *From Hiroshima to Glasnost: At the Center of Decision*. New York: Grove Weidenfeld, 1989.
Rostow, Walt W. *The Diffusion of Power: An Essay on Recent History*. New York: The Macmillan Company, 1972.
Rusk, Dean. *As I Saw It: As Told to Richard Rusk*. Edited by Daniel S. Papp. New York: W.W. Norton, 1990.
Seaborg, Glenn T., with Benjamin S. Loeb. *Stemming the Tide: Arms Control in the Johnson Years*. Lexington, MA: Lexington Books, 1987.
Sharp, U.S. Grant. *Strategy for Defeat: Vietnam in Retrospect*. San Rafael, CA: Presidio Press, 1978.
Taylor, Maxwell D. *Swords and Plowshares*. New York: W.W. Norton & Company, Inc, 1972.
Westmoreland, William C. *A Soldier Reports*. Garden City, NY: Doubleday, 1976.

BOOKS

Abu-Lughod, Ibrahim. *The Arab-Israeli Confrontation of June 1967: An Arab Perspective*. Evanston, IL: Northwestern University Press, 1970.
Addington, Larry H. *America's War in Vietnam: A Short Narrative History*. Bloomington: Indiana University Press, 2000.
Anderson, James E. and Jared E. Hazleton. *Managing Macroeconomic Policy: The Johnson Presidency*. Austin, TX: University of Texas Press, 1986.
Anderson, Mary E., Leo P. Holliday, and Richard B. Rainy, Jr. *Alternative Force Structures for the U.S. Army in Europe*. RAND Project 9489. November 1966.
Appelbaum, Henry and Wendy Hilton-Jones, eds. *Studies in Intelligence: 45th Anniversary Special Edition*. Center for the Study of Intelligence, Central Intelligence Agency, 2000.
Art, Robert J. *The TFX Decision: McNamara and the Military*. Boston: Little, Brown and Company, 1968.
Atlantic Council Working Group on the International Monetary System, ed. *The International Monetary System: Progress and Prospects*. Boulder, CO: Westview Press, 1977.
Barrett, David M. *Uncertain Warriors: Lyndon Johnson and His Vietnam Advisers*. Lawrence, KS: University Press of Kansas, 1994.

Barton, John H. and Lawrence D. Weiler, eds. *International Arms Control: Issues and Agreements*. Stanford, CA: Stanford University Press, 1976.

Baucom, Donald R. *The Origins of SDI, 1944–1983*. Lawrence, KS: University Press of Kansas, 1992.

Belden, David Leigh. *Defense Procurement Outcomes in the Incentive Contract Environment*. Stanford, CA: Stanford University, Department of Industrial Engineering, Technical Report No 69-2, May 1969.

Berman, Larry. *Planning a Tragedy*. New York: W.W. Norton, 1982.

____. *Lyndon Johnson's War: The Road to Stalemate in Vietnam*. New York: Norton, 1989.

Bernstein, Irving. *Guns or Butter: The Presidency of Lyndon Johnson*, New York: Oxford University Press, 1996.

Binkin, Martin, et al. *Blacks and the Military*. Washington, DC: The Brookings Institution, 1982.

Bird, Kai. *The Color of Truth: McGeorge Bundy and William Bundy: Brothers in Arms*. New York: Simon & Schuster, 1998.

Blechman, Barry M. and Stephen S. Kaplan, et al. *Force Without War: U.S. Armed Forces as a Political Instrument*. Washington, D.C.: The Brookings Institution, 1978.

Bolger, Daniel P., *Scenes from an Unfinished War: Low Intensity Conflict in Korea, 1966–1969*, (Leavenworth Papers No. 19). Ft Leavenworth, KS: Combat Studies Institute, 1991.

Boutwell, Jeffrey D., Paul Doty, and Gregory F. Treverton, eds. *The Nuclear Confrontation in Europe*. Dover, MA: Auburn House Publishing Company, 1985.

Bradley, Charles E. and Clayton C. McCuistion. *Contractor Decision Making and Incentive Fee Contracts*. Washington: George Washington University, NASA Economic Research project, 22 December 1965.

Brands, H.W. *The Wages of Globalism: Lyndon Johnson and the Limits of American Power*. New York: Oxford University Press, 1995.

Brecher, Michael. *Decisions in Israel's Foreign Policy*. New Haven: Yale University Press, 1975.

____. *Decisions in Crisis: Israel, 1967 and 1973*. Berkeley, CA: University of California Press, 1980.

Bregman, Ahron and Jihan El-Tahri. *The Fifty Years' War: Israel and the Arabs*. New York: TV Books, 1999.

Brigham, Robert K. *Guerrilla Diplomacy: The NLF's Foreign Relations and the Viet Nam War*. Ithaca, NY: Cornell University Press, 2000.

Brundage, Percival Flack. *The Bureau of the Budget*. New York: Praeger Publishers, 1970.

Bunn, George. *Arms Control by Committee: Managing Negotiations with the Russians*. Stanford, CA: Stanford University Press, 1992.

Burke, John P. and Fred I Greenstein, et al. *How Presidents Test Reality: Decisions on Vietnam, 1954 and 1965*. New York: Russell Sage Foundation, 1989.

Buteux, Paul. *The Politics of Nuclear Consultation in NATO, 1965–1980*. Cambridge: Cambridge University Press, 1983.

Buzzanco, Robert. *Masters of War: Military Dissent and Politics in the Vietnam Era*. Cambridge: Cambridge University Press, 1996.

Califano, Joseph. *The Triumph & Tragedy of Lyndon Johnson: The White House Years*. New York: Simon & Schuster, 1991.

Campagna, Anthony S. *The Economic Consequences of the Vietnam War*. New York: Praeger, 1991.

Carbaugh, Robert J. and Liang-Shing Fan. *The International Monetary System: History, Institutions, Analyses*. Lawrence: The University Press of Kansas, 1976.

Carland, John M. *The United States Army in Vietnam: Combat Operations: Stemming the Tide, May 1965 to October 1966*. Washington, DC: U.S. Army Center of Military History, 2000.

Carter, Ashton B. and David N. Schwartz, eds. *Ballistic Missile Defense*. Washington, DC: The Brookings Institution, 1984.

Castle, Timothy N. *At War in the Shadow of Vietnam: U.S. Military Aid to the Royal Lao Government, 1955–1975*. New York: Columbia University Press, 1994.

Ciano, Galeazzo. *The Ciano Diaries, 1939–1943*, edited by Hugh Gibson. Garden City: Doubleday & Company, Inc., 1946.

Clarke, Jeffrey, J. *The U.S. Army in Vietnam: Advice and Support: The Final Years, 1965–1973*. Washington, DC: U.S. Army Center of Military History, 1988.

Cleveland, Harlan. *NATO: The TransAtlantic Bargain*. New York: Harper & Row, Publishers, 1970.

Clodfelter, Mark. *The Limits of Airpower: The American Bombing of North Vietnam*. New York: The Free Press, 1989.

Cohen, Warren I. and Nancy Bernkopf Tucker, eds. *Lyndon Johnson Confronts the World: American Foreign Policy, 1963–1968*. Cambridge: Cambridge University Press, 1996.

Condit, Doris M. *The Test of War, 1950–53*. Vol. II in History of the Office of the Secretary of Defense. Washington, DC: Historical Office, Office of the Secretary of Defense, 1988.

Cosmas, Graham A. *The United States Army in Vietnam: MACV: The Joint Command in the Years of Escalation, 1962–1967*. Washington, DC: U.S. Army Center of Military History, 2006.

_____. Cosmas, Graham A. *The United States Army in Vietnam: MACV: The Joint Command in the Years of Withdrawal, 1968–1973*. Washington, DC: U.S. Army Center of Military History, 2006.

Cristol, A. Jay. *The Liberty Incident: The 1967 Israeli Attack on the U.S. Navy Spy Ship*. Washington, DC: Brassey's, Inc, 2002.

Crossland, Richard B. and James T. Currie. *Twice the Citizen: A History of the United States Army Reserve, 1908–1983*. Washington, DC: Office of the Chief, Army Reserve, 1984.

Daalder, Ivo H. *The Nature and Practice of Flexible Response: NATO Strategy and Theater Nuclear Forces Since 1967*. New York: Columbia University Press, 1991.

Dallek, Robert. *Flawed Giant: Lyndon Johnson and His Times, 1961–1973*. New York: Oxford University Press, 2003.

Daum, Andreas W., Lloyd C. Gardner, and Wilfred Mausbach. *America, The Vietnam War, and the World*. Cambridge: Cambridge University Press, 2003.

Dawisha, Karen. *The Kremlin and the Prague Spring*. Berkeley: University of California Press, 1984.

Dawson, David A. "The Impact of Project 100,000 on the Marine Corps." *Occasional Paper*. Washington, D.C.: History and Museums Division Headquarters U.S. Marine Corps, 1995.

DeBenedetti, Charles with Charles Chatfield. *An American Ordeal: The Antiwar Movement of the Vietnam Era*. Syracuse, NY: Syracuse University Press, 1990.

Divine, Robert A., ed. *The Johnson Years, 1, Foreign Policy, the Great Society, and the White House*. Lawrence, KS: University Press of Kansas, 1981.

_____. *The Johnson Years, 2, Vietnam, the Environment, and Science*. Lawrence, KS: University Press of Kansas, 1987.

_____. *The Johnson Years, 3, LBJ at Home and Abroad*. Lawrence, KS: University Press of Kansas, 1994.

Duffield, John S. *Power Rules: The Evolution of NATO's Conventional Force Posture*. Stanford, CA: Stanford University Press, 1995.

Enthoven, Alain C. and K. Wayne Smith. *How Much Is Enough: Shaping the Defense Program, 1961–1969*. New York: Harper & Row, Publishers, 1971.

Finkbeiner, Ann K. *The Jasons: The Secret History of Science's Postwar Elite*. New York, NY: Viking Penguin, 2006.

Fisher, Irving N. *Cost Incentives and Contract Outcomes: An Empirical Analysis*. Santa Monica, CA: The Rand Corporation, RM-5120-PR, September 1966.

Fitzgerald, Ernest A. *The High Priests of Waste*. New York: Norton, 1972.

Flynn, George Q. *The Draft, 1940–1973*. Lawrence, KS: University Press of Kansas, 1993.

Ford, Harold P. *CIA and the Vietnam Policymakers: Three Episodes, 1962–1968*. Washington, DC: History Staff, Center for the Study of Intelligence, Central Intelligence Agency, 1998.

Freedman, Lawrence. *US Intelligence and the Soviet Strategic Threat*. Boulder, CO: Westview Press, 1977.

Gaiduk, Ilva V. *The Soviet Union and the Vietnam War*. Chicago: Ivan R. Dee, 1996.

Gallucci, Robert L. *Neither Peace Nor Honor: The Politics of American Military Policy in Viet-Nam*. Baltimore: The Johns Hopkins University Press, 1975.

Gardner, Lloyd C. *Pay Any Price: Lyndon Johnson and the Wars for Vietnam*. Chicago: Ivan R. Dee, 1995.

_____. and Ted Gittinger, eds. *International Perspectives on Vietnam*. College Station, TX: Texas A&M University Press, 2000.

_____. and Ted Gittinger, eds. *The Search for Peace in Vietnam, 1964–1968*. College Station, TX: Texas A&M University Press, 2004.

Garfinkle, Adam. *Telltale Hearts: The Origins and Impact of the Vietnam Antiwar Movement*. New York: St. Martin's Press, 1995.

Gelb, Lesile H. and Richard K. Betts. *The Irony of Vietnam: The System Worked*. Washington, DC: Brookings Institution, 1979.

Gerhardt, James M. *The Draft and Public Policy: Issues in Military Manpower Procurement, 1945–1970*. Columbus, OH: Ohio State University Press, 1971.

Gibbons, William C. *The U.S. Government and the Vietnam War: Executive and Legislative Roles and Relationships, Part 3: January–July 1965*. Washington, DC: U.S. Government Printing Office, 1988.

_____. *The U.S. Government and the Vietnam War: Executive and Legislative Roles and Relationships, Part 4: July 1965-January 1968*. Washington, DC: U.S. Government Printing Office, 1994.

Gittinger, Ted, ed. *The Johnson Years: A Vietnam Roundtable*. Austin, TX: Lyndon B. Johnson School of Public Affairs and Lyndon Baines Johnson Library, 1993.

Gleijeses, Piero. *The Dominican Crisis: The 1965 Constitutionalist Revolt and American Intervention*. Trans. by Lawrence Lipson. Baltimore: The Johns Hopkins University Press, 1978.

Goldman, Eric F. *The Tragedy of Lyndon Johnson*. New York: Alfred A. Knopf, 1969.

Graves, Ernest and Steven A. Hildreth, eds. *U.S. Security Assistance: The Political Process*. Lexington, MA: Lexington Books, 1985.

Greenberg, Lawrence M. *United States Army Unilateral and Coalition Operations in the 1965 Dominican Republic Intervention*. Washington, D.C.: U.S. Army Center of Military History, 1987.

Greenwood, Ted. *Making the MIRV: A Study of Defense Decision Making*. Cambridge, MA: Ballinger Publishing Company, 1975.

Gregory, Shaun R. *Nuclear Command and Control in NATO: Nuclear Weapons Operations and the Strategy of Flexible Response*. New York: St. Martin's Press, Inc., 1996.

Gunston, Bill. *F-111*. New York: Charles Scribner's Sons, 1978.

Haftendorn, Helga. *NATO and the Nuclear Revolution: A Crisis of Credibility, 1966–1967*. Oxford: Clarendon Press, 1996.

Halberstam, David. *The Best and the Brightest*. New York: Random House, 1969.

Hammond, Paul Y. *LBJ and the Presidential Management of Foreign Relations*. Austin, TX: University of Texas Press, 1992.

Hammond, William M. *The United States Army in Vietnam: Public Affairs: The Military and the Media, 1962–1968*. Washington, DC: U.S. Army Center of Military History, 1988.

_____. *The United States Army in Vietnam: Public Affairs: The Military and the Media, 1968–1973*. Washington, DC: U.S. Army Center of Military History,

Hargrove, Edwin C. and Samuel A. Morley, eds. *The President and the Council of Economic Advisors: Interviews with CEA Chairmen*. Boulder, CO: Westview Press, Inc., 1984.

Harrison, Michael M. *The Reluctant Ally: France and Atlantic Security*. Baltimore: The Johns Hopkins University Press, 1981.

Helsing, Jeffrey W. *Johnson's War/Johnson's Great Society: The Guns and Butter Trap*. Westport, CT: Praeger, 2000.

Herken, Gregg. *Counsels of War*. Expanded ed. New York: Oxford University Press, 1987.

_____. *Cardinal Choices: Presidential Science Advising From the Atomic Bomb to SDI*. New York: Oxford University Press, 1992.

Herring, George C. *LBJ and Vietnam: A Different Kind of War*. Austin: University of Texas Press, 1994.

_____., ed. *The Secret Diplomacy of the Vietnam War: The Negotiating Volumes of the Pentagon Papers*. Austin, TX: University of Texas Press, 1983.

_____. *America's Longest War: The United States and Vietnam, 1950–1975*. New York: Alfred A. Knopf, 1993.

Heuser, Beatrice. *NATO, Britain, France and the FRG: Nuclear Strategies and Forces for Europe, 1949–2000*. London: MacMillan Press Ltd. 1997.

Hewes, James E. Jr. *From Root to McNamara: Army Organization and Administration, 1900–1963*. Washington, DC: U.S. Army Center of Military History, 1975.

Hilsman, Roger. *To Move a Nation: The Politics of Foreign Policy in the Administration of John F. Kennedy*. Garden City, NY: Doubleday & Company, 1967.

Holloway, David. *The Soviet Union and the Arms Race*. New Haven: Yale University Press, 1983.

Hovey, Harold A. *United States Military Assistance: A Study of Policies and Practices*. New York: Frederick A. Praeger, 1965.

Hunt, Michael H. *Lyndon Johnson's War: America's Cold War Crusade in Vietnam, 1945–1968*. New York: Hill and Wang, 1996.

Hunt, Richard A. *Pacification: The American Struggle for Vietnam's Hearts and Minds*. Boulder, CO. Westview Press, 1995.

Janis, Irving L. *Victims of Groupthink: A Psychological Study of Foreign-Policy Decisions and Fiascoes*. Boston: Houghton Mifflin Company, 1972.

Jeffreys-Jones, Rhodri. *Peace Now! American Society and the Ending of the Vietnam War*. New Haven: Yale University Press, 1999.

Joint Chiefs of Staff. Joint Secretariat. Historical Division. *The History of the Joint Chiefs of Staff: The Joint Chiefs of Staff and the War in Vietnam, 1960–1968*, Parts 2 and 3, 1970.

Jordan, Robert S., ed. *Generals in International Politics: NATO's Supreme Allied Commander, Europe*. Lexington, KY: The University Press of Kentucky, 1987.

Kahin, George McTurnan. *Intervention: How American Became Involved in Vietnam*. Garden City, NY: Anchor Press/Doubleday, 1987.

Kaiser, David. *American Tragedy: Kennedy, Johnson, and the Origins of the Vietnam War*. Cambridge, MA: The Belknap Press of Harvard University Press, 2000.

Kanter, Arnold. *Defense Politics: A budgetary perspective*. Chicago: The University of Chicago Press, 1979.

Kaplan, Fred. *The Wizards of Armageddon*. New York: Simon & Schuster, Inc., 1983.

Kaplan, Lawrence S. ed. *American Historians and the Atlantic Alliance*. Kent, Ohio: The Kent State University Press, 1991.

_____. *NATO and the United States Updated Edition, The Enduring Alliance*. New York: Twayne Publishers, 1994.

_____., et al eds. *NATO After Forty Years*. Wilmington, DE: Scholarly Resources, Inc.,1990.

_____., Ronald D. Landa, and Edward J. Drea. *The McNamara Ascendancy 1961–1965*. Vol. V in *History of the Office of the Secretary of Defense*. Washington, DC: Historical Office, Office of the Secretary of Defense, 2006.

Karnow, Stanley. *Vietnam: A History*. New York: The Viking Press, 1983.

Kearns, Doris. *Lyndon Johnson and the American Dream*. New York: Harper & Row, Publishers, 1976.

Kelleher, Catherine M. *Germany & the Politics of Nuclear Weapons*. New York: Columbia University Press, 1975.

Kerr, Malcolm H. *The Elusive Peace in the Middle East*. Albany, NY: State University of New York Press, 1975.

Kinnard, Douglas. *The Secretary of Defense*. Lexington, KY: The University Press of Kentucky, 1980.

Knaack, Marcelle Size. *Encyclopedia of U.S. Air Force Aircraft and Missile Systems, 1, Post-World War II Fighters 1945-1973*. Washington, D.C.: Office of Air Force History, 1978.

Kunz, Diane B. *Butter and Guns: America's Cold War Economic Diplomacy*. New York: The Free Press, 1997.

Laurence, Janice H. and Peter F. Ramsberger. *Low-Aptitude Men in the Military: Who Profits, Who Pays?* New York: Praeger, 1991.

_____. _____. Monica A. Gribben. *Effects of Military Experience on the Post-Service Lives of Low-Aptitude Recruits: Project 100,000 and the ASVAB Misnorming*. Alexandria, VA: Human Resources Research Organization, December 1989.

Lerner, Mitchell B. *The Pueblo Incident: A Spy Ship and the Failure of American Foreign Policy*. Lawrence, KS: University Press of Kansas, 2002.

Lewy, Guenter. *America in Vietnam*. New York: Oxford University Press, 1978.

Lind, Michael. *Vietnam: The Necessary War*. New York: The Free Press, 2000.

Logevall, Fredrik. *Choosing War: The Lost Chance for Peace and the Escalation of War in Vietnam*. Berkeley: University of California Press, 1999.

Love, Robert William, Jr., ed. *The Chiefs of Naval Operations*. Annapolis, MD: Naval Institute Press, 1980.

Lowenthal, Abraham F. *The Dominican Intervention*. Cambridge, MA: Harvard University Press, 1972.

Mahon, John K. *History of the Militia and the National Guard*. New York: Macmillan Co., 1983.

Marolda, Edward J., and Oscar P. Fitzgerald. *From Military Assistance to Combat, 1959–1965*. Vol 2 in *The United States Navy and the Vietnam Conflict*. Washington, DC: Naval Historical Center, Department of the Navy, 1986.

McMaster, H.R. *Dereliction of Duty: Lyndon Johnson, Robert McNamara, The Joint Chiefs of Staff, and the Lies that Led to Vietnam*. New York: HarperCollins, 1997.

McNamara, Robert S. *Blundering into Disaster: Surviving the First Century of the Nuclear Age*. New York: Pantheon Books, 1986.

McNamara, Robert S, James G. Blight, and Robert Brigham. *Argument Without End: In Search of Answers to the Vietnam Tragedy*. New York: Public Affairs, 1999.

McNaugher, Thomas L. *The M16 Controversies: Military Organizations and Weapons Acquisition*. New York: Praeger, 1984.

_____. *New Weapons, Old Politics: America's Military Procurement Muddle*. Washington, DC: The Brookings Institution, 1989.

_____. *Collaborative Development of Main Battle Tanks: Lessons for the U.S.-German Experience, 1963-1978*. Santa Monica, CA: The Rand Corporation, N-1680-RC, August 1981.

Military History Institute of Vietnam. *Victory in Vietnam: The Official History of the People's Army of Vietnam, 1954-1975*. Trans. by Merle L. Pribbenow. Lawrence, KS: University Press of Kansas, 2002.

Mollenhoff, Clark R. *The Pentagon: Politics, Profits and Plunder*. New York: G.P. Putnam's Sons, 1967.

Momyer, William M. *Airpower in Three Wars (WWII, Korea, Vietnam)*. Reprint. Maxwell Air Force Base, AL: Air University Press, April 2003.

Moyer, Mark. *Triumph Forsaken: The Vietnam War, 1954-1965*. New York: Cambridge University Press, 2006.

Mueller, John E. *War, Presidents and Public Opinion*. Lanham, MD: University Press of America, 1985.

Nalty, Bernard C. *The War against Trucks: Aerial Interdiction in Southern Laos, 1968–1972*. Washington, D.C.: Air Force History and Museums Program, United States Air Force, 2005.

_____. *Air War over South Vietnam, 1968–1975*. Washington, D.C.: Air Force History and Museums Program, United States Air Force, 2000.

Newhouse, John. *Cold Dawn: The Story of SALT*. New York: Holt, Rinehart and Winston, 1973.

Oren, Michael B. *Six Days of War: June 1967 and the Making of the Modern Middle East*. New York: Random House, 2003.

Osgood, Robert Endicott. *Limited War: The Challenge to American Strategy*. Chicago: University of Chicago Press, 1957.

Palmer, Bruce, Jr. *The 25-Year War: America's Military Role in Vietnam*. Lexington, KY: The University Press of Kentucky, 1984.

____. *Intervention in the Caribbean: The Dominican Crisis of 1965*. Lexington, KY: The University Press of Kentucky, 1989.

Palmer, Gregory. *The McNamara Strategy and the Vietnam War, Program Budgeting in the Pentagon, 1960–1968*. Westport, CT: Greenwood Press, 1978.

Pape, Robert A. *Bombing to Win: Air Power and Coercion in War*. Ithaca: Cornell University Press, 1996.

Parker, Richard B. *The Politics of Miscalculation in the Middle East*. Bloomington, IN: Indiana University Press, 1993.

____, ed. *The Six-Day War: A Retrospective*. Gainsville, FL: University Press of Florida, 1996.

Parker, Thomas F., ed. *Violence in the U.S., 1968–71*, Vol 2. New York: Facts on File, 1974.

Perry, Mark. *Four Stars*. Boston: Houghton Mifflin, 1989.

Pierce, Lawrence C. *The Politics of Fiscal Policy Formulation*. Pacific Palisades, CA: Goodyear Publishing Company, Inc., 1971.

Poole, Walter S. *The Joint Chiefs of Staff and National Policy, 1961–1964* and *1965–1968*. Vols. 8 and 9, in *The History of the Joint Chiefs of Staff*. Washington, DC: Historical Division, Joint Secretariat, Joint Chiefs of Staff, 1985.

Potter, William C. *Nuclear Power and Nonproliferation: An Interdisciplinary Perspective*. Cambridge, MA: Oelgeschlager, Gunn & Hain, Publishers, Inc., 1982.

Prados, John. *The Soviet Estimate: U.S. Intelligence Analysis and Soviet Strategic Forces*. Princeton: Princeton University Press, 1982.

____. *The Blood Road: The Ho Chi Minh Trail and the Vietnam War*. New York: John Wiley & Sons, Inc., 1999.

Preston, Andrew. *The War Council: McGeorge Bundy, the NSC, and Vietnam*. Cambridge, MA: Harvard University Press, 2006.

Qiang Zhai. *China and the Vietnam Wars, 1950–1975*. Chapel Hill: University of North Carolina Press, 2000.

Quandt, William B. *Peace Process: American Diplomacy and the Arab-Israeli Conflict Since 1967*. 3d ed. Washington, D.C.: Brookings Institution Press, 2005.

Redford, Emmette S. and Richard T. McCulley. *White House Operations: The Johnson Presidency*. Austin: University of Texas Press, 1986.

Rogers, Bernard W. *Cedar Falls-Junction City: A Turning Point*. Washington, DC: Department of the Army, 1974.

Roherty, James M. *Decisions of Robert S. McNamara: A Study of the Role of the Secretary of Defense*. Coral Gables, Fla: University of Miami Press, 1970.

Sapolsky, Harvey M. *The Polaris System Development: Bureaucratic and Programmatic Success in Government*. Cambridge, MA: Harvard University Press, 1972.

Schandler, Herbert. *Unmaking of a President: Lyndon Johnson and Vietnam*. Princeton, NJ: Princeton University Press, 1977.

Scheips, Paul J. *The Role of Federal Military Forces in Domestic Disorders, 1945–1992*. Washington, DC: U.S. Army Center of Military History, 2005.

Schelling, Thomas C. *The Strategy of Conflict*. Cambridge, MA: Harvard University Press, 1960.

____. *Arms and Influence*. New Haven: Yale University Press, 1966.

Schlight, John. *The War in South Vietnam: The Years of the Offensive, 1965–1968*. Washington, DC: Office of Air Force History, 1988.

Schoenbaum, Thomas J. *Waging Peace & War: Dean Rusk in the Truman, Kennedy, & Johnson Years*. New York: Simon and Schuster, 1988.

Schoonmaker, Herbert G. *Military Crisis Management: U.S. Intervention in the Dominican Republic, 1965*. New York: Greenwood Press, 1990.

Schwartz, David N. *NATO's Nuclear Dilemmas*. Washington, DC: The Brookings Institution, 1983.

Schwartz, Thomas Alan. *Lyndon Johnson and Europe in the Shadow of Vietnam*. Cambridge, MA: Harvard University Press, 2003.

Shapley, Deborah. *Promise and Power: The Life and Times of Robert McNamara*. Boston: Little, Brown and Company, 1993.

Shulimson, Jack and Charles M. Johnson, *U.S. Marines in Vietnam: The Landing and the Buildup, 1965*. Washington, D.C.: History and Museums Division, Headquarters U.S. Marine Corps, 1978.

Shulimson, Jack, Leonard A. Basil, Charles R. Smith, and David A. Dawson. *U.S. Marines in Vietnam: The Defining Year, 1968*. Washington, D.C.: History and Museums Division, Headquarters U.S. Marine Corps, 1997.

Slater, Jerome. *Intervention and Negotiation: The United States and the Dominican Revolution.* New York: Harper & Row, Publishers, 1970.

Small, Melvin. *At the Water's Edge: American Politics and the Vietnam War.* Chicago: Ivan R. Dee, 2005.

____. *Covering Dissent: The Media and the Anti-Vietnam War Movement.* New Brunswick, NJ: Rutgers University Press, 1994.

____. *Johnson, Nixon, and the Doves.* New Brunswick, NJ: Rutgers University Press, 1988.

Smith, Bromley K. *Organizational History of the National Security Council during the Kennedy and Johnson Administrations.* Washington, DC: National Security Council, 1988.

Sorley, Lewis. *Honorable Warrior: General Harold K. Johnson and the Ethics of Command.* Lawrence, KS: University Press of Kansas, 1998.

____. *Thunderbolt: General Creighton Abrams and the Army of His Times.* New York: Simon and Schuster, 1992.

____. *A Better War: The Unexamined Victories and Final Tragedy of America's Last Years in Vietnam.* New York: Harcourt Brace and Co., 1999.

Spector, Ronald, H. *After Tet: The Bloodiest Year in Vietnam.* New York: Vintage Books, 1994.

Stevens, Robert Warren. *Vain Hopes, Grim Realities: The Economic Consequences of the Vietnam War.* New York: New Viewpoints, 1976.

Stevenson, Charles A. *SECDEF: The Nearly Impossible Job of Secretary of Defense.* Washington, D.C.: Potomac Books, Inc., 2006.

Sticht, Thomas G., et al. *Cast-off Youth.* New York: Praeger, 1987.

Stromseth, Jane E. *Origins of Flexible Response: NATO's Debate over Strategy in the 1960s.* New York: St. Martin's Press, 1988.

Taylor, Maj Gen Leonard B. *Financial Management of the Vietnam Conflict, 1962-1972.* Vietnam Studies, No. 13, Washington: Department of the Army, 1974.

Telfer, Gary L., Lane Rogers, and V. Keith Fleming, Jr. *U.S. Marines in Vietnam: Fighting the North Vietnamese, 1967.* Washington, D.C.: History and Museums Division, Headquarters U.S. Marine Corps, 1984.

Thompson, James Clay. *Rolling Thunder: Understanding Policy and Program Failure.* Chapel Hill, NC: The University of North Carolina Press, 1980.

Thompson, Wayne. *To Hanoi and Back: The United States Air Force and North Vietnam, 1966–1973.* Washington, DC: Air Force History and Museums Program, United States Air Force, 2000.

Tilford, Earl H., Jr. *Setup: What the Air Force Did in Vietnam and Why.* Maxwell Air Force Base, AL: Air University Press, 1991.

Trask, Roger R. and Alfred Goldberg. *The Department of Defense, 1947–1997: Organization and Leaders.* Washington, DC: Historical Office, Office of the Secretary of Defense, 1997.

Trewhitt, Henry L. *McNamara.* New York: Harper & Row Publishers, 1971.

Valenta, Jiri. *Soviet Intervention in Czechoslovakia, 1968: Anatomy of a Decision.* Baltimore: The Johns Hopkins University Press, 1991.

Valenti, Jack. *A Very Human President.* New York: W.W. Norton & Company, Inc., 1975.

VanDeMark, Brian. *Into the Quagmire: Lyndon Johnson and the Escalation of the Vietnam War.* New York: Oxford University Press, 1991.

Van Staaveren, Jacob. *Gradual Failure: The Air War Over North Vietnam, 1965–1966.* Washington, DC: Air Force History and Museums Program, United States Air Force, 2002.

Vogel, Stephen F. *The Pentagon: A History: The Untold Story of the Wartime Race to Build the Pentagon — And to Restore it Sixty Years Later.* New York: Random House, 2007.

Watson, Robert J. *Into the Missile Age, 1956–1960.* Vol. IV in *History of the Office of the Secretary of Defense.* Washington, DC: Historical Office, Office of the Secretary of Defense, 1997.

Weidenbaum, Murray L. *Economic Impact of the Vietnam War.* The Centre for Strategic Studies, Special Report Series No. 5, June 1967, Washington, D.C.: Georgetown University, 1967.

White, Theodore H. *The Making of the President, 1968.* New York: Atheneum Publishers, 1968.

Whiting, Allen S. *The Chinese Calculus of Deterrence: India and Indochina.* Ann Arbor: University of Michigan Press, 1975.

Woods, Randall B. *LBJ: Architect of American Ambition.* New York: Free Press, 2006.

Worden, Simon P. *SDI and the Alternatives.* Washington, DC: National Defense University Press, 1991.

Yanarella, Ernest J. *The Missile Defense Controversy, Strategy, Technology, and Politics, 1955–1972.* Lexington: University Press of Kentucky, 1977.

Yates, Lawrence A. *Power Pack: U.S. Intervention in the Dominican Republic, 1965–1966,* (Leavenworth Paper No. 15). Ft Leavenworth, KS: Combat Studies Institute, 1988.

York, Herbert F. *Making Weapons, Talking Peace: A Physicist's Odyssey from Hiroshima to Geneva.* New York: Basic Books, Inc., 1987.

Zeiler, Thomas W. *Dean Rusk: Defending the American Mission Abroad*. Wilmington, DE: SR Books, 2000.

Zimmermann, Hubert, *Money and Security: Troops, Monetary Policy, and West Germany's Relations with the United States and Britain, 1950–1971*. Cambridge: Cambridge University Press, 2002.

ARTICLES

"After the Pentagon Papers: Talk with Kistiakowsky, Wiesner." *Science*, 174 no. 4012 (26 November 1971):923-28.

Ang Cheng Guan. "Decision-making Leading to the Tet Offensive (1968)—The Vietnamese Communist Perspective." *Journal of Contemporary History*, 33:3 (1998):341–53.

____. "The Vietnam War from Both Sides: Revisiting 'Marigold', 'Sunflower' and 'Pennsylvania.'" *War & Society*, 24:2 (2005):93–125.

Bowen, William. "The Vietnam War: A Cost Accounting." *Fortune*, 73:4 (April 1966):119–23, 254, 259.

Brands, Hal. "Progress Unseen: U.S. Arms Control Policy and the Origins of Détente, 1963–1968." *Diplomatic History*, 30:2 (April 2006):253–85.

Brower, Charles F., IV. "Strategic Reassessment in Vietnam: The Westmoreland 'Alternate Strategy' of 1967–1968." *Naval War College Review*, 44:2 (Spring 1991):20–51.

Bozo, Frederic. "Detente versus Alliance: France, the United States and the Politics of the Harmel Report (1964–1968)," *Contemporary European History*, 7:3 (1998):343–60.

Brodie, Bernard. "Why Were We So (Strategically) Wrong?" *Foreign Policy*, 5 (Winter 1971-72):151–61.

____. "The McNamara Phenomenon." *World Politics*, 17:4 (July 1965):672–86.

Bunn, George. "The Nuclear Nonproliferation Treaty." *Wisconsin Law Review*, 1968:3 (Fall 1968):766–785.

Carland, John. "Documents of Note: Winning the Vietnam War: Westmoreland's Approach in Two Documents." *The Journal of Military History*, 68 (April 2004):553–74.

Chen Jian. "China's Involvement in the Vietnam War, 1964–1969." *The China Quarterly*, 142 (June 1995):356–87.

Clifford, Clark. "A Viet-Nam Reappraisal: The Personal History of One Man's View and How It Evolved." *Foreign Affairs*, 47:4 (Summer 1969):601–22.

____. "Annals of Government - III, Serving the President: The Vietnam Years." *The New Yorker*, 67:13 (May 20, 1991):59–92.

Collins, Robert M. "The Economic Crisis of 1968 and the Waning of the 'American Century.'" *The American Historical Review*, 101:2 (April 1996), 396–422.

Cooper, Charles G. "The Day It Became the Longest War." *U.S. Naval Institute Proceedings*, 122:5 (May 1996):77–80.

Dallek, Robert. "Presidential Address: Lyndon Johnson and Vietnam: The Making of a Tragedy." *Diplomatic History*, 20:2 (Spring 1996):147–62.

Dare, James A. "Dominican Diary." U.S. *Naval Institute Proceedings*, 91 (December 1965):37–44.

"Defense Fantasy Come True: In an Exclusive Interview Secretary McNamara Explains in Full the Logic Behind the ABM System." *Life* 63, (September 29, 1967):28 A-C.

Duffield, John S. "The Evolution of NATO's Strategy of Flexible Response: A Reinterpretation." *Security Studies*, 1:1 (Autumn 1991):132–56.

____. "The Soviet Military Threat to Western Europe: US Estimates in the 1950s and 1960s." *Journal of Strategic Studies*, 15:2 (June 1992):208–27.

Fielding, Jeremy. "Coping with Decline: US Policy Toward the British Defense Reviews of 1966." *Diplomatic History*, 23:4 (Fall 1999):633–56.

Filgstein, Neil D. "Who Served in the Military, 1940-1973." *Armed Forces and Society*, 6:2 (Winter, 1980):297–312.

Ford, Harold P. "Thoughts Engendered by Robert McNamara's *In Retrospect*." *Studies in Intelligence*, 39:1(Spring 1995):37–51.

Gavin, Francis J. "The Myth of Flexible Response: United States Strategy in Europe during the 1960s." *The International History Review*, 23:4 (December 2001):847–75.

Gelb, Leslie H. "The Pentagon Papers and The Vantage Point." *Foreign Policy*, 6 (Spring 1972):25–41.

____. "Vietnam: The System Worked." *Foreign Policy*, 5 (Summer 1971):140–67.

Golan, Galia. "The Soviet Union and the Outbreak of the June 1967 Six-Day War." *Journal of Cold War Studies*, 8:1 (Winter 2006):3–19.

Garbo, Cynthia M. "Soviet Deception in the Czechoslovak Crisis." *Studies in Intelligence*, Special Unclassified Edition, (Fall 2000):71–86.

Greene, Gen Wallace M., USMC (Ret). "The Bombing 'Pause': Formula for Failure." *Air Force Magazine*, 59:4 (April 1976):36–39.

Glass, Andrew J. "Defense Report/Draftees Shoulder Burden of Fighting and Dying in Vietnam." *National Journal*, 33:2 (15 Aug 1970):1747–55.

Halberstam, David. "How the Economy Went Haywire." *Atlantic Monthly*, 230:3 (September 1972):56–60.

Halperin, Morton H. "The Decision to Deploy the ABM: Bureaucratic and Domestic Politics in the Johnson Administration." *World Politic*, 25:1 (October 1972):68–83.

Hershberg, James G. and Chen Jian. "Reading and Warning the Likely Enemy: China's Signals to the United States About Vietnam in 1965," *The International History Review*, 27:1 (March 2005):47–84.

____. "The President and the Military." *Foreign Affairs*, 50 (January 1972):310–24.

Hotz, Robert. "The War Budget." *Aviation Week & Space Technology* (January 31, 1966):9.

Hughes, Thomas L. "Experiencing McNamara." *Foreign Policy*, No. 100 (Fall 1995):154–71.

Humphrey, David C. "Tuesday Lunch at the Johnson White House: A Preliminary Assessment." *Diplomatic History*, 8:1 (Winter 1984):81–101.

____. "NSC Meetings during the Johnson Presidency." *Diplomatic History*, 18:1 (Winter 1994):29–45.

Jervis, Robert. "Realism, Game Theory, and Cooperation." *World Politics*, 40 (April 1988):317–49.

Kennedy, Floyd D., Jr. "David Lamar McDonald 1 August 1963 – 1 August 1967." In *The Chiefs of Naval Operations*, edited by Robert William Love, Jr., 333–350. Annapolis, MD: Naval Institute Press, 1980.

Kim J. Yi. "In Search of a Panacea: Japan-Korea Rapprochement and America's 'Far Eastern Problems.'" *Pacific Historical Review*, 71:4 (2002):633–62.

____. "The U.S.-Korean Alliance in the Vietnam War: The Years of Escalation, 1964-68." In *International Perspectives on Vietnam*, edited by Lloyd C. Gardner & Ted Gittinger, 154-175. College Station, TX: Texas A&M University Press, 2000.

____. "The Making of Tigers: South Korea's Military Experience in the Vietnam War." In *The Australian Army and the Vietnam War, 1962–1972*, edited by Peter Dennis and Jeffrey Grey, 152-179. Canberra: Department of Defence, Army History Unit, 2002.

King, Ronald F. "The President & Fiscal Policy in 1966: The Year Taxes Were Not Raised." *Polity*, 17:4 (Summer 1985):685–714.

Kuklick, Bruce. "McNamara's Struggle for Understanding." *Orbis*, 44:1 (Winter 2000):166–74.

Lerner, Mitchell. "A Dangerous Miscalculation: New Evidence from Communist-Bloc Archives about North Korea and the Crises of 1968." *Journal of Cold War Studies*, 6:1 (Winter 2004):3–21.

Mastny, Vojtech. "Was 1968 a Strategic Watershed of the Cold War?" *Diplomatic History*. 29:1 (January 2005):149–77.

McConnell, J. P. "Some Reflections on a Tour of Duty." *Air University Review*, 21:6 (Sep-Oct 1969):3–11.

McNamara, Robert S. "The Military Role of Nuclear Weapons: Perceptions and Misperceptions." *Foreign Affairs*, 62:1 (Fall 1983):59–80.

Milne, David. "'Our Equivalent of Guerrilla Warfare': Walt Rostow and the Bombing of North Vietnam, 1961–1968." *The Journal of Military History*, 71:1 (January 2007):169–203.

Morris, Thomas D. "Robert S. McNamara: Pentagon Genius." In *Giants in Management*, edited by Robert L. Haught, 35–50. Washington, D.C.: National Academy of Public Administration, 1985.

Moskos, Charles C., Jr. "Minority Groups and Military Organization." In *The Military in American Society: Essays and Readings*, edited by Stephen E. Ambrose and James A. Barber, 192–201. New York: The Free Press, 1972.

Moyers, Bill. "One Thing We Learned." *Foreign Affairs*, 46 (July 1968):657–64.

Moynihan, Daniel P. "Who Gets in the Army?" *The New Republic*, 155:32 (5 Nov 66):19–22.

Palmer, Bruce, Jr. "US Intelligence and Vietnam." *Special Issue: Studies in Intelligence*, 28 (1984).

Parker, Richard B. "The June 1967 War: Some Mysteries Explored." *Middle East Journal* 46:2 (Spring 1992):177–97.

Poole, Walter S. "Acquisition in the Department of Defense, 1959–1968: The McNamara Legacy." *In Providing the Means of War: Perspectives on Defense Acquisition 1945–2000*, edited by Shannon A. Brown, 79–96. Washington, D.C.: U.S. Army Center of Military History and Industrial College of the Armed Forces, 2005.

Pribbenow, Merle L., II. "The -Ology War: Technology and Ideology in the Vietnamese Defense of Hanoi, 1967." *The Journal of Military History*, 67:1 (January 2003):175–200.

Quandt, William B. "Lyndon Johnson and the June 1967 War: What Color Was the Light?" *The Middle East Journal* 46:2 (Spring 1992):198–228.

Quello, J. I. and N. Isa Conde. "Revolutionary Struggle in the Dominican Republic and its Lessons." Part I *World Marxist Review* 8:12 (December 1965):91–103 and Part II *World Marxist Review* 9:1 (January 1966):53–56.

Quiang Zhai. "Beijing's Position on the Vietnam Peace Talks, 1965–1968: New Evidence from Chinese Sources," Working Paper #18, Cold War International History Project, Internet Copy.

Rosen, Stephen Peter. "Vietnam and the American Theory of Limited War," *International Security.* 7:2 (Fall 1982):83–113.

Sarantakes, Nicholas Evan. "In the Service of the Pharaoh? The United States and the Deployment of Korean Troops in Vietnam, 1965–1968." *Pacific Historical Review*, 68:3 (1999):425–449.

Shipler, David K. "Robert McNamara and the Ghosts of Vietnam." *New York Times Magazine*, (August 10, 1997):30-35, 42, 50, 56–57.

Sloan, John W. "President Johnson, The Council of Economic Advisers, and the Failure to Raise Taxes in 1966 and 1967." *Presidential Quarterly Series*, 15:1 (Winter 1985):89–98.

Stiles, David. "A Fusion Bomb over Andalucia: U.S. Information Policy and the 1966 Palomares Incident." *Journal of Cold War Studies*, 8:1 (Winter 2006):49–67.

Stucky, John D. and Joseph H. Pistorius. "Mobilization for the Vietnam War: A Political and Military Catastrophe." *Parameters*, XV:I (Spring 1985):26–38.

Taylor, Jack H. "Wohlsetter, Soviet Strategic Forces, and National Intelligence Estimates." *Studies in Intelligence*, 19:1 (Spring 1975):1–8.

"The Fairy-Tale Figures on Defense." *Business Week*, (October 29, 1966):182–84.

Wenger, Andreas. "Crisis and Opportunity: NATO's Transformation and the Multilateralization of Détente, 1966-1968." *Journal of Cold War Studies*, 6:1 (Winter 2004):22–74.

White, Theodore H. "Revolution in the Pentagon." *Look*, 27:8 (April 23, 1963):31–48.

Woods, Randall B. "The Politics of Idealism: Lyndon Johnson, Civil Rights, and Vietnam." *Diplomatic History*, 31:1 (January 2007):1–18.

Zimmermann, Hubert. "Who Paid for America's War? Vietnam and the International Monetary System, 1960–1975." In *American, the Vietnam War, and the World: Comparative and International Perspectives*, edited by Andreas W. Daum, Lloyd C. Gardner, and Wilfried Mausbach, 151–73. Cambridge: Cambridge University Press, 2003.

Zuckert, Eugene M. "The Service Secretary: Has He a Useful Role?" *Foreign Affairs* 44 (April 1966):458–79.

UNPUBLISHED SOURCES

Bundy, William P., "Manuscript of Vietnam War." Papers of William P. Bundy, LBJL Library [copy at OSD Historical Office].

Cahn, Anne Hessing. "Scientists and the ABM." Ph. D. Dissertation, Massachusetts Institute of Technology. 1971.

Cole, Alice C., et al. "History of the Strategic Arms Competition 1945–1972: Chronology." 3 vols. Washington, DC: Historical Office, Office of the Secretary of Defense, 1974.

"Draft Administrative History of the Department of Defense, 1963–1969." nd. [Compiled in late 1968 and early 1969 by the Office of the Assistant Secretary of Defense (Administration), with contributions by various DoD components, in response to a request from the White House.]

Duffield, John S. "The Evolution of NATO's Conventional Force Posture," Ph.D. Dissertation, Princeton University, 1989.

Fuller, Jon Wayne. "Congress and the Defense Budget: A Study of the McNamara Years." Ph.D Dissertation, Princeton University, 1972.

Gorn, Michael H. "The TFX: Conceptual Phase to F-111B Termination (1958–1968)." Andrews Air Force Base, MD: Office of History, Air Force Systems Command, nd.

Jayne, Edward R. II., "The ABM Debate: Strategic Defense and National Security," Ph. D. Dissertation, Massachusetts Institute of Technology, 1969.

Janicik, E.C. "Southeast Asia Force Deployments Buildup, pt 1, 1965." Critical Incident No. 13, IDA Report R-137, 1968.

_____. "Evolution of Missions for US Land Forces (March 1965–July 1966)." IDA Document TS/HQ 68-235, 1968.

Joint Logistics Review Board Report. *Logistic Support in the Vietnam Era, II, Appendix A, Impact of the Vietnam Conflict on Readiness in Other Areas of the World. (1970).*

_____. *Logistic Support in the Vietnam Era.* Monograph 2, "Ammunition," appx C through H. (1970).

May, Ernest R., John D. Steinbruner, and Thomas W. Wolfe. "History of the Strategic Arms Competition, 1945–1972." 2 Parts. Washington, DC: Historical Office, Office of the Secretary of Defense, 1981.

Office of the Assistant Secretary of Defense (Manpower). "Reference Materials: Department of Defense Study of the Draft." July 1966.

Office of the Director of Defense Research & Engineering, Weapons Systems Evaluation Group. "The Domini-
    can Republic Crisis of 1965," 16 August 1966.
Poole, Walter S. "An Overview of Acquisition, 1959–1968: The McNamara Legacy," 10 September 2001.
Rearden, Steven L. "The Secretary of Defense and Foreign Affairs." December 1995, OSD Hist.
Scheips, Paul J. and M. Warner Stark. "Use of Troops in Civil Disturbances Since World War II." Supplement II
    (1967), April 1969, OCMH.
Tyszkiewicz, Mary T. and Daggett, Stephen. "A Defense Budget Primer," 9 Dec 98, Congressional Research
    Service Report for Congress.
U.S. Air Force, Headquarters. "Air Force Project *Blue Lance* -- Interrelationships Between Strategic Offensive and
    Defensive Forces." December 1965.
U.S. District Court, Southern District of New York. "Deposition of Robert S. McNamara," 26 Mar 1984.
____, ____. "Continuation of Deposition of Robert S. McNamara," 27 Mar 1984.
Wainstein, L. "Some Aspects of the U.S. Involvement in the Middle East Crisis, May–June 1967." Critical Inci-
    dent No. 14, IDA Report R-132, February 1968.
Yackiel, Thomas F. and Robert W. Menestrina. "A Study of Selected Legislative Restrictions and Their Effect on
    the Administration of the United States Military Assistance and Foreign Military Sales Programs in Latin
    America (1959–1970)." MA Thesis, Air Force Institute of Technology, 1970.
Yoshpe, Harry B. "Our Missing Shield: The U.S. Civil Defense Program in Historical Perspective." Washington,
    D.C.: Federal Emergency Management Agency, 1981.

U.S. CONGRESS: GENERAL

Congressional Record. 1965–1968.

U.S. CONGRESS: HOUSE HEARINGS

Committee on Appropriations. Subcommittee on Department of Defense Appropriations. *Department of Defense
    Appropriations for 1965.* 88 Cong, 2 sess, 1964.
____. ____. *Hearings: Department of Defense Appropriations Act 1966,* 89 Cong, 1 sess, 1965.
____. ____. *Hearings: Department of Defense Appropriations for 1967,* 89 Cong, 2 sess, 1966.
____. ____. *Hearings: Department of Defense Appropriations for 1968,* 90 Cong, 1 sess, 1967.
____. ____. *Hearings: Department of Defense Appropriations for 1969,* 90 Cong, 2 sess, 1968.
____. ____. *Hearings: Department of Defense Appropriations for Fiscal Year 1970,* 91 Cong, 1 sess, 1969.
____. ____. *Hearings: Foreign Assistance and Related Agencies Appropriations for 1966,* 89 Cong, 1 sess, 1965.
____. ____. *Hearings: Foreign Assistance and Related Agencies Appropriations for 1967,* 90 Cong, 2 sess, 1966.
____. ____. *Hearings: Foreign Assistance and Related Agencies Appropriations for 1968,* 90 Cong, 1 sess, 1967.
____. ____. *Hearings: Foreign Assistance and Related Agencies Appropriations for 1969,* 90 Cong, 2 sess, 1968.
____.____. *Hearings: Supplemental Defense Appropriation for 1966,* 89 Cong, 2 sess, 1966.
____.____. *Hearings: Supplemental Defense Appropriations for 1967,* 90 Cong, 1 sess, 1967.
Committee on Armed Services. *Hearings: Military Posture and H.R. 13456,* 89 Cong, 2 sess, 1966.
____. *Hearings: Authorization for Military Procurement, Research and Development, FY 1969, and Reserve Strength,*
    90 Cong, 2 sess, 1968.
____. *Hearings: FY 1967 Supplemental Authorization for Southeast Asia,* 90 Cong, 1st sess, 1967.
____. *Hearings: Authorization for Military Procurement, Research, and Development Fiscal Year 1969, and Reserve
    Strength,* 90 Cong, 2 sess, 1968.
____. Subcommittee for Special Investigations. *Hearings: Examination of DoD Cost Reduction Program,* 89 Cong,
    2 sess, 1966.
____. Subcommittee No 2. *Hearings: Department of Defense Decision to Reduce the Number and Types of Manned
    Bombers in the Strategic Air Command,* 89 Cong, 2 sess, 1966.
Committee on Banking and Currency. *Hearings: Export-Import Bank and Credit Sales of Defense Articles,* 90 Cong,
    1 sess, 1967.
Committee on Foreign Affairs. *Hearings: Foreign Assistance Act of 1966,* 89 Cong, 2 sess, 1966.
____. *Hearings: Foreign Military Sales Act,* 90 Cong, 2 sess, 1968.
____. *Hearings: Foreign Assistance Act of 1969,* 91 Cong, 1 sess, 1969.

U.S. CONGRESS: SENATE HEARINGS

Committee on Appropriations. *Hearings: Foreign Assistance and Related Agencies Appropriations for Fiscal Year 1968*, 90 Cong, 1 sess, 1967.
____. *Hearings: Second Supplemental Appropriation FY 1968*, 90 Cong, 2 sess, 1968.
Committee on Appropriations. Subcommittee on Department of Defense Appropriations. *Hearings: Department of Defense Appropriations,1966*, 89 Cong, 1 sess, 1965.
____.____. *Hearings: Department of Defense Appropriations for 1966*, 89 Cong, 1 sess, 1966.
____.____. *Hearings: Department of Defense Appropriations for Fiscal Year 1967*, 89 Cong, 2 sess, 1967.
____. ____. *Hearings:Department of Defense Appropriations for FY 1969*, 90 Cong, 2 sess, 1968.
____. ____. and Committee on Armed Services, *Hearings: Department of Defense Appropriations,1966*, 89 Cong, 1 sess, 1965.
____. ____. and Committee on Armed Services. *Hearings: Military Procurement Authorizations for Fiscal Year 1967*, 89 Cong, 2 sess, 1966.
____. and Committee on Armed Services. *Hearings: Supplemental Defense Appropriations for Fiscal Year 1966*, 89 Cong, 2 sess, 1965.
____. ____. *Hearings: Supplemental Defense Appropriations for Fiscal Year 1966*, 89 Cong, 2 sess, 1966.
____. ____. and SCAS. *Hearings: Supplemental Defense Appropriations and Authorizations, Fiscal Year 1967*, 90 Cong, 1 sess, 1967.
____.____. and SCAS. *Hearings: Military Procurement Authorizations for FY 1967*, 89 Cong, 2 sess, 1966.
____. ____. *Hearings: Military Procurement Authorizations for Fiscal Year 1968 on Defense Budget*, 90 Cong, 1 sess, 1967.
____. ____. *Hearings: Department of Defense Appropriations for FY 1967*, 90 Cong, 1st sess, 1967.
Committee on Armed Services. *Hearings: Authorization for Military Procurement, Research and Development, Fiscal Year 1969*, and Reserve Strength, 90 Cong, 2 sess, 1968.
____. Preparedness Investigating SubCommittee. *Hearings: Proposal to Realign the Army National Guard and the Army Reserve Forces*, 89 Cong, 1 sess, 1965.
____. ____. *Hearings: Air War Against North Vietnam*, 90 Cong, 1 sess, 1967.
Committee on Foreign Relations. *Hearings: Foreign Assistance, 1965*, 89 Cong, 1 sess, 1965.
____. *Hearings: Foreign Assistance, 1966*, 89 Cong, 2 sess, 1966.
____. *Hearings: Foreign Assistance Act of 1967*, 90 Cong, 1967.
____. *Hearings: The Foreign Assistance Act of 1968*, Part 2, 90 Cong, 2 sess, 1968.
____. *Report of Proceedings*, 89 Cong, 2 sess, 1966, vol 1, Congressional Information Service, Unpublished U.S. Senate Cte Hearings, Cte on Foreign Relations, 1965-1966   (89) Sfo-T.21, (microfiche).
____. *Executive Sessions of the SFRC together with Joint Sessions with the SASC (Historical Series)*, XIX, Made Public 2007.
____. Subcommittee on US Security Agreements and Commitments Abroad. *Hearings: United States Security Agreements and Commitments Abroad, Republic of Korea*, 91 Cong, 2 sess, 1970.
Committee on Government Operations. Subcommittee on National Security and Internal Operations. *Hearings: The Atlantic Alliance*, 89 Cong, 2 sess, 1966.
____. Permanent Subcommittee on Investigation. *Hearings: TFX Contract Investigation, (Second Series)*, 91 Cong, 2 sess, 1970.
Joint Committee on Atomic Energy. *Hearings: S. Res. 179 Nonproliferation of Nuclear Weapons*, 89 Cong, 2 sess, 1966.
Joint Economic Committee. Subcommittee on Federal Procurement and Regulations. *Hearings: Economic Impact of Federal Procurement*, 89 Cong, 2 sess, 1966.
Joint Economic Cte, *Hearings: Economic Effects of Vietnam Spending*, 90 Cong, 1 sess, 1967.

HOUSE DOCUMENTS AND REPORTS

HCA, *Department of Defense Appropriation Bill, 1968*, H Rpt 349, 9 Jun 67.
HCA, *Appropriations for the Department of Defense for 1968*, H Rpt 595, 23 Aug 67.
HCA, *Foreign Assistance and Related Agencies Appropriation Bill, 1967*, H Rpt 2045, 16 Sep 66.
HCA, *Supplemental Defense Appropriation Bill, 1966*, H Rpt 1316, 11 Mar 66,
HCA, *Department of Defense Appropriation Bill, 1967*. H Rpt 1652, 24 Jun 66.
HCA, *Second Supplemental Appropriation Bill, 1968*, H Rpt 1531, 7 Jun 68.
HCA, *Department of Defense Appropriation Bill, 1968*, H Rpt 349, 9 Jun 67.

HCA, *Appropriations for the Department of Defense for 1968*, H Rpt 595, 23 Aug.
HCA, *Department of Defense Appropriation Bill, 1966*, H Rpt 528, 17 Jun 65.
HCA, *Department of Defense Appropriations, 1969*, H Rpt 1970, 10 Oct 68.
HCA, *Foreign Assistance and Related Agencies Appropriations Bill, 1968*, H Rpt 891, 6 Nov 67.
HCA, *Second Supplemental Appropriation Bill, 1968*, H Rpt 1531, 7 Jun 68.
HCA, *Department of Defense Appropriation Bill, 1969*, H Rpt 1735, 18 Jul 68.
HCAS, *Reserve Bill of Rights*, H Rpt 13, 13 Feb 67.
HCAS, *Foreign Assistance and Related Agencies Appropriation Bill, 1967*, H Rpt 2203, 6 Oct 66.
HCAS, *Report of the Special SubCte on the M-16 Rifle Program*, H Rpt 26, 19 Oct 67.

SENATE DOCUMENTS AND REPORTS

SCA, *Department of Defense Appropriation Bill, 1966*, S Rpt 625, 18 Aug 65.
SCA, *Supplemental Defense Appropriation Bill, 1966*, S Rpt 1074, 17 Mar 66.
SCA, *Department of Defense Appropriation Bill, 1967*, S Rpt 1458, 12 Aug 66.
SCA, *Department of Defense Appropriation Bill, 1968*, S Rpt 494, 4 Aug 67.
SCA, *Foreign Assistance and Related Agencies Appropriation Bill, 1968*, S Rpt 807, 28 Nov 67.
SCA, *Foreign Assistance and Related Agencies Appropriation Bill, 1968*, S Rpt 1663.
SCA, *Supplemental Defense Appropriations Bill, 1967*, S Rpt 74, 17 Mar 67.
SCA, *Second Supplemental Appropriation Bill, 1968*, S Rpt 1269, 19 Jun 68.
SCA, *Department of Defense Appropriation Bill, 1969*, S Rpt 1576, 19 Sep 68.
SCAS, *Authorizing Appropriations During Fiscal Year 1967 for Procurement of Aircraft, Missiles, Naval Vessels, and Tracked Combat Vehicles, and Research Development, Test, and Evaluation for the Armed Forces*, S Rpt No. 76, 20 Mar 67.
SCF, *Public Debt Limit*, S Rpt 357, 26 Jun 67.
SCFR, *Foreign Assistance Act of 1965*, S Rpt 170, 28 Apr 65.
SCFR, *Military Assistance and Sales Act*, S Rpt 1358, 7 Jul 66.
SCFR, *Arms Sales and Foreign Policy*, S Staff Study, 25 Jan 67.
SCFR, *Foreign Assistance Act of 1967*, S Rpt 499, 9 Aug 67.
SCFR, *Foreign Assistance Act of 1968*, S Rpt 1479, 26 Jul 68.

CONFERENCE DOCUMENTS AND REPORTS

H Committee of Conference, *Conference Report on Foreign Assistance Act of 1966, H.R. 15750 To Amend Further the Foreign Assistance Act of 1961, as Amended, and for Other Purposes*, 31 Aug 66.
H Committee of Conference, *Foreign Assistance and Related Agencies Appropriations Bill, 1967*, H Rpt 2203, 6 Oct 66.
Conference Report on Foreign Assistance Act of 1965, Conf H Rpt 811, 18 Aug 65.
Conference Report on the Foreign Assistance Act of 1967, H Rpt 892, 7 Nov 67.

INTERVIEWS

LYNDON B. JOHNSON LIBRARY, AUSTIN, TEXAS
Ackley, Gardner. Interviewed by Joe B. Frantz, Ann Arbor, Mich, 13 Apr 73, AC 76-20, and 7 Mar 74, AC81-23.
Bundy, William P. Interviewed by Paige E. Mulhollan, Washington, DC, 29 May 67 (AC 74-181).
Clark, Ramsey. Interviewed by Harri Baker, Falls Church, VA, 16 Apr 69, [Internet Copy].
Clifford, Clark M. Interviewed by Paige E. Mulhollan, Washington, DC, 2 Jul 69, 14 Jul 69, 14 Aug 69, [Internet Copy].
Clifford, Clark. Interviewed by Joe B. Frantz, 15 Dec 69, Washington, DC, 24 Apr 70, [Internet Copy].
Enthoven, Alain. Interviewed by Dorothy Pierce, Washington, DC. 27 Dec 68 (AC 74-16).
Hebert, Edward F. Interviewed by Dorothy Pierce McSweeney, Washington, DC, 15 Jul 69 (AC 79-60).
Horwitz, Solis. Interviewed by Paige E. Mulhollan, Pittsburgh, PA, 9 Jan 69.
Johnson, Lyndon B. Interviewed by William Jorden, LBJ Ranch, Tex, 12 Aug 69, (AC 66-1).
Katzenbach, Nicholas DeB. Interviewed by Paige E. Mulhollan, Washington, DC, 11 Dec 68, [Internet Copy].

Mann, Thomas C. Interviewed by Joe B. Frantz, Washington, DC, 4 Nov 68, [Internet Copy].

McConnell, John P. Interviewed by Dorothy Pierce McSweeny, Washington, DC, 28 Aug 69, (AC 79-71).

McNamara, Robert S. Interviewed by Walt W. Rostow, Washington, DC, 8 Jan 75.

Mills, Wilbur. Interviewed by Michael L. Gillette, Washington, DC, 15 May 87 (AC 94-19).

Palmer, Bruce. Interviewed by Ted Gittinger, Washington, DC, 28 May 82 (AC 92-49).

Read, Benjamin H. Interviewed by Paige E. Mulhollan, Washington, DC, 13 Jan 69 and Mar 70, [Internet Copy].

Rostow, Eugene. Interviewed by Paige E. Mulhollan, Washington, DC, 2 Dec 68, (AC 74-72).

Rostow, Walt. Interviewed by Paige E. Mulhollan, Austin, TX, 21 Mar 69, (AC 74-242).

Rusk, Dean. Interviewed by Paige E. Mulhollan, Washington, DC, 28 Jul 69, 26 Sep 69, 2 Jan 70, 8 Mar 70, [Internet Copy].

Smith, Bromley. Interviewed by Paige E. Mulhollan, Washington, DC, 25 Sep 69, [Internet Copy].

Vance, Cyrus. Interviewed by Paige E. Mulhollan, New York, NY, 3 Nov 69, 29 Dec 69, 9 Mar 70, [Internet Copy].

Warnke, Paul C. Interviewed by Dorothy Pierce McSweeny, Washington, DC, 8 Jan 69, (AC 74-264).

Westmoreland, William C. Interviewed by Dorothy Pierce McSweeny, Washington, DC, 8 Feb 69, (AC 77-32).

Wheeler, Earle G. Interviewed by Dorothy Pierce McSweeny, Washington, DC, 21 Aug 69, (AC 78-87), 7 May 70, (AC 78-88).

OSD HISTORICAL OFFICE, ARLINGTON, VA

Ailes, Stephen. Interviewed by Maurice Matloff, Washington, DC, 6 Jun 86, 2 Jul 86.

Brown, Harold. Interviewed by Alfred Goldberg and Maurice Matloff, Washington, DC, 20 Apr 90.

Brown, Harold. Interviewed by Alfred Goldberg and Roger F. Trask, Washington, DC, 4 Dec 81.

Bundy, McGeorge. Interviewed by Alfred Goldberg and Maurice Matloff, Washington, DC, 15 Apr 91, OSD Hist.

Enthoven, Alain. Interviewed by Maurice Matloff, Stanford, CA, 3 Feb 86.

Frank, Benis. Interviewed [telephone] by Edward J. Drea, 26 Feb 03.

Gilpatric, Roswell L. Interviewed by Maurice Matloff, New York, NY, 14 Nov 83.

Glass, Henry. Interviewed by Alfred Goldberg, Lawrence Kaplan, Robert Watson, and Maurice Matloff, Washington, DC, 28 Oct 87, 4 Nov 87.

Glass, Henry. Interviewed by Edward J. Drea, Washington, DC, 22 Oct 97.

Goldberg, Alfred. Interviewed by Diane Putney, Arlington, Va, 14 Apr 03.

Goodpaster, Andrew. Interviewed by Edward J. Drea, Washington, DC, 29 Jul 99.

Lemnitzer, Lyman L. Interviewed by Maurice Matloff, 24 Jan 84, Washington, DC.

McNamara, Robert S. Interviewed by Alfred Goldberg and Maurice Matloff, Washington, DC, 3 Apr 86.

McNamara, Robert S. Interviewed by Alfred Goldberg, Lawrence Kaplan, and Maurice Matloff, Washington, DC, 22 May 86, 24 Jul 86.

McNamara, Robert S. Interviewed by Edward Drea, Alfred Goldberg, and Lawrence Kaplan, Washington, DC, 8 Jan 98.

McNamara, Robert S. Interviewed [telephone] by Edward J. Drea, 6 Mar 2000.

Morris, Thomas D. Interviewed by Alfred Goldberg and Maurice Matloff, Washington, DC, 4 Jun 87.

Nitze, Paul H. Interviewed by Roger Trask and Maurice Matloff, Arlington, VA, 9 Oct 84.

Packard, David. Interviewed by Alfred Goldberg and Maurice Matloff, Washington, DC, 9 Nov 87.

Pursley, Robert E. Interviewed by Alfred Goldberg and Roger Trask, Washington, DC, 6 Sep 95, 7 May 1996, 15 Aug 97.

Rostow, Walt. Interviewed by Edward J. Drea, Austin, TX, 21 Sep 98.

Schultze, Charles L. Interviewed by Edward J. Drea, Washington, DC, 14 Jan 98.

Warnke, Paul C. Interviewed by Maurice Matloff and Roger Trask, Washington, DC, 10 Sep 84, 10 Nov 84.

Zuckert, Eugene M. Interviewed by Alfred Goldberg and Maurice Matloff, Washington, DC, 10 Oct 84.

US ARMY MILITARY HISTORY INSTITUTE, CARLISLE BARRACKS, PA

Johnson, Harold K. Interviewed by Col George H. Gray, Valley Forge, Penn, 1 Aug 74, Senior Officer Oral History Program.

Palmer, Bruce. Interviewed by James E. Shelton and Edward P. Smith, 1976, Senior Officers Debriefing Program.

US NAVY HISTORICAL CENTER, WASHINGTON, DC

McDonald, David L. Interviewed by John T. Mason, Jr., Washington, DC, 7 Oct 75 and 24 Jan 76.

Moorer, Thomas H. Interviewed by John T. Mason, Jr., Washington, DC, 8 Jun 81.

INDEX